LAWYERS IN 21ST-CENTURY SOCIETIES

The world's legal professions have undergone dramatic changes in the 30 years since publication of the landmark three-volume *Lawyers in Society*, which launched comparative sociological studies of lawyers. This is the first of two volumes in which scholars from a wide range of disciplines, countries and cultures document and analyse those changes.

The present volume presents reports on 46 countries, with broad coverage of North America, Western Europe, Latin America, Asia, Australia, North Africa and the Middle East, sub-Saharan Africa, and former communist countries. These national reports address: the impact of globalisation and neoliberalism on national legal professions (the relationship of lawyers and their professional associations to the state and tensions between state and citizenship); changes in lawyer demography (rapidly growing numbers and the profession's efforts to retain control, the entry of women and obstacles to full gender equality, ethnic diversity); legal education (the proliferation of institutions and pedagogic innovation); the regulation of lawyers; structures of production (especially the growth of large firms and the impact of technology and paraprofessionals); the distribution of lawyers across roles; and access to justice (state-funded legal aid and pro-bono services). The juxtaposition of the reports reveals the dramatic transformations of professional rationales, labour markets, and working practices and the multiple contingencies of the role of lawyers in societies experiencing increasing juridification within a new geopolitical order.

Vol 1: National Reports

Lawyers in 21st-Century Societies

Volume 1: National Reports

Edited by
Richard L Abel
Ole Hammerslev
Hilary Sommerlad
and
Ulrike Schultz

·HART·
OXFORD · LONDON · NEW YORK · NEW DELHI · SYDNEY

HART PUBLISHING

Bloomsbury Publishing Plc

Kemp House, Chawley Park, Cumnor Hill, Oxford, OX2 9PH, UK

1385 Broadway, New York, NY 10018, USA

HART PUBLISHING, the Hart/Stag logo, BLOOMSBURY and the Diana logo are
trademarks of Bloomsbury Publishing Plc

First published in Great Britain 2020

Copyright © The editors and contributors severally 2020

The editors and contributors have asserted their right under the Copyright, Designs and Patents
Act 1988 to be identified as Authors of this work.

All rights reserved. No part of this publication may be reproduced or transmitted in any form or by any means,
electronic or mechanical, including photocopying, recording, or any information storage or retrieval system,
without prior permission in writing from the publishers.

While every care has been taken to ensure the accuracy of this work, no responsibility for loss or damage
occasioned to any person acting or refraining from action as a result of any statement in it can be
accepted by the authors, editors or publishers.

All UK Government legislation and other public sector information used in the work is Crown Copyright ©.
All House of Lords and House of Commons information used in the work is Parliamentary Copyright ©.
This information is reused under the terms of the Open Government Licence v3.0 (http://www.
nationalarchives.gov.uk/doc/open-government-licence/version/3) except where otherwise stated.

All Eur-lex material used in the work is © European Union,
http://eur-lex.europa.eu/, 1998–2020.

A catalogue record for this book is available from the British Library.

ISBN: HB: 978-1-50991-5-149
       ePDF: 978-1-50991-5-163
       ePub: 978-1-50991-5-156

Typeset by Compuscript Ltd, Shannon
Printed and bound in Great Britain by CPI Group (UK) Ltd, Croydon CR0 4YY

To find out more about our authors and books visit www.hartpublishing.co.uk.
Here you will find extracts, author information, details of forthcoming events
and the option to sign up for our newsletters.

To Philip SC Lewis (1933–2019), who founded the Working Group for Comparative Study of Legal Professions and guided it through publication of the three volumes of Lawyers in Society.

Preface

THE STORY OF the project on *Lawyers in 21st-Century Societies* goes back almost 50 years. At the end of the 1970s Philip Lewis from Wolfson College, University of Oxford and Richard Abel from University of California, Los Angeles decided to launch an international comparative project on the history, constitution and role of lawyers in society. After preliminary meetings at conferences of the Law and Society Association (LSA) and the International Sociological Association's Research Committee on Sociology of Law (RCSL), the group gathered for a week in the summer of 1984 at the Rockefeller Foundation's Villa Serbelloni in Bellagio, Italy, ultimately producing the three volumes on *Lawyers in Society*: one on the common law world, one on the civil law world, and one on comparative theories (Abel and Lewis 1988a; 1988b; 1989; 1995). These pathbreaking books became the foundation of socio-legal research and teaching about lawyers for decades.

Because the successful collaboration created an intense identification with a common intellectual enterprise, the contributors decided to found a Working Group (WG) on Comparative Studies of Legal Professions within the framework of the RCSL. The WG has met biennially since 1986, mainly in France, and has a blog;[1] its work is described on the RCSL website.[2]

The WG has grown from the 32 contributors to the original volumes to more than 300 members, 60–70 of whom attend any given meeting. Developments in various countries are presented and discussed in the WG's 12 subgroups on Ethics and Deontology; Family, Policy and the Law; International Lawyering and Large Law Firms; Judiciary; Lawyers and Clients; Legal Aid; Legal Education; Legal Professional Values and Identities; Regulatory Reform; Women/Gender in the Legal Profession; Histories of Legal Professions; and Lawyers and Imperialism. This collaborative enterprise has produced many monographs, articles and international comparative volumes, including three comprehensive books on women in the legal profession (Schultz and Shaw 2003; 2013; Schultz et al 2019). Several subgroups have held their own meetings, often as workshops at the International Institute for the Sociology of Law (IISL) in Oñati. William Felstiner (2005), then WG chair, published an update of changes in ten countries. At the fifteenth WG meeting in Frauenchiemsee, Germany, Hilary Sommerlad and Ole Hammerslev suggested that, given the dramatic transformation of the geo-political order since 1989 and its impact on national societies and their legal professions, the 1988/89 project should be revisited. Ulrike Schultz, then WG chair and contributor to the 1988/89 volumes, lent her full support, and the three of them recruited Richard Abel. Because socio-legal scholarship has flourished globally in the intervening three decades, we have been able to involve colleagues from many more countries (46 rather than the original 19),

---

[1] See iwglp.wordpress.com/.
[2] At rcsl.iscte.pt/rcsl_wg_professions.htm.

including categories that were omitted or barely covered: Africa and the Middle-East, Latin America, Asia, and former communist countries. This new project has been greatly facilitated by the enormous technological improvements since the time when contributors wrote on typewriters, corrected with Wite-Out, rarely made the very expensive international phone calls, and were limited to snail mail for communicating and transmitting drafts. The contributions have been presented and discussed at the annual LSA conferences in Seattle (2015), New Orleans (2016), and Washington, DC (2019) the third ISA Forum of Sociology in Vienna, Austria (2016), the international socio-legal meeting in Mexico City (2017), a special workshop at IISL in 2017, the RCSL meetings in Canoas, Brazil (2015), Lisbon, Portugal (2018), and Oñati (2019), the joint LSA/Canadian Law and Society Association conference in Toronto, Canada (2018), and the WG meetings in Andorra (2016 and 2018).

We are grateful to LSA (which obtained funding from the US National Science Foundation) for generously supporting the travel expenses of colleagues who otherwise would have been unable to attend the meetings in Mexico City, Oñati, and Washington, DC, and to Hart Publishing for subsidising the Oñati meeting. Richard Abel is grateful to the UCLA Academic Senate's Council on Research for support in organising and attending some of the above conferences. Hilary Sommerlad thanks the University of Leeds for making her attendance at project meetings possible through its 'Dowry' system. Ole Hammerslev is grateful to the Department of Law, University of Southern Denmark, for generous strategic funding. And the editors wish to thank all the contributors who have invested so much time and effort in writing and revising their national reports. For quite a few, time-consuming field work was necessary to excavate data on their legal professions. We also wish to thank the contributors for their engagement at all the meetings and conferences, which made these volumes truly collaborative in the spirit of the original project.

The present volume contains reports by 76 authors on legal professions in 46 countries. In the companion volume, 45 authors will make use of those reports and other data to engage in cross-national comparisons (in Africa, Asia, former communist countries, Latin America, and the Islamic world) and address a wide variety of theoretical issues, including: comparative methodology, lawyers in the EU and international tribunals, large firms, emerging economies, ethics and regulation, state production, gender, ethnicity, the construction of law, access to justice, legal education, the rule of law, corruption, casualisation, masculinity, information technology, cause lawyers, and sociology of the professions. We had invited an eminent legal historian, Wes Pue, to contribute to Volume 2 but sadly Wes was already extremely ill and consequently declined. He died 3 April 2019. His scholarship on the legal profession was inspirational and a contribution from him would have greatly enhanced our project. He is sorely missed.

REFERENCES

Abel, RL and Lewis, PSC (eds) (1988a) *Lawyers in Society: Vol I The Common Law World* (Berkeley, University of California Press).

—— (1988b) *Lawyers in Society: Vol II The Civil Law World* (Berkeley, University of California Press).

—— (1989) *Lawyers in Society: Vol III Comparative Theories* (Berkeley, University of California Press).
—— (1995) *Lawyers in Society: An Overview* (Berkeley, University of California Press).
Felstiner, WLF (2005) *Reorganisation and Resistance: Legal Professions Confront a Changing World* (Oxford, Hart Publishing).
Schultz, U and Shaw, G (eds) (2003) *Women in the World's Legal Professions* (Oxford, Hart Publishing).
—— (2013) *Gender and Judging.* (Oxford, Hart Publishing).
Schultz, U, Shaw, G, Thornton, M and Auchmuty, R (eds) (2019) *Gender and Careers in the Legal Academy* (Oxford, Hart Publishing).

Richard Abel, Santa Monica, California, United States
Hilary Sommerlad, Leeds, United Kingdom
Ole Hammerslev, Odense, Denmark
Ulrike Schultz, Hagen, Germany
1 September 2019

Table of Contents

Preface vii
Contributors xv

1. *Lawyers in a New Geopolitical Conjuncture: Continuity and Change* 1
   Hilary Sommerlad and Ole Hammerslev

PART I
ANGLO-AMERICAN COMMON LAW

2. *Australia: A Legal Profession Globalised and Magnified* 45
   Margaret Thornton and Asmi Wood

3. *Canada: Continuity and Change in a Modern Legal Profession* 65
   Ronit Dinovitzer and Meghan Dawe

4. *England and Wales: A Legal Profession in the Vanguard of Professional
   Transformation?* 89
   Hilary Sommerlad, Andrew Francis, Joan Loughrey and Steven Vaughan

5. *Scotland: Caught between Nationalism and the Market: What Does the
   Future Hold for Scots Lawyers?* 117
   Alan Paterson and Peter Robson

6. *United States: Out of Many Legal Professions, One?* 127
   Scott L Cummings, Carroll S Seron, Ann Southworth, Rebecca L Sandefur,
   Steven A Boutcher and Anna Raup-Kounovsky

PART II
WESTERN EUROPEAN CIVIL LAW

7. *Belgium: A Law Degree Opens the Door to a Lot of Occupations,
   Even the Bar* 157
   Steven Gibens, Bernard Hubeau, Stefan Rutten, Jean Van Houtte
   and Margot Van Leuvenhaege

8. *Denmark, Sweden and Norway: Liberalisation, Differentiation
   and the Emergence of a Legal Services Market* 175
   Ole Hammerslev

9. *France: The Reconfiguration of a Profession* 193
   Christian Bessy and Benoit Bastard

10. *Germany: Resistance and Reactions to Demands of Modernisation* 209
    Matthias Kilian and Ulrike Schultz

11. *Italy: A Delicate Balance between Maintenance and Change* 235
    Evelyn Micelotta and Gabrielle Dorian

12. *Netherlands: Developments and Challenges* 253
    Nienke Doornbos and Leny de Groot-van Leeuwen

13. *Switzerland: The End of Prosperity in the Age of Globalisation?* 271
    Isabel Boni-Le Goff, Eléonore Lépinard, Grégoire Mallard and Nicky Le Feuvre

PART III
EASTERN EUROPE AND RUSSIA

14. *Czech Republic: Legal Professions Looking for Serenity and Stability* 289
    Jan Kober

15. *Poland: Opening the Legal Professions* 309
    Kaja Gadowska

16. *Russia: Challenges of the Market and Boundary Work* 331
    Ekaterina Moiseeva and Timur Bocharov

17. *Serbia and Bosnia and Herzegovina: Challenges of Liberalisation
    and Democratic Consolidation* 353
    Danilo Vuković, Valerija Dabetić and Samir Forić

PART IV
LATIN AMERICA

18. *Argentina: The Long Transition of the Legal Profession* 377
    Martin Böhmer

19. *Brazil: Fragmentary Development, Democratisation, and Globalisation* 391
    Maria da Gloria Bonelli and Pedro Fortes

20. *Chile: Lawyers Engage with the Market, Specialisation, and Rights* 411
    Cristián Villalonga

21. *Mexico: Significant Growth and Under-Regulation of the Legal Profession* 429
    Luis Fernando Perez-Hurtado

22. *Venezuela: A Despatch from the Abyss* 449
    Manuel Gómez and Rogelio Pérez-Perdomo

PART V
AFRICA

23. *Burundi: Middlemen and Opponents in the Shadow of the Ethno-state* 473
    Sara Dezalay

24. *Kenya: Between Globalisation and Constitutionalism* 495
    Winifred Kamau

25. *Nigeria: An Account of Adaptation* 515
    Enibokun Uzebu-Imarhiagbe

26. *South Africa: A Profession in Transformation* 535
    Jonathan Klaaren

27. *Zimbabwe: Legal Practitioners, Politics and Transformation Since 1980* 547
    George H Karekwaivanane

PART VI
NORTH AFRICA AND MIDDLE EAST

28. *Egypt: The Long Decline of the Legal Profession* 565
    Nathalie Bernard-Maugiron and Menna Omar

29. *Iran: A Clash of Two Legal Cultures?* 581
    Reza Banakar and Keyvan Ziaee

30. *Israel: Numbers, Make-Up and Modes of Practice* 601
    Eyal Katvan, Limor Zer-Gutman and Neta Ziv

31. *Libya: Lawyers between Ideology and the Market* 619
    Jessica Carlisle

32. *Palestine: Lawyering between Colonisation and the Struggle
    for Professional Independence* 639
    Mutaz M Qafisheh

33. *Tunisia: A Political Profession?* 657
    Eric Gobe

34. *Turkey: Emergence and Development of the Legal Profession* 675
    Seda Kalem

PART VII
ASIA

35. *China: A Tale of Four Decades* 697
    Sida Liu

36. *India: Present and Future: A Revised Sociological Portrait* 713
    Swethaa S Ballakrishnen

37. *Indonesia: Professionals, Brokers and Fixers* 735
    Santy Kouwagam and Adriaan Bedner

38. *Japan: Towards Stratification, Diversification and Specialisation* 753
    Masayuki Murayama

39. *Myanmar: Law as a Desirable and Dangerous Profession* 775
    Melissa Crouch

40. *South Korea: Reshaping the Legal Profession* 789
    JaeWon Kim

41. *Taiwan and Hong Kong: Localisation and Politicisation* 801
    Ching-Fang Hsu

42. *Thailand: The Evolution of Law, the Legal Profession and Political
    Authority* 831
    Frank W Munger

43. *Vietnam: From Cadres to a 'Managed' Profession* 855
    Pip Nicholson and Do Hai Ha

44. *Comparative Sociology of Lawyers, 1988–2018: The Professional Project* 879
    Richard L Abel

Index 917

Contributors

Richard L Abel, Connell Distinguished Professor of Law Emeritus and Distinguished Research Professor, University of California, Los Angeles (US)

Swethaa S Ballakrishnen, Assistant Professor, School of Law, University of California, Irvine (US)

Reza Banakar, Professor, Sociology of Law, Lund University (Sweden)

Benoit Bastard, Director of Research Emeritus, CNRS and Institut des sciences sociales du politique, ENS Paris-Saclay (France)

Adriaan Bedner, Professor of Law and Society in Indonesia, Van Vollenhoven Institute, University of Leiden (Netherlands)

Nathalie Bernard-Maugiron, Director of Research, Institute of Research for Development (IRD), Centre for Population and Development (CEPED) (France), nathalie.bernard-maugiron@ird.fr

Christian Bessy, Director of Research, Centre nationale de la recherche scientifique (CNRS), and Director, IDHES ENS Paris-Saclay (France)

Timur Bocharov, Researcher, Institute for the Rule of Law, European University at St. Petersburg (Russia)

Martin Böhmer, Professor of Law, Universidad de Buenos Aires (Argentina), martin.bohmer@gmail.com

Maria da Gloria Bonelli, Titular Professor of Sociology, Universidade Federal de São Carlos (Brazil)

Isabel Boni-Le Goff, Lecturer in Sociology, University of Lausanne (Switzerland)

Steven A Boutcher, Senior Research Fellow, Institute for Social Science Research, University of Massachusetts, Amherst (US)

Jessica Carlisle, Research Fellow, Department of Visual Cultures, Goldsmiths University (UK)

Melissa Crouch, Associate Professor of Law, University of New South Wales (Australia), Melissa.crouch@unsw.edu.au

Scott Cummings, Robert Henigson Professor of Legal Ethics and Professor of Law, University of California, Los Angeles (US)

Valerija Dabetić, Teaching Assistant, Faculty of Law, University of Belgrade (Serbia)

Meghan Dawe, Research Social Scientist, American Bar Foundation (US)

Leny de Groot-van Leeuwen, Emerita Professor of Sociology and Migration Law, Radboud University (Netherlands)

Sara Dezalay, Senior Lecturer in International Relations, Cardiff University (UK)

Ronit Dinovitzer, Professor of Sociology, University of Toronto (Canada), ronit.dinovitzer@utoronto.ca

Do Hai Ha, Research Fellow, Asian Law Centre, Melbourne Law School, University of Melbourne (Australia), doh@unimelb.edu.au

Nienke Doornbos, Assistant Professor of Legal Sociology, University of Amsterdam (Netherlands)

Gabrielle Dorian, PhD Candidate, Anderson School of Management, University of New Mexico (US)

Samir Forić, Senior Teaching Assistant, Sociology, University of Sarajevo (Bosnia and Herzegovina)

Pedro Fortes, CSLS Associate, Centre for Socio-Legal Studies, University of Oxford (UK), pfortes@alumni.stanford.edu

Andrew Francis, Head and Professor of Law, Manchester Law School, Manchester Metropolitan University (UK)

Kaja Gadowska, Associate Professor of Sociology, Jagiellonian University (Poland)

Steven Gibens, Lecturer in Law, Karel de Grote University College and Research, University of Antwerp (Belgium)

Eric Gobe, Director of Research, Centre nationale de la recherche scientifique (CNRS), Institut de recherches et d'études sur les mondes arabes et musulmans, Aix-en-Provence (France), jbheuman@gmail.com

Manuel Gómez, Professor of Law and Associate Dean for International and Graduate Studies, Florida International University (US)

Ole Hammerslev, Professor of Sociology of Law, University of Southern Denmark (Denmark)

Ching-Fang Hsu, PhD Candidate, Political Science, University of Toronto (Canada), chingfang.hsu@mail.utoronto.ca

Bernard Hubeau, Professor of Sociology of Law, University of Antwerp and University of Brussels (Belgium)

Seda Kalem, Assistant Professor of Sociology, Istanbul Bilgi University (Turkey)

Winifred Wambui Kamau, Associate Professor of Law, University of Nairobi (Kenya), wkamau@uonbi.ac.ke

George H Karekwaivanane, Lecturer in African Studies, University of Edinburgh (Scotland)

Eyal Katvan, Senior Lecturer, Law School, Peres Academic Center (Israel)

Matthias Kilian, Hans-Soldan Professor, Faculty of Law, University of Cologne (Germany)

JaeWon Kim, Professor of Law, Sungkyunkwan University Law School (South Korea)

Jonathan Klaaren, Professor of Law, University of the Witwatersrand (South Africa), Jonathan.Klaaren@wits.ac.za

Jan Kober, Researcher, Institute of State and Law, Czech Academy of Sciences, Prague (Czech Republic), jan.kober@law.cas.cz

Santy Kouwagam, PhD Candidate, Van Vollenhoven Institute University of Leiden (Netherlands), s.u.kouwagam@law.leidenuniv.nl

Nicky Le Feuvre, Professor of Sociology, University of Lausanne (Switzerland)

Eléonore Lépinard, Professor of Sociology, University of Lausanne (Switzerland)

Sida Liu, Associate Professor of Sociology and Law, University of Toronto (Canada)

Joan Loughrey, Professor of Law, University of Leeds (UK)

Grégoire Mallard, Professor of Sociology, Graduate Institute of Geneva (Switzerland)

Evelyn Micelotta, Assistant Professor of Strategic Management and Organization, University of New Mexico (US)

Ekaterina Moiseeva, PhD Candidate, University of California, Irvine (US) and Researcher, Institute for the Rule of Law, EUSP (Russia)

Frank W Munger, Professor of Law, New York Law School (US)

Masayuki Murayama, Professor of Law, Meiji University (Japan), masayuki.murayama@gmail.com

Pip Nicholson, Dean and William Hearn Professor of Law, Melbourne Law School, University of Melbourne (Australia), p.nicholson@unimelb.edu.au

Menna Omar, PhD Candidate, École doctorale de droit comparé, Université de Paris 1 – Panthéon Sorbonne (France), meena.omar2@gmail.com

Alan Paterson, Professor of Law, Strathclyde University (Scotland)

Luis Fernando Pérez-Hurtado, Director, Centro de Estudios sobre la Enseñanza y el Aprendizaje de Derecho – CEEAD (Mexico), luisph@ceead.org.mx

Rogelio Pérez-Perdomo, Professor of Law, Universidad Metropolitana (Venezuela)

Mutaz M. Qafisheh, Dean, College of Law and Political Science and Associate Professor of Law, Hebron University (Palestine), mutazq@hebron.edu; mmqafisheh@gmail.com

Anna Raup-Kounovsky, PhD Candidate, School of Social Ecology, University of California, Irvine (US)

Peter Robson, Professor of Law, Strathclyde University (Scotland)

Stefan Rutten, Professor of Law, University of Antwerp (Belgium)

Rebecca Sandefur, Associate Professor of Sociology and Law, University of Illinois, Urbana-Champaign (US)

Ulrike Schultz, retired senior academic, FernUniversität in Hagen (Germany) Ulrike.Schultz@FernUni-Hagen.de

Carroll Seron, Professor Emerita of Criminology, Law & Society, University of California, Irvine (US)

Hilary Sommerlad, Professor of Law and Social Justice, University of Leeds (UK)

Ann Southworth, Professor of Law, University of California, Irvine (US)

Margaret Thornton, Emerita Professor of Law, Australia National University (Australia), margaret.thornton@anu.edu.au

Enibokun Uzebu-Imarhiagbe, Lecturer, Department of History and International Studies, University of Benin (Nigeria), enibokun.uzebu@uniben.edu

Jean Van Houtte, Emeritus Professor of Sociology and Sociology of Law, University of Antwerp (Belgium)

Margot Van Leuvenhaege, PhD Student, University of Antwerp (Belgium)

Steven Vaughan, Professor of Law and Professional Ethics, University College London (UK)

Cristián Villalonga, Assistant Professor of Law, Pontificia Universidad Católica de Chile (Chile), cvillalt@uc.cl

Danilo Vuković, Associate Professor of Sociology, University of Belgrade (Serbia)

Asmi Wood, Professor of Law, Australian National University (Australia)

Limor Zer-Gutman, Senior Lecturer, COMAS Law School (Israel)

Keyvan Ziaee, Sociology of Law, Lund University (Sweden)

Neta Ziv, Professor of Law, Tel-Aviv University (Israel)

1
Lawyers in a New Geopolitical Conjuncture
Continuity and Change

HILARY SOMMERLAD AND OLE HAMMERSLEV*

I. INTRODUCTION

IN CLASSICAL WESTERN sociology the view of law as a master discourse through which rational authority, social solidarity and the moral foundations of society are articulated assigns the legal profession a central role in the construction of modernity (Durkheim 1957; Weber 1978; Parsons 1954b, 1962; Aubert 1976; Luhmann 1981).[1] The performance of this socially constitutive role rested on lawyers' claims to systematic, rational knowledge, political neutrality and social detachment, denoted by a distinctive ethical code, service ethos and lengthy, standardised training (Carr-Saunders and Wilson 1933; Parsons 1954a). These traits grounded lawyers' moral, cultural and intellectual authority, facilitating and legitimising professional closure and lawyers' consequent capacity to extract monopoly rents and enjoy a special, relatively autonomous, status in the institutional environment of the modern Western state (Weber 1978; Larson 2013).[2]

The intimate connection between this professional model and the processes of state formation in the West[3] was the outcome of particular historical, cultural and political

---

* We are very grateful to Richard Abel and Ulrike Schultz for their close readings of this chapter, and helpful comments. We also thank Andrew Francis and Joan Loughrey for taking the time to read an early draft, and for their helpful comments.

[1] This is not to overlook such classical legal sociologists as Eugen Ehrlich (1936), whose understanding of law extended beyond state law to encompass informal (or unofficial) forms of normativity and regulation generated within groups, associations and communities. Modernity is an equally complex concept (Bayly 2004; Eisenstadt 2000), related to the fact that both it and Europe are 'reference cultures' (Delanty 2015).

[2] The multiple definitions of the state range from a centralised set of institutions wielding coercive power to conceptualisations of it as a cultural process, a (contingent) assemblage of rationalities and technologies, practices, techniques, programmes, knowledges, rationales and interventions (Miller 1990: 317). Weber's work on the construction of rational-legal authority in modern Western states exemplifies this understanding of the state as always in formation, and this view informs the present project, which similarly conceptualises the profession as a social process (Liu 2013).

[3] The labelling of geo-political divisions is ideological and increasingly meaningless as globalisation fragments national societies, eroding some of the characteristics once believed to define different world regions,

conditions which made lawyers' claims credible and ensured the superiority of state consecrated normative judgements over competing ones (Cotterrell 1998: 177).[4] Nevertheless, diverse histories, socio-economic contexts and political institutions generated different paths to modernity and a positivist legal order (see eg Jerneck et al 2005), and corresponding variations in professional forms. Most notably, whereas the Glorious Revolution in England and Wales (1688–89) enabled the profession to claim and link its autonomy to the (circumscribed) role of the liberal state (Sugarman 1996), the historical trajectories of civil law countries led to the establishment of professional service as part of a state bureaucracy, resulting in different forms of regulation and qualifying processes.

However a unifying feature in the development of Western modernity, frequently overlooked in classical and subsequent mainstream sociologies of the profession (Delanty 2015), was its grounding in relationships of domination with most of the rest of the globe (Johnson 1973; Bhambra 2016). It is correspondingly vital to recall how the colonial experience shaped the development of modernity in non-Western societies.[5] Even allowing for the huge variations *between* these societies, a common feature was the sharp divergence between their pre-modern modes of legitimacy and governance models and those in the West (Eisenstadt 2000; and see, eg Harrison 2001 and Pomerantz 2002 on China; Gordon 2009 on Japan), and these divergences were not entirely eradicated by formal or informal colonialism. For instance, while both types of imperial domination entailed the importation of Western institutions, local dispute resolution forms generally persisted (see eg Aiyedun and Ordor 2016 on Africa). A further common, distinguishing feature was the relative lack of autonomy of the formal legal order from the state: the combined and uneven development suffered by societies subject to imperialism (Hilferding 1981: 322–23) and frequent absence or weakness of an indigenous bourgeoisie (Alavi 1972) constricted the base for professional practice. Consequently, where Western style professions developed, the state was usually its primary client (Johnson 1973), and post-independence reforms generally failed to eradicate the 'over-developed administrative/military apparatus' (Alavi 1972) and weak internal structural interdependence characteristic of the colonial era.

---

such as political stability. It is also problematic for our aim of capturing the nuances in the development of different states and their professions. However, the need to reference longstanding debates mandates these shorthand terms (and their conventional meanings). By the West, therefore, we refer to those states which, from roughly the late eighteenth century until recently, dominated the globe and which include most of Europe, North America and Australasia. Global South refers to those regions which were, overwhelmingly, subject to Western economic and cultural imperialism; it includes most countries in Africa and Central and South America and parts of Asia. However, the term originally encompassed states which are now global economic powers such as China, South Korea, Indonesia and India. An alternative shorthand term for technologically advanced, economically developed and dominant societies is the Global North, encompassing Europe, North America, Australia, Israel, South Africa, and some other wealthy states. There are also the terms First, Second and Third World.

[4] As Terence Johnson (1995) argued, following Foucault, the professionalisation of legal expertise represented a fundamental technique of liberal governance. Olgiati (2006) similarly describes the professional form as particular to Western development.

[5] There is of course an extensive literature – apart from mainstream sociologies of the state and profession – on both the relationship between modernity and colonial domination (eg Fitzpatrick 1992; Duncanson 2003; Dezalay and Garth 2011) and on non-Western 'roads to modernity' (eg Moore 1966; Jaguaribe 1973) and an extensive post-colonial and international law literature (eg Sinclair 2015).

In short, the complex, variable relationship between professionalism and modernity underlines Abbott's warning that 'thinking about professions developing independently [is] ... foolish' (2001: 9): it is only by considering both the domestic and global socio-economic and cultural context that we can gain insight into the consequences for legal professionalism of the entanglement of different historical traditions with exogenous forces. Such 'connective sociologies' (Bhambra 2016) are essential if we are to deepen our understanding of the dynamics shaping contemporary meanings of legal professionalism (Bellini and Maestripieri 2018).

The project which this chapter introduces is grounded in such a connective sociology. Modelled on Richard Abel and Philip Lewis's landmark comparative work *Lawyers in Society* (1988a; 1988b; 1989b), it comprises a two-volume comparative analysis of contemporary forms and meanings of the legal profession. In the intervening three decades since the Abel and Lewis volumes 'inherited professional forms' have been 'daily assailed by forces associated with globalisation, the centrifugal pulls of the new market economy and the disintegration of cultural or national bonds' (Pue 1998: 127). This volume seeks to map how these forces impacted on national professions through 42 chapters which report on a total of 46 jurisdictions. Volume Two then addresses the key themes which these reports disclose. This chapter introduces the project, beginning with a brief outline of some key features of the Abel and Lewis volumes. We then consider the main dimensions of the transformation which marked the period between 1988 and 2014, when this project was conceived. The subsequent sections summarise the research design of the project, followed by a discussion of the data.

II. LAWYERS IN SOCIETY: THE ORIGINAL PROJECT

The three-volume collection *Lawyers in Society* edited by Abel and Lewis (1988a; 1988b; 1989b) represents a seminal, and enduring, contribution to connective sociology. The profession's contingency was exposed through explorations of the histories and status of lawyers in both common law and civil law jurisdictions, which elucidated 'the demographic, economic, ideological, and cultural background to the ways in which lawyers are organized and choose and carry on their work as well as to the changes that have affected or are likely to affect them' (Lewis 1988: 2). The authors' concern, therefore, extended beyond analysis of the distinctive relationships between lawyers, the state, civil society and the market to encompass such issues as the impact of national patterns of social stratification, culture and educational environment on the composition, practice and functions of the profession.

The scale and depth of the collection's comparisons were one of its major strengths: eleven civil law and seven common law countries were studied – substantially more than those covered by other ground breaking studies, such as those by Larson (1977), Rueschemeyer (1973; 1983) and Abbott (1988), and this was achieved despite the lack of large scale quantitative data and difficulties in identifying national reporters for some societies (Abel and Lewis 1988b: xi). However, the primary problem for the project was the semantic and conceptual difficulty of comparing different 'families' of legal professions. 'Profession' has long been a contested term, even within the Anglo-American field, where its distinctiveness from other occupational categories has been primarily asserted

(Saks 2012; Larson 1977). Furthermore, as discussed above, its generic use occludes its origin in Western environments and trajectories. While culturally specific terms such as 'attorney', 'barrister' and 'solicitor' serve to signal structural and functional differences, this proliferation of designations and categories hampered the identification of commonalities in the social and political meaning of the profession (Schultz 2003: xxxi; see also Abel 1989: 101). Yet, since the project's comparative approach centred on engaging with that meaning and exploring its differentiated forms by situating lawyers in the space-time conditions of the social systems in which they were embedded, it was vital to establish a conceptualisation that could work cross-culturally but was neither too confining nor empty. The solution was a definition of legal profession with two components: a credential (whether conferred by profession, state, or university) and a set of functions (which also varied across societies). This approach made it possible to engage with the profession's status project and examine its jurisdictionally specific patterns. Abel (1989) described the highly privileged relationship between the profession and state in common law jurisdictions, which resulted from the construction of the professional autonomy essential to the rule of law; and by deploying a neo-Weberian interpretation of the data from these jurisdictions, he showed how lawyers' consequent right to self-regulation and market shelters gave them control of entry through the apprenticeship mode of legal training. By contrast, in civil law countries the profession's origins as a university-educated state service meant that it only later developed as a private profession. The data from these countries confirmed that this 'professionalisation from above' (Siegrist 1990) made practitioners dependent upon, and regulated by, the state. Thus, the project not only delineated the key characteristics of professional institutions in common and civil law countries but also succeeded in deepening our understanding of the contingent relationship between lawyers and society – and hence of the distinction between the rule of law and the Rechtsstaat.[6] In this way it shed light on the professional project's various modalities – such as differing entry and closure mechanisms and ways of structuring and controlling the market for legal services. The significance of the state-lawyer relationship for shaping these key structural elements was fundamental to generating research questions about, and theories of, the professions (Abel 1988: 8; see also Heinz and Laumann 1982; Halliday and Karpik 1997).[7]

As a product of an epoch of counter-hegemonic engagement and critical scholarship, *Lawyers in Society* itself exemplifies the historical and geographical contingency of both the profession and its sociology. Written against the backdrop of the Cold War and the dramatic socio-economic and political upheavals and ideological challenges to the post World War II settlement, the collection engaged with many of the processes that were beginning to de-construct the basic tenets of the professional model that, in the West, had enjoyed a 'golden age' until at least the early 1960s (Freidson 2001: 182; Galanter and

---

[6] The position of the civil law profession reflects the near-identity of the law and state in the civil law tradition: the continental Rechtsstaat was not only subject to law but also its legal source. By contrast, English constitutional jurisprudence comprises plural and competing conceptions of the sources of law, and by tradition the 'common law' was preferred to the commands of the King (ie the state) (Krygier 2013).

[7] Some issues examined in the Abel and Lewis volumes have developed into distinct research fields with their own conferences and journals, and comparative studies have been undertaken by members of the original Legal Profession Working Group, which came out of the Lawyers in Society project; see, eg, Schultz and Shaw (2003); Felstiner (2005a).

Palay 1991: 20–36). Concluding that the professional project was in 'serious disarray', Abel (1989:189) and other contributors speculated on the likely future for professionalisation. Szelenyi and Martin (1989) enriched the volume's predominantly structural analysis by drawing attention to the significance and extent of critical discourse in the legal field to reflect on Larson's 'collective mobility project' and Gouldner's (1978) 'new class project'. This approach echoed Weber's view of the profession as particularly suited to 'the role of representative of the under-privileged' (1978: 875). The Janus-faced character of the profession is also a feature of Halliday's (1989) discussion of the state/profession relationship and the variable types of collective organisation by, and political behaviour of, national professions.

Other chapters focused on such drivers of change as the impact of developments in higher education (Neave 1989), the growing participation of women in the profession (Menkel-Meadow 1989) and the changing nature of law, legal representation and the trend to de-professionalisation (Larson 1989; Falcão 1988). While recognising that change was occurring unevenly across both jurisdictions and the profession, Abel argued that national professions would increasingly display institutional isomorphism as a result of these drivers and other developments

> some ... [of which are] economic: progressive concentration within industry and commerce, the expansion of the service sector and the internationalization of business (accelerated by the EEC). Some are political: the increased role of the state in all economies, the growth of welfare programs, and the emergence of movements to oppose the growing dominance of the state and to equalize access to law. Some are cultural: the availability of divorce, the demand by racial and ethnic minorities for equal opportunity. (Abel 1988: 43)

It is a mark of the ambition and richness of *Lawyers in Society* that it provided both a benchmark for assessing the strength of these theoretically grounded predictions concerning professional change and a resource, in the form of the country reports, for scholars to develop their own comparative frameworks and investigations. The reports in the present volume provide the raw materials for a similar framing of the transformations currently affecting legal professions and are thus the basis for in-depth explorations in the second volume.

III. LAWYERS IN A NEW WORLD ORDER: GLOBALISATION AND NEOLIBERALISM[8]

By 2014, when the current project was conceived, some of Abel's predictions had been fulfilled, but others had been confounded. Business had been progressively internationalised and concentrated: the deregulation of financial markets had led to an exponential growth in the size and political and economic power of transnational corporations

---

[8] Contingent, complex and therefore ambiguous concepts, globalisation and neoliberalism have generated multiple interpretations – for instance, neoliberalism encompasses a policy framework, a political discourse and ideology, and a form of governmentality (Larner 2000). Nevertheless, they do have sufficient common features to give them conceptual validity, and as the primary drivers behind the new world order, must be deployed. We understand globalisation as the intensification of world-wide relationships, including trade, culture and technologies, leading to both internationalisation and de-nationalisation. Also viewed as the latest phase of imperialism, it entails economic and cultural penetration by hegemonic states (the 'core') of the Global South (the 'periphery'), based on and reinforcing their asymmetrical relationship – for instance, JK Galbraith described

(TNCs) (Strange 1996; Crouch 2011)[9] and associated super-clusters of producers, technological infrastructures and institutional networks. These 'private sector quasi states' (Beck 2005: 75) generated a multiplicity of laws, quasi-laws, other forms of regulation, and new fora and procedures for litigation, arbitration and 'cross-sanctioning' (Scott 2001). The creation of this patchwork of transnational jurisdictional geographies and virtual regulatory spaces by international (primarily Anglo-American) corporate law firms greatly expanded their size, reach and wealth (Trubek et al 1994: 407; Dezalay and Garth 2002; Dezalay and Sugarman 1995; Halliday et al 2007; Wilkins 2013).[10] Their interdependence with corporate clients also dismantled the traditional professional form, logics and production techniques,[11] while their location in different jurisdictions dissolved their characteristic national and local embeddedness.[12] Furthermore, although the new legal order was implemented by *national* legislatures, judiciaries and lawyers, it was harmonised through transnational institutions, subject to a *non-national* organising logic and temporal frame.

This de-nationalisation (Sassen 1999) fractured 'the coherence, wholeness and unity of individual societies' (Urry 1989: 97), dividing and commercialising national sovereignty (Picciotto 2008: 457) and weakening states' capacity to pursue an independent economic policy. Once relatively self-contained geographical units, national economies and institutions have splintered, rescaled into new configurations tailored to the needs of global capital. The systematic concentration of developmental capacities within certain geographical zones has consigned peripheral regions to chronic marginalisation (Brenner 2004).[13] These fissiparous tendencies are mirrored in the legal profession, while legal monism has weakened in the face of new centres of power (such as financial markets and independent central banks) and consequent proliferation of normative orders within nation states. Once a master discourse which, by articulating state theory, political values, and collective ideology, crystallised the state/society/citizen relationship, national law has come to assume 'the characteristics of contemporary society … open,

---

globalisation as a 'term invented to conceal the current policy of economic penetration' (1997). However, it also has a humanitarian face, in the form of the globalisation of human rights. A key feature of neoliberalism, which facilitates the penetration of global capitalism, is the installation of markets as the organising principle of political-economic governance (Birch 2017), grounded in the principle of possessive individualism and anti-statism (Hall 2011: 10–11).

[9] As our above comments indicate, we frame this phase of capitalism as imperialism (Hirst and Thompson 1996), its key agents being not only the most developed market economies and powerful states such as the US and China but also TNCs.

[10] US-style corporate law firms proliferated between 1988 and 2008, and the number of overseas offices in the National Law Journal's list of the 250 largest US firms nearly quadrupled, while the number of lawyers working in these offices increased by a factor of 12 (Silver 2011: 1–2).

[11] Although, evidently, the traditional professional form varied between the common and civil law worlds, and between jurisdictions, the professional project was grounded in its attempt to establish itself as a distinctive autonomous field – detached from the world of business (and politics) thereby legitimising the profession in the name of the common good and the rule of law or Rechtsstaat.

[12] The disembedding of sectors of once deeply-rooted, local professions is also apparent in the increasing mobility of individual lawyers, both between firms and regions (Dinovitzer and Hagan 2006) – since, of course the structure of the profession mirrors the structure of the economy.

[13] Marginalisation has been exacerbated in many societies as a result of the austerity programmes adopted following the financial crisis of 2008.

decentred, fragmented, nebulous and multiform' (Douzinas and Warrington 1994: 3).[14] In the process it has lost the 'metaphysical dignity' (Douglas-Scott 2013: 56) which made it central to the foundation of the modern Western state.[15]

The profession's constitutional role of boundary-agent between the state and civil society (Loughlin 2000; Olgiati 2010) has also been undermined by popular scepticism about its claims to special ethicality (Leicht 2015). This evaporation of lawyers' moral, cultural and intellectual authority[16] justified the removal of the monopolies which, in many jurisdictions, supported the private client sector, while the commoditisation and marketisation of domestic legal services infused that sector with the commercial/entrepreneurial ethos characteristic of international corporate firms, generating the concepts of commercialised and corporate professionalism (Hanlon 1998; Muzio et al 2011). Concurrently, in jurisdictions where neoliberalism had become particularly dominant (such as England and Wales) discursive constructions of public sector professionals as a *rentier* class eroded the legitimacy which accrued to the legal aid or public service sector, facilitating its subjection to new public management measures (Sommerlad 2008). The related managerialisation/de-politicisation of governance (Cerny 1996) dissolved the 'complex inter-dependencies between rights and obligations, power and the law' characteristic of the Keynesian nation state (Sassen 2006: 3). As a result, rather than the predicted expansion of welfare programmes (Abel 1988: 43), socio-economic rights have been cut and/or transformed into conditional benefits, even while the significance of (individual) human rights has increased in political discourse and law making.

All of the above indicates the need to modify the traditional focus on state, power and national law (Teubner 1997) and highlights the fact that even former imperial powers are now objects of neo-imperialism, exercised primarily by the US, China and TNCs (Bakan 2005). However, globalisation and neoliberalism are multi-faceted, uneven processes, and these characteristics are accentuated by their imbrication with other forces, including those that result from historically specific trajectories, posing problems for generalising about their impact on national professions.

The complex analytics of change are illustrated by contrasting the English profession with that of Northern Italy. As one of the first adopters of the neoliberal policies required by globalised capitalism, the expansion and enrichment of the corporate sector and decline of the private client and 'social service' sectors of the profession in England and Wales took place early and swiftly. By contrast, Italian law firms largely retained their traditional kinship structure and resisted globalising forces (Muzio and Faulconbridge 2013), successfully lobbying governments to obtain re-regulation and protect their jurisdictions (Bellini and Maestripieri 2018). Access to justice offers another instance

---

[14] These processes of fragmentation, inherent in the dynamics of neoliberalism, have been all encompassing, fracturing both social bonds and 'our sense of ourselves as integrated subjects' (Hall 1992: 275). The rich scholarship generated by these 'liquid times' (Bauman 2000) includes concern with their impact on the self – see eg theories of psycho-social fragmentation (Sennett 1999) and the 'extended reflexivity thesis' (Giddens 1990).

[15] Again, however, the differences between jurisdictions must be noted; for instance, in Germany administrative law only started to be systematised in the course of the 1960s and needed at least two decades to develop a dogmatically clear structure.

[16] We are not asserting that lawyers were always distinctively ethical but that their claim to possess particular moral, cultural and intellectual authority was a fundamental component of the professional project and their position in the social order.

of national variation, even within the same region. Whereas generously supported legal aid systems suffered significant cuts (eg in England and Wales and the Netherlands), they either remained stable in other comparable states or were outsourced to private practitioners, through legal expenses insurance providers, and the 'third sector', as in Scandinavia (Hammerslev and Rønning 2018),[17] while in Belgium and Brazil provision was expanded. The differential trajectories of East European states after the fall of communism underscore this patterning of change by both endogenous and exogenous factors (Mrowczynski 2012; Hammerslev 2011) and hence the fallacy of assuming that the importation of capitalist law will naturally generate liberal democratic state forms and professions (Fukuyama 1989: 3).

The impact of globalisation on former colonies (both formal and informal) underscores the fact that the last 30 years have been characterised by continuity as well as change. The articulation of different modalities of power and economic and cultural production is a longstanding feature of the colonial state, where the national space was never unitary even if institutionally constituted as such (Sassen 2006: 381). Indigenous law and the profession were articulated with Western legal and institutional frameworks, developed in the Age of Empire – in those colonies with resources – to support extraction by the West. The current policy of economic penetration has been underpinned by re-colonisation by Anglo-American law and forms of practice and the co-option of indigenous lawyers as negotiators of transnational relationships (Dezalay and Garth 2011). The legal field in the Global South has thus been a key site in the current stage of imperialism and dependency.

However, law's capacity to act as a mechanism for social justice and political contestation (Sinclair 2015) is also evident, as transnational law and legal institutions based on human rights – representing a 'humanist' form of globalisation – have been deployed as counter-hegemonic forces to counteract neo-colonial power hierarchies (Santos and Rodríguez-Garavito 2005), fostering professional political activism. For instance, Ghai (cited in Douglas-Scott 2013: 327) has argued that the universalism and inherent diversity of human rights discourse and legal forms have provided a basis for intercultural dialogues and consensus in post-conflict societies and protection against the state, which sectors of the profession in post-colonial societies have exploited.[18]

Neither globalisation nor neoliberalism can fully account for the development of contemporary professional forms and practices. Technological developments have been fundamental to the processes of neoliberalism and globalisation, including their impact on 'the space of flows' (Castells 1996: 405). Sassen (2006: 378) argues that globalisation's digital networks changed the micro-level features of the state's spatio-temporal

---

[17] The widespread use of insurance schemes to provide access to justice is consistent with the neoliberal ideology of individual responsibility. Furthermore, the pressure to reduce expenditures in these countries is strong, and the move to digitise services is a common solution.

[18] Bolivia's experiment with pluri-national constitutions that accorded the legal systems of subordinated indigenous populations parity with state law appears to illustrate Ghai's contention; however, it is argued that human rights law has been 'colonised' by neoliberal discourses, resulting in a commercial, de-politicised humanism (Douglas-Scott 2013: 298). As a result human rights have been critiqued as a new form of oppression (Barrantes Reynolds 2016). This interpretation is supported by Pue's (1998) argument that American Bar Association and Canadian Bar Association 'missions' to teach the virtues of the rule of law to the Chinese represented neo-colonial agents; see too Gilroy 2004 and Ranciere 2004.

order and that the organisational logic of the global, largely electronic, market circulates through the public domain where it emerges as de-nationalisation. The cumulative effect is to accentuate the incoherence of national society. Correspondingly, technological developments underpinned the reconfiguration of professional work, in particular its decomposition, economisation and commodification (Susskind 2013). This has intensified the stratification of the legal field within and between firms both nationally and internationally, facilitating the consolidation of firms, and the practices of off- and nearshoring, entrenching the dependency of professions in the Global South.

Incomplete transformations from the previous era represent another variable in the processes of change. By 1988 many Western jurisdictions had expanded and (to a degree) democratised their higher education systems, due in part to the Keynesian state's equal opportunity programmes, reinforced by the demands of civil rights movements including anti-racists and second wave feminists,[19] and in part to governments' concern to reconstruct their economic base by building a 'knowledge economy'. While the abandonment of the Keynesian agenda de-politicised this modernising impulse, neoliberal discourses of pure market rationality, together with the demand for professional labour generated by globalisation, furthered the opening of both higher education and the profession across the globe. As a result, from the late 1980s onwards legal professions in the overwhelming majority of jurisdictions expanded and underwent a rapid process of feminisation (Schultz and Shaw 2003; 2013) and, later, the progressive inclusion of other subordinated groups. However, lawyers drawn from 'non-normative'[20] categories have largely been incorporated into the profession as 'semi-professional' adjunct labour (Hagan and Kay 1995; Thornton 1996; Sommerlad and Sanderson 1998; Sommerlad 2016; Wilkins and Gulati 1996; Carbado and Gulati 2000), a role legitimised by the resilience of traditional stereotypes. Evidently, this confounds the argument that markets dissolve traditional social categories and enhance the potential for individual agency and meritocracy (Giddens 1994). Nevertheless, the neoliberal discourse of the classless, post-racial, post-gender society has made diversity a key criterion for establishing the legitimacy of social institutions in many jurisdictions, placing pressure on BigLaw[21] – whose global business depends on an increasingly multicultural client base – to ensure that at least a proportion of these 'outsiders' occupy prominent roles in their firms.

Yet, the counter-hegemonic political movements and thought which developed in the 1960s have not been extinguished and, together with the growing presence of women and those drawn from other non-normative groups (for instance racial minorities in the US), continued, in many jurisdictions, to stimulate radical (explicitly socially embedded) lawyering and scholarship. This has contributed to the erosion of the traditional

---

[19] Although the phrase civil rights is generally associated with the US, here we use it as a shorthand term to describe the democratic wave and counter-hegemonic struggles that swept many parts of the world from the late 1960s – for instance the West German '68er Studentenbewegung', the Prague Spring, the Paris 'événements', and the civil rights movement in Northern Ireland.

[20] Since professions are preeminent 'status groups' – that is, communities based on ideas of proper lifestyles who 'had honour' and were hence owed deference by wider society (Weber 1946: 180) – a common feature has been their relatively homogeneous class, ethnic and gender profile, achieved through closure. We therefore use the term 'non-normative' to refer to the diverse groups which have entered the profession as a result of the changes described in this book; however, we also deploy the term 'outsiders', used by Carbado and Gulati (2013).

[21] Originally a US nickname for the largest firms, now in general usage as a shorthand term for the mega-law firms.

professional paradigm in two ways: first by challenging the material and ideological conditions which support white male dominance of the profession; and second by exposing the artificiality of law's masculinity (Rackley 2009) (and race and class). Similarly, 'political' lawyering, committed to the use of law as a social justice mechanism (Sarat and Scheingold 1998), contributed to the fracturing of a unitary professional paradigm, including its traditional collegial form (Evetts 2014). The resulting fissures have formed part of the more general social and value fragmentation (Bauman 2000; see also Pue 1998; Santos 2000), which, as noted, have been accentuated by neoliberal globalisation.

IV. NEW THEORETICAL TURNS

Since 1988, when neo-Weberian approaches to the profession were dominant, social theorising has taken new turns. Postmodern scepticism (identified by Leicht (2015) as a key factor in the profession's changed status) forms part of a wider epistemological turn away from meta-narratives (Lyotard 1984: xxiv), including, it is argued, the sociology of the professions (Gorman and Sandefur 2011: 281). In its place, stimulated by changes (outlined above) such as those in the profession's structure, markets and demographic profiles, there has emerged a rich scholarship in other fields. For instance, feminist theory since 1988 has made a major contribution to thinking about professions and their role in maintaining the wider status order (Walby 1990; see also Glucksman 1995), underlining such factors as the temporal frame of globalised capitalism (see eg Epstein et al 1999) and how the relationship between 'on-demand' professional practice and the gendered division of labour sustains the patriarchal order. Critical race theory (CRT) (eg Crenshaw 1991) has illuminated the salience of 'race' to law and professional structures and organisational practices, shaping individuals' careers (see eg Payne-Pikus et al 2010; Wilkins and Gulati 1996 on the US legal profession) and reinforcing wider patterns of social stratification. The later embrace by both feminist and CRT scholarship of post-structural insights about the role of language, symbolism, and culture in exclusionary processes sheds light on the role of the law and profession in constituting the meaning of gender and 'race' (Smart 1992; Butler 1990; Ramji 2009; Brubaker 2009).

Contra Gorman and Sandefur's argument, neo-institutionalism is directly concerned with professionalism. Arguing that the general erosion of self-regulation has meant that occupational (professional association) professionalism has been displaced by organisational professionalism, neo-institutionalists focus particularly on large law firms (now more closely resembling other professional services firms than traditional law firms). In this perspective, the market has become a primary regulatory force, and the distinctive actors in the processes of professional identity production are employing organisations. Pointing to the blurring of professional boundaries and hybridity of logics within large law firms, this perspective challenges the classical view of the profession as a discrete, bounded realm (see eg Noordegraaf 2007; Muzio et al 2013). The insight that a range of different logics co-exist within contemporary professions is compatible with Foucauldian perspectives, which focus on the discursive strategies professions use to motivate and control staff 'at a distance'. Contemporary professionalism is thus conceptualised as a disciplinary strategy (Fournier 1999), which realigns individual identities with organisational priorities (Tomlinson et al 2013). This concern with processes of normalisation and subjectification[22] has been deployed in a range of studies (eg Ashley et al 2015) to explore the professional workplace as a site 'where professional identities are mediated, formed and transformed' (Cooper and Robson 2006: 416), producing subjectivities which conform to neoliberal rationality (Newman 2005). And this approach sheds light on how professional closure continues to operate but *within* the profession, as the restructuring of large law firms and the elongation of professional hierarchies have facilitated the confinement of 'outsiders' to lower status labour markets as transient employees (Tomlinson et al 2013).

Another lens for investigating the profession is offered by Bourdieu's theory of social fields (1977a; 1984; 1990). Loosely defined as a structured autonomous social space or network of objective relations between agents and institutions, with rules of practice and logic, a field has its own mechanisms of production and reproduction. The agents in the field are occupied with the meta-issues produced historically in that field and with struggles over the different forms of capital – economic, social, symbolic, and cultural – through which power relations crystallise (Bourdieu and Wacquant 1992: 97). The characteristics of a field are produced and naturalised through its cultural practices, especially actors' interrelationships and struggles over the economy of symbolic goods. Bourdieu's (1987) application of this concept to the profession overcomes the dichotomy between theories that understand it as socially embedded and idealist theories that focus on law's closed, abstract character.[23] The apparent contradiction between law's relative autonomy and its proximity to the field of state power is expressed in and managed by the field's constitution (Arnholtz and Hammerslev 2013), which in turn is determined by its characteristic power relations, modes of communication and social practices, all of which are disciplinarily and professionally defined. This patterning by traditions, pedagogies, discourses, practices, and codes is a major source of law's legitimacy and therefore its power, giving it universal value and performative force (which other expert professions cannot rival) and endowing it with a sacral quality. These qualities also rest on law's autonomy, which is fundamental to rule of law ideology, since it is legal formalism that makes law appear to transcend conflicts of interests. Boundary work between law and society, practitioner and client, is thus intrinsic to the legal field. Both the legitimacy of the legal enterprise and the success of the professional project therefore depend on lawyers' demarcation of the legal as the domain of detachment and rationality, characterised by a logic distinct from either the market or bureaucracy (Freidson 2001), and hence able (apparently) to transcend the favouritism of politics, the corruption of personality, and the exclusiveness of partisanship (Pue 1998). Evidently, the changes which have taken place in the nation state and the legal field since 1988 have made this difficult.

---

[22] These terms are rooted in Foucauldian theory of governmentality, and allude to how the 'subject' is constituted through discourses which normalise asymmetrical power relationships.

[23] In the attempt to overcome this dichotomy, Bourdieu bases his sociology on the fact that the very notion of profession is a 'folk concept', which was uncritically 'smuggled' into sociology; in other words, a 'profession' is neither a natural group of people nor a neutral term. Rather it 'is the *social product* of a historical work of construction of a group and of a *representation* of groups that has surreptitiously slipped into the science of this very group', which is then used to justify its monopoly of certain societal tasks. Moreover, the term hides differences among the members of the profession, whether derived from socio-economic status, gender or race (Bourdieu and Wacquant 1992: 242).

V. REVISITING LAWYERS IN SOCIETY IN A NEW WORLD ORDER

The decision (taken in 2014) to revisit the Abel and Lewis project was stimulated by the unprecedented scale of the material changes of the previous three decades and the theoretical work they inspired, sketched above. However, these developments also accentuated the difficulty of devising a workable concept of profession. Yet, despite the destabilising impact of 30 years of denationalising processes, both national and international socio-economic orders continue to rest on lawyers' traditional function of negotiating the interchange between social relations and law. The legal professions' scientifically grounded form of esoteric but socially useful knowledge (Olgiati 2010) equips them to contribute solutions to the social 'co-ordination problems' (Finnis 1980: 245–52) generated by the increasingly complex structural and functional differentiation characteristic of the new orders. Furthermore, the professions' claim to exercise key social functions remains an active property of the field, while the capacity to perform these functions rests on social recognition (through state certification) of lawyers' special knowledge and fitness to practise (Parsons 1954a; Freidson 1970). We therefore adopted the original project's definition, which was based on functions and credentials. However, the question of definition is a central theme of this project: the contingency of professions and professionalism is related to their shaping by contests over systems of meaning – and their functions and credentials are only one part of these contests.

Our sample comprised 46 jurisdictions, drawn from all over the world. It therefore encompasses countries that have experienced multiple ruptures – from colonialism to independence, communism to capitalism and civilian to military rule – as well as tensions between secular and religious law and authorities, and includes countries drawn from both common and civil law traditions. This variety required us to allow contributors to develop research questions appropriate to their particular jurisdictions, a 'federated' research strategy which, emulating the original project, was grounded in 'the notion that ... comparative work should consist of research separately conducted in different countries, but taking into account common concerns and following common guidelines' (Felstiner 2005b: 1). In order to foster this coherence we therefore also asked all authors to address the following research questions:

- What is the contemporary relationship between the international order, the state, market, civil society and law and lawyers?
- How has this relationship changed over the last 30 years?
- What forces have produced that change?

These generated a number of subsidiary questions related to the developments outlined above. In addition, in order to facilitate comparisons, our authors were asked to include data on certain fundamental issues, such as demographic profile and size of the profession.

As the project progressed through regular meetings at international conferences our contributors raised other themes which their research was disclosing. These included: the capitalisation of firms; their transformation into service industries and penetration by managerialist discourses; the trend to outsourcing and increasing casualisation of the working conditions of many lawyers and increase in paralegal labour; the use of women and other non-normative lawyers as a sub-professional, transient labour force;

the intensification of work; changing modes of regulation; the decline in public deference towards the profession; and an erosion of access to justice (both civil and criminal).[24]

These, then, are some of the issues and themes that contributors to this volume have considered. Some hewed closely to our research agenda, but others followed their own theoretical and empirical interests. We see this as a strength, since it highlights the socio-institutional complexity and contingency of different jurisdictions and the significance of their histories in shaping their articulation with global capital and the reconfiguration of their professions. Yet all the national reports indicate that the forces of globalisation and neoliberalism, together with other macro-level developments such as technological innovations and the disintegration of cultural or national bonds, have ruptured state-centric governance and traditional understandings of lawyers' functions and credentialing. Nevertheless, the data also demonstrate the profession's retention of its socially constitutive role, as activists, moral entrepreneurs and brokers between TNCs and domestic state or private companies (Dezelay and Garth 2011). Much of the data is presented in Richard Abel's conclusion to this volume (2020). In a rich, theorised synthesis of the differences *among* countries (drawn from both the 1988/89 and the current sample), *within* them and *over time*, he focuses on fluctuations in the profession's size, their causes and the profession's response. Considering both supply and demand factors, he analyses the numbers of lawyers; their growing diversity; how they are 'made'; how competition is controlled and the structures of practice (including the decline in solo practice and the increase in the numbers of large law firms). His discussion encompasses variations in policies towards the surge in foreign lawyers as a result of globalisation and the growing competition from non-lawyers. The chapter is another rich contribution to the historically informed structural tradition initiated by Weber.

However, Weber's sociology also engages with rational action and the complex composites of calculative and value rationality, affective and habitual action, which enable actors to make sense of their activities in the social world. The thick descriptions contained in the country reports make this lens for viewing legal professionalism particularly attractive. Together with Geertz's semiotic understanding of culture as, following Weber, a web of inherited conceptions of social relations, institutions and discourses in which everyone is suspended (1973: 89), and Bourdieu's theory of cultural practice, this perspective permits an understanding of the practice of segments of the profession and individual lawyers as counter-hegemonic and value-driven.

In the following discussion based on data from this volume's chapters[25] we bear this perspective in mind, seeking to illuminate aspects of both structural and cultural changes of the last 30 years. While the data underline the fact that there is no typical country, our authors' responses to our research questions disclose patterns resulting from, for instance, shared histories and common legal systems.[26] We identify these patterns by sketching

---

[24] Our methodology is discussed in depth in volume two (Hammerslev and Sommerlad forthcoming).
[25] References to the data chapters are made without full citation beyond the authors' names.
[26] These shared histories and legal systems determined our categorisation of countries, which is thus intended to facilitate comparison (which will be done explicitly by contributors to the second volume and, we hope, encourage readers to do the same). We recognise that all categories are potentially over- and under-inclusive. For instance, Nigeria's legal system could have been placed in the Anglo-American law category; both Asia and North Africa and the Middle East are very diverse.

some of the most striking aspects of the relationship between different geo-political groups of states and the global order, including the periodisation of individual states' embrace of globalisation and neoliberal policies and the primary mechanisms deployed to liberalise their economies and professions. We then discuss the data on corporate law firms, their key role in the processes of globalisation, and the effect of this role both on their structure and logics and on the wider profession, including the relationship between their expansion and the profession's diversification. Finally, we consider how the above changes are crystallised in the legal education field.

VI. THE DATA: VARIATIONS IN IMPACT OF GLOBALISATION

It is notable that the common law world was the vanguard in embracing globalisation and neoliberal policies. The UK[27] and US led the field, due in part to their histories as leading imperialist powers and the consequent dominance of the common law in global transactions and in part to the decline of manufacturing and their tradition of anti-statist ideologies (Gamble 1988; Hartz 1952; Somers 2008), which pre-disposed both states to neoliberal market policies. In economic and cultural conditions increasingly shaped by globalisation, they reconfigured the public realm, promoting individualism and entrepreneurship, furthering the privatisation and marketisation of both national industries and welfare provision, and accelerating the de-regulation of their legal professions. In England and Wales this extended beyond increasing competition among service providers, liberalising fee structures and ending the right to self-regulate: restrictions on law firm ownership were also removed, authorising Alternative Business Structures (ABSs) in which lawyers could practise with non-lawyers. Concurrently, the private client sector was weakened by further dismantling the profession's monopolies, and by 2014 the legal aid sector had been virtually destroyed. Though the US profession has not adopted ABSs,[28] its lawyers have been pivotal in globalising legal practice, creating new arenas of legal conflict, de-regulating economic activity, promoting corporate growth and leading the push to open new markets in areas of rapidly expanding legal business. Australian firms have also been leaders in the new global order, adopting ABSs and establishing law firms as public companies, while the state has cut back and reconfigured welfare. Although the Canadian profession is currently threatened with losing its monopoly over legal services provision and the number of legal outsourcers offering systematised, standardised, or routinised legal services is rising, it has otherwise been slower to adopt neoliberal policies; for instance, the Bar has retained its right to 'unfettered self-regulation' and multi-disciplinary partnerships are virtually non-existent. In Scotland, too, the profession has successfully resisted the extremes of liberalisation adopted in England and Wales, staving

---

[27] The UK comprises three jurisdictions: England and Wales, Scotland, and Northern Ireland; but the Supreme Court of the UK is the final court for interpreting law for all three. The UK government also retains its primacy; however, the limited devolution of power to Scotland and Northern Ireland enabled their governments to pursue less neoliberal policies in some arenas such as higher education and also with regard to the legal services market. Most of the reforms of the English profession, therefore, were not applied to the Scottish profession, which has generally resisted liberalisation. The two jurisdictions are discussed in separate chapters.

[28] Reflecting the conservatism of the non-global/non-international firms which comprise the large bulk of US firms, tend to dominate the ABA, and rely on a deep domestic market.

off the threat of ABSs by stressing the vital importance of professional independence. In all these states progressive policies on some human rights issues (eg LGBTQ[29]) co-exist with the dismantling of collectivist welfare policies.

The statism of the civil law professions and traditions of other Western societies made them initially more resistant to the market imperatives of globalisation. Italy has been described as a case of exceptional resistance. Micellota and Dorian write that its profession's 'most enduring characteristics ... are products [of nineteenth century] institutional upheavals', resulting in a 'complicated relationship between the state, professional associations, and legal professionals'. The political, social and economic traditions of both France and Germany also generated strong resistance to liberalisation and de-nationalisation and the marginalisation of welfare. However, by the end of the twentieth century the reconstruction of capitalism in the absence of colonies – through globalisation and neoliberal policies – had become fundamental to the European Union project, driving the creation of an internal market for legal services and requiring member states to adopt liberalising measures. Bessy and Bastard report the transformation in France of societal rights into conditional benefits, just as the growth of finance capitalism and economic globalisation was making law more procedural and complex and, in tandem with the 'juridification' of social relations and expansion of alternative dispute resolution, increasing the complexity of the types of practice and organisation in law firms. Similar patterns are reported elsewhere in Western Europe. Hammerslev narrates the ideological shift in Scandinavia towards neoliberal policies focused on austerity, financial control, and efficiency, reconfiguring the welfare state through market solutions. Boni-Le Goff et al recount how globalisation and the interdependence of national and international economic regulations have generated dramatic changes in Swiss legal practice, ranging from the ending of regional jurisdictions, the concentration of law firms, new forms of legal practice and competition from other professions, to the internationalisation of corporate management and relative decline in the centrality of lawyers and law graduates in the economic and political spheres. Van Houtte et al describe the growing hegemony of market discourses and de-regulation in Belgium and how the disintegrative impact on the profession mirrors wider social polarisation. Doornbos and de Groot-van Leeuwen comment on the increased hybridity of the Dutch legal services market[30] resulting from mergers and associations of law firms with other legal service providers and the emergence of other service providers (eg accounting firms opening legal departments). By contrast, sole practitioners and small firms are still predominant in Germany, whose profession appears to have resisted 'Europeanisation', largely preserving its 'guild-like' status.

The impact of neoliberal globalisation in other parts of the world suggests that there is *some* validity in the link Fukuyama (1989) posited between free trade and the spread of Western style democracy – or at least a thin version of the rule of law (Raz 1977). Although the predicted 'spillover' between laws designed to produce economic liberalisation has been limited, the data nevertheless suggest that the twin prongs of this stage of

---

[29] LGBTQ: that is lesbian, gay, bisexual and transgender; the Q stands for either queer or questioning.
[30] The description of the Dutch legal services market as increasingly hybrid is broadly applicable to all of the societies described above (and we discuss this in more detail in the next section) and the data suggest that it has even more relevance in other parts of the world.

imperialism – the pressure to open up to global capital combined with a discourse that links capitalist penetration to the rule of law and human rights – have, in some jurisdictions, generated a move towards a more substantive rule of law. Despite the evidence that where democratic measures have been implemented their impact has been relatively superficial, the data suggest that their provision of a vocabulary for contestation has stimulated resistance to state oppression by groups of lawyers, sometimes at risk of severe repression.[31]

The varied nature and impact of liberalisation and globalisation and the relevance of previous power structures are clearly illustrated by the former Soviet bloc's integration into the new global order. The fall of the Soviet Union inaugurated a dramatic intensification of globalised, financialised capitalism, which – as elsewhere – both facilitated great material progress and generated huge levels of economic inequality. Throughout the region, driven in large part by foreign investment in legal assistance projects and the ingress of American and British law firms, domestic lawyers were transformed from Communist Party cadres into independent practitioners, and new Bar associations were established, based on Western organisational models. The commercialisation of legal services in Russia is described as 'intense', leading to a proliferation of unlicensed practitioners who provide their services through commercial entities like limited liability companies and individual enterprises while lacking any professional attributes, such as educational and work credentials, an ethical code, licences, associations, or even a specific title. This swift embrace of the principles of economic rationality, marketisation, and neoliberalism, displacing the principles of equality and solidarity, also characterised Serbia, whose 1988 Law on Advocacy created a marketised legal profession, thereby transforming it into an independent field based on new logics and practices. The change to a market based system in Poland is depicted as having been a huge challenge. For many lawyers it marked the beginning of a boom period with an increased need for their services, leading to a significant increase in the number of qualified lawyers and the supply of legal services. For others, however, it entailed a transition to another legal profession or even an end to their legal careers. Access to justice is also extremely limited, with the free legal aid serving less than 3 per cent of eligible citizens in its first year.

Although independent judiciaries and other rule of law features were adopted throughout the region, these reforms have been largely subverted (eg in Poland, following the election of the Law and Justice party). Moreover, the kleptocratic setting into which Western legal forms were sometimes introduced (eg in Russia) has facilitated the use of law as an instrument not simply of capitalist development but also of dispossession. The Czech Republic provides another illustration of how insertion into the global system generated unregulated and highly predatory forms of capitalism and legal practice. Its high inward rates of return swiftly attracted foreign investment, leading to the privatisation of the entire economic and property sector as well as the bailiff's profession. The vigour with which bailiffs now pursue debt collection is reported to be exacerbating the

---

[31] See eg Koskenniemi 2005. This emphasis on the Janus face of law – which does not simply mystify and apologise for power, but also holds out the promise of constraining it – echoes EP Thompson's description of the rule of law as an 'unqualified human good' (1975). The law's ambivalence is mirrored in the contradictory yet symbiotic relationship between the profession's 'aptness for justice' (Green 2008) and the fact that it is a commercial and status project.

vulnerability of private citizens resulting from the dismantling of the formerly extensive welfare system.

There are parallels between the adjustments made in the former Soviet bloc following its opening to the global economy and those adopted in China and Vietnam (which remain communist). The revival in 1980 of the Chinese legal profession, based on the Soviet model, made all lawyers state employees. However, from the late 1980s to 1999 the Chinese Bar was transformed into an almost fully private profession. As in Russia, modernisation and economic growth rather than political liberalism drove the reforms. Restrictions on handling 'Chinese legal affairs' limited foreign law firms' expansion, stimulating the development of local firms, and the lawyer population virtually tripled between 2000 and 2017. However, politically embedded lawyers continue to enjoy significant advantages in their practice, including greater business opportunities. It is anticipated that the 'Belt and Road Initiative' (launched in the mid-2010s) will mean that more Chinese law firms will become global. In Vietnam, the impact of increasing integration into the global economy on demand for legal services and law's role in state governance led to some institutional restructuring, including constitutional reform and commitments to human rights. Nevertheless, as in China, the party-state retained leadership of economic, political and legal institutions.

This state-centric model of development is the norm throughout the region; one of its primary functions is to manage the articulation of two apparently contradictory modalities of social relations: pre-modern, patron-client relations of reciprocity (such as *guanxi*), manifest in the significance of political embeddedness, and the development of Anglo-American style professions and rule of law reforms. The Indonesian profession is exemplary: on one hand, globalisation has promoted human rights, stimulating public interest litigation and civil society organisations while also generating the growth of the sector that serves the globalised world of investment, business and finance; on the other, the traditional 'fixer who cares little about law and uses any means, including bribes and thugs, to resolve the client's problem' remains a feature of the profession. Kouwagam and Bedner present this divide as characteristic of developing countries – although, as the reports indicate, it has various manifestations. Myanmar has also seen both the emergence of lawyers who advocate for rule of law and social reforms (thereby risking imprisonment, physical harm and death) and, following the shift to a market economy in 2011, the establishment of the first generation of commercial lawyers and a corporate law market, which is described as the most crowded and least regulated market in Southeast Asia. South Korea's incorporation into the US informal empire shaped its globalising policies from the 1980s, leading to the importation of American legal professionalism and consequent modification of traditional legal professions. At the same time, lawyers' sense of social responsibility and commitment to the rule of law and human rights were stimulated by the 'candlelight revolution' against state authoritarianism: lawyers played pivotal roles, helping citizens understand the constitution and impeachment process and challenging those lawyers more closely aligned with state power.

The persistence of (layers) of Western legal imports also provides the basis for anti-authoritarian struggles even while they mould legal fields in the interests of global capitalism. Hong Kong exemplifies this pattern, which is found in other non-Western parts of the world. 'Foreign' or expatriate lawyers have long dominated Hong Kong; today increasing numbers are Hong Kong people, as China's booming economy shapes the evolution of the profession, inducing its glocalisation.[32] Although Thailand was never a formal colony, its early economic development was shaped by foreign domination, including the establishment of international firms (the first in 1894) by Western-trained foreign lawyers. This pattern of foreign ownership has persisted but in partnership with Thai lawyers and there has been a shift in international legal services towards Asia. The influence of the World Bank and IMF on Thailand's adoption in the 1990s of liberalisation and modernisation reforms highlights the imperialist role played by transnational entities in the Global South.[33]

Japan's trajectory is distinctive. US pressure in the early 1980s to liberalise and open its legal services market to American lawyers was resisted until the late 1990s, when the economy, especially finance, was deregulated. The increased demand for business lawyers led to a rise in the number of practising attorneys. By contrast, India was an early adopter of economic market reforms (1991), which made 'the Indian economy one of the fastest growing in the world'. Ballaskrishnen's description of the reshaping of the legal profession emphasises lawyers' centrality to this process:

> The dramatic expansion of international trade and transactions, an essential by-product of this liberalisation, required new laws and regulations and, consequently, lawyers to implement them ... [O]ver the last three decades, India has seen the burgeoning of both new kinds of legal practice and new kinds of lawyers who could perform such transactions.

Many of the features and patterns of development described above – including the emergence of an external facing corporate/commercial/international sector and of human rights lawyers, and the struggles between those who challenge the state versus those who are politically embedded – characterise other non-Western states. For instance, our group of North African and Middle Eastern countries generally exhibit the co-existence of Western style professions and jurisprudence with Islamic systems and the conjunction of strong authoritarian states (albeit now collapsed in Libya), a profession that lacks autonomy, and close relationships between ruling powers and the state. The colonial legacy which marks this region is of course most evident in Palestine's subordination to Israeli control. Its mixed legal system comprises Jordanian law in the West Bank, largely derived from the Egyptian/French legal system, and British law in Gaza with some Egyptian-influenced legislation. This legal pluralism, professional factionalism, and the physical separation of the two regions delayed the emergence of a Palestinian Bar Association until 1999. A free trade agreement with the EU and the presence of some international firms, including major banks, link Palestine with the global capitalist order. There is also a strong global non-governmental organisation (NGO) presence, closely connected to the Muslim Brotherhood and including European countries' aid agencies.

Mixed legal systems deriving from the colonial past also co-exist with Sharia courts in Libya, Iran and Egypt. Libya exemplifies the pattern found in other resource rich economies, where the demand for lawyers generated by multi-national domination of the

---

[32] For further discussion of the concept of glocalisation, see Bauman 1998.

[33] As noted throughout this chapter, while the growth of international organisations was and continues to be posited as integral to the ongoing process of modern state construction on a broadly Western model, others conceptualise it as an extension of colonial domination, the latest form of imperialism (see eg Koskenniemi 2001; Pahuja 2011).

extractive sector unleashed a (limited) process of modernisation and secularisation of the legal profession, eroding the dominance of the Sharia courts in civil, criminal and family cases. However, Gaddafi's nationalist and socialist policies and consequent ambivalence towards Western-style modernisation and, by extension, 'modern' legal professions, generated contradictory policies, which included nationalising the profession in 1981. As a result, the domestic legal services market dramatically expanded and continued to grow during the final decade and a half of the Gadafi regime, despite subsequent relaxation of the nationalisation policy. The concurrent rise in international investment following the lifting of sanctions led to a massive boom for firms serving the oil industry, dividing them from the mass of lawyers representing domestic clients.

The struggle in Egypt between secularism and Islam and the relapse into authoritarian rule following the demise of the Arab Spring have affected the legal profession. As elsewhere in the region, Egypt's legal system is a hybrid and its profession polarised between generalist private practitioners and the small minority of elite lawyers employed by American and British firms established after the 1980s privatisation reforms. However, relatively strong civil society traditions have generated human rights activity supported by humanist globalisation (for instance, the Center for Human Rights Legal Aid depends mainly on foreign funding). Human rights NGOs engage in disputes over labour and social and economic rights, and their lawyers suffer harassment and restrictions on their freedom of expression. The divisions within the profession (intensified by the increased power of the Muslim Brotherhood) are illustrated by the Bar association's failure to defend these lawyers or protect human rights, despite the association's long history of confrontation with the government in defence of the rule of law.

Tunisia's colonial legacy includes its French civil law system and secular tradition: Sharia courts are used only in some family cases. The tension between the liberal tendencies inherent in French law and the Ben Ali regime's authoritarianism stimulated the divisions found elsewhere in the global South between politically embedded lawyers who had enjoyed a virtual monopoly of state litigation, lawyers seeking to enlarge their market share based on their expertise, lawyers engaged in defensive cause lawyering (eg to end torture and protect workers' rights), and a small group specialising in commercial law, acting for American and European professionals who cannot settle in Tunisia or plead before Tunisian courts.

Islamisation of laws and legal institutions was a priority following the 1979 Iranian revolution: the new Constitution required all laws to be consistent with 'Islamic criteria', and the judiciary was replaced by Islamic jurists and clerics. After the end of the war with Iraq, repression of human rights and attacks on lawyers diminished, and defendants were granted the right to representation, though not necessarily by a qualified lawyer. The profession struggled to remain a civil society organisation, as clerics have repeatedly attempted to subordinate it to the Ministry of Justice. Nevertheless, a few corporate law firms exist, operated by small groups of international lawyers who are often educated and trained abroad, associated with foreign international law firms and deal exclusively with shipping and international trade law.

In Turkey, rapid economic liberalisation after 1983 was accompanied by the reorganisation and further centralisation of the state apparatus but also a growth of civil society; and the new century saw the most comprehensive legal reform since the early Republican period. Turkey's bid for EU membership generated further democratic and market reforms, liberalising rules on advertising and opening the profession to competition in dispute resolution processes. However, Erdogan's incremental authoritarianism and the erosion of state-imposed secularism and rise in threats to judicial independence since 2009 have increasingly provoked clashes between the state and the legal profession.

While Israel's legal system is also a hybrid and includes Ottoman jurisprudence, it most closely resembles English common law. The country's wealth and advanced technology, intimate links with the US, and colonising policies make it unique in the region. However, its exceptionalism also rests on strong social democratic traditions that have made public interest lawyering an important part of the profession's identity.

The influence of history on the response to and relationship with global capital and neoliberal policies is also evident in Latin America, which is again characterised by mixed legal systems (generally borrowed from continental traditions and, more recently, the US), weak civil society institutions, and the importance of patronage. For instance, Böhmer explains how judicial careers in Argentina involve an ongoing exchange of favours, which are later translated into such privileges as the capacity to influence the appointment of law officers. Democratic and rule of law reforms have been impeded by US informal colonialism and military dictatorship; yet these reforms have also stimulated strong human rights movements, exemplified by participation in international instruments such as the Inter-American Convention on Human Rights. The transformation of the Argentinian political system following the end of the dictatorship in 1983 was particularly legal, constitutional, and lawyerly, generating corresponding changes in the profession and the law, including the nature, scope and litigation of rights. Public interest law clinics were established in Argentina, as they have been in Chile following its liberalisation over the last two decades, similarly transforming lawyers into spokespersons on rights issues. In Brazil, too, there has been an increase in rights groups and greater access to justice, delivered through the Office of Public Defender and the expansion of small claims courts.

However, globalisation's impact on the (legitimation) crisis of democracy is also reported: the growing importance of extra-national rule creation and enforcement has multiplied the loci within which legal professionals may act but simultaneously limited the regulatory capacity of domestic democratic institutions by allowing external deliberation. Bilateral and multilateral agreements in the areas of international trade and foreign investment under the aegis of transnational agents (World Bank, IMF, WTO, etc) have furthered this globalisation of public policy issues and consequent subversion of national sovereignty. In Mexico, for instance, GATT and NAFTA acted as constitutional substitutes for democratically elected political bodies, enforcing techno-political programmes, reinforcing dependent, subaltern relations with the US and Canada and opening Mexico to the global economy. As occurred elsewhere, liberalisation policies extended to the legal profession, leading to expansion, diversification and polarisation. Chile offers the most striking example of the region's dependent relationship with the US; as the testing ground for Chicago School economics under the Pinochet dictatorship, it occupied the vanguard of the neoliberal revolution and globalisation. The 1980s boom, based on mass privatisations and the ingress of numerous international investors, encouraged the development of large firms on the US model. By contrast, Brazil began liberalising and privatising its economy in the 1990s; thereafter, growing demand from TNCs for specialised legal knowledge initiated a rapid expansion of both the domestic profession and international law firms. The history of Venezuela and its legal profession resembles that of other

Latin American states in its asymmetrical relationships with global capital, oligarchic politics and struggles for democracy. As in Brazil, the abundance of natural resources led to an influx of TNCs and mega law firms in the 1990s. However, the intensification of inequality following the 'Oil Opening', together with human rights violations, led to the 1989 riots and, ultimately, the election of Hugo Chávez in 1998. The early promise of structural reform degenerated into an increasingly uncertain institutional landscape accentuating the need to 'know who' in order to conduct legal work. The legal profession (which, as elsewhere, has undergone, a dramatic expansion) extended along a spectrum from the international corporate sector to human rights lawyers and 'revolutionary lawyers' produced by government-sponsored law schools, and large numbers of Venezuelan lawyers have left the country.

Our African sample was also characterised by the co-existence of Western systems of law (facilitating the persistence of asymmetrical relationships with global capital) and traditional dispute resolution processes in 'a fabric of pluralism' (Aiyedun and Ordor 2016). In South Africa the role played by a handful of lawyers in the struggle against apartheid exemplifies the split between law's functional significance for capitalism and the state and its capacity to act as a tool for and symbol of social justice (Abel 1995). However, the inequalities stemming from prioritising the drive to meet the demands of the global economy are mirrored in the divisions within the legal profession between the corporate and private client sectors. The failure to fulfil the post-apartheid promise of social democracy has stimulated the current de-colonisation movement, which includes greater efforts to diversify the profession.

The trajectories of the legal professions of Zimbabwe, Nigeria, Ghana and Kenya have been shaped by a range of factors. These encompassed indigenisation as governments sought to create national professions; oscillations between dictatorship and moves to establish liberal democratic institutions and the rule of law; political manipulation and patronage to control and destabilise Bar associations, causing intense internal friction and reducing lawyers' moral authority; and the significance of both human rights and economic globalisation. For instance, the Zimbabwean report highlights the impact of the 'democratic wave' that supplanted military regimes, personal dictatorships, and one-party states across Africa in the 1990s and how this, together with the increased legitimacy and currency of human rights discourse, led to the rise of lawyers' organisations focused on human rights. Lawyers also engaged in human rights struggles in Nigeria when, in the first decades following independence, the military harassed and detained them even while recognising their potential to legitimise military rule. The Kenyan postcolonial experience is also characterised by tensions between championing justice and the rule of law on one hand and the 'bread and butter issues' that require lawyers to respond to market forces and globalisation on the other. The unregulated nature of globalisation and the mixed benefits for the domestic profession are illustrated by the Nigerian report: while TNCs import legal services from international law firms (without regard for municipal licensing laws), this activity has nevertheless spawned a domestic corporate sector. In Ghana,[34] globalising policies date from early 2000, although President Nkrumah warned against

---

[34] JJ Dawuni (2017) 'Lawyers in Ghana', presented at the International Meeting on Law and Society, Mexico City.

this new imperialism as early as 1970. Dawuni recounts how neoliberalism and globalisation shaped the Ghanaian legal corporate sector, establishing a symbiotic (junior partner, subaltern) relationship with the growing numbers of multinational law firms, since, as in Nigeria, foreign lawyers cannot practise in Ghana.

Burundi offers an extreme example of the trends that characterise the legal field in the Global South. Dezalay explains how external interests and interventions have produced a patrimonial state built on ethnic affiliation and extraversion. She shows how this (typically colonial) intensely bureaucratic state contributed to the rising demand for lawyers and how massacres, wars and dictatorship generated formidable investment by NGOs from the mid-1990s, focused on reforming a justice sector seen as both a root cause of the 1993 massacres and a potential vector for peace and development. As a result, the domestic market suffers from 'a double bind: dependent on and vulnerable to the volatile demand from international donors and organisations and weakened as a buffer between international diplomacy and a repressive government'. Dezalay's conclusion, which highlights the ambivalence of human rights interventions (and see eg Sinclair 2015), applies – as she notes – elsewhere in the Global South:

> the coupling of structural adjustment policies and political liberalisation echoed the contradictory dimensions of the impact of neoliberal globalisation found elsewhere in the world ... while opening the possibility of a domestic space for human rights activism attuned to the international market for human rights, liberal reforms in Burundi also deepened the capacity of the state to shape and neutralise political opposition.

VII. ETHOS, LOGICS AND NEW INSTITUTIONAL AND SOCIAL STRUCTURES

As the above summary of the data indicates, international corporate law firms are primary engines of economic globalisation. They also act as vectors of cultural imperialism, transmitting neoliberalism's market dogma and thereby, as Thornton and Wood note, profoundly affecting the structure of private legal practice, shifting its logics from professionalism (denoted as lawyers' work autonomy, collegiality and public service) to profit maximisation, accentuating law's business orientation, and generating its re-organisation according to contractual relationships or managerial hierarchies. The profession's expansion and diversification are also related to this transformation. However, as the above outline of the data indicates, the degree and pace of the impact on private practice is highly variable, and change is also driven by other forces (such as the increasing complexity of society). Furthermore, some of the traditional claims of professionalism are still invoked by BigLaw (Muzio and Faulconbridge 2013). In this section we sketch the expansion of BigLaw and then consider some of the challenges this poses for traditional professionalism.

Thirty years ago, BigLaw was a US phenomenon (Abel 1989), but in 2015 just four of the world's ten largest firms were US based. Nevertheless, US law firms were critical in furthering US imperialism, as Murayama's reference to Americanisation illustrates. He recounts the demand in the early 1980s that Japan open its legal services market to US firms and how, following adoption in the late 1990s of deregulation policy, large

Anglo-American firms established offices in Tokyo. This pattern is repeated across the world. For example, global firms led by Baker McKenzie entered the Russian market as soon as the borders were opened. Corporate law firms operated by small groups of international lawyers (often educated or trained abroad and associated with foreign international law firms, and dealing exclusively with shipping and international trade law) exist even in Iran, as noted above.

This global dominance depended on the dramatic expansion of US and UK corporate firms over the last 30 years: by 2015, the UK corporate legal services sector accounted for more than two fifths of total turnover of the UK legal services market and included firms with over 550 partners worldwide, half of whose lawyers work outside the UK. While there are fewer international mega law firms in other Western countries (constraining the impact these firms have had on those legal markets), the twenty-first century did see their numbers increase: for example, by 2016, eight law firms in Canada had over 500 lawyers, two of which are merged with foreign firms, and the Netherlands (which has a long tradition of international firms) had 13 law offices with 100 or more lawyers, the largest with 301.

However, the growth of international corporate firms in China, reflecting its extraordinary economic boom, is now outpacing growth in the US, UK and other Western nations. The restriction on foreign lawyers handling Chinese legal affairs and practising Chinese law has supported this expansion. By the mid-2010s, there were Chinese megafirms (modelled on UK and US global firms) with thousands of lawyers, and Liu describes how this expansion has continued in the years since then. For instance, in 2012 an elite Chinese law firm with more than a thousand lawyers announced a merger with a large Australian law firm with 800 lawyers, creating King & Wood Mallesons, and in 2015, Dacheng made an alliance with the global law firm Dentons, creating the largest law firm in the world with over 7,000 lawyers and more than 100 offices around the globe. With the launch of the Belt and Road initiative, China is now a major rival to Western-centric imperialism.

The ingress of international mega-law firms has stimulated the development or expansion of domestic corporate firms, which then work in partnership with BigLaw and shape the host state's integration into the global system. Protectionist regulation requiring foreign-owned firms to refer litigation to the domestic profession (as in China) is in weaker states either being diluted or abandoned (as in Thailand) or circumvented, entrenching the 'comprador' status of their firms. For instance, large foreign law firms (mainly from Austria) operate in Serbia through partnerships with domestic offices, which are *de facto* (if not *de jure*) their country offices. Nigerian firms subcontract unfamiliar subject matters to overseas law firms and then superficially comply with the Local Content Law requirement by rubber-stamping their work. Domestic firms are also used as sources of cheap labour, receiving outsourced projects from global law firms. Nevertheless, even junior partner corporate firms occupy a different domain from the rest of the national profession, which everywhere is divided into two hemispheres (Heinz and Laumann 1982: 319 ff; Galanter and Palay 1991: 1), exemplifying the dependent development that results from the spatially and temporally uneven processes and outcomes characteristic of, and functional to, global capitalism (Gregory et al 2009).

A. Impact on Structure, Logics and Coherence of the Profession

Many reports describe how Anglo-American law firms have acted as conduits for a new form of profession: for example, Indonesian firms have adopted the Cravath model,[35] and Hammerslev notes the influence exercised on Danish firms by the ABA, lawyers who had worked in the US, management consultants and legal economists. Descriptions of the (interlinked) features of this new form of profession (such as the intensification of work, a commercial ethos, specialisation and technicisation,[36] the commoditisation of legal services, loss of autonomy, routinisation and stratification) recur throughout the data. Villalonga (describing Chile) writes of the departmentalisation of competences and the employment of large numbers of salaried lawyers and non-lawyers, facilitating the provision of services through scale economies.[37] Bonelli and Fortes similarly comment on the repetitive mass litigation of small claims in Brazil and note that it is accelerating the casualisation of professional labour. New regulatory forms – such as computational methods based on top down standardised procedural grids for assessing quality through algorithms and information technology – underpin these industrialising and de-professionalising processes. The displacement of the professional doxa of expertise and contextual knowledge, tailored to complexity and variability, by technicised, standardised knowledge is facilitated by new technology, and in many Western jurisdictions (eg England and Wales; the Netherlands) by the colonisation of the public sector by managerialism and penetration of the public realm by entrepreneurial discourses.

Evidently, traditional professionalism is also eroded by specialisation. As a key way in which professional expertise is becoming unbundled, specialisation compromises the ideal of equal professional competence and claim to mastery of the whole field. This in turn erodes the profession's capacity to establish and maintain the confidence of its clients, the state, and overlapping professions, thereby challenging the profession's legitimacy and ethics (Moorhead 2010). Specialisation also contributes to the field's internal differentiation, and hence its ongoing fragmentation. However, again there are wide variations in the extent to which specialisation is taking place; for instance, the data suggest that it is more marked in Germany than in England and Wales.

The threat to the profession's coherence posed by specialisation has been intensified by the incremental juridification of societies as a consequence of their increasing differentiation. Kalem illustrates this development in Turkey by pointing to the creation of specialised jurisdictions like consumer courts.[38] In England and Wales, juridification

---

[35] In the early twentieth century, the Cravath firm hired graduates from top universities on the understanding that they might progress to partnership after an extended probationary period (during which they would be assigned to a partner and/or specialised practice) or would leave (Galanter and Palay 1991).

[36] Technicisation is the shorthand term used in adult education to describe the shift to training professionals to perform their jobs as 'lifelong learning technicians', effectively renouncing the humanistic, critical and transformative dimensions of their work (see eg Broek et al 2010). See too Caserta and Madsen's (2019) discussion of how the processes of change associated with digitalisation are further accelerating the economisation and commodification of the practice of law.

[37] Though this is not always true; for instance the trend in Germany to specialised boutique firms is found elsewhere.

[38] Although the creation of multiple specialised courts in other substantive areas, such as family, juvenile, small claims and patent, is a longstanding and widespread feature of legal development, as society itself becomes more complex.

has greatly expanded (and differentiated) the legal services market and, together with liberalisation measures, exposed the profession to competition from non-lawyers, eg will writers. In France, lawyers also face competition from 'law-related' practitioners and accountants. In Russia, as in many other civil law countries, rather than a single profession, there are several discrete legal occupations administered by different agencies and following different professional rules, as well as practitioners who have no legal qualifications, all of whom compete in the legal services market. Other reports (eg Germany) focus on the emergence of highly specialised boutique law firms. In the US the last 20 years have also seen this development, as both the number of firms and types of expertise offered have grown: small groups of elite lawyers leave big firms to set up lower-priced, lower-overhead specialty shops, sometimes trading income for greater control over hours, fewer disqualifying conflicts of interest, and less formal work environments. Boutiques challenge large firm dominance in practice areas such as real estate, information technology, intellectual property licensing, defence-side employment, trial work, and complex litigation. Another developing form of practice, described in the Australian report, is termed NewLaw and entails remote-working technology, replacing the billable hour with alternative pricing structures, such as fixed pricing or risk-reward billing, and utilising cloud-based computing and storage systems, together with task-oriented apps.

The concentration of the new mega-law firms and their domestic corporate partners in one or two large (global) cities (and particular zones within those cities) represents a further dimension of professional polarisation and fragmentation. This pattern mirrors the generally uneven concentration of economic activity and wealth which has followed the 'unbundling' of the nation state (Urry 1989; Sassen 1999). The de-nationalisation of domestic corporate firms is also illustrated by their external referent; the decreased relevance of national professional codes of conduct (Loughrey 2011) and the firms' focus on international rather than national law creation – even while, as noted above, much of the law they practise remains national. This spatial concentration of the corporate sector is widely reported; for instance, in South Africa it is primarily located in Johannesburg, with the six largest firms (each employing 250–600 lawyers) based in the suburb of Sandton. In Zimbabwe, both corporate and private law practices are concentrated in the two main towns: 263 law firms are based in Harare and 41 in Bulawayo, while the other 111 firms are spread among 26 towns and cities. In Brazil, the growing presence of international law firms is concentrated in São Paulo and Rio de Janeiro. While China's size and the vibrancy of its regional economies mean that at least four or five cities boast a corporate legal sector, in many rural counties in western China non-lawyers are the main providers of legal services. The split in the Indonesian profession is more profound than those in most other jurisdictions. At one extreme is the modern corporate law firm in South Jakarta, whose professionals deal mainly with large foreign clients and operate according to international standards, serving the globalised world of investment, business and finance; at the other are the 'fixers', who deal with corrupt bureaucracies, incomplete registers, and inconsistent laws.

The mass ingress of women represents a further way in which the profession is fragmenting. Over the course of the last 30 years, the demographic profile of virtually all the professions in our sample has gone from being largely male to being diverse and in some jurisdictions, majority female. However, while in many jurisdictions women have developed professional niches to suit their needs there is nevertheless an intricate reciprocal relationship between this numerical feminisation (and, to a lesser extent, ethnic diversification) of law graduates and practitioners and the profession's need for more labour, the de-composition of professional work, and its re-constitution into a number of hierarchically organised tasks. This relationship is reflected in the elongation of professional structures to facilitate this new mode of professional production and the disproportionate placement of women and other non-normative practitioners in lower level professional strata. The reconfiguration of professional work through the processes of standardisation and specialisation discussed above make possible this occupational segmentation and segregation; 'low value' work is allocated to different strata through outsourcing, on-shoring, subcontracting and the use of 'contract' lawyers on zero hours, fixed-term contracts. The reports overwhelmingly indicate that women (regardless of intersections with other identity categories) and, more recently, lawyers not drawn from the jurisdiction's dominant ethnic group and those from lower socio-economic groups are over-represented in the lower status specialisms in the large corporate firms and also in small, less profitable forms of practice. For instance: the execution of routine tasks in Brazilian corporate firms is highly feminised; while Chilean women have increased their participation in practice, they have not gained an equal share in the higher positions; the Belgian professional culture is described as deeply masculine; and the US report points to ongoing disparities in compensation, barriers to partnership, and higher exit rates from the profession, all of which they attribute to organisational structures and biases favouring men's success in private practice. However, women's increased presence has led some sectors of the profession in some jurisdictions (eg England and Wales) to develop diversity and inclusion initiatives designed to support caring responsibilities. Nevertheless, the data point to a number of mechanisms that enforce gendered divisions and serve to legitimate them, such as the impact of work intensification on work-life balance, which complements the concern with and maintenance of 'natural' gender roles (in Zimbabwe private practice is deemed too demanding for women), reinforced by breadwinner ideologies (Switzerland). There is also evidence of bullying and sexual harassment (eg South Korea; China; Australia; US), racism (eg England and Wales and the US), and misrecognition of class affinity as merit (eg England and Wales).

The profession is also fragmented in that alongside the corporate law firms there remains, in most societies, a predominance of small practices and/or sole practitioners, complicating the picture of BigLaw dominance.[39] The size of this sector is related to several factors, including a country's culture (this type of practice is traditional in many societies – eg Germany, Italy, and Tunisia) and the resilience of the private client market (related in turn to juridification). The commercialisation and consequent growth of legal education and individuals' social mobility projects have also led to a proliferation of lawyers (Katvan et al 2016), many of whom cannot find employment with the big firms. In South Africa nearly 40 per cent of attorneys practise alone; in England and Wales in 2016, 86 per cent of firms had fewer than five partners, and sole practitioners were the largest category of firms; in the US, 63 per cent of private practitioners work in very small firms (1–5 lawyers); in Canada in 2014, about three-quarters of all establishments

---

[39] Although not all sole practitioners practise alone; in some jurisdictions (eg England and Wales) some sole partners will preside over firms with other qualified lawyers/employees.

of lawyers and notaries with employees were 'micro' sized, with one to four employees; in Italy, where a substantial number of lawyers may never practise, only 4.7 per cent of lawyers work in firms of more than 10, while the majority are in studios of 6–8, and the kinship structure of business persists. In Denmark in 1998, more than a third of the nearly 1,800 law firms were solo practitioners, and only one per cent had more than 50 employees. In Tunisia, almost 90 per cent of lawyers are self-employed generalists representing individual clients and, to a lesser degree, enterprises; the few law firms (about 100 in 2010) containing 5 per cent of the Bar were often composed of just two or three lawyers, sometimes belonging to the same family, three-quarters of those firms with 1–4 employees. In Palestine, most lawyers practise alone, although some belong to firms, groups or companies; only 12 law offices are formally registered.

Cummings et al prefer to describe the contemporary US profession as 'disaggregated' rather than 'fragmented', arguing that this term better captures the differentiated impact of globalisation, technological innovation, and neoliberalism. Their argument – that this professional disaggregation mirrors the disintegrative impact of these forces on society and its occupational structures, creating a significant growth in inequality since the 1970s – applies to many other jurisdictions. However, as indicated above, the resulting fissures are cultural as well as structural. Commercialisation challenges the classical view of the profession as a discrete, bounded realm, a distinct occupational form with unique advantages over markets and business, and a value system that socialises new professionals and maintains, stabilises and legitimises the normative order of the state. Resistance to commercialisation features in several reports; for instance, in Brazil there is competition between traditional and new business elites. Boni-Le Goff et al recount how a declaration that law firm incorporation was compatible with the principle of lawyers' independence exposed opposing visions of the profession in Switzerland. Other reports (eg Belgium) focus on concerns about the impact of the contractual relationships and managerial hierarchies which characterise highly stratified forms of practice on traditional collegiality and practitioners' capacity to exercise discretion in decision-making and hence control the content of their labour. Bessy and Bastard reflect on the ways in which the collegial organisation and social networks enabled by the *Ordre Professionnel* encouraged cooperation among lawyers, essential to the development and consolidation of high professional standards, and how competition is eroding this positive externality and widening the divide between the business law and traditional Bars. The challenge posed by neoliberal regulatory regimes to traditional legal professionals in dispute resolution processes in Turkey is also framed as a threat to their values. Kalem's account of how these regimes have entailed the introduction of a more 'complex system of rules whose legality is more often than not assessed in terms of its technicality and only secondarily in terms of metaphysical legal concerns such as justice and legitimacy' echoes our earlier discussion of the displacement of creative professional expertise by technicised, standardised knowledge.

But variations in the patterns and time frames of and resistance to the dissolution of traditional forms of professionalism are also visible. For instance, Micellotta and Dorian note that while Italian business law firms have started advocating for changes in organisational forms and professional rules in order to maintain their international competitiveness, Bar associations and other institutions constrain change by shaping professional practices and structures, successfully obstructing multiple attempts by governments since 1994 to update and reform the codes, rules, and practices that regulate lawyers. The complex motivations behind these conflicts, the class struggles that underpin them and their relationship to different visions of the future and the power to make law are captured by Banakar and Ziaee's description of Iran as:

> a clash between two legal cultures over the most valuable symbolic capital of the juridical field – the authority to determine the law – grounded in political conflicts between reformist political groups seeking the separation of state and religion and supporters of the hierocracy. What is at stake is no less than the future of Iranian modernity ... Our IBA attorneys are agents in the juridical field, competing with the judiciary for the 'monopoly of the right to determine the law' .... But they are also members of the middle class and the intellectual elite in Iranian civil society – a segment that continues to argue for the rule of law in a country organised under clerical rule in accordance with Islamic ideology.

VIII. LEGAL EDUCATION AND STATE (RE-)CONFIGURATIONS

Since lawyers' capacity to perform key social functions rests on socially recognised certification of their special knowledge and fitness to practise, possession of credentials was one of the components of our working definition of profession. The key role played by legal education in the production and reproduction of social hierarchies and the conceptions and categorisations of professionals is underscored by the reciprocal and recursive relationship between changes in the educational field and the transformations of traditional professionalism generated by neoliberalism, globalisation and technological innovations.

The majority of chapters report a massive expansion of legal education. This is driven in part by governments' recognition of the centrality of the knowledge economy to success in the global order and in part by law's market appeal as an avenue of social mobility. Furthermore, because law degrees are cheap to deliver, they are very attractive to profit oriented higher education institutions. Expansion has therefore not only taken the form of increases in the numbers of public law schools but also has generated substantial private sectors. For instance, the 'virtually unstoppable demand for law places' in Australia has resulted in 40 law schools, several of which are private, serving a population of less than 25 million.

This increase in private legal education, facilitated by higher education deregulation and marketisation, is reported elsewhere. For instance in Mexico in 1970, 5,953 students were taking advanced law degrees; by 2003, they numbered 139,669. Russia offers an extreme illustration of unregulated private provision: any university can launch a law programme, and two-thirds of law students pursue their degrees through correspondence courses involving minimal classroom attendance. Alongside this 'Wild West education', mirroring the disaggregation of the profession, is the separate system for state legal professionals and other lawyers (for example, law schools whose students are trained specifically to work for law enforcement agencies).

This disaggregation is widespread, but its form varies. For instance, in Chile the types of school are shaped not only by the range of markets (affecting enrolments, whether classes are day or evening, quality of the professoriate and socio-economic background of the students) but also by traditional political or religious affiliations: the Universidad La

República is linked to the Masonic movement and Universidad ARCIS to the Communist Party. The significance of tradition in legal education is evident elsewhere. For instance, Kober describes how Czech students are overwhelmed by historical and theoretical disciplines including legal history, Roman law, legal theory, and legal philosophy. The Turkish curriculum is highly positivistic and doctrinal, despite recent (cautious) ventures into private legal education. Nevertheless, in general classical models of education have been or are being eroded. In many jurisdictions this erosion was originally driven by the egalitarianism generated by the 1960s/70s civil rights struggles – for instance, in the Netherlands, Latin and Greek ceased to be entrance requirements in the 1960s. By the 1990s a more common driver of change was the need to harmonise jurisdictions with the global order by adopting (usually) American models of education. In South Korea, growing military, diplomatic and economic ties with the US led to the replacement of a Japanese model of legal education by a US model. Similarly in Japan, US style law schools were adopted in order to qualify students for globalised legal practice (although this change is now being reversed); and in the late 1980s, India established a 'Harvard of the East', supported by wide range of institutions and external agents such as the Ford Foundation, with the explicit aim of achieving global competitiveness.

However, legal education is also central to state-building projects. This is most evident in Africa, where legal education policies were shaped not only by the pressures of international capital but also by the need to reconfigure the state following the end of colonial rule, leading to the establishment of law schools and a drive to create an indigenous profession. For instance, the University of Zimbabwe enrolled more black students in order to weaken the dominance of non-black lawyers. At independence in 1957, Ghana had no law faculties; one of the first acts of the post-colonial government was to establish a Department of Law, the first in sub-Saharan Africa (outside South Africa). The tenth Ghanaian law faculty was opened in 2014.[40] Colonisation had similarly offered limited educational opportunities for Libyans, but the growth of the oil sector following independence in 1950 stimulated a demand for lawyers (mainly driven by foreign companies), leading to the founding of the University of Libya in 1955 and the emergence of a secular legal profession. However, the Libyan report also reveals the persistence of other forms of legal education as non-commercial legal issues continued to be settled by traditional or Sharia courts presided over by tribal authorities. Law schools were prohibited under the Israeli occupation of Palestine; the first year after it was established, the Palestinian Authority founded a law school, and there are now 11. Venezuela also demonstrates the centrality of legal education to state construction projects: under Chávez, new public universities were launched and the curriculum infused with political ideology to create loyal state bureaucrats. This significance of education as a political site is underscored by the closure in 1988 of all universities in Myanmar following the military coup. The University of Yangon did not reopen until 1993, when the military introduced a strategy of expanding higher education, including law. Similarly, in post-unification Vietnam the need for legal expertise in state building led to the reopening of law schools in the late 1970s. These links between major political shifts (and related changes in legal systems)

---

[40] JJ Dawuni (2017) 'Lawyers in Ghana', presented at the International Meeting on Law and Society, Mexico City.

characterise developments in legal education in other jurisdictions. In Bosnia and Herzegovina, for example, legal education has been deeply affected by the radical transitions between Sharia and civil law, socialism and capitalism.

Even in those parts of the world that have not suffered the sorts of major disruptions described above, the centrifugal tendencies generated by neoliberal globalisation have influenced the direction of legal education policy. For instance, Canada has implemented legal education reforms with the aim of restoring a 'sense of common cause and common culture amongst new entrants'; and Paterson and Robson describe how Scotland has resisted the extreme market model of education adopted by England and Wales in favour of a more consensual (neo-contractual) model. The aim of building a 'supra-national' entity prompted the harmonisation of the European educational market, although the reforms were motivated less by concerns with social solidarity than with economic reconstruction. As Doornbos and de Groot-Van Leeuwen note, their primary objective was to make 'European higher education more competitive with other world regions' and thereby impede domination by BigLaw. As a result, 29 European countries created the European Higher Education Area (EHEA) and implemented the Bologna model of a three-tier structure. However, although Bologna also aimed to facilitate European cultural and legal interchange,[41] the impact of national traditions is again apparent, exemplified by Germany's and Norway's retention of their own models. The distinctive system of German legal education, centred on the concept of the *Einheitsjurist* (unified jurist), continues to entail training students in the Roman law tradition with a focus on doctrinal law.

Shifts in the curriculum reflect these multiple drivers of educational change, some of which pre-date the 1980s. The social democratic dimension of legal education's expansion, in part a result of the late 1960s/70s civil rights movements, generated critique – in some Western jurisdictions – of legal positivism and the development of socio-legal, critical and feminist studies, courses which addressed almost every field of social activity, and a focus on professional skills. This flowering of socio-legal scholarship is attributable not only to social democratic rationalities but also to the increased significance of human rights, legal education's contribution to increased political activism, and struggles against theocratic powers and colonial legacies. The general expansion of legal clinics (eg in South Africa, Palestine, Turkey, Argentina, Chile, Germany, the Czech Republic) is also connected to this move away from the traditional positivist focus; but their perceived capacity to fill some of the gaps in the provision of legal services following cuts to legal aid has provided another reason for their popularity. The spread of the clinic movement is also due to the influence of US models of legal education, exemplifying their role as a key vector of imperialism, transmitting Western forms of law and values (including entrepreneurialism and individualism). The Canadian report describes the increased use of clinics as representing a shift in pedagogic practice away from an 'intellectual approach to law' and towards 'experiential learning', making graduates 'ready to practise' when leaving law school, and suggests that they thus form part of the move away from the apprenticeship model of learning, which underpinned traditional professionalism. The emphasis on experiential learning can also be linked to a utilitarian conception

---

[41] According to the four pillars of the European Treaty, here: movement of labour.

of education, the corollary of its commodification and the related 'mercantilization of knowledge' (Lyotard 1984: 51).[42] England and Wales illustrates how this has driven curriculum change focused on enhancing employability/entrepreneurialism and privileging the teaching of skills and 'appropriate' values and an increased focus on commercial law.[43]

Doornbos and de Groot-Van Leeuwen also report a shift to commercial law in the Netherlands; from the end of the 1990s there were cutbacks in education funding, a backlash against the democratisation of the legal curriculum, and a reversion to the narrow positivist focus on civil, criminal, constitutional, administrative and procedural law, supplemented by international and European law. This policy of educational expansion and greater accessibility combined with inadequate funding is reported elsewhere. Doornbos and de Groot-Van Leeuwen argue that it indicates the co-existence of a 'leftist' agenda of access with a 'rightist' agenda of cuts. Alternatively, these two dimensions may be seen as reflecting the conjuncture of the neoliberal market ideology of category-blind meritocratic selection processes and global capitalism's need for skilled labour, with education's commodification and hence the withdrawal of the state from responsibility for its funding. This latter interpretation is supported by the clear correlation between enthusiasm for neoliberal policies and the marketisation of higher education and imposition of fees. Thus, in states which have generally been slow to liberalise, the public sphere funding regimes have been unaffected; for instance in Germany, Scandinavia, France, Slovakia, Serbia, the Czech Republic and Austria, higher education is free for EU citizens, and other countries (for instance Switzerland) have very moderate fees. However, both Australia and England and Wales have instituted high fees, with a concomitant shift to a user-pays regime comprising government-funded, low interest loan schemes and income-contingent repayment, and across Canada law school tuition doubled between 2006 and 2016. The resulting rise in high levels of student debt is justified as engendering individual responsibility and has reinforced the importance of employability in the curricula and intensified the stratification of legal education. The expensive, elite institutions tailor their education to serve the global world order, and their graduates occupy a different space from graduates of middle and lower tier institutions. These inequalities have then been accentuated by the creation of international markets, particularly located in the US, UK and Australia, and the high fees charged to international students in the UK and Australia.

This disaggregation and stratification of legal education can also be interpreted as a reaction by elite groups and institutions to the threat to their social and cultural capital posed by educational expansion and the usurpationary projects pursued by non-normative groups (Witz 1992). The data indicate that the diversification of legal education has been a virtually universal trend, primarily in the form of an exponential increase in the number of women students – whose low social standing evidently threatens the profession's status. This is most clearly illustrated in Myanmar where feminisation of the profession (women *already* make up a majority of the legal profession, a majority of judges and *all* law professors) has been part of the military's strategy to reduce its status. In most Western

---

[42] Grounded in turn in the neoliberal economisation of the public sphere (Brown 2015).
[43] But see Francis (2015) for a nuanced evaluation of the increased significance of employability in the curriculum in England and Wales, where the shift to commercial law may be largely designed to cater to international students.

jurisdictions the percentage of women law students has equalled or exceeded 50 per cent for several years (for instance, in Australia, England and Wales, Poland and Belgium). This pattern is also found in Latin America; for example, in Mexico female students rose from 33.3 per cent in 1985 to 48.1 per cent in 2000, reaching 50.1 per cent in 2015. It is clear that diversification in terms of socio-economic background and ethnicity is also taking place. However, the data show that poorer and ethnically diverse[44] students are concentrated in low status schools, and the asymmetrical terms on which these 'outsiders' are included are legitimated by the stratification of the institutions from which they graduate. Katvan et al apply the two hemispheres metaphor to Israeli legal education, which is then reproduced in the profession. A similar divide characterises Venezuelan legal education: out of its 26 law schools, just two attract the best students and professors; they offer a curriculum that includes foreign language skills and problem-based learning, and their graduates constitute the vast majority of the corporate legal sector. This link between educational stratification and the bifurcation of careers is widespread. For example, Chilean legal education is described as a hierarchical market of law schools and programmes, reflecting the social capital and skills of students and instructors, thereby reproducing the profound segmentation of primary and secondary education. In Brazil, too, despite both dramatic expansion and the adoption of affirmative action policies, higher education is deeply stratified. Indonesia reports enormous status differences among its more than 300 law faculties; students seeking to enter a corporate law firm must attend one of the two most prestigious state universities or a few expensive private universities. It appears, therefore, that everywhere massification is shaped by pre-existing social hierarchies; for instance, there is a clear correlation between the status of Belgian institutions, their intake from higher socio-economic groups, and the success of their graduates in the legal labour market. The role played by this stratified system in reproducing social hierarchies, while apparently offering the possibility of social mobility, is formalised through national and international university league tables (eg US, UK, and Australia).[45]

In summary, the data underline the intimate relationship between the changes to legal education and legal professions across the world in their response to neoliberalism and globalisation. These forces have produced a system stratified in a way that responds to the needs of deeply polarised national professions, despite the evidence that diversity and inclusion initiatives and human rights and rule of law issues are important features in many law schools. The traditional curriculum and teaching methods in the most disadvantaged parts of the system have generally been modernised (and Westernised in the Global South and Asia), standardised, and technicised and involve transmission to large numbers of students, sometimes conducted on-line, completely free of regulation. By contrast, while the most prestigious parts of the system are oriented towards the global order and thoroughly modernised, some have retained elements of the classical curriculum and include foreign language courses and in-depth instruction, all of which represent

---

[44] This patterning is, however, very nuanced: ethnicity is as an extremely fluid term and its intersection with other categories, particularly class, accentuates pre-existing ethnic hierarchies. But although higher class minorities, and also women, are more likely to attend high status schools, the demerit of belonging to an ethnic minority or being female tends to undermine the advantage of attending a prestigious school.

[45] Again we see a difference from some civil law countries; for instance in Germany rankings featured in tabloids for a while but were found not to work.

valuable cultural capital. However, a unifying feature of both hemispheres of the education system is the capitalist logic which now informs them and their shaping by the global legal order.

IX. CONCLUSION

The legal order was the key capability for the development of the Western nation state and the inter-state system, making law the 'cutting edge' of Western imperialism (Chanock 1985). Yet law is also central to state construction in former colonies (both formal and informal). The characteristics that equipped it for this role included the grounding of the profession's expertise in formal training and credentialing (that is, in achievement rather than ascription); its (relative) autonomy from state, society and capital and the law's related 'eternalisation' (Bourdieu 1987) and connection to the ideals of liberty and justice. All these interlinked dimensions, which underpinned the profession's legitimacy and 'social magic' (Sommerlad 2015), were eroding by 1988 as the institutional forms of both nation states and the global order were transforming. Since then the rate of change has been exponential and, as the conceptive ideologists (Cain 1979) and agents of neoliberal global capitalism, (some) lawyers, supported by technological innovations, have been central players in this transformation. As a result, the contemporary legal field is everywhere splintered and the meaning of the profession contested. As the data indicate, such fundamental traditional characteristics as professional autonomy (and the illusion of objectivity) have eroded, and the doxa of the legal field has been challenged by the discourse of entrepreneurialism, which has re-shaped the logics and organisational practices of the corporate legal sector, and, in many jurisdictions, marketised the legal academy.

The national chapters attest to these transformations. However, even while they depict socially constitutive roles played by the profession (both nationally and internationally), they also reveal the inflection of these transformations by pre-existing socio-structural capacities in the national fields of power, exemplifying specific dynamics which shape the profession across time and space. The result is a fluid, 'messy' social reality (Law and Urry 2005). The data reveal other continuities; for instance, how – despite the struggles of subordinate groups – the profession remains patterned by social hierarchies and instrumental in their reproduction, and yet how traditional ideals of justice, equity and the rule of law continue to inspire some lawyers, who are prepared, at great risk to their lives (or livelihoods), to struggle for social justice.

Our aim in this project, as in the 1988 collection, was to explore these transformations and continuities through a comparative, connective sociology of contemporary legal professions, thereby contributing to a deeper understanding of their current forms, meaning(s) and roles. This chapter's outline of the reports' accounts of the key consequences of incorporation into the global order and impact of neoliberal rationalities cannot do full justice to their rich data, which, like the original collection, represent a resource for further research. Although each report can be read alone, their riches will unfold only when read together.

The reports did not devote much space to the global financial crisis of 2008–09 and subsequent worldwide recession. Yet the crisis can be directly attributed to the interlinked processes of globalisation, liberalisation, financialisation and new technologies – processes in which, as we have noted throughout this chapter, corporate lawyers are deeply implicated. It has been predicted that the crisis will be 'known as an inflection point in world history because of huge revolutions under way in the world', which make 'this an electrifying time to be in the legal profession' (Minow 2010). Wald (2010), writing about the US profession, describes the immediate impact of the economic meltdown as devastating; however the 'huge revolutions' clearly extend beyond such effects as 'unprecedented layoffs'.[46] Birch (2017) speaks of a challenge to both market liberalisation, including from the IMF, and financial globalisation. However, the most striking aspect of the major political-economic shift resulting from the crisis is the resurgence of nativist ethnonationalism in much of Europe, the US, Australia and Brazil, where it challenges the rule of law (described as at risk in the Netherlands). As austerity continues to bite, the position of populist politicians appears to strengthen, and the political tone hardens on issues such as immigration, security and law enforcement. It seems likely that continuing global instability, the climate crisis and consequential resource scarcity will produce further mass human displacement, which in turn will fuel populist movements (Semple 2019) – a scenario which raises new questions about the potential role of the profession.

The ongoing impact of the financial crisis, the related policies of austerity and increasing precarity in labour markets and the implications for liberal democracy and the profession thus form the backdrop to Volume Two, which will include a chapter on the rule of law. The volume will generally deepen the insights revealed by the data reported here by comparing central features of the impact on lawyers of neoliberal globalisation, and the development of new technologies such as AI, and will consider themes which refer back to the original collection and which are central to understanding how law and the profession have developed during the last 30 years. It includes chapters by the most eminent legal profession scholars comparing legal professions within rubrics (Africa, Latin America, the Islamic world, emerging economies, and former communist regimes) and addressing state production, regional bodies and international courts, large law firms, access to justice, technology, legal education, ethics and regulation, casualisation, cause lawyers, corruption, gender, masculinity, diversity, and sociologies of the legal, medical and accountancy professions. It is our hope that, taken together, these two volumes will inform and challenge our conceptions of the contemporary profession, stimulate and support further research and – at best – encourage reform.

REFERENCES

Abbott, A (1988) *The System of the Professions* (Chicago, University of Chicago Press).
—— (2001) *Time Matters: On Theory and Method* (Chicago, University of Chicago Press).
Abel, RL (1988) 'Lawyers in the civil law world' in RL Abel and PSC Lewis (eds), *Lawyers in Society: Vol II The Civil Law World* (Berkeley, University of California Press) 1–53.
—— (1989) 'Comparative Sociology of Legal Professions' in RL Abel and PSC Lewis (eds), *Lawyers in Society: Vol III Comparative Theories* (Berkeley, University of California Press) 80–153.
—— (1995) *Politics by Other Means: Law in the Struggle against Apartheid, 1980–1995* (New York, Routledge).

---

[46] See Bellini and Maestripieri's discussion (2018) of how the crisis has magnified pre-existing trends within the professional labour market.

—— (2019) 'Comparative Sociology of Lawyers, 1988–2018: The Professional Project' in R Abel, O Hammerslev, H. Sommerlad and U Schultz (eds), *Lawyers in 21st-Century Societies: Vol 1* (Oxford, Hart Publishing).
Abel, RL and Lewis, PSC (eds) (1988a) *Lawyers in Society: Vol I The Common Law World* (Berkeley, University of California Press).
—— (1988b) *Lawyers in Society: Vol II The Civil Law World* (Berkeley, University of California Press).
—— (1989a) 'Putting Law Back into the Sociology of Lawyers' in RL Abel and PSC Lewis (eds), *Lawyers in Society: Vol III Comparative Theories* (Berkeley, University of California Press) 478–526.
—— (1989b) *Lawyers in Society: Vol III Comparative Theories* (Berkeley, University of California Press).
Aiyedun, A and Ordor, A (2016) 'Integrating the traditional with the contemporary in dispute resolution in Africa' 20 *Law Democracy and Development* 1.
Alavi, H (1972) 'The State in Post-Colonial Societies: Pakistan and Bangladesh' I/74 *New Left Review*.
Arnholtz, J and Hammerslev, O (2013) 'Transcended power of the state: the role of actors in Pierre Bourdieu's sociology of the state' 14 *Distinktion: Scandinavian Journal of Social Theory* 42–64.
Ashley, L, Duberley, J, Sommerlad, H and Dora, S (2015) *A Qualitative Evaluation of Non-educational Barriers to the Elite Professions* (London, Social Mobility and Child Poverty Commission).
Aubert, V (1976) 'The Changing Role of Law and Lawyers in Nineteenth- and Twentieth-Century Norwegian Society' in DN MacCormick (ed), *Lawyers in Their Social Setting* (Edinburgh, Green) 1–17.
Bakan, J (2005) *The Corporation: The Pathological Pursuit of Profit and Power* (Robinson Publishing).
Barrantes-Reynolds, M (2016) *Legal Pluralism in the Constitution of Bolivia of 2009: Between multiculturalism and plurinationalism* PhD thesis, University of Leicester, unpublished.
Bauman, Z (1998) *Globalization: The Human Consequences* (Cambridge, Polity Press).
—— (2000) *Liquid Modernity* (Cambridge, Polity Press).
Bayly, C (2004) *The Birth of the Modern World* (Oxford, Oxford University Press).
Beck, U (2005) *Power in the Global Age* (Cambridge, Polity Press).
Bellini, A and Maestripieri, L (2018) 'Professions Within, Between and Beyond. Varieties of Professionalism in a Globalising World' 8(16) *Cambio* 5–14.
Bhambra, GK (2016) 'Whither Europe?: Postcolonial versus Neocolonial Cosmopolitanism' 18 *Interventions* 187–202.
Birch, K (2017) *A Research Agenda for Neoliberalism* (Cheltenham, Edward Elgar).
Bourdieu, P (1977) *Outline of a Theory of Practice* (Cambridge, Cambridge University Press).
—— (1984) *Distinction: A Social Critique of the Judgment of Taste* (Cambridge, MA: Harvard University Press).
—— (1987) 'The Force of Law: Toward a Sociology of the Juridical Field' 38 *Hastings Law Journal* 805.
—— (1990) *The Logic of Practice* (Stanford, Stanford University Press).
—— (1996) *The Rules of Art* (Cambridge, Polity Press).
Bourdieu, P and Wacquant, L (1992) *An Invitation to Reflexive Sociology* (Chicago, University of Chicago Press).
Brenner, N (2004) *New State Spaces: Urban Governance and the Rescaling of Statehood* (Oxford, Oxford University Press).
Broek, SD, Buiskool, BJ and Hake, B (2010) *Impact of Ongoing Reforms in Education and Training on the Adult Learning Sector (2nd phase) ANNEX report* (Zoetermeer, 17 December).

Brown, W (2015) *Neo-liberalism's Stealth Revolution* (New York, Zone Books, MIT Press).
Brubaker, R (2009) 'Ethnicity, Race, and Nationalism' 35 *Annual Review of Sociology* 21–42.
Butler, J (1990) *Gender Trouble: Feminism and the Subversion of Identity* (London, Routledge).
Cain, M (1979) 'The General Practice Lawyer and the client: Towards a radical conception' 7(4) *International Journal of the Sociology of Law* 331–54.
Carbado, D and Gulati, M (2000) 'Working Identity' 85(5) *Cornell Law Review* 1259–1308.
—— (2013) *Acting White? Rethinking Race in 'Post-Racial' America* (Oxford, Oxford University Press).
Carr-Saunders, AM and Wilson, P (1933) *The Professions* (Oxford, Clarendon Press).
Caserta, S and Madsen, MR (2019) 'The Legal Profession in the Era of Digital Capitalism: Disruption or New Dawn?' 8 *Laws* 1–17.
Castells, M (1996) *The Rise of the Network Society, The Information Age: Economy, Society and Culture Vol I* (Oxford, Blackwell).
Cerny, P (1996) 'Globalization and the erosion of democracy' 36 *European Journal of Political Research* 1–26.
Chanock, M (1985) *Law, Custom and Social Order: the Colonial Experience in Malawi and Zambia* (Cambridge, Cambridge University Press).
Cooper, DJ and Robson, K (2006) 'Accounting, professions and regulation: Locating the sites of professionalization' 31(4) *Accounting, Organizations and Society* 415–44.
Cotterrell, R (1998) 'Why must legal ideas be interpreted sociologically?' 25(2) *Journal of Law and Society* 171–92.
Crenshaw, K (1991) 'Mapping the margins: Intersectionality, identity politics, and violence against women of color' *Stanford Law Review* 1241–99.
Crouch, C (2011) *The Strange Non-death of Neo-liberalism* (Cambridge, Polity Press).
Delanty, G (2015) 'Europe and the Emergence of Modernity. The Entanglement of Two Reference Cultures' 3(3) *International Journal for History, Culture and Modernity* 9–34.
Dezalay, Y and Garth, B (2002) *The Internationalization of Palaces War: Lawyers, Economists, and the Contest to Transform Latin American States* (Chicago, University of Chicago Press).
—— (2011) *Lawyers and the Rule of Law in an Era of Globalization* (New York, Routledge).
Dezalay, Y and Sugarman, D (1995) *Professional Competition and Professional Power: Lawyers, Accountants and the Social Construction of Markets* (London, Routledge).
Dinovitzer, R and Hagan, J (2006) 'Lawyers on the move: the consequences of mobility for legal careers' 13 *International Journal of the Legal Profession* 119–35.
Douglas-Scott, S (2013) *Law after Modernity* (Oxford, Hart Publishing).
Douzinas, C and Warrington, R (1994) 'The Face of Justice: a Jurisprudence of Alterity' 3(3) *Social and Legal Studies* 428.
Duncanson, I (2003) 'Writing in the Postcolonial: Postcolonial Legal Scholarship, Law' *Social Justice and Global Development Journal* (LGD) 1.
Durkheim, E (1957) *Professional Ethics and Civic Morals* (London, Routledge).
Ehrlich, E (1936) *Fundamental Principles of the Sociology of Law* (Cambridge, MA, Harvard University Press).
Eisenstadt, SN (2000) 'Multiple Modernities' 129 *Daedalus* 1–29.
Epstein, CF, Seron, CB, Oglensky, B and Saute, R (1999) *The Part Time Paradox: Time Norms, Professional Life, Family and Gender* (London, Routledge).
Evetts, J (2014) 'Professionalism, Enterprise and the Market: contradictory or complementary?' in H Sommerlad, L Harris-Short, S Vaughan and R Young (eds), *The Futures of Legal Education and the Legal Profession* (Oxford, Hart Publishing).
Falcão, J (1988) 'Lawyers in Brazil' in RL Abel and PSC Lewis (eds), *Lawyers in Society: Vol II The Civil Law World* (Berkeley, University of California Press) 400–42.
Felstiner, WLF (2005a) *Reorganisation and Resistance: Legal Professions Confront a Changing World* (Oxford, Hart Publishing).

—— (2005b) 'Reorganisation and Resistance' in WLF Felstiner (ed.), *Reorganisation and Resistance: Legal Professions Confront a Changing World* (Oxford, Hart Publishing) 1–12.

Finnis, J (1980) *Natural Law and Natural Rights* (Oxford: Clarendon Press).

Fitzpatrick, P (1992) *The Mythology of Modern Law* (London, Routledge).

Fukuyama, F (1989) 'The End of History' 16 (Summer) *The National Interest* 3–18.

Fournier, V (1999) 'The appeal to "professionalism" as a disciplinary mechanism' 47 *The Sociological Review* 280–307.

Francis, A (2015) 'Legal Education, Social Mobility and Employability: Possible Selves, Curriculum Intervention and the role of Legal Work Experience' 42(2) *Journal of Law and Society* 173–201.

Freidson, E (1970) *Professional Dominance: The Social Structure of Medical Practice* (New York, Atherton).

—— (2001) *Professionalism: the Third Logic* (Chicago, University of Chicago Press).

Galanter, M and Palay, T (1991) *Tournament of Lawyers: The Transformation of the Big Law Firm* (Chicago, University of Chicago Press).

Galbraith, JK (1997) Interview, *Folha de Sao Paulo* (2 October).

Gamble, A (1988) *The Free Economy and the Strong State: The Politics of Thatcherism* (London, Palgrave Macmillan).

Geertz, C (1973) *The Interpretation of Cultures* (New York, Basic Books).

Giddens, A (1990) *Consequences of Modernity* (Cambridge, Polity Press).

—— (1994) *Beyond Left and Right: the Future of Radical Politics* (Cambridge, Polity Press).

Gilroy, P (2000) *Against Race: Imagining Political Culture beyond the Color Line* (Cambridge, MA, Harvard University Press).

—— (2004) *Postcolonial Melancholia* (New York, Columbia University Press).

Glucksmann, M (1995) 'Why "work"? Gender and the "total social organisation of labour"' 2(2) *Gender, Work and Organization* 63–75.

Gordon, A (2009) *A Modern History of Japan* (Oxford, Oxford University Press).

Gorman, EH and Sandefur, RL (2011) '"Golden Age", Quiescence, and Revival: How the Sociology of Professions Became the Study of Knowledge-Based Work' 38 *Work and Occupations* 275–302.

Gouldner, AW (1978) 'The New Class Project, I' 6 *Theory and Society* 153–203.

Green, L (2008) 'Positivism and the Inseparability of Law and Morals' 83 *New York University Law Review* 1035.

Gregory, D, Pratt, R and Pratt, G (2009) *Dictionary of Human Geography*, 5th edn (Hoboken, Wiley-Blackwell).

Hagan, J and Kay, F (1995) *Gender in Practice: A Study of Lawyers' Lives* (New York, Oxford University Press).

Hall, S (1992) 'The Question of Cultural Identity' in S Hall, D Held and A McGrew (eds), *Modernity and Its Futures* (Cambridge, Polity Press) 274–316.

—— (2011) 'The neoliberal revolution' 48 *Soundings* 9–28.

Halliday, TC (1989) 'Legal professions and the state: neocorporatist variations on the pluralist theme of liberal democracies' in RL Abel and PSC Lewis (eds), *Lawyers in Society: Vol III Comparative Theories* (Berkeley, University of California Press) 375–426.

Halliday, TC and Karpik, L (1997) *Lawyers and the Rise of Western Political Liberalism: Europe and North America from the Eighteenth to Twentieth Centuries* (Oxford, Clarendon Press).

Halliday, TC, Karpik, L and Feeley, M (2007) *Fighting for Political Freedom: Comparative Studies of the Legal Complex and Political Liberalism* (Oxford, Hart Publishing).

Hammerslev, O (2011) 'The European Union and the United States in Eastern Europe: Two ways of exporting law, expertise and state power' in Y Dezalay and B Garth (eds), *Lawyers and the Rule of Law in an Era of Globalization* (New York, Routledge) 134–55.

Hammerslev, O and Rønning, OH (2018) 'Outsourcing Legal Aid in the Nordic Welfare States' in O Hammerslev and OH Rønning (eds), *Outsourcing Legal Aid in the Nordic Welfare States* (London, Palgrave).

Hammerslev, O and Sommerlad, H (forthcoming) 'Studying lawyers comparatively in the 21st century: outline of a methodological approach' in R Abel, H Sommerlad, O Hammerslev and U Schultz (eds), *Lawyers in 21st-Century Societies: Vol II Comparative Perspectives* (Oxford, Hart Publishing).

Hanlon, G (1998) 'Professionalism as Enterprise: Service Class Politics and the Redefinition of Professionalism' 32(1) Sociology 43–63.

Harrison, H (2001) *China; Inventing the Nation* (New York, Oxford University Press).

Hartz, L (1952) 'American Political and the American Revolution' XLVI(2) *The American Political Science Review* 321–42.

Heinz, JP and Laumann, EO (1982) *Chicago Lawyers: The Social Structure of the Bar* (Chicago, Northwestern University Press).

Hilferding, R (1981) *Finance Capital. A Study of the Latest Phase of Capitalist Development* (London, Routledge and Kegan Paul).

Hirst, P and Thompson, G (1996) *Globalization in Question: The International Economy and the Possibilities of Governance* (Cambridge, Polity Press).

Jaguaribe, H (1973) *Political Development* (New York, Harper and Row).

Jameson, F (1996) 'Five theses on actually existing Marxism' 47(11) *Monthly Review* 1–10.

Jerneck, M, Morner, M, Tortella, G and Ackerman, S (eds) (2005) *Different Paths to Modernity: a Nordic and Spanish Perspective* (Lund, Nordic Academic Press).

Johnson, T (1973) 'Imperialism and the professions: notes on the development of professional occupations in Britain's colonies and the New States' 20 *Sociological Review Monograph* 281–309.

—— (1995) 'Governmentality and the institutionalization of expertise' in T Johnson, G Larkin and M Saks (eds), *Health Professions and the State in Europe* (London, Routledge) 7–24.

Katvan, E, Silver, C, Ziv, N and Sherr, A (eds.) (2016) *Too Many Lawyers? The Future of the Legal Profession* (London, Routledge).

Koskenniemi, M (2001) *The Gentle Civilizer of Nations: The Rise and Fall of International Law 1870–1960* (Cambridge, Cambridge University Press).

—— (2005) *From Apology to Utopia: The Structure of International Legal Argument* (Cambridge, Cambridge University Press).

Krygier, M (2013) *Rule of Law (and Rechtsstaat)* University of New South Wales Faculty of Law Research Series 52.

Larner, W (2000) 'Neo-liberalism: policy, ideology, governmentality' 63 *Studies in Political Economy* 5–26.

Larson, MS (1977) *The Rise of Professionalism: A Sociological Analysis* (Berkeley, University of California Press).

—— (1989) 'The Changing Functions of Lawyers in the Liberal State: Reflections for Comparative Analysis' in RL Abel and PSC Lewis (eds), *Lawyers in Society: Vol III Comparative Theories* (Berkeley, University of California Press) 427–77.

—— (2013) *The Rise of Professionalism: Monopolies of Competence and Sheltered Markets* (New Brunswick, Transaction Publishers).

Law, J and Urry, J (2005) 'Enacting the Social' 33(3) *Economy and Society* 390–410.

Leicht, K (2015) 'Market fundamentalism, cultural fragmentation, post-modern skepticism, and the future of professional work' *Journal of Professions and Organization* 1–15.

Lewis, PSC (1988) 'Introduction' in RL Abel and PSC Lewis (eds), *Lawyers in Society: Vol I The Common Law World* (Berkeley, University of California Press) 1–22.

Liu, S (2013) 'The Legal Profession as a Social Process: A Theory on Lawyers and Globalization' 38(3) *Law and Social Inquiry* 670–93.

Loughrey, J (2011) *Corporate Lawyers and Corporate Governance* (Cambridge, Cambridge University Press).

Loughlin, M (2000) *Sword and Scales; An Examination of the Relationship between Law and Politics* (Oxford, Hart Publishing).
Luhmann, N (1981) *Ausdifferenzierung des Rechts. Beiträge zur Rechtssoziologie und Rechtstheorie* (Frankfurt am Main, Suhrkamp Verlag).
Lyotard, JF (1984) *The Postmodern Condition: A Report on Knowledge* (Manchester, Manchester University Press).
Menkel-Meadow, C (1989) 'Feminization of the Legal Profession: The Comparative Sociology of Woman Lawyers' in RL Abel and PSC Lewis (eds), *Lawyers in Society: Vol III Comparative Theories* (Berkeley, University of California Press) 196–255.
McGrew, A and Lewis, PG (1992) *Global Politics: Globalization and the Nation-state* (Cambridge, Polity Press).
Miller, P (1990) 'On the Interrelations between Accounting and the State' 15 *Accounting, Organizations and Society* 315–38.
Minow, M (2010) 'Foreword: The Great Recession and the Legal Profession' in E Wald (ed), 'Symposium: The economic downturn and the legal profession' 78 *Fordham Law Review* 2051–66.
Moore, B (1996) *Social Origins of Dictatorship and Democracy* (Boston, Beacon).
Moorhead, R (2010) 'Lawyer Specialization – Managing the Professional Paradox' 32 *Law and Policy* 226–59.
Mrowczynski, R (2012) 'Self-Regulation of Legal Professions in State-Socialism: Poland and Russia compared' 20 *Rechtsgeschichte Legal History* 170–88.
Muzio, D, Brock, DM and Suddaby, R (2013) 'Professions and Institutional Change: Towards an Institutionalist Sociology of the Professions' 50(5) *Journal of Management Studies* 699–721.
Muzio, D and Faulconbridge, J (2013) 'The Global Professional Service Firm: "One Firm" Models versus (Italian) Distant Institutionalized Practices' 34(7) *Organization Studies* 897–925.
Muzio, D, Hodgson, D, Faulconbridge, J, Beaverstock, J and Hall, S (2011) 'Towards Corporate Professionalization: The Case of Project Management, Management Consultancy and Executive Search' 59(4) *Current Sociology* 443–64.
Neave, G (1989) 'From the Other End of the Telescope: Deprofessionalization, Reprofessionalization, and the Development of Higher Education, 1950–1986' in RL Abel and PSC Lewis (eds), *Lawyers in Society: Vol III Comparative Theories* (Berkeley, University of California Press) 154–95.
Newman, J (2005) *Remaking Governance: Peoples, Politics and the Public Sphere* (Bristol, The Policy Press).
Noordegraaf, M (2007) 'Boundaries of Professionalism: The Institutionalization of Managerial Professionalism in Public Sectors' 5th International Critical Management Studies Conference www.mngt.waikato.ac.nz/ejrot/cmsconference/2007/proceedings/newperspectives/noordegraaf.pdf.
Olgiati, V (2006) 'Shifting Heuristics in the Sociological Approach to Professional Trustworthiness: The Sociology of Science' 54(4) *Current Sociology* 533–47.
—— (2010) 'The Concept of Profession Today: a disquieting misnomer?' 9 *Comparative Sociology* 804–42.
Pahuja, S (2011) *Decolonising International Law* (Cambridge, Cambridge University Press).
Parsons, T (1954a) 'The Professions and Social Structure' in T Parsons, *Essays in Sociological Theory* (New York, The Free Press) 39–49.
—— (1954b) 'A Sociologist Looks at the Legal Profession' in T Parsons, *Essays in Sociological Theory* (New York, The Free Press) 370–85.
—— (1962) 'The Law and Social Control' in WM Evan (ed), *The Sociology of Law* (New York, The Free Press) 60–68.
Payne-Pikus, M, Hagan, J and Robert, N (2010) 'Experiencing discrimination: race and retention in America's largest law firms' 44(3) *Law & Society Review* 553–83.

Picciotto, S (2008) 'Constitutionalizing multilevel governance?' 6 *International Journal of Constitutional Law* 457–79.
Pomerantz, K (2002) *The Great Divergence: China, Europe and the Making of the World Economy* (Princeton, Princeton University Press).
Pue, W (1998) 'Lawyering for a fragmented world; professionalism after God' 5(2/3) *International Journal of the Legal Profession* 125–40.
Rackley, E (2009) 'Detailing Judicial Difference' 17(1) *Feminist Legal Studies* 11–26.
Ramji, H (2009) *Researching Race: Theory, Methods and Analysis* (Milton Keynes, Open University).
Ranciere, J (2004) 'Who is the Subject of the Rights of Man?' 103(2/3) *South Atlantic Quarterly* 297–310.
Raz, J (1977) 'The Rule of Law and its Virtue' 93 *Law Quarterly Review* 195–211.
Rueschemeyer, D (1973) *Lawyers and Their Society: A Comparative Study of the Legal Profession in Germany and in the United States* (Cambridge, MA, Harvard University Press).
—— (1983) 'Professional Autonomy and the Social Control of Expertise' in R Dingwall and P Lewis (eds), *The Sociology of the Professions: Lawyers, Doctors and Others* (London, Macmillan Press) 38–58.
Saks, M (2012) 'Defining a Profession: The Role of Knowledge and Expertise' 2(1) *Professions and Professionalism* 1–10.
Sarat, A and Scheingold, SA (1998) *Cause Lawyering: Political Commitments and Professional Responsibilities* (Oxford, Oxford University Press).
Santos, BdS (2000) 'Law and Democracy: (Mis)trusting the Global Reform of Courts' in J Jenson and B de Sousa Santos (eds), *Globalizing Institutions: Case Studies in Regulation and Innovation* (Aldershot, Ashgate).
Santos, BdS and Rodríguez-Garavito, CA (2005) *Law and Globalization from Below: Towards a Cosmopolitan Legality* (Cambridge, Cambridge University Press).
Sassen, S (1999) *Globalization and its Discontents* (New York, New Press).
—— (2006) *Territory, Authority, Rights: From Medieval to Global Assemblages* (Princeton, Princeton University Press).
Schultz, U (2003) 'Introduction: Women in the World's Legal Professions: Overview and Synthesis' in U Schultz and G Shaw (eds), *Women in the World's Legal Professions* (Oxford, Hart Publishing) xxv–lxii.
Schultz, U and Shaw, G (eds) (2003) *Women in the World's Legal Professions* (Oxford, Hart Publishing).
—— (2013) *Gender and Judging* (Oxford, Hart Publishing).
Scott, C (2001) 'Analysing Regulatory Space: Fragmented Resources and Institutional Design' *Public Law* 329–53.
Semple, K (2019) 'Central American Farmers Head to the U.S., Fleeing Climate Change' *New York Times* 13 April.
Sennett, R (1999) *The Corrosion of Character: The Personal Consequences of Work in the New Capitalism* (London, WW Norton).
Siegrist, H (1990) 'Professionalisation as a process: patterns, progression and discontinuity' in M Burrage and R Torstendahl (eds), *Professions in Theory and History: Rethinking the Study of the Professions* (London, Newbury Park) 177–202.
Silver, C (2011) 'The Variable Value of U.S. Legal Education in the Global Legal Services Market' 24(1) *Georgetown Journal of Legal Ethics* 1–57.
Sinclair, GF (2015) 'State Formation, Liberal Reform and the Growth of International Organizations' 26(2) *European Journal of International Law* 445–69.
Smart, C (1992) 'The Woman of Legal Discourse' 1 *Social and Legal Studies* 29–44.

Somers, M (2008) *Genealogies of Citizenship: Markets, Statelessness, and the Right to Have Rights* (Cambridge, Cambridge University Press).

Sommerlad, H (2008) 'Reflections on the reconfiguration of access to justice' 15(3) *International Journal of the Legal Profession* 179–93.

—— (2012) 'Minorities, Merit, and Misrecognition in the Globalized Profession' 80 *Fordham Law Review* 2481–12.

—— (2015) 'The "social magic" of merit: diversity, equity and inclusion in the English and Welsh Legal Profession' 83 *Fordham Law Review* 2325–47.

—— (2016) '"A pit to put women in": professionalism, work intensification, sexualisation and work-life balance in the legal profession in England and Wales' 23(1) *International Journal of the Legal Profession* 61–82.

Sommerlad, H and Sanderson, P (1998) *Gender, Choice and Commitment: Women Solicitors and the Struggle for Equal Status* (Aldershot, Dartmouth).

Strange, S (1996) *The Retreat of the State: the Diffusion of Power in the World Economy* (Cambridge, Cambridge University Press).

Sugarman, D (1996) 'Bourgeois Collectivism, Professional Power and the Boundaries of the State: The Private and Public Life of the Law Society, 1825–1914' 3 *International Journal of the Legal Profession* 81–135.

Susskind, R (2013) *Tomorrow's Lawyers: An Introduction to Your Future* (Oxford, Oxford University Press).

Szelenyi, I and Martin, B (1989) 'The Legal Profession and the Rise and Fall of the New Class' in RL Abel and PSC Lewis (eds), *Lawyers in Society: Vol III Comparative Theories* (Berkeley, University of California Press) 256–88.

Teubner, G (1997) *Global Law without a State* (Aldershot, Dartmouth).

Thompson, EP (1975) *Whigs and Hunters: The Origin of the Black Act* (Harmondsworth, Penguin).

Thornton, M (1996) *Dissonance and Distrust: Women in the Legal Profession* (Melbourne, Oxford University Press).

Tomlinson, J, Muzio, D, Sommerlad, H, Webley, L and Duff, L (2013) 'Structure, agency and career strategies of white women and black and minority ethnic individuals in the legal profession' 66 *Human Relations* 245–69.

Trubek, DM, Dezalay, Y, Buchanan, R and Davis, JR (1994) 'Global restructuring and the law: studies of the internationalization of legal fields and the creation of transnational arenas' 44 *Case Western Reserve Law Review* 407–98.

Urry, J (1989) 'The End of Organized Capitalism' in S Hall and M Jaques (eds), *New Times: The Changing Face of Politics in the 1990s* (London, Lawrence and Wishart).

Wald, E (2010) 'The Great Recession and the legal profession: symposium: the economic downturn and the legal profession' 78 *Fordham Law Review* 2051–66.

Walby, S (1990) *Theorizing Patriarchy* (Basil Blackwell, Oxford).

Weber, M (1946) 'Class, Status, Party' in HH Gerth and C Wright Mills (eds), *From Max Weber: Essays in Sociology* (New York, Oxford University Press).

—— (1978) *Economy and Society* (Berkeley, University of California Press).

Wilkins, DB (2013) 'The Rise of the Corporate Legal Elite in the BRICS: Implications for Global Governance' 54(3) *Boston College Law Review* 1149–84.

Wilkins, DB and Gulati, GM (1996) 'Why are there so few black lawyers in corporate law firms? An institutional analysis' *California Law Review* 493–625.

Witz, A (1992) *Professions and Patriarchy* (London, Routledge).

Part I

Anglo-American Common Law

2

Australia
A Legal Profession Globalised and Magnified

MARGARET THORNTON AND ASMI WOOD*

I. INTRODUCTION

As suggested in the Introduction to this collection, the fissures that appeared in the legal profession 30 years ago have deepened as a result of the twin variables of neoliberalism and globalisation, the impact of which has been striking in Australia. Once regarded as an exemplar of social liberalism because of its commitment to egalitarianism and the public good, Australia soon became a passionate supporter of neoliberalism and its 'market dogma' (Self 2000). The adoption of competition policy, the linchpin of the market, has profoundly affected the structure of private legal practice, tipping the scales away from professionalism and service in favour of profit maximisation. Whereas professionalism formerly denoted autonomy, collegiality and public service on the part of lawyers (Holmes et al 2012: 29), competition has infused the concept with new meanings, making legal practice more like a business, organised according to contractual relationships or managerial hierarchies.

Although deregulation normally goes hand-in-glove with neoliberalism, Australian governments have somewhat paradoxically sought to increase the regulation of legal practice in the interests of consumers. In addition, the contraction of the public purse – another key characteristic of neoliberalism – has severely affected access to justice, including legal aid, community legal centres, Aboriginal legal services and legal education.

Beyond these substantive changes, the Australian legal profession is becoming less overtly the preserve of Anglo-Celtic masculinity. In 1988, the law student body had already been feminised, a phenomenon that is changing the composition of legal practice, although feminisation is more likely to be found in the managed base of organisations than in authoritative positions, such as law firm partnerships. Also notable is the increasing number of Indigenous lawyers and the youthful age profile of the profession due to the exponential growth in the number of law graduates.

---

* Thanks to Tony Foley and Vivien Holmes for reading and commenting on the draft and to Ian McRae for assistance with census data.

II. COMPETITION POLICY AND THE TRANSFORMATION OF LEGAL PRACTICE

The restructuring of the economy by Labor Prime Minister Paul Keating following enactment of the Competition Policy Reform Act 1995 (Commonwealth) resulted in the liberalisation of legal practice. Competition between service providers was intended to benefit consumers. The legal profession lost some of its traditional monopolies to non-lawyers, such as conveyancing specialists. While professional associations were initially sceptical about the benefits of competition policy, they were soon persuaded otherwise (Parker 1997: 43). Under the new regime, the Australian Competition and Consumer Commission, the independent statutory authority responsible for promoting competition and fair trading, assumed oversight of the legal profession.

The legal profession itself initiated a constellation of reforms at the turn of the twenty-first century, placing Australia in the vanguard in developing innovative business structures. A national competition policy review had found the partnership, the most common law firm structure, to be anti-competitive. Initiatives included the incorporation of legal practices, multidisciplinary practices and listing on the stock exchange, all emphasising the commercial and competitive aspects of legal practice, consistent with the neoliberal turn. The commitment to commercialisation is underscored by the official phrase 'the legal services industry' (Lamb et al 2015: 132).

The incorporation of a legal practice involves registration as a company, which offers the benefits of limited liability, taxation set-offs and the distribution of profits based on merit rather than seniority, although the model suits small single-jurisdiction law firms rather than large multi-jurisdiction firms (Mark and Gordon 2009: 511; Parker 2010). Incorporation requires the appointment of a practitioner director with an unrestricted practising certificate and audits by the relevant State or territory regulator. While incorporation conferred limited liability, the suite of reforms did not include limited liability partnerships, restricting the ability of Australian law to compete with international firms (Law Council 2016: 11).

Nevertheless, incorporation paved the way for the most innovative business structure of all – the establishment of a law firm as a public company – a world first when Slater & Gordon was listed on the Sydney Stock Exchange in 2007 (Mark and Gordon 2009: 515). Slater & Gordon had been seen as a radical law firm committed to social justice and involved in numerous high-profile personal injury cases involving asbestos, silicone breast implants and tobacco (Cannon 1998). While listing represents unequivocal evidence of the market embrace, the New South Wales (NSW) regulator, the Office of the Legal Service Commissioner (OLSC), was very aware of the tensions between legal practitioners' ethical obligations to their clients and a company's duty to its shareholders to maximise profits. The OLSC sought to resist commodifying legal practice while acknowledging that the practice of law is both a profession and a business and the two roles have merged in the new business structures. Recognising the need for a heightened degree of vigilance, the Slater & Gordon prospectus, drafted in consultation with the OLSC, expressly stated that in the case of conflict, the duty to the client would prevail over that to shareholders (Mark and Gordon 2009: 524).

Despite a promising beginning that included expansion and listing in the UK, Slater & Gordon soon began to falter because of the global financial crisis (GFC) and its acquisition of Quindell's professional services in the UK, burdening it with additional debt and poor cash flows. In early 2016, Slater & Gordon revealed that its share price fell more than 95 per cent in 12 months and it lost AUD1 billion in six months, prompting lawsuits against it, including a substantial class action by shareholders. Few firms have followed Slater & Gordon down the listing path.

The internationalisation of the Australian economy, another key plank of the Keating Government's competition policy, had a profound effect on the legal profession. Expansion of Australian law firms into the Asia-Pacific region began in the 1980s, but formal adoption of competition policy in the 1990s saw Australian firms establish offices all over the world. The most dramatic expansion involved the amalgamation of the leading Australian law firms with elite London-based firms in 2011–12 (Thornton 2014: 294).[1] The imperative was intensified by the GFC of 2009, from which Australia emerged relatively unscathed compared to the downturn suffered by European and North American economies. In addition, Australia was enjoying a resources boom: China was paying high prices for Australian iron ore; Australian lawyers had considerable expertise in natural resources and energy; and Australia was seen by other advanced capitalist nations as a stepping stone to Asia. These factors, together with the suggestion that the UK legal profession wanted to be more competitive with Wall Street, made Australia look very attractive to the global firms of the Northern Hemisphere. After this flurry of activity, however, the price of iron ore slumped, and the global firms began to look elsewhere.

Globalisation markedly changed the culture of the Australian legal profession, accentuating the division into 'two hemispheres' – the large corporate and small law firms (*cf* Galanter and Palay 1991: 1; Heinz and Laumann 1982: 319 ff). Income maximisation became the raison d'être of the large firms competing for international rankings based on profit per firm or partner and number and value of deals. These firms eagerly sought to maximise profits while responding to client demands to pay less for process work, cutting overheads by 'off-shoring' routine legal services to cheaper jurisdictions like India or 'nearshoring' them to cheaper organisations within the region.

The export of legal services emerged as another source of revenue since Australia shares its common law system with many other jurisdictions and is competitively priced. The export of legal services has also been fostered by the expansion of international business, including mergers and acquisitions. Legal services are the second highest component after engineering services in the export of professional and technical services (Law Council 2017). This global world, however, is remote from the many small firms that still operate much as they always have done, graphically underscoring the 'two hemispheres' thesis. The influential large corporate firms, with their global orientation and high-flying clients, do little to bridge the gap with the sole practitioners and small firms in the suburbs or regional, rural and remote (RRR) firms (*cf* Heinz and Laumann 1982: 347).

While the neoliberalising imperative privileging profit-making has been advantageous for large law firms and equity partners, increased competition has had more equivocal implications for legal associates. The rapid expansion and bureaucratisation of firms have exacerbated dissatisfaction and attrition because fewer associates can now expect

---

[1] They included Ashurst, Allens Linklaters and Herbert Smith Freehills. Mallesons was the first western firm permitted to amalgamate with a Chinese firm to form King & Wood Mallesons.

to become equity partners, confirming Galanter and Palay's prediction (1991: 122) that the loyalty of associates is likely to be tested in the 'promotion-to-partner tournament' if the time to partnership is lengthened. No figures are available for the proportion of associates promoted to partner, however, and the 'up or out' policy is not strictly applied in Australian firms.

The culture of long hours and relentless billing pressures has induced high rates of depression, stress and addiction among employed lawyers (Hickie et al 2009). Demands for constantly increasing productivity in this highly competitive world have also contributed to increasing reports of uncivil behaviour within law firms, such as bullying and harassment (eg Baron 2015; Bagust 2014; Le Mire and Owens 2014). The Law Council of Australia found that 50 per cent of female and 38 per cent of male legal practitioners had been subjected to bullying or intimidation (Law Council 2014: 76).

The level of dissatisfaction is clearly revealed by the high attrition of female associates from private law firms. A NSW study of women who entered private practice over a 20-year period found that 50 per cent left within five years (Law Society of NSW 2011: 14). The high rate of attrition led the Law Council of Australia to conduct a national study of the phenomenon (Law Council 2014). While associates represent a crucial source of profitability for firms (Campbell and Charlesworth 2012), they can be replaced relatively easily given the large number of graduates emerging from a demand-driven law school environment (discussed below), although the high attrition rate raises law firms' training costs. To retain their best associates, some large corporate firms now offer structured programmes and executive coaching for senior lawyers with partnership potential.

A choice of pricing structures, including task-based billing, is available to clients, but law firms continue to make billable hours the central mechanism to motivate associates. Some associates who lose the tournament leave law altogether, but the majority who leave large firms go to small firms, the public sector or in-house, where working conditions are thought to be more congenial. Key 'push' factors expressed by those leaving private law firms or the Bar include lack of work/life balance, stress and the pressure of work (Law Council 2014: 57).

Some young lawyers who leave have expressed frustration with the conservatism of law firms and their inability to adapt to new technology. The more entrepreneurial have turned to NewLaw or innovative 'start-ups'. The increasing popularity of alternative forms of practice among Millennial lawyers suggests that they are less wedded to the traditional 'high-overhead pyramid, with a core number of partners supported by a larger cohort of associates … all charging clients at hourly rates' (Lim 2016). NewLaw introduces a nimbler model based on remote-working technology, replacing the billable hour with alternative pricing structures, such as fixed pricing or risk-reward billing, and utilising cloud-based computing and storage systems, together with task-oriented apps. Some have predicted a 'tidal wave' of 'start-ups' whose 'legal engineers' deploy IT to enhance efficiencies with clients' specific requirements in mind. An example is Salvos Legal, a commercial law firm owned by the Salvation Army, whose profits are devoted to humanitarian work. Larger firms also are investing in new technologies and buying equity in start-ups (Law Society of NSW 2017), fulfilling Richard Susskind's prediction (2013) that technology will rapidly change the face of legal practice.

A notable aspect of NewLaw is its exceptionally flexible work schedules, which are particularly appealing to lawyers with family responsibilities. Cyber law and the development of Law Apps are now included in some law school curricula to teach students to design and build websites to provide fast and inexpensive solutions to basic legal problems. Artificial intelligence is being deployed in areas such as disputes and corporate transactional work (Mahlab 2016: 4).

III. DEMOGRAPHIC SNAPSHOT OF THE AUSTRALIAN LEGAL PROFESSION

On completion of a law degree and a short period of practical legal training (PLT) (discussed below), candidates are eligible to be admitted in a State or territory Supreme Court as an 'Australian lawyer'. (Australia has nine jurisdictions: six States, two territories, and a federal jurisdiction.) Despite the common roll (an important step towards uniformity), lingering elements of the historic division between solicitors and barristers – a relic of British colonialism – contribute to the fragmentation of the profession. NSW and Queensland retain separate Bars, whereas Victoria and the other States are fused, though they have either a de facto Bar or a small number of lawyers who perform mainly an advocacy role.

Australian lawyers wishing to work in a law firm must apply to a State or territory admitting authority. After satisfying the 'fit and proper person' character requirement, they will be eligible for a restricted practising certificate, usually for two years, requiring them to work under supervision, after which they are entitled to an unrestricted practising certificate. Australian lawyers who wish to practise at the Bar undertake a specialised advocacy course before applying to a State or territory Bar Association for a practising certificate.

The professional associations that provide data on the legal profession invariably underestimate the number of lawyers by focusing on those who have current practising certificates or belong to professional associations, thereby overlooking those who work for government, academia, in-house, or in other positions where a practising certificate may not be required (Weisbrot 1988).

A. Solicitors

In 2016, there were 71,509 practising solicitors/lawyers in Australia, 69 per cent in private practice (signifying the domination of this branch), 15.9 per cent in-house, and 10 per cent in government. There were equal numbers of men and women, but men predominate in the private sector (54.7 per cent) and women in the corporate sector as in-house counsel (57.2 per cent), government (63.9 per cent) and 'other' categories (65 per cent) (Urbis 2017).

Of the 15,539 private law firms operating in Australia in 2016, the overwhelming majority (73 per cent) were sole practitioner firms. Furthermore, almost one-third (30.3 per cent) of all private practice solicitors worked as sole practitioners and 19.6 per cent in firms with 2–4 partners, while 22.4 per cent worked in firms with 40 or more partners (Urbis 2017). In 2015, six of the 23 large commercial firms were global firms. Another 25 international law firms operate in Australia, contributing to the highly competitive market. Foreign lawyers may practise foreign law to facilitate the internationalisation of legal services in accordance with Part 3.4 of the *Legal Profession Uniform Law* 2014 (LPUL) (as enacted in NSW and Victoria). High calibre lawyers, particularly from the UK, Canada and the US, are encouraged to immigrate, and Australian and foreign firms may provide the necessary visa sponsorship. Foreign lawyers may not practise Australian law and must be registered in order to practise foreign law. If they wish to be admitted, they apply to a State or territory admitting authority for an evaluation of their academic and legal qualifications; NSW admitted 117 in 2016 (Legal Profession Admission Board of NSW 2015–16: 7).

In 2015, the main practice areas for the large corporate firms were dispute resolution (22 per cent), corporate (13 per cent), banking and finance (13 per cent) and real estate (10 per cent) (Melbourne Law School and Thomson Reuters 2015: 5). These firms generally do not handle individual matters, such as personal injury, wills, probate and estates, criminal and family law, the 'bread and butter' of sole practitioners and small suburban and RRR firms.

More than half the solicitors (52.7 per cent) were practising in a capital city, 32.7 per cent in a suburban location and 10.5 per cent in a country or rural area. There is concern about the continuing viability of the practices in RRR areas, particularly as they conduct a disproportionate amount of legal aid work (Law Council 2009: 16–18). Because the shortage is partly attributable to generational change, a succession plan has been on the agenda for some time (Mundy 2008). RRR shortages are so acute that the Law Council has called for a national summit on the issue (Law Council 2016a: 5). Despite the demand for RRR lawyers, law graduates prefer to work in the capital cities where incomes are higher and the lifestyle is more appealing, even though the labour market is significantly more competitive (McDougall and Mortensen 2011). Sydney and Melbourne lead the way; Brisbane also is strong because of Queensland's substantial resources industry. Perth's legal profession has grown dramatically but is volatile because the Western Australia (WA) economy is dependent on the price of iron ore.

Table 1 The Big 6 Australian Law Firms (Global Elites) (2016)

Firm Name	Partners	Other Lawyers	Australian offices	Revenue (AUD millions)	Leverage
Allens	140	614	4	440	1/4
Ashurst	149	664	5	319	1/4
Clayton Utz	177	803	6	398	1/4
Freehills	178	733	4	565	1/4
King & Wood Mallesons	160	837	5	424	1/5
Minter Ellison	202	981	8	456	1/5

NB: The volatility of the composition of the large corporate firms due to amalgamations and takeovers means that these figures are constantly changing; the salary of equity partners is approximately AUD 1.5m (Mahlab 2016: 3); firms have traditionally driven profits based on a high leverage of fee earners per partner, but the trend is to a lower leverage that gives greater access to partners; many smaller boutique firms consistently outperform the Big 6 in niche areas (Mahlab 2016: 8).

B. Barristers

In 2015, there were 6,005 practising barristers in Australia: 76.9 per cent male and 23.1 per cent female. Senior barristers are known as Senior Counsel (SC), formerly Queen's Counsel (QC). They are able to charge higher fees and wear silk gowns. Of the 843 Senior Counsel, 89.2 per cent were male and 10.8 per cent female.[2] Ninety-four barristers (1.6 per cent), including seven SCs (0.73 per cent) were Asian Australian (Asian Australian Lawyers Association 2015); the first Indigenous SC was appointed in 2016.

Bar Associations generally appoint SCs in consultation with the profession and the judiciary. NSW abolished the title 'QC' in 1992, followed by other States, but Victoria and Queensland re-introduced the title in 2014 on the ground that it had greater public recognition. In Victoria, barristers who 'take silk' have the option of becoming either a QC or an SC, whereas QC is the only option in Queensland.

C. Judges

Australian courts are arranged hierarchically at the federal, State and territory levels, although it is estimated that 90 per cent of proceedings are conducted in the lower courts (Lamb et al 2015: 96). In addition, a host of generalist and specialist tribunals have been established to hear civil disputes in a relatively informal, economical and expeditious manner. Legal representation is not required in these tribunals, although it may be desirable in the more complex cases.

In 1988, courts were bastions of Anglo-Celtic masculinity. While the appointment of judges was the prerogative of the executive, demographic changes led to criticism and the creation of advisory panels, merit criteria, greater consultation with stakeholders and the advertising of vacancies. Around the turn of the millennium, the Attorneys-General of Queensland and Victoria began appointing more women. The initial backlash from conservative male lawyers subsided (Thornton 2007), and in 2016 the Chief Justices of the Supreme Courts of Victoria and Queensland were female. In 2016, women comprised 350 of the 1,014 judges and magistrates (34.5 per cent), including three of the seven judges on the High Court of Australia, one of whom was appointed Chief Justice in 2017.

It is notable that the percentage of female judges is considerably higher than that of female barristers (23.1 per cent), from whose ranks judges are normally appointed. In recognition of the bias in briefing women barristers, the Law Council of Australia (2016b) has developed a Gender Equitable Briefing Policy. While women have entered the judiciary in increasing numbers, there is relatively little racial or ethnic diversity (Roach Anleu and Mack 2017: 22). In 2015, there was just one Indigenous judge and eight Asian Australian judges (0.89 per cent), while the first Muslim magistrate was appointed in Victoria in 2016.

---

[2] See austbar.asn.au/.

IV. REGULATION OF THE LEGAL PROFESSION

Although a unified legal profession might make good sense in a country with nine jurisdictions serving a population of 25 million, historical and geographical fragmentation has militated against unification (Weisbrot 1988: 248–60; Thornton 2005). Successive federal governments have worked with the legal profession on developing a national legal services market for more than two decades, but unanimity has proven elusive. In 2009, the Council of Australian Governments decided to put regulation of the profession on its microeconomic agenda. It established a National Legal Profession Reform Taskforce, which drafted the Legal Profession Uniform Law (LPUL). The law was designed primarily to promote interjurisdictional consistency but has been adopted only by the two most populous States – Victoria and NSW.[3]

The federal Legal Services Council and a Commission for Uniform Legal Services Regulation oversee the scheme.[4] The Council ensures it is applied consistently and remains efficient, targeted and effective, maintaining professional standards and promoting the interests of clients. The Law Society of NSW and the Law Institute of Victoria continue to perform their traditional roles of regulating trust accounts and practising certificates. LPUL requires only that the complaint-handling function be vested in an independent statutory body, which can delegate some of its powers to the local professional bodies. Critics have pointed to this as evidence that the profession 'was more responsive to practitioners' concerns than those of the general public' (Briton 2015).

LPUL also took what some saw as a retrograde step in ethics regulation. The earlier Legal Profession Act 2004 (NSW), which enabled the incorporation of law firms, sought to improve ethical conduct by requiring management systems based on self-assessment. This proactive model was emulated by other jurisdictions but has been discarded by LPUL. That decision was blamed on the Law Society of NSW and the Law Institute of Victoria, which represent approximately 70 per cent of Australian lawyers; but there was also concern about the increased 'red tape' accompanying additional regulation.

While LPUL may promote more consistent regulation, the disciplinary framework remains jurisdiction-specific with differences in how complaints are recorded and handled, as the 2016 annual reports for each jurisdiction reveal, although the types of complaint and areas of practice in which they arise are remarkably similar (Office of the Legal Services Commissioner (NSW) 2016; Victorian Legal Services Board 2016; Legal Services Commission (Qld) 2016; Legal Profession Complaints Committee 2016 (WA); Legal Profession Conduct Commissioner (SA) 2016; Legal Profession Board of Tasmania 2016; ACT Law Society 2016; Northern Territory Law Society 2016). The majority of complaints were lodged against solicitors, ranging from 2.6 per cent of solicitors a year in WA to 12.2 per cent in SA. This compared with a complaint rate for barristers ranging from 0.14 per cent in WA to five per cent in NSW. The most common causes of complaints related to costs, negligence and personal conduct. The main areas of practice in which complaints arose were family law, probate and civil litigation. The majority were

---

[3] Legal Profession Uniform Law Application Act 2014 (NSW); Legal Profession Uniform Application Act 2014 (Vic).
[4] See www.legalservicescouncil.org.au.

dealt with summarily or closed, with less than two per cent proceeding to formal hearing before a tribunal. Sanctions imposed included an order for costs, compensation or an apology, the payment of a fine or, very rarely, removal from the roll of solicitors. In most jurisdictions, the gender breakdown was not reported but where it was, slightly more complaints were made about male practitioners.

V. LEGAL AID

The establishment of a publicly-funded national system of legal aid and community legal centres (CLCs) was a key element of the commitment to distributive justice in the 1970s. There are about 190 CLCs across Australia, dedicated to assisting the most vulnerable citizens, including the homeless, prisoners and older people. In addition, there are a range of specialist services designed to assist Indigenous people, those with disabilities, youth and women. In accordance with the neoliberal philosophy of reducing public expenditure, however, legal aid has been subject to successive funding cuts over two decades. With the legal aid budget of AUD10.88 per capita in 1996–97 projected to fall to AUD7.80 per capita in 2019–20, only eight per cent of Australian citizens presently qualify (Law Council 2016a: 3). The Productivity Commission (the government's independent advisory body on microeconomic policy), in a thoroughgoing report on access to justice, found that Commonwealth expenditure on legal aid was completely inadequate (Productivity Commission 2014).

Although the massive cuts to legal aid have coincided with the embrace of competition policy and increased profits earned by large law firms, the Productivity Commission found that pro bono contributions by the practising profession in 2014 were modest, representing only about one per cent of the legal market (Productivity Commission 2014: 32).

VI. LEGAL EDUCATION

Disinvestment in public higher education is one of the most dramatic manifestations of the retreat from social liberalism; but perversely it has led to a marked increase in the number of law graduates. The Dawkins reforms (Dawkins 1988) replaced free higher education with a user-pays regime, which eschewed the language of 'fees' in favour of the euphemistic 'contribution' (the Higher Education Contribution Scheme or 'HECS', now 'FEE-HELP'[5]), a government-funded, low interest loan scheme with income-contingent repayment (emulated in other parts of the world, including the UK). If a graduate does not obtain employment or works part-time, the loan is not repayable until circumstances change and income reaches a specified threshold. Because HECS was initially set at a modest AUD1,800 a year across all disciplines and the income-contingent element occluded the tuition debt, prospective students were not deterred from enrolling in law, even when differential disciplinary rates were subsequently

---

[5] See studyassist.gov.au.

introduced and law students were charged the top rate while their discipline received the lowest subsidy. A significant outcome of the deferred repayment scheme is that legal education is not dependent on wealth. But because FEE-HELP does not cover the cost of living, many students need to find paid employment whilst studying and Indigenous students from remote communities require scholarship assistance.

The Dawkins reforms fostered significant expansion of higher education to accommodate the shift from agriculture and manufacturing to a knowledge economy. Like polytechnics in the UK, all colleges of advanced education became universities or were amalgamated with existing universities. Sixteen new universities were established in Australia in four years (Marginson and Considine 2000: 29), but because government funding did not rise proportionately universities sought to supplement the modest amount students paid by offering the most lucrative courses (Thornton 2012). When law tuition was set at the highest rate, vice-chancellors of the new universities were keen to establish law schools, which they believed could teach 'on the cheap', generating profits to subsidise other university activities (Thornton 2012: 29; cf Tamanaha 2012: 127). Because universities could decide which disciplines to offer (except for medicine, which affects the cost of health care), the virtually unstoppable demand for law places encouraged a proliferation of new law schools.

After the government cap on student enrolments was lifted in 2012, universities were free to increase them based on demand (Kemp and Norton 2014). With the abolition of the Commonwealth Tertiary Education Commission (CTEC), at the time of the Dawkins reforms (1988), there was no national body to address issues of supply and demand. CTEC had authorised a thoroughgoing review of the discipline of law shortly before its demise, which had recommended against establishing more law schools, except perhaps in Queensland (Pearce et al 1987: 998). Instead, quasi-deregulation allowed the number of law schools to more than triple, from 12 in 1988 to 42 in 2016, including three not-for-profit private university law schools (Bond, Notre Dame and the Australian Catholic University) and the first for-profit law school (Sydney City School of Law). Because demand has not slowed, some law schools have established or are proposing additional campuses. Many schools also offer a range of online courses to generate additional income, and the Legal Profession Admission Board of NSW provides a part-time diploma course. Partial deregulation, together with university autonomy over course offerings, helps to explain why Australia, with a population of 25 million, has 42 law schools, whereas Canada, with a population of 35 million, has 25 schools, only three of them established in the last 40 years.

While there was relatively little stratification among law schools in 1988 (Weisbrot 1988: 266), this has changed with 'massification'. The original cluster of universities had more than a century to accumulate positional goods, allowing them to claim elite status as the 'Group of Eight' (Go8).[6] The new universities, some of them less well-resourced former colleges of advanced education located in regional areas (eg Charles Sturt, Southern Cross, Southern Queensland and Central Queensland) and less affluent suburban areas (eg Western Sydney), occupy a secondary position. Stratification and competition have

---

[6] The eight research-intensive universities are Adelaide, the Australian National University, Melbourne, Monash, Queensland, Sydney, University of NSW and the University of WA.

been accentuated by domestic and international university league tables, virtually unknown in the twentieth century.

A. 'Too Many Lawyers'

The proliferation of law schools has led to this refrain being frequently heard (Law Society of NSW 2015: 28; *cf* Katvan et al 2017). Because there are little more than 70,000 lawyers in private law firms (Urbis 2017), it is impossible to absorb more than 8,000 new graduates a year. Like the UK training contract, the mandatory period of supervised employment after admission constitutes a barrier for those seeking employment in law firms, some of which even seek to charge graduates for this (so far unsuccessfully).

Despite the employment bottlenecks, a survey by Graduate Careers Australia in 2015 revealed that 74.1 per cent of law graduates were in full-time employment within four months of graduation, albeit not necessarily law-related (compared with 83 per cent two years earlier). The majority of graduates gravitate to in-house, government and community organisations, as well as business and financial institutions. According to an analysis of the 2011 Australian census, law graduates enjoy high incomes throughout their lives (Norton and Cakitaki 2016: 82), and the transferability of legal skills continues to make the law degree an attractive qualification.

B. The Law School Experience

Entry to law school is competitive, particularly among the Go8, where the Australian Tertiary Admission Rank, based on secondary school examination results, may exceed 99 per cent. The University of NSW was the first to introduce an aptitude test, the Law Admission Test, in 2017 (although Indigenous students undertaking a Pre-Law program are assessed differently).

The JD (Juris Doctor), which replaced the LLB (Bachelor of Laws) in North America in the 1970s, was first introduced in Australia in the early twenty-first century as a mechanism to circumvent the government prohibition on universities charging undergraduates full fees (Cooper et al 2011: 45–46). The JD has now replaced the LLB as the basic law degree at both Melbourne and the University of WA Law Schools; most other schools offer both degrees. Apart from the possibility of raising additional revenue, the JD is believed to have greater currency internationally, making it more attractive to overseas students (who pay higher fees). Whereas the undergraduate LLB is commonly completed in conjunction with a second undergraduate degree, such as arts or commerce, over a period of five years, the JD, like its North American counterpart, is designed for graduates from non-law backgrounds and is normally completed in three years.

Under the Tertiary Education Quality and Standards Agency, the JD falls within the Master's Degree (Extended) category of the Australian Qualifications Framework (2013), which requires a greater degree of specialised knowledge and/or scope for research than a bachelor's degree like the LLB (Australian Qualifications Framework 2013: 59). The LLB and JD curricula have to be approved by the relevant State or territory admitting authority; law graduates do not undertake a separate professional examination. To be approved, the LLB and JD must include the standardised eleven compulsory subjects known as the Priestley Eleven.[7] The decreasing proportion of graduates embarking on traditional law-related employment has not prompted a review of the law curriculum.

Similarly, the globalisation of legal practice has not led to a concerted attempt to internationalise the curriculum, although a few law schools have sought to do so. Nevertheless, exchange programmes are encouraged to develop cross-cultural competence. In view of Australia's geographical location, Universities Australia urges students to undertake part of their degree in Asia, as well as in Europe and North America, although a Eurocentric bias persists. Australia is also a popular destination for exchange students from Europe, with some students electing to undertake their entire programme in Australia.[8]

Clinical programmes that allow the opportunity for experiential learning are offered by several law schools, but because they are expensive not all schools offer quality programmes (Evans et al 2017). Such programmes enable a small cohort of students to work on actual cases with real clients and reflect on the experience under the guidance of a qualified lawyer at a CLC, Aboriginal legal service or a clinic specialising in an area such as youth law, environmental law or international social justice. Internships in a parliamentary or legal aid office offer a cheaper option for a hands-on experience with a social justice orientation. A small number of international internships are available at the International Court of Justice in The Hague or the United Nations in Geneva or New York.

Since the mid-1970s, PLT has replaced articles of clerkship (except for a small number registered each year in WA) (Legal Practice Board of WA 2016: 32). The College of Law in Sydney is the main PLT provider, but there are several others, including the ANU School of Legal Practice. PLT is generally undertaken on-line in conjunction with work experience for about six months after the completion of a law degree. The Law Admission Consultative Council (LACC) specifies the skills and competencies to be satisfied for admission,[9] which include the practice areas of civil litigation, property, commercial and corporate practice, and ethics and professional responsibility. A few law schools, such as Flinders and Newcastle (NSW), integrate the PLT skills and competencies into their law degrees so that their students are ready to be admitted as Australian lawyers on graduation. This does not affect the additional requirement to undertake a period of supervised employment (usually for two years) in order to practise.

A four-year undergraduate LLB normally costs students approximately AUD44,000 (which eligible citizens can borrow under FEE-HELP). The deferred-repayment scheme means that Australian law graduates do not face as much debt-related stress as Americans (Tamanaha 2012: 107 ff). But because the three-year JD is technically a postgraduate degree, universities may set their own fees at what the market will bear, normally about AUD100,000 (although some Commonwealth-supported places, such as those offered by the University of WA, are treated like the LLB). The Commonwealth Government contributes approximately 15 per cent towards the cost of a supported LLB/JD place,

---

[7] After Justice Priestley who chaired the Law Admissions Consultative Committee in 1992, requiring Criminal Law and Procedure, Torts, Contracts, Property, Equity, Company Law, Administrative Law, Federal and State Constitutional Law, Civil Dispute Resolution, Evidence, and Ethics and Professional Responsibility.

[8] More than 1,000 Canadian students have completed a bespoke JD program at Bond University in Queensland.

[9] Available at www.lawcouncil.asn.au/LACC/images/212390818_8_LACC_Model_Admission_Rules_2015.pdf.

with students paying the remainder. Law is subsidised at the lowest level of the disciplinary cluster on the assumption that students will receive higher salaries on graduation. A PLT course costs approximately AUD12,000, varying with the number of electives taken and the length of a placement.

Inspired by the prevailing neoliberal philosophy, the Australian government proposed in 2014 to deregulate all university fees, potentially allowing fees for all undergraduate degrees in Commonwealth-supported places, including the LLB, to rise to AUD100,000 or more. But a public outcry at the prospect of 'American-style' tuition debts forced the government to shelve the proposal, although the 2017 Federal Budget announced modest fee increases together with a lower loan repayment threshold.

A number of studies have found significantly higher levels of stress and depression among law students compared with the general population (Hickie et al 2009: 12; Larcombe and Fethers 2013). The transformation of legal education from a public to a private good within a highly competitive labour market may have contributed to the high levels of stress, although the evidence is ambiguous (Larcombe and Fethers 2013: 398; Thornton 2016c).

VII. DIVERSITY

Following publication in 2014 of the *National Attrition and Re-engagement Study (NARS) Report*, the Law Council adopted a Diversity and Equality Charter, which undertook to 'treat all people with respect and dignity regardless of sex, sexuality, disability, age, race, ethnicity, religion, culture or other arbitrary feature' (Law Council 2015). Although the Charter did not include any mechanism for taking action, it represented an important symbolic step. The Law Society of South Australia went further by introducing gender quotas to ensure an equal number of male and female members on its council and at least three female members on its eight-person executive. Diversity is supported and promoted by many societies and networks, such as Women Lawyers, the Asian Australian Lawyers Association and the Muslim Legal Network (Law Society of NSW 2017: 90).

A. Race

The key changes concerning 'race' since 1988 arguably have been the discovery and recognition by the High Court that the Australian continent was not *terra nullius* and that native title remains a burden on the Crown's radical title (*Mabo v Queensland (No 2)*;[10] see also Keating 1992). This notion of native title codified as the Native Title Act 1993 (Commonwealth) has generated significant litigation, making this a specialised area of legal practice. Since then, the Australian Parliament commissioned an Expert Panel to consider how Indigenous people might be recognised in the Constitution (Commonwealth of Australia 2012). The High Court has further recognised that where native

---

[10] *Mabo v Queensland (No 2)* (1992) 175 CLR 1, 52.

title has not been extinguished, Indigenous people may sometimes be entitled to take commercial quantities of marine resources.[11]

Recent constitutional and legislative activity has encouraged Indigenous people to study law, although the number of practitioners remains just 621 (53.1 per cent female and 46.9 per cent male), mostly in public and community sectors (Urbis 2017), up from six in 1981 (Australian Council of Churches 1981). Positive measures have been developed, such as the NSW Law Society's Indigenous Reconciliation Strategic Plan 2016, which articulates broad-ranging objectives for the profession (Law Society of NSW 2017: 90).

Indigenous people were largely excluded from schools until the 1960s and barred from universities. Consequently, the 'pipeline' necessary to achieve parity at tertiary levels is still growing. While law schools do not have affirmative action policies for Indigenous students, several offer places to Indigenous students who are close to the 'cut off' mark. The aim of many universities is to raise the proportion of Indigenous students from the present one per cent to population parity (approximately 2.4 per cent) (Wood 2011: 256); 92 Indigenous students graduated in law in 2009 (Rodgers-Falk and Vidler 2011: 2). Although scholarships for legal studies are scarce, government schemes like the Indigenous Tutorial Assistance Scheme assist the transition of Indigenous students into higher education through one-to-one and group support (Wilks et al 2017). Most Indigenous law students come from the middle or upper socio-economic classes. A few providers of PLT, such as the ANU, offer scholarships for Indigenous students (Australian National University 2016). PLT completion rates are close to 100 per cent, with no statistically significant difference between Indigenous and non-Indigenous lawyers.

B. Lawyers Born Overseas

The 2011 census revealed that 23.5 per cent of Australian lawyers were born overseas, which included 21.9 per cent of solicitors and 16.3 per cent of barristers (Australian Bureau of Statistics 2011). In 2015, Asian Australians comprised 9.6 per cent of the population but just 3.1 per cent of law firm partners, reflecting the 'bamboo ceiling', and just 2.4 per cent of barristers compared with 10.3 per cent of solicitors (Asian Australian Lawyers Association 2015).

C. Gender

Women are 63.4 per cent of law students and reached gender parity with men among private practitioners in 2016. The number of female solicitors grew by 34.2 per cent between 2011 and 2016, while the number of male solicitors grew less than half as much (15.6 per cent). As elsewhere, however, it is only the base of the organisational pyramid that is feminised. Thus, while women are a majority of associates in private law firms, they are only 17.8 per cent of equity partners (22.4 per cent if salaried partners are included).

---

[11] *Akiba v Commonwealth* (2013) 252 CLR 209.

As mentioned, the attrition of women from law firms after five years is striking, a phenomenon noted in respect of a range of countries in the 1988 study (Menkel-Meadow 1988: 214). In a 2014 survey, the lack of work/life balance, particularly for those with caring responsibilities, was the reason given for leaving private law firms by 76 per cent of women who went to government positions, 65 per cent who went to corporate legal positions, and 49 per cent who left the legal profession altogether (Law Council 2014: 42, 57). Culture, leadership and the nature of the work were also important reasons male and female practitioners left (Law Council 2014: 7).

The provision of flexible work was thought to be the solution to the high female attrition rate (eg Victorian Women Lawyers, 2015; Law Council of Australia 2017). Nevertheless, lawyers working flexibly may have even less control over their hours of work than those in an office: 'being connected' by mobile phone and/or computer may signal an expectation of 24/7 availability (Thornton 2016b). Although law firms claim to support parental leave and flexible work to accommodate caring responsibilities, women may still be prejudiced when pursuing non-normative careers that include working part-time and 'not being seen' (Lamb et al 2015: 86; Law Council 2014: 30). While flexible work policies are ostensibly gender-neutral, they are under-utilised by men, who fear stigmatisation for being the primary carers of children (Thornton 2016a: 33). Indeed, women in law firms earn 34.4 per cent less than men, a greater pay gap than elsewhere in the Australian workforce. The gender pay gap for women barristers is considerably higher, even though barristers work fewer hours. Women find academia an attractive alternative to practice, partly because of the flexible hours, although the same gendered organisational pyramid prevails. Women are more than half of those occupying the lower ranks, but just 39.5 per cent of the professoriate.

D. Age

The profession is growing younger because of the exponential increase in law graduates. Millennials are believed to change employers frequently, contributing to the volatility of the profession. In 2016, 32.6 per cent of solicitors were under 35: 42.4 per cent of women and 25.7 per cent of men. At the other end of the age spectrum, 11.2 per cent of male solicitors are over 64, compared with 2 per cent of female solicitors, which could partly account for the gender pay gap. The mean age of female solicitors (38.8 years) is considerably lower than that of male solicitors (46 years). Nevertheless, a 14.9 per cent decline in solicitors under 25 occurred in 2014–16 (Urbis 2017: 2), possibly attributable to changes in legal practice.

E. Class

Lawyering is a middle-class occupation that relies on a predominantly middle-class client base. Nevertheless, the 'hereditary and tribal aspects' of the legal profession that once prevailed (Sexton and Maher 1983: 8) have been diluted by the proliferation of new law schools, some in regional and outer suburban areas. Indeed, a social profile of law students conducted in 15 law schools in 1996, after the first tranche of new law schools had been established, revealed a marked shift from private independent school graduates to government secondary school graduates, whose parents had lower incomes and occupational status (Goldring and Vignaendra 1997: 102–103, 112–17).

As the number and size of large firms increased in the US, recruitment became more competitive and meritocratic, lowering the barriers against women and racial minorities (Galanter and Palay 1991: 57). While all vestiges of homosociality associated with university attended may not have dissipated in Australia, especially with the increased stratification of law schools, the introduction of HECS and the 'massification' of legal education have undoubtedly reduced class bias, although racial barriers remain.

VIII. LAWYERS AND CONTEMPORARY POLITICS

Australian lawyers are overrepresented among politicians, prime ministers, premiers, governors and other prestigious public office-holders. In 2017, 30.4 per cent of the Australian Parliament possessed legal qualifications, compared with approximately 0.4 per cent of the general population. While the legal profession is generally regarded as conservative, the Law Council of Australia has not refrained from criticising the federal government for rule of law violations. The Law Council's 2016 Federal Election Policy Platform urged the abolition of mandatory sentencing and drew attention to the 'catastrophic' rate of Indigenous incarceration. It also called for caution regarding post-sentence administrative controls on convicted terrorists. In addition, the Council has been critical of the indefinite off-shore detention of asylum seekers and refugees and has recommended a review of detention policies and immigration laws more generally (Law Council 2016a).

The Law Council (2016a) favours a progressive stance regarding a range of issues, both domestic (such as constitutional recognition of Aboriginal people and same-sex marriage) and international (the death penalty, particularly in Indonesia and the US, and the removal of judges in Turkey following the failed military coup). Numerous 'radical' lawyer activist groups (such as the Human Rights Law Centre and Refugee Legal) lobby governments and engage in strategic 'test cases' on issues such as abortion, Muslim immigration, racial vilification, children in adult prisons, prisoners with disabilities and deaf jurors.

Despite the profession's ostensibly progressive attitudes on political issues, the public remains ambivalent toward lawyers (Weisbrot 1990: 16 ff). In a poll of Australian citizens (n=598) conducted in 2015, only 31 per cent rated lawyers as either 'high' or 'very high' on ethics and honesty, ranking them just 15th out of 30 professions (Morgan 2015).

IX. CONCLUSION

The dramatic changes in the Australian legal profession outlined above occurred in the context of the larger movement from social liberalism to neoliberalism, which significantly reduced public goods, as shown by the contraction of legal aid and state disinvestment in legal education. The number of law schools more than tripled, and the number of law graduates increased sevenfold. The embrace of competition policy and globalisation has strengthened the domination of large corporate law firms. While many small firms continue to typify RRR practice, their numbers are slowly dwindling.

The profession has grown increasingly diverse: equal numbers of women and men, the substantial proportion of lawyers born overseas, the exponential growth of young lawyers (many of whom are sceptical about the norms of traditional private practice) and the relatively small but increasing number of Indigenous lawyers. These changes prefigure what is likely to be an even more radical transformation of the Australian legal landscape in the next 30 years.

REFERENCES

ACT Law Society (2016) Annual Report 2015–16 https://www.actlawsociety.asn.au/documents/item/2648.

Asian Australian Lawyers Association (2015) *The Australian Legal Profession: A Snapshot of Asian Australian Diversity in 2015* www.legalpracticeintelligence.com.au/asian-australian-lawyers-diversity-study-released-2/.

Australian Bureau of Statistics (2011) *2011 Census of Population and Housing* (Canberra: Commonwealth of Australia).

Australian Council of Churches (1981) *Justice for Aboriginal Australians: Report of the World Council of Churches Team Visit to the Aborigines June 15 to July 3, 1981* (Sydney: Australian Council of Churches).

Australian National University (2016), ANU Legal Workshop, Indigenous Student Scholarships www.legalworkshop.law.anu.edu.au/sites/all/files/flyer_a5_indigenous_student_scholarship_scheme_2016.pdf.

Australian Qualifications Framework Council (2013) *Australian Qualifications Framework*, 2nd edn.

Bagust, J (2014) 'The Culture of Bullying in Australian Corporate Law Firms' 17(2) *Legal Ethics* 177.

Baron, P (2015) 'The Elephant in the Room? Lawyer Wellbeing and the Impact of Unethical Behaviours' 41(1) *Australian Feminist Law Journal* 87.

Briton, J (2015) 'Between the Idea and the Reality falls the Shadow' law.anu.edu.au/sites/all/files/briton_between_the_idea_and_the_reality_falls_the_shadow_2016.pdf.

Campbell, I and Charlesworth, S (2012) 'Salaried Lawyers and Billable Hours: A New Perspective from the Sociology of Work' 19(1) *International Journal of the Legal Profession* 89.

Cannon, M (1998) *That Disreputable Firm … The Inside Story of Slater & Gordon* (Melbourne, Melbourne University Press).

Commonwealth of Australia (2012) *Recognising Aboriginal and Torres Strait Islander Peoples in the Constitution: Report of the Expert Panel* www.pmc.gov.au/sites/default/files/publications/Recognising-Aboriginal-and-Torres-Strait-Islander-Peoples-in-the-constitution-report-of-the-expert-panel_0.pdf.

Cooper, DM, Jackson, S, Mason, R and Toohey, M (2011) 'The Emergence of the JD in the Australian Legal Education Marketplace and its Impact on Academic Standards 21 *Legal Education Review* 23.

Dawkins, JS (1988) *Higher Education: A Policy Statement* ('White Paper') (Canberra, Australian Government Publishing Service).

Evans, A, Cody, A, Copeland, A, Giddings, J, Joy, P, Noone, MA and Rice, S (2017) *Australian Clinical Legal Education: Designing and Operating a Best Practice Clinical Program in an Australian Law School* (Canberra, ANU Press).

Galanter, M and Palay, T (1991) *Tournament of Lawyers: The Transformation of the Big Law Firm* (Chicago, University of Chicago Press).

Goldring, J and Vignaendra, S (1997) *A Social Profile of New Law Students in the Australian Capital Territory, New South Wales and Victoria* (Sydney, Centre for Legal Education).

Heinz, JP and Laumann, EO (1982) *Chicago Lawyers: The Social Structure of the Bar* (New York, Russell Sage and Chicago, American Bar Foundation).

Hickie, I, Kelk, N, Luscombe, G and Medlow, S (2009) 'Courting the Blues: Attitudes towards Depression in Australian Law Students and Lawyers' (Sydney, Brain and Mind Research Institute, University of Sydney).

Holmes, V, Foley, T, Tang, S and Rowe, M (2012) 'Practising Professionalism: Observations from an Empirical Study of New Australian Lawyers' 15 *Legal Ethics* 29.

Katvan, E, Silver, C and Ziv, N (eds)(2017) *Too Many Lawyers* (Abingdon, Routledge).

Keating, PJ (1992) One Nation: Statement by the Prime Minister, 26 October (Canberra, Australian Government Publishing Service).

Kemp, Hon Dr D and Norton, A (2014) *Review of the Demand Driven Funding System* (Canberra, Department of Education, Australian Government).

Lamb, A, Littrich, J and Murray, K (2015) *Lawyers in Australia* (Leichhardt, Federation).

Larcombe, W and Fethers, K (2013) 'Schooling the blues: An investigation of factors associated with psychological distress among law students' 36 *University of New South Wales Law Journal* 390.

Law Council of Australia (2009) Report into the Rural, Regional and Remote Areas Lawyers Survey (Canberra, Law Council of Australia) www.rrrlaw.com.au/media/uploads/RRR_report_090709.pdf.

—— (2014) 'National Attrition and Re-engagement Study (NARS) Report' (Canberra, Law Council of Australia).

—— (2015) Diversity and Equality Charter www.lawcouncil.asn.au/lawcouncil/index.php/current-issues/diversity-and-inclusion.

—— (2016) 2016 Federal Election Policy Platform (Canberra, Law Council of Australia).

—— (2017) 'Legal and Related Services Export Survey 2014–15' (Canberra, Law Council of Australia) www.lawcouncil.asn.au/policy-agenda/international-law/legal-and-related-services-export-survey-2014-15.

—— (2019) National Model Gender Equitable Briefing Policy (Canberra, Law Council of Australia) www.lawcouncil.asn.au/policy-agenda/advancing-the-profession/equal-opportunities-in-the-law/national-model-gender-equitable-briefing-policy/terms-and-conditions-equitable-briefing-policy-policy.

Law Society of NSW (2011) *Thought Leadership 2011: Advancement of Women in the Profession* (Sydney, Law Society of NSW).

—— (2017) *The Future of Law and Innovation in the Profession: Flip Report 2017* (Sydney, Law Society of NSW) www.lawsociety.com.au/sites/default/files/2018-03/1272952.pdf.

—— (2018) *Future Prospects of Law Graduates: Report and Recommendations* (Sydney, Law Society of NSW) www.lawsociety.com.au/sites/default/files/2018-04/Future%20prospects%20of%20Law%20Graduates.pdf.

Legal Practice Board of WA (2016) Annual Report 2015–16 www.lpbwa.org.au/Documents/For-The-Public/Annual-Reports/Legal-Practice-Board-of-WA-Annual-Report-2015-2016.aspx.

Legal Profession Admission Board of NSW (2016) Annual Report 2015–16 (Sydney: NSW Dept of Justice), www.lpab.justice.nsw.gov.au/Documents/Annual%20Report%202015-16.pdf.

Legal Profession Board of Tasmania (2016) Annual Report 2015–2016 www.lpbt.com.au/resources/lpbt_annual_report_2015_2016/.

Legal Profession Complaints Committee (WA) (2016) 2016 Annual Report www.lpbwa.org.au/Documents/Complaints/Forms-and-Publications/Annual-Reports/LPCC-Annual-Report-2015_16.aspx.

Legal Profession Conduct Commissioner (SA) (2016) Annual Report 2015–2016 www.lpcc.sa.gov.au/upload/PDFs/Annual%20Report%202015%20-%202016%20-%20Website.pdf.

Legal Services Commission (Qld) (2016) Annual Report 2015–16 www.lsc.qld.gov.au/__data/assets/pdf_file/0010/492850/LSC-Annual-Report-2015-2016.pdf.

Le Mire, S and Owens, R (2014) 'A Propitious Moment? Workplace Bullying and Regulation of the Legal Profession' 37 *University of New South Wales Law Journal* 1030.

Lim, R (2016) 'What is a true NewLaw firm? Insight, Thomson Reuters, 8 December insight.thomsonreuters.com.au/posts/true-newlaw-firm.

Mahlab (2016) *Mahlab Report 2016: Private Practice* (Melbourne, Mahlab Recruitment Pty Ltd).

Mark, S and Gordon, T (2009) 'Innovations in Regulation: Responding to a Changing Legal Services Market' 22 *Georgetown Journal of Legal Ethics* 501.

McDougall, K and Mortensen, R (2011) 'Bush Lawyers in New South Wales and Queensland: A Spatial Analysis' 16(1) *Deakin Law Review* 75.

Melbourne Law School and Thomson Reuters Peer Monitor (2015) *Australia: State of the Legal Market 2015* www.thomsonreuters.com/en/press-releases/2015/september/2015-australia-state-of-the-legal-market-report-issued.html.

Menkel-Meadow, C (1988) 'Feminization of the Legal Profession: The Comparative Sociology of Women Lawyers' in RL Abel and PSC Lewis (eds), *Lawyers in Society: Vol III Comparative Theories* (Berkeley, University of California Press).

Morgan, R (2015) *Image of Professions Survey* www.roymorgan.com/findings/6188-roy-morgan-image-of-professions-2015-201504280343.

Mundy, T (2008) *Recruitment and Retention of Lawyers in Rural, Regional and Remote NSW: A Literature Review* (Lismore, Northern Rivers Community Legal Centre).

Northern Territory Law Society (2016) Annual Report 2015–16 (Darwin, NT Law Society).

Norton, A and Cakitaki, B (2016) *Mapping Australian Higher Education 2016* (Melbourne, Grattan Institute).

Office of the Legal Services Commissioner (NSW) (2016) 2015–2016 Annual Report www.olsc.nsw.gov.au/Documents/2015%202016%20OLSC%20AnnRep%20accessible.pdf.

Parker, C (1997) 'Converting the Lawyers: The Dynamics of Competition and Accountability Reform' 33 *Australia and New Zealand Journal of Sociology* 39.

—— (2010) 'An Opportunity for the Ethical Maturation of the Law Firm: The Ethical Implications of Incorporated and Listed Law Firms' in K Tranter, F Bartlett, L Corbin, M Robertson and R Mortensen (eds), *Reaffirming Legal Ethics: Taking Stock and New Ideas* (Abingdon, Routledge).

Pearce, D, Campbell, E and Harding, D (1987) *Australian Law Schools: A Discipline Assessment for the Commonwealth Tertiary Education Commission* (Pearce Report) (Canberra, Australian Government Publishing Service).

Productivity Commission (Australian Government) (2014) Access to Justice Arrangements: Productivity Commission Inquiry Report (Canberra: Productivity Commission).

Roach Anleu, S and Mack, K (2017) *Performing Judicial Authority in the Lower Courts* (London, Palgrave).

Rodgers-Falk, P and Vidler, R (2011) *Growing the Number of Aboriginal and Torres Strait Islander Law graduated: Barriers to the Profession* (Canberra, Department of Education and Training, Australian Government).

Self, P (2000) *Rolling Back the Market: Economic Dogma and Political Choice* (Basingstoke, Macmillan).

Sexton, M and Maher, L (1982) *The Legal Mystique* (Sydney, Angus & Robertson).

Susskind, R (2013) *Tomorrow's Lawyers: An Introduction to Your Future* (Oxford, Oxford University Press).

Tamanaha, B (2012) *Failing Law Schools* (Chicago, University of Chicago Press).

Thornton, M (2005) 'The Australian Legal Profession: Towards a National Identity' in WLF Felstiner (ed), *Reorganisation and Resistance: Legal Professions Confront a Changing World* (Oxford, Hart Publishing).

—— (2007) '"Otherness" on the Bench: How Merit is Gendered' 29 *Sydney Law Review* 391.
—— (2012) *Privatising the Public University: The Case of Law* (Abingdon, Routledge).
—— (2014) 'Hypercompetitiveness or a Balanced Life? Gendered Discourses in the Globalisation of Australian Law Firms' 17 *Legal Ethics* 153.
—— (2016a) 'Work/life or Work/work? Corporate Legal Practice in the 21st Century' 22 *International Journal of the Legal Profession* 13.
—— (2016b) 'The Flexible Cyborg: Work-Life Balance in Legal Practice' 38(1) *Sydney Law Review* 1.
—— (2016c) 'Law Student Wellbeing: A Neoliberal Conundrum' 58 *Australian Universities Review* 42.
Urbis Pty Ltd (2017) *National Profile of Solicitors 2016 Report* (Sydney, Urbis & NSW Law Society).
Victorian Legal Services Board + Commissioner (2016) *Annual Report 2016* lsbc.vic.gov.au/documents/Report-Victorian-Legal_Services_Board_and_Commissioner_annual_report_2016.PDF.
Victorian Women Lawyers (2015) *Flexible Work Protocols: A Best Practice Guide for Productive and Engaged Legal Workplaces* (Melbourne, Victorian Women Lawyers).
Weisbrot, D (1988) 'The Australian Legal Profession: From Provincial Family Firms to Multinationals' in RL Abel and PS Lewis (eds), *Lawyers in Society: Vol I The Common Law World* (University of California Press, Berkeley).
—— (1990) *Australian Lawyers* (Melbourne, Longman Cheshire).
Wilks, J, Radnidge Fleeton, E and Wilson, K (2017) 'Indigenous Tutorial Assistance Scheme, Tertiary Tuition and beyond Transitioning with Strengths and Promoting Opportunities' 59 *Australian Universities Review* 14.
Wood, A (2011) 'Law Studies and Indigenous Students' Wellbeing: Closing the (Many) Gap(s)' 21 *Legal Education Review* 25.

3

Canada

Continuity and Change in a Modern Legal Profession

RONIT DINOVITZER AND MEGHAN DAWE

I. BACKGROUND

CANADA'S LEGAL PROFESSION evolved out of a nation-building project aimed at unifying a vast and heterogeneous land through the legitimacy of law and professionalism. Early Canadian legal professionalism developed at the intersection between England's gentlemanly barristers and its more practical solicitors (Pue 2016; Sommerlad 2017). Although the profession today retains some of its early roots (Pue 2016: 76), it is in a state of flux due to significant transformations in the local and global political economies. This chapter situates Canada's legal profession within the context of demographic shifts that are, to some extent, rendering 'old mythologies irrelevant' under conditions of rapid technological change and significant upheaval in the market for legal services and the business models of both large and small law firms (Arthurs 2017: 15).

II. POPULATION AND DISTRIBUTION

Although Canada has the world's second largest land mass, it is home to a population of just 36 million, the majority concentrated in a handful of cities. For example, the Toronto metropolitan census area alone contained 17 per cent of the population in 2014. It is not surprising to find a parallel concentration among lawyers: 42 per cent in Ontario, almost a quarter in Quebec, and 11 per cent in each of Alberta and British Columbia (BC) (see Table 1).

Expanding primarily through international migration, Canada's population growth has been more rapid than other developed countries' (Statistics Canada 2016), but the legal profession's growth rate has outstripped that of the population. Between 1971 and 2014, the legal profession expanded from 16,130 lawyers to 125,190 at a rate of 667 per cent, far outpacing the 65 per cent population growth. Consequently, the ratio

Table 1 Distribution of Canadian Lawyers by Law Society, 1981–2014

Province/Territory	Percentage of National Total					
	1981	1996	2002	2006	2010	2014
Newfoundland	0.7	0.9	0.9	1.2	0.9	0.8
Prince Edward Island	0.3	0.3	0.3	0.4	0.3	0.3
Nova Scotia	2.6	2.3	2.8	3.9	2.9	2.6
New Brunswick	2.3	1.9	1.7	2.2	1.5	1.4
Barreau du Québec	26.9	25.5	22.4	28.7	21.3	19.9
Chambre des Notaires du Québec			4.1	4.9	3.8	3.7
Ontario	37.5	40.5	39.1	50.9	38.9	42.2
Manitoba	13.5	0	0	0	0	0
Saskatchewan	3.35	2.2	2.6	2.8	2.2	2
Alberta	10.1	9.2	9.9	15.1	11.7	11.3
British Columbia	12.5	14.1	12.2	14.8	11.4	10.9
Nunavut	N/A	N/A	0.2	0.3	0.2	0.2
Northwest Territories	0.1	N/A	0.5	0.5	0.5	0.4
Yukon	0.1	N/A	0.3	N/A	0.2	0.3

Source: FLSC statistics; census data from Statistics Canada; Barreau du Québec.

of people per lawyer fell from 1,337 in 1971 to 284 in 2014, close to the 250 reported by the US, Canada's southern neighbour (see Table 2). The pace of growth was dramatic in the early years: the profession doubled in 1971–81 but then took the next 30 years to double again.

Table 2 Canadian and Lawyer Populations, 1971–2014

Year	Lawyers	Population of Canada	People per Lawyer	Annual Rate of Growth: Lawyers (%)	Annual Rate of Growth: Population (%)
1971	16,130	21,568,000	1,337		
1981	34,205	24,343,000	712	112	13
1996	59,970	28,847,000	481	75	19
2001	82,740	30,007,000	363	38	4
2006	75,115	31,613,000	421	−9	5
2011	112,417	33,477,000	298	50	6
2014	125,190	35,540,400	284	11	6

Source: Statistics Canada; Arthurs et al 1988.

This growth has not been evenly distributed (see Table 3). Between 1981 and 2014 (the years for which provincial data are available), the most rapid growth occurred in newly-established jurisdictions, such as Northwest Territories and Yukon. Yet the sheer size of

Table 3 Law Society Membership in Canada, 1981–2014

Province/Territory	1981	1996	2002	2006	2010	2014
Newfoundland	195	535	771	857	929	1,021
Prince Edward Island	80	170	249	273	324	320
Nova Scotia	680	1,370	2,368	2,896	3,120	3,308
New Brunswick	615	1,125	1,483	1,602	1,628	1,708
Barreau du Québec	7,040	15,315	19,207	21,374	23,083	24,923
Chambre des Notaires du Québec			3,501	3,651	4,087	4,580
Ontario	9,830	24,275	33,593	37,907	42,169	52,819
Manitoba	950	1,670	2,006	2,037	3,914	4,335
Saskatchewan	865	1,300	2,191	2,117	2,416	2,550
Alberta	2,650	5,500	8,501	11,272	12,674	14,163
British Columbia	3,270	8,435	10,448	11,036	12,382	13,625
Nunavut	N/A	N/A	181	190	219	308
Northwest Territories	20	N/A	430	407	564	515
Yukon	25	N/A	268	238	174	334

Source: FLSC statistics; census data from Statistics Canada; Barreau du Québec.

the profession in Ontario and Quebec remains unparalleled, with Ontario having an even larger share of the lawyers by 2014 and the lowest number of people per lawyer. One of the outliers in this recent story is Alberta, which overtook the more populous BC in 2006 as the province with the third lowest ratio of people per lawyer, no doubt largely due to the oil boom, which literally fuelled the growth of Alberta's legal profession.

III. PRACTICE SETTINGS

A. Small Firms

The vast majority of Canadian lawyers practise alone or in small firms.[1] From 1988 to 2014, about three-quarters of all establishments employing lawyers and notaries[2] were 'micro' sized, containing 1–4 employees (Statistics Canada 2017b).[3] Data from Ontario

---

[1] Gathering statistics on lawyers' practice settings is challenging in Canada, especially since 2001, when lawyers were allowed to register as a professional corporation, because law societies do not report firm size statistics for lawyers registered as working within a professional corporation. Although FLSC data show a decline in the proportion practising alone (from 58 per cent in 1998 to 47 per cent in 2014), these data are not ideal for tracking the patterns of lawyers in law firm settings.

[2] Notaries here do not include notaries public (which we discuss below).

[3] Employees need not be lawyers; a sole practice could employ a secretary. However, about 56 per cent of all law offices did not have formal employees in 2014.

confirm these patterns: between 1980 and 2015, just under a quarter of lawyers practised alone (see Figure 2). Furthermore, a third of lawyers in firms have been sole practitioners, and another 40 per cent worked in firms of less than 25 lawyers (see Figure 3). Small firms continue to be the practice setting for the plurality of recent law graduates, with 31 per cent in firms of 20 or fewer lawyers and 5.6 per cent in solo practice (Dinovitzer 2015).[4]

Figure 1 Percentage of Ontario Lawyers by Type of Employment, 1990–2014

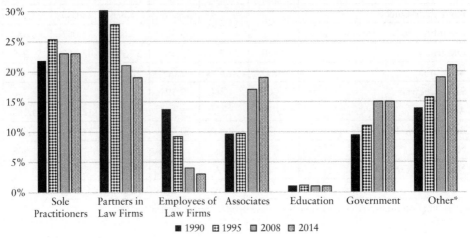

Source: LSUC Annual Reports.
Note: In 2014, the 'other' figure was disaggregated to indicate that 12 per cent were working as in-house counsel.

Figure 2 Distribution of Ontario Lawyers Working in Private Law Firms by Firm Size, 2008–2015

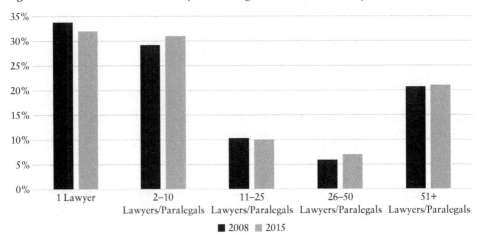

Source: LSUC Annual Reports.

---

[4] Data from Dinovitzer (2015) rely on a nationally representative survey of lawyers admitted to practice in 2010.

B. Large Firms

Mirroring global trends, Canadian law firms have been growing. In 1980, only one firm had more than 100 lawyers, followed by 19 firms in 1989 (Daniels 1993: 155), and 33 in 2016 (Martindale 2016). Yet the 17 largest law firms have reported stagnant growth since at least 2009 (Wiffen 2015). Because there are over 30,000 firms nationwide, large firms do not dominate the legal landscape. Even relying on the more expansive Federation of Law Societies of Canada (FLSC) definition of large firms as 51+ lawyers, they accounted for less than 1 per cent of firms in 2014. Still, they employ a significant proportion of lawyers. In 2014, the 30 largest firms (all with over 100 lawyers) employed 9,500 lawyers, about 10 per cent of practising lawyers (Lexpert 2016).

A small handful of Canadian firms have also joined the stratosphere of global law firms. In 2016, eight had over 500 lawyers (Lexpert 2016), and two had merged with foreign firms (Dentons and Norton Rose). It is noteworthy that none of the foreign mergers involved the dominant Toronto-based firms known as the 'Seven Sisters' (Hasselbeck 2015). Because Toronto is the home and hub of corporate practice, 27 per cent of its lawyers work in firms of over 100 lawyers, up from 19 per cent in 2010 (LSUC 2014; 2009).[5] This concentration is likely due to the increasing number of firms of more than 100 lawyers rather than the further growth of such firms, suggesting that there is declining incentive to grow above this threshold.

Given the large firm's pyramidal structure, with a smaller number of partners depending on the cheaper labour of a larger number of associates (Galanter and Palay 1994), the distribution of lawyers is age graded. 15.4 per cent of new lawyers work in the largest firms (251+) and another 4.6 per cent in slightly smaller ones (101–250 lawyers). Calgary has the highest concentration (41.3 per cent) of new lawyers working in large firms (101+), followed by Toronto (25.8 per cent) (Dinovitzer 2015).

C. Public Sector

A substantial proportion of Canadian lawyers work in the public sector. The 2011 National Household Survey (NHS)[6] found that 15 per cent of Canadian lawyers were employed in the public sector (federal and provincial governments). There is some provincial variation: 15 per cent in Ontario (LSUC, 2008; 2015a), 17 per cent in Quebec (NHS) and 11 per cent in BC (NHS). Among new lawyers, 16.6 per cent work in government, two-thirds for the local or provincial bodies and one-third for the federal government.

---

[5] These data are derived from a voluntary survey, with approximately 50 per cent of lawyers reporting.

[6] The National Household Survey (NHS) replaced the mandatory long-form census in 2011. Although their contents are identical, NHS was a voluntary survey with a lower response rate. Whereas the 2006 long-form census had a 94 per cent response rate, the unweighted NHS response rate was only 68.6 per cent for Canada as a whole and even lower in some of the smaller provinces (Statistics Canada 2015a; 2015b). This makes the NHS less reliable, and 'in some areas with smaller populations and for some population groups, the response rate may be insufficient to provide a valid statistical picture' (Jackson 2016). As a result, many (including government agencies) are not comparing the NHS 2011 to prior census data. Since it is the most recent source of national statistics on lawyers, we draw on these data for a general picture of the legal profession in 2011 but limit our use of the NHS to the national and provincial level.

About half the lawyers working for the federal government are in Ottawa (Dinovitzer 2015).

D. Corporate Counsel

According to surveys by the Counsel Network (2016), the majority of in-house counsel work for corporations, just over half of which are publicly owned, and 13 per cent work for Crown corporations.[7] The remainder work in the non-profit sector. While these corporations include a wide swath of industries, the largest proportion are in financial services, insurance, or banking, though there was a substantial drop in this sector between 2010 and 2012 (from 24 per cent to 16 per cent) and an increase in the proportion working in oil and gas. Although half of corporate counsel reported in 2012 that their departments had grown over the previous two years, only 41 per cent reported that in 2016, when an increasing number reported shrinking legal departments. Most of those in-house counsel (89 per cent) came from a law firm, after an average of 5.3 years in that setting.

E. Not Practising Law

An increasing proportion of lawyers are not practising (25 per cent in 2014, up from 20 per cent in 2002), including those working for business (outside legal departments), educational institutions, and labour unions (see Table 4).[8] The proportion, unsurprisingly, varies by seniority: 92 per cent of new lawyers are practising law in their primary jobs (Dinovitzer 2015).

Table 4 Percentage of Lawyers Practising Law by Geography, 2002–2014

Province/Territory	2002	2006	2010	2014
Newfoundland	79.6	76.7	74.4	75.4
Prince Edward Island	83.5	80.2	68.5	73.4
Nova Scotia	72.8	63.5	60.6	59.2
New Brunswick	82.5	80.1	85.1	76.3
Barreau du Québec	89.2	85.0	82.4	81.3
Chambre des Notaires du Québec	89.1	88.5	87.5	85.3
Ontario	75.3	75.0	74.0	75.7
Manitoba	88.2	79.0	48.6	92.8
Saskatchewan	73.1	73.8	79.8	80.2

(continued)

[7] Crown corporations are wholly owned by the government but operate at arm's length.
[8] The category is based on Law Society fee categories and thus varies across the country. Ontario lawyers who do not practise law pay reduced fees; but those who choose to be suspended are not counted in the practising statistics. As a result, this is a conservative estimate of the proportion not practising.

Table 4 (*Continued*)

Province/Territory	2002	2006	2010	2014
Alberta	82.4	70.4	67.8	66.4
British Columbia	85.3	87.6	84.0	82.6
Nunavut	78.5	82.1	90.9	89.0
Northwest Territories	67.4	70.0	67.0	75.9
Yukon	73.9	97.5	71.8	87.4

Source: FLSC statistics; census data from Statistics Canada; Barreau du Québec.

IV. DEMOGRAPHICS

A. Gender

Feminisation is one of the most significant transformations of modern legal professions. Yet even with the rapid entry of women, very few professions report gender parity (eg Bulgaria, Portugal, Nicaragua, Puerto Rico, Romania, Uruguay, and Venezuela) (Michelson 2013). In Canada, women have increased from 12 per cent of lawyers in 1981 to 42 per cent in 2014, compared with 34 per cent in the US (see Table 5; American Bar Association 2014). Notably, women are half or more of lawyers and notaries in Quebec (see Kay 2002), which also has nearly attained gender parity in its medical doctor workforce (Canadian Medical Association 2017). It is a fair prediction that gender parity is only a matter of time for the legal profession, since in 2006, 52 per cent of lawyers under 44 were women, compared to 39 per cent ten years earlier; and in 2015, 55 per cent of lawyers called to the Bar were women.

Table 5 Percentage of Female Lawyers by Province/Territory, 1981–2014

Province/Territory	1981	1996	2002	2006	2010	2014
Newfoundland	0.0	30.8	32.2	34.6	37.6	39.6
PEI	21.4	26.5	39.8	42.5	51.9	43.8
Nova Scotia	8.8	23.8	34.3	37.1	39.0	40.8
New Brunswick	9.8	23.1	30.8	35.1	36.3	38.2
Barreau du Québec	13.8	36.8	42.1	45.0	47.9	50.5
Chambre des Notaires du Québec			46.4	44.6	50.0	55.2
Ontario	9.5	30.1	33.2	36.4	38.7	40.3
Manitoba	10.1	24.0	27.5	31.1	32.3	34.1
Saskatchewan	12.2	25.8	29.5	31.6	35.3	37.4
Alberta	12.6	27.0	30.9	32.0	34.4	36.6
British Columbia	13.6	28.5	31.8	35.2	37.3	39.2

(*continued*)

Table 5 (Continued)

Province/Territory	1981	1996	2002	2006	2010	2014
Nunavut	N/A	N/A	26.0	29.5	N/A	N/A
Northwest Territories	0.0	N/A	29.3	30.0	31.4	36.3
Yukon	33.3	N/A	28.4	29.8	49.7	39.5

Source: FLSC statistics; census data from Statistics Canada; Barreau du Québec.
Notes: There are no available data for 1981 and 1996 for Barreau du Québec and Chambre des Notaires du Québec; non-practising notaires are excluded from the 2002 data.

B. Gender by Setting

Women have increased their representation in all sectors of the profession over recent decades. By 2006, they accounted for well over half of lawyers in educational institutions and government, with a more modest increase among those working in legal services (from 27.8 per cent in 1996 to 34.0 per cent in 2006) (Statistics Canada 2009a; 2009b).

Between 1996 and 2006, women increased their representation among all classes of legal workers other than those self-employed without help (Statistics Canada 2009c). The growth rate was highest (7.7 per cent) among employees and paid workers (and comprised more than half of employees by 2006), with the result that nearly three-quarters of women were employees.

Among new lawyers, women are less likely than men to work in private firms (63.3 versus 72.1 per cent), more likely to work in the public sector (26.8 compared to 19.5 per cent), and equally likely to work in business and other settings (just under 10 per cent) (Dinovitzer 2015). Within private firms, women are more likely to be working in the smallest firms (2–20 lawyers) and men are more likely to be working in larger firms. Men are also more than twice as likely to be working in solo practice (7.7 compared to 3.5 per cent).

C. Ethnicity and Immigration

The proportion of visible minority[9] lawyers in Canada also has steadily increased, from 2.4 per cent in 1981 to 11.3 per cent in 2011 (see Figure 3). It is important to place this within the larger context of diversity in Canada: 4.7 per cent of Canadians were members of a visible minority group in 1981 (Statistics Canada, 2009d), and by 2011 it was close to 20 per cent (Statistics Canada, 2013).

Canada's major urban centres have seen substantial growth in diversity: visible minorities accounted for nearly one in five lawyers in Vancouver in 2006 and nearly 15 per cent

---

[9] Statistics Canada defines visible minorities as 'persons, other than Aboriginal peoples, who are non-Caucasian in race or non-white in colour. The visible minority population consists mainly of the following groups: Chinese, South Asian, Black, Arab, West Asian, Filipino, Southeast Asian, Latin American, Japanese and Korean': www23.statcan.gc.ca/imdb/p3Var.pl?Function=DEC&Id=45152.

Figure 3 Percentage of Visible Minority Lawyers by Province/Territory and City, 1981–2011

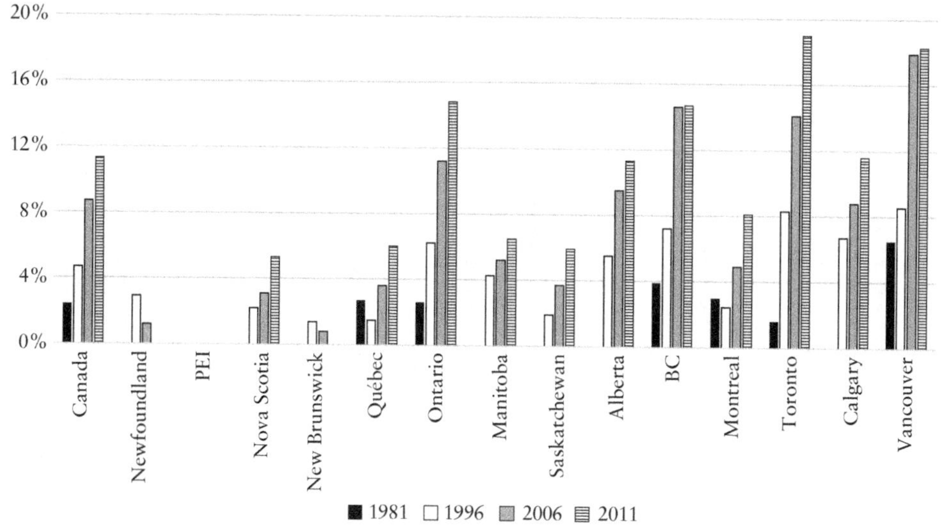

■ 1981 □ 1996 ▦ 2006 ▤ 2011

Source: Statistics Canada.

in Toronto, whereas Montreal had the lowest proportion (4.9 per cent), followed by Calgary (8.8 per cent). The legal profession is substantially less diverse than other professions: in 'Ontario in 2006, members of a visible minority accounted for 30.7 per cent of all physicians, 31.7 per cent of engineers, 17.6 per cent of academics and 11.8 per cent of high-level managers' (Ornstein 2010: ii).

Diversity is growing more rapidly in younger cohorts. Among Ontario lawyers 25–34 years old, visible minorities were '2 per cent in 1981, 3 per cent in 1986, 6 per cent in 1991, 11 per cent in 1996, 17 per cent in 2001 and 20 per cent in 2006' (Ornstein 2010: i). A more recent study found that 22.4 per cent of new lawyers were non-white: 3.7 per cent black, 6.6 per cent Asian, 5.8 per cent South or Southeast Asian, and 6.3 per cent members of other racial minority groups (Dinovitzer 2015).

The share of immigrants has also increased since 1981, despite the fact that entry barriers based on citizenship persisted in some provinces until the mid-2000s (Adams 2016). In 2006, 13.5 per cent of Canada's lawyers were immigrants, a modest increase from 11.4 per cent in both 1981 and 1996 (see Figure 4). The distribution of immigrant lawyers in 2006 was similar to that of visible minorities, with the highest proportions in BC and Ontario (about one in five), followed by Alberta (12.7 per cent). Vancouver and Toronto had by far the highest proportions (22.0 and 20.5 per cent), while Calgary and Montreal were at the low end (13.8 and 10.9 per cent). These fall short of the overall population: the percentage of foreign born was 47.5 in Toronto, 39.6 in Vancouver and 20.6 in Montreal. Again, immigrants are better represented among the recent cohort of lawyers (16.4 per cent) (Dinovitzer 2015). Country of origin is important. As Ornstein (2010: 11) notes, '[b]eing an immigrant from a country whose majority population is defined as a visible minority in Canada does more to decrease a person's chances of being a lawyer than being a member of that visible minority group'.

Figure 4 Immigrants as a Percentage of Lawyers by Province/Territory and City, 1981–2011

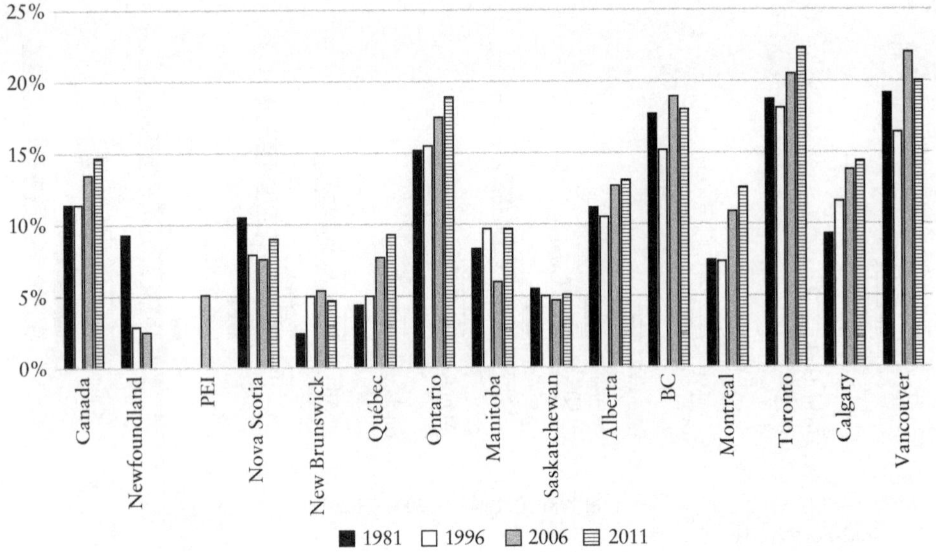

■ 1981   ☐ 1996   ■ 2006   ☰ 2011

Source: Statistics Canada.

V. EARNINGS

Lawyers' earnings[10] have risen considerably over the past 30 years: median income increased from $76,939 in 1981 to $107,324 in 2011 and the average from $107,303 to $153,320 (Statistics Canada 2016b; 2016c). These figures are substantially higher than in other industries (Statistics Canada 2009b). Average earnings are, of course, also shaped by local labour markets: Toronto and Calgary lawyers earned above $225,000 in 2006 compared to about $150,000 in Montreal and Vancouver.

New lawyers working full-time reported a median income of $78,000, but data demonstrate the variation by practice setting (see Figure 5): $105,000 in firms with over 250 lawyers, $85,000 in firms of 101–250 and house counsel, $70–80,000 in smaller firms and government, $60,000 in solo practice, and $64,000 in NGOs (Dinovitzer 2015). They earned most in Alberta ($90,000), BC ($83,000) and Ontario ($81,350) and least in New Brunswick ($36,000).

The data also indicate a declining yet persistent gender gap: women earned 56 per cent as much as men in 1981 and 78 per cent in 2011, with the narrowing attributed to the fact that women's earnings increased faster than men's (Statistics Canada 1981; 2011; see Figure 6). Yet even among the newer generation women earn 93 per cent of men's salary, and the gender gap is larger in firms, business and in-house counsel, although close to parity in the public sector (Dinovitzer 2015).

In contrast, the racial/ethnic earnings gap appears to be widening. In 1981, visible minorities' median earnings roughly equaled those of white lawyers, but by 2011 white

---

[10] All income data are in Can$; those from 1981 and 2006 have been adjusted to 2010 constant dollars using the Cost Price Index: www.bankofcanada.ca/rates/related/inflation-calculator/.

Figure 5 Median Salary of New Lawyers by Gender and Practice Setting (Canadian Dollars)

■ Women ▒ Men

Source: Law and Beyond Study (Full-time Workers Only, N=1031).

Figure 6 Women's Earnings as a Percent of Men's

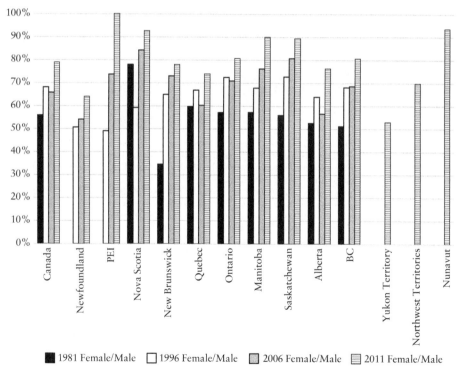

■ 1981 Female/Male   ☐ 1996 Female/Male   ▒ 2006 Female/Male   ☰ 2011 Female/Male

Source: Statistics Canada.

lawyers were earning 31 per cent more.[11] The recent cohort of lawyers displays differences between ethnic groups (Dinovitzer, 2015). Among those in law firms, for example, black respondents report the lowest median earnings and Asians the highest because the former are more likely to be solo practitioners and the latter in the largest firms.

A similar pattern of growing inequality is found among immigrant lawyers, whose earnings dropped from close to parity in 1981 to 87 per cent of Canadian-born lawyers' earnings in 2011. Yet the recent cohort of immigrant lawyers working full time earned 95.7 per cent of the earnings reported by Canadian-born lawyers (Dinovitzer 2015). One hypothesis for this discrepancy is that new immigrant lawyers are generally educated in Canada, while the older cohorts of immigrant lawyers trained abroad.

VI. LEGAL EDUCATION

A. Demographics

Entry to the Canadian legal profession is regulated by provincial and territorial governing bodies (generally called Law Societies), which almost always require a law degree followed by an apprenticeship.[12] As Arthurs, Weisman and Zemans noted (1988), given the low failure rate in law schools and the generally high pass rates for the Bar exam,[13] admission to a Canadian law school virtually guarantees entry into law practice. The real competition for entry is fought on the battleground of law school admissions.[14] Canada has 17 common law schools[15] and another four offering civil law degrees in Quebec (while Ottawa and McGill offer both degrees and thus comprise part of the 17). Admission to law school is highly competitive: the bottom Law School Aptitude Test (LSAT) scores and undergraduate grade point averages (UGPA) of Canadian common law schools are about the same as those of the US law school ranked 64th out of 197.[16] Competition is also enhanced by the fact that only two law schools have been established in Canada since 1978, in interior BC and Northern Ontario, both far from large urban centres.

---

[11] This varies by ethnicity. Japanese-Canadian lawyers were the lowest paid in 1981 but the highest paid in 2011.

[12] As we discuss below, Ontario has recently experimented with an alternative process, the Legal Practice Program. Furthermore, the newly-opened Bora Laskin Faculty of Law has been allowed to replace articling with a 15-week Practice Placement for third-year law students.

[13] Pass rates are not routinely published, but we have estimated them at 85–100 per cent by comparing those who enroll for the Bar admission course with those called to the Bar in each province. Quebec is an exception, with rates as low as 45 per cent for University of Ottawa graduates (École du Barreau 2015).

[14] While the number of US law school applicants has decreased dramatically over recent years, this has not occurred in Canada: 'In the last few years, between 5,000 and 7,000 applicants have competed for approximately 2,350 first-year places in Canada's common-law law schools': www.lsac.org/jd/choosing-a-law-school/canadian/law-schools-select-applicants. Comparing the numbers who apply and enroll reveals the intensity of competition for admission; only 37.3 per cent of first-year applicants in 2015 enrolled in an Ontario law school in the autumn of 2016. This proportion varied significantly between schools: 10 per cent at University of Toronto and just over 6 per cent at Lakehead University: www.ouac.on.ca/statistics/law-school-application-statistics/.

[15] Université de Moncton offers a common law degree in French and does not require the LSAT for admission.

[16] The lowest median LSAT score reported by a Canadian law school is 159, and the lowest GPA is 3.46: www.lsac.org/choosing-law-school/find-law-school/canadian-law-schools.

Growth in the profession has come from two sources: existing Canadian law school enrolments and lawyers trained abroad. The entering classes at most law schools have expanded, producing an average of 32 per cent[17] more graduates in 2014 than in 2002. Data from Ontario, which provides statistics on enrolments by law school, reveal that growth is uneven. The University of Toronto and Osgoode Hall displayed only marginal increases, whereas the University of Ottawa had a dramatic increase, followed by significant increases at Windsor and Queen's.

Enrollment growth has not occurred at the expense of student credentials. The mean LSAT score for Canadian test takers increased from 151.6 in 2007/08 to 152.67 in 2013/14, whereas US scores were constant (150.51 and 150.59).[18] And though the number of LSAT takers declined in the US after 2008, it has continued to increase in Canada (Dalessandro et al 2014: 9). The difference is no doubt due to the fact that the Canadian economy and legal profession experienced a milder blow from the 2008 recession and a quicker recovery (Bouvin 2011).

Competition for entry to law school has become so fierce that, in addition to the 7 per cent of Canadian LSAT takers who matriculate in ABA-approved US law schools, other Canadians are enrolling in UK and Australian law schools, which are creating programmes catering to them. Those educated abroad and wishing to practise in Canada must submit their credentials for verification by the National Committee on Accreditation (NCA), which may require additional courses and/or exams. Once the NCA issues a Certificate of Qualification, individuals can begin the process of licensing through a provincial law society.[19] The number of NCA certificates increased almost tenfold from 2008 to 2014 (89 to 810), representing 16 per cent of all Bar admissions in Canada that year.[20] (These figures include both Canadian students trained abroad and new immigrants who obtained a law degree abroad.)

B. Curriculum

Since the 1960s, legal education has been only lightly regulated by provincial law societies (Arthurs et al 1988). This led to a high degree of variation between the provinces, including McGill's combined programme of common and civil law and other legal systems. In 2015, FLSC established a national standard for Canadian law schools, the 'National Requirement', outlining the academic programme and learning resources law schools must offer and the knowledge and skills they must impart for graduates to be

---

[17] There are no general statistics on law school enrolments outside Ontario. These data are from the FLSC's Students Admitted to Bar Admission Course numbers as a rough proxy for law graduates.

[18] At University of Toronto, the most competitive school, the median GPA for the incoming classes of 1994 and 2014 rose from 83 to 86, while median LSAT scores rose from 163 to 167: 68.media.tumblr.com/eb273bef3f43629ed34ed46c26251d18/tumblr_ncounh4RiE1slek2no1_1280.png; 68.media.tumblr.com/8fe44a6 6beb92275c55dfa072732cf80/tumblr_ncoupq7Ute1slek2no1_1280.png.

[19] The NCA does not assess the legal credentials of individuals who want to become members of the Barreau du Québec or the Chambre des notaires du Québec, which have their own evaluation procedures.

[20] Data for 2013 indicate the national origins of those receiving certificates: 26 per cent UK, 24 per cent US, 14 per cent Australia, 10 per cent India, and 5 per cent Nigeria: www.canadianlawyermag.com/legalfeeds/1886/dentons-imperial-launch-program-for-lawyers-from-abroad.html.

eligible for law society admission programmes.[21] As Arthurs (2016: 16) notes, 'the clear intention is to restore some sense of common cause and common culture amongst new entrants to practice' (see also Arthurs 1998; Tong and Pue 1999; Pue 2016). Yet Arthurs also cautions:

> These and other law society policies have helped to legitimate a shift in pedagogic practice in law faculties away from an intellectual approach to law and towards 'experiential learning,' in part in the hope that new graduates will indeed be 'practice ready' when they are licensed.[22]

Legal education has recently experienced two major transformations. Most law schools followed the University of Toronto's 2001 decision to change the name of the common law degree from an LLB to a JD. The primary justification has been that the LLB signified an undergraduate degree, whereas the Canadian common law degree requires prior undergraduate education. Some have countered that the retitling was simply another example of isomorphism in which Canada has mimicked its southern neighbour (Arthurs 2000). The second transformation has been a steady and significant rise in tuition – a trend affecting most professional education in the country, including medicine, management, and dentistry (Statistics Canada 2017b). Law school tuition doubled between 2006 and 2016, reaching a peak of $30,000 at University of Toronto and $16,000 in Ontario, compared to the national average of $11,000. There are, of course, deviations from this pattern, notably in Quebec. McGill's common law programme remains an LLB; and law school tuition is low throughout the province, which has a long history of social action relating to postsecondary education dating to the 1960s, coupled with greater government financing.

C. Entry to the Profession

Because of the growth in law school enrolments and increasing numbers entering the profession after studying abroad, some jurisdictions have had difficulty placing students in the articling positions required for admission to the bar. Ontario has experienced the greatest pressure. Since 2011, approximately 11–15 per cent of those beginning the licensing process have not obtained articles. The Law Society of Upper Canada (LSUC) (ie Ontario) created a pilot alternative, the Legal Practice Program, a four-month training course and four-month work placement.[23] The Law Society of BC (2015: 32) has stated there are enough articling positions for its graduates, while young lawyers in Quebec have reported problems with the articling process (Young Bar of Montreal 2016: 11); but there do not seem to be other reports of major strain (Neshevich 2012).

Articling remains a major feeder for lawyers' careers. 63.4 per cent of the recent cohort of lawyers started their first jobs with the employers with whom they articled (although this varied widely by province and setting). Respondents who articled for private law

---

[21] At flsc.ca/law-schools/.
[22] Under the new regulatory framework law schools are reviewed annually by the Canadian Common Law Program Approval Committee.
[23] It will expire with the 2018/19 licensing year.

firms were more likely to be hired back compared to those who had articled in the public sector; and hire-back rates were highest in the larger law firms (93 per cent in firms of 101–250 lawyers, 82.9 per cent in firms of 251+) (Dinovitzer 2015).

VII. ACCESS TO JUSTICE: LEGAL AID AND PRO BONO

Canada's legal aid programme has been co-sponsored by the federal and provincial/territorial governments since 1973 (Government of Canada 2017a). In 1982, the Canadian Charter of Rights and Freedoms expanded legal aid by identifying legally protected groups, leading to a steady increase in successful applications (Government of Canada 2017b). The range of services has also expanded. For example, Legal Aid Ontario (LAO) provides services in Aboriginal, criminal, family, mental health, and refugee law and is now one of the largest legal services providers in North America.[24] Legal aid spending has also grown considerably, from $15 million in 1973 to $856 million in 2014/15 ($162 million in 1973 dollars) (Government of Canada 2017b; Statistics Canada 2016d).

Most Canadians cannot afford the formal justice system because of rising legal services costs and underfunded legal aid programmes (Farrow et al 2016). Many do not qualify due to low income ceilings, even though Legal Aid Ontario significantly expanded eligibility and increased funding for clinics in 2015/16 (LAO 2016). However, the majority of litigants in family courts are self-represented, and they are an increasing minority in other civil courts (Semple 2014: 373), suggesting that Canada's legal aid system has failed to resolve the current access to justice crisis. As several scholars have noted, many shortcomings of legal aid derive from the definition of legal needs (Mosher 1997; Mossman et al 2010).

Some law firms have responded by offering 'unbundled' legal services, allowing litigants to retain lawyers for certain tasks rather than full representation; and some simple legal services are now available by telephone and online. Partly in response to access to justice needs, formal pro bono organisations have also been established in five provinces, with more flexible eligibility criteria than legal aid (CBA 2016). Pro bono services are also provided by private law firms (Sossin 2008) and by law students through Pro Bono Students Canada. But these bodies also are unable to meet the growing demand for their services.[25]

VIII. REGULATION A: COMPETITION AND THE FUTURE OF LEGAL PRACTICE

Canadian lawyers and Quebec's notaires are legally required to join one of the 14 provincial and territorial law societies authorised by law to govern the legal profession in the public interest. The public's right to seek legal advice from professionals operating at arm's length from the government is an important part of the Canadian legal system;

---

[24] See www.legalaid.on.ca/en/about/historical_overview.asp.
[25] See www.cba.org/Sections/Pro-Bono/Pro-Bono-Resources-in-Canada/Resources.

and the self-regulation of the legal profession is enshrined in law. The law societies are charged with controlling entry to the profession, regulating members' conduct, tracking and auditing the use of client trust funds, handling complaints and sanctioning members who violate standards of conduct.[26]

Canada's legal professionals may represent the sole remaining case of 'unfettered self-regulation' in the common law world (Rhode and Woolley 2012: 2774). Judges exercise little control over lawyers. Courts cannot sanction misconduct or suspend or disbar lawyers. And while other regulatory agencies, such as the securities commission, may impose practice requirements, this has had limited effects on the legal and ethical commitments of Canadian lawyers.

In recent years, globalisation, technology, and changes in the regulatory structures of foreign legal professions have created new challenges for Canadian lawyers and their regulators. Developments such as the outsourcing of legal services,[27] globalisation of law firms, and authorisation of alternative business structures by the UK and Australia have forced Canadian law societies to consider changes to the structure and regulation of the legal profession (Terry et al 2012).

A. Changes in the Regulation of Paralegals

In 2014 there were 24,400 individuals working in paralegal and related occupations, including notaries public (Government of Canada 2016). Historically, direct competition with lawyers' services has been prohibited by 'unauthorised practice' clauses in the legislation creating law societies; and no jurisdiction regulated independent practice by legal paraprofessionals (Stager and Arthurs 1990: 210–11). The status quo has come under significant pressure because of concerns over access to justice generated by the rise in self-representation, high cost of legal services, and inadequate funding of legal aid (Terry et al 2012: 2674). To bridge this 'justice gap', some law societies have considered shrinking lawyers' monopoly over the provision of legal services, allowing paralegals, notaries public, and other licensed agents to perform particular functions, either autonomously or under lawyer supervision. Some provincial law societies are considering focusing on oversight of legal work rather than lawyers.

Ontario took the lead in 2007 by giving LSUC the power to train, certify, and regulate paralegals' conduct (Woolley and Farrow 2016: 549–50). Paralegals may provide legal services independently for a limited range of matters, including traffic tickets, small claims courts, administrative tribunals, and some criminal charges.[28] Practising paralegals must carry professional liability insurance; and LSUC handles complaints against and discipline of paralegals violating its by-laws and the *Paralegal Rules of Conduct* (Cameron 2016). The Law Society had issued 2,311 paralegal licences by the end of 2008 and about 7,700 by 2015 (LSUC 2008; 2015a). The Law Societies of Nova

---

[26] See flsc.ca/about-us/our-members-canadas-law-societies/.
[27] For the remainder of the chapter, the term 'legal services' simply refers to legal work or practice, not necessarily services provided by lawyers (ie it refers to the substance of the service, not the provider).
[28] ibid.

Scotia and BC have also considered regulating paralegals (Perry 2015: 5). In 2014, a Task Force advised BC's Law Society to establish classes of legal service providers who could represent clients in arbitration and mediation and practise independently in such areas as debtor-creditor, employment, and family law (Law Society of BC 2014).

B. Notaries: Quebec versus Others

It is important to distinguish between notaries and Quebec's notaires, more accurately described as lawyers (Stager and Arthurs 1990: 20). Like lawyers, notaires must be members of a law society, which regulates their behaviour (FLSC 2016). Notaires must graduate from law school and write a formal entrance exam in order to join the Chambre des Notaires du Québec (CNQ). They also complete an extra year of law school to earn a diploma in notarial law (DDN) and article for a longer period than lawyers (Kay 2009: 91). The number of notaires grew from 3,510 in 1998 to 4,580 in 2014 (85.3 per cent of whom were practising) (FLSC 1998; 2014).

Notaries (or notaries public), by contrast, are unregulated in every province except BC, which passed the Notaries Act in 1956 (Stager and Arthurs 1990: 20–21). In 1929, BC had more notaries than lawyers (approximately 1,000 and 600), but the number of notaries had fallen to 332 by 1981 and has fluctuated around that level ever since (Brockman 1997: 197; Gourley 2014: 2). BC notaries can provide legal services independently in a range of matters, including conveyancing and administering real estate and drafting contracts, wills, liens, and affidavits. They must be members of the Society of Notaries Public of BC and have completed a Master's degree in Applied Legal Studies.[29] Outside of Quebec and BC, unregulated notaries may only collect affidavits and notarise or authenticate documents (Brockman 1997: 225; Stager and Arthurs 1990: 20–21).

C. MDPs and Relations with Other Professionals

Recent research suggests the public consults lawyers on just 11.7 per cent of legal matters, individuals doing so primarily for real estate issues, family and criminal matters, wills, and powers of attorney (CBA 2014: 19). Financial planners, accountants, human resource consultants, and other professionals are increasingly providing advice and services. The number of enterprises offering systematised, standardised, or routinised legal services requiring limited legal expertise is rising, and competition from international law firms or legal process outsourcers is further reducing the demand for lawyers in Canada. About half of Canadian law firms outsource legal processes (Ammachchi 2016). Although multi-disciplinary practices (MDPs) are expanding in other countries, they are virtually non-existent in Canada, where they are subject to strict and cumbersome controls (CBA 2013: 30; CBA 2014: 19). In Ontario, for example, lawyers and licensed

---

[29] See www.notaries.bc.ca/becomeANotary/index.rails.

paralegals must apply to LSUC to form an MDP, assume responsibility and carry professional liability insurance for their partners, and submit annual reports to the law society.[30]

D. The Rise of Legal Alternatives

The term alternative business structure (ABS) encompasses both traditional law firms and alternative ways of providing legal services, including firms owned in whole or part by non-lawyers or non-paralegals, firms providing both legal and other professional services, and firms offering a variety of products ranging from sophisticated technology and business applications to automated legal forms that can be completed by individual clients (LSUC 2014). Lawyer-owned entities still have the exclusive right to provide legal services, and regulators have limited profit sharing between lawyers and non-lawyers and the joint provision of legal and non-legal services (CBA Alberta 2015). However, pressure to reduce the cost of legal services, rising competition, and limited growth in certain areas of legal practice have resulted in a reassessment of how lawyers organise their operating practices and business structures (CBA 2013: 5). Paquin (2017: 2) argues that given the crisis in access to justice, the cost of legal services, and technological innovations,

> the question remains whether the Canadian legal profession is on the verge of an incremental evolution aimed at adjusting the modes of delivery of legal services to new economic realities, or a more fundamental revolution involving the reconsideration of the 'professional' nature of legal work and the special status granted to lawyers as professionals, including the privilege to self-regulate.

Wooley and Farrow (2016) agree that new legal services providers are an essential part of addressing the access to justice crisis.

In 2014, a Canadian Bar Association (CBA) study recommended that provincial regulators begin letting non-lawyers own law firms (Hasselback 2015), and provincial regulatory bodies are grappling with the possibility of permitting ABSs. In Ontario, however, an LSUC working group decided against considering majority non-lawyer ownership, citing the modest improvements in innovation and access to justice realised by Australia and England and Wales (which allow it) (LSUC 2015b).

The 'Big Four' accounting firms have been gradually moving into legal services since the 1990s. An early merger between Ernst & Young and a Canadian firm ultimately failed, prompting a decade-long pause in the Big Four's movement into legal services. Accounting firms have regained interest but with the more restrained goal of providing 'complementary' instead of 'comprehensive' legal services. Nonetheless, they have consistently encountered 'the intransigence of the Canadian legal profession' (Melnitzer 2017: 48). Thus, the fate of MDPs and other ABSs in Canada rests primarily on the ongoing regulation of legal services. However, two of Canada's mega law firms (Dentons and Bennett Jones) have recently recruited executives from the 'Big Four', suggesting a potential shift in how law firms are relating to both the threat and the promise of accounting firms (Melnitzer 2017: 44–46).

---

[30]See www.lsuc.on.ca/For-Paralegals/Manage-Your-Practice/Practice-Arrangements/Multi-Discipline-Practice-and-Multi-Discipline-Partnership/.

IX. REGULATION B: ETHICS

Although Canada's provincial and territorial law societies are responsible for regulating the practice of lawyers licensed in their respective jurisdictions, the CBA's[31] Code of Professional Conduct has historically shaped the activities of Canadian lawyers (Arthurs et al 1988). Citing the interprovincial mobility[32] of lawyers and the globalisation of legal practice, law societies have begun to cooperate to institute national guidelines for professional conduct (Rhode and Woolley 2012). In 2011, FLSC published a national Model Code of Professional Conduct, which most provincial law societies have adopted (with some local modifications) and the rest are considering (FLSC 2015).

A. Complaints and Discipline

Although the provincial/territorial law societies are responsible for hearing complaints and disciplining their members, FLSC

> is working with Canada's law societies to develop high national standards for how they handle complaints to ensure that members of the public are treated fairly and openly and their concerns addressed promptly, wherever in Canada they have used the services of members of the legal profession.[33]

FLSC's (2016) National Discipline Standards outline sanctions for lawyers who have violated law society rules, including fine, reprimand, practice restrictions, suspension, and disbarment.

Statistics collected from provincial and territorial law societies by FLSC indicate that the number of complaints they received decreased between 2002 and 2014 (eg from over 6,000 to just under 5,000 in Ontario). Many of those filed in 2002–14 did not make it past the screening stage. For example, in 2006 over half the complaints received by the Law Society of BC were screened out (though in other years the proportion was 10–47 per cent). However, the Barreau du Québec (BQ), CNQ, and the Prince Edward Island and Yukon Law Societies screened out relatively few complaints during this time (perhaps because complaints to BQ and CHQ are pre-screened by a third party). Most of the complaints that made it past the screening stage led to informal resolutions or disciplinary action; very few led to acquittals. The proportion of complaints resulting in a conviction is generally less than 3 per cent.

In addition to the number of complaints received, the law societies also track who is targeted by these complaints. In Ontario, the proportion of lawyers subject to complaints has declined over time (LSUC 2015a), from 6.4 per cent of all lawyers

---

[31] CBA is Canada's largest professional association for lawyers. Lawyers in New Brunswick must join the CBA; membership is voluntary in all other jurisdictions: www.cba.org/Who-We-Are.

[32] Canada's provincial law societies recognise lawyers' credentials from the province in which they were initially admitted to practice, and members of the legal profession may transfer between jurisdictions on a temporary or permanent basis. Interprovincial mobility is facilitated by the National Mobility Agreement, the Territorial Mobility Agreement, and the Quebec Mobility Agreement and Addendum: flsc.ca/national-initiatives/national-mobility-of-the-legal-profession/.

[33] See flsc.ca/national-initiatives/national-discipline-standards/.

in 2009 to 5.5 per cent in 2014 and from 12.4 per cent of private practitioners in 2009 to 10.9 per cent in 2014 (Cameron 2016). Sole practitioners are just a third of Ontario practitioners, yet they receive more than half (53 per cent) of the complaints. Although unethical behaviour might be attributed to inexperience, complaints actually vary *directly* with age. The 20 per cent of lawyers who have been practising for up to five years receive just 12 per cent of complaints, while the 20 per cent practising more than 30 years receive 29 per cent. The majority of complaints received by LSUC refer to service issues, followed by integrity and governance; elsewhere they commonly cite quality, delay, lawyers' fees and attitudes. They relate primarily to family law, estates, real estate, civil litigation, and criminal law (Law Society of Saskatchewan 2014; Law Society of Manitoba 2015; Law Society of BC 2011; Nova Scotia Barristers' Society 2016).

When lawyer dishonesty inflicts economic loss, clients may be entitled to payments from a compensation fund to which all lawyers contribute.[34] Both the number and value of these payments have fluctuated across the provinces over the past several decades. For example, while payments in Ontario totalled $2,443,707 for 216 claims in 1984[35] (an average of $11,313 per claim), they fell to $1,768,783 for 102 claims in 2014 (an average of $17,341 per claim) (Legge 1985; FLSC 2014). Between 2002 and 2014, the average cost per claim rose from $33,892 to $228,603 in Alberta, $6,451 to $12,746 for Quebec lawyers, and from $43,620 in 2006 to $66,450 in 2014 in BC. Meanwhile, Saskatchewan, Manitoba, and PEI each made payments from their compensation funds in 2002 but not in 2014 (FLSC 2014).

X. CONCLUSION

Canada is in the midst of profound transformations. Its population is becoming more diverse, with projections that by 2036, 28 per cent of its population will be foreign born. Its cities, which are home to the majority of the legal profession, are even more diverse: in 2016, 46 per cent of Toronto's population was foreign born, while over half identified as a visible minority. There are signals that the legal profession is struggling to adapt to this diversity, but at the same time these transformations are providing a unique opportunity. There are other sources of pressure, both internal and external, which have the potential to produce important transformations in the decades ahead, including alternative licensing structures, innovative forms of practice, technology and artificial intelligence, and the pressures of the global marketplace.

REFERENCES

Adams, T (2016) 'When "Citizenship is Indispensable to the Practice of a Profession": Citizenship Requirements for Entry to Practise Professions in Canada' 29 *Journal of Historical Sociology* 550.

---

[34] www.lsuc.on.ca/with.aspx?id=428.

[35] All compensation fund payment data are in Can$; those from 1984 and 2002 have been adjusted to 2014 constant dollars using the Cost Price Index: www.bankofcanada.ca/rates/related/inflation-calculator/.

American Bar Association 'A Current Glance at Women in the Law July 2014' (2014) www.americanbar.org/content/dam/aba/administrative/women/current_glance_statistics_july2014.pdf.

Ammachchi, N (2016) 'Nearly Half of Canada's Law Firms Are Outsourcing Legal Processes: Study' www.nearshoreamericas.com/canadian-lawyers-happy-legal-process-outsourcing-study/.

Arthurs, HW (1998) 'The Political Economy of Canadian Legal Education' 25 *Journal of Law and Society* 14.

—— (2000) 'Poor Canadian Legal Education: So Near to Wall Street, So Far from God' 38 *Osgoode Hall Law Journal* 381.

—— (2017) 'The Commonwealth of Lawyers?' 24 *International Journal of the Legal Profession* 13.

Arthurs, HW, Weisman, R, and Zemans FH (1988) 'Canadian Lawyers: A Peculiar Professionalism' in RL Abel and PSC Lewis (eds), *Lawyers in Society: Vol I The Common Law World* (Berkeley, University of California Press).

Bouvin, J (28 March 2011) 'The "Great" Recession in Canada: Perception vs. Reality' www.bankofcanada.ca/2011/03/great-recession-canada-perception-reality/.

Brockman, J (1997) '"Better to Enlist their Support than to Suffer their Antagonism": The Game of Monopoly between Lawyers and Notaries in British Columbia, 1930–81' 4 *International Journal of the Legal Profession* 197.

Cameron, L (2016) 'Executive Director's Report: Analysis of Complaints Received by Professional Regulation in 2014' lawsocietyontario.azureedge.net/media/lso/media/legacy/pdf/c/convocation-april-2016-professional-regulation.pdf.

Canadian Bar Association (2013) 'The Future of Legal Services in Canada: Trends and Issues' www.cba.org/CBAMediaLibrary/cba_na/PDFs/CBA%20Legal%20Futures%20PDFS/trends-isssues-eng.pdf.

—— (2014) 'Futures: Transforming the Delivery of Legal Services in Canada' www.cba.org/cbamedialibrary/cba_na/pdfs/cba%20legal%20futures%20pdfs/futures-final-eng.pdf.

—— (2016) 'Study on Access to the Legal System – Legal Aid' www.cba.org/CMSPages/GetFile.aspx?guid=8b0c4d64-cb3f-460f-9733-1aaff164ef6a.

Canadian Bar Association Alberta (2015) 'Alternative Business Structures and the Modern Regulatory Dilemma' www.cba-alberta.org/Publications-Resources/Resources/Law-Matters/Law-Matters-Fall-2015-Issue/Alternative-Business-Structures-and-the-Modern-Reg.

Canadian Medical Association (2017) 'Number of Active Physicians by Age, Sex and Province/Territory, Canada, 2018' www.cma.ca/sites/default/files/pdf/Physician%20Data/04-age-sex-prv.pdf.

Chambre des Notaires du Québec (2016) 'Rapport Annuel 2015–2016' www.cnq.org/DATA/TEXTEDOC/2015-2016.pdf.

Dalessandro, SP, Anthony, LC, and Reese, LM (2014) 'LSAT Performance with Regional, Gender, and Racial/Ethnic Breakdowns: 2007–2008 Through 2013–2014 Testing Years' www.lsac.org/docs/default-source/research-(lsac-resources)/tr-14-02.pdf.

Daniels, R (1993) 'Growing Pains: The Why and How of Law Firm Expansion' 43 *University of Toronto Law Journal* 147.

Dinovitzer, R (2015) 'Law and Beyond: A National Study of Canadian Law Graduates' individual.utoronto.ca/dinovitzer/images/LABReport.pdf.

École du Barreau (2015) 'Formation Professionnelle 2014–2015: Taux de Réussite par Provenance Universitaire' www.ecoledubarreau.qc.ca/media/cms_page_media/127/statistiques-universite-2014-2015.pdf.

Farrow, TC, Currie, A, Aylwin, N, Jacobs, L, Northrup, D, and Moore, L (2016) 'Everyday Legal Problems and the Cost of Justice in Canada: Overview Report' Osgoode Legal Studies Research Paper No 57.

Federation of Law Societies (1998) '1998 Law Societies' Statistics' flsc.ca/wp-content/uploads/2015/03/1998-statistical-report.pdf.

—— (2014) '2014 Law Societies' Statistics' docs.flsc.ca/2014-Statistics.pdf.

—— (2015) 'Federation of Law Societies of Canada Launches Interactive Model Code of Professional Conduct' (9 December) flsc.ca/federation-of-law-societies-of-canada-launches-interactive-model-code-of-professional-conduct/.

—— (2016) 'National Discipline Standards' (June) flsc.ca/wp-content/uploads/2014/10/DisciplineStandardsJune2016.pdf.

Galanter, M and Palay, T (1994) *Tournament of Lawyers: The Transformation of the Big Law Firm* (Chicago, University of Chicago Press).

Gourley, A (2014) 'The Professionalization of BC Notaries 1981–2010: From the Brink of Elimination to the Brink of Expansion' 49 *UBC Law Review* 339.

Government of Canada (2016) 'Job Market Report: Paralegal and Related Occupations' www.jobbank.gc.ca/report-eng.do?area=9219&lang=eng&noc=4211&ln=n&s=2.

—— (2017a) 'Legal Aid Program' www.justice.gc.ca/eng/fund-fina/gov-gouv/aid-aide.html.

—— (2017b) 'Riding the Third Wave: Rethinking Criminal Legal Aid within an Access to Justice Framework' www.justice.gc.ca/eng/rp-pr/csj-sjc/ccs-ajc/rr03_5/p2.html.

Hasselback, D, 'Why that Proposal to Let Non-Lawyers Own Canadian Law Firms is Probably Toast' *Financial Post* (12 August 2015) business.financialpost.com/legal-post/drew-hasselback-that-proposal-to-open-canadian-law-firm-ownership-to-non-lawyers-is-probably-toast.

Jackson, H, 'The Long-Form Census is Back, It's Online – And This Time, It's Mandatory' *CBC News* (2 May 2016) www.cbc.ca/news/politics/mandatory-census-mail-out-1.3557511.

Kay, F (2002) 'Crossroads of Innovation and Diversity: The Careers of Women Lawyers in Quebec' 47 *McGill Law Journal* 699.

—— (2009) 'The First Legal Profession of New France in Jeopardy or Revival?: History and Futures of the Quebec Notariat' 16 *International Journal of the Legal Profession* 87.

Law Society of British Columbia (2011) 'Top Complaint Against Lawyers Is Rude or Uncivil Behaviour' 2 *Benchers' Bulletin*.

—— (2014) 'Report of the Legal Services Regulatory Framework Task Force 4-5' (5 December) www.lawsociety.bc.ca/Website/media/Shared/docs/publications/reports/LegalServicesRegulatoryFrameworkTF.pdf.

—— (2015) 'Admission Program Review Report' (4 December) www.lawsociety.bc.ca/Website/media/Shared/docs/publications/reports/LawyerEd_2015.pdf.

Law Society of Manitoba (2015) '2015 Annual Report'.

Law Society of Saskatchewan (2014) 'Annual Report 2014' www.lawsociety.sk.ca/media/113643/AR2014op.pdf.

Law Society of Upper Canada (2008) '2008 Annual Report Performance Highlights' lawsocietyontario.azureedge.net/media/lso/media/legacy/pdf/a/arep_full_08.pdf.

—— (2014) 'Alternative Business Structures and the Legal Profession in Ontario: A Discussion Paper' www.lsuc.on.ca/uploadedFiles/abs-discussion-paper.pdf.

—— (2015a) '2015 Annual Report' www.annualreport.lsuc.on.ca/2015/en/index.html.

—— (2015b) 'Professional Regulation Committee Report to Convocation' lsuc.on.ca/uploadedFiles/For_the_Public/About_the_Law_Society/Convocation_Decisions/2015/convocation-january-2015-professional-regulation.pdf.

Legal Aid Ontario (2016), 'Minutes of Legal Aid Ontario clinic law advisory committee, on March 10, 2016' www.legalaid.on.ca/en/publications/boardac/2016-03-10-cliniclaw-advisorycommittee.asp.

Legge, L (1985) 'The Treasurer's Report to the Annual Meeting' (Law Society of Upper Canada).

Lexpert (2016) 'Canada's Largest Law Firms' www.lexpert.ca/500/canadas-largest-law-firms/.

Melnitzer, J (2017) 'Accounting Firms in Law: The Long Game' *Lexpert Magazine*, www.lexpert.ca/article/the-long-game/.

Michelson, E (2013) 'Women in the Legal Profession, 1970–2010: A Study of the Global Supply of Women' 20 *Indiana Journal of Global Legal Studies* 1071.

Mosher, J, 'Poverty Law – A Case Study' (1997) Paper 82, digitalcommons.osgoode.yorku.ca/reports/82.

Mossman, MJ, Schucher, K and Schmeing, C (2010) 'Comparing and Understanding Legal Aid Priorities: A Paper Prepared for Legal Aid Ontario' 29 *Windsor Review of Legal and Social* 149.

Neshevich, C (2012) 'Does Articling Need an Overhaul?' *CBA National Magazine*.

Nova Scotia Barristers' Society (2016) '2016 Annual Report' nsbs.org/sites/default/files/cms/publications/annual-reports/2016annualreport.pdf.

Ornstein, M (2010) *Racialization and Gender of Lawyers in Ontario: A Report for the Law Society of Upper Canada* (Toronto, The Law Society of Upper Canada).

Paquin, J (2017) 'From partners to team leaders: tracking changes in the Canadian legal profession through discourse analysis' (unpublished manuscript).

Perry, J (2015) 'Access-to-Justice Priorities at the Root of Regulatory Overhaul' 33 *The Society Record* 5.

Pue, WW (2016) *Lawyers' Empire: Legal Professions and Cultural Authority, 1780–1950* (Vancouver, UBC Press).

Rhode, DL and Woolley, A (2012) 'Comparative Perspectives on Lawyer Regulation: An Agenda for Reform in the United States and Canada' 80 *Fordham Law Review* 2761.

Semple, N (2014) 'Depending on the Kindness of Strangers: Access to Civil Justice in Canada' 16 *Legal Ethics* 373.

Sommerlad, H (2017) 'Lawyers, Legal Education and Nation Building: Lessons from Lawyers' Empire: Legal Professions and Cultural Authority 1789–1950' 24 *International Journal of the Legal Profession* 47.

Sossin, L (2008) 'The Public Interest, Professionalism, and Pro Bono Publico' 46 *Osgoode Hall Publico* 131.

Stager, DAA and Arthurs, HW (1990) *Lawyers in Canada* (Toronto, University of Toronto Press).

Statistics Canada (2009a) 'Custom Tabulation from 1996 Census'.

—— (2009b) 'Custom Tabulation from 2006 Census'.

—— (2009c) 'More Information on Class of Worker' www12.statcan.gc.ca/census-recensement/2006/ref/dict/pop017a-eng.cfm.

—— (2009d) 'Number and Share of Visible Minority Persons in Canada, 1981 to 2006' www12.statcan.gc.ca/census-recensement/2006/as-sa/97-562/figures/c1-eng.cfm.

—— (2013) 'Immigration and Ethnocultural Diversity in Canada' www12.statcan.gc.ca/nhs-enm/2011/as-sa/99-010-x/99-010-x2011001-eng.pdf.

—— (2015a) 'NHS: Data Quality' www12.statcan.gc.ca/NHS-ENM/2011/ref/about-apropos/nhs-enm_r005-eng.cfm.

—— (2015b) 'National Household Survey: Final Response Rates' www12.statcan.gc.ca/NHS-ENM/2011/ref/about-apropos/nhs-enm_r012.cfm?Lang=E.

—— (2016a) 'Canadian Demographics at a Glance: Second Edition', published 19 February 2016 www.statcan.gc.ca/pub/91-003-x/91-003-x2014001-eng.pdf.

—— (2016b) 'Custom Tabulation from 1981 Census'.

—— (2016c) 'Custom Tabulation from 2011 National Household Survey'.

—— (2016d) 'Legal Aid Statistics (Revenues)' www.statcan.gc.ca/tables-tableaux/sum-som/l01/cst01/legal18a-eng.htm.

—— (2017a) 'Employer Establishments by Employment Size Category and Province/Territory (2015)' www.ic.gc.ca/app/scr/app/cis/businesses-entreprises/54111.

—— (2017b) 'Tuition and Living Accommodation Costs: Detailed Tables from CANSIM' www5.statcan.gc.ca/COR-COR/COR-COR/objList?lang=eng&srcObjType=SDDS&srcObjId=3123&tgtObjType=ARRAY.

Terry, LS, Mark, S and Gordon, T (2012) 'Trends and Challenges in Lawyer Regulation: The Impact of Globalization and Technology' 80 *Fordham Law Review* 2661.

The Counsel Network (2016) 'In-House Counsel Compensation & Career Survey Report 2016'.

Tong, D and Pue, WW (1999) 'The Best and Brightest?: Canadian Law School Admissions' 37 *Osgoode Hall Law Journal* 843.

Wiffen, M (1 June 2015) 'Large Firm Growth – 2015 Edition' wiffenlaw.ca/blog/item/107-large-firm-growth-2015-edition.

Woolley, A and Farrow, T (2016) 'Addressing Access to Justice through New Legal Service Providers: Opportunities and Challenges' 3 *Texas A&M Law Review* 549.

Young Bar of Montreal, 'Employment and Young Lawyers in Quebec' (16 February 2016) ajbm.qc.ca/wp-content/uploads/2016/03/report-employment-and-young-lawyers-in-quebec-web.pdf.

4

England and Wales

A Legal Profession in the Vanguard of Professional Transformation?

HILARY SOMMERLAD, ANDREW FRANCIS,
JOAN LOUGHREY AND STEVEN VAUGHAN*

I. INTRODUCTION

UNTIL THE LATE 1970s the legal profession of England and Wales[1] largely preserved its core traditional traits. However, by the time *Lawyers in Society* was published in 1988, complex, interlocking forces were beginning to erase the conditions supporting the classical profession, including the radical politics generated by post-war social citizenship, the neo-liberal challenge to Keynesian economics, technological innovation, the emergence of the 'new legal order' under the European Court of Justice (ECJ) (Loughlin 2000: 150–57), and the impact of globalisation on networks of finance, employment, media, communication, and travel. From the 1960s, social modernisation was weakening the profession's control over the reproduction of lawyers. The expansion of higher education (a response to the decline in traditional, male-dominated industry) together with civil rights discourses was fostering women's entry into higher education and elite professions and a 'new breed of lawyers interested in human rights' (Lester 2017: 3–4), whose radical and capacious approach to law work challenged traditional lawyering and legal positivist scholarship. The increasing pace of globalisation was reconfiguring the state, and private institutional orders, especially those linked to the

---

*Thanks to our research assistants, Opemiposi Adegbulu (University of Leeds) and Lloyd Brown (University of Birmingham) for their sterling efforts in navigating a significant amount of data. We are also grateful to the research teams at the Law Society, the Legal Services Board (LSB) and the Bar Standards Board (BSB) for their help.

[1] The United Kingdom (UK) is a unitary sovereign state which comprises four countries: England, Wales, Scotland, and Northern Ireland, and is divided into three legal jurisdictions: England and Wales; Scotland; and Northern Ireland. Although the Supreme Court is the highest civil appeal court for all three systems (and the Westminster Parliament is the primary legislature), the histories of the three jurisdictions generated differences in their laws and professions, and in many ways they remain distinct. This chapter describes the legal profession of England and Wales (generally termed the English legal profession); however, some policy reports (eg on the size of the legal services market) consider the UK as a whole; we make this clear when referring to these.

global economy, were displacing the centrality (and monism) of state law (Sassen 1999). Margaret Thatcher's neo-liberal government was a response to, and active agent of, this new order, introducing a range of liberalisation policies, including de-regulation of the City of London financial markets in 1986. Finally, the authority of traditional expert knowledge and the profession's claim to a distinctive ethicality were starting to crumble in the face of the normative fragmentation generated by these changes. In sum, the professional project was in 'serious disarray' (Abel 1988: 189).

Since 1988, the disintegration of the traditional professional model has accelerated.[2] For instance, the expansion and (partial) democratisation of higher education diversified the law student population, ending the profession's relative homogeneity, while the continuation of Thatcherite de-regulation policies has supported the reconstruction of the state and legal order in the interests of global capital (Douglas-Scott 2013). The corporate hemisphere of the profession (both barristers' chambers and law firms) has been a leading player in the new global order (Flood 1995). Large firm lawyering now represents one of the UK economy's most profitable sectors,[3] employs a majority of lawyers, and is highly feminised – at the lower levels. In-house lawyering has also increased in size, power and capabilities, reorienting some sites of professional practice and regulation and reinforcing a more general shift in the balance of power from legal services producers to consumers. However, while the corporate sector's dominance and wealth have increased, neo-liberal policies have tended to impoverish the high street sector. The monopolies enjoyed by firms dealing primarily with individual private clients and small businesses have been dismantled, forcing them to compete with regulated and unregulated entities, qualified and unqualified law workers. At the same time, 'the de-nationalization of the state agenda – namely the Keynesian agenda' (Sassen 1999: 2) has generated successive reforms of legal aid, reconstructing the sector as a market, constraining practitioner autonomy, re-organising service delivery, and reducing scope, eligibility and funding. These measures culminated in the Legal Aid, Sentencing and Punishment of Offenders Act 2012 (LASPO 2012), which effectively ended legal aid as a viable source of business, creating 'advice deserts' and a crisis in criminal justice.

The last 30 years, therefore, have seen changes in the profession's work (and hence in the skills, forms of knowledge and technologies entailed in legal practice) and in its work sites, size, composition, coherence, and traditional values. One consequence has been a blurring of professional boundaries. This is due, in part, to government marketisation policies, ending restrictions on law firm ownership, allowing solicitors and barristers to practice together (Legal Disciplinary Partnerships (LDPs)) and with non-lawyers (Alternative Business Structures (ABSs)). But it is also the result of a general de-differentiation of professional work exemplified by similarities between the work of corporate lawyers and business (Mueller et al 2011) and the entry of other players, such as accountants, into the legal services market.

---

[2] This process of disintegration has been comprehensively described and analysed by Abel, who summarises it in his description of the profession as caught 'between market and state' (2003).

[3] Turnover in the legal services sector grew by 60 per cent between 1995 and 2003 to £19bn and by another 35 per cent by 2010 (despite the recession) to £25.6bn (LETR 2013: 77). By 2016 the total UK legal services market (including private practice firms, barristers, patent agents, and other legal services providers) was valued at £31.5bn, and by 2018 had risen to £32.7bn: www.businesswire.com/news/home/20180301006274/en/UK-Legal-Services-Market-Report-2018--.

In summary, many of the profession's traditional structures and strategies are obsolete, leaving it 'factionalised, heterogeneous and fragmented' (Paterson 2011: 9). Yet the changes have been neither uniform nor uncontested. In sites of multi-professional work strong disciplinary connections to law survive, despite regulatory liberalisation and increased external control. Furthermore, the profession retains a large proportion of legal work, and the global corporate sector is a world leader – although its future has been thrown into doubt by the UK's exit from the European Union (Brexit). The radical approach to law engendered by civil rights movements persists in some firms and barristers' chambers and also parts of the academy. Finally, vestiges of traditional professionalism remain – for instance in its imagery, certain archaic rituals, and the cultural and social capital the profession values.

II. MAPPING THE LEGAL PROFESSION OF ENGLAND AND WALES

A. Size and Shape of the Legal Services Market in England and Wales

We focus primarily on the two traditional English professions – solicitors and barristers – and, to a lesser extent, legal executives. However, the opening of the field to non-lawyer competition and such innovations as LDPs and ABSs require us to discuss the new legal services providers.

i. Solicitors

In 1988, 66,380 solicitors were registered on the Roll, 50,247 of whom held practising certificates (known as PC holders). On 31 July 2018 there were 188,868 solicitors on the Roll and 143,167 PC holders.[4] The 230,000 people employed in solicitor firms represents 69.9 per cent of the estimated 329,000 employed in the legal services sector. This expansion, however, varies by region, sector, specialism, demography, and organisational type, and by differences in working practices, structure, cultures and income.

Traditionally, solicitors' firms were small partnerships whose kinship character represented the primary form of (collegial) regulation and means of occupational closure. Typically, they consisted of two or three lawyers: equity partners, assistant solicitors (most of whom could expect to become equity partners), and trainees (originally termed articled clerks). Solicitors had direct access to clients, enjoyed a monopoly over land transactions (conveyancing) and, apart from criminal practitioners, generally worked outside courts (for instance handling the pre-trial stages of litigation or non-contentious matters).

In July 2018 of the total of 9,452 firms, the majority were still small, general practices catering to private clients and small and medium-sized businesses: 86.6 per cent had fewer than five partners, and just under half of all PC holders practised in firms of fewer than 11 partners. Furthermore sole practitioners (4,174) remained the largest category of firms; however they are a smaller proportion than in 1988, and liberalisation policies

---

[4] Unless otherwise referenced, this statistic and the subsequent ones in this section were supplied through private communication with the Law Society Research Unit.

have made their future precarious. By contrast, the corporate sector has thrived under liberalisation. The 0.6 per cent of firms with over 80 partners[5] employ 29 per cent of all PC holders, account for more than two-fifths of the legal services market's total turnover, and are better understood as Professional Service firms (PSFs) rather than law firms. The City of London (hereafter the City) hosts 73 per cent of their head offices. The general dominance of the UK economy by London and the South East is exemplified by the fact that the region contains over two-fifths of all private practice firms. London was home to half of all trainee solicitors starting in 2017–18, and firms with more than 80 partners offered 35.5 per cent of all training contracts.

Globalisation has resulted in the largest City firms developing a network of overseas offices or 'best friend arrangements': about half their lawyers work outside the UK. Some PSFs have also opened regional UK offices to conduct 'back office' and commoditised work, retaining high value bespoke work in London. Their main competitors are other UK-based global firms, international firms (primarily from the US, with over 200 offices in London), and the large accountancy firms (The City UK 2016). Regional commercial law firms have also internationalised, though to a lesser degree. In sum, it is the extraordinary growth of the corporate legal services sector that drove the expansion of the legal profession by almost 70 per cent between 1995 and 2015 (Galanter and Roberts 2008). In-house counsel now account for just under a quarter of all solicitors; a handful of in-house teams, such as those at large banks, each employ more than 1,000 solicitors (Law Society 2017).

ii. Barristers

Traditionally, barristers enjoyed higher status than solicitors, partly because they were the specialists, insulated from clients on whose behalf solicitors sought 'opinions', and partly because their monopoly over litigation in the higher courts made them the only source of judges. Excellence in advocacy is recognised by the award of Queen's Counsel (QC), consistently restricted to 10 per cent of the practising Bar. A majority of barristers, 13,171 out of 16,598, are self-employed[6] and grouped in 'chambers' serviced by a clerk (Flood 1983). Their representative body is the Bar Council. Most chambers are located in London, varying significantly in size from one or two barristers to 200 in the largest commercial sets. As of 1 August 2019, the largest chambers had around 250 currently practising barristers, and the three next largest had between 180 and 200. Other barristers registered with the Bar Standards Board (BSB) as practising in England and Wales are at the employed Bar and work for a wide variety of employers. These include the Government Legal Department (GLD), which employs 10 per cent of employed currently practising barristers; the Crown Prosecution Service (CPS), which has just over 20 per cent, and law firms and businesses, which employ almost 30 per cent.

The Bar nearly trebled between 1960 and 1990 and then virtually doubled by 2004 (LETR 2013) but grew only 4.85 per cent between 2007 and 2015 (Bar Council 2016).

---

[5] The largest firms are considerably bigger. Slaughter and May – the smallest 'Magic Circle' firm – has 106 UK partners, and DLA Piper has 492. Clifford Chance has 392 partners worldwide: www.thelawyer.com/top-200-uk-law-firms/.

[6] Both this figure and the following statistics were provided by the BSB research team. Dataset used was the BSB data warehouse as of 1 August 2019.

Like the solicitors' profession, it became more and more differentiated and stratified between regional and London practices and between the corporate Bar (which increasingly resembles corporate PSFs) and chambers specialising in legal aid (primarily criminal) and/or private client work, which have seen revenues plummet. The ending of barristers' monopoly of advocacy in the higher courts and of solicitors' intermediary role (barristers now have the option of 'direct access' to clients) has affected both barristers' traditional roles and their relationship with solicitors (Flood and Whyte 2009).

iii. Legal Executives

Legal Executives were originally solicitors' assistants, known as Managing Clerks. Towards the end of the nineteenth century they began to pursue their own professional project, establishing the Solicitors Managing Clerks Association (SMCA) in 1892 (Francis 2002). With Law Society support, this became the Institute of Legal Executives (ILEX) in 1963, introducing regulations on training, including examinations and a qualifying period of employment. It is now the Chartered Institute of Legal Executives (CILEX), and its members can qualify as solicitors, apply for judicial office and become partners in LDPs and ABSs (exemplifying the erosion of professional boundaries). Nevertheless, they continue to be overshadowed by solicitors despite the recent (state driven) enhancement of their status. Their numbers remained quite steady between 2012 and 2018, rising slightly from 7,467 to 7,587.[7]

iv. Licensed Conveyancers

Because the conveyancing monopoly was the bedrock of high street firms, the creation of licensed conveyancers (by the Administration of Justice Act 1985) represented a far more significant attack on solicitors' professional privilege than legal executives' elevated status. Regulated by the Council of Licensed Conveyancers (CLC), these practitioners qualify via diploma and 1,200 hours of practical experience. In 2018, the approximately 1,400 licensed conveyancers practised in 228 regulated conveyancer firms, which had a median of four managers and 16 employees: a mix of licensed conveyancers, solicitors and non-authorised persons. Although licensed conveyancers can also be authorised to undertake probate, in 2015 88 per cent of their work was residential conveyancing (LSB 2016). However, this represented only 10.3 per cent in value of property transactions at the Land Registry (CMA 2016), while solicitors (through advertising and new pricing practices) retained 66 per cent of the market and other legal professionals, including Chartered Legal Executives, served the rest (LSB 2016). Overall, in 2018, regulated conveyancer firms accounted for a total turnover of £233 million.

v. Paralegals

The expansion of the profession's supply base and technological innovations have fostered the casualisation of legal services, and whereas once paralegals were not lawyers

---

[7] This statistic and, unless otherwise referenced, the data on licensed conveyancers were provided by the LSB on 7 August 2019, collated from data from approved legal services.

an increasing proportion are law graduates who may also have the Legal Practice Course (LPC) or Bar Professional Training Course (BPTC)[8] qualification (some are even qualified lawyers) (Sommerlad 2015a). Their position is generally precarious, but although much of their work remains routinised and low level, paralegals increasingly cross work boundaries and take on more advanced tasks previously restricted to qualified lawyers. However, this work augmentation rarely translates into greater opportunities to obtain a training contract or pupillage (Gustafsson and Empson 2018). Nevertheless, the increasing significance of paralegals and change in their composition prompted a professionalisation project and in 2005 the Department of Trade & Industry granted institute status to the Institute of Paralegals, recognising it as a professional body.[9] It is thought that there are currently 60,000 paralegals in solicitor's firms and 6,000 paralegal law firms,[10] and some even estimate the number at 300,000, depending on the definition of the paralegal role.[11]

vi. Government Lawyers

The GLD employs 2,000 lawyers, 1,600 of whom are solicitors or barristers, who provide legal advice (including drafting legislation) and conduct litigation. The Civil Service Code requires them to act on the instructions of the relevant minister but remain politically impartial and observe their professional code of conduct. The CPS employs 2,131 frontline prosecutors and 2,970 legal caseworkers and support staff. Both institutions are accountable to the Attorney General, a political appointee, government minister, and chief legal adviser to the government. The ancient role of the Lord Chancellor (now Justice Secretary) is legally responsible for the efficient functioning and independence of the courts. However, the Lord Chancellor is also a political appointee, and, controversially, since 2012 non-lawyers have occupied the role and have been criticised for failing to defend judges from media and political criticism and for presiding over cuts to legal aid and the judiciary that have threatened its efficiency (Logan Green and Sandbach 2016).

Judges are neither government lawyers nor political appointees but, since 2005, are selected by the independent Judicial Appointments Commission (JAC), whose recommendations the Lord Chancellor must accept or reject.[12] Supreme Court appointments, however, are made by a separate selection commission created by the Lord Chief Justice.[13]

---

[8] The LPC and BPTC are the professional education courses for solicitors and barristers respectively, followed by the training contract or pupillage.
[9] See theiop.org/.
[10] See www.clt.co.uk/qualifications/paralegal.aspx and www.ltckent.co.uk/nalp-qualifications/.
[11] See www.allaboutlaw.co.uk/law-careers/paralegal/the-paralegal-profession-explained.
[12] Established by the Constitutional Reform Act (CRA) 2005 in response to criticism of the archaic practice of using informal soundings to appoint judges, the JAC failed to fulfil its mandate to increase judicial diversity (Gee and Rackley 2017). As part of New Labour's modernising project, the Act also modified the office of Lord Chancellor, abolished the appellate jurisdiction of the House of Lords and established the Supreme Court.
[13] This is governed by the CRA 2005, ss 25–31 and Sch 8, as amended by the Crime and Courts Act 2013, and is usually chaired by the President of the Supreme Court.

vii. LDPs, ABSs and Other New Entrants to the Market

The creation of LDPs and ABSs as a result of the relaxation of professional rules on law firm ownership by the Legal Services Act 2007 (LSA 2007) exemplifies the destruction of traditional forms of professionalism and embrace of the market. LDPs are partnerships of different types of lawyer and up to 25 per cent non-lawyers (though non-lawyers who are not managers cannot hold ownership interests). ABSs allow multi-disciplinary practices, non-lawyer ownership and outside investment. The rationale for this liberalisation was that integrating legal and other professional activities and attracting investment by corporations (such as insurance companies and supermarkets) would produce economies of scale, lowering prices and generally improving consumer service (SRA 2009).

In April 2019, there were 1,306 ABSs,[14] concentrated in high-volume, commoditised markets, particularly wills, trusts and probate,[15] conveyancing, corporate restructuring and finance, and personal injury. In 2018, SRA licensed ABS firms together with LDPs represented 7.6 per cent of the market (then comprising 9,452 law firms) (Law Society 2018). They tend, however, to be conversions of existing law firms rather than new entrants; the handful that have received outside investment have overwhelmingly drawn upon a parent firm (Aulakh and Kirkpatrick 2016). Other innovative business models include practitioners working as freelancers and virtual and dispersed law firms. For instance, Carbon Law Partners is an umbrella company providing 'a secure hosted platform, state of the art practice management system, compliance management tools, a comprehensive online legal library and precedent services' for self-employed lawyers, all of whom form their own limited companies.[16] There are also numerous online providers of bundled services, including legal documentation, in a range of areas such as criminal and family law.[17]

B. Regulatory Architecture

Abel's prediction that the patterns of differentiation and stratification described above threatened 'the capacity of lawyers to engage in self-governance' (1988: 188) has been vindicated. The dissolution of solicitors' and barristers' associations as autonomous, self-regulating entities was formalised by the LSA 2007, which effectively reduced the Law Society and Bar Council to representative bodies. The Act also created an 'oversight regulator', the Legal Services Board (LSB), empowered to ensure that regulatory and representative functions were exercised independently. The former were allocated to 'front line regulators', including the Solicitors Regulation Authority (SRA) and the Bar Standards Board (BSB), which regulate both individual lawyers and the chambers/law firms in which they work (known as entity-based regulation), and three accountancy bodies, which license probate activities. Although the LSB must approve rule changes, set

---

[14] This statistic was provided by the LSB on 7 August 2019, collated from data from approved legal services.
[15] In 2014 the Institute for Chartered Accountants in England and Wales licensed over 100 accountancy firms to offer non-contentious probate services (LSB 2016).
[16] See www.carbonlawpartners.com.
[17] See www.cambridge-news.co.uk/news/cambridge-news/cambridge-university-students-design-interactive-12077890; www.divorce-online.co.uk/.

performance targets and sanction defaults (including removing the regulator's licence), the SRA and BSB produce professional Codes of Conduct and are responsible for prosecuting misconduct allegations. Complaints about poor service are handled separately by the Legal Ombudsman, established by the Office for Legal Complaints (OLC) (again subject to LSB oversight) to provide an independent form of consumer redress for unresolved complaints. However, the fact that several of the front-line regulators – including the SRA and BSB – are operationally but not structurally independent of their representative bodies has created concerns (LSB 2017a; 2017b), and the SRA has complained that its lack of structural independence has impeded pro-competitive regulatory initiatives (SRA 2013; CMA 2016). The Ministry of Justice (MoJ) nevertheless rejected calls from the Competition and Markets Authority (CMA 2016) for an overview of the regulatory framework and full independence for the regulatory bodies (MoJ 2017), though the LSB is likely to initiate reform within the current regulatory framework.

C. Key Developments in the Regulatory Landscape

i. Regulatory Fragmentation and Private Forms of Regulation

The complexity of the new regulatory architecture is compounded by the existence of other regulatory mechanisms – hard and soft, public and private – generated by the profession's fragmentation. The plurality of normative orders includes both norm-making by powerful corporate clients, which tend to express dissatisfaction by threatening to litigate to remove their business (or actually doing so), and complaints by high street clients to the Legal Ombudsman (OLC Annual Report 2015). Other important sources of norms include 'soft' professional bodies (eg specialist interest and lobbying groups, often linked to particular practice areas) and firms themselves. Lawyers in large corporate firms have little awareness of the SRA Code of Conduct's provisions (Vaughan and Coe 2015; Vaughan and Oakley 2016) because the firm itself is the primary site of normative control. This latter development may be accentuated by the SRA's focus on entity regulation and its recent requirement that law firms have 'Compliance Officers for Legal Practice' (Loughrey 2014; Aulakh and Loughrey 2017). Law firm insurers and LEXCEL, a quality standard awarded under Law Society auspices, also play a regulatory role, encouraging firms to institute systems and processes that reduce the likelihood of a breach of regulatory norms (including competence requirements), thereby affecting premium levels.

ii. Regulation of Competition in the Legal Services Market

Competition as a regulatory mechanism has been largely driven by front-line regulators using powers delegated by primary legislation (eg the Courts and Legal Services Act 1990, Access to Justice Act 1999 and LSA 2007). The SRA has been particularly dynamic, reforming the 'separate business rule' which prohibited solicitors from owning or managing unregulated businesses, and initiating changes that will let solicitors offer legal services in other business forms, for instance on a 'freelance basis' (SRA 2017). However, competition is constrained by the maintenance of 'reserved' activities – probate, immigration, conveyancing, notarial functions, rights to litigate, and rights of audience – which can be conducted only by persons authorised by the approved regulators. Such authorisation operates at both an individual and firm level. If, however, a firm is authorised it is possible for non-authorised employees within that firm to conduct reserved work. The extension of authorisation for conveyancing and probate work to multiple actors (notaries, chartered accountants, and others) has intensified intra-professional competition. The ending of solicitors' traditional monopoly over client access has also generated competition with barristers and re-shaped how both work.

Lawyers also compete with non-lawyers for unreserved work. While immigration advice, claims management and insolvency work are subject to separate regulation and authorisation requirements, will writing and a range of other legal services (including employment advice, family law, and much transactional work) is entirely ungoverned by legal services regulation, covered instead by consumer protection. Non-lawyers operating in the unregulated sector include paralegals, claims agents, 'McKenzie Friends' (who assist litigants-in-person),[18] will writers, and accountants. Lawyers, who are regulated by title, remain subject to regulation of *all* their work, whether or not reserved. Despite this, in 2013 only 15 per cent felt pressure from competition (LSB 2016b), and the for-profit unregulated sector comprises only 5.5 per cent of the legal services market, though a higher proportion in family, property and construction, wills, intellectual property, and employment (LSB 2016; LSB 2016a).

The current regulatory regime is further complicated by the uneven implementation of marketisation. For instance, the 'client' (rather than the 'consumer') still figures in professional codes of conduct; the promotion of the public interest remains an objective of legal services regulation; and entity regulation potentially strengthens the power of professional regulators. Also, despite the discursive mobilisation of the 'sovereign consumer', the information asymmetry between clients and providers has been neglected. Consequently, the current regime is described as a 'regulatory maze' (Dixon 2016), and research suggests consumers are confused about avenues of redress (Graham et al 2011). There is also evidence that consumers tend to assume that all legal services are regulated (LSB 2016), less than a quarter 'shop around' (CMA 2016), and legal services remain unaffordable for most (LSB 2016). Further, data is lacking on the quality differential between regulated and unregulated legal service providers (LSB 2011). And while the greater availability of fixed-price work may be reducing the cost of some services, and for-profit unregulated providers may charge lower prices than regulated firms (LSB 2016), the services provided by the two sectors are not always directly comparable.

However, current policy is guided by 'the rigid belief that unfettered and unregulated free markets will deliver higher quality professional services at lower prices' (Leicht 2016: 1). The SRA in particular has prioritised competition to the neglect of the other regulatory objectives in the LSA 2007 (which include promoting the public interest by supporting the rule of law and access to justice). Yet the ability of competition

---

[18] The origin of the term is the divorce case *McKenzie v McKenzie* [1970] 3 All ER 1034 (CA). Unable to represent Mr McKenzie due to the refusal of legal aid, his solicitor enlisted the services of a barrister who, having no UK rights of audience, hoped to provide McKenzie with 'quiet assistance'; the Trial Judge refused to allow this, but on appeal it was held that this had deprived McKenzie of the assistance to which he was entitled.

to raise the quality of credence goods like legal services is questionable. Declaring that 'competition in legal services ... is not working well' (CMA 2016), the CMA proposed a range of measures to empower the consumer. Meanwhile, the marketisation agenda suffered a setback when the MoJ rejected an accountancy regulator's application to further regulate legal activities, despite support for it from both the LSB and the CMA (Hyde 2017).

D. Professional Associations

Because a key characteristic of traditional professionalism was the coherent, single-discipline, self-regulating association, their displacement by the complex constellation of representative bodies, regulators, specialist sections, campaigning organisations and large law firm private regulation is one of the most obvious manifestations of 'post-professionalism' (Kritzer 1999). Front-line regulators and representative bodies (eg the Law Society and Bar Council) are complemented by the Inns of Court (an archaic residue of the Bar's history, offering barristers and students educational activities and dining facilities) and a range of special interest associations grounded in demographics (eg the African Women Lawyers' Association and the Society of Asian Lawyers), practice areas (eg the City of London Law Society and the Association of Personal Injury Lawyers (APIL)) and geographic locations (eg Birmingham Law Society). These several dozen groups represent and further the fragmentation of the profession, including its knowledge base.

While the traditional professional paradigm rested on mastery of the 'whole field' – an essential element of the claim to profession-wide competence – globalisation and the growing complexity and juridification of society (Teubner 1998) require increasing specialisation. Many special interest associations are sites of education, representation and socialisation, often setting and operationalising the norms governing members' day-to-day practices. Their most significant segments are relatively old (eg APIL was founded over 25 years ago). All specialisation disrupts the myth of equal professional competence, and although the Law Society has attempted to manage disciplinary differentiation and maintain unity through its Accreditation Schemes, these tend to underline the benefits of consulting an expert rather than a generalist. Moreover, the Society's capacity to utilise these schemes to manage the fragmentation of members' interests and knowledge is further undermined by the development by discipline-specific associations of accreditation and training schemes (Moorhead 2010; Francis 2011). However, regulators have sought to re-establish standards for shared expert knowledge through reforms to legal education and training.

E. Legal Education, the Academy and the Relationship to the Legal Profession

The traditional links between the profession and the academy, underpinned by the latter's role in certifying entrants, have ensured that legal education has been influenced by developments affecting the profession. Successive governments' liberalisation and marketisation of the university sector (BiS 2016) have represented another source of change. However, the latest SRA proposal to liberalise the solicitors' labour market is likely to utterly transform the relationship between the profession and the academy.

The frequently troubled nature of this relationship (Cocks and Cownie 2009) largely stemmed from disagreement about whether law should be a free standing liberal arts degree or a vocational course (ACLEC 1996), a dissension expressed in the profession's sporadic attempts to gain greater control over degree content (CLLS 2010), provoking defence of academic freedom (Bradney 2003). The existing qualification framework is the regulatory exemplification of these tensions and ambiguities. The undergraduate LLB – the qualifying law degree (QLD) – is a certified route into the profession (although not required), but while most enrol in it with the objective of becoming a lawyer, very significant numbers (varying between institutions, but up to 80 per cent) do not enter the profession (Hardee 2012; Francis and Sommerlad 2009; Law Society 2017). Although this appears to be largely the result of the dramatic expansion of legal education since 1988 (LETR 2013) and ongoing employer control of legal graduate opportunities (Sommerlad et al 2013), other factors contribute including the increasing diversity of professional fields open to law graduates and, as we discuss below, the cost of qualifying.

Both Conservatives and New Labour aimed to open higher education through marketisation and expansion, leading to the re-badging (in 1992) of polytechnics as universities and the introduction (in 1998) of tuition fees, with the result that the number of LLB degrees doubled between 1989 and 2011 (and increased 24 per cent between 2006 and 2016). In 2009, 19,882 of the 29,211 applicants to study first-degree courses in law were accepted (68.1 per cent) (Law Society 2010; 2017). In 2015/16, there were just over 50,000 undergraduate law students (HESA 2016). Governments also sought to encourage access by previously excluded groups. However, whereas in 1980 local authority grants were provided to almost three quarters of students at the College of Law (Abel 1998: 3), at the end of the 1980s these grants were eliminated for all but the poorest. As a result, the proportion of lower socio-economic groups at universities (particularly the most selective) remains very low. By contrast, the last 30 years have seen a progressive feminisation of the student body, with women now comprising about 60 per cent of law students (Law Society 2017). In the early 1990s the numbers of Black, Asian and Minority Ethnic (BAME) law students also began to rise, reaching 32.1 per cent of students starting a first degree in law in 2008, significantly above their representation in the population and above average for BAME participation in higher education generally (ECU 2010: 87).

The law degree (or its equivalent) represents only the first stage of professional qualification. It must be followed by the one-year LPC and two-year training contract (which includes a Professional Skills Course) for solicitors or a one-year BPTC and one-year pupillage (apprenticeship) for barristers. Non-law graduates can qualify by taking a one-year law 'conversion' course (the Common Professional Exam), followed by the stages described above. In 2013–14, 77 per cent of admitted solicitors had a QLD (3,095) or were graduates of the conversion course (1,973). A further 17.6 per cent were overseas qualified lawyers, and others were admitted through cross-qualification routes (eg barrister to solicitor) (Law Society 2015). In 2015, 1,096 students on the BPTC were law graduates, and 270 were graduates of a conversion course (BSB 2017: 109). Traditionally, however, a degree was not required to become a solicitor, and a minority still take a non-graduate route: 3–4 per cent qualify as CILEX Fellows and then transfer; and 1 per cent qualify through 'equivalent means' whereby paralegals gain exemptions from various stages of the qualification process. Finally, in an effort to assist individuals from lower socio-economic groups to enter the profession, 'Trailblazer' solicitor apprenticeships have been developed which enable qualification after six years of working while studying at a law firm. However, the shift from occupational to organisational professionalism (Evetts 2013) is reflected in the fact that individual firms (and barristers' chambers) control the numbers and types of people who qualify through training contracts and pupillages (Francis 2011), and research suggests that the corporate sector, which offers most contracts and pupillages, continues to prefer trainees or pupils with the cultural and/or social capital acquired at elite universities (Sommerlad 2011; Sommerlad et al 2013; Ashley and Empson 2013). Further, the policies of massification, diversification and marketisation have intensified the pre-existing stratification of higher education and its students. As a result, neither the diversification and expansion of the student body nor non-graduate qualification routes have greatly affected the class composition of the profession, especially its upper echelons (Kirby 2016).

Competition for contracts (generally beginning before the LPC application) is intense, and many fail to gain a traineeship.[19] In 2014 there were 4,382 applications for the LPC (Hall 2014); after a decline following the 2008 financial crisis, training contract numbers had recovered by 2018 to 5,249 (Law Society 2019). Attrition of law and non-law graduates before the LPC application stage is a further reason why people who want to be solicitors are unable to achieve this. Becoming a barrister is even more competitive: in 2015, 2,910 applied for 1,500 BPTC places; 1,092 students graduated,[20] but only about 450 obtained pupillages (BSB 2016). Given the importance of fee income to all university providers and the dominance of professional legal education by a handful of private providers, students who can pay for the LPC or BPTC are unlikely to be turned away even if it is clear that they may struggle to obtain a contract or pupillage. However, as at the undergraduate stage, finance plays a major role in excluding those from a lower socio-economic background: the BPTC costs £13–19,000 and the LPC around £12,000. The Inns of Court offer some scholarships and grants for the BPTC, and larger law firms sponsor their future trainees on the LPC, but the majority must self-fund. And while training contracts are paid, in 2012 the SRA determined that setting a minimum salary level above the national minimum wage was 'not in the public interest' and from 2014 only required firms to pay this rate (£7.83 per hour),[21] leading to a sharp rise in trainees paid less than the recommended Law Society minimum (£20,913 a year in London) (Walters 2018). Trainee barristers (pupils) earn a minimum of £12,000 a year (significantly more in commercial chambers).[22]

Despite the continuing barriers to professional diversification, the Legal Education and Training Review (LETR), set up by the SRA, BSB and CILEX, concluded in broad terms that the current system worked well (2013: ix). In 2015, however, partly

---

[19] While the relationship between training contracts and LPC numbers fluctuates (Moorhead 2013), the general disparity between them has raised concerns about encouraging students to undertake the LPC without having secured a contract (Fouzder 2015).
[20] The non-pass outcomes are: Not Yet Complete (11 per cent); Fail (14 per cent); Withdrawn (4 per cent): www.barstandardsboard.org.uk/media/1835435/bptc_key_statistics_report_2017_-_all_parts.pdf.
[21] See www.sra.org.uk/sra/consultations/review-minimum-salary-trainee-solicitors.page.
[22] From September 2019, the minimum pupillage award in London will rise to £18,436 per annum and £15,728 per annum outside London: www.barstandardsboard.org.uk/qualifying-as-a-barrister/becoming-a-barrister/.

in a further effort to widen access to the profession, the SRA proposed a new qualification route for solicitors termed the Solicitors Qualifying Examination (SQE). This comprises: (i) possession of a degree (not necessarily in law), apprenticeship, or equivalent; (ii) success in stages 1 and 2 of a centrally set SQE (combining the law degree's knowledge content with the content of the current vocational stage); and (iii) a requisite period of workplace training (likely, in most cases, to resemble the existing training contracts). A law degree would offer no exemptions, effectively abolishing the QLD. Stage 1 of the SQE (which mostly consists of multiple choice questions) could be taken after graduation and Stage 2 any time after Stage 1.

The SRA's rationale that the SQE will create a 'more open market' articulates its conviction about the benefits of liberalisation: 'competitive pressures raise standards and reduce costs' (SRA 2016: 6). However, these claims have been questioned by law schools, employers, and representative bodies, which criticised the proposals on grounds of cost, likely impact on standards, and access to the profession (Bindman 2016). The City of London Law Society concluded that the proposals failed 'to demonstrate high standards of learning or to deliver a modern and relevant syllabus of study which provides newly qualified solicitors with a knowledge base and the skills to be effective in providing a broad range of advice in the most appropriate areas of practice' (CLLS 2017: 140). A survey (commissioned by BPP, a major private legal trainer) of 59 firms ranging from small practices 'to the biggest in the City' found they had 'not become more receptive to the SQE' and those 'feeling negative about it outnumber those feeling positive by more than two to one' (trendence UK 2017: 3). Despite this opposition, in March 2018 the LSB approved the application for the SQE framework and will later be asked to approve specific SRA rule changes to introduce it.

However, it appears that if the SQE is introduced, many firms (particularly the largest) are likely to continue recruiting based on university performance, and that their strong preference for elite universities is unlikely to change (CLLS 2017: 143; Francis 2015). The general higher education policy is important. Successive reforms, including the rise in undergraduate fees (£9,250 per year in 2017,[23] to be repaid at rates above inflation) and the use of proxies to measure teaching quality through a new government initiated Teaching Excellence Framework (TEF) (including graduate destination statistics) have intensified the 'employability' discourse (Browne 2010), reconstructing universities as markets whose ultimate function is 'wealth creation' (Collini 2012; Bradney 2011: 60). The concomitant transformation of law degrees into positional goods and the rise of audit has intensified emphasis on law school rankings, accentuating the stratification of higher education (as in the US). As a result, irrespective of the formal qualification framework, market imperatives require law schools to present a compelling narrative of their capacity to facilitate students' access to the profession (Thornton and Shannon 2013).

For teachers and researchers in the legal academy, the story of the last 30 years is less straightforward. On the one hand, the commodification and privatisation of knowledge and impact of managerialism on the academy represents a growing constraint on the potential for critical socio-legal work (Hillyard 2007: 276; Sommerlad 2013). On the

---

[23] What will happen to fee levels is uncertain: one of the recommendations of a recent review into post-18 education was that 'Universities should find further efficiency savings over the coming years, [and] maximum fees for students should be reduced to £7,500 a year' (Augar 2019).

other hand, Cownie's study of legal academics led her to conclude that 'we're all socio-legal now' (2004). This discrepancy is due in part to the protracted and uneven processes of social change (radical social movements of the 1970s influencing the academy even as neo-liberalism was becoming hegemonic in the political and economic spheres), and in part to the increased stratification of higher education, with elite institutions enjoying greater academic freedom. Parallel with the strengthening of rights' struggles in wider society, the 1980s onwards saw the development of legal scholarship that challenged insular positivist thought. Supported by the Institute of Advanced Legal Studies, which played a fundamental role in making law a proper object of inquiry in the liberal arts, critical and socio-legal scholarship in several law schools was fostered by the Critical Legal Conference (established 1984) and the formation in 1990 of the Socio-Legal Studies Association. The desire of New Labour administrations to ground policy in evidence further supported the development of socio-legal research. Finally, the significance of both socio-legal and critical scholarship was, ironically, reinforced by one of the key mechanisms deployed to marketise the academy. Introduced in 1986 as part of New Public Management reform of the public sector (Pollitt 1990), the Research Excellence Framework (REF) is an external audit intended to introduce transparency and accountability into the allocation of university funding. The belief was that the effect on reputation and indirectly on finances would generate significant changes in academic culture and practice, making it more business-like (Blackmore et al 2016). However, as the most recent REF Law panel reflected, traditional black letter law scholarship did not lend itself easily to this exercise: 'the volume of outputs submitted in property law and more traditional areas of mercantile law was surprisingly low, given their importance in undergraduate and postgraduate [and practice] areas'; instead, 'the field as a whole is shaped by socio-legal research methods and techniques' (REF 2014: 71).

The diversity of intellectual and methodological perspectives over the last three decades have made English legal research and education highly successful on a global stage. Other developments include the increasing importance of clinical legal education and experiential learning (Thomas et al 2018), and a growing focus on ethics (Moorhead et al 2016; Vaughan and Oakley 2016), the result of increasing concerns about the effect of the profession's shift to an explicitly commercial rationality (Muzio et al 2013). However, research into, and university courses on, the legal profession remain rare (for instance, the first sustained study of large law firm lawyers is Loughrey 2011). Also apparent is the impact of globalisation in law schools' attempts to internationalise their profiles and activities through research and educational exchange, study abroad, and the recruitment of international students (who represented 26.4 per cent of registered law students in 2016) (HESA 2016).

Whereas the majority of law teachers used to come from practice, today most have a PhD – a further indicator of the shift from a narrowly positivist approach to law and reflective too of the academy's changing relationship with the profession. Teaching qualifications have also gained greater significance and are now held by 47 per cent of academics (HEFCE 2016). However, this percentage varies; those institutions which possess most cultural capital (largely grounded in research excellence but also in traditional association with high class status) have little need to be concerned with teaching qualifications: only 3 per cent of academics at the University of Cambridge hold such a qualification, whereas the proportion in 'new' universities can be as high as 82 per cent (eg Chester University).

Nevertheless, data on the teaching qualifications of staff at all universities are likely to become an increasingly important feature of the TEF (BIS 2016a: 30).

The dramatic increase in female participation in formerly male dominated professions also characterises the legal academy, which now has 2,780 women and 2,665 men (HESA 2016). Furthermore, whereas women are 23 per cent of all professors they are 30 per cent of law professors (Vaughan 2016). However, as in the legal profession, women (and other 'non-traditional' workers) are more likely to occupy less remunerative and prestigious positions: women comprise only about a third of law academics paid the highest 'Contract Salary Range 6' (any figure above £57,032). And although 3 per cent of legal academics are 'Black' (HESA's catch-all term), they are only 1 per cent of law professors; similarly, Asians are 5 per cent of legal academics but comprise only 3 per cent of law professors (ibid). As in other labour markets, academic work is increasingly casualised through short, fixed-term or hourly-paid teaching contracts, and research has indicated that managerial pressures are having a deleterious impact on legal academics' wellbeing (Collier 2014).

III. KEY DEVELOPMENTS

A. Changing Work Patterns in the Profession

Some of the most striking changes since 1988 are found in the nature, organisation and ethos or logics of professional work. The financialisation of the large PSFs and the increasing capabilities of information technology have furthered the routinisation and commodification of professional work. Artificial Intelligence (AI) has facilitated the decomposition of professional labour into discrete packages (Susskind 2010), presenting one of the greatest challenges to traditional professionalism and its claims to expert knowledge (Abbott 1988).

The resulting reconfiguration of professional work and the division of labour has entailed a change from what Weber termed value rationality to calculative rationality or capitalist logic (Hanlon 1998; Boon 2014: 63–75). Sophisticated clients are seen as 'connected consumers', more likely to seek recommendations from peer-users of social media than to rely on traditional signifiers of quality and reputation (Solis 2014). Client-driven considerations of price, quality and the timing of service delivery have gained primacy (Hanlon 1999). There is also a direct relationship between the profession's capitalist logic and industrialised processes, its expansion and diversification, and the need for a variety of (skilled, semi-skilled and relatively unskilled) workers (Sommerlad 2015).

B. Diversity in the Legal Profession

Changes in the nature of legal work, the profession's growing need for workers, and the diversification of the law student body combined to weaken closure from the late 1970s. Abel described the consequent transformation of the profession's demographic profile as 'revolutionary' (1988: 202). The change has been most dramatic in the solicitors' profession, particularly in its corporate sector. Yet this sector exposes the fact that continuities also mark the profession, including its traditional rituals and status symbols, and dominance by white men.

The entry of women and BAME groups was a pivotal factor in the solicitors' profession's increase by almost 70 per cent between 1995 and 2015 (Law Society 2016: 10). Women comprised 24 per cent of newly qualified solicitors in 1978/79, 41 per cent by 1991/92, and 60 per cent by 2008/09, and this remains the pattern. Despite high levels of attrition, they were nearly half of all solicitors (48.8 per cent) by 2015 (Law Society 2016). In 1998/99, 13 per cent of newly qualified solicitors self-classified as BAME (compared to 9 per cent in the overall working population); ten years later they were 28 per cent. In 2007/08, 18.7 per cent of pupil barristers were BAME, and 53 per cent were women. However, these 'non-normative' professionals were incorporated not as potential partners but as transient, 'adjunct' employees (Hagan and Kay 1995), effectively technicians (Dezalay 1995). Statistics reveal the persistence of this gender, race and class gap between the profession's hemispheres and the increasing horizontal and vertical segregation that accompanied the profession's expansion (Aulakh et al 2017). In the solicitors' profession the restructuring of legal work entailed the elongation of occupational structures, so that standardised, specialised components could be assigned to different strata of the legal profession's hierarchy through outsourcing, on-shoring, subcontracting and the use of 'contract' lawyers and paralegals on zero hours[24] fixed term contracts. This development reflected the reciprocal relationship between the need for more low-level labour and the expansion and diversification of law graduates. Women (regardless of intersections with other identity categories), BAME lawyers and those from lower socio-economic groups are over-represented in these forms of work, and also in private client and 'female typed' specialities and under-represented in the prestigious specialisms in large corporate firms. In 2016, women assistant/associate solicitors were paid on average 6.3 per cent less than their male counterparts (Law Society 2017a) and in 2018, 18.6 per cent of all women solicitors were partners, compared to 40.8 per cent of all men (Law Society 2018). Although BAME solicitors are 12.9 per cent of all partners, they are just 5.7 per cent of those in 81+ partner firms (ibid). Illustrating intersectionality, the BAME female solicitor is more likely than her white peer to work in low-status, less profitable sectors and to be a solo practitioner. Similar patterns characterise the Bar. Women and BAME barristers are over-represented in less prestigious chambers and specialisms and under-represented at QC level. In 2017 only 4.4 per cent of female barristers were QCs, and accounted for 14.8 per cent of all QCs. Some 7 per cent of BAME barristers are QCs, making up 7.1 per cent of the total number of QCs. By contrast, 11.5 per cent of white barristers and 13.9 per cent of male barristers are QCs (BSB 2019).

We have already alluded to the significance of class in legal careers. As noted above, class proxies like attendance at a fee-paying school and high-status university (Oxford, Cambridge or what is known as a 'Russell Group' university) vastly increase chances of obtaining training contracts or pupillages. Although just 7 per cent of the population attended fee-paying schools, their graduates were 33 per cent of solicitors in corporate firms compared to 16 per cent in criminal law firms, 26 per cent of law firm partners and

---

[24] Where the employer is not obliged to provide any minimum working hours, and the worker is not obliged to accept any work offered.

37 per cent of large firm partners (Kirby 2016). A disproportionate amount of the Bar is also drawn from privileged backgrounds (ibid; BSB 2018).

Nevertheless, the meritocratic ideology of commercialised professionalism, with its bureaucratic recruitment and promotion processes, combined with pressure from 'outsiders' for inclusion on equal terms, has reduced *direct* discrimination. However, commercialised professionalism has also generated the 'business case for diversity', characterised by an individualised, de-politicised approach to equality (in contrast with the equal opportunities policies of the 1960s and '70s). As a result, the bureaucratisation of PSFs has proved double-edged: vindicating the neo-liberal discourse of the intrinsic rationality (and hence fairness) of labour markets while justifying the failure to recognise systemic causes of inequality, such as the constraints placed on women's agency by traditional gendered divisions of labour, the role of cultural practices in identifying insiders and outsiders, and the highly masculinised character of law firm networking and socialising, including practices that sexualise and de-professionalise women (Sommerlad 2016; and see survey in *The Lawyer*: Bernal, 2018). As a result, initiatives like the Law Society Diversity Charter and flexible working policies have been largely ineffective (Aulakh et al 2017).

In summary, while non-normative groups have gained entry to the profession, they continue to be disproportionately relegated to sub-professional roles and less prestigious work, while the commodification of work and outsourcing practices facilitate the exclusion of some altogether, resulting in rising numbers of paralegals, the majority of whom are law graduates, some with the LPC or BPTC.

C. Access to Justice and Legal Aid

1973 to 1986 has been described as a golden era when justice for all seemed an attainable goal (Hynes and Robins 2009: 26). Building on the activism of earlier social justice and human rights, non-governmental organisations (NGOs) such as Liberty (established 1934), JUSTICE (1957), and the Child Poverty Action Group (1965), this period saw the foundation of Law Centres, radical barristers' chambers and firms such as Bindman & Partners (1974), and the Legal Action Group (1972), and inspired the establishment of new NGOs (such as Shelter) committed to using law to pursue social justice. The re-election of a Conservative government in 1987 and its enactment of the Legal Aid Act 1988 is generally viewed as ending this period (ibid). Nevertheless, it took several years and further legislation to reduce access to justice to the current skeletal system, available only to the poorest, and to destroy the networks of organisations listed above and those of ordinary (non-political) high street firms, for which legal aid had become an important source of income.

The solicitors' profession was initially most concerned about the transfer, in 1988, of the administration of legal aid from The Law Society to the Legal Aid Board (LAB). But a more important development for access to justice was the abolition of the connection between legal aid fees and the market rate and the subsequent erosion of professional autonomy through LAB control over the type of work and how it was delivered. The managerial techniques (applied across the public sector as New Public Management) were grounded in a franchising scheme specifying a set of (auditable) criteria for the conduct of transactions. Driven by 'supplier induced demand theory' (Bevan 1996) and justified by a discourse demonising lawyers as 'fat cats' and 'state funded Rottweilers', these measures (mimicking the transformation of the corporate sector) were designed to achieve the systematisation and routinisation of legally aided work and its delegation to low cost labour, and effect a change from a professional to a commercial rationality through the development of a market (Sommerlad 1995; Smith 1996: 574).

The policy of marketisation and cutbacks was largely continued by New Labour after 1997: the Access to Justice Act 1999 replaced the LAB with the Legal Services Commission (LSC), split the provision and delivery of legally aided services into the Community Legal Service (CLS) and the Criminal Defence Service (CDS), imposed a budget cap, replaced legal aid for some matters (eg personal injury) with conditional fee agreements and imposed contracts that further constrained practitioner autonomy with the aim of creating a 'market of providers'. However, New Labour's programme for civil legal aid also initially aimed to enhance access to justice through support for specialist, quality certified firms and Not for Profit agencies and a focus on welfare law. This policy was largely abandoned in 2003, and a programme of progressive cuts in eligibility and scope and the institution of fixed fees (and reductions in fee levels) adopted. Through their obligation to assess eligibility, legal aid lawyers were made gatekeepers to the justice system on behalf of the taxpayer, attenuating their capacity to act as their client's advocate. Over time these reforms produced a collapse in morale, and drove firms and individual practitioners out of the sector (Sommerlad 2001).

The evisceration of civil legal aid culminated in LASPO 2012, enacted by the Coalition Government as part of its assault on the welfare state following the global financial crisis. Despite overwhelming opposition from the profession (Sommerlad 2015b), LASPO 2012 removed most areas of civil law from the CLS, except where that would breach the Human Rights Act 1998, further tightened eligibility criteria and reduced lawyers' fee levels (Bach Commission 2017). The Act also replaced the LSC – a non-departmental public body – with an executive agency, the Legal Aid Agency (LAA), with the express purpose of achieving greater ministerial control.

The impact of LASPO 2012 has been compounded by other cuts and also by the 'reform' of judicial review, with the result that between 2007 and 2016 the number of civil legal aid providers halved (LCN 2017) and the number of practices committed to 'cause lawyering' has been decimated. MoJ figures showed that in 2016, 846,000 people had not been helped by legal aid who would have been in 2013 (ibid), and the LAA has acknowledged a countrywide lack of 'access' for those with housing and debt problems (Hyde 2017a). The impact on family law has been particularly severe, generating widespread criticism, including from senior judges who have described the LASPO 2012 cuts as 'a false economy' (Lady Hale), a 'huge burden on judges, lawyers and litigants' (Lady Justice Hallett), and 'shaming' (Mr Justice Bodey) (Bowcott 2017). The numbers of providers continue to drop, and government's plea that the profession increase its pro bono work has gone largely unheeded; instead, the main resources for the expanding numbers of unrepresented litigants are McKenzie Friends and law students.

The CDS has also been restructured through marketisation based on competitive tendering, cuts and fixed fees. Research indicates that this combination of low resources and the commercialisation of the sector's ethic has led criminal lawyers to increase pressure on clients to plead guilty (McConville and Marsh 2014: 167; Newman and

Welsh 2019). There has also been a dramatic drop in supply: in 2010/11 1,861 firms and 2,598 offices offered legally aided criminal defence advice and representation; in 2018/19 these numbers had declined to 1,271 firms and 1,921 offices (Law Society 2019). The drop in junior barristers' fees by 8 per cent between 2012 and 2016 (Smith and Cape 2017: 76–77) has made a career at the Criminal Bar increasingly unviable, provoking warnings about the profession's age profile (Law Society 2019). Continued cuts led to repeated strikes and boycott of new legal aid work (The Independent 2015) and a High Court challenge by the Law Society in 2018. In June 2019 the Criminal Bar voted overwhelmingly for another strike over legal aid fees.[25]

In 2018 the impact of LASPO 2012 on both civil and criminal legal aid was subjected to trenchant criticisms by Parliament,[26] and, early in 2019, following an MoJ review, the government set out some proposals designed to address some of these criticisms. However, these have been described as amounting 'to no more than a sticking plaster' (Fouzder 2019[27]) and the justice system as a whole has been described by a barrister as 'broken' (Anonymous, 'The Secret Barrister' 2018).

D. Lawyers and Contemporary Politics

The intimate connection between the legal profession and political power is manifest in the disproportionate representation of lawyers among politicians and other prestigious public office-holders. But whereas in modernity the law legitimated the power of the nation state and underpinned the profession's 'license and mandate' (Hughes 1981), the fragmentation of the contemporary profession and de-centering of state law have produced a more complex and often antagonistic relationship. Increasing government violations of democratic norms and the rule of law have prompted individual lawyers, sectional groups and professional bodies to intervene on such core issues as judicial independence and human rights; for instance both the Law Society and Bar Council played prominent roles in challenging LASPO 2012.

The willingness to adopt a more independent and politically engaged stance also emerged in the priorities drafted by The Law Society prior to the 2017 General Election, including maintaining legal certainty in light of Brexit and safeguarding effective access to justice and human rights for every individual (Law Society 2017a). This stance was most evident following attacks on the judiciary in response to the High Court ruling requiring the Government to secure parliamentary approval before triggering Article 50 of the Lisbon Treaty (which establishes the right to leave the EU). Noting that the Justice Secretary's silence contravened her statutory obligation to defend judicial independence, the Bar Council called for strong condemnation of the 'serious and unjustified' attacks on senior judges, and the Law Society President reminded ministers of the need to offer an unequivocal defence of the rule of law.

---

[25] See www.legalcheek.com/2019/06/criminal-barristers-vote-in-favour-of-strike-action/.
[26] See hansard.parliament.uk/Commons/2018-11-01/debates/9886E282-3B9E-4F2B-8F03-0A3494228ED8/FutureOfLegalAid; and see Pratt et al 2018.
[27] See www.theguardian.com/law/2019/feb/07/we-need-the-system-rebooted-verdicts-on-the-legal-aid-review.

Government willingness to support or even provoke antipathy to 'political' lawyers (and experts in general) has long been evident with respect to legal aid lawyers. The denigration of public sector lawyers – an integral component of New Public Management reforms – recurred in 2014 when, days before a strike by criminal barristers against legal aid cuts, the MoJ published the legal aid earnings of top QCs, encouraging 'fat cat' headlines. Popular antipathy has also been fomented by depictions of human rights lawyers as disloyal, exemplified by the then Prime Minister's denunciation of the representatives of Iraqis pursuing torture claims against British troops,[28] leading to SRA disciplinary proceedings. Although several lawyers were exonerated, the charges had a chilling effect on recourse to strategic litigation. Nevertheless, some firms have survived LASPO 2012, and sectional groups remain active: for example, after the tower block fire in London causing multiple fatalities, BME Lawyers 4 Grenfell warned the Prime Minister about her failure to observe the Inquiries Act 2005 and the Equality Act 2010. Concern about the government's apparent disregard for the rule of law has also been articulated by former Lord Chancellors (eg Falconer 2018) and the judiciary. However, the most damning critique was recently delivered in a Supreme Court judgment finding that Employment Tribunal fees were discriminatory and had impeded access to justice and hence the rule of law.[29]

IV. CONCLUSION

We have situated our analysis of the legal profession in the socio-economic and political transformations since 1988, especially the hegemony of globalised neoliberalism, which has reconfigured both state and law, leading to the de-regulation and marketisation of the profession (and legal education), the establishment of new legal services providers, and drastic restrictions in access to justice. This transformation, together with new technologies, has resulted in an expanded but highly fragmented and diverse legal services field and an industrialised mode of legal services production.

Because solicitors and barristers have been at the core of this revolution, we have focused on them, especially the corporate sector of the solicitors' profession, which now dominates the legal landscape, making it a central player in the UK economy. Transformations in the organisational structure of corporate firms have underpinned this sector's economic significance (leading it to employ the highest percentage of diverse lawyers, concentrated in its lowest tiers). However, the traditional sites of legal practice – the high street firm and regional Bar – have also been transformed. These practices – self-employed lawyers who, in 1988, still enjoyed monopoly rents and consciously reproduced other pre-capitalist traits – were destabilised by their loss of market shelters, especially that of the conveyancing monopoly, and by incremental cuts in legal aid funding.

The increasing juridification of society, diversification of clientele, and proliferation of normative orders have accentuated the 'competing conceptions of the role of law and

---

[28] See www.theguardian.com/uk-news/2016/sep/23/theresa-may-british-troops-uk-protect-abuse-legal-system-soldiers-war-crimes-iraq.
[29] *R (on the application of UNISON) v Lord Chancellor (Respondent)* [2017] UKSC 51.

of justice within the profession' (Johnson 1972: 60). The contemporary English legal profession is so disaggregated that the most appropriate unit of analysis is the legal services provider. However, the field also is characterised by continuities, notably the significance of class, gender and ethnicity in career trajectories and the cultural practices and ideologies that naturalise and support professional hierarchies. Professional bodies, firms and individual lawyers continue to deploy the discourse of traditional professionalism, including the values of justice, the public interest, and the rule of law. Even though the services now delivered by some of the largest commercial firms overlap with those offered by other PSFs, they still claim to 'offer top quality *legal* advice' and describe themselves as 'globally minded *lawyers*'.

However, the transformations we describe may pale in the wake of Brexit. Implementing the EU (Withdrawal) Act 2018 will transplant relevant EU law into British law (omitting the Charter of Fundamental Rights) and repeal the European Communities Act 1972. The extensive primary and secondary legislation this will require has led to predictions of a surge in demand for legal expertise and guidance. Some also argue that London will remain the jurisdiction of choice for commercial disputes. Others dispute this, expressing concern about lawyers' loss of the right to practise and base themselves in EU Member States: *Oxford Economics* reported (2015) that legal services would be disadvantaged disproportionately by Brexit, and The Law Society warned that the legal services sector could be damaged by a post-Brexit free trade deal, arguing that 'the inevitable reintroduction of trade barriers with EU countries would hit legal services' (Walters 2017). The outlook for the corporate sector depends on 'the ultimate agreement relating to free movement of trade, people and financial services between the UK and the EU' (Croft 2016). At the other end of the professional spectrum, some fear the exclusion of the Charter of Fundamental Rights will let the government kindle a 'bonfire of rights' (Peers 2016; LCN 2017). The threatened resort by government to use its prerogative powers to prorogue parliament in order to force through a no-deal Brexit represents a further challenge to fundamental rights. Furthermore, such an exclusion of Parliament from this matter of historic constitutional importance could break up the UK. Finally, the deep polarisation characterising both profession and society is reflected in the commodified and exclusionary nature of contemporary justice, especially the fragility of the legal aid sector, ongoing court closures, massive increases in court fees, and the drive to ADR. The future of professionalism, the law and British democracy is thus highly uncertain.

REFERENCES

Anonymous ('The Secret Barrister') (2018) *Stories of the Law and How It's Broken* (London, Macmillan).
Abbott, A (1988) *The System of Professions: An Essay on the Division of Expert Labour* (London, University of Chicago Press).
Abel, RL (1988) 'England and Wales' in RL Abel and PSC Lewis (eds), *Lawyers in Society: Vol I The Common Law World* (Berkeley, University of California Press).
—— (2003) *Between Market and State* (Oxford, Oxford University Press).
ACLEC (1996) *First Report on Legal Education and Training* (London, Lord Chancellor's Advisory Committee on Legal Education and Conduct).

Allaboutlaw (2017) 'Paralegals: The backbone of legal sector', www.allaboutlaw.co.uk/law-careers/paralegal/paralegals-the-backbone-of-legal-sector.

Ashley, L and Empson, L (2013) 'Differentiation and discrimination: understanding social class and social exclusion in leading law firms' 66(2) *Human Relations* 21.

Augar, P (2019) *Independent panel report to the Review of Post-18 Education and Funding* (London, Department for Education).

Aulakh, S and Kirkpatrick, I (2016) 'Changing regulation and the future of the professional partnership: the case of the Legal Services Act, 2007 in England and Wales' 23 *International Journal of the Legal Profession* 277.

Aulakh, S and Loughrey, J (2018) 'Regulating Law Firms from the Inside: The Role of Compliance Officers for Legal Practice in England and Wales' 45(2) *Journal of Law and Society* 254.

Aulakh, S, Charlwood, A, Muzio, D, Tomlinson, J and Valizade, D (2017) *Mapping Advantages and Disadvantages: Diversity in the Legal Profession in England and Wales* (University of Leeds and Newcastle University Business School).

Bach Commission (2017) *The Right to Justice: the Final Report of the Bach Commission* (London, Fabian Society).

Bar Council (2016) *Snapshot Report: The Experience of Employed Barristers at the Bar* (London, Bar Council).

Bar Standards Board (BSB) (2019) *Diversity at the Bar* www.barstandardsboard.org.uk/media/1975681/diversity_at_the_bar_2018.pdf.

Bernal, N (2018) '#Me Too: Lawyers share their worst experiences of sexual harassment' *The Lawyer*, 1 March www.thelawyer.com/metoo-worst-experience-sexual-harassment/.

Bevan, G (1996) 'Has there been supplier-induced demand for legal aid?' 15 *Civil Justice Quarterly* 98.

Bindman, D (2016) 'Widespread concern about training proposals, SRA acknowledges' *Legal Futures* 11 March www.legalfutures.co.uk/latest-news/widespread-concern-about-training-proposals-sra-acknowledges.

BIS (Department for Business, Innovation and Skills) (2016) *Success as a Knowledge Economy: Teaching Excellence, Social Mobility and Student Choice*, CM9258.

—— (2016a) *Teaching Excellence Framework: Technical Consultation for Year 2*, BIS/16/262.

Blackmore, P, Blackwell, R and Edmondson, M (2016) *Tackling Wicked Issues: Prestige and Employment Outcomes in the Teaching Excellence Framework* (Occasional Paper 14).

Boon, A (2014) *The Ethics and Conduct of Lawyers in England and Wales* (Oxford, Hart Publishing).

Bowcott, O (2017) 'Senior Judge warns over "shaming" impact of legal aid cuts' *The Guardian*, 13 October www.theguardian.com/law/2017/oct/13/senior-judge-warns-over-shaming-impact-of-legal-aid-cuts.

Bradney, A (2003) *Conversations, Choices and Chances: The Liberal Law School in the Twenty-first Century* (Oxford, Hart Publishing).

—— (2011) 'English university law schools, the age of austerity and human flourishing' 18 *International Journal of the Legal Profession* 59.

Browne, J (2010) *Securing a Sustainable Future for Higher Education: An Independent Review of Higher Education Funding and Student Finance* www.gov.uk/government/uploads/system/uploads/attachment_data/file/422565/bis-10-1208-securing-sustainable-higher-education-browne-report.pdf.

BSB (Bar Standards Board) (2014) *Bar Barometer* (London, Bar Standards Board).

—— (2016) *BPTC Key Statistics 2016* (London, Bar Standards Board).

—— (2017) 'BPTC Key Statistics 2017: An analysis of students over three academic years' (Bar Standards Board Report, June) www.barstandardsboard.org.uk/media/1835435/bptc_key_statistics_report_2017_-_all_parts.pdf.

—— (2018) 'Report on Diversity at the Bar 2017 A summary of the latest available diversity data for the Bar' (London, Bar Standards Board).
CLLS (City of London Law Society) (2010) *Response to SRA's Consultation on Outcomes Focused Regulation* (20 August) www.citysolicitors.org.uk/attachments/article/108/20100820-1550-(Final)-Response-to-SRA-Handbook-consultation-(2).pdf.
—— (2017) 'City of London Law Society Training Committee Response to SRA's Consultation' in SRA Consultation Responses: A New Route to Qualification: The Solicitors Qualifying Examination www.sra.org.uk/documents/SRA/consultations/sqe2-consultation-responses-list.pdf.
The City UK (2016) *UK Legal Services 2016* www.thecityuk.com/research/uk-legal-services-2016-report/.
CMA (Competition and Markets Authority) (2016) *Legal Services Market Study: Final report* (London, CMA).
Cocks, R and Cownie, F (2009) *A Great and Noble Occupation! The History of the Society of Legal Scholars* (Oxford, Hart Publishing).
Collier, R (2014) '"Love Law, Love Life": Neo-Liberalism, Wellbeing and Gender in the Legal Profession – The Case of Law School' 17 *Legal Ethics* 202.
Collini, S (2012) *What Are Universities For?* (London, Allen Lane).
Cownie, F (2004) *Legal Academics: Cultures and Identities* (Oxford, Hart Publishing).
Croft, J (2016) 'Brexit: law firms set for the great EU demerger' *Financial Times*, 6 October www.ft.com/content/5a653770-83eb-11e6-8897-2359a58ac7a5.
Dezalay, Y (1995) 'Introduction: professional competition and the social construction of transnational markets" in Y Dezalay and D Sugarman (eds), *Professional Competition and Professional Power: Lawyers, Accountants and the Social construction of Markets* (London, Routledge).
Dixon, C (2016) 'The government must take a holistic approach to reforming the Legal Services Act, says the Law Society's chief executive' *Law Society Gazette*, 15 February www.lawgazette.co.uk/features/regulation-the-end-of-our-profession/5053623.article.
Douglas-Scott, S (2013) *Law after Modernity* (Oxford, Hart Publishing).
ECU (Equality Challenge Unit) (2010) 'Equality in higher education: Statistical report 2010' (London, Equality Challenge Unit) www.ecu.ac.uk/publications/equality-in-he-stats-10/.
Evetts, J (2013) 'Professionalism: Value and ideology' 61 *Current Sociology* 778.
Falconer, C (2018) 'British Justice is in flames. The MOJ's fiddling is criminal', *The Guardian* 6 February www.theguardian.com/commentisfree/2018/feb/06/british-justice-collapse-moj-prisons-probation-legal-aid-lord-chancellor-charles-falconer.
Flood, J (1983) *Barristers' Clerks: The Law's Middlemen* (Manchester, Manchester University Press).
Flood, J (1995) 'The Cultures of Globalization: Professional Restructuring for the International Market' in Y Dezalay and D Sugarman (eds), *Professional Competition and Professional Power: Lawyers, Accountants and the Social construction of Markets* (London, Routledge).
Flood, J and Whyte, A (2009) 'Straight there, no detours: direct access to barristers' 16 *International Journal of the Legal Profession* 131.
Fouzder, M (2015) 'LPC graduates toil to find training contracts' *Law Society Gazette*, 23 February www.lawgazette.co.uk/news/lpc-graduates-toil-to-find-training-contracts/5046948.article.
—— (2019) 'LASPO review: the profession reacts' *Law Society Gazette*, 7 February www.lawgazette.co.uk/law/laspo-review-the-profession-reacts/5069191.article.
Francis, A (2002) 'Legal Executives and the phantom of legal professionalism: The rise and rise of the third branch of the legal profession?' 9 *International Journal of the Legal Profession* 5.
—— (2011) *At the Edge of Law – Emergent and Divergent Models of Legal Professionalism* (Aldershot, Ashgate).

—— (2015) 'Legal Education, Social Mobility and Employability: Possible Selves, Curriculum Intervention and the role of Legal Work Experience' 42 *Journal of Law and Society* 173.

Francis, A and Sommerlad, H (2009) 'Access to legal work experience and its role in the (re)production of legal professional identity' 16 *International Journal of the Legal Profession* 63.

Galanter, M and Roberts, S (2008) 'From kinship to Magic Circle: the London commercial law firm in the twentieth century' 15 *International Journal of the Legal Profession* 143.

Gee, G and Rackley, E (2017) *Debating Judicial Appointments in an Age of Diversity* (London, Routledge).

Graham, C, Lennard, L and Sommerlad, H (2011) 'Mapping potential consumer confusion in a changing legal market' report for the Legal Ombudsman, Centre for Consumers and Essential Services, University of Leicester www.legalombudsman.org.uk/downloads/documents/publications/Consumer-Confusion-Report.pdf.

Gustafsson, S and Empson, L (2018) '"Climbing invisible walls": The construction of career (im)mobility in liminal professional roles' 1 *Academy of Management Proceedings*.

Hagan, J and Kay, F (1995) *Gender in Practice: A Study of Lawyers' Lives* (New York, Oxford University Press).

Hall, K (2014) 'LPC applications down by 10%' *Law Society Gazette*, 7 July www.lawgazette.co.uk/practice/lpc-applications-down-by-10/5042040.article.

Hanlon, G (1998) "Professionalism as Enterprise: Service Class Politics and the Redefinition of Professionalism" 32 *Sociology* 43.

—— (1999) *Lawyers, the State and the Market: Professionalism Revisited* (Basingstoke, Macmillan).

Hardee, M (2012) 'Career Expectations of Students on Qualifying Law Degrees in England and Wales' www.heacademy.ac.uk/system/files/resources/hardee_interimreport_2014final.pdf.

HEFCE (2016) 'Academic Teaching Qualifications' webarchive.nationalarchives.gov.uk/20160702214224/http://www.hefce.ac.uk/media/HEFCE,2014/Content/Learning,and,teaching/Wider,information/Academic_teaching_qualifications_statement_July_15.pdf.

HESA (2016) 'Data and Analysis' www.hesa.ac.uk/data-and-analysis.

Hillyard, P (2007) 'Law's Empire: Socio-Legal Empirical Research in the Twenty-First century' 34(2) *Journal of Law and Society* 266.

Hyde, J (2017) 'MoJ says no to accountancy body regulating all legal services' *Law Society Gazette* 21 September, www.lawgazette.co.uk/law/moj-says-no-to-accountancy-body-regulating-all-legal-services/5062929.article.

—— (2017a) 'MoJ reveals massive budget cut as new advice deserts open' *Law Society Gazette* 20 November www.lawgazette.co.uk/news/moj-reveals-massive-budget-cut-as-new-advice-deserts-open-/5063763.article.

Hynes, S and Robins, J (2009) *The Justice Gap* (London, Legal Action Group).

Hughes, E (1981) *Men and their Work* (Glencoe, Free Press).

The Independent (2015) 'Legal aid cuts: Criminal barristers' strike will go ahead despite last-minute feud with solicitors', 26 July www.independent.co.uk/news/uk/home-news/legal-aid-cuts-criminal-barristers-strike-will-go-ahead-despite-last-minute-feud-with-solicitors-10417351.html.

Johnson, TJ (1972) *Professions and Power* (London, Macmillan).

Kirby, S (2016) *Leading People 2016: The educational backgrounds of the UK professional elite* (London, Sutton Trust).

Kritzer, H (1999) 'The Professions Are Dead, Long Live the Professions: Legal Practice in a Postprofessional World' 33(3) *Law & Society Review* 713.

Law Society (2010) *Trends in the Solicitors Profession: Annual Statistical Report 2009* (London, Law Society).

—— (2015) *Trends in the Solicitors Profession: Annual Statistical Report 2014* (London, Law Society).

—— (2016) *Trends in the Solicitors Profession: Annual Statistical Report 2015* (London, Law Society).
—— (2017) *Trends in the Solicitors Profession: Annual Statistical Report 2016* (London, Law Society).
—— (2017a) *Private Practice Solicitors' Salaries: PC Holder Survey* (London, Law Society).
—— (2017b) *Election Manifesto* (London, Law Society).
—— (2019) *Justice on Trial 2019: Fixing our Criminal Justice System* (London, Law Society).
Law Centres Network (2017) *Annual Review 2016/17* (Law Centres Network).
Leicht, K (2016) 'Market fundamentalism, cultural fragmentation, post-modern skepticism, and the future of professional work' 3 *Journal of Professions and Organization* 103.
Lester, A (2017) *Five Ideas to Fight For* (London, Oneworld Publications).
LETR (2013) *Legal Education and Training Review: Final Report* letr.org.uk/.
Logan Green, L and Sandbach, J (2016) *Justice in free fall: a report on the decline of civil legal aid in England and Wales* (London, Legal Action Group) www.lag.org.uk/article/201911/justice-in-free-fall--a-report-on-the-decline-of-civil-legal-aid-in-england-and-wales.
Loughlin, M (2000) *Sword and Scales* (Oxford, Hart Publishing).
Loughrey, J (2011) *Corporate Lawyers and Corporate Governance* (Cambridge, Cambridge University Press).
—— (2014) 'Accountability and the Regulation of the Large Law Firm Lawyer' 77 *Modern Law Review* 732.
LSB (2011) *Quality in legal services: a literature review* (London, Legal Services Board).
—— (2016) *Evaluation: Changes in the legal services market 2006/07 – 2014/15* (London, Legal Services Board).
—— (2016a) *Unregulated Legal Services Providers: Understanding Supply-Side Characteristics* (Economic Insight) (London, Legal Services Board).
—— (2017) *ABS and investment in legal services* (London, Legal Services Board).
—— (2017a) *Formal investigation into the governance arrangements between the Law Society and the Solicitor's Regulation Authority* (London, Legal Services Board).
—— (2017b) *Reviewing the Internal Governance Rules Consultation* (London, Legal Services Board).
McConville, M and Marsh, L (2014) *Criminal Judges: Legitimacy, Courts and State-Induced Guilty Pleas in Britain* (Cheltenham, Edward Elgar).
Ministry of Justice (2014) 'Legal Aid Statistics in England and Wales Legal Aid Agency 2013–2014' (Ministry of Justice Statistics bulletin).
—— (2017) 'Legal Services Market Study, Letter to Competition and Markets Authority' (London, Ministry of Justice).
Moorhead, R (2010) 'Lawyer Specialization – Managing the Professional Paradox' 32 *Law and Policy* 226.
—— (2013) 'LPC and Training Contract Numbers: Market Corrections?' 11 December lawyerwatch. wordpress.com/2013/12/11/lpc-and-training-contract-numbers-market-corrections/.
Moorhead, R, Denvir, C, Cahill-O'Callaghan, R, Kouchaki, M and Galoob, S (2016) 'The ethical identity of law students' 23 *International Journal of the Legal Profession* 235.
Mueller F, Carter C, and Ross-Smith, A (2011) 'Making sense of career in a Big Four accounting firm' 59 (4) *Current Sociology* 551.
Muzio D, Brock DM, and Suddaby R (2013) 'Professions and institutional change: towards an institutionalist sociology of the professions' 50(5) *Journal of Management Studies* 699.
Newman, D and Welsh, L (2019) 'The practices of modern criminal defence lawyers: alienation and its implications for access to justice' 48 (1–2) *Common Law World Review* 64.
Office for Legal Complaints (2015) 'Annual report and accounts 2014 to 2015' (London).
Oxford Economics (2015) *The UK Legal Services Sector and the EU* (London, The Law Society).

Paterson, A (2011) *Lawyers and the Public Good: Democracy in Action?* (Cambridge, Cambridge University Press).

Peers, S (2016) 'EU Referendum Briefing 6: A Bonfire of Rights? EU Employment and Equality Law after Brexit', *EU Law Analysis*, 21 June eulawanalysis.blogspot.co.uk/2016/06/eu-referendum-briefing-6-bonfire-of.html.

Pollitt, C (1990) *Managerialism and the Public Services: The Anglo-American Experience* (Oxford, Basil Blackwell).

Pratt, A, Brown, J and Sturge, G (2018) *The Future of Legal Aid: Debate Pack* (House of Commons Library no CDP-2018/0230).

REF (2014) Panel C: Overview Report www.ref.ac.uk/media/ref/content/expanel/member/Main%20Panel%20C%20overview%20report.pdf.

Sassen, S (1999) *Globalization and its Discontents* (New York, New Press).

Smith, R (1996) 'Legal Aid on an Ebbing Tide' 23 *Journal of Law and Society* 570.

Smith, T and Cape, E (2017) 'The rise and decline of criminal legal aid in England and Wales' in A Flynn and J Hodgson (eds), *Access to Justice and Legal Aid: Comparative Perspectives on Unmet Legal Need* (Oxford, Hart Publishing).

Solis, B (2014) *The Connected Consumer and the New Decision-Making Cycle* (IBM – ZZU12352-USEN-02).

Sommerlad, H, Webley, L, Muzio, D, Tomlinson, J and Duff, L (2013) *Diversity in the legal profession in England and Wales: a qualitative study of barriers and individual choices* (London, University of Westminster Law Press).

Sommerlad, H (1995) 'Managerialism and the legal profession: A new professional paradigm' 2 *International Journal of the Legal Profession* 159.

—— (2001) '"I've lost the plot": an everyday story of legal aid lawyers' 28(3) *Journal of Law and Society* 335.

—— (2011) 'The commercialisation of law and the enterprising legal practitioner: continuity and change' 18 (1–2) *International Journal of the Legal Profession* 73.

—— (2013) 'Socio-legal studies and the cultural practice of lawyering' in D Feenan (ed), *Exploring the 'Socio' of Socio-legal Studies* (Palgrave Macmillan).

—— (2015a) 'The new "professionalism" in England and Wales: Talent, diversity and a legal precariat' in S Headworth, R Nelson, R Dinovitzer and D Wilkins (eds), *Rhetoric and Reality* (Cambridge, Cambridge University Press).

—— (2015b) 'Access to Justice in hard times and the deconstruction of democratic citizenship" in M Maclean, J Eekelaar and B Bastard (eds), *Delivering Family Justice in the 21st Century* (Oxford, Hart Publishing).

—— (2016) '"A pit to put women in": professionalism, work intensification, sexualisation and work-life balance in the legal profession in England and Wales' 23(1) *International Journal of the Legal Profession* 61.

SRA (2009) *Regulating alternative business structures* (London, Solicitors Regulation Authority) www.sra.org.uk/sra/consultations/regulating-alternative-business-structures-june-2009.page.

—— (2013) 'Solicitors Regulation Authority response to Ministry of Justice – Call for evidence on the regulation of legal services in England and Wales' (Birmingham, Solicitors Regulation Authority).

—— (2016) 'Consultation: A new route to qualification: the Solicitors Qualifying Examination' (London, Solicitors Regulation Authority).

—— (2017) www.sra.org.uk/sra/consultations/lttf-phase-two-handbook-reform.page.

Susskind, R. (2010) *The End of Lawyers* (Oxford, Oxford University Press).

Teubner, G (1998) 'Juridification: Concepts, Aspects, Limits, Solutions' in R Baldwin, C Scott and C Hood (eds), *A Reader on Regulation* (Oxford, Oxford University Press).

Thomas, L, Vaughan, S, Lynch, T and Malkani, B (2018) *Reimagining Clinical Legal Education* (Oxford, Hart Publishing).

Thornton, M and Shannon, L (2013) '"Selling the Dream": Law School Branding and the Illusion of Choice' 23 *Legal Education Review* 249.

Trendence UK (2017) 'The law training survey: How firms and students are responding to the challenge of the SQE, BPP.

Vaughan, S (2016) 'The state of the nation: diversity and the British legal academy' 50 *The Law Teacher* 255.

Vaughan, S and Coe, C (2015) *Independence, Representation and Risk* (commissioned by the Solicitors Regulation Authority).

Vaughan, S and Oakley, E (2016) 'Gorilla Exceptions and the Ethically Apathetic Corporate Lawyer' 19 *Legal Ethics* 50.

Walters, M (2017) 'Brexit: UK legal services could be left 'high and dry', Society warns' *Law Society Gazette*, 15 December www.lawgazette.co.uk/law/brexit-uk-legal-services-could-be-left-high-and-dry-society-warns/5064070.article.

—— (2018) 'Sharp rise in trainees paid less than minimum salary' *Law Society Gazette*, 17 January www.lawgazette.co.uk/law/sharp-rise-in-trainees-paid-less-than-minimum-salary-/5064351.article.

5

Scotland

Caught between Nationalism and the Market: What Does the Future Hold for Scots Lawyers?

ALAN PATERSON AND PETER ROBSON

JUST AS THE Scots legal profession did not fit neatly into the dominant paradigm of market control in the original Abel and Lewis collection (Paterson 1988), so too the Scots legal profession of today appears to have escaped the excesses of marketisation depicted in the account of the evolution of the legal profession in England and Wales since 1988 (chapter four, above). As we will see, both branches of the Scots legal profession, for different reasons, have avoided (at least until 2019) the threat posed by alternative business structures (ABSs) or other significant players in the market, save one – the English City law firm. Yet these intruders, like a latter-day Norman invasion, may pose a real threat in the long run to the independent legal system of Scotland so cherished by the forces of nationalism.

I. INTRODUCTION

Scotland has a population of 5.6 million and has retained its separate laws and legal institutions since the Act of Union 1707 but shares some UK political institutions.[1] Its legal profession resembles that of its southern neighbour in many ways. Both have a varied legal practice, ranging from large corporate firms to small partnerships of self-employed lawyers. Women are now significantly represented in the lower ranks of the profession, and ten Law Centres offer poorer clients an alternative to private practitioners or salaried

---

[1] The United Kingdom (UK) consists of four countries: England, Wales, Scotland, and Northern Ireland, and is divided into three jurisdictions: England and Wales; Scotland; and Northern Ireland. The histories of these jurisdictions generated differences in their laws and professions, some of which have persisted over the centuries. While the Supreme Court is the highest civil appeal court for all three systems, and the Westminster Parliament is the legislature for all countries within the UK for all matters which are not devolved, the Scots and Northern Irish professions retain a significant degree of regulatory autonomy.

public defenders. A major difference concerns legal aid. Although legal aid spend shrank in the last decade in proportions similar to those in England and Wales, this was due much more to a decline in litigation than to austerity based cuts (Evans 2018: 15–16). As a result, Scots legal aid remains one of the most generous in the world in terms of scope (largely intact), eligibility (70 per cent of the population), independence and per capita expenditure (ibid). High Street firms that do little legal aid work or operate in towns or cities with an oversupply of providers and too little business will struggle like some of their English and Welsh counterparts. However, there is research evidence suggesting that firms that are geared up to do reasonable amounts of legal aid work in an efficient manner can make an adequate living (Otterburn 2017).

In other areas of the legal market competition is less intense than in England and Wales. Economic liberalism and de-regulation have made less progress. ABSs have yet to arrive in Scotland. Estate agents may dominate conveyancing in the West of Scotland, but solicitors retain a substantial portion of such work in the East of Scotland as the property pages of the major Scottish newspapers show. Licensed conveyancers were tried and failed as a way of breaking the profession's conveyancing monopoly. Legal executives do not exist. Paralegals are overseen by the Law Society of Scotland (LSS), and the legal profession retains the lion's share of will making and estate administration. Moreover, there has been no significant entry by other players, such as accountants or will writers, into the legal services market in Scotland. Price transparency and price competition outside the conveyancing field still have a long way to go.

Entry into the profession is almost wholly through the universities. In Scotland the law degree normally takes four years, with one or two years spent doing more advanced work on the core subjects covered in the early years. Teaching has altered in the past 30 years to encompass a more socio-legal approach. The split between a professional and an academic focus, encountered in England and Wales, exists north of the border too. Students who study the core professional subjects are not required to take further courses other than the practical training of the Diploma in Legal Practice provided in six of the 10 law faculties.[2] The five 'new' universities offering LLB degrees since 1988 – Abertay, Napier, Robert Gordon, Stirling and the West of Scotland – have largely sought to replicate the approach of the original five – Aberdeen, Dundee, Edinburgh, Glasgow and Strathclyde. Annually more than 1,200 students embark on programmes that will allow them to enter the profession as trainee lawyers. The number of training places available over the past five years has varied from 530 to 585. The other students go to work in commerce, academe and the civil service, where a legal qualification is prized.[3]

II. MAPPING THE LEGAL PROFESSION OF SCOTLAND

A. Size and Shape of the Legal Services Market in Scotland

As in England and Wales there is a split profession: solicitors principally office-based and advocates very largely working in courts, although solicitor advocates have made serious

---

[2] The number taking the Diploma ranged from 540 to 690 in the five years to 2018.
[3] See www.lawscot.org.uk/qualifying-and-education/qualifying-as-a-scottish-solicitor/the-traineeship/trainee-statistics/.

inroads into the criminal advocacy market, prompting resistance by both the Bar and (some) of the judiciary.

i. Solicitors

In 2018, there were 11,952 solicitors with practising certificates and a further 2,178 who were not practising.[4] About 8,000 practitioners worked in the private sector, nearly half (3,977) in large firms with 10 or more partners, 36 per cent (2,828) in small to medium firms with 2-9 partners, and 14 per cent (1,147) in 603 sole principal firms. In the last five years these percentages have not greatly changed.[5] However, the 4,000 or so in-house solicitors now represent a third of the practising profession and are the fastest growing sector of the profession.[6] Some expect this sector to grow to half of the practising profession within a decade, both because of the growth in compliance jobs in medium-sized businesses and the work-life balance that in-house positions offer.

Thirty years ago, 75 per cent of practising solicitors were male, but times were already changing and today 53 per cent of the practising profession is now female. This reflects the fact that female students have outnumbered their male counterparts for nearly 30 years: by 2018, 65 per cent of entrants to the profession were female, and 67 per cent of those taking the Diploma in Legal Practice.[7] Yet it is premature to say the glass ceiling has been shattered. Five female LSS Presidents and several prominent female managing partners in top large law firms cannot disguise the fact that progress on the partnership front is less impressive. The percentage of female practising solicitors who are partners in private firms has dropped consistently over the last decade and is now below 20 per cent, but there have been signs of an upturn in the last year or so. One long-established law firm in Edinburgh in 2019 proudly announced that it had become the first firm with more than 20 partners in which a majority (13/24) were female. Part of the problem is that a LSS study found that while flexitime was valued more by women, its availability was perceived to have a negative effect on career prospects (as did career breaks for child rearing). In fact, flexible working practices had led to an endemic overtime culture, which was perceived to disadvantage women particularly (Law Society 2013). Nevertheless, the follow-up survey (Law Society 2018) found that achieving an acceptable work-life balance was very important to a considerable majority of respondents. Even though the survey reported that the gender pay gap within the profession had declined from 42 per cent in 2013 to 23 per cent in 2018, the concern with an appropriate work-life balance may partly explain the reluctance of some female lawyers to become a partner.

The 2011 census revealed that 96 per cent of the population was white and 2.7 per cent Asian/Asian Scottish/Asian British, figures that were virtually unchanged in the 2015 Scottish Government Equality Evidence Finder. A higher proportion of law students are ethnic minority in origin.[8] Yet class remains a major entry barrier. Private education facilitates law school entry. There have been determined efforts to enhance access for

---

[4] Data obtained from the LSS Registrar.
[5] See the LSS Annual Reports at www.lawscot.org.uk.
[6] As can been seen from successive LSS Annual Reports.
[7] The equivalent of the English LPC and BVC.
[8] Although Scottish university law faculties avoid asking about applicants' ethnicity, observations of classes over the past two decades make this abundantly clear.

lower income students, such as the wider access programmes and financial support of Strathclyde, Edinburgh and Glasgow Universities and the LSS Fair Access to the Legal Profession initiative.[9] Doubling the number of law schools has facilitated entry by lower income students.[10] The cost of tuition for the Diploma in Legal Practice (the main route to the profession) and maintenance during that year exceeds the available government loans.[11] That this can be problematic for lower income students (Justice Committee of the Scottish Parliament 2018: 8)[12] led the LSS to accept trainees with part-time diplomas, distance learning diplomas, and even no law degree or diploma. However, Scotland's stakeholders in the legal education community[13] have resolutely rejected the marketised SQE model being pushed by the SRA in England and Wales, preferring a more consensual (neo-contractual) model of legal education and training. When the number of Diploma graduates significantly exceeds the training contracts available in the profession,[14] voices are raised in Parliament and elsewhere demanding a cap on Diploma places. However, such market control initiatives tend to be viewed as anti-competitive and have yet to succeed.

ii. Advocates

The composition of the pleading branch of the profession – advocates – is more traditional. The Faculty of Advocates (the Scots Bar) has about 700 persons, of whom about 100 are judges or academics not active at the Bar and another 175 are doing other jobs or retired. The practising Bar at the start of 2019[15] consisted of 425 advocates, of whom 115 (27 per cent) were female – a major jump from 1988, when the figure was below 10 per cent. At the same date 128 of the 425 (30 per cent) were practising senior counsel (or Queen's Counsel), of whom 28 (22 per cent) were female. These figures suggest that women are making slower progress at the Bar than in the solicitors' branch. All practising advocates are self-employed and share a clerk; but rather than being distributed among 'chambers', as in England and Wales, they are grouped in stables,[16] which have no physical location since most of the Bar practises from the Faculty Library located between the Court of Session and the National Library.[17]

---

[9] See LSS website Action Plan 31 January 2014, www.lawscot.org.uk/news-and-events/news/fair-access-programme-to-be-taken-forward/.

[10] Although most are underfunded, this is unlikely to lead to rationalisation because law schools confer prestige on a university and may be valuable 'cash cows'.

[11] Typical fees for the Diploma are £7,500 in 2019/20 plus £450 for professional materials. The maximum government loans for that year are £4,500 for living costs and £5,500 for tuition.

[12] LSS evidence to this committee showed that the proportion of students from disadvantaged backgrounds taking the Diploma was the same as that among those taking an LLB degree in Scotland.

[13] The Bar, the LSS, the Law Schools, the Diploma providers and the Scottish Judicial Institute. They are all represented on the Joint Standing Committee on Legal Education and Training.

[14] This has occurred several times in the last 20 years.

[15] Statistics obtained from the Clerk to the Faculty of Advocates in January 2019. See also the latest volume of the Scottish Annual Law Directory.

[16] There are nine principal stables in 2019.

[17] This building was originally owned by the Faculty; when it was sold to the state in 1925 the Faculty retained preferential rights to access the books within the National Library.

iii. Other Providers

Legal executives and licensed conveyancers have not made headway in Scotland. Paralegals, by contrast, have had their own training and professional association since 1993, with several hundred members. There is also, under the auspices of the LSS, a voluntary Accredited Paralegal Status, which has been attained by about 450 people. It provides a defined professional status and a career path for paralegals.

B. Legal Education, the Academy and the Relationship to the Legal Profession

Like the practising profession, the legal academy has experienced dramatic change since the 1980s (as recorded in the annual Scottish Law Directory). While the number of full-time staff increased from 147 in 1980 to 281 in 2015, female staff increased from 16 to 103 (from 11 to 37 per cent). At the professorial level, the change was most marked. In 1988 amongst the 40 professors of law in Scottish Law Faculties, there were no female law professors. By 2018, there was an increase in the professoriate to 84, of whom nearly a third (27) were women.

However, as in England and Wales, the academic imperative from Principals because of the REF means that many more academics now have PhDs than a practising qualification. This has done nothing to bring the profession and the academy any closer. It is harder to find academics to teach the professional subjects and no easier to persuade the profession to sponsor activities within the law schools (Paterson 2012). In the longer term, the shortage of academics with a professional qualification will make academic appointments to the judicial bench even rarer than they already are.

C. Regulatory Architecture

Perhaps because these patterns of differentiation and stratification are less pronounced than those in England and Wales or because of the continuing strength of neo-contractualism (Paterson 1988; 2012), in contrast to England and Wales, Abel's suggestion (Abel 1988: 188) that lawyers would lose much of their ability to self-govern has not been realised in Scotland in the last 30 years. The Scots did pay close heed to the Clementi Review (2004), introducing an independent complaints body, the Scottish Legal Complaints Commission (SLCC) in the 2007 Legal Profession and Legal Aid (Scotland) Act, but in neither that Act nor the Legal Services (Scotland) Act 2010 were the regulatory and representative functions of the LSS split, as they were in England and Wales. Scotland has no super regulator equivalent to the LSB, whose role in approving regulators of ABSs in Scotland is performed by the chief judge, the Lord President. The Law Society has changed its internal structure to comply with the 2010 Act, creating Regulatory Sub Committees (50 per cent lay members) reporting to a Regulatory Committee (50 per cent lay members and a lay chair), which deal with the regulation of the profession and protection of the public, and Membership Committees (consisting mostly of solicitors), which focus on the interests of the Society's members. Technically, however, the LSS Council remains its governing body. Although tensions sometimes arise if regulatory matters are mistakenly diverted to a membership committee, recent annual surveys of the profession have suggested that it is becoming less supportive of splitting into two bodies, one regulatory and one membership.

D. Key Developments in the Regulatory Landscape

i. Regulatory Fragmentation?

The regulatory architecture in Scotland, while representing an attempt at co-regulation, is not nearly as complex as in England and Wales. The profession has changed but is not dramatically more fragmented than it was 30 years ago, nor are there many more regulators. The large firms – even those controlled by English firms – are aware of the LSS Code of Conduct, the essence of which has not greatly changed since 1988, and there is neither entity regulation nor other private regulation. Although the City of London firms persuaded the SRA and the Law Society of England and Wales to relax the conflict of interest rules such that clients can be deemed (by the acceptance of the firm's terms of engagement letter) to consent to their lawyer acting in a conflict situation, the same rule change was not accepted in Scotland. Indeed, the ethical rules of Scotland still do not allow client consent as a defence to an ethical accusation of acting in a conflict of interest.

ii. Regulation of Competition in the Legal Services Market

In England and Wales, the LSB and SRA have made competition the foremost of the eight regulatory objectives in the Legal Services Act 2007, even though there is no statutory basis for this. The LSS has shown no such inclination. Competition is one of six regulatory objectives in the Legal Services (Scotland) Act 2010, but the LSS has evinced little enthusiasm for it. Price transparency may be pushed by the Competition and Markets Authority (CMA), but there are few signs of this being welcomed by either the profession (when it was consulted by the LSS) or the Society. Nor is there any pressure to alter the scope of the reserved areas. Moreover, the market position of the larger law firms has been strengthened by the arrival of limited liability partnerships, which combine limited liability for their members with the tax treatment of a traditional partnership.

Indeed, marketisation has a long way to go in Scotland. The profession has done little to address the continuing information asymmetry between clients and lawyers. Except in the conveyancing sector, price competition and shopping around have made remarkably little headway. It is true that by 1988 accountants and estate agents had made significant inroads into the non-reserved legal market. Since then, however, only a few other competitors have emerged, eg commercial attorneys, conveyancing practitioners, and executory practitioners; but less than a total of 20 work in these three occupations. Will writers, some employed in banks, have had a slightly greater impact, as have paralegals, mostly working in law firms.

iii. Regulatory Reform

However, the LSS has sought a review of its founding legislation to remove anomalies, eg an inability to protect the public from lawyers whose competence is threatened by illness or to prevent unqualified individuals from claiming to be lawyers, as well as the option to engage in entity regulation. Accordingly, in April 2017, the Scottish Government established an independent review of legal services regulation, chaired by a person with links to the world of medicine. When she reported in October 2018 (Roberton 2018), some of the LSS requests had been granted, but (to its dismay) the report also recommended a General Medical Council (GMC)-style independent regulator, covering not only complaints and entity regulation but also education and training. The Ministry of Justice had rejected the CMA proposal to introduce such a model in 2017, and the initial response of the Scottish Government (published in late June 2019) was more cautious as to the review than some had feared – promising a consultation paper which will seek to build a consensus between the various stakeholders.[18] Although there may be logical arguments for such a radical reform, the report lacks an evidentiary base in several areas, including education and training, which had not appeared to be within the Review's interpretation of its remit at any stage. Moreover, the reform would probably lead to the evisceration of the LSS as a national body, becoming instead just one of several voluntary membership organisations, including the Writers to the Signet Society, the Society of Scottish Law Agents, and various Royal Faculties and Bar Associations, all competing to set standards for their members. Such fragmentation of the professional associations is unlikely to enhance the strength or status of the legal profession. In consequence, it is possible that neo-contractualism will lead the profession to seek to trade certain reforms, eg periodic re-validation of practitioners or a totally independent complaints body, in return for rejection of the nuclear option of an independent regulator. The more astute option, however, would be for the profession to recognise that the SLCC was a blind alley – ineffective co-regulation – rather than effective co-regulation, and to replace it with an oversight Ombudsman with teeth, a single gateway for all complaints, most of which would be handled by the professional bodies subject to monitoring and correction by the Ombudsman.

III. CONCLUSION

In the last decade the Scots legal profession has tended to embrace change less rapidly than its larger counterparts south of the border, perhaps not unconnected with their relative sizes.[19] Clementi and ABSs are a clear example. The Scots Bar staved off the threat of ABSs, partnerships with solicitors or even partnerships at the Bar by stressing the need for an independent referral Bar[20] and by an 'agreement' with the Government (now quietly forgotten about) to permit ease of transfer between the Bar and the solicitor advocate's branch of the profession. The solicitors' branch fought off a rear-guard action by smaller firms and rural solicitors[21] to resist ABSs but was unable to prevent a

---

[18] Independent review of legal services regulation in Scotland: our response, www.gov.scot/publications/scottish-government-response-fit-future-report-independent-review-legal-services-regulation-scotland/.
[19] The turnover of a single City firm, Clifford Chance, may exceed that of the entire Scots profession.
[20] See the Scottish Parliament's briefing paper for the Legal Services (Scotland) Bill in 2009 www.parliament.scot/SPICeResources/Research%20briefings%20and%20fact%20sheets/SB09-78.pdf.
[21] Presaged in the Parliament's briefing paper for the Legal Services (Scotland) Bill in 2009, ibid, p 10.

provision that lawyers must own a majority of the law firm's equity. This dampened some of the impetus for the reform.[22] Although ABSs were permitted by the Legal Services (Scotland) Act 2010, the then Lord President (the ultimate regulator for both branches of the legal profession) appeared unenthusiastic, and the relevant regulations to allow them were introduced only in 2019.

Ironically the LSS embraced ABSs in part to appease the country's largest law firms, which feared unfair competition from their London competitors (mid-ranked law firms in the top 100) since they would have greater chances of borrowing money if they could be ABSs, while their Scots counterparts would be disadvantaged by not being ABSs. Yet the delay in implementing ABSs in Scotland allowed eight large English law firms to take over leading Scottish firms accounting for more than 16 per cent of the privately practising profession. The Act of Union has sometimes been thought to guarantee the Scots their own legal system, including aspects of their legal profession. This posed no market threat to the much larger English and Welsh legal system (although for over a century after the Union the Scots did monopolise legal appeals to the House of Lords).[23] However, repeated attempts by Scots-based lawyers and politicians in the last 15 years to claw back legal work to Scotland and its commercial courts have largely failed. Corporate clients vote with their feet, and the movement of business and client headquarters to London has proved irresistible. Scotland may have delayed the arrival of ABSs, but by taking over the bulk of Scotland's most significant law firms in the last five years, English large firm raiders may be achieving through the side door what the Act of Union was seeking to prevent through the front – loss of control of key aspects of the Scots legal system. Most of the lawyers in these law firms do not practise in the areas reserved for Scots law and do not need a Scots practising certificate or a Scots legal qualification. ABSs may have been delayed or neutered, and the SRA's threat to law degrees may have been avoided, but capitalism and the market may yet pose a greater threat to the more lucrative aspects of Scotland's independent legal system in the long run. A lot will depend on how much commercial clients and the Scots-based professionals continue to value the brand of the Scots solicitor.

REFERENCES

Abel, RL (1988) 'England and Wales' in RL Abel and PSC Lewis (eds), *Lawyers in Society: Vol I The Common Law World* (Berkeley, University of California Press).

Clementi, D (2004) *Review of the Regulatory Framework for Legal Services in England and Wales*.

Evans, M (2018) *Rethinking Legal Aid: An Independent Strategic Review* (Edinburgh, Scottish Government).

Justice Committee of the Scottish Parliament, 'Training the next generation of lawyers: professional legal education in Scotland', 23 September.

Law Society of Scotland (2013) *Demographics and work patterns of Scottish solicitors* (Profile of the Profession, Edinburgh, LSS).

---

[22] See eg the LSS website, www.lawscot.org.uk/members/membership-and-fees/licensed-legal-service-providers/ (2010).

[23] The rise of political nationalism in the last 20 years heightened opposition to Anglicisation of Scots law through Scots appeals to the top UK court (Paterson 2013).

Law Society of Scotland (2018) *Profile of the Profession*, 5 December.
Otterburn Legal Consulting (2017) 'Financial health of legal aid firms in Scotland, a report for the Law Society of Scotland'.
Paterson, AA (1988) 'The Legal Profession in Scotland – An Endangered Species or a Problem Case for Market Theory?' in RL Abel and PSC Lewis, *Lawyers in Society: Vol I The Common Law World* (Berkeley, University of California Press) ch 3.
—— (2012) 'Lawyers and the Public Good' (2010 Hamlyn Lectures, Cambridge, Cambridge University Press).
—— (2013) *Final Judgment: The Last Law Lords and the Supreme Court* (Oxford, Hart Publishing).
Roberton, E (2018) *Fit for the Future: Report of the Independent Review of Legal Services Regulation in Scotland* (Edinburgh, Scottish Government).

6

United States
Out of Many Legal Professions, One?

SCOTT L CUMMINGS, CARROLL S SERON, ANN SOUTHWORTH,
REBECCA L SANDEFUR, STEVEN A BOUTCHER
AND ANNA RAUP-KOUNOVSKY*

I. INTRODUCTION

MANY OF THE profound changes that have shaped the American legal profession over the past three decades were well underway 30 years ago (Abel 1988), including the enormous expansion, increased specialisation and fragmentation, rise of competing Bar associations, and growth and increased stature of in-house counsel. Since the 1970s, the demographic transformation has been nothing short of 'revolutionary' (ibid: 202), as a predominantly white male profession incorporated women and minorities. New entrants were part of an ongoing challenge to elite control, producing greater diversity and inequality. The latter phenomenon, reflecting and reinforcing broader social trends, is at the centre of our analysis.

The contest over control of the profession and its relation to patterns of exclusion and stratification have a long and complex history. By the late 1970s, longstanding patterns of 'differentiation and stratification' had 'undermine[d] the sense of professional community and threaten[ed] the capacity of lawyers to engage in self-governance' (ibid 1988), leaving 'the professional project in the first half of the twentieth century [in] serious disarray' (Abel 1989). Our account begins at that moment. While we find a persistence and amplification of differentiation and stratification, we also identify emergent structural forces that have transformed the contemporary profession in multifaceted and contradictory ways: globalisation, innovation, and neoliberalism. Globalisation – associated with greater cross-border movement of goods, services, and people – has reshaped labour markets with direct consequences for the structure of firms and relations with clients across professional sectors. Innovation, including the expansion of the Internet and growing capabilities of artificial intelligence, challenges professional expertise and permits new models of legal

---

* The authors would like to thank Swethaa Ballakrishnen, Andrew Francis, and Charles Epp for their feedback and suggestions on earlier drafts of this chapter.

practice and service delivery. Neoliberalism in the domestic political sphere – a set of policies and practices associated with declining government regulation of the market and diminished redistributive programs, coupled with a greater role for private actors in public governance – has been linked to a rise in social inequality, with direct consequences for the quantity and quality of legal services for those of different means.

Our central claim is that while these three forces are a challenge to the profession as a whole, they have influenced different sectors of the profession in distinct ways. The contemporary profession is not so much in 'disarray' as it is disaggregated, with change proceeding differently in sectors at the heart of our analysis: the private practice sector, composed of solo and small firms, boutiques, large firms, and in-house counsel; the government sector, with prosecutors, public defenders, agency lawyers, and the judiciary; the nonprofit sector, consisting of legal services and public interest law organisations; and the legal academy.

Globalisation, innovation, and neoliberalism have transformed American society and its occupational structure, significantly increasing inequality since the 1970s, whether measured by income (McCall and Percheski 2010; Piketty 2014; Stiglitz 2013) or wealth (Hacker and Pierson 2010, 2014; Keister 2014). The American legal profession is a microcosm of this broader trend, revealing persistent structural inequality between the 'haves' who represent 'repeat players' and the 'have nots' who represent 'one-shot' players (Galanter 1974). As we demonstrate, this dichotomy has become more complicated as fractures within the two 'hemispheres' of practice have produced new categories of winners and losers.

II. GENERAL DEMOGRAPHIC TRENDS

Figure 1 Active Resident Lawyers in the US, 1990–2015

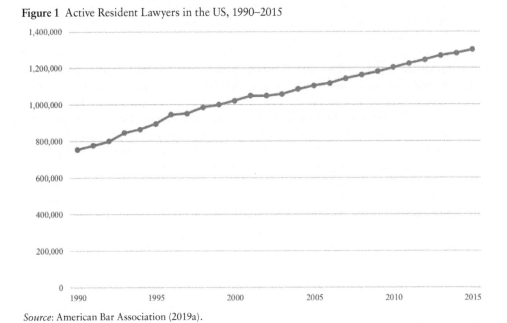

Source: American Bar Association (2019a).

The profession is large, with over 1.3 million active lawyers in 2015, and has grown by roughly two-thirds since 1990, fairly steadily except for a dip in 2003.[1] Large states such as California and New York experienced the largest increases. The growth of the profession has tracked that of the population, of which the profession has consistently represented 0.3–0.4 per cent.

Figure 2 Practice Sectors of Practising Lawyers, 1991–2005

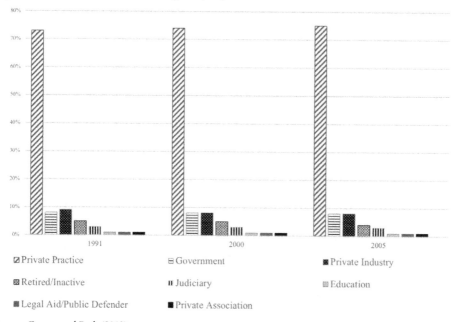

Source: Carson and Park (2012).

The largest sector of the Bar has always been private practice. The next two most common practice sites are private industry (as in-house counsel) and government. Legal aid/public defender, public interest law (included in the private associations category), and education have long constituted a small percentage.

III. FORCES OF CHANGE

Demographic trends reflect a picture of gradual growth, but this image obscures more complex developments within professional sectors shaped by structural forces that amplify inequality.

---

[1] Estimates of the profession's size vary by the methodology for collecting data. We rely primarily on ABA data (based on reports by Bar associations and licensing agencies), which provide the greatest detail for the categories that interest us.

A. Globalisation

Legal practice has been 'remade by the emerging global order' as American lawyers are 'actively trying to remake it' (Trubek et al 1993: 407). Increasing global trade and investment as well as new communication technologies have expanded the scope of law practice 'across provincial, national, and regional boundaries, culminating in the internationalization of business law firms and the formation of global legal institutions' (Liu 2013). Globalisation also increases the significance of supranational legal institutions, such as the United Nations, World Trade Organisation, and European Union, which require cross-border expertise (Abel 1994). The push to open new legal markets in areas of rapidly expanding legal business has led US firms to create offices not only in centres of business and finance in the global North, such as London and Berlin, but also in so-called 'emerging' markets in the global South, where demand for legal services has increased significantly (Papa and Wilkins 2011).

Globalisation has also allowed efficiencies in the production of legal services, particularly through legal process outsourcing (LPO), a broad term for 'sending [overseas] legal work traditionally handled inside a company or firm' (Papa and Wilkins 2011). LPOs generally charge 'one-tenth to one-third what a traditional western law firm charges per hour' (ibid: 184). LPO services include '[c]ontract attorneys [who] are employed by temporary staffing agencies' (Sechooler 2008) to perform legal research, provide litigation support, and submit patent and trademark applications (D'Angelo 2007; Regan and Heenan 2010; Robers 2010; Silver and Daly 2006). LPOs can also cut administrative costs by outsourcing tasks like office operations, word processing, finance and accounting, and human resources. Together, these services were estimated at nearly $20 billion in 2004 (Krishnan 2007).

The spread of foreign law firm affiliates and the growth of transnational practice are not limited to for-profit law. The 'internationalisation' of public interest practice has included legal work for immigrants, cross-border advocacy around regional labour and environmental standards, litigation against multinational corporations, and human rights work within domestic legal systems (Cummings 2008). A key driver of cross-border advocacy has been regional market integration, which accelerated the transnational flow of workers and spread of pollution while providing mechanisms like NAFTA's labour and environmental side agreements to address them (ibid). Transnational public interest practice has been integral to the expansion of human rights institutions like the UN and Inter-American Commission on Human Rights, which have created opportunities for advocacy and litigation around domestic issues such as the death penalty, welfare reform, and detentions.

B. Innovation

In law, as in other service industries, technological developments have disrupted traditional practice. LPO changes which people do the work, but technology questions whether people perform it at all. Some traditional lawyers' services are now automated and delivered by computers. The most successful of the web-based consumer-oriented platforms,

LegalZoom, enables clients to prepare downloadable legal documents such as wills, real estate deed transfers, leases, and articles of incorporation (Lanctot 2011; Moxley 2015). Some 'virtual law firms' communicate with clients, firm members and co-counsel through secure online interfaces and deliver legal services to clients over the Internet (Williams et al 2015). Access to justice apps provide information about law and legal services to the public via smart phones (Carter 2015).

The Internet has introduced new online marketing methods, including law firm websites, social and professional networking sites, blogs, pay-per-click ads, and lead generation services. Artificial intelligence and data analytics are changing how lawyers manage documents, conduct legal research, test theories, predict litigation outcomes, and manage workflows (Sobowale 2016; Susskind 2013).

Comparative data have become easily available, not only for consumers but also competitors. The rise of rankings has driven professional change, from the *American Lawyer* magazine's publication of partner salaries and rankings of per partner profits (Harper 2013) to rankings of law schools by *US News and World Report* (Espeland and Sauder 2016; Tamanaha 2012). Both law firms and law schools prioritise activities and time investments with an eye to these rankings.

C. Neoliberalism

A broad and contested concept, neoliberalism at its core signifies the related ideas of a reduced role for government, laissez faire economic policy, and free trade. Its signal policies are austerity in social welfare spending, deregulation of markets and commerce, and privatisation of public functions (Goldsmith and Eggers 2004; Hacker 2004; Kamerman and Kahn 2014; Kettl 1994). Reagan's 1980 election marked the ascendance of a neoliberal agenda, which has persisted through all subsequent administrations. Lawyers have played a pivotal role in shaping this broad agenda (Southworth 2008; Teles 2008), which has in turn created new arenas of legal conflict, for example around religious rights, corporate influence in politics, and de-regulation of economic activity.

IV. SECTORAL ANALYSIS

The forces of globalisation, innovation and neoliberalism have shaped inequality and differentiation in an already disaggregated profession.

A. Private Practice

Private practice is divided between lawyers in corporate firms representing large organisations and those in small or solo practices representing individuals and small businesses (Heinz et al 2005; Heinz and Laumann 1982). As Figure 3 shows, nearly two-thirds (63 per cent) of private practitioners work in very small firms (1–5 lawyers). By contrast, less than a fifth (16 per cent) work in firms of 101 or more.

Figure 3 Firm Size for Private Practitioners, 1991–2005

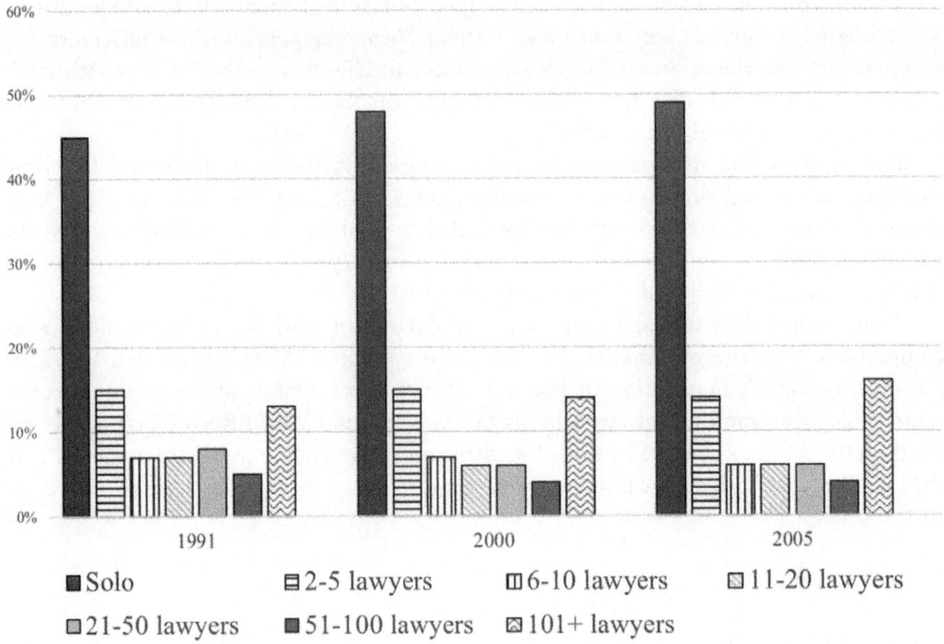

■ Solo ▤ 2-5 lawyers ▥ 6-10 lawyers ▧ 11-20 lawyers
▤ 21-50 lawyers ■ 51-100 lawyers ▨ 101+ lawyers

Source: Carson and Park (2012).

i. Solo and Small Firm Lawyers

Solo and small firm lawyers tend to represent clients with relatively small, discrete legal problems and limited experience with the law. The one-off nature of these lawyer-client relationships contributes to what is consistently shown to be a precarious professional niche (Carlin 1962; Heinz et al 2005; Seron 1996; Van Hoy 1997). As the profession has grown, more solo practices and small firms have marketed their services, but this has not produced greater demand.

One study of Chicago lawyers (Heinz et al 2005) found that between 1975 and 1995 the demand for individual-client services was relatively stagnant and specialisations were relatively fixed, offering limited opportunities for new areas of work. Some legal needs are fairly constant, such as divorce and criminal defence. But technological innovation and neoliberal trade policies have driven employees to cheaper labour markets, depressing real wages and benefits among the middle and working classes. Some traditional clients of solo and small firm lawyers can no longer afford legal services. The numerous contingent fee lawyers offering access to legal services for injuries and other cases promising a money judgment (Daniels and Martin 1999) are stratified into a food-chain of highly visible lawyers who attract such claims and refer them to smaller players (Parikh 2006). Indeed, most low- and middle-income people with legal problems never see a lawyer (American Bar Association 1994; Legal Services Corporation 2017; Sandefur 2014).

Reflecting the relative continuity in their professional activities over the past 20 years, many solo and small-firm lawyers feel their work is not 'cutting-edge' or innovative (Heinz et al 2005; Seron 1996), which is reflected in lower prestige and incomes (Dinovitzer et al 2009).

Nevertheless, these lawyers take seriously their responsibility for public service and pro bono activities (Heinz et al 2005; Seron 1996). Advertising, legal insurance, and solicitation opened new ways to obtain clients, but many solo and small firm lawyers continue to rely on more traditional methods like personal networking through family, friends, and local associations. Access to these networks is unequal: women do not have the same breadth of networks as men (Kay and Gorman 2016; Seron 1996), and the likelihood that minority clients will retain minority lawyers reflects the racial segregation of many Americans social networks (Lempert et al 2000). The expansion of the Internet and the emergence of new technologies has had both positive and negative effects on solo and small firm practices. The ready availability of information and document assembly applications online has challenged the traditional way individuals and small businesses obtain legal services, moving some of the work from law offices to the Internet (Cabral et al 2012). Globalisation has opened opportunities to tap new markets but also intensified competition, even among small firms, which observers postulate lose clients to offshore lawyers in the 'Globalisation 3.0 world' (Terry 2007).

ii. Boutique Firms

Boutique firms are generally small and focused, intentionally 'cultivat[ing] their comparative advantage in selected specialties' and 'suppress[ing] any push to more general coverage in order to maintain their attractiveness for referral work' (Galanter and Palay 1990). The last 20 years have seen growth in both the number of firms and types of expertise offered, as small groups of elite lawyers leave big firms to set up lower-priced, lower-overhead specialty shops, sometimes trading income for greater control over hours, fewer disqualifying conflicts of interest, and less formal work environments (Burk and McGowan 2011). Boutiques challenge large firm dominance in practice areas such as real estate, technology firm transactions, intellectual property licensing, defence-side employment, trial work, and complex litigation (Williams et al 2015). Replacing some human labour with technology and outsourcing other work allow firms to lower production costs. Outsourcing permits flexible expansion and contraction depending on work flow (Krishnan 2007), enabling some firms to handle the large complex matters previously the exclusive domain of large firms (Williams et al 2015).

Some boutique firms are 'private public interest law firms', commited to promoting political causes while balancing economic return and social impact. This sector has grown significantly over the last 40 years (Cummings and Southworth 2009), with a recent compilation listing 671 firms (Cummings 2012). Civil rights, criminal, and employment law have become more popular, while environmental and consumer protection have declined (ibid), which may reflect the influence of fee-shifting statutes that make civil rights and employment cases economically viable for private practitioners as well as the availability of federal funding for private lawyers defending indigent clients.

iii. Large Firms

Large law firms grew even larger in the 1980s as they added both lawyers and geographic reach. In 1985, the largest law firm, Baker McKenzie, had 755 lawyers (Abel 1989), but in 2015 it employed over 6,000 (Johnson 2016). The median number of lawyers in the 200 largest firms was 205 in 1987 (Abel 1989); by 2015 it was 445 (The National Law Journal 2016), and 44 firms had more than 1,000 (Johnson 2016). Thirty years ago, the large firm was a US phenomenon (Abel 1989). In 2015, just 64 of the 100 largest and four of the ten largest were based in the US. The world's largest law firm, Dentons, employed 6,568 lawyers in 54 countries, most of them in China (Johnson 2016).

As they have grown, firms have globalised. By 2007, only about half (52 per cent) of the lawyers in overseas offices of US firms were in EU countries, while about a third (34 per cent) were in the Asia-Pacific region (Silver et al 2009), many in China, where there 'are now American and British law firms in Hong Kong, Shanghai, and Beijing' (Krishnan 2010: 58). US firms now employ more foreign than American lawyers in their overseas offices (Silver et al 2009). In 1990, less than half of US firms with London offices had more than five London-based lawyers, most of whom were US lawyers providing US legal advice (Silver 2007). However, once restrictions on solicitor and foreign lawyer collaboration were lifted, British solicitors quickly outnumbered US lawyers in those offices (ibid). The 'vast majority of lawyers working in overseas offices earned their legal education outside the United States', suggesting that 'US JDs are important as symbols of the US identity of the firms, rather than (or in addition to) simply as mechanisms for performing legal work' (Silver et al 2009: 1462).

The global expansion of US firms has been motivated, in part, by the pull of a global legal services market projected to be worth $762.2 billion by 2019 (Wilkins and Esteban 2016). US law firms compete not only with other global law firms but also with other types of professional services firms – including international accounting firms, multidisciplinary partnerships (MDPs), management consulting firms, and LPOs. The Big Four accounting firms, for example, have retooled their legal practices in response to Bar regulatory challenges and the accounting scandals of the dot-com era. They have expanded beyond tax advising and taken advantage of technology to offer 'truly integrated legal services and innovative business solutions' around the world, including fast-growing emerging economies in Asia Pacific, Latin America and Africa (ibid).[2]

Large firms' relationships with their corporate clients have changed, as comprehensive long-term retainers have given way to less enduring or exclusive relationships and more task-specific assignments (Galanter and Palay 1990; Ribstein 2010). These pressures from corporate clients, in turn, have affected the market for junior associates. Over the past 20–30 years, in-house counsel have become more engaged in monitoring the work their corporations send to firms. As one put it, 'You don't need a $500-an-hour associate to do things like document review and basic due diligence' (Timmons 2010). These pressures lead associates to compete for assignments that will let them meet billable hours targets (Fortney 2005) and motivate partners to skimp on non-billable activities, such as mentoring and training (Galanter and Henderson 2008; Wilkins 2010). Recent evidence suggests that elite law graduates view a stint in a large firm as an apprenticeship leading to highly valued positions elsewhere in the legal profession or business world, many leaving before being considered for partnership (Garth and Sterling 2009).

---

[2] In 2015, Price Waterhouse Cooper provided legal services in 85 countries, Deloitte in 69, KPMG in 53, and Ernst & Young in 69.

Under these highly competitive conditions, large firms rely heavily on lateral hiring to expand to new locations, add new practice specialties, and acquire rainmakers (Galanter and Palay 1990). Public ranking of per partner profits has contributed to lateral defections by both lawyers and clients (Galanter and Henderson 2008). With so many practice areas and so many lawyers in large firms, conflicts of interest among current and potential clients become more common, generating tension between partners and provoking defections (Shapiro 2002).

Increased monitoring by in-house counsel, the breakdown of retainer relationships, competition with alternative service providers, and more lateral hires and departures have eroded law firm culture and promoted commercial values. Compensation formulas tied to hours worked and business-getting ability make 'economics rather than culture' the 'glue that holds the firm together' (Galanter and Henderson 2008). To boost per partner profits and rankings, attract laterals and discourage defections, many large firms have increased leverage by reducing the proportion of equity partners and expanding non-equity positions (ibid). The Great Recession spurred additional restructuring, making firms more heavily leveraged (Yoon 2014).

In the early 1990s, the *American Lawyer* began reporting data on firms' pro bono work and ranking them accordingly. Large firms formalised pro bono policies, in part to bolster those rankings and more generally to appeal to law students and improve their public image at a time when the competitive environment and long hours for associates were making it difficult for law firms to compete with start-ups, investment banks, venture capital firms and consulting firms for top talent (Cummings 2004).

iv. In-House Counsel

In-house corporate law departments have grown substantially in size, budget, authority, and stature over the past several decades. Between 1997 and 2008, the 2,000 largest law departments grew an average of 4.8 per cent per year (Schwarcz 2008). Corporations have moved much of their legal work in-house, including more of the complex matters and some transactional work previously delegated to outside firms (Daly 1997; Nelson and Nielsen 2000; Schwarcz 2008). Today's general counsel typically serves as manager for all the corporation's legal services, responsible for hiring outside counsel, controlling their cost, and ensuring that the corporation complies with the law (Danzig 2009).

Globalisation and the rise of multinational corporations have increased the risk of legal scandals (Simmons and Dinnage 2011). Legislatures have addressed corporate misconduct with regulations giving corporations incentives to adopt compliance programs and offering whistle-blowers immunity. This has increased the responsibility and authority of in-house counsel to monitor legal risk, which has elevated its status (Deloitte 2011; Heineman 2012). From 2006 to 2012, the proportion of in-house lawyers serving on senior management teams grew from 47 to 62 per cent (Deloitte 2011). It has become commonplace for corporations to recruit big firm senior partners to lead their legal departments (Rostain 2008). A 2010 survey of 130 general counsel and 80 law firm partners around the world concluded that general counsel had acquired substantially greater status and influence since the 2008 recession (Eversheds 2010).

B. Nonprofit Sector

The nonprofit sector is distinguished by the organisational form in which law is practised, which shapes what lawyers do in pursuit of noncommercial goals. This sector is divided between legal aid groups serving the poor and public interest law groups focused on advancing causes across the political spectrum. The growth of clinical legal education has meant that significant public interest-oriented legal services are rendered by law professors and students working in clinics housed in law schools, themselves nonprofit organisations. There is some overlap between nonprofit groups and boutique law firms specialising in civil and labour rights or other underrepresented causes; the key distinction is that nonprofit groups must be devoted exclusively to advancing a public mission and cannot distribute profits to lawyers, whereas boutique firms may combine cause lawyering with fee-generating work.

i. Legal Services Organisations

Since its inception in 1965 as part of the war on poverty, the federal legal services programme has been an important source of free civil legal services to the poor. From the outset, it generated conflict between those who believed it should focus on individual dispute resolution and those who favoured law reform. By the mid-1980s, the neoliberal backlash secured substantial reductions in funding and new restrictions on lobbying and representation of undocumented immigrants (among others). In 1981, the Legal Services Corporation (LSC) required its grantees to make a 'substantial amount' of funds available for Private Attorney Involvement (PAI). While in other nations such funds might be used for 'judicare' services (paying private lawyers to represent indigent clients), the major effect of this mandate in the US was to stimulate the expansion of programmes designed to recruit, train, and connect pro bono volunteers with low-income clients. Spurred by the PAI mandate, the number of organised pro bono programmes rose from about 50 in 1980 to over 500 in 1985 (McBurney 2003).

The backlash reached a peak in the 1994 election, when Republicans gained control of Congress. In 1996, Congress cut the LSC budget by a third and banned class actions, the collection of attorneys' fees, prisoner representation, and political advocacy, while prohibiting LSC-funded offices from using non-LSC funds to engage in those activities. To meet the shortfall, legal services organisations diversified their funding. In the mid-2000s, state and local government funds contributed about one-third, Interest on Lawyers' Trust Accounts about 10 per cent, foundations about 7 per cent, and private lawyer donations roughly 4 per cent (Houseman 2005), with some minor variation in recent years (Houseman 2013). Reliance on private funding, from individuals and corporations, has increased (Sandefur and Smyth 2011).

ii. Public Interest Law Organisations

In 1969, there were only 15 public interest law groups, which together had fewer than 50 full-time lawyers (Council for Public Interest Law 1976). A 2004 study reported slightly more than 1,000 public interest law organisations (including legal aid organisations) with an average of 13 lawyers each, for an estimated total of 13,715 attorneys (Nielsen and Albiston 2006)[3] – approximately 1.3 per cent of the Bar (Carson and Park 2012).

Since its inception, public interest lawyering has secured resources from philanthropic foundations. While this remains important, public interest law organisations now also receive support from state and local governments, individual donations, and corporations (Nielsen and Albiston 2006; Rhode 2008). Public interest groups supplement their personnel with volunteer lawyers from private firms (Boutcher 2013) and collaborate with private public interest law firms. No longer in a 'fragile alliance' with the organised Bar (Scheingold and Sarat 2004), public interest law now is a stable and strongly supported occupational category. This is reflected, in part, in the status of clinical education, launched in the 1970s as the academic counterpart to the public interest law movement with a $10 million grant from the Ford Foundation. Since that time, clinical education – hands-on legal training typically through faculty-supervised representation of clients unable to afford private counsel – has grown significantly and become an important source of legal services for underserved clients and causes. In 1999, the AALS Section on Clinical Education's database showed 183 law schools with clinics staffed by over 1,700 clinicians – 80 per cent of whom taught in live-client clinics primarily serving the needs of underserved clients in areas like criminal defence, immigration, housing, environmental law, and civil rights (Barry et al 2000). The lawyer-hours devoted to public interest oriented legal work in law school clinics in the early 2010s was equivalent to the work of nearly 300 full-time attorneys per year (Cummings 2012).

Perhaps the most striking development in public interest law since the 1980s has been the representation of conservative and libertarian causes. Beginning in the 1970s, conservative movement leaders recognised the need to institutionalise their legal goals with support from conservative foundations and corporate interests (Southworth 2008). First-wave efforts in the 1970s, focused on creating regional groups like the Pacific Legal Foundation, were limited by close alliances with corporate sponsors, undermining those groups' claim to serve the public good. The next wave of organisations, like the Institute for Justice, publicly distanced themselves from corporate backers, realising that by '[r]epresenting traditionally liberal clients, ... it would be possible for conservatives to gain a hearing on a wide range of issues' (Teles 2008: 239). The field of conservative public interest organisations might best be described as a coalition spanning a wide range of interests – including conservative Christians, Libertarians, and business elites – held together by important institutions like the Federalist Society and Heritage Foundation, which work to bridge these disparate constituencies (Heinz et al 2003).

C. Government

A robust federalist tradition defines lawyers' roles in government. Whether at the federal, state, county, or city levels, lawyers are employed by courts, executives, administrative agencies, and legislatures. The proportion of all lawyers employed in government

---

[3] The Legal Services Corporation (2007) reported that in 2002 there were 3,845 lawyers in LSC-funded programmes and an estimated 2,736 lawyers in non-LSC funded programmes.

(approximately 10 per cent) is small compared to their private practice counterparts (75 per cent) and remained relatively constant between 1980 and 2005 (Carson and Park 2012). Lawyers in the federal government declined from 4 per cent of the profession in 1980 to 3 per cent in 2005. Lawyers in state and local government (excluding legal aid and public defenders) declined from 9 per cent in 1980 to 6 per cent in 2000 and rose slightly to 7 per cent in 2005. While these proportions are relatively small, the lawyers nonetheless play a significant role in shaping American policy, both domestically and globally, in a highly fragmented context characterised by federalism, separation of powers, and the circulation of political appointees representing the values and orientations of elected officials at all levels.

i. Judges

Most judges are fully qualified attorneys, though some federal administrative law judges and others working in state and local tribunals and courts (often in rural areas) are not (Ford 2017). Judges are selected by election, appointment, or some combination (American Judicature Society 2015). Three per cent of all lawyers served as state or local judges in 1980, declining to 2 per cent in 2005 (Carson and Park 2012). Even this small fraction masks the deterioration of support for the state judiciary, especially the impact of the 2008 recession, which further reduced funding for courts, resulting in pay freezes and furloughs, unfilled positions opened by retirement and other departures, and courts operating for fewer hours or even closing (Flango and Clarke 2014). The length of time from case filing to first hearing to resolution increased for both civil and criminal cases.

All federal judges are appointed by the President, confirmed by the Senate, and enjoy lifetime tenure. During the Reagan administration, Attorney General Meese and his team of political appointees at the Department of Justice worked to appoint conservative judges and executive branch officials in order to generate and diffuse conservative ideas. They received support from the Federalist Society, a fledgling lawyer debating group that has since groomed a generation of conservative lawyers for senior positions in government, the bench, and the private bar. Conservative lawyers and legal academics promoted 'originalism', a jurisprudential approach invoking an original understanding of the Constitution to legitimate conservative ideas (Teles 2009). Meese's tenure as Attorney General also created a path for conservative lawyers to move between government service, advocacy organisations, and private practice (ibid), in much the same way that President Roosevelt's New Deal, Kennedy's New Frontier, and Johnson's Great Society institutionalised this career path on the left (Auerbach 1976). The Obama administration took steps to appoint judges with a more liberal jurisprudential philosophy, though opposition from the Republican Senate meant that many federal seats were kept vacant and have been filled by President Trump at the fastest pace in modern history.

ii. Prosecutors and Public Defenders

Prosecutors play critical roles in the criminal justice system at the federal and state levels. Each of the 94 federal district courts has an appointed US Attorney who serves at the pleasure of the President while overseeing a staff of career attorneys who manage the government docket. In 2007, there were 2,330 prosecutors offices with 25,000 assistant prosecutors and a total operating budget of close to $6 billion (Bureau of Justice Statistics 2011: 2). Of elected prosecutors, 95 per cent are white and 79 per cent white men. In contrast, although the Supreme Court in *Gideon v Wainwright*[4] and *Argersinger v Hamlin*[5] interpreted the Constitution to confer a right to counsel in all felony and most misdemeanour cases, this unfunded mandate has produced a highly variable system of public defenders. Federal public defenders are funded through the judicial branch and serve as the counterparts of the US Attorney's offices. Many state and local jurisdictions have never funded public defenders at a level that would permit the zealous advocacy legal ethics requires. In 2007, there were 15,000 state public defenders in 957 offices handling over 5.5 million cases on a budget of just over $2 billion (Bureau of Justice Statistics 2010).

iii. Agency Lawyers

There is a division of labour between the civil service or career staff and political appointees who serve at the pleasure of elected officials. Because the top tier of administrative agencies is staffed by political appointees, cause lawyers have sought them as a way to influence government policy from the inside. In filling those positions at the federal level, Democratic administrations have treated public interest credentials and social movement activism, such as work at the ACLU and NAACP, as a 'marker of relevant expertise' (Banaszak 2009; Epp 2009; NeJaime 2012). The Reagan presidency opened its doors to Federalist Society members (Southworth 2008; Teles 2009), a pattern that persists as President Trump fills appointed positions (Toobin 2017).

In a marked change from their traditional, relatively limited role in overseeing a state's criminal and civil docket, state Attorneys General (AGs) have recently become significant players in national policymaking. Drawing on expanded capacity and jurisdiction, they have developed strategies to launch 'coordinated litigation [across various states] to promote the expansion of national regulation' (Nolette 2015: 11), upsetting the traditional balance of power in the federal polity. For example, in the 1990s, state AGs coordinated investigations and litigation with private attorneys and public interest advocates to successfully challenge the pharmaceutical industry, fundamentally revamping drug pricing, particularly for Medicare and Medicaid (federally-funded health care programmes for the elderly and the poor). During the Obama administration, state AGs on the right deployed the same robust strategy to challenge environmental regulations and roll back the Affordable Care Act. Recently states have sought to override the Trump administration's withdrawal from the Paris Agreement on climate and opposed reductions of support for cities and states offering sanctuary to undocumented immigrants.

Career lawyers in local, state, and federal government play a pivotal role in the day-to-day execution of government regulation and policy. At the municipal level, for example, lawyers develop expertise in law enforcement regulations as well as

---

[4] *Gideon v Wainwright*, 372 US 335 (1963).
[5] *Argersinger v Hamlin*, 407 US 25 (1972).

the relevant constitutional law. At the state level, lawyers draft regulations on topics ranging from agriculture and labour relations to fair employment and housing. At the federal level, lawyers are employed across the bureaucracy, including in departments of labour, housing and urban development, state, homeland security, and treasury. Lawyers in state and local government tend to be graduates of less prestigious law schools, whereas those from prestigious law schools gravitate toward federal agencies, where some take first jobs before moving to large firm practice (Heinz et al 2005).

D. The Legal Academy

Though the popular press declares that legal education is currently in crisis, a longer view reveals that its mission has been contested within the academy and among key stakeholders since at least the Progressive Era (Llewellyn 1948; Solomon 1992). The key question is whether the object is to institutionalise law as a scholarly discipline or to impart knowledge essential to future practitioners (Stevens 1983). The slowdown of large firm hiring in 2009 exacerbated this tension as the legal academy faced a corresponding contraction of resources after years of growth.

In 2015, there were 37,058 first-year JD students and 113,900 students at the 207 ABA-approved law schools. JD enrolment fell after the 2008 recession, but it is unclear whether this contraction will be permanent (and recent enrolment trends upward). Tuition has risen continuously since 1990: an inflation-adjusted 46 per cent at private and 132 per cent at public law schools between 1999 and 2014 (American Bar Association 2015b). But the proportion of students paying full tuition has fallen from 58 per cent in all law schools in 1999 to 38 per cent in private and 40 per cent in public law schools in 2013 (ibid), reflecting an increase in merit-based aid to recruit top students from the smaller post-recession pool.

The professoriate is small (1 per cent of the profession). Among those teaching in 1996–2001, 67.5 per cent had attended one of the top 25 law schools; the proportion was 81 per cent at elite institutions. Most had also practised (Redding 2003). The proportion of new hires with PhDs (who were less likely to have practised) increased from 13 per cent in 1996–2000 to 27 per cent in 2010 and 48 per cent in 2011–15 (LoPucki 2015).

In response to critiques of the usefulness of a law degree (particularly difficult to ignore after the 2008 recession), the ABA adopted standards in 2015 requiring law schools to provide experiential learning (through law clinics, field placements, or simulation courses) and students to take one or more experiential courses totalling at least six credit hours.

As the profession has become more global, law schools have introduced curricular changes and study abroad opportunities to promote global education (Carrillo 2004; Hurwitz 2003; Sexton 1996; Silver 2013). Perhaps the most significant change has been the growth of foreign student to 3,200 in 2004 (about five per cent of first-year JD students), 50 per cent more than in 1998 (Silver 2005). In 2005, over 100 law schools offered LLMs, and nearly 60 had other programmes exclusively for foreign lawyers (Lazarus-Black and Globokar 2015; Papa and Wilkins 2011; Sechooler 2008). The absence of ABA regulation of LLM programmes and the fact that foreign students pay full tuition (without financial aid) but do not count for *US News* rankings have encouraged this growth (Silver 2005).

V. INEQUALITY IN A DISAGGREGATED PROFESSION

The development of the legal profession over the past 30 years has exacerbated long-standing structural patterns of inequality, including the persistent problem of diversity in entry and promotion, economic inequality across professional sectors, unequal access to justice, and inequities in professional regulation.

A. The Persistent Problem of Diversity: Inequality in Entry and Promotion

While the legal profession may profess common values regardless of where its members attended law school (Kronman 1993; Linowitz and Mayer 1994), sociologists have repeatedly debunked this claim. Legal education has been highly stratified since the late nineteenth century, a hierarchy exacerbated by *US News* rankings. Social background remains a highly significant predictor of where one goes to law school, which affects where one practises (Dinovitzer et al 2009).

i. Entry to the Profession

Perhaps the biggest exogenous shock to legal education in recent decades has been the *US News* rankings (Espeland and Sauder 2016). Because students' undergraduate grades and LSATs have significant weight in that algorithm, law schools have shifted financial support to recruit those with the highest numbers, who often have the least need, further disadvantaging students who are Black or Latino and first generation college graduates, all of whom are more likely to assume increased educational debt (Taylor and Christensen 2017).

Women have reached numerical parity in law schools but ethnic and racial minorities continue to be underrepresented compared to the population at large and the undergraduate pipeline, and are significantly more likely to graduate with greater debt. Legal constraints on affirmative action have contributed to this trend. For example, after California passed Proposition 209 in 1996, eliminating affirmative action at the University of California, its four law schools experienced a significant drop in applications from underrepresented minorities (Lempert et al 2000).

ii. Promotion within the Profession

Patterns of inequality persist after entry into the profession. As Figure 4 illustrates, the proportion of women grew steadily over the past 25 years. Greater parity, however, should not be confused with equal status. Sterling and Reichman (2016) point to ongoing disparities in compensation, barriers to partnership, and higher exit rates from the profession, all of which they attribute to organisational structures and biases favouring men's success in private practice.

Figure 4 Changes in Gender Composition of the Legal Profession, 1991–2015

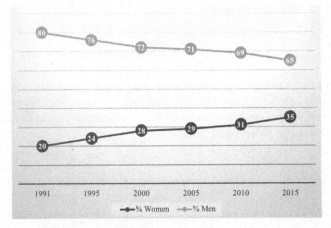

Source: American Bar Foundation (2009; 2019b).

As Figure 5 shows, historically underrepresented racial minority (URM) lawyers (Blacks, Latinos, and American Indians/Alaskan natives) still represent just 9 per cent of the profession, nearly unchanged between 2000 and 2010, although they are more than 30 per cent of Americans (US Census Bureau 2015). Minority representation is greatest in larger firms but still lags at their top tiers (Kay and Gorman 2016).

Figure 5 Percentages of Racial Groups in the Legal Profession, 1990–2010

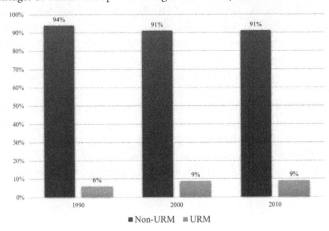

Source: American Bar Association (2009; 2019b).

The legal academy presents a microcosm of these broader trends. Despite overall gains in female and URM representation, most tenured or tenure-track professors and law school deans are men (primarily white), while other full-time instructors (whether of legal skills or writing) are disproportionately women (also primarily white) (American Bar Association 2013). Women also comprise a disportionate percentage of lower level administrative positions. URM faculty representation resembles that of the student body, meaning that it is remains low relative to the general population.

There are modest diversity gains in other areas. The National Association for Law Placement (2015c) reported that the proportion of lawyers identifying as lesbian, gay, bisexual, or transgender increased from 1 per cent in 2002 to 2.34 per cent in 2015, while those identifying as disabled changed little between 2003 (0.1 per cent) and 2005 (0.13 per cent) (National Association for Law Placement 2005). More US lawyers are immigrants, increasing from 6 per cent of the profession in 2000 to 8 per cent by 2012 (Michelson 2015). One reason has been the expansion of LLM programmes, which provide exposure to US law for foreign-trained lawyers, some of whom remain after completing their degrees (Silver 2002). At the same time, many immigrant lawyers are 'home-grown'. As a generation of 'Dreamers' – undocumented immigrants brought to the US by parents when young – has begun to attend law school and seek admission to practice, state bars have had to rule on their eligibility, with California leading the way by admitting undocumented lawyers.[6]

B. A Disaggregated Profession: Inequality across Sectors

In 2015, the Bureau of Labor Statistics reported that the mean annual wage for a lawyer was $136,260. But there are deep economic fault lines within the profession, notably between the 'two hemispheres' of private practice (Heinz and Laumann 1982). Starting salaries for recent law school graduates show a bimodal distribution, which produces a lifetime 'earnings gap between law graduates who take a job in a large law firm and graduates who take a job in just about any other sector or in small firms' (National Association for Law Placement 2015b). While starting salaries resembled a bell-shaped curve in 1990, a bimodal distribution emerged in 2000 as large law firms began to raise starting salaries. According to the 'After the JD I' study, the median salary of entry-level large firm lawyers in 2003 was $135,000, compared to $50,000 for solo practitioners, $55,000 for those in firms of 2–20 lawyers, and $110,000 for in-house counsel; it was $70,500 for federal government lawyers compared to $43,000 for legal services lawyers or public defenders and $48,000 for public interest lawyers (Dinovitzer et al 2009). Fewer graduates obtained the highest salaries after the 2008 recession curtailed large firm hiring. The distribution of earnings for the class of 2014 synthesises these trends: most graduates received starting salaries of $40–65,000, while just 17 per cent earned $165,000 (National Association for Law Placement 2015a). Lawyers in federal, state and local government earned 23 per cent less (in inflation-adjusted dollars) in 1995 than they had in 1975 (Heinz et al 2005).

C. The Distribution of Legal Services in the US: Unequal Access to Lawyers

There is chronically unequal access to justice, measured by the gap between the legal needs of the poor and the number of lawyers serving them. The problem is not a labour shortage (though restrictive Bar entry practices contribute) but the lack of funding for lawyers who serve low-income people, compounded by geographic mismatch (too few lawyers in rural and small-town areas) and the Bar's resistance to letting qualified non-lawyers offer services (Rhode and Cummings 2017; Sandefur 2014).

---

[6] *In re Garcia on Admission*, 315 P 3d 117 (Cal 2014).

This has reached crisis proportions in indigent criminal defence. Despite the constitutional right to counsel, the 'war on crime' launched in the 1980s has resulted in increasingly harsh treatment of offenders because declining '[p]ublic defender budgets ... [have] suffered crippling blows from the government's fiscal axe' (Taylor-Thompson 1996). In some places, absurdly large caseloads have undermined the public defender's capacity to provide effective assistance of counsel. In 2008, the Miami-Dade County public defender refused to accept new cases after average lawyer caseloads reached 500 felonies or more than 2,000 misdemeanours; other jurisdictions have followed suit. Nationwide, funding for public defence has fallen by 2 per cent since 1995, while the number of felony cases has increased by 40 per cent (Pfaff 2017). As the Department of Justice concluded: 'Heavy caseloads, insufficient resources, and inadequate oversight make it difficult for many attorneys representing indigent clients to completely fulfil their legal and ethical obligations' (Office of Justice Programs 2011).

On the civil side, the picture is equally dire. Although legal needs surveys consistently show that poor people experience 1–3 legal needs per year, only a small fraction of which receive legal advice or representation (Legal Services Corporation 2007), federal support for legal aid through the Legal Services Corporation (LSC) declined 60 per cent (in real terms) between 1980 and 2013 (Houseman 2013), forcing LSC-funded organisations to turn away at least as many clients as they serve (LSC 2007, 2009, 2016). In 2015, 5,000 LSC-funded lawyers closed 750,000 cases (91,618 with help of pro bono lawyers) (Legal Services Corporation 2016); President Trump's 2018 budget proposed eliminating all of them, and the Department of Justice has closed the Office for Access to Justice created under Obama. Among LSC organisations, family law cases dominate the docket, accounting for one-third of closed cases in 2015, followed by housing (28 per cent), and consumer and income maintenance cases (10 per cent each) (Legal Services Corporation 2016). Even these meagre resources were unequally distributed: '[s]tates differ substantially in the resources available to support legal assistance, in the kind of services that are available, and in the groups served by existing programs' (Sandefur and Smyth 2011).

Table 1 Civil Legal Aid Attorneys Per 10,000 People Below 200% of the Federal Poverty Level

California	0.44
Florida	0.46
Georgia	0.31
Illinois	0.79
Massachusetts	0.88
New Jersey	0.56
New York	2.65
Pennsylvania	0.59
Texas	0.30
Washington, DC	9.33

As Table 1 shows, the access to justice problem is acute even in states whose lawyer populations grew over the last decade. While Washington, DC and New York are outliers, in populous states like California there is barely half an attorney per 10,000 poor people, compared with approximately 40 lawyers for 10,000 non-poor people.

Figure 6 Ratio of Civil Legal Aid Attorneys to All Other Attorneys, 2016

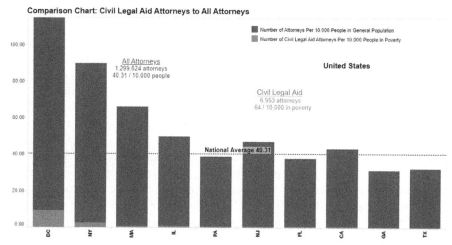

Source: NCAJ (2016).

The decline of federal support for civil legal aid has coincided with increases in pro bono services to poor and underrepresented clients, particularly by large law firms (Boutcher 2017). In 2005, pro bono's contribution to civil legal aid was worth at least $246 million, three-quarters as much as LSC funding that year (Sandefur 2007). Large firm pro bono hours increased by nearly 80 per cent between 1998 and 2005 (Boutcher 2009) and pro bono hours by all lawyers by nearly 50 per cent between 2005 and 2008 (the per-lawyer average growing by 10 hours) (Cummings and Rhode 2010). While impressive, commentators have questioned the wisdom of relying on private lawyer charity to address civil justice needs (Cummings and Sandefur 2013; Sandefur 2009). Overall, as American society grows more unequal, these efforts are insufficient to fill the justice gap (Hadfield 2016).

D. The Role of Regulation in a Disaggregated Bar

Just as the economic fortunes of the corporate and individual hemispheres of the Bar have diverged, so too have professional regulations governing them, loosening to accommodate corporate client interests while preserving boundary-maintenance practices affecting the supply of law-related services, thereby limiting access to justice for lower-income Americans.

In 2009, the ABA created the Ethics 20/20 Commission to identify and offer solutions for a growing number of regulatory issues arising from globalisation and technological change. It updated the ABA Model Rules of Professional Conduct to address issues such as cross-border practice by foreign lawyers, outsourcing, the delivery of legal services through the Internet, and online marketing of lawyers' services (Terry 2014).

Recognising the greater role of foreign lawyers advising multinational corporate clients, the Commission expanded multijurisdictional practice rules to permit foreign lawyers to appear in court pro hac vice and provide in-house services to the affiliates of an organisational client. The Commission also approved the growing use of outsourcing, while emphasising lawyers' duty to ensure that the outsourced work is performed competently and to avoid assisting unauthorised practice of law or breaching client confidences. Although the organised Bar has largely succeeded in defeating proposals to permit domestic MDPs and other types of alternative business structures, the relaxation of professional boundaries abroad has given multinational corporations access to MDPs there (Wilkins and Esteban 2016). Some commentators have raised concerns about the adequacy of global professional regulation, arguing that global firms have used their power to liberalise professional regulation in ways that are potentially damaging to clients, third parties, and the public (Flood 2011; Silver 2016).

By contrast, the ABA has justified its continued monopoly over the provision of legal services in the name of consumer protection. The Commission considered but rejected a proposal to let lawyers share fees with non-lawyers in alternative business structures – something the UK permitted under its Legal Services Act 2007 and which is considered to be one way to promote investment in lower cost legal services. The District of Columbia is the only US jurisdiction permitting such arrangements.[7] This effectively bans MDPs, in which experts from professions such as law, accounting, and management consulting collaborate to serve a single client.

More significant for individual consumers is the organised Bar's resistance to letting non-lawyers provide law-related services in simple routine matters. A few states have begun to 'nibble' at this monopoly (Sandefur and Clarke 2016). Washington State allows Limited License Legal Technicians to deliver a narrow set of family law services.[8] In most states, however, non-lawyers working independently are limited to selling and typing legal forms for self-represented individuals. Many state Bar associations actively prosecute or threaten non-lawyer providers who offer services proscribed as the unauthorised practice of law (Rhode 2016). Legal Zoom and similar web-based consumer-oriented platforms have sought to avoid such charges by characterising their services as self-help rather than law practice. But Legal Zoom has tangled repeatedly with state Bar organisations over whether it is violating unauthorised practice rules or the Bars are violating antitrust laws. Courts and NGOs are experimenting with using non-lawyer personnel with limited training and no certification to assist in problems like divorce, eviction, and debt collection.[9]

VI. CONCLUSION

The forces driving the growth of the American legal profession also encourage increasing fragmentation. Globalisation opens new markets for American lawyers' services and contributes to professional diversification. Technological and regulatory innovation

---

[7] DC Rules of Professional Conduct, 5.4.
[8] See Wash Sup Ct R: Admission to Practice r 28.
[9] See eg California's Justice Corps, Colorado's Self-Represented Litigant Coordinators, New York's Court Navigators, and Family Court Facilitators in many states.

reshape how lawyers work and introduce new competitors, some human, others not. Neoliberal policies support a dramatic rise in social inequality and governmental retreat. Developments in the broader society are reflected in the profession, enhancing markets for corporate and high-end personal services while undermining those for routine personal legal services and some types of government legal employment. Growth has allowed the entry of historically excluded groups – particularly women and racial and ethnic minorities – but has not created equal opportunity across the professional hierarchy. Professional segments differ not only in the work they do but also in their conditions of work, levels of income, and types of clients, fostering increasingly divergent interests. Cross-cutting inequalities and powerful structural forces have created not one but many American legal professions.

REFERENCES

Abel, RL (1988) 'United States: The Contradictions of Professionalism' in RL Abel and PSC Lewis (eds), *Lawyers in Society: Vol I The Common Law World* (Berkeley, University of California Press).
—— (1989) *American Lawyers* (Oxford, Oxford University Press).
—— (1994) 'Transnational Law Practice' 44 *Case Western Reserve Law Review* 737–870.
American Bar Association (1994) 'Legal Needs and Civil Justice – A Survey of Americans: Major Findings from the Comprehensive Legal Needs Study'.
—— (2009) 'Lawyer Demographics'.
—— (2013) 'Data from the 2013 Questionnaire: ABA Approved Law School Staff and Faculty Members, Gender and Ethnicity' www.americanbar.org/content/dam/aba/administrative/legal_education_and_admissions_to_the_bar/statistics/2013_law_school_staff_gender_ethnicity.xlsx.
—— (2015a) 'Lawyer Demographics'.
—— (2015b) 'Report of the ABA Task Force on Financing Legal Education' www.americanbar.org/content/dam/aba/administrative/legal_education_and_admissions_to_the_bar/reports/2015_june_report_of_the_aba_task_force_on_the_financing_of_legal_education.authcheckdam.pdf.
—— (2019a) 'ABA National Lawyer Population Survey: Historical Trend in Total National Lawyer Population, 1878–2019' www.americanbar.org/content/dam/aba/administrative/market_research/total-national-lawyer-population-1878-2019.pdf.
—— (2019b) 'ABA National Lawyer Population Survey: 10-Year Trend in Lawyer Demographics' www.americanbar.org/content/dam/aba/administrative/market_research/national-lawyer-population-demographics-2009-2019.pdf.
American Judicature Society (2015) 'Methods of Judicial Selection'. web.archive.org/web/20150222053432/http://judicialselection.us/judicial_selection/methods/selection_of_judges.cfm?state.
Auerbach, JS (1976) *Unequal Justice: Lawyers and Social Change in Modern America* (New York, Oxford University Press).
Banaszak, LA (2009) *The Women's Movement Inside and Outside the State* (Cambridge, Cambridge University Press).
Barry, MM, Dubin, JC and Joy, PA (2000) 'Clinical Education for This Millennium: The Third Wave' 7 *Clinical Law Review* 1.
Boutcher, SA (2009) 'The Institutionalization of Pro Bono in Large Law Firms: Trends and Variation Across the AmLaw 200' in R Granfield and L Mather (eds) *Private Lawyers and the Public Interest: The Evolving Role of Pro Bono in the Legal Profession* 135–44 (New York, Oxford University Press).

—— (2013) 'Lawyering for Social Change: Pro Bono Publico, Cause Lawyering, and the Social Movement Society' 18(2) *Mobilization: An International Quarterly* 179–96.

—— (2017) 'Private Law Firms and the Public Good: The Organizational and Institutional Determinants of Law Firm Pro Bono Participation, 1993–2005' (42) *Law & Social Inquiry* 543–64.

Bureau of Justice Statistics (2010) 'State Public Defender Programs, 2007' (US Department of Justice) www.bjs.gov/content/pub/pdf/spdp07.pdf.

Burk, B and McGowan, D (2011) 'Big but Brittle: Economic Perspectives on the Future of the Law Firm in the New Economy' *Columbia Business Law Review* 1–117.

Cabral, JE, Chavan, A, Clarke, TM, Greacen, J, Hough, BR, Rexer, L, Ribadeneyra, R and Zorza, R (2012) 'Using Technology to Enhance Access to Justice' 26 *Harvard Journal of Law & Technology* 241–324.

Carlin, J (1962) *Lawyers on Their Own: A Study of Individual Practitioners in Chicago* (New Brunswick, NJ, Rutgers University Press).

Carrillo, AJ (2004) 'Bringing International Law Home: The Innovative Role of Human Rights Clinics in the Transnational Legal Process' 35 *Columbia Human Rights Law Review* 527–88.

Carson, CN and Park, J (2012) *The Lawyer Statistical Report: The US Legal Profession in 2005* (Chicago, American Bar Foundation).

Carter, T (2015) 'Professor Tanina Rostain Has Her Students Developing Access-to-Justice Apps' *ABA Journal*, 23 September www.abajournal.com/legalrebels/article/tanina_rostain_profile/.

Council for Public Interest Law (1976) *Balancing the Scales of Justice: Financing Public Interest Law in America* (Washington, DC, Council for Public Interest Law).

Cummings, SL (2004) 'The Politics of Pro Bono' 52 *UCLA Law Review* 1–150.

—— (2008) 'The Internationalization of Public Interest Law' 57(4) *Duke Law Journal* 891–1036.

—— (2012) 'Privatizing Public Interest Law' 25 *Georgetown Journal of Legal Ethics* 1.

Cummings, S and Rhode, D (2010) 'Managing Pro Bono: Doing Well by Doing Better' 78(5) *Fordham Law Review* 2357.

Cummings, SL and Sandefur, RL (2013) 'Beyond the Numbers: What We Know – And Should Know – About American Pro Bono' 7 *Harvard Law & Policy Review* 83–112.

Cummings, SL and Southworth, A (2009) 'Between Profit and Principle: The Private Public Interest Firm' in R Granfield and L Mather (eds), *Private Lawyers and the Public Interest: The Evolving Role of Pro Bono in the Legal Profession* 183–210 (New York, Oxford University Press).

Daly, MC (1997) 'The Cultural, Ethical, and Legal Challenges in Lawyering for a Global Organization: The Role of the General Counsel The Randolph W. Thrower Symposium: The Role of General Counsel – Perspectives' 46 *Emory Law Journal* 1057–1112.

D'Angelo, C (2007) 'Overseas Legal Outsourcing and the American Legal Profession: Friend or "Flattener"?' 14 *Texas Wesleyan Law Review* 167–96.

Daniels, S and Martin, J (1999) '"It's Darwinism – Survival of the Fittest:" How Markets and Reputations Shape the Ways in Which Plaintiffs' Lawyers Obtain Clients' 21(4). *Law & Policy* 377–99 https://doi.org/10.1111/1467-9930.00078.

Danzig, C (2009) 'Inside Job' *Inside Counsel* 1 November.

Deloitte (2011) 'Global Corporate Counsel Report 2011: How the Game Is Changing' www.deloitte.com/ContentPages/2513816748.pdf.

Dinovitzer, R, Nelson, RL Plickert, G, Sandefur, RL and Sterling, JS (2009) 'After the JD II: Second Results from a National Study of Legal Careers' (NALP Foundation for Law Career Research and Education and the American Bar Foundation) www.law.du.edu/documents/directory/publications/sterling/AJD2.pdf.

Epp, CR (2009) *Making Rights Real: Activists, Bureaucrats, and the Creation of the Legalistic State* (Chicago: University of Chicago Press).

Espeland, WN and Sauder, M (2016) *Engines of Anxiety: Academic Rankings, Reputation, and Accountability* (New York: Russell Sage Foundation).

Eversheds (2010) 'Law Firm of the 21st Century, The Clients' Revolution' gould.usc.edu/assets/docs/contribute/Eversheds21CClientsRevolution.pdf.
Flango, VE and Clarke, TM (2014) *Reimagining Courts: A Design for the Twenty-First Century* (Philadelphia, Temple University Press).
Flood, J (2011) 'The Re-Landscaping of the Legal Profession: Large Law Firms and Professional Re-Regulation' 59(4) *Current Sociology* 507–29 doi.org/10.1177/0011392111402725.
Ford, M (2017) 'When Your Judge Isn't A Lawyer' *The Atlantic* 5 February www.theatlantic.com/politics/archive/2017/02/when-your-judge-isnt-a-lawyer/515568/.
Fortney, SS (2005) 'The Billable Hours Derby: Empirical Data on the Problems and Pressure Points' 33 *Fordham Urban Law Journal* 171–92.
Galanter, M (1974) 'Why the "Haves" Come out Ahead: Speculations on the Limits of Legal Change' 9(1) *Law & Society Review* 95–160 doi.org/10.2307/3053023.
Galanter, M and Henderson, W (2008) 'The Change Agenda: Tournament Without End' *The American Lawyer*, 1 December.
Galanter, M and Palay, TM (1990) 'Why the Big Get Bigger: The Promotion-to-Partner Tournament and the Growth of Large Law Firms' 76(4) *Virginia Law Review* 747–811 doi.org/10.2307/1073211.
Garth, BG and Sterling, J (2009) 'Exploring Inequality in the Corporate Law Firm Apprenticeship: Doing the Time, Finding the Love' 22 *Georgetown Journal of Legal Ethics* 1361–94.
Goldsmith, S and Eggers, WD (2004) *Governing by Network: The New Shape of the Public Sector* (Washington, DC, Brookings Institution Press/Ash Center).
Hacker, JS (2004) 'Privatizing Risk without Privatizing the Welfare State: The Hidden Politics of Social Policy Retrenchment in the United States' 98(2) *American Political Science Review* 243–60 doi.org/10.1017/S0003055404001121.
Hacker, JS and Pierson, P (2010) *Winner-Take-All Politics: How Washington Made the Rich Richer – and Turned Its Back on the Middle Class* (New York, Simon and Schuster).
—— (2014) 'After the "Master Theory": Downs, Schattschneider, and the Rebirth of Policy-Focused Analysis' 12(3) *Perspectives on Politics* 643–62 doi.org/10.1017/S1537592714001637.
Hadfield, GK (2016) *Rules for a Flat World: Why Humans Invented Law and How to Reinvent It for a Complex Global Economy* (New York, Oxford University Press).
Harper, SJ (2013) *The Lawyer Bubble: A Profession in Crisis* (New York, Basic Books).
Heineman, BW Jr (2012) 'The Rise of the General Counsel' *Harvard Business Review* 27 September.
Heinz, JP and Laumann, EO (1982) *Chicago Lawyers: The Social Structure of the Bar* (New York, Russell Sage Foundation and Chicago, American Bar Foundation).
Heinz, JP, Nelson, RL, Sandefur, RL and Laumann, EO (2005) *Urban Lawyers: The New Social Structure of the Bar* (Chicago: University of Chicago Press).
Heinz, JP, Southworth, A and Paik, A (2003) 'Lawyers for Conservative Causes: Clients, Ideology, and Social Distance' 37(1) *Law & Society Review* 5–50.
Houseman, AW (2005) 'Civil Legal Aid in the United States: An Overview of the Program in 2003' (Center for Law and Social Policy) www.clasp.org/sites/default/files/public/resources-and-publications/publication-1/0153.pdf.
—— (2013) 'Civil Legal Aid in the United States: An Update for 2013' (Center for Law and Social Policy) www.clasp.org/sites/default/files/public/resources-and-publications/publication-1/CIVIL-LEGAL-AID-IN-THE-UNITED-STATES-3.pdf.
Hurwitz, DR (2003) 'Lawyering for Justice and the Inevitablity of International Human Rights Clinics' 28 *Yale Journal of International Law* 505–50.
Johnson, C (2016) 'The Global 100: The World's Top-Ranked Law Firms by Revenue, Lawyers and Partner Profits' *LegalWeek*, 25 September www.legalweek.com/sites/legalweek/2016/09/26/the-global-100-the-worlds-top-ranked-firms-by-revenue-lawyers-and-partner-profits/.
Kamerman, SB and Kahn, AJ (2014) *Privatization and the Welfare State* (Princeton, Princeton University Press).

Kay, FM and Gorman, EH (2016) 'Which Kinds of Law Firms Have the Most Minority Lawyers? Organizational Context and the Representation of African-Americans, Latinos, and Asians' in S Headworth, RL Nelson, R Dinovitzer and DB Wilkins (eds), *Diversity in Practice: Race, Gender, and Class in Legal and Professional Careers* (New York, Cambridge University Press) 263–300.

Keister, LA (2014) 'The One Percent' 40(1) *Annual Review of Sociology* 347–67 doi.org/10.1146/annurev-soc-070513-075314.

Kettl, DF (1994) *Sharing Power: Public Governance and Private Markets* (Washington, DC, Brookings Institution Press).

Krishnan, JK (2007) 'Outsourcing and the Globalizing Legal Profession' 48 *William and Mary Law Review* 2189–2246.

—— (2010) 'Globetrotting Law Firms' 23 *Georgetown Journal of Legal Ethics* 57–102.

Kronman, A (1993) *The Lost Lawyer: Failing Ideals of the Legal Profession* (Cambridge, Mass, Belknap Press).

Lanctot, CJ (2011) 'Does Legalzoom Have First Amendment Rights: Some Thoughts about Freedom of Speech and the Unauthorized Practice of Law' 20 *Temple Political & Civil Rights Law Review* 255–96.

Lazarus-Black, M and Globokar, J (2015) 'Foreign Attorneys in US LLM Programs: Who's In, Who's Out, and Who They Are' 22(1) *Indiana Journal of Global Legal Studies* 3–65.

Legal Services Corporation (2007) 'Documenting the Justice Gap in America' (2nd edn) www.lsc.gov/sites/default/files/LSC/images/justicegap.pdf.

—— (2016) '2015 Annual Report' www.lsc.gov/media-center/publications/2015-annual-report.

—— (2017) 'The Justice Gap: Measuring the Unmet Civil Legal Needs of Low-Income Americans' www.lsc.gov/media-center/publications/2017-justice-gap-report.

Lempert, RO, Chambers, DL and Adams, TK (2000) 'Michigan's Minority Graduates in Practice: The River Runs Through Law School' 25(2) *Law & Social Inquiry* 395–505 doi.org/10.1111/j.1747-4469.2000.tb00967.x.

Linowitz, SM and Mayer, M (1994) *The Betrayed Profession: Lawyering at the End of the Twentieth Century* (New York: Charles Scribner's Sons).

Liu, S (2013) 'The Legal Profession as a Social Process: A Theory on Lawyers and Globalization' 38(3) *Law & Social Inquiry* 670–93 doi.org/10.1111/lsi.12007.

Llewellyn, KN (1948) 'Current Crisis in Legal Education, The Education for Professional Responsibility' 1 *Journal of Legal Education* 211–20.

LoPucki, LM (2015) 'Dawn of the Discipline-Based Law Faculty' 65 *Journal of Legal Education* 506–42.

McBurney, M (2003) 'The Impact of Legal Services Program Reconfiguration' (Minnesota Bar Assosciation) www.mnbar.org/committees/lad/impact-reconfiguration.pdf.

McCall, L and Percheski, C (2010) 'Income Inequality: New Trends and Research Directions' 36(1) *Annual Review of Sociology* 329–47 doi.org/10.1146/annurev.soc.012809.102541.

Michelson, E (2015) 'Immigrant Lawyers and the Changing Face of the US Legal Profession' 22 *Indiana Journal of Global Legal Studies* 105–20.

Moxley, L (2015) 'Zooming Past the Monopoly: A Consumer Rights Approach to Reforming the Lawyer's Monopoly and Improving Access to Justice 9 *Harvard Law & Policy Review* 553–84.

National Association for Law Placement (2005) 'Still Relatively Few Openly GLBT or Disabled Lawyers Reported' NALP Bulletin www.nalp.org/2005decfewopenlyglbtdisabled.

—— (2015a) 'Class of 2014 Bimodal Salary Curve' www.nalp.org/class_of_2014_salary_curve.

—— (2015b) 'Salary Trends for New Law Graduates – 1985–2013' www.nalp.org/0115research.

—— (2015c) 'LGBT Representation Among Lawyers in 2015' NALP Bulletin www.nalp.org/1215research.

NeJaime, D (2012) 'Cause Lawyers inside the State' 81 *Fordham Law Review* 649.

Nelson, RL and Nielsen, LB (2000) 'Cops, Counsel, and Entrepreneurs: Constructing the Role of Inside Counsel in Large Corporations' 34(2) *Law & Society Review* 457–94 doi.org/10.2307/3115090.

Nielsen, LB and Albiston, CR (2006) 'The Organization of Public Interest Practice: 1975–2004' 84 *North Carolina Law Review* 1591.

Nolette, P (2015) *Federalism on Trial: State Attorneys General and National Policymaking in Contemporary America* (Lawrence, University Press of Kansas).

Office of Justice Programs (2011) 'OJP Fact Sheet: Indigent Defense' (US Department of Justice) ojp.gov/newsroom/factsheets/ojpfs_indigentdefense.html.

Papa, M and Wilkins, DB (2011) 'Globalization, Lawyers and India: Toward a Theoretical Synthesis of Globalization Studies and the Sociology of the Legal Profession' 18(3) *International Journal of the Legal Profession* 175–209 doi.org/10.1080/09695958.2011.679797.

Parikh, S (2006) 'How the Spider Catches the Fly: Referral Networks in the Plaintiffs' Personal Injury Bar' 51 *New York Law School Law Review* 243.

Pfaff, J (2017) *Locked In: The True Causes of Mass Incarceration – and How to Achieve Real Reform* (New York, Basic Books).

Piketty, T (2014) *Capital in the Twenty First Century* (trans by A Goldhammer) (Cambridge, Mass, Belknap Press).

Redding, RE (2003) '"Where Did You Go to Law School?" Gatekeeping for the Professoriate and Its Implications for Legal Education' 53(4) *Journal of Legal Education* 594–614.

Regan, MC Jr and Heenan, PT (2010) 'Supply Chains and Porous Boundaries: The Disaggregation of Legal Services Symposium: The Economic Downturn and the Legal Profession: The Transformation of Large Law Firm Organization and Structure' 78 *Fordham Law Review* 2137–92.

Rhode, DL (2008) 'Public Interest Law: The Movement at Midlife' 60(6) *Stanford Law Review* 2027–84.

—— (2016) 'What We Know and Need to Know about the Delivery of Legal Services by Nonlawyers White Papers' 67 *South Carolina Law Review* 429–42.

Rhode, DL and Cummings, SL (2017) 'Access to Justice: Looking Back, Thinking Ahead' 30(3) *Georgetown Journal of Legal Ethics* 485–500.

Ribstein, LE (2010) 'The Death of Big Law' *Wisconsin Law Review* 749–816.

Robers, B (2010) 'The Firm Is Flat: Ethical Implications of Legal Offshoring Current Developments 2009–2010' 23 *Georgetown Journal of Legal Ethics* 799–812.

Rostain, T (2008) 'General Counsel in the Age of Compliance: Preliminary Findings and New Research Questions' 21 *Georgetown Journal of Legal Ethics* 465–90.

Sandefur, RL (2007) 'Lawyers' Pro Bono Service and American-Style Civil Legal Assistance' 41(1) *Law & Society Review* 79–112 doi.org/10.1111/j.1540-5893.2007.00292.x.

—— (2009) 'Lawyers' Pro Bono Service and Market-Reliant Legal Aid' in R Granfield and L Mather (eds), *Private Lawyers and the Public Interest: The Evolving Role of Pro Bono in the Legal Profession* (New York, Oxford University Press).

—— (2014) 'Bridging the Gap: Rethinking Outreach for Greater Access to Justice' 37 *University of Arkansas at Little Rock Law Review* 721.

Sandefur, RL and Clarke, TM (2016) 'Designing the Competition: A Future of Roles beyond Lawyers: The Case of the USA Symposium: Advancing Equal Access to Justice: Barriers, Dilemmas, and Prospects' 67 *Hastings Law Journal* 1467–92.

Sandefur, RL and Smyth, AC (2011) 'Access Across America: First Report of the Civil Justice Infrastructure Mapping Project'. American Bar Foundation www.americanbarfoundation.org/uploads/cms/documents/access_across_america_first_report_of_the_civil_justice_infrastructure_mapping_project.pdf.

Scheingold, S and Sarat, A (2004) *Something To Believe In: Politics, Professionalism and Cause Lawyering* (Stanford, Stanford University Press).

Schwarcz, SL (2008) 'To Make or to Buy: In-House Lawyering and Value Creation' 33 *Journal of Corporation Law* 497.

Sechooler, A (2008) 'Globalization, Inequality, and the Legal Services Industry' 15(3) *International Journal of the Legal Profession* 231–48 doi.org/10.1080/09695950902785861.

Seron, C (1996) *The Business of Practicing Law: The Work Lives of Solo and Small-Firm Attorneys* (Philadelphia, Temple University Press).

Sexton, JE (1996) 'The Global Law School Program at New York University Symposium on Globalization' 46 *Journal of Legal Education* 329–35.

Shapiro, SP (2002) *Tangled Loyalties: Conflict of Interest in Legal Practice* (Ann Arbor, University of Michigan Press).

Silver, C (2002) 'The Case of the Foreign Lawyer: Internationalizing the US Legal Profession' 25 *Fordham International Law Journal* 1039–84.

—— (2005) 'Winners and Losers in the Globalization of Legal Services: Situating the Market for Foreign Lawyers' 45 *Virginia Journal of International Law* 897–934.

—— (2007) 'Local Matters: Internationalizing Strategies for US Law Firms' 14(1) *Indiana Journal of Global Legal Studies* 67–93.

—— (2013) 'Getting Real about Globalization and Legal Education: Potential and Perspectives for the US' 24 *Stanford Law & Policy Review* 457–502.

—— (2016) 'What We Know and Need to Know about Global Lawyer Regulation White Papers'. 67 *South Carolina Law Review* 461–84.

Silver, C and Daly, MC (2006) 'Flattening the World of Legal Services? The Ethical and Liability Minefields of Offshoring Legal and Law-Related Services' 38 *Georgetown Journal of International Law* 401 works.bepress.com/carole_silver/1/.

Silver, C, De Bruin Phelan, N, and Rabinowitz, M (2009) 'Between Diffusion and Distinctiveness in Globalization: U.S. Law Firms Go Glocal' 22 *Georgetown Journal of Legal Ethics* 1431–72.

Simmons, OS and Dinnage, JD (2011) 'Innkeepers: A Unifying Theory of the In-House Counsel Role' 41 *Seton Hall Law Review* 77–152.

Sobowale, J (2016) 'How Artificial Intelligence Is Transforming the Legal Profession' *ABA Journal* 1 April www.abajournal.com/magazine/article/how_artificial_intelligence_is_transforming_the_legal_profession/.

Solomon, RL (1992) 'Five Crises or One: The Concept of Legal Professionalism, 1925–1960' in RL Nelson, DM Trubek and RL Solomon (eds), *Lawyers' Ideals/Lawyers' Practices: Transformations in the American Legal Profession* (Ithaca, Cornell University Press) 144–73.

Southworth, A (2008) *Lawyers of the Right: Professionalizing the Conservative Coalition* (Chicago, University of Chicago Press) www.press.uchicago.edu/ucp/books/book/chicago/L/bo5928619.html.

Sterling, JS and Reichman, N (2016) 'Overlooked and Undervalued: Women in Private Law Practice' 12(1) *Annual Review of Law and Social Science* 373 doi.org/10.1146/annurev-lawsocsci-120814-121705.

Stevens, RB (1983) *Law School: Legal Education in America from the 1850s to the 1980s* (Chapel Hill, University of North Carolina Press).

Stiglitz, JE (2013) *The Price of Inequality: How Today's Divided Society Endangers Our Future* (New York, WW Norton & Co).

Susskind, R (2013) *Tomorrow's Lawyers: An Introduction to Your Future* (Oxford, Oxford University Press).

Tamanaha, BZ (2012) *Failing Law Schools* (Chicago, University of Chicago Press).

Taylor, AN and Christensen, C (2017) 'Law School Scholarship Policies: Engines of Inquity (LSSSE Annual Results 2016)' (Bloomington, Indiana University).

Taylor-Thompson, K (1996) 'Individual Actor v. Institutional Player: Alternating Visions of the Public Defender' 84 *Georgetown Law Journal* 2419–72.

Teles, SM (2008) *The Rise of the Conservative Legal Movement: The Battle for Control of the Law* (Princeton, Princeton University Press).

—— (2009) 'Transformative Bureaucracy: Reagan's Lawyers and the Dynamics of Political Investment' 23(1) *Studies in American Political Development* 61–83 doi.org/10.1017/S0898588X09000030.

Terry, LS (2007) 'The Legal World Is Flat: Globalization and Its Effect on Lawyers Practicing in Non-Global Law Firms' 28 *Northwestern Journal of International Law & Business* 527.

—— (2014) 'Globalization and the ABA Commission on Ethics 20/20: Reflections on Missed Opportunities and the Road Not Taken' 43 *Hofstra Law Review* 95–138.

The National Law Journal (2016) 'NLJ 500: A Robust Portrait of Big Law', 27 June www.nationallawjournal.com/id=1202759306590/NLJ-500-A-Robust-Portrait-of-Big-Law?slreturn=20170728164351.

Timmons, H (2010) 'Outsourcing to India Draws Western Lawyers' *The New York Times*, 4 August www.nytimes.com/2010/08/05/business/global/05legal.html.

Toobin, J (2017) 'The Conservative Pipeline to the Supreme Court' *The New Yorker*, 10 April www.newyorker.com/magazine/2017/04/17/the-conservative-pipeline-to-the-supreme-court.

Trubek, DM, Dezalay, Y, Buchanan, R and Davis, JR (1993) 'Global Restructuring and the Law: Studies of the Internationalization of Legal Fields and the Creation of Arenas Symposium: The Future of the Legal Profession' 44 *Case Westerm Reserve Law Review* 407–98.

US Census Bureau (2015) 'Population Estimates, July 1, 2015' www.census.gov/quickfacts/.

Van Hoy, J (1997) *Franchise Law Firms and the Transformation of Personal Legal Services*. (Westport, Conn, Praeger).

Wilkins, DB (2010) 'Team of Rivals – Toward a New Model of the Corporate Attorney-Client Relationship' 78 *Fordham Law Review* 2067–2136.

Wilkins, DB and Esteban, MJ (2016) 'The Rise, Fall, and Re-Emergence of the Big 4 in Law' blogs.thomsonreuters.com/answerson/wp-content/uploads/sites/3/2014/04/infographic-re-emergence-big-4-accounting-firms-law.pdf.

Williams, JC, Platt, A and Lee, J (2015) 'Disruptive Innovation: New Models of Legal Practice' 67 *Hastings Law Journal* 1–84.

Yoon, A (2014) 'Competition and the Evolution of Large Law Firms' 63 *DePaul Law Review* 697–718.

Part II

Western European Civil Law

7

Belgium

A Law Degree Opens the Door to a Lot of Occupations, Even the Bar

STEVEN GIBENS, BERNARD HUBEAU, STEFAN RUTTEN,
JEAN VAN HOUTTE AND MARGOT VAN LEUVENHAEGE

I. OVERVIEW

A. Law Degree Programmes

LBs AND LLMs can be earned in the law faculties of private or public universities. Although the LLB offers some opportunities in the labour market, it is primarily intended to prepare for an LLM, which alone affords access to the classic professions: attorney, magistrate, notary, bailiff and corporate lawyer. More than 10 universities offer law degrees (though Mons awards only an LLB). Because they are comparable in educational quality and offer similar opportunities for specialisation, further studies and exchange projects, there is very little competition in curricula and none in tuition, which is fixed by the government (VLIR 2006). Belgium does not distinguish between elite and other universities, although each institution has distinctive characteristics, eg internationalisation, student orientation, or metropolitan character.

University colleges (*hogescholen* in Dutch) offer a professional bachelor's degree in legal practice. But though this does not provide access to the classic professions, legal practitioners may perform important preparatory legal and administrative work, including drafting official documents, providing information to applicants, and taking notes during court sessions. Legal practitioners find jobs in the private sector (30 per cent, primarily with banks and insurance companies, as well as in real estate and industry), government (18 per cent, primarily as clerks), and as employees of attorneys, notaries and bailiffs (20 per cent); 4 per cent are self-employed, and the rest work in diverse fields (Van Delm 2012).

B. Growth in the Number of Law School Graduates

The number of law school graduates has been increasing ever since the emergence of Belgium, if not always in a linear pattern (see Figure 1). Following a small decrease at the end of the nineteenth century (to 130), the number increased steadily until shortly before World War II (267) and then more rapidly from the end of the war until the mid-1960s (615), when there was a major decrease. There was another rapid increase until 2002 (1,896), followed by a sudden decrease until 2013 (1,808).

Figure 1 Number of Law School Graduates

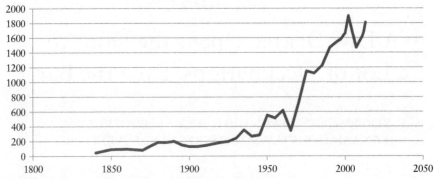

Source: Belgian University Foundation and the University of Antwerp.

Among the social and human sciences, law programmes offer some of the best employment opportunities: only 4.7 per cent of newly graduated law students were still unemployed one year after graduation (VDAB 2016). Several broader societal movements have also played important roles in the rising number of law students and graduates.

Flemish emancipation generated a continuing increase in the proportion of Dutch-speakers among law students and graduates. In 1965, the majority of law school graduates were French-speaking; now the majority are Flemish. Growth in the number of Dutch-speaking lawyers reached a high point between 1960 and 1975, after which the number remained relatively stable, even declining in some years (eg 2010) (see Figure 2).

Figure 2 Proportions of French- and Dutch-speaking Law School Graduates

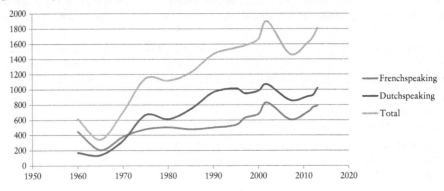

Source: Belgian University Foundation and the University of Antwerp.

Another factor was feminisation. While women constituted barely 3 per cent of law students before 1940, they reached 57.5 per cent between 2000 and 2009. After the 1960s, the number of women law school graduates has increased faster than the number of men. Since the early 1990s women have been 50 per cent to more than 60 per cent of law graduates each year (see Figure 3).

Figure 3 Male-Female Ratio of Law School Graduates

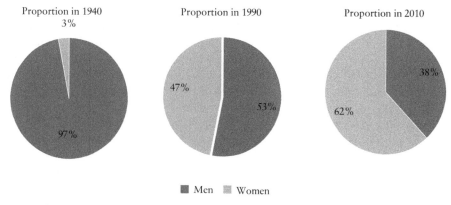

Source: Hardyns et al 2014.

Internationalisation and globalisation promote student mobility but do not increase the number of graduates, since most students return home to complete their degrees after studying abroad for several months to a year. Roughly equal numbers of students enter and leave Belgium.

C. Law School Graduates and the Democratisation of the Educational System

Although students today have many more educational opportunities than their predecessors, sociological research shows that higher education has been massified rather than democratised. Since 1965, government policy has heavily emphasised greater participation in education, but the proportions of the various social strata remained unchanged (Groenez 2008; 2010). Some institutions attract disproportionate numbers of native-born students from the upper classes. The educational level and employment of parents are related to the likelihood their children will enter higher education. In 2003–04, nearly 90 per cent of students with at least one highly educated parent began higher education, compared to 40 per cent of those whose mothers had little education and 48 per cent of those whose fathers had little education. Fathers' position in the labour market also plays a role in their children's decisions to pursue advanced studies. Only a third of the sons and two-fifths of the daughters of unemployed fathers continued to higher education, compared with three-fifths of the sons and three-quarters of the daughters of employed fathers (Vranken et al 2013; Van Haarlem 2011). The increase in the number of students is a consequence not of the democratisation of education but of the increase in wealthy families. Democratisation has actually declined in law and medicine, whose graduates come from more privileged backgrounds than those of other faculties.

D. The Diversification of Lawyers

Not all law school graduates practise a legal profession. But though law degrees provide access to positions outside law, they are primarily oriented towards the traditional legal professions: attorneys, notaries, bailiffs and magistrates. Non-traditional professions include government officials, corporate lawyers, and professions that may have no legal component (Van Houtte and Gibens 2002). Despite the rise of non-traditional professions, the continuing attraction of the Bar is shown by the fact that in 2013 there were just 639 residents for each attorney, the lowest number ever (Van Houtte and Gibens 2002; Van Houtte and Gibens 2003; Hardyns et al 2014). The size of the other traditional professions – magistrates, notaries and bailiffs – is fixed by the government (a type of *numerus clausus*). Because these professions require greater maturity, their members tend to be older (except for public prosecutors) (Van Houtte and Gibens 2002). If the traditional professions (particularly the Bar) may have reached a saturation point, the non-traditional legal professions have become more attractive, increasing their proportion of law graduates from a low of 31 per cent among members of the Flemish lawyers' association in the 1960s to 55 per cent in the 1990s (Van Houtte and Gibens 2002).

Nineteenth-century society was directed largely by lawyers. In addition to playing a dominant role in government and public administration, they were also well represented in trade and industry (Aubert 1971). This was less a response to the need for legal knowledge than a reflection of the value society placed on higher education, where law graduates predominated (Van Houtte 1973–74). In the twentieth century, however, there was a growing need for technical legal knowledge as a result of the increasing juridification and legalisation of social relationships (Huyse and Sabbe 1997).

E. Legal Aid

Established in 1998, the Commission for Legal Aid was the federal government's initial answer to the fragmented and unstructured offering of front-line legal aid. There were many providers of such aid but no central body to help coordinate their services or to enhance the level of collaboration between the various providers. At the same time, the Bar Association was given an opportunity to strengthen its position in the provision of front-line aid. The policy of the Commission is influenced by topics that concern the Bar because half of the members are attorneys appointed by the local Bar presidents (the other half are appointed by welfare organisations or public services). Whereas the Commission used to be subsidised by the federal government (Department of Justice), since 2015 it (like the welfare organisations) has been financed by the regional Flemish or Walloon governments. The primary task of the commission is to organise the front-line legal aid provided by attorneys in private practice.

Front-line legal aid under the 1998 Legal Aid Act is restricted to information and advice. Further support, eg with letter-writing or negotiating a contract with the opposing party, is available only to clients of limited means covered by the second-line legal aid. This contrasts with the services offered by the welfare organisations devoted to specific legal areas such as housing and debt, which open files, try to resolve users' legal problems by writing letters or through mediation, and provide a broad range of specialised legal services.

The annual number of consultations in Flanders varied between 30,000 and 35,000 (except in 2009–10), rising from 2006 to 2010 and then declining, perhaps because consulting hours were cut or fewer people sought front-line assistance. In the period 2006–13, family law and property law (particularly rent and ownership cases) were the most common areas in which users sought advice (60 per cent); criminal law, consumer law and consumer debts, and immigration law each accounted for 6 per cent.

The majority of consultations end with the provision of information or advice. If clients are referred, the referral is usually to an attorney (acting pro bono for clients of limited means). Referrals to other specialised organisations, such as tenants' associations, consumer groups or trade unions, are unusual. The fact that clients are rarely referred to non-lawyers is probably due to lawyers' unfamiliarity with the welfare organisations and available social legal aid services. It also suggests that attorneys trust their peers more.

While front-line legal aid is open to every citizen, second-line legal assistance depends on a means and merits test. Those who are not eligible must pay for an attorney, unless they have legal expenses insurance. Requests for free legal assistance are handled by Bureaux for Legal Aid. There is one in every legal district, operated by the local Bar association and free to determine its own policy. Since the 1980s, the federal government has been subsidising the costs of the second-line legal aid.

There are three ways to apply for legal aid: in person; through an attorney; or by referral from a front-line organisation. In special areas, such as criminal law cases, the bureau may grant legal aid at the request of the investigating magistrate or the criminal court. Since the *Salduz* decision of the European Court of Human Rights[1] and the promulgation of the Salduz Act 2011 (No 2011009606, effective 1 January 2012 but replaced by the Salduz bis Act 2016 (No 2016009565)), the presence of an attorney during police interrogations has become common practice. A special duty attorney scheme has been set up to represent suspects before the investigating magistrate. The Flemish Bar Association has provided software to schedule the presence of a lawyer during the initial police interrogation. The system requires police to telephone a number that will assign and summon a lawyer.

The budget for second-line legal aid steadily increased over the last decade (except for one year), reaching €77,923,000. About 44 per cent of attorneys in private practice in Flanders handled at least one legal aid case. The number of cases handled by private lawyers in Flanders increased from 99,008 in 2003–04 to 220,238 in 2012–13.

II. THE DIVERSE LEGAL PROFESSIONS

A. The Bar

i. The Organisation of the Bar: Institutional Independence

Although the Justice Department continues to operate as a federal institution, the Bar was officially regionalised in 2001 into the Flemish Bar Association (in Dutch, *Orde van Vlaamse Balies* or OVB) and the Association of the French-speaking and German-speaking Bars (in French, *Ordre des barreaux francophones et germanophones* or OBFG)

---

[1] *Salduz v Turkey*, ECtHR 27 November 2008, ECLI:CE:ECHR:2008:1127JUD003639102.

(Article 488 of the Judicial Code). The regional Bar associations have assumed the duties of the National Bar Association established in 1967 to promote uniformity of rules and customs, which had differed from Bar to Bar. The regional Bars monitor the rights and common professional interests of attorneys (Article 495 of the Judicial Code) and take initiatives relating to education, discipline and ethical rules, loyalty within the profession and protection of the interests of attorneys and citizens. They also organise internships and conduct professional training for interns and continuing education of attorneys. Because their regulations are not binding until approved by the King, regulatory authority remains with the executive.

Local Bar associations (subordinate to the two Regional Associations) are primarily involved in monitoring enrolments on the Roll of Attorneys as well as deletions (disbarments, resignations, deaths).[2] They also supervise internships, are responsible for the ex officio appointment of a private attorney as defence counsel if a suspect or defendant does not have one, and organise legal aid. Local Bar presidents receive complaints and initiate disciplinary investigations. In 2006 the legislature transferred discipline from the Boards of the local Bar associations to six Disciplinary Boards (composed of attorneys) and a Disciplinary Board of Appeals (a professional magistrate and four attorneys) (Stevens 2006: 584).

ii. Access to the Profession

Anyone wishing to become an attorney must hold a master's degree in law and work as an 'attorney-intern' for three years under a supervisor. During the first year, interns must follow the professional training programme and pass its examinations. During their three-year internship attorney-interns participate in pro bono legal aid.[3] Every attorney on the Roll or list of interns must pay an annual Bar fee (Article 443 of the Judicial Code), which supports the local and regional Bar associations, including the platform that facilitates electronic litigation. It also contains the premium for the collective insurance policies: insurance for professional and non-contractual liability for damages to third parties and clients and an insolvency policy protecting third parties or clients from whom the attorney has embezzled and cannot repay (Rutten et al 2017). Finally, the fee includes the social security contributions paid by the Bar for its members and sometimes hospitalisation insurance (Stevens 2015: 838). Attorneys must complete 20 hours of continuing education each year. Although not a legal condition for remaining on the Roll, failure to fulfil this duty can subject the attorney to disciplinary sanctions (the most severe being suspension).

Although all attorneys (intern or licensed) must be self-employed, many actually are employed under conditions resembling those of clerks. Requiring attorneys to adhere to a strict hourly schedule with limited holiday leave, receive instructions concerning their work, or submit reports raises questions about their independence, especially in light of the Court of Cassation's 'qualification rulings', which give primacy to the actual context of the employment relationship (see eg Court of Cassation 4 January 2010, 23 May 2011

---

[2] Court of Cassation 26 June 2014, D.13.0012.N and Constitutional Court no 117/2008, 31 July 2008.
[3] See www.attorney.be.

and 10 October 2013). In legal terms, however, attorneys are professionals who should act with complete independence (Articles 429 and 444 of the Judicial Code) (Matthys 2003; 2004).

The number of attorneys increased 2,200 per cent between 1850 (813) and 2014 (18,099) (Hardyns et al 2014). The number of Dutch-speaking interns increased 37 per cent between 2012 and 2016. One possible explanation is that many large law firms are headquartered in Brussels. Flemish-speakers rank fourth globally in English-language skills; and Flemish law graduates are likely to specialise in commercial law (whereas French and German speakers are more likely to focus on family and criminal law).

iii. Codification of Attorney Ethics

The Flemish Bar Association (in 2015) and the Association of the French-speaking and German-speaking Bars (in 2013) formulated new codes of conduct to harmonise the ethics of attorneys by bringing together all previous regulations and codifying matters that had been regulated only by local bars, if at all. This eliminated the power of local bars to issue rules on matters regulated by one of the regional Bar associations. In contrast to the Code of Conduct established by the UK Solicitors Regulation Authority, neither of these codes is outcome-based. Both establish a few general principles, which are then elaborated, sometimes into highly detailed regulations. These are posed primarily in terms of rights and obligations, rarely specifying the desired results. Both begin with an overview of the attorney's essential duties: independence and partiality, avoidance of conflicts of interest, expert professional practice, rectitude, dignity, discretion and professional secrecy (Article 1 of the Flemish code and Articles 1.1 and 1.2 of the French-speaking code). Some principles are not elaborated further, such as the duty of expert professional practice (Lamon and Hofströssler 2014). Violations of the code are subject to disciplinary sanctions ranging from warning or reprimand to suspension and disbarment. In principle, disciplinary action occurs only in response to a complaint, although attorneys have a duty to submit annual reports of client accounts, subject to random checks.

The codes continue to be modified to address recent phenomena. In 2016, regulations were promulgated to organise secondment: arrangements whereby attorneys are temporarily reassigned to a client's legal department (acting not as an employee of the client but as an attorney). The Bars are expected to regulate limited non-lawyer ownership of attorney partnerships. As these examples show, the regional Bar associations are more reactive than proactive, perhaps because of their relatively cumbersome decision-making process and the highly diverse concerns of the local associations represented within them (Van Moorleghem 2017). Although both codes continue to focus on the individual attorney, they acknowledge that attorneys can practise in partnership and impose rules for partnerships. The duties always address the individual attorney, sometimes specifying those belonging to law firms. Law firms are not enrolled in the Roll of Attorneys and not subject to disciplinary sanctions.

Neither code is client-centred. They are primarily oriented towards establishing the rights and obligations of individual attorneys. The OBFG code says nothing about the attorney-client relationship. The OVB code section entitled 'Relationships with regard to clients' addresses money-laundering, exoneration clauses and publicity, none of which could be considered client-centred. The only substantive provision describing the attorney-client relationship is Article 4 of the OVB Code, which declares that attorneys are always obligated to represent the interests of their clients to the best of their ability and place those interests above their own or those of third parties, taking into account the rules prescribed by law and by professional codes and codes of conduct. But there is no consensus in Belgian law concerning the extent to which attorneys must seek to establish the truth in a legal proceeding or what they can do in devising a litigation strategy (Stevens 2015: 1150). Although attorneys may go to the limits of the law in defending their clients' interests, clients may not require attorneys to test those limits. In their oath, attorneys promise 'not to defend any case that they in good conscience do not believe to be just' (Article 429 of the Judicial Code). This suggests that an attorney may not be required to represent a client (as the UK barristers' 'cab rank' rule required) (Van den Heuvel and Du Mongh 2004). However, the Judicial Code does guarantee the right to legal representation by allowing the Bar president to assign attorneys to represent parties whom no attorney is willing to represent (Article 446 of the Judicial Code). Despite the attorney's duty of loyalty, assigned attorneys may declare that they do not endorse the strategies and positions of their clients.

iv. Legislative Amendments

Under the influence of European consumer protection guidelines and competition law, the Belgian legislature is increasingly treating attorneys like any other enterprise, as shown by the Code of Economic Law (implemented in 2013–14 and revised in 2018). This is probably the most important change in the past 30 years. Very recently, attorneys were subjected to commercial insolvency law and allowed to seek protection from their creditors through a reorganisation procedure or be declared bankrupt (Book XX of the Code of Economic Law). Although the Court of Justice left open the possibility of restricting cooperation between attorneys and other independent professionals,[4] a general prohibition on multidisciplinary partnerships would conflict with European competition law. For this reason, the Court of Cassation also vacated an OVB regulation containing a quasi-prohibition on multidisciplinary partnerships.[5] In response to market demand, attorneys increasingly draft written agreements with clients specifying fees. Until very recently, attorneys' services were not subject to VAT. Despite the Bar's strong resistance, the legislature decided to eliminate this exception. For consumers, this translated into a 21 per cent increase in the cost of attorneys, since most raised their fees by that amount. The Constitutional Court upheld the tax over the Bar's objections.[6]

Another important trend has been the emergence of alternative dispute resolution. Since 1972, the Judicial Code has contained regulations concerning arbitration, which are updated regularly in light of the UNCITRAL Model Law on International Commercial Arbitration. Mediation was introduced in the 1990s, primarily in family cases, resulting in the Act of 19 February 2001 concerning court ordered mediation in

---

[4] Case C-309/99 *Wouters et al v Algemene Raad van de Nederlandse Orde van Advocaten* [2002] ECR-I 1653.
[5] Court of Cassation 25 September 2003, C.03.0139.N.
[6] Constitutional Court 23 February 2017, No 27/2017.

family cases. Because of its success, the legislative framework was soon extended to all civil, commercial and labour disputes. The Act of 21 February 2005 added a seventh section to the Judicial Code, dedicated to mediation. The current Minister of Justice has far-reaching plans for integrating mediation into other legal proceedings and anchoring the principles of collaborative law in the Judicial Code. As alternative dispute resolution permeated procedural law, attorneys' tasks also changed (Warson 2016).

The Bar often has successfully resisted legislation restricting professional privilege. The Constitutional Court invalidated laws requiring attorneys to inform the debt mediator, report transactions suspected of money laundering, or disclose sexual abuse or domestic violence.[7] The Court repeatedly emphasised the uniqueness of the legal professional privilege, intended to protect the privacy of individuals who have taken attorneys into their confidence, sometimes concerning highly personal matters. The information entrusted to attorneys may also enjoy the protections derived from the guarantees of Article 6 of the European Convention on Human Rights. The Constitutional Court therefore views attorneys as fundamentally different from other professionals.

v. Feminisation

Women did not have access to the Bar until 1922; in 1969, only 10 per cent of attorneys were women (Huyse and Sabbe 1997). But in 2011, 78 women were sworn in as attorneys in Antwerp compared to 36 men, and 74 were enrolled in Brussels compared to 54 men (Hardyns et al 2014). Women still encounter a glass ceiling in advancing to higher positions (eg becoming a partner) because of the belief that mothers must prioritise children over careers (Wyckaert 2006). If one parent decides to work less in order to care for children, it is usually the mother. Men have traditionally regarded themselves as breadwinners. This creates a self-reinforcing system in which attorney fathers earn more than attorney mothers and invoke that difference to justify the gendered division of household labour (Ietswaart 2003). The culture of the traditional legal professions is deeply masculine. Lawyers feel the need to be available to clients at all times and to work long hours (Bacik and Drew 2006).

vi. Partnership Forms and Specialisation

Based on data concerning University of Leuven graduates, Huyse found that before 1940, 80 per cent of lawyers were solo practitioners. By the late 1980s, however, half of all economically active lawyers were employed in relatively large organisations or, in the case of attorneys, were members of associations and partnerships (Huyse 1988: 242). In 1997, only 25 per cent of attorneys were solo practitioners (Huyse and Sabbe 1997).

Today, Belgian attorneys can choose between three kinds of collective practice. Partners in an association contractually specify how profits and losses will be divided. Members of a grouping share costs but not profits. Members of a network merely recommend work to each other. The Code of Ethics lets attorneys decide whether to establish

---

[7] Constitutional Court 3 May 2000, 46/2000; Constitutional Court 28 July 2006, No 129/2006; 23 January 2008, No 10/2008; Constitutional Court 26 September 2013, No 127/2013; Constitutional Court 5 December 2013, No 163/2013.

a legal entity and, if so, whether to choose full or partial incorporation, a partnership, or a capital company (Stevens 2015: 936–37). In 2007, 40 per cent of Flemish attorneys were affiliated with associations, while solo practitioners had once again increased to 34.8 per cent. In 2012–13, the same proportion of attorneys practised in associations, but solo practitioners had decreased to 30.3 per cent. Attorneys in groupings increased from 17.2 per cent in 2007 to 28.8 per cent in 2012/13 (see Figures 4 and 5). The tendency to work in a grouping or association is even more notable amongst Flemish attorney-interns, not less than 58 per cent of whom are active within an association. Partnerships facilitate cost savings and specialisation while keeping work pressures at an acceptable level. But they also create risks, including conflicts of interest (Parmentier and Ponsaers 2008; see also Van Houtte et al 2007). Similar trends can be found in the French and German speaking regions (Gothot 2013–14), where almost 29 per cent of attorneys are in associations and 24 per cent are in groupings, while only 23.5 per cent are solo practitioners (OBFG and Université de Liège 2013). In addition, 13.9 per cent of law firms are part of an international structure, most of them located in Brussels (Franssen et al 1999; OBFG and Université de Liège 2013).

Figure 4 Solo Practice or Nature of Partnership among Flemish Attorney-Interns

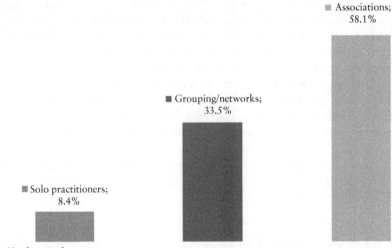

Source: Hardyns et al.

Both the OBFG and the OVB are considering whether and to what extent borrowed capital should be allowed in attorney firms. Many UK firms are active in Belgium, especially in Brussels. The UK Legal Services Act introduced Alternative Business Structures, which permit non-lawyers to partner with lawyers and invest in law firms. But Belgian law currently denies attorneys from other EU countries the right to practise in Belgium as members of an association whose capital is held by non-attorneys (Article 477 octies, §5, of the Judicial Code). Some Belgian attorneys (especially younger ones) feel that the prohibition on non-lawyer capital restricts their economic possibilities by preventing parents from investing in their children's law firms in exchange for a security interest. Both regional Bar associations seem likely to go as far as possible to prohibit or limit non-lawyer shareholding consistent with European competition rules and freedom of establishment.

Figure 5 Solo Practice or Nature of Partnership amongst Flemish Attorneys

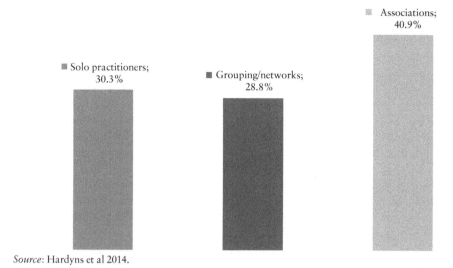

Source: Hardyns et al 2014.

Flemish attorneys are most likely to practise civil, commercial and family law. Attorney-interns in both regions are more likely to practise immigration law (to fulfil their obligation to take a minimum number of *pro bono* cases) (Hardyns et al 2014; Gothot 2013–14; OBFG and Université de Liège 2013). Men are more likely to work in administrative, commercial, tax and corporate law, while women are more likely to practise social and family law. The extent of specialisation varies directly with firm size (Ponsaers and Parmentier 2008).

vii. Is Lawyering in Belgium a Profession?

The Belgian Bar calls itself a profession on several grounds (Mok 1973: 104; Huyse 1980). First, lawyering is part of the system of justice. Ethical duties are imposed on the Bar by law. Second, the two regional Bar associations are authorised to formulate rules of professional practice and operate disciplinary systems. There are also regulations concerning admission and disbarment, although there is no *numerus clausus*. But several factors threaten professionalism: growing competition among the increasing number of attorneys; internationalisation, which complicates control and leads to diversification; specialisation and the emergence of niches, which contribute to fragmentation within the Bar; an increase in the number and size of law firms containing partners, employees and interns, eroding the independence of attorneys and creating subordination; and the fact that law firms are increasingly assuming the form of an ordinary enterprise (eg through branding and advertising).

B. Notarial Practice

To become a notarial candidate one must obtain an LLM and then a Master's degree in notarial practice and complete a three-year internship in a notarial firm. Notarial interns then take an examination set by the Appointments Committee for the Notarial Profession, which generates the ranking from which the King will issue notarial candidate appointments to fill the *numerus clausus*.[8] Notarial candidates can become notaries by associating with an incumbent notary or applying to be appointed as an incumbent notary in a vacant position. They also can act as a deputy notary with a temporary title.[9] Given the limited opportunities to establish themselves as notaries, many candidates become associate notaries, and many notary firms employ a substantial number of legal assistants (Huyse and Sabbe 1997). This ensures that graduates in notarial practice have a good chance of finding notarial jobs quickly, making the profession more attractive, even for those who do not immediately aspire to positions as notaries.

Belgium currently has approximately 1,500 notaries – just 200 more than 20 years ago. As in the Bar, there is an increasing trend towards partnership: in 2015, 323 of the 1,172 notary firms were associations (28 per cent), whereas two decades ago only 2 per cent of notaries were part of an association. Notary firms have merged, leading to greater concentration. Since 2014, notaries could also form a corporation (Act of 25 April 2014). Women have entered the notarial profession, if not as rapidly as the Bar (see Figure 6). The first woman notary was appointed in 1955 (Huyse and Sabbe 1997). In the period 2006–16 women increased from 18 to 31 per cent of notaries. The total number of notaries and associate notaries has increased (from 1,227 in 2001 to 1,519 in 2014) in parallel with the number of female notaries (from 57 in 2002 to 355 in 2014), suggesting that the option to associate has made the profession more attractive to women. At the same time, we see a small decrease of male notaries from 1,105 in 2002 to 1,076 in 2014.

Figure 6 Change in the Number, Gender Composition, and Practice Structure of Notaries

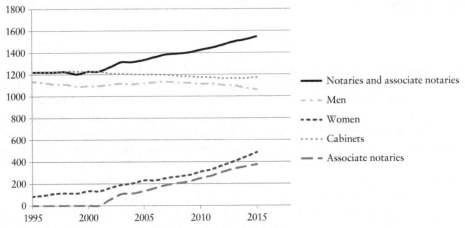

Source: Royal Federation of Belgian Notaries and University of Antwerp.

---

[8] See www.bcn-not.be/nl/opdrachten/examen.
[9] See www.notaris.be.

C. The Magistracy

After acquiring a law degree those aspiring to become magistrates may follow three routes.[10] The first is through the judicial internship. Candidates selected after an open competition complete a unique two-year judicial internship, qualifying them to become public prosecutors or judges. Until their appointment as magistrates, judicial interns serve as judicial attachés in a court or public prosecutor's office. The number of judicial interns is determined by decree each year. More experienced lawyers can enter the magistracy directly by passing a professional competence examination, whose graduates can apply for a position as a judge if they have sufficient experience (10 years for attorneys, 12 for other lawyers practising in the private sector) or a public prosecutor (five years of experience). Finally, anyone who has worked 20 years as an attorney (or 15 years as an attorney and five in another profession requiring substantial legal knowledge) may enter the magistracy by passing an oral examination. All selections are made by the Council for the Judiciary.

The number of magistrates increased from 1,155 in 1988 to a high of 1,614 in 2015; the number of prosecutors increased from 674 in 1988 to a high of 860 in 2016 – both much more slowly than the number of attorneys. Changes in the number of positions offered are usually related to exceptional circumstances (eg war or a new Judicial Code). Spontaneous waves of recruitment are less common (Huyse and Sabbe 1997).

Figure 7 Male-Female Ratio among Magistrates

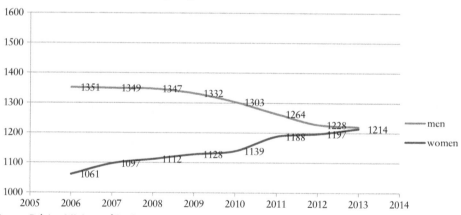

Source: Belgian Ministry of Justice.

Between 2006 and 2016 the number of male magistrates decreased 12 per cent and the number of female increased 12 per cent, with the result that women gained parity with men in 2013 (see Figure 7). Women are the majority in labour courts (60 per cent), courts of first instance (57 per cent) and parole boards (53 per cent), whereas 86 per cent of the judges in the Belgian Supreme Court are men. Only three of the 35 judges who ever served

---

[10] See justitie.belgium.be.

on the Constitutional Court have been women, and only one of the 12 now serving is a woman. Some have argued that women magistrates are more responsive to context and oriented towards reconciliation and thus give less weight to legal precedents (Ponet and Lamon 2013).

Lay judges play a variety of roles in the Belgian legal system. A 12-person jury in the Court of Assizes decides questions of guilt in cases involving serious crimes and then, with the judge, passes sentence (by majority vote). Each of the five Belgian parole boards consists of one professional judge and two lay judges, one specialised in re-integration and the other in incarceration. These boards determine whether convicts are entitled to a transfer to an open prison, conditional release or electronic surveillance. On the labour courts and labour courts of appeal the professional judge is assisted by one lay judge representing the employees and another representing employers. Finally, lay judges assist the professional judges in the court of commerce, performing important tasks such as that of delegated judge in bankruptcy proceedings.

D. Bailiffs

Bailiffs are public and ministerial officials, whose number is subjected to a quota (536 in 2017). A candidate must hold an LLM, complete a two-year internship with one or more bailiff firms, and pass an examination before the appointments committee, which generates a ranking of candidate bailiffs. After working as a bailiff candidate for five years, an individual may be appointed as a bailiff. Bailiff candidates who have not yet been appointed may act only as deputies to incumbent bailiffs.[11] There is a trend towards partnership: the 326 firms are organised as associations or groupings.

In recent years, the number of interns has quintupled even though the number of incumbent bailiffs has remained relatively constant, while the number of candidate bailiffs has decreased, partly because recent legislation tightened access to the status of candidate. Only 15 per cent of bailiffs are women, a figure that has increased little (although it will do so soon, since 61 per cent of candidate bailiffs are women). The profession has aged, from an average of 49 years old in 1995 to 55 in 2009. In 2015, only 0.5 per cent of bailiffs were in their thirties, while 40 per cent were in their fifties, 33.5 per cent in their sixties, and 10 per cent in their seventies.

E. The Corporate Lawyer

The number of corporate lawyers increased rapidly between 1960 and 1975 (Van Houtte et al 1995). In 1997, the corporate legal sector was the second largest employer of law graduates from the University of Leuven (after the Bar) (Huyse and Sabbe 1997). In the last decade the number of corporate lawyers almost doubled from 1,006 in 2004 to 1,923 in 2016 (see Figure 8). To be accepted by the Institute of Corporate Lawyers (IBJ in Dutch)[12]

---

[11] See www.gerechtsdeurwaarders.be.
[12] See www.ibj.be.

the individual must: possess a Master's degree in law; have an employment contract with an enterprise, joint venture or other legal entity in which the lawyer bears primary legal responsibility; and perform functions such as conducting studies and making recommendations, preparing documents, and offering legal advice. Membership of the Institute is not compulsory.

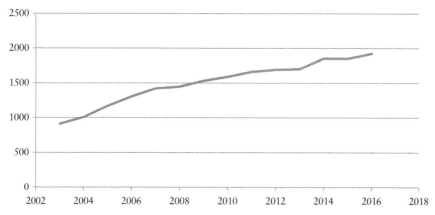

Figure 8 Number of Corporate Lawyers

Source: Institute of Company Lawyers.

The number of corporate lawyers increased rapidly after the creation of the IBJ in 2000 (Van Houtte and Gibens 2002). Men slightly outnumber women, and Dutch-speakers significantly outnumber French- and German-speaking lawyers.

III. CONCLUSION

The numbers of attorneys and corporate lawyers are increasing substantially, as are the proportions of women and of lawyers working in collectivities. The Bar displays increasing specialisation, internationalisation and globalisation, the impact of European regulations, and the growth of entrepreneurship. These trends are less marked among notaries and bailiffs, partly because of the *numerus clausus* and because these professions are more likely to be passed from father to son (Huyse and Sabbe 1997). The trend towards Flemish emancipation appears to be largely complete: the proportions of linguistic groups in the legal professions now correspond much more closely to those in the larger population.

REFERENCES

Aubert, JV (1971) 'De jurist en zijn beroepsrollen' in B Peper and K Schuyt (eds), *Proeven van rechtssociologie* (Rotterdam, Universitaire Pers Rotterdam).

Bacik, I and Drew, E (2006) 'Struggling with juggling: gender and work/life balance in the legal professions' 29 *Women's Studies International Forum* 136.

Franssen, G, Van Wambeke, W and Van Loon, F (1999) 'Internationalisering van de juridische dienstverlening in Brussel. Een kwantitatief beeld van de internationale advocatenkantoren' in F Van Loon and K Van Aeken (eds), *60 Maal recht en 1 maal wijn. Liber Amicorum Prof. Dr. Jean Van Houtte* (Leuven, Acco) 595.

Gothot, S (2013–2014) 'Présentation du baromètre des avocats belges francophones et germanophones (Ordre des Barreaux Francophones et Germanophones)' 42-43-44-45-46 *La Tribune* avocats.be/fr/tribune.

Groenez, S (2008) *Onderwijsexpansie en – democratisering in Vlaanderen* (Kuleuven, Dag van de sociologie).

—— (2010) 'Onderwijsexpansie en – democratisering' 31(3–4) *Tijdschrift voor sociologie* 199.

Hardyns, W, Gudders, D, Parmentier, S, Pauwels, I and Verhage, A (2014) *De advocatenbarometer 2012/2013. Een beschrijvende analyse van het profiel van de Vlaamse advocaat* (Den Haag, Boom Juridische Uitgevers).

Huyse, L and Sabbe, H (1997) *De mensen van het recht* (Leuven, Van Halewijck).

Huyse, L (1980) 'Preadvies. Sociologie van de advocatuur. Proeven van trendrapport' *Nieuwsbrief voor Nederlandstalige rechtssociologen* 12.

—— (1988) 'Legal experts in Belgium' in RL Abel and PSC Lewis (eds), *Lawyers in Society: Vol II The Civil Law World* (Berkeley, University of California Press) 225.

Ietswaart, H (2003) 'Choices in context: life histories of women lawyers in the Netherlands' in U Schultz and G Shaw (eds), *Women in the World's Legal Professions* (Oxford, Hart Publishing) 353.

Lamon, H and Hofströssler, P (2014) 'Brussel, we hebben een (deontologisch) probleem' 300 *De Juristenkrant* 16.

Matthys, D (2003) 'De advocaat: zelfstandige of schijnzelfstandige?' 3 *Ad Rem* 17.

—— (2004) 'Schijnzelfstandigheid en advocatuur' 4 *Ad Rem* 30.

Mok, AL (1973) *Beroepen in actie: bijdrage tot een beroepensociologie* (Meppel, Boom).

Ordre des Barreaux Francophones et Germanophones de Belgique (OBFG) and Université de Liège (2013) *Baromètre des avocats Belges francophones et germanophones: étude 2013*.

Parmentier, S and Ponsaers, P (eds) (2008) *De Vlaamse advocaat. Wie, wat, hoe* (Den Haag, Boom Juridische Uitgevers).

Ponet, B and Lamon, H (2013) 'Vrouwen in toga (steeds meer vrouwelijke advocaten en magistraten)' 261 *Juristenkrant* 13.

Rutten, S, Hubeau, B and Van Houtte, J (2017) 'Legal malpractice in Belgium: redress from a client perspective' *IJLP* 145.

Stevens, J (2006–07) 'Het tuchtprocesrecht voor advocaten vernieuwd: De wet van 21 juni 2006' *RW* 582.

—— (2015) *Advocatuur. Regels & deontologie* (Mechelen, Kluwer).

Van Delm, J (2012) 'Wie zijn de Belgische rechtspractici' 257 *Juristenkrant* 6.

Van Den Heuvel, J and Du Mongh, J (2004) 'De waarheidsplicht van de advocaat – Bedenkingen bij artikel 444, lid 1, Ger.W' in JP De Bandt (ed), *Liber Amicorum Jean-Pierre de Bandt* (Brussels, Bruylant) 233.

Van Haarlem, A (2011) 'Armoede en sociale uitsluiting ontcijferd' in D Dierckx et al (eds), *Armoede in België. Jaarboek 2011* (Leuven, Acco).

Van Houtte, J (1973–74) 'De plaats van de jurist in de komende samenleving' *RW* 2351.

Van Houtte, J and Gibens, S (2002) 'Waar komen afgestudeerden in de rechten terecht?' 66(1) *Rechtskundig Weekblad* 1.

—— (2003) 'Traditional and non-traditional occupations of law graduates: which jobs do law graduates enter?' 10 *International Journal of the Legal Profession* 55.

Van Houtte, J, Duysters, J and Thielman, V (1995) *Gebruik van het recht in de zakenwereld: over juristen in grote industriële ondernemingen* (Leuven, Acco).

Van Houtte, J, Dvorak, C and Vermeiren, M (2007) *Belangenconflicten in (middel)grote advocatenkantoren in België* (Mechelen, Kluwer).

Van Moorleghem, S (2017) 'Dringend nood aan hervorming Orde van Vlaamse Balies' 344 *Juristenkrant* 11.

VDAB (2016) *Werkzoekende schoolverlaters in Vlaanderen* (online) www.vdab.be/sites/web/files/doc/schoolverlaters/Schoolverlatersrapport2016.pdf.

VLIR (2016) *De onderwijsvisitatie Rechten – Notariaat* (online) www.vlir.be/media/docs/Visitatierapporten/2005/kv05z3-rechtennotariaat.pdf.

Vranken, J, Van Hoortegem, G, Henderickx, E and Vanmarcke, I (2013) *Het speelveld, de spelregels en de spelers* (Leuven, Acco).

Warson, M (2015–16) 'De advocaat als performante viertrapsraket in vijf dimensies' *RW* 1574.

Wyckaert, M (2016) 'De vrouwelijke braindrain in de advocatuur' 1 *Ad Rem* 6–8.

8

Denmark, Sweden and Norway
Liberalisation, Differentiation and the Emergence of a Legal Services Market

OLE HAMMERSLEV

THE SCANDINAVIAN LEGAL professions have been called the 'midwives' of the state. In the nineteenth century, legal professions dominated all parts of Danish, Norwegian and Swedish political and commercial life. Members of the legal profession were not only well represented in Scandinavian parliaments but also had important positions in both the state administration and commerce, and devised crucial legal innovations that laid the foundations for markets and modern state bureaucracies. They belonged to the 'upper social strata', as Jon J Johnsen (1988) noted in the Norwegian chapter in *Lawyers in Society*. Legal education not only implied general training in running a society and becoming a jack-of-all-trades but also established and manifested social networks in the upper classes, with which the legal profession could construct society (Aubert 1976: 2).

The Danish welfare state, as well as those in the other Nordic countries, expanded after World War II, driven by a link between the trade union movement and the Social Democratic Party. It became a universal welfare state, founded on principles of solidarity, equality and individual autonomy, which attempts to give all citizens clearly defined rights and distribute specific, equal and sufficient benefits. The state advises citizens about their welfare rights and ensures they receive them. It relies on a tax-financed public sector as the main protector of citizens' rights and promotor of universal benefits and services in areas such as education and care for the sick, disabled, children and the elderly (Francis et al 2010; Esping-Andersen 1990). It became the state's responsibility to remedy its own failures by helping citizens resolve their problems with the public administration through complaints commissions, appeal committees, consumer councils, ombudsmen, and housing complaints commissions. Moreover, legislation concerning disputes between private individuals has developed clear rules that cannot be supplanted by agreement between the parties. The regulation and dispute commissions and committees address complaints against the public administration and disagreements about private housing, health care, education, social security, family matters, and landlord-tenant conflicts (Bryde Andersen 2005: 55). The number of jurists working in public administration expanded to deal with these issues.

However, since the 1980s the Danish welfare state – like its Scandinavian counterparts – has been challenged by economic crises and neoliberal reforms, whose focus on austerity, financial control, efficiency, and market solutions with new private actors, public-private collaborations and contracting out traditional welfare services – all legitimised as ensuring resources for welfare (Bonoli and Natali 2012) – ended the 'golden welfare years' (Petersen et al 2006; Erikson 1987). This reconfiguration of the welfare state, globalisation, layers of increasing legal complexity and juridification (partly attributable to the harmonisation of the EU's internal market) together with deregulation transformed the legal market and the organisation and practices of law firms, expressing the new spirit of capitalism (Boltanski and Chiapello 2007). Since the 1980s, many Danish governments have liberalised the lawyers' market, constantly asking if regulatory changes could increase competition and lower prices for the benefit of consumers, including businesses (thereby enhancing their competitiveness). Mergers have concentrated capital (especially in the financial sector), and new forms of public-private ownership have developed. The legal profession differentiated internally: several large firms (inspired by global Anglo-American firms' organisational structures and practices) comprise a legal elite counselling the corporate sector and large organisations, while a majority of generalist small law offices and solo practitioners serve individuals and small businesses.

This chapter examines the changes and continuities in the legal profession in Denmark, a country with a population of just over 5.7 million, and then compares developments in Norway and Sweden. It begins with the demographic changes before turning to the impact of liberalisation and globalisation on the lawyers' market. Then it discusses legal education and gender and the trajectory of legal aid in relation to developments in the welfare states.

The chapter is based on different sources. First on official statistics and reports from the Scandinavian Bar associations. Second on a qualitative document analysis (Prior 2003) of 464 issues of the Danish Bar and Law Society (DBLS) magazine *Advokaten (The Lawyer)* from 1983 to 2018. Each magazine was manually examined to identify the discussions, content, and contextual changes and continuities concerning the lawyers. The aim was to develop empirical knowledge about the structures and rationale that have dominated and defined the trajectory of field of lawyers over the last 35 years. Third, to strengthen the validity of the document analysis and thus make a stronger argument for the interpretation of the trajectory of the legal field (Bowen 2009), 18 semi-structured interviews were conducted with lawyers and central actors in Denmark, Norway and Sweden, selected to represent different positions in the lawyers' field (Bourdieu 1996). The interviews were transcribed and have been anonymised. All quotations below come from the interviews.

I. CHANGES IN THE DEMOGRAPHY AND STRUCTURE OF THE LEGAL PROFESSION

The origins of the Danish legal profession lie in the absolute monarchs' establishment of a state in 1660. Harmonisation of the law and university education for legal professionals who could judge, advise and administer legal affairs paved the way for the emergence of civil servants who could legitimate and strengthen the power of the king and the state (Tamm 2005; Hammerslev 2008). Though closely related to the civil law systems of continental Europe, with whose professions they have similar and interconnected trajectories, the Scandinavian jurisdictions (together with Iceland and Finland) are often categorised as a distinct 'Nordic legal family' (Zweigert and Kötz 1998).

In Denmark today, anyone with a master's degree in law is called a 'jurist' and considered a member of the legal profession. The title opens the doors to many careers and, with further training, grants access to monopolised positions as lawyers (or advocates), judges (magistrates and high court and supreme court judges) and public prosecutors. Each sector is entitled to join the union The Danish Association of Lawyers and Economists, although most of its members are public jurists.

A. The 'Replacement' of Jurists

The legal profession was central to the development of the modern state in Denmark (and the rest of Scandinavia). But from the 1960s, while it continued to attract a large number of students pursuing a variety of careers both in private practice and as civil servants, it slowly lost its exclusivity. The Danish government invested in education to enhance the knowledge base of the large post-war generation and the increasing number of women entering higher education and the job market. This was part of the democratisation project, which used education to strengthen democracy and promote economic growth. Social science professionals with non-legal expertise multiplied, displacing jurists (whose numbers also increased) in many positions in politics, the state and commerce. With the rise of the welfare state, welfare law became more elaborated and complex, creating space for non-lawyer professionals, such as psychologists and social workers, to participate in decision-making (Aubert 1976; Sand 1996; Bertilsson 1995). The 'power base of law' shifted from central to local civil servants and from clearly written rules to discretionary decisions based on general legal frameworks and face-to-face interaction with citizens, thereby replacing traditional legal methods with other forms of expertise and methods (Luhmann 1985). Nevertheless, law remained one of the largest professions (Aubert 1976; Hammerslev 2003; 2013).

The decline of the dominance of the legal profession can be seen in changes in the enrolments in social science disciplines in Denmark during the twentieth century (see Table 1). Whereas law was the most popular degree until the 1980s, when welfare state reforms were introduced and the lawyers' markets began its transformation, other social science degrees started to challenge it, and business economics eventually became the largest discipline.

Table 1 Enrolment of University Students in Social Science Disciplines in Denmark, by Percentage and (Number), 1928–97

	1928	1958	1978	1988	1997
General social sciences	(0)	(0)	6 (959)	9 (2,135)	11 (2,923)
Business economics	(0)	0 (8)	7 (1,125)	25 (5,700)	28 (7,725)
Economy	15 (195)	23 (383)	12 (1,889)	14 (3,268)	13 (3,511)
Law	84 (1,116)	74 (1,233)	27 (4,321)	21 (4,960)	20 (5,383)
Political science and sociology	(0)	(0)	18 (2,867)	10 (2,384)	11 (3,013)
Psychology	(0)	(0)	22 (3,568)	15 (3,432)	12 (3,248)
Other social sciences	1 (24)	3 (48)	8 (1,239)	6 (1,344)	6 (1,681)
Total	100 (1,335)	100 (1,672)	100 (15,968)	100 (23,223)	101 (27,484)

Source: Hammerslev 2003.

However, the number of jurists also increased. Not only did enrolments rise at the two old universities of Copenhagen and Aarhus (where law degrees had been introduced in 1736 and 1936, respectively), but law departments were established at two newer universities (University of Southern Denmark in 2004 and Aalborg University in 2007). Moreover, degrees in business administration and law were launched in 1984 and are now found at four universities, and other interdisciplinary degrees involving law have emerged.

With the growth of the public sector, the number of jurists in the state administration increased, but the most dominant and policy-oriented positions were filled by other professions (see Table 2). Moreover, the number of judges almost stagnated and, relative to the entire legal profession, actually declined, showing that the law was developing on new platforms outside the courts.

Table 2 Occupations of Jurists, by Percentage and (Number), 1928–2014

Year	1928	1952	1985	2000	2014
Central Administration	13 (431)	21 (1,289)	28 (2,575)	21 (3,215)	27 (4,221)
Counties and Municipalities	6 (191)	8 (464)	10 (969)	9 (1,309)	9 (1,456)
Lawyers and assistant attorneys-at-law (including in-house lawyers)	39 (1,304)	35 (2,170)	36 (3,400)	27 (4,153)	34 (5,337)
Courts (judges and staff)	16 (523)	9 (527)	6 (527)	4 (625)	4 (648)
Public prosecutors and police	3 (107)	4 (268)	4 (391)	3 (512)	4 (606)
Teaching and research	1 (17)	1 (32)	2 (212)	2 (293)	2 (287)
Private sector and others	23 (790)	23 (1,404)	13 (1,250)	35 (5,277)	20 (3,175)
Total	100 (3,363)	100 (6,154)	100 (9,324)	100 (15,384)	100 (15,730)

Sources: Hammerslev 2003, Dalberg-Larsen and Lehmann Kristiansen 2014.

About one third of those with a law degree work in public administration as civil servants. The ongoing process of juridification, the complexity of welfare entitlements, EU requirements for procurement law, increasing rights consciousness, and the merging of municipalities into larger entities have all increased the employment of jurists.

The growing number of jurists, the specialisation of many, and the development of the welfare state have reduced the cohesiveness of the profession. Social differentiation also has emerged in the Danish judiciary, which is increasingly divided between provincial lower courts and those in Copenhagen (both district and higher courts) (Hammerslev 2003). The higher the court, the more elite the social background of recruits. Furthermore, in the later twentieth century the judicial elite were increasingly recruited from the Ministry of Justice and its institutions, including the prosecutor's office and police, where they received their initial training.

II. THE LAWYERS' PROFESSION

To become a lawyer it is usually necessary to have a Danish master's degree in law, which takes five years, followed by three years as assistant attorney-at-law consisting of practical legal experience and professional training, including mandatory courses and theoretical and practical exams. The path to the judiciary is similar but generally requires three years as a magistrate's clerk or similar position.

In the 1980s the DBLS sought to require supplemental training in order to address the growing quantity and complexity of legislation. A 2008 law mandated supplemental training, thereby further demarcating lawyers' work and qualifications and protecting their market from other consultants, especially accountants. However, many lawyers are unhappy with the requirement because they have difficulty finding time for it, and the supply of specialised courses is limited. The largest law firms operate their own courses, DBLS also provides them, and a market for supplemental training has developed.

With the implementation of the EU directives, those holding a master's degree in law from another Member State can become lawyers in Denmark. The Ministry of Justice requires a trial period of law practice (no more than three years) to ensure the necessary knowledge of Danish procedural law and mastery of the Danish language at a level suitable for conducting oral proceedings. After this the foreign lawyer must work as an assistant attorney-at-law and pass the mandatory exams. However, EU citizens may also practise under their home country professional title. Citizens from non-EU Member States may become lawyers in Denmark only after obtaining a law degree from an EU Member State. In 2014, 30 foreign lawyers had established themselves in the country, just 0.5 per cent of the lawyer population (the average for EU countries) (Economics 2014: 89).[1]

A. Liberalisation of the Market and New Competitive Structures

The state has shaped the legal profession and played a role in the professional project by legislating the framework for competition, legal education and law firm ownership, while the DBLS had engaged in more detailed regulation and promulgated a code of conduct. Since the 1980s, however, the Monopolies and Mergers Commission has attempted to deregulate the field and open it to competition.

In 1990, the Administration of Justice Act was amended to eliminate the prohibition against lawyers having offices in more than one jurisdiction. This paved the way for larger firms with branches in different cities. Law firms were allowed to adopt a corporate form with limited liability; ownership initially was restricted to lawyers (including foreign lawyers registered in Denmark), but now 10 per cent of the shares may be owned by non-lawyers.

One landmark change was the 2006 repeal of the 'Pettifogger Act', which prohibited non-lawyers from advertising legal advice, suggesting they or their firm had been publicly approved or supervised, or using terms such as legal aid, legal consultant, or legal office. At the same time a new law regulated commercial legal counselling (other than by law firms and financial companies), requiring legal counsellors to comply with good practices under the supervision of the Consumer Ombudsman. With this market liberalisation, other advisers – such as estate agents, third sector employees (in membership organisations, organisations with volunteers and non-lawyers), accountants, bank employees, and company agents – could compete with law firms in providing legal services.

---

[1] Sweden, with one per cent, has the highest proportion in the EU.

The 2007 reform of the judicial system merged 82 jurisdictions into 24, served by fewer and larger district courts, motivating law firms and lawyers to move from provinces to cities with district courts. In 2008 the lawyers' monopoly over rights of audience was relaxed, allowing other advisers to appear in court in smaller cases. Liberalisation encouraged the expansion of law firms, differentiating the industry in terms of their organisation and practices.

B. From Law Offices to Law Firms

i. Before the 1980s

Until the early 1980s most lawyers practised alone or in small offices with senior partners and a few employees; few firms had more than ten lawyers. Speaking of the 1970s, a lawyer from one of the top five Copenhagen law firms said the

> characteristic for law firms of the time was that they were not firms, as we know them today, but isolated businesses, even though the larger firms ... had the character of a firm. It has been a part of the identity of the lawyers' industry that the relationship to clients is strongly driven by single persons. And specialisation did not exist, not at all.

Another lawyer from a small-to-middle size firm noted that the law office then

> was, in fact, something of a mixed bag, you know, where you had a little of this and a little of that.... Even in other larger offices with which I was in contact, you would realise that they had different mixed bags where they all sat together and handled the entire palette of legal issues and areas.

Firms bore their partners' names. The top Copenhagen firms were located in the noble *Frederikstaden*, which also houses the Queen (Madsen 2008). Lawyers were generalists, taking any case that came into the office. Lawyers entitled to plead before the Supreme Court or the High Courts had a distinctive title.

ii. External Changes Affecting the Lawyers' Market

In the 1980s the commercial field was fundamentally restructured. Mergers created larger financial institutions and companies, and the economy became more dependent on foreign trade. At the same time the EU harmonised the market, and IT solutions developed in both law firms and the public sector, reducing the cost of transactions such as digital land registration. Larger companies and financial institutions slowly began to develop in-house legal departments to cut costs and increase efficiency. The number of in-house lawyers increased from fewer than 400 in 2000 (8 per cent of the profession) to 1,400 in 2014 (22 per cent) (Economics 2014: 15). The increasing number followed both the creation of branches by large companies and the recognition by smaller companies that lawyers could create added value.

Market pressures forced the leading firms to specialise in order to develop the expertise to advise large companies. A lawyer from one of the top five Copenhagen law firms explained the rationale for law firm mergers, which is also represented in the DBLS magazine *Advokaten*:

> [I]t is the clients' growth that necessitates the growth of advisors. You saw the mergers and larger companies in, e.g. the financial sector and in the industrial companies as the key reason and a specialisation which also began in the 1980s. You could say that the entire EU (EC at the time) area of law has increased the complexity of the legislation in the entire competition law area. Another area that developed in a way that required continuous specialisation was tax law and environmental law, which started in the beginning of the 80s. So specialisation and an appropriate number of personnel were necessary to manage larger cases and larger clients.

Law firm mergers, starting in the 1980s, created a distinct top five. After the first wave of mergers, firms that were not included had to reflect on their size and future in the new legal market. An interviewed lawyer from a top five firm said:

> The fact that the other firms had grown so much made us relatively smaller, and that can be a bad place to end up, neither big nor small, because you don't really have the strength to compare yourself with the big and don't really have the strength to develop many specialties, unless you want to become a niche company. Thus, it is very difficult to keep up in terms of competences. So that was the rationale and it was also the rationale in the mergers we joined, namely that we wanted to establish a firm which could be in a position to develop thorough areas of specialisation because that is the part of the economic life we wanted to serve.

This accords with other interviews and articles in *Advokaten*. The elite firms whose advocates had rights of audience in the Supreme Court developed into business counsellors. The mergers led to increased competition and the reorganisation of law firms with managing partners, foreign offices, international inter-firm collaboration, greater specialisation and increasing differentiation from the large group of solo practitioners.

These developments followed neo-liberal trends and were strongly influenced by the model of Anglo-American law firms. From the early 1980s, the DBLS magazine *Advokaten* covered and endorsed the development in articles by and about management consultants, legal economists, lawyers from the American Bar Association, and Danish lawyers who had worked in the US. These showed how to manage firms strategically, making them more professional and competitive through specialisation and managing partners, and explained how to create a corporate management culture with clear goals, a focus on budgets, and new methods for calculating fees. Other articles advised on how to behave professionally, both personally and in terms of office aesthetics; for instance, one warned against having only women's magazines in the reception area, which could suggest the firm dealt exclusively with women's divorces (*Advokaten* 1986). In a few years the recommendations evolved from good ideas to imperatives for survival. Making a virtue of necessity, the DBLS repeatedly stressed that law firms should specialise because of the increasing number and complexity of laws, merge into larger offices like those in the US, be more efficient, and use IT to reduce the cost of secretaries. The issues can be illustrated with titles of some articles: 'We have to specialise', 'Ten years with EDP [electronic data processing]' (article from the *American Bar Journal* about the experiences of American lawyers), 'Good advice to start-up firms', 'American Law Firms Earn So Much' (list of top 10), 'The law firm is also a business'.

In 1998 more than a third of the nearly 1,800 law firms were solo practitioners, and only one per cent had more than 50 employees (most having 2–19 lawyers). By 2004 the field was increasingly differentiated into two poles, with a few large law firms on one hand and many small law offices and an increasing number of solo practitioners on the other. With the financial crisis in 2007 many of the youngest lawyers in the largest law firms who did not have a chance to become a partner tried to establish their own firms. Over time, however, the number of large law firms continued to grow. Since the 1980s law firms have concentrated in the largest cities. In 2000, two-thirds of firms were based in the two largest cities, and in 2006 more than half of all lawyers worked in Greater Copenhagen.

Table 3 Composition of Law Firms, 1998–2017

Size of firm	1998	2004	2017
Solo practitioners	654	969	
2–19	1,098	540	
20–49	54	17	
50+	18	2	1
100+		3	8

Source: Estimated on the basis of figures in Advokatsamfundet (2000; 2006).

The reconfiguration of the legal field can also be seen in the distribution of revenue, which grew from a total of 7.5 billion DKK (€1 billion) in 2004 to 12 billion DKK (€1.61 billion) in 2012 (Danske advokater 2014), an annualised growth of approximately 6 per cent.

Table 4 Distribution of Revenue among Law Firms, 2000–14

Firms	2000	2010	2014	Number in 2014	Revenue Growth 2000–14
Top 5	18%	24%	26%	5	166%
Next 6–10	6%	10%	12%	5	251%
Other firms with DKK50+m (€6.7m) in revenue	-	13%	11%	13	-
Firms with DKK 10–50m (€1.3–6.7m) in revenue	28%	26%	25%	150	65%
Firms with DKK 1–10m (€0.13–1.3m) in revenue	43%	25%	25%	1,004	6%
Firms with max DKK 1m (€0.13 m) in revenue	4%	2%	3%	688	13%

Source: Danske Advokater (2017: 8).

In 2000, domestic clients (including the largest Danish companies) accounted for 98 per cent of the market for legal services. By contrast, in 2014, foreign clients accounted for 68 per cent of revenues in the 10 largest firms. The financial and business sectors produced 40 per cent of total lawyer revenues in 1997. A 2014 study from Statistics Denmark found that the most important kinds of work for lawyers (in descending order) were advising companies, real estate, advising individuals, and liquidation; together they accounted for 68 per cent of lawyers' revenues. Only 10 per cent of lawyers' work concerned litigation (in which lawyers had a monopoly), which meant that lawyers earned 90 per cent of their revenue delivering the kinds of services that other professional groups could provide (Economics 2014).

Another issue mentioned in both interviews with lawyers and the DBLS journal *Advokaten* is that American contracts are much longer – or 'rich in words' (*Advokaten* 1984: 214). A lawyer said that mergers and acquisitions

> have always been a large part of the lawyers' sector ... but M&A was not as complex previously, as they have been later, even relatively large M&As or deals in real property for that matter, it could be done with relatively short contracts until the Americans told us how contracts should be very long and detailed ... That affected, clearly, the number of employees.

iii. Competition from Foreign Firms and Lawyers

Competition from foreign law firms has increased. However, after several foreign law firms and the big accountancy firms failed to establish offices in Denmark, the main competition was from the so-called 'fly-in-fly-out' counsel. A 2012 survey found that foreign legal services from EU countries mainly came from Sweden, to a lesser degree from Finland, England and Wales, and even less from France, Germany and the Netherlands (Economics 2014: 90). In recent years, however, both global (Anglo-American) law firms and accountancy firms have again tried to establish offices, the former by incorporating Danish firms and the latter by opening legal departments.

C. Lawyers under Cross-Pressures

Lawyers have represented themselves as the foundation of the *Rechtsstaat* and claimed that their independence plays a central role in preserving democracy. However, with deregulation, liberalisation of the legal services market and more intense competition, lawyers are increasingly compared with other consultancy services. Lawyers have responded by differentiating themselves from competing occupations and seeking closure within specific profitable areas.[2] At the same time, they need to market themselves to clients, who increasingly define the services they want from lawyers. As the power relationship between lawyer and client has changed, lawyers have asked if they have 'lost a part of our soul during this process? Has the result on the bottom line become the decisive landmark?' (*Advokaten* 1999). The quotation illustrates the conflicting pressures on lawyers at the end of the 1980s. Lawyers' privileged position and legitimacy was based partly on their alleged independence, which was threatened by increasing competition. This transformation can be illustrated by the reflections of an elderly solo practitioner on law practice in the 1970s:

> Knowledge was of the utmost importance. You really needed to know your law, as it was always called. And if you didn't, then you could not be used. That is, you should not bawl and be smart. It would not happen. Well, maybe it would, but then it was the dregs of lawyers with offices in Istegade [a Copenhagen street notorious for pornography shops, strip clubs, sex workers, and pubs] but not in the decent offices. In these offices you needed to know your law, you had to be able to express yourself, you needed to be on time and prepared, you had to be dressed properly,

---

[2] As a form of market closure (Abel 1988).

and as a woman not wear exceptionally high heels or low-cut tops at work, nor could you be dressed indecently and all those norms, which are poorly known today. You behaved properly against the adversary – you did not approach his client directly. You are not allowed to do that now, but nowadays nobody is really restricted by that norm, at the time you were. The rules of conduct were important. They were a kind of yoke of your practice ... You were not allowed to fish for clients, you needed to live by your knowledge, not by your impudence.

In addition to the conflicting pressures on lawyers, the solidarity that used to characterise the profession has been eroded by the differentiation and individualisation caused by mergers, specialisation and the relaxation of competition rules. Interviewed lawyers contrasted the ignorance large firm lawyers acknowledged about their colleagues with the old firm lunches where everybody knew each other, which engendered solidarity. This change is visible in articles and book reviews in the DBLS journal focusing on personal profiles, personal development, how to handle stress, sales competence and mindfulness. This represents a shift from an emphasis on working procedures and firm organisation towards innovation, optimisation and individual excellence (see eg Bagger and Hjortshøj 2012).

D. Gender Differences

A key impact of the democratisation project was the rising enrolment in higher education of women students, whose numbers exceeded those of men by the late 1980s and reached 63 per cent by 2015. Women increased from 20 per cent of lawyers in 2000 to 24 per cent in 2004 and 32 per cent in 2015 (*Danske Advokater* 2017). Indeed, women now outnumber men among district court judges (Hammerslev 2003). Yet despite the rising number of women lawyers, gender differences remain. Women are overrepresented among those lawyers leaving law firms after 4–5 years, which often is explained by the difficulty of combining the long working hours in a law firm with starting a family. In 2004 more women lawyers than men were employed in entities other than law firms, which offer better work-life balance. And women are a third of lawyers in law firms other than the largest (Advokatsamfundet 2007).

Gender inequality is even more striking in the ownership structures of the large law firms. A 2017 survey shows that after more than three decades of there being more female than male law students, 93 per cent of the owners of capital (ie partners) in the three largest law firms were men. In the rest of the 20 largest law firms that replied to the survey, women were only 5–30 per cent of shareholders and were more than 15 per cent in just three (Hyltoft 2017).

E. *Kammeradvokaten* (Junior Council to the Treasury)

Representation of the state is the monopoly of one law firm, now the largest. This was an arrangement devised during the sovereign state (the term goes back to 1684), when the Junior Counsel to the Treasury was a civil servant. However, in 1936 that government post was replaced by a private lawyer appointed by the King. From 1936 to 2014 the *Kammeradvokaten* was a partner of the law firm now called Advokatfirmaet Poul Schmith. That firm has followed the general trend of specialisation and growth in order to provide highly qualified legal services to the state and public authorities. The firm had 42 lawyers in 1994; but by 2016 it had grown to 212, opened an office in the second largest city (Aarhus), and become the largest in Denmark. The monopoly of the *Kammeradvokaten* has been strongly criticised, and several political parties wanted to liberalise the function. In 1995 this led to a change in the agreement, making *Kammeradvokaten* a legal entity and authorising the state or public authorities to litigate cases themselves or refer them to state legal departments or even other law firms (Waage 2017).

F. The Danish Bar and Law Society

The DBLS was founded in 1886 on models drawn from England, Germany and France, with the goal of ensuring that lawyers enjoyed professional status and independence from the state. It assumed its present form in 1919. All lawyers were automatically members of the DBLS, which was responsible for maintaining their competence and ethical standards. However, the DBLS has had to deal with liberal reforms. The 2006 judgment of the European Court of Human Rights in *Sørensen and Rasmussen v Denmark*[3] found that forcing a person to belong to a specific union in order to be employed in a Danish enterprise violated the European Convention on Human Rights (Article 11 on freedom of association). The government responded by transforming the DBLS into an institution established and regulated through law and including all lawyers. It has supervisory and disciplinary authority and responsibility for education and strives to support the *Rechtsstaat*. But it can no longer advocate for the interests of lawyers.

In 2008 a group of lawyers decided to establish a new organisation, the *Association of Danish Law Firms* (Danske Advokater), to promote their interests. One of the lawyers involved explained the rationale behind the association.

> In a way it has always been an impediment to lawyers that they did not have an advocate for their interests in the same way as our counsellor competitors did. Thus, you could say that it was a lucky circumstance that they [the European Court of Human Rights] wanted to abolish the possibility of operating the bar association as an association. In a way it was a good result that we, finally, could establish a professional association, and that was what we did. That was the rationale behind the establishment of *The Association of Danish Law Firms*, a long overdue institution, which we had not worked for or been in agreement about, but suddenly the circumstances were there more or less of necessity.

The two associations still observe a division of labour. There are other associations for lawyers specialising in the purchase or lease of real estate and family law, which can promote their interests and discuss professional issues.

III. LEGAL EDUCATION

As part of the universal welfare state all students get a grant from the state, free tuition and can borrow on favourable terms. All universities are public. Like other European

---

[3] Application nos 52562/99 and 52620/99, 11 January 2006.

countries, Denmark followed the Bologna model by offering a three-year BA followed by a two-year master's degree. More than 95 per cent of BA graduates complete their master's degree. They can then do a three-year PhD, during which they will be paid a salary comparable to that in public administration. With the Bologna model it became easier to study in other European countries and use the European Credit Transfer System to complete a Danish degree.

Even though a law degree may lead to a job with an international profile, most courses at the bachelor's level are still in Danish and concern Danish law, with a leavening of EU law, human rights, international law and social-legal, historical and jurisprudential approaches depending on the individual university. However, an increasing number of courses at the master's level are taught in English, partly to attract students from other countries.

Legal education is closely related to the field of practice, with many adjunct instructors coming from law firms, the public sector or the courts. Moreover, large law firms have adopted recruitment practices like those of US firms to recruit the best students before they finish their degrees, offering them study jobs, scholarships, and workshops and office space while they are writing their dissertations.

In recent decades the state has increasingly curtailed the independence of universities. First, via the introduction of top-down leadership structures through which deans and department heads, instead of being elected by staff and students, were appointed by the rector who was appointed by the university board with internal and external university members. Second, universities increasingly compete for students and external funding. The Danish Accreditation Institution was established in 2007 as a state institution to evaluate the quality of universities and degrees in terms of staff/student ratio, productivity, and number of classes available to students. This new public management turn has forced universities and departments to shift resources from scientific and educational work to administrative staff capable of providing figures and managerial schemes for evaluations. Third, the universities and their degrees need to have formalised recruitment panels to advise about educational questions.

IV. LEGAL AID

Legal aid has been affected by the reconfiguration of the welfare state and the marketisation of law. Danish lawyers have a long tradition of providing legal advice on a voluntary basis. The first legal aid clinic, *Københavns Retshjælp*, was founded in 1885 and became a model for legal aid offices in the US (Wilson 2018). When Aarhus began offering a law degree in 1936, a legal aid office opened in the city as well. However, Denmark also developed a judicare legal aid scheme, paying private lawyers for their services. During the golden years of the welfare state in the 1960s and 1970s several volunteer legal aid institutions were established. In 1978, progressive lawyers launched 'lawyers on call', providing free basic legal aid to needy citizens. The DBLS publicised the fact that lawyers and assistant attorneys-at-law were 'on call' in public libraries or law firms to supplement the existing legal aid offices. These 'legal emergency rooms' provided 'legal first aid', offering basic advice. The approach was less structured than the legal aid offices and independent of the government. However, the reconfiguration of the welfare state, the consolidation of jurisdictions motivating lawyers and law firms to relocate to the larger cities, and the marketisation of law made it more difficult to recruit lawyers for 'lawyers on call'. Moreover, government budget cuts meant tightened eligibility criteria for extended legal aid. This led to a restructuring of legal aid based increasingly on legal expenses insurance and the third sector, ie membership organisations and volunteer institutions.

Membership organisations (such as unions, health care providers, the DanAge association, sports and hobby groups, and tenant associations) and third sector organisations based on volunteer work (such as legal aid institutions, *The Street Lawyer, Refugees Welcome*) provide legal aid in an increasing number of cases, even though not all organisations employ lawyers. Thus, legal aid moves from lawyers as the exclusive providers to a more heterogeneous field of lawyers, law students, social workers and volunteers (Olesen and Hammerslev 2018).

In the early 2000s, voluntary assistance was slowly transformed and redefined by large law firms as pro bono services and corporate social responsibility programmes modelled on those of US firms. Lawyers in these firms (who rarely served individuals) targeted organisations and institutions that needed their specialist expertise. Individual legal aid remained largely the province of solo practitioners and smaller law firms (Olesen and Hammerslev forthcoming).

V. CONCLUSION AND PERSPECTIVES ON SWEDEN AND NORWAY

Denmark has seen intensified competition between different professions. Jurists, who dominated all sectors of nineteenth-century society, have been displaced from their important positions in the state administration and the market. However, they have found new arenas and expanded their domain. Since the 1980s, law has faced greater liberalisation. The competition authorities forced lawyers to become more competitive and liberalised their markets so that other professional groups could offer legal advice. This laid the foundation for the emergence of large law firms delivering specialised services on the Anglo-American model. Similar tendencies can be seen in Sweden and Norway. But though all the Scandinavian countries are universal welfare states, their different sizes (Sweden has nearly twice as many people as either Denmark or Norway) and economies have produced different developmental paths.

A. Norway

The Norwegian legal profession has been studied in much greater detail than the other Scandinavian professions (Espeli et al 2008; Papendorf 2002; Johnsen 1987; Aubert 1976). Espeli et al (2008) note that when social democracy was replaced by neo-liberalism, lawyers played a central role in creating legal structures for an effective market and helping businesses adjust to it. The legal profession also contributed to increasing rights consciousness and the process of juridification, as well as the changes following the Norwegian agreement with the EU. After Norway began extracting North Sea oil in the 1960s, the new industry became the focus of the new large law firms. The petroleum industry and government investment in education also explain the increasing number of lawyers and assistant attorneys-at-law, which rose slowly from fewer than 2,500 in 1974 to under than 2,800 in 1990 but then jumped to almost 6,700 in 2006 and 7,781 in 2015. Norway also saw internal differentiation between solo practitioners and small firms on one hand and a small number of large firms earning a disproportionate share of the total revenue on the other (Espeli et al 2008: 373 ff; Advokatforeningen 2016: 33). Although the large firms emulated the Anglo-American model, they did not reach the size of their Danish and Swedish counterparts (Espeli et al 2008; Papendorf 2002). In 2002, approximately 10 per cent of lawyers' income came from publicly financed legal aid (4 per cent from criminal cases).

i. Legal Education

Despite close collaboration between the Nordic universities, the structures of legal education are different. Only Oslo, Bergen and Tromsø offer a master's degree in Law, but in 2007 the Universities of Agder and Stavanger, Høyskolen in Lillehammer and Høyskolen in Buskerud and Vestfold began offering LLBs. Those of their graduates who wish to practise must take an LLM, but the universities offering the degree cannot guarantee enrolment for all.

Although the increase in the number of law students facilitated a more diverse social recruitment, the parents of law and medical students at University of Oslo were more educated than those of other students. At the end of 1990s, 10 per cent of law students had one parent educated in law, and these students received better grades and earned higher incomes after graduating. Espeli et al (2008) argue that higher grades offer an even greater advantage today than they did a century earlier. In 1999, 18 per cent of lawyers had a father who graduated in law – the same proportion as in 1932 and 1950 (see also Olaussen 2015).

ii. Legal Aid

As in Denmark, more legal aid has been supplanted by legal expenses insurance and the third sector (Rønning 2018). However, Norway has more student-run legal aid clinics affiliated to universities. The oldest and most renowned is *Juss-Buss* (Law Bus). The clinic was established at the Faculty of Law, University of Oslo in 1971, inspired by US innovations, and was part of the Norwegian radical student movement of the 1970s. Juss-Buss provides legal aid from an office and does outreach to groups that otherwise would have difficulty securing access to justice, such as prison inmates or Romani people. The staff consists of about 30 law students who voluntarily spend a year working full time on legal aid and then work part time for one semester, for which they receive credit. The students are paid a small salary comparable to the student loan. Juss-Buss also does policy work for groups that would otherwise lack a voice in public debates (Hammerslev et al 2018).

B. Sweden

Because Sweden accords the title 'lawyer' only to jurists employed in law firms (whereas in Denmark and Norway the term includes jurists in the in-house legal departments of companies), statistics about who is a lawyer are not comparable across Scandinavian countries. Nevertheless, Sweden may have the most liberalised legal market, in the sense that anyone can offer legal advice or represent parties in civil cases.

In some ways the Swedish legal profession has experienced a more profound transformation than those in other Scandinavian countries, again inspired by the organisation, practice and understanding of Anglo-American law firms (Modéer 2012). That Sweden was conscious of the magnitude of this transformation may be seen in an observation by the editor-in-chief of *Svenska Dagbladet*: 'Our society is not a very good market for free lawyering. We are a consensus society. We are not an adversary society as you say in the USA' (Zetterberg 1987: 492). Another impetus for the transformation was membership in the EU and implementation of the Maastricht Treaty in 1992, which not only increased the mobility of lawyers across member nations in Europe but also affected Swedish legal culture (Modéer 2012).

The Swedish private sector has larger companies and more international companies than those of the two other Scandinavian countries. Moreover, Swedish companies own more subsidiaries and employ about 66 per cent more people abroad than Danish companies. Foreign investment also is higher in Sweden, which has more international arbitration cases; and more Finnish law firms have been established in Sweden because of the close relationship between the Swedish and Finnish corporate sectors. These features affected the Swedish lawyers' market in different ways.

As in Denmark and Norway, law firm mergers began in the 1980s, differentiating lawyers into two hemispheres (Heinz and Laumann 1994). However, the second wave of mergers during the 1990s was stronger in Sweden, creating the largest law firms in Scandinavia – with approximately 400 lawyers – twice the size of Danish and Norwegian firms. They serve the increasingly international market, which demands fast, specialised legal services. In addition, the large firms, some of which already had offices in several Swedish cities, saw the mergers as a way of systematising their internal processes (Modéer 2012: 20). Global law firms based in the US, UK and Germany entered the Swedish market faster and more aggressively than they did in Denmark and Norway. Some established offices, other merged with or acquired Swedish offices. Finnish law firms also established offices in Stockholm. During the 1990s smaller law offices developed collaborative relationships to reduce administrative costs and share expertise.

The similarities among the countries are illustrated by the following statement from a Swedish lawyer:

> Earlier, in 1976 when I began practising in a law office, we were only three lawyers who did everything from family law to criminal law to civil litigation, acquisitions, estate administration and trusteeship. You have to look carefully to find such offices today. They do not exist in Stockholm and Goteborg, but you might find them in the countryside. But even there it only develops in one direction.

With the new millennium, a debate began about the large accountancy firms' entry to the legal market. As in the other Nordic countries, the big five accountancy firms sought to offer legal services. However, the Swedish Bar Association managed to prevent them from using the title 'law firm'. Even though some accountancy firms created quite large legal departments, they then drastically contracted, ending up by employing only a few legal experts. In recent years some accountancy firms have tried to re-establish legal departments.

i. Legal Aid

From the heyday of the welfare state through the mid-1990s Sweden had 'probably the most generous and comprehensive [legal aid] scheme internationally' (Kilian and Regan 2004), although this comparison included legal expenses insurances (part of household insurance), which other Nordic legal aid researchers excluded (Schoultz 2018). In contrast to Denmark and Norway, Sweden established 26 state-financed legal aid bureaux staffed by more than a hundred public-sector lawyers in the 1970s as a part of the universal welfare programme designed to redress economic inequalities. However, in an attempt to cut costs in the wake of the worst recession since the 1930s and as a response to arguments that public offices should not compete with the private market, which was said to allocate legal services adequately, the bureaux were closed in 1997 and replaced by a judicare system with stringent eligibility requirements, making it secondary to legal expenses insurance. The Swedish Bar Association responded by organising free legal advice in 1998, offered by volunteer lawyers in local libraries and civic centres in 38 cities in Sweden (30 sites in the Stockholm area) (Schoultz 2018). As in Denmark, large Swedish law firms performed pro bono work as a part of their corporate social responsibility programmes. Swedish firms began to do more strategic work after the 2004 tsunami catastrophe in South East Asia, in which more than 500 Swedish citizens died or went missing. That pro bono project, organised by the Swedish Bar Association, became the largest ever in Sweden, involving 275 law firms of all sizes. Lawyers contributed 24,400 pro bono hours to cases involving foundation law, corporate law, family law, estate law and insurance law (Olesen and Hammerslev forthcoming).

C. Scandinavian Lawyers

In all the Scandinavian countries the changes in the legal profession have to be seen in light of the gradual transition from social democratic to neoliberal governance and regulation. Whereas the legal profession played a central role in building modern states and markets, it was displaced after World War II when the social democratic universal welfare state developed, complicating legislation and increasing discretion, thereby allowing other professions to participate in decision making.

Yet, the reconfiguration of welfare states and an increasing emphasis on market solutions transformed the lawyers' market. The complexity of the law and the growth of new (international) markets increased demand for legal services. To enhance competition, the lawyers' market was liberalised, allowing other consultants to compete in corporate counselling. The legal profession responded with mergers creating modern firms inspired by Anglo-American models to counsel the corporate sector and large institutions based on a new spirit of capitalism.

REFERENCES

Abel, RL (1988) *The Legal Profession in England and Wales* (Oxford, Basil Blackwell).
Advokatforeningen (2016) *Rapport fra BRANSJEUNDERSØKELSEN 2016* (Oslo, Advokatforeningen).

Advokatsamfundet (2007) *Advokatrådets beretning 2005–2007.*
Aubert, V (1976) 'The Changing Role of Law and Lawyers in Nineteenth- and Twentieth-Century Norwegian Society' in DN MacCormick (ed), *Lawyers in Their Social Setting* (Edinburgh, Green).
Bagger, E and Hjortshøj, C (2012) *Excellens i advokatbranchen: Personlige virkemidler til succes* (København, Jurist- og Økonomforbundets Forlag).
Bertilsson, M (ed) (1995) *Rätten i Förvandling. Jurister mellan stat och marknad* (Stockholm, Nerenius & Santerus Förlag).
Boltanski, L and Chiapello, E (2007) *The New Spirit of Capitalism* (New York, Verso).
Bonoli, G and Natali, D (eds) (2012) *The Politics of the New Welfare State* (Oxford, Oxford University Press).
Bourdieu, P (1996) 'Understanding' 13(2) *Theory, Culture & Society* 17–37.
Bryde Andersen, M (2005) *Advokatretten* (København, Advokaternes Serviceselskab).
Dalberg-Larsen, J and Lehmann Kristiansen, B (2014) *Lovene og livet: En retssociologisk grundbog* (København, Jurist- og Økonomforbundets Forlag).
Danske Advokater (2017) *Kvartalsstatistik nr. 1 2017* (Danske Advokater).
Economics, C (2014) *Konkurrence og regulering i advokatbranchen* (København, Advokatsamfundet & Danske Advokater).
Erikson, R (1987) *The Scandinavian Model: Welfare States and Welfare Research* (New York, ME Sharpe).
Espeli, H, Næss, HE and Rinde, H (2008) *Våpendrager og veiviser: advokatenes historie i Norge* (Oslo, Universitetsforlaget).
Esping-Andersen, G (1990) *The Three Worlds of Welfare Capitalism* (Cambridge, Polity Press).
Francis, GC, Stephan, L, Jane, L, Herbert, O, Christopher, P, Wil, AA and John, G (2010) *Models of the Welfare State* (Oxford, Oxford University Press).
Hammerslev, O (2003) *Danish Judges in the 20th Century: A Socio-Legal Study* (Copenhagen, DJØF Publishing).
—— (2008) 'The Development of the Danish Legal Profession' in P Wahlgren (ed), *Scandinavian Studies in Law*, vol 53: Law and Society (Stockholm: Stockholm Institute for Scandinavian Law).
—— (2013) 'Studies of the Legal Profession' in Banakar, R and Travers, M (eds) *Law and Social Theory* (Oxford, Hart Publishing).
Hammerslev, O, Olesen, A and Rønning, OH (2018) 'JussBuss' in O Hammerslev and OH Rønning (eds), *Outsourcing Legal Aid in the Nordic Welfare States* (London, Palgrave).
Heinz, JP and Laumann, EO (1994) *Chicago Lawyers: The Social Structure of the Bar* (New York, Russell Sage Foundation and Chicago, American Bar Foundation).
Hyltoft, V (2017) 'Mænd sidder på magten i landets 20 største advokatfirmaer' 4 *Berlingske Business* December p 8.
Johnsen, JT (1987) *Retten til juridisk bistand* (Oslo, Tano).
—— (1988) 'The Professionalization of Legal Counseling in Norway' in in RL Abel and PSC Lewis (eds), *Lawyers in Society: Vol II The Civil Law World* (Berkeley, University of California Press).
Kilian, M and Regan, F (2004) 'Legal expenses insurance and legal aid – two sides of the same coin? The experience from Germany and Sweden' 11 *International Journal of the Legal Profession* 233.
Luhmann, N (1985) 'The Self-Reproduction of Law and its Limits' in G Teubner (ed), *Dilemmas of Law in the Welfare State* (Berlin, Walter de Gruyter).
Madsen, MR (2008) 'Return to the Copenhagen "Magic Circle": First Elements of a Longitudinal Study of Large Law Firms in Denmark' 53 *Scandinavian Studies in Law* 303.
Modéer, KÅ (2012) 'Den kämpande och gränslösa advokaten: Från modernitetens till senmodernitetens svenska advokatroll 1987–2012' in A Ramberg, T Knutson and M Andersson (eds), *Sveriges advokatsamfund 125 år – 1887–2012* (Stockholm: Sveriges advokatsamfund).

Olaussen, LP (2015) 'Juristprofesjonen – en lagdelt sosial elitegruppe' 41 *Kritisk Juss* 134.

Olesen, A and Hammerslev, O (2018) 'Nye udbydere af retshjælp i Danmark' in R Banakar, K Dahlstrand and L Ryberg-Welander (eds), *Festskrift til Håkan Hydén* (Lund, Juristförlaget).

—— (forthcoming) 'Legal Pro Bono Work in Denmark' in SL Cummings, F de Silva, and L Trubek (eds), *Global Pro Bono: Causes, Consequences, and Contestation* (Cambridge, Cambridge University Press).

Papendorf, KE (2002) *Advokatens århundre? Globaliseringen og dens følger for advokatmarkedet* (Oslo, Unipub Forlag Rapportserie, UiO).

Petersen, K, Edling, N, Haave, P and Christiansen, NF (2006) *The Nordic Model of Welfare: A Historical Reappraisal* (Copenhagen, Museum Tusculanum Press).

Prior, L (2003) *Using Documents in Social Research* (London, Sage).

Rønning, OH (2018) 'Legal Aid in Norway' in O Hammerslev and OH Rønning (eds), *Outsourcing Legal Aid in the Nordic Welfare States* (London, Palgrave).

Sand, I-J (1996) *Styring av kompleksitet. Rettslige former for statlig rammestyring og desentralisert statsforvaltning* (Bergen-Sandviken, Fakbokforlaget).

Schoultz, I (2018) 'Legal Aid in Sweden' in O Hammerslev and OH Rønning (eds), *Outsourcing Legal Aid in the Nordic Welfare States* (London, Palgrave).

Tamm, D (2005) *Retshistorie. Danmark – Europa – globale perspektiver* (København, Jurist- og Økonomforbundets Forlag).

Wilson, RJ (2018) 'Legal Aid and Clinical Legal Education in Europe and the USA: Are They Compatible?' in O Hammerslev and OH Rønning (eds), *Outsourcing Legal Aid in the Nordic Welfare States* (London, Palgrave).

Waage, F (2017) *Det offentlige som procespart* (København, Karnov Group Denmark).

Zetterberg, H (1987) 'Advokaten, samfundet, samhället' *Advokaten* 429.

Zweigert, K and Kötz, H (1998) *An Introduction to Comparative Law* (Oxford, Clarendon Press).

9

France

The Reconfiguration of a Profession

CHRISTIAN BESSY AND BENOIT BASTARD

WHAT HAS HAPPENED to the legal profession since Anne Boigeol and other researchers, including Lucien Karpik, published their analyses 30 years ago? All the trends they identified have been confirmed and extended. Over the past three decades, the legal profession has continued to be transformed from a purely judicial profession, practised by individual lawyers grouped in Bar associations close to the various courts.[1] Every aspect of the profession has been affected. There are many more lawyers and women. The Bar now incorporates new professionals: legal advisers and *avoués* (solicitors).[2] The types of practice and organisation in law firms have become much more diverse and complex. The profession's representative bodies were transformed by the creation in 1990 of the *Conseil National des Barreaux* (National Bar Council, CNB), which has become the main interlocutor of the government with respect to projects to reform law practice.

These changes have occurred in the context of the growth of finance capitalism and the move towards economic globalisation. They accompany a transformation of law itself (which is becoming more procedural and complex), in tandem with the 'juridification' of social relations. At the same time, the state has contracted: societal rights that used to be guaranteed are becoming conditional. Alternative dispute resolution has expanded, offering the profession new opportunities. These changes reflect and extend reforms that affect all European professions. The European Commission's plan to build an internal market for legal services, launched in the 2000s, liberalised the market by eliminating restrictions seen as constraints on competition.[3] Although deregulation has

---

[1] The American lawyer's field of activity is wider than that of the French *avocat* and includes functions performed by other members of the French legal profession, such as magistrates, notaries, and in-house counsel of corporations and insurance companies (Boigeol 1988). Nevertheless, we use the term lawyer to designate the French *avocat*.

[2] The English solicitor resembles the French *avoué*: a lawyer who does not argue before a judge but performs other legal work, such as drafting contracts.

[3] European Commission, Rapport sur la concurrence dans le secteur des professions libérales, COM(2004) 83. See also Progress by Member States in renewing and eliminating restrictions to competition in the area of professional services, COM(2005) 405.

not been total, representatives of the legal profession have had to renegotiate some of its rules under ever-increasing pressure from the political elite, which seeks to promote the competitiveness of French law firms against foreign firms (Darrois 2009; Prada 2011).[4] The most recent Loi Macron of 2015 is a perfect illustration, especially by making it easier to capitalise law firms. Large law firms favour such deregulation.

All these changes have had massive consequences. Differentiation within the profession, already seen 30 years ago as a remarkable phenomenon, has increased. The gaps have widened: between the work done by business lawyers and litigators, large and small firms, and the major Bars (Paris in particular) and those of the provinces. The diversification of activities and income levels, disconnection among different sectors of the profession, pressure for deregulation, the effect of information technology, and the encroachment of the state on confidentiality all create fear that lawyers' distinctive roles will disappear even if the profession does not disintegrate. These centrifugal forces are resisted by the Bars, which seek to maintain and promote the 'identity of the profession', if not its unity, in order to preserve its independence from state and the market (Karpik 1995).

What gives the legal profession staying power? What is the outcome of its battles? Is it sufficient for lawyers to assert their unique functions, to champion human rights, to emphasise their respect for professional ethics and practices in order to maintain their autonomy and preserve their activity and social status as professionals? To answer these questions, we first describe some recent socio-demographic changes. Next, we highlight the segmentation of the profession and emergence of new forms of law firm organisation. Lastly, we analyse the effects of this segmentation and discuss the threats facing the profession and its response.

I. CHANGES IN THE DEMOGRAPHY AND STRUCTURE OF THE PROFESSION

In 1983 there were 15,757 lawyers in France, in addition to 80 at the *Conseil d'Etat* (Council of State) and *Cour de Cassation* (High Court) (Boigeol 1988). By 1988 there were 17,683 lawyers and 4,825 legal advisers (*conseils juridiques*), according to the Ministry of Justice.

A. The Increase in the Number of Lawyers Since the 1991 Admission of Legal Advisers

The profession subsequently expanded with the admission of legal advisers, who had been excluded from the 'minor merger' of lawyers and solicitors in 1971 (Boigeol and Dezalay 1997).[5] This inclusion both enlarged and diversified the profession, adding advising functions (especially consulting for businesses) to the traditional activity of dispute resolution. Legal advisers even organise their work in a more entrepreneurial way, relying more on salaried employees and limited companies (*Sociétés de capitaux*).

---

[4] These reports include proposals for improving the quality of French law (and the civil law tradition generally), which they view as insufficiently 'attractive'.
[5] The 1971 reform merged the profession of *avocats*, *agréés* of the commercial courts, and solicitors of the lower courts (Boigeol 1988).

The inclusion of legal advisers increased the number of lawyers to 25,399 and introduced the first collective agreement in 1995 regulating the employment contracts of salaried lawyers in legal adviser firms. Statistics (of the Ministry of Justice, see Figure 1) became more reliable and extensive in 1997, documenting the growth in the number of lawyers from 32,997 that year to 62,073 in 2015, an increase of 85.2 per cent or 5 per cent a year, about the same as in the years 1973–90 (Vauchez and Willemez 2002).

Figure 1 Number of Lawyers

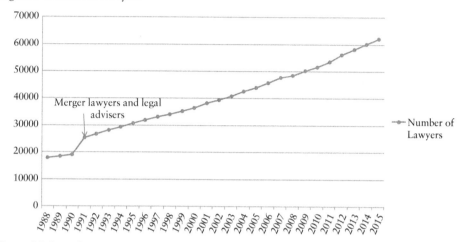

Source: Ministry of Justice.

The 2011 merger with the 430 solicitors of the appeal courts (*avoués auprès des cours d'appel*) did not significantly increase the number of lawyers.[6] That year there were 9,147 notaries and 3,237 bailiffs, making lawyers close to 80 per cent of all workers in law-related occupations, a proportion that has increased continually since the 1991 merger.

Legal advisers on patent and trademark matters (*propriété industrielle*) and corporate in-house counsel have not been admitted to the legal profession despite proposals to that effect, especially the *Rapport Darrois* (2009), which argued for a 'broadly defined legal profession'. The debate on the inclusion of in-house counsel (estimated at 15,800 in 2012 by *Association Française des Juristes d'Entreprise*) was revived in the draft Loi Macron of 2015, but at the date of writing it has not been adopted, the CNB being opposed. Negotiations to integrate patent and trademark counsel (1,000 members in 2017), which started in 2004, have stopped because some law firms specialising in intellectual property rights feared competition from patent and trademark experts.

This sustained expansion of the legal profession has been accompanied by a growing feminisation, more rapid than in some other European countries.[7] Women lawyers first

---

[6] Once integrated into the profession, solicitors (*avoués*) continued to exercise their privileged role as intermediaries with the appellate courts. Other lawyers have also assumed this role, which includes following the specific procedures for drafting appeals. The integration of solicitors coincided with simplifying and expediting appellate procedures, as well as their computerisation, which imposed additional constraints on lawyers.

[7] In 2011, women were 52 per cent of lawyers in France, 42 per cent in Italy, and only 32 per cent in Germany (where women's labour force participation is generally low). Women comprised less than 40 per cent of French medical doctors in 2011.

outnumbered men in 2009, reaching 54 per cent in 2015, whereas they comprised barely a third of the profession in 1983 (Boigeol 1988), 43 per cent in 1995, and 46 per cent in 2000. Feminisation accelerated in the 1990s, along with the expansion of litigation between individuals (divorce being the most typical) and other less prestigious work. This is one reason why male lawyers' income is twice that of female lawyers: €79,125 and €37,365 in 2000, €100,740 and €51,101 in 2008 (Vauchez and Willemez 2002). The average income of French lawyers, €74,586 in 2011, is significantly higher than that of their European counterparts, enhancing their status in French society (even though an increasingly large number of lawyers on the fringes of the profession earn relatively little – about as much as other workers in law-related occupations).

Another factor affecting the number of lawyers is the proliferation of foreign lawyers in France, increasing from 2.0 per cent in 1995 to 2.7 per cent in 2000, 3.1 per cent in 2006, and 3.4 per cent in 2015. Almost half come from the EU, especially the UK. More than a quarter come from Francophone Africa, but these highly qualified lawyers have encountered problems integrating into the profession. In 2015, 2,433 French lawyers practised abroad, 95 per cent of them attached to the Paris Bar.

B. Lawyers' Careers

This growth in the number of lawyers was accompanied by a reform of their training. The decree of 21 December 2004 eliminated the requirement that they present a contract of collaboration with a law firm in order to practise as a lawyer.[8] Once enrolled at a regional training centre (*L'Ecole des Avocats*), the future lawyer undergoes 18 months of training, including a six-month law firm internship, after which the trainee is examined for the CAPA (*Certificat d'aptitude à la profession d'avocat*).[9] Lawyers who pass this examination take the formal oath and register in the Bar where they plan to practise.[10] The new rules reduce the length of both graduate study and the mandatory internship. However, the reduction is somewhat illusory, since large law firms' new hires are increasingly expected to have pursued a double course of study (in law and another field, such as management or banking and finance), as shown by the age at which they enter the profession (Observatoire du CNB 2010).

Other avenues into the legal profession are quite marginal, for example the option for in-house counsel to join the Bar after eight years of practice. While this transition used to occur toward the end of a career, business experience is becoming obligatory in niche firms specialising in highly technical areas of law, such as NICT (information technology). There also is greater crossover of the political and administrative elite to the major business law firms in Paris (which employ similar performance and results-based management standards) to serve a clientele at the intersection of the public and private sectors

---

[8] The elimination of this requirement was justified by the difficulty young lawyers experienced in finding such contracts because established practitioners were becoming more prosperous and resented the expense of trainees. In 2010, there were 3,356 law graduates enrolled in the various training centres, compared to 2,547 in 2000 (Observatoire du CNB 2010).

[9] Before 2004, training lasted for three years, including a two-year internship in a law firm.

[10] The pass rate at CAPA is high (99 per cent) and constant from one year to the next.

(with the increasing importance of public law in the business domain). Pierre France and Antoine Vauchez (2017), for example, show that the *Conseil de l'Ordre*[11] of the Paris Bar has encouraged these transitions.[12] This raises questions about the transformation of relations between the professions of politics and law, especially the emergence of conflicts of interest inconsistent with the former 'Independent Republic of Lawyers' (Karpik 1995: 211–27).

Specialisation naturally reduces the occupational mobility of lawyers and other law-related occupations. Competition is intensifying among the increasing number of new lawyers, who encounter greater difficulty in practising their profession and becoming a partner. These factors, combined with extra-professional ones (maintaining work-life balance), may explain why some are leaving the profession: one quarter of lawyers (and a third of women) quit the profession in their first ten years, most often between years two and six (CNB Observatoire 2007). Informants indicate that close to half the departing lawyers go to work in business. Whatever the reason, these premature departures are troubling in a profession that underwrites much of the cost of training, especially by funding the graduate training centres.[13]

But what *Observatoire du CNB* also shows is that these exit rates increased between 1994 and 2005, reflecting not only the difficulty of getting a foothold in the profession but also poor career expectations when law graduates begin studying at the training centres, since they are leaving the profession earlier and earlier. Although the favourable economic climate up to 2009 had reduced exit rates substantially, this trend resumed at the end of the 2000s. Over the period 1994–2009, slightly less than one in five men and one in four women left the profession, confirming the finding that women represent a more transient workforce (Observatoire du CNB 2010).

This increase in lawyers' occupational mobility depends on the emergence of new recruitment intermediaries not controlled by the profession (private agencies specialising in law-related occupations, websites, and digital social networks). Their increasing involvement tends to blur the boundaries between the various legal occupations (lawyer, in-house counsel, notary[14] and, further removed, chartered accountant). It parallels the emergence of a European market in legal services, for it is the conception of what constitutes law as a profession (increasingly seen as globalised) that affects the training, assessment, and recruitment of new lawyers and, more generally, the organisation of their practice.

C. Geographical Polarisation

The ratio of population to lawyers has recently declined steadily to 1,053 in 2015 from 1,471 ten years earlier. But it remains far higher than in other European countries such as

---

[11] The elected governing body within each bar.
[12] They found nearly 200 instances in 1988–2014 compared with just 16 in 1979–87. Nearly a third of those in the more recent group made the transition before they were 40.
[13] Ten per cent of the cost is paid by the state and the rest by the profession and trainees' fees. There is a proposal to raise the latter from €1,600 to €3,000.
[14] By contrast with an American notary, who has limited responsibilities, a French *notaire* carries out many routine legal procedures, such as writing wills and transferring property.

Italy, Spain, and Germany (although in the last two count in-house counsel as lawyers). Moreover, there is a significant disparity among the 161 Bars in France, with the Paris and largest provincial Bars enrolling most of the profession. Indeed, lawyers continue to concentrate in Paris, which contained 42 per cent in 2015, up from 36 per cent in 1983. However, the largest law firms have opened subsidiary offices in increasing numbers since 1997 in other cities with large Bars.

All these disparities (of gender, region, increased consulting activity, and specialisation) are related to an entrepreneurial approach within the profession, which has developed greatly since the 1990s, as we will see by reviewing the diversity of types of practice, especially the rise of law firms organised as 'independent professional companies' (*sociétés d'exercice liberal*, SEL), whose effect is to deepen the division between business law and the traditional Bars.

D. Sharp Contrasts among Law Firms

For a long time, lawyers could only practise as solo practitioners. After 1954 they could join group practices organised as private entities – partnerships. In 1966, another type of organisation was created: civil professional societies (*Sociétés Civiles Professionnelles*, SCP).[15] When lawyers incorporated legal advisers in 1991, they also permitted multiple ways of organising group practices to enable law firms to expand in an increasingly competitive international market.

i. The Rise of Law Firms Organised as Independent Professional Companies

The Law of 31 December 1990 allowed lawyers to create commercial companies of independent professionals (SELs) (meaning that partners with shares in the company could also practise law outside the company).[16] The French legislature encouraged these more corporate forms of organisation in response to the growing concentration of all sorts of professionals, in both Europe and the US, and the establishment of these firms in France. The law also allowed legal advisers to practise with lawyers and represent clients in court. It was endorsed by the future elite among French legal professionals (the founders of the business law Bar) as well as the *Conseil de l'Ordre* of the Paris Bar, supported by the most innovative members of the professional associations (*Fédération National de l'Union des Jeunes Avocats* (FNUJA) and *Syndicat des Avocats Français*) (Dezalay 1990). The then Bâtonnier[17] had no hesitation in invoking the Anglo-Saxon model of the versatile 'law firm', able to meet the diversified needs of a business clientele and thus resist the encroachment of foreign competitors. In 1987, the revenue of the

---

[15] Unlike the partnership, the SCP is the joint exercise of the profession. The client is dealing with a company consisting of its lawyer and several others, who share fees according to their previous agreement.

[16] In addition to their different statutory functions, these firms are differentiated in terms of their origin (inherited family income versus earned professional income), taxable status (individual or corporate), social function, and responsibilities.

[17] The president of the *Conseil de l'Ordre*.

400 US and UK lawyers in France equalled that of the 7,000 lawyers registered with the Paris Bar (Dezalay 1990).[18]

The internationalisation of lawyers' work, as well as the increased establishment of large Anglo-Saxon law firms in France, accelerated after the 1991 merger of legal advisers and lawyers. Unlike their American counterparts, which had just a few representatives of the parent firm in a small office, British firms created branch offices with a substantial number of lawyers (Morgan and Quack 2005).

The number of group practices (with at least two lawyers) has constantly increased, from 3,268 in 1997 (the first year statistics were kept) to 8,116 in 2015, a growth of 148 per cent during a period when the total number of lawyers increased 88 per cent. However, the vast majority of group practices are relatively small, and the proportion of lawyers belonging to them actually decreased slightly, from 30.7 per cent in 1997 to 29.4 per cent in 2015 (see Table 1).[19]

Table 1 Distribution of Lawyers by Type of Practice (%)

	1997	2015
Solo practitioners (*avocat exerçant à titre individuel*)	32.0	36.3
Partners (*avocat exerçant en qualité d'associé*)	30.7	29.4
Associates (*avocat exerçant en qualité de collaborateur*)	28.7	29.4
Salaried associates (*avocat exerçant en qualité de salarié*)	8.5	4.7
Total	100.0	100.0
Number of lawyers	32,997	62,073

Source: Ministry of Justice.

At the same time, the proportion of lawyers with solo practices increased slightly during this period, from 32.0 per cent in 1997 to 36.3 per cent in 2014. Conversely, the proportion of associates (*collaborateurs*) decreased from 37.2 per cent to 34.1 per cent, which partly corresponds to the decrease in the proportion of salaried lawyers from 8.5 per cent to 4.7 per cent. Nonetheless, apart from the decline in wage-earning associates[20] and the increase in the number of lawyers practising individually, the distribution of types of legal practice was relatively stable during this period.

In 2012, 43.6 per cent of group practices were a *Société d'Exercice Liberal à Responsabilité Limitée* (SELARL) (independent limited professional company) and 34.0 per cent a SCP (civil professional society); just 12.6 per cent took the form of partnerships (19.2 per cent in 1997). This is a dramatic change from 1997, when only 12.8 per cent of groups practised as SELARL, while 61.1 per cent practised as SCP. This expansion of the SELARL demonstrates the law firms' shift towards commercial forms of organisation and a business model, which is confirmed by the fact that these large companies employ the greatest number of salaried lawyers and non-lawyers

---

[18] In 2010, foreign firms accounted for almost two-thirds of the turnover of all business law firms operating in France (Barszcz 2012).

[19] The average number of partners in each practice gradually decreased from 3.1 to 2.2 during this period.

[20] Unlike the 'liberal' associates, salaried lawyers cannot have a personal clientele.

(Vauchez and Willemez 2002: 74). Opening up the capital of these firms to non-lawyers is likely to reinforce their commercial character and desire for profit, with the risk that their services will become more standardised, while also offering opportunities for growth. The Law of 28 March 2011 on the modernisation of the regulated legal and judicial professions, which allows the creation of capitalised companies by members of different professions, only came into force very recently, with the Decree of 19 March 2014. It also allows financial participation in SEL companies by legal, accounting, and industrial property professionals. More recently, the Loi Macron of 2015 proposes to allow the creation of true multi-professional companies in law and accounting.

ii. Widening the Gap between Business Law and Traditional Bars

Drawing on a representative sample of more than 200 law firms, we have constructed a typology based on the distribution of their revenue across 20 domains.[21] By adopting this type of variable, we can see a clear dichotomy among the eight categories our study has identified.[22]

(i) on one side, business law is central, practised with tax, bankruptcy, and information technology law. Most are group practices, primarily offering consulting services to a business clientele. Revenue per lawyer is very high. We might compare these firms with specialists in intellectual property, whose practitioners charge the highest hourly rates;

(ii) on the other side, the dominant fields are family and (to a lesser extent) criminal law, together with immigration and asylum law. Most are solo practices conducting litigation for individuals. Revenue per lawyer is lower, in part because 30 per cent of cases are paid by legal aid. The concentration of new graduates on family disputes and small claims has intensified competition in this sector.

These two categories, which resemble the hemispheres of the Chicago Bar (Heinz and Laumann 1982), account for almost two-thirds of firms and have grown substantially more numerous since the 1990s (Karpik 2003). In France, they are also gendered: men dominate counselling activities and women litigation. In between these 'business law firms' and 'traditional individual practices' there is an intermediate category containing three types of firm (focused on public, labour, and property law), whose clientele is equally divided between companies and individuals (and public entities); litigation accounts for nearly three-quarters of their revenue. Thus, we now see a clear distinction

---

[21] The survey data for 2010 were collected during the second half of 2011 through a questionnaire posted on a website, except in the case of large firms (with revenues of over €7 million), where face-to-face interviews were conducted to obtain qualitative data. In addition to general information on each firm, the questionnaire covered activity and competitiveness in the market, advertising and consumer information, organisation and type of operations (staffing, methods of recruitment, remuneration and partnership, and organisation of work). This survey was funded by CNB, which also helped us construct the sample of 205 representative law firms broken down by type of practice (group or individual) and Bar (Paris or elsewhere in France). For more details, see Favereau et al (2013).

[22] The network of joint practices across the different legal domains is related to additional variables: principal activity (consultation/litigation), clientele (businesses, individuals, or public entities), and average revenue per lawyer, as well as the hourly rate charged (Bessy 2015).

between firms that function as colleagues in planning their business clients' legal strategy and firms that traditionally enjoyed some autonomy in constructing a case for individuals who have a problem that must be solved by litigation (and may want it to cost as little as possible).

This dichotomy is paralleled by differences in firm size. According to the results of our 2011 survey, 49 per cent of the firms are solo practices, 40 per cent have 2–5 lawyers, and 11 per cent have more (20, 34, and 46 per cent of lawyers belong to the respective categories). Except for the 0.5 per cent of firms with over 100 lawyers, containing nearly 5 per cent of lawyers, the distribution is dominated by small firms, even more so than 'ordinary' businesses.

The reason for this unequal distribution lies in their different growth strategies. The largest firms include the big Anglo-Saxon business law firms established over the last two decades, which engage in intense 'head-hunting,' systematically bidding up the salaries of associates, not always participating in their training, and taking advantage of high staff turnover (Henderson and Galanter 2008; Bessy 2015).[23] Moreover, the length of time to partnership tends to increase. By contrast, preserving the traditional model of solo practice or limiting the firm's growth may reflect a desire for autonomy or even an outright rejection of the business model. This may explain the repeated fractures of French law firms, which have hindered their growth.[24]

iii. The Proliferation of Interlocking Organisations

Another factor limiting the size of law firms is the development of interlocking organisations of firms pooling resources. These complement groups created earlier to cope with economic conditions while preserving the individual lawyer's independence (Boigeol 1988). The adoption of 'resource sharing associations' allows firms to pool administrative resources. Twenty-five per cent of firms in our survey belonged to such associations, which were slightly over-represented among provincial solo practices (30 per cent) and under-represented among Parisian group practices (17 per cent). Premises are shared in over 94 per cent and documentation is pooled in 52 per cent, secretarial support in 41 per cent, and other resources in 33 per cent; only 5 per cent share accounts payable and receivable.

Links between firms can also take the form of alliances for the exchange of dossiers and clients. Of the firms we surveyed, 2.6 per cent belonged to a national network and 5.2 per cent to an international one; these ranged from 50 to 15,000 lawyers. Network membership is more typical of group practices than solo; indeed, 17 per cent of group practices belong to an international network, compared to 2 per cent of solo practices. These networks are expanding by using information technology and taking an increasingly organised form. This can be explained both by the firms' desire to accommodate

---

[23] One of our subjects (interviewed in 2008) working at this kind of firm noted that turnover among his colleagues had increased in recent years, reducing the average tenure to 18 months. Our statistical study showed that in 2010 turnover (of both partners and other lawyers) in the group practices averaged 13.5 per cent, suggesting that a lawyer moves to a different firm roughly every 7–8 years.

[24] This pattern based on repeated fractures, specific to France, was emphasised by several respondents and noted by Karpik (2003). It explains why there are very few long-established law firms in France (Chatudeau 2014).

corporate clients, which are diversifying geographically, and by the rapidity of changes in the law, which require highly specialised expertise, for instance in the area of social law. This hybrid type of organisation is developing not only in response to extreme specialisation but also to promote cross-selling among firms in the network, allowing each member to take advantage of the opportunities presented by a national or international market for legal services.

Recently, networks of firms have adopted the franchise business model, serving needs not met by traditional firms by actively targeting clients unaccustomed to dealing with lawyers (Wickers 2014). To attract this new clientele they have adopted the marketing techniques of retail distribution: storefronts, information centres, and other methods that encourage prospective clients to seek legal advice. Their creators claim they are responding to a demand for simplified access to the law. This hybrid organisation has created an online presence, joining the proliferation of platforms offering basic legal services at 'low cost' in the face of hostility from the Bars (which are launching their own platforms).

This more fluid approach to the organisation of law firms can be seen in the stabilisation in the number of non-lawyers in each firm. While non-lawyer staff have been increasing, from almost 31,000 salaried employees in 2002 to 39,742 in 2012, their proportion of all staff declined slightly, from 44 to 41 per cent.[25] This may be partly attributable to the fact that solo practices, which employ few non-lawyers, increased from 35.8 per cent in 2002 to 36.5 per cent in 2012.

In conclusion, the establishment of large law firms in France has reinforced the professional dichotomy and normalised the business model of legal services, whose market is becoming increasingly international.[26] This model is leading to greater integration of resources, especially in the larger firms, although this varies with lawyer turnover within each firm and the use of subcontracting.[27] Smaller firms and solo practitioners have the option of joining networks of firms or, now that actively seeking clients has been authorised (Loi Hamon, 17 March 2014) and information technology is expanding, working for low-cost legal service providers. That there are few firms between the two extremes is unsurprising and found in other occupations. It is more worrying that these medium-sized 'intermediate firms' seem to be losing ground since they mitigate the polarisation of the profession by combining the public sphere and the world of the market, corporate clients and private individuals, and also facilitate lawyers' career mobility.

---

[25] These data are drawn from INSEE statistics, restated by CNB Observatoire (2010). The ratios are higher in other regulated professions, such as notaries and chartered accountants.

[26] Barszcz (2012) identifies four groups of firms among the 150 largest operating mainly in business law. In 2010, they had revenues close to €3.2 billion (about a quarter of the legal profession's total revenue) and employed more than 10,600 lawyers (one-fifth of the total). The 77 national firms in Paris and the 23 in the provinces have grown substantially over the last 20 years but do not compare in size to the big international firms. Indeed, although there are twice as many large national firms as large international firms, the former account for no more than a third of total revenue.

[27] Business law firms can always enlist niche firms when they need specialised expertise, introducing a division of labour based on outsourcing – for example, of the 'social component' of a merger and acquisition deal managed by a large business law firm. This specialised outsourcing differs from that used to offset fluctuations in the demand for standard legal services (Bessy 2015). Although the latter is still relatively undeveloped in France, it began in the US about 30 years ago with New York or Chicago firms billing for legal services performed by lawyers in developing countries (Wilkins 1992).

iv. Publicly Funded Work

Another professional dichotomy is the concentration of legal aid work (*Aide juridictionnelle*, AJ) among a shrinking number of lawyers. In 2011, 24,450 lawyers were reimbursed at least once for handling nearly 745,000 legal aid cases costing the state nearly €227 million (Union Nationale des Caisses d'Avocats 2012). In 2014, 26,174 lawyers (41.5 per cent of the profession) handled 791,448 basic legal aid cases and 71,731 more partly subsidised by legal aid. Lawyers' unions are constantly lobbying for re-appraisal of reimbursement levels, an issue that regularly leads to strikes. At the time of the 1972 reform (harshly criticised by the profession as an effort to control the cost of legal services) the number of subsidised cases had decreased from the level of the 1950s (Boigeol 1988). A 1991 reform extended AJ, allowing the number of cases to increase from 348,587 that year to 698,779 in 2000 (when 79 per cent of lawyers took at least one) (Vauchez and Willemez 2002). But by 2014, when the number of lawyers had almost doubled, the proportion taking AJ cases dropped dramatically, reflecting the concentration of such work among less well-off lawyers. At the same time, business law firms also take pro bono cases, enabling their staff to share the symbolic authority enjoyed by trial lawyers (Diener 2016).[28]

II. A RECONFIGURED PROFESSION

On the basis of the data presented here, we can return to our initial question about the forces affecting the profession. On one hand, there are signs of increased segmentation and centrifugal forces leading to deregulation and diffuse activity. On the other, there are strategies for enhancing the profession's internal unity and preserving at least a façade of common purpose.

A. Does Segmentation Portend the Dissolution of the Profession?

Except in the most standardised cases, the quality of lawyers' services can be assessed only by their peers. The collegial organisation and social networks enabled by the *Ordre Professionnel* encourage many kinds of cooperation among lawyers, which is essential to the development and consolidation of high professional standards. But increasingly intense competition within the profession is eroding this positive externality, at least in the larger Bars (Favereau et al 2010). Similarly, intense competition in the other law-related and accounting professions widens the divide between the business law and traditional Bars. Lucien Karpik (1995; 2003: 208) identified the growing heterogeneity of professional skills, practices, interests, ideologies, and goals. We draw an analogy to the business model governing the largest law firms.[29] These observations highlight the importance of the unity of the profession, whose regulatory role is being supplanted by

---

[28] The lawyers in our statistical survey had an average of seven pro bono files in progress; but this figure must be interpreted with caution because only a hundred answers were collected.

[29] A growing number of lawyers feel a stronger commitment to their firm than to the profession (CSA/CNB 2014).

large firms and market intermediaries deploying information technology. These partially replace *Conseils de l'Ordre* in the areas of client confidence, recruiting lawyers and assessing their competence, connecting lawyers to clients, settling disputes, and helping firms expand. Through our statistical survey we have begun to identify the role of different market intermediaries in recruiting lawyers and putting them in contact with clients (Bessy 2015).

B. The Mechanics of the Governing Bodies: Who Represents Lawyers?

The disintegration of the legal profession is also the result of its organisational structure. The 160 Bars in France, each independent and governed by an elected *Conseil de l'Ordre* and *Bâtonnier*, range in size from a few dozen lawyers to several hundred in the larger cities. The Paris Bar alone contains over 25,000 lawyers, more than 40 per cent of the total in 2015, giving it a disproportionate role, especially because it includes the elite of the business law bar. The dominance of one Bar claiming to represent the interests of all lawyers makes the profession difficult to manage. On one hand, smaller Bars consider their internal proximity and collegiality paramount for guaranteeing the effectiveness of the law; on the other, the Paris Bar's wealth and size enhances its influence. This tension makes it difficult to reach consensus on issues affecting the organisation of the profession.

Other governing bodies also manage and represent the profession. The CNB became the main interlocutor of the government concerning its plans to reform the profession after the Law of 31 December 1990 officially merged lawyers and legal advisers (Wickers 2014). But it shares representation and lobbying with the Bars (especially the Paris Bar) and the *Conférence des bâtonniers*, whose three working committees examine each important dossier. Professional unions also play an influential role in representing, advising and training their members. The three most important trade unions differ ideologically. FNUJA had 4,000 active members in 2011. ACE (*Avocats Conseils d'Entreprises*/Business Consultancy Lawyers) claims to be the primary lawyers' union in France, with at least as many active members as FNUJA. SAF (*Syndicat des Avocats de France*/Union of French Lawyers) shares the left-wing politics of its nearly 1,500 members. But less than a quarter of the profession is unionised.[30]

The individuality of the provincial Bars has been eroded by CNB's expanding activities, such as its competition with the major Bars in computer technology, especially implementation of the 'e-bar' (for electronic communication with the courts). CNB also contributed to transforming CAPA from a regional to a national examination and helped to pass the Loi Macron of 6 August 2015, eliminating the substitution system (*postulation*), which had required lawyers seeking to appear in a court associated with a Bar to which they did not belong to pay a local lawyer to act for them. The CNB claimed that by standardising legal practice it served the interests of the greatest number of lawyers.

---

[30] Boigeol (1988) attributed the emergence of lawyers' unions to the state's growing interference in the legal profession's business. Since her study was conducted the percentage of unionised lawyers has decreased even though state intervention has not declined.

C. Affirmations of Unity and Preservation of the Profession's Façade

In order to mitigate the segmentation of lawyers and the weakening of their governing bodies, the Bars have sought to promote the profession's image in the eyes of the judiciary and other state authorities by maintaining the competence of their members and the quality of their services. *Conseils de l'Ordre* organise specialised legal training and take a leadership role in the legal and social spheres. But most lawyers remain unenthusiastic. Many abstain from elections to *Conseils*, believing their activities are too expensive and relevant only to those directly involved in governance. That is less true in smaller Bars, where lawyers regularly participate in the activity of *Conseils*. Even in the major Bars, like Paris, business lawyers previously uninvolved in these governing bodies are now represented and active.

Collective affirmation of shared values such as discretion, integrity, honesty, and collegiality can also preserve professional unity.[31] However, a more detailed study shows that the profession's segments do not value the same basic principles (Bastard 2016). For business lawyers, confidentiality is a categorical imperative, essential to the negotiations and other operations they perform for their large corporate clients; litigators, by contrast, are more interested in rules concerning collegiality in their sphere of activity, which is characterised by increased litigiousness and competition.

The *Ordre Professionnel* is heavily invested in preventing malpractice. The disciplinary process, which is handled by lawyers themselves, has been reformed to more closely resemble a judicial procedure. It deals with the 'penniless' (lawyers in extreme difficulty due to illness or bankruptcy) and the 'rogues' (lawyers whose misconduct ranges from minor opportunistic offences to large-scale but inevitably unsuccessful swindles). Remarkably, none of the work of the disciplinary bodies concerns the business law sector (Bastard 2016). Yet even though discipline by the *Ordres* concerns only litigators, it still helps the profession legitimise self-regulation and differentiate it from other professions (such as medical doctors), which exercise little control over their members. This is particularly true when it comes to confidentiality, whose protection extends well beyond litigation and thus benefits business lawyers.

The *Ordre* also supports the defence of rights, including those against discrimination and of the accused. These activities express law's traditional function as protector of rights, justice, and freedoms – a cornerstone of the profession. The profession's ability to mobilise and unify its membership is particularly important today because all segments of the Bar are feeling constraints on their freedom to practise their profession. Lawyers have expressed opposition to money-laundering laws and unanimously condemn the wiretapping and searches conducted during tax and national security investigations. Lastly, the increasing importance of rights following the contraction of the state (Vauchez 2012) offers new opportunities for the profession to expand, which may also help to preserve its unity and social status (see also Karpik 1995: 463–64).

---

[31] The recent study by Chaserant and Harnais (2016), drawing on a corpus of disciplinary measures and judicial decisions, shows that departure from collegial values is the infraction most often punished. This is linked to support for appropriate behaviour and professional cohesion. By contrast, violations of rules concerning lawyer-client relations are punished much less often.

III. CONCLUSION

Despite its internal disunity, the legal profession in France is thriving, even though it (like other professions) is the object of suspicion and pressure, especially due to the EU push for deregulation. Nonetheless, the profession has continued to develop actively in directions visible 30 years ago. Its strength lies in its ability to reconfigure itself, expand, and incorporate new features without fundamentally changing, while continuing to enjoy public confidence. In this process, it relies on the social and economic capital it can mobilise, as well as its narrative resources. By operating on several levels, it draws strength from the very segmentation that may look like weakness or disunity. The Bar is supported by its impressive history, its image as the representative of human rights and the rights of the accused, and its central role in democratic discourse. It emphasises the preservation of basic principles and self-regulation. At the same time, it has made itself indispensable to business, reinforcing its inclusion in multinational networks, its authority, and the appeal of large firms to new generations of lawyers. By combining these activities and exploiting its multifaceted image, the Bar overcomes the menacing centrifugal forces. New forms of state regulation of markets, especially the independent administrative authorities defining the rules of competition, as well as public-private partnerships have created opportunities for the business Bar (France and Vauchez 2017). Business law firms participate in reforming the state in pursuit of a new public good, reducing the divide with litigation firms and thus the dichotomy between the two spheres. Nonetheless, the legal profession (like others) suffers from a lack of medium-sized firms, whose practices bridge the professional divide by addressing both the public sphere and the market, corporate and individual clients, while facilitating lawyers' career mobility.

In conclusion, we may ask what new challenges will face the profession and propose several responses (see also Assier-Andrieu 2011). What changes will result from the massive expansion of information and communication technologies, which offer new vehicles for legal and judicial activity, facilitating access to law as well as internationalising professional cooperation? How will the legal profession respond to the emergence of market intermediaries, which threaten to degrade the quality of legal services while reducing their cost (Hadfield 2014)? Will lawyers' careers become more insecure and the profession decline due to increased regulation and malfunctioning of the legal services market? The expansion of electronic communication between the Bars and jurisdictions (the 'e-bar') is profoundly changing legal proceedings (to the detriment of the oral hearings to which lawyers are wedded) and how trial lawyers operate (Dumoulin and Licoppe 2011). How can lawyers reform the way their Bars are organised? Can differentiation within and between Bars be bridged by combining them regionally or introducing a single national Bar? How should lawyers respond to wiretapping, seizure of evidence, and rejection of defence strategies? Do these represent an erosion of the profession's unique role in a world that is more pervasively policed by a state appropriating the dispensation of justice? The final challenge is the plan to expand the legal profession by incorporating new categories of lawyer, as has happened with corporate counsel. Should we encourage 'interprofessionality', as recommended by the *Rapport Darrois* of 2009, seeking to reduce jurisdictional conflicts among professionals? And should we encourage interdisciplinary networks and partnerships across law, accounting, and intellectual property consulting?

REFERENCES

Assier-Andrieu, L (2011) *Les avocats, identité, culture et devenir* (Paris, Lextenso).
August, G (2012) 'L'internationalisation des cabinets d'avocats' 140 *Pouvoirs* 49, 57.
Barszcz, C (2012) 'La typologie de la profession d'avocats: l'exemple des avocats d'affaires' 140 *Pouvoirs* 21, 32.
Bastard, B (2016) *Ethique et TIC. A quoi sert l'Ordre des avocats?* (Paris, ENS Paris-Saclay).
Bessy, C (2015) *L'organisation des activités des avocats, entre monopole et marché* (Paris, LGDJ, Lextenso).
Boigeol, A (1988) 'The French Bar: The Difficulties of Unifying a Divided Profession' in RL Abel and PSC Lewis (eds), *Lawyers in Society: Vol II The Civil Law World* (Berkeley, University of California Press).
Boigeol, A and Dezalay, Y (1997) 'De l'agent d'affaires au barreau: les conseils juridiques et la construction d'un espace professionnel' 27 *Genèse* 49, 68.
Chaserant, C and Harnay, S (2016) 'La déontologie professionnelle en pratique. Enquête sur l'activité disciplinaire de la profession d'avocat' 16 *Revue française de socio-économie* 119, 140.
Chatudeau, O (2014) 'Les cabinets d'avocats d'affaires en France' 147 *Commentaire* 597, 604.
CSA (Conseil Supérieur de l'Audiovisual)/CNB (2014) *Quels avocats pour quels marchés demain?*, Etude N° 1400436 (Paris, CSA/CNB).
Darrois, J-M (2009) *Rapport Darrois: 'Vers une grande profession du droit'* (Paris, La Documentation Française).
Dezalay, Y (1990) *"Big Bang" sur le marché du droit. La restructuration du champ du professionnel des affaires* (Paris, Commissariat Général au Plan).
Diener, L (2016) 'Avocats des droits de l'homme: la pratique du pro bono en France' 1 *Les cahiers de la justice* 139, 149.
Dumoulin, L and Licoppe, C (2011) 'Technologies, droit et justice' 61 *Droit et Cultures* 13, 36.
Favereau, O, Bessis, F, Bessy, C, Chaserant, C, Harnay, S, and Lazega E (2010) *Les avocats entre ordre professionnel et ordre marchand – Concurrence par la qualité et socio-économie d'une réglementation professionnelle* (Paris, Lextenso).
Favereau, O, Bessis, F, Bessy, C, Chaserant, C and Harnay, S (2013) *Enquête statistique sur la profession d'avocat: modes d'organisation des activités et identité professionnelle* (Paris, CNB).
France, P and Vauchez, A (2017) *Sphère publique, intérêts privés. Enquête sur un brouillage*, (Paris, Science Po les presses).
Hadfield, GK (2014) "Innovating to Improve Access: Changing the Way Courts Regulate Legal Markets" 143 *Daedalus* 83–95.
Heinz, J and Laumann, E (1982) *Chicago Lawyers: The Social Structure of the Bar* (New York, Russell Sage Foundation and Chicago, American Bar Foundation).
Karpik, L (1995) *Les avocats entre l'Etat, le public et le marché: XIIIème-XXème siècles*, (Paris, Gallimard).
—— (2003) 'Est-ce que les avocats peuvent affronter les défis posés à leur profession' 35 *Hermès* 203, 211.
Morgan, G and Quack, S (2005) 'Institutional Legacies and Firm Dynamics: The Internationalisation of UK and German Law Firms' 26 *Organization Studies* 1765–1785.
Observatoire du CNB (2007) *Regards sur une nouvelle generation d'avocats* (Paris, CNB).
—— (2010) *Regard sur la démographie des avocats* (Paris, CNB).
Prada, M (2011) *Rapport sur certain facteurs de renforcement de la compétitivité juridique de la place de Paris* (Paris, Ministère de l'Economie, des Finances et de l'Industrie and Ministère de la Justice).
Union Nationale des Caisses d'Avocats (2012) *Statistique aide juridictionelle 2011* (Paris, UNCA).

Vauchez, A (2012) 'Elite politico-administrative et barreau d'affaires. Sociologie d'un espace-frontière' 140 *Pouvoirs* 71, 81.

Vauchez, A and Willemez, L (2002) *Contribution à la connaissance statistique de la profession d'avocat* (Paris, CNB).

Wickers, T (2014) *La grande transformation des avocats* (Paris, Dalloz).

Wilkins, DB (1992) 'Who Should Regulate Lawyers?' 105 *Harvard Law Review* 799, 871.

10

Germany
Resistance and Reactions to Demands of Modernisation

MATTHIAS KILIAN AND ULRIKE SCHULTZ

I. PROFESSIONALISATION FROM ABOVE: THE STATE

HISTORICALLY, GERMANY'S LEGAL profession[1] has been characterised by professionalisation from above, by the state, resulting in a bureaucratic model (McClelland 1990). Because the profession was subject to state regulation, autonomy had to be found within the limits of bureaucratic rights and privileges. German legal professionals differ from the Anglo-American ideal-type (Schultz 2003c). Although the profession has adapted to economic and political developments over the past 150 years, basic features have remained unchanged.

The strong influence of the state in shaping the legal profession is rooted in history (Weißler 1905; Bleek 1972; Hartstang 1986). In 1871, the German Empire was created under the hegemony of Prussia, whose emperors viewed legal and judicial services as part of the government machinery. At the end of the eighteenth century advocates representing clients at court became for some time civil servants (*Assistenzräte*) charged with assisting the parties while helping the judges investigate the facts. Their number was limited by a *numerus clausus*. Others were allowed to work as judicial commissioners (*Justizkommissare*), offering advice and representation in non-contentious legal matters and performing notarial functions. Courts defined the examination requirements and admitted advocates and Commissioners of Justice. The 1878 Act on Advocates (*Rechtsanwaltsordnung*, RAO), passed after the creation of the German Empire, introduced a uniform profession of *Rechtsanwälte* throughout the empire[2] and abolished the *numerus clausus*. But lawyers remained the backbone of German bureaucracy. At the same time, the Act on

---

[1] Detailed descriptions of the status of the German legal profession can be found in Blankenburg and Schultz (1988; 1995); Schultz (1997; 2003a; 2005; 2011; 2013); Schultz et al (2018) and many publications by Kilian. See also Gerold (2008); Rüschemeyer (1973).

[2] Some subdivisions had had a split profession, influenced by the Roman model of procurator charged with procedural tasks and a learned advocatus entrusted with oral representation in court.

the Constitution of the Judiciary (*Gerichtsverfassungsgesetz*) made the judiciary autonomous. The RAO remained in force until replaced in West Germany by the 1957 Federal Advocates' Act (*Bundesrechtsanwaltsordnung*).

II. THE TRADITIONAL LEGAL PROFESSIONS

A. Advocates

This new act retained the traditional features of the advocates' profession, modelled on a litigator representing clients in court, but adapted them to constitutional requirements rooted in the 1949 Basic Law (*Grundgesetz*) of the Federal Republic of Germany. Rechtsanwälte still had to be admitted by the appeal courts to a court of the ordinary jurisdiction (localisation principle) and maintain an office within that jurisdiction. They were compensated by a monopoly over representing litigants in court and dispensing legal advice. Ever since 1878 the Federal and State Ministries of Justice have regulated entry, requiring advocates, judges, notaries and higher civil servants to pass two examinations set by them. Until three decades ago the second legal examination was the prerequisite for many leading civil service positions and some in the private sector, and it remains a desirable qualification for higher positions. This has led to the notion of the jurists' monopoly in Germany (Dahrendorf 1965).[3]

With the rise in the number of Rechtsanwälte from 18,214 in 1959 to 164,656 in 2018, the demands of a society increasingly oriented toward individual rights, and the growing importance of consultancy work, the scope of legal practice has changed. The necessary modification of professional regulations was less a result of German government or professional policy initiatives than of landmark decisions by the Federal Constitutional Court, European Court of Justice, and German Supreme Court and policy initiatives of the European Commission in the 1980s and 1990s, all of which the Bundestag had to transform into law (Schultz 2005). Many ethical rules have been liberalised, such as the ban on advertising. The strict system of scale fees based on a Federal Advocates Fee Act (*Rechtsanwaltvergütungsgesetz*) has become more flexible;[4] and advocates are now admitted by the Chambers of Advocates. But disciplinary control is still exercised by Advocates Courts, which are part of the administration of justice in the courts of ordinary jurisdiction[5] and staffed by advocates as lay judges and, on appeal, professional judges. The court administration still controls entry through the state examinations.

The profession is organised in 27 regional chambers of advocates (*Rechtsanwaltskammern*, RAK) in which membership is compulsory (German *Kammerprinzip*), ranging

---

[3] The 2017 Bundestag has 115 lawyers among its 709 members (16 per cent). In recent decades, as many as half of federal government ministers were lawyers.

[4] The 2004 *Rechtsanwaltsvergütungsgesetz* (RVG) still sets rules for charging fees based on scales for representation and advocacy, but hourly rates and contingency fees (quota litis) are permitted, and the statutory fees only apply by default in the absence of an individual fee agreement. Output-based fees are permissible in individual cases if the client would otherwise refrain from pursuing a legal proceeding for economic reasons (Kilian and Kothe 2015).

[5] The judicial system is highly developed, with separate jurisdictions for civil and criminal matters (ordinary jurisdiction, *ordentliche Gerichtsbarkeit*), labour, administrative, social and tax law. All but tax law have three instances, with further appeals to state constitutional courts and the Federal Constitutional Court. The first and second instances are state courts, the third are federal courts.

in size from 1,423 to 21,416, and a 42-member Chamber of Advocates at the Federal Supreme Court. Their umbrella organisation is the Federal Chamber of Advocates (*Bundesrechtsanwaltskammer*, BRAK) in Berlin. 64,382 advocates (39 per cent) belong to the German Advocates Association (*Deutscher Anwaltverein*), with local associations at the level of the regional courts of ordinary jurisdiction, which offers support services and represents the profession at the federal level in policy matters. In questions concerning the profession and legislation, the *Kammern* tend to be more conservative and the *Deutscher Anwaltverein* more liberal.

Reunification of West and East Germany in 1990 did not affect the regulatory regime or the characteristics of the profession since the five states of the former German Democratic Republic (GDR) simply joined the Federal Republic of Germany (FRG), accepting its legal system. Because the GDR lacked an independent judiciary and had very few advocates (592 in 1989 for about 17 million people), reunification opened a new market for legal professionals, temporarily alleviating the tension in the legal market caused by a tripling of the number of advocates between 1981 and 2001. To continue working, former GDR legal professionals had to undergo a test of personal qualifications. Besides GDR's advocates, many of its former judges, prosecutors and civil servants, who could not pass the more demanding FRG admission test for the judiciary and civil service, applied for membership as Rechtsanwälte in one of the newly established regional Bars in Eastern Germany (Schultz 1997).

B. Anwalt Notaries and Solo Notaries

Following the Prussian model of legal commissioner, Rechtsanwälte in many parts of Western Germany can be admitted as notaries (*Anwaltsnotare*). In 1981, 18.2 per cent of Rechtsanwälte were also Anwaltsnotare, which offered financial security. Because the number of Anwaltsnotare has declined and that of Rechtsanwälte has increased, the former were only 3.4 per cent of the latter in 2018. Anwaltsnotare are still governed by a *numerus clausus*. Admission used to depend mainly on years of practice, but an entry examination was introduced in 2011.[6] In other parts of Germany and, since reunification, all of Eastern Germany, the notary is a separate profession (*Nur-Notare*).[7]

The functions of the German notariat resemble those of the Roman law influenced Latin notariat.[8] They charge fees according to a fixed scale. In recent decades there was a steady increase in the number of notaries, which peaked in 1998 at 9,045 Anwaltsnotare and 1,656 solo notaries. Due to stricter entry controls and a limitation on places by federal states seeking to improve the quality of notarial services by guaranteeing each Anwaltsnotar more notarisations, the number of Anwaltsnotare decreased to 5,558 in 2018. After stagnating for a couple of years the number of solo notaries also decreased to 1,479 in 2017.

---

[6] In consequence of a 2004 decision of the Federal Constitutional Court.
[7] As of 2018 also in Baden-Württemberg, in parts of which notaries had been civil servants. After reunification the number of solo notaries rose from 1,014 in 1989 to 1,463 in 1991 and then declined.
[8] In parts of Germany the Code Napoléon had been introduced under French occupation in the early nineteenth century.

C. Judges

Germany traditionally has had a high ratio of professional judges to population[10] because German legal culture is strongly judge-centred. In the civil law inquisitorial system, procedural law gives judges a dominant role: they control the proceedings, suggest settlements, pass judgments, and write detailed opinions. The judiciary is a lifetime career until retirement at 65–67, normally starting right after the second qualifying examination, at an average age of 29. The status resembles that of a civil servant, and promotion to higher courts is the usual career expectation. Although each court's president supervises its personnel, the state ministries of justice are involved in promotions (Schultz et al 2011).

In the early years of the German Empire the number of judges greatly exceeded that of Rechtsanwälte. In 1883 there were 7,052 judges, but only 4,342 advocates. In 1909 the number of advocates had grown to equal that of judges. In the 1970s, favourable economic conditions permitted an expansion of the judiciary to increase access to justice and strengthen citizens' legal rights. Since the turn of the millennium the number of judges has declined slightly.[9] But the ratio of judges to population has remained remarkably stable over almost 130 years. As the number of prosecutors increased from 1,873 in 1955 to 5,503 in 2007, their ratio to population rose slightly.

Table 1 Development of the Number of Advocates, Notaries and Judges

Year	Advocates	Solo Notaries/ Advocate-Notaries	Judgeships*	Population (in millions)
1883	4,342		7,052	46.0
1909	9,608		9,798	63.7
1915	13,051		10,719	67.9
1933 Third empire	19,200		10,069	66.0
1959	18,214		8,909 (11,502)	54.9
1971	23,599		9,926 (12,954)	60.7
1981	37,314	959/6,803	12,298 (16,657)	61.6
1989	54,108	1,014/8,724	(17,627)	60.5
2001	116,305	1,665/8,897	15,464 (20,880)	82.4**
2011	155,679	1,561/6,373	14,929 (20,411)	82.3
2018	164,156	1,719/5,460	15,161 (20,739)***	82.8****

Various sources: eg Federal Statistical Office, Federal Ministry of Justice (Judicial Statistics); Bundesrechtsanwaltskammer; historical literature on advocates and the judiciary.
*Number of judgeships (not a head count) in the ordinary civil and criminal law jurisdiction;[10] number in brackets is judgeships in all jurisdictions.
**Rise in numbers due to reunification in 1990.
***Data for 2016.
****Increase through refugees.

[9] With population growth due to migration and refugees since 2015, the judiciary has obtained new positions, mainly in administrative courts for asylum and refugee cases.

[10] Because a considerable number of judges (mainly women) work part-time, their actual number is higher. Part-time work for family reasons was made possible through a change in the Civil Service Act in 1969.

III. UNIFORM LEGAL EDUCATION FOR TRADITIONAL LEGAL PROFESSIONALS: JUDGE, ADVOCATE, NOTARY, PROSECUTOR, ADMINISTRATIVE LAWYER

The system of legal education is distinctive (Schultz 2011; Kilian 2012a; 2015a).[11] It is centred on the concept of the *Einheitsjurist* (unified jurist), allowing jurists to work in all traditional legal professions without additional training. Subject to passing two state legal examinations, those who complete legal studies at university law faculties and a two-year legal traineeship (*Rechtsreferendariat*), organised and funded by the appeal courts and Ministries of Justice of the federal states, qualify as *Volljuristen* (full-fledged jurists), enabling them to become a judge (*Richter*), public prosecutor (*Staatsanwalt*), advocate (*Rechtsanwalt*), notary (*Notar*), in-house-counsel (*Syndikusrechtsanwalt*) or administrative lawyer in the higher civil service (*Verwaltungsjurist*).

Law students are trained in the Roman law tradition as legal technicians by learning to apply positive law to hypothetical cases (the process of *Subsumtion*). During their practical training they get to work on real files. Legal education is focused on writing opinions on cases and judgments, skills required for judicial office but not necessarily for practice as an advocate. Legal studies[12] do not result in graduation with a university degree but rather confer the right to take a state legal examination (*Erste Juristische Prüfung*); law has resisted the so-called Bologna process unifying European university education based on bachelor's and master's degrees. Every successful examinee is guaranteed a position as a legal trainee (*Rechtsreferendar*) and will be paid a subsistence income from the public purse. Over the course of the two-year traineeship, *Referendare* work a couple of months in each of the following – the civil branch of a court of ordinary jurisdiction, a public prosecutor's office, the civil service, and a law firm – giving them insight into all aspects of legal practice and preparing them to choose a career. The traineeship ends with a second state legal examination (*Zweite Juristische Staatsprüfung*). Only future notaries must undergo another two years of specialised training, and there is no additional Bar exam for future advocates.

Because performance in the state exams is treated by employers as an objective measure of quality, it is the most important influence on legal careers, which are not significantly shaped by performance at university.[13] The advocates' profession has no control over supply: everyone who passes the second state examination has a constitutional right to be admitted as long as there are no personal incompatibilities.

In 2017/18, 21,646 students entered law faculties, which enrolled a total of 116,217. In 2016, 9,353[14] passed the first examination and 8,693 the second. The number of law students rose following reunification (which increased demand for lawyers), fell in the 2000s, and recently started rising again, although most of the growth is not in legal

---

[11] The only European country with a similar system is Slovenia (Kilian 2010).

[12] The average duration of legal studies is five years. Those who take the exam after four years can do so three times, all others twice. Since 2003, students had to choose a specialist subject at university, which counted for 30 per cent of the first examination. Because university grades were higher and deemed less reliable than those in the state examination, most employers only used the latter. The Conference of the Ministers of Justice is considering giving the university examinations less weight.

[13] Unlike the situation in most countries, the reputation of law faculties therefore has relatively little impact on employment opportunities and career development in Germany.

[14] This low figure is due to low enrolment in the preceding decade.

programmes that allow students to sit the state examinations. About 30 per cent of those taking the first examination fail; overall, half of those who begin legal studies drop out. Ten per cent of the successful candidates do not continue to the second examination, where the pass rate is 82–88 per cent (Schultz et al 2018: 214 ff; Kilian and Dreske 2018). The top mark – which used to be the entrance ticket for the judiciary and positions in international law firms[15] – is achieved by only 17 per cent in the first examination and slightly more in the second. Although women were 56 per cent of law students, a higher proportion of them fail the first state exam, and more men get top marks (Schultz et al 2018; Towfigh et al 2014). Each year, between 1,300 and 1,700 students (60 per cent of them male) earn a doctorate (a prerequisite for an academic career[16] and a significant advantage in the legal labour market).

Although advocates have outnumbered judges for more than 100 years, and today there are roughly eight advocates for each judge (see Table 1), legal education has not shifted its focus to the legal practice of advocates. State legal education legislation and the Federal Statute on Judges (*Deutsches Richtergesetz*) set the rules for the examinations and the expected outcome. There are no curricula that use competence-oriented definitions of pedagogic objectives. Because law professors are primarily scholars, students experience a theory-practice gap, or rather a teaching-examination gap, which is filled by commercial *Repetitoren* (private coaches).[17] For many years, the German Advocates Association argued that practical training should be divided into different branches for the legal occupations, each of which would end with a qualifying examination, but this failed to attract support from policymakers and other stakeholders. The main argument against differentiation into specialised training systems is that it is beneficial for members of each legal profession to get a better understanding of the legal practice in the others.

Law students tend to be highly motivated to study a subject they view as difficult (RuhrUniversität 2012: 9). Students experience deficits in communication with teachers and fellow students (Schultz et al 2018; Schultz 2018b). Compared with other faculties, law receives the least favourable scores in categories such as competitive behaviour among students, overcrowding, disintegration, isolation and depersonalisation (Ramm et al 2014). Rigid marking of tests and examinations intensifies pressure. Final oral examinations have been described as a 'conformity test' to see whether the candidate's thought processes fit the appropriate pattern of 'perceiving, thinking and judging' (Schultz 2011; 2018b; Böning 2017). The state examinations serve as particularly powerful status transitions or rites of passage (Schultz 2011). The 8–10 years of legal education socialise students to internalise the qualities expected from civil servants and create a strong *esprit de corps*. And German jurists are socially homogeneous, traditionally coming from the middle and upper-middle class, with an overrepresentation of parents in the civil service (Schultz et al 2018: 205 ff).

---

[15] A decline in the number of law students and thus legal clerks (of about 30 per cent since 2001) has forced employers to lower the bar when hiring.
[16] The academy remains a male bastion in which women occupy only 15 per cent of the full chairs (Schultz et al 2018).
[17] 86 per cent of all law students attend (and pay for) commercial *Repetitoren* in preparation for the first state examination (Kilian 2015a).

Although law graduates do not have to choose a career until they complete their traineeships, typically in their late 20s, subsequent career changes are rare (except for transfers between advocates and in-house counsel). Due to age limits in the civil service,[18] only junior advocates can switch careers during the first years in practice to become a career judge, prosecutor or civil servant. And after working for several years, the latter three rarely become advocates for fear of losing the vested rights enjoyed by civil servants.

Passing the state examinations has traditionally been regarded as a sufficient quality stamp for life, resulting in a lack of formalised continuing legal education. Only recently have the German Advocates Association and the Federal Chamber of Advocates begun to lobby for the introduction of CLE for advocates to guarantee the quality of legal services and thereby justify the high access barriers to the legal services market that result from the two state examinations (Kilian 2016b; 2017b).[19]

IV. OTHER LEGAL PROFESSIONALS AND LEGAL OCCUPATIONS

A. *Syndikusrechtsanwälte*

A subspecies of advocates who serve as in-house counsel was created in 2016 through an amendment of the Federal Advocates' Act (Kilian 2014a). Previously, in-house counsel could be members of the chamber of advocates but could not represent employers in court, claim legal privilege for their in-house work, or belong to the advocates' pension fund[20] (as a result of a 2014 decision of the Federal Social Court, see Kilian 2014a). All this is now permitted, but once admitted, *Syndikusrechtsanwälte* may work in that capacity only for their employers and in criminal proceedings and may not claim legal professional privilege. Providing legal services to third parties requires admission as a traditional advocate (which about 90 per cent of *Syndikusrechtsanwälte* have). On 1 January 2018, 14,054 *Syndikusrechtsanwälte* had been admitted (although a much larger number work as in-house counsel without admission, providing legal services solely to an employer).

B. Bachelor's and Master's in Law

In the 1990s, universities of applied sciences (*Fachhochschulen/polytechnics*) created bachelor's and master's programmes for commercial law and, later, for general legal

---

[18] In order not to discriminate against women who start careers in the judiciary or civil service later or interrupt their careers to bear and raise children, the age limits have been raised from 32–35 to 40–45 in three federal states and 50 in the federal government.

[19] Until the advocate's rule-making body obtains statutory authority to regulate CLE, advocates have been encouraged by the German Advocates Association and the Federal Chamber of Advocates to attend courses on a voluntary basis. Both issue an icon attesting attendance at CLE courses, which can be used for marketing.

[20] Which offers generous compensation and pensions because few lawyers are rendered redundant or incapacitated, and the life expectancy of advocates is lower than that in the general population.

studies (which has grown in popularity). Law faculties at universities and ministries of justice initially resisted, fearing that the state's control over legal education could erode. University law faculties now also offer those degrees, some as an intermediate examination, others as a degree course for a specific area of law. Those holding a bachelor's and/or master's degree may not sit the state legal exams. Degree holders cannot offer legal services to the general public under the Legal Services Act, be admitted as advocates, or appear before courts that mandate legal representation.

In 2017, 17,098 students were enrolled in such programmes at universities of applied sciences (almost twice as many as ten years earlier) and 5,494 at universities (where they were less than 5 per cent of all law students). An increasing number of universities of applied sciences offer these programmes, some through distance study.[21] In 2017, 86 per cent of law students at universities of applied sciences were studying commercial law, hoping for employment as a *Wirtschaftsjurist* in-house counsel or employment by advocates, tax advisers, and insolvency practitioners, all of which would find them cheaper than *Volljuristen* (whose training in criminal, public or procedural law is of little relevance to such employers).

Universities of applied sciences also offer work-integrated courses for assistant judges and prosecutors (*Rechtspfleger*), focusing on procedural law, cost calculation, and probate and other non-contentious procedures. *Rechtspfleger* (whose numbers approximately equal those of judges and prosecutors) may leave the judiciary to work in law firms and other positions in the civil service, although such a move is rare.

C. *Rechtsbeistände*

For a hundred years non-academic legal advisers could be licensed by the court administration to provide legal services to the public on proof of their legal knowledge and reliability. The last licences were issued in 1980, when the profession was abolished. On 1 January 2018, only 222 legal advisers remain licensed.

D. *Registrierte Rechtsdienstleister*

Registered legal service providers are a variant of legal advisers, limited to the three areas (foreign law, pension law and debt collection) designated in the Legal Services Act of 2008 (Kilian 2012c). Their licences are based on proof of knowledge of one of those areas and a test of reliability. In December 2018, 244 were licensed for foreign law, 854 for pension law and 2,131 for debt collection. Registered legal service providers cannot represent clients in court.

---

[21] Studying law at universities of applied sciences may have become more attractive because the programmes are shorter, more structured and practice-oriented and have lower drop-out rates. They may also appeal to many secondary school graduates belonging to Generations Y and Z (Kilian 2015a), who are considered less career-oriented, less interested in financial rewards and more focused on work-life balance and meaningful work than the members of Generation X or baby-boomers, who currently dominate the legal professions.

E. Para-Professionals (*Rechtsanwaltsfachangestellte*)

Paralegals trained in both legal matters and law practice management also perform tasks requiring knowledge of the law and legal procedures, mostly in cost law and debt collection, as well as secretarial functions (Kilian 2018b). Based on the German tradition of a dual education system, the three-year intensive training combines apprenticeship with vocational education, which is regulated by law and controlled by the chambers of advocates. After a couple of years of practice legal assistants can qualify as senior legal assistants (*Fachwirt*), who generally become practice managers in smaller firms.

Despite the fact that the number of advocates (and therefore potential employers) doubled between 1997 and 2017, the number of new paralegal apprenticeship contracts nearly halved, from almost 9,000 to 4,611. Relatively low salaries, the emergence of other apprenticeship career tracks and the rise of legal studies at universities of applied sciences have contributed to the decline of paralegal apprenticeships. Traditionally it was a poorly remunerated women's occupation in solo practices and small firms. Many paralegals leave employment for better paid jobs in the legal departments of banks and insurance companies or in the public sector, forcing law firms to employ mostly older, unskilled office staff without legal training.

V. THE PRACTICE OF ADVOCATES

A. Changing Scope of Practice

In recent decades there has been a shift of advocates from traditional general legal practice in small firms operating at a strictly local level engaged mostly in litigation to specialised legal practice on a national, sometimes even international, level in larger law firms with a stronger focus on legal advice. The number of solo practitioners remains high, however, and litigation is an important part of the legal work of general practitioners. Although the Federal Advocates' Act, fee regulation, and rules about specialist accreditation emphasise representation in court, advocates spend an average of just 26 per cent of their time on court-related cases, 33 per cent on out-of-court representation, 35 per cent on giving legal advice, providing legal opinions or drafting legal documents, and the rest mostly on alternative dispute resolution. A total of 9 per cent of advocates do no court work, and only 8 per cent spend the majority of their time on it. On average, German advocates attend court only six times a month, the majority of them only once or twice a month (Kilian 2016a).

The declining importance of court-related work can be explained partly by the fact that between 2000 and 2016, litigation declined 32 per cent while the number of advocates grew 57 per cent. In civil, family and employment law, which generate 80 per cent of German advocates' caseload, the number of lawsuits fell 30.5 per cent during this period. Cases in criminal and fiscal courts have also declined. These changes are attributable to the growing complexity of the legal system and litigation caused by the expanding legal literature and number of precedents, which increase the cost and length of proceedings, making out-of-court settlements more attractive. The Ministries of Justice have started to discuss simplified procedures for small claims (eg up to €2,000) to improve access to justice and generate more court work.

Table 2 Number of Court Cases Filed and Number of Advocates

Year	Civil (incl Family)	Employment	Criminal	Administrative	Advocates
2000	1,452,245	524,845	840,325	366,397	104,067
2005	1,400.724	521,769	874,703	405,522	132,569
2010	1,213,093	692,298	776,447	391,460	153,251
2015	1,093,454	654,382	664,867	329,639	163,513
2016	986,139	617,859	670,036	347,169[22]	163,779

Source: Federal Statistical Office, Federal Ministry of Justice (Judicial Statistics).

The declining importance of court work for advocates has created challenges. It constituted the core of advocates' identity: what they are trained for and where they still enjoy a monopoly (albeit one that has shrunk). The Federal Advocates Fees Act stipulates higher fees for court work than for the often time consuming out-of-court representation. Legal expenses insurance policies and state legal aid focus on court work and either do not cover legal advice or pay low fees.[23]

B. Data[24]

The average age of German advocates is 50. Men have an average of 21 years of professional experience, women have 17, and 34 per cent of advocates are female. Some 60.5 per cent of advocates practise in cities of 100,000 or more, where only a third of Germans live. Advocates work an average of 51 hours a week; 24 per cent (most of them women) work part-time. A total of 39 per cent of advocates work in a law firm owned by one person. Of those working in a partnership, 74 per cent are in a local partnership, 26 per cent in a transregional partnership. The majority of law firms are small: 43 per cent have 2–5 practitioners, 12 per cent have 6–10, and 6 per cent each have 11–20 and more than 20. The balance (33 per cent) are solo practitioners. Only 7,471 advocates (4.5 per cent) work at the 30 largest firms. In 2018, 551 advocates practised at the largest German law firm, CMS Hasche Sigle, which would barely make it into the UK's TOP 30; the tenth largest had 266.

In terms of employment status, 81 per cent of advocates are owners or partners of their firms, 14 per cent are employees, and 5 per cent are freelancers. However, two-thirds of new entrants begin their careers as law firm employees. That employment generally is a transitional role is shown by the fact that employees are on average 39 years old, while partners are 52. After eight years in practice only a third of those who began as employees are still employed advocates, since most firms follow the 'up or out' principle (Kilian 2012a).

---

[22] Since 2015 the number of cases has started to rise in administrative courts because of migration and the refugee crisis and in social courts due to new social legislation.
[23] Clients can also avoid financial risks from litigation by involving litigation funders who ask for approximately 30 per cent of the recovery. Litigation funding, however, is still a niche phenomenon in Germany (where losing parties must pay their own costs, court fees, and the other party's costs based on full scale fees).
[24] Based on empirical data published in Kilian (2016a); see also Prognos (2013).

Larger transregional and international firms now have several career steps: (1) associate; (2) non-equity or salaried partner or counsel; and (3) partner (fixed-share/regional/associated/junior or full). In response to Generation Y demands, large firms have started to introduce positions with a fixed number of working hours for a reduced salary, adjustable up or down, which are occupied mainly by women.

The type of client varies: 50 per cent are consumers, 42 per cent businesses and 8 per cent institutions (public service or non-profit organisations). The largest sub-group are repeat customers with infrequent legal problems, followed by those with recurring legal problems. Advocates deal with about 200 matters per year, more than half of them court cases. They spend an average of 42 per cent of their working time on files, 21 per cent on interviews and meetings with clients, 11 per cent on meetings and interviews with third parties, 11 per cent on court appearances, 8 per cent on law practice management, and 6 per cent on continuing legal education. Around 50–60 per cent of advocates use information technology, mainly management and voice recognition software, and 75 per cent use legal research tools; 70 per cent have a website.

The majority of firms are still organised as general partnerships (*Gesellschaften bürgerlichen Rechts*) (Kilian 2018a). In 2018, 893 firms were incorporated as private limited companies (GmbH or UG) and 24 as public limited companies (*Aktiengesellschaften*). 2,669 were limited partnerships (*Partnerschaftsgesellschaften*), 1,983 limited liability partnerships (*Partnerschaftsgesellschaft mit beschränkter Berufshaftung*) and 145 UK/US LLPs. Shareholders and partners must be advocates, tax advisers and accountants. The rules on multi-disciplinary partnerships (MDPs) will be relaxed soon as a result of a Constitutional Court ruling on the lawfulness of an MDP between advocates and health care professionals (Kilian 2016c). The relaxation of professional rules on external ownership has been discussed but is strongly resisted by the Federal Chamber of Advocates and the German Advocates Association (Kilian 2018a).

C. Liability, Fees and Income

Advocates are liable for breach of contractual duties. They are under a statutory duty to carry malpractice insurance (*Berufshaftpflicht*) with a minimum coverage of €250,000; 86 per cent take out additional cover: an average of €1.7m and a median of €1m (Kilian 2015b). A waiver of liability can be agreed with a client but is rare because of the stringent requirements; only 12 per cent of advocates use it more than occasionally (Kilian 2015b). The incidence of liability claims is not published by the insurance industry; anecdotal evidence suggests that on average an advocate refers a liability case to an insurer every four years (Kilian 2015b).[25]

In terms of average turnover for advocates, 42 per cent derives from court work and 57 per cent from extrajudicial work. They earn 33 per cent of their income from hourly fees, 17 per cent from flat-rate agreements and the rest according to scale fees. The overall turnover generated on the German legal services market by law firms was €18.2bn in 2016 (Kilian and Dreske 2018). Legal aid expenditure of the federal states was approximately

---

[25] For 1997 see Schultz (1997).

€500m in 2016,[26] with almost 90 per cent spent on cases in civil courts (and 50 per cent of those on family law) (Kilian and Dreske 2018).[27] Legal expenses insurers paid out €3.83bn in the same year (this figure also contains – to a lesser extent – expenditure on court fees) (Kilian and Dreske 2018), making Germany the largest legal expenses insurance market in the world.[28] As both legal aid and legal expenses insurance are almost exclusively relevant in the consumer submarket, advocates serving this type of client generate a significant portion of their income from third-party funding of legal services.

In 2016, 13 per cent of advocates had an annual turnover of less than €50,000, 20 per cent €50,000–99,999, 30 per cent €100,000–199,999, 18 per cent €200,000–299,999, and 19 per cent higher. The average turnover was €172,000 (median €107,000) for solo practitioners, €885,000 (median €494,000) for local firms, and €12,897,000 (median €1,000,000) for transregional and international law firms. The figures are much lower in the former GDR.[29] An average of 51 per cent of the turnover is spent on overheads. In 2016, employed advocates working 41–57 hours per week earned an average of €66,000 a year, those working less than 40 hours a week earned €53,000 and those working more than 58 hours per week €121,000. Freelancers earned €50,000 and in-house lawyers (*Syndikusrechtsanwälte*) €94,000. The average personal hourly pre-tax profit in law firms is €50 (€53 in the West and €41 in the East). The disparity between East and West is mainly due to differences in economic structure. Advocates in the East are also less specialised and have fewer commercial clients; more are solo practitioners, and the average partnership is much smaller.[30]

D. Specialisation

Advocates have experienced a shift from general practice to specialisation (Kilian 2017c). Although specialisation began in the 1920s, until recently most advocates offered services in several areas, often to both individuals and businesses (Hommerich and Kilian 2011; Kilian 2017c). In 1986, the legislature responded to pressure from professional organisations by creating an accreditation scheme for specialisation in administrative, employment, social security, and tax law, mirroring the four specialised courts. After the power to create accreditations was delegated to the profession's rule-making body, other specialties were

---

[26] Unlike other countries, Germany did not expand legal aid in the 1970s. It remains demand driven, but it is means tested, and parties must repay the costs if their financial situation improves and pay the other party's advocate if they lose.

[27] Criminal legal aid in the traditional sense, ie subject to a means test, does not exist in Germany. Instead, there is a system of 'forced representation' in place regardless of the means of a defendant.

[28] With 22 million contracts in 2017. Source: de.statista.com/statistik/daten/studie/6599/umfrage/vertragsbestand-der-rechtsschutzversicherung-seit-1990/.

[29] Figures for former West Germany: solo practitioners €164.000 (median €113.000), local firms €976,000 (median €550,000), transregional and international firms €19,684,000 (median €1,400,000). For the former East Germany the respective turnovers are: €187,000 (median €96,000), €516,000 (median €340,000), and €1,506,000 (median €530,000). In the West average turnover in all law firms rose from €413,000 in 2001 to €673,000 in 2016, while in the East it increased from €260,000 to €308,000.

[30] Data from STAR 2018 (*Statistisches Berichtssystem für Rechtsanwälte*), representative empirical research on the professional situation of advocates, commissioned every three years by the Federal Chamber of Advocates) available at www.brak.de/fuer-journalisten/star-bericht/.

added in 1994 and 2003, including traffic, insurance, information technology, intellectual property and banking law. In 2018, there were 23 accredited specialties, 18 in areas handled by courts of general jurisdiction. The latest, designated in 2016, was immigration law, when the rule-making process was fast-tracked in response to the European refugee crisis (two years later 66 advocates had been accredited). Accreditation requires theoretical training, examinations, and proof of work on a specific number of matters over a three-year period, some in court. In 2018, 55,274 accreditations were current, held by 43,419 advocates (8,864 advocates held two and 895 the maximum of three). Accreditation has been found to make advocates more attractive to clients, increase turnover, and narrow the scope of practice. It is most common in mid-sized firms, large enough to permit specialisation but too small to create a brand based on the reputations of the firm (or its rainmakers), rather than those of individual advocates (Kilian 2017b). Accredited advocates must give proof of relevant further education annually. Other advocates do not have that obligation.

Accredited specialisation, however, is only the visible tip of the iceberg. Among practising advocates (estimated at fewer than 110,000 of the 164,156 registered advocates), two-thirds regard themselves as specialists, but less than a third hold an accreditation (Kilian 2016a; 2017b). Some advocates specialise by clientele rather than legal area (Kilian 2013a), an approach that is more profitable and better serves client needs (Kilian 2016a).

The number of *Rechtsanwälte* with a dual qualification as auditors (*Wirtschaftsprüfer*) (639), tax advisers (2,151), and certified accountants (402) also has risen in the last two decades, probably due to the increased demand from the growing number of larger and multidisciplinary firms.

The shift to specialisation by judges started later (Kilian 2017c). Since 2018, regional courts of first instance and appeals courts must create specialised chambers for a number of legal areas (before that they had no such obligation but could do so if they saw a need).

E. Women Advocates[31]

Since 2005, more women than men have studied law. Over the last 30 years women ranked law 2–4 among preferred subjects, whereas men ranked it 4–6. Law students increased from 5.2 to 6.9 per cent of all women students between 1975 and 2015 but decreased from 8.7 to 5.9 per cent among men. Although women used to be much more likely than men to drop out, there is not much difference now.

Feminisation of the profession started late. The first woman was admitted in 1922. In 1933, just 114 of the 18,766 advocates were female. After seizing power in 1933, the National Socialists expelled all women from practice and barred them from the state-controlled practical training and the judiciary.

Their numbers rose slowly in the first three decades after World War II, gaining speed only in the 1980s with the deterioration of job prospects in the public sector, which women traditionally had preferred (Schultz 2003a). In 2017, women were, for

---

[31] See Schultz (2003b; 2003c; 2013; 2018).

the first time, more than half of newly admitted *Rechtsanwälte* (52 per cent), although at the end of that year only 35 per cent of *Rechtsanwälte* were women. The number of women who are *Anwaltsnotare* is rising while the total number declines. Solo notaries were a very male profession, with high marks in the second examination constituting an entry barrier in the former West Germany. The socialist notariat in Eastern Germany had been feminised (67.8 per cent in 1989) but enjoyed little prestige, and notaries were poorly paid (Shaw 2003). At reunification the Western-style notariat was extended to the East.

Table 3 Increase in Women in the *Rechtsanwaltschaft* and *Notariat*

	Women as percentage of Advocates (*Rechtsanwältinnen*)	Increase in all Advocates: percentage and (absolute)	Increase in female Advocates: percentage and (absolute)	Women as percentage of Advocate-notaries (*Anwaltsnotarinnen*)	Women as percentage of solo notaries (*Nur-Notarinnen*)
1985	12.0			4.4	
1991	16.1			4.9	14.4
1997	21.2	96–97: 8.0 (6,283)	14.3 (2,261)	7.9	18.7
2000	24.6	99–00: 6.4 (6,276)	10.6 (2,450)	8.4	18.4
2005	28.6	04–05: 4.6 (5,776)	7.8 (2,759)	9.7	19.6
2010	31.5	09–10: 1.9 (2,874)	3.6 (1,657)	10.5	
2015	33.6	14–15: 0.5 (875)	1.4 (773)	12.7	
2016	33.9	15–16: 0.2 (259)	1.0 (562)	13.8	
2018	34.8	17–18: 0.2 (303)	1.3 (749)	16.5 (904)	24*

Source: Official Statistics of the Federal Chamber of Advocates and the Federal Chamber of Notaries published annually in *BRAK-Mitteilungen*.
*Data for 2017.

The proportion of judges and public prosecutors who are women has been rising faster than the proportion of the *Rechtsanwaltschaft* for many years. In 2017, 52 per cent of newly admitted advocates were women, compared with 58 per cent of probationary judges and 59 per cent of probationary prosecutors (those in the first three years of practice after admission). Women prefer the judiciary and civil service for their social status, predictable workload, and benefits, including parental leave, the right to part-time work, inexpensive insurance for private healthcare and a generous pension.

Table 4 Proportion of Women in the Legal Professions

	Women (*Anwältinnen*) as percentage of Advocates	Women (*Richterinnen*) as percentage of Judges	Women (*Staatsanwältinnen*) as percentage of Public Prosecutors
1960	<2.0	2.6	
1970	4.5	6.0	5.0
1980	8.0	13.0	11.0
1989	14.7	17.6	17.6
2001*	25.3	27.7	30.9
2011	38.5	41.0	32.0
2017	34.4	44.5	45.9

Source: Federal Ministry of Justice (Judicial Statistics).
*In 1997 the judicial statistics changed from counting heads to counting full-time equivalents. Because many women judges work part-time, the actual percentage of judges who are women is higher.

Women advocates are younger, have fewer years of practice, and prefer to work in big cities or small towns (Kilian and Hoffmann 2018). A higher proportion of women than men leave the profession. Women plan more career breaks and try to find employment in less conventional settings, such as associations (non-profit societies, service organisations, interest groups, and trade unions). Women are overrepresented among in-house counsel.[32] Compared with men, women are more often solo practitioners and less often partners (ibid). In the 200 largest firms, women comprised 43 per cent of associates, 31.2 per cent of counsel, 27.4 per cent of non-equity partners, and 10.7 per cent of equity partners (Schultz et al 2018).

A higher proportion of female advocates than male characterise themselves as specialists (75 versus 69 per cent) (Kilian and Hoffmann 2018). This does not translate into a higher share of official accreditations for specialisation: only 29.5 per cent of all accredited specialisations are held by women, who make up 35 per cent of advocates. Because accreditation for specialisation is based on work on a defined number of cases over a three-year period, women are at a disadvantage since they work part-time more often than men (Kilian and Hoffmann 2018; Schultz 2018a). When women receive accreditation, it is in less rewarding fields, such as family law (where 58 per cent of all accreditations in 2018 were held by women), social law (43 per cent) and health law (39 per cent). Men specialise in tax, administrative, insolvency, business, building, IP, copyright, IT and banking law (areas where women hold less than 20 per cent of the accreditations) (Kilian and Hoffmann 2018; Schultz 2018a).

There is a marked gender pay difference associated with other variables: age, place of work, form of practice, specialisation, share of notarial functions, and positions in partnerships and companies. Among full-time advocates in 2016, men earned €123,000 and women €74,000 The income gap has widened in recent years. Women

---

[32] In 2017, women were 43 per cent of *Syndikusrechtsanwälte* and 54 per cent of *Syndikusanwälte*.

have fewer corporate clients and more legal aid cases; a higher proportion of their income is derived from statutory fees, less from fee arrangements, and a lower proportion from hourly fees, which are also lower than those of men (Kilian and Hoffmann 2018; Schultz 2018a).

The profession only recently started to address these differences. In the past, women had simply been expected to integrate. Professional rules ignore them, speaking and thinking of *Rechtsanwälte* (male form) not of *Rechtsanwältinnen* (female form). There are no specific anti-discrimination rules[33] or official recommendations on how to combine family and work, maternity leave, part-time work, the workplace or flexible working hours. Some of the larger international firms offer special working conditions for members with family obligations. But those who exercise these options (especially men) may jeopardise their reputations as high performers. Some firms have created positions for knowledge or professional support lawyers, who perform back-office work, enjoying family-friendly working hours and workloads but at the expense of career advancement and pay. Women's participation became a general subject of the national advocates conference for the first time in 2018 (Schultz 2018a).

Women also hit the glass ceiling in the judiciary, although their share of higher positions (presiding judges at appeal courts, court presidents, federal court judges) and comparable positions among prosecutors has increased to 25–33 per cent in recent years (Schultz 2013; Schultz et al 2018: 187 ff). The entire German civil service has gender quotas and European anti-discrimination rules administered by equal opportunities officers, but these are not very effective in filling leading positions.

F. Diversity

Few children of former *Gastarbeiter* (guest workers recruited in the 1960s–80s) have entered the legal profession. Most of them practise alone or in small firms, often serving their ethnic communities. Overall, immigrants form 20–25 per cent of the population in the former West Germany and 6 per cent in the former East Germany and are increasing rapidly as a result of massive migration from poorer European countries and the refugee crisis.

Germany was slow in addressing LGBTI issues. As late as 1974 a man was refused admission as an advocate for being homosexual. Decades ago a federal prosecutor founded a group of gay jurists, which lobbied for gay rights but was generally ignored. After the turn of the millennium the situation changed, with the election of a gay mayor in Berlin and appointment of a gay foreign minister, greatly raising public awareness. In line with Western European developments, LGBTI are socially accepted, and discriminatory rules have been abolished. After employers found that the rainbow factor offered a competitive advantage,[34] LGBTI career fairs have been held since 2014 and a LGBTI network and career portal has been created.[35]

---

[33] Of course, the general anti-discrimination rules apply; but there are only a handful of cases where these are known to have mattered.
[34] www.lto.de/recht/job-karriere/j/homosexualitaet-lgbt-arbeitsmarkt-juristen-anwaelte-kanzleien-diversity/.
[35] See alice.lgbt.

VI. REGULATORY REFORM

The 1980s and 1990s saw the emergence of significant tensions within the profession as a result of the growing gap between the more conventional solo practitioners and small firms on one side and the international and big firms on the other, which had different regulatory needs. Many of the questions which have been raised in the last 30 years have been solved by landmark decisions of the Federal Constitutional Court, European Court of Justice, and German Supreme Court and by policy initiatives of the European Commission in the 1980s and 1990s (Kilian 2017a; Schultz 2005), which were the drivers of reform. The professional organisations played a minor role in this process, and the Bundestag basically followed the court decisions (Kilian 2012c). We discuss three of the main points of dispute, which led to profound change.

A. Practice Rules and Legal Ethics: The End of a Self-Limiting Self-Regulation

Advocates, like many professions, had promulgated a code of conduct (so-called guidelines) regulating legal practice and forming the basis for disciplinary sanctions ranging from reprimand to disbarment (Kilian 2017b; Schultz 1997). The first code published in 1929 by the German Advocates Association merely restated and clarified legislation and case law for the benefit of newly admitted advocates, without offering a binding set of rules. After World War II the German Federal Chamber of Advocates enacted rules of conduct (most recently in 1982) based on a vote of the then 23 regional chambers, which had been tasked with identifying good legal practice. The code was still a small booklet but complemented by more than a thousand pages of commentary by practitioners. Discipline was based on it (Kilian 2017b; Schultz 1997). Over time it had prevented the profession from adapting to an expanding legal services market and offering careers to the rapidly multiplying new advocates. In a landmark ruling on 14 July 1987 (colloquially known as the Bastille judgement, Kilian 2012b), the Federal Constitutional Court held that decisions of the disciplinary courts[36] violated the 'guarantee of occupational freedom' in Article 12 of the Basic Law because any infringement of a constitutional right had to be based on a law passed by the democratically elected Parliament representing the will of the people (*Gesetzesvorbehalt*) (Kilian 2017a). This effectively ended self-regulation by advocates (Kilian 2012b). In 1994, Parliament finally passed the new Federal Advocates' Act (*BRAO*),[37] leaving limited scope for regulatory action by the profession. A statutory assembly of the profession (*Satzungsversammlung*) may pass rules on matters enumerated in the *BRAO* but can only supplement and implement that statute, subject to a test of constitutionality. These Rules of Professional Conduct (*Berufsordnung BORA*) have just 34 provisions, most concerning issues of little importance to or impact on the legal services market (eg rules on how law firm members' names may be displayed on a letterhead).

---

[36] Disciplinary courts (*Anwaltsgerichte* or advocates' courts) are independent from the chambers of advocates and a branch of the judiciary, although advocates serve as lay judges. For data on disciplinary proceedings resulting from unethical behaviour, see statistics compiled by Kilian and Dreske (2018). In 2016, advocates' courts had to deal with 710 procedures.

[37] For an English version see www.brak.de/w/files/02_fuer_anwaelte/berufsrecht/brao-stand-6-12-2011-mit-korr-191f-2014.pdf.

In more than 100 cases, the new *BRAO* was closely scrutinised by the Federal Constitutional Court, which annulled some of its provisions and their application by regional chambers of advocates and lower courts, forcing Parliament to rectify their constitutional shortcomings (Kilian 2017a). The court invalidated (for restricting the occupational freedom of advocates) the prohibition of MDPs,[38] limitations on advocates' freedom of expression, the rule against directly contacting an adversary represented by another advocate, the sale of legal services on eBay, the duty to maintain a law office, rules about advertising content, the use of slogans by law firms, imputed disqualification as a result of a conflict of interest, and the century-old system of admitting advocates to either civil courts of first instance or courts of appeal (Kilian 2017a). A good example of how the court compelled the profession to change was its 1993 decision about which professional activities were incompatible with the practice of law (*Zweitberufsentscheidung*). Although the chambers had traditionally allowed only activities whose prestige was comparable to that of advocates, the court held that all activities enjoyed the constitutional guarantee of occupational freedom and thus were permissible, absent a conflict of interest in the individual case. A disadvantage of the central role of the Federal Constitutional Court in these reforms is that it can hear only cases that are submitted by a complainant (or lower court judge) and meet rather complex procedural requirements; this results in a patchwork of decisions instead of coherent policy-based development. An advantage is that the court is much less subject than the Bundestag to lobbying by a profession resisting change, particularly since advocates are not represented on the bench. (Of more than 100 judges appointed to the court since 1949, only four have been former advocates.)

The erosion of the profession's self-regulatory power contrasts with the important role it plays in legislation. The German Advocates Association and the Federal Chamber of Advocates are among the organisations and interest groups that provide the largest number of evaluations of government bills. Over a three-year period in 2014–17, the German Advocates Association rendered 92 advisory opinions; only the Association of German Chambers of Industry and Commerce, the Federation of German Industries and the German Trade Union Confederation were more active. During the same period, the Federal Chamber of Advocates offered comments 84 times, making it the seventh most active interest group in Parliament.

B. Authorised and Unauthorised Practice of Law

Another example of the Constitutional Court shaping professional practice was its decision on the 'Law to Prevent Malpractice in the Provision of Legal Services' (*RBerG*). Over the course of 70 years, regulation of legal services evolved from a very liberal approach to an iron-clad monopoly and back to a more liberal model. Before 1935, the provision of legal services, like any other business or profession, was not governed by specific

---

[38] Although interprofessional partnerships with pharmacists and doctors are permitted: decision of the Federal Constitutional Court, 12 January 2016.

regulations but subject only to a 'test of reliability' of the provider under the 1869 Code of Commerce (*Gewerbeordnung*) (Rücker 2007). Only court-related work and notarial services were reserved for admitted advocates or notaries. The economic crisis of the late 1920s led to calls from the German Advocates Association (DAV) to introduce a licensing system linked to qualification requirements (Ostler 1982). The Nazi government finally passed a 'Law to Prevent Malpractice in the Provision of Legal Services' (RBerG), which prohibited Jews from being admitted as legal advisers[39] and allowed the government to control legal service providers' representation of citizens by requiring a licence from the court administration. As a result, for decades thereafter legal services remained a reserved activity for admitted advocates, notaries and tax advisers; non-lawyers were hardly ever licensed.

In 2008, a new Legal Services Act (*Rechtsdienstleistungsgesetz*) came into force, relaxing the rules on unauthorised practice of law and letting alternative service providers offer legal services on the fringes of the market (Kilian 2012c). Beginning in the late 1980s, unlicensed legal service providers had invoked the constitutional guarantee of occupational freedom under Article 12 of the Basic Law to challenge the rules on unauthorised practice of law in cases involving property developers unlawfully assisting buyers to transfer title, probate researchers dealing with inheritance law, the operation of a monitoring system tracking the expiration of patents, debt collection, radio call-in shows offering legal advice, and retired judges advising conscientious objectors (Schönberger 2003). While accepting that unauthorised practice rules could promote the common good, the Federal Constitutional Court identified a number of cases where it did not. It found that fully-trained law graduates, even if not admitted as advocates, should be able to offer free legal advice. It also ruled that incidental legal advice was lawful if essential for the provision of non-legal professional service. Because the Constitutional Court's decision addressed only out-of-court legal services, the rules on the right of audience in court remained unchanged by the ensuing reforms: court work is still a reserved activity for advocates, and parties still must be represented by advocates in most court proceedings (except local civil courts of first instance and first instance social, administrative and labour courts).

Advocates had expected or even feared that the 2008 reform might adversely affect the legal services market, but relatively few non-advocates have been willing to take the risk of giving legal advice to their customers in conjunction with another service (eg architects in building and construction law matters, car repair shops in traffic law matters, undertakers about inheritance law) since they would be liable for malpractice and lack insurance coverage. An unexpected effect, however, was that the reforms opened the door to law students' legal clinics under the supervision of a qualified lawyer. In 2017, 64 law clinics offered legal services at 37 of the 39 law faculties in Germany (Kilian and Wenzel 2017).

---

[39] An April 1933 Act on Admission to the Legal Profession, passed just three months after the Nazis came to power, excluded Jews from entering legal practice. A 1934 Amendment to the Legal Profession Act banned Jews from using the title Rechtsanwalt; and from 1938, Jewish jurists were only allowed to work as legal advisers for Jews. Law had been a preferred subject for Jews. In 1930, of the approximately 18,500 admitted Rechtsanwälte, 4,394 (22 per cent) were of Jewish descent; in 1933 in Berlin, 60 per cent of Rechtsanwälte had at least one Jewish grandparent (so-called 'quarter Jews') (Müller 1987).

C. Parochialism and Transregional and International Lawyering

Until well into the 1980s, legal practice was strictly local. Advocates in most federal states were admitted to either a regional court of ordinary jurisdiction or a court of appeal, resulting in distinct local sub-groups at these two levels, active in different professional spheres. An advocate had to instruct an out-of-town colleague to represent clients before any other court. The justification was to distribute advocates evenly across Germany, create trust between courts and advocates, and ensure knowledge of local peculiarities and efficient management of litigation (Kilian 2012c). Advocates had to maintain an office in the district where they were admitted and a private residence in the Court of Appeal district where they were admitted. They could belong to only one partnership, and branch offices and supraregional partnerships were forbidden. This produced strong cohesion among advocates, who also knew local judges professionally and personally.

With 60,000 advocates admitted at 115 regional courts of first instance, only a relatively small, socially coherent group of advocates practised together, even in the larger courts. But the Federal Constitutional Court invoked the right of free movement by advocates from other EU member states (pursuant to Directive 77/249/EC) to abolish the localisation principle and singular admission rule in 2000 and 2001 (Schultz 2005; Kilian 2012c). The only remaining court with a singular admission is the *Bundesgerichtshof* (BGH), the Federal Supreme Court (for civil and criminal law), with a separate Bar of just 42 members.[40]

In the 1990s, supra-regional law firms began to emerge as the result of a 1989 Federal Supreme Court ruling (Schultz 2005; Kilian 2017a). In 2007, a change in legislation also allowed branch offices of law firms for the first time (Kilian 2012c). By 2014, 15 per cent of advocates were working in a local law firm with one or more branch offices (Kilian 2016). Nevertheless, due to the late relaxation of the practice rules, in 2017 there were only 40 law firms with 100 or more advocates, and just 7 per cent of advocates worked in the 75 largest firms (Kilian 2018a).

Organisational structures of law firms also began to change during that period (Kilian 2018a). Traditionally, law firms could be established only as civil law partnerships. In 1994, advocates were allowed to incorporate in limited companies (*Gesellschaften mit beschränkter Haftung*), and in 1995 limited partnerships (*Partnerschaftsgesellschaften*) became available. Case law of the European Court of Justice at the turn of the century opened the door for UK Limited Liability Partnerships, which became the preferred organisational structure for many international law firms operating in Germany. Limited Liability Partnerships (*Partnerschaftsgesellschaften mit beschränkter Haftung*) under German law were finally introduced in 2013 (Kilian 2013b).

While the turn of the millennium saw many mergers of large German commercial law firms with even larger US or UK law firms and rapid expansion of the resulting international law firms (Henssler and Terry 2001), growth levelled off the following decade, mostly as a result of dissolutions, spin-offs and the emergence of highly specialised boutique law firms. A clash of corporate cultures between US and UK firms and the traditional attitudes and values of German professionals also contributed to this development.

---

[40] Of whom just seven (16 per cent) are women.

EU rules on freedom of establishment allow advocates from EU (and EEA) Member States to practise in Germany. If they do not pass an aptitude test (*Eignungsprüfung*)[41] or prove that the test (or part of it) is superfluous because they possess adequate knowledge of German law, they may practise in Germany only under their home professional title during the first three years. After three years of regular and effective practice in German law they can be admitted as a German *Rechtsanwälte*. In 2017 there were 659 'registered European advocates' (*niedergelassener europäischer Rechtsanwalt*) as members of the German Bar. Many specialise in particular fields of law, in both their home countries and Germany, and few represent clients in court. Advocates from WTO countries may practise only their home country's law under their home professional title (§ 206 BRAO). In 2018, 331 WTO advocates were registered, including 135 from the US, 63 from Turkey, and 21 from China.

VII. WHERE TO?

A. Numbers: From Growth to Decline?

After the end of World War II it took the profession 40 years to grow from 10,000 to 50,000 members and another 13 years to double its size. It had 100,000 members at the turn of the millennium and more than 150,000 nine years later. Since the 1980s the vast majority of those passing the second state examination became advocates (three-quarters of them in recent decades).[42] But growth in the number of advocates declined after the millennium, to 0.16 per cent[43] a year in 2017. When in-house counsels (*Syndikusrechtsanwälte*) are excluded, the number of advocates actually declined in 2017 and 2018, for the first time in more than 80 years.

Supply and demand are never perfectly synchronised. When demand was rising, school leavers were encouraged to study law; but other generations of law students and *Referendare* heard the mantra of too many lawyers. While at the turn of the millennium 10–11,000 *Referendare* passed the state examination each year, that number has declined by about a third to just 7,400, and only 4,757 new advocates were admitted in 2017.[44] Because the general population increased by 17 million through reunification in 1990, the ratio of admissions to population has fallen to the level of the early 1980s. As the large cohort of advocates who entered the profession in the late 1970s and early 1980s retire, replacements will be needed. There will be a short reprieve in the first half of the 2020s as university enrolments recover, but the demographic factor has already begun to kick in because the number of high school graduates peaked in 2013 and will (probably) decrease 20 per cent by 2025 and more thereafter. The supply of new legal professionals can be

---

[41] From 1991 to 2016, 342 advocates from other EU Member States passed the German aptitude test (and 181 failed).
[42] In the 1970s, 30 per cent joined the judiciary, but over the last three decades less than 10 per cent have done so.
[43] 1.02 per cent for women.
[44] Not all successful examinees immediately enter practice, and some advocates are admitted after a career in another profession.

maintained at present levels only if a higher percentage of high school graduates enrol in law, which is unlikely because law has become less attractive in recent decades. As law firms, courts and businesses compete for lawyers, the job market will start to favour sellers rather than buyers. Because recruitment of judges, prosecutors and notaries is based on performance in the state exams, law firms will be forced to raise salaries to attract talent. And to hire women, who constitute 57 per cent of law students, they will have to offer favourable working conditions.

There are signs that the legal market is moving from expansion to contraction. The question has never been how many lawyers are needed by society, because lawyers will create their clientele (although some professional sectors may encounter difficulties). But the advocates' knowledge monopoly has been broken. The *Wirtschaftsjuristen* have occupied a significant part of the market of in-house lawyers. Databases increase access to legal knowledge. Automated mass-processing of cases reduces specialist work; electronic files rationalise legal work. Together with electronic communication between advocates, clients and courts, legal processes are accelerated and depersonalised. Nevertheless, the profession has held its ground and opened new fields of work.

B. The German Advocate in 2030?[45]

The cohesion of advocates as a local peer group has weakened. Participation in professional governance has decreased, eg service on the board of the local bar, attendance at its general assemblies, voting in Bar elections, or volunteering as a disciplinary court judge. Participation in social events like the annual general meeting of the German Advocates Association has lost much of its appeal. Because of progressive internal differentiation and stratification, advocates no longer engage in similar work or share professional values. The common ground of a traditional (upper) middle-class ethic has been lost as the profession has become less exclusive and homogeneous. The professional ethos of total commitment is questioned by Generation Y, and the increasing proportion of women is forcing a rethinking of organisational structures.

To know who they are and where they want to go, advocates will have to examine their self-concept and self-image, resist influences and inroads from above, take responsibility, and gain self-respect as an independent force able to adapt to changing social conditions.

REFERENCES

Blankenburg, E and Schultz, U (1988) 'German Advocates: A Highly Regulated Profession' in R Abel and PSC Lewis (eds), *Lawyers in Society: Vol II The Civil Law World* (Berkeley, University of California Press) 124–59.

—— (1995) 'German Advocates: A Highly Regulated Profession' in R Abel and PSC Lewis (eds), *Lawyers in Society. An Overview* (Berkeley, University of California Press) 92–127.

Bleek, W (1972) *Von der Kameralausbildung zum Juristenprivileg* (Berlin, Colloquium).

---

[45] For the German Advocates Association's take on the profession in 2030 see the Prognos study (2013), summarised and criticised in Kilian (2014b).

Böning, A (2017) *Jura studieren. Eine explorative Untersuchung im Anschluss an Pierre Bourdieu* (Weinheim, Beltz Juventa).

Böning, A and Schultz, U (2018) 'Juristische Sozialisation' in C Boulanger and J Rosenstock (eds), *Studienbuch Interdisziplinäre Rechtsforschung* (Baden-Baden, Nomos) 191–203.

Dahrendorf, R (1965) *Gesellschaft und Demokratie in Deutschland* (Munich, Piper).

Gerold, L (2008) *The Legal Profession in Germany. Background Report for ODIHR Workshop on Reform of the Legal Profession* (Warschau) www.osce.org/odihr/36304?download=true.

Hartstang, G (1986) *Der deutsche Rechtsanwalt. Rechtsstellung und Funktion in Vergangenheit und Gegenwart* (Heidelberg, CF Müller).

Henssler, M and Terry, LS (2001) 'Lawyers Without Frontiers – A View from Germany' 19 *Dickinson Journal of International Law* 269–99.

Hommerich, C and Kilian, M (2011) *Fachanwälte* (Bonn, Anwaltverlag).

Kilian, M (2010) *Modelle der Juristenausbildung in Europa* (Bonn, Anwaltverlag).

—— (2012a) *Die junge Anwaltschaft: Ausbildung, Berufseinstieg und Berufskarrieren* (Bonn, Anwaltverlag).

—— (2012b) 'Bastille Day – the German Way' 15(1) *Legal Ethics* 123–28.

—— (2012c) *Developments in the German Legal Profession 2000–2010* (Bonn, Anwaltverlag).

—— (2013a) *Rechtsanwälte als Spezialisten und Generalisten* (Bonn, Anwaltverlag).

—— (2013b) 'Imitation is the Sincerest Form of Flattery – The New German LLP' (2013) 16(1) *Legal Ethics* 232–35.

—— (2014a) 'To Be a Lawyer or Not To Be a Lawyer, That is the Question: The German Federal Social Court's Views on In-House Lawyers' 17(3) *Legal Ethics* 448–53.

—— (2014b) 'The Future of the Lawyers' Profession' 17(1) *Legal Ethics* 138–42.

—— (2015a) *Juristenausbildung: Die Ausbildung künftiger Volljuristen in Universität und Referendariat* (Bonn, Anwaltverlag).

—— (2015b) 'Managing Liability Risks in German Law Firms in Times of Doomsday Claims' 18(1) *Legal Ethics* 87–92.

—— (2016a) *Anwaltstätigkeit der Gegenwart: Rechtsanwälte, Kanzleien, Mandate und Mandanten* (Bonn, Anwaltverlag).

—— (2016b) *Fortbildung zwischen Freiheit und Zwang – Eine Studie zur Reform der anwaltlichen Fortbildungspflicht* (Bonn, Anwaltverlag).

—— (2016c) 'All hail the MDP: the German Federal Constitutional Court paves the way for multidisciplinary service firms' 19(1) *Legal Ethics* 163–68.

—— (2017a) 'The Constitutional Court as the Driver of Change in the Regulation of Legal Professions' in A Boon (ed), *International Perspectives on the Regulation of Lawyers and Legal Services* (London, Bloomsbury).

—— (2017b) 'Legal Ethics Training Between a Rock and a Hard Place in Germany' 20(1) *Legal Ethics* 147–50.

—— (2017c) 'Germany: towards a legal profession of specialists? 20(2) *Legal Ethics* 271–77.

—— (2018a) *Die Reform des anwaltlichen Gesellschaftsrechts: Empirische Grundlagen zu einer großen BRAO-Reform* (Bonn, Anwaltverlag).

—— (2018b) *Personal in Anwaltskanzleien: Eine empirische Studie zu nicht-juristischen Mitarbeitern in deutschen Rechtsanwaltskanzleien* (Bonn, Anwaltverlag).

Kilian, M and Dreske, R (2018) *Statistisches Jahrbuch der Anwaltschaft 2017/18* (Bonn, Anwaltverlag).

Kilian, M and Hoffmann, H (2018) *Rechtsanwältinnen* (Bonn, Anwaltverlag).

Kilian, M and Kothe, F (2015), 'Speculative fees and their impact on access to justice: German experiences' 22(3) *International Journal of the Legal Profession* 244–71.

Kilian, M and Wenzel, L (2017) 'Law Clinics in Deutschland: Zahlen, Typologien und Strukturen' *Anwaltsblatt* 963–65.

McClelland, CE (1990) 'Escape from freedom? Reflections on German professionalization 1870–1933' in R Torstendahl and M Burrage (eds), *The Formation of Professions: Knowledge, State and Strategy* (London, Sage) 97–113.

Müller, I (1987) *Furchtbare Juristen* (München, Kindler).

Ostler, F (1982) *Rechtsanwälte 1871–1971* (Essen, Ellinghaus).

Prognos (2013) *Prognos Studie: Der Rechtsdienstleistungsmarkt 2030. Eine Zukunftsstudie für die deutsche Anwaltschaft* (Berlin) anwaltverein.de/de/anwaltspraxis/dav-zukunftsstudie.

Ramm, M, Multrus, F, Bargel, T and Schmidt, M (2014) *Studiensituation und studentische Orientierungen*. 12 Studierendensurvey an Universitäten und Fachhochschulen (Berlin, BMBF) www.bmbf.de/de/der-studierendensurvey-1036.html.

Roloff, J and Schultz, U (2016) *Vom Studium zur Juraprofessorin – ein Werdegang aus statistischer Sicht* (Hamburg, Dashöfer Verlag).

RuhrUniversität Bochum (2012) *Studierendenmonitoring*. Steckbrief der juristischen Fakultät. Studieneingangsbefragung WS 11/12 www.zefir.ruhr-uni-bochum.de/mam/content/fakultaetsbericht_jura_ws_11_12.pdf.

Rücker, S (2007) *Das Rechtsberatungswesen von 1919–1945 und die Entstehung des Rechtsberatungsmissbrauchgesetzes von 1935* (Tübingen, Mohr Siebeck).

Rüschemeyer, D (1973) *Lawyers and Their Society: A Comparative Study of the Legal Profession in Germany and the United States* (Cambridge, Mass: Harvard University Press).

Schönberger, C (2003) 'Rechtsberatungsgesetz und Berufsfreiheit' *Neue Juristische Wochenschrift* 249–56.

Schultz, U (1997) 'Legal Ethics in Germany' 4 *International Journal of the Legal Profession* 55–87.

—— (2003a) 'The Status of Women Lawyers in Germany' in U Schultz and G Shaw (eds), *Women in the World's Legal Profession* (Oxford, Hart Publishing) 271–91.

—— (2003b) 'Women Lawyers in Germany: Perception and Construction of Femininity' in U Schultz and G Shaw (eds), *Women in the World's Legal Profession* (Oxford, Hart Publishing) 295–321.

—— (2003c) 'Die deutsche Anwaltschaft zwischen staatlicher Gebundenheit und freiem Markt' in S Machura and S Ulbrich, *Recht, Gesellschaft, Kommunikation. Festschrift für Prof. Dr. Klaus Röhl* (Baden-Baden: Nomos) 103–17.

—— (2005) 'Regulated Deregulation – The Case of the German Legal Profession' in W Felstiner (ed), *Reorganization and Resistance: Legal Professions Confront a Changing World* (Oxford, Hart Publishing) 93–131.

—— (2011) 'Legal Education in Germany – an ever (never?) ending story of resistance to change' 4 *Revista de Educación y Derecho* 1–24 revistes.ub.edu/index.php/RED.

—— (2013) '"I was noticed and I was asked …" Women's Careers in the Judiciary. Results of an Empirical Study for the Ministry of Justice in Northrhine-Westfalia, Germany' in U Schultz and G Shaw (eds), *Gender and Judging* (Oxford, Hart Publishing) 145–66.

—— (2018a) 'Haben Frauen in der Anwaltschaft schlechte Karten? Eine rechtssoziologische Betrachtung' in *BRAK-Mitteilungen*, 223–31 www.brak.de/w/files/newsletter_archiv/berlin/2019/tn3.pdf.

—— (2018b) 'Also ward ich ein Juriste… Sozialisatorische Bedingungen und Auswirkungen des Jurist Werdens und Seins' in S Berghahn and U Schultz (eds), *Rechtshandbuch für Frauen- und Gleichstellungsbeauftragte* (Hamburg, Dashöfer).

Schultz, U, Peppmeier, I and Rudek, A (2011) *Frauen in Führungspositionen der Justiz. Eine Untersuchung der Bedingungen von Frauenkarrieren in den Justizbehörden in Nordrhein-Westfalen* (Hagen, Institut für Geschlechterforschung und Gleichstellungsrecht und – politik).

Schultz, U, Böning, A and Peppmeier, I (2017) 'Biographie und Recht' in H Lutz, M Schiebel and E Tuider (eds), *Handbuch Biografieforschung* (Wiesbaden: Springer-VS-Verlag) 339–51.

Schultz, U, Böning, A, Peppmeier, I and Schröder, S (2018) *De jure und de facto: Professorinnen in der Rechtswissenschaft. Geschlecht und Wissenschaftskarriere im Recht* (Baden-Baden, Nomos).

Shaw, G (2003) 'Women Lawyers in the New Federal States of Germany: from Quantity to Quality?' in U Schultz and G Shaw (eds), *Women in the World's Legal Profession* (Oxford: Hart Publishing) 323–39.

Towfigh, E, Traxler, C and Glöckner, A (2014) 'Zur Benotung in der Examensvorbereitung und im ersten Examen. Eine empirische Analyse' 1 *Zeitschrift für Didaktik der Rechtswissenschaft* 8–27.

Weißler, A (1905) *Geschichte der Rechtsanwaltschaft* (Leipzig, Pfeffer; reprinted Frankfurt, Sauer und Avermann 1967).

11

Italy
A Delicate Balance between Maintenance and Change

EVELYN MICELOTTA AND GABRIELLE DORIAN

I. INTRODUCTION

IN THE CONTRIBUTION by Olgiati and Pocar to *Lawyers in Society* (1988), the Italian legal profession is described as an 'institutional dilemma', highlighting two peculiar elements of modern legal professionalism in Italy. First, national institutions have played a critical role over a thousand years in shaping the profession, while maintaining a striking continuity between past and present, modernity and tradition. As Olgiati and Pocar (1988: 337) emphasise: 'the essential attributes of modern legal professions are not a direct function of economic and technological processes'. The Italian profession's 'most enduring characteristics ... are historical products of the *institutional* upheavals', such as the insurrectional movement, the Wars of Independence (the *Risorgimento*), and the proclamation of the Kingdom of Italy in 1861. These historical events have deeply affected the development of the modern legal profession in Italy, particularly through legislation affecting lawyers' interests and responsibilities.

Second, Italian lawyers' claims to practise a 'free' profession are clouded by duality, ambivalence, and ambiguity because of their 'organic dependence on the bureaucratic-administrative apparatus of the state'. In Italy, lawyers play a 'boundary role' (1988: 343). They perform a public function and enjoy a professional monopoly over a set of activities, granting them prestige and social status. Yet their role is inherently ambiguous, both public and private, enabling the state to control lawyers' activities. For example, state-controlled professional associations (ie *Ordini* and *Consiglio Nazionale Forense* or National Bar Council) complicate professional self-regulation. Similarly, bureaucratic formalities (eg taxes paid by lawyers to file documents) enable the state to derive revenue from the administration of justice.

In this chapter, we build on and extend the valuable insights of Olgiati and Pocar to show that Italy is still an unusual environment for the legal profession. We draw on an emerging body of management research on professional service firms to understand how the legal sector has evolved in the past three decades. Taking an institutional perspective, the chapter highlights the distinctiveness of the Italian legal context and the complicated contemporary relationship between the state, professional associations, and legal professionals. We focus on the challenges and opportunities that the emergence of a national and international market for corporate law firms has created for Italian and foreign legal enterprises.

We unpack these dynamics and relationships in the two sections. The first presents an overview of the legal profession in Italy: statistical data on the size and demographics of the profession, education, training, and selection, and lawyer employment. The second explores the persistence of national institutional features and professional resistance to institutional change. Italian lawyers seek to maintain autonomy and independence to meet changing social demands and respond to increasing competition. The state seeks to tie lawyers' practices to state functioning and use the Ordini to control professionals. We draw on Scott's (1995) analysis of how regulatory, normative, and cognitive institutions are maintained to explain how Italian institutions enable and constrain change by shaping professional practices and structures. We also discuss the transformation of the legal industry since the mid-1990s – deregulation and Europeanisation, internationalisation, and the entry of English and American firms – which dramatically altered the competitive landscape and created ongoing tensions in the legal profession. On one hand, Italian professionals have been able to deflect pressure for radical change and resist threats from increasingly aggressive Anglo-Saxon global law firms. On the other, the growth of a national corporate legal sector has intensified internal pressures for the profession to 'modernise'. Italian business law firms have started advocating for changes in organisational forms and professional rules in order to maintain their international competitiveness.

II. THE LEGAL PROFESSION IN ITALY: AN OVERVIEW

A. Size and Demographics of the Profession

Law historically was seen as one of the most prestigious and (potentially) lucrative professions in Italy. Lawyers used to be drawn mainly from the upper-middle classes (Prandstraller, 1967), and the profession used to be perceived as the 'social and political representative of the ruling class' because of its political and cultural prestige (Olgiati and Pocar 1988: 349). Aspirations for upward mobility still make law an attractive profession despite the difficulty of entry. Italy has the third lowest number of inhabitants per lawyer (272) of the 47 Council of Europe countries, after Greece (258) and Luxembourg (258) (CEPEJ 2016). The distribution of lawyers varies greatly across regions (see Figure 1).

There is an interesting anomaly: regions in the South (ie Calabria and Campania) have far lower than average ratios of population/lawyer (150 and 153 respectively), while those in the North (Trentino Alto Adige and Val d'Aosta) have much higher than average ratios (719 and 631). Although there is no simple explanation, the difference in economic

Figure 1 Distribution of Lawyers across Italian Regions (Population/Lawyer)

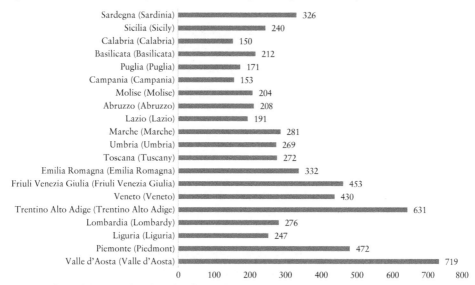

Source: Author's elaboration based on data from online sources.

development and employment opportunities between the regions may contribute. In Calabria and Campania, the legal profession may offer one of the few employment possibilities and represent a stepping-stone to public sector employment (Bellini 2014). The demand for legal advice is not always sufficient to guarantee employment in these overcrowded regions; indeed, the number of lawyers in a region has been inversely correlated with their average annual income (Bellini 2014) (see Figure 2).

Despite high entry barriers, the number of lawyers has steadily increased, spiking in the mid-1990s (see Figure 3 and Table 1) and prompting debates over whether there are 'too many lawyers' (Calamandrei 1921; Carmignani and Giacomelli 2009).

Bellini (2014) argues that the growth of all professions is driven by the increasing professionalism of the workforce. Yet the Italian legal profession may be experiencing a 'crisis'. A substantial number of lawyers may never practise (Giovannini 1969). Others may struggle to earn enough income and save for retirement (by enrolling in the Cassa di Previdenza Forense and making the required annual contributions). Owners of small law firms assume most of the financial risk of running a business. According to ISTAT (2011a) (census data from the National Institute of Statistics), 80 per cent of owners use their own funds, 13 per cent rely on short-term bank credit, 14 per cent on medium or long-term credit, and 18 per cent find other sources.

In 2015, 19.1 per cent of 2011 law graduates began working before obtaining a law degree, 48.9 per cent had been working since graduation, 24 per cent were seeking employment, and 8 per cent were not seeking employment (ISTAT 2011b). Of those employed in 2015, 57.2 per cent were working as 'senior officials, managers and highly skilled workers', 20.2 per cent as 'technicians and associate professionals', 20.8 per cent

Figure 2 Average Annual Income for Lawyers by Region (Euros) and Women's Income as Per Cent of Men's

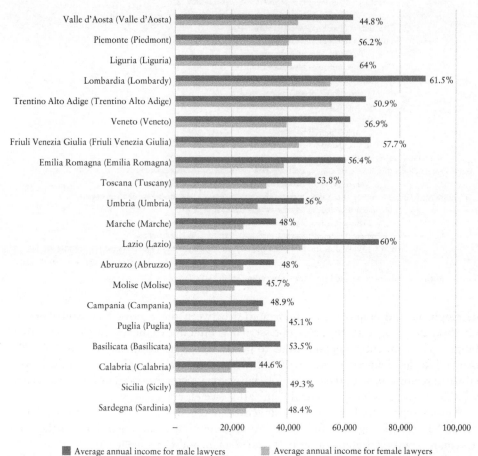

Source: Author's elaboration based on data from online sources.

as 'clerks, service workers and shop and market sales workers', and 1.8 per cent in 'blue collar, artisans, and elementary occupations'.

The proportion of 19 to 25-year-olds enrolled in university rose from 12 per cent in 1970 to 20 per cent in 1990 and 42 per cent in 2008 (ISTAT 2011c). However, the number of law graduates actually declined nearly a quarter from 2007 to 2011 throughout Italy. The difference in enrolment rates between the specific regions is shown in Table 2. Campania was the only region that saw an increase in enrolment at the end of the period.

The percentage of women in the legal profession has increased substantially, from 9.2 per cent in 1985 to 41.1 per cent in 2006. According to the CCBE (2015), 47 per cent of the 246,786 lawyers in 2015 were women. In fact, women law graduates have outnumbered men every year from 1998 to 2012, constituting 59 per cent during that period (see Figure 4). As Bellini (2014) reports, however, Italy is still far from achieving gender equality: men earn 54.6 per cent more than women (62 per cent more in Calabria) (see Figure 2).

Figure 3 Number of Lawyers Enrolled in Law Lists, 1880–2014

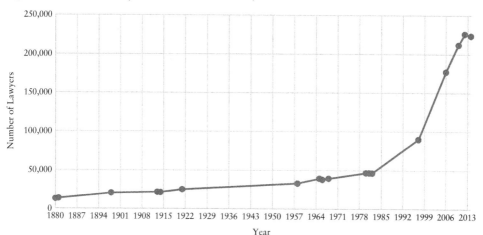

Sources: Author's elaboration based on combined data from Olgiati and Pocar (1988); CEPEJ report (2016); Bellini (2014).

Table 1 Size of the Profession, 1880–2014

Year	Number of Lawyers Enrolled	Population	Population/Lawyer
1880	12,885	28,709,000	2,228
1881	13,518	29,953,000	2,216
1898	20,361	32,554,000	1,599
1913	21,488	36,178,000	1,684
1914	21,163	36,707,000	1,734
1921	25,000	38,449,000	1,538
1958	33,059	49,640,000	1,502
1965	39,415	52,931,000	1,343
1966	37,859	52,317,900	1,382
1968	39,415	53,080,900	1,347
1980	46,620	56,388,481	1,210
1981	46,610	56,479,287	1,212
1982	46,401	56,590,000	1,220
1997	89,880	57,460,977	639
2006	177,162	58,064,214	328
2010	211,962	59,190,143	279
2012	226,202	59,394,207	263
2014	223,842	60,782,668	272

Source: Author's elaboration based on data from online sources.

Table 2 Total Law Graduates

Total law graduates	2007	2008	2009	2010	2011
Italy	44,096	40,172	38,114	34,582	35,199
All Northwest regions	7,311	6,669	5,845	6,016	5,972
Piemonte	1,803	1,599	1,528	1,538	1,303
Liguria	691	588	488	488	631
Lombardia	4,817	4,482	3,829	3,990	4,038
All Northeast regions	6,871	6,386	6,054	5,361	5,519
Trentino Alto Adige / Suditrol	639	554	571	529	595
Provincia Autonoma Trento	639	554	571	529	595
Veneto	1,466	1,500	1,445	1,352	1,378
Friuli-Venezia Giulia	807	731	543	491	457
Emilia-Romagna	3,959	3,601	3,495	2,989	3,089
All Central regions	11,178	10,602	10,139	8,929	8,247
Toscana	3,120	2,780	2,713	2,028	1,953
Umbria	540	633	665	619	532
Marche	2,039	1,727	1,724	1,274	1,092
Lazio	5,479	5,462	5,037	5008	4,670
All Southern regions	13,324	11,787	11,459	10,217	11,282
Abruzzo	956	738	585	604	576
Molise	799	866	399	430	637
Campania	6,186	5,408	5,556	5,259	6,765
Puglia	3,789	3,133	3,062	2,600	2,215
Calabria	1,594	1,642	1,857	1,324	1,089
All Island regions	5,412	4,728	4,617	4,059	4,179
Sicilia	4,279	3,752	3,608	3,393	3,427
Sardegna	1,133	976	1,009	666	752

Source: Author's compilation of data from ISTAT (2011d).

The seeming over-production of lawyers does not mean that work gets done quickly; Italy's judicial system has the third worst performance record in the EU (after Malta and Cyprus). Civil and commercial cases take an average of 600 days to reach court and can take more than five years to complete the appeals process and obtain a final decision from the Court of Cassation. Nevertheless, the Italian legal profession strives to provide public service and promote access to justice. The legal aid budget grew from €115,938,469 in 2008 to €127,055,510 in 2010 and €153,454,322 in 2012 before declining to €143,915,571 in 2014 (CEPEJ 2016). To participate in the legal aid programme, a lawyer who has been a member of the Bar for at least two years and meets other requirements may register to be assigned cases for a fee determined by the court that decides the case (an amount that may not exceed the average for similar professional services).

Figure 4 Law Graduates by Gender

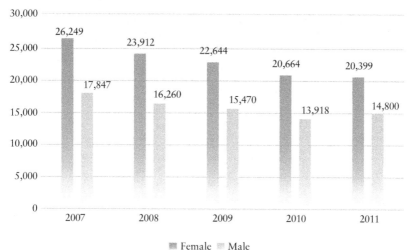

Source: Author's compilation of data from ISTAT.

B. Education, Training, and Selection

Lawyers must obtain a university degree in '*giurisprudenza*' from an Italian law faculty, which takes five years, requiring successful completion of 32 exams and a dissertation. Many universities have increased their international offerings by giving students the opportunity to take a few exams in English. The curriculum is very traditional, focusing on theory, philosophy, history and doctrine rather than practical skills (Faulconbridge and Muzio 2016). A few elite schools, such as Bocconi University School of Law, focus on preparing graduates for corporate practice.

Those who wish to practise as lawyers must complete an 18-month apprenticeship in a lawyer's office (*praticantato*) The '*praticante*' must attend at least 20 court proceedings a semester, evidence of the emphasis on contentious legal practice (Faulconbridge and Muzio 2013). An apprenticeship is difficult to obtain for those without connections to a prestigious office (Pellizzari et al 2011). Apprentices are unpaid; at best, they are entitled to reimbursement of expenses. After the apprenticeship, lawyers must take the state examination (*esame di stato*): three written papers over three consecutive days and an oral examination for those who pass the written exams. Only 26 per cent passed in 2011, a much lower proportion than those taking the state exam for doctors (98 per cent), journalists (78 per cent), and architects (49 per cent), though higher than that for notaries (6 per cent) (Pellizzari et al 2011). Examinations are held in regional courts (*Corte d'Appello*), which vary in pass rates (see Table 3). Some candidates travel to a court where the exam is supposed to be less difficult. Pass rates tend to be higher in districts in the Northern regions. For example, in 2005, 21 per cent of all candidates who took the exams in Milan were found suitable to practise, while 69 per cent of those who took the exams in Messina passed (Negri 2008). Others seek admission in European countries where it is said to be easier (eg Spain or Romania) and invoke European legislation to have their titles accepted in Italy and enrol in the register of lawyers in their city

Table 3 State Examination Results (2013)

Courts	Registered for Written Examination	Admitted to Oral Examination	Percentage Admitted to Oral Examination
Ancona	649	268	41.29
Bari	1,675	635	37.91
Bologna	1,911	894	46.78
Brescia	737	290	39.35
Cagliari	655	270	41.22
Caltanissetta	375	170	45.33
Campobasso	248	43	17.34
Catania	1,255	424	33.78
Catanzaro	1,521	637	41.88
Firenze	1,351	675	49.96
Genova	634	383	60.41
L'Aquila	701	274	39.09
Lecce	1,221	608	49.79
Messina	518	271	52.32
Milano	3,258	1,031	31.65
Napoli	5,688	174	30.59
Palermo	1,100	599	54.45
Perugia	411	120	29.19
Potenza	410	121	29.51
Reggio Calabria	820	247	30.12
Roma	3,089	1,344	43.51
Salerno	1,114	640	57.45
Torino	1,442	773	53.61
Trento	172	52	30.23
Trieste	352	125	35.51
Venezia	1,544	572	37.04
Total Italy	31,596	11,640	40.74

Source: Author's compilation of data from Altalex (2013).

(*Ordine degli Avvocati*). The similarity in language and culture increased the attraction of Spain, which did not have a state exam until 2013. Even now that it has aligned its requirements with other European countries, the 'Spanish path' still allows aspiring lawyers to circumvent the 'dreaded' Italian state exam.[1]

[1] Candido (2013).

C. Lawyers' Employment

In the past two decades the legal profession has experienced a slow transformation, which some interpret as a process of delegitimation and impoverishment (Festi and Malatesta 2011). Olgiati and Pocar (1988: 352) described a transition from social stratification to functional differentiation, a situation in which the legal profession is perceived as offering a technical service; professionals become 'entrepreneurs of legal services'; marketing, advertising prices, and competition become increasingly important; and the lawyer-client relationship embodies a new model of social interaction. These authors predicted 'an increasing homology between the professional office and that of the business firm'.

These expectations have been at least partially confirmed. Since the mid-1990s, the Italian legal field has experienced important changes in organisational practices, structures and relationships (Faulconbridge and Muzio 2016; Micelotta and Washington 2013; Muzio and Faulconbridge 2013). Three are particularly salient: (1) growth in the size and formalisation of the organisational structures within which legal professionals operate; (2) state reforms intensifying competition and encouraging internationalisation; and (3) the still limited but growing interest among lawyers in being employed by companies rather than practising as 'free' professionals.

The legal profession historically was organised in small offices, often just one lawyer and an assistant or apprentice (Consorzio Aaster 2011). Even today only 4.7 per cent of lawyers work in firms of more than 10; the majority are in studios of 6–8 (Guastella 2009). This is true of firms serving both individuals and businesses. Small studios headed by prestigious well-known lawyers (boutiques) are in demand by important clients. One well-known example is Franzo Grande Stevens, a small Turin firm, which used to be the primary adviser of the large automobile manufacturer Fiat (Fairclough and Micelotta 2013; Stefanoni 2011). There is relatively little specialisation, and the relationship between clients and lawyers is often a 'stewardship' built on trust and mutual respect. There are many possible motivations for keeping a law firm small. The Code of Conduct declares that the lawyer-client relationship is based on trust, which is easier to build on a personal relationship. Furthermore, it is not uncommon for a law firm to be inherited. Although only 4 per cent of small firms in 2011 were family-owned, 13 per cent of firms were expected to be inherited in the next five years (ISTAT 2011e). That 38.1 per cent of lawyers and 34.2 per cent of architects have parents who were professionals shows the heritability of class privilege (Consorzio Aster 2011).

Even though small legal practices and prestigious boutique firms remain important forms of employment for legal professionals (TopLegal 2014), changes in the legal landscape have transformed the organisation of legal professional service firms. The opening of the Italian market has intensified competition from UK and US firms. In order to secure and keep a larger and increasingly international clientele, Italian studios have begun to grow while attempting to preserve their distinctive identity and autonomy against threats of acquisition by larger players (Muzio and Faulconbridge 2013). Once the largest firm in Italy, Bonelli Erede Pappalardo recently ranked at the top of Italian firms in terms of total revenue and profit per equity partner, although it is nowhere near the largest in the country (see Table 4).

Although major English law firms began entering the Italian market in 1993, mainly through alliances with local firms, mergers were either never completed or short-lived;

Table 4 Largest Italian Law Firms by Revenue and Number of Partners

	Law firm	Revenue (€ 000,000s)	Profit per equity partner (€ 000s)	Revenue per partner (€ 000s)	Number of partners: equity	Number of partners: non-equity	Number of associates
1	Bonelli Erede Pappalardo	130	2,432	2,321	37	19	141
2	Chiomenti	123	1,538	2,365	52		225
3	Gianni Origoni Grippo & Partners	94	1,351	1,649	27	20	222
4	Priola Pennuto Zei	88	1,375	880	32	68	270
5	NCTM	70	977	752	43	50	150
6	Freshfields	57.5	921	3,026	19		70
7	Clifford Chance	46	794	2,706	17		84
8	Allen & Overy	42	919	2,625	16		67
9	Cleary Gottlieb	40	1,700	3,636	11		50
10	Legance	40	962	1,538	26		108
11	DLA Piper	37	3,033	1,276	6	23	60
12	Baker McKenzie	35	972	1,029	18	16	73
13	Simmons & Simmons	34.7	1,625	2,313	8	7	77
14	CBA	31	845	705	22	22	137
15	Pavia e Ansaldo	28.6	1,069	894	16	16	73
16	Linklaters	28	1,089	3,111	9		39
17	Trifrio & Partners	27	1,238	2,077	13		47
18	Tonucci & Partners	26.5	757	981	14	13	136
19	Grimaldi e Associati	26	1,600	1,368	10	9	38
20	Sutti	25.3	540	1,012	25		65
21	Lovells	25	690	1,250	20		85
22	Maisto e Associati	25.3	2,143	3,571	7		23
23	Dewey & LeBoeuf	24	833	1,043	15	8	37
24	LS LexJus Sinacta	23	133	256	90		67
25	Vitali Romagnoli Piccardi	21	1,200	2,100	10		26

Source: Top Legal (2009).

by 2002–04, many founding or crucial partners left the firms, and many mergers collapsed or failed (Faulconbridge and Muzio 2016). Nevertheless, some foreign firms survived, often after relocating to cities better suited to their operations and needs. A few domestic firms, mainly in large cities like Milan and Rome, have grown bigger than the foreign 'mega-firm' subsidiaries (Fairclough and Micelotta 2013). The largest Italian firms are significantly smaller than their counterparts in the UK, Continental Europe and the US, where the largest have thousands of lawyers. Nevertheless, they have remained independent and maintained their revenue leadership in the local market. The overwhelming majority of small firms (over 99 per cent) are owned by Italian citizens and are local: 97 per cent describe their region as their primary market; and though 43 per cent practise outside their region, less than 7 per cent do so outside Italy (ISTAT 2011f).

Some of the changes highlighted above have been stimulated or supported by increasingly forceful state intervention. Since 1994, the Italian government has embarked on multiple attempts to comprehensively update and reform the codes, rules, and practices that regulate professions (Bellini 2014; Fiorenza 2009; Sereni 1949). Despite the apparent agreement by the state and representatives of the profession on the need for such reform, the process has been tumultuous, obstructed by the profession's resistance to what it sees as threats to self-regulation. The distinctive configuration of Italian professionalism is one of the main factors insulating it from competitive market dynamics (Fiorenza 2009).

In 1994 the Authority for Competition and the Market ('*Autorita' Garante della Concorrenza e del Mercato*) began an analysis of Italian professions, producing a report on 'Activities Aimed at Liberalising Professional Services in 2004–2005' urging broad reform of the regulation of professional services. In 2005, a joint directive by the European Council and the European Parliament (Directive 2005/36/EC) required all Member States to review domestic legislation for compatibility with EU guidelines. The objective was a transparent system to compare qualifications across EU Member States and promote competition in professional services. The Italian Government responded by issuing the 2006 Bersani decree (no 248/06), Bolkestein decree (2006/123/CE) and 'stability decree' (2011), culminating in the final decree (247/2013), crafted with the guidance of the National Forensic National Bar Council, which regulates and represents Italian lawyers.

The legislation sought to modify practices seen as obstacles to a competitive environment. The reforms included abolishing the fixed fee structure (the minima and maxima lawyers could charge), letting lawyers specialise, allowing advertisements, and permitting professionals to associate in a 'corporate' organisational form and offer multidisciplinary services (as long as each lawyer belonged to just one association).

For years, professionals and politicians have tried to update anachronistic legislative codes, some of which date to the founding of the Kingdom of Italy in 1861. However, prior attempts succumbed to arguments that institutionalised practices were necessary to protect 'professionalism' and guarantee the highest standards of conduct. Opponents insisted that major changes be made cautiously and only under the leadership of the profession's representatives (Micelotta and Washington 2013). Nevertheless, although 98 per cent of lawyers still practise in the traditional organisational form of an association of independent professionals, some service providers have created franchises offering relatively low fixed fees (Consorzio Aaster 2011; Bellini 2014). A prominent example is ALT (*Avvocati Per Tutti* – Lawyers For All), which now has 15 offices.[2] There has been much dispute about whether the promotional message used by this company – legal

---

[2] See www.alassistenzalegale.it.

services for all, with transparent fees – is consistent with professional norms. In fact, this law firm has been disciplined by the Italian Court (*Cassazione*) for disseminating a 'suggestive' and 'deceitful' promotional message.

Very few lawyers are employed by companies. A 2005 survey of 271 lawyers enrolled in the Milan registry revealed that 70 per cent identified being a lawyer as a 'free profession', 13 per cent as an autonomous economic activity, 8 per cent as a mission, and only 7 per cent as just like any other occupational activity (Bertozzi and Zanderighi 2005); 19.3 per cent would never consider being part of a law firm (*studio legale associato*). This helps explain why in-house lawyers have been classified as an unregulated profession by Decree 2005/36/CE. Italy formally distinguishes between regulated and unregulated professions, conferring on each different rights and autonomy. Under a system established in 1804, the core professions (eg law, medicine, and engineering) are regulated professions. To practise them, each professional must join the regional affiliate of the state-sanctioned association (*Ordine*). Other occupations (eg chiropractors, marriage counsellors, and public relations consultants) are unregulated professions, whose members are free to join private associations. Neither the associations nor their members enjoy the status and privileges of regulated professions (eg autonomy and self-regulation).

The Association of In-House Counsel (*Associazione Italiana Giuristi di Impresa*, AIGI), founded in 1976, has sought to promote its members' interests and gain legal status (granted in 2013). Although AIGI reported 1,000 members in 2016, it claims that the number of lawyers employed by companies is much higher and growing rapidly (Root and AIGI 2016). In-house lawyers must have the degree in *giurisprudenza* but need not take a state examination or complete an apprenticeship and are not registered in the Law Lists. A survey found that 92 per cent were happy or very happy with their in-house positions because the job was stimulating, (combining legal advice with business expertise) and offered greater job security than independent practice. However, salaries were 20–30 per cent lower. An in-house counsel with no experience typically has a starting salary of €15–20,000, earning €40–60,000 after five years and €150–200,000 after 20 (see Tables 5 and 6).

Table 5 Average Salary Range by Years of Experience

Years of experience	Salary range (€ 000s)
0–1	15–20
2–3	20–35
4–5	40–60
6–7	65–75
8–9	75–95
10–11	95–130
12–13	130–150
14–15	150–160
16–20	160–200
21+	155–250

Source: Root and AIGI (2016).

Table 6 Average Salary Range by Professional Level

Professional level	Salary range (€ 000s)
Praticante	15–25
Junior	25–35
Associate	35–50
6–8 years	50–85
8–10+ years	75–120
Senior Associate, or Senior counsel with 10+ years	120+

Source: Root and AIGI (2016).

III. THE PERSISTENCE OF NATIONAL INSTITUTIONAL FEATURES AND PROFESSIONAL RESISTANCE TO INSTITUTIONAL CHANGE

The above overview reveals some peculiarities or 'anomalies' (Olgiati and Pocar 1988: 353) of the Italian legal system and the legal profession's practices and structures. Here we draw on Scott (1995) to understand how institutions have shaped the Italian profession (see also (Greenwood and Suddaby 2006; Micelotta and Washington 2013; Muzio and Faulconbridge 2013; Reay and Hinings 2005; Smets, Morris and Greenwood 2012). Scott (1995: 33) defines institutions as

> *regulative*, *normative*, and *cognitive* structures and activities that provide stability and meaning to social behavior. Institutions are transported by various carriers – culture, structures, and routines – and they operate at multiple levels of jurisdiction.

As we will show, the legal profession's practices, rules, norms, behavioural patterns, social interactions, and power hierarchies have been reproduced over a long period of time.

The *regulatory* pillar refers to the (typically formal) laws and rules that prescribe and proscribe organisational behaviours. In professional settings these include rules regulating access to the profession, mandatory training, and professional conduct and those influencing lawyers' strategic and operational choices (Micelotta 2010; Muzio and Faulconbridge 2013). Because of the arduous entry barriers, Italian lawyers tend to qualify to practise in their late 20s or early 30s, older than in many other countries (Faulconbridge and Muzio 2013). In addition to those discussed above, Italian regulations limit law firm names (with rare exceptions) to one or more lawyer working in the firm, further strengthening the profession's individualistic character. Governance of lawyers has been decentralised to the local Bar associations. The 2014 Code of Conduct for Italian lawyers applies to all those practising or registered to practise in Italy (including foreign lawyers) and requires them to conform to EU regulations. The state exercises informal control over the profession through the *Ordini*, whose responsibilities and privileges are granted by the state and whose governance is monitored by the EU.

The *normative* pillar refers to norms defining appropriate and desirable behaviour by specifying the criteria institutions use for evaluations. The definition of appropriate behaviour lies at the core of professional codes of conduct and permeates notions of what is 'professional'. In the Italian context, the most salient are norms governing the lawyer-client relationship. Lawyers serve their clients by offering expertise acquired through their lengthy training, extending from the beginning of the university degree through apprenticeship. Even *praticanti* consider themselves autonomous professionals; and law firm partners remain individually responsible to clients (Micelotta 2010). Client relationships are typically enduring and based on personal ties as well as commercial interests. Clients choose a lawyer they believe will understand their specific needs and circumstances because the lawyer is an acquaintance or recommended by one. The behaviour of Italian lawyers is strongly influenced by the pervasive family logic of Italian life, which nurtures robust networks of colleagues and clients and shapes institutional and regulatory contacts. 'Just as familial social networks support the operation of Italian business relationships more generally, partners of Italian law firms develop a close "family" of trusted peers and associates, underpinned by personal trust and knowledge among the partners' (Fairclough and Micelotta 2013: 392). Clients have come to expect this degree of familiarity (Faulconbridge and Muzio 2013). Individual firm owners and large firm corporate partners make themselves personally available and customise services, taking account of the client's preferences as well as the legal circumstances. For this reason, clients are reluctant to hire a firm that uses a bureaucratic organisation to deliver standardised services.

Finally, the *cognitive* pillar refers to shared systems of belief, frames, schemas, and taken-for-granted assumptions through which individuals understand and interpret their reality. This affects how professionals 'see the world' and the cultural underpinnings of their relationships with the law, clients and other professionals. In Italy, this has two dimensions (Faulconbridge and Muzio 2013). First, the intellectual roots of the law emphasise a comprehensive knowledge of the legal code. Second, Italian lawyers see their profession as an individual activity. Although associating with others may offer advantages in exploiting market opportunities and confronting competitive pressures, many lawyers still feel the disadvantages are greater. Italian law firms often fail to grow. Efforts to do so are reversed because lawyers defect and launch their own practices. Italian lawyers believe that modest size signals quality, while large Anglo-Saxon firms are impersonal and bureaucratic.

Scott's framework enabled us to describe salient features of the Italian institutional context. But the insights are less informative about the dynamics encouraging or obstructing change. In the next section, we draw on theories of institutional maintenance work to understand what drives or impedes change in the institutionalised practices and structures of the Italian legal profession (Lawrence and Suddaby 2006; Lawrence et al 2009; 2011).

A. The Delicate Balance between Maintenance and Change

The concept of institutional work refers to 'the practices of individual and collective actors aimed at creating, maintaining and disrupting institutions' (Lawrence et al 2011: 52). Institutions can be reproduced through individual or collective action. This theoretical lens enables us to understand why, in Italy, the discourse about professions is typically based on narratives of change and yet change is fraught with hurdles and challenges.

There are interesting connections between the work of maintaining institutions and the notion of a professional project (Abel 1988). The professional project literature (Abbott 1988; Larson 1977) argues that professions seek to maintain their social positions and financial rewards by restricting entry to an elite circle. Professions seek to preserve exclusivity through entrance exams, training, an ethical code, and socialisation processes, (Abbott 1988). Professions also use entry barriers to define the meaning of membership: the authority, responsibility, and especially expertise of members (Lawrence et al 2009).

An exploratory investigation by the Institute for Advanced Studies in Vienna observed:

> [R]egulatory changes in Italy take a very long time to be decided, and if they are decided, it takes even longer to implement them, if they are implemented at all (and not abolished at a later stage). … In such a situation it appears to be rather difficult to deregulate the market, especially as far as market entry, the questions of business-forms and inter-professional cooperation is concerned. Nonetheless, in the long run, the small-scale structure of legal (and accounting) services will not be competitive, even more in an increasingly internationalized market. (Paterson et al 2003)

Despite repeated efforts to reform the Italian legal profession, 'plus ça change, plus c'est la même chose.' This final section analyses why this is so.

B. Who Can Make Change Happen? What Change is Possible?

Because professions enjoy the prerogatives of self-regulation they are expected to be the primary agents of institutional change. Many studies confirm that professionals and professional service firms often propose, enable and drive change. Major changes (eg multidisciplinary practices) were introduced by elite Canadian accounting firms and then legitimised and accepted by professional associations (Greenwood, Hinings and Suddaby 2002; Greenwood and Suddaby 2006; Suddaby and Greenwood 2005). Large US law firms introduced innovative human resources practices, rejecting traditional up-or-out career trajectories. To manage the cross-jurisdictional complexity of a merger of a British and German law firm, teams of lawyers improvised in their day-to-day activities, creating a hybrid organisation and significantly modifying the German lawyers' practices (Smets et al 2012).

But few examples of change driven by professionals and professional service firms are found in Italy. In civil law countries like Italy, the profession has evolved as a branch of the civil service and is thus dependent on the state (Bellini 2014; Olgiati and Pocar 1988). In the past two decades, the state has been the primary proponent of legislation to reform the professions, provoking conflict between the two. Whether change can happen is determined by the outcome of this 'battle' between professions and the state, in which professions seem to have the advantage (Micelotta and Washington 2013).

Since the 1990s, the Italian Government has been encouraged by European authorities to ensure that domestic legislation complies with EU guidelines. Because representatives of the Italian legal profession (*Ordini* and *Consiglio Nazionale Forense*) are extremely conservative, the government initiated reforms in 2006 without consulting or negotiating with either. The new legislation (Bersani Decree) required all professions to comply with EU guidelines and modify their codes of conduct to promote competition in professional markets. After two years, however, the President of the Italian Authority for Competition and the Market (Antitrust) criticised the legal profession for its reluctance 'to implement competitive practices, in terms of prices for services provided and advertising through the abolition of the prohibition to promote services' (Antitrust Authority 2008). As the government sought to enact changes, the Italian professions vigorously resisted, defending their right to self-regulate.

Representatives of all regulated professions, including lawyers, condemned the government, encouraging their members to mobilise and protest. Professionals suspended their work to demonstrate in the streets and even strike, delaying some trials. The government, weakened by internal division, appointed a committee to hold hearings to address the profession's concerns and present new legislation to Parliament. The situation was further complicated by support for the Bersani Decree from representatives of unregulated professions. When, after protracted hearings, it became clear to the Council that the government's new proposal would be unacceptable, representatives of the professions proposed their own reform. The government capitulated, allowing the Council to submit its reform to Parliament.

Regulated professions were able to 'repair' the disruption caused by the government by re-asserting the norms of institutional interaction, re-establishing the balance of institutional powers, and regaining institutional leadership (Micelotta and Washington 2013). The professions and the state will continue to pursue their divergent institutional projects; though the balance of power may shift, the state's top-down efforts to reform the professions are unlikely to succeed. Cooperative strategies of mutual understanding and compromise to define spaces for negotiation are more likely to yield durable, if incremental, change.

As the Italian legal profession resists state-initiated change, it is also subject to economic, political, and cultural convergence processes fostering greater homogeneity in professional work practices. Italy has not been insulated from deregulation and globalisation, as the entry of English and American firms reveals. But despite changes in the competitive landscape, international law firms have not fully secured their market or propagated rapid bottom-up change. In order to acquire knowledge of the local context and develop connections with the local clientele in other countries, American and English firms have made alliances and merged with local firms. These strategies, however, have proved challenging in the Italian context. Mergers between Italian and American or English firms have encountered internal difficulties and typically failed. Foreign firms have had to adopt 'relocation' strategies and modify their Italian subsidiaries in order to 'adapt' to the Italian context (Faulconbridge and Muzio 2016; Muzio and Faulconbridge 2013). Italians are reluctant to embrace Anglo-Saxon models of professionalism. The lawyers' Code of Conduct prohibits contingent fees, negotiating compensation, and most advertising of professional services and limits multidisciplinary practices. Indeed, the legal profession is regarded as one of the most conservative, allegedly because of its strenuous commitment to perpetuating a caste system.

Although the preservation of these institutionalised practices has reinforced the belief that efforts to inject competition into the Italian professional services sector is futile, corporate law firms will continue to play a major role in promoting changes to professional codes and practices. The 2013 reform of the profession encourages specialisation, legitimises corporate organisational forms, and allows lawyers to use new channels of communication with prospective clients (including websites). These changes are partly a response to the growth of a more sophisticated market for legal services, primarily in Milan, where Italian firms have had to offer customised specialised services to their international clients in order to be competitive. The distinctive pressures experienced by corporate lawyers are evident in their creation of a new professional association (*Associazione Studi Legali Associati*, ASLA)–for law firms adopting corporate forms. The changes embraced by the corporate world may have important effects for all lawyers.

REFERENCES

Abel, RL (1988) 'Lawyers in the civil law world' in in RL Abel and PSC Lewis (eds), *Lawyers in Society: Vol II The Civil Law World* (Berkeley, University of California Press).
Abbott, A (1988) *The System of the Professions* (London, University of Chicago Press).
Antitrust Authority (2008) *Il Sole 24 Ore*.
Bellini, A (2014) 'Gli avvocati e i paradossi della regolazione delle professioni: Un esercizio autoriflessivo' 135(3) *Sociologia del Lavoro* 91–108.
Bertozzi, P and Zanderighi, L (2005) 'Professione avvocato: Tendenze evolutive degli studi legali milanesi' in *TradeLab per Ordine degli avvocati*.
Calamandrei, P (1921) *Troppi avvocati!* (La Voce, Firenze).
Candido, A (2013) 'L'incompiuta liberalizzazione dei servizi professionali. Federalismi.it: Rivista di diritto pubblico italiano, comunitario e comparato' in Quaderno della Collana del 'Dipartimento di Scienze Economico-Aziendali e Diritto per l'Economia' of Milan University, Bicocca.
Carmignani, A and Giacomelli, S (2009) 'Too many lawyers? Litigation in Italian civil courts' (Bank of Italy, Research Department).
CCBE (2015) 'CCBE Laywers Statistics 2015' www.ccbe.eu/actions/statistics.
CEPEJ (2016) 'European judicial systems. Efficiency and quality of justice' *CEPEJ Studies No 23*.
Consorzio Aaster (2011) 'Vecchie e nuove professioni a Milano: Monadi, corporazioni o terzo stato in cerca di rappresentanza?' (Milan).
Fairclough, S and Micelotta, E (2013) 'Beyond the family firm: Reasserting the influence of the family institutional logic across organizations' in *Research in the Sociology of Organizations* Institutional Logics in Action, Part B (Emerald Group Publishing Ltd) 63–98.
Faulconbridge, J and Muzio, D (2012) 'Professions in a globalizing world: Towards a transnational sociology of the professions' 27(1) *International Sociology* 136–52.
—— (2013) 'The global professional service firm: "One Firm" models versus (Italian) distant institutionalized practices' 34(7) *Organization Studies* 897–925.
—— (2016) 'Global professional service firms and the challenge of institutional complexity: "Field relocation" as a response strategy' 53(1) *Journal of Management Studies* 89–124.
Festi, D and Malatesta, M (2011) 'Il discorso pubblico sulle professioni' 60(5) *Il Mulino* 788–95.
Fiorenza, C (2009) 'La riforma della disciplina della professione tecnica: Rapporto per l'80^0 anniversario delle professioni di Geometra, Perito Agrario e Perito Industriale (1929–2009)' 46(4) *Il Perito Agrario* 15–30.
Giovannini, P (1969) 'La professione di avvocato in una fase di transizione' 3(3) *Sociologia* 209–286.
Greenwood, R, Hinings, C and Suddaby, R (2002) 'Theorizing change: The role of professional associations in the transformation of institutionalized fields' 45(1) *Academy of Management Journal* 58–80.
Greenwood, R and Suddaby, R (2005) 'Rhetorical strategies of legitimacy' 50(1) *Administrative Science Quarterly* 35–67.
—— (2006) 'Institutional entrepreneurship in mature fields: The big five accounting firms' 49(1) *Academy of Management Journal* 27–48.

Guastella, G (2009) 'Avvocati, un futuro di piccolo studi' *Corriere della Sera* (29 April).
ISTAT (2011a) 'Finance' www.istat.it/en/national-accounts.
—— (2011b) 'Graduates and Work' www.istat.it/en/files/2012/09/SintesiIEnglish.pdf?title=Graduates+and+work+2011++-+21+Sep+2012+-+Full+text.pdf.
—— (2011c) 'Italy in Figures' www.istat.it/en/files/2011/06/Italy2011.pdf.
—— (2011d) 'University education – graduates' www.istat.it/en/education-and-training.
—— (2011e) 'Ownership and governace – past events' www.istat.it/en/enterprises.
—— (2011f) 'Competitiveness and market' www.istat.it/en/external-trade.
Larson, M (1977) *The Rise of Professionalism: A Sociological Analysis* (Berkeley, University of California Press).
Lawrence, TB and Suddaby, R (2006) 'Institutions and institutional work' in H Clegg, TB Lawrence and W Nord (eds.), *Handbook of Organization Studies* (London, Sage) 215–54.
Lawrence, TB, Suddaby, R and Leca, B (2009) *Institutional Work: Actors and Agency in Institutional Studies of Organizations* (Cambridge, Cambridge University Press).
—— (2011) 'Institutional work: refocusing institutional studies of organization' 20(1) *Journal of Management Inquiry* 52–58.
Micelotta, E (2010) *Professional Service Firms between Resistance and Change: Business Law Firms in Italy* (Saarbrücken, Lambert Academic Publishing).
Micelotta, E and Washington, M (2013) 'Institutions and maintenance: The repair work of Italian professions' 34(8) *Organization Studies* 1137–70.
Negri, G (2008) 'Avvocati, l'esame resta un incubo' *Il Sole 24 Ore*.
Olgiati, V and Pocar, V (1988) 'The Italian legal profession: an institutional dilemma' in RL Abel and PSC Lewis (eds), *Lawyers in Society: Vol II The Civil Law World* (Berkeley, University of California Press).
Paterson, I, Fink, M and Ogus, A (2003) 'Economic impact of regulation in liberal professions in different member states' (Vienna, Institute for Advanced Studies).
Pellizzari, M, Basso, G, Catania, A, Labartino, G, Malacrino, D and Monti, P (2011) *Legami familiari ed accesso alle professioni in Italia*.
Prandstraller, GP (1967) *Gli avvocati italiani: Inchiesta sociologica* (Edizioni di Comunità).
Reay, T and Hinings, CRB (2005) 'The recomposition of an organizational field: Health care in Alberta' 26(3) *Organizational Studies* 351–84.
Root, T and AIGI (2016) 'Legali in house stipendi al palo' *Legal Community*.
Scott, WR (1995) *Organizations and Institutions* (Thousand Oaks, CA, Sage).
Sereni, AP (1949) 'The legal profession in Italy' 63 *Harvard Law Review* 1000.
Smets, M, Morris, T and Greenwood, R (2012) 'From practice to field: A multilevel model of practice-driven institutional change' 55(4) *Academy of Management Journal* 877–904.
Stefanoni, F (2011) *I veri intoccabili: Commercialisti, avvocati, medici, notai, farmacisti. Le lobby del privilegio* (Chiarelettere).
Top Legal (2009) 'Centro Studi: Periodo di riferimento'.
Top Legal (2014) 'Rapporto TopLegal Amministrativo, *Guida Top Legal*'.

12

Netherlands

Developments and Challenges

NIENKE DOORNBOS AND LENY DE GROOT-VAN LEEUWEN*

I. INTRODUCTION

THE NETHERLANDS IS one of the leading countries in the Rule of Law Index of the World Justice Project (based on interviews with more than 110,000 households and 2,700 expert surveys in 113 countries and jurisdictions). It ranks fifth (after the Scandinavian countries) with respect to adherence to the rule of law, especially on indicators such as access to justice, absence of corruption and independence of the judiciary (World Justice Project 2016: 108). The Netherlands also has a strong international reputation for peace and justice because it hosts several international courts and tribunals, including the International Court of Justice and the International Criminal Court.

The excellent international reputation of the Netherlands, however, conceals concerns about its commitment to the rule of law. These were strongly articulated in 2014 during an expert meeting in the Senate with prominent lawyers, including the president of the Supreme Court, the national ombudsman and several law professors.[1] Some said the Netherlands is not as democratic as it seems because legislative and executive powers are closely intertwined. Others pointed to the detrimental effects on access to justice of the proposed budget cuts in the legal aid system and the rise of court fees. The new public management principles in the judicial system were thought to place too much emphasis on output figures and budget controls.

Thirty years ago, Schuyt (1988) showed that Dutch society was still only moderately juridified, despite increases in the number of lawyers and the quantity of legal services. A robust network of legal aid bureaux had been established. However, the economic crisis of the 1980s led to stricter eligibility criteria and lower budgets for many aspects of the Dutch welfare state, including legal aid. The country remained prosperous until the financial crisis in 2008. As in many countries, the aftermath of

---

* The authors would like to thank Marijke ter Voert and Jonathan Soeharno for their useful comments and insights.
[1] Expert meeting on the adherence of the Netherlands on the Rule of Law in the Senate, 4 February 2014, *Parliamentary Notes I* 2013/14, 33750 VI, O, p 19.

the terrorist attacks on 9/11 polarised the political debate. Although the Netherlands has been spared a major terrorist attack, two political murders deeply shocked Dutch society.[2] The threat of terrorist attacks not only restricted civil rights but also shifted political debate to issues of security. In recent years, populist politicians have gained more adherents and proposed the introduction of minimum sentences and the elimination of lifetime appointments for judges. Although neither was enacted, the political tone on issues such as immigration, security and law enforcement has hardened. The rule of law, though still strong, is at risk.

Data from 2009 show that approximately 36 per cent of law graduates (in Dutch: *juristen*) go into law firms, notarial work or tax firms, 28 per cent become judges, prosecutors or other government workers, 10 per cent are employed by banks, insurance companies or other commercial enterprises, and 4 per cent pursue academic careers (Wilson 2012: 175–176). It is estimated that at the present only 20–30 per cent become attorneys (*advocaten*) licensed to practise law alone or in a law firm, in government, or as in-house counsel (Wilson 2012: 174, 176).

Attorneys, including apprentice attorneys, who are members of the Dutch Bar Association, have two main tasks: to give legal advice and to represent clients before district and higher courts. They have no monopoly on giving legal advice. Even in legal representation, their monopoly is restricted to civil cases worth €25,000 or more and all criminal cases (though parties can represent themselves in both kinds of cases). In all other cases, including administrative law, representation in court is open for bailiffs, lawyers (not members of the Bar) from legal expenses insurance companies, legal aid bureaux, and anyone else. The limited monopoly has led to the development of a substantial number of law clinics (non-profit law practices run by law students) and strong competition from other professions and paralegal services.

Whereas in 1986 there were only 5,124 attorneys (Schuyt 1988: 201), their number has more than tripled in 30 years to 17,498 on 1 January 2017 (Annual Report Dutch Bar Association, 2016) (see Table 1). The Netherlands, being a small country of 17 million, has one lawyer for 976 people, a high ratio compared to the neighbouring countries of Belgium (617) and Germany (495) (CEPEJ 2016: 160). This contrast has much to do with the different tasks of attorneys. German attorneys, for instance, enjoy a statutory monopoly over legal advice and representation (Blankenburg 1998: 6). The difference could also stem from the fact that Dutch attorneys are not allowed to convey real estate or register mortgages, which is the sole competence of notaries.[3] Finally, the Dutch legal profession does not distinguish between solicitors and barristers, as in the UK.

---

[2] The assassinations of politician Pim Fortuyn on 6 May 2002 and film-maker Theo van Gogh on 2 November 2004.

[3] Notaries are specialised contract lawyers appointed by the Crown under the supervision of the Ministry of Security and Justice, holding a professional monopoly on family services, such as drawing up wills, marriage contracts and donations; real estate services, such as conveying real property, creating and altering mortgages; and corporate services, such as establishing public and private limited liability companies (Nahuis and Noailly 2005). At the end of 2016, 1,286 notaries and 1,799 candidate notaries were active in the Netherlands, according to the Royal Dutch Association of Civil-law Notaries (KNB) 2016 annual report.

Table 1 Number of Attorneys and Percentage of Women, Compared to the Population (1960–2017)

Year	Population (1,000s)	Number of attorneys	Percentage of women	Population per attorney
1960	11,417	1,931	8.1	5,912
1970	12,958	2,063	10.3	6,281
1980	14,091	3,726	18.1	3,782
1990	14,893	6,381	25.8	2,334
2000	15,864	11,033	34.5	1,438
2010	16,575	16,275	41.7	1,018
2017	17,082	17,498	43.6	976

Sources: Kester and Huls (1992: 35); Bruinsma (2003: 34); Annual reports Dutch Bar Association; Central Bureau for Statistics.

The Netherlands is a civil law country based on Roman and French law. It has 11 district courts, four courts of appeal and a supreme court.[4] Judges are appointed by royal decree for life, until they retire voluntarily or after reaching the age of 70. The number of judges has increased at the same pace as attorneys: from 696 in 1986 (Schuyt 1988: 201) to 2,357 in 2016 (2,169 FTE; Annual Report Council for the Judiciary 2016).[5]

II. LEGAL EDUCATION

A. Law Faculties, Staff and Student Numbers

Higher education is offered at two types of institutions: universities of applied sciences and classical universities. In 1960, legal education in the Netherlands was provided by seven law faculties. In 2015 this number had grown to ten at the classical universities, the only ones that offer entry to the legal professions (the *effectus civilis* certificate).[6]

To study for a classical university law degree, students must have a diploma from an athenaeum (without classical languages) or gymnasium (with classical languages) or have completed the first year of a bachelor's programme at a university of applied sciences. The law faculties of classical universities have a three-cycle degree system, awarding bachelor's, master's and PhD degrees. Enrolment rose rapidly from 3,000 in 1960 to 32,000 in 1990 and then stabilised. Because budgets did not rise at the same pace, funding

---

[4] There are three separate highest courts for administrative law.
[5] In the Netherlands, public prosecutors are also members of the judiciary, appointed by royal decree. However, they are not appointed for life and do not enjoy the same independence as judges. As civil servants carrying out their functions under the authority of the Ministry of Security and Justice, they have an intermediate position between the executive and judiciary (Marguery 2008: 100). The Netherlands had approximately 800 public prosecutors on 1 January 2016 (Openbaar Ministerie 2017).
[6] In 2002, universities of applied science introduced a new type of legal education, a four-year vocational programme leading to an LLB certificate. But though it has the same name as the certificate offered by the universities, graduates are expected to work as paralegals or court registrars. These programmes are attractive to students who do not qualify for a classical university.

per student declined. Moreover, the neoliberal funding model emphasised 'output financing' (ie payment per successful graduate), constricting the ability of law students to study for more than the obligatory four years.

The rising student numbers were mirrored in the faculty, which grew from 193 in 1959 to 1,376 in 2002 (Roos 1981: 24; QANU 2004). In 1959, three out of five faculty members were full, associate or assistant professors. The rapid expansion created an entirely new category of junior members: lecturers without a doctorate or any other academic or educational qualifications, appointed by the holder of a chair. Today, however, all faculty must have a doctoral degree and a university teaching qualification.

B. Student Backgrounds

The enrolment jump is related to shifts in the population from which law faculties draw their students. Reflecting a deliberate government policy to increase the number of university graduates, law faculties dropped Latin and Greek as entrance requirements in the 1960s. At the same time, the system of open entry (common in most continental European countries) was maintained for all applicants meeting the basic qualifications. Baccalaureates without Latin and Greek filled law schools in the next 10 years (Roos 1981: 16–17). Gymnasium graduates fell from more than 80 per cent of law students in 1960 to just 25 per cent in 1971. The social backgrounds of students also changed, but not as dramatically, the proportion from higher social status families falling from 66 per cent in 1961 to 40 per cent in 1971 (though it was still above the average in other academic fields 20 years later) (Koppen 1991).

As everywhere in Europe, universities historically were a male bastion. In 1900, just 2 per cent of law students were women. But the proportion increased gradually to 9 per cent in 1910, 12 per cent in 1920, and 20–30 per cent between 1950 and 1980 before breaking even in the 1990s and reaching 60 per cent today (VSNU 2017). Law (as well as medicine) appeals to young Dutch people of 'non-Western' origin (who constitute 11.9 per cent of the population) (CBS 2014; Böcker and De Groot-van Leeuwen 2007). The four largest minority groups (Surinamese, Turks, Moroccans and Antilleans) were 8 per cent of the entering law students in 1997–2001. The drop-out rates for students from 'non-Western' backgrounds were not much higher than for their indigenous fellow students, and those for Turkish and Moroccan law students were below the average of all law students (Crul and Wolff 2002; Wolff and Crul 2003).

C. Curriculum Unification

Because none of the legal professions sets a national examination, each faculty determines the qualifications to enter a legal profession and conducts its own exams. Faculties historically had considerable autonomy in shaping their curricula, since state prescriptions were phrased in very general terms. This changed, however, at the end of the 1990s. Education ministers from 29 European countries created a European Higher Education Area (EHEA). This Bologna process sought to make European higher education more competitive with other world regions by ensuring that the educational systems of the participating countries followed a three-tier structure consisting of bachelor's degree, master's degree and PhDs. The Netherlands complied in 2002 by establishing a three-year bachelor's and one-year master's degree, enabling students to transfer to another law faculty after their bachelor's degree.

Because every enrolled student brings money to the universities, either directly (tuition fees) or indirectly (government support), internationalisation has become lucrative and competitive. One side effect is the growth of English-language courses. In 2016, 60 per cent of courses at Dutch universities were taught in English, and 70 per cent of master's degrees. The proportions are lower at law faculties because of the national character of law and the fact that the labour market for those holding Dutch law degrees is largely limited to the Netherlands (Zwemmer and Bosch-Boesjes 2012). Nevertheless, programmes in international and European law are offered in English. Contemporaneously, an accreditation system was made a condition for receiving public funding and the right to award officially recognised degrees. The diversity of the student population and unification of the curricula also prompted a reaction in favour of diversification, especially in the honours programmes, which offer extra courses and moot courts for a select group of highly talented and motivated students.

D. Curriculum Content

Since legal education sought to be academic as well as to prepare students to practise law, the classic law education was a combination of vocational, academic and personal development. Traditionally, it began with the study of Roman law and legal theory, viewed as the foundation for a proper understanding of the ever-changing positive law. This was questioned in the 1970s, as law expanded to address almost every field of social activity (eg construction law and labour law), introducing many new subjects to the curriculum. Critics argued that legal education paid too much attention to obsolete legal theory and too little to the practice of law. They wanted the curriculum to focus more on professional skills. Because the social sciences were considered an important part of the legal curriculum (Lokin and Jansen 1995: 225), courses on law and economics and law and society were introduced (VSNU 1997: 32).

Since the end of the 1990s, the law curriculum has been narrowed to focus on the main subjects of positive law: civil, criminal, constitutional, administrative and procedural law, supplemented by international and European law and some training in legal skills and a limited degree of specialisation. Legal theory, legal history, philosophy, law and economics, and the psychology and sociology of law were usually offered as electives. In 2016, an agreement was reached between the law faculties, the Council for the Judiciary, the Public Prosecution and the Bar Association concerning the minimum requirements for the *effectus civilis*.

Nevertheless, debate has continued about whether studying law is high-level vocational training or an academic education (Bruinsma 2000; Stolker 2003; Kortmann 2010; Ashmann 2011; 2015). Some authors have emphasised the importance of applied knowledge. Others have argued that the study of law should challenge students to think critically about law. They believe the present curriculum is too simple and thin: future lawyers need a broad academic education to develop their own notions of what is fair and just, considering the circumstances of a constantly changing society. The nuts and bolts of the legal procedure can be learned in practice. Yet others have decried the whole current situation of mass education, low expenditures per student, and disincentives for in-depth study. In a recent report on the education of lawyer-trainees by a committee of the Bar association, its chairman stated that law graduates not only lack a command of positive law but also cannot address questions such as 'What is law?', 'What is its relation to justice?' and 'Can or should the law be otherwise?'

E. Entry to the Bar and Bench

Law graduates can be admitted to the Bar and appear in court as attorneys after they have been sworn in before a district court. From the first day an attorney has the right to act in all kinds of cases. Admission to the Bar, however, is conditional, meaning that it necessitates a successful traineeship of three years, which must include some litigation experience and passing an examination.

A law degree is also necessary to become a judge. Until 2016, there were two entry routes: the internal judicial training programme immediately after graduation and the route for experienced lawyers drawn from the practising Bar or other legal professions. Today, only the latter remains. The period of required training for prospective judges is determined on an individual basis depending on the candidate's work experience. In addition to a minimum of two years' work experience, candidates should also demonstrate their involvement in socially relevant work, either professional or voluntary.

The evolution of legal education in the Netherlands has resulted in a combination of a 'leftist' agenda of access for all and a 'rightist' agenda of inadequate funding. One result has been a greater diversity of students and staff. Another is a loss of depth in legal study for most students but an increase of depth for honours students.

III. THE DUTCH BAR AND BENCH: SIZE AND COMPOSITION

In retrospect, the 'juridification' of Dutch society started only 30 years ago. The ratio of population to attorneys dropped dramatically from 5,912 in 1960 to 976 today, and the number of judges showed a similar trend. Now we take a closer look at the size and composition of the Dutch Bar and bench.

A. Office Size

The 'two hemispheres', which Heinz and Laumann (1982) identified in the Chicago Bar, are clearly visible in the Netherlands, with large, internationally oriented commercial law firms representing large organisations and small firms and solo practitioners working mainly for individuals and small businesses. Nevertheless, 'large' is a relative notion in a small country like the Netherlands. Today, 13 law offices have 100 or more lawyers, the largest being De Brauw, Blackstone and Westbroek (301 attorneys) (De stand van de advocatuur en het notariaat 2016) (see Tables 2 and 3).

Table 2 Attorneys (%) by Office Size 1960–2017

	1960	1972	1980	1991	2001	2017
1	40.3	29.3	18.1	14.6	11.9	17.2
2–5	48.0	38.9	42.7	39.9	27.6	30.1
6–20	11.6	22.0	24.5	29.3	29.4	26.5
21–60	-	9.5	12.4	9.4	12.8	13.0
> 60	-	-	0.1	0.3	18.4	13.3
Total	100	100	100	100	100	100

Sources: Klijn et al 1992: 41; Bruinsma and Gunst 2004: 1020–1026; Annual Report of the Dutch Bar Association 2016: 18. Numbers may not add up due to rounding.

Table 3 Number of Lawyers and Number of Law Offices by Law Firm Size on 1 January 2017

Office size	Number of lawyers	%	Number of offices	%
Solo practitioners	3,004	17.2	3,004	55.0
2–5 lawyers	5,266	30.1	1,864	34.1
6–20 lawyers	4,630	26.5	504	9.2
21–60	2,272	13.0	71	1.3
60 +	2,326	13.3	20	0.4
Total	17,498	100	5,463	100

Source: Annual Report of the Dutch Bar Association 2016: 18–19. Numbers may not add up due to rounding.

The proportion of solo practitioners is still substantial (17.2 per cent of lawyers and 55 per cent of offices) and has even grown during the last decade, despite the fact that the Dutch Bar Association strongly urges collaboration in its internal rules and publications. For instance, lawyers must make arrangements with colleagues for replacement during holidays or illness. Working in a small law firm continues to be preferred by most Dutch lawyers: 30.1 per cent work in firms of 2–5 lawyers and 26.5 per cent in firms of 6–20 (see Tables 2 and 3). The intense competition among lawyers in large law firms may also explain why so many lawyers work in solo or small firms. In the last decade 'work-life balance' has become one reason why some 'millennials' leave large firms to start boutique firms specialising in a niche area. Surveys of young lawyers (up to seven years' experience) reveal growing dissatisfaction with long working hours (approximately 20 per cent work 50–60 hours a week); 55 per cent of young lawyers do not feel their work and personal lives are in balance (SJBN 2016).

The top 20 law firms have either an unwritten 'up or out' policy (requiring those not made partner to leave) or performance-based profit sharing (De Haas 2013: 31). The mobility of lawyers between law firms has increased (Dullaert et al 2015: 12). The vast majority of law firms still bill by the hour (with discounts), although fixed or flat fees, risk-sharing arrangements and hybrid fee arrangements are becoming more common (for an overview, see De Brauw, Blackstone and Westbroek 2014).

B. The Internationalisation of Law Firms

As law practice has become increasingly international, cooperation between national and foreign firms and attorneys has taken different forms. Some firms choose to remain independent and concentrate on the Dutch market, often collaborating with a group of firms abroad called 'corresponding offices' or 'best partner for the job'. Some of these firms are affiliated with the Association of European Lawyers. Others belong to multi-national partnerships with offices in different countries. Some smaller firms (eg in the human rights area) have strategic partnerships with one or more firms abroad.

The internationalisation of law firms has been accompanied by the development of full service firms through associations with notarial, tax and accountancy firms (De Haas 2013: 18). The Dutch Bar Association prohibits attorneys from entering into partnerships with accountants or consultants, which it fears would curtail legal privileges (eg client confidentiality) and attorney independence. However, the rules do not forbid members of the Dutch Bar Association from registering as accountants.[7]

Although some feared at the end of the 1990s that multidisciplinary and multinational partnerships would fundamentally change the character of the Dutch legal profession – subordinating classical rule of law values to commercial profit – collaboration and mergers did not materialise to the extent expected (Bruinsma and Gunst 2004). Despite the changes in the legal services market, large (international) accounting firms have been expanding their legal services divisions.

C. Diversity: Gender and Ethnic Background

Although only a quarter of attorneys were women in 1990, they were 43.6 per cent on 1 January 2017 (see Table 1). Feminisation has been even more successful in the judiciary, from one-fifth of judges in 1990 to more than half today (see Table 4) and 89 per cent of judges under 35 (see Table 5). More women (69 per cent) than men (31 per cent) are employed as judicial assistants (Council for the Judiciary, Annual Report 2016), making the judiciary – especially the district courts – a female environment.

Table 4 Number of Judges and Percentage Female (1960–2016)

Year	Number of judges	Women (%)
1960	453	>1
1970	503	3
1980	578	?
1990	778	20
2000	1,546	41
2010	2,502	53
2016	2,357	58

Sources: De Groot-van Leeuwen 1991; Annual reports Council for the Judiciary.

---

[7] The Disciplinary Committee for Accountants is unhappy with this situation and urges attorneys-in-law to withdraw as accountants (*Financieel Dagblad* 16 August 2017).

Table 5 Age Distribution of Judges (Total and Female) on 31 December 2016

Age	Number of judges		Women
	Absolute	Percent	Percent
< 35	36	2	89
35–39	171	7	73
40–44	255	11	74
45–49	391	17	69
50–54	465	20	60
55–59	505	22	50
60–64	346	15	45
65–70	159	7	26
Total	2,328	100	58

Attempts to increase the number of ethnic minorities in the Bar and bench have been less successful. Very few have entered the ranks of the judiciary (Böcker and De Groot-van Leeuwen 2007; Van der Raad 2015). It is estimated that less than 2 per cent of lawyers have a non-Western minority background, much lower than the estimated 8 per cent of law students and 12 per cent of the population (Van der Raad 2015: 11, 14).

D. Other Developments within the Legal Profession

As predicted by Susskind (2010), the processes of specialisation, division of labour and digitisation have changed the legal profession. There are 29 specialist associations. However, outside the urban areas, many solo practitioners or small law firms continue to conduct a general practice.

Mid-sized and large law firms employ an increasing number of paralegals. Contrary to expectations, most paralegals have graduated from classical university law faculties rather than universities of applied sciences. The same phenomenon is visible within the judiciary. Holvast (2014: 54; see also 2017) noted that 'judicial assistants currently play a prominent role in the Dutch judicial decision-making process: they often write the first draft of judgments, they provide judges with memoranda that reflect their views on the merits of a case and they regularly actively participate in deliberation'.

On 12 July 2016, the Senate passed four Bills to digitise, improve and simplify civil and administrative procedures. For legal entities and professional attorneys (but not parties appearing pro se), digital litigation will be mandatory in district courts.

The role of legal professionals will probably also be changed by the introduction of new technologies, such as blockchains and computer programmes acting as artificially intelligent attorneys, helping professionals analyse and solve legal problems. In the Netherlands, however, these systems are in their infancy (Ter Voert 2016). There also are tools to help unrepresented individuals, such legal aid websites and online dispute resolution. The capability for online dispute resolution has existed for years, but the legal community is just beginning to bridge the gap between that potential and actual use (Lodder and Van Kralingen 2001; Van Aeken 2014).

IV. THE TENSE RELATIONSHIP BETWEEN THE GOVERNMENT AND THE LEGAL PROFESSION

Lawyer regulation (admission to the Bar, education and disciplinary proceedings) remains largely in the hands of the Dutch Bar Association, whose authority is firmly rooted in law and protected by the government. But it is not unchallenged. Abel predicted 30 years ago that legal professions would become more fragmented, a trend that is certainly visible in the Dutch legal services market. This section describes how regulatory reform has contributed to developments within the Dutch legal profession.

A. Liberalising the Legal Services Market

The first regulatory reform took place in 1997 after the Committee on the Reappraisal of Compulsory Representation proposed to restrict the attorneys' monopoly in civil commercial cases to claims above €5,000. In July 2011, this limit was raised to €25,000. These measures were primarily aimed at enhancing competition and improving access to justice. Both reforms led to increased litigation and greater diversity of legal representation (Shinnick et al 2003; Eshuis and Geurts 2016). Today, only 27 per cent of plaintiffs retain an attorney in cases claiming €5,000–25,000. Most hire less expensive representatives, such as bailiffs (53.5 per cent), debt collectors (9 per cent) or – newcomers in the Dutch legal landscape – lawyers from legal expenses insurance companies (7 per cent) (Eshuis and Geurts 2016: 184). Half of defendants simply default because most cases concern debt collection, which they know they will lose. Among those who defend themselves, almost half do so without a representative, while 80 per cent of the rest choose a lawyer.

Also in 1997, employed lawyers were allowed (under certain conditions) to register as attorneys. Although the Bar feared an influx of 2,000 new attorneys, fewer than 300 were admitted in the following two to three years (Shinnick et al 2003: 254). Today, more than 500 in-house lawyers are believed to have been admitted to the Bar (Piersma 2013), including those working for (legal expenses) insurance companies, trade unions and corporations. Admission is attractive to the lawyers because it allows them to represent clients in court in all cases; and it saves their employers the cost of hiring outside attorneys. The Dutch Bar Association has always been somewhat ambivalent about employed lawyers, fearing they do not enjoy the same degree of independence as outside counsel.

B. Debate about the Attorneys' Role

We have already seen that the legal services market has become more hybrid through mergers and associations of law firms with other legal service providers, the emergence of other service providers (eg accounting firms opening legal departments), and the Dutch Bar Association's admission of in-house lawyers. Together with the fact that attorneys specialise more in legal advice rather than litigation, these developments have raised questions within the Bar, such as: 'What is the role of an attorney?' 'Should all attorneys enjoy legal privilege or only those engaged in litigation?' 'Should the profession and its disciplinary system be modernised?' Debate over these questions began in 2005, culminating in legislation implemented in 2015.

A committee (*Commissie advocatuur* 2006) concluded – unsurprisingly – that independent attorneys were still indispensable in the Dutch democratic *rechtsstaat* and there were no good reasons to revise the rules on legal privilege. The committee advised codifying six core principles for lawyers (independence, partisanship, expertise, integrity, confidentiality and public responsibility). But the new Act on Advocates included only the first five because the Bar insisted that the sixth (public responsibility) was a more general obligation, which should defer to the core principle of partisanship in specific cases. Although the influence of these principles on lawyer behaviour is unknown, the debate focused greater attention on legal ethics.

The committee also concluded that supervision of the profession and the disciplinary system needed modernisation. In an early draft of the new Bill, responsibility for the Dutch Bar Association's compliance with the Act on Advocates was entrusted to a new independent committee composed of three members, only one of whom could be a lawyer and Association member. But the Association declared it 'unacceptable' for this committee to review the files of individual attorneys, which would undermine their independence from the government (since almost a third of all law suits are filed against government agencies).[8] The Bill was only adopted after it was amended five times over ten years. Supervision of the Association was still vested in an independent Supervisory Committee, but the deans of the local Bar associations remained responsible for the conduct of individual lawyers (Doornbos and De Groot-van Leeuwen 2014). After an intense period of turmoil, peace and quiet returned when the new legislation came into force in January 2015.

C. Managing the Courts

During the last two decades, the Dutch judiciary has undergone extensive transformations. In the 1980s, management was almost completely absent. Virtually all decisions were made by each court's judges, who performed their management duties part-time alongside their judicial duties. After experiments with different management arrangements, an integrated management structure was introduced in 2002. Many features reflected neoliberal policies and demonstrated a preoccupation with new public management principles (Mak 2008). Each court now has an executive board responsible for administration and management. Since 2012, membership on it has become a full-time occupation. The management of all courts is overseen by the Council for the Judiciary.

The creation of the Council in 2002 was part of a trend visible in European judiciaries over the last few decades (Voermans 2003). The Dutch Council for has far-reaching responsibilities, including the coordination and supervision of administration and policy, as well as daily management, acting as the link between the ministry and the courts (Voermans and Albers 2003: 102–03). It also controls the budget and

---

[8] Reaction of the Dutch Bar Association to the proposal of law, 18 November 2011, www.advocatenorde.nl.

distribution of resources among the courts (after which each court's executive board distributes resources internally). Although the Council was intended to enhance the independence of the judiciary, it is frequently criticised for being too closely aligned with the Ministry of Security and Justice (Bovend'Eert 2003; De Groot-van Leeuwen 2014: 173–80).

Following the new management model, a financing structure of output-based funding was established in 2005, a reorganisation of jurisdictions was implemented in January 2013, and preparations for the Bill on digitising litigation caused disruption and increased work pressure on judges. In a survey of 684 judges and prosecutors, 53 per cent felt pressured to meet production targets, especially judges in the criminal divisions of district courts (Fruytier et al 2013: 35). In December 2012, discomfort among judges overflowed when a group of them issued a manifesto summing up their objections to the management structure and heavy work load. Within two weeks, it was signed by approximately 700 out of 2,500 judges and supported by the President of the Dutch Supreme Court. Although this number (less than a third) might not seem significant, Dutch judges are usually reluctant to voice any public criticism (it is an implicit rule that judges express their views exclusively through their judgments) (Holvast and Doornbos 2015). Although the Council took some actions in response, budget cuts were also announced, provoking new anger among judges (Berendsen et al 2016).

V. ACCESS TO JUSTICE

A. Access to Legal Aid

The Netherlands has had a balanced and robust statutory system of legal aid since 1957. The current Legal Aid Act of 1994 (amended on 1 February 2015) seeks to provide representation to those who need professional assistance but are unable to (fully) bear the costs. Approximately 36 per cent of the population would qualify. The system has three components: (1) online digital help by means of an interactive application called Roadmap to Justice; (2) primary help by legal services counters (information, advice and, if necessary, referral to the next step); and (3) secondary help by private attorneys and mediators. In 2014, approximately 44 per cent of the Dutch Bar Association participated, 90 per cent of whom remained active within the system for at least five consecutive years (Legal Aid Board 2015: 27).

Although generally regarded as one of the major achievements of the Dutch *rechtsstaat*, the legal aid system has also proven to be vulnerable because it operates with an open-ended mandate. Legal aid expenditures doubled in 20 years, creating a major problem for successive governments (see Table 6). Rising costs are mainly attributable to increases in hourly legal aid fees and the number of people seeking recourse in the system. According to the Legal Aid Board, governments have contributed to the problem by promulgating complex laws and regulations (Legal Aid Board 2015: 30). To address the costs, the Parliament decided in 2008 and 2010 to cut the legal aid budget €50 million each year (approximately 11 per cent; see Table 6). A recent proposal for more radical cutbacks has been postponed.

Table 6 Dutch Population and Expenditure on Legal Aid

	1994	1998	2002	2006	2008	2010	2012	2014
Total Dutch population (1000s)	15,300	15,650	16,105	16,334	16,405	16,575	16,656	16,829
Total expenditure on legal aid in Euros (1000s)	184,000	195,000	315,000	398,000	440,000	472,000	486,000	432,000
Expenditure per capita in Euros	12	12	20	24	27	28	29	26

Source: Legal Aid Board 2015: 6. NB: The Central Bureau for Statistics estimates the average annual inflation rate between 1994 and 2015 at 2.05 per cent.

B. Access to Courts

Measures both to improve access to courts and to discourage litigation have been implemented, making courts more accessible to some and less accessible to others. Courts themselves have sought to improve access and make their decisions more comprehensible. For instance, judges have sought to write criminal judgments in plain language. Administrative law judges have devised more responsive approaches by placing legal conflicts within a broader context and using mediation to explore potential solutions (Verburg and Schueler 2014).

Digitalisation of court procedures and other technological developments have made legal services cheaper, faster and simpler. However, these developments do not help vulnerable clients, such as the computer illiterate and less well-educated (Ter Voert 2016). Even in the Netherlands, approximately 2.5 million people 16 or older (14–15 per cent of the population) have difficulties reading and calculating and lack digital skills (Algemene Rekenkamer 2016).

In the past, government sought to alleviate caseload pressures on the courts by removing routine cases. Traffic offences and misdemeanours carrying penalties of six years imprisonment or less were transferred from the criminal courts in 1992 and 2013, respectively, to public prosecutors, to be handled through an accelerated procedure. The belief was that with a faster process (in Dutch: ZSM, which initially stood for 'as fast as possible' but later became 'fast', 'meaningful' and 'meticulous) more efficient and effective action could be taken against common crimes (Thomas et al 2016).

As administrative sanctions became more widely available, the role of criminal courts in imposing penalties has diminished, and some of the tasks of civil and administrative courts have been transferred to governmental or other non-judicial institutions (Böcker et al 2016). For example, some of the civil courts' dispute-resolution tasks moved to dispute-resolution committees and mediators, leaving the courts with fewer cases and reducing their role to that of evaluator. These reforms were believed to offer a low-cost alternative to courts, resolve disputes more effectively, relieve caseload pressures, and reduce the costs for the government and parties.

VI. CONCLUSION

In this final part, we reflect on three themes relevant to cross-national comparisons: internationalisation, neoliberal policies, and access to justice. We also consider how these themes illuminate the extent to which countries like the Netherlands adhere to fundamental principles of the rule of law.

A. Internationalisation

Internationalisation is certainly visible in legal education and the legal profession, but it has not had the impact expected 30 years ago. Although the educational system has been harmonised by introducing a bachelor/master structure to make it compatible with those of other European countries, the number of international exchanges of law students remains modest. The majority of courses are still taught in Dutch and concern the national legal system. Internationalisation profoundly affects large law firms operating in global markets, such as those for corporate law, finance and insurance law. The Netherlands also host international law firms and companies with in-house counsel. However, the majority of Dutch lawyers still work in solo or small practices focused on domestic issues.

B. Neoliberal Policies

An 'efficiency takeover' is visible in the legal professions of the Netherlands, as manifested by output-based funding of law faculties and the judiciary, measured by the production of degrees and decisions. The second aspect is the 'redistribution' of legal work from attorneys and judges to paralegals, mediators and public prosecutors. A similar phenomenon is visible at the top of the judiciary, where roles of supervision, management and regulation have been transferred from legal professionals to specialised bodies. The new public management values, however, have been hotly debated. Judges have realised that a one-sided focus on 'output figures' may lead to a deterioration in the quality of adjudication. They are also acutely aware that the new management styles may affect their independence from court managers and the Council for the Judiciary. As a result, judges and lawyers are placing more emphasis on professional standards and autonomy.

C. Access for All?

We have addressed concerns about access at several levels. Legal education is accessible to all strata of Dutch society. Higher education was limited to the elite for a long time; but since the 1960s, 'education for all' has become a political ideal, gradually transforming the population of law students and the composition of the Bar and bench. However, whereas feminisation has changed the composition of the legal profession (in the lower ranks more than the higher), the participation of minorities remains low.

Access to legal aid has been constricted, though the budget cuts were not as radical as in countries like the UK. The government advocates self-help and alternative dispute resolution. Access to courts displays a mixed picture. On one hand, measures have made it easier for litigants to file claims and render judicial procedures and judgments more comprehensible. On the other, some types of cases have been removed from the courts, subjecting parties to administrative procedures and blurring the boundaries between criminal and administrative law.

These developments raise important questions for the rule of law. How will Dutch lawyers (private practitioners and in-house lawyers) balance commerce with independence? Will the judiciary be able to maintain its independence from court managers and the Council for the Judiciary? Future challenges will come from technological innovations that support self-help and standardise legal procedures (Ter Voert 2016). Access to justice will be threatened: will court procedures remain accessible for digital illiterates and the less well-educated? These debates are very much alive in Dutch society, where lawyers occupy a key position. Both attorneys and judges have shown their teeth in attempts to safeguard their independence within the Dutch Rule of Law (*democratische rechtsstaat*).

REFERENCES

Aeken, K van (2014) 'E-justice in the Low Countries' in B Hubeau and A Terlouw (eds), *Legal Aid in the Low Countries* (Cambridge, Intersentia) 307–29.

Algemene, R (2016) *Aanpak van laaggeletterdheid* (Den Haag, SDU).

Ashmann, MJAM (2011) *Over meesters en priesters: feit en fictie in de rechtswetenschap en rechtspleging* (The Hague, Boom).

—— (2015) 'Civiel effect: keurslijf of keurmerk?' *Nederlands Juristenblad* 66–69.

Berendsen, R, Creutzberg, A, van Holten, A, van Lieshout, S, Phaff, H, Schuman, A, Slootweg, M, Steenberghe, H and Veldhoen, G (2015) 'Tegenlicht, de rechterlijke organisatie tegen het licht' *Nederlands Juristenblad* 2800–803.

Blankenburg, E (1998) 'Patterns of Legal Culture: The Netherlands Compared to Neighboring Germany' 46(1) *American Journal of Comparative Law* 1–41.

Böcker, A and Groot-van Leeuwen, LE de (2007) 'Ethnic Minority Representation in the Judiciary: Diversity among Judges in Old and New Countries of Immigration' *The Judiciary Quarterly* 2007 (The Hague, Council for the Judiciary).

Böcker, A, Groot-van Leeuwen, LE de and Laemers, M (2016) *Verschuiving van rechterlijke taken: Een verkennend onderzoek op civiel- en bestuursrechtelijk terrein* (Den Haag, WODC).

Bovend'Eert, PPT (2003) 'De Raad voor de Rechtspraak, de Minister van Justitie en de Hoge Raad: drie kapiteins op een schip. Over toezicht en rechters' in Bovend'Eert, PPT et al (eds), *De rechter bewaakt* (Deventer, Kluwer).

Bruinsma, JF (2000) 'De ondraaglijke lichtheid van de rechtenstudie' *Nederlands Juristenblad* 1371–74.

—— (2003) *Dutch Law in Action* (Nijmegen, Ars Aequi Libri).

Bruinsma, JF and Gunst, JP (2004), 'Hoe commercieel zijn advocaten? MNP en MDP' in ieder geval een brug te ver' 79 *Nederlands Juristenblad* 1020–1026.

CBS (2010) 'Rechtsbescherming en veiligheid; Historie' www.statline.cbs.nl.

CEPEJ (2016) *European Judicial Systems: Efficiency and Quality of Justice* (Brussels, European Commission for the Efficiency of Justice).

Crull M and Wolf R (2002) *Talent gewonnen. Talent verspild? Een kwantitatief onderzoek naar instroom en doorstroom van allochtone studenten in het Nederlands Hoger Onderwijs 1997–2001* (Utrecht, ECHO).

De Brauw, Blackstone and Westbroek (2014) 'A Guide to Alternative Fee Arrangements' (Amsterdam, De Brauw).

De Groot-van Leeuwen, LE (1997) 'De feminisering van de juridische beroepen: een overzicht van onderzoeksresultaten' 23 *Justitiële Verkenningen* 103–117.

—— (2003) 'Women in the Dutch Legal Profession (1950–2000)' in U Schultz and G Shaw (eds), *Women in the World's Legal Professions* (Oxford, Hart Publishing).

—— (2006) 'Merit selection and diversity in the Dutch Judiciary' in PH Russell and K Malleson (eds), *Appointing Judges in an Age of Judicial Power: Critical Perspectives from around the World* (Toronto, University of Toronto Press) 145–58.

—— (2014) 'Judicial Reform in the Netherlands: Perception and Reception in the Judiciary' in B Hess (ed), *Judicial Reforms in Luxembourg and Europe, Studies of the Max Planck Institute Luxembourg for International, European and Regulatory Procedural Law* (Luxembourg, Nomos) 173–80.

Doornbos, N and de Groot-van Leeuwen, LE (2014) 'Modernising the Napoleonic Structure of Bar Regulation' in B Hubeau and A Terlouw (eds), *Legal Aid in the Low Countries*, (Antwerpen, Intersentia).

Dullaert, CM van de, Griendt, HFM and Mensch, J (2015) *De nieuwe advocaat. Nieuwe kansen voor ondernemende advocaten* (Den Haag, SDU).

Eshuis, RJJ and Geurts, T (2016) *Lagere drempels voor rechtzoekenden, Evaluatie van de verhoging van de competentiegrens 2011* (Den Haag, WODC).

Fruytier, BGM, Dikkers, J, Keesen, M, Janssen, J, Berg, I van den, Valeton, N and Schouteten, RLJ (2013) *Werkdruk bewezen. Eindrapport werkdrukonderzoek rechterlijke macht* (Utrecht, Hogeschool Utrecht).

Haas, M.J.O.M. de (2013), *Up or Out? Archetypes and Person-Organization fit in Dutch Law Firms* (PhD thesis, University of Amsterdam).

Heinz, JP and Laumann, EO (1982) *Chicago Lawyers; The Social Structure of the Bar* (New York/Chicago).

Henssen, EWA (1998) *Twee eeuwen advocatuur in Nederland 1798–1998* (Deventer, Kluwer).

Holvast, NL (2017) 'In the shadow of the judge; the involvement of judicial assistants in Dutch district courts' (dissertation) (The Hague, Eleven).

—— (2014) 'Considering the Consequences of Increased Reliance on Judicial Assistants: A Study on Dutch Courts' 21 *International Journal of the Legal Profession* 39–59.

Holvast, NL and Doornbos, N (2015) 'Exit, Voice and Loyalty within the Judiciary, Judges' Responses to New Managerialism in the Netherlands' 11 *Utrecht Law Review*, 49–63.

Kester, JGC and Huls, FWM (1992) 'Veertig jaar advocatuur. Veranderingen in de beroepsgroep, de bedrijfstak en de dienstverlening, 1952–1992' *Kwartaalbericht rechtsbescherming en veiligheid*, CBS, 9–42.

Klijn, A, Kester, JGC and Huls, FWM (1992) 'Advocatuur in Nederland 1952–1992' 18 *Justitiële Verkenningen* 10–44.

Koppen, JK (1991) *Een kwestie van discipline; over de externe democratisering van het wetenschappelijk onderwijs* (Amsterdam, Thesis).

Kortmann, SCJJ (2010) *Met recht advocaat. Een nieuwe opleiding: de Stagiaire-opleiding*, Advies van de Commissie Stagiaire-opleiding onder voorzitterschap van prof. mr. S.C.J.J. Kortmann (Nijmegen).

Legal Aid Board (2015), *Legal Aid in the Netherlands – a broad outline* (Den Bosch: Legal Aid Board).

Lodder, AR and Van Kralingen, RW (2001) 'Dossier online geschiloplossing' *Computerrecht* 231–60.
Lokin, JHA and Jansen, CJH (1995) *Tussen droom en daad: de Nederlandse Juristen Vereniging 1870–1995* (Zwolle, Tjeenk Willink).
Mak, E (2008) 'The European Judicial Organisation in a New Paradigm: The Influence of Principles of New Public Management on the Organisation of the European Courts' 14(6) *European Law Journal* 718–34.
Marguery, TP (2008) *Unity and Diversity of the Public Prosecution Services in Europe, A Study of the Czech, Dutch, French and Polish Systems* (PhD thesis, University of Groningen).
Nahuis, R and Noailly, J (2005) 'Competition and Quality in the Notary Profession' 94 *CPB Document* (The Hague, Netherlands Bureau for Economic Policy Analysis).
Openbaar Ministerie (2017) Netherlands Public Prosecution Service at a glance, www.om.nl/algemeen/english/@25162/brochure-the-public/.
Piersma, J (2013) Bedrijfsjuristen hebben toch recht op geheimen, *Financieel Dagblad* 22 March.
Raad, S van der (2015) *Othering and Inclusion of Ethnic Minority Professionals, A Study on Ethnic Diversity Discourses, Practices and Narratives in the Dutch Legal Workplace* (PhD thesis, Amsterdam, Free University).
Roos, NHM (1981) *Juristerij in Nederland: Sociale ontwikkelingen in de opleiding en de beroepen van juristen* (Deventer, Kluwer).
Schuyt, CJM (1988) 'The Rise of Lawyers in the Dutch Welfare State' in RL Abel and PhSC Lewis (eds), *Lawyers in Society: Vol II The Civil Law World* (Berkeley, University of California Press).
Shinnick, E, Bruinsma, F and Parker, C (2003) 'Aspects of Regulatory Reform in the Legal Profession: Australia, Ireland and the Netherlands' 10(3) *International Journal of the Legal Profession* 237–67.
SJBN (2016), *Enquête Stichting Jonge Balie Nederland* (Utrecht, SJBN).
Simon Thomas, MA, van Kampen, PTC and van Lent, P (2016) *Snel, betekenisvol en zorgvuldig, een tussenevaluatie van de ZSM-werkwijze* (Den Haag, WODC).
Stolker, C (2003) 'Ja, geleerd zijn jullie wel!, Over de status van de rechtswetenschap' *Nederlands Juristen Blad* 766–78.
Susskind, RE (2010) *The End of Lawyers?* (Oxford, Oxford University Press).
Ter Voert, M (2016) *Trends juridische beroepen in de toekomst: Ontwikkelingen binnen advocatuur en notariaat* (Den Haag, WODC).
Verburg, A and Schueler, B (2014) 'Procedural Justice in Dutch Administrative Court Proceedings' 10 *Utrecht Law Review* 56–72.
Voermans, W (2003) 'Councils for the Judiciary in Europe: Trends and Models' in FR Segado (ed), *The Spanish Constitution in the European Constitutional Context* (Madrid, Dykinson).
Voermans, W and Albers, P (2003) *Councils for the Judiciary in EU Countries* (Strasbourg, Council of Europe).
Wilson, RJ (2012) 'Practical Training in Law in the Netherlands: Big Law Model or Clinical Model, and the Call of Public Interest Law' 8 *Utrecht Law Review* 170–88.
Wolff, R and Crul, M (2003) *Blijvers en uitvallers in het hoger onderwijs, Een kwalitatief onderzoek naar de sociale en academische integratie van allochtone studenten* (Utrecht, Echo).
World Justice Project 2016. *Rule of Law Index 2016* (Washington, WJP).
Zwemmer, JW and Bosch-Boesjes, JE (2012) *Kwaliteit ondanks massaliteit* (QANU).

13

Switzerland

The End of Prosperity in the Age of Globalisation?

ISABEL BONI-LE GOFF, ELÉONORE LÉPINARD, GRÉGOIRE MALLARD AND NICKY LE FEUVRE

I. INTRODUCTION

FOR MORE THAN 30 years, scholars and analysts of the Swiss legal profession have predicted that inevitable changes would soon affect Swiss lawyers. Josephine Carr (1986) was quite positive about the forthcoming difficulties for Swiss lawyers, who had:

> been used to a comfortable life, with a codified law to apply, bank secrecy attracting overseas clients, easy fee income from hundreds of directorships, and international work the domain of a small number of sole practitioners and firms.

Benoit Bastard and Laura Caria-Vonèche (1988) predicted that a changing environment might trigger new rules of the game for Switzerland but found that the situation was still very advantageous in Geneva. While the authors acknowledged the diversity of legal practice in the 24 Swiss regions, each with its own training rules, Bar organisation and legislation, they insisted Geneva was exceptional because the canton was one of the most economically dynamic regions (as were Basel and Zurich). Geneva lawyers would have to deal with the 'emergence of businesses requiring broader knowledge and foreign contacts, which confer[red] an international dimension on the occupation of the lawyer' (ibid: 296). But they believed the legal profession would adapt well to the evolution of legal practice in an economy open to international influences and new legal initiatives.

Despite the early fears of some researchers, the contemporary Swiss legal profession still seems prosperous. The number of lawyers affiliated to the different Swiss Bars has increased significantly: 194 per cent from 1984 to 2016, an annual average increase rate of 3.4 per cent for the past ten years (Fédération Suisse des Avocats 2017). This steady growth is linked to what seems to be continuing economic prosperity. In 2012 the average annual income of Swiss lawyers was more than 140,000 CHF (US$147,000) (Bergmann and Frey 2014).

However, while Swiss lawyers' financial situation remains comfortable, this does not mean things have remained the same with respect to legal rules, practice settings, working standards or professional culture. On the contrary, Swiss legal practice is in many ways quite different from what it was 30 years ago. One of the most important changes occurred in 2002: the federal law on lawyers' free movement (*Loi fédérale sur la libre circulation des avocats*, LLCA) led to the unification of lawyers' practices in the different Swiss regions. Benoit Chappuis (2016a: 107), a renowned Geneva lawyer and law professor at the University of Geneva, declared that if 'the (LLCA) law is not a comprehensive legislation on lawyers', it has ended 'a regime of exclusively cantonal laws regulating the legal profession' in Switzerland. To facilitate practice throughout Switzerland, LLCA Article 12 exhaustively listed the professional rules every Swiss lawyer must observe to practise anywhere in the country. They concern litigation as well as transactional work (where lawyers do not have a monopoly). This was followed in 2011 by the unification of both criminal and civil procedure, reaffirming the desire to simplify law practice. These movements towards unification occurred at a time when the Swiss Bars were confronting many other changes, symbolising a new era for Swiss lawyers: 'the development of new regulations affecting the legal profession, new competition in the field of legal counseling, the development of new technologies, the burgeoning of new legal domains, new ways of practising the law' (Bydzovsky 2014).

The contemporary situation of the Swiss legal profession and its ongoing transformations reflect wider economic and geopolitical trends affecting the country, making it more difficult for Switzerland to preserve its status as a financial haven. We argue that the legal profession has not completed its adaptation to this more uncertain and volatile context. In the first section of this chapter, we analyse the dynamic demography of the Swiss legal profession over the last 30 years, emphasising some of the processes that have combined to fuel this growth. In the second section, we examine how this period of steady growth was accompanied by deep changes in the structure of Swiss capitalism, with important consequences for the nature and the division of legal labour and the organisation and the polarisation of practice settings. While offering data on the entire country, this paper will also present a more detailed description and analysis of French-speaking Switzerland, especially the regions of Geneva and Lausanne, where we have been doing empirical research on the early careers of young lawyers and the intersecting effects of globalisation and feminisation.[1] Our research is based on a mixed methods approach combining quantitative and qualitative data and analysing the professional lives and early careers of lawyers who entered the legal profession after 1998 in French-speaking Switzerland (as well as France). In this chapter, we will draw on the quantitative survey administered in Geneva (N=317) and Lausanne (N=156) in 2016 and 16 qualitative interviews with Swiss lawyers.

---

[1] The project 'Gendered Globalisation of the Legal Profession' is financed by the Fonds National Suisse (FNS) and is collecting and comparing data from three countries, Switzerland, France and Germany.

II. A RESILIENT PROSPERITY IN A TIME OF FEMINISATION AND UNIFICATION?

A. A Dynamic Demography

Because of a deeply rooted culture of cantonal independence (Chappuis 2009), the Swiss legal profession does not offer easy access to many statistics and records. However, recent statistics of the Federal Lawyers' Association (*Fédération Suisse des Avocats*, or FSA) give an overview of the demographic evolution of the profession. They show a very significant increase in the number of lawyers in every canton. The total number of Swiss lawyers increased almost threefold between 1984 and 2016, from 3,383 to 9,962, 32.1 per cent in the last decade (2006–16) (Fédération Suisse des Avocats 2017; Bastard and Cardia-Vonèche 1988), while the Swiss population grew only 29.5 per cent between 1984 and 2016 and 11.6 per cent between 2006 and 2016.[2]

The disproportionate numbers of lawyers in regions like Geneva, Zurich, Ticino, Bern and Vaud (Lausanne) persisted over the last three decades; in 2016 they contained two-thirds of all lawyers. These are the most economically dynamic regions, and Zurich and Geneva are the two largest economic centres. The Zurich Bar grew 293 per cent between 1984 and 2016, 34.2 per cent in the last decade (from 2,324 to 3,119). The Geneva Bar grew 44 per cent in the last decade (from 907 to 1,310). While the economic strength of German-speaking Zurich lies in its industrial sector and banking industry, French-speaking Geneva is one of the leading sites in the world for commodity trading, finance, wealth management and private banking. But even if Geneva and Zurich still rank first and second in the number of lawyers, other cantons have experienced even more rapid growth. The Lausanne Bar is one of the most demographically dynamic regions, with an increase of 340 per cent between 1984 and 2016 (from 147 to 648), 83.1 per cent in the last decade.[3] This numerical expansion has occurred in the context of legal, demographic and technological changes, which have accelerated in the past 15 years.

B. Almost a Unified Practice of Law

The 2002 LLCA allowing free movement of lawyers outside their cantonal Bar represents a major shift from an 'inner' protectionism inherited from the political history of Switzerland. Cantonal rules have been replaced by a federal code of ethics issued by the FSA. Furthermore, the 2011 law unifying both civil and criminal procedure has opened a new era for lawyers. During the same period, both the new principles of civil procedure and the progress of the Internet have increased public access to many legal forms, gradually changing Swiss citizens' relations to their judicial system.

---

[2] Office Fédérale de la Statistique/Bundesamst für Statistik.
[3] The population growth rate was 15.8 per cent for the Zurich region, 12.9 per cent for Geneva and 18.4 per cent for the Vaud region in the last decade (Office Fédérale de la Statistique/Bundesamst für Statistik) www.bfs.admin.ch/bfs/de/home/statistiken/bevoelkerung/stand-entwicklung/bevoelkerung.assetdetail.5886171.html.

If these new rules have transformed the practice of the law, Bar associations (*Ordres des Avocats*) have been less affected because these are private voluntary associations (Bar registration is administered by the local judicial authority). However, the unification of legal practice effected by the new regulations has changed the balance of power between the FSA (whose members are both the 24 cantonal Ordres and individual lawyers) and the cantonal Ordres, which remain focused on social networking. However, some Bar associations have become think tanks to address questions about the future of the profession (Elkaïm and Demierre 2014). For example, the Ordre des Avocats de Genève (ODAGE) recently created a committee dealing with the 'modernisation of the profession' and addressing issues like gender equality and the development of legal marketplaces.

C. A (Slow) Movement towards Feminisation, Without Gender Equality

The feminisation of the legal profession is a social phenomenon affecting many countries (Epstein et al 1995; Schultz and Shaw 2003). Switzerland is no exception, and Swiss women have actively contributed to the demographic growth of the last decades. In little more than a decade, the proportion of the FSA who were women increased significantly from 17 per cent in 2002 to 28 per cent in 2016 (Bergmann and Frey 2014; *Anwalts/Revue de l'Avocat* 2017). Even if it remains much lower than in other European countries like France, we might expect a convergence since women represented 61 per cent of University of Lausanne students with a bachelor's degree in law in 2016 and 59 per cent of students with a master's degree in law.

The representation of women in the legal profession differs significantly among cantons, ranging from 12.8 per cent to 38 per cent, partly as a result of local history and the way each region regulated entry before the LLCA. For instance, a PhD in Law could be required in certain regions (like Vaud), even if exceptions were made in the 1990s for law graduates who had practised as a court clerk (Burger et al 1989). Confronted by such restrictions, women had greater difficulty entering the profession, since very few had PhDs. In 1984, the representation of women among lawyers was twice as high in the Geneva region (15 per cent) as it was in Lausanne (the Vaud canton) (7 per cent). With the new federal regulation in place, however, women's representation in the Lausanne Bar (34.6 per cent) slightly surpassed that in the Geneva Bar (34.4 per cent) in the 2000s (*Anwalts/Revue de l'Avocat* 2017).

If women's greater access to the legal profession has wrought a major change in its demography, several factors combine to maintain rampant gender inequalities in their working conditions and careers and a thick glass ceiling. In the Geneva and Lausanne Bars, women are much less likely to be partners than men, even in the youngest generations (Boni-Le Goff et al 2019). Among lawyers who passed the Bar exam after 1998, women represented 64 and 61 per cent of associates respectively in Geneva and Lausanne, but only 21 and 29 per cent of equity partners (Boni-Le Goff et al 2017a).

Switzerland's modified male-breadwinner gender regime weighs heavily on the careers of women lawyers. Combined with a conception of state-family relations that assigns child-rearing responsibility to mothers, this leads to high rates of female part-time employment in the labour market in general and the legal profession in particular (Giraud and Lucas 2009). In 2016, 15 and 35 per cent of women lawyers in Lausanne and Geneva worked part-time compared with 2 and 10 per cent of men. Part-time work is likely to block women from partnerships and maintain them in subaltern positions in their practices.

Organisational practices embedded in a culture of 24/7 availability and long working hours[4] and a masculine ethos also contribute to producing gender inequalities by making it difficult to balance family life and work, especially for women. Indeed, many young lawyers we surveyed saw the culture of long hours as a major issue. Asked 'what would you like to change in your present job position?', 'more time flexibility to balance personal and professional life' was chosen first by Geneva and Lausanne lawyers (39 and 45 per cent) and 'fewer working hours' second (26 and 28 per cent). In this context, 26 per cent of women lawyers in Lausanne and 28 per cent in Geneva reported having experienced gender discriminations during the past five years (compared with just 1 and 3 per cent of men lawyers) (Boni-Le Goff et al 2017b).

Until recently, the increase in both the number of women lawyers and gender inequality received little attention from Bar associations, despite the creation of women's associations like ALBA[5] in the Vaud canton, dedicated to women lawyers' networking, support and promotion, or Women's Business Society founded in 2012 for women executives, a significant proportion of whose board were lawyers. But in the past two years, some symbolic changes have helped put the question of women's careers and equal access to partnership on the agenda, like the fact that the newly elected head of the Lausanne Bar association in 2016 was – for the first time in its history – a woman (a *Bâtonnière* instead of a *Bâtonnier*) (Maspoli 2016).[6] However, even if gender inequality has gained visibility, a complex set of social and organisational processes impedes rapid improvement, and firms are just beginning to address the problem. While American-based firms like Baker McKenzie have brought their gender equality programmes to Switzerland (albeit with negligible results), Swiss firms are just now timidly assessing the situation. Some medium-size firms have implemented a set of informal policies to encourage women to stay on the partnership track, and bigger firms have started discussing the issue, but there are no systematic schemes to promote women's access to partnership or improve work-life balance for employees.

D. A Persistent Prosperity?

Even if Swiss legal markets offer unequal opportunities to women and men, the financial situation of the profession is good, reflecting the nation's persistent economic prosperity. For the last decade, while the number of lawyers increased significantly,

---

[4] Lawyers in our survey reported working an average of 47.1 hours a week in Geneva and 46.4 hours in Lausanne.
[5] Femmes à la Barre (Women at the Bar) founded in 2001.
[6] *24 Heures*, 11 March 2016, see www.24heures.ch/vaud-regions/Une-bâtonnière-feministe-de-gauche-mais-indépendante/story/11982529.

economic stability has assured them steady business growth and stable average revenues. According to Bergmann and Frey (2014), the average income before taxes for full-time associates (*avocats collaborateurs*) amounted to 141,000 CHF (US$94,000 or €95,300)[7] in 2002 and 143,000 CHF (US$153,000 or €117,500) in 2012.[8] This exceeds the average income for all categories of lawyers (including partners and solo practitioners) in most European countries, for instance, €74,586 in France and €46,042 in Belgium in 2009. This is due in no small part to the Swiss economy, where the mean annual gross income in 2010 was €59,800, the highest in Europe. These high incomes must be seen in the context of the high cost of living in Switzerland. Still, in 2010 the average Swiss income in relation to purchasing power was 1.2 times higher than in Germany and 1.4 times higher than in France (*Enquête Suisse sur la structure des salaires 2012* 2015). Such persistent economic prosperity appears particularly impressive not only in the context of the rapid demographic growth of the profession but also because the population per lawyer has significantly declined from 1,389 in 1986 to 840 in 2016 (see Table 1). That ratio was much lower in 2016 in Geneva (370) and Zurich (472) than in rural cantons like Fribourg (1,923) and Thurgovie (2,222). Even if the ratios are lower in other European countries,[9] the very prosperity of the profession during a period of rapid growth is striking.

Table 1 Population per Lawyer in Switzerland and Select Cantons, 1986, 2006 and 2016

	1986	2006	2016
Switzerland	1,389	990	840
Geneva	595	510	370
Zurich	980	549	472
Vaud (Lausanne)	2,632	1,887	1,205
Fribourg	2,326	2,174	1,923
Thurgovie	2,941	2,273	2,222

Source: Burger et al (1989); FSA/SAV and Office Suisse de la Statistique.

Nonetheless, significant changes have occurred in the national and international economic environment during the last decade, raising concerns about the future of Switzerland as a financial haven and questioning lawyers' centrality in Swiss capitalism. These have accelerated a transformation in the structure and division of labour within the profession.

---

[7] Partly due to the nation's economic prosperity, the Swiss Franc appreciated against other currencies between 2002 and 2015. For instance, one CHF equalled €0.6894 in August 2002 and €1.033590 in August 2015. Since the end of 2015, the Swiss currency has undergone significant fluctuations and an overall slight depreciation – one CHF equalled €1.011936 in August 2018 and 1.013144 in July 2019).The growing uncertainties surrounding banking secrecy have played a role: fxtop.com/fr/historique-taux-change.php?A=1&C1=CHF&C2=USD&TR=1&DD1=29&MM1=07&YYYY1=2018&B=1&P=&I=1&DD2=29&MM2=07&YYYY2=2019&btnOK=Chercher.
[8] The average income of full-time partners in 2012 was 626,531 CHF.
[9] For instance, Germany (523), Belgium (598) and Italy (370). Conseil National des Barreaux (2013).

III. A LESS PROTECTED HAVEN

A. The Transformation of the Swiss Business Elites

> [T]he Swiss corporate networks underwent a strong dynamic of disintegration between 1980 and 2000 [because of the] transformation of the social composition and the strategies of the three fractions of the Swiss business elite. (Bühlmann et al 2012: 208)

First, corporate management became more international, as a significant proportion of top management positions were occupied by foreigners. At the same time, there were changes in the strategies deployed by different fractions of the Swiss business elite to achieve and maintain economic power. Whereas they were once 'well represented in integrating institutions, such as the army, and in wider political networks', members of the Swiss business elite disengaged from politics and increasingly completed their education with an MBA abroad (ibid: 212). Even if 'the dominant fraction maintains rather strong ties to political worlds and accumulates several mandates', the density and cohesion of corporate networks have clearly weakened, with fewer interlocking directorates and 'neo corporatist control mechanisms' (ibid: 218).

Second, this important shift in the business culture was accompanied by a relative decline in the centrality of lawyers and law graduates in the economic and political spheres. Swiss law requires 'any company set up in Switzerland to have the majority of its board be both Swiss nationals and residents' (ibid). For a long time this requirement allowed Swiss lawyers to earn large incomes in directors' fees. However, decisions of the Federal court in the 1980s forced lawyers to take a more active role in the businesses, making them 'more careful in their choice of directorships' (Carr 1986). This may partly explain the declining representation of law graduates in the Swiss business elite (Bühlmann et al 2012). Another study found that the proportion of members of Parliament who were law graduates fell from 73 per cent in 1910 to 46 per cent in 2010, while the proportion that were lawyers fell from 26 per cent to 20 per cent (Pilotti et al 2010). Nevertheless, lawyers and law graduates remain a higher proportion of legislators in Switzerland than in most other European countries.

B. The 'Real' End of Bank Secrecy?

Along with the transformation of the domestic economy, successive international regulations of and institutional pressures on money laundering, insider trading, illicit assets and tax evasion increasingly threatened the Swiss banking system by gradually limiting the extent and security of Swiss bank secrecy. These gradual limitations, which alter 'all three institutional dimensions [of bank secrecy]: banker confidentiality, nondisclosure to foreign authorities, and the clarification of customer identity by self-regulation' (Steinlin and Trampusch 2012: 252), are having major consequences for the Swiss economy and particularly the legal profession because of the strong dependence of most business law firms on the financial and banking industry (Carr 1986).

While bank secrecy had already been challenged in the 1970s with the first demand by the United States 'to prevent insider trading in the US through the use of Swiss banks' (Steinlin and Trampusch 2012; see also Pagano 2017), international pressure intensified in the 1980s following several financial and political scandals concerning dictators' illicit assets, such as President Marcos's accounts (Carr 1986; Sommaruga 2008; Pagano 2017). But until recently, the 'end of bank secrecy' was not seen as a very serious threat by economic and political actors in Switzerland and abroad. However, pressure from politically and economically significant countries like the United States has dramatically increased over the last 20 years (Cassani 2008). Furthermore

> the [financial] crisis [that began in 2007] has indirectly affected the Swiss financial market: government debt in several countries has increased heavily since the crisis, and this has led to a high level of international political pressure on untaxed money in Swiss bank accounts and therefore on the principle of Swiss banking secrecy itself. (Steinlin and Trampusch 2012: 252)

This political pressure

> led the [Swiss] Federal Council to decide on 13 March 2009, along with Austria, Belgium, and Luxembourg, that it would now accept Art. 26 of the OECD Model Tax Convention. Hence, the Federal Council announced that concerning foreign bank clients, administrative assistance would in future also be offered in individual cases of well-founded suspicion of tax evasion and not only in cases of tax fraud. (ibid: 254)

While Swiss political and financial elites 'vehemently' opposed most of the regulations recommended by the Financial Action Task Force (FATF), founded in 1989,

> the legislative history shows that important parts of the FATF recommendations have been implemented because international pressure defeated resistance. This is the case, for example, for the duty to report suspected money laundering activities. (Cassani 2008: 398)

Cassani predicted that Switzerland's growing dependence on a more globalised financial industry and transnational money circulation would weaken its ability to resist new limitations on bank secrecy. She was proved right. In 2013, the Swiss parliament approved a law known as FATCA, requiring Swiss banks to cooperate with US tax authorities (Leadersleague 2016b). This law initiated a long expensive legal process costing Swiss banks US$1.4 billion in penalties between August 2013 and December 2016. The US crackdown on tax evasion in Switzerland not only recovered a large amount of money but also inspired similar actions and strategic political pressure from the European Union and OECD (Peillon and Monteboug 2001). From 2018, no EU resident may hide undeclared income (Atkins 2016).

The recent vote for a more proactive and innovative regulation of illicit assets shows that Swiss politics on bank secrecy has substantially changed. The Federal Law on Recovery of Illicit Assets of Politically Exposed Persons (*Loi fédérale sur la restitution des valeurs patrimoniales d'origine illicite de personnes politiquement exposées*, or LRAI) came into force in 2011, offering a new political and administrative mechanism for recovering illicit assets and symbolising a new Swiss paradigm on bank secrecy (Cassani 2010; Pagano 2017).

These successive regulations have had quite damaging effects on Swiss financial institutions, with a vast majority of banks suffering stagnant or declining performance.[10]

---

[10] '59 out of the 94 banks that were analyzed reported that they either stabilized their poor performance levels or they continued to decline. In terms of International Market Volume (IMV), Hong Kong ranked highest with

But if the image and reputation of the Swiss financial system as a tax haven has been fading (Song 2015; Farine 2017), the consequences for the Swiss legal profession remain unclear. The new regulations have important implications for law practice, raising questions about confidentiality and the attorney-client privilege. The importance of these issues and the uncertainties surrounding lawyers' practices are visible in the number of recent professional publications on the topic. Some underline potential contradictions between Swiss federal law and the new recommendations and FATCA regulations to fight money laundering and tax evasion (Chappuis 2016). Others analyse (and criticise) the 'inflation' and extension of international recommendations and how they may affect lawyers' civil and criminal responsibilities in law practice (Cassani 2008; Montmollin 2014; Béguin 2015). The fact that several Geneva lawyers in one of the most prestigious Swiss law firms were implicated in the 2013 'offshore leaks' scandal for having provided important clients with anonymous bank accounts in various tax havens confirmed that the new regulatory context could negatively affect lawyers as well (International Consortium of Investigative Journalists; Duvillard 2013; Pagano 2017).

However, even if this uncertainty may increase lawyers' professional stress, it also generates new sources of business (Bydzovsky 2016; Boni-Le Goff 2017b). Indeed, the US FATCA 'tax programme' represented a significant increase in billable hours, especially for the largest Swiss firms, five of which handled 80 per cent of the FATCA cases (Leadersleague 2016b).

Victoria Pagano provides evidence of a similar specialisation in illicit assets recovery, which has gradually become a profitable niche for certain firms. She quotes a Geneva law firm partner who built a reputation in illicit assets recovery procedures during the previous 10 years: 'There is a rather limited circle of lawyers with a reputation on the matter of economic crimes, you find more or less always the same persons' (Pagano 2017: 54). Large law firms are clearly privileged in developing such niches because defendants incriminated in financial and economic crimes often contact the firm that manages their other legal matters.

C. Increased Competition in a More Polarised Profession

As shown in the last two sections, both the domestic economic structures and the international context have profoundly altered with the growing globalisation and interdependence of national and international economic regulations. The changes in the rules of the Swiss game have recently accelerated, but the legal profession had already entered an important restructuring process before this. In this last section, we emphasise two consequences of these transformations: the growing concentration of law firms and the gendered polarisation of law practice.

---

an increase of 47% from the years 2012–2014 while Switzerland increased only by 2% of their IMV' (*Deloitte Wealth Management Ranking, 2015*).

i. The Concentration of Law Firms

In the 1980s, the small size of Swiss law firms was considered appropriate for the small size of the domestic market and even as an asset: *'intuitu personae'* (personal services) and 'small is beautiful' were key phrases defining relations between lawyers and clients. As Carr (1986: 8) wrote: 'Banks and companies ... are still happy to adhere to the tradition of using a sole practitioner in Zurich or Geneva'. But she already perceived what Guertchakoff would later call 'increased pressure to expand' on Swiss law firms (Guertchakoff 2015).

Thirty years later, a wave of mergers and acquisitions has substantially increased the concentration of legal business and built new bridges between the two main Swiss legal markets, Geneva and Zurich. One of the landmarks was the creation in 1991 of the first Swiss law firm with more than 200 lawyers, Lenz & Staehelin, by the merger of a Zurich firm founded in 1917 by Conrad Staehelin with a Geneva competitor founded in 1951 by Raoul Lenz. Many other mergers followed and have not yet ceased (Mabut 2014). For instance in 2015, Carrard Associés, a Lausanne medium-size business law firm, merged with Kellerhals Anwälte, a Zurich firm (Meyer 2015). A few months later, in January 2016, Walder Wyss, a Zurich law firm, expanded and opened offices in Geneva and Lausanne, incorporating 18 lawyers from its competitor Froriep (Besson 2016). These structural transformations have not been limited to Geneva and Zurich but have also affected smaller Bars, especially those in regions experiencing dynamic economic and demographic growth, like Vaud. Indeed, after the 1991 merger, Lenz & Staehelin decided to open a new office in Lausanne.

Table 2 illustrates the transformation of the market by comparing the leading Geneva law firms in 1986 and 2017. Among the eight leading firms in 2017, three were not present in the Geneva market 30 years earlier (Bär & Karrer, Schellenberg Wittmer, and Homburger) and the largest– Lenz & Staehelin – had not yet merged (Ruche 2017; Bloch 2017).

Table 2 Major Geneva Law Firms (1986–2017)

Firm	Founded	Number of lawyers (1986)	History	Present position in the legal market	Number of lawyers (2017)
Etienne Blum Stehle & Manfrini	1968	11	Acquired by Baker McKenzie	Top 10	42
Froriep Rengli & ass.	1966	5	Members of the Geneva team left for Walter Wyss (2016). Offices abroad: Madrid and London	Top 10	80
Lalive Budin	1965	19		Top 10 (specialised in international arbitration)	77

(continued)

Table 2 *(Continued)*

Firm	Founded	Number of lawyers (1986)	History	Present position in the legal market	Number of lawyers (2017)
Lenz Schluep Briner & de Coulon	1951	26	Merger with Staehelin in 1991	Top 10 (1st)	200
Pirenne Python Schifferli Peter & Partners	1981	12	Python	Top 10	69
Poncet Turrettini Amaudruz & Neyroud	1940	19	Poncet Turrettini		31
Secretan Troyanov Terracina & Fichter	1967	8	Secretan Troyanov		16
Tavernier Gillioz de Preux Dorsaz	1981	9	Gillioz Dorsaz opened Hong Kong office in 2014		12
Bär et Karrer	1968	Not present in Geneva in 1986; 14 in Zurich	Opened office in Geneva in 2000	Top 10 (specialised in white collar crime)	150
Schellenberg Wittmer		Not present in Geneva in 1986 (founded 2000)	Merger of Brunschwig Wittmer and Schellenberg Haissly in 2000	Top 10	140
Homburger Achermann Müller & Heini	1958	Not present in Geneva in 1986; 22 in Zurich	Homburger opened an office in Geneva in DATE	Top 10	140

Sources: Bastard and Cardia-Vonèche 1988; Favre 2017; Ruche 2017; *Le Temps* 2017; Dossier spécial 'Avocats' (28 April), *Leadersleague* 2016a.

Although this concentration created larger firms, the average size of the largest Swiss firms remains quite modest compared with those in other countries. Lenz & Staehelin, ranked first, has only 200 lawyers (partners and associates), while Baker McKenzie has 4,800 worldwide (Meyer 2015). The size of the domestic market imposes some limitations arising from the growing number of conflicts of interest, especially for the biggest firms (Le Temps 2017).

However, this move towards concentration constitutes a major turning point for the Swiss legal market. It leads to a more rationalised and profit-driven approach. A former managing partner of one of the largest Swiss law firms has described the consequences of merging his Geneva firm with one in Zurich.

> We first merged with a practice from Zurich, so we became one of the largest practices in Switzerland. Which makes everybody laugh, well, in the States ... when you have reached the maximum size maybe you reach 300 people, so obviously for an American it's funny, but still, that's very, very big for the Swiss market, it's also a change of concept under the influence of Zurich ... much more geared towards money than us, clearly. And we moved, which sounds anecdotal, but it had a great impact, because we moved into a modern building, very functional, very beautiful, that encourages all sorts of communications, so it led to a stronger structuring of the team, we really became an entity.[11]

New information technologies have facilitated a more industrialised and standardised law practice. In this respect, Swiss firms are playing catch-up. The recently founded 'commission de modernisation' of the Geneva Bar Association is one example of the concern about the professional transformation and the intensified competition engendered by these technological changes (Alberini et al 2017).

While the profession has undergone a profound reorganisation since the 1980s, its relation to economic globalisation appears paradoxical. On one hand, very few law firms – even the largest – have expanded abroad. Froriep represents the rare Swiss firm with an international dimension (offices in Madrid and London), while the top-ranked Lenz & Staehelin remains exclusively domestic. On the other, the major Swiss firms have all developed international training and career standards inspired by the Cravath system because a large portion of their clients are not Swiss. Most of these firms encourage or even require young associates to obtain an LLM degree early in their careers, preferably in the US, in order to learn US practices and develop what V, a young woman associate in a prestigious business firm, called 'a bilingual approach to the law'. Such complementary training turned out to be particularly useful to her when she had to deal with important complex cases for Swiss banks during the US FATCA 'tax programme'. She does not regret having personally financed her very expensive LLM at Columbia University immediately after passing the Geneva Bar exam.

ii. A More Polarised Profession?

These changes in the practice of law along with the wave of concentration have consequences for the structure of the legal market. They have contributed to widening the gap between small and solo practices and large law firms. This is multi-faceted: small and large firms differ in how they practise law (the latter are much more specialised) and their revenues; but the divide also seems to be cultural. Chappuis (2016a: 106) describes the intense controversies surrounding a new regulation enabling law firms to become corporations.[12] The Federal Court ended this long-lasting debate in 2013 by finding that

---

[11] Interview with D, solo practitioner, former managing partner of a major Swiss law firm (6 August 2016).
[12] 'For two years after the law was passed, a segment of the profession, including heads of Bar Associations, challenged it in court. Meanwhile, several large firms favouring the law rapidly incorporated and took the risk

incorporating law firms was compatible with the principle of lawyers' independence. However, Chappuis (see n 12) emphasised how the possibility that the law might be invalidated sowed division and conflicts revealing opposing visions of the profession when the vast majority of the largest firms chose to become limited companies.

The chasm between small and large firms is particularly visible in their revenues. While solo practitioners earned an average of 234,000 CHF (gross before interest and taxes) in 2012, partners of incorporated law firms (public limited companies or limited liability companies) made an average of 546,000 CHF (Bergmann and Frey 2014). Compared with large firms, solo practitioners and small firms engage in more litigation and represent more individuals, as shown by the fact that 17 per cent of cases handled by solo practitioners were financed by legal aid (assistance judiciaire), more than three times the 5 per cent of cases handled by incorporated law firms (Bergmann and Frey 2014: n 9). Thus, the division resembles the two hemispheres described by Heinz and Laumann (1994).

Not surprisingly the divide between the wealthiest firms engaged in business and corporate law and the more precarious law practices is gendered. Almost half of women lawyers (49 per cent) but only 27 per cent of men depend on legal aid for more than 20 per cent of their cases (Bergmann and Frey 2014: n 9). This is consistent with our survey of young lawyers in Geneva and Lausanne, which shows that women are still overrepresented in the traditionally 'feminine' legal domains, such as family law and labour law.[13] In Lausanne, 69 per cent of women respondents practised family law compared to 51 per cent of men, 68 per cent of women practised labour law compared to 54 per cent of men, and just 30 per cent of women practised business law compared to 50 per cent of men. In Geneva the relative percentages were 58 and 37, 56 and 47, and 45 and 68.

Dependence on legal aid increased recently: in 2003, 23 per cent of men and 44 per cent of women depended on legal aid for more than 20 per cent of their cases; by 2012, these percentages had increased to 27 and 49 (Bergmann and Frey 2014: n 9). This means that outside the very profitable domains of business law (especially representing international business), many lawyers are facing less prosperous times. And because of the horizontal division of labour, those lawyers are more likely to be women.

Even if a larger number of young women are entering prestigious firms offering high incomes and high-powered careers, they confront many obstacles and fewer opportunities to get on the partner track and become partners. In this context, the survey revealed paradoxical data about job satisfaction and the intention to leave the profession. While equally high percentages of women and men are satisfied or very satisfied with their decision to become a lawyer (83 and 88 in Lausanne, 76 and 75 in Geneva), higher proportions of women than men intended to leave the Bar in the short or medium term (30 versus 15 in Lausanne, 36 versus 30 in Geneva). This 'paradox of satisfaction' among women lawyers has already been described in the US (Hull 1999). Although it has multiple causes, our study points to the central role of the high level of discrimination experienced by women lawyers. Being exposed to discrimination in income, promotions and access to partnership can provoke a high rate of attrition among women, even if they feel a great sense of accomplishment in the practice of law.

---

of having to return to their former legal status if the law were annulled': interview with Professor B Chappuis, 11 September 2017.

[13] Women were 54.6 per cent of the Geneva survey respondents and 50 per cent of the Lausanne respondents.

IV. CONCLUSION

Over the past three decades many important changes have affected Switzerland, its economy and its legal profession. One of the most important is the growing international pressure on bank secrecy and the Swiss federal decision to limit it. While this can generate business for lawyers who are seen as 'mediating the country out of bank secrecy' (Leadersleague 2016b), it also creates uncertainty and prompts new ways of practising law.

Both the Swiss Federation and the legal profession have taken many initiatives in recent decades to modernise and adapt legal practices to this changing environment, from the unification of the different cantonal professional rules to a succession of organisational transformations, mergers and acquisitions. But while the dynamic demography and sustained level of lawyers' incomes seem to portray a positive picture of the overall profession, the changing environment and legal practices tend to increase polarisation, with less favourable prospects for small firms and lawyers practising non-business law. This widening gap between different types of law practice is gendered and may contribute to the persistence of gender inequalities. Whether the demographic trends and prosperity of the profession will continue is unknown.

REFERENCES

Alberini, A, Bernard, F and Bugmann, L (2017) 'Legal marketplaces: opportunités ou menaces pour les avocats et les ordres d'avocats' 6 *Anwalts/Revue de l'Avocat* 253.

Anwalts/Revue de l'Avocat, Dossier 2016 'Anwaltspraxis/Pratique du Barreau', 2016/10 *Anwalts/Revue de l'Avocat*.

Atkins, R (2016) 'Switzerland moves further to end bank secrecy' *Financial Times* (29 December).

Bastard, B and Cardia-Vonèche, L (1988) 'The Lawyers of Geneva: An Analysis of Change in the Legal Profession' in RL Abel and PSC Lewis (eds), *Lawyers in Society: Vol II The Civil Law World* (Berkeley, University of California Press).

Béguin, N (2015) 'L'avocat face à la révision GAFI 2012' 2015/6 *Anwalts/Revue de l'Avocat* 256.

Bergmann, H and Frey, U (2014) 'Etude sur les frais professionnels de la Fédération Suisse des Avocats (Année de référence: 2012)' Université de Saint-Gall, Institut suisse de recherche pour les petites et moyennes entreprises.

Besson, S (2016) 'Razzia zürichoise chez les avocats d'affaires romands' *Le Temps* (6 January).

Bloch, G (2017) 'Une plongée au cœur du bureau d'avocats Schellenberg Wittmer' *Le Temps* (27 April).

Boni-Le Goff, I, Mallard, G, Lépinard, E, Le Feuvre, N and Morel, S (2017a) 'Powerlessness, Unfairness and Conflict. Explaining Three Ways of Experiencing Alienation in European Legal Professions' Paper presented at the Law and Society Conference, Mexico City.

Boni-Le Goff, I, Lépinard, E, Le Feuvre, N and Mallard, G (2017b) 'A case of love and hate. The Four Faces of Alienation Among Young Lawyers in France and Switzerland' Paper presented at the Law and Society Conference, Mexico City.

Boni-Le Goff, I, Le Feuvre, N, Mallard, G and Lépinard, E (2019) 'Do Gender Regimes Matter? Converging and Diverging Career Prospects Among Young French and Swiss Lawyers' in T Adams and M Choroszewicz (eds), *Gender, Age and Inequality in the Professions* (London, Routledge).

Bühlmann, F, David, T and Mach, A (2012) 'The Swiss business elite (1980–2000): How the Changing Composition of the Elite Explains the Decline of the Swiss Company Network' 41 *Economy and Society* 199.

Burger, M, Busino, G, Chaghaghi, F, Gendre, F, Hofer, G and Tschannen, O (1989) *Les avocats vaudois. Recherche Sociologique* (Lausanne, Université de Lausanne, Institut d'Anthropologie et de Sociologie).
Bydzovsky, C (2014) 'L'Ordre des Avocats de Genève' 1 *Anwalts/Revue de l'Avocat* 11.
— (2016) 'Les avocats, le stress et la prévention des conflits au travail' 1 *Anwalts/Revue de l'Avocat*, Anwaltspraxis/Pratique du Barreau, 10.
Carr, J (1986) 'The Discreet Charm of the Swiss Lawyer' 5 *International Financial Law Review* 7.
Cassani, U (2008) 'L'internationalisation du droit pénal économique et la politique de la Suisse: la lutte contre le blanchiment d'argent' 2 *Revue de Droit Suisse* 280.
— (2010) 'Les avoirs mal acquis, avant et après la chute du potentat' 20 *Swiss Review of International and European Law* 465.
Chappuis, B (2009) *La profession d'avocat. Tome 1 Le cadre légal et les principes essentiels*, 2nd edn (Geneva, Schultess Editions Romandes).
— (2016a) *La profession d'avocat. Tome 2 La pratique du métier. De la gestion d'une étude et la conduite des mandats à la responsabilité de l'avocat*, 2nd edn (Geneva, Schultess Editions Romandes).
— (2016b) 'Le secret de l'avocat. Quelques questions actuelles', 2016/2 *Anwalts/Revue de l'Avocat* 55.
Conseil National des Barreaux (2013) *Profession avocat. Les chiffres-clés de 6 pays de l'Union Européenne. Vers une connaissance statistique de la profession d'avocat en Europe* (Paris, Observatoire du Conseil National des Barreaux).
Deloitte Wealth Management Ranking, 2015.
Duvillard, L (2013) ' Plusieurs avocats suisses sont impliqués dans les Offshore Leaks' *La Tribune de Genève* (7 April).
Elkaïm, E and Demierre, B (2014) 'L'Ordre des Avocats Vaudois' 5 *Anwalts/ Revue de l'Avocat*, Thema/Question du jour 202.
Epstein, C, Sauté, R, Oglensky, B and Gever, M (1995) 'Glass Ceilings and Open Doors: Women's Advancement in the Legal Profession' 64 *Fordham Law Review* 306.
Farine, M (2017) 'La Suisse exclue du top 10 des places financières mondiales' *Le Temps* (27 May).
Favre, A (2017) 'Lenz et Staehelin, géant à taille humaine' *Le Temps* (27 April).
Fédération Suisse des Avocats (FSA) (2017) 'Mitgliederstatistik' SAV 2006–2016. *Anwalts/Revue de l'Avocat* 4.
Giraud, O and Lucas, B (2009) 'Le renouveau des régimes de genre en Allemagne et en Suisse: bonjour néo-maternalisme?' 46 *Cahiers du genre* 17.
Guertchakoff, S (2015) 'Les études d'avocats ne cessent de grandir' *Bilan* (2 March).
Leadersleague (2016a) 'Homburger's partners: "Banking regulation will bring law firms more work in regulatory and compliance areas"' (10 April).
Leadersleague (2016b) 'Law Firms in Switzerland: Mediating Banks out of Secrecy' *Leadersleague* (6 January).
Heinz, J and Laumann, E (1994) *Chicago Lawyers: The Social Structure of the Bar* (New York: Russell Sage Foundation and Chicago: American Bar Foundation).
International Consortium of Investigative Journalists (ICIJ) 'Panama Papers. Offshore Leaks Database' offshoreleaks.icij.org/.
Mabut, J (2014) 'L'étude Ziegler Poncet Grumbach fusionne avec des Zurichois', *La Tribune de Genève* (10 January).
Maspoli, P (2016) ' Une bâtonnière féministe, de gauche, mais indépendante' *24 Heures* (11 March).
Meyer, T (2015) 'De Zurich à Lausanne, les raisons d'une alliance' *24 Heures* (1 September).
Montmollin (de), D (2014) 'Lutte contre le blanchiment d'argent: les exigences supplémentaires prévues sont-elles vraiment indispensables ?' 2 *Anwalts/Revue de l'Avocat*, Anwaltspraxis/ Pratique du Barreau 65.
Office Fédéral de la Statistique (2015) *Enquête Suisse sur la structure des salaires 2012* (Neuchâtel: Office Fédéral de la Statistique).

Pagano, V (2017) 'Pour que le crime ne paie pas. Trajectoire Suisse de la problématique des avoirs illicites de personnes politiquement exposées' (MA dissertation) (Geneva, Graduate Institute Geneva, Institut de Hautes Etudes Internationales et du Développement).

Peillon, V and Montebourg, A (2001) *La lutte contre le blanchiment des capitaux en Suisse: un combat de façade. Mission d'information commune sur les obstacles au contrôle et à la répression de la délinquance financière et du blanchiment des capitaux en Europe. Rapport d'information* (Paris, Editions des arènes. Assemblée nationale).

Pilotti, A, Mach, A and Mazzoleni, O (2010) 'Les parlementaires suisses entre démocratisation et professionalisation, 1910–2000' 16 *Swiss Political Science Review* 211.

Ruche, S (2017) 'Bär et Karrer, le spécialiste du contentieux' *Le Temps* (27 April).

Schultz, U and Shaw, G (eds) (2003) *Women in the World's Legal Professions* (Oxford, Hart Publishing).

Sommaruga, C (2008) 'Le blocage des fonds Marcos en Suisse (1986) – Colloque Edouard Brunner' Presentation to Forum suisse de politique internationale (24 June).

Song, J (2015) 'The End of Secret Swiss Accounts? The Impact of the US Foreign Account Tax Compliance Act (FATCA) on Switzerland's Status as a Haven for Offshore Accounts' 35 *Northwestern Journal of International Law and Business* 687.

Steinlin, S and Trampusch, C (2012) 'Institutional shrinkage: The deviant case of Swiss banking secrecy' 6 *Regulation & Governance* 242.

Le Temps (2017) Dossier spécial 'Avocats' (28 April).

Part III

Eastern Europe and Russia

14

Czech Republic
Legal Professions Looking for Serenity and Stability

JAN KOBER*

I. INTRODUCTION

A. The Aim of the Chapter

AFTER LEAFING THROUGH the three brick-coloured volumes of Abel and Lewis (1988a; 1988b; 1989) lying on my desk, a colleague suddenly asked: 'But where is the volume covering the socialist countries?' Unfortunately, that was never written or planned. The 1988 work focused on developed capitalist countries (plus India, Venezuela, and Brazil); other countries were omitted because of 'limited resources and lack of national reporters' (Abel and Lewis 1988c: xi). The absence of Czechoslovakia, as well as the whole community of socialist countries,[1] in the 1988 book makes my situation complicated but challenging. I will provide information about developments during the three decades since the Abel and Lewis volumes were published and sketch a more complex background. A historical perspective makes sense because the developments of the last 30 years have been strongly influenced by the past.

B. Legal Professions and Lawyers

Unlike the occupational identities of lawyers in common law countries, those in the Czech Republic[2] are connected with particular legal professions, not a unitary 'legal profession'. Compared to the primary identity of the particular legal profession (eg judge, advocate,

---

* This work was created under subsidies for long-term conceptual development of the Institute of State and Law of the Czech Academy of Sciences (RVO: 68378122).
[1] About the notion, see Zweigert and Kötz (1971: 349 ff).
[2] The Czech Republic is a developed country in Central Europe with 10.6 million inhabitants. It has a high sustainable development index (7th worldwide) (Sachs 2019), a high inequality-adjusted human development index (27th worldwide), an income equality level (Gini coefficient) similar to those in Scandinavia, and one

prosecutor), the general 'lawyer'[3] identity is rather unimportant and subsidiary, merely a function of a common legal education in a law faculty; many legal professions require at least three years of additional specialised training.[4] Occupational identities based on the several legal professions are traditional in the Czech Lands, as they are throughout continental Europe.[5] Historically, the only manifestation of a common 'lawyer' identity was the emphasis on the Czech language as opposed to the official German, a position shared by all the legal professions.[6] After 1900, especially after 1918, the different professional associations became more important in legal life (and published their own journals). Legal professionals often devote their whole lives to a single legal profession. Transfers among them were uncommon during nineteenth and twentieth centuries with two exceptions: young practitioners becoming university law teachers, and transfers compelled by political ruptures (eg 1848/1850s, 1938/39, 1948/49, 1969/1970s, 1990s). Lifelong careers within a particular legal profession help build a stable internal culture, inculcate and informally enforce professional ethics, and socialise new entrants. The present situation is still influenced by the large-scale migrations between the legal professions during the 1990s, but it is slowly reverting to the traditional model of a lifetime career in a single legal profession.

C. The Historical Transitions in the Development of Legal Professions

Instead of presenting a comprehensive history of legal professions, I will concentrate on developments in recent decades.[7] Nevertheless, a brief overview of the historical context

---

of the lowest levels of religiosity in the world (14 per cent of inhabitants feel affiliated to a church/religious organisation, 2014 census). The Czech state has existed for 12 centuries, since the defence of Czechs (Bohemians by an older name derived from Latin) against military attack by Charlemagne in 805. In the fifteenth century, the country became the cradle of Protestantism (the Hussites after 1415, the Unity of Brethren after 1457) and successfully defended itself against much stronger armies during five consecutive crusades organised by the Pope. Under the Kings of the Habsburg dynasty (1526, 1621), the Lands of the Bohemian Crown were later subordinated to the common administration with Austrian Duchies (1749) but never completely lost their statehood. The position of Catholic Habsburgs as Bohemian Kings led to a brutal re-Catholisation of the mostly Protestant nation in the seventeenth and eighteenth centuries and a gradual Germanisation, displacing the Czech language, especially in the administration. In order to defend the language, the Czech revival movement (with an important role by lawyers) emerged in the late eighteenth and nineteenth centuries, inspiring profound Czech patriotism. During World War I, Czech volunteers formed Legions fighting against Austria-Hungary and Germany as allies of the *Entente Cordiale* on the French, Russian and Italian fronts. In 1918, the Lands of the Bohemian Crown recovered their full independence and merged with the Slovak region of former Hungary to become the Republic of Czechoslovakia. (The Czech and Slovak languages are extremely close and mutually comprehensible.) The country had a socialist economic and political system between 1948 and 1990. In 1993 Czechoslovakia (a federation since 1969) peacefully dissolved into the Czech Republic and the Slovak Republic.

[3] The word *právník/právnička* (lawyer; masculine, feminine), meaning a 'person educated in law', simply denotes someone who completed a five-year university education in law (*právo*) but may not be practising any legal profession.

[4] Unlike Moiseeva and Bocharov (see Chapter 16), who seem to adopt the US unitary legal profession as their standard, I do not interpret the Czech legal professions as a 'fragmentation', a negative feature or a problem. Moreover, the unitary 'lawyer' identity is not a useful concept for analysing the frequently contradictory or differentiated roles within many legal professions.

[5] See, eg Chapter 9 on France, by Bessy and Bastard, comparing the US term 'lawyer' with French legal professions.

[6] Eg the journal *Právník* (The Lawyer) founded in 1861 (which served all lawyers because it was the only Czech legal journal of that time), the Union of Lawyers founded in 1864, and the later Czech Lawyers' Convention and Slavonic Lawyers' Convention.

[7] For extended histories of legal professions, see Jireček (1903); Vaněček (1953); Kindl and Skřejpek (2016).

is indispensable,[8] focused on the important ruptures that influenced the legal professions. The shift to a republican regime (First Republic, 1918–38) had a limited impact on law but an important one on legal professions. Legal education and the legal professions were opened to women. The newly established state offices employed many lawyers, and the legal academy expanded, requiring more teachers and attracting many more students. The rise of international trade created new jobs for company lawyers as well as advocates.

In September 1938, after being betrayed by France (Czechoslovakia's key military ally), the Republic capitulated to the threats of Hitler's Germany, and predominantly German-speaking border districts of the Czech Lands were occupied by Hitler. (Czechs, antifascists and those suffering racial persecution, including many lawyers, had to flee to inner Czech Lands.) The profound political and refugee crisis led to the collapse of the First Republic and the establishment of the anti-democratic, anti-Semitic and anti-socialist regime of the Second Republic (1938–39). The conservative regime sidelined Parliament with rule by governmental decrees, initiating the persecution of Jews, communists and other groups; it also expelled married women from state employment. The persecutions deeply affected the legal professions. In March 1939, Hitler occupied the inner regions of the Czech Lands, reducing them to the colonial status of 'Protectorate' of the Reich; the Slovak region became a puppet state. In autumn 1939, after Czech-led street demonstrations against the Reich, the occupiers executed nine students and sent 1,200 others to concentration camps as hostages; all Czech universities were closed as part of the plan to Germanise the Czech Lands and eliminate future generations of Czechs (Čelovský 2005). Czech legal academia lost its institutional bases. Many legal professionals were murdered because of their alleged 'racial origins', executed or tortured to death as members of the underground resistance, or killed during the uprising in Slovakia. Some lawyers also died as members of the Czechoslovak army units fighting against Germany in France, Britain, Russia, the Middle East and Africa.

After the victory over Nazi Germany in 1945, law schools were overwhelmed by students, including the war generation who had missed university studies. Another transformation accompanied the government crisis of February 1948, after which illegal Action Committees (dominated by communists) ousted right-wing officials and politicians, including some lawyers. The Action Committees began the transition towards the power monopoly of the Communist Party (CP). Many legal professionals were pillars of the old regime: civil servants selected for their political conformity (judges, prosecutors, state service counsel, university professors). Many advocates were connected with the economic power groups. Some were removed and some relocated to other positions after 1948 as the new regime sought to install loyal legal professionals (new law graduates or those educated in extraordinary short-term courses). All professions formerly independent (advocate, notary) were transformed into public employees (although advocates retained some organisational independence). Lawyers employed by private corporations became counsel to state-owned companies.

Another major change occurred between 1968 and 1971. After August 1968, those who had sought political change (including some lawyers) feared repression. Some fled the country; others were discharged or relocated. Both 1948 and 1968 produced profound

---

[8] Standard works on Czech legal history are Jireček (1863–64; 1903); Čelakovský (1900–12); Kapras (1935); Vaněček (1975); Malý (1976; 2010); Soukup (2002); Beňa (1998); Kuklík (2015); Vojáček et al (2016); and Schelle and Tauchen (2016); Kober (2019); the most important works are large collective monographs Bianchi (1971) for the period 1848–1948 and Malý and Soukup (2004) for the period 1948–1989.

discontinuity and instability, which affected the legal professions. As part of the dissolution of the socialist bloc 20 years later, the CP power monopoly in Czechoslovakia collapsed during political negotiations following the wave of demonstrations (mostly in Prague). The period of transition started with roundtables and the mixed 'Government of National Understanding' and continued with the co-optation of the opposition into Parliament, ending the power monopoly ('leading role') of the CP. But while that monopoly was viewed as 'unnecessary' by 67 per cent of Czech respondents and 'less necessary' by another 18 per cent (and by 44 and 32 per cent of Slovak respondents, respectively) (Slejška and Herzmann 1990: 56), the socialist economic system and the idea of a 'third way' probably still enjoyed widespread support. When public opinion polls in November–December 1989 asked 'which way should the society [country] develop?', 3 per cent of respondents selected the 'capitalist way', 45 per cent the 'socialist way', and 47 per cent 'somewhere between capitalism and socialism' (5 per cent could not answer) (Slejška and Herzmann 1990: 51).

New political parties won the 1990 elections (the first pluralist elections in 40 years) and initiated a rapid transformation towards capitalism. First the entire economic and property sector (except for banks) was quickly privatised, but the extensive welfare system (social, health, housing and work security) was preserved to prevent discontent that might endanger privatisation. Then the banks were privatised. And finally the welfare system was constrained, underfinanced and dismantled. In economic terms, a country that had had almost no foreign investment now offered one of the highest inward foreign direct investment rates of return among developed countries (13 per cent) (UNCTAD 2013: 33). The legal professions underwent unprecedented changes. Advocates and notaries privatised; bailiffs were created and privatised; arbitrators were abolished; and prosecutors, judges, company lawyers, and state service counsel experienced changes in personnel. Advocacy boomed under capitalism: its numbers grew more than twelvefold between 1989 and 2017.

II. LEGAL PROFESSIONS

A. Overview of the Present Legal Professions

University legal education takes five years and ends with a master's degree. Another three years of professional training is required for advocates, notaries, private bailiffs, prosecutors and judges. The other legal professions, like corporate counsel, civil servants, local government counsel, and non-governmental organisation (NGO) counsel require no additional training. This chapter will focus on selected legal professions.

B. Advocates

Despite a long tradition of advocacy in the Czech Lands, modern regulation began with the 1848–49 reforms.[9] The *numerus clausus* for advocates was abolished when the

---

[9] For the history of advocacy see Balík (2009; 1998; 2005–08); Kober (1994); Tarabrin (1936); Kerecman and Manik (2011), Gajdošová and Kerecman (2015).

new advocates and disciplinary orders were published in 1868 and 1872. The profession required a seven-year traineeship. The prestige of advocates in the nineteenth century was high, and many were also active in municipal politics, state parliaments or the imperial Parliament. When municipal and district self-government became an instrument of the Czech political and economic revival, advocates played an important role. The number of advocates grew from 1,100 in 1890 to 1,789 in 1917 and 3,845 in 1938. Women were admitted in 1922, and the traineeship was shortened to six years and then to five in 1924 but reverted to six in 1936, following the economic crisis. Despite various efforts, the advocacy laws of the Czech Lands and Slovakia have never been unified.[10]

Major changes occurred between 1948 and 1951. The Advocacy Act of 1948 unified Czech and Slovak advocates and abolished their private economic character. The profession was restructured into a Supreme Association of Advocacy (SAA) and Regional Associations of Advocacy (RAAs), the latter consisting of the members and an elected board and president. Only some former advocates were allowed to continue practising; the selection was made by the SAA Administration Committee, whose criteria were mostly political. The number of advocates in each region was regulated and the total reduced to 570 in 1951. The Advocacy Act of 1951 made the district Advocacy Advisory Bureau (AAB) the primary unit, which employed advocates, trainees and administrative staff. The traineeship was shortened to two years. The structure was reformed by the Advocacy Act of 1963. The main units became the RAAs, whose members elected their boards, which chose the President. The Supreme Board of the Czech Advocacy (SBCA) consisted of delegates elected by members of the RAAs.

In 1989, there were 826 advocates in the Czech Lands. After the political changes in November and December 1989, opposition groups gained control over the SBCA on 21–22 February 1990, having been elected by the Extraordinary Advocates Conference. Their goal was the restoration of the capitalist model of advocacy existing before 1948. The Advocacy Act of 1990 recreated advocacy based on the principles found in capitalist countries. A contemporary advocate called it 'one of the first privatisations' (Stewart 1991). The AABs and RAAs were abolished and their property vested in the new Czech Chamber of Advocacy (CCA), which sold most of it to individual advocates. The CCA also became the only advocates organisation.

The principal feature of the new model was its extreme centralisation and militant opposition to self-government by advocates in the districts and regions. The reason was probably political: the abolition of regional self-government liquidated the opposition and prevented reversion to the regional and district advocacy structures or to a different design of the profession. All district and regional organisations disappeared. Today the CCA is a self-governing body vested with the power to issue regulations and discipline advocates. Although advocate trainees also belong, only advocates have voting rights. The CAA has a managing board (11 members, led by president), control board and disciplinary board, all elected by the Assembly of advocates. Voting is not obligatory. The election assemblies rotate between Prague and Brno and are dominated by advocates in those cities.

---

[10] Between 1939 and 1945, 642 Czech advocates were persecuted on racial grounds; only a few survived fascist rule. Others were murdered for political reasons. Many advocates and other lawyers were active in the underground resistance, and about 100 advocates were imprisoned.

In 1993–94, CCA started negotiations with the Chamber of Commercial Counsel (CCC), which concluded with both chambers supporting a change in the law and the incorporation of CCC members into CCA (implemented in 1996). After the 1994 attempt by the Thatcherite Prime Minister Václav Klaus to abolish all professional chambers as obstacles to the 'free market', the CCA mounted a successful defence. This included the 'revival' of its traditions: publishing books on the history of the profession (Kober 1994), reconstructing its traditional seat (Kaňka house), even bizarre imitations of the lost portraits of old Chamber presidents inspired by black and white photographs (Balík 2009: 251).

The influx of newcomers profoundly destabilised the whole profession: its traditions, ethical standards and, significantly, traineeship. Trainers had been deeply devoted to their role and proud of it. Decades later, many former trainees still recall their trainers with gratitude. The commitment of trainers to their role was inspired and nourished by professional tradition, and the absence of economic pressure before 1990 helped them avoid being distracted by the desire for profit. Those who entered advocacy from other legal professions in the 1990s were not subjected to any advocate training. Because all advocates (including the newcomers) may become trainers, this influx nearly destroyed the traditional methods and good practices of traineeship.[11] Whereas historically most trainers had a single trainee, the new act did not regulate this, allowing some advocates to operate 'legal factories' employing many trainees. Some of the new advocates were interested only in using trainees as modern-day serfs working for very low salaries (approaching the minimum wage); some trainers even hindered them from attending the obligatory classes organised by the CCA. Despite a request by the Ministry of Work and Social Affairs that the CCA set a decent minimum wage for trainees, the Chamber refused to interfere. In September 2017 there was a slight reform: trainers, who had to have practised at least a year, could have no more than five trainees.

The Advocacy Act confers various self-governmental and self-regulating powers on the chamber. It may organise the advocacy exams, control entry to the profession and promulgate a code of ethics. The chamber is very active in legal training, offering mandatory and voluntary courses and classes and opening its library to members. The chamber administers legal aid, helping those whose cases have been rejected by advocates find one willing to serve them. The chamber organises short free legal consultations for poor people at both its main office and in the regions. (More extensive legal aid is provided by NGOs, legal clinics of the law faculties, and individual advocates working pro bono.) The chamber's disciplinary board investigates complaints and can impose punishment ranging from fines to expulsion.

In 2016, there were 11,310 advocates (39.3 per cent women). Nearly 62 per cent had been born between 1966 and 1985. Most are solo practitioners (9,826); others practise in association (786), as partners in a public commercial company (126), in a limited liability company (856) and as employed advocates (246). The largest concentrations of advocates are in Prague (5,677) and Brno (1,129), with smaller numbers in Ostrava (356) and Pilsen (338).

---

[11] Because of the small number of advocates before 1990, the role of trainer was more or less obligatory for senior advocates (and conferred prestige). Since 1990, the great majority of advocates (especially solo practitioners) have taken no trainees at all, while other advocates take many in order to exploit their low-wage work – in which case there is little actual training.

The largest law firms are located in Prague, both local Czech firms and subsidiaries of large international firms. The foreign firms predominantly serve foreign investors but also work for large Czech corporate clients, especially in international cases. The largest Czech law firms developed from small local law firms after 1990 and serve large Czech and foreign corporate clients. Their size varies between 40 and 200 lawyers (advocates and trainees), but few have more than 100. Another group of mid-sized law firms (8–40 lawyers) serve a mostly Czech clientele as well as foreign clients, especially when they focus on a particular area of law or clients from a particular region or language (eg Spanish, German, Russian), often in accordance to the language skills of the firm's founder. The third category is small law firms (fewer than eight lawyers), often with one or two advocate partners and few employees, mostly serving medium or small local corporate clients and local individuals. The last and largest category (86.8 per cent) is solo practitioners, often working for individual clients and small local corporate clients. Small firms and solo practitioners often have a general practice, and many take cases by assignment (eg criminal defence paid by the state).

Table 1 Number of Advocates in the Territory of the Present Czech Republic (1890–2017)

Year	1890	1917	1938	1948	1951	1984	1986	1989	1990
Advocates	1,100	1,789	3,845	1,913	570	660	770	826	1,117
Year	1991	1995	1999	2000	2002	2005	2011	2016	2017
Advocates	1,208	4,969	6,554	6,207	7,343	7,553	9,526	11,310	11,520

Source: Kober (1994); Balík (2009); information from the Chamber; own research.

Table 2 Number of Advocate Trainees in the Territory of the Present Czech Republic (1990–2017)

Year	1990	1995	2000	2005	2010	2012	2015	2016	2017
Trainees	2,671	1,955	2,020	2,344	3,134	3,639	3,305	3,111	2,907

Source: Information from the Chamber; own research.

C. Judges

The 1991 judiciary reform radically changed the position of judges.[12] Despite the new pluralist political situation, election and dismissal of judges were abolished, and the old judicial system, based on the institutions of the Habsburg monarchy, was restored. After three years of traineeship or practice and the judicial exam, the candidate could be appointed as a judge with lifetime tenure by the President of the Republic. There are 3,018 judges (60.7 per cent women). The court system consists of four levels: District Courts (DC) (1,838 judges), Regional Courts (RC) (946), two High Courts (HC) (Prague and Olomouc, 91 and 44 judges) and the Supreme Court (SC) in Brno (64). Regional Courts have administrative panels, with an appeal to the Supreme Administrative Court (SAC)

---

[12] For the history of judges and the judiciary see Hlavsa (2002); Schelleová and Schelle (2004; 2004a); Adamová et al (2005); Princ (2015); Soukup (2002a); Šolle (1968–71).

D. Prosecutors

The modern 'procurator', called the State Prosecutor's Office (SPO), was founded in 1848, following the introduction of the indictment in criminal procedure. The structure of SPOs resembled that of the courts.[13] Prosecutors and their administrative assistants had to be politically reliable. After 1948, the SPO was reformed and renamed the Prosecution (P). Its power was gradually expanded, for instance by authorising it to intervene in civil matters and arbitration. In 1952 the P was transformed into an office to control legality in administrative matters (partly replacing the abolished SAC) and freed from supervision by the Ministry of Justice. The General Prosecutor was appointed by the President and responsible to the government.

Profound changes in P occurred in 1990; some staff were forced to leave the profession (Kuchta and Schelle 1994: 62). The old name, State Prosecutor's Office, was restored, and its role in civil and administrative matters was limited (and the SAC re-established). The transition from socialism to capitalism led to a marked rise in criminality, not only in Czechoslovakia (a threefold increase in reported crime between 1989 and 1994) but also in all former socialist countries (Levay 2000: 38). Criminality took new forms, including complex economic crimes and crimes with foreign elements and new organisational forms (mafia), and its brutality intensified. These developments, together with an increasing workload, made the profession of public prosecutor less attractive. The work of the SPO became more demanding and dangerous. There are 1,255 public prosecutors (nearly 54 per cent women). Because the profession has no chamber, its members created a professional association (Union of State Prosecutors) in 1995.

E. Notaries

The public notary was adopted from Italy in the thirteenth century.[14] The modern notary profession was based on the Notary Act of 1871, influenced by French law: it was an independent profession with a *numerus clausus*, territorial offices, and a strict separation between notary and advocacy. Notaries were independent public officers subject to control by the courts. Candidates were required to have a law degree and four years of training (at least two in a notary's office) and pass the notary exam. Notaries were appointed by the Minister of Justice with lifetime tenure. Notaries had boards and chambers with elected heads. In 1929, Czechoslovakia had 453 notary offices (422 in the Czech Lands, 61 in Slovakia and 10 in Subcarpathia). The first woman passed the notary exam in 1930 and was appointed to the notary office in 1938.

During the legal reforms at the end of the 1940s, some wanted to abolish the notary profession and divide its functions between advocates and the courts, as was the case in

---

[13] For more details see eg Kuchta and Schelle (1994); Flegl (1979); Vlček (2004); Fenyk (2001); Růžička (2005).
[14] For detailed information see eg Brázda et al (1976); Balík (2014); Bičovský (1968); Jireček (1903).

Yugoslavia and some Scandinavian countries. Tradition prevailed, however, and within a few years a form of notary consistent with socialism was adopted. In 1949, notaries lost their independence, becoming officers of the state (State Notaries) organised into regional notary boards; by 1950, there was one in every court district. In 1954, State Notaries were given primary decision-making powers over inheritance cases, acting as an administrative adjunct to the courts. Because notaries were viewed as doing merely administrative work, the profession was less attractive than that of a judge or advocate and became dominated by women.

Rapid privatisation in the 1990s profoundly changed the role of notaries, who became economically independent but regulated actors with a *numerus clausus* and their own chambers (national and regional) and were limited to practising within their districts. This independence and the new notary fee schedule made the profession quite attractive almost overnight. There were 316 notaries in 1995 (72.8 per cent women), 450 in 2009 (73.8 per cent women), and 442 in 2017 (74.2 per cent women).[15] The *numerus clausus* preserved the high number of women because the number of people with notary qualifications was limited during the transition from socialism, and the majority were women.

Notaries are organised into eight chambers (following the old regions). The largest number of notaries (67) are in Prague and its surroundings (the Municipal chamber). The Central Bohemian chamber serves the rest of that region except Prague, with 17 notaries exclusively in Prague, six outside Prague but with a branch office there, and 36 outside Prague. There are large chambers in Brno (80), Ostrava (65), Hradec Králové (55) and Pilsen (48) and smaller ones in Ústí nad Labem (37) and České Budějovice (31).

F. Private Bailiffs

The profession of private bailiff (*soudní exekutor/soudní exekutorka*)[16] was established in 2001 under the influence of neoliberalism and remains highly controversial. Compared to court bailiffs (*vykonavatel/vykonavatelka*), who are the court employees, the new profession of private bailiffs represented an unprecedented privatisation of state power. The reform was criticised by eminent scholars of civil procedure (Alena Winterová and Petr Hlavsa), as well as human rights NGOs. Like notaries, bailiffs have a *numerus clausus* but are not territorially limited. There is intense market competition among bailiffs. Some offices adopt aggressive tactics, becoming giant 'firms' operating throughout the country and employing a large number of candidates, trainees and others, whereas other offices have limited their activities to the district of their seat. Attempts to reform the law and limit bailiffs to their districts failed. Discipline is handled by the disciplinary body of the SAC.[17] The main powers of private bailiffs are seizing property or enforcing court decisions after judicial authorisation. Bailiffs also provide deposits (of money, deeds or

---

[15] Because the register does not specify gender, I used the female surname suffix ová as a surrogate. Since not all women use this, the figures are minima.

[16] The Czech term literally means 'court bailiff', which is misleading. Court bailiffs are court employees, and most have no legal education. For more about the profession see eg Winterová (1998; 2001).

[17] Discipline was originally vested in the bailiffs' chamber but was transferred to the court following scandals and criticism.

movables) and write 'bailiff's deeds' proving they have witnessed certain acts. Bailiffs earn a law degree, complete three years of training, pass the bailiffs exam and then wait to be selected for a vacant office. Like the Chamber of Advocates, the Chamber of Bailiffs is a centralised organisation (with its seat in Prague) whose Assembly elects the Board; the Chamber exercises control over the bailiffs. In 2017 there were 154 bailiffs (26.62 per cent women); information about bailiff candidates and trainees is secret.[18]

The role of private bailiffs in debt collection is one of the most serious social and political issues. The entire profession is reviled by the public. Bailiff practice has been criticised by human rights NGOs. But the profession is just one part of a complex of problems: debt collection, non-bank lenders, gambling machines and social dysfunction in some regions. The best solution might be abolition of the private profession and re-integration of private bailiffs and bailiff trainees as court employees.

G. Corporate Counsel

The profession of corporate counsel is among the least researched. Because they were treated like other employees and had no special regulations or chamber, we know very little about their development (Hajn 1968). In early 1990s, their numbers dwindled with the decline of state enterprises. Some switched to the profession of commercial counsel, created in 1990, which had its own chamber and merged with the advocacy in 1996 (Balík 2009: 234). Commercial counsel were limited to commercial and corporate ('entrepreneurial') matters by law; but in this area they were entitled to provide all the services of advocates (offering legal advice, drafting legal deeds, appearing in court). Their chamber and three-year traineeship resembled those of advocates. The profession of commercial counsel sought to privatise corporate counselling and encourage employed counsel to become economically independent – often with comical consequences: most of the new private counsel were just re-hired by their former employers (state companies) and often remained in their old offices, now rented from their former employer.

Advocates and commercial counsel were competitors in the field of corporate and commercial law. But advocates enjoyed greater prestige (for historical reasons) and a stronger legal position. The strategic 'takeover' of commercial counsel by the advocates in 1996 was profitable for both. The former enhanced their status and market (without taking three years of advocacy traineeship and the advocates exam), and the latter eliminated their only competitor and critic, while retaining market dominance. Only the demand for legal services in the 1990s made the deal possible: there were so few advocates that they were not economically threatened by the sudden increase in numbers. During and after the privatisation of state corporations (a process that often failed as many declared bankruptcy, suffered embezzlement by the new private owners[19] or were bought by foreign competitors only to be shut down) some of the corporate counsel who did not become commercial counsel also migrated into advocacy after 1996. But other lawyers remained active in old and new corporations. Since the wild 1990s, the profession

---

[18] The Chamber of Bailiffs refused to give me any statistical data about its members. The numbers given were calculated from the official list of bailiffs.

[19] The new Czech verb *vytunelovat* (to tunnel out or steal something) has been used ever since.

of corporate counsel has become more stable. It has a voluntary professional association, the Union of Corporate Counsel, but no chamber or special regulation.

H. State Service Counsel

The State Service is the largest employer in the Czech Republic, 422,445 employees in 2015, of whom about 150,000 are employed by self-governing bodies (regions and municipalities) and the rest by government or public contributory institutions financed by the public budgets, such as schools, libraries,[20] museums, archives, hospitals, and social services. The exact number of legal counsel in the state service is unknown. Every office has a legal department, from the large departments of ministries and special legal offices like the Ombudsman (*Ochránce*) to individual legal counsel in the offices of small towns. State Service counsel have no chamber or association. The Czech Republic lacks good education for State Service lawyers or non-legal administrators. One source of the country's problems is the absence of a strong stable State Service whose employees (including legal counsel) are fearlessly devoted to the public interest. The vulnerability of the service may be due to the lack of an *esprit de corps*, which could be instilled by special education and training.

I. Legal Academia: A Tribe of Teachers and Researchers

i. Faculties of Law

Legal education began at the Faculty of Charles University in Prague, founded in 1348.[21] During the eighteenth and nineteenth centuries, legal studies also were offered at the University of Olomouc (abolished for political reasons in 1855). In November 1918, a motion was tabled to fulfil an old Czech goal – the foundation of a second university in Brno – which was approved in January 1919. A few months later, the third university was established in the Slovak capital, Bratislava. Both had law faculties. The most important changes in their structure date from the 1950s: the old model of a professorial chair and assistants was replaced by the modern model of specialised departments following the Soviet pattern (Litsch 2004: 84). The change had positive consequences, including a better work environment, greater equality for the former assistants and more opportunities for women. The department model is still regarded as a good solution (Kučera 2016: 22). Efforts to increase student-teacher contact in the 1950s led to a rise in the number of teachers. During the 1990s, faculties were opened in Olomouc and Pilsen. But weak control mechanisms and the lack of standards, planning, centralised coordination and

---

[20] The Czech Republic has one of the highest number of public libraries per capita in the world (618.8 libraries per 1 million inhabitants; the number does not include the school libraries: IFLA 2018). The dense net of libraries goes back to the Libraries Act of 1919 which obliged every municipality to have a public library and to spend a standard amount of money per capita every year for its books.
[21] For the history of legal education and legal scholarship see, eg Litsch (2004); Adamová (1998); Maršálek (2004); Pavlíček (1991). About the reforms see Kuklík (2009); Kristková (2012); Tomoszek (2013) and Bobek (2005).

support in the new faculties created many problems. Today the four faculties have 431 teachers (many part-time) (Prague 170, Brno 107, Olomouc 79, and Pilsen 75). Women are 30.85 per cent of the total, ranging from 20 per cent in Pilsen to 37.38 per cent in Brno.

ii. Legal Research Facilities

Legal research remained the exclusive domain of universities until 1953, when the Czechoslovak Academy of Sciences was founded as a national research institution. The Research Centre for the History of State and Law in Prague was established in 1953 as one of the first non-university legal history research institutions in the world. Two other legal research centres followed, for International Law and Comparative Law of the Socialist Countries. These were later unified under the umbrella of the Institute of State and Law (ISL); a similar Slovak Institute was established in Bratislava. Both institutes retain their central role. After 1989, some former ISL employees who had suffered political discrimination after 1968 were rehabilitated. During the 1990s, the ISL experienced a kind of shock treatment, suffering severe budget cuts, losing about two-thirds of its employees, and seeing parts of its large library devastated and one of its buildings privatised. It took years to overcome the crisis. In 2019, the Institute has 46 research employees (many part-time and some financed through grants), about 33 per cent of whom are women.

iii. Common Problems

The most serious problem of Czech legal academia is the far-reaching influence that business exerts through some researchers' parallel careers in large law firms or companies. According to Tomáš Richter (2013), an independent legal academy simply does not exist in areas important to business. Because many academics write scholarly opinions and belong to the Legislative Council or various legislative commissions, they can influence legal policies. When those scholars are practising advocates working (directly or indirectly) for the largest businesses, they cannot divide themselves into two separate persons with competing views and opinions. Some scholars misuse their scholarly positions to benefit their clients or the interests of powerful corporations or individuals.

One problematic feature of Czech legal academia is the multiplicity of work contracts. Instead of holding one full-time job at a single institution, many academics combine several (sometimes full-time) contracts at different institutions. This has two main causes. Before 1990, nearly all law faculty positions were full-time and permanent. Since then there has been a growing trend toward part-time temporary positions, engendering the phenomenon of 'flying professors', who spend their week wandering like itinerant peddlers among various universities. This is paralysing the inner life of the institutions. One reason for the multiplication of work contracts may be the exaggerated income expectations[22] of young lawyers, shaped by their perception of the legal professions and pressure from peers, parents or partners. Because most PhD students have part-time poorly paid positions in legal academia they have to get another principal work contract.

---

[22] This might be a reflection of the hunger for legal services during the 1990s. The popular image of the legal professional among the Czech public is a wealthy person, whereas the real situation of advocates outside the large Prague law firms may be very different.

Even many senior lawyers in comfortable economic positions still try to accumulate the greatest number of work contracts and maximise their income.

III. THE INTERSECTIONS

A. Gender and Legal Professions

Women were excluded from legal studies until the end of the Habsburg monarchy. As part of the equalisation reforms, legal studies were opened to women in November 1918,[23] women in the state service (teachers, administrators) were no longer forced to resign when they married (1919), and women could become advocate trainees and advocates (1922). The first woman advocate was inscribed by the Chamber after five years of training in 1929, and the number of women advocates rose to 71 in 1938 (59 in the Czech Lands, 12 in Slovakia). In 1948, 40 of the 61 women advocates, ie 67.2 per cent of all those in the Czech Lands, lived in Prague (compared to 44.2 per cent of men advocates). Women advocates remained scarce until the early 1970s.

The presence of women in the legal professions was officially praised as a sign of equality and social modernisation (eg the Slovak movie *The Women Advocate* (1977), whose subtitle was: 'The story of a young modern woman in an unusual and demanding profession').[24] The representation of women in all legal professions greatly increased during the 1970s and the 1980s, when women born in the 1950s (the large baby-boom generation) and educated in the socialist era began their legal careers. The early 1980s constituted a final breakthrough, as women became commonplace in legal academia and the judiciary. For example, the advocacy had 660 professionals in 1984, serving to 10.3 million inhabitants, ie 15,625 people per advocate. A quarter of advocates were women (25.75 per cent), but their numbers varied between 30.7 per cent (Prague) and 15.9 per cent (Pilsen). Many Advocacy Advisory Bureaus (AABs) had no women at all, whereas some had high proportion, eg 75 per cent in AAB Třebíč (South Moravia), 66.7 per cent in AAB Prague-West, 50 per cent in both AAB No 7 in Prague and AAB Mladá Boleslav (Central Bohemia), and 46 per cent in AAB Karviná (Ostrava region). Women rarely were appointed as AAB leaders (partly because women tended to be younger than their male colleagues). Eleven out of 80 AABs had women leaders in 1984,[25] three in the Ostrava region, which also elected a woman as president of the Ostrava Regional Association of Advocacy (RAA);[26] another three were in the Hradec Králové. In the highest advocacy council, the Supreme Board of the Czech Advocacy, a woman has been one of two vice-presidents. After 1989, the number of women in advocacy did not change dramatically. In May 1991, nearly one year after the new Advocacy Act opened the

---

[23] Women also secured the franchise and legal equality with men.
[24] *Advokátka* (ČSSR 1977) 87 min. The Czech and Slovak nouns have masculine and feminine forms.
[25] Although women formed a high proportion of lawyers in Prague, they had better chance of bcoming an AAB leader in the eastern regions (Ostrava and Hradec Králové) than in Southern Moravia (where there were two), Prague (one), Central Bohemia (one), and Southern Bohemia (one).
[26] Women comprised 25.5 per cent of this RAA. This might be explained by the fact that the regional economy of industry and mining opened more non-traditional roles to women. Since 1989, the Ostrava region has been known as the political citadel of the left (Social Democratic Party and Communist Party).

profession, women accounted for 27.6 per cent, ie only 1.85 per cent higher than in 1984 (334 out of 1,208) but 34.9 per cent in Prague.

The socialist decades greatly improved gender equality, especially with respect to work and education. Yet the culture changed more slowly, continuing to make women responsible for housework and childcare. Even though the 1948 Constitution decreed equality in wages and the state wielded complete power over the nationalised economy, the wages of men and women were never equalised (Havelková 2007; 2017; Kober 2018). After 1990, the gender wage gap persisted and even grew.[27] The public discourse of the 1990s and 2000s was dominated by local neoconservative and neoliberal journalists hostile to equality issues, gender research and feminism (calling it 'Marxist') and even sexual harassment complaints (Osvaldová 2004).

Although the situation of women is probably better in Czech legal professions than in those of other countries, many Czech legal professions still have a significant gender imbalance. Other and perhaps more important imbalances characterise the internal hierarchy of each profession. The most feminised profession is the notary (73 per cent women), while the most masculine is the private bailiff (26.62 per cent women). Women are 25–40 per cent of legal academia and 39.3 per cent of advocates. Women comprise 60.7 per cent of judges (65.88 per cent of DC judges, 56.76 per cent of RC judges, and 43.7 per cent of HC judges), 34.28 per cent of SACs and 20.31 per cent of SCs. Women are underrepresented among court presidents and vice-presidents (46.8 per cent in DCs, 29.54 per cent in RCs, 28.57 per cent in the HC, and none on the SAC and SC, the highest judicial positions). Women are 58.92 per cent of the DP and 49.23 per cent of the RP but much less in the highest bodies (31.46 per cent in the HP and 31.48 per cent in the SP). An important question is how much the remaining differences are attributable to disproportions among the older generations and how much to subconscious gender stereotypes. No gender data are available about corporate counsel or State Service counsel.

B. Legal Education

The Czech Republic offers a university education along continental European lines based on traditional universities, not colleges. The basic principles of the Czech educational system are solidarity and equality: since 1945, university education (undergraduate, postgraduate, and PhD) has been, in principle, free of charge. The study of law takes five years and leads to a master's degree[28] after the state exams and defence of the master's thesis. The law degree allows its holder to enter any unregulated legal or other profession (eg corporate counsel, state service counsel, NGO counsel, and social workers). Regulated legal professions require further professional training (three years) and professional exams. Historically, the study of law was open to every person with a grammar school leaving

---

[27] Data exclusively on legal professions are not available. In 2017, the median monthly income for the entire working population was 24,896 CZK (€954). Gender unequality is still high: the median income is 27,181 CZK for men and 22,300 CZK for women.

[28] There are no bachelor's degrees in law. The country was urged to adopt the market-oriented Bologna model (including the division of studies into bachelor's and master's degrees), but law and medicine retained their traditional forms.

exam (as in Austria or Germany). In 1948, a *numerus clausus* was introduced, leaving each faculty free to determine its selection procedure. The scarcity of advocates and the booming market for legal services after 1990 created a durable popular image that legal professions promised a 'golden bonanza', ensuring that the number of applications would remain high.

The structure and methods of legal education resemble those of a hundred years ago. Students are overwhelmed by historical and theoretical disciplines – legal history, Roman law, legal theory, and legal philosophy – which would be more meaningful after they studied the living law. Unlike students in other countries (eg Germany), Czech students are not encouraged to move between universities during their studies,[29] a problem that is closely connected to inbreeding (*Inzucht*) (discussed below).

Yet promising innovations include the clinical legal education and legal skills education projects initiated by teachers at the Palacký University in Olomouc (Tomoszek 2013), which have inspired other faculties (Kristková 2012). Another new phenomenon is legal moots and mock trials. Some practical legal courses have been organised outside the universities, such as the Human Rights School of the NGO Pro Bono Alliance, which has attracted students from various law faculties by its interactive teaching.

C. Education and Training of Law Teachers and Scholars

The faculties also offer internal and external PhD programmes for new teachers and scholars. Internal candidates are typically required to teach and are given a small bursary.[30] Most candidates are external, incurring no teaching obligation but receiving no financial support. Both internal and external candidates must pass several exams and produce some publications. Supervisors often have more candidates than they can supervise effectively; and most supervisors also have to counsel or lead some master's and *rigorosum*[31] theses and serve as examiners. The number of PhD candidates is too high. However, some candidates are more interested in obtaining the title[32] than in conducting research or teaching.

The key problem seems to be the belief that training to be a scholar is not a full-time occupation. Insufficient funding is the most severe obstacle for candidates, most of whom must obtain another work contract. Although a PhD requires only a minimum of three years, many students take longer (up to the eight-year maximum) because of inadequate time and financial support. Candidates submitting a thesis at the last possible moment are not uncommon.

---

[29] The only exception is short-term international mobility under the Erasmus programme, after which students return to their Czech home faculty. National mobility is almost nonexistent.

[30] Because this is not an employment contract, the university does not pay for health or social insurance.

[31] The rigorosum is a voluntary procedure of conferring of the title JUDr (doctor of universal law), which is worthless because it has nothing in common with the real PhD. The requirements are a thesis (often a slightly extended former master's thesis), an oral exam, and payment of about €450. The purpose of the rigorosum is to generate income for the faculties.

[32] Under the influence of the former Habsburg Empire and as in the present-day Austria, academic titles are still widely used in Czech social life, even in election campaigns, where the title improves the candidate's electoral chances (Jurajda and Münich 2014: 27).

Another serious problem is faculty 'inbreeding'. Students typically take their habilitation at the faculty where they completed their master's and PhD and worked as PhD students and then for many years as post-doctorate researchers and remain as teachers. This makes faculties resemble brotherhoods, isolated from each other. Quite often, students have the same adviser for their master's, *rigorosum* and PhD theses. Sometimes the subject of these theses is the same or similar, with the earlier theses just rewritten, extended and improved.[33] Faculties use their PhD students as an inexpensive teaching and examination force as well as to increase the number of publications attributable to the faculty because academic departments are financed in proportion to the number and types of publications, creating a 'publication horse race'.

D. Professional Legal Training

Regulated legal professions (advocacy, judiciary, prosecution, notaries, bailiffs) require three years of training, which each profession organises. Trainees learn skills, professional rules, and ethics and deepen their practical knowledge of the law related to their field (Kober 2016). The training consists of an apprenticeship under a practitioner, usually the trainee's work superior, and classes organised by their respective professional chamber (or by the Judicial School in the case of judges and prosecutors). The professional exams, organised by each of the respective chambers (advocates, notaries, bailiffs) or by the Judicial School in the case of the judiciary and prosecution, are comparable but specific to the field.

IV. CONCLUSION

Since 1988–89, Czech legal professionals have experienced difficult years of transformation from one economic and political system to another. The changes created a great deal of uncertainty, stress, and migration between professions, as well as an enormous increase in earnings in some professions, partly because of political decisions (in the case of judges, notaries, and private bailiffs) but also because of genuine demand for legal services (from advocates). But that 'golden bonanza' also produced an influx of students seeking money, power and domination over others more than justice and fairness. After 30 years of change, some of the professions have achieved stability (advocates and notaries). However, the disparity between the centralisation of advocacy and the decentralisation of notaries is striking. The other professions (judiciary and state prosecution) have problems (eg excessive workloads and threats to independence), but some of these have deep historical roots. After the reform of the state service, the situation of its legal counsel seems to have improved. The most serious issues pertain to the profession of private bailiff and the entire debt collection system, which has been sharply criticised for violating human rights. The unstable political situation after the 2017 elections and the serious political and economic split in Czech society will probably not permit a consensus

---

[33] The Olomouc faculty recently prohibited the rigorosum thesis from containing more than 50 per cent of the text of the diploma thesis.

on substantial changes. After 30 years of changes, Czech lawyers are exhausted, not only by the transformation of their professions but also by the many other legal reforms (not all of which were essential or desirable). Many lawyers probably have just one wish: more stability and tranquility.

REFERENCES

Abel, RL and Lewis, PSC (1988a) *Lawyers in Society: Vol I The Common Law World* (Berkeley, University of California Press).

—— (1988b) *Lawyers in Society: Vol II The Civil Law World* (Berkeley, University of California Press).

—— (1988c) 'Preface' in R Abel and P Lewis, *Lawyers in Society: Vol I The Common Law World* (Berkeley: University of California Press) xi–xii.

—— (1989) *Lawyers in Society: Vol III Comparative Theories* (Berkeley, University of California Press).

Adamová, K (1998) 'The Development of Legal Scholarship in the Czech Lands between 1945 and 1989' in H Mohnhaupt and H-A Schönfeldt (eds), *The Promotion of the Norms in the East European Societies after the War (1944–1989) Vol 4, Czechoslovakia (1944–1989)* (Frankfurt, Vittorio Klostermann) 5–21 (in German).

Adamová, K et al (2005) *History of the Czech Judiciary from the Beginning of the Czech Statehood to 1938* (Prague, Lexis Nexis) (in Czech).

Balík, S (1998) *Past, Present and Perspectives of the Advocacy* (Pilsen, Vydavatelství Západočeské University) (in Czech).

—— (2005–2008) *From the Past Times of the Advocacy* Vols I–II (Prague, Linde) (in Czech).

Balík, S et al (2009) *History of Advocacy in Bohemia, Moravia and Silesia* (Prague, Czech Chamber of Advocacy) (in Czech).

—— (2014) *History of Notary in the Czech Lands* (Prague, Chamber of Notary) (in Czech).

Beňa, J (1998) 'An Outline of the History of State and Law of Czechoslovakia after WW2' in H Mohnhaupt and H-A Schönfeldt (eds), *The Promotion of the Norms in the East European Societies after the War (1944–1989) Vol 4, Czechoslovakia (1944–1989)* (Frankfurt, Vittorio Klostermann) 447–76 (in German).

Bianchi, L (1971) *History of State and Law in the Area of Czechoslovakia during the Era of Capitalism* Vols I–II (Bratislava, Slovak Academy of Sciences) (in Czech and Slovak).

Bičovský, J (1968) *The Position of the State Notary in the Judicial Structure* (Socialistická zákonnost) 346–53 (in Czech).

Bobek, M (2005) 'Knocking on the Heaven's Door: On the Impossibility of Reforming the Legal Studies in the Czech Republic' *Právní rozhledy* 10, 365–70, 12, 446–51, 14, 523–29, 16, 601–606 (in Czech).

Čelakovský, J (1900–1912) *General Czech Legal History*, 2nd edn (Prague, Bursík & Kohout) (in Czech).

Čelovský, B (2005) *Germanisation and Genocide: Hitler's Final Solution of the Czech Question. The German Documents 1933–1945* (Dresden, Neisse Verlag) (in German).

Brázda, J, Bébr, R and Šimek, P (1976) *Notaries. Their Development, Organisation and Competences (a Comparative Study)* (Prague, Academia) (in Czech).

Fenyk, J (2001) *Public Prosecution (History, Present Time and Possible Development of Public Prosecution)* (Prague, Ministry of Justice) (in Czech).

Flegl, V (1979) *Czechoslovak Judiciary and Prosecution* (Prague, Ústav státní správy) (in Czech).

Gajdošová, M and Kerecman, P (2015) *The First Women in the Slovak Advocacy* (Bratislava, Veda) (in Slovak).

Hajn, P (1968) *The Corporate Counsel* (Prague, Orbis) (in Czech).
Havelková, B (2007) *Rovnost v odměňování žen a mužů* (Prague, Auditorium) (in Czech).
—— (2017) *Gender Equality in Law. Uncovering the Legacies of Czech State Socialism* (Oxford, Hart Publishing).
Hlavsa, P (2002) 'A Sketch of the Legal Development of Civil Procedure and of the Court Structure in the Territory of the Czech Republic after the WW2' in L Soukup, *Chapters in the Development of Law in Czechoslovakia 1945–1990* (Prague, Charles University, Karolinum) 263–92 (in Czech).
IFLA (International Federation of Library Associations) (2018) *Library Map of the World* librarymap.ifla.org/map/Metric/Number-of-libraries/LibraryType/National-Libraries,Academic-Libraries,Public-Libraries,Community-Libraries,School-Libraries,Other-Libraries/Weight/Per-Capita-by-Country.
Jireček, H (1863–64) *Slavonic Law in Bohemia and Moravia* (Prague, Karel Bellmann) (in Czech).
—— (1903) *Lawyer's Life in Bohemia and Moravia during 1000 years from the 9th until the end of the 19th century* (Prague, Jireček) (in Czech).
Jurajda, Š and Münich, D (2014) *Candidate Ballot Information and Election Outcomes: The Czech Case* (Prague, CERGE-EI).
Kapras, J (1935) *An Overview of the Czech Legal History* Vols I–II, 5th edn (Prague, Jan Kapras) (in Czech).
Kerecman, P and Manik, R (2011) *History of Advocacy in Slovakia* (Bratislava, Eurokódex) (in Slovak).
Kindl, V and Skřejpek, M et al (2016) *Legal Social Groups and Legal Professions of the Past*, 2nd edn (Prague, Wolters Kluwer) (in Czech).
Kober, J (Brno) (1994) *Advocacy in the Czech Lands between 1848 and 1994* (Prague, Czech Chamber of Advocacy) (in Czech).
—— (2016) *Lawyers' Ethics in the University Curriculum and in the Professional Schooling of Advocates* (Prague, Pro bono alliance) (in Czech).
—— (2018) 'Equality of Men and Women – in Wages or Another Way? The Underground Programme "For Freedom into the New Czechoslovak Republic" between the Older Political Demands and Post-War Legal Development' in K Koldinská (ed), *Liber amicorum for Věra Štangová* (Pilsen, Aleš Čeněk) pp 146–60 (in Czech).
—— (2020) *Czech Legal History* (Academia Publishing house).
Kristková, V (2012) 'Clinical Legal Education' in V Kristková (ed), *The Skills in Legal Education. Forms and Methods of Developing of the Lawyers Skills* (Brno, Masaryk University) 73–104.
Kuchta, J and Schelle, K (1994) *History and Presence of the State Prosecutor's Office* (Brno, Masarykova univerzita) (in Czech).
Kuklík, J (2009) *Reform of the Lawyer's Education at the Beginning of the 21th Century* (Prague, Auditorium) (in Czech).
—— (2015) *Czech Law in Historical Contexts* (Prague, Karolinum).
Levay, M (2000) 'Social Changes and Rising Crime Rates: The Case of Central and Eastern Europe' 8 *European Journal of Crime, Criminal Law and Criminal Justice* 35.
Litsch, K (2004) 'Changes in the Education of Lawyers 1945–1989' in K Malý and L Soukup (eds), *The Development of Law in Czechoslovakia in the Years 1945–1989* (Prague, Karolinum) 84–118 (in Czech).
Malý, K et al (1976) *The Emergence and Development of the Socialist Law* Vols I–II (Prague, Charles University) (in Czech).
—— (2010) *History of the Czech and Czechoslovak Law before 1945*, 4th edn (Prague, Leges) (in Czech).
Malý, K and Soukup, L (eds) (2004) *The Development of Law in Czechoslovakia in the Years 1945–1989* (Prague, Karolinum) (in Czech).

Maršálek, P (2004) 'The Changes in the Czech Legal Scholarship between 1945 and 1989' in K Malý and L Soukup (eds), *The Development of Law in Czechoslovakia in the Years 1945–1989* (Prague, Karolinum) 29–58 (in Czech).

Osvaldová, B (2004) *Czech Media and Feminism* (Prague, Libri/Slon) (in Czech).

Pavlíček, V (1991) 'The Conception of the Educational Reform at the Law Faculty of the Charles University in Social Context' 130(2) *Právník* 97–112 (in Czech).

Princ, M (2015) *Judiciary in the Czech Lands between 1848 and 1938* (Prague, Wolters Kluwer) (in Czech).

Richter, T (2013) 'He Who Pays the Piper: the Conflicts Involved in Combining Careers in Legal Academia and Legal Practice' 152(2) *Právník* 124–37 (in Czech).

Růžička, M (2005) *Public Prosecution and the Bodies of Preparatory Procedure* (Prague, CH Beck) (in Czech).

Sachs, J et al (2019) *Sustainable Development Report 2019* (New York, Bertelsmann Stiftung and Sustainable Development Solutions Network) s3.amazonaws.com/sustainabledevelopment.report/2019/2019_sustainable_development_report.pdf.

Schelle, K and Schelleová, I (2004) 'The Development of Judicial Organisation in the Years 1945–1989' in K Malý and L Soukup (eds), *The Development of Law in Czechoslovakia in the Years 1945–1989* (Prague, Karolinum) 343–83 (in Czech).

Schelle, K and Tauchen, J (eds) (2016) *Encyclopedia of the Czech Legal History* Vols I–VI Pilsen; Ostrava: Aleš Čeněk (Key Publishing) 2016 ff (in Czech).

Schelleová, I and Schelle, K (2004a) *The Judiciary (History, Present Time and the Future Perspectives)* (Prague, Eurolex Bohemia) (in Czech).

Soukup, L (2002) *Chapters in the Development of Law in Czechoslovakia 1945–1990* (Prague, Charles University; Karolinum).

Stewart, P (1991) 'Czechoslovakia's Lawyers Post-Privatisation' 10 *International Financial Law Review* 21.

Slejška, D and Herzmann, J (1990) *Sondy do veřejného mínění* (Prague, Nakladatelství Svoboda).

Šolle, V (1968 and 1971) 'The Beginnings of the Bourgeois Judiciary in the Czech Lands I-II' 18(1) *Sborník archivních prací* 86–141 and 21(1) *Sborník archivních prací* 93–170 (in Czech).

Tarabrin, E (1936) *A Sketch of the Development of Advocacy in the Lands of the Bohemian Crown (13th to 18th Century)* (Prague, Jednota advokátů československých) (in Czech).

Tomoszek, M (2013) *Complex Law Teaching: Knowledge, Skills and Values* (Olomouc, Palacký University).

UNCTAD (2013) *World Investment Report 2013. Global Value Chains: Investment and Trade for Development* (Geneva, United Nations) 33 (figure I.32) unctad.org/en/PublicationChapters/wir2013ch1_en.pdf.

Vaněček, V (1953) *Czech Lawyers During Capitalism* (Prague, Nakladatelství Československé akademie věd) (in Czech).

—— (1975) *History of the State and Law in Czechoslovakia before 1945*, 3rd edn (Prague, Orbis) (in Czech).

Vlček, E (2004) 'Development of the Prosecution Office 1945–1990' in K Malý and L Soukup (eds), *The Development of Law in Czechoslovakia in the Years 1945–1989* (Prague, Karolinum) (in Czech).

Vojáček, L, Schelle, K and Knoll, V (2016) *Czech Legal History*, 3rd edn (Pilsen, Aleš Čeněk) (in Czech).

Winterová, A (1998) 'A Bailiff – a Tradesman?' 2 *Právní praxe* 115–18 (in Czech).

—— (2001) ' The First Consideration of the New Bailiff Order' 49(7) *Právní praxe* 394–402 (in Czech).

Zweigert, K and Kötz, H (1971) *Introduction to Comparative Law* Vol I (Tübingen, JCB Mohr) (in German).

15
Poland
Opening the Legal Professions

KAJA GADOWSKA

I. INTRODUCTION

With the transformation of 1989, Polish lawyers faced the monumental challenge of helping to build the new structures of a democratic state based on the principles of a social market economy. Many also experienced fundamental changes in their professional lives, sometimes entailing a transition to another legal profession or even an end to their legal careers or a move to the public sphere. The new economic system increased the demand for lawyers, convincing many young people that a law degree was a passport to professional success.

During the planned economy in 1945–89, demand for legal services was limited because the political decisions of the Polish Workers' Party played the dominant role in creating the rules of social and economic life, which the state administration executed. At the transition in 1989, there were approximately 4,000 advocates (*adwokaci*) and 14,000 attorneys at law (*radcowie prawni*)[1] with rights to appear before ordinary courts (NRA 2018; KRRP 2018; MS 2018a), which represented a ratio of 2,128 people per lawyer. Because attorneys at law could not appear in court on behalf of individuals who were not pursuing business activities, the ratio of population to lawyers who could represent them was 10,000:1. Now, nearly 30 years later, there are 17,000 advocates and 34,000 attorneys at law, or approximately 758 people per lawyer (ibid).

This chapter describes the rules governing qualified lawyers during the period 1989–2017, focusing on how changes in the recruitment of new members of self-governing councils of lawyers affected the availability of legal services for commercial and non-commercial operations and entry to the profession by law graduates. The 'opening of legal professions' refers to the approximately 15-year process of social negotiations and statutory changes that increased access to the profession and to legal services.

The term 'qualified lawyer' includes advocates and attorneys at law who have the statutory right to appear in ordinary courts. The profession of attorney at law was regulated by the Act of 6 July 1982, which established their self-governing council.

---

[1] Also translated as 'legal adviser' or 'legal counsel'.

Over the last 25 years, their professional rights have gradually approached those of advocates, the remaining difference being that only attorneys at law may be employed. Attempts at statutory unification have failed because of resistance by the self-governing council of advocates, which reveres its traditions and fears being swallowed by the much larger number of attorneys at law. As a result, the structure of legal professions in Poland is characterised by the co-existence of two separate self-governing organisations and two different professional titles, although their members have the same professional qualifications.

II. THE LEGAL EDUCATION SYSTEM

The size of the legal market, meaning the number of people with legal training who are working as lawyers, is a function of the legal education system, which has remained essentially unchanged for the last 30 years. A five-year programme and successful completion of an examination lead to the title of master of law, which is a requirement for working in a profession involving provision of legal support and applying or creating the law as well as for taking the entrance examinations for judge, prosecutor, advocate, attorney at law, notary public, bailiff and tax adviser trainee.

Following passage of the Law on Higher Education a year after the 1989 transformation, it became possible to study at private universities offering fee-based law degree programmes,[2] which complemented the free degrees offered at state universities such as the Faculty of Law at the Jagiellonian University, founded in 1364. The economic transformations of the 1990s reignited young people's educational aspirations. In the 2005/06 academic year, there were 1,953,800 students in higher education (68 per cent at the 130 public universities and 32 per cent at the 315 private institutions, only a quarter of which were authorised to offer master's programmes), almost five times the 403,800 enrolled in 112 institutions in 1990/91. During these 15 years, the proportion studying full-time during the day declined from 77 per cent to 49 per cent.

In the 2004/05 academic year, 56,500 were studying law (53 per cent women). At state universities, which enrolled almost 85 per cent, 45 per cent were full-time day students, 11 per cent were taking evening classes, and 44 per cent were enrolled in weekend programmes; in private institutions, which enrolled 15 per cent, 64 per cent were day students, and 35 per cent were taking weekend classes. In 2005, 8,662 completed law degrees (58 per cent women), 86 per cent from public universities. The fact that this was the largest number ever increased the pressure for access to the legal professions. For demographic reasons the number of students in higher education has steadily declined since 2006/07. However, the number of law students continued to rise through 2008/09, when there were almost 60,000 (55 per cent women). Among the 80 per cent at public universities, 48 per cent were full-time and 52 per cent part-time; among the 20 per cent in private institutions, 58 per cent were full-time and 42 per cent part-time. Because the 19–24-year-old age cohort contracted 31 per cent between 2005 and 2016, the proportion studying at private institutions declined. In 2016, out of 390 universities, only 132

---

[2] The Law on Higher Education of 27 July 2005 distinguishes between public and private universities.

were private. In the 2016/17 academic year, public universities enrolled 75 per cent of the 53,200 law students (60 per cent women), 63 per cent full-time (compared with 40 per cent of private students). In 2016, there were 8,632 law graduates, 72 per cent from public universities and 62.5 per cent women (see Figure 1). The number of law doctoral candidates increased from 2,356 (48 per cent women and 30 per cent full-time) in 2005/06 to 3,860 (55 per cent women and 45 per cent full-time) in 2016/17 (GUS 1990, 1991, 2005, 2006a, 2006b, 2008, 2017a; 2017b).

Figure 1 Number of Law Graduates 1990–2015

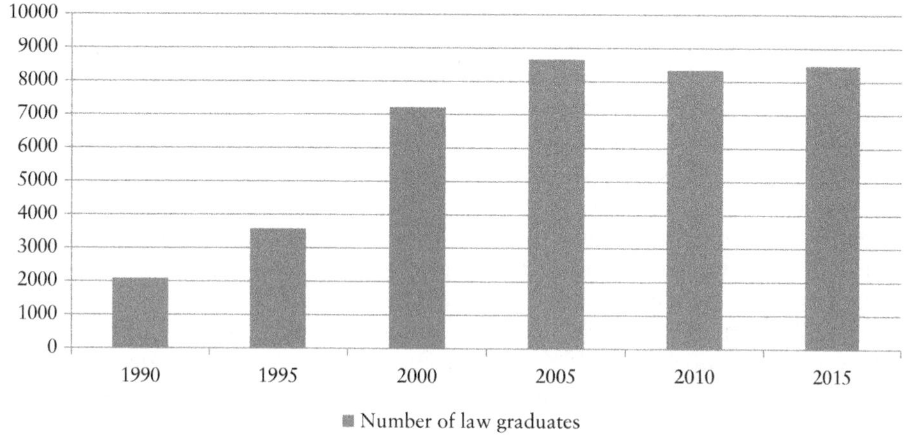

■ Number of law graduates

Source: GUS 1991, 1996, 2001, 2006, 2011, 2016.

III. LEGAL PROFESSIONS IN POLAND: GENERAL OVERVIEW

Legal professions consist of qualified lawyers entitled to represent parties in court, ie advocates and attorneys at law, as well as notaries public and tax advisers (defined as professions of public trust in the Constitution of the Republic of Poland of 1997) and lawyers who are public officials in the judiciary, ie judges and prosecutors and bailiffs operating under court supervision. Article 17 of the Polish Constitution provides for self-governing bodies representing people in professions of public trust, which are responsible for protecting the professions and ensuring that they operate in the public interest.

A. Judges

After the changes of 1989, there was no break in the functional continuity of the judiciary. But there was a 'self-lustration' by the community of judges to eliminate those who had betrayed the independence of the judiciary during the period of 'real socialism'. Since then, there has been a debate about whether judges should be recruited through a judicial traineeship immediately after completion of law studies or chosen from the best advocates, attorneys at law or prosecutors.

At present, the main path to the judiciary – on the basis of the Law of 27 July 2001 on the System of Ordinary Courts, as amended, which replaced the Law of 20 June 1985 – is a three-year judicial training period following graduation in legal studies.[3] This culminates in a judicial examination, followed by appointment by the Minister of Justice to the position of judge's assessor, entrusted with the duties of a judge for a limited period (the National Council of the Judiciary of Poland may raise objections), and finally appointment by the President of Poland as judge upon nomination by the National Council of the Judiciary. Court referendars (ie clerks) and assistant judges who have taken the judicial examination may also apply for the position of judge. Since 2009, the judicial training course and examination have been organised by the National School of the Judiciary and Public Prosecution in Krakow, which coordinates judicial training throughout the country. This replaced decentralised judicial training conducted by individual appellate courts. Trainees receive scholarships. Prosecutors, attorneys at law, advocates and notaries with more than three years' experience, as well as law professors and those with a habilitation in law (a postdoctoral academic degree) may apply for positions as judges. In practice, however, the first model, which dominated Poland for 30 years, still does so. Therefore, judges in low-ranking courts tend to be young people without previous professional experience. Interest in the position of judge among more experienced lawyers is relatively low, although recent changes in the legal services market have augmented it.

In late 2016, there were 9,867 judges in ordinary courts (6633 in district courts, 2759 in regional courts, and 475 in appellate courts), 83 in the Supreme Court (29 per cent women), 110 in the Supreme Administrative Court (45.5 per cent women), 504 in voivodeship administrative courts (62.5 per cent women), and 15 in the Constitutional Tribunal (13.5 per cent women). Since the beginning of the transformation, the number of judges has more than doubled. Currently, there are 27.5 judges per 100,000 citizens. At the same time, the number of new cases has grown more than sevenfold, from approximately 2 million in 1990 to almost 15 million in 2016 (GUS 1991; 2017a; MS 2017a; 2017b). Lawyers in other legal professions earn more than judges, especially in large cities, making the judiciary less attractive to men; but greater job security and stability make it more attractive to those seeking to combine work with family responsibilities (KRS 2012). On the other hand, politically motivated changes introduced to the judiciary system since 2015 undermined the professional position of judges, prompting some experienced judges to leave the profession (for discussion of changes see Mazur and Żurek 2017).

B. Prosecutors

The prosecutor's office underwent significant changes after 1989. For many years, there was vociferous debate about the relationship between the Minister of Justice and the Prosecutor General. The two positions were combined in 1990–2010, divided between 2010 and 2016, and re-combined in 2016.

---

[3] In 2018 a new form of 18-month supplementary traineeship was introduced to facilitate entry to the profession of judge by court referendars, assistant judges and assistant prosecutors.

The profession of prosecutor is regulated by the Law of 28 January 2016 on Prosecutors, which replaced the Law of 20 June 1985. Prosecutors are appointed by the Prosecutor General on the recommendation of the National Public Prosecutor (previously the National Prosecutors Council) on the basis of a competition; at present, however, the Prosecutor General may waive this procedure in justified cases. The position is open to candidates who have passed a prosecutor's or judge's examination and have at least one year's experience as a prosecutor's or court assessor, as well as to judges, advocates and attorneys at law with three years' experience and law professors and those with a habilitation. Until recently, few legal professionals were interested in becoming prosecutors, but changes in the legal services market led to increased applications from advocates and attorneys at law. In practice, however, the main path to becoming a prosecutor remains completion of a three-year prosecutor's training (supported by a scholarship), following a law degree and culminating in the prosecutor's examination.[4] After this comes appointment as a prosecutor's assessor, and then as a prosecutor, by the Prosecutor General. Since 2009, the prosecutor's traineeship and examination have been organised by the National School of the Judiciary and Public Prosecution in Krakow, which replaced individual appellate prosecutor's offices.

Since the beginning of the transformation, the number of prosecutors has grown by almost 90 per cent. At the end of 2016, 5,834 prosecutors (52.5 per cent women) were employed in the National (previously General) Public Prosecutor's Office and supra-regional (previously appellate) and regional and district prosecutor's offices. There are 15.2 prosecutors per 100,000 citizens (GUS 1991; 2017a).

C. Court Bailiffs

The Law of 29 August 1997, amended by the Law of 18 September 2001, transformed court bailiffs from state officials to public officials working under the auspices of a court but on their own terms. Court bailiffs must complete a law degree and a two-year paid training period as a bailiff, pass the bailiff's examination and work as a bailiff's assessor for at least two years. Applicants may be judges, court assessors, prosecutors, advocates, attorneys at law, notaries and those with a habilitation. Bailiffs are appointed and dismissed by the Minister of Justice following consultation with the relevant council for the chamber of bailiffs. Bailiffs belong to the National Bailiffs Council (NBC) and 11 bailiffs' chambers in the districts of appellate courts.[5] The NBC is consulted on significant professional matters, while chambers oversee bailiffs and organise training. Recruitment used to be conducted by individual bailiffs' chambers, while the professional examination was organised by the NBC and the Ministry. Since 2008, both recruitment and examinations have been organised by the Ministry, which appoints the commission responsible for setting test questions and oversees bailiff's examinations and the examination committees. Each bailiff must employ at least one trainee every three years.

---

[4] In 2018 a new form of 18-month supplementary traineeship was introduced to facilitate entry to the profession of prosecutor by court referendars, assistant judges and assistant prosecutors.

[5] Bailiffs are liable for the damages caused by their enforcement activities and subject to a disciplinary action by the disciplinary committee.

The number of bailiffs increased from 459 in 1990 to 1,574 by the end of 2016 (GUS 1991; MS 2017c), or four bailiffs per 100,000 citizens. The marked increase in the number of bailiffs after 2008 coincided with a new law allowing creditors to choose a bailiff from anywhere in Poland rather than (as previously) only within the jurisdiction of the appellate court. At the same time, the number of cases grew dramatically, from 1,912,792 in 2008 to 2,503,442 in 2009 and 7,958,864 in 2015. Increased competition between bailiffs has led to a stratification of bailiffs' firms by size and less efficient enforcement as firms handled more cases. Almost half the cases became concentrated among 100 bailiffs. In 2013, nearly 23 per cent of cases went to just 11 firms (draft bill explanatory statement, Sejm printed matter no 2561 of 28 May 2014). A 2015 amendment restricted the number of cases bailiffs can take annually to 5,000 for firms whose efficiency did not exceed 35 per cent and 10,000 for more efficient firms. The goal was to limit the sharp rise in large bailiffs firms, each with several dozen employees, serving mass creditors, and to increase the efficiency of small and medium-sized firms. Currently, new Laws of 22 March 2018 on Court Bailiffs and 28 February 2018 on Bailiffs' Costs have been implemented to improve the efficiency and effectiveness of enforcement of judgments and to rationalise and reduce the fees and reinforce supervision of bailiffs. These laws limit how bailiffs may rely on others, including bailiffs' assessors, when engaging in official activities. The explanatory statement for the Bill on Court Bailiffs emphasised that a bailiff is not a profession of public trust although it possesses certain characteristics of these professions (Sejm printed matter no 1582 of 24 May 2017). This contradicts the binding Court Bailiff Ethics Code, which defines a bailiff as a public official pursuing a profession of public trust.

D. Notaries Public

The Law of 14 February 1991 on Notaries[6] refers to pre-war traditions, ie the 1933 Resolution of the President of the Republic of Poland unifying notaries, but the profession has undergone fundamental change. Notaries, who had previously been officials employed in state notary bureaux responsible for keeping land registers and drafting notarial acts, have regained the status of a profession of public trust. They must be members of the notarial self-governing council, comprising 11 notarial chambers and the National Notarial Council (NNC) and conduct notarial work[7] in their firms concerning land transactions, inheritance, company and family law. They are entrusted with the security and safety of legal transactions and are required to have liability insurance. The NNC is the consultative organ for the Minister of Justice and responsible for traineeship. Notary chambers oversee notaries, assistant notaries (assessors until 2013) and trainee notaries and are consulted on the appointment and dismissal of notaries. Notaries are subject to disciplinary proceedings, which may be initiated by the Minister of Justice or the council of the relevant notary chamber and heard by notary chambers' disciplinary tribunals, with appeal to the High Disciplinary Court.

---

[6] The Law of 24 May 1989 preserved state notary bureaux but also allowed individuals to open notary offices.
[7] The fees are set by contract but may not exceed those established by the Minister of Justice in agreement with the Minister for Financial Affairs, following consultation with the National Notarial Council.

A notary must complete a law degree and 3.5-year paid notarial traineeship and pass the notary examination. Until 2013, to become a notary one had to complete a 2.5-year training and work as a notary assessor for at least two years. Law professors and those with a habilitation, judges and prosecutors, and advocates and attorneys at law with three years' experience may also qualify. There has been a steady expansion of those eligible to take the notary examination without completing the notary traineeship. Notaries are appointed by the Ministry of Justice (MoJ), which also designates where they may practise after consultation with the council of the relevant notary chamber. In 2013 the Ministry was authorised to refuse to appoint a candidate whose previous conduct raised doubts about the candidate's reliability, honesty or commitment to the rule of law.

The organisation and content of the traineeship is determined by the MoJ after consultation with the NNC and managed by the notary chamber council on the basis of a programme determined by the NNC. Competitions for traineeships were conducted by councils of notary chambers in a manner determined by the MoJ, and trainees were examined by a committee appointed by the MoJ, which also determined the scope of the notary examination after consultation with the NNC. Since 2006, both the traineeship entrance examination and the notary examination are conducted by MoJ exam committees, and the MoJ also appoints groups responsible for drafting the examination. In 2013, notaries were required to accept at least one notary trainee every 3.5 years in order to enable trainees to gain the necessary work experience to open their own firms. Before 2013, a notary trainee who had passed the notary examination and presented a notary's declaration of readiness to sign a work contract was appointed by the MoJ as an assessor, after consultation with the council of the relevant notary chamber. Owing to the difficulty in finding employment as an assessor, the legislature abandoned this format. Currently, a trainee who has passed the notary examination becomes an assistant notary and may apply for appointment as a notary.

In 1990 there were 862 notaries and notary assessors employed in state notary bureaux, as well as 116 trainees. At the end of 2015 there were 3,293 notaries. There was a 40 per cent increase in numbers between 2013 and 2015, which is related to the abolition of the assessorship requirement. In the following year, this trend slowed (GUS 1991; MS 2018a). There are almost 9 notaries for every 100,000 citizens. The average pass rate of the notary examination in 2009–17 was 49 per cent (MS 2018b). In 1995 notaries prepared 1,020,000 notary acts and carried out 2,273,000 notarial actions; in 2016 these numbers increased to 2,139,000 and 11,833,000 (GUS 1996; 2017a). Because the number of notaries rose faster than that of notarial acts, firms have become less profitable and more competitive.

E. Tax Advisers

The development of the legal services market has increased the autonomy of lawyers offering specialist services, the most numerous of whom are tax advisers. The profession of tax adviser is regulated by the Law of 5 July 1996 on Tax Advisory Services. A tax adviser's licence requires higher education, not necessarily in law, and passing a professional examination covering fiscal law, preceded by six-months' work experience. Tax advisers must belong to their self-governing body, the National Chamber of Tax Advisers, which provides compulsory professional indemnity insurance and possesses disciplinary power; unlicensed provision of tax advice is subject to financial penalties. Tax advisers are authorised to act as legal representatives in fiscal cases in administrative courts.

At the end of 2017, there were 8,920 registered tax advisers in 492 firms (KRDP 2017). Attorneys at law, advocates and statutory auditors also may offer tax advice without registering as tax advisers.

F. Other Forms of Work for Lawyers

In addition to the professions of public trust discussed above, which require affiliation to a professional self-governing council, law graduates also work as legal advisers for collection agencies, compensation firms or other businesses, and offices of public authorities.

Inadequate state regulation has allowed the emergence of a market for legal services by people calling themselves legal advisers, most of whom have a legal education. In 2011, the website of the Association of Legal Advisers estimated their number at about 20,000, which is probably exaggerated (SDP 2017). The code of civil procedure limits what legal advisers can do in ordinary courts. For many years legal advisers have lobbied in vain for recognition as a profession of public trust.

The limitations on how lawyers, as a profession of public trust, may advertise their services have contributed to the development of businesses seeking to collect debts, especially in mass claims, some of which employ qualified lawyers as subcontractors. Because of inadequate regulation by government bodies responsible for protecting competition and consumers, these companies acquired significant financial power, and some were even listed on stock exchanges. The market for debt collection is currently estimated at 105 billion PLN (approximately €25 billion), compared to 20 billion PLN (approximately €4.8 billion) in 2010 (KPFwP 2017).

For similar reasons, an unregulated market has developed for compensation firms handling claims of road accident victims, mainly addressed to insurance companies. Here, too, qualified lawyers are often subcontractors or employees as well as shareholders. The largest compensation firms, listed on the stock market, have an annual income of around 100 million PLN (approximately €24 million) (Inwestinfo.pl 2017).

IV. ADVOCATES AND ATTORNEYS AT LAW

A. 1989–97: New Challenges. Economic Freedom

The return to a market economy in 1989 necessitated the revival of an infrastructure, including legal services. The number of entities engaged in business increased from 1,135,492 in 1990 to 2,968,786 in 2016, while the number of commercial law companies rose from 36,267 to 501,056 and the number of cases examined by ordinary courts jumped from 2,767,000 to 17,210,000 (GUS 1991; 2017a; 2017c; MS 2017a; 2017b).

In 1989 there were about 4,000 advocates and 14,000 attorneys at law (NRA 2018; KRRP 2018; MS 2018a). Control over their education was left in the hands of professional self-governing councils because of the perceived need to restore their autonomy, as well as the trend, starting in 1982, of increasing the rights of self-governing councils for attorneys at law. Based on the Bar Profession Act of 26 May 1982, and the Act of 6 July 1982 on Attorneys at Law, as amended, legal self-governing councils had statutory independence in performing their functions and were subject only to legal regulation; all advocates, attorneys at law, and their trainees had to belong to one of these councils.

Such systemic solutions have been confirmed by the provisions of Article 17 Para 1 of the Constitutional Act of 2 April 1997, indicating that 'the Law stipulates the establishment of professional self-governing councils to represent persons executing professions of public trust and supervising the due execution of these professions within the limits of the public interest and for its protection'.

The institutions of the Bar are the National Bar Congress, Supreme Bar Council, High Disciplinary Court and Bar Disciplinary Ombudsman. The National Bar Congress is responsible for representing advocates, supervising the activity of district advocates' councils, and educating trainees through these councils, as well as consulting on legislation and making recommendations for the creation and implementation of laws. There are 24 district advocates' chambers based on the jurisdiction of district courts.

The institutions of the self-governing council of attorneys at law are the National Attorneys at Law Congress, National Attorneys at Law Council, High Disciplinary Court, Chief Disciplinary Ombudsman, district councils of attorneys at law chambers, and disciplinary ombudsmen. They represent attorneys at law and their trainees, protecting their professional interests, participating in the creation and implementation of the law, ensuring that trainee attorneys at law have the skills necessary for the profession, and providing continuing education for attorneys at law, as well as supervising the work of attorneys at law and trainees. There are 19 district attorneys at law chambers, whose jurisdiction is defined by the National Attorneys at Law Council, consistent with the fundamental territorial division.

The professional self-governing councils of advocates and attorneys at law (actually the local chambers) previously formulated the rules for preliminary examinations for legal training and recruitment criteria. Candidates must have completed a five-year university-level law degree and be accepted for training (for an average of 3.5 years)[8] after passing the entrance examination. The training included theoretical classes and practical aspects, such as observing the judiciary and performing professional activities under the supervision of a lawyer with the relevant experience. The advocate traineeship was free, but the attorney at law traineeship required a fee determined by the district chambers. Both traineeships culminated in professional examinations, coordinated by the self-governing councils, which could be retaken only once. Only professors and habilitated doctors of law, as well as judges, prosecutors, notaries, attorneys at law or advocates with three years' experience, were exempt from the traineeship and examination.

B. 1997: Expansion of the Scope of Professional Rights of Attorneys at Law

The legislature was under pressure to address growing demand in the legal services market by expanding the professional rights of attorneys at law, given the opposition

---

[8] The advocate traineeship initially lasted four years and the attorney at law traineeship three. In 1997, the duration of the two traineeships was equalised at 3.5 years and shortened to three years in 2009.

by advocates to merging the two groups. The Act of 22 May 1997 allowed attorneys at law who were not employed to provide representation in ordinary courts for individuals not engaged in business. The restriction on employed attorneys at law was eliminated in 2005. As a result, the professional rights of attorneys at law and advocates were identical except for the fact that only advocates could engage in defence in criminal and fiscal penal proceedings. Since 1997, therefore, apart from criminal defence, individuals not involved in business had access to both 4,594 advocates and attorneys at law (6,692 at that date because 7,345 of the 14,037 attorneys at law were employed).

During the first seven years of the new social order the number of advocates increased by just 17 per cent (from 2,932 in 1990 to 4,594 in 1997), and the number of attorneys at law remained practically unchanged. After the statutory changes in 1997, legal services were provided by about 18,600 qualified lawyers, giving a ratio of 2,083 people per lawyer. However, there were only about 11,300 lawyers for individuals not engaged in business, and there has been no major increase in the number of lawyers for business entities (NRA 2018; KRRP 2018; MS 2018a; see Figures 2 and 3). Considering the increase in the number of cases filed in ordinary courts and the number of business enterprises, maintaining the availability of legal services at the level of the early 1990s would require doubling the number of lawyers.

Figure 2 Number of Advocates 1999–2017

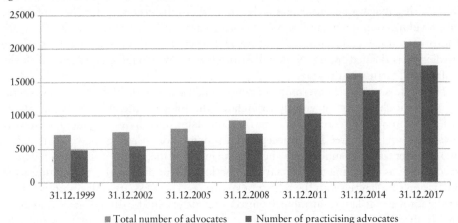

Source: NRA 2018; KRRP 2018; MS 2018a.

C. 1997–2005: Efforts to Open up the Legal Professions

Between 1995 and 2005 the number of law graduates increased from 2,582 to 8,662 (GUS 1996; 2006; see Figure 1). The number of graduates admitted to the first year of attorney at law training increased from 514 in 1997 to 1,003 in 2004, the last year in which traineeship entrance examinations were administered by self-governing councils. In a judgment on 18 February 2004, the Constitutional Tribunal held that legislation empowering the Supreme Bar Council and National Attorneys at Law Council to define traineeship competitions violated the Constitution because self-governing councils could

Figure 3 Number of Attorneys at Law 1999–2017

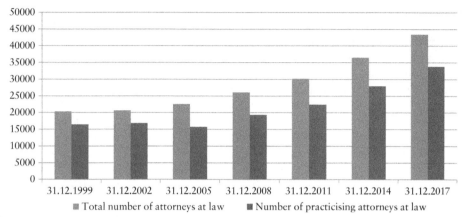

Source: NRA 2018; KRRP 2018; MS 2018a.

not benefit from specifying the requirements for traineeships. The selection and qualification of candidates had to be based solely on the statutory principles and specified criteria.

The number of practising advocates increased 35 per cent between 1997 and 2005 and the number of trainees 122 per cent, the number of practising attorneys at law 25 per cent and the number of trainees 93.5 per cent (NRA 2018; KRRP 2018; MS 2018a; see Figures 2 and 3).

There was growing social and political pressure to open up the legal professions by increasing recruitment for legal training programmes. Opposition parties criticised self-governing councils for limiting the number admitted to trainee programmes and favouring candidates related to council members, thereby frustrating the aspirations of hundreds or thousands of law graduates. Abolition of these limitations was supposed to result in 'market verification' of the knowledge and skills of a much larger number of lawyers after they completed their training under the supervision of the Minister of Justice. The state would be responsible for ensuring equal opportunities for law graduates while simultaneously increasing the recruitment of graduates by training programmes.

Those supporting the changes wanted legislation allowing law graduates who were not members of self-governing legal councils to practise independently without being part of a profession of public trust. In judgments on 21 May 2002 and 26 November 2003, the Constitutional Tribunal confirmed that law graduates not affiliated with self-governing councils could practise until this was regulated by law. As a consequence, lawyers operating outside the standards of European Union legislation began practising law in simple civil law and business cases, debt collection, and damage claims for injury or ill-health brought by 'compensation firms'.

Reform advocates insisted on transferring control over recruitment for training from the self-governing professional councils to the MoJ and establishing criteria that would increase recruitment for training programmes. By virtue of its responsibility for organising preliminary examinations, the MoJ was to have the decisive say over the number of legal trainees and, therefore, the number of lawyers. The reform also considered allowing lawyers with professional experience or an academic degree to take professional examinations or be qualified without either training or examination.[9] Representatives of self-governing legal councils invoked the risk to clients from lawyers without the relevant legal training and warned against weakening the independence of self-governing councils, making it more difficult for them to meet their constitutional obligation to supervise professions of public trust (Agacka-Indecka 2005).

After turbulent discussions in parliament and among the public, the Act of 30 June 2005 amended the laws governing advocates, attorneys at law, and notaries. The Minister of Justice became responsible for entrance examinations for training and for professional examinations, advised by the self-governing legal councils. The committee responsible for the preliminary examination consisted of three members designated by the MoJ and two by the relevant self-governing councils; they were directed to ensure the same level of knowledge for all candidates. The seven-person examination commissions comprised three representatives of the MoJ, two of self-governing councils, one professor or habilitated doctor of laws, and one prosecutor. The statute fixed the passing grade at 190/250 points (76 per cent correct answers). There were no annual limits on the number of places in the training programmes. In practice, the difficulty of test questions and preparation of candidates determine the number of legal trainees in the programmes conducted by local chambers of attorneys at law or advocates. At the same time, self-governing legal councils were required to organise and conduct training courses for a larger and variable number of legal trainees.

The annual state examinations for advocates and attorneys at law were supposed to be set by the MoJ, with the Supreme Bar and National Attorneys at Law Councils limited to a consultative role. Those who had been involved in applying or creating the law, either as an employee or independently, were admitted to exams without having completed traineeship, and those who had passed the examinations for judges or notaries, attorneys at law or advocates could apply for entry regardless of whether they were able to demonstrate any professional experience or how long ago they had passed the exam. The 2005 amendment introduced fees for the advocates' traineeship, which were four times the minimum wage in 2006 and 2.6 times in 2018. The attorney at law traineeship fee has, since 2005, been set at the same level as the fee for advocate training.

Some of the statutory changes were challenged by the Constitutional Tribunal in judgments of 19 April 2006 and 8 November 2006, which revoked the regulations applying to self-governing councils.[10] It held that allowing one who had a law degree but did not belong to the self-governing councils of advocates or attorneys at law to perform the functions reserved to these professions could mislead potential clients about the lawyer's qualifications. The Constitutional Tribunal judgments also invalidated the statutes for failing to require professional experience or specify the maximum time between the completion of other professional examinations and application for entry on the registers of advocates and attorneys at law and the regulations admitting to the advocate's and attorney at law's examinations those whose professional capacities had not been verified objectively and who had not completed a traineeship. The Tribunal also found

---

[9] The Act on amending the Bar Profession Act and some other acts, drafted by the Law and Justice Party Parliamentary Club and Fair Play Association (Sejm printed matter no 1694 of 6 March 2003).

[10] The Constitutional Tribunal judgment of 26 March 2008 also questioned some of the articles of the Law on Notaries Public, amended by the 2005 law.

it unconstitutional to strip the self-governing councils of the power to determine the requirements for taking professional examinations.

D. 2005–11: Implementation of Changes and the 2009 Act

The first traineeship entrance examination was organised by the MoJ in 2006. Between 2006 and 2017, 48,749 law graduates became entitled to register for advocate and attorney at law traineeships. In the same period, 40,627 took the advocate traineeship examination (47.9 per cent passing), and 67,234 took the attorney at law traineeship exam (43.6 per cent passing). The difficulty varied annually, however. In 2007, the pass rates for the examinations were 11.7 and 11.8 per cent respectively, whereas a year later they were 78 and 76.5 per cent (MS 2018c; see Figures 4 and 5). Analysis by the MoJ shows that in 2008–17, an average of about 53 per cent of law graduates took entrance examinations for advocate, attorney at law, notary and bailiff traineeships. Yet the total number of those taking traineeship examinations annually was (and remains) considerably higher. Graduates completing their degree programmes in the year in which the exam took place were 28–46 per cent of candidates for traineeship examinations. The chances of passing diminish with each attempt (MS 2018c).

Figure 4 Entrance Exam Results for Advocate Traineeship 2006–2017

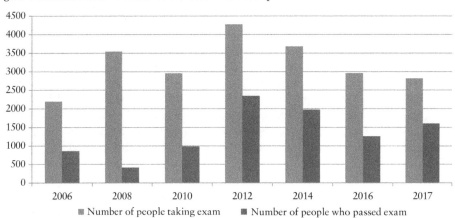

Source: MS 2018c.

In response to the Constitutional Tribunal judgments, the legislature made further changes in the laws on self-governing councils, by passing the Act of 20 February 2009, specifying the formal requirements for professional practice required for registration as advocate or attorney at law for those who had completed judges' or prosecutors' traineeships and for admission to the professional examination of lawyers of those who had work experience in applying the law but had not completed a legal traineeship. Exemptions from the requirement to complete the traineeship and pass the professional examination in order to register as advocate and attorney at law were granted to those who held the position of judge or prosecutor or practised the profession of notary, advocate or attorney at law.

Figure 5 Entrance Exam Results for Attorney at Law Traineeship 2006–2017

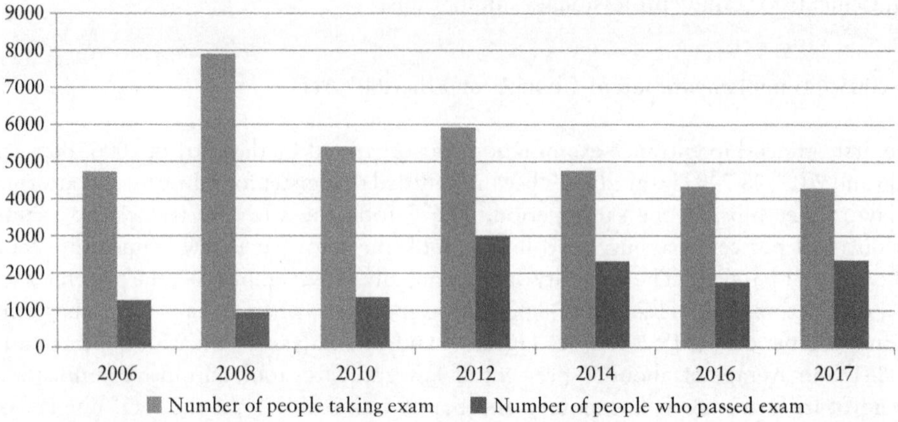

■ Number of people taking exam ■ Number of people who passed exam

Source: MS 2018c.

The number of questions in the entrance exam was reduced from 250 to 150 and the pass threshold lowered to 100 (or 66 per cent). A list of the legal acts forming the basis of the test questions also was published in advance. In addition to responding to the demand for greater transparency and predictability, these changes loosened the requirements for qualifying for legal traineeships.

Furthermore, the duration of the advocate and attorney at law traineeships was shortened from 3.5 years to three, and the form of the professional exam was changed. The legislature eliminated the oral exam. The written exam consisted of 100 questions followed by problems in four legal fields: penal, civil, economic and administrative. Between 2010 and 2015, the pass rate for the advocate examination ranged from 68.4 to 83.6 per cent and that for the attorney at law exam from 62.2 to 82.4 per cent, with a considerably higher pass rate among those who had completed a traineeship (MS 2018b). Those who failed could take the examination again as often as they wanted.

The number of active advocates and attorneys at law was 24 per cent higher in 2010 than in 2005, an annual growth rate 1.4 times higher than it had been between 1997 and 2005. In 2013, 2,585 sat the advocate exam and 4,840 the attorney at law exam, a dramatic increase resulting from the greater intake for traineeships following new rules from 2009. The consequence was a marked growth in the number of lawyers in 2013, 19.8 per cent more advocates and 12.4 per cent more attorneys than the previous year (NRA 2018; KRRP 2018; MS 2018a; see Figures 2 and 3).

E. Further Deregulation of Legal Professions on the Basis of the 2013 Act

In early 2012 the ruling Civic Platform and Polish People's Party coalition government sought to further open up the professions of advocate, attorney at law and notary (Nalewajko et al 2016). The most significant change based on the Act of 13 June 2013 was continued expansion of the number entitled to be registered as advocates or attorneys at law by exempting some from both the traineeship and the professional examination and allowing others to take the examination without completing a traineeship. (For the latter, the length of experience was shortened from five years to four, and the list of activities was expanded.) The professional examination was modified by eliminating the 100 questions and adding a problem concerning ethical rules.

The government explained its Bill as an effort to increase competitiveness among the legal professions by facilitating mobility between them, thereby lowering costs and increasing quality, in response to society's expectations (Sejm printed matter no 806 of 8 October 2012). But by offering a way to take a professional examination without completing a traineeship, the Bill questioned the desirability of preserving a traineeship organised by professional self-governing councils as the main access point to a legal profession. Implementation of these changes may lead to increased divergence between two groups of qualified lawyers: those with and without a traineeship under the supervision of a patron and professional councils.

The system for training lawyers, therefore, is facing changes that may constitute a rejection of the educational model based on the master–student relationship (dominant in Europe since the Middle Ages), whose current form entails a legal traineeship with mandatory patronage. It may also represent a shift from the influence of professional self-governing councils on training to a model based upon testing the knowledge of lawyers through state examinations, often preceded by a period of practising law, whose varied activities make it difficult to evaluate what was learned.

F. Advocates and Attorneys at Law: the Situation of the Legal Services Market

Between 2005 and 2016, the number of advocates increased by 160 per cent, the number of attorneys at law by 77 per cent, and the total number of qualified lawyers (in these two groups) by 99 per cent, for a ratio of 758 people per lawyer, slightly above the EU average of 671 (NRA 2018; KRRP 2018; MS 2018a; CEPEJ 2016; 2018; see Figures 2 and 3).[11] The large number of lawyers currently completing traineeships means that the market saturation indicator for qualified lawyers will rise dramatically, and Poland will soon become one of the ten EU countries with lowest ratio of population per lawyer.

Attorneys at law are the legal occupation securing the largest number of registrations as advocates. In 2009–17, 363 attorneys at law, 134 prosecutors, 63 judges, 15 notaries and 139 bailiffs were registered as advocates, with the greatest interest occurring in 2009 and 2010, when 72 and 57 attorneys at law as well as 46 and 34 prosecutors were added to the advocates register. Between 2009 and 2017 a total of 652 advocates, 27 prosecutors, 9 notaries, 19 judges and 10 bailiffs were registered as attorneys at law, with a steady increase in interest among advocates, from 7 in 2009 to 160 in 2017. The professions of advocate and attorney at law do not seem to be financially attractive to judges and prosecutors. In 2009–17, 162 attorneys at law and 68 advocates switched to the profession

---

[11] A major hurdle in correct interpretation of the statistics on legal services in Poland arises from the fact that the number of lawyers entitled to use the title of attorney at law or advocate is used interchangeably with the number of attorneys at law and advocates currently practising the profession. As we have seen, the latter number is smaller since it does not include retirees or people who, for various reasons and especially at the lawyer's request, have had their right to practise the profession suspended.

of notary, a higher proportion in 2009–11 (MS 2018d). The increased flow of advocates to the profession of attorney at law can be explained by the imbalance of supply and demand in the legal services market, particularly for natural persons. Attorneys at law engage in a broader spectrum of professional activities and may be employed while offering services in chambers. In recent years, employment has become increasingly attractive. In late December 2016, 44 per cent of attorneys at law were employed, and another 27 per cent were both employed and in chambers or firms (KRRP 2018).

There are several reasons for the changes in the legal services market. The opening of the legal professions, and especially the increased recruitment for traineeships, have resulted in a significant increase in the number of qualified lawyers and the supply of legal services. At the same time, technological changes, which have increased access to the content of legal acts and documents concerning the law and legal advice, have reduced the demand for lawyers' services. Contrary to expectations, growing prosperity has not encouraged Poles to use legal services. One might expect that the increased number of qualified lawyers combined with a flat demand for services will prompt changes in the rules of professional conduct, for example greater acceptance of advertising for legal services.

G. Realisation of Statutory Aims: Evident Weaknesses

A comparison of the two research periods – 1997–2005 and 2005–17 – indicates that the changes in 2005, opening up the field and easing access to legal careers, accelerated the growth of the profession. The ratio of population per lawyer now puts Poland in the centre of EU rankings. Recruitment for traineeships has been made more transparent through reliance on written national examinations graded by anonymous examiners.

The legislative goals of 2005 have been realised: traineeships are more accessible; the process of getting them is transparent; and professional legal services are more available for the average citizen. These effects intensified over the next few years as several thousand legal trainees completed their traineeships. Those changes would not have occurred without the organisational effort undertaken by the Bar and other legal professional associations, which accepted the challenges associated with training a much higher number of trainees.

The absence of a cap on traineeships, however, means that the commission appointed by the MoJ is responsible for shaping the procedures by which candidates are accepted for traineeships, drafting exam questions and organising the exam. The difficulty of the exam keeps changing, leading to pendulum swings in the number who pass annually.

The rising number of lawyers has not been accompanied by state engagement and social partnerships to create new routines among individuals and businesses to take advantage of the legal services now available. Because of their legal culture and limited financial resources, Poles are not accustomed to consulting lawyers about crucial financial transactions or life decisions. Consequently, citizens and businesses blame the state for their own failures. For instance, people bought apartments through contracts making the buyer financially responsible for construction costs; when developers went bankrupt before completing the project, buyers expected the state to bail them out. Others borrowed in foreign currencies; when the złoty plummeted in 2008, borrowers expected the government to cover their losses.

The plans of subsequent governments to provide free legal aid for the poor were postponed. Only after years of debate and preparation did legislation introduce legal assistance, together with legal education reforms. Regulations promised free, pre-trial legal assistance to low-income individuals and universal access to free legal information in order to increase legal awareness and transform legal culture (see Sejm printed matter no 3338 of 16 April 2015). The new Law of 5 August 2015 was also a response to the dramatic increase in the supply of legal services. Nevertheless, reports found that the free legal aid system was ineffective, serving less than 3 per cent of eligible citizens in its first two years. Each legal aid office served an average of just one client a day, usually offering information rather than legal assistance (see ISP 2016; MS 2018e; Winczorek 2019).

At the same time, a boisterous political and media campaign accompanied the 2005 expansion of legal services. As of early 2001 this blitz contributed to undermining the authority of both legal associations and lawyers (Tatomir 2008; Kopania 2012; TNS OBOP 2009a; 2009b; Łojko 2011). The image of the lawyer as worthy of public trust was supplanted by that of an exclusive corporation, a privileged elite. Rather than seeing lawyers as performing services requiring expert knowledge and scrupulous compliance with ethical principles, the public saw them as a self-interested group obstructing transparent rules of entry and constricting the supply of legal services. This, not surprisingly, did not lead to an increased demand for legal services; it retarded the market's development and harmed potential clients, whose cases went unheard or unresolved.

Advocate and attorney at law trainees incur substantial organisational, intellectual, and financial costs. They must pass an entry exam, complete the lengthy traineeship, and then pass their professional examination. If traineeships are seen as both expensive and ineffective pathways to a professional career, without any guarantee of a place in this labour market, aspirants will seek alternative (lawfully permitted) pathways.

At the same time, the average earnings of attorneys at law or advocates in the first three years after passing their Bar exam fall far below expectations (Banasik 2012; Jaraszek 2011; Rojek-Socha 2018). Before 2005, unemployment among lawyers was almost unknown. However, representatives of the association for attorneys at law in Krakow noticed a few years ago that 'one can ascertain with great likelihood that close to 20% of those now qualified as attorneys at law have not found a place on the legal services market' (Grelewicz-La Mela and Wyszogrodzka 2011: 5). This association also pointed out that:

> statistical analyses show that demand for professional legal services is not growing proportionately to the supply of legal services. It appears that 'absorption' of so many attorneys at law will no longer be possible. This tendency is indirectly confirmed by information relayed by 'new' attorneys at law to the District Chamber of Attorneys at Law in Krakow; they request exemptions from membership and insurance fees due to their remaining unemployed or inform [the chamber] that they are not working in their field. (ibid)

Furthermore, officers of the relevant national association reported that, according to 2012 data, several hundred attorneys at law (those of pre-retirement age as well as young, recent admits) are registered as unemployed (Sałajewski 2012).

Therefore, the first years of the implementation of the new system displayed symptoms of maladaptation. Either the specialised knowledge of a significant proportion of lawyers was underutilised, or the career profile of many lawyers was ill suited to the needs of the market.

The number of lawyers is influenced by decisions of the MoJ Commission, which determines the difficulty of the entry exam. Neither the state nor the Bar associations possess mechanisms to control the number of young lawyers. The new legislation expects the market to evaluate the ability of a lawyer. Newly certified lawyers continue to encounter inadequate demand, wasting the time and money invested in specialised studies and traineeships. Because of inadequate career counselling, far too many students enter public and private law schools in Poland and elsewhere in Europe.

Lack of effective cooperation by the state and its social partners in the process of increasing the recruitment of law graduates to the advocates and attorneys at law self-governing councils in 1990–2005 resulted in opening up the legal professions without taking into account the need to ensure that young advocates and attorneys at law had realistic opportunities to find a place in the legal services market. Such a match between supply and demand was essential for efficient practice of the profession, given the economic and social costs incurred by entrants, and for the preservation of the social capital acquired by professional self-governing councils.

V. CONCLUSIONS: THE CONSEQUENCES OF TRANSFORMATION AND PREDICTIONS FOR THE FUTURE

Sometime around 2003, politicians began to characterise professional associations of lawyers as exclusive and elitist. The self-governing councils were depicted as limiting the constitutional rights of citizens to freely choose a legal career or retain legal counsel. At the same time, those councils were unable to discuss the situation or undertake changes themselves. Unwilling to increase the number of available traineeships, the professional self-governing councils could influence neither the number of law graduates nor public opinion. The legal establishment was perceived by politicians and the media as a corporation that overwhelmingly favoured its own interests over those of newly qualified lawyers and clients. This weakening image and reputation led to a loss of crucial social capital accumulated over the years by the legal professions. Francis Fukuyama (2000: 98) sees social capital as 'an instantiated set of informal values or norms shared among members of a group that permits them to cooperate with one another' allowing them to 'build bonds of trust (and hence social capital) outside their own memberships' (ibid: 102).

The more than 50,000 Polish lawyers are described by the 1997 Constitution as a vocation of public trust (see Skuczyński 2016: 31–44). But politics has undermined social trust in legal professions. At the same time, some political leaders have assured those embarking on a legal career that demand for their services is basically unlimited and the only barrier to their fulfilling this demand is the limited number of traineeships. Yet a significant increase in professional council membership for advocates and attorneys at law accompanied by limited demand for legal services creates great risks. Trust would diminish, and bonds among the members of autonomous professional councils would erode; these two elements are formally anchored not only in a professional ethos but also in a common experience of years of study and traineeship. Without specialised traineeships supervised by professional councils, the sole link tying newly inducted members to self-governing councils would be their professional examination and formalised ethical principles.

An increase in the number of lawyers in excess of market demand could undercut the means by which social capital is spontaneously generated. In conjunction with the end of clear and identical procedures for socialising all lawyers, this could lead to weak or broken bonds between council members as well as between lawyers and their clients.[12] The consequences might be particularly painful for those who have incurred significant financial and other expenses: the cost of years of university study and fees for traineeship procedures. Discontent among these individuals would probably lead to conflict when they compete in an open market with colleagues who took advantage of other, less expensive, less rigorous pathways to professional qualification.

Increased supply and stable demand generate heightened competition and reduced prices. But another effect could be lower quality and loss of faith in lawyers among clients dissatisfied with case outcomes. Such a situation imposes increased transaction costs on clients, who must engage in a more thorough verification of a potential attorney's qualifications.

Noting the emerging risks as well as the expectations of trainees, the independent council of attorneys at law passed a resolution (No 73/VIII/2011, 9 November 2011) introducing changes to the traineeship programme, including increased emphasis on trainee familiarity with the practical aspects of legal work: rhetorical, negotiation, and conflict management skills as well as continuing education regarding ethical principles and proper execution of duties. It also restored oral exams. In turn, the Supreme Bar Council passed a resolution (No 55/2011, 19 November 2011) modifying advocate traineeships by replacing the traditional lectures with more workshops focused on practical learning.

Further change in the process by which people are recruited into legal careers must attend to the views of professional self-governing councils and take account of market reality. Without input from those already working in this specialised field, the government's social partners would be no more than atomised, isolated lawyers without any real influence over the socialisation of new members into autonomous, professional entities; and there would be lower levels of trust within these organisations. Lawyers and their self-governing councils would find it difficult to maintain their independence vis-à-vis the state and its agencies when representing ordinary citizens. Heightened competition (which could lead to battling for clients in certain market segments) would negatively affect the predisposition to uphold the ethical principles of the profession. A consequence would be further erosion of the social capital accumulated over years (see Putnam 1994; 2000; Fukuyama 1995; 2000).

The aim is to preserve coherence and cohesion and ensure proper functioning of independent professional self-governing councils. It seems justified to regulate and restrict the pathways to the various legal professions to, in principle, traineeship in order to ensure that apposite relationships and bonds are formed among members. That process (lasting three years) – under the supervision of autonomous professional councils and

---

[12] Fukuyama (2000: 109) notes that excessive increase in size of a group inevitably leads to less commitment to the public good.

based on intense cooperation between trainees and their patrons – should facilitate the newly-qualified lawyer's entry into the market for legal services. This lengthy procedure should promise entry into the profession at the moment the candidate passes the qualifying examination for traineeship. Participants in this process should acquire a meaningful chance to build a market position and professional reputation under the tutelage of their masters as well as the supervision of a functioning independent council. Such participants will gain a much greater chance of success in the market than a lawyer whose contact with the practice of the profession and the professional association is limited to a single professional examination.

As the number seeking traineeships increases it is becoming harder for patrons to perform their functions under the current guidelines. The more desirable law offices are accepting only trainees willing to work for little or no pay, creating obstacles for law graduates who cannot count on financial support from their families.

After the reforms of 2005, 2009, and 2013, which sought to increase access to traineeships, the time has come to consider new solutions that will allow newly qualified lawyers to find a place for themselves in the legal services market. For several years, officers of professional councils have pointed out the urgent need to change university law studies. Sociological research among law students reveals their desire to have more practical coursework as well as workshops enhancing interpersonal skills (Łojko 2011).

The latest traineeship programmes prepared by the councils of attorneys at law and of advocates are a step in the right direction. Still, that move should be accompanied by endeavours to stabilise the number of trainees accepted annually so that the councils can guarantee an appropriate level of coursework and assigned tasks alongside an effective system of supervision by patrons.

To protect the social capital accrued by the self-governing councils, the regulations governing the professions must find a middle ground between the state and the councils.

REFERENCES

Agacka-Indecka, J (2005) 'W sejmie i w senacie. Sprawozdanie z zakończenia prac parlamentarnych nad zmianami ustawy – Prawo o adwokaturze' [In the Sejm and in the Senate. Report on the completion of parliamentary work on amendments to the Bar Profession Act] 9–10 *Palestra*.

Banasik, M (2012) 'Dużo prawników, ale nie wykształconych' [Numerous lawyers, but not educated], *Gazeta Wyborcza* 2 March.

Fukuyama, F (1995) *Trust: The Social Virtues and the Creation of Prosperity* (New York, Free Press).

—— (2000) 'Social capital' in LE Harrison and SP Huntington (eds), *Culture Matters* (New York, Basic Books) 98–111.

Grelewicz-La Mela, M and Wyszogrodzka M (2011) 'Nowi radcowie prawni na start' [New attorneys at law ready] 4 Oct–Dec *Biuletyn Informacyjny Okręgowej Izby Radców Prawnych w Krakowie* [The Newsletter of the Regional Chamber of Attorneys at Law in Krakow].

Jaraszek, A (2011) 'Aplikacja nie gwarantuje dobrej pracy w zawodzie' [Training does not guarantee a good job in the profession] *Rzeczpospolita* 13 July.

Kopania, B (2012) 'Studenci prawa w badaniach socjologicznych' [Law students in sociological research] 123 *Radca Prawny* March.

Łojko, K (ed) (2011) *Studenci prawa o studiach i perspektywach zawodowych* [Law students on studies and career perspectives] (Warsaw, University of Warsaw, Department of Law and Administration).

Mazur, D and Żurek, W (2017) 'Wymiar sprawiedliwości w Polsce u progu 2017 r. – wyzwania i zagrożenia'[Judicial system in Poland at the beginning of 2017 – challenges and threats] LXXIX (1) *Ruch Prawniczy, Ekonomiczny i Socjologiczny* 25–38.

Nalewajko, E, Post B, Radiukiewicz, A and Maranowski, P (2016) *Społeczne światy elity administracji państwa* [Social worlds of the state administration elite] (Warsaw, Instytut Studiów Politycznych PAN).

Putnam, R (1994) *Making Democracy Work: Civic Traditions in Modern Italy* (Princeton, New Jersey, Princeton University Press).

—— (2000) *Bowling Alone: The Collapse and Revival of American Community* (New York, Simon & Schuster).

Rojek-Socha, P (2018) 'Prawnicy skarżą się na małe zarobki, MS wierzy w wolny rynek' [Lawyers complain about low earnings, MoJ believes in free market] *Prawo.pl* 21 November 2018.

Sałajewski, D (2012) 'Deregulacja bez dezorientacji' [Deregulation without confusion] 124 *Radca Prawny* April.

Skuczyński, P (2016) *Etyka adwokatów i radców prawnych* [Ethics of advocates and attorneys at law] (Warsaw, Wydawnictwo CH Beck).

Tatomir, T (2008) 'Zmniejsza się zaufanie do prawników' [Trust in lawyers is diminishing] *Gazeta Prawna* 5 February.

Winczorek, J (2019) *Dostęp do prawa. Ujęcie socjologiczne* [Access to the law. Sociological approach] (Warsaw, Wydawnictwo Naukowe Scholar).

Primary Resources

CEPEJ (European Commission for the efficiency of Justice) (2016) *European Judicial Systems. Efficancy and Quality of Justice*. CEPEJ Studies no 12, available at www.coe.int/t/dghl/cooperation/cepej/evaluation/2016/publication/CEPEJ%20Study%2023%20report%20EN%20web.pdf.

—— (2018) *European Judicial Systems. Efficiency and Quality of Justice* CEPEJ Studies no 26, available at rm.coe.int/rapport-avec-couv-18-09-2018-en/16808def9c.

GUS (Główny Urząd Statystyczny) [Central Statistical Office of Poland] (1990, 1991, 1996, 2001, 2006a, 2011, 2016, 2017a) 'Rocznik Statystyczny Rzeczypospolitej Polskiej'. [Statistical Yearbook of the Republic of Poland], Warsaw.

—— (2005, 2006b, 2008, 2017b) 'Szkoły wyższe i ich finanse w 2004 r./2005 r./2007 r./2016 r.' [Higher education and its finances in 2004/2005/2007/2016], Warsaw.

—— (2017c) 'Zmiany strukturalne grup podmiotów gospodarki narodowej w rejestrze REGON' [Structural changes in groups of subjects of national economy in REGON Register], available at stat.gov.pl/obszary-tematyczne/podmioty-gospodarcze-wyniki-finansowe/zmiany-strukturalne-grup-podmiotow/, Warsaw.

Inwestinfo.pl (2017) 'Wyniki finansowe spółek giełdowych' [Financial results of listed companies], available at www.inwestinfo.pl/analiza-finansowa/wyniki-finansowe/.

ISP (Instytut Spraw publicznych) [Institute of Public Affairs] (2016) 'Raport końcowy z monitoringu funkcjonowania systemu nieodpłatnej pomocy prawnej' [Final report on monitoring of the free legal aid system], Warsaw, December.

KPFwP (Konferencja Przedsiębiorstw Finansowych w Polsce – Związek Pracodawców) [Conference of Financial Companies in Poland – Association of Employers] (2017) 'Wielkość polskiego rynku wierzytelności' [The size of the Polish debt market], available at kpf.pl/badania-i-publikacje/raporty-cykliczne/wielkosc-polskiego-rynku-wierzytelnosci.

KRDP (Krajowa Rada Doradców Podatkowych) [The National Council of Tax Advisers] (2017) 'Lista doradców podatkowych. Rejestr osób prawnych uprawnionych do wykonywania czynności doradztwa podatkowego' [List of tax advisers. Register of legal entities authorised to perform tax advisory activities], available at krdp.pl/doradcy.php.

KRRP (Krajowa Rada Radców Prawnych) [The National Council of Attorneys at Law] (2018) 'Ruch kadrowy radców prawnych i aplikantów radcowskich 1998–2017' [Staff changes: attorneys at law and attorney at law trainees 1998–2017]. Data made available by KRRP at the author's request.

KRS (Krajowa Rada Sądownictwa) [National Council of the Judiciary of Poland] (2012) 'Komunikat Krajowej Rady Sądownictwa' [Statement of the National Council of the Judiciary], Warsaw, 15 November.

MS (Ministerstwo Sprawiedliwości) [Ministry of Justice], Departament Strategii i Funduszy Europejskich [Department of Strategy and European Funds] (2017a) 'Podstawowa informacja o działalności sądów powszechnych – 2016 rok na tle poprzednich okresów' [Basic information on the activities of ordinary courts – 2016 as compared to previous statistical periods].

—— (2017b) 'Ewidencja spraw 2011–2016' [The number of cases in 2011–2016] available at isws.ms.gov.pl/pl/baza-statystyczna/opracowania-wieloletnie/.

—— (2017c) 'Wykaz komorników sądowych na dzień 31.12.2016' [List of court bailiffs as at 31 December 2016] available at dane.gov.pl/dataset/927,wykaz-komornikow-sadowych/resource/9860.

—— (Departament Zawodów Prawniczych) [Department of Legal Professions] (2018a) 'Dane dotyczące liczby adwokatów, radców prawnych i notariuszy wpisanych na listy w latach 1999–2017' [Data on the number of advocates, attorneys at law, and notaries public entered on the lists in the years 1999–2017]. Data made available by MS at the author's request.

—— (Departament Zawodów Prawniczych) [Department of Legal Professions] (2018b) 'Analiza wyników zawodowych egzaminów prawniczych 2010–2017' [Analysis of the results of professional legal examinations 2010–2017]. Data made available by MS at the author's request.

—— (Departament Zawodów Prawniczych [Department of Legal Professions] (2018c) 'Analiza wyników egzaminów wstępnych na aplikację adwokacką, radcowską, notarialną i komorniczą 2006–2017' [The analysis of preliminary examination for advocate, attorney at law and notary training 2008–2017]. Data made available by MS at the author's request.

—— (Wydział Komunikacji Społecznej i Promocji) [Division of Social Communication and Promotion] (2018d) 'Dane dotyczące liczby osób wykonujących inne zawody prawnicze przed uzyskaniem wpisu na listy adwokatów, radców prawnych i notariuszy' [Data on the number of persons practicing other legal professions before being entered on the lists of advocates, attorneys at law and notaries public]. Data made available by MS at the author's request.

—— (Departament Zawodów Prawniczych) [Department of Legal Professions] (2018e) 'Ocena wykonywania zadań z zakresu nieodpłatnej pomocy prawnej oraz edukacji prawnej za rok 2017' [Assessment of the performance of tasks in the field of free legal aid and legal education for 2017] Warsaw, June.

NRA (Naczelna Rada Adwokacka) [The Supreme Bar Council] (2018) 'Stany osobowe adwokatury za okres 1989–2017' [The Bar profession headcount for the period 1989–2017]. Data made available by NRA at the author's request.

SDP (Stowarzyszenie Doradców Prawnych) [Association of Legal Advisers] 'Doradca prawny – nowoczesny prawnik' [Legal adviser – a modern lawyer] (2017), available at www.doradcyprawni.org/.

TNS OBOP (Public Opinion Research Center) (2009a) to the order of the National Council of Attorneys at Law 'Zawody prawnicze w opinii i doświadczeniu Polaków' [Legal professions in the opinion and experience of the Poles], Warsaw, February.

TNS OBOP (Public Opinion Research Center) (2009b) to the order of the National Council of Attorneys at Law 'Opinie studentów prawa na temat przyszłości zawodów prawniczych' [Opinions of law students of law on the future of legal professions], Warsaw, October.

16

Russia

Challenges of the Market and Boundary Work

EKATERINA MOISEEVA AND TIMUR BOCHAROV

I. AN OVERVIEW OF THE RUSSIAN LEGAL PROFESSION

THE MAIN FEATURE of the legal profession in Russia is its high degree of fragmentation. Like many other civil law countries, Russia would more accurately be described as having several discrete legal occupations rather than a single profession. Judges, prosecutors, police investigators, notaries, advocates, unlicensed practitioners, and in-house counsel are loosely connected groups, administered by different agencies and following different professional rules. Russia's legal occupations include 31,000 judges, 65,000 judicial assistants and secretaries, 45,000 prosecutors, 80,000 police investigators, 35,000 notaries, 72,000 advocates, and an unknown number of unlicensed practitioners. A common name for all practising law graduates is 'jurist' (*iurist*), a term similar to the American 'lawyer'. However, Russian judges and law enforcement personnel would rarely call themselves 'jurists'. The professional identity of these two groups is shaped by their workplaces – courts, criminal investigative departments, and public prosecutor's offices – rather than by academic training. Neither do advocates or notaries refer to themselves as 'jurists'. The only people who use the word 'jurist' for self-designation are unlicensed legal representatives or unlicensed practitioners, since they do not have a specific professional designation.

The Russian legal profession's fragmentation manifests itself in different ways. First, mobility between its sub-groups is severely limited. For example, an advocate has basically no chance of being appointed to the bench because judges are mainly recruited from judicial assistants, who have no experience outside the courts (Volkov and Dzmitryieva 2015). Fragmentation of the legal profession also characterises education, for several reasons. First, there is an abundance of part-time study programmes for lawyers. Two-thirds of law students pursue their degrees through correspondence courses, which involve minimal classroom attendance. Second, state legal professionals and other lawyers are educated differently. For example, law enforcement agencies have their own law schools, where students are trained specifically to work in those agencies. Third, there is a disparity between theory and practice: because students do not get sufficient practical experience at university, professional socialisation occurs in the workplace. Thus, even a law degree – the only element various legal occupations share – does not unite the profession.

The Russian advocate community (*advokatura*) is the most 'professionalised' group in the Russian legal community because it enjoys self-governance. An advocate (*advokat*) must have earned a law degree, practised for two years, passed the Bar exam, taken an oath, and been granted an advocate's licence. Every advocate must be a member of a regional chamber (*palata*) and pay a monthly fee towards the general needs of the community. The Federal Chamber of Advocates is a nationwide professional association that represents the interests of advocates vis-à-vis officialdom, oversees the work of the regional chambers, holds annual meetings, and establishes professional standards. The Federal Bar Act (2002) defines entry barriers, rights and obligations of advocates, types of professional activity, and the structure of the Bar. The Code of Ethics (2003) regulates the relations of advocates with clients, colleagues, and professional associations. A violation of ethical norms leads to a disciplinary hearing, whose most severe penalty is disbarment. Advocates can neither be employed – except as academics or teachers – nor involved in commercial activities. They work in 25,000 non-commercial organisations, 30 per cent alone, with the rest in collective entities.

The advocates' profession is less feminised than other legal occupations: 40 per cent of advocates and 25 per cent of the regional Bars' leaders are women (Kazun et al 2015). In comparison, 70 per cent of investigators and 65 per cent of judges are women (Titaev and Shklyaruk 2016; Volkov et al 2015). The gender balance of the *advokatura* remains the same as in the 1980s. In Soviet times women were well represented in the advocate profession. They did not want to work in the 'masculine atmosphere' of the law enforcement agencies, and the *advokatura* became a respectable alternative (Huskey 1982). Nowadays, the judiciary and law enforcement sectors have become more feminised due to recruitment policy and the prevalence of paper work (Volkov and Dzmitryieva 2015).

The exclusive jurisdiction of Russian advocates is limited to representing defendants in criminal cases. In civil cases, any citizen, even without a law degree, can act as a legal representative. In administrative cases, the representative must have a law degree but does not have to be a licensed advocate. Civil and administrative cases are the principal jurisdictions where advocates compete with unlicensed practitioners. The difference between the two groups is their institutional status. Advocates work through non-commercial (public) organisations, while unlicensed practitioners provide their services through commercial entities, such as limited liability companies and individual enterprises, although the difference is rather technical, since both groups offer paid legal services and profit from their professional activity. Unlicensed practitioners do not possess any professional attributes, such as educational and work credentials, an ethical code, licences, associations, or even a specific title. Table 1 summarises the differences between advocates and unlicensed practitioners.

Table 1 A Comparison of Licensed and Unlicensed Legal Representatives

	Licensed representatives	Unlicensed representatives
Title	Advocates	No specific title. Variously referred to as 'legal business', 'unlicensed practitioners', 'lawyers in private practice', 'law firm employees', or simply 'lawyers'
Workplaces	Advocates' organisations	Law firms and individual enterprises
Type of activity	Non-entrepreneurial	Entrepreneurial
Exclusive jurisdiction	Representing defendants in criminal cases	None
Educational and work credentials	Law degree, two years of legal practice	Law degree necessary only in administrative cases (disputes with the state); nevertheless, most unlicensed practitioners have a law degree
Professional credentials	Bar exam, professional oath	None
Professional associations	Federal Chamber of Advocates and its regional bars in which membership is mandatory	Several minor professional unions in which membership is voluntary
Professional obligations	State appointed criminal cases	None
Professional oversight	Disciplinary hearings by Bar associations, convened at the request of clients, officials, and other advocates	None

There are no accurate data on the number of unlicensed practitioners; estimates vary from 100,000 to 1,000,000. They work in 47,000 law firms and 27,500 individual entrepreneurships (Moiseeva and Skougarevskiy 2016). Advocates operate in 25,000 non-commercial organisations. Another 1,800 non-commercial organisations, such as human rights groups, labour unions, and professional unions, deliver legal services outside the advocate profession. Table 2 highlights the main differences between advocates' organisations and commercial enterprises.

Russian advocates work in a highly competitive environment. Courts hear about one million criminal cases annually, half of them misdemeanours, which are adjudicated in magistrate courts, often without the involvement of legal representatives. Thus, the monopoly of 70,000 advocates is limited to about 500,000 criminal cases. By contrast, courts hear 13,000,000 civil and 4,000,000 administrative cases annually.[1] Given the

---

[1] Official statistics of the Judicial Department of the Russian Federation for 2016. We have not included figures for appellate hearings.

Table 2 A Comparison of Organisational Forms within which Lawyers Practise

	Advocates' organisations (25,000)	Commercial enterprises (74,500)
Types of activity	Non-commercial; contain only advocates	Commercial; advocates must terminate their licences
Types of organisations	Three forms of collective practice (colleges of advocates, legal consultation offices, advocates' bureaux) and solo practice	Law firms, 97 per cent registered as limited liability companies (collective practice), and individual entrepreneurships (solo practice)
Simplified taxation system	May not be used	May be used
Extra expenses	Entry fee and monthly membership	None
Year of incorporation	57 per cent before 2006 26 per cent 2006–11 17 per cent after 2012	Law firms: 22 per cent before 2006 27 per cent 2006–11 51 per cent after 2012 Individual entrepreneurships: 14 per cent before 2006 27 per cent from 2006–11 59 per cent after 2012
Frequency of liquidation (2012–16)	Less than one per cent	Law firms: 15 per cent Individual entrepreneurships: less than one per cent
Registered in the largest cities (Moscow and St. Petersburg)	10 per cent	Law firms: 33 per cent Individual entrepreneurships: 16 per cent

absence of a professional monopoly, it is unsurprising that such a large market encourages the emergence of a huge number of 'non-professional' unlicensed practitioners.

Advocates present themselves as the most qualified providers of legal services, claiming a special position within the legal community by fashioning their profession into a 'collective honorific symbol' (Becker 1962). Their public discourse is built around professional institutions, such as qualification commissions (administering entrance examinations and disciplining unethical behaviour), attorney-client privilege, ethical norms, and Bar exams. However, ordinary Russians often cannot tell the difference between licensed and unlicensed legal representatives, lumping them together as 'advocates' or 'lawyers'. When seeking legal assistance, laypersons pay less attention to formal professional credentials than to recommendations from those they trust (Bocharov and Moiseeva 2016). Paraphrasing Everett Hughes (1963), the state grants advocates the exclusive 'licence' to practise in a narrow jurisdiction, criminal law, while the public does not give advocates the 'mandate' to control the legal field fully.

Advocates pursue a professional project by attempting to expand their jurisdiction to *all* spheres of legal representation and convincing the 'army' of anonymous competitors to join the Bar. However, unlicensed practitioners are not eager to obtain an advocate's licence, which they see as an unconditional obligation imposed on criminal lawyers. In fact, only 40 per cent of advocates specialise in criminal cases, while 30 per cent work primarily on civil cases and the rest have mixed specialisations. The practices of advocates and unlicensed practitioners in civil cases are nearly identical. As one advocate put it:

> There is no difference in terms of quality of the services provided by advocates and other lawyers. Say, today you are an advocate, but tomorrow you decide to suspend your license for some reason and work as an entrepreneur. So does your IQ immediately drop? Is your knowledge of the law diminished? No, it doesn't work this way.[2]

The impending reform of the judicial system has provoked heated debate about the regulation of the legal services market. The state's primary concern is to improve the quality of legal representation enjoyed by ordinary people. This can be achieved, advocates insist, only by extending their professional jurisdiction and establishing high entry barriers for all market actors. Unlicensed practitioners perceive that extension as a threat, arguing that bar associations should become more market-oriented *before* extending their monopoly. As the debate continues, the parties are seeking compromise solutions.

Recently, the Justice Ministry proposed making Bar membership more attractive for unlicensed practitioners and only then extending advocates' professional monopoly to civil and administrative cases.[3] Meanwhile, a group of unlicensed practitioners and public figures introduced a Bill to require that all legal representatives have a law degree.[4] Because liberal institutions have found it hard to survive in Russia's autocratic environment, it is useful to trace the historical trajectory of the advocate's profession.

II. THE HISTORICAL BACKGROUND OF THE RUSSIAN LEGAL PROFESSION: PROFESSIONALISATION FROM ABOVE AND THE PROBLEM OF PUBLIC RECOGNITION

A. Advocates in the Russian Empire

The development of the legal profession in pre-revolutionary Russia was part of the intelligentsia's political programme (Levin-Stankevich 1996; Novikov 2012). Whereas in the US and Europe professionalisation was associated with the emergence of the bourgeoisie, in Russia, which basically lacked a middle class, the intelligentsia played the most important role (Balzer 1996).[5]

---

[2] This and the following quotations are drawn from the interviews with 54 Russian advocates and 9 unlicensed practitioners (two-thirds in St Petersburg and the rest in Moscow, Vladimir, Kazan, and Irkutsk) conducted in 2014–16 by researchers of the Institute for the Rule of Law at the European University in St Petersburg. The study was supported by the Russian Scientific Foundation under Grant No 14-18-02219.

[3] The Project on the Regulation of the Market of Professional Legal Services issued on 1 November 2017.

[4] The Bill was introduced by the President of the Association of Russian Lawyers, a non-professional voluntary association of practising lawyers, academicians, state officials, and businessmen, established in 2005 with the support of the President, Vladimir Putin, to monitor the quality of legal education and rank law departments.

[5] Balzer (1996) defines the intelligentsia in terms of a focus on public service, social responsibility, a distrust of the state, a critical attitude toward society, and sympathy for liberal ideas.

Russian advocates were not a professional group until 1864, when the Judicial Statutes of Emperor Alexander II were implemented, completely reorganising the judicial system, introducing new legal concepts and techniques, and generating demand for legal experts who could apply them (Levin-Stankevich 1996). There were few professional lawyers in Imperial Russia, since legal education was elitist.

The first law school, the Imperial School of Jurisprudence, was founded in 1835.[6] After graduating from it, lawyers had to work in the Justice Ministry for six years (Levin-Stankevich 1996). Many alumni later held senior positions in the state apparatus or became legal scholars (*pravovedy*). Often travelling to Europe, they 'became imbued with a sense of mission, a desire to change Russia's backward system of justice, and in 1864 they would play a pivotal role in the drafting of the Judicial Reforms' (Pomeranz 1993: 322–23). Those alumni constituted the core of the newly formed legal profession, becoming the main disseminators of a liberal legal culture and engineers of the 1864 Judicial Reforms.

The professionalisation of legal representation was one of the goals of the judicial reform, since legal assistance was being provided mostly by unqualified laypersons. The Judicial Statutes gave legal representatives a professional title, 'sworn attorneys' (*prisiazhnye poverennye*), although they were commonly called 'advocates' (*avocats*), in the French manner. The structure of the Russian legal profession also resembled the French model, which was eagerly discussed in contemporaneous newspaper articles (Blagodeteleva 2015). To become an advocate, a person needed a law degree and five years of legal practice. Because few people met these qualifications, there were only 1,617 advocates in 1886 (a third of whom lived in Moscow and St Petersburg) and just 2,656 in 1900 and 5,658 in 1914 (Gilmutdinov 2013).

Advocates were financially and institutionally independent from the state. They had self-regulating institutions: councils of advocates (*sovety prisiazhnykh poverennykh*), which established ethical rules, reviewed applications, held qualification commissions, organised annual meetings and conferences, developed a comprehensive training programme for legal assistants, and allocated financial resources.[7] Yet relations with the state remained ambiguous. The new legal techniques were not easily assimilated by the traditional legal culture, and the judicial reforms soon started unravelling (Levin-Stankevich 1996).

Professionalisation from above does not automatically create a professional community. In Russia, collective action and professional discourse emerged in response to the state's restriction of professional autonomy and increasing competition. In 1874, advocates lost control over disciplinary procedures, which were transferred to district courts. In 1889, the government imposed a moratorium on the creation of new councils of advocates (which lasted until 1904) and restricted the admission of Jews to the Bar.

---

[6] Besides the Imperial School of Jurisprudence, which served only nobles, a few state universities had established law departments by the mid-nineteenth century.

[7] The councils were not full-fledged membership associations but rather bodies for managing the professional community. As in nineteenth-century France, Russian advocates were registered with regional appellate courts (*sudebnye palaty*). If there were enough of them, they could obtain permission to establish an autonomous council, whose members were elected annually. Since the criterion for a 'sufficient number' was never defined, councils were founded only in a few major cities. Elsewhere, district courts oversaw the work of advocates.

In 1878, political trials were moved to military courts (from which advocates were practically excluded). A national meeting was allowed only once. Advocates ascribed resistance to reform to the state's fear that the *advokatura* might become a strong political institution.

In 1874, the shortage of qualified lawyers forced the state to establish a group of 'private attorneys' (*chastnye poverennye*), who needed neither a law degree nor legal training. They were attached to district courts, from which they obtained permission to practise (Poznyshev 1913). Laypersons also could dispense legal advice and represent people in court. The so-called 'underground *advokatura*' or 'street' lawyers greatly outnumbered advocates, and their shady practices cast a shadow on the entire legal profession (Pomeranz 1993).

Ordinary Russians (especially the peasantry) could not distinguish between the new advocates and the old legal representatives. To gain public recognition, advocates tried to distance themselves from both 'street' lawyers and private attorneys (Blagodeteleva 2013). Gradually, they earned trust by providing free legal aid to indigent defendants and participating in the landmark political trials of the 1870s and 1880s. Even though advocates did not have exclusive rights to all legal work, they were obliged to represent indigent people. On one hand, this was more a burden than a privilege: since advocates worked without payment for such clients, their expenses had to be covered by membership fees. On the other, in their public declarations and statements advocates characterised free legal aid to indigents as a professional vocation. Legal representation of political defendants accused of crimes against the emperor, the government or state officials also contributed to the profession's prestige (Barry and Berman 1968; Novikov 2013).

Created as a liberal institution that could publicly defend the rule of law in pre-revolutionary Russia, the *advokatura* inevitably became a persistent critic of autocracy and quickly found itself in the opposition, even though its arena was the courtroom rather than the political system (Pomeranz 1997: 326). Active involvement in defending indigent people and political dissenters helped advocates win public trust and recognition. The counter-reforms further consolidated the advocates' community. Advocates' main concerns were gaining a professional monopoly and eliminating 'underground' lawyers.

B. Advocates in the Soviet Union

The Revolution of 1917 thoroughly disrupted the legal system. Legal representation was collectivised: private practice eliminated and legal services delivered exclusively in legal consultation offices (*iuridicheskie konsul'tatsii*). Seen as a 'relic of bourgeois society', pre-revolutionary advocates did not blend into socialist society. At first the Soviet government tried to abolish the legal profession by letting anyone act as a legal representative, which corresponded well with Marx's hypothesis that the state would wither away in the future communist society. However, the Soviet government soon realised the judicial system could not function without professional lawyers. The legal profession re-emerged with a new mission: advocates were supposed to function as assistants of the courts, helping judges establish the 'objective truth' (Undrevich 1928). The plan was to attract young members of the working class to the profession and gradually slough off the old advocates.

The transformation of advocates into officers of the court was only partly successful. Neither legislation nor media campaigns could engender the new Soviet advocate envisaged by the state. Instead, pre-revolutionary advocates took senior positions in the executive committees of the Soviet bar associations and were the main recruiters of new members. The 1930s Stalinist purges transformed the Soviet legal profession: many Tsarist-era advocates emigrated or were exiled,[8] while the number of Party members increased (Lubshev 2002; Huskey 1986).[9] However, the norms of professional conduct and work practices of pre-revolutionary advocates had already shaped the Soviet legal profession. Moreover, even though the Soviet state did not formally adopt the pre-revolutionary regulation of the legal profession, legislation and unofficial manuals on professional ethics were virtual replications. Dina Kaminskaya (1982), who joined the Moscow Bar Association in the late 1930s, remembered that the pre-revolutionary advocates constituted the core of the Bar, maintaining old attitudes toward the legal profession and legal culture, and exemplifying declamatory skills and ethical standards for the new members.

The position of Soviet advocates was contradictory. On one hand, they operated under the umbrella of the Justice Ministry, which issued guidelines for their work, established rates for legal services, and oversaw elections to the executive committees of local Bars. Despite the liberal ideals inherited from their pre-revolutionary predecessors, Soviet advocates were not immune to collectivisation and bureaucratisation. In a sense, they did become the court's assistants: advocates' professional autonomy was limited by their lack of procedural power vis-à-vis law enforcement personnel, especially in criminal cases. Advocates faced difficulties when they needed to examine case files or introduce evidence (Kaminskaya 1982; Luryi 1977). According to Kaminskaya (1982), the state controlled all political utterances in the public arena: any advocate who did not demonstrate political loyalty could not appear in court. The executive committees of the local Bars, in coordination with the KGB (Committee for State Security), selected the advocates eligible to work on politically sensitive cases.

At the same time, advocates enjoyed an autonomy other Soviet professionals could only dream about (Huskey 1982; Mrowczynski 2012). Advocates were not state employees working for a flat wage, unlike other legal occupations. Soviet Bars (*kollegii advokatov*) were local associations, financially independent from the state and endowed with elements of self-governance (recruiting and disciplining members, allocating financial resources).[10] Clients paid the attorney's fees through a consultation office, which distributed them to the advocates. Even under the Soviet command economy, relations between advocates and clients preserved the features of a free market economy. In addition to the official fee, calculated at a fixed rate, advocates also received informal payments called MIKST, an acronym translated as 'maximum utilization of the client above the statutory fees' (Jordan 2005; Kaminskaya 1982). These equalised the difference between the cost of legal services estimated by the state and that defined by advocates themselves. But though a national association representing the professional community in relations with

---

[8] According to Huskey (1986), the number of advocates decreased by 21 per cent between 1935 and 1936.
[9] By 1951, Communist Party members had become 60 per cent of advocates (Devitsyna 2015) and remained at that level until the 1980s (Barry and Berman 1968; Jordan 1998).
[10] The Soviet bars were professional associations, in contrast to the pre-revolutionary councils of advocates, which were more similar to the executive committees of the bars.

the state was always a priority for the local bar leaders, the Union of Soviet Advocates was established only in 1989.[11]

Soviet advocates had a monopoly on representation of *individual* clients in all types of cases at all stages. Soviet companies and enterprises obtained legal services from a special professional group, state corporate counsel (*iuriskonsulty*). Advocates did not regard them as competitors since they were state employees, whose credentials and salaries were generally lower (Mrowczynski 2012). By the end of the Soviet period, advocates could represent companies, thereby invading the jurisdiction of state corporate counsel.

Soviet advocates were deeply concerned about their image. Advocacy was the least prestigious occupation for law school graduates, most of whom became judges, prosecutors, and police investigators. It was also disreputable in the eyes of society for two reasons. First, advocates were seen as bourgeois; second, they defended people accused of committing crimes against the Soviet people. The image of advocates as 'class enemies' gradually changed during Khrushchev's thaw. Part of his political program was strengthening the role of legal professionals in building a socialist society (Barry and Berman 1968). As criminal defenders, advocates strove to present themselves as mediators between the state and the accused, arguing that only a universal right to legal representation could guarantee fair trials.

This brief historical overview identified two challenges stemming from top-down professionalisation, which shaped the evolution of advocates: the struggles for autonomy (which they enjoyed on paper but not in practice) and for the public's trust and social prestige. Russian advocates still confront the shadows of the past. Renowned for their passionate speeches in defence of revolutionaries and political prisoners, pre-revolutionary advocates remain a role model for modern advocates. In their public discourse, the profession's elite still invokes the ethical norms of their pre-revolutionary predecessors. Telling examples of such a heritage are the 150th anniversary of the Russian advokatura, celebrated in 2014 with emphasis on its prerevolutionary dawn, and a special lapel badge of advocates, established in 2015, which closely reproduces that of the pre-revolutionary advocates. At the same time, Bar associations have maintained the stance of their Soviet-era bureaucratic forebears, remaining more preoccupied with preserving the status quo than modernising the profession in response to the market-based economy. This generates tension between advocates and other legal representatives and obstructs discussion of regulatory reform. The procedural disparities with and dependence on law enforcement personnel are another unfortunate relic of the Soviet period, which tarnishes the public image of advocates.

III. ADVOCATES AFTER PERESTROIKA

A. The Rise of Professional Competition and the Failure to Unify

During the Soviet era, advocates cared more about social benefits than economic gain, since the problem of monopoly was not pressing. Radical changes in the legal profession

---

[11] Because membership in the Union of Soviet Advocates was voluntary and it had to compete with other emerging professional associations, the Union never had real clout (Jordan 1998). The local Bars thus remained the main professional entities until passage of the Federal Bar Act in 2002.

took place in the late 1980s and early 1990s, with the first blooms of the market-based economy. During Perestroika, Russian advocates faced the same challenges as their Western colleagues: the marketability of the legal services and the need for a professional monopoly. In a market economy, the success of professionalisation depends on the ability of service providers to convert specialised knowledge into social and economic benefits (Larson 1977).

The capitalist economy has generated new specialisations in the Russian legal profession for those who had an intimate knowledge of economics and management and could keep up with the rapid changes in commercial legislation. The two very important Perestroika regulations, the Law on Individual Labour Activity (1986) and the Law on Cooperation (1988), authorised small and medium businesses. The legal profession rapidly commercialised. The Soviet Bars were forced to compete with the so-called alternative Bar associations and unlicensed practitioners operating through commercial enterprises. By February 1989, there were 370 legal cooperatives employing 2,500 people (Jordan 2005). In the 1990s, legal cooperatives were reorganised as individual entrepreneurships and limited liability companies. Since the provision of legal services was not subject to licensing, unlicensed practitioners did not adhere to any professional standards, and their work did not differ from that of other service-oriented enterprises.

The alternative Bars have been another source of concern for advocates. In 1989, the year the first national association of Soviet advocates was formed, the Justice Ministry approved the establishment of alternative Bar associations, justified by the shortage of professional lawyers during Perestroika. The policy draws a parallel with the creation of private attorneys in the late nineteenth century (Jordan 2005). The alternative Bars promoted themselves as innovators serving business interests by adopting Western organisational models (Lubshev 2002). They combined the features of professional associations (admission, training, disciplinary practices) and commercial companies (entering into contractual relationships with clients).

Viewing the existing Bars as Soviet-era holdovers, the new Bars shaped their image in opposition to the past. The alternative Bars had better economic and managerial assets, while Soviet-era organisations often could not see the opportunities offered by the market-based economy. As the renowned Russian advocate Genri Reznik put it (2001: 16), the older generation had 'a natural fear of free floating in a highly competitive environment'. Unable to exploit these new realms, the post-Soviet advocates' organisations were shunted aside. Unlicensed practitioners and alternative Bars took over representation in civil cases and advising business clients, while the old Bars handled 90 per cent of criminal cases, mostly by court appointment (Jordan 1998).

The alternative Bars were registered as public organisations and viewed as part of the advocate's profession. In 1995, they established their own national professional association, the Guild of Russian Advocates, to represent their interests nationwide. Both original and alternative Bars were dissatisfied with the growth of the commercial sector and the quality of services provided by unlicensed practitioners. From the mid-nineties, the advocate community sought to control the legal market and introduce entry barriers for all those offering legal services, but their campaign failed for several reasons. First, advocates were insufficiently unified and organised to prevent the invasion of the law firms, which spread like wildfire. Second, professional lawyers could not meet the growing market demand: post-Soviet advocates did not upgrade their skills in disputes between economic actors quickly enough, and there were too few alternative Bars. When the Justice Ministry banned the registration of new alternative Bars in 1995, there were just 40. Third, the leaders of the Bars lacked the political power and public support to obtain a monopoly over all legal representation (Jordan 1998).

The inability of old and new generations of advocates to cooperate legitimised the state's intervention. In 1995, the state issued a resolution requiring every legal practitioner who was not a Bar member to obtain a permission to practise from the Justice Ministry. This was a form of bureaucratic enforcement rather than a bottom up initiative lobbied by *advokatura*. The state supported the growth of the legal market but also sought to control it (Jordan 2005). Both advocates and unlicensed practitioners perceived this policy as hostile interference. Advocates were afraid to lose control over admissions, while unlicensed practitioners resented state authority. The resolution was revoked two years later (after the issuance of just 8,000 permissions), not through the efforts of lawyers but because the state adopted a new law on state licensing, which did not regulate legal services.

In 2002, after passage of the Federal Bar Act, the alternative and original Bars merged into a new professional body, the Federal Chamber of Advocates and its regional branches. This legislation had been in the works for ten years. Advocates were heavily involved in drafting it in cooperation with the Justice Ministry. Determining their rights and obligations required compromises between private and public interests. Russian professionals historically were the losers in such regulatory haggling, since fostering civil society institutions has never been a state priority. Consequently, the project of unifying all legal representatives under one roof, as the advocates proposed, failed. Currently, the profession of advocates is based on their exclusive right to represent *criminal* defendants, precisely where the state has the strongest stake in supporting qualified lawyers. In civil cases, advocates compete with an army of unlicensed practitioners.

B. The Professional Hallmarks of Today's Advocates

The Federal Chamber of Advocates, representing all advocates, and their regional chambers, is their regulatory body. Every advocate must belong to a regional chamber. The governing body of each regional chamber includes a president (who represents advocates' interests vis-à-vis state agencies and other public organisations), a board (an elected executive body dealing with day-to-day issues), an assembly of all chamber members (that takes crucial decisions but meets irregularly), an audit committee (overseeing finances), and a qualification committee.

The Code of Professional Ethics of Advocates, adopted in 2003, is not very detailed compared with those in Western countries. It contains 18 articles outlining the norms and principles of professional behaviour and nine establishing procedural rules for disciplining members. Most of the ethical norms are universal, such as a ban on advertising, attorney-client privilege, respect for the court, and avoidance of conflicts of interest. Complaints of unethical behaviour can be submitted to the qualification committee by other advocates, clients, the chamber's vice-president, regional offices of the Justice Ministry, and judges. Disciplinary proceedings resemble court hearings: oral and adversarial, with submission of evidence and cross-examination of the parties, but closed to the public. If found guilty, an advocate can receive a reprimand, a warning or licence termination. Disbarred advocates can apply for a new licence after three years, provided they repass the examination. In 2015, regional chambers received 12,814 complaints against advocates; qualification committees reviewed 4,894, finding 2,942 advocates guilty and revoking 507 licences.[12]

The formal requirements for admission to the Bar are a law degree, two years of legal practice,[13] a clean criminal record, and passage of an examination set by the qualification committee, which includes a computer-based written test and an oral interview. The list of 236 questions is provided to candidates in advance. Qualification committees pay attention not only to candidates' knowledge of the law but also to their familiarity with the profession's ethical norms, organisation, and history. Moreover, candidates should be prepared to draft a legal document or decide a legal case during the examination. In 2015, 3,793 out of 5,827 applicants (65 per cent) passed the exam. Candidates who fail can try again after a year. After passing the examination, candidates take a professional oath, a formal ritual of admission to the professional community.

Within three months of taking the oath, advocates must decide where they are going to practise. In addition to solo practice, there are three collective structures: colleges of advocates (*kollegii advokatov*),[14] legal consultation offices (*iuridicheskie konsul'tatsii*), and advocates' bureaux (*advokatskie biuro*), which differ in terms of collegial relationships and responsibilities to clients. More than 60 per cent of advocates work in colleges of advocates, and another third are solo practitioners (*advokatskie kabinety*). All these modes are non-commercial.

Internships and assistantships are important stages on the road to joining the *advokatura*. Interns (who must have a law degree) may practise law under an advocate's supervision, while assistants (who may be law students) perform mostly clerical work. Both must honour the attorney-client privilege; and both sign work contracts with the advocates' organisations and are paid a wage.

Because advocates have the exclusive right to represent defendants in criminal cases they must accept appointments from the state, which guarantees anyone charged with a crime free representation during both the pre-trial investigation and the trial itself. The regional chambers of advocates are responsible for assigning cases to their members and pay them fees set by the Justice Ministry. Defendants can choose to pay for private counsel. Since the majority of criminal defendants are unemployed (62 per cent) or members of the working class (23 per cent) (Volkov et al 2014), most have appointed counsel. In 2015, approximately 37,000 advocates accepted at least one legal aid appointment. Because fees in the state legal aid system are considerably lower than market prices, many advocates accept state appointment only at the beginning of their careers, when they need experience.[15]

Advocates can avoid state appointments in several ways. Some regional chambers ask members to pay a special fee to be excluded from the list of appointed counsel.

---

[12] Official statistics of the Federal Chamber of Advocates (2015).

[13] Two years of legal practice are required if the candidate previously worked as a judge, notary, law enforcement officer, corporate lawyer, court clerk, advocate's assistant, legal scholar or legal researcher. However, an exception is made for advocates' interns, who need only one year.

[14] In Soviet times, 'colleges' referred to the local Bars; nowadays, the term refers to group practices.

[15] Fees are US$10–40 for a single investigative procedure or court hearing, depending on the complexity of the case, time of day, and type of court adjudicating the case.

Others add advocates to the list only on request. There is a belief in the legal community that advocates assigned the most cases – who are called 'pocket' counsel – are controlled by police investigators. 'Pocket' counsel may force the accused to plead guilty, act passively when vigorous action is required, or sign police investigative documents without having participated in investigative procedures. These practices reflect several problems in the criminal justice and state legal aid systems. The accusatory bias and managerial problems of law-enforcement agencies, both derived from the inquisitorial nature of Soviet criminal justice, generate demand for predictable and loyal defence counsel. Ineffective regulation and insufficient funding of appointed cases permit shady and collusive practice. 'Pocket' behaviour is widely discussed and harshly criticised both inside and outside the legal community (Moiseeva 2016).

The hallmarks of Russian advocates – Bar associations, entry examinations, disciplinary proceedings, traineeships, and free legal aid – are the way they distinguish their organised professional community from amorphous unlicensed practitioners. References to history are another means of erecting symbolic borders. In their public statements, elite advocates repeatedly emphasise that the modern profession has maintained the traditions of the pre-revolutionary *advokatura*, adhering to its high ethical standards. The paradox is that the professional standards of advocates remain invisible to the public and meaningless to unlicensed practitioners. Average Russians asked to explain the difference between advocates and unlicensed practitioners would not know what to say. At best, they might mention that advocates work on criminal cases. Unlicensed practitioners exhibit deep scepticism about the need for and efficiency of advocates' self-regulation. And though advocates point to their provision of free legal aid, the problem of 'pocket' counsel has gone unsolved for years. Furthermore, the prosecutorial bias of the Russian justice system limits what advocates can accomplish in criminal cases (Khodzhaeva and Rabovski 2016) and impairs their reputation. Our interviews reveal that work practices of advocates and unlicensed practitioners in civil cases are identical, suggesting that the discrepancy between these groups is institutional rather than practical.

C. The Turbulent Forces of the Legal Market

Perestroika introduced conflict between market, professional, and bureaucratic logics, fostering divisions within the legal profession. In the late 1980s, the state stopped constricting the growth in the number of lawyers, seeking instead to satisfy the demand for legal services by letting unlicensed practitioners enter the market. Former state corporate counsel (*iuriskonsulty*), risking extinction from the wave of privatisation, migrated to neighbouring occupations: in-house counsel, advocates in alternative Bars, law firm employees, and solo practitioners. Retired law enforcement personnel became the main source of new cadres for the original Bars: as the incomes of public servants declined, they looked for more lucrative employment.[16]

---

[16] The difference in career trajectories remains an important feature of the advocate's profession. Only 20 per cent of lawyers join the *advokatura* after graduation, while most advocates have prior work experience in other legal fields. A third work in law enforcement, 23 per cent as unlicensed practitioners, 12 per cent as in-house counsel, and 8 per cent as court personnel (Khodzhaeva et al 2015).

In the 1990s, the legal profession was divided into clusters. The former Soviet advocates and new recruits from law enforcement worked primarily on criminal cases, mostly following on state appointment. Fearing change, they adhered to inherited work practices and earlier institutional models. The liberal members of the Soviet *advokatura*, who successfully established a national association in 1989, pursued their professional project. Favouring innovation and development, they sought to transform the *advokatura* into a true civil society institution. Alternative Bars moved in the same direction, although the old Bars did not recognise their leadership and refused to cooperate. Ordinary Bar members were more concerned with extracting financial benefits from the market economy than with professional matters.

In 2002, after the Federal Bar Act was enacted, legal representation split into different segments. Representation in criminal cases remained a closed jurisdiction with high entry barriers, while the remaining areas of legal practice were open to everyone, leaving advocates in a paradoxical situation. On one hand, the advocate community had increased fivefold. The Soviet Union had always kept the numbers low. In 1939, there were just 8,000 advocates in the entire country; 20 years later the number had increased to 13,000 (more than half of them in the Russian Soviet Federative Socialist Republic), and it remained approximately the same until the late 1980s (Barry and Berman 1968; Jordan 1998). That represented one advocate for every 16,000 people. Perestroika caused intense commercialisation of legal services and an increase in the number of lawyers. The number of advocates doubled in the early 1990s and doubled again by 2002 (Burrage 1990; Jordan 1998). In 2016, there were 72,000 advocates with valid licences and another 5,000 with terminated licences, cutting the ratio of people to lawyers to 1:2,000.

On the other, these figures are dwarfed by the thousands of unlicensed practitioners. Over the past decade, the legal services market has grown enormously from 114 billion roubles in 2003 to 222 billion roubles by 2015. The number of people seeking legal advice is also growing. Russian courts heard 4,800,000 civil cases in 2000, 10,600,000 civil cases in 2008, and 13,000,000 civil and 4,000,000 administrative cases in 2016.[17] Unlicensed practitioners handle most civil and administrative cases. Today there are 47,000 law firms (97 per cent registered as limited liability companies), 27,500 individual entrepreneurships, 21,500 advocates' solo practices, and 4,500 collective advocates' organisations. Unlicensed practitioners operate in commercial enterprises, both law firms and individual businesses. There are three times as many commercial enterprises as advocates' organisations (Moiseeva and Skougarevskiy 2016). Commercial enterprises are more flexible, dynamic, and competitive than advocates' organisations.[18] For example, advocates' organisations cannot use tax preferences; and only individual advocates, not their organisations, can contract with clients. The only significant advantage of being an advocate is the attorney-client privilege, which unlicensed practitioners lack.

---

[17] Official statistics of the Judicial Department of the Russian Federation. Until 2015, administrative cases were grouped with civil but then were counted separately.

[18] More than half of existing law firms and individual businesses were incorporated after 2012; one out of seven such companies was dissolved within five years. Advocates' organisations are less vulnerable: 17 per cent were incorporated after 2012, and less than 1 per cent were dissolved within five years (Moiseeva and Skougarevskiy 2016).

Foreign law firms invaded the Russian market at the beginning of the 1990s, as soon as the borders were opened. The pioneer was Baker McKenzie, which came to Russia in 1989. Foreign law firms introduced new business models and an organisational culture, which leaders of the national market eagerly adopted. On one hand, top-rated advocates' organisations and law firms established close ties with foreign companies. On the other, foreign law firms became the main competitors of national mega-law firms. The relatively few foreign firms occupy top positions in the professional rankings. But in the interviews we conducted, lawyers from the biggest national law firms and advocates' organisations expressed resentment of foreign companies for 'stealing' clients and attracting the most promising graduates.

Under the Federal Bar Act, foreign lawyers can practise only their national law. To practise Russian law, they must pass a bar exam and join the *advokatura*. As of the January 2017, only 125 foreign advocates were registered by the Justice Ministry.

The regulation of legal services has been the subject of intense debate between the state, advocates, and unlicensed practitioners. In 2014, the government approved a reorganisation of the judicial system, including reform of the legal market aimed at improving the quality of legal services and developing unified standards for all lawyers. The Justice Ministry, which implemented the reform, held meetings with advocates and unlicensed practitioners to outline scenarios that would satisfy both.

In November 2017, the Justice Ministry announced its plan to reform the legal services market by extending the advocates' monopoly to non-criminal cases by 2023. The reform will occur in two steps. First, to make the *advokatura* more attractive to unlicensed practitioners, advocates will be allowed to work in commercial enterprises and use tax preferences. During this transitional period, bars will simplify entry exams and abolish membership fees. Only after that will all legal representatives be integrated into the *advokatura*. Despite this gradual process, many unlicensed practitioners still view the extension of the advocates' jurisdiction as a hostile takeover that would lead to a loss of income and autonomy.

Opponents of the advocates' monopoly argue that the easiest and most effective way to solve the problem of malpractice in civil cases is to oblige every legal representative to have a law degree. They argue that because a law degree demonstrates that the holder is well qualified to practise law, there should be no additional requirements. A week before the Justice Ministry announced its reform proposal, a group of unlicensed practitioners and public figures introduced a Bill to require all legal representatives to have a law degree; it has a good chance of passing.

IV. LEGAL EDUCATION: THE PRODUCTION OF PROFESSIONALS AND ITS INCONSISTENCIES

A. Legal Education in the Soviet Union

Legal education reveals a great deal about the legal profession. In the Russian Empire, a law degree was a status symbol distinguishing advocates from their principal competitors, private attorneys, whose competence was certified by district court judges rather than universities or the professional community. In Soviet times, influenced by the new proletarian culture, the importance of a legal education in shaping the legal profession declined as legal training became less elite. In the early years, legal training was almost abolished, although industrial growth and the burgeoning administrative bureaucracy soon convinced the Soviet government that its judicial system could not be efficient without legal professionals. By the late 1940s, legal education had been re-established. In 1946, the Central Committee of the Communist Party adopted a special resolution on the importance of higher education for Soviet lawyers. Still, it was not until the 1960s that a law degree was required for advocates (Razi 1960).

The peculiarities of Soviet legal education were attributable to the position of lawyers in socialist society. First, the state guaranteed employment for every citizen, assigning people to workplaces in accordance with its own needs. Law graduates had to work at the assigned jobs for at least three years before looking for one on their own (Granik 1993). Law school grades could significantly affect graduates' professional trajectories. The most promising lawyers were assigned to the major cities, while the least promising were dispatched to less attractive regions (Sahlas and Chastenay 1998). Courts and prosecutors' offices were the most desirable workplaces, while working as an advocate was one of the least prestigious jobs (Finder 1989).

Second, Party membership was an asset for progress up the career ladder, especially for jobs in official institutions and managerial positions. Party membership was less important for ordinary advocates than for Bar leaders, since the latter had to be informally approved by the Justice Ministry before the elections (Pipko and Pipko 1987).

Third, many legal professionals studied by correspondence. In the early years of the Soviet state, large numbers of people were admitted to the legal profession based on their ideological reliability, not because they had university educations (Finder 1989). To increase the professional competence of judges and law enforcement personnel, universities and colleges launched a variety of short-term programmes and correspondence courses, which gained widespread acceptance.[19]

Fourth, because correspondence programs encouraged state officials to combine work with study, their professional identity was shaped by the workplace rather than at university. Courts and law enforcement agencies paid more attention to candidates' personal traits and political loyalty than to the university from which they had graduated. It was believed that all the necessary skills could quickly be obtained on the job.

Fifth, there were few law programmes. In the late 1930s, only three classical universities and seven specialised law colleges trained lawyers. In the late 1980s, there were 30 universities with law programmes, in which 70 per cent of law students studied by correspondence.

To conclude, lawyers did not enjoy high standing in the Soviet hierarchy. A law degree conferred neither economic nor social benefits. Within the legal community, reputation was based not on income but proximity to the state's primary functions and needs; criminal law was thus more prestigious than civil law (Shelley 1991). Accordingly, judges and law enforcement personnel were more respected than advocates, and jurisconsults had the lowest professional status.

---

[19] Courses varied in length: a year for rural lawyers and two for employees in the Commissariat of Justice, but just three months for court clerks (Hazard 1938).

B. Legal Education Today

Now any Russian university can launch a law programme at minimal cost. In 2012, almost 1,000 universities and colleges (including their regional branches) had undergraduate law programmes (Moiseeva 2015). In other words, every other higher education institution in the country could train lawyers.[20] Every year, Russian universities and colleges enrol 150,000 undergraduate students, admitting about half the applicants. The vast majority of law undergraduates (72 per cent) study by correspondence with only brief classroom attendance.[21] Correspondence courses last longer than full-time programmes, five years instead of four. Since legal education does not serve to rank law graduates, they see correspondence courses as a more convenient option, letting them combine work and study, rather than a 'second-class' option.

As these statistics show, many Russians pursue law degrees. However, only few of them go on to practise law. The are 330,000 legal professionals whose jobs require them to have a law degree (judges, investigators, prosecutors, police, advocates, judicial assistants, and notaries). Even if we add unlicensed practitioners and in-house counsel, the total will still be significantly less than the 2 million who obtained law degrees during the last 20 years.

Legal training has different advantages for various social groups. For young people, it is a form of symbolic capital. In the labour market, a law degree is prized more than many other degrees because it is relatively easily converted into economic capital; parents, therefore, encourage their children to enrol in law school. A law degree helps state officials climb the career ladder. Because legal education is easily accessible, businessmen and managers often get a second degree in law to navigate Russia's chaotic legal environment.

C. Legal Education as the Basis of the Legal Profession

Those criticising attempts to expand the advocates' monopoly tend to assume that universities should set the parameters of the modern legal profession. Russian law departments have uniform educational standards and a national curriculum determined by the Ministry of Education. Therefore, a law degree can be viewed as an entry ticket to legal practice. This paradigm is shared not only by unlicensed practitioners but also by state officials, as shown by the recent regulation of legal representation in administrative cases. Since 2015, legal representatives may not litigate administrative cases without a law degree. Lawyers must bring their diplomas to court, where judges are responsible

---

[20] Half of these universities and colleges have fewer than 100 students per year. Five per cent of law programmes admit more than 500 students per year. The most prestigious places to get a law degree (and the largest) are the classical state universities and state law schools (such as Lomonosov Moscow State University, St Petersburg State University, Moscow State Institute of International Relations, and Moscow University of Finance and Law). There are no law schools founded by foreign organisations, although several Russian universities offer joint degrees with foreign universities.

[21] At the beginning of the semester, students attend several introductory lectures and receive homework for the next six months. At the end of the semester, they sit for exams.

for checking them.[22] Thus, an alternative to extending the advocates' monopoly to non-criminal cases (justified as a way to improve the quality of legal representation) would be to require every litigator to have a law degree. However, problems in the Russian legal education system make implementing this alternative untenable.

The divide between theory and practice is one of the most pressing issues in Russian legal education. Theoretical training prevails in the universities, while employers are concerned about newly minted graduates' insufficient practical experience. The older generation of legal academics believes universities should not have to respond to the demands of the labour market: privileging practical skills over theoretical knowledge would engender narrow-minded technicians incapable of critical legal thinking. Since university education does not encourage translating theoretical knowledge into practical experience, the professional socialisation of new lawyers occurs where they are employed.

Special higher education institutions for law enforcement personnel (*vedomstvennye vuzy*) also encourage fragmentation of the Russian legal profession: 37 per cent of police investigators graduate from special law schools (Titaev and Shklyaruk 2016). The curriculum and the lecturers' background at these universities differ from those of other law departments. There is a significant amount of physical conditioning, drilling, and weapons training. Students are required to wear uniforms and strictly obey rules. After graduation, they must work in government agencies for at least five years or repay their educational fees to the state (a legacy of the Soviet workplace assignment system).

The third reason why legal education cannot create unity among Russian lawyers is the predominance of correspondence courses, which prepare 40 per cent of judges, police investigators, and advocates (Kazun et al 2015; Volkov et al 2015; Titaev and Shklyaruk 2016). Tuition fees are generally half those of full-time law programmes, and the state pays for a small subset of students. Correspondence course students are usually older and have families and steady jobs. Advocates of correspondence courses emphasise their role in expanding access to the legal profession. But there are significant differences in students' engagement with the learning process. Debates over this issue have become more intense. The lobby for abolishing the correspondence courses includes the leading law schools, prestigious law firms and advocates' organisations. Nevertheless, there is a strong demand for this form of education from other segments of the legal profession, mainly court clerks and law enforcement personnel, who need to work while studying law.

To summarise, Russian legal education does not provide a venue for consolidating the legal profession. Different legal professionals are accountable to different agencies and thus have different professional values and notions of what being a lawyer means. Organisational affiliation has a greater impact on the self-identification of Russian lawyers than educational backgrounds.

---

[22] The legislation benefiting all graduate lawyers was not secured by lawyers' efforts but suddenly introduced by the state, without any lobbying.

V. CONCLUSION

The Russian legal profession (like those of many other civil law countries) consists of different legal occupations administered by different agencies and following different professional rules. It is highly fragmented. There is neither a professional association unifying all lawyers nor a common platform for discussing interprofessional issues. The deterioration of legal education has further eroded the professional identity of being a 'lawyer'. Judges and law enforcement personnel work under the pressure of an accusatory bias, and the interests of the organisations they serve have priority over professional norms.

Advocates occupy a unique place among other legal occupations and are the most autonomous. They were not part of the state bureaucracy in either the late imperial period or the Soviet Union. Today, by law, the *advokatura* is a civil society institution, enjoying full autonomy from the state. However, it is difficult to speak about the legal profession as a part of civil society when the very existence of civil society in Russia is questionable. As Levin-Stankevich (1996: 237) noted, the Russian state has always reminded advocates that being members of a free profession and working as free professionals are different things. While advocates are institutionally autonomous, they have never been truly independent.

Advocates have always been more modern and better educated than state lawyers, but they have never enjoyed political influence. On the contrary, they have constantly lost in negotiations with the state. Their current position is highly ambiguous. Even though advocates *de jure* are independent of the state, *de facto* they have little autonomy within their exclusive jurisdiction: representation in criminal cases. The institutional incentives of law enforcement personnel and judges demand cooperative defence counsel and limit the opportunities for advocates to conduct their own investigations, introduce evidence, or present arguments in court (Moiseeva 2016).

Advocates lack social prestige among the public and other legal representatives. They compete with other legal professionals to represent clients in civil and administrative cases. The work practices of advocates and unlicensed practitioners are identical, as are their professional credentials since most unlicensed practitioners have law degrees. Every profession would like to gather all the members who meet its criteria under a single umbrella – what Robert Merton (1968) called 'completeness'. In Russia, many civil litigators prefer to remain outside the *advokatura* since the licence is difficult to convert into social prestige or financial benefits. As a result, advocates are surrounded by competitors who greatly outnumber them. Advocates try to erect symbolic borders and separate themselves from unlicensed practitioners, who are allegedly less ethical, organised, and qualified. But laypersons often do not see the difference between advocates and other lawyers and choose legal representatives mostly on the recommendations of those they trust.

The current position of Russian advocates and ongoing debates about regulating legal representatives offer unique insights into how professional markets emerge. For the past 25 years, the Russian market for legal services has operated without entry barriers. Everyone agrees reforms are highly desirable and inevitable. The state's official position is to seek a balance between protecting clients' rights and maintaining competition among the providers of legal services.

The Justice Ministry recently announced a reform that will unify all legal representatives under the umbrella of *advokatura*. But before integration starts, the state intends to make advocates' organisations more competitive in the market and thus more attractive to unlicensed practitioners. Adapting to a professional market would be least painful for top-rated law firms, which are willing to embrace the logic of professionalism and join the *advokatura*. However, small and medium-sized commercial enterprises are comfortable in the present circumstances. They insist the free market can regulate itself, since it is clients who decide which lawyers provide better services.

The erosion of professionalism by market forces, often called 'deprofessionalisation,' is visible in many countries. It accelerates with the growth of mega-lawyering, the transition from individual practice to teamwork, and the entry of foreign law firms into national markets. Such transformations are inevitable, since the practice of law is changing significantly. Russia's legal market is undergoing similar changes. The collision among professional, market, and bureaucratic logics in the ongoing debates on regulating the Russian legal profession exposes the vulnerabilities of professional markets, forcing us to question the future of professionalism and the role of lawyers in modern society.

REFERENCES

Balzer, HD (1996) 'Introduction' in HD Balzer (ed), *Russia's Missing Middle Class: The Professions in Russian History* (Armonk, NY, ME Sharpe).

Barry, DD and Berman, JH (1968) 'The Soviet Legal Profession' 82 *Harvard Law Review* 1.

Becker, HS (1962) 'The Nature of a Profession' in *Education for the Professions: Sixty-first Yearbook of the National Society for the Study of Education* 24.

Blagodeteleva, E (2013) 'Grazhdanskaia i professional'naia identichnost' rossiiskoi advokatury vtoroi poloviny XIX – nachala XX veka' [The civil and professional identity of Russian lawyers in the late nineteenth and early twentieth centuries] in N Proskuriakova (ed), *Grazhdanskaia identichnost' rossiiskoi intelligentsii v kontse XIX – nachale XX veka* [The civic identity of the Russian intelligentsia in the late nineteenth and early twentieth centuries] (Moscow, Novii Khronograf).

—— (2015) 'The French Bar and the Emerging Legal Profession in Russia' Working Paper No 110, Higher School of Economics.

Bocharov, T, and Moiseeva, E (2016) *Byt' adkovatom v Rossii: sotsiologicheskoe issledovanie professii* [Being a lawyer in Russia: a sociological study of the legal profession] (St Petersburg, EUSP Press).

Burrage, M (1990) 'Advokatura: In Search of Professionalism and Pluralism in Moscow and Leningrad' 15 *Law & Social Inquiry* 433.

Devitsyna, I (2015) 'Tip provintsial'nogo sovetskogo advokata v pervye poslevoennye gody: opyt istoriko-biograficheskogo issledovaniia' [Provincial Soviet advocates in the early postwar years: a historical and biographical study] 3 *Gramota* 71.

Finder, S (1989) 'Legal Education in the Soviet Union' 15 *Review of Socialist Law* 197.

Gilmutdinov, N (2013) 'Istoriia sozdaniia Kazanskogo soveta prisiazhnykh poverennykh' [A history of the founding of the Kazan Council of Sworn Attorneys] 3 *Izvestiia vysshikh uchebnikh zavedenii. Povolzhskii region* 5.

Glos, GE (1989) 'Soviet Law and Soviet Legal Education in an Historical Context: An Interpretation' 15 *Review of Socialist Law* 227.
Granik, LA (1993) 'Legal Education in Post-Soviet Russia and Ukraine' 72 *Oregon Law Review* 963.
Hazard, JN (1938) 'Legal Education in the Soviet Union' 1938 *Wisconsin Law Review* 562.
Hughes, E (1963) 'Professions' 92 *Daedalus* 655.
Huskey, E (1982) 'The Limits to Institutional Autonomy in the Soviet Union: The Case of the Advokatura' 34 *Soviet Studies* 200.
—— (1986) *Russian Lawyers and the Soviet State: the Origins and Development of the Soviet Bar, 1917–1939* (Princeton, NJ, Princeton University Press).
Jordan, P (1998) 'The Russian Advokatura (Bar) and the State in the 1990s' 50 *Europe-Asia Studies* 765.
—— (2005) *Defending Rights in Russia: Lawyers, the State, and Legal Reform in the Post-Soviet Era* (Vancouver & Toronto, UBC Press).
Kaminskaya, D (1982) *Final Judgment: My Life as a Soviet Defence Attorney* (New York, Simon and Schuster).
Kazun, A, Khodzhaeva, E and Yakovlev A (2015) *Advokatskoe soobshchestvo Rossii* [The Russian advocate community] (Moscow & St Petersburg, International Centre for the Study of Institutions and Development at the Higher School of Economics & Institute for the Rule of Law).
Khodzhaeva, E and Shesternina Rabovski, Y (2016) 'Strategies and Tactics of Criminal Defenders in Russia in the Context of Accusatorial Bias' 54 *Russian Politics & Law* 191.
Larson, M (2013) *The Rise of Professionalism: Monopolies of Competence and Sheltered Markets* (New Brunswick & London, Transaction Publishers).
Levin-Stankevich, BL (1996) 'The Transfer of Legal Technology and Culture: Law Professionals in Tsarist Russia' in HD Balzer (ed), *Russia's Missing Middle Class: The Professions in Russian History* (Armonk, NY, ME Sharpe).
Lubshev, Y (2002) *Advokatura v Rossii* [Advocates in Russia] (Moscow, Profobrazovanie).
Luryi, Y (1977) 'The Right to Counsel in Ordinary Criminal Cases in the USSR' in DD Barry, G Ginsburgs, and P Maggs (eds), *Soviet Law after Stalin. Part 1. Citizens and the State in Contemporary Soviet Law* (Leyden, AW Sijhoff).
Merton, R (1968) *Social Theory and Social Structure* (New York, Free Press).
Moiseeva, E (2015) *Iuridicheskoe obrazovanie v Rossii. Analiz kolichestvennykh dannykh* [Legal education in Russia: a statistical analysis] (St Petersburg, Institute for the Rule of Law).
—— (2016) 'Plea Bargaining in Russia: The Role of Defence Attorneys and the Problem of Asymmetry' 41 *International Journal of Comparative and Applied Criminal Justice* 163.
Moiseeva, E and Skougarevskiy, D (2016) *Rynok iuridicheskikh uslug v Rossii: chto govorit statistika* [The legal services market in Russia: what the statistics say] (St Petersburg, Institute for the Rule of Law).
Mrowczynski, R (2012) 'Self-Regulation of Legal Professions in State-Socialism: Poland and Russia Compared' 20 *Journal of the Max Plank Institute for European Legal History* 170.
Novikov, A (2012) 'Prisiazhnye poverennye kak predstaviteli intelligentsii' [Sworn attorneys as members of the intelligentsia] 2 *Izvestiia Tul'skogo gosudarstvennogo universiteta* 158.
—— (2013) 'Vliianie predstavitelei iuridicheskoi intelligentsii na otnoshenie obshchestva k sudu vtoroi poloviny XIX v.' [Influence of the legal intelligentsia on social attitudes towards the courts in the late nineteenth century] 2 *Izvestiia Tul'skogo gosudarstvennogo universiteta* 239.
Pipko, S and Pipko, R (1987) 'Inside the Soviet Bar: A View from the Outside' 21 *The International Lawyer* 853.
Pomeranz, W (1993) 'Justice from Underground: The History of the Underground Advokatura' 52 *Russian Review* 321.
Poznyshev, S (1913) Elementarnyi uchebnik russkogo ugolovnogo protsessa [Elementary textbook on Russian criminal justice] (Moscow, Leman).

Razi, GM (1960) 'Legal Education and the Role of the Lawyer in the Soviet Union and the Countries of Eastern Europe' 48 *California Law Review* 776.

Reznik, G (2001) 'Advokatskaia deiatel'nost'' i advokatura' [The work of advocates and the bar] 8 *Rossiiskaia iustitsiia* 9.

Sahlas, PJ and Chastenay, C (1998) 'Russian Legal Education: Post-Communist Stagnation or Revival?' 48 *Journal of Legal Education* 194.

Shelley, LI (1991) 'Lawyers in the Soviet Union' in A Jones (ed), *Professions and the State: Expertise and Autonomy in the Soviet Union and Eastern Europe* (Philadelphia, Temple University Press).

Titaev, K, and Shklyaruk, M (2016) *Rossiiskii sledovatel': prizvanie, professiia, povsedvenost'* [Russian investigators: vocation, profession, and everyday practice] (Moscow, Norma).

Undrevich, VS (1928) 'Sovetskii sud i zashchita' [Soviet courts and defence counsel] 5 *Revolutsiia prava* 14.

Volkov, V and Dzmitryieva, A (2015) 'Recruitment Patterns, Gender, and Professional Subcultures of the Judiciary in Russia' 22 *International Journal of the Legal Profession* 166.

Volkov, V, Dzmitryieva, A, Pozdniakov, M and Titaev K (2015) *Rossiiskie sud'i: sotsiologicheskoe issledovanie professii* [Russian judges: a sociological study of the profession] (Moscow, Norma).

Volkov, V, Dzmitryieva, A, Skugarevskii, D, Titaev, K, Chetverikova, I and Shesternina, Y (2014) *Ugolovnaia iustitsiia v Rossii v 2009 godu. Kompleksniy analiz sudebnoi statistiki* [Russian criminal justice in 2009: a complex analysis of court statistics] (Moscow, Statut).

17
Serbia and Bosnia and Herzegovina
Challenges of Liberalisation and Democratic Consolidation

DANILO VUKOVIĆ, VALERIJA DABETIĆ AND SAMIR FORIĆ

I. INTRODUCTION

THIS CHAPTER FOCUSES on legal *professions* rather than a single unified legal profession (*cf* Kober; Schultz and Shaw 2003). These professions – practising lawyers or advocates, judges, and prosecutors – are sometimes referred to as juridical professions (Spasić et al 2011; Sibinović 2011). As in other civil law jurisdictions, being a lawyer is not an identity. The term 'lawyer' (*pravnik* in Serbian/Croatian/Bosnian) simply denotes someone who has completed a legal education, which qualifies the holder for various jobs, including administration, civil service, and management. It is the forms of legal practice that create professional identities – such as advocates (Serbian: *advokat*; Bosnian/Croatian: *odvjetnik*), judges, prosecutors, and notaries – defined by admission rules, career paths, and institutional structures.

This chapter focuses on central socio-legal questions about legal professions, such as the construction and defence of monopoly, occupational unity, independence and self-regulation, feminisation, and globalisation. But it also addresses issues specific to the region, such as political pressures and threats to the independence of the judiciary or the peculiar role of legal academics. The chapter is based on official statistics, legal documents and media, as well as previous socio-legal studies conducted in Serbia and Bosnia and Herzegovina (Zvekić 1985; Studija 2000; Spasić et al 2011; Sibinović 2011; Grozdić 2016). An important source are data gathered by the 'Legal Professions in South Eastern Europe' project[1] and in-depth interviews with Serbian practising lawyers, as well as previous research on Serbian judges.[2] We begin by discussing legal education before

---

[1] The research was conducted in 2018 by a team of sociologists and lawyers from Serbia, Croatia and Bosnia and Herzegovina headed by Danilo Vuković of the University of Belgrade and Marko Mrakovčić of the University of Rijeka. Data were collected through an online questionnaire from May to July in Serbia and Croatia and September and October in Bosnia and Herzegovina. The sample consisted of 660 legal professionals in Serbia, 393 in Croatia and 441 in Bosnia and Herzegovina. The first results were presented in Vuković et al 2018.

[2] Ten semi-structured in-depth interviews with practising lawyers were conducted in Belgrade in September–November 2018. In addition, we rely on transcripts from 20 interviews with randomly chosen Serbian judges from different courts and localities conducted in June and July 2016.

describing advocates (their history and contemporary situation), judges, and other legal professions (primarily legal academics and notaries), paying particular attention to gender composition.

II. LEGAL EDUCATION

A. Serbia

Higher education began with the emerging independent Serbian state in the early nineteenth century. The Belgrade Higher School (1808–13) was opened with a predominantly legal curriculum, a modification of the prevailing Austro-Hungarian pedagogical system (Mirković 2008: 213–14; Avramović 2013). The decades following its closure were marked by military and political struggles to liberate Serbia from Ottoman rule and establish a modern system of administration and education. The Lyceum was established in 1838 and incorporated into the University of Belgrade when it opened in 1905.

In 1920 the University of Belgrade launched a second law faculty in the northern city of Subotica. After World War II, law faculties were established in Novi Sad (1955), Niš (1960), Priština[3] (1961), Kragujevac (1976) and most recently Novi Pazar (2006). With the liberalisation of higher education in recent decades, there are now five private law faculties enrolling approximately 16 per cent of university students.[4] Despite the recent growth of private higher education, we focus on public faculties, which preserve academic traditions and represent the nursery for future academics, judges, prosecutors and practising lawyers, as well as leading politicians, civil servants and business people.

Serbian law faculties offer four-year undergraduate law courses, selecting secondary school graduates based on their grades and an admission exam. Tuition is free for a number of students set by the government, while the rest pay fees of up to the €800 per year. The tradition of free education and open admissions to promote social mobility, so characteristic of the socialist period (Stanojević 2013), has survived but in tension with the educational policies focused on academic merit (Đorđević 2009: 65).

Most subjects are compulsory, and students have little freedom in designing their course of study. Serbian legal education seeks to provide the broadest theoretical foundation, not to prepare for legal practice. Vocational training takes place after the completion of university studies, in law offices, courts, and prosecutors' offices (Đorđević 2009: 67). In recent years, however, law faculties have been introducing compulsory practical courses, moot courts, and legal clinics.

In order to overcome the shortcomings of the practical training, the Government of the Republic of Serbia and the Judges Association of Serbia founded the Judicial Centre for Training and Professional Development in 2001. Because the Centre was not part of the judicial system's mandatory institutional framework it was unable to provide initial lectures and obligatory continuous education for judges (Kmezić 2017: 115). In 2009, therefore, the Centre was transformed into the Judicial Academy, with the goal

---

[3] University of Priština was temporarily moved to Kosovska Mitrovica after NATO occupied the Serbian province of Kosovo and Metohija in 1999 and it declared its independence in 2008.
[4] According to the Statistical Office of Serbia, this figure has been constant during the last decade.

of 'providing professional, independent, and impartial and efficient performance of the judicial and prosecutorial function' (Law on Legal Academy, Article 2).[5] As we shall see, the Academy has been the object of contestation among Serbian professionals.

Women started entering legal education and the profession in the early twentieth century. However, it was socialism that fundamentally changed their position, transforming the traditional 'gender regimes' in south-eastern Europe. This was attributed not only to ideology but also to the important role of women in the (communist) liberation movement against the Nazi occupation in World War II, rapid post-war modernisation, and urbanisation. All this has led to women's heightened participation and greater visibility in the economy, public administration and political life, though patriarchal patterns have prevailed in private life (*cf* Gudac-Dodić 2006; Milić 1994; Marcus 1994).

In Serbia, women started entering legal education at the beginning of twentieth century. The first woman graduated from the Faculty of Law in 1914 (Kandić 2002). The proportion of students who were women gradually rose, but the feminisation of legal studies did not occur until recently (see Figure 1), first at the undergraduate level and later in magister/MA studies.[6] However, men remain the majority amongst PhD students.

Figure 1 Women as a Proportion of Graduate Students at Public Law Faculties

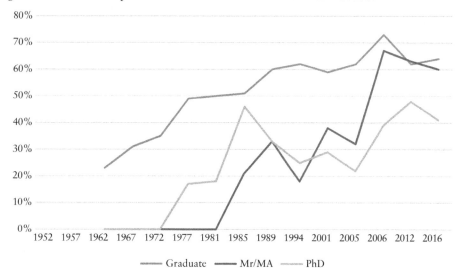

Source: Federal Statistical Office of the Socialist Federal Republic of Yugoslavia, bulletins on higher education; Republican Statistical Office, bulletins on higher education; Kandic 2002.

---

[5] The Centre provides two types of training for judges, prosecutors and auxiliary staff of the judiciary. During the initial 30-month course participants are temporarily employed and receive 70 per cent of their salary (Art 40). All those who have not completed the initial course must take continuous training, during which their work duties and working hours will be reduced up to 30 per cent (Law on Legal Academy, Art 45).

[6] Prior to the Bologna Process, the magister was a postgraduate degree offered after graduate studies lasting four to six years. The 2–3-year programme required coursework and a thesis. These highly selective courses typically led to writing a PhD thesis and were followed by future researchers and academics.

Despite the feminisation of higher education, the trend has not extended to academia, where women represent 37 per cent of academic staff at public law faculties. However, there is a clear trend of progressive feminisation: whereas women are 30 per cent of professors (33 per cent of associate and 28 per cent of full professors), they are 40 per cent of lecturers (*docent*) and 52 per cent of teaching assistants. Historical data also point to gradual feminisation, with some disruptions during the 1960s and 1970s, probably reflecting the creation of new male-dominated faculties in the provinces.

Table 1 Percentage of Academic Staff Who Are Women

Year	1956	1961	1966	1973	1980	1984	2018
Per cent female	3	11	8	7	11	20	37

Source: Federal Statistical Office of Socialist Federal Republic of Yugoslavia, bulletins on higher education; Republican Statistical Office, bulletins on higher education; official web sites of law faculties for 2018.

B. Bosnia and Herzegovina

At first, legal education in Bosnia and Herzegovina (BiH) was predominantly religious. After the conquest of BiH by the Ottoman Empire in 1463, Sharia was the only legal subject taught in over 100 madrasas (high schools) until the Austro-Hungarian occupation in 1878 (Durmišević 2012: 90). The Sharia Judges School (established in 1887), besides training future khadi judges, also offered European law courses, enabling students to continue their legal education at the Faculty of Law in Zagreb (today Croatia, then Austro-Hungary).[7] Legal education in Franciscan monasteries was transformed into the Lyceum in the first half of the twentieth century. After 1882 both Roman Catholic and Eastern Orthodox high schools were established and taught canon law. At the same time (and until the end of the Austro-Hungarian occupation in 1918), technical high schools and academies were developed all over the country, offering courses in business and administrative law.

In the interwar period, Sharia legal education was institutionalised in the Sharia gymnasium (1918–44) and the Higher Islamic-Sharia-Theological School (1938–45), which preceded the establishment in 1946 of secular legal education in the University of Sarajevo, the first modern university in Bosnia and Herzegovina. Since the first class of 334 students, about 14,000 students have graduated. The first PhD was defended in 1952 (Durmišević 2012: 95). The university later established law faculties in Banja Luka, Mostar, Zenica and Tuzla. After BiH became an independent state in 1992, following the war in Bosnia (1992–95),[8] and adopted the Bologna model of higher education in 2005,

---

[7] From 1913 to 1930 the Law Faculty at University of Zagreb had a chair (cathedra) for 'Bosnian Law' (Durmišević 2012: 93).

[8] The peace settlements also resulted in a new political and administrative structure. Bosnia and Herzegovina is now composed of two entities: Republika Srpska (RS) and the Federation of Bosnia and Herzegovina (FBiH) and District Brčko of Bosnia and Herzegovina. FBiH is composed of 10 cantons. In this decentralised setting, many administrative units (entities, districts, cantons) have substantial responsibilities in fields relevant to the legal professions, including education, the judiciary, and the regulation of practising lawyers.

legal education was institutionalised in 21 law faculties, 8 public and 13 private. Other aspects of legal education (tuition fees, feminisation and pedagogy) resemble those in Serbia.

Legal education in BiH has been deeply affected by the radical changes in the legal system, which have happened every 15–20 years as the system transitioned between Sharia and civil law, socialism and capitalism. This requires students, and especially practising lawyers, to adapt to new legal regimes without having acquired the necessary experience (Gradaščević-Sijerčić 2012: 128).

In recent years, legal education has also occurred outside higher education. Judicial and prosecutorial training centres were established as part of a comprehensive judicial reform between 2002 and 2004. They operate on the entity level, under the supervision of the High Judicial and Prosecutorial Council (HJPC), which coordinates their work, creates educational programmes, and approves the instructors. Judges in BiH need not complete a preparatory training programme,[9] but they must be law graduates, have three years of experience after successfully passing the judicial exam, and then pass an additional qualifying exam before the HJPC. Judges must complete an eight-day programme in the first year after being appointed. Other judges and prosecutors must attend 3–10-day training programmes every year. Unlike judicial academies, judicial and prosecutorial training centres provide practical training for a variety of specialisations. Only in 2018 did the HJPC acknowledge the importance of an initial training programme for new judges and prosecutors and those who aspire to such positions (HJPC Decision no 07-13-3-2195-6/2018), and they have yet to yield palpable results. The HJPC made it clear in July 2018 that improvements in the existing educational and training system will be made by strengthening the capacities of the two entity-based judicial and prosecutorial training centres and implementing the initial training programme (Trlin 2018).

III. ADVOCATES IN SERBIA AND BOSNIA AND HERZEGOVINA

A. Historical Background

Although the modern Serbian legal system emerged at the beginning of the nineteenth century following liberation from Ottoman rule, the role of practising lawyers or advocates was first regulated by the 1862 Law on Legal Representatives (*Zakon o pravozastupnicima*). Advocates had to be legally educated, pass an exam administered by five members of the Higher Court, and then be enlisted by the Ministry of Justice.[10] The first association of advocates was created in 1886 to protect the moral reputation of advocates and nurture legal science (Regulation of the Association of Legal Representatives, Article 1). The first professional magazine, *Branič*, was launched in 1887 and has appeared ever since, with minor disruptions.

---

[9] Interns, intern-volunteers and expert associates working in courts and prosecutorial offices in BiH may opt to attend the initial training programme but need not do so even if they choose to pursue judgeships (Training Programme for 2018, Judicial and Prosecutorial Centre of F BiH, 2018: 10, available at www.fbih.cest.gov.ba/index.php/dokumenti-centra/category/9-programi-obuke).

[10] Those without legal education were allowed to appear in court between 1865 and 1871. Retired court clerks could practise law between 1896 and 1929 (Spasić et al 2011: 29–30).

The nineteenth century witnessed the emergence of professional legal advocacy in BiH as well. During the Ottoman occupation, khadi judges administered justice as civil servants (Bahtijarević and Čizmović 2017: 14). After it occupied BiH in 1878, the Austro-Hungarian Empire reformed the judicial system. From 1881 the courts were 'part of the organisation of the state but independent, subjected only to law' (ibid: 17), and professional advocates were introduced to the reformed courts. Advocates were defined as a 'profession of the public order', but having previously been part of the judiciary and under government control their status was closer to that of civil servants (ibid: 18).

The 1883 Law on Attorney Order introduced new entry requirements: passing the advocates' exam,[11] a year of experience in BiH courts, and taking an oath at the BiH Supreme Court. Even if the law 'made a viable attempt to bring the legal space of Bosnia and Herzegovina closer to the Middle European legal circle', the profession still lacked a crucial feature: autonomy (ibid: 24). A 1909 law created the Bar Association and charged it with maintaining the list of advocates. However, the national government and the BiH Supreme Court retained ultimate powers to appoint and control advocates, reflecting the idea that they were civil servants. Nevertheless, advocates were given a monopoly over legal services, and unauthorised paralegal services were criminalised (ibid: 29–38).

The next step in the professionalisation of advocates occurred in the early days of the Kingdom of Yugoslavia, as part of the legal unification of the former territories of the Austro-Hungarian Empire (Slovenia, Croatia and Bosnia and Herzegovina) and the Ottoman Empire with the independent states of Serbia and Montenegro. The 1929 Law on Advocacy (*Zakon o advokaturi*) made advocates an independent 'public order' profession (Spasić et al 2011: 30). They had to have a legal education and pass an exam administered by the Bar Associations, which were in turn responsible for enrolling new members (Article 6). But though advocates were defined as an independent profession (Article 49), the Minister of Justice retained authority over the Bar Associations and could dissolve them (Article 50). This law placed some limits on marketisation. The Minister of Justice set the fees for simple legal tasks (Article 28). Advocates were banned from advertising (Article 51), having a branch office, or working with non-lawyers (Article 20). The law also created a pension fund for lawyers in 1931, which operated until 1959.

During World War II, Jewish advocates and those associated with the communist resistance suffered persecution by the German occupation forces and the Nazi Independent State of Croatia. After liberation, the position of lawyers was transformed by the prevailing socialist ideology and regulated by a changing sequence of federal and republican laws (eg in BiH in 1957, 1971, 1977 and 1989; in Serbia in 1971 and 1977).

The 1946 federal Law on Advocacy (*Zakon o advokaturi*) is considered a 'step backwards' from the 1929 law since it stripped lawyers of the prerogatives of independence and autonomy (Bahtijarević and Čizmović 2017: 26–104; Sibinović 2011: 42). Advocates were no longer designated as a 'profession of public order'. They could work as either individuals or in an 'advocates' community', a voluntary association of practising lawyers with the status of a legal person (Article 9), but were still forbidden to have branch offices (Article 15). The state's role was strengthened since the Bar exam was administered by the Minister of Justice (Article 4), who was also charged with confirming the Bar's decisions

---

[11] The advocates' exam was introduced in 1883 and the judges' exam three years later.

on enrolling new advocates and resolving complaints (Article 7). The Minister could also dissolve some organs of the Bar and annul its decisions (Article 39).[12]

According to the 1957 law, advocates held the status of civil servants. Bars effectively lost their autonomy, and the position of advocates was equated to that of other civil servants who provided free legal aid, thereby significantly reducing professional autonomy (Bahtijarević and Čizmović 2017: 79). This trend continued in the 1971 Law on Attorney and Other Legal Aid, which formally equated advocates with other legal aid providers (ibid: 90). From then until the late 1980s the legal profession focused on improving its material status, and the national Bar Association sought to displace its decentralised components. Both goals were achieved in 1989, when the last law was enacted before independence (ibid: 104).

The 1971 Serbian Law on Advocacy and Other Legal Aid defined advocates (*advokatura*) as independent in their work (Article 4) and autonomous in their provision of social services (Article 5). Advocates were organised in local Bars, which enjoyed autonomy in accepting new members (Article 13) and regulating themselves, eg by adopting the Code of Ethics (Article 12). This law also envisaged the creation of municipal legal aid services and in-house lawyers (Articles 79–83). The 1977 Law on Advocacy and Legal Aid Services sought to apply the principles of socialist self-management (incorporated into the 1974 Constitution) to the legal profession. It provided for detailed regulation of 'advocates' communities' (Articles 10–28), enabling the state to retain control in many areas, such as setting the prices for advocates' services (Article 44) and approving the Statute of the Bar (Article 93).

Throughout this period, legal professions had little prestige. The dominant professions in former (socialist) Yugoslavia were economists, engineers and graduates of political schools (Šporer 1990: 107, 113). In 1977, the prestige of the legal profession ranked below that of engineers, medical doctors and university professors, whereas it ranked highest in the US (Treiman 1977; Županov and Šporer 1984: 38; Šporer 1990: 122). The lower prestige of law and other professions in Yugoslavia at that time reflected the egalitarian ideology and the anti-intellectual climate it fostered, eventually leading to various forms of deprofessionalisation (Županov and Šporer 1984: 40).

B. Bosnia and Herzegovina

The independence of BiH was soon followed by a war (1992–95), which effectively dissolved the BiH Bar Association. Today there are Bars in two BiH entities: the Bar Association of RS and the Bar Association of the FBiH. In 2002, each entity passed a new law to regulate advocates. The Bars cooperate closely and have had a joint membership in the Council of Bars and Law Societies in Europe (CCBE) since 2009. That year an attempt to create a common law on advocates and a BiH Bar Association failed because of reservations by the RS Bar Association (Bahtijarević and Čizmović 2017: 144–47).

Compared to the socialist period, the two Bar Associations seem to be more energetic in their struggles to improve the status of advocates, but their collective efforts have not

---

[12] One result of those legal provisions was that many advocates joined the public service, reducing the BiH Bar's membership by 43 per cent (Bahtijarević and Čizmović 2017: 71).

produced significant results. However, the RS Bar Association is better situated than its FBiH counterpart, since its authority has enabled it to be deeply involved in setting fees and participating in discussions of constitutional and legislative changes in RS affecting the judiciary and rule of law (ibid: 133). Its influence was tested when it sought to be the exclusive provider of free legal aid to citizens. But this failed, and the 2016 national Law on Providers of Free Legal Aid (Official Gazette of BiH, No 83/2016) left little scope for Bar Association regulation, although it did require that advocates who provide free legal aid belong to their respective Bar Associations.

The FBiH Bar Association, unlike its RS counterpart, was quite vocal on several occasions, accusing both the Office of the High Representative (OHR) and HJPC of 'generally unacceptable stances toward the state of advocacy in FBiH' (ibid: 158). The main reason for the FBiH Bar Association's concerns arises from its lack of involvement in the legislative process, including the promulgation of fee schedules. In 2010 the Bar openly threatened a general strike in response to the FBiH Government's decision subjecting advocates to fiscal regulation. Support from other Bar Associations, including the RS Bar Association and CCBE, appeared to be decisive in reversing the Government's decision in late 2011, and this remains the greatest success of the many struggles by the FBiH Bar Association since 2002 (ibid: 165–70).

Throughout the period we have analysed, the profession has undergone demographic changes, growing in size (see Table 2), while recent decades have witnessed feminisation. Even if Bosnian advocates remain predominantly male, in 2018 almost 30 per cent were women, as were 58 per cent of advocate trainees (ibid: 196). Although women were allowed to become advocates in 1929, the first woman did so only in 1951. Six joined over the next two decades and four in 1971–72, but the next five joined only in 1981–83. The pace then accelerated slightly: five in 1984, seven in 1985, 13 in 1986–89, and 44 in 1989–91 (ibid: 198). There has been only one woman president of FBiH (Amila Kunisić-Ferizović 2008–12) and two women presidents of the Executive Board of the RS Bar Association (Marija Stanković-Vukmirica 2011–15 and Irena Puzić-Obradović in 2015).

Table 2 Number of Advocates and Population per Advocate in Bosnia and Herzegovina

Year	Number	Population	Population per advocate
1883	6	1,158,440	77,229
1895	15	1,336,091	70,321
1909	26	1,889,044	34,346
1927	167	1,890,440	37,067
1945	21	2,564,308	10,017
1975	256	3,746,111	10,493
1983	357	4,124,008	10,059
1987	410	4,267,000	7,196
1990	593	4,376,403	2,752
2018	1,590	3,531,159	2,220

Sources: Bahtijarević and Čizmović 2017: 26–104; registries of the RS and FBiH Bar Associations for 2018.

C. Contemporary Serbia

The professional issues in post-Yugoslav Serbia differ from those in BiH. The transition from socialism marked a break with the dominant ideology, discourse and institutions; principles of equality and solidarity were replaced by economic rationality, marketisation, and neoliberalism. This was reflected in the 1998 Law on Advocacy, which defined it as the independent and autonomous professional activity of providing legal aid (Article 1). The law retained the prohibition on incorporating a legal practice since advocates could work only as individuals, in joint offices or in partnership (Article 38). Although the basic principles of the 1998 law were retained in the 2011 Law on Advocacy, the influence of global capitalism led to some adjustments. The new law extends the right to be registered as an advocate to foreign law graduates whose diplomas have been validated by a domestic university (Article 6). It also enables domestic lawyers to work abroad (Article 16) and foreign citizens to be registered as advocates in Serbia after they pass the bar and judicial exams and work in association with a domestic advocate for three years (Articles 14, 25). Other limits on marketisation are still in place: partnerships and joint offices may not have branch offices (Article 50); there are restrictions on advertising legal services (Article 24); and non-lawyer ownership of law firms is forbidden (Articles 44–52).

Advocates are individual professionals; even those in large offices are officially referred to as individual advocates practising in cooperation with the office. Qualitative research confirms the widespread belief that incorporation will endanger ethical practice by lawyers. This argument has also been advanced in other jurisdictions (*cf* Evetts 2015; Parker 2004; Webersraedt 2014). In Serbia, the alleged tax advantages of incorporation seem less relevant since advocates enjoy a preferential tax status: they register as entrepreneurs and pay a lump-sum tax unless their turnover exceeds approximately €50,000 per year (in the Serbian context a rather high income), in which case they must maintain a business register and pay corporate taxes. Apparently, the majority of Serbian advocates stay below this threshold by not reporting or registering transactions.[13] Our interviews suggest that the resistance to new tax legislation and cash registries, which led to the first strike of advocates in 2014, was an attempt to preserve their preferential tax status but damaged the public perception of lawyers.

Despite the resistance to incorporation, large foreign law firms (mainly from Austria) opened several representative offices in the form of limited liability companies in the early 2000s, but they were banned after a late, mild reaction by the Serbian Bar Association. Now they operate in the Serbian market through partnerships with domestic offices, which are *de facto* though not *de jure* their country offices.[14] According to our respondents, many of these offices have been and still are involved in marketing practices banned by the Law on Advocacy (Article 24). This has caused dissatisfaction and a perception of

---

[13] This seems to be another example of a widely accepted informal practice in the Serbian economy (FREN 2013; SELDI 2016).

[14] In these instances, the office is identified by the name of the domestic law office 'in cooperation with' the name of the foreign law office.

unfair competition. These firms have also introduced a corporate culture and management practices that are alien to the vast majority of practitioners.[15]

Table 3 Advocates, Apprentices, and Population per Advocate (Serbia)

	Advocates	Apprentices	Population	Population per Advocate
1931	1,402	357	5,737,000	4,092
1947	829	189	6,528,000	7,875
1958	1,405	249	7,425,000	5,284
1968	1,645	233	8,235,000	5,006
1978	1,402	94	9,030,000	6,441
1989	2,360	620	9,874,000	4,184
1990	2,588	1,084	9,923,000	3,834
1998	Data not available			
2009	Data not available			
2018	9,228		7,020,858	761

Sources: Statistical Yearbook of the Socialist Federal Republic of Yugoslavia (1947, 1958, 1968, 1978, 1989); archive of the Serbian Bar Association for later years; online database of the Statistical Office of Serbia (www.stat.gov.rs).[16]

Recent years have witnessed a rapid increase in the number of advocates (see Table 3).[17] This has been attributed to the growth of higher education and rising demand for legal services, as well as the peculiar situation of the Serbian judiciary, which faced political pressures and low pay, motivating many judges (particularly men) to become advocates. We lack a comprehensive picture of the socio-economic position and internal stratification of the profession.[18] However, limited data suggest that recent years have led to internal stratification of the legal profession: individual practitioners report lower incomes than advocates who work in large firms and mainly serve business clients.[19] Most advocates (80 per cent) report that their income is above the average for the entire

---

[15] One respondent vividly depicted these differences: 'Once I was interviewed for the job in one of those firms. It was so funny! I was interviewed by someone who is younger than me and has less experience and knowledge. Then at the end I was supposed to be interviewed by a foreigner ... as if he knows something about our law .... Big firms, this is not "advokatura", this is legal consulting' (interview, October 2018).

[16] After 1998 statistical data do not include the provinces of Kosovo and Metohija.

[17] As indicated by Tables 2 and 3, Serbia seems to have a larger and more developed market for legal services, while the BiH market is not only smaller but also divided between two bar association in two entities.

[18] Qualitative research reveals a deep divide in the socio-economic position, interests and perceptions of the profession among practising lawyers. There seem to be three tiers: (1) a small number of criminal defence advocates; (2) a small number of corporate or big firm lawyers; and (3) a majority of sole practitioners working in various fields (called 'corridor lawyers' by one respondent). Advocates generally feel that the first two groups have higher social status, professional prestige and income.

[19] The qualitative survey also indicates that most individual practitioners are dependent on the low socio-economic status of ordinary clients. The interviews suggest that the official fee schedule of the Serbian Bar Association is high compared to the living standard and average income in Serbia. For instance, the fee for a written complaint in civil cases such divorce and labour issues represents 70 per cent of the average pre-tax salary, and the fee for traffic accidents is 94 per cent. Advocates negotiate lower prices for their services or face problems obtaining payment.

population, while 16 per cent say it is average and only 6 per cent that it is below average. Nevertheless, lawyers who represent international companies, banks and investment funds report a much higher income (150 per cent of the average), while those who rarely or never work for such clients report just 73 per cent of the average.

The Serbian Bar still controls entry to the profession and enjoys a monopoly over the delivery of legal services. This monopoly is strengthened by the RS Constitution, which states that 'legal assistance shall be provided by legal professionals [*advokatura* in Serbian], as an independent and autonomous service, and legal assistance offices established in the units of local self-government in accordance with the law' (Article 67). On a few recent occasions, advocates engaged in collective actions aimed at protecting their professional status and market and excluding competitors (Abbott 1991). Two actions were of particular importance: the struggle to preserve the monopoly from incursions by notaries in 2013; and almost two decades of resistance to reforms of the free legal aid system.

The notary case started in summer 2014 when advocates called a strike over increased tax burdens on practising lawyers. The initially mild response evolved into a more serious one lasting five months to protest the introduction of notaries. One of the contested issues was whether notaries should be given a monopoly over the authentication and verification of real estate transactions (Rakić Vodinelić 2014). The rationale was that this would enhance legal certainty in an under-regulated real estate market and give the new profession an adequate incentive to make a substantial investment in office and personnel (Živković and Živković 2013: 440–41). Since the real estate market was a significant source of income for many practising lawyers, the Serbian Bar Association reacted by suspending the activities of advocates almost completely. Of course, the strike's official rationale was not the financial interests of the estimated 4,000 practising lawyers (out of a total of 8,000) whose main source of income came from drafting contracts, but rather the alleged weakening of the *advokatura* and the rule of law (*cf* interview with one the most prominent Serbian lawyers in Peščanik 2014). The strike was compulsory: advocates who continued to work were threatened with exclusion from the Bar Association, and some were banned from practice for three years (Šarić 2015). The strike resulted in a retreat by the legislature, which accepted all the Bar Association's demands.

The second case expressed resistance to allowing civil society organisations to provide free legal aid services. In various forms, most often through in-house lawyers and external consultants, these organisations had been doing this for at least two decades. However, legalising that practice faced strong resistance from the Bar Association, which insisted that no 'negotiations with the civil sector will take place' and argued that the use of civic associations to provide legal services was unconstitutional[20] (Jeremić 2018; Bjeletić and Arsić 2017). The existing system of free legal aid was often criticised as ineffective and unresponsive to the needs of the poor and socially excluded (Uzelac and Preložnjak 2012; Reljanović and Knežević-Bojović 2014). Proponents of more liberal policies for free legal aid argued for solutions that would enable civic associations and free legal aid clinics established within law faculties to offer these services.

---

[20] This remark relates to Art 67 of the Serbian Constitution.

Rising poverty and inequality,[21] the high costs of trials, and the belief among judges and prosecutors that social and economic capital could significantly affect the ability of litigants to obtain justice strongly supported these claims (*cf* Vuković et al 2011; Vuković et al 2018). More than a decade after the issue was joined, however, the deadlock remains unresolved.

During the last decade, the Serbian and Belgrade Bar Associations have been sites of fierce contestations and power struggles between competing fractions of practising lawyers. This was reflected in the low level of trust expressed by members of both Bars: just 34 per cent of respondents trusted the Serbian Bar Association, 38 per cent were undecided, and 28 mistrusted it. Nearly twice as many believed the Bar was representing the interests of the most powerful law offices and advocates rather than protecting the interests of all its members (62 versus 37 per cent). Lawyers' narratives about the Bar are consistent: it is perceived as a self-referential system composed of 'advocates who talk to each other', 'are not dealing with the true interests of the profession' and 'further embarrass Serbian advocates' (interviews, Belgrade, October 2018). One of the remarks appearing in all interviews relates to the lack of participation in law-making processes, where the profession's expertise is underutilised.

In Serbia, women started entering the advocates' profession under socialism in the late 1960s. In 1967, just 4 per cent of enrolled practising lawyers were women; that share remained fairly constant for a decade, rising to 9 per cent in 1982 and 14 per cent in 1989.[22] At present, 35 per cent of enrolled practising lawyers are women. The feminisation of the judiciary is far more advanced. Out of 2,573 judges working in Serbia at the end of 2018, 71 per cent are women.

IV. JUDGES

A. Historical Background

Cyclical changes of legislative and executive officials, which occur every four or five years through regular elections, represent a democratic verification of their legitimacy. But similar changes in the judiciary are neither desirable nor effective and would open the door to illegal political influences (Orlović 2010: 165). For these reasons, the tenure of judges – one of the universal guarantees of institutional (*de jure*) independence – should last a lifetime, or at least longer than that of those who appointed them. The other two principal mechanisms affecting judicial independence are the appointment process, in which judicial bodies need to participate, and the dismissal procedure, which needs to be independent of political actors. These operate conjunctively: one without the other cannot ensure independence (Melton and Ginsburg 2014: 190).

The development of a modern, independent and professionalised Serbian judiciary began in the nineteenth century but was not a linear process. Throughout the nineteenth

---

[21] Serbia has a higher rate of income inequality than any EU country, with a Gini coefficient of 38.26 per cent of the population is at risk of poverty, and 39 per cent are at risk of poverty or social exclusion (2016 data).

[22] Data for the period from 1961 to 1989 are from Statistical Yearbooks of the Federal Statistical Office of the Socialist Federal Republic of Yugoslavia. The source of the later data is the Serbian Bar Association archive.

and twentieth centuries authoritarian political leaders, wars and internal power struggles strongly influenced the judiciary. The 1835 Constitution and 1881 Law on Judges guaranteed a degree of independence, since judicial appointments were permanent and immovable. According to the 1881 law, the Government appointed only first instance judges, while presidents of first instance courts and judges of the Appellate Courts and Court of Cassation could be appointed only from lists submitted by those courts (Marinković 2010: 140–43). The 1888 Constitution was the first to clearly limit the role of the monarch and proclaim the permanence and immovability of judges. Although its guarantees of judicial independence followed prevailing European standards, political influence was pervasive, and the government transparently and systematically sought to fill the judiciary with its supporters. The 1903 Constitution was an improvement, rendering the monarch's role in the appointment process merely symbolic (Marinković 2010: 143–45). But the normative framework of the judicial system created an image of a well-functioning state, which did not correspond to reality. This was particularly true for the Kingdom of Yugoslavia, which was riven by internal grievances and dysfunctionalities. Judges were guaranteed independence and permanence, but their appointments depended on the executive power, excluding the judiciary from this process. Above all, the executive continued to interfere with and influence judicial decision-making (Mirković 2017: 259–60).

In socialist Yugoslavia after World War II, the judiciary was seen as a political instrument of the Communist Party. At the same time, judges enjoyed lifetime tenure (unlike those in other communist legal systems), and the government was committed to the professionalisation and modernisation of the judiciary (Kmezić 2017: 40–41). The 1963 and 1974 Constitutions proclaimed the independence of the judiciary, but 'political suitability' was decisive in appointments and dismissals. Judges were appointed for eight years with no guarantee of re-appointment. All this was reflected in cases of 'higher interest' to the state, when the ruling party used courts and judges to deal with political opponents. This was easy to do because in 1979 about 90 per cent of judges and public prosecutors were Party members (ibid: 42–43).

B. Contemporary Serbia

The politicisation of the judiciary continued after the end of socialism. The 'long 1990s' permitted various modes of political influence. The whole period, up to the present, can be viewed as a constant battle to secure political control over the judiciary, waged through the appointment of court presidents (*cf* Dallara 2014; Kmezić 2017: 43–45). According to our data, this still occurs in Serbia: one-third of judges in our sample reported direct or indirect pressure from the executive, court presidents, or colleagues. Most respondents were suspicious about the way court presidents were chosen and saw them as a source of pressure. One judge said 'They are being elected in a different way from other judges, and this is a clear proof that the state expects something from them! They are the "extended hand" of the authorities through which the executive power orders the verdicts' (interview, Belgrade, June 2016).

The 2006 Constitution of the Republic of Serbia guarantees the separation of powers and independence of the judiciary (as had previous modern constitutions). However, as we have seen, Serbia has a long tradition of pressure on the courts and unwillingness by the political elite to respect their independence. This is particularly relevant in light of the growing corruption, asset stripping and other types of official misconduct. Some of the legal provisions also jeopardise judicial independence (*cf* Dabetić 2018: 383). The procedure for the initial appointment of a judge is inconsistent with the Constitution's proclamation of judicial independence. The High Judicial Council (HJC)[23] proposes judges, whom Parliament appoints for a three-year probationary period (Law on Judges, Article 51).[24] Those whose work is deemed 'very successful' receive a lifetime appointment (Law on Judges, Article 52).

There have been several important judicial reforms in Serbia, but the consequences of the last one (2008–12) were far-reaching, leading to the dismissal of 837 judges and about 200 prosecutors and deputy prosecutors. This process has often been condemned as not transparent (Dallara 2014: 96 ff), unconstitutional and illegal (Rakić-Vodinelić 2012), and it had a negative impact on judicial efficiency (EC 2010: 10). It violated the guarantee of lifetime tenure (Law on Judges, Articles 47–52) and was conducted by the HJC when it had a temporary and controversial membership.[25] After the Constitutional Court decision on the unconstitutionality of the re-election procedures, judges and prosecutors who had not been re-elected were reintegrated into the judiciary (Marković 2014: 156–58).[26] As a result, only 8 per cent of judges are satisfied with the reforms, and just 13 per cent are satisfied with the present condition of the judiciary. In deciding cases, judges are more inclined to self-censorship, and their faith in the rule of law is weakened. One judge said: 'I learned that I could be dismissed without knowing why. Who guarantees me that it will not be repeated? Therefore, I will be careful in the decision making process' (interview, Belgrade, June 2016). The re-appointment process also intensified judges' insecurity and dissatisfaction, discrediting the entire profession. Interpersonal relations were affected, as mistrust was sown between judges who were and were not reappointed. One said: 'There is tacit animosity among colleagues, a division between "us" and "them", and I think it will persist until retirement' (interview, Belgrade, June 2016).

One issue concerning the election of judges in Serbia involves the role of the Judicial Academy. Although it was created to redress gaps in legal education, the question of whether it should be the exclusive means of entry into the judiciary has been hotly contested. The strongest opponents of this idea – civil society groups and associations representing judges, prosecutors, and legal academics – warn that it will perpetuate

---

[23] A similar process governs the appointment of court presidents and the Supreme Court of Cassation President. HCJ is also in charge of granting lifetime tenure and dismissing judges (Law on the High Judicial Council, Art 13). HJC consists of 11 members: three with permanent positions (President of the Supreme Court of Cassation, Minister in charge of the judiciary and President of the Justice Committee of the National Assembly) and eight elected by Parliament (six judges with lifetime tenure, one distinguished lawyer with at least 15 years' experience, and one university law professor) (Law on the High Judicial Council, Art 5).

[24] Even though this compromises the principle of the permanence of the judicial function, it can also be found in France, Greece, the Netherlands, Germany, and Austria (Marinković 2009: 285). However, one should bear in mind that the procedures are implemented differently in different professional and political cultures.

[25] Judges who were serving their three-year probationary period were illegally elected members of the temporary HJC; after the HJC was dissolved, those judges were guaranteed higher ranking professional positions; court presidents were also elected to the temporary HJC, although this was illegal (for details, see Rakić-Vodinelić 2012: 47–58).

[26] Data obtained through the research project 'Legal Professions in South Eastern Europe'.

political influence over the judiciary (Jeremić 2018) since the executive would retain a strong role in the selection of judges.[27]

Finally, a word on material position of judges. Like immovability, the material position of judges was not ensured until the late nineteenth or early twentieth centuries (Mirković 2017: 189). Under current law, judges are entitled to a salary suitable to the dignity and responsibility of their function, thereby guaranteeing their independence and the well-being of their families (Law on Judges, Article 4). Despite the views of some that judicial salaries in Western Balkan countries 'meet satisfactory standards' (Kmezić 2017: 136), a survey found that 87 per cent of Serbian judges believe they are not adequately paid, while only 8 per cent find their salary satisfactory (Društvo sudija Srbije 2017: 41).

C. Contemporary Bosnia and Herzegovina

The professional status of judges in BiH was particularly affected by its recent history. The aftermath of the Bosnian war (1992–95) left the judicial system devastated. Every level of government – state, entity and canton – had a say in the matters concerning judicial politics. While several reforms were adopted to strengthen the judiciary and ensure its independence, autonomy, competence and integrity, only one of them managed to establish a functional self-regulating judiciary at the state level – the High Judicial and Prosecutorial Council of Bosnia and Herzegovina (HJPC). The international community (ie the European Commission) was and still is very involved in judicial reforms directed at rebuilding the post-conflict society through law.

However, this effort was hampered by ethnic and entity divisions. As the first socio-legal study on the BiH legal profession indicates,[28] the inefficacy and corruption of the post-war judiciary 'reflect the transition from the communist system based on patronage and control, along with the deep consequences of a war that damaged infrastructure and economic stability' (Studija 2000: 7–8). One of the study's central findings was the lack of qualified judicial candidates from the beginning of the war until late 1990 (ibid: 15).

The declining professionalism of the Bosnian judiciary impelled influential members of the international community[29] to develop a strategic approach to legal reform. The first step was the introduction of the Independent Judicial Commission in 2001, which coordinated the reform process until 2004, when HJPC was established.[30]

---

[27] The Board of the Academy contains three government appointees in addition to four judges and two prosecutors. Consequently, representatives of the executive become permanent members of the body responsible for the pre-selection of future judges, because 'to become a judge, you could only enter through that door' (interview with the judge of Appellate Court Miodrag Majić, Insajder, 2018, available at www.insajder.net/sr/sajt/vazno/9588/).

[28] This study, the only one of its kind, sought to collect all relevant data on the Bosnian judiciary through in-depth interviews with 26 judges and six prosecutors from all three ethnic groups in Bosnia and Herzegovina.

[29] Namely the Office of High Representative for Bosnia and Herzegovina (OHR), UN Mission to BiH, International Crisis Group (ICG) and Initiative for European Stability (ESR).

[30] The period 2001–04 demonstrated the value of reforms, which nevertheless proved to be unsuccessful until key members of the international community joined forces to develop a systematic approach. The legal framework for judges and prosecutors was reformed, along with other relevant legislation. Three HJPCs were created and then supplanted by a single state institution. The BiH Court and Office of the Prosecutor were also established, as were judicial and prosecutorial training centres in the entities (A Decade 2014: 8–12).

HJPC exercised jurisdiction over the election and appointment of judicial office holders, training, ethical guidelines, disciplinary procedures and the budgets of courts and prosecutorial offices. It has 15 members: five judges, five prosecutors, and five elected members (one by the Judicial Commission of Brčko District BiH, two by the entity Bar Associations, and two by the state legislature and executive) (Law on High Judicial and Prosecutorial Council, *Official Gazette of BiH*, No 25/04, Articles 4, 17). In 2001 there were about 868 judges; but since the reform also restructured the network of courts and prosecutors offices – reducing the number of municipal and basic courts from 78 to 47 and prosecutors offices from 103 to 19 – the number of judges fell to 629 (A Decade 2014: 13).

By 31 March 2004, 878 positions had been filled. After the reappointment process was complete some 30 per cent of the judges and prosecutors were not reappointed, and some 18 per cent of the candidates who were appointed had not previously held office, judicial or prosecutorial. Significantly, only 21 per cent of the candidates who were court presidents or chief prosecutors at the time were reappointed. The reappointment process also had a major influence on the establishment of an appropriate ethnic balance in the BiH judiciary (A Decade 2014: 18). The HJPC Annual Report for 2017 indicates that there are 1,394[31] judicial office holders (555 men and 839 women), including 99 heads of courts and prosecutorial offices (54 men and 45 women) (HJPC Annual Report for 2017, 2018: 33). BiH judges seem to be less critical of the reforms and the situation of the judiciary than their Serbian counterparts: 25 per cent were satisfied with the situation of the judiciary, and 29 per cent were satisfied with the reforms. Still, this left 38 per cent dissatisfied with the situation and 31 per cent with the reforms.

The overall reform proved successful, and establishment of the HJPC gave the Bosnian judiciary an unprecedented level of independence. Since the whole purpose was to insulate the judiciary from the ruling political parties and establish the rule of law and an efficient and professional judiciary, the major BiH political parties tried to change the Law on HJPC in 2011 to vest power over the judiciary in the Ministry of Justice. The international community, now represented by the European Commission, immediately reacted by developing the EU-BiH Structured Dialogue on Justice – a mechanism designed to safeguard judicial independence through a collaborative methodology requiring that all future legal changes be approved by both the EC and HJPC (A Decade 2014: 61). The European Union was and remains the main financial supporter of the HJPC (ibid: 67). However, the efficiency of the judicial system in BiH remains questionable, given the ongoing battle against corruption; the fact that all chief prosecutors of the Prosecutorial Office of BiH prematurely resigned in scandalous circumstances[32] failed to inspire

---

[31] A decade earlier (2007) there were 1,149 judicial office holders: 856 judges and 293 prosecutors (HJPC Annual Report for 2007 2008: 23). Unfortunately, the 2007 report failed to indicate the gender composition (AR HJPC 2007), and the 2017 report failed to indicate the judicial office holder composition (AR HJPC 2017).

[32] First Chief Prosecutor Marinko Jurčević (2003–08) resigned under media pressure. His successor, Milorad Barašin (2009–11), was removed by the HJPC for 'innapropriate contacts with the members of the criminal milieu'. The same thing happened to Barašin's successor, Goran Salihović (2011–16), who is under both disciplinary investigation (by the HJPC) and criminal investigation (by the prosecutorial body he headed for five years) (available at www.faktor.ba/vijest/kontroverzne-biografije-tuilaca-istrage-i-optunice-u-rukama-podobnih-i-ne-sposobnih-216888).

confidence that the reformed judiciary will succeed in establishing the rule of law and securing public trust.

V. OTHER LEGAL PROFESSIONS: PUBLIC NOTARIES, BAILIFFS AND LEGAL ACADEMICS

In both countries, the notariat was abandoned during socialism and was reintroduced in 2006 in Bosnia and Herzegovina and in 2013 in Serbia. As we have seen, the introduction of the notariat in Serbia was contested by advocates, provoking a battle over professional status, autonomy and market. At present there are 176 public notaries in Serbia, 106 (60 per cent) of them women. In BiH professional notary associations were established in the FBiH in 2007 and RS in 2008. The market for their services threatened the monopoly of advocates, who challenged the Law on Notaries before the FBiH Constitutional Court in 2006, which decided in 2016 that some provisions of the law were unconstitutional; but that did not significantly affect the scope of services provided exclusively by notaries (Bahtijarević and Čizmić 2017: 172–73). There are now 131 notaries in BiH: 53 men and 78 women.

Legal academics played an important role in public and political life in the former Yugoslavia and continue to do so in Serbia and Bosnia and Herzegovina. Throughout modern history, boundaries have been blurred between free professionals and academics on one side and politicians and civil servants on the other. Cultural, scientific and political elites were not differentiated, and writers, scientists, university professors, practising lawyers and medical doctors have been actively engaged in political life (Stojanović 2008: 180–93). Today, legal academics serve as ministers, members of parliament, ambassadors, and Constitutional Court judges.[33] With the rise of modern civil society from the early 1990s, legal academics found themselves involved in various legal reform projects promoted by both the civil sector and the state. Legal academics are occasionally involved in drafting legislation when governmental bodies seek their expertise. In BiH, legal academics also disseminate expert analyses through the Foundation Centre for Public Law in BiH, which brings together legal academics, judges, practising lawyers and members of the government to discuss the challenges of the existing legal framework and propose solutions.[34]

Serbian legal academics are also deeply involved in lawmaking and policymaking processes, which are often outsourced to expert bodies and working groups, allowing middle class and professional groups (including legal academics) to capture public resources. Those groups use their positional and political capital to secure access to markets and control public finances and governing structures (Vuković 2016). Lawmakers sometimes amplify the social and political influence of these actors by granting them membership quotas in the bodies governing the judiciary, such as the High Judiciary Council.

---

[33] Six of the Serbian Constitutional Court's 15 judges are legal academics and professors. Professors also serve on HJC. The BiH Constitutional Court has one professor, the RS Constitutional Court has three, and the FBiH Constitutional Court has one.

[34] See www.fcjp.ba/index.php. This nongovermental institution is funded by Deutsche Gesellschaft für Internationale Zusammenarbeit and has worked in Serbia on constitutional reform.

VI. CONCLUSION

In this chapter we have outlined the historical background of legal professions in Serbia and Bosnia and Herzegovina and the most important issues they face today, focusing primarily on advocates and judges. These issues stem from the interplay of changes in global capitalism and politics with internal structures and power relations in both countries. For example, the position of advocates in Serbia and Bosnia and Herzegovina has been influenced by the transformation of global capitalism and internal legislative and market changes. According to our data for Serbia, this has resulted in the internal stratification of the profession. The socio-economic position of solo practitioners who primarily work with individual clients is affected by the low living standard of the general population, while advocates in the field of corporate law, who work for large clients, are in a much more favourable situation. The profession has been struggling to maintain autonomy and preserve the market for its services in light of the introduction of notaries and various providers of free legal aid services. Resistance on behalf of Serbian advocates represents a striking example of professional mobilisation. At the same time, judges and prosecutors were struggling to maintain professional autonomy from political influences. All this was happening in an environment marked by unconsolidated democracy and strong authoritarian impulses. In Bosnia and Herzegovina – a post-conflict society in which peace and state-building processes are still ongoing – international actors have played a key role in reforming the judiciary and safeguarding it from political pressures, even if judicial independence does not ensure an effective judiciary, especially in battling corruption. Serbia, by contrast, suffered from internal power struggles, which have resulted in an unsuccessful and unfinished reform of the judiciary, whose final outcome remains to be seen.

REFERENCES

A Decade (2014) *A Decade of High Judicial and Prosecutorial Council in Bosnia and Herzegovina: The Judicial Reforms and its Achievements* www.pravosudje.ba/vstv/faces/pdfservlet?p_id_doc=27870.

Abbott, A (1991) 'The order of professionalization: an empirical analysis' 4(18) *Work and Occupations* 355.

Avramović, S (2013) 'Nastanak i razvitak pravnoistorijskih predmeta na Pravnom fakultetu u Beogradu' 5–6(63) *Zbornik Pravnog fakulteta u Zagrebu* 921.

Bahtijarević, S and Čizmović, J (2017) *Advokatura u Bosni i Hercegovini 1883–2013* (Sarajevo, Advokatska/Odvjetnička komora Federacije BiH).

Bjeletić, B and Arsić, T (2017) 'Subjekti prava pružanja besplatne pravne pomoći' *Blog AKS* blog. aks.org.rs/subjekti-prava-pruzanja-besplatne-pravne-pomoci/.

Constitution of the Republic of Serbia, Službeni Glasnik RS, no 98/2006.

Dabetić, V (2018) 'Normative endangerment of institutional independence of judiciary in contemporary Serbia' in Z Pavlović (ed), *Yearbook Human Rights Protection – From Unlawfulness to Legality* (Novi Sad, Provincial Protector of Citizens –Ombudsman – Institute for Criminological and Sociological Research in Belgrade).

Demographic Research Center, Institute of Social Sciences (1974) *The Population of Yugoslavia* (Belgrade, DRC).

Društvo sudija Srbije (2017), *Jačanje nezavisnosti i integriteta sudija u Srbiji* (Belgrade, Društvo sudija Srbije).
Durmišević, D (2012) 'Razvoj pravnog obrazovanja i pravne nauke u Bosni i Hercegovini' in B Petrović (ed), *Savremene tendencije u razvoju pravne nauke i pravnog obrazovanja* (Sarajevo, Pravni fakultet Univerziteta u Sarajevu).
Đorđević, M (2009) 'The Export of American Legal Education and Its Impact in Serbia' in A Brand Ronald and D Wes Rist (eds), *The Export of Legal Education: Its Promise and Impact in Transition Countries* (New York, Ashgate).
European Commission (2010) 'Serbia 2010 Progress Report' SEC(2010) 1330 (Brussels, 9 November).
Evetts J (2015) 'Professionalism, Enterprise and the Market: contradictory or complementary?' in H Sommerland et al (eds), *The Futures of Legal Education and the Legal Profession* (Oxford, Hart Publishing).
FREN (2013) *The Shadow Economy in Serbia: New Findings and Recommendations for Reform* (Belgrade, Foundation for the Advancement of Economics).
Gradaščević-Sijerčić, J (2012) 'Pravno obrazovanje: izazovi i ogledi' in B Petrović (ed), *Savremene tendencije u razvoju pravne nauke i pravnog obrazovanja* (Sarajevo, Pravni fakultet Univerziteta u Sarajevu).
Grozdić, V (2016) 'Odnos države prema profesionalnom udruživanju sudija – slučaj Društva sudija Srbije' 10–12 *Pravo i privreda* 54, 89.
Gudac-Dodić, V (2006) *Žena u socijalizmu: položaj zene u Srbiji u drugoj polovini 20. veka* (Belgrade, Institut za noviju istoriju Srbije).
HJPC (2007) Annual Report for 2007 vstv.pravosudje.ba/vstv/faces/pdfservlet?p_id_doc=28709.
Jeremić, V (2017) 'Da li je Akademiji mesto u Ustavu?' *Danas* 7 September www.danas.rs/drustvo/da-li-je-akademiji-mesto-u-ustavu/.
—— (2018) 'No negotiations with civil sector' *Danas* 1 February www.danas.rs/drustvo/vladavina-prava/nema-pregovora-sa-civilnim-sektorom/.
Kandić, Lj (2002) *Istorija Pravnog fakulteta 1905–1941* Vols I–II (Belgrade, Zavod za udžbenike i nastavna sredstva).
Kmezić, M (2017) *EU Rule of Law Promotion – Judiciary Reform in the Western Balkans* (London, Routledge Taylor & Francis Group).
Kober, J (2020) 'Czech Republic: Legal Professions Looking for Serenity and Stability' in this volume.
Law on Judges, Službeni Glasnik RS, no 116/2008, 58/2009 – decision of the Constitutional Court (CC), 104/2009, 101/2010, 8/2012 – decision of the CC, 121/2012, 124/2012 – decision of the CC, 101/2013, 111/2014 – decision of the CC, 117/2014, 40/2015 i 63/2015 – decision of the CC, 106/2015, 63/2016 – pru of the CC and 47/2017.
Law on Legal Academy, Službeni Glasnik RS, no 104/2009, 32/2014, decision of the Constitutional Court 106/2015.
Law on the High Judicial Council, Službeni Glasnik RS, no 116/2008, 101/2010, 88/2011 and 106/2015.
Marcus, I (2014) 'The "Woman Question" in Post-Socialist Legal Education' 36(3) *Human Rights Quarterly* 507.
Marinković, T (2009) 'O ustavnosti opšteg reizbora' 57(1) *Anali Pravnog fakulteta u Beogradu* 283.
—— (2010) 'Jemstva sudijske nezavisnosti u Ustavima Kneževine i Kraljevine Srbije' 58(2) *Anali Pravnog fakulteta u Beogradu* 134.
Marković, Đ (2014) 'Doprinos Visokog saveta sudstva (ne)zavisnosti pravosuđa u Republici Srbiji' in E Šarčević (ed), *Ko bira sudije redovnih sudova? – Regionalni bilans teorije i prakse: BiH, Hrvatska, Srbija* (Sarajevo, Foundation Public Law Centre).

Melton, J and Ginsburg, T (2014) 'Does De Jure Judicial Independence Really Matter? – A Reevaluation of Explanations for Judicial Independence' *Coase-Sandor Institute for Law & Economics Working Paper No 612*.

Milić, A (1994) *Žene, politika, porodica* (Belgrade, Institut za političke studije).

Mirković, Z (2008) 'Belgrade Higher School (1808–1813) and Legal Education in Serbia' 3 *Annals – Belgrade Law Review* 195.

—— (2017) *Srpska pravna istorija* (Belgrade, Univerzitet u Beogradu – Pravni fakultet).

Orlović, S (2010) 'Stalnost sudijske funkcije vs. opšti reizbor sudija u Republici Srbiji' 58(2) *Anali Pravnog fakulteta u Beogradu* 163.

Parker, C (2004) 'Law Firms Incorporated: How Incorporation Could and Should make Firms more Ethically Responsible' 23(2) *University of Queensland Law Journal* 347.

Peščanik (2015) 'Pobuna advokata' *Peščanik* www.pescanik.net/emisija-10-10-2014/.

Rakić-Vodinelić, V (2014) 'Advokatura i notarijat danas' *Peščanik* www.pescanik.net/advokatura-i-notarijat-u-srbiji-danas/.

Rakić-Vodinelić, V, Knežević-Bojović, A and Reljanović, M (2012) *Reforma pravosuđa u Srbiji 2008–2012* (Belgrade, Pravni fakultet Univerziteta Union – Službeni glasnik).

Reljanović, M, and Knežević-Bojović, A (2014) 'Judicial reform in Serbia and negotiating chapter 23: A critical outlook' 5(1) *Pravni zapisi* 241.

Schultz, U (2003) 'Women in the World's Legal Professions: Overview and Synthesis' in U Schultz and G Shaw (eds), *Women in the World's Legal Professions* (Oxford, Hart Publishing).

SELDI (2016) 'Hidden Economy and Good Governance in Southeast Europe – Regional Assessment Report 2016' *Sofija: Southeast Europe Leadership for Development and Integrity* www.seldi.net/publications/publications/hidden-economy-and-good-governance-in-southeast-europe-regional-assessment-report/.

Sibinović, Đ (2011) *Pravo advokature* (Belgrade, Službeni glasnik).

Spasić, S, Šarkić, N and Sibinović, Đ (2011) *Pravosudne profesije* (Belgrade, Službeni glasnik).

Stanojević, D (2008) *Kaldrma i asfalt: urbanizacija i evropeizacija Beograda 1890–1914* (Belgrade, Udruženje za društvenu istoriju, 2008).

—— (2013) 'Međugeneracijska obrazovna pokretljivost u Srbiji u XX veku' in M Lazić and S Cvejić (eds), *Promene osnovnih struktura društva Srbije u periodu ubrzane transformacije* (Belgrade, ISI FF).

Studija (2000) 'Pravda, odgovornost i socijalna rekonstrukcija u Bosni i Hercegovini: studija o bosanskim sudijama i tužiteljima na osnovu intervjua' (Berkeley/Sarajevo: Centar za ljudska prava, Međunarodna pravna klinika za ljudska prava Univerziteta Kalifornija, Berkeley/Centar za ljudska prava Univerziteta u Sarajevu).

Šarić, M (2015) 'Mali broj postupaka protiv advokata rezultirao kaznama' *CINS* www.cins.rs/srpski/news/article/mali-broj-postupaka-protiv-advokata-rezultirao-kaznama.

Šporer, Ž (1990) *Sociologija profesija: ogled o društvenoj uvjetovanosti profesionalizacije* (Zagreb, Hrvatsko sociološko društvo).

Trlin, D (2018) 'Da li je Bosni i Hercegovini potrebna pravosudna akademija?' 4(3) *Iustitia* 47.

Uzelac, A and Preložnjak, B (2012) 'The Development of Legal Aid Systems in the Western Balkans. A Study of Controversial Reforms in Croatia and Serbia' 38(3–4) *Kritisk Iuss, Utgitt av Rettspolitisk Forening (Liber amicorum–Jon T Johnsen)* 261.

Verheijen, TJG and Rabrenović, A (2015) 'Civil Service Development in Central and Eastern Europe and the CIS: A Perfect Storm?' in FM van der Meer, J Raadschelders and T Toonen (eds), *Comparative Civil Service Systems in the 21st Century* (New York, Palgrave Macmillan UK).

Vuković, D (2016) 'Capturing Resources: The Role of Professional Communities and Middle Classes in Fostering Social Reforms within Serbia' 58(2) *Sociologija* 253.

—— (2017) 'The Hollowing Out of Institutions: Law and Policymaking in Contemporary Serbia' in B Fekete and F Gárdos-Orosz (eds), *Central and Eastern European Socio-Political and Legal Transition Revisited* (Frankfurt am Main, Peter Lang).

Vuković, D, Antonijević, M, Golubović, K, Milenković, M and Vujić, K (2011) *Access to Justice and Free Legal Aid in Serbia: Challenges and Reforms* (Belgrade, YUCOM and SeConS).

Vuković, D, Mrakovčić, M and Forić, S (2018) 'Legal Professions in South East Europe: From Post-Socialist Transformation to Globalization', paper presented at the Law and Citizenship beyond the State RCSL and SDJ Annual Meeting, Lisbon, Portugal.

Weberstaedt, J (2014) 'English Alternative Business Structures and the European Single Market' 21(1) *International Journal of the Legal Profession* 103.

Zvekić, U (1985) *Profesija sudija – Sociološka analiza* (Belgrade, Institut za kriminološka i sociološka istraživanja).

Živković, M, and Živković, V (2013) 'O uvođenju javnog beležništva u Srbiji' 23(2) *Zbornik Pravnog fakulteta u Zagrebu* 433.

Županov, J and Šporer, Ž (1984) 'Profesija sociolog' 50–51(1–2) *Revija za sociologiju* 14, 11.

Part IV

Latin America

18

Argentina
The Long Transition of the Legal Profession

MARTIN BÖHMER

SINCE THE END of the last and bloodiest military dictatorship in December 1983, the legal profession in Argentina has been undergoing a major transition. Although any regime change affects the entire political system, Argentina's was especially legal, constitutional, and lawyerly. Accordingly, every aspect of the profession has changed or is changing, including legal education, the authoritative sources of law, the routines and practices of legal professionals, legal procedures (from written to oral, from inquisitorial to adversarial, the introduction of jury trials), the nature and scope of rights, the role of lay people (standing for collectivities, the creation of legal NGOs), and the extension of law in both time (statutes of limitations) and space (international law and its adjudication and enforcement within Argentina).

This chapter addresses three domains of action by the profession. The first is the role of the legal profession in administering social conflicts, mainly through judicial processes. Its main feature is the profession's monopoly over access to the justice system and the rendering of judicial decisions. The second is the judiciary. The third is the role of the profession in government, where it monopolises one branch and deeply influences the others. I will begin by describing the profession before this transition began.

The creation of a constitutional order has always been linked to the idea of limits on power. In that sense Argentina's political system, as defined in its first Constitution enacted in 1853, can only loosely be related to constitutionalism. In effect, the political project of the founding fathers aimed not to limit power but to create almost unbounded power.

The diagnosis of Argentina's weaknesses centred on its long history of confrontation (a war of independence from Spain in 1810–20, a civil war in 1820–35 and a dictatorship in 1835–52), which led elites to believe that pervasive anarchy and chronic poverty were responsible for the country's lamentable condition. Anarchy was blamed on the refusal of provincial warlords to accept a formal, written Constitution, which created an unstable system of atomised power without processes to resolve conflicts other than wars and assassinations. Poverty was attributed to the deserted *pampas* and its few resident *gauchos* (peasants-soldiers-cowboys), who could not be turned into civilised citizens. The political project of the founding generation, which sought to achieve order and promote growth, proposed two main policies: concentration of power to curb anarchy and Northern European immigration and education to end poverty. This was written into the 1853 Constitution, which borrowed ideas from both Continental European and US traditions to create a quasi-centralist monarchy – a hyper-presidential system within the restrictions (and under the guise) of a federal republic.

From the US the Argentine Constitution borrowed the role of the President (while endowing it with greater discretionary power), a bicameral Congress (which favoured the Senate, representing the provincial elites), a Supreme Court with judicial review powers, and a federal system. From the Continental tradition it borrowed the Federal Code (which took most of the legislative power away from the provinces), a formalist dogmatic legal culture and legal education, no *stare decisis*, and the methods of Continental legal science. Thus, an almost unconstrained President, a handful of Senators, and three out of five justices (nominated by the President and confirmed by the Senate in secret deliberations) were able to rule Argentina. The political culture mirrored this scheme: fraudulent elections and political assassinations were the norm in most of the second half of the nineteenth century. And the economic project was successful: Argentina grew very fast. By the turn of the century it was one of the world's top ten economies; and half the population, some two million people, were immigrants. Although most did not speak Spanish, an impressive public educational policy enabled their children to become lawyers and physicians; and illiteracy rates were the lowest in the world.

But the immigrants were not hard working, obedient Northern European peasants. Most came from Southern Europe, and some were political dissidents. Anarchists, socialists, unionists, and communists fleeing persecution established many of the first labour unions and led violent strikes and uprisings. Their struggle was not new to Argentine culture. Even before they arrived, those excluded by the political system resisted, creating a political party, which (after many unsuccessful revolutionary attempts to overthrow the government) forced Congress to pass legislation ending fraudulent elections. The majority party, the Radicals, won the first clean election in 1916 and subsequent elections, using every bit of concentrated power the system offered. The conservatives, having lost the Presidency three times, orchestrated the first military coup in the midst of the 1930 economic depression, followed by those in 1943, 1955, 1962, 1966 and 1976. In 1930 the Supreme Court obliged with an infamous decision creating the *de facto* doctrine: it would admit as legitimate any authority that could produce social order.

Law's function was reduced to ensuring stability in society and certainty in market transactions. Law was depoliticised, de-constitutionalised – excluded from political deliberations and any role in limiting the power of the political branches. The Code and the culture of codification provided the necessary arrangements, creating a self-sufficient set of rules, written by one individual, enacted without congressional deliberation, taught literally, learned by rote in law schools, and dogmatically enforced by the judiciary. When the Codes grew inadequate to regulate an increasingly complex economy, professors wrote treatises, and when those offered insufficient scaffolding, the Code was reformed substantially (by a military government in 1968).

In the 1960s and 1970s politics unrestrained by law and contemptuous of constitutional rights, together with a violent, terrorist, subversive attempt to oppose illegitimate authority in the international context of the Cold War, prompted the 1976 military coup. It invoked the customary justification that it was necessary to curb chaos and eliminate the communist threat of the armed groups. But this time the violation of human rights, which had accompanied earlier coups, changed qualitatively: the State not only closed Congress and banned electoral politics and freedom of expression but also became a terrorist itself, engaging in a systematic program of kidnappings, torture and murder. Argentina thus created its own radical evil.

I. LEGAL PROFESSION

Because of the hegemony of dogmatic training, a homogeneous legal community read the same texts, interpreted them according to the same criteria and applied them consistently. Lawyers and judges, trained by the same legal education system, created a common legal culture, allowing Argentine civil society to navigate difficult times without too much stress. This was the result of a deliberate educational policy that transformed a long process of university training in civil and canon law, simulations and apprenticeship (the Bourbon system of legal education) into five years of learning the letter of the Codes by heart through intensive black-letter law pedagogy. Thus, ever since 1872 (two years after the enactment of the Civil Code) the only requirement to become a lawyer has been the five-year law school course.

Since the judicial process dealt with conflicts between either private parties or individuals and the State, courts rarely discussed the legality or constitutionality of public policies. The scope of a judicial decision was restricted to the case in question. The exceptional judgment addressing larger questions of regulatory authority did so for reasons unrelated to formal rules, such as the need to increase the prestige of the court or economic utility. The creation of an injunction to defend constitutional rights (the individual *amparo*), for example, occurred under a military government. Here, the court tried to distinguish itself and find a more legitimate place in an illegitimate political environment. Similarly, the need to alleviate the impact of inflation and balance the rights of the parties in contracts during the economic turmoil of the 1960s also became a reason for courts to intervene. These were exceptions that confirmed the general rule of judicial restraint.

This conception of law was consistent with a particular mode of legal practice. Lawyers still enjoy a virtually unregulated legal monopoly: there is no *pro se* representation; a lawyer is required in every legal proceeding. Admission to law schools is open to any secondary school graduate. Law is a five to six year undergraduate programme; the curriculum is determined autonomously by each law school (accreditation of law schools started in 2016). There is neither a final university exam nor a Bar exam. There is no mandatory continuing legal education, and lawyer discipline rests with autonomous Bar Associations that are more lawyer unions than regulators.

Lawyers are divided into three categories: government, house counsel, and private practitioners. Although a small minority work for big law firms, most are solo practitioners. They should belong to the Bar Association of the province where they practise. There are 23 provinces and an autonomous city, Buenos Aires, which is also the federal district. Each province is divided in judicial districts, and almost all have a Bar Association. There are

80 public Bar Associations created by law but autonomous from state institutions and funded by member fees. They organise disciplinary procedures, enact a Code of ethics, and provide pro bono assistance for the poor. The only requirement to be a member is to hold a law degree. Officers are elected by the members. Bar Associations have become a sort of union for lawyers, which may be why they are uninterested in creating entry barriers: the more members, the bigger their budget. Their web pages are preoccupied with information on members' benefits, from parking permits to discounts in gyms. By contrast, there is no information on pro bono services and no account of discipline beyond the mandatory publication of the names of lawyers suspended or expelled from practice. This is unsurprising since legal ethics is not taught at law schools. When lawyers become members of a Bar Association, they take an oath to obey a Code about which they know nothing.

It is very difficult to obtain information about the legal profession, which is either not collected or kept secret. The *Reporte sobre la Justicia de las Américas 2006–2007* (CEJA 2006), though dated, is the source most often cited. It states that there are 305.53 lawyers per 100,000 population. If we take the 2010 population of 40,117,096 from the national census,[1] there are 122,491 lawyers in Argentina.

The Public Bar of the City of Buenos Aires is the largest Bar Association. It includes lawyers who work in the private sector and in the federal judiciary, since the federal government is located in the city. It contains 86,432 active members, equally divided between men and women (43,419 and 43,013). 12,994 work in the national government (6.6 per cent of its 196,923 employees; lawyers working in the armed forces are not included).[2] 5,157 lawyers litigate for the administration; most are tax lawyers (44.8 per cent), followed by administrative lawyers (27.9 per cent).

Martindale-Hubbell lists 13 law firms with more than 29 lawyers and five with more than 50.[3] According to Bergoglio (2005), who uses the same source, there were nine firms with more than 50 lawyers in 1999 and 16 Argentine and four foreign firms with more than 50 in 2005.

The legal services market functions as a filter, excluding both frivolous lawsuits and conflicts that should have been addressed elsewhere. Given the fact that many people cannot pay lawyers' fees, sacrifice the time required for a judicial proceeding, or travel for hours to find a lawyer or courtroom, and they do not know their rights or how to defend them, the distribution of legal resources limits access to justice by the disadvantaged.

The professionals who should remedy these deficiencies include public defenders (always inadequately staffed or financed), public prosecutors,[4] and, in the private sector, Bar Associations (which are legally obligated to create legal aid offices but do very little),

---

[1] Instituto Nacional de Estadistica y Censos (INDEC) 2010, accesible at www.indec.gov.ar.
[2] Base Integrada del Empleo Público (BIEP), Secretaria de Empleo Público, Ministerio de Modernización. 2018 (Integrated base of public employment, Secretary of Public Employment, Ministry of Modernisation).
[3] Martindale-Hubbell online at www.martindale.com/.
[4] There were 0.8 prosecutors and 0.6 public defenders per 100,000 population in 2006 (CEJA 2006). The national budget in 2019 allocates Arg$10,684,874,896 (about US$300,000,000) and 5,633 staff members to the federal prosecutor's office and Arg$5,936,457,934 (about US$165,000,000) and 3,266 staff for the federal public defender's office.

lawyers (mandated to perform pro bono services) and law schools (though only a few have legal clinics).

These institutions are clearly insufficient. In the case of the public defenders and prosecutors, the lack of funds, current maps of legal resources (which could rationalise the distribution of legal services), unmet legal needs analyses, and inadequate public policies all leave disadvantaged people without ways of enforcing their constitutional rights. Because Bar Associations perceive pro bono work as unfair competition they evade their legal obligation to provide it. Law schools see their function as purely pedagogical, not as a means of expanding access to justice. Lawyers do not believe that their monopoly obligates them to provide services to those who cannot pay.

II. JUDICIARY

The judiciary is divided into two jurisdictions, federal and provincial, both with trial, intermediate appellate and Supreme Courts. The federal judiciary is a virtual embassy of the federal government in each province. The communicating mechanism between the two jurisdictions is an extraordinary federal appeal, a way to enforce the federal constitution and federal laws, even against the judgments of provincial courts.

Until 1994 the judiciary depended on the political branches for appointments. Federal judges were nominated by the Executive and appointed with the consent of the Senate; provincial judges were nominated by the Governors with the agreement of the provincial legislatures. Until the 1940s the tenure of judges was relatively secure because of their close relationship with the political branches and the deference they showed the latter. After the first Peronist government impeached the Supreme Court judges who had tolerated previous *coups d'état*, each new government, democratic or authoritarian, modified the composition of the Court. At this level, one of the crudest forms of dependence of the judiciary on the Executive was the removal of sitting judges and appointment of new members of the highest courts (federal and provincial).

This did not occur with the same virulence in the lower courts, which function as a 'judicial family'. This is a complex phenomenon interweaving formal rules of conduct, rules of procedure and the allocation of powers with informal rules about how to comply with or evade the formal rules. The beliefs, attitudes and habits of the judicial family derive from the practices of two interconnected careers: judicial and academic. This intertwining starts at the beginning of the legal career. Law students work as law clerks in courts and rise in the judiciary as they progress through law school. The recommendation of law professors makes it easier to obtain positions, not only in courts but also in law firms. Law school faculty recruit students for their firms, and students see faculty as a conduit to professional networks. This is why practising lawyers are eager to teach despite the meager salaries and why students become teaching assistants.

Law lacks a critical perspective because part-time law professors have no incentive to engage in research, identify problems and propose solutions without fear of retaliation. No client hires a lawyer who has criticised the judge; rather, clients want lawyers who can persuade the judge of the rightness of their claim. Practitioners who teach and publish on the subject – or, even better, have taught at judicial training centres or institutions where judges teach as adjuncts – can exploit their proximity to the courts to get clients for their law firms.

The judicial career involves a permanent exchange of favours, which are later translated into privileges, such as the possibility of influencing the appointment of law officers, issuing orders to them, or intervening in cases. These exchanges begin with appointment to the judiciary. Different kinds of skills, knowledge, titles and personal, family or political contacts are required, depending on the position the applicant is seeking. The career starts with a request from a relative or acquaintance or sometimes sponsorship by a law professor. The first step consists of free provision of basic services in the court without a formal appointment. Entry into the formal career requires a permanent position as administrative assistant, the lowest rank. The next step, which necessitates a law degree and appointment by the judge, is a clerkship, a fundamental role given the widespread practice of delegation. A clerk virtually becomes the judge in charge, handling the court's day-to-day business. Judges enjoy many privileges: lifetime tenure, 13 months' pay for ten months' work, and no income tax.

III. POLITICS

Since 1983 every president has been a lawyer except for Puerta (an engineer who held office for just a few hours) and Macri (another engineer). Throughout Argentina's history, 23 of its 38 democratically-elected presidents were law graduates. Lawyers also have been about 30 per cent of Representatives and 40 per cent of Senators. Given the limited ability of political parties to organise and support professional politicians and law makers, lawyers generally keep their law firms open while occupying public positions and return to those firms when they leave office. The capacity of the majoritarian branches to control the judiciary is limited by this conflict of interest. Lawyers cannot be on bad terms with judges. This is not a minor obstacle to judicial reform. The lack of politicians willing and able to advocate for reforms is a well-known cause of their failure.

Judicial power was curtailed by other means. The belief in codification and the Continental tradition justified the rejection of *stare decisis* and trust in the ability of a fragile legal science and ad hoc equity to provide certainty. But the strong ideological consensus among lawyers and judges prevailing when the Codes were enacted in the late nineteenth century gradually succumbed to doctrinal debates, ideological dissent and eventually simple disagreement about the meaning of law, which increased the arbitrariness of the decisions and eroded the capacity of judges to limit the actions of the other branches of government. This situation undermined the prestige of the profession and the legitimacy of the courts.

A. Transition to Democracy and the Reconfiguration of Law

Nobody could have predicted the demise of this political system. The radicalisation of the authoritarian project, its exclusionary character, the concentration of power, and its denial of constitutional rights all culminated in an apotheosis of massive and systematic violations of human rights orchestrated by the state.

Nothing will ever be the same after these events. They required tangible gestures, unprecedented social and political practices that defined what had happened as radically evil, thereby linking Argentina, tragically and irrevocably with the Holocaust. The initial gesture came from civilians, relatives of the first 'disappeared', particularly those who became the Mothers of Plaza de Mayo, who demanded to know the whereabouts of those who had been kidnapped. The *de facto* authorities criminally and persistently denied their existence, leading to the victims being called the 'disappeared'. This was how the dictator Videla cynically defined them: 'The disappeared are just that: disappeared. They are neither alive nor dead. They are disappeared'.

The miracle of the Mothers and the human rights movement in Argentina, their semantic achievement in laying the foundation of what would become Argentine democracy, consisted of transforming that merciless, cynical, criminal definition first into a complaint, then into a lawsuit, next into an international legal claim, and finally into a crime codified in international treaties: the forced disappearance of persons. But more importantly, it redefined political and especially legal practices in Argentina, advancing rights from a marginalised space to a central role, displacing the idea that the common good, unilaterally defined by the State, is superior to all rights.

This hopeful proposal was embraced by politics following President Alfonsín's victory in the first post-military election. His triumph was imbued with a strong feeling of constitutional mysticism. His electoral victory was related to his affirmation that the military dictatorship's self-amnesty had no legal force because it lacked the presumption of legitimacy enjoyed by democratically deliberated decisions. The end of the *de facto* doctrine paved the way for the trials and criminal sentences of those responsible for the human rights violations, marking the beginning of a reconfigured constitutional democracy.

What moral, legal and political resources engendered this response to the military dictatorship? Part of the answer lies in the practice of lawyers who survived the persecution and fled into exile. They were essential to the ability of human rights organisations to raise international awareness about what had been suspected as, and was later confirmed to be, a terrorist and criminal strategy orchestrated by the State. Abroad, these reports had to adopt the language of rights and democracy, a language alien to Argentine political activists and lawyers.

The institutions that heard and understood the demands were those responsible for defending and enforcing international human rights treaties, such as the Office of the UN Under-Secretary for Human Rights and the Inter-American Commission on Human Rights. This set the course of politics and law in Argentina for future decades. Because many of these lawyers were criminal defenders, they characterised rights violations as crimes under national and international law, which called for an accusation, criminal trial and punishment, a translation of the famous demand by human rights organisations for '*juicio y castigo*' (trial and punishment).

The government's answer included not only the criminal prosecutions ordered by President Alfonsín but also the signing of international human rights treaties enlarging the list of rights and the number of fora that could adjudicate them. During the new government's first year, and a few months after the signing of the Pact of San José, Argentina ratified the jurisdiction of the Commission and the Inter-American Court of Human Rights.

Thus, shortly after the restoration of democracy, the main features of the reconfiguration of law in Argentina were already in place: the mobilisation of groups of people united around the violation of their rights, the creation of social organisations to institutionalise their activities, and the articulation of their demands to the authorities. These efforts were directed not only at the legislative and executive branches but also at the judicial system, articulating claims by reference to laws, Codes and the newly acquired language of human rights. In order for this translation to occur, victims had to find lawyers and eventually associations of lawyers. The judiciary responded by accepting the demands and the authority of these rules. Many of their decisions affected public policies, starting an institutional dialogue among those concerned with rights, policies and budgetary decisions. This new social and political practice radically modified the previous understanding of law, including the following features.

(1) Judicialisation of politics: the need to resort to the judiciary to initiate or accelerate the implementation of a public policy adopted by majoritarian institutions or to continue discussion of that policy. In the traditional logic of rights, judicialisation supplements the courts' traditional task of enforcing the law (respecting and enforcing majoritarian decisions) by requiring them to determine the law's constitutionality (decide whether it violates rights or procedures in ways that could erode the legitimacy of the system) without arbitrariness (honouring previous decisions by deciding similar cases in similar ways, thereby increasing predictability).

(2) Politicisation of the judiciary: the acknowledgment that in making decisions (within the aforementioned limits) the judiciary must adjudicate complex, often deliberately ambiguous, texts, which becomes an essential part of its role in a constitutional democracy. Admitting this engenders arguments about the appointment, tenure and removal of judges, especially the role of the legal profession (including Bar Associations and law schools) and the balance of power between the profession and the Executive and Legislative branches.

(3) Constitutionalisation: scepticism about the constitutionality of decisions by majoritarian institutions expands the scope of judicial review and the jurisdiction of lawyers in politics. Issues that formerly had been finally decided by the Executive (justified by the presumption of legitimacy of administrative acts) or Legislature (because of the horizontal deference owed by judges) now proceed to the courts through the invocation of constitutional texts.

(4) Fragmentation: the creation of relatively autonomous systems of rules about diverse topics (such as environmental torts, consumer rights, or domestic violence), which sometimes contradict each other and the principles embodied in the Codes. Fragmentation refers to the erosion of unity in the law, perceived as a coherent system of rules that could consistently resolve matters like liability, causation and damages, determination of the aggrieved party, legal standing or capacity to contract.

(5) De-codification: constitutionalisation and fragmentation decentred the Codes, reducing them to just one source of law among others. The Codes had articulated a monotheistic practice, which now has become polytheistic in the sense that multiple sources of law compete for authority: the Constitution, international treaties, domestic laws, domestic, foreign, regional or international judicial decisions, commercial or political customs, economic efficiency, and academic opinions. Each bases its legitimacy on public deliberation and votes, sometimes invoking the counter-majoritarian logic of rights, sometimes asserting the need to maintain legal consistency over time.

(6) Globalisation: the growing importance of the complex process of rule creation and enforcement outside national borders by foreign or national actors, with consequences within the nation state. This phenomenon limits the regulatory capacity of the traditional democratic institutions by allowing deliberation to extend outside national boundaries. Globalisation multiplies the arenas for politics and therefore the loci within which legal professionals may act.

This reconfiguration of politics and law has influenced how lawyers can practise their profession. In addition to serving traditional individual clients, lawyers are now approached by collective actors such as civil society organisations, the office of the Ombudsperson or international organisations (and public interest lawyers can proactively engage these entities). Many of these organisations have legal standing to initiate collective litigation, challenging public policies or private practices that violate collective rights. The success of human rights organisations during the democratic transition offered an example to the rest of society. An unprecedented number of groups followed that path, creating civic associations with an explicit mandate to use litigation to advocate for their rights or the cause they represent. These include women, sexual orientation, people with disabilities, indigenous peoples, the environment, reproductive rights, consumers, and health.

This proliferation of actors was accompanied by the multiplication of procedures allowing public actors to participate in litigation. In 1957 the Supreme Court had created an accelerated procedure for individuals to defend their constitutional rights (the *amparo*). This became part of the Constitution in the 1994, which also authorised standing for collectivities and NGOs and the collective *amparo*. These produced judicial decisions that challenged public policies and structural violations of constitutional rights.

Another key feature was the ratification of international human rights treaties, especially the dramatic constitutional gesture of incorporating a dozen in the 1994 Constitution. These also increased the range of institutions able to enforce such rights, including international courts, commissions, and committees.

The transition to new modes of legal practice is highlighted by the emergence of public interest law. It is interesting to track the origin of these movements. Having secured the prosecution of those responsible for crimes against humanity, human rights organisations sought to expand their agendas (partly in response to shifts in international sources of financial support). A new generation of civil society leaders used what had been built in the previous decade to defend other rights, including social, economic and cultural rights, which required new strategies.

The privatisation of public services in the 1990s was one stimulus for this change. It prompted the emergence of new social actors and opportunities for public deliberation about public policies, challenging a tradition of state privilege and an administrative law dismissive of citizens' rights. The deregulation and privatisation of public services and the creation of public goods compelled the state to find new ways of controlling the now private suppliers. This led to the emergence of new regulatory agencies, as well as consumers' associations, which deployed the new tools of public interest litigation.

Traditional human rights organisations like the Centre for Legal and Social Studies (*Centro de Estudios Legales y Sociales*) litigated cases for the recognition of prisoners' rights, health access and social inclusion. The Public Interest Law Clinic of the University of Palermo Law School represented indigenous communities in cases involving land and bilingual education, LGBTQ people in cases of discrimination, consumers, persons with disabilities, and women, among others. The Civil Association for Equality and Justice (*Asociación Civil por la Igualdad y la Justicia*) dedicates most of its efforts to using collective litigation and negotiation in pursuit of equality of access to public utilities for disadvantaged communities. The Association for Civil Rights (*Asociación por los Derechos Civiles*) has litigated issues of transparency and citizen participation.

These practices transcend national borders. The inclusion of human rights treaties in the Constitution and the many other bilateral and multilateral agreements in the areas of international trade and foreign investment protection coincided with the globalisation of many public policy issues that had been regulated only by sovereign nations. These treaties and agreements not only defined rights and obligations but also regulated the procedures for interpreting them, generating new global actors charged with adjudicating the language of the agreements and empowered to enforce their decisions. Examples include the Inter-American Human Rights System, the dispute resolution system of the World Bank, the arbitration system of the International Center for the Settlement of Investments Disputes, and the dispute settlement procedure in the World Trade Organisation; Argentine lawyers have become frequent actors in all of them.

Although globalisation expands the opportunities for political deliberation and places the administration of justice in a new context, three deficits traditionally attributed to the judiciary are even more acute in the global arena: democratic, semantic, and implementation. Some systems have multiplied deliberative opportunities to mitigate the democratic deficit, such as *amici curiae*, oral proceedings, and expert witnesses. The semantic deficit calls on courts to speak with a clear voice and maintain the stability of their decisions. Some courts make an effort to publish and explain their decisions, even offering courses to teach the decisions to practitioners. Finally, some see the enforcement deficit not as a problem but as an opportunity. The need to follow convoluted procedures to enforce a global decision within a domestic jurisdiction is generally regarded as a deficit, a means by which national states evade global decisions. But if these obstacles were regarded as opportunities, then the enforcement efforts of skilful lawyers could strengthen democracy by expanding opportunities for inclusive deliberation, discussing the place of rights in a plural society, multiplying public goods, and increasing the legitimacy of the authority. This opportunity is twofold: for global actors to strengthen their legitimacy and effectiveness, and for States to use the decisions of global actors as levers to compel further deliberation.

The successful implementation of the decisions of these actors depends on their clarity, consistency, permanence, sensitivity to the necessary pace of the proposed changes (not imposing counter-majoritarian decisions abruptly in an elitist way or letting rights violations continue indefinitely), knowledge of the context in which the decision must be implemented, and perception of the consequences of the decision for those affected. The many challenges of globalisation are complicated by a national tradition hostile to participation, deliberation and the defence of human rights. Argentines have had to become globalised in order to secure from external institutions what domestic majoritarian politics and legal decisions denied them for decades. However, which national actors can rise to these challenges?

This question forces us to re-examine the pre-democratic legal culture described above. It takes longer to instil new legal habits, skills, beliefs, attitudes, and modes of reasoning than it does to reform the legal texts that embody the agreements to embrace these new practices. The imbalance this transition produces emerges in the recurrent criticisms of the judiciary for its lack of independence and failure to gain citizen trust, and of the legal profession for failing to perform its legal duties to ensure equal access to justice and behave ethically.

B. Legal Profession

Critics of the legal profession invoke its three obligations in a constitutional democracy. The first is efficacy: solving conflicts in order to avoid violence and enforcing democratic decisions within the limits of the Constitution in order to create a legal practice people can rely on to freely plan their lives.

The legal process was seen as the primary obstacle to efficacy. A written, inquisitorial system was blamed for the impossible caseloads, long delays in judicial decisions, and absence of judges at key moments (examination of witnesses, interrogation of experts, gathering of documents). Since the transition to democracy, therefore, there have been persistent calls for an oral, adversarial process and even a jury trial. Codes of procedure have been reformed (mainly in criminal cases and gradually in the different provinces), and many jurisdictions are starting to create the necessary infrastructure. Courtrooms, jury boxes, new software, and scientific laboratories are being built, connected, and tested. Nevertheless, the legal training of lawyers and judges remains unchanged.

There are 70 law schools: 29 public and 41 private. There were 209,959 law students in 2004 and 213,915 in 2014. Law schools collectively had an incoming class of 46,699 students in 2004 and 47,043 in 2014 and graduated 12,120 lawyers in 2004 and 16,895 in 2014.[5] The largest law schools are the national ones: Buenos Aires, La Plata, Rosario, Córdoba, Tucumán, Litoral and Cuyo enroll a third of all law students. A few small private law schools are implementing different teaching strategies and hiring full-time professors.

Law schools in Argentina have just started a process of evaluation and accreditation, which had been promised in 1995. Many have changed their curricula, incorporating new courses, such as legal writing, legal research, evidence, legal ethics, negotiation and mediation, lawyering skills, moot courts, legal reasoning and sentencing, and clinical legal education. They are involved in a complex struggle to reduce or modify the usual black letter, codified courses to make room for a more skills-oriented, critical legal training.

There are many obstacles. The undergraduate course must educate teenagers with serious learning deficiencies. It is difficult to provide adequate training because there are no admission requirements (beyond a secondary school diploma) and no fee for public law schools, the largest of which (University of Buenos Aires) has 20,000 students. Graduation rates are very low: about 30 per cent. A majority of law students work, as do most of their professors: lawyers and judges who teach in their spare time for very low salaries. There is no tradition of legal research and no highly respected law review.

---

[5] Source: Secretary of University Policies, National Ministry of Education.

It is not clear who will teach the new courses, where they will be trained, whether law schools will find the resources to hire full-time faculty, or how the part-time faculty will react to a possible loss of prestige and power. In recent decades many lawyers earned LLMs and JSDs from prestigious foreign institutions, but they may be reluctant to dedicate themselves to teaching. The demand for legal educators is increasing exponentially, not only as law schools seek to reform but also from the proliferation of graduate courses and programmes to train lawyers and judges in the new professional skills in institutions other than law schools.

The second obligation of a monopolistic legal profession in a constitutional democracy is to provide access to justice for all. The lack of alternative systems of conflict resolution leads those with know-how and resources to assert their rights in court. But the entry barriers to the legal system are extremely high for most people. The few empirical studies find that two out of five people report unmet legal need, a third of the population had at least one legal problem in the last three years, and more than half of respondents admitted not having enough expertise to solve legal problems on their own. The level of unmet legal need increases with poverty, disability or social disadvantage (such as indigenous people).

Paradoxically, Argentina has ample resources to supply justice for the most disadvantaged. There are more than 100,000 lawyers registered in the country and more than 200,000 law students. The former have a legal obligation to provide services to those who need them, regardless of their ability to pay; and the latter need internships and clinics to be properly trained. There are public defenders and prosecutors paid by the government, private organisations that offer free legal aid, and community leaders eager to acquire the knowledge and skills to be part of an equal and effective system of access to justice. In this process of transition the pressure on law schools to provide clinical legal education, on the state to provide clearinghouses, and on public defenders and prosecutors to decentralise their offices is gradually having results.

The third obligation of the legal system in a constitutional democracy is the creation and protection of the rule of law. Lawyers must not take decisions that may destroy the tools democracy gives them to practise their profession. Lawyers must help judges balance their three main obligations: respect for majoritarian decisions, defence of constitutional rights and procedures, and preservation and improvement of the language of the law. This is why the double monopoly of lawyers – over access to and the production of justice – is justified only when it is exercised in the defence of the client and offered equally to all but without destroying the delicate balance between those obligations and respect for the rule of law. Lawyers violate that mandate when they defend the private interests of their clients at the expense of the public interest.

An obvious example is corruption. There is a pervasive public belief that judges and lawyers collude in corrupt activities, for instance the payment of bribes to affect the outcome of a case, accelerate a procedure, influence the selection of a friendly official in a bankruptcy case, or ensure that the case finds its way to the desk of the 'appropriate' judge.

There are also flagrant conflicts of interest, for instance when a lawyer serves on the examination board of judges in the Council of Magistrates or holds a chair or teaches in a law school where the judge is a colleague.

The lack of social distance between lawyers or judges and law professors, and the consequent absence of a body of independent legal scholarship capable of offering critical perspectives on legal practice without fear of professional retaliation, open the door to the emergence of an 'academic lobby', which produces legal scholarship to disguise as scientific what actually is an argument on behalf of a case or a client.

C. Judiciary

The diverse political groups that engaged in the constitutional reform of 1994 had no alternative but to reach a difficult consensus with results that were sometimes contradictory, one of which is the creation of a Council of Magistrates (CM) in the Continental European tradition. Since the CM's inception, the Federal judiciary has become a two-headed beast, with the National Supreme Court of Justice (CSJN) as the jurisdictional head and the CM in charge of administration, including the selection and removal of judges and district attorneys from within its ranks. Even though CSJN members are exempt from these procedures and the CM proposes a shortlist of three candidates, from which the President chooses (with the Senate's consent), the CM's powers to decide budgetary issues, make appointments, and discipline judges and district attorneys suffice to make it a central political actor.

However, the CM has its roots in Europe, where ordinary judges do not exercise judicial review, which is entrusted exclusively to a political body, a Constitutional Court, because of the belief that the judge's functions are strictly technical. In Europe, therefore, the CM ensures that judges possess the necessary technical ability through an open public examination, similar to that taken by all other state officials.

In Argentina, by contrast, every judge can exercise judicial review. Thus, the necessary knowledge and skills are fundamentally different from those required in Continental systems. In the constitutional reform of 1994, the political role of the judiciary was hotly debated. The main argument for the inclusion of the CM in the Constitution was that technically qualified judges would be less dependent on political power, less corruptible, and therefore more reliable. The Constitution states that the CM should include representatives of the political branches, the judiciary, lawyers and the scientific community.

It is important to emphasise the problem of judicial corporatism because it is related to the serious conflict of interest discussed above. Most (if not all) CM members are lawyers and judges. Lawyers argue in front of judges who, in turn, handle cases that affect the interests of the political branches (public budgets, public policies, the government's financial capacity or, more bluntly, individual criminal cases involving the political class). Since legal scholarship is not a full-time occupation in Argentina, the lawyers who produce it experience the same conflicts as their colleagues. The fact that the CM decides on the appointment, promotion, discipline, and removal of judges should be a source of institutional concern. The training and evaluation of judicial candidates (some of whom already sit as judges) is conducted not by professional academics devoted to full-time teaching but by judges, lawyers and prosecutors. CM lawyers can teach and evaluate judges before whom they litigate, a clear conflict of interest raising suspicions about the transparency and legitimacy of the selection process.

D. Politics

The transition to a constitutional democracy affected the role of the courts, especially the Supreme Court. From a position of deference to the political branches, the Court tried to find a new place in the separation of powers. Changes in the Court's size and composition modified the conception of its role several times. The first Court regarded itself as active and liberal. It showed its willingness to hear constitutional challenges to statutes and responded with historical decisions that changed well-established rules dealing with divorce, recreational drug use, and the military draft. Finding itself in the midst of an economic emergency, the second Court deferred to the authority of the President and overruled some of its predecessor's decisions. Nevertheless, it sat during the transition to the newly reformed Constitution and was very sympathetic to the globalisation of Argentine law, thereby restraining itself and deferring to international legal authorities. In 2003 another economic crisis again changed the composition of the Court, which adopted a third strategy: oral hearings, *amicus curiae* and dialogic decisions. Seeking neither to impose its own will nor to submit to that of the other branches, it offered them time to reconsider legislation that seemed constitutionally dubious, asked them for more information, or exhorted them to move in a particular direction.

Lawyers were centrally involved in all three phases. They gave the Court the opportunity to try out its changing roles; they challenged the Court's decisions abroad, returning with resolutions from international bodies, which they tried to enforce domestically; they organised civil society and incorporated the associations so they had standing in court; they framed their own interests in the language of constitutional democracy; they spoke in hearings; they amended laws; they challenged the formalist legal culture; and they reconfigured Argentina's legal practice. The impact of this legal revolution requires ongoing institutional reforms and the articulation of this new practice in lawyers' habits, skills and common understanding. The scale of the challenge can only be compared to the creation of the Argentine nation state a century and a half ago.

REFERENCES

Bergoglio, MI (2005) 'Cambios en la profesión jurídica en América Latina' 5(10) *Revista sobre Enseñanza del Derecho* 9.

Centro de Estudios de Justicia de las Américas (CEJA) (2006) *Reporte sobre la Justicia de las Américas 2006–2007* (Santiago, CEJA).

19

Brazil

Fragmentary Development, Democratisation, and Globalisation

MARIA DA GLORIA BONELLI AND PEDRO FORTES

I. INTRODUCTION

THE PURPOSE OF this chapter is to conduct a dialogue with research completed 30 years ago (Falcão 1988). Most Brazilians then had no access to justice because they lacked the resources to hire a lawyer. Courts monopolised dispute resolution, and lawyers monopolised legal representation. The legal profession was not the exclusive occupation of many lawyers. Public prosecutors could advocate on behalf of private interests. Today, after three decades of democratic government, access to justice is provided through the Office of Public Defender (OPD) and the expansion of small claims courts. Litigation is not the only way to resolve conflicts, especially because of the growth of alternative dispute resolution (ADR). Yet better access to justice did not eliminate pervasive inequalities; and, ironically, corporations now often prefer arbitration to courts, seeking a dispute resolution process that reproduces social inequalities in new ways. The expansion of legal services and the demands of mass justice also further professionalised Brazilian lawyers. This chapter explains the transformations of the legal profession since 1988.

The twenty-first century has seen the proliferation of private legal counselling, the growth and institutionalisation of public legal careers, and the expansion of international networks. Hybrid professionalism, combining the world view of big business, bureaucratic hierarchies, and a more diverse legal profession, is another important dimension. The legal profession has been transformed by political democratisation, economic development, and the globalisation of law. Between 1988 and 2017, lawyering became more accessible, professionalised, and international. The demography of the profession changed significantly with the growing numbers of minority lawyers. Yet social hierarchies continue to shape the legal market, lawyers' reputations, and access to justice. However, contemporary lawyering does not correspond to the class analysis that dominated the literature in the 1980s: a legal profession divided into two hemispheres of lawyers serving either corporations or individual clients (Heinz and Laumann 1982) and a legal clientele similarly divided into elites and the poor (Falcão 1988).

Instead, the hierarchical structure of the legal profession and its clientele is complex, multidimensional, and diversified, not just the result of a 'professional project' (Abel and Lewis 1988a) or state project (Falcão 1988). Multiple institutional actors influence the job market, supply and demand for legal services, and professional positions of lawyers, judges, prosecutors, public defenders, police chiefs, and law professors. Control of the legal profession is not concentrated in the hands of the state or the Brazilian Bar Association (*Ordem dos Advogados Brasileiros*, OAB) but rather fragmented among relevant stakeholders representing competing professional groups. The OAB Bar examination, for instance, is regularly modified in response to political pressures, judicial challenges, and legislative proposals. Professional associations of judges, prosecutors, public defenders, and lawyers are constantly promoting their collective interests and adopting strategic behaviour to influence public policy.

Although the OAB seeks to influence professional development, it does not control the market for legal services. The Brazilian State also shapes lawyering by establishing the OPD and enacting legislation. True, Brazil is unique among Latin American jurisdictions in requiring a special professional exam for aspiring lawyers (Gómez and Pérez-Perdomo 2018). However, other forces affect the market for legal services. Universities, corporations, and law firms also shape the legal profession. The OAB did not restrict its project to promoting lawyers' market interests but also contributed to state construction and civic professionalism (Halliday and Karpik 1997). The pendulum of professional legitimacy is not fixed, but oscillates in response to civic and corporate disputes, the challenges of inclusion and inequality, and the fragmentation caused by professional diversification and the emergence of new legal elites.

This chapter is based on research conducted by socio-legal scholars, a richer and more relevant literature than the few publications available in the 1980s. We also collected our own data, especially on legal academics and students.[1] We pose two main questions: what have been the principal transformations in the legal profession since 1988? And how have democratisation, economic development, and globalisation reshaped legal education, public careers, and private practice?

II. HISTORICAL TRANSFORMATIONS: DEMOCRATISATION, DEVELOPMENT, AND GLOBALISATION

The 1988 Constitution and 1989 direct elections institutionalised democracy after 21 years of a military regime (1964–85) and a civilian government elected indirectly by Congress (1985–89). Falcão (1988) reviewed the professional situation of lawyers in private practice and the public sector, as well as legal education, focusing not only on the labour market but also on political-juridical activities. The dominant professional ideology of political liberalism did not prevent lawyers from formulating legal strategies to support authoritarian regimes. According to Falcão, legal professions in the 1980s were embedded in a dual social reality, divided between those who could hire lawyers

---

[1] Research made with support from FAPESP (Grant no 2016/08850-1) and CNPQ (Grant no 443416/2015-0). This chapter was completed on 7 February 2018.

and solve their conflicts with the assistance of experts and those whose disputes were decided outside the formal legal system according to unofficial 'laws' applied by informal 'courts' located on the margins of society.

In this binary conception, legal professionals were defined by their positions in the market and state (whether their practices consisted of technical services or legal-political activity) and their clients' locations in a dual society divided by more or less access to justice. We argue that this duality has imploded because of the fragmentation of practices, discourses, organisational forms and professional identities, hybridising local differentiations, homogenising globalisation of legal business, and encouraging international circulation in the legal professions. Professions once seen as producing fixed, unified, and cohesive ideals, possessing a singular identity, are now viewed as competing with other identifications, changeable, fragmentary, and shaped by difference. Brazil has experienced powerful processes of social inclusion, economic growth, and institutional development since 1988. As part of the project for socio-economic development and democratisation of opportunity, the country witnessed the expansion of university education, nearly tripling the proportion of 18–24-year-olds enrolled, from 7 to 19 per cent between 1995 and 2009 (Andrade 2012). Ironically, most students in the prestigious free public universities came from upper middle class families because their private secondary schools prepared them better for the competitive university entrance examination. Therefore, ever since the pioneering initiative of the State Universities of Rio de Janeiro and Bahia in 2002 and the Federal University of Brasília in 2004 public universities have gradually adopted affirmative action policies to increase the number of students from racial minorities and poor families. Since the passage of the Quotas Act (2012), federal universities have been legally obligated to reserve half their places for students educated in public secondary schools and from racial minorities. These policies transformed access to education and promoted the incorporation of a significant number of poor black students into the workforce.

The deregulation of higher education by the Guidelines for Education Act (1996) facilitated the expansion of private legal education. With investments from private entrepreneurs and support from the government and international investors, the number of law schools grew exponentially, from 130 in 1980 to 1,171 in 2015. The increase was especially rapid in the most recent decade because of the governmental agenda, the opening of education to foreign investors, and initial public offerings of shares of higher education companies in the stock market. Consequently, the number of lawyers accredited by OAB quintupled between 1980 and 2017, exceeding one million in 2016. The substantial presence of women in the legal profession (now 47.7 per cent) also explains this extraordinary growth.

Another factor was the globalisation of law and the growing presence of international law firms in São Paulo and Rio de Janeiro. Attracted by economic growth and the development of new legal fields, foreign law firms established partnerships with Brazilian counterparts. However, a dispute between traditional legal elites and the new business legal elites resulted in the OAB's decision to restrict the activity of foreign lawyers to consulting on foreign law and to prohibit partnerships between Brazilian and international law firms (Almeida and Nassar 2018). The OAB sought to reserve the legal market for Brazilian law firms, which may only collaborate with international law firms on specific matters. However, globalisation continues to transform the legal profession

A. The Professional Limbo of Bachelors of Law: Unlicensed Law Graduates

OAB estimates that 30 per cent of lawyers do not practise law. Even if this is correct, there are 700,000 active lawyers. Economic growth and institutional development explain the expansion of the market for legal services. With the establishment of a liberal democracy, Brazil passed legislation to reorganise the political regime, regulate the economy, promote sustainable development, and protect individual and social rights. With these new rules of the game, there was a growing demand for lawyers to defend not only the interests of business and government but also those of workers, consumers, and society generally. Law became the most attractive undergraduate course: because of this perception of job opportunities, about 10 per cent of university students study law, and approximately 100,000 students receive their LLBs every year.[2]

In this context, OAB revived its effort to control the professional market by making the Bar exam mandatory in 1994, thereby responding to the proliferation of law schools by denying access to law practice for a significant fraction of graduates. Unable to overcome the strength of interest groups and private entrepreneurs organised around higher education, OAB blocked the access of those with less power – failed LLBs – who were portrayed as incompetent and devoid of the value conferred by the social magic of merit (Sommerlad 2015). These failed LLBs fell into a professional limbo, where professional opportunities were limited to working as cheaper assistants to qualified lawyers. There may be millions of LLBs who cannot practise law because they failed the Bar exam. Some of them formed the National Association of Bachelors of Laws (NABL), whose mission is to raze the entry barriers erected by the OAB. This controversy reached the Brazilian Supreme Court when some LLBs claimed that the Bar examination violated their constitutional rights, especially the free exercise of a profession, equal protection, and the principle of human dignity. A unanimous court rejected their claim in 2011, upholding the authority of OAB to assess lawyers' professional credentials on behalf of society's collective interests.[3]

In response to criticism of the Bar exam, the House of Representatives considered legislative project 5749/2013[4] on the regulation of the paralegal profession. This would allow a paralegal to work for three years as a lawyer's assistant but not act as a lawyer or represent a party in a judicial proceeding. Paralegals who did not pass the Bar exam during this period would revert to being mere LLBs. Although approved by the Committee on the Constitution and Justice, this project did not succeed. OAB organised resistance, arguing there was no need to produce unqualified professionals who would be unmotivated to study and pass the Bar exam. And in 2016 the Institute of Brazilian Lawyers (IAB) approved four motions opposing the creation of a paralegal profession.[5]

---

[2] See jota.info/carreira/brasil-o-pais-dos-bachareis-um-em-cada-dez-universitarios-estuda-direito-18102016.
[3] *João Antônio Volante v OAB and Federal Union* (Extraordinary Appeal no 603.583, Rapporteur Justice Marco Aurélio, decided 26 October 2011).
[4] Available at www.camara.gov.br/proposicoesWeb/fichadetramitacao?idProposicao=580518.
[5] Available at www.iabnacional.org.br/noticias/quatro-pareceres-contrarios-a-criacao-do-paralegal.

That year, however, the Brazilian Institute for Research and Education of Paralegals (Inbrapa) was established in São Paulo to lobby for the legislation.[6]

III. LEGAL EDUCATION: EXPANSION, PROFESSIONALISATION, AND INTERNATIONALISATION

Legal education has also been transformed in the last 30 years. The traditional public university law faculties now face competition from a few small private law schools, which invested significantly in empirical research, participatory pedagogy, and international partnerships (Vieira et al 2014; Falcão 2014). Global law schools developed special programmes oriented to business, international legal practice and promotion of the democratic rule of law (Alviar 2014). However, these law schools have little capacity to transform Brazilian legal education because they are very expensive and not easily replicated (Trubek 2012). Yet their relative success encouraged traditional faculties to innovate as well, especially through international exchange programmes and empirical research (Cunha and Ghirardi 2018; Fortes 2019). By contrast, most private law schools provide low-cost standardised courses offering basic legal training to tens of thousands of students from lower-middle class and poor backgrounds. Most law schools provide basic courses of study, focused primarily on domestic law (Cunha and Ghirardi 2018). For most law students, therefore, legal education remains largely generalist, doctrinal, and formalist – incapable of providing the legal knowledge needed by privately practising lawyers and in-house counsel, some of whom pursue further professional training through post-graduate study abroad (Oliveira and Ramos 2018). Yet the trend toward multidisciplinary and international legal education is found not only at elite law schools but also elsewhere in response to globalisation, democratisation and market competition (Gómez and Pérez-Perdomo 2018a). Similarly, empirical legal research expanded in legal academia after 2008, changing the environment at many law schools (Fortes 2017a). However, these innovations remain marginal and are not always valued by students, most of whom are more concerned about learning the traditional subjects tested by the OAB exam.

A. Quality of Legal Education and Regulatory Efforts of OAB

Between 2010 and 2015, 639,000 people took the OAB examination, 56 per cent of whom passed (40 per cent on their first attempt, 75 per cent after two or three) (FGV Projetos 2016). In 2012–15, pass rates varied by law school attended: 40 per cent for graduates of public schools compared with 18 per cent for those from private schools (but because 93 per cent of those taking the exam were from private schools, they accounted for 86 per cent of those passing). However, 19 of the 20 law schools with the highest pass rates were public (FGV Projetos 2016). A survey of 5,541 candidates qualified for the second phase of the 2015 examination found that 52 per cent were women, 64 per cent white, 56 per cent had attended public secondary schools, 42 per cent were 20–25 years

---

[6] Available at www.inbrapa.com.br/.

old, 29 per cent of their parents had received higher education, 64 per cent took a preparatory course for the examination, and 41 per cent wanted to take the entrance exams for a public legal career (FGV Projetos 2016). These data showed the difference in the quality of education offered by public and private schools and the need of most candidates to take preparatory courses for the bar examination.

Concerns about the quality of legal education grew with the proliferation of institutions. Since the mid-1990s, changes in the regulatory framework for higher education led the Ministry of Education (MEC) to produce criteria for evaluating and accrediting courses and institutions. OAB collaborated with MEC to influence its decisions, opining on the programme of study, the evaluation of legal education, and creation and supervision of courses. Since 2001, OAB has developed its own evaluation of law schools, annually publishing a list of recommended schools. This effort to certify the quality of legal education through an 'OAB recommendation stamp' exerts pressure on MEC and supports its policy of restraining the multiplication of law schools. OAB recommended 52 courses its first year (2001) and 146 (11.3 per cent of those offered) in 2016.[7]

Table 1 Percentage Distribution of Law Student Entrants in 2015 by Race, Gender, Law School Attended and Financing, and Secondary School

	Race			Gender	
	White/Asian	Black/Brown/Indigenous	NA	Women	Men
Law School					
Public	8	8	8	8	9
Private non-profit	55	41	36	46	44
Private for profit	37	51	56	46	47
Law school financing					
None	57	50	49	52	53
Some	43	50	51	48	47
Secondary school					
Private	43	33	42	40	40
Public	57	67	58	60	60
Number	84,489	60,739	65,354	116,487	94,095

Source: Bonelli (2107), based on data from the Higher Education Census (INEP 2015).

In spite of OAB's efforts to guide students and warn them about the low quality of education in most Brazilian law schools, most candidates simply look for schools that will accept them, as revealed by data from the Census of Higher Education (INEP). The 2015 census gathered information from 1,107,405 law students: 67 per cent were active students, 10 per cent concluded their courses, and 23 per cent interrupted their studies. Of the 210,582 entering students in 2015, 60 per cent had attended public secondary school and 55.3 per cent were women. Whites and Asians were 41 per cent of women and 39 per cent

[7] OAB's examination in numbers, V. III, April 2016, p 41.

of men, while black and indigenous students were 30 per cent of men and 28 per cent of women (there was no information on race for 31 per cent of this population). Even if comprehensive empirical research on the impact of affirmative action programmes on Brazilian legal education still needs to be done, racial minorities have much more access to legal education than they did in 1988.

Table 2 LLB Degrees and Legal Professionals, by Year, Gender, and Race

	Year	Men (%)	White (%)	Number
Bachelor in Law	2010	53.9	79.7	1,300,000
Lawyers	2016	52.8	–	956,740
Legal academics	2014	60.0	77	32,249
Judges	2013	64.1	82.8	16,812
Public prosecutors	2014	–	–	12,676
Public lawyers	2016	58.1	–	5,703
Public defenders	2015	52.5	74.5	6,052
Federal police officers	2014	85.0	–	1,690
Civil police officers	2013	75.0	–	11,479

Source: Bonelli (2017).

46.3 per cent of students were enrolled in private for-profit institutions, 45.3 per cent in private non-profit institutions, and 8.4 per cent in public and free private institutions. The number of black and indigenous students has gradually increased, mainly in private for-profit institutions (see Table 1). Nearly two-thirds of students attend law school mainly at night, with no difference by race. Women are a smaller proportion of evening students. The national programmes that reserve places for minorities, students with disabilities, graduates of public secondary schools, and those from poor families enrolled less than 2 per cent of all students in 2015. That year 45 per cent of students took out loans, mostly from the government, mediated by MEC. In contrast to 1988, social inclusion policies implemented through quotas and public funding enhanced access to legal education by poor students and racial minorities.

B. Professionalisation of Legal Academia: Full-Time Law Professors

The expansion of legal education and the growth of post-graduate programmes increased the proportion of those teaching full time. In 2013, there were 54 masters and 30 doctoral programmes. In 2016, there were 103 and 34, employing 1,774 professors and (in 2017) enrolling 6,954 and 2,644 students.[8] Because these programmes are geographically concentrated and recruit their own graduates as faculty, their influence is limited (Varela 2016).[9]

---

[8] Data from students obtained from a consultation with the Sucupira Platform, Capes at sucupira.capes.gov.br/sucupira/public/consultas/coleta/discente/listaDiscente.jsf.

[9] See www.rdb.org.br/ojs/index.php/rdb/article/view/213.

Table 3 Percent Distribution of Legal Academics by Employment Status, Law Degree, Law School, Gender and Race (2015)

	Women	Men	White/Asian	Black/brown/Indigenous	NA
Employment status					
Hourly wage	23	28	28	26	21
Part Time	38	38	39	41	34
Full time	30	27	28	28	30
Full Time Exclusive Dedication	9	7	5	5	15
Degree					
Doctorate	30	27	28	24	32
Specialist	22	27	25	31	22
LLB	0	1	0	1	2
LLM	48	45	47	44	44
Law School					
Private	84	82	88	86	70
Public	16	18	12	14	30
Number	12,918	19,331	18,342	5,393	8,514

Source: Bonelli (2017), based on data from the Higher Education Census (INEP 2015).

Of the 32,249 legal academics recorded by the 2015 Census of Higher Education, 60 per cent were men. Of the 73 per cent who reported race, 57 per cent were white or Asian (see Table 3). Although doctorates are becoming more common, only 27 per cent of men and 30 per cent of women had one (more in public universities). In the previous five years, the percentage teaching full-time increased, but a significant number still work part-time.

Table 4 Percentage Distribution of Legal Academics and Entering Students by Gender and Race (2015)

Gender and race	Faculty	Students
Women (White/Asian)	23	23
Men (White/Asian)	34	17
Women (Black/brown/indigenous)	6	15
Men (Black/brown/indigenous)	10	14
Women (no information)	11	17
Men (no information)	16	14

Source: Bonelli (2107), based on data from the Higher Education Census (INEO 2015).

The expansion of post-graduate programmes could become an important mechanism for social inclusion in academic leadership of minority groups and the lower middle class.

But legal academics from the private sector complain they lack opportunities to pursue doctorates. Post-graduate programmes are expensive (given law professors' salaries at private schools), and entrance examinations seems to favour applicants who studied in public universities and belong to their relatively closed academic social networks.

IV. THE PUBLIC CAREERS OF LEGAL PROFESSIONALS

In the past 30 years, the public careers of legal professionals have changed significantly. In the 1980s, judges were predominantly male and had a monopoly on dispute settlement but faced the challenge of deciding cases under laws enacted by a military dictatorship (Falcão 1988). Now there are more women, including the President of the Brazilian Supreme Court and the Chief Prosecutor of the Federal Attorney General's Office (AGO). Courts no longer monopolise dispute settlement because of laws regulating arbitration in 1996 and the growth of ADR mechanisms.

A. The Judiciary: National Council of Justice and Judicial Careers

Public legal careers have also multiplied and diversified, becoming an attractive career for lawyers. The roles of judges, prosecutors and public defenders have grown more demanding and complex. Because of the expansion of access to justice, courts receive tens of millions of new cases every year. In 2005, the creation of the National Council of Justice (CNJ) transformed discipline and promoted transparency within the judiciary. Each Brazilian judge must decide thousands of cases annually, and the CNJ constantly evaluates judicial efficiency (Fortes 2015). Judges must work collaboratively with a team of clerks and assistants, develop case management techniques, and embrace more flexible routines. Courts have gradually adopted e-processes, expediting the disposition of cases. Experiences with small claims courts and class actions have influenced judicial culture and discussions about the challenges of mass produced justice. The legal discourse also changed, incorporating concerns about the social, economic, and political impact of the law. More judges are looking beyond the text of the black letter law, employing an interdisciplinary approach to understand the living character of the law.

The judiciary nearly tripled in size between 1983 and 2013, from 6,057 magistrates to 16,812. There are more women and racial minorities on the bench. But though the proportion of new judges who were black or mixed race increased from 15.5 to 19.1 per cent between 2002–11 and 2012–13, the proportion of women fell from 38.9 to 35.9 per cent. Multiple studies confirm the persistent glass ceiling in judicial careers, especially in state courts that managed to structure their hierarchy before women entered. Therefore, in addition to the smaller number of women in most of these professional groups, the pipeline problem concentrates men at the top (Junqueira 1998; Sadek 2006; Barbalho 2008; Bonelli 2013; Marques 2014; Campos 2015). A recent study concluded that the increasing number of female judges in administrative positions has not made it more egalitarian since it remains controlled by a 'gender system' dominated by a male paradigm to which women must conform in order to demonstrate their competence (Fragale et al 2015).

B. Defence of Society and the Poor: New Roles for Prosecutors and Public Defenders

Professionalisation has also transformed the AGO and OPD. The democratic regime institutionalised lawyers' careers within those institutions and enhanced their autonomy. Public prosecutors lobbied for significant changes in the AGO's structure. Since adoption of the Constitution, prosecutors have become advocates for society rather than defenders of the state (Mazzilli 2014). The role of defending state interests is assigned only to state attorneys (*Procuradores do Estado, Procuradores do Município*, and *Advogados da União*), not prosecutors (*Promotores de Justiça* and *Procuradores da República*). The Constitution recognised the role of the latter as ombudsmen and plaintiffs in class actions on behalf of groups of workers and consumers, as well as the environment and other social interests. Professionalisation barred prosecutors from engaging in private practice, holding another public office, or belonging to a political party. The expansion of collective justice radically transformed the role of prosecutors, who became actively involved in protecting new social rights to education, healthcare, and citizenship.

Inspired by the success of prosecutors as champions of collective interests, public defenders lobbied to be legally recognised as plaintiffs with a similar mandate (Fortes 2017). OPD also needed to adjust to the demands of class actions and mass produced justice. In contrast to the austerity measures and restrictions on legal aid experienced by other jurisdictions, access to justice increased in Brazil over the last three decades (Gidi and Zaneti 2015). Free justice is more widely available through expansion of the OPD, elimination of court fees in small claims courts, and litigation on behalf of poor parties. Some states provide greater access to justice. For instance, only in 2006 did São Paulo create its OPD, whose structure, funding, and capacity are insufficient to provide legal assistance for its tens of millions of citizens (Tonche 2016). Rio de Janeiro's OPD, by contrast, is older and better resourced and organised (Madeira, 2014). Competition for institutional space, professional prestige, and higher salaries also stimulated the professionalisation of public defenders, whose work became more collaborative, efficient, and pragmatic. Professionalisation occurred throughout the state bureaucracy in response to public demands, reshaping legal practices at the police, central bank, and tax revenue services, for instance.

These changes are visible in the performance of the judiciary, Public Prosecutor's Office and Federal Police investigating corruption among politicians and businessmen in financing electoral campaigns and misusing public resources. Because of their fragmentary professional identifications, these officials seem to exercise great autonomy in such investigations, despite expectations that their careers would produce internal cohesion. Media visibility blurs boundaries between the professions and politics: there are frequent reports of magistrates, prosecutors and federal police officers involved in such cases being invited to participate in legislative and executive elections (even if they are prevented by professional regulations).

C. Public Interest Litigation and Pro Bono Services: Private Lawyers Pursuing Public Good?

During the military regime, a few private lawyers and organisations engaged in public interest litigation, notably criminal lawyers serving pro bono on behalf of political dissidents and Catholic organisations representing the poor (Falcão 1988). Following the transition to democracy there were at least 136 rights groups in 2013, including non-governmental organisations (NGOs) and social movements providing access to justice and mobilisation for excluded individuals (Rodriguez 2013). These professionals were trained as cause lawyers by participating in human rights courses, discussion groups, student organisations, and other extracurricular activities. Motivated by religion, family, and ideology, they joined professional networks through post-graduate courses and internships in NGOs and other rights groups. They were not strongly influenced by foreign models, although they did compete for scarce foreign resources (Rodriguez 2013). These groups generally offered advice and support in filing a lawsuit but rarely provided continuous legal assistance throughout the action; and few were prepared to conduct class actions.

The limited role of these private associations is explained by the reorganisation of lawyers' public careers in the last 30 years. Because public prosecutors have standing to file collective actions on behalf of consumers, citizens, and the environment, the AGO invested resources, provided technical support, and assumed leadership in promoting public interest litigation. From 1990 to 2010, public prosecutors from the Rio de Janeiro consumer protection department filed 405 class actions, many affecting the enforcement of consumer law (Fortes 2017). This inspired OPD and the State Assembly's Commission for Defence of Consumers to invest resources to develop their own structure for filing class actions for consumer protection (Fortes 2017). This institutional competition between public organisations preempted the space for private organisations to pursue public interest litigation, encouraging them instead to refer cases to the public actors (Fortes 2017). In contrast to the US class action and EU model of collective redress, Brazilian public interest litigation is conducted by public organisations like the AGO, not by 'private attorneys general' motivated by potential economic rewards to pursue the public good (Fortes 2017).

The expansion and professionalisation of OPD in the last 30 years also explains why Brazilian law firms are not significant providers of pro bono legal services. Whereas legal aid budgets have declined in Europe and the US (Maclean 2015), Brazil expanded free legal services by reorganising, professionalising and funding OPD (Madeira 2014). Every year tens of thousands of cases are filed with the assistance of public defenders. But there are still limitations and regional differences in the coverage and quality of their work (Madeira 2014). In 1990, only seven states had OPDs, but 18 new OPDs were created in the next two decades. By 2009, OPD was present in 43 per cent of judicial districts (*comarcas*) and completely absent only in the southern states of Paraná (until 2011) and Santa Catarina (until 2012). Caseloads varied greatly: public defenders assisted an average of 4,604 poor individuals a year in Bahia but only 190 in Paraíba and Amapá (Secretaria da Reforma do Judiciário 2009). And there is still a deficit of public defenders. São Paulo would need to hire 2,471 new public defenders to provide full coverage to its poor population; with only 717, it must ration assistance.[10]

Since the 1990s, the traditional and business legal elites have promoted pro bono legal services by law firms. Influenced by globalisation, boutique law firms have been pressured by their international clients to promote corporate social responsibility by

---

[10] See www.ipea.gov.br/sites/en-GB/mapadefensoria/deficitdedefensores.

pursuing the public interest. Aspiring jurists attempting to become notable lawyers, in turn, are motivated by the inspirational examples of iconic predecessors who challenged torture by the military regime, patronage under the old republic, and slavery during the monarchical empire (Silva 2018). This alliance led to the establishment of the Institute Pro Bono (IPB) in 2001, which was supported by the Centre for Studies on Law Firms (CESA), a think tank sponsored by business legal elites (ibid). In 2002, however, the organisational elites of the São Paulo OAB limited pro bono work to legal counselling for NGOs, fearing the expansion of free legal services could hurt solo practitioners, many of whom receive public money to provide legal assistance for the poor. Only after federal public prosecutors intervened in 2015 did the national OAB change the rules and authorise pro bono work for individuals, including litigation (ibid). Compared with other Latin American countries, however, Brazilian pro bono practice remains small and less than international partners expect (ibid).

V. PRIVATE LAWYERING: DIVERSIFICATION, STRATIFICATION, AND FRAGMENTATION

In 1988, private lawyering consisted primarily of solo practitioners and small firms led by a notable jurist, as well as in-house counsel (Falcão 1988). Since then the number of solo practitioners has contracted in the urban capitals. For instance, of the 13,461 firms registered in 2016 at the state Bar of São Paulo (the largest in the country), just 1.6 per cent of lawyers were solo practitioners, 92.3 per cent in firms with 2–5 partners, 3.1 per cent in firms with 6–10, 1.6 per cent in firms with 11–20, and 1.4 per cent in larger firms. By contrast, corporate legal departments grew enormously. Although companies have an average of 11 in-house counsel, major banks like CEF, Itaú, and Bradesco have 1,000, 450, and 361 lawyers respectively. In-house lawyers have become more involved in making business decisions and allocating work to outside firms. General Counsel are expected to have international experience and develop an intimate knowledge of the business, working more as counsellors than traditional lawyers. But unlike their US counterparts, Brazilian General Counsel are not normally responsible for government relations (lobbying), corporate social responsibility, or entrepreneurship (Oliveira and Ramos 2018).

Private law firms also experienced growth. In 1988, a law firm with 20 lawyers was considered large, and few had 50 (Falcão 1988). Now there are at least 92 law firms with over 50 lawyers, and two have more than 600 (Gabbay et al 2018). Economic development encouraged firms to diversify their functions. The wave of privatisations in the 1990s led to the establishment of regulatory agencies, creating opportunities for experts on energy, infrastructure and telecommunications law, and regulation generally. The business legal elite collaborated with government to shape the regulation of telecommunications during the neoliberal Cardoso administration and the new developmental state promoted by Lula (Silva and Trubek 2018). Commercial arbitration grew exponentially after enactment of the Arbitration Act in 1996. In 2011, the five major arbitration chambers of São Paulo decided 122 cases worth a total of about US$1 billion. Every major corporate law firm became competent in commercial arbitration (Chasin 2016). In-house counsel also developed expertise to support the growing demand of multinational corporations, especially for specialised legal knowledge in fields like taxation, antitrust, and mergers and acquisitions (while spending most of their budget on hiring outside firms).

Massification also has transformed the legal market, engendering a division of labour in which boutique firms defend corporations in class actions, while generalist firms handle individual cases in small claims courts (Fortes 2017). With the expansion of ADR, lawyers have been trained to mediate disputes before litigating. Lawyering has become less adversarial and more collaborative, less dogmatic and more pragmatic, less formalistic and more concerned with the law in action. As mass litigation becomes a repetitive task with less value, the threat to the legal profession is not just the proletarianisation of lawyers (Falcão 1988) but even the risk of displacing lawyers by information technology capable of producing legal documents (Susskind 2010; 2013).

A. Hierarchy, Status, and Competition among Private Lawyers

Social inequalities are reproduced in the stratification of lawyers as income, race and gender shape careers that are far more differentiated than they were in the 1980s, when small firms predominated. Privatisation of public companies in the 1990s, globalisation of business, and internationalisation of professions have contributed to this transformation. Both the traditional ideology of market control and the duality of the technical and political activities of lawyers are under strong pressure from the business legal elites, who criticise the prohibition of international partnerships and domestic lawyers' efforts to protect their market, exposing the clash of interests between legal elites and their corporate clients.

Legal practice is differentiated into solo practitioners and small, medium, and large firms. But these also vary by type of service: one-stop-shops catering to individuals; large firms serving corporate clients; highly specialised boutique firms offering prime services at high prices; and mass litigation firms operating an assembly line. Contracts also define the status of private practitioners, who may be partners, associates, salary-based employees, house counsel, and advocates.

The old hierarchical duality of the Brazilian legal profession is gone. Before 1988, competitors in the legal market invested their resources to become notable jurists, who would be both respected professionals in a law firm and respected academics in a traditional law faculty. Today, some rising stars in academia are full-time professors with doctorates and extensive bibliographies of innovative scholarship. Leading practitioners now need to produce serious research in order to establish an academic reputation, because the symbolic capital of their practice is not automatically translatable to the academic environment. In legal practice, the complexity of contemporary legal knowledge requires collaborative teams with international experience, interdisciplinary skills, and the capacity to negotiate in order to devise innovative legal solutions for new problems. Paradoxically, lawyers must cooperate competitively, demonstrating both that they are team members and that they can add individual value to the legal product. The hierarchical organisation of the legal profession has changed as traditional elites compete with the new business and academic elites.

Globalising processes in private law practice are not restricted to the professional elites that circulate worldwide. They have also affected mass law practice, such as the routine work involved in mass litigation. Such processes reproduce the inequalities between men's and women's careers, constructing the gender stratification of the profession (Thornton 1996; Schultz and Shaw 2003; Feuvre and Lapeyere 2005; Bolton and Muzio 2007; Kay and Gorman 2008) while also creating new opportunities for those women who enter the internationalised legal elite (Ballakrishnen 2012), especially when they share the male view of professionalism (Bonelli 2013).

B. The Challenge of Social Inclusion: Gender, Race, Class, and Sexual Orientation

Analytical gender perspectives emphasising the diversification of the profession and its internal fragmentation influenced research in Brazil. In the 1990s, the concepts of the glass ceiling and the gender gap appeared in studies of women in legal practice and of public legal careers (Junqueira 1998). Examining contemporary Brazilian socio-legal studies, Madeira and Engelmann (2013) showed how jurists used the sociology of law to critique legal tradition and translate social issues into the judicial arena.

The growth of global legal practice in São Paulo allowed a larger number of women to join these firms while reproducing gender hierarchies (Bonelli and Benedito 2018).[11] Medium and large law firms were more open to incorporating female professionals, where they were nearly 30 per cent of partners (gender representation among associates varied less by firm size) (see Figure 1). Small law firms resemble traditional legal practices, mostly run by men (83 per cent of partners), incorporating female lawyers in less prestigious career positions focused on routine work.

Figure 1 Distribution of Partners and Associates in Law Firms Affiliated with CESA, by Firm Size and Gender

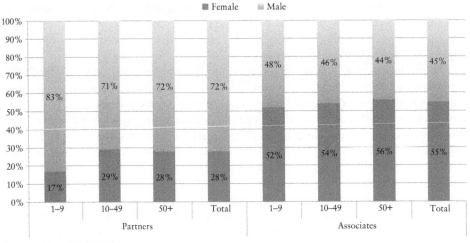

Source: Bonelli (2013)

---

[11] This study used information on 864 partners and 2,457 associates found on the websites of 198 São Paulo law firms affiliated with the Centro de Estudos das Sociedades de Advogados (CESA).

Corporate mass litigation may be conducted in house or outsourced to law firms. Most of this growing work is performed by women, particularly the execution of routine tasks, thereby reproducing gender hierarchies. A striking example is JBM, the largest Brazilian law firm in terms of litigation volume (Bonelli and Benedito 2018). This firm considers itself an extension of its corporate clients, emphasising managerial values instead of professionalism and diversified expertise. Most lawyers perform repetitive generalist tasks requiring no specialised skills. In March 2014, 65 per cent of the firm's 535 lawyers were salaried women. JBM regulates work and disciplines employees through organisational professionalism, not the typical collegial values of boutique law firms. The hierarchical format and standardised production of legal briefs are controlled by managers. Partner J Bueno[12] claims that perceptions of mass litigation are changing, and JBM is adapting to transformations of legal practice effected by the market and globalisation. He justifies hiring lawyers as employees by questioning the traditional relationship between partners and associates. JBM lawyers work 40 hours per week for a monthly salary of less than US$900 plus benefits.

In 1988, there was gender discrimination, even at the most prestigious law firms (Falcão 1988). Despite changes in the demography of the legal profession, such discrimination is still pervasive. Black lawyers have fewer professional opportunities than whites. Favela residents are unlikely to become members of the legal elite. LGBT lawyers traditionally stayed in the closet to retain their clients and social prestige, but since at least 2011 there has been a growing movement of legal activists within OAB and private NGOs to protect sexual orientation minorities and fight homophobia (Araújo and Bonelli 2013). Evidence of persistent discrimination can be found in the prestigious profession of *commercial arbitrate*, almost entirely composed by old white men – a professional club closed to minorities (Chasin 2016).

VI. CONCLUSION

The forces of democracy, development, and globalisation have transformed the Brazilian legal profession since 1988. Legal education expanded to more than 1,000 law schools, producing more than a million licensed lawyers. Unlicensed LLBs remain in professional limbo, litigating and lobbying to eliminate the OAB exam and regulate paralegals. OAB regulation was followed by stricter MEC evaluations of law schools. The expansion and professionalisation of legal education led to the growth of post-graduate education and establishment of full-time professorships, international partnerships, and empirical legal research. New public management forced the judiciary, AGO, and OPD to increase efficiency and transformed the role and potential social impact of judges and prosecutors. Private lawyering also experienced diversification, stratification, and fragmentation with the emergence of new professional elites, restructuring of professional hierarchies, and fragmentation of professional power among multiple individuals and stakeholders. Legal professionals creatively explored the opportunities revealed by these changes, adopting strategic behaviour to promote their work, transform their status, and resist or embrace internationalisation, stratification, and fragmentation.

---

[12] See www.conjur.com.br/2013-out-06/entrevista-jose-edgard-bueno-socio-fundador-jbm-advogados.

The dualism prevailing before 1988 has been replaced by complex multidimensional networks with their own scale of hierarchies and prestige symbols. The binary distinction between elite and non-elite (Falcão 1988; Heinz and Laumann 1982) is insufficient to explain the complexity of the contemporary profession. Big Law can no longer be identified with powerful corporate clients because the massification of legal disputes and pressure to reduce the cost of legal services have led corporations to hire law firms and lawyers, many of whom cannot be classified as elite (Craveiro and Gómez 2018). The era of the notable jurist (Falcão 1988) seems to be over, not only because the elite is fragmented into academic, organisational, traditional, and economic domains but also because transnational legal knowledge is no longer concentrated in a few lawyers (Gómez and Pérez-Perdomo 2018a). Moreover, the legal profession has changed from an unequal, masculine, hegemonic, national, fixed singular identity into something more fragmented, globally stratified, diversified, mutable and plural, without eliminating the persistent inequalities.

The present situation poses important questions, suggesting directions for socio-legal research on the future of the Brazilian legal profession. On one hand, the contemporary political crisis stimulates reflections on the capacity of democracy and globalisation to promote political liberalism, economic growth, and social inclusion. On the other, there is potential for innovation in legal education and the use of information technology to deliver legal services. Some law schools have introduced courses on law and technology. Public prosecutors are investigating the ethics of algorithms in e-commerce and exploring the use of big data to collect evidence for litigation through the programme 'AGO in maps' ('*MP em Mapas*') in Rio de Janeiro. Public defenders in São Paulo are experimenting with digital document production to increase their capacity to provide legal assistance to the poor. Private lawyers also face competition from the digital provision of legal services by start-ups (Falcão 2017). When these new technologies are deployed competitively by lawyers, they may result in the fracture of an already fragmented legal profession, reducing the scope, reach, and verticality of professional power and reinforcing democratic practices that valorise lay opinion over legal expertise and replace legal knowledge with practical knowledge.

REFERENCES

Abel, RL and Lewis, PSC (eds) (1988a) *Lawyers in Society: Vol 1 The Common Law World* (Berkeley, University of California Press).

—— (1988b) *Lawyers in Society: Vol 2 The Civil Law World* (Berkeley, University of California Press).

Almeida, F and Nassar, P (2018) 'The Ordem dos Advogados do Brasil and the politics of professional regulations in Brazil' in L Cunha et al (eds), *The Brazilian Legal Profession in the Age of Globalization: The Rise of the Corporate Legal Sector and its Impact on Lawyers and Society* (Cambridge, Cambridge University Press).

Alviar, H (2014) 'Quando ideais viajam: algumas reflexões sobre a globalização do ensino jurídico e a circulação da crítica' in P Fortes (ed), *A Globalização do Ensino Jurídico*. (Rio de Janeiro, FGV).

Andrade, C (2012) 'Acesso ao Ensino Superior no Brasil: equidade e desigualdade social' www.revistaensinosuperior.gr.unicamp.br/edicoes/ed06_julho2012/Cibele_Yahn.pdf.

Araújo, D and Bonelli, M da Glória (2013) 'A construção de identidades homossexuais na advocacia paulista: uma abordagem sociológica de profissionalismo e diferença' in M da Glória Bonelli and M Landa (eds), *Sociologia e Mudança Social no Brasil e na Argentina* (São Carlos, Compacta).

Ballakrishnen, S (2012) 'Breaking bad: Gender inequality in the Indian legal profession and the advantage of new institutional frameworks' Paper presented at LSA.

Barbalho, R (2008) 'A feminização das carreiras jurídicas e seus reflexos no profissionalismo' PhD thesis deposited at UFSCar.

Bolton, S and Muzio, D (2007) 'Can't live with 'em; Can't live without 'em: Gendered segmentation in the Legal Profession' 41 *Sociology* 47–64.

Bonelli, M da Glória (2013) *Profissionalismo, gênero e diferença nas carreiras jurídicas* (São Carlos, EDUFSCar).

—— (2017) 'Changes in the Brazilian legal professions' International Meeting on Law and Society, Mexico City.

Bonelli, M da Glória and Benedito, C (2018) 'Globalizing processes for São Paulo attorneys: gender stratification in law firms and law-related businesses' in L Cunha et al (eds), *The Brazilian Legal Profession in the Age of Globalization: The Rise of the Corporate Legal Sector and its Impact on Lawyers and Society* (Cambridge, Cambridge University Press).

Campos, V (2015) 'A chegada das meritíssimas: agência individual e mudança social no processo de feminização da magistratura' PhD thesis deposited at UFPE.

Chasin, A (2016) 'A institucionalização da arbitragem comercial e a formação de uma nova elite jurídica no Brasil' Paper presented at ANPOCS 2016.

Conselho Nacional do Judiciário (2014) *Censo do Poder Judiciário* (Brasília) sidneibjr.jusbrasil.com.br/noticias/303545941/censo-judiciario-2014.

Conselho Nacional do Ministério Público (2015) 'MP: Um retrato' www2.cnmp.mp.br/portal/images/MP_Um_retrato_WEB_FINAL.pdf.

Craveiro, M and Gómez, M (2018) 'Big Law in Brazil: Rise and Current Challenges' in M Gómez and R Pérez-Perdomo (eds), *Big Law in Latin America and Spain: Globalization and Adjustments in the Provision of High End Legal Services* (London, Palgrave Macmillan).

Cunha, L and Ghirardi, J (2018) 'Legal Education in Brazil: The Challenges and Opportunities of a Changing Context' in L Cunha et al (eds), *The Brazilian Legal Profession in the Age of Globalization: The Rise of the Corporate Legal Sector and its Impact on Lawyers and Society* (Cambridge, Cambridge University Press).

Falcão, J (1988) 'Lawyers in Brazil' in RL Abel and PSC Lewis (eds), *Lawyers in Society: Vol II The Civil Law World* (Berkeley, University of California Press).

—— (2014) 'Ensino jurídico Local Global' in P Fortes (ed), *A Globalização do Ensino Jurídico* (Rio de Janeiro, FGV).

Falcão, João (2017) 'Startup Law Brasil' Master thesis deposited at FGV.

Feuvre, N Le and Lapeyre, N (2005) 'Les "scripts sexués" de carrière dans les professions juridiques en France; in M Giannini (ed), *The Feminization of the Professions, Thematic Issue, Knowledge, Work & Society* 101–126.

FGV Projetos e Conselho Federal da OAB (2016) *Exame da Ordem em números* fgvprojetos.fgv.br/publicacao/exame-de-ordem-em-numeros.

Figueiredo, I and Camilo, G (eds) (2014) 'Pesquisa Perfil das Instituições de Segurança Pública 2013 (ano-base 2012)' (Brasília, Ministério da Justiça, Secretaria Nacional da Segurança Pública) www.justica.gov.br/central-de-conteudo/senasp/anexos/pesquisa-perfil-2013_ano-base_2012.pdf/view.

Fortes, P (2015) 'How Legal Indicators Influence Judicial Behaviour: The Brazilian National Council of Justice and "Justice in Numbers" 47(1) *Journal of Legal Pluralism and Unofficial Law* 39–55.

—— (2017) 'Collective Action in Comparative and Empirical Perspective: Towards a Socio-Legal Theory' PhD thesis deposited at Oxford.

—— (2017a) 'The Rise of Empirical Socio-Legal Studies in Brazil' paper presented at LSA/RCSL Conference in 2017.

—— (2019) 'An Agenda for Latin American Law and Development' in R Sieder, K Ansolabehere and T Alfonso (eds), *Routledge Handbook of Law and Society in Latin America* (London, Routledge).

Fórum de Segurança Pública (2015) *9º Anuário Brasileiro de Segurança Pública* (São Paulo) www.forumseguranca.org.br/storage/download//anuario_2015.retificado_.pdf.

Fragale Filho, R, Moreira, R, Sciammarella, A (2015) 'Magistratura e gênero: um olhar sobre a mulheres nas cúpulas do judiciário brasileiro' eces.revues.org/1968.

Gabbay, D, Ramos, L, Sica, L (2018) 'Corporate Law firms: the Brazilian case' in L Cunha et al (eds), *The Brazilian Legal Profession in the Age of Globalization: The Rise of the Corporate Legal Sector and its Impact on Lawyers and Society* (Cambridge, Cambridge University Press).

Gidi, A and Zanetti, H Jnr (2015) 'Brazilian Civil Procedure in an Age of Austerity' *Erasmus Law Review no 04*.

Gómez, M and Pérez-Perdomo, R (2018) 'Corporate Lawyers and Multinational Corporations in Latin America and Spain: 1990–2015' in M Gómez and R Pérez-Perdomo (eds), *Big Law in Latin America and Spain: Globalization and Adjustments in the Provision of High End Legal Services* (London, Palgrave Macmillan).

—— (2018a) 'Conclusion' in M Gómez and R Pérez-Perdomo (eds), *Big Law in Latin America and Spain: Globalization and Adjustments in the Provision of High End Legal Services* (London, Palgrave Macmillan).

Halliday, T and Karpik, L (1997) *Lawyers and the Rise of Western Political Liberalism* (Oxford, Clarendon Press).

Heinz, J and Laumann, E (1982) *Chicago Lawyers: The Social Structure of the Bar* (New York, Russell Sage Foundation and Chicago: American Bar Foundation).

Junqueira, E (1998) 'A mulher juíza e a juíza mulher' in C Bruschini and H Holanda, *Horizontes plurais: Novos estudos de gênero no Brasil* (São Paulo, Fundação Carlos Chagas e Editora) 34.

Kay, F and Gorman, E (2008) 'Women in the legal profession' 4 *Annual Review of Law and Social Sciences* 299–332.

Maclean, M (2015) 'Delivering Family Justice: New Ways of Working for Lawyers in Divorce and Separation' in H Sommerlad et al (eds), *The Futures of Legal Education and The Legal Profession* (Oxford, Hart Publishing).

Madeira, L (2014) 'Institutionalization, Reform, and Independence of the Public Defender's Office in Brazil' 8(2) *Brazilian Political Science Review* 48–69.

Madeira, L and Engelmann, F (2013) 'Estudos sociojurídicos: apontamentos sobre teorias e temáticas de pesquisa em sociologia jurídica no Brasil' 15(32) *Sociologias* 182–209.

Marques Jr, G (2014) 'Espaço, profissões e gênero: mobilidade e carreira entre juízes e juízas no Estado de São Paulo' 43 *Cadernos Pagu* 265–297.

Mazzilli, H (2014) *Regime Jurídico do Ministério Público* 8th edn (São Paulo, Saraiva).

Oliveira, F and Ramos, L (2018) 'General (in-house) counsels in Brazil: Career, professional profile and a new role' in L Cunha et al (eds), *The Brazilian Legal Profession in the Age of Globalization: The Rise of the Corporate Legal Sector and its Impact on Lawyers and Society* (Cambridge, Cambridge University Press).

Rodriguez, JR (2013) 'Advocacia de interesse público no Brasil: atuação das entidades de defesa de direitos da sociedade civil e sua interação com órgãos de litígio do Estado' (CEBRAP, Brasília, Ministério de Justiça) www.justica.gov.br/seus-direitos/politicas-de-justica/publicacoes/Biblioteca/dialogos-ssobrejustica_advocacia_popular.pdf/.

Sadek, MT (2006) *Magistrados: uma imagem em movimento* (Rio de Janeiro, FGV).

Secretaria da Reforma do Judiciário (2009) *III Diagnóstico da Defensoria Pública no Brasil* (Brasília, Ministério da Justiça).

—— (2011) *I Diagnóstico da Advocacia Pública no Brasil* (Brasília, Ministério da Justiça) www.justica.gov.br/seus-direitos/politicas-de-justica/publicacoes/Biblioteca/diagnostico-advocacia.pdf/.

—— (2015) *IV Diagnóstico da Defensoria Pública no Brasil* (Brasília, Ministério da Justiça) www.anadep.org.br/wtksite/downloads/iv-diagnostico-da-defensoria-publica-no-brasil.pdf.

Silva, F (2018) 'Doing well and doing good in emerging economy: the social construction of pro bono among corporate lawyers and law firms in Sao Paulo' in L Cunha et al (eds), *The Brazilian Legal Profession in the Age of Globalization: The Rise of the Corporate Legal Sector and its Impact on Lawyers and Society* (Cambridge, Cambridge University Press).

Silva, F and Trubek, D (2018) 'Lawyering in New Developmentalism: Legal Professionals and the Construction of the Telecom Sector in the Emerging Brazil (1980s–2010s)' in L Cunha et al (eds), *The Brazilian Legal Profession in the Age of Globalization: The Rise of the Corporate Legal Sector and its Impact on Lawyers and Society* (Cambridge, Cambridge University Press).

Sommerlad, H (2015) 'The "Social Magic" of Merit: Diversity, Equity, and Inclusion in the English and Welsh Legal Profession' 83 *Fordham Law* Review 2325–2347.

Schultz, U and Shaw, G (eds) (2003) *Women in the World's Legal Professions* (Oxford, Hart Publishing).

Susskind, R (2010) *The End of Lawyers? Rethinking the Nature of Legal Services* (Oxford, Oxford University Press).

—— (2013) *Tomorrow's Lawyers: An Introduction to Your Future* (Oxford, Oxford University Press).

Thornton, M (1996) *Dissonance and Distrust: Women in the Legal Profession* (Oxford, Oxford University Press).

Tonche, J (2016) 'Defensoria Pública do Estado de São Paulo: a emergência de um novo ator em um campo de conflitos e os significados do ativismo' paper presented at ANPOCS.

Trubek, D (2012) 'Reabrindo o arquivo do CEPED: o que podemos aprender de um "caso do arquivo morto" in G Lacerda, J Falcão and T Rangel (eds), *Aventura e legado do ensino jurídico* (Rio de Janeiro, FGV).

Vasconcelos, M (2013) 'É preciso rever regras regulatórias da advocacia' www.conjur.com.br/2013-out-06/entrevista-jose-edgard-bueno-socio-fundador-jbm-advogados.

Vieira, O, Lima, M and Ghirardi, J (2014) 'Ensino do Direito para um mundo em transformação: a experiência da FGV Direito' in P Fortes (ed), *A Globalização do Ensino Jurídico* (Rio de Janeiro, FGV).

20

Chile

Lawyers Engage with the Market, Specialisation, and Rights

CRISTIÁN VILLALONGA*

I. INTRODUCTION

Had I been asked to describe Chilean lawyers at the end of the 1970s, my assessment would have been very different from what I will say about the profession today. Virtually all were *licenciados en derecho* who graduated from the five law schools. Almost all would be registered in the *Colegio de Abogados* (Chilean Bar Association or CBA), a guild responsible for professional discipline. A significant number would have combined representing private litigants with a part-time civil service job. Most would have practised in a small law firm organised as a family office sharing expenses but not income, without the limited liability conferred by legal personhood. These would have dealt with cases ranging from criminal law to contracts. They would also share overarching assumptions about legal expertise, cementing a relatively unitary legal culture (Lowenstein 1970: 21–53). None of that fully describes the contemporary profession.

By the mid-twentieth century, Chile had a robust administrative state structured by political bargaining and had attempted to industrialise the economy by an import substitution strategy. That regime had a substantial effect on the legal profession. For instance, the large public bureaucracy offered jobs for law graduates, generated corporatist links with interest groups like the organised Bar, and produced a weak economic growth that influenced the demand for legal services (Villalonga Torrijo 2017). Nevertheless, a new political and economic cycle in the late-1970s initiated a transformation of the profession.

After a profound political crisis, a military dictatorship took control in 1973. Besides repressing dissidents with an iron fist, this regime embraced a modernisation process based on a market economy and gradual political liberalisation. From the late-1970s,

---

* The author expresses his gratitude to Marianne González Le Saux and Agustín Barroilhet, who provided valuable feedback on earlier versions of this chapter.

the government applied monetarist shock policies, relaxing the stringent labour and tax safeguards on domestic businesses and privatising most public corporations and social security. In the same spirit, it adopted regulatory norms to monitor the emerging market economy. Forestalling a gradual transition to democracy, in 1980 it enacted a new constitution that reestablished the Constitutional Court and expanded judicial review, facilitating the control of administrative action and protecting private property. During the second half of the decade, especially after losing a 1988 plebiscite on its future, the military designed institutional devices and compromised with the opposition on some constitutional matters in order to preserve its most significant structural reforms (Huneeus 2000: 242–55, 604–608).

After the restoration of democracy in 1990, Chile accelerated several changes instituted during the authoritarian period. Through free market policies and targeted social expenditure the country generated an economic bonanza that peaked in the mid-1990s, driven mostly by foreign investment. In response to the Washington consensus, the new governments preserved free trade to integrate Chile into global markets and gained political legitimacy by subscribing to international instruments, such as the Inter-American Convention on Human Rights (Sehnbruch and Seavelis 2014). Over the following years, this led to the substitution of written for oral procedures in criminal, family, and labour cases, requiring a transformation of those courts. Seeking to modernise an expanding state and correct market failures, the new regime also enacted numerous regulatory norms in areas like the provision of social services and consumer protection and created new administrative tribunals for public acquisitions and environmental safeguards. All those reforms significantly modified legal practice (Peña 2003).

Chilean society also underwent a profound transformation through the institutional reforms initiated about 1980. As in most Latin American countries, market forces and democratisation have unsettled traditional forms of sociability and reinforced personal autonomy. An increasing fraction of the population has grown less conservative, embracing a wider variety of choices about sexuality, religion, and lifestyle. Poverty has diminished, and cultural codes of material consumption have invaded many realms, from food to higher education. During the last 20 years, a growing demand for accountability and the assertion of individual rights have replaced social class hierarchies and political passivity. Technological development, predominantly internet and global communications, has accelerated this shift (Tironi 1999; Peña 2002). All these changes have altered the relation of society to authority, critically reshaping the life of the law.

These political, economic, and social changes represent a wave of modernisation that rejects the domination of the administrative state. Responding to the new context, lawyers have gradually transformed the profession in three major domains: market, specialisation, and mobilisation of rights.

II. THE MARKET ECONOMY: ITS EFFECT ON LEGAL EDUCATION AND PROFESSIONAL CONTROL

The path to becoming a lawyer still resembles what it had been in the mid-twentieth century. The Supreme Court bestows a licence upon any individual who receives an undergraduate law degree (*licenciado en derecho*), completes an unpaid six-month apprenticeship in a free legal clinic, demonstrates good behaviour and has no criminal record.[1] Nevertheless, what seems like the same procedure on the books has dramatically changed in reality. The economic liberalisation conducted by the military dictatorship had a profound impact on the legal system. The gradual infiltration of a free-market logic into higher education permitted the establishment of new law schools, making law a striking example of greater access to the university. At the same time, market-oriented measures limited the possibility of restricting professional labour, contracting the jurisdiction of the organised Bar, which had exercised broad control over legal practice until 1980. Thus the market economy has been a principal factor in transforming the demography of lawyers and their social differentiation.

A. Law Schools in a Time of Mass Higher Education

The expansion of higher education constitutes a social revolution fostered by the market, allowing almost anyone to aspire to get a professional certificate. Among the 707,000 students enrolled in university in 2015, almost 43,000 (6.2 per cent) were law students (Zapata and Tejada 2016: 8, 10). Even though law schools enrol a relatively small proportion of the total, they have been criticised as demonstrating the failure of free-market logic (Espinoza 2005: 49). Such a perception reflects both nostalgia for a career previously reserved for the elite and the difficulties graduates from the less prestigious academic institutions face in finding jobs.

Military rule initiated a broad structural reform of the university system in around 1980, incorporating the freedom to establish educational centres into the new constitution and implementing this by statute.[2] This reform was not driven exclusively by a free market ideology but also reflected other motives, such as defusing politics within public universities, enhancing regionalisation, and expanding geographic access. Although the regulations prohibited for-profit institutions, many of the new institution began to behave like market actors. For example, most universities organised their academic personnel and admissions in response to demand, and some employed loopholes to generate profits (eg by renting infrastructure to related corporations). Diverse public agencies were established to certify programmes and oversee the emerging system but without the institutional capacity to exert effective control (Brunner 2009: 220–337). As expected, these developments had a significant impact on the expansion of legal education.

Until 1980, there were only five law schools: University of Chile (in Santiago and Valparaíso), Pontifical Catholic University of Chile and Valparaíso, and University of Concepción. Their curricula emulated the University of Chile, which was responsible for approving the classes and degrees of all students. Although centralised examinations were abolished in the early 1950s, this has had an enduring legacy. Even today, the core of the curriculum is an encyclopedic knowledge intended to prepare graduates to represent litigants in private law, procedure, and criminal law. By the early 1970s, these universities had begun to expand their enrolment beyond the upper and middle classes in order to increase access (Lowenstein 1970: 121–75).

---

[1] Government of Chile, Código Orgánico de Tribunales 1943, Art 523.
[2] Government of Chile, DFL N°1 1981 establishes regulations on universities.

Since the early 1980s, new law schools have opened their doors, increasing the number of admissions and student diversity. Like many careers in the humanities and social sciences, legal training requires little investment compared with engineering or science. Government does not control enrolment, although schools seek government certification to attract students. Between 1982 and 1993, 25 new law schools were established in public and private universities. By 2014, there were 49 law schools, some offering programmes in several cities. By 2006, there were more than 140 programmes leading to an undergraduate law degree (Guzmán Brito 2005: 282–89). At the same time, traditional law schools increased their admissions from about 100 to as many as 350 students. Consequently, the number of law graduates grew exponentially. From 197 admitted to practice in 1977 to 815 in 1997 and 3,487 in 2015 (Pérez-Perdomo 2006: 114; Dolmestch 2016: 24). Most of that expansion was concentrated between 1990 and 1999, levelling off in 2010 (Rolando et al 2010: 11.19; Zapata and Tejada 2016: 10).

Chilean records do not always eliminate dead professionals or law graduates who are not practising or include the small number of graduates from countries like Spain and Ecuador, whose law degrees Chile recognises. The statistics on law graduates, however, reveal how their numbers have grown. Census data show there were 1,724 people per lawyer in 1982; scholars estimate this had dropped to 435 in 2014 (more slowly than in other Latin American countries). Some studies find about 40,000 lawyers today (Pérez-Perdomo 2006: 105, 114; De la Maza et al 2016: 22).

Law students have become more diverse in gender, geographic origin, and class background. Women have increased from about 27 per cent in 1970 to 53 per cent in 2010 (Lowenstein 1970: 123; Zapata and Tejada 2016: 10). Although law schools are still concentrated in the three largest cities (Santiago, Valparaíso, and Concepción), their presence outside those cities has increased access for regional students. And the number of students from middle and lower class backgrounds has mushroomed in a highly stratified system of higher education (Elgueta et al 2015).

The new law schools have diversified pedagogically. At first, they were mere copies of the traditional institutions, which retained control over examinations. But after receiving the authority to grant law degrees and competition for students, most have tried to emphasise research or teaching in particular areas (Guzmán Brito 2005: 282–89). For example, some have developed an active research agenda with full-time professors, journals, and a strong presence in the public sphere (eg Universidad Diego Portales and Universidad de Los Andes). Others have chosen massive enrolments, night-time classes, and freelance law professors paid on an hourly basis (eg Universidad Bolivariana). Some have focused on human rights, exerting significant influence on legal reforms (eg Diego Portales University). Others have concentrated on business and corporate issues (eg Universidad Adolfo Ibáñez). Several take their identity from the university to which they belong: Catholic (eg Universidad Alberto Hurtado), regional development (Universidad Católica del Norte and Universidad Austral) or political (eg Universidad La República for the masonic movement or ARCIS linked to the Communist Party). These orientations emerge mostly in the focus of research and the relation to society. Only recently have such projects tried to change the educational curriculum and pedagogy. However, efforts to create academic concentrations by way of certificates have failed. Most schools continue to offer a generalist education through lectures and a traditional curriculum, provoking criticism within legal academia (Benfeld 2016).

The spread of higher education has created a mismatch between expectations, academic skills, and instruction, causing significant difficulties inside and outside of law schools. Most secondary school students dream of getting a university degree because economic development has increased the possibility of achieving social mobility by obtaining symbolic credentials. However, few students possess the necessary academic skills. That gap is especially great in law, which remains the most prestigious and profitable career in the humanities, attracting a large number of students who must follow a rigid curriculum and pass difficult examinations. Universities have been unable to cope with this challenge because they are structured around mass instruction and impersonal relations. As a result, there is a belief that the quality of legal training has declined, even in traditionally elite institutions like the University of Chile (Jocelyn-Holt 2015: 376–77). This constitutes an increasing problem throughout law schools but is most pronounced at the less prestigious ones established in recent decades, which have tended to enrol students with lower academic abilities.

The length of training constitutes another hurdle. Although the formal curriculum lasts ten semesters, in order to practise students must pass a difficult exam covering the principal subjects. Since there is no national exam, universities have substantial control over access to the profession. Examinations range from traditional oral interrogations on civil law and procedure to general tests that include addressing a case. Anecdotal evidence suggests that some students who fail in more rigorous law schools transfer to others with lower standards (Marré Velasco 2009: 10–15; Jocelyn-Holt 2015: 367). Besides the delays caused by courses they fail to pass, students spend about six months preparing for their final exam. Those who fail can usually retake it twice after paying additional fees. This involves an extended period of cramming, with the uncertainty and living expenses that entails. It is common for students to work as *procuradores* in low-skilled legal tasks before taking the exam, both to support themselves and to improve their job prospects. Because of the enormous pressure to secure the licence, an informal industry has developed of law graduates who prepare students for the examination. The average time to get the most basic law degree is 17 semesters (Arriagada and Naranjo 2016).

Objective measures confirm the shortcomings in legal education. During 2007, for example, about 32 per cent of law students dropped out during their first year (Rolando et al 2010: 18). That is similar to the attrition rate in other subjects, but it increases over time to give law one of the highest drop-out rates: only 21 per cent of first-year students earn a law degree (Zapata and Tejada 2009: 29).

Many have criticised mass education for producing too many poorly trained lawyers. Although there are no data on how the new lawyers are affecting the price of the legal services, elite professionals complain that law schools are producing more graduates than the market can absorb. Such protests seem to be prompted by the depreciation of the economic and symbolic value of the undergraduate law degree. The CBA has asserted that universities are not preparing graduates for practice. The Supreme Court has also declared the need for a national Bar examination or, at least, a national programme to certify the competence of law graduates, suggesting it would refuse to grant licences without assurances about the quality of legal education. The Pontifical Catholic University of Chile and the University of Chile have proposed basic guidelines for a voluntary national exam (Marré Velasco 2009: 12–14; Jocelyn-Holt 2015: 367–424). But attempts at standardisation have been seen as efforts by elite schools, the guild and the judiciary to become gatekeepers of the profession, restricting the freedom of law teachers.

In response to the depreciation of the first law degree, law schools have expanded their graduate programmes (which did not exist before 1980), seeking to meet the demand from lawyers eager to improve their job opportunities. The late 1990s saw the emergence of a prosperous market for brief classes targeted at professional specialisation (*certificados*, *diplomados*). Law schools have also created more than 30 master's programmes, graduating 219 in 2010 and 589 in 2014 (Guzmán Brito 2005: 306). Eight doctoral programmes at the most prestigious law schools grant about nine degrees a year (far less than those in other fields) (Comisión Nacional de Acreditación 2017; Zapata and Tejeda 2016: 42).

Since the late 2000s, domestic graduate programmes have been complemented by study abroad, mostly financed by the National Commission for Sciences and Technology. By 2012, 67 Chilean students were taking a foreign LLM and 48 a foreign doctorate in law. Such financial support has benefited the best students, who frequently derive substantial amounts of social and academic capital from their family backgrounds (López Barrera 2012). Most of these LLM graduates hope to be hired by big law firms, international corporations, and, to a lesser extent, government agencies. For instance, 39 per cent of large firm lawyers with a master's degree obtained them from well-respected law schools in the UK and US (De la Maza et al 2016: 53). Doctoral graduates have tended to become full-time professors, supplementing their incomes with legal advising. Having instructors with doctoral degrees is said to be a valuable asset in obtaining certification of law programmes from the national educational authorities (Muñoz León 2014: 14–15).

Legal education has become a hierarchical market of law schools and programmes reflecting the social capital and skills of students and instructors, thereby reproducing the profound segmentation of primary and secondary education. The strongest evidence for this is that each market segment tends to draw from different demographic sectors and sends graduates to different professional strata. The Pontifical Catholic University of Chile and the University of Chile head the upper segment, which has the highest concentration of students with the most social and academic capital and send some of their best graduates to the most prestigious settings in practice, the judiciary, and politics. A second tier includes the other traditional schools and some emerging centres that have demonstrated their research capabilities and attracted talented students who were not admitted to elite institutions. Their graduates tend to concentrate in mid-level occupations. At the bottom are schools with lower reputations, which enrol students with fewer skills and less social capital (Revista Qué Pasa 2015: 42–43; Con 2006: 14–17). Their students have higher attrition rates, and their graduates face considerable uncertainty in the job market.

B. The Organisation of the Bar: Governance, Discipline, and Legal Aid

Lawyers require a licence granted by the Supreme Court to perform certain tasks, principally litigation.[3] By the mid-twentieth century, that monopoly was associated with a

---

[3] Government of Chile, Código Orgánico de Tribunales 1943, Art 520.

system of professional control exercised by the CBA (established in 1925). The guild had public law status, managed a legal aid programme, disciplined lawyers, and made them public employees for retirement purposes. All lawyers had to be registered in the CBA to practise, and that collective experience was critical to understanding their identity (Pardo Valencia 1969).

As a part of its promotion of free market policies, however, the 1980 constitution incorporated the rights of freedom of association and freedom to work, ending the structures of compulsory corporatist control that characterised the previous decades.[4] The constitution and implementing legislation banned restrictive practices such as mandatory enrolment and minimum prices. Despite attempts to modify this for professional groups, the organised Bar became a private guild of voluntary members, terminating a more than 50-year monopoly on legal services dominated by elite lawyers.

The CBA still represents an important setting for elite lawyers, both old-school practitioners and large firm partners, who typically win the 19 places on the general board in biannual elections of half of its members fought openly along political lines (Couso 2007: 329; Revista del Abogado 2017: 31). The CBA chair still enjoys significant status, but the organised Bar has maintained a low profile in the public arena, framing its positions in technical language.

The CBA offers members several benefits, such as a library, a journal, and continuing education. More than 15 committees study critical aspects of law and professional life (Colegio de Abogados 2017). Most activities are conducted in Santiago, although there are branches throughout the country. Nevertheless, the market revolution curtailed several of its functions, and it has abandoned efforts to ensure lawyers' social status. For instance, lawyers lost their right to be treated as civil servants for retirement proposes; and the more diverse universe of law schools offer better post-graduate education. Because the association no longer acts as gatekeeper, young lawyers join it to certify to clients and potential employers that they adhere to a high ethical standard (Con 2017: 36–39).

The organised Bar has also lost its power to discipline all lawyers. In 1949, the CBA drafted a Code of Ethics for the generalist lawyer, which had the force of law. After legislation on professional groups in 1981, however, courts held that the CBA exercised control only over its voluntary members; the judiciary was responsible for the rest of the profession. As a result, disciplinary complaints handled by the CBA fell from 100 a year in the late 1970s to an annual average of about 88 between 1998 and 2010, at a time when the profession was expanding rapidly. Between 1990 and 2010, the CBA lobbied to recover its former powers and tried to update its Code by re-interpreting rules concerning advertising, participation in directories, and money laundering. After several years of negotiation with the judiciary and executive, the CBA issued a new Code of Ethics in 2011, taking account of lawyers' increasingly diverse occupations. Though it binds only members, courts have sometimes employed it in disciplining other lawyers (Sierra and Fuenzalida 2014: 430; Chaparro 2016: 16–21).

The number of complaints resolved by the CBA's disciplinary panel remains small. Although they take about two years to resolve, and a substantial number are dismissed, fear of exposure by the media influences lawyers to change their behaviour. Of the

---

[4] Government of Chile, Constitution of the Republic 1980, Art 19 N° 15 and 16; DFL N° 3.621 1981 that establishes regulations on professional associations.

226 complaints filed with the CBA between January 2014 and April 2016, the most common alleged malpractice (70 per cent), followed by inadequate information, undue touting, and fees conflicts. Suspension of membership and written admonitions were the most frequent sanctions, and only two lawyers were expelled under the new disciplinary procedure (Chaparro 2016: 16–21). However, most of the profession remains under the control of the judiciary, which is believed to exert almost no supervision.

Legal aid also has been hived off from the CBA. Until the late 1970s, the CBA operated a national legal aid scheme financed by public funds. By providing legal services to the poor, the programme helped to shape the public image of lawyers and offered an opportunity to socialise new graduates during the transition from law school to practice (González Le Saux 2017). In 1981, the Ministry of Justice assumed that responsibility, creating three regional agencies in Valparaiso, Concepción and the Santiago Metropolitan area. After finishing their studies, law graduates must spend six months working in a free legal clinic before receiving their licences.[5] These agencies have been criticised for their inadequate budget, delay in assigning graduates to positions, and lack of physical infrastructure (Balmaceda Jimeno 2000). Recent judicial reforms have granted poor clients access to licensed lawyers, limiting the role of unlicensed graduates to providing information, mediation, and assisting senior lawyers (Corporación de Asistencia Judicial 2015: 6).

These reforms established structures to guarantee access to justice in certain areas of practice, particularly criminal defence and workers' representation in labour courts. The state created different systems of public tenders in which private practitioners bid to offer legal aid at the lowest cost. The National Criminal Defence Office and the Regional Agencies of Legal Aid supervise these attorneys and provide some training. This system seeks to assure legal representation as a fundamental right while preserving the model of a market economy. The results are still being evaluated (Instituto Nacional de Derechos Humanos 2013: 59–72).

Other initiatives have sought to enhance access to justice. Under earlier legislation, courts could order a lawyer (*abogado de turno*) to provide free legal assistance for a month under penalty of licence suspension for refusing without cause.[6] In a well-known case filed by the CBA in 2008, the Constitutional Court declared that this violated the fundamental rights of freedom of work and equal distribution of public duties (Humeres 2008). At the same time, a significant number of law schools have established clinics to provide legal aid, and elite lawyers offering pro bono services have played a modest role (Fundación Pro Bono 2015: 21).

The traditional organisation of the Bar has lost ground since the 1980s, a direct and indirect effect of the market economy. First, new regulations on professional activity eliminated most of the CBA's responsibilities as the steward of lawyering; and most of the benefits and services it offered can be obtained outside its domain. Second, the growth of the market economy and special courts has produced a more segmented legal practice (discussed below). As a result, a growing number of lawyers are no longer unified by

---

[5] Government of Chile, Ley N° 17.995 1981 that bestows legal personhood to Public Corporations of Legal Aid.
[6] Government of Chile, Código Orgánico de Tribunales 1943, Art 595.

offering a generalist practice. Finally, a mass profession, produced by rapidly increasing cohorts of new law graduates, seems incapable of collective action. Mass lawyering is unsuited to a rigid hierarchical guild controlled by elite professionals akin to the corporatist arrangement of the mid-twentieth century.

Quantitative evidence confirms these impressions. While 257 out of the 297 lawyers admitted to practise in 1981 enrolled in the CBA, only 574 of the 2,860 admitted in 2009 did so (Sierra and Fuenzalida 2014:430). Specialisation has generated competitors, such as the Association of Labor Lawyers (established in the 1980s) and the Family Lawyers Guild (2008) (Fundación Pro-Bono 2014). Low profile attorneys have formed an Association of Lawyers of Chile to engage in mutual support (Asociación de Abogados 2017). Nevertheless, none of those specialist associations has enrolled a significant number of members. The fragmentation of the organised Bar seems to be a persistent legacy of these recent developments.

III. SPECIALISATION AND ITS RELATIONSHIP WITH SOCIAL SEGMENTATION

Free market policies and state reforms have forced a restructuring of legal practice, creating incentives for lawyers to adapt. The global market and mushrooming regulations have increased the demand for more sophisticated legal services. Meanwhile, specialised judicial procedures encourage similar specialisation by lawyers. De la Maza (2002: 22) argues that large firm lawyers adjusted to the new milieu through specialisation, competition, and bureaucratisation. These strategies transcend the division of labour, also influencing social, gender and geographic segmentation. As a result, the allocation of expertise, social capital, and economic rewards has become highly stratified.

At the top of the hierarchy are law firms organised on the Wall Street model. Some emerged as loose associations of attorneys at the beginning of the twentieth century by serving the nitrates industry and copper mining (eg Claro & Cía, and Carey). Others appeared decades later, usually as groups of politically influential lawyers representing foreign capital (eg Alessandri). However, there were no large firms before 1970 (Lowenstein 1970: 36). These emerged during the economic boom of the 1980s. Following privatisations, local industries reorganised their corporate structures, and numerous international investors came to Chile, participating in areas such as mining, utilities, and public works. This juncture triggered several partnerships that adopted the American model. Although no law firm had more than 20 attorneys in 1985, at least six had more than 40 by the next decade. Carey, the largest, had almost 152 in 2013, and three other firms reached about 100 that year (De la Maza et al 2016: 28). Some international companies offering legal and accounting services have established branches staffed by Chilean professionals (eg Deloitte). And there have been a few mergers of local and international partnerships. Although the large Chilean firms are smaller than their counterparts in other Latin American countries, like Brazil and Mexico, they all follow the Wall Street model (Pérez-Perdomo 2006: 118).

This new elite is defined not only by size. Some firms are relatively small boutique offices offering highly specialised services. Employing Chambers Latin America indexes, De La Maza, Mery and Vargas (2016: 33, 49–53) systematically analysed their characteristics. They strongly institutionalise internal careers, hiring young lawyers or even senior law students, who ascend within the firm over many years. Lateral hiring of senior professionals is rare, in order to avoiding disrupting the firm's internal culture and the relationship between associates and partners (whose 3:1 ratio create the leverage that inflates partner incomes). They offer premium salaries to attract talent and discourage defections to other firms (Lavín 2014: 31). They employ other professionals for recruitment, management, and advertising. One goal of this complex structure is to departmentalise competences, providing sophisticated services through scale economies. The other is to ensure the fidelity of clients, mostly big corporations.

Large firms recruit the most skilled law graduates, or at least those with the greatest social capital: almost 42 per cent got their first law degrees from Pontificia Universidad Católica de Chile. Other data show that only 10 per cent of large firm attorneys come from law schools outside Santiago (Guerrero 2014: 34). Lawyers at these firms have acquired highly specialised expertise: 27.5 per cent of the 1,571 lawyers in large firms completed graduate studies abroad, usually LLMs in the US. Moreover, 84 per cent of the sample reported English as their second language. Surprisingly, there are very few foreign lawyers in these firms: 98.8 per cent of them received their undergraduate law degree in Chile (De la Maza et al 2016: 42–43, 50). As expected, partners in these firms have the highest prestige and earn the most money.

Just below this stratum we find general counsel of large industries. Local corporations and branches of international companies have created in-house legal departments that conduct most of their daily legal work (eg quotidian regulatory issues, labour relations), to the dismay of big firm partners, who performed such tasks two decades ago (El Mercurio Legal 2014: 25). These departments used to be headed by generalist lawyers with significant social capital, who could count on the trust of corporate directors, but some general counsel now have acquired specialist expertise through LLMs (Lavín 2014: 31). The size of these departments varies with the company. For instance, CMPC, a traditional paper-mill corporation, has 12 lawyers managing its legal affairs. Because most services provided by big law firms have been commodified, in-house counsel play a crucial role in allocating tasks to outside firms, usually based on price competition. Recently, some general counsel have emerged as strategic actors in corporate governance and decision-making, acquiring a substantial amount of authority (Pontificia Universidad Católica de Chile, School of Law 2017). The social capital and prestige of legal counsel are closely related to the industry they serve, varying from complex international organisations (eg mining companies) to local medium-size industries.

In the middle of this hierarchy are lawyers providing legal services to small businesses and individuals, who constitute most of the profession according to anecdotal evidence. By the mid-twentieth century, a substantial number of them practised in small informal associations organised as family offices in urban downtowns. They combined advocacy and private counselling, collecting debts, establishing title to land, and conducting general civil litigation. Most came from the middle class and received their law degrees from elite and second-tier law schools.

This middle group also includes the significant number of lawyers who joined the public bureaucracy as clerks and counsel. Since at least the 1930s, many lawyers have worked in the public sector (Lowenstein 1970: 39–40). As more regulatory agencies were established in recent decades, this field offered greater job opportunities but with some degree of segmentation. Agencies such as the Antitrust Prosecution Office

(*Fiscalía Nacional Económica*) and the Superintendence of Insurance and Securities resemble sophisticated elite legal practice (Pardow 2015). These and other institutions responsible for regulating specific markets offer competitive salaries and may provide talented young lawyers with a stepping stone to big law firms or lucrative counselling and litigation. But most agencies offer rank-and-file jobs handling more monotonous quotidian matters. Lawyers are a minority in most agencies, even those whose functions are primarily legal. In 2015, lawyers are only about 230 of the 2,400 employees of the General Comptroller of the Republic, responsible for monitoring the legality of all government actions (Merino 2015).

Chile has a long tradition of public lawyers engaged in litigation. For instance, the State Defence Council (established 1895), a prestigious agency that litigates on behalf of the national interest, contained some of the most outstanding legal minds of the twentieth century, although its prestige has decreased (Vial 1995). Recent legal reforms have created new settings for lawyering in the public interest, such as the National Prosecution Office (*Ministerio Público*), which operates under the new penal procedure introduced in 1998. Other public agencies, like the National Institute of Human Rights and the Human Rights Program in the Ministry of Interior, have developed institutional mechanisms for public interest litigation. All these constitute an attractive setting for young lawyers. For instance, the National Prosecution Office had 709 lawyers in 2017, recruiting mostly from first-tier law schools or those that emphasise criminal law: University of Chile (18 per cent), Universidad de Concepción (12 per cent), Universidad Central (7 per cent), Universidad Católica de Chile (5 per cent), and Universidad de Talca (5 per cent) (La Tercera 2017). The most successful and best known of its lawyers, like the former Chief of the National Prosecution Office, Sabas Chauán, often move to criminal defence to earn more (El Mercurio Legal 2016: 12). The system of public tenders, which pays private practitioners to provide legal aid in the areas of criminal defence and labour courts, also represents the lower stratum of this middle ground.

At the bottom of this stratification are graduates of less prestigious law schools, usually from lower class backgrounds. Many have great difficulties finding jobs; and many of those who do are underemployed in notaries offices, banks, or municipalities. Many provide services to underprivileged sectors or are hired by more established lawyers, who informally delegate touting for clients and tedious tasks like transcription of documents and revisions of folders. These lawyers compete in a micro-market against those who have not completed legal law training (*tinterillos*), untitled law graduates (*egresados*), and even senior law students. Many are situated near jails and urban farmers markets and in the outskirts of cities. Their incomes vary widely, but even those who make US$400 per month cannot live on that (Lavín 2014: 31). This process of proletarisation intensified after the mid-1990s. The Chief Justice of the Supreme Court and the CBA have denounced the proliferation of law graduates without proper training, who are believed to reduce the price of services and the profession's social status (Marré Velasco 2009: 12).

Santiago, the centre of political and economic power, offers lawyers the greatest economic rewards and highest social status. It contains all the big law firms, although their lawyers travel or delegate tasks for work outside the city (De la Maza et al 2016: 33). The same is true of the in-house legal departments of big corporations, even when they conduct operations in the provinces. Almost all public administrative agencies have their headquarters in Santiago, while maintaining minor branches outside it. Only a small percentage of attorneys who trained outside the capital enter the upper strata of the profession (Guerrero 2014: 33–34).

Women have increased their participation in practice but have not gained an equal share in the more senior positions. In 2014 they were only 32 per cent of large firm lawyers and just 6 per cent of partners (De la Maza et al 2016: 48–49) and earned only 77 per cent as much as men in similar positions (Lavín 2014: 31). Women were just 3 of the 18 members of the CBA board for 2017–21 (Revista del Abogado 2017: 31). They tend to work in some of the least prestigious areas, such as family law, whose allegedly 'soft' expertise carries a lower status (Azócar 2015). The few leading female attorneys, such as Nicole Nehme, a founding partner of the successful antitrust law firm Ferrada-Nehme, and the influential tax expert Carolina Fuensalida, are exceptions to the general pattern (Revista Capital 2017).

IV. THE NEW POLITICS OF RIGHTS: FROM POWER BROKERS TO SPOKESPERSONS?

Modernisation has had a significant influence on lawyers' political roles. Traditionally, they functioned as clerks and power brokers in the political process, enjoying a near monopoly of statecraft. Most congressmen and presidents were aristocratic law graduates, who continued to practise law while serving in government (Dezalay and Garth 2002: 18–22). From the mid-twentieth century, however, lawyers became concerned they were losing influence over socioeconomic reforms to competitors (Novoa Monreal 1972: 36–68). Legal credentials were no longer enough to participate in governance, and dogmatic juridical expertise seemed too rigid to be relevant. Empirical data confirm a growing division of governmental labour and the need for additional investment to gain prominent positions. Elite lawyers do not necessarily enjoy a comparative advantage in the political arena anymore (Villalonga Torrijo 2017).

Elite lawyers' political power declined and other forms of expertise (eg economists and social scientists) consolidated theirs through the new technocracy that dominated liberalisation and social policy from the 1980s to the 2000s (Silva 2012: 143–216). Competition among law graduates and the demand for specialisation have created incentives for lawyers to stay focused on their legal careers, which require continuous attention and offer more stable prospects. As a result, elite lawyers have limited their participation in government and administrative agencies to brief periods.

In 2017 lawyers (mostly from centre and right parties) were 37 per cent of the Senate and the 28 per cent of the Chamber of Deputies, far below the 60 per cent they represented in the early 1970s (Cámara de Diputados 2017; Senado 2017). For most of them, politics is a full-time activity. Lawyers were presidents of the Republic for only two of the seven administrations between 1990 and 2018, whereas all presidents elected democratically during the first half of the twentieth century were law graduates. Agencies of economic decision-making, such as the Central Bank, also have been headed by economists since the 1950s. Lawyers have lost control of the boards of the main business federations, to engineers in the field of manufacturing (Villalonga Torrijo 2017: 11–19). Many lawyers with clear partisan identities serve in the government bureaucracy; and Bar Association elections are fought along political lines. Nevertheless, legal professionals now occupy a subordinate position in the sphere of power.

At the same time, young elite law graduates participate in the political process by offering legal advice and helping to design institutions. Multidisciplinary think tanks, such as Libertad y Desarrollo and Fundación Jaime Guzmán on the right and Instituto Igualdad on the left, compensate for the lack of legal and economic expertise in public debates, especially because politicians are preoccupied with partisan and electoral issues. The first of these has developed a comprehensive legal agenda, including regular legislative bulletins and annual reviews of judicial decisions (Libertad y Desarrollo 2017). The Congress Library and private economic federations have created departments offering legal advice. In all these settings, a few lawyers engage in the first step in their careers in politics, the academy or private practice. Many of those join law schools to teach constitutional law and human rights or big law firms to litigate on economic regulation.

The new political milieu has also opened the door to cause lawyering, which evolved from political dissidence to strategic litigation directed at producing legal reform. The Vicariate of the Solidarity, established by the Catholic Church to seek accountability for human rights violations during military rule, was the first example (in the 1970s–1980s). Military rule itself expanded the possibilities for judicial review (*recursos de protección*), which became an important procedure in ordinary courts. After 1990, ratification of the Inter American Convention on Human Rights and a limited repertoire of administrative remedies also contributed to this phenomenon. But above all it was the liberalisation of Chilean society over the last two decades that increased the demand for this kind of mobilisation. Public interest litigation has turned lawyers into spokespersons in hotly contested areas like LGBT advocacy, indigenous affairs, and religious freedom.

Several law schools pioneered a new style of lawyering before national and international courts. In the 1990s, for example, the Universidad Diego Portales developed an outstanding clinic of public interest litigation related to the areas where its scholars proposed legal reforms, (eg criminal procedure) (González 1999: 21–59). Recently the Pontificia Universidad Católica de Chile engaged in litigation to protect immigrants, an issue that has become controversial. Outside law schools, groups engage in other legal activities, such as producing reports and acting as *amici curiae*. Libertades Públicas, a network of liberal elite lawyers, even sponsored candidates for the CBA board. The LGBT NGO Fundación Iguales and the feminist organisation Humanas have developed an active cause lawyering agenda. The NGO Obeservatorio Ciudadano has litigated on issues like indigenous rights. Conservative attorneys have established Comunidad y Justicia, a cause lawyering group that participates in the cultural wars. This kind of mobilisation has gained legitimacy and even been institutionalised through state-run programmes such as the National Institute of Human Rights and the Human Rights Deputy Secretariat of the Ministry of Interior. In this, Chile followed other Latin American nations (Huneeus et al 2014: 3–20).

These campaigns have often led to litigation before the Inter-American Court of Human Rights. In 1998, the activist Marcel Claude and others filed a constitutional writ against the Foreign Investment Committee, which refused to disclose information about the forestry company Trillium and the environmental effects of its project Río Cóndor. When Chilean courts failed to provide a remedy the plaintiffs filed a petition before the

Inter-American Commission, supported by the NGO Terram, and the Public Interest Litigation Program of the Universidad Diego Portales, among other organisations. In 2005, the case was reviewed by the Inter-American Court, which found for the plaintiffs, declaring that the Chilean state had violated the right to information guaranteed by the American Convention on Human Rights.[7] In response, the Chilean state developed a comprehensive system to assure the transparency and accessibility of publicly held information, which has had a significant impact on political and administrative accountability.[8]

Other examples include anti-terrorism legislation and freedom of expression. Recently, the Chilean state reached an agreement with LGBT NGO Movilh, after it filed a petition with the Commission arguing that the ban on same-sex marriage constituted undue discrimination.[9] This new kind of mobilisation is likely to expand with the emergence of more diverse interest groups and the success of previous campaigns.

Human rights discourse and constitutionalisation are not the sole focus of cause lawyering. Rights-oriented discourse has expanded to areas such as political violence and environmental damage and influenced traditional areas of practice, such as property and contracts, for example litigation challenging price increases in health insurance and labour disputes (García and Verdugo 2013: 81–107). The final result has been a transformation in legal culture. Some lawyers are still attached to positivist jurisprudence and deference to political power. But others increasingly embrace a new understanding of rights and adversarial litigation for political ends.

V. CONCLUSION

Chilean lawyers mirrored the institutional and social changes initiated in the early 1980s. Liberalisation of the economy expanded access to legal training and freed lawyers from the structures of professional governance. The market has encouraged specialisation by lawyers, particularly among those with more social and academic capital. The division of governmental labour and the emergence of competing interest groups have modified the value of a legal credential in politics while opening new spaces for political engagement by lawyers.

Such a transformation has not been free of difficulties, however. Underemployment and insufficient rigour in the certification of legal expertise have fed lawyers' status anxiety. The allocation of prestige and income according to social origin, gender, and geography has generated discomfort. Mobilisation through public interest lawyering and the courts' response have divided the profession and provoked political conflict. Clearly, lawyers have lost the common ethos they once enjoyed.

Lawyers' current challenges reflect the same logic since they are inexorably associated with Chile's economy and political culture. It would be inconceivable to revive the profession's mid-twentieth century model. Indeed, mass education and the technological revolution are likely to produce even greater changes in the future.

---

[7] Inter-American Court of Human Rights, 19 September 2006, Series C 151.
[8] Government of Chile Ley N° 20.285 2009, Statute on Transparency and the Right to Access to Public Hold Information.
[9] Inter-American Commission of Human Rights, Acuerdo de Solución Amistosa, Caso P-946-12.

REFERENCES

Arriagada, I and Naranjo, JP (2016) 'Enseñanza del Derecho fuera de las Aulas Universitarias. Oficinas de Interrogadores y Educación Legal en Chile' 2 *Derecho y Crítica Social* 1.

Asociación de Abogados (2017) www.asociacionabogados.cl.

Azócar Benavente, MJ (2015) 'Expertos en derecho: profesión legal, género y reformas judiciales en Chile' XXVIII(2) *Revista de Derecho* (Valdivia) 9.

Balmaceda Jimeno, N (2000) 'Corporación de Asistencia Judicial y Abogados de Turno ¿Incumplimiento de una garantía constitucional?' 27(4) *Revista Chilena de Derecho* 721.

Benfeld, J (2016) 'La Discusión sobre la Enseñanza del Derecho en Chile dentro del Nuevo Paradigma Universitario: Una Tarea Pendiente' 23(1) *Revista de Derecho Universidad Católica del Norte* 143.

Brunner, JJ (2009) *Educación Superior en Chile. Instituciones, Mercados y Políticas Gubernamentales (1967–2007)* (Santiago, Universidad Diego Portales).

Cámara de Diputados www.camara.cl.

Chaparro, A (2016) 'Los Juicios a los abogados' *El Mercurio Legal* (April) 16.

Colegio de Abogados AG (2017) www.abogados.cl.

Comisión Nacional de Acreditación, 'Buscador de Acreditaciones' www.cnachile.cl/Paginas/buscador-avanzado.aspx.

Corporación de Asistencia Judicial Región Metropolitana (2015) (*Cuenta Pública*. Santiago).

Con, D (2016) 'Nuevos Abogados ¿Cómo los está tratando el mercado?' *Revista del Abogado* (November) 14.

—— (2017) 'Abogados jóvenes ¿por qué afiliarse al colegio de abogados?' *Revista del Abogado* (May) 36.

Couso, J (2007) 'When the Political Complex takes the Lead: The Configuration of the Moderate State in Chile' in L Karpik, T Halliday and M Feeley (eds), *Fighting for Political Freedom. Comparative Studies of the Legal Complex and Political Liberalism* (Portland, Hart Publishing).

De la Maza, I (2002) *Los abogados en Chile: desde el Estado al Mercado* (Santiago, Centro de Investigaciones Jurídicas, Universidad Diego Portales).

De La Maza, I, Mery, R and Vargas, JE (2016) 'Big Law en Chile. Un Vistazo a las Firmas de Abogados' in I De La Maza, R Mery and JE Vargas (eds) *Big Law: Estudios de Abogados en Chile* (Santiago, Thomson Reuters).

Dezalay, Y and Garth, B (2002) *The Internationalization of Palace Wars. Lawyers, Economists, and the Contest to Transform Latin American States* (Chicago, University of Chicago Press).

Dolmestch, H (2016) 'Discurso de Inauguración del Año Judicial 2016' *El Mercurio* (2 March) static.elmercurio.com/Documentos/Legal/2016/03/01/20160301184844.pdf.

Elgueta MF, Zamorano, F and Palma, E (2015) *Primer Estudio Nacional de Caracterización de Estudiantes de Derecho* (Santiago, Unidad de Pedagogía Universitaria y Didáctica del Derecho. Facultad de Derecho, Universidad de Chile).

El Mercurio Legal (2014) 'Tendencias y Perfiles en el Mercado Jurídico Chileno' (December) 25.

Espinoza, O (2005) 'Privatización y Comercialización de la Educación Superior en Chile: Una Visión Crítica' 135 *Revista de Educación Superior* 41.

Fundación Pro-Bono (2014) 'Acuerdo Fundación Pro-Bono y Asociación de Abogados de Familia' probono.cl/2015/home.php/?tag=asociacion-de-abogados-de-familia.

—— (2015) *Memoria Anual* (Santiago).

García, JF and Verdugo, S (2013) *Activismo Judicial en Chile ¿Hacia el Gobierno de los Jueces?* (Santiago, Libertad y Desarrollo).

González Le Saux, M (2017) 'Legal Aid, Social Workers, and the Redefinition of the Legal Profession in Chile, 1925–1960' 42 *Law & Social Inquiry* 347.

González, F (1999) 'Evolución y perspectivas de la Red Universitaria Sudamericana de Clínicas de Interés Público' in F González and F Viveros (eds), *Defensa Jurídica del Interés Público. Enseñanzas Estrategias, y Experiencias* (Santiago, Universidad Diego Portales).

Guerrero, JL (2014) 'Desde la Academia y la Periferia' *El Mercurio Legal* (December) 34.

Guzmán Brito, A (2006) 'La Enseñanza del Derecho. Historia y Perspectivas' XXV N°2 *Anales del Instituto de Chile* 273.

Humeres, H (2008) 'El Abogado de turno: Un trabajo forzoso' in A Fermandois and R Delaveau (eds), *Sentencias Destacadas 2008* (Santiago, Libertad y Desarrollo).

Huneeus, A, Couso, J and Sieder, R (2014) 'Introduction' in J Couso, A Huneeus and R Sieder (eds), *Cultures of Legality: Judicialization and Political Activism in Contemporary Latin America* (New York, Cambridge University Press).

Huneeus, C (2000) *El Régimen de Pinochet* (Santiago, Sudamericana).

Instituto Nacional de Derechos Humanos *Informe Anual 2013* (Santiago, INDH).

Jocelyn-Holt, A (2015) *La Escuela Tomada. Historia/Memoria. 2009–2011* (Santiago, Taurus).

La Tercera (12 June 2017) 'El 70% de los fiscales egresó de universidades del consejo de rectores' www.latercera.com/noticia/fiscales-consejo-rectores.

Lavín, F (2014) 'Cuanto ganan los abogados: el secreto mejor guardado' *El Mercurio Legal* (December) 31.

Libertad y Desarrollo (2017) www.lyd.org.

López Barrera, R (2012) 'Abogados Jóvenes. Postgrados en el extranjero y servicio público' *El Mercurio Legal* (March) www.elmercurio.com/Legal/Noticias/Noticias-y-reportajes/2012/03/16/Abogados-jovenes-perfeccionamiento-y-servicio-publico.aspx.

Lowenstein, S (1970) *Lawyers, Legal Education and Development. An Examination of the Process of Reform in Chile* (New York, International Legal Center).

Marré Velasco, X (2009) 'Calidad de la Abogacía ¿Cómo mejorarla?' *Revista del Abogado* (April) 12.

Merino, V (2015) 'El derecho administrativo no se limita solo a demandar al estado' (Universidad de Valparaíso School of Law) www.uv.cl/pdn/?id=7205.

Muñoz León, F (2014) '¿Hacia una academización de las facultades de derecho en Chile? Un análisis teórico y comparado del conflicto de profesiones' Vol XXVII No 1 *Revista de Derecho (Valdivia)* 9.

Novoa Monreal, E (1972) 'La crisis del derecho y de la profesión de abogado' 10 *Boletín de Docencia e Investigación Jurídica* 39.

Pardo Valencia, F (1969) *Ética y Derecho de la Abogacía en Chile* (Santiago, Editorial Jurídica de Chile).

Pardow, D (2015) 'El Desempeño en Juicio de la FNE: ¿Es realmente un mejor litigante que los demandantes privados?' 22(2) *Revista de Derecho de la Universidad Católica del Norte* 419.

Peña, C (2002) '¿Modernidad Irreflexiva o malestar de las élites?' 5 *Perspectivas* 275.

—— (2003) 'Economic and Political aspects of Judicial Reform: The Chilean Case' in E Jensen and T Heller (eds), *Beyond Common Knowledge. Empirical Approaches to the Rule of Law* (Stanford, Stanford University Press).

Pérez-Perdomo, R (2006) *Latin American Lawyers. A Historical Introduction* (Stanford, Stanford University Press).

Pontificia Universidad Católica de Chile, School of Law (2017) *Program on Legal Corporative Sustainability*, Document of Work.

Revista Capital (2017) 'Especial Abogadas' (July) 25.

Revista del Abogado (2017) 'Elecciones colegio de abogados' (May) 31.

Revista Qué Pasa (2015) 'Ranking de Universidades Chilenas' (11 December) 42.

Rolando, R, Salamanca, J and Aliaga, M (2010) *Evolución Matricula de Educación Superior en Chile. 1990–2010* (Santiago, Ministerio de Educación).

Rolando, R, Salamanca, J and Lara, A (2010) *Retención de Primer Año de Pregrado. Descripción y Análisis de la Cohorte 2007* (Santiago, Ministerio de Educación).

Sehnbruch, K and Seavelis, P (eds) (2014) *El Balance. 20 años de Concertación* (Santiago, Catalonia).

Senado, www.senado.cl.

Sierra, L and Fuenzalida, P (2014) 'Tan lejos, tan cerca: La profesión legal y el Estado en Chile' in P Grez et al (eds) *Una vida en la Universidad de Chile. Celebrando al profesor Antonio Bascuñán Valdés* (Santiago, Thomson Reuters).

Silva, P (2012) *In the Name of Reason. Technocrats and Politics in Chile* (University Park, Penn State University Press).

Tironi, E (1999) *La Irrupción de las Masas y el Malestar de las Élites* (Santiago, Grijalbo).

Vial, G (1995) *Consejo de Defensa del Estado. 100 años de historia* (Santiago, CDE).

Villalonga Torrijo, C (2017) 'Dwindling Professional Authority: Legal Elites and the Division of Governmental Labor in the Administrative State (Evidence from Chile: 1932–1970)' (unpublished manuscript).

Zapata, G and Tejeda, I (2009) *Educación Superior y Mecanismos de Aseguramiento de la Calidad – Informe Nacional, Chile* (Santiago, CINDA).

—— (2016) *La Educación Superior en Chile. 2010–2015* (Santiago, Universia – CINDA).

21

Mexico

Significant Growth and Under-Regulation of the Legal Profession

LUIS FERNANDO PEREZ-HURTADO*

I N THE 30 years since *Lawyers in Society* was published, Mexico has undergone major changes in almost every sphere, including the legal profession. The number of higher education institutions offering a Bachelor of Laws degree (LLB) has grown at a rate of a new law school a week, rising from 93 to 1,715. The number of licences issued annually to practise law increased by 848 per cent, climbing from 3,549 to 33,631.

However, regulation of the legal profession has remained limited, confusing, and disjointed, despite several reform efforts. A 2011 United Nations report on the independence of judges and lawyers in Mexico found that

> the standards that individuals are required to meet in order to become members of the legal profession are not uniform and that there is no independent oversight mechanism for upholding the quality, integrity, ethics and good repute of the profession. (UN General Assembly, 2011)

The professional licence to practise law represents only a proof issued by the Ministry of Education that a valid LLB diploma has been registered at its office. Once lawyers obtain their professional licences, they are entitled to give legal advice as lawyers in relation to any matter and represent clients in proceedings before any local or federal administrative authority or court, including the Mexican Supreme Court. There is no additional requirement to maintain the validity of the licence and practise as a lawyer: no mandatory Bar Association membership, vocational course, apprenticeship, periodic fee or contribution, insurance, continuing legal practice, or continuing legal education.

---

* For further information concerning this chapter, please email luisph@ceead.org.mx. Special thanks to Sandra Escamilla and Hedilberto Rivera for their research support and Marcela Barrio and Leticia Partida for their editing.

I. RECENT DEVELOPMENTS IN THE LEGAL CONTEXT

Over the past 30 years, three major economic, political, and social transformations have especially affected the professional practice of law: trade liberalisation; structural reforms; and democratisation.

A. Trade Liberalisation

In the 1980s, Mexico started a neoliberal transition towards an open economy. In 1986, it adhered to the General Agreement on Tariffs and Trade (GATT), initiating the gradual and reciprocal elimination of tariffs, simplifying importation procedures, opening to foreign investment, and promoting exports by domestic industries. Most of this *apertura* (a term that denotes the opening of markets) occurred after the signing of the 1994 North American Free Trade Agreement (NAFTA) by Mexico, the US, and Canada. NAFTA gradually removed commercial restrictions on trade and investment among those three countries. Today, Mexico is part of 12 free trade agreements granting preferential access to 46 countries and a market representing 58 per cent of the world's GDP (Malpica Soto 2016).

This *apertura* did not significantly affect most legal professionals, who practised in traditional areas, such as civil, criminal, family, commercial or labour law. Nonetheless, it did affect the professional practice and organisation of legal counsellors of companies, as well as domestic and foreign investors. According to Meneses and Caballero (2014), the economic *apertura* 'seems to be the root of two great transformations. On the one hand, the entry of foreign law firms into the national market; and, on the other, the possibility of Mexican law practitioners entering the international market' (p 12). It initiated the arrival of foreign corporate firms and increased commercial agreements between them and Mexican corporate law firms to serve the corporate and financial transactional market.

International firms in Mexico include Baker McKenzie, Greenberg Traurig, Holland & Knight, Jones Day, and White & Case (Chambers & Partners 2017). Their practice usually includes corporate law, securities, antitrust litigation, competition regulation, energy and natural resources, banking, finance, mergers and acquisitions, restructuring, and bankruptcy. Other international law firms are based in convenient locations for specific practices, such as US firms Snell & Wilmer, focused on real estate and commercial finance in San Jose del Cabo, or Maldonado Myers, focused on cross-border disputes in Tijuana. Mergers between international and Mexican firms combine international coverage and local strength, eg Dentons López Velarde, Hogan Lovells BSTL, or AvaLerroux. Some Mexican firms join international networks of independent law firms to reach international clients, like BGI Villarreal, which is part of BGI (Balms Group International) with partner offices in many countries.

Currently, Baker McKenzie (2017) is the largest law firm in Mexico, with 184 lawyers in five cities. By comparison, the largest Mexican law firm is Creel, García-Cuéllar, Aiza y Enríquez, with 150 lawyers in two cities, followed by Santamarina y Steta (135 lawyers), Basham, Ringe y Correa (126), González Calvillo (104), Galicia Abogados (98),

Ritch Mueller (96), and Von Wobeser y Sierra (83). The remaining international and merged law firms have no more than 80 lawyers (The Legal 500 2017).

B. Structural Reforms

During recent decades, Mexican norms, institutions, and structures have been reformed in fundamental areas. According to a 2014 study, the 1917 Mexican Constitution was amended 573 times through 214 reform decrees, but almost two-thirds of those changes occurred in the previous 30 years (Fix-Fierro 2014).

These reforms have significantly affected law practice. In response to more technical and extensive regulations, practitioners and firms have specialised to gain a competitive advantage over generalists (Meneses and Caballero 2014: 21). Because there are no formal certifications, lawyers can advertise as specialists in any field, based mainly on practical experience or advanced law degrees. Another outcome has been increasing opportunities for legal professionals (Fix-Fierro and Lopez-Ayllon 2006: 48–49). New institutions require legal experts to advise and represent clients before them.

A further repercussion is the necessity of continuing legal education (ibid: 22–26). Often, what students learn in law school has been substantially modified by the time they graduate. The market demands that legal advisers remain up-to-date in matters of professional practice. This has benefited law schools and vocational education institutions offering continuing education, diplomas, or master's degrees in areas where law is changing rapidly. For example, in 1970 there were 5,953 students taking advanced law degrees in Mexico; by 2003 the number had risen to 139,669 (ibid: 23). In 2017, 687 law schools offered advanced degrees in various fields, with different modalities, duration, costs, and quality standards (CEEAD 2017a). In addition to their interest in remaining current in a specific field, lawyers pursue these degrees as a marketing tool to attract future clients or as a way to network with colleagues.

C. Mexico's Democratisation

Another important transformation concerns the political-electoral domain. The Institutional Revolutionary Party (PRI) dominated Mexican politics since its creation as the National Revolution Party in 1929, ruling Mexico until 2000. During that period, as Dezalay and Garth (2006: 203) pointed out, '[t]he people in government with legal training based their careers primarily on political contacts. Technical expertise was not highly valued, and institutionally it was subordinate to politics'.

The recent political-electoral fluctuations, combined with economic and social changes, have affected legal norms and institutions. According to López-Ayllón and Fix-Fierro (2003: 504):

> these changes correspond to a new social awareness of the significance of law to achieve modernity, since both the government and major sectors of society have come to believe that, more and more, law is a crucial instrument for the consolidation of a democratic political system and an open market economy.

The new role of law strengthened the judiciary and reinforced the indispensability of law in drafting agreements and resolving conflicts. The professional practice of lawyers became particularly relevant. The success of legal practitioners began to depend more on technical capability than connections within the legal system or involvement in certain social circles. Although it will be a long time before the legal profession is free, responsible, and professional and bases its success on merit, significant steps have been taken.

II. LEGAL EDUCATION[1]

A. Law Schools

In the 2015–16 academic year, there were 1,715 institutions of higher education offering an LLB programme to 312,429 law students (CEEAD 2017a). The 8 per cent (135) that were public law schools enrolled 46 per cent (143,677) of LLB students, while the 92 per cent (1,580) that were private enrolled 54 per cent (168,752). The law schools with the highest enrolment were public; the *Universidad Nacional Autónoma de México* (UNAM), a public institution located in Mexico City, has the largest enrolment with 11,603 LLB students (CEEAD 2017b).

Public law schools are established by federal or state governments and are mainly financed with public resources. They charge low tuition fees (US$1 to US$700 per year) and seek to provide educational opportunities to the largest number of students possible. In most of these institutions, the demand for admission far exceeds their capacity. Each university defines its admission requirements and student selection process, which typically require a standardised admission test assessing general knowledge and ability for any bachelor's degree and, in some cases, specifically for the social sciences. In most of these universities, the test is administered by the National Centre for the Evaluation of Higher Education (CENEVAL), an independent, non-profit institution focused on developing and delivering assessment tools (CENEVAL 2017). Available places are assigned to those with the highest scores. In 2015, 65,290 people applied for the 31,974 places in LLB programmes in public universities; 31,166 enrolled, 51.5 per cent of whom were women.

Private law schools are founded by individuals, religious groups or private entities, and financed primarily by tuition and student fees. Most have a non-profit legal status, but some are for-profit institutions. In 2015, 53,230 students began the LLB programme in private law schools, 48.3 per cent of them women.

Private law schools could be divided informally into two groups: elite and non-prestigious. Elite are characterised by high academic quality, professors with good reputations, adequate infrastructure, and financial resources. Their tuition and fees are

---

[1] All figures in this section, such as law schools, law students and their characteristics, are uploaded annually to a database and displayed as an infographic elaborated by CEEAD from the following sources: SEP, Estadística de Educación Superior, por Carrera, Módulo de Docencia 911.9A [Higher Education Statistics, by degree, Teaching Module 911.9A] (institutional archives); ANUIES, Anuarios Estadísticos de Educación Superior 1985, 1990, 1995, 2000, 2005–2006, 2010–2011, and 2015–2016 [Statistical Yearbooks for Higher Education (by term)].

the highest (up to US$12,000 per year). Since their financial resources come mainly from tuition and fees, their admission policies seek to balance enroling the best students and guaranteeing sufficient tuition income. To select students, they typically conduct admission and psychometric exams, look at high school grades, and conduct interviews.

Most private law schools are not prestigious. They have an 'open door' admission policy, seeking to enrol the largest number of students. Tuition and fees are affordable for middle and middle-low income students (US$1,000 to US$4,000 per year). The admission requirement of these institutions is usually only a high school diploma and a very modest GPA.

Most of these private institutions owe their existence to the limited capacity of public universities and the high tuition fees in private elite universities. Almost 60 per cent of their students would rather study in another institution but either were not admitted or could not afford it (Perez-Hurtado 2009: 121–26). However, for many students (especially those not from conventional professional backgrounds), these institutions offer a good option since they have shorter programmes, more flexible schedules (including night and weekend classes), several modalities (including open and online programmes), and more practical subjects. Besides, these institutions are usually located close to large working areas, in easily accessible centres, or in localities with few – if any – other higher education opportunities. The vast majority of these private institutions are small; in 2015, most had fewer than 80 students.

In 2000, the federal government implemented an accreditation system to assess the quality of all higher education programmes and introduce uniform educational policies (COPAES 2017a). In 2006, two accreditation bodies were created specifically for law programmes: Consejo Nacional para la Acreditación de la Educación Superior en Derecho (CONFEDE) and Consejo Nacional para la Acreditación de la Enseñanza en Derecho (CONAED). To date, only 114 law schools have been accredited: 59 private and 55 public (COPAES 2017b). Accreditation gives public institutions access to additional public funding but has no substantial effect on private institutions. Most private law schools do not have the qualifications to obtain accreditation, although a few have done so to differentiate themselves and promote their graduates among potential employers. Even some elite law schools have chosen not to seek accreditation.

B. Law Students and Faculty

There were 312,429 law students in the 2015–16 academic year, 50.1 per cent female. According to a 2004 study, their average age was 21.3 years; 63 per cent considered themselves middle class; 41 per cent spoke a language other than Spanish (predominantly English and only 1.2 per cent an indigenous language); and 75 per cent were studying in the city where they had attended high school (Perez-Hurtado 2009: 66–79).

There are some differences among law schools. The proportion of women was higher in public institutions (52.4 per cent) than private (48.1 per cent). Students in elite private law schools come from more privileged backgrounds; the vast majority speak a language in addition to Spanish; and the percentage of students who relocate to attend law school is higher. Students in non-prestigious private law schools are slightly older (Perez-Hurtado 2009).

A total of 41.3 per cent of law students work and study at the same time (ibid: 160). However, in elite private law schools, only 33.4 per cent work, and they work an average of 25 hours a week, mostly in law-related jobs with the purpose of becoming familiar with legal practice (ibid: 159–67). In contrast, in non-prestigious private law schools 55.3 per cent work, an average of 34 hours a week, mostly in jobs unrelated to law, and almost 70 per cent for economic reasons (ibid). A high percentage of them had jobs unrelated to law before entering law school and decided to stay in them (ibid: 165). Public law schools fall between these extremes: 40.5 per cent of their students also work, an average of 29 hours per week in law-related jobs, but mainly for economic reasons (ibid: 159–67).

LLB programmes have a high attrition rate. An average of one in five students drops out, suspends temporarily or delays studies during the first year, and almost one in three does so during the first two years (ibid: 81).

Regarding faculty, over 90 per cent of law teachers are lecturers, combining pedagogy with professional practice (ibid: 26). Legal practice remains their principal professional activity, but they dedicate a few hours per week to teaching one or two courses in order to earn additional income (usually very little), keep current with the law, fulfil an academic vocation (ibid: 54–55), or even to recruit the best students for their law firms, courts, companies, or legal offices.

Interestingly, the professors are what students like most in their law programmes, valuing their instructors' practical experience and prestige, as well as their support in obtaining legal jobs or further professional development (ibid: 146–47). Paradoxically, the changes students would most like to see are a more practical focus and better professors (ibid: 151). Although faculty possess practical experience, they are prevented from transmitting it by the curriculum, course materials, and teaching methodologies.

Most law schools prefer lecturers because they are cheaper and easier to find and hire. The disadvantage is that very little research is done in Mexican law schools. Most full-time research-oriented faculty are found in public and elite private law schools, and even there they represent a small percentage of all professors. In appointing full-time faculty, law schools consider teaching and professional experience, publications, advanced degrees, and professional support. For lecturers, they usually consider only the basic law degree and some professional experience in the field, although the better law schools have higher requirements.

C. Increase in Law Schools and Law Students

In the last 30 years, there has been an enormous increase in the number of law schools and law students. While in 1985 there were 93 higher education institutions offering LLB degrees, in 2015 there were 1,715. This means that during this period, the number of law schools grew at a rate of one new law school every week.

The number of LLB students rose from 85,418 in 1985 to 312,429 in 2015,[2] a 266 per cent increase (see Table 1). The proportion of female students rose from 33.3 per cent in 1985 to 48.1 per cent in 2000 and 50.1 per cent in 2015.

---

[2] The total number of students for 2015 is based on what 1,118 higher education institutions reported to the Ministry of Education (SEP). The almost 600 institutions that did not report their data are very small or recently founded, so the actual number of students could be around 10 per cent higher.

Table 1 Enrolment in LLB and all Bachelor's Degree Programmes, by Year and Gender

	1985	1990	1995	2000	2005	2010	2015
LLB enrolment	85,418	106,268	134,576	202,054	231,308	244,015	312,429
# women	28,416	41,588	61,441	97,022	114,313	120,501	156,437
% women	33.3	39.1	45.7	48.1	49.4	49.4	50.1
BA enrolment	966,384	1,078,191	1,217,431	1,585,408	2,070,311	2,530,925	3,632,189
# women	334,087	434,803	549,840	748,307	NA	1,236,794	1,791,102
% women	34.6	40.3	45.2	47.2	NA	48.9	49.3
LLB/BA (%)	8.8	9.9	11.1	12.7	11.2	9.6	8.6

Source: elaborated by the author and CEEAD with information from ANUIES and SEP.

This accelerated growth has several causes (Perez-Hurtado 2009: 50–64). One is the general expansion of higher education.[3] Indeed, enrolment grew slightly faster in all BA programmes (276 per cent) than in LLB programmes (266 per cent). The ratio of LLB students as a proportion of all BA students has remained quite constant over these years, between 8.6 and 12.7 per cent.

Another contributing factor is the boom in private education, which offers easy access. Since the economic *apertura* in the 1980s and Mexico's participation in international organisations like the World Bank and the Organisation for Economic Co-operation and Development (OECD), the country has sought to diversify higher education financing (Maldonado 2000). This has greatly simplified the process for obtaining authorisation to offer higher education degrees (called RVOE), resulting in a great expansion of private higher education.[4] In 1985, half the institutions offering LLBs were private (47 of the 93) and enrolled only 13 per cent of students (11,263). By 2015, 92 per cent of law schools were private (1,580 out of 1,715) and enrolled 54 per cent of students (168,752).

Another cause for growth is the wide variety of reasons why students study law. According to research led by Perez-Hurtado (2009: 55) surveying almost 22,000 Mexican law students in 2004, a legal profession means:

> professionally, a broad range of opportunities for different types of professional practice and locations in which to work; personally, it represents an appropriate income, access to certain social networks, as well as prestige; and socially, it offers the opportunity to expand democracy, social justice, and the common good.

One or more of those motives can easily attract a high school graduate. Furthermore, the study reveals that one of the main experiences fuelling students' interest in studying law was 'that they were victims of violations of their rights or perceived their environment as characterised by injustice, corruption and impunity' (ibid: 93). Almost one in five law students gave that response, and the proportion was significantly higher among those at

---

[3] In 2016, 37.1 per cent of those 18–22 years old were enrolled in bachelor's degree programmes (SEP 2017).
[4] See Acuerdo número 243 por el que se establecen las bases generales de autorización o reconocimiento de validez oficial de estudios [Agreement Number 243 which Establishes the General Bases for Authorisation or Recognition of Official Validity of Studies] (1998); Acuerdo número 279 por el que se establecen los trámites y procedimientos relacionados con el reconocimiento de validez oficial de estudios del tipo superior [Agreement Number 279 which Establishes the Formalities and Procedures Related to the Recognition of Official Validity of Studies] 2000.

public and non-prestigious private universities, women, and students from middle-low or low socioeconomic backgrounds (ibid: 95). The perceived weakness of the rule of law will continue to provoke interest in studying law as both a defence of rights and a transformational mechanism.

D. Contents of the LLB Programme

In Mexico, there is no regulation specifically for law studies or the content of their programmes. If each public university can freely design its law programmes, and private universities need only to establish programmes consistent with their objectives and graduate profiles to obtain the RVOE, we might expect a great diversity of programmes. However, this is not the case. The curriculum is quite homogeneous across law schools. Most programmes include 50 to 70 mandatory subjects, approximately 80 per cent of which are similar across schools. The main differences concern the institution's identity or specialisations offered in the programmes' later years. The most common subjects relate to legal context (Roman law, Mexican legal history, introduction to the study of law, philosophy of law); the traditional practice areas (criminal, civil, commercial, procedural, constitutional, international, administrative, tax, and labour law); and the professional context (legal ethics, legal methodology). However, this education is criticised as too 'encyclopaedic', shallow, lecture-centred, focused on doctrine, and remote from practice.

Environmental, electoral, and international trade law, as well as alternative dispute resolution and legal clinics, have been incorporated recently. Otherwise, however, the academic content and didactic materials have barely changed for decades. One of the reasons is that most faculty are part-time lecturers, who are preoccupied with practising law and do not conduct academic research. Since there is little research, concentrated mainly in public and elite private universities, legal scholarship has stagnated.

Overall, public law schools offer the widest range of law courses, while elite private law schools offer more interdisciplinary, skill-based, business and international law courses, and non-prestigious private law schools offer merely basic law courses. Ultimately, all provide a similar basic legal training.

The main differences in what students learn depend on faculty backgrounds, the quality of academic resources available to students, and the structure of programmes. The last varies in modalities (direct instruction, blended learning, online or distance learning), flexibility (rigid, flexible or specialised programmes), academic terms (annual, semi-annual, four-monthly, quarterly, or bimonthly), duration (2.5 to 5 years), and class schedules (morning, intermediate, evening, night, mixed, or flexible) (Perez-Hurtado 2009: 45–50). Each law school decides the programme's duration, which must include at least 4,800 hours of instruction, whether independent study or under academic supervision, its academic terms, the number of hours per subject, and length of their vacations.

E. Bachelor of Laws Diploma

There is at least one requirement for an LLB besides passing all the courses. All undergraduates must perform at least 480 hours of pro bono work, a requirement established by federal law in 1945.[5] Each university determines the rules for its students' pro bono work, approves the sites where it may be performed, and issues the completion certificate once it receives a letter from the institution confirming the number of hours worked. The main purpose is to offer students professional training and strengthen their social commitment.[6] In practice, however, law students consider this requirement a burden rather than an opportunity, mainly because most already have paid jobs by the end of their programme.

Many non-prestigious law schools require only the minima described above in order to attract students who want to finish the programme as soon as possible. However, other schools, mainly public and elite private, have additional requirements, most often a thesis, a general examination, mastery of a foreign language, or an internship. In 2015, 49,650 students finished their LLB programmes but only 38,214 obtained their diploma. Many students take another year or more to complete all the requirements and receive the diploma. Once they do, they need to obtain a professional licence to practise law.

III. LAW GRADUATES[7]

A. Professional Licence to Practise Law

The Mexican Constitution (1917, Article 5 para 2) allows each state to determine which professions require a licence to practise; all 32 local jurisdictions require one for legal practice (for local laws, see CEEAD 2016). Obtaining a licence to practise law is an administrative procedure before the Federal Ministry of Public Education, which, after verifying a diploma's authenticity, registers it and issues the licence, as proof of the validity of a diploma and its record in the issuing authority's registry of professionals.

Other countries impose additional requirements, including examinations focused on legal practice and professional ethics, a supervised internship, or evidence of practical skills. Mexico requires none of these. As explained below, possession of this licence is the only requirement to practise as a lawyer before any federal or state court, including the Supreme Court.

B. The Increase of Licences to Practise Law

Because there has been an explosion in the number of law schools and students in the last 30 years, the number of professional licences to practise law has also experienced an

---

[5] See Reglamento para la Prestación del Servicio Social de los Estudiantes de las Instituciones de Educación Superior en la República Mexicana [Regulation for the Provision of Pro bono Services by Students in Higher Education Institutions in Mexico], 1981; and Ley Reglamentaria del Artículo 5° Constitucional, Relativo al Ejercicio de las Profesiones en el Distrito Federal [Statutory Law under Article 5 of the Constitution, Related to Professional Practice in the Federal District] 1945.

[6] Reglamento para la Prestación del Servicio Social de los Estudiantes de las Instituciones de Educación Superior en la República Mexicana [Regulation for the Provision of Pro bono Services by Students in Higher Education Institutions in Mexico] 1981.

[7] The information on professional licences for LLB graduates was collected by CEEAD with data from Dirección General de Profesiones (DGP) 2017.

enormous increase. While 3,549 licences were issued to LLB graduates in 1985, 33,631 licences were granted in 2015, an 848 per cent increase in the number issued annually (see Table 2). The proportion issued to women has significantly increased as well, from 27.8 per cent in 1985 to 49.9 per cent in 2015.

Table 2 Professional Licences Issued to LLB Graduates, by Year and Gender

	1985	1990	1995	2000	2005	2010	2015
Professional licences	3,549	7,015	11,573	16,465	25,503	32,791	33,631
Men	2,564	4,690	6,985	9,247	13,252	16,091	16,850
Women	985	2,325	4,588	7,218	12,251	16,700	16,781
% Women	27.8	33.2	39.6	43.8	48.0	50.9	49.9
Population (millions)	75.82	81.25	91.16	97.48	103.26	112.34	119.53
Population/licences	21,364	11,582	7,877	5,921	4,049	3,426	3,554

Source: elaborated by the author and CEEAD with information from SEP and INEGI.

Because the population grew at a slower rate than the number of licences, the ratio of people per licence issued dropped sixfold during this period.

IV. LEGAL PROFESSIONS

The professional licence issued to LLB graduates authorises its holder to engage in the following legal professions.

A. Lawyer

Everyone with an LLB diploma becomes a *licenciado en derecho* or *abogado* (lawyer). However, within the legal professions the term commonly refers only to trial and transactional attorneys and in-house counsel, as discussed below.

B. Public Notary and Public Broker

The *notarios públicos* (public notaries) are legal experts authorised by a state government to give legal form to the people's intentions (eg contracts and wills) as well as to authenticate and give legal certainty to the acts and facts they endorse. Each state has its own notary law, and some also allow notaries to practise as lawyers. All 2,930 public notaries must join a public notary association (Colegio Nacional del Notariado Mexicano 2017).[8]

The *corredores públicos* (public brokers) are legal experts authorised by the federal government to give legal certainty exclusively to commercial transactions and other matters within that government's jurisdiction (Ley Federal de Correduría Pública [Federal

---

[8] There is no limit to the number of public notaries. See Ley del Notariado del Estado de Nuevo León [Notary Law of the State of Nuevo Leon], 1983.

Law of Public Brokerage], 1992).[9] The requirements for qualification and tenure for all 380 public brokers are defined in the Federal Law of Public Brokerage and its regulations (1993),[10] including brokers' obligation to be affiliated to their regional public brokers association.[11]

C. Prosecutor

An *agente del Ministerio Público* or *fiscal* (prosecutor) works in a federal or state attorney general's office prosecuting criminal cases.[12] Hiring and security of employment are governed by law, but personal relations and political contacts heavily influence appointments in many states. In 2013, there were 2,665 federal prosecutors, 43 per cent women (INEGI 2014: 18). At the state level, in 2015 there were 9,248 local prosecutors (INEGI 2016b: 11).

D. Public Defender

A *defensor público* (public defender) works in federal or state public defenders offices representing defendants unable to afford private counsel, mainly in criminal cases.[13] Appointments, like those of prosecutors, follow internal promotions, in some states based on personal and political factors. The Federal Institute of the Public Defender is part of the Council of the Federal Judiciary. Local Institutes of the Public Defender are part of the judicial branch in seven states and the executive branch in the others. In 2015, there were 810 federal and 3,475 local public defenders (INEGI 2016: 20; 2016b: 11; 2016c).

E. Lawyer in the Public Administration

Lawyers in public administration work in federal or local executive branches in positions that require a law degree, mainly in legal departments, advising on a variety of legal issues and the scope and legality of government actions.

F. Judge

Judges sit on federal and local courts, some of which have age or residence requirements for candidates. The judiciary is administered, monitored, and disciplined by the Council

---

[9] See also Secretaría de Economía (2016).
[10] There is no limit to the number of public brokers (Secretaría de Economía, 2017).
[11] Ley Federal de Correduría Pública [Federal Law of Public Brokerage] 1992, Art 15 section IX.
[12] See generally Ley Orgánica de la Procuraduría General de la República [Organic Law of the Attorney General's Office] 2009. For a local example, see Ley Orgánica de la Procuraduría General de Justicia del Estado de Guerrero [Organic Law of the Attorney General of Justice in the State of Guerrero] 2004.
[13] See generally Ley Federal de Defensoría Pública [Federal Law of the Public Defender Office] 1998. For a local example, see Ley de Defensoría Pública para el Estado de Tamaulipas [Law of Public Defender Office in the State of Tamaulipas] 2009.

of the Federal Judiciary (except for the Supreme Court and the Electoral Tribunal) and state Judiciary Councils, whose role is to protect the autonomy of the judicial branch and ensure the impartiality and independence of its members (Political Constitution of the United Mexican States, 1917, Article 94). Recent decades have seen significant advances in judicial independence and professionalism, especially at the federal level. In some states, however, the executive branch still exerts strong influence in the local courts. In 2015, there were 1,281 federal judges, including 11 Supreme Court Justices, and 4,349 local judges, including 577 judges in the 32 Superior Courts of Justice. Women were only 20 per cent of federal and 31 per cent of state judges (INEGI 2016a: 5–6; 2016b: 9).

G. Number of Legal Professionals

The National Survey on Employment (ENOE) of the National Institute of Statistics and Geography (INEGI) provides the only data available regarding legal professionals. Unfortunately, the information is not very accurate because of the ambiguity of occupational categories and the difficulty of making comparisons over time.

According to ENOE, in 2017 there were 862,853 people with an LLB, 47 per cent of whom were women.[14] Of these 862,853 professionals, 79.3 per cent (684,094) were employed, 16.4 per cent (141,211) inactive and 4.3 per cent (37,268) unemployed. Of the 141,211 economically inactive, the majority were women homemakers (60.4 per cent), law graduates pursuing other studies (12.7 per cent), or pensioned or retired (9.6 per cent).

Of the 684,094 people holding an LLB and employed, only 51.3 per cent were engaged in a law-related activity: 83.1 per cent of them as lawyers, 8.2 per cent as professors, 4.6 per cent as area coordinators of legal services, lower court judges or prosecutors, 2.9 per cent as legal assistants, and 1.2 per cent as high governmental or jurisdictional authorities, judges, or directors and legal services managers (INEGI 2011b).[15]

The categories are crude: lawyers include practitioners, legal advisers, corporate lawyers, and public defenders; professors include those at any level, not just higher education. Nevertheless, the ENOE data do reveal that only 40.7 per cent of those with an LLB work in law-related activities and 41.9 per cent of the latter are women. And though there are 141.7 people for every LLB holder, there are 348.2 people for every LLB holder working in law-related activities (INEGI 2016d). During the decade 2005–15, the number of people holding an LLB increased 44.5 per cent, women by 71 per cent and men by 27.2 per cent; but the number of unemployed or economically inactive women increased even more, by 87 per cent (see Table 3).

---

[14] The source of the following data on those with an LLB diploma by gender, activity condition, reason for inactivity and occupation, is the National Survey on Employment (ENOE) (INEGI 2016d). Data are of the fourth quarter of ENOE in 2005, 2010, 2015 and 2016, on those 22 to 65 years old that obtained the LLB diploma. Data for 2005 and 2010 also include a bachelor's degree in criminology because occupational data are constructed from the Mexican Classification of Occupations (CMO) (INEGI 2011a). In 2015 and 2016 data only include the LLB programme because occupational data are constructed from the National Occupational System (SINCO) 2011 (INEGI 2011b). Special thanks to Mónica Chávez Elorza for her support to obtain these data.

[15] It corresponds to the SINCO 2011 classification, which is based mainly on hierarchical structures rather than on career fields.

Table 3 Professionals with an LLB by Activity Status and Reasons for Inactivity, Year and Gender

	2005		2010		2015		Increase
		%		%		%	%
LLB diploma	550,988	100	707,143	100	795,977	100	44.5
Women	213,057	38.7	313,700	44.4	366,040	46.0	71.8
Employed	442,363	80.3	564,445	79.8	620,294	77.9	40.2
Women	151,733	34.3	216,430	38.3	247,070	39.8	62.8
Unemployed	28,749	5.2	34,888	5.0	42,547	5.4	48.0
Women	8,119	28.2	16,469	47.2	19,811	46.6	144.0
Economically inactive	76,263	13.8	106,919	15.1	133,136	16.7	74.6
Women	52,958	69.4	80,339	75.1	99,159	74.5	87.2
Homemakers	35,761	67.5	58,920	73.3	73,202	73.8	104.7
Not available	3,613	0.7	891	0.1	0	0	

Source: Author's estimates based on the fourth quarter of ENOE 2005, 2010 and 2015.

In absolute terms, employed professionals with an LLB grew 40.2 per cent, but in relative terms the economically inactive grew 74.6 per cent.

Among those holding an LLB and performing a professional activity, the proportion engaged in a law-related activity fell slightly, from 54 to 52 per cent (see Table 4). However, the percentage of lawyers and women engaged in law-related activities increased.

Table 4 Employed Professionals with an LLB Diploma, by Occupation, Year and Gender

	2005		2010		2015		Increase
		%		%		%	%
Employed	442,363	100	564,445	100	620,294	100	40.2
Women	151,733	34.3	216,430	38.3	247,070	39.8	62.8
Non-law related	203,347	46.0	267,540	47.4	297,696	48.0	46.4
Women	71,835	35.3	101,525	38.0	117,827	39.6	64.0
Law-related	239,016	54.0	296,905	52.6	322,598	52.0	35.0
Women	79,898	33.4	114,905	38.7	129,243	40.1	61.8
Lawyers	189,128	79.1	254,910	85.9	269,313	83.5	42.4
Women	62,518	33.1	98,103	38.5	98,325	36.5	57.3
Professors	19,678	8.2	15,589	5.2	26,721	8.3	35.8
Women	6,962	35.4	6,618	42.5	15,594	58.4	124.0
Others	30,210	12.7	26,406	8.9	26,564	8.2	-12.1
Women	10,418	34.5	10,184	38.6	15,324	57.7	47.1

Source: Author's estimates based on the fourth quarter of ENOE 2005, 2010 and 2015.

Note: The information included in 'others' cannot be unbundled since the functions included in 2005 and 2010 differ from those in 2015.

In summary, the number of people with an LLB increased 44.5 per cent in the decade but the proportion of those working in law-related activities has decreased from 43.4 to 40.5 per cent.

V. LAWYERS

A. Context

According to ENOE, the 291,767 professionals practising as lawyers (60.2 per cent of them men) represent 83.1 per cent of professionals with an LLB engaged in law-related activities (INEGI 2016d).

B. Regulation and Disciplinary Mechanisms

Regulation of the legal profession in Mexico is limited, confusing, and disjointed, generating several problems for the practice of law.

Anyone can practise as adviser, consultant, or representative in legal matters outside federal or local courts, but no one can claim to be a lawyer without having an LLB. The criminal and civil procedure codes govern litigation and the relationship between lawyers and clients. State laws specify the duties of all professions, such as respecting the confidential nature of communications with clients (with certain legal exceptions) and professionals' obligation to devote their knowledge and technical resources to the client's interests.[16]

There is no code of legal ethics. Federal and state criminal codes prohibit some lawyer behaviour, such as knowingly alleging false facts, submitting false documents, or calling perjurious witnesses; assisting parties with opposed interests; or harming a client by abandoning representation without justification (American Bar Association's Rule of Law Initiative 2011: 16). There are no separate legal proceedings or tribunals for lawyer misconduct. Anyone can complain to the Attorney General about a lawyer's alleged crime, which can be punished by a fine, 2–6 years in prison, and suspension from practice for 2–6 years, but no lawyer has ever been suspended (ibid: 44–46).

After a comprehensive study of the Mexican legal profession in 2011, the Legal Practice Reform Index for Mexico (LPRI) concluded: 'the general consensus among interviewees was that violations of the ethical rules are not infrequent in practice and that the rules are generally not enforced' (ibid: 45). It blamed the lack of interest among victims in prosecuting, the inability of the General Office of Professions and local counterparts to monitor and sanction violations (because staff were over-burdened with administrative tasks), and the absence of incentives for most associations to pursue the frequent violations of their ethics codes (ibid: 45–46).

---

[16] Statutory Law under Art 5 of the Constitution, Related to Professional Practice in the Federal District, 1945, Arts 33–34, 36.

C. Professional Bar Associations

About 6 per cent of legal professionals belong to a Bar Association (American Bar Association's Rule of Law Initiative 2011: 2). The percentage is low because membership is not required to practise law and most lawyers see no benefits in it. The vast majority of Bar Associations function as social clubs or political societies to secure government positions for their leaders and special benefits for their members (ibid: 2).

The Bar Associations with good reputations operate as independent, self-governing bodies, discipline unethical behaviour, promote their members' interests, offer continuing legal education, encourage networking, seek to improve the legal profession, and have criteria for becoming and remaining a member (ibid: 63–65). Most of their members are regarded as competent lawyers. Membership fees vary considerably among Bar Associations but are usually less than US$300 for admission and US$400 annually.

The three Bar Associations with the best reputations are *Ilustre y Nacional Colegio de Abogados* (INCAM), founded in 1760 (the oldest in America); *Barra Mexicana Colegio de Abogados* (BMA), founded in 1922; and *Asociación Nacional de Abogados de Empresa* (ANADE), founded in 1970. BMA has the largest membership with 4,172 lawyers (3,843 men and 282 women), but only 1,644 are active members who pay fees and fulfil all other requirements (information provided by the institution).

D. Reforming the Regulation of Lawyers

Several studies have identified the inadequate regulation of legal practice as one cause for the rule of law's weakness in Mexico. A 2001 report by the UN Human Rights Commission concluded that

> [the] total disorganization of law teaching, and the lack of training to practice the legal profession, as well as the lack of coordination of the profession, without disciplinary procedures that guarantee accountability, may have been the cause of many evils that have afflicted the administration of justice in Mexico for years. (UN Economic and Social Council 2002: 41)

Another example is *Justicia Cotidiana* (Everyday Justice), conducted in 2015 by a group of universities to propose ways to strengthen day-to-day justice in Mexico, which recommended giving priority to improving accountability in professional legal services (Justicia Cotidiana 2015):

> [T]he notorious quality of professional legal services was a recurring and serious problem. Its improvement involves reviewing legal education and the regulation of the legal practice. Although there is consensus on this point, there is no agreement on how to regulate the legal profession, because each proposal presents significant problems. It is therefore essential for future discussion to make this issue a priority. The most critical topic to be analysed is the creation of effective mechanisms for professional accountability and public and accurate reports of their performance. (CIDE 2015: 155)

For several years there has been a search for ways to improve the regulation of legal practice because of studies like these, combined with the rapid increase in the number of law schools, law students, and professional licences, as well as concern within the profession about the quality of legal services.

On 19 October 2010, a constitutional amendment concerning professional practice was submitted to the Senate of the Republic by a group of senators, led by the parliamentary coordinators of the main political parties and lobbied by professional associations, including the leading Bar Associations discussed above. They proposed a general law of professions stipulating which careers require a licence and affiliation to a professional association; regulations for professional associations; mandatory continuing education and periodic renewal of the professional licence; the certification of professionals; the creation of the National Council of Professional Certification; and mechanisms to discipline professional misconduct (Senado de la República 2015). However, this initiative was never considered by the Plenary of the Senate, primarily because of strong opposition from professional groups concerning the distribution of powers between the Federation and states, the proposed mechanisms for monitoring compliance, antipathy to professional monopolies, and aversion to overregulating all professions.

Similar initiatives were submitted to the House of Representatives on 13 July 2011, 10 September 2013, and 27 November 2014 (Senado de la República 2015). Parties representing different political views proposed them, and the same groups lobbied for them, but they failed for similar reasons. A new group of senators, also from the main political parties, submitted another initiative to the Senate on 18 February 2014, lobbied by the same professional associations. They proposed constitutional amendments concerning professions and included a draft General Law of Professional Practice subject to Mandatory Association and Certification (Senado de la República 2015). As the title implies, this initiative focused on establishing the basis for professional associations and certification of certain professional activities, defining the minimum requirements to be observed throughout the country, and distributing powers between the Federation and the states. The law was focused on professions dealing with life, health, freedom, security, and property. Forums were held across the country to discuss these initiatives.

Recognising the difficulty of drafting a single regulation for all professions, however, the three leading Bar Associations mentioned above joined the same group of senators to promote a proposal specifically for lawyers. On 21 May 2015 this group submitted the draft of the General Law of Mexican Advocacy, which seeks to require the association and certification of lawyers as advocates (RENACE 2015). It defines advocacy as representation in any dispute before authorities, courts or alternative means of dispute resolution. Only those with an LLB, the corresponding professional licence, and proof of association and certification could perform this activity. Forums were held throughout the country to discuss and improve both the proposed constitutional amendments and the bill. But nothing more has happened. This failure is due mainly to the rejection of a mandatory Bar Association by most lawyers, who fear it will be exploited for political purposes to limit the activities of those who oppose the government or powerful economic interests, or to create monopolistic market enclaves for the elite (see Cruz Angulo 2016; Revilla 2015; Corta and Reyes Retana 2015). Critics of the reform also noted that the vast majority of professional Bar Associations do not meet the minimum standards of quality, transparency, and professionalism, while the proposed criteria to become a registered Bar Association are 'tailor-made' for the three leading Bar Associations.

Nonetheless, leading proponents, such as the Bar Associations mentioned above, are convinced that mandatory affiliation is essential to improve legal practice (Patiño Jimenez

2015). They believe that lawyers can practise freely, independently and with dignity only if they are affiliated with an effective professional association that represents and protects them, especially against harassment or discrimination. Therefore, they are not willing to consider abandoning the mandatory Bar Association.

These different visions have frustrated efforts to regulate the legal profession. It is evident that many Mexicans agree on the need to improve the quality of the legal profession and ensure that practice adheres to high ethical and professional standards. In the current situation, however, this would be possible only through a clear, comprehensive, and precise regulatory scheme focusing on professional certification, continuous education, and high ethical and professional standards, without a mandatory Bar Association. Until that is created, the limited, confusing, and disjointed regulation for lawyers will persist.

REFERENCES

American Bar Association's Rule of Law Initiative (2011) *Legal Profession Reform Index for Mexico* www.americanbar.org/content/dam/aba/directories/roli/mexico/mexico_legal_profession_reform_index_2011_en.authcheckdam.pdf.

ANADE (nd) *Acerca de ANADE Colegio* (Asociación Nacional de Abogados de Empresas) www.anademx.com.

Baker McKenzie (2017) 'México' www.bakermckenzie.com/en/locations/latin-america/mexico/.

BMA (2017) Information received directly from the BMA by email, 3 July.

—— (nd). '¿Quiénes Somos?' (Barra Mexicana de Abogados) www.bma.org.mx.

CEEAD (2016) *Leyes estatales del ejercicio professional* www.ceead.org.mx/ej-leyes-de-los-estados.html.

—— (2017a) *Infografía, Las escuelas de derecho en México, Ciclo académico 2016–2017* [Law schools in Mexico, Academic year 2016–2017 infographic] (30 May) (Centro de Estudios sobre la Enseñanza y el Aprendizaje del Derecho) www.ceead.org.mx/infograficos/CEEAD_InfografiaLED_2016_2017.pdf.

—— (2017b) *Base de datos de instituciones de educación superior en México que ofrecen la Licenciatura en Derecho* [Mexican Higher Education Institutions which offer a Bachelor of Laws Degree Database] (February) (Centro de Estudios sobre la Enseñanza y el Aprendizaje del Derecho) www.ceead.org.mx/base-de-datos.html.

CENEVAL (2017) *Perfil Institucional* (Centro Nacional de Evaluación para la Educación Superior) www.ceneval.edu.mx/web/guest/perfil-institucional.

Chambers & Partners (2017) *Directory of the Legal Profession* www.chambersandpartners.com.

CIDE (2015) *Informe de resultados de los Foros de Justicia Cotidiana* imco.org.mx/wp-content/uploads/2015/04/Documento_JusticiaCotidiana_.pdf.

Colegio Nacional del Notariado Mexicano (2017) *Directorio de Notarios de la República Mexicana* [Directory of Public Notaries in Mexico] www.notariadomexicano.org.mx/directorio-de-notarios/.

Constitución Política de los Estados Unidos Mexicanos (1917) [Political Constitution of the United Mexican States].

COPAES (2017a) *Proceso de acreditación* (Consejo para la Acreditación de la Educación Superior) www.copaes.org/proceso_acreditacion.php.

—— (2017b) *Consulta de Programas Acreditados* [Database of Accredited Programmes] (Consejo para la Acreditación de la Educación Superior) www.copaes.org/consulta.php.

Corta, V and Reyes Retana, I (2015). *Por qué no es buena idea la colegiación obligatoria* [Why mandatory affiliation is not a good idea] (El Mundo del Abogado) www.elmundodelabogado.com/revista/posiciones/item/por-que-no-es-buena-idea-la-colegiacion-obligatoria.

Cruz Angulo, J (2016) '25 errores de la Ley general de abogacía mexicana' [25 mistakes of the Mexican General Advocacy Law] (Derecho en Acción) (11 February) www.derechoenaccion.cide.edu/25-errores-de-la-ley-general-de-abogacia-mexicana/#_ftn4.

Dezalay, Y and Garth, BG (2006) 'De elite dividida a profesión cosmopolita: los abogados y las estrategias internacionales en la construcción de la autonomía del derecho en México' in H Fix-Fierro, *Del gobierno de los abogados al imperio de las leyes: Estudios sociojurídicos sobre educación y profesión jurídicas en el México contemporáneo* (Mexico City, IIJ UNAM) 185–253 https://archivos.juridicas.unam.mx/www/bjv/libros/5/2261/9.pdf.

Dirección General de Profesiones (2017) *Base de datos de cédulas profesionales* [Professional Licenses Database] (Institutional archive).

Fix-Fierro, H (2014) 'Engordando la Constitución' [Fattening the Constitution] *Nexos* (1 February) www.nexos.com.mx/?p=18375.

Fix-Fierro, H and Lopez-Ayllon, S (2006) '¿Muchos abogados, pero poca profesión? Derecho y Profesión Jurídica en el México Contemporáneo' [Many lawyers, but little profession? Law and legal profession in contemporary Mexico] in H Fix-Fierro, *Del gobierno de los abogados al imperio de las leyes: Estudios sociojurídicos sobre educación y profesión jurídicas en el México contemporáneo* (Mexico City, IIJ UNAM) https://archivos.juridicas.unam.mx/www/bjv/libros/5/2261/4.pdf.

INCAM (nd) 'Historia' (Ilustre y Nacional Colegio de Abogados de México) www.incam.org/historia.

INEGI (2011a) *Clasificación Mexicana de Ocupaciones* (CMO) [Mexican Classification of Occupations] vol II (Instituto Nacional de Estadística, Geografía e Informática) www.inegi.org.mx/contenidos/clasificadoresycatalogos/doc/clasificacion_mexicana_de_ocupaciones_vol_ii.pdf.

—— (2011b) *Sistema Nacional de Clasificación de Ocupaciones 2011* (SINCO) [National Occupational System 2011] www.colef.mx/emif/eng/metodologia/catalogos/emifnte/2013/Catalogo%20del%20Sistema%20Nacional%20de%20Clasificacion%20de%20Ocuapciones%20(SINCO-2011).pdf.

INEGI (2014) *Censo Nacional de Procuración de Justicia Federal 2014: Resultados* [2014 National Census on Federal Prosecution: Results] (Instituto Nacional de Estadística y Geografía) internet.contenidos.inegi.org.mx/contenidos/Productos/prod_serv/contenidos/espanol/bvinegi/productos/nueva_estruc/702825080853.pdf.

—— (2016a) *Censo Nacional de Impartición de Justicia Federal 2016: Resultados* [2016 National Census on the Federal Justice System: Results] internet.contenidos.inegi.org.mx/contenidos/Productos/prod_serv/contenidos/espanol/bvinegi/productos/nueva_estruc/702825091569.pdf.

—— (2016b) *Censo Nacional de Procuración de Justicia Estatal 2016: Resultados* [2016 National Census on State Prosecution: Results] internet.contenidos.inegi.org.mx/contenidos/Productos/prod_serv/contenidos/espanol/bvinegi/productos/nueva_estruc/702825091576.pdf.

—— (2016c) *Censo Nacional de Gobierno, Seguridad Pública y Sistema Penitenciario Estatales 2016* [2016 National Census of State Government, Public Safety and Penitentiary System] www.inegi.org.mx/programas/cngspspe/2016/.

—— (2016d) *CONAPO, Proyecciones de la Población en México, 2010–2030* [Projections of the Population in Mexico, 2010–2030] from *Anuario estadístico y geográfico de los Estados Unidos Mexicanos 2016* [Statistical and geographical yearbook of the United Mexican States] www.beta.inegi.org.mx/app/biblioteca/ficha.html?upc=702825087340.

—— (2016d) *Encuesta Nacional de Ocupación y Empleo* (ENOE) [National Survey on Employment] www.inegi.org.mx/programas/enoe/15ymas/default.html#Microdatos.

Justicia Cotidiana (2015) www.gob.mx/justiciacotidiana.
Lopez-Ayllon, S and Fix-Fierro, H (2003) '"¡Tan Cerca, Tan Lejos!" Estado de Derecho y Cambio Jurídico en México (1970–2000)' ["So Close, So Far!" State of Law and Legal Change in México (1970–2000)] in H Fix-Fierro, LFM and RP Perez (eds), *Culturas jurídicas latinas de Europa y América en tiempos de globalización* [Latin legal cultures of Europe and America in times of globalization] (Mexico City, IIJ UNAM) 503–603.
Maldonado, A (2000) 'Los organismos internacionales y la educación en México. El caso de la educación superior y el Banco Mundial' 87 *Perfiles Educativos*.
Malpica Soto, G (2016) 'Presentación en la Dirección General de Profesiones' [Presentation at the General Office of Professions] (16 November) (author's archives).
Meneses, R and Caballero, J (2014) *Globalizados y tradicionales: el perfil de los abogados corporativos en México* (Mexico City, CIDE) 12.
Patiño Jimenez, S (2015) '*BMA, ANADE e INCAM: unidos por la colegiación obligatoria*' [BMA, ANADE and INCAM: united for mandatory affiliation] (Abogado Corporativo) studylib.es/doc/5447457/bma--anade-e-incam--unidos-por-la-colegiaci%C3%B3n-obligatoria.
Perez-Hurtado, L (2009) *La futura generación de abogados mexicanos. Estudio de las escuelas y los estudiantes de derecho en México* [The future generation of Mexican lawyers. Study of law schools and law students in Mexico] (Mexico City, IIJ UNAM-CEEAD).
RENACE (2015) *Proyecto Final de Ley General de la Abogacía Mexicana* [Final Draft of the General Law of Mexican Advocacy] (21 May) www.renace.org.mx/renace2015/wp-content/uploads/2015/12/Ley-General-de-la-Abogac%C3%ADa-Mexicana-PROYECTO-FINAL.pdf.
Revilla, E (2015) 'Colegiación obligatoria y certificación periódica de abogados' [Mandatory affiliation and periodical lawyer certification] *El Economista* (15 October) www.eleconomista.com.mx/opinion/Colegiacion-obligatoria-y-certificacion-periodica-de-abogados-20151015-0005.html.
Secretaría de Economía (2016) 'Correduría Pública' [Public Brokerage] www.correduriapublica.gob.mx/correduria/?.
—— (2017) 'Directorio de Corredores Públicos' [Directory of Public Brokers] www.gob.mx/cms/uploads/attachment/file/157916/Directorio_Corredores_P_blicos.pdf.
Senado de la República (2015) *Proyecto de iniciativa de reformas constitucionales en materia de ejercicio de actividades profesionales y calidad de los servicios de abogados.*
SEP (2017) *Estadística del Sistema Educativo en la República Mexicana, Ciclo Escolar 2015–2016* [Statistics of the Education System in Mexico, Academic Year 2015–2016] (Secretaría de Educación Pública) September www.snie.sep.gob.mx/descargas/estadistica_e_indicadores/estadistica_e_indicadores_educativos_33Nacional.pdf.
The Legal 500 www.legal500.com.
UN Economic and Social Council (2002) *Civil and Political Rights, Including Questions of: Independence of the Judiciary, Administration of Justice, Impunity*, E/CN.4/2002/72/Add.1 (24 January) undocs.org/E/CN.4/2002/72/Add.1.
UN General Assembly (2011) *Report of the Special Rapporteur on the independence of judges and lawyers. Addendum: Mission to Mexico*, A/HRC/17/30/Add.3 (18 April) undocs.org/A/HRC/17/30/Add.3.

22

Venezuela
A Despatch from the Abyss

MANUEL GÓMEZ AND ROGELIO PÉREZ-PERDOMO

I. INTRODUCTION: ON THE EDGE OF THE ABYSS

VENEZUELAN LAWYERS ARE in a state of flux. The deep political, economic and social crisis their country has suffered for more than a decade has provoked an unprecedented exodus, and legal professionals are no exception. By early 2018 about four million Venezuelans – or more than 10 per cent of the population – had emigrated since the beginning of the Chavista revolution in the late 1990s (Forero 2018). This so-called Bolivarian diaspora (Wyss 2017) has included people from different socio-economic strata and backgrounds. During the first wave the majority of émigrés had college degrees, and many were professionals (Olivares 2014), causing a serious brain drain (Gillespie 2017). The massive numbers fleeing the hardships of the Maduro regime on foot to Colombia have prompted comparisons with the mass exoduses from Cuba and El Salvador during the 1980s and 1990s and the ongoing humanitarian crises of Syria and Myanmar (Londoño 2018; Long and Schipani 2018).

Although we do not know how many lawyers, law students or other legal professionals have left the country, a recent study of the professional trajectory of 2006–16 graduates of Universidad Metropolitana Law School showed that more than half reside in another country, the majority of whom are doing law-related work (Capriles and Pérez-Perdomo 2019). These results are consistent with our own observations and preliminary discoveries from data collected in a comprehensive study of the professional occupations and challenges faced by Venezuelan expatriate lawyers (Gómez et al 2020), which found that many have been able to join the legal professions of other nations but also face significant challenges, including immigration status, foreign language proficiency, restrictive licensing requirements, and local market conditions. The successful are usually employed by the legal departments of multinational corporations, international organs or intergovernmental agencies, global law firms and, to a much lesser extent, universities and other institutions as law professors or researchers (ibid).

Émigrés have often attended just two of 26 law schools: Universidad Católica Andrés Bello (UCAB) and Universidad Metropolitana de Caracas (Unimet), whose graduates also constitute the vast majority of the corporate legal sector in Venezuela (Gómez and

Pérez-Perdomo 2018). These schools attract the best students and professors, and Unimet also offered a curriculum geared to contemporary needs, including foreign language skills, legal skills, and problem-based learning (Capriles and Pérez-Perdomo 2019).

With a few exceptions, *Ucabistas* and *Unimetanos* (as they call themselves), dominated the local law firm market until recently. The public sector, including the judiciary, was mostly populated by graduates of the Universidad Central de Venezuela (UCV) and to a lesser extent the Universidad Santa María (USM), as well as those from other regional law schools, such as Universidad de Los Andes (ULA) or La Universidad del Zulia (LUZ) (depending on the region). In the last few years, however, the majority of judicial appointees have been graduates of Universidad Bolivariana (UBV), founded by the Chavista regime in 2003 to reshape higher education by infusing curricula with its political ideology in order to groom future generations of unconditionally loyal state bureaucrats.

The erosion of the rule of law, extreme politicisation of the judiciary, widespread repression of political dissidents, persecution of ordinary citizens, and mounting economic crisis have contributed to reshaping the legal profession both internally and with respect to society. Venezuelan lawyers have had to learn to navigate an uncertain institutional landscape, where the 'know-who' has become much more important than the 'know-how', even for something as trivial as paying court fees or obtaining a certified birth certificate. The division between Chavistas or Maduristas and their opponents has become a challenge for legal professionals, who cannot avoid being labelled one or the other and suffering scorn and even physical violence. The mounting levels of police and other government abuse have propelled a growing number of lawyers into human rights advocacy and activism, which they must juggle with their other professional commitments (Gómez 2010).

The current landscape is difficult to understand and describe because, despite the government's disdain for the rule of law, human rights, separation of powers and other tenets of democracy, the Maduro regime, like its precursor under Chávez, still seeks the appearance of legality. Law, however, has been seen more as an instrument to seize and wield political power regardless of its legitimacy than as a concept that embodies justice, equality and other democratic ideals (Gómez 2015). As we explain below, there has been an exponential increase in the number of government-sponsored law schools and their graduates. The regime has packed the courts from top to bottom with ideologues and political operatives appointed without regard to academic merit or professional accomplishment (Pérez-Perdomo and Santacruz 2017). The representation of the Venezuelan state before international organisations and through the diplomatic corps has also involved lawyers, although to a much lesser extent than previously. These 'revolutionary lawyers' have created professional organisations to advance their own conception of what it means to be a lawyer.

II. ONCE UPON A TIME: LAWYERS IN A PACTED DEMOCRACY

During the second half of the twentieth century, Venezuela was a model of stability, progress, and upward social mobility. From 1958 to 1998, the Republic was nominally a democracy. The transition to democracy after years of military dictatorship was facilitated by a declaration of principles, the *Pacto de Punto Fijo*, by which the leaders of the major political forces affirmed their willingness to uphold fundamental democratic principles, defend the Constitution, and form a government of national unity representing all sectors of society. In the following decades, elections were held regularly, the executive, legislature, and judiciary enjoyed a degree of independence, and civil society played an important role. The system is described as a 'pacted' democracy (Gómez 2009) since it was dominated by two major parties, which alternated in power. *Acción Democrática* (AD), the social-democratic or white party (*La tolda blanca*), won the election five times. The *Comité de Organización Política Electoral Independiente* (COPEI), the Christian-democratic party, held office for only two terms (1969–74 and 1979–84) but was part of a coalition with AD in the first constitutional term. As the two traditional parties lost most of their power during the early 1990s, the last period of pacted democracy (1993–98) was governed by a coalition of former COPEI leaders and left-wing parties.

During the pacted democracy, the party occupying the presidency or having a majority in Congress did not necessarily dominate the other. Rather, the major parties often relied on coalitions with smaller parties to advance their legislative agendas. The pact was a living arrangement allocating political power through the distribution of key government positions, congressional seats, judicial appointments, and public contracts and requiring respect for opposition parties (Gómez 2011).

Lawyers became important players. They possessed not only the technical expertise to deal with the legal system – the know-how – but also the necessary connections – the know-who – to navigate the complicated relationship between the private and public sectors. Law graduates populated the entire state apparatus, from top cabinet positions to routine bureaucratic jobs. Congress was also filled with lawyers (Pérez-Perdomo 1981; 2003). The advent of democracy coincided with industrialisation, nationalisation of the oil industry, and an unprecedented level of economic prosperity, earning the country the moniker of Saudi Venezuela (*Venezuela Saudita*). Yet Venezuelan democracy had its blemishes, one of the most visible of which was the weakness of the rule of law. The police were abusive, especially toward the lower socio-economic strata and those who fit the 'profile' of an offender. There was a significant judicial backlog, and courts were not very committed to upholding human rights or due process. Prisons were overcrowded and lacked the most basic sanitary conditions, and a significant number of prisoners were awaiting sentence. Most problematic was the pervasive corruption. Bribes and influence peddling of judges and high-ranking public officials became rampant by the 1980s (Pérez-Perdomo 2003; 2011).

In the absence of trustworthy legal institutions, the stability of the political system depended on agreements among elites, the driving force behind the political parties (Rey 1991). Their tentacles influenced every aspect of life, including the selection of judges, university presidents, deans, and even beauty queens. Given that parties were the main vehicles through which elites exercised power, the country really was a parties' democracy (*democracia de partidos*) or 'partidocracy', rather than a traditional democracy. Other groups also had an important voice in running the country: business associations and trade unions, the Catholic Church, and high-ranking members of the military. The networks of influence that developed between these and other influential players were the lubricant that greased the squeaky wheels of the legal system and the rest of the state

(Gómez 2011). Lawyers, predictably, were at the epicenter of political elites, and some benefited from the power they accumulated.

The economic system during the pacted democracy depended mostly on the production and export of hydrocarbons and protectionist policies shielding domestic enterprises from outside competition through tariffs and non-tariff barriers. The 1960s and 1970s were marked by government policies fostering industrialisation, nationalisation of strategic industries (eg oil and other hydrocarbons, minerals) and restrictions on foreign investors regarding activities like banking. These policies produced economic growth and the highest per capita income in Latin America until 1980 (Karl 1986), as well as an unprecedented volume of work and wealth for legal professionals. Despite the comparatively small size of the Venezuelan corporate legal sector, the local, mostly family-owned, law firms became very prosperous.

During the years of Saudi Venezuela there was enough legal work for everyone. Since most was inbound, lawyers did not feel the need to internationalise or worry about liaising with foreign colleagues unless their clients or the type of work demanded this, or if they wanted to specialise in a field for which a foreign graduate degree was desirable. There was only one foreign law firm – Baker McKenzie – although a number of foreign lawyers affiliated with big local firms, and a small but growing number of local lawyers had pursued graduate studies overseas and worked in foreign firms (Mézsaros and Pérez-Perdomo 2017).

Since politics permeated social life, leadership of the Bar Associations (*Colegios de Abogados*) was also influenced by the political pact to ensure that legal professionals did not make waves. Because of the economic prosperity, social mobility and relative progress, lawyers were not very engaged in social change, human rights activism or the transformation of the legal profession. Nevertheless, the government responded to the severe economic difficulties of the 1980s with strict economic measures, including currency exchange restrictions, which, for the first time, exposed the vulnerability of the country's democratic foundations.

In 1989, soon after being reelected president, Carlos Andrés Pérez – one of the traditional AD leaders – tried to jettison traditional party politics through a bold reform dubbed 'the great turnaround' (*El gran viraje*), which sought to open the economy to international markets and align it with International Monetary Fund recommendations. These policies produced economic growth benefiting the upper and middle class but not the poor, raising social tensions and provoking major protests, including riots, looting and extreme violence, forcing the government to suspend its plans. The political crisis paved the way for an unexpected transition to a populist regime (López Maya 2005). Pérez faced two attempted coups d'état, including one in 1992 led by lieutenant colonel Hugo Chávez, and was finally removed from office amidst a political scandal. The next five years were marked by growing uncertainty, a profound banking crisis and political turmoil, which, despite a seemingly stable term led by COPEI's founder, Rafael Caldera, proved fatal to Venezuelan democracy. In 1993 Caldera had split from COPEI, winning the election and becoming president one more time but on behalf of a coalition of small leftist and centre-right political parties called *Convergencia*.

Despite enormous political uncertainty and mounting social discontent, the 1990s were a good decade for corporate lawyers. A government plan dubbed 'The Oil Opening' (*La Apertura Petrolera*) encouraged powerful multinational companies to re-enter the country through special contracts to explore and exploit its untapped hydrocarbon reserves–some of the largest in the world. The once small and predominantly local corporate law firm market grew exponentially to handle the influx of work from powerful foreign clients and their Wall Street firms. This caused some of the leading Venezuelan corporate firms to hire associates, open new offices around the country, and imitate the organisational structure of their foreign counterparts. Hourly fees paid in US dollars became the norm for foreign or corporate clients, and acquiring a foreign graduate law degree (ideally an LLM from a top US law school) became essential for any lawyer seeking to climb the partnership ladder of the leading firms. Many lawyers with foreign master's degrees also worked as summer associates at large US firms, exposing them to US law practice and law firm internal structure. Returning to Venezuela, these lawyers transmitted their experience to their respective firms and replicated some of the skills they learned. Some described the ecstasy of the Venezuelan Big Law sector during the 1990s by saying it felt 'as if instead of oil, the multinational companies had struck holy water, and the lawyers were carrying buckets of it' (Gómez and Pérez-Perdomo 2018: 303).

The euphoria experienced by those in the higher echelons of the legal profession did not trickle down to other lawyers or ordinary people. The financial crisis meant the collapse of several important banks, causing thousands to lose their life savings overnight. The government responded with emergency legislation placing the affected institutions under special management and receivership and creating a separate jurisdiction for financial matters. Since many big law firms had a close relationship with the banks and served on their boards, these lawyers became the targets of criminal investigations and prosecutions, and some went to jail. There were growing accusations of police abuse and human rights violations, some going back as far as the 1989 riots known as 'El Caracazo'. These events prompted a small group of lawyers to represent the victims, becoming Venezuela's first human rights advocates (Gómez 2010). The judiciary was also plagued by widespread allegations of corruption, backlog and inefficiency; but since the World Bank had chosen Venezuela as one of the first beneficiaries of its judicial reform efforts and involved local scholars, policymakers and experts, there was hope the crisis would soon be resolved.

III. THE ADVENT OF THE CHAVISTA REVOLUTION AND JUSTICE'S MISFORTUNES

In December 1998, Hugo Chávez, a political outsider and former army officer who had led an unsuccessful coup d'état six years earlier, won the presidential election after being pardoned by President Caldera. His first electoral promise included overhauling the Constitution and restructuring the state apparatus. A Constituent Assembly appointed during his first year in office produced a new Constitution, which created two additional branches of government, transformed the legislature into a unicameral body, and changed the country's name to the 'Bolivarian Republic of Venezuela'.

Chávez claimed to be leading a democratic and socialist revolution, which he called 'Bolivarian' to evoke Simón Bolívar, the Venezuela-born hero who led five South American colonies to independence. During the heyday of his popularity, Chávez achieved international legitimacy by calling and winning numerous elections and referenda. It was less evident, however, that these electoral processes were being manipulated to strengthen an authoritarian and personalistic government of *Comandante Chávez* [Commander Chávez], as his followers called him. From its early days, the regime forged a close alliance with Cuba and claimed to be on the verge of war with the United States. An unexpected upsurge in global oil prices lasting several years gave Chávez enough economic power to build alliances throughout the global south and embark on an unprecedented expansion of the state bureaucracy through a web of politically controlled social programmes named 'missions to save the people' (Gómez, 2015). Unlike the windfall of corporate legal work during the 1990s, the only lawyers benefiting were the handful the government did not link to the opposition.

Like its predecessors, the Chávez administration distributed privileges and perks to its political network, whose members pledged unconditional loyalty to the ruling party; those outside this circle were treated as enemies and banished. In the wake of the massive oil strike that paralysed the Venezuelan oil sector in 2002–03, Chavez purged PDVSA, the state-owned oil company, by firing tens of thousands of employees and replacing them with political cronies. The traditional Venezuelan law firms that had represented PDVSA and other government-controlled entities for decades were called 'radioactive'. As supporters of the opposition they were enemies of the Revolution, and all government entities stopped retaining them and treated their lawyers as pariahs. None of their clients could get government contracts or participate in the incredibly lucrative deals involving the state or its partners (Gómez and Pérez-Perdomo 2018).

Notwithstanding the ultra-nationalist political discourse, the complexity of oil transactions and related business demanded sophisticated legal advisers, which the government lacked. This created valuable opportunities for new players in the corporate legal sector, including a handful of foreign law firms that had established offices in the country or whose members had forged personal contacts at the highest levels of government. During the subsequent years, these new business lawyers shared in the bonanza created by skyrocketing oil prices, which in turn financed the export of the Chavista revolution. Given the government's new international partners and political allies, its lawyers had to familiarise themselves with and provide legal services to entities from countries such as Brazil, China, Russia, Iran, Argentina, Ecuador and Bolivia.

Not all legal work came from new business ventures, assisting with project finance or advising on mergers and acquisitions. An upsurge in international arbitration claims against Venezuela arising from confiscations occupied the administration's legal advisers, including such US firms as Arnold & Porter, Foley Hoag and Curtis Mallet Prevost & Mosle. Venezuela also sought legal assistance from nontraditional newcomers, such as the Buenos Aires-based boutique law firm Guglielmino & Asociados, founded by members of the team that represented Argentina against a similar wave of foreign-investment related claims. Because the claimants in most of these cases were the foreign companies that had entered Venezuela during the 1990s, they retained the lawyers who had assisted them during the days of Caldera's oil opening. For the embattled Venezuelan corporate law firms spurned by the Chavista regime, this string of lucrative cases brought respite from the mounting hardships.

In December 2012, Chávez traveled to Cuba in a shroud of secrecy and speculation to seek cancer treatment and died soon after his return in March 2013. His hand-picked successor was Nicolás Maduro, a member of Chávez's inner circle who had held several key posts, including President of the National Assembly, Vice-President, and Minister of

Foreign Affairs. The Constitution required an election, which he won by only a narrow margin despite the enormous resources the government invested in the campaign. His administration vowed to build on Chávez's legacy, but the reality was very different. The year Chávez died oil prices plummeted. The huge bureaucracy and populist machinery created by Chávez, including the *Misiones* social programmes, coupled with billions of dollars in foreign aid to political allies, left the government heavily indebted to foreign creditors from China and Russia. Maduro also lacked his predecessor's popularity and appeared to have no control over his party or international allies.

As a result, Venezuela is suffering a very serious humanitarian crisis. The staggering inflation, which was 27,364 per cent in May 2018 (Forbes 2018) and could reach a million per cent by the end of the year (Casey 2018), coupled with failed economic policies and a deep political crisis, have placed the country among the worst performing in the region and the world. More than 80 per cent of the population is under the poverty line, and the scarcity of food, medicines, and consumer goods is dramatic. It has become much harder, if not impossible, to import raw materials for manufacturing, machinery, and other components needed to run the country's commercial and industrial sectors. During the first trimester of 2017, numerous protests flooded the streets of Venezuela's main cities, leaving behind an unprecedented death toll and hundreds of detained civilians, many of whom have been tortured or held incommunicado. In 2018, protests continued but on a much smaller scale, in part because of police and military repression.

The systematic violation of human rights has prompted many countries and international organisations to criticise the Venezuelan government. The European Union and the United States imposed severe sanctions on a growing number of high-profile Venezuelan officials, including eight Justices of the Supreme Justice Tribunal and the Vice-President, for playing 'a significant role in international narcotics trafficking' (US 2017). The number of political prisoners continues to grow (CSIS 2018; Human Rights Watch 2018; López Maya 2016; Pérez-Perdomo 2014). There were at least 234 by the end of March 2018 according to a recent report from the human rights group Foro Penal Venezolano (2018). This astonishing figure, coupled with the thousands of citizens detained for political reasons since Chávez took power (Silva Franco 2014), have made Venezuela one of the worst countries in the western hemisphere for human rights, democracy, and the rule of law. According to the same report, ordinary citizens are sometimes charged in military courts and detained for long periods without bail, access to counsel or other basic guarantees. The response of the Maduro regime has been to deny any wrongdoing and accuse the opposition of conspiring to overthrow the government. The military – together with paramilitary groups and government-sponsored militias – has continued to repress all forms of protest, often with excessive force. The armed forces have also been tasked with overseeing the distribution of food and other goods in order to ensure that these reach only those who demonstrate unconditional allegiance to the ruling party. Corruption has attained a level far beyond that in the worst times of the partydocracy.

The once-prominent local law firms, whose offices occupied the most expensive real estate in Caracas, have downsized significantly, and some have closed. Every month more partners and associates emigrate. Some have made the transition with ease, but others have had to enrol in law school, supplement their income with non-lawyer activities, or change their profession (Faiola 2018). The country's law schools – mainly the private and public-autonomous ones – are struggling to survive. University libraries have not been able to acquire new publications, and publishing houses have significantly reduced their production schedules. Faculty hiring and retention is more difficult every day.

Some émigré law professors still teach their Venezuelan students via Skype or other remote communication platforms, but Internet service is unreliable. Law students are more engaged in social justice causes than their predecessors, leading anti-government protests and fighting for human rights and the release of political prisoners. Nonetheless, the incredible uncertainty and lack of career prospects have taken a toll. The majority of law students are planning to leave the country when they graduate, consistent with a study finding that more than 88 per cent of the recent graduates of four universities wanted to emigrate as soon as possible (Pimentel and Herrera 2017).

IV. THE COMMANDER'S JUSTICE

Before Chávez's ascent to power, the Pérez and Caldera administrations attempted to address some of the most serious problems affecting the justice system. During Pérez's last term the government obtained World Bank funds to modernise the Supreme Court and embark on a comprehensive judicial reform agenda. These and other initiatives were temporarily interrupted by the political crisis leading to Pérez's impeachment, but the Caldera government was able to resume them. One significant step was a Justice of the Peace statute (*Ley Orgánica de la Justicia de Paz*) in 1995, seeking to improve access to justice by launching small claims courts.

Another initiative was the Organic Code of Criminal Procedure of 1998, which introduced two important innovations – oral proceedings and the jury system for some cases – in order to reduce the enormous backlog in the criminal courts and make trials fairer and more efficient. Unfortunately, the Code had to be amended several times (Alguíndigue and Perez-Perdomo 2008; 2013). Only a few municipalities have implemented the justice of peace system, which is generally deemed a failure (Zubillaga Gabaldón 2007). At the same time armed militias known as *círculos bolivarianos* were created to suppress the opposition or anyone believed to pose an obstacle to the so-called Bolivarian revolution. The new criminal procedure, intended to guarantee freedom, was amended to become an instrument of repression, endowing prosecutors with increased discretion, which they used to cover up crimes and police abuses (Alguíndigue and Pérez-Perdomo 2008; 2013).

An important innovation of the 1990s was the promotion of alternative dispute resolution mechanisms in labour and employment cases and matters involving children and adolescents (Pérez-Perdomo 2011; Gómez and Pérez-Perdomo 2006). One of the most important milestones was the Commercial Arbitration Act (CAA) of 1998, which, with international treaties ratified around that time, brought the legal framework for protecting and promoting international trade up to international standards. The rash of investor-state arbitration claims against Venezuela, prompted the Chavista government to mount a fierce defence, denouncing the International Convention on the Settlement of Investment of Disputes between States, which it had signed, and promoting an alternative international arbitration forum under the auspices of the Union of South American Nations, UNASUR (Gómez 2017).

In the wake of the 1999 constitutional reform, the Constituent Assembly enacted detailed rules for appointing judges, especially on the Supreme Court, now called the Supreme Justice Tribunal (*Tribunal Supremo de Justicia*). The selection of ordinary judges occurred after a comprehensive evaluation requiring candidates to compete against each other (*concurso de oposición*). Those selected were granted tenure for 12 years to guarantee their independence. A judge could be removed from office only for grave misconduct, through a procedure in a special court. The National Assembly could appoint Supreme Justice Tribunal Justices only after a complex procedure entailing a nomination, public scrutiny and confirmation hearings. Unlike the lower court judges, justices were appointed for a 12-year term. The process was entrusted to the Judicial Appointments Committee, composed of representatives from government and civil society. The Citizens Branch (*Poder Ciudadano*), created by the 1999 Constitution, was charged with nominating justices (Pérez-Perdomo and Santacruz 2017). The judiciary also underwent an administrative overhaul to increase information about court cases through an Internet platform offering public access to the docket and case management software (Pérez-Perdomo 2011).

Although some of these reforms occurred during Chávez's early years, the result of his vow to re-legitimise and democratise the justice system, in practice his government was very hostile to the changes since they impeded the control and use of judges to thwart the opposition. Consequently, the Judicial Appointments Committee was never established, and the National Assembly, following Chávez's instructions, appointed Supreme Justice Tribunal members. The competitive evaluation processes for appointing ordinary judges occurred only in 1999 and 2000. In 2004 more than 500 trial court judges – a third of the judiciary – were removed (Louza 2011; Chavero 2011; Pérez-Perdomo and Santacruz 2017), and about half of the Supreme Justice Tribunal Justices were forced to retire or forcibly removed. Furthermore, a new Organic Law of the Supreme Justice Tribunal (2004) increased the number of Justices from 20 to 32 to pack the Court with regime loyalists (Louza 2011; Chavero 2011; Pérez-Perdomo and Santacruz 2017). Of the 84 Justices appointed, only seven have completed their constitutionally mandated 12-year terms. It is believed that about half the current Justices might not meet the minimum qualifications, though we cannot know because their selection process was too opaque (Observatorio Venezolano de la Justicia 2017; Pérez-Perdomo and Santacruz 2017).

In short, the Supreme Tribunal has become an 'instrument in the service of the Revolution' (Canova et al 2014). A close look at how the Court decides illustrates this. Between 2006 and 2012, it did not rule against the government in a single case. All this time the President routinely announced on his weekly television show that opposition leaders should be jailed, the assets of private companies, farms and industries confiscated, and government employees summarily dismissed unless they demonstrated unconditional loyalty to the regime. Unsurprisingly, all of this happened. One of the most dramatic cases involved Maria Lourdes Afiuni, a criminal judge arrested in 2009 on charges of corruption for ordering the conditional release of Eligio Cedeño, a Venezuelan banker who had been held in pre-trial detention for more than three years (a term greatly exceeding the statutory limits). Cedeño's detention was deemed arbitrary by the UN Working Group on Arbitrary Detention (UN 2008). Judge Afiuni was arrested almost immediately after President Chávez learned of her order. In a nationally televised speech – Chávéz's preferred means for issuing orders – he urged law enforcement officers to arrest and detain her, saying she should be convicted and receive the maximum penalty because 'a judge who frees a criminal is much, much, much more serious than the criminal himself' (Carroll 2009). During that broadcast, the President boasted he had discussed the matter with the President of the Supreme Justice Tribunal.

Judge Afiuni was swiftly arrested, jailed for three-and-a-half years, and released in June 2013, only after an incredible amount of international and domestic pressure (Newman and Díaz 2013). During her ordeal, she was kept in inhumane and degrading prison conditions, forced to share a cell with those she had convicted, and denied medical treatment for cancer (Human Rights Center 2011). The international community, including organisations like the International Commission of Jurists and Human Rights Watch, followed her case with great attention; its sordid details are documented by Olivares (2012).

In 2003, the government improperly dismissed three judges of the First Administrative Contentious Court of Caracas. The Inter-American Court of Human Rights decided in their favour, but the government ignored the order to reinstate them. Even though unconditional loyalty became the norm, some Chavista judges have been caught in factional crossfire. Justices Luis Velázquez Alvaray and Eladio Aponte Aponte, once greatly esteemed by the regime, were removed and fled the country after being charged criminally. Velázquez Alvaray was accused of corruption, but the real reason for his fall was rumoured to be rivalry with then-Chief Justice Omar Mora. Aponte was accused of protecting members of a drug cartel, but the real cause of his disgrace was allegedly another internal fight among top Chavista officials. He fled the country in 2012 and subsequently alleged undue influence and political manipulation at the highest levels of government (Tablante and Tarre 2013; Petit 2018; Pérez-Perdomo and Santacruz 2017).

Although one sign of the modernisation of the judiciary was the dissemination of information about cases through publicly accessible online platforms, those now lack data about either individual cases or judicial statistics. There is no public information about the number of judges, how many decisions they issue in a given time period, how long a case takes from beginning to end, or any other basic data. Some non-governmental organisations like the Venezuelan Justice Observatory (*Observatorio Venezolano de la Justicia*) have attempted to collect information. According to their reports, there were 2,162 judges in 2015, 56 per cent provisory (*jueces provisorios*), 10 per cent temporary (*jueces temporales*), and only 33 per cent permanent (*jueces titulares*). But these distinctions have little practical importance because in March 2009 the Supreme Justice Tribunal suspended the tenure of all Venezuelan judges (SJT, Resolution 2009–2008).

The mixture of apparently democratic and rule-of-law features with abusive and arbitrary government behaviour (selective prosecution of political adversaries, total control of judges) is what Sánchez-Uribarri (2011) has called a 'hybrid system'. Venezuelan judges are expected to sanctify government abuse and have become de facto political operatives, whose allegiance to the regime is not discreet or *sotto voce* but rather open and public. Judges proclaim their fidelity to the Chavista revolution not only during solemn speeches (Arias Castillo 2012) but also in rulings justifying their actions in terms of political ideology rather than legal standards.

The rule of law façade has eroded under Maduro, whose regime has been labelled a dictatorship by most governments in the Americas and Europe. The US Treasury Department has put many Venezuelan high officials, including members of the Supreme Justice

Tribunal, on the list of those subject to sanctions, and the US Justice Department has charged former Venezuelan government officials and others with money laundering and other offences. During the political crisis of early 2017, the National Assembly – controlled by the opposition – appointed a new set of justices to the Supreme Justice Tribunal. The government retaliated by persecuting them, forcing most to flee to Panama, Chile, Colombia and the US. The Organisation of American States supported the exiled members by hosting the Court in their Washington, DC headquarters. Both the European Parliament and the Inter-American Bar Association recognised the Tribunal in exile, which has held virtual sessions and issued several rulings, including one declaring the unconstitutionality of the Constituent Assembly, which Maduro created to redraft the Constitution and enhance his power. In the meantime, the Maduro regime has continued attacking the legitimacy of the exiled judges, who would be imprisoned if they returned. The situation has reached a political and institutional stalemate, in which each side questions its adversary's legitimacy.

Despite these setbacks, Venezuelan lawyers have remained visible and active. Courts still receive petitions and actions to defend human rights and the rule of law. Even though the rulings are almost always against the petitioner, legal professionals believe court battles should not be abandoned. The legal fight against the Maduro regime has expanded to foreign courts and international tribunals, where Venezuelan lawyers have joined forces with their foreign counterparts to bring claims and defend cases.

V. THE LANDSCAPE AND DEMOGRAPHY OF LAW STUDENTS AND LAWYERS

One of the most significant challenges of studying the contemporary Venezuelan legal profession and legal education is the lack of official statistics and other reliable data. The Planning Office of Higher Education (*Oficina de Planificación del Sector Universitario*, or *OPSU*) is in charge of compiling and publishing statistics about universities, but it last reported in 2001 and has stopped collecting data.

The traditional means to count the number of lawyers has been the registry of the Institute of Social Welfare for Lawyers (*Instituto de Previsión Social del Abogado*, or *Inpreabogado*), where law graduates must register to practise. Almost all graduates register whether or not they intend to practise since the cost is low and membership confers benefits, including insurance. Since the Inpreabogado database classifies new lawyers by law school, we can learn how many are graduating from each university (see Table 1).

Table 1 Law Graduates Registered with Inpreabogado (1986–2017)

Period	Total	Annual Average
1986–89	14,395	3,599
1990–99	38,043	3,804
2000–09	65,713	6,573
2010–17	138,909	17,369
Total 1986–2017	257,060	8,292

Source: Inpreabogado.

Before 1995, there were seven law schools. The number increased to 13 by 2000, 23 by 2005, and 37 by 2015. During the earlier years, all law schools were in either Caracas (the capital) or other major cities, forcing many aspiring law students to leave home. Now, law schools are more dispersed. Deducing the population of law students is difficult; our rough estimate based on the attrition rate and other factors is that the ratio of students to graduates is about seven to one. Law is an undergraduate degree and ordinarily takes five years to complete. Depending on the university, coursework is divided by year, semester or quarter, and students must pass several examinations for each course. Some universities are considered more difficult, for example Universidad Metropolitana, which requires a comprehensive examination and a final research paper.

Law schools are departments of a university. The establishment of a new school starts with a petition filed with the National Council of Universities (*Consejo Nacional de Universidades*, or *CNU*), part of the Ministry of Higher Education. From the early 1960s to 1980, CNU did not authorise the establishment of any new law school. Between 1980 and 2000, several private universities were authorised to open law schools; after 2000, the government authorised new law schools only at public universities it controls. Traditionally, Venezuelan universities have always had considerable independence from the government and could elect their administrators and regulate internal governance. The newer public universities have little or no autonomy and are directly controlled by the Ministry of Higher Education, which also is in charge of appointing university administrators and overseeing their activities.

Tuition is free or nominal at public universities, which are supported entirely by the government, creating the danger of political manipulation. Private universities depend on tuition as well as philanthropic contributions and other private funding. Tuition varies greatly depending on class size, facilities and infrastructure like libraries, access to technology, faculty and staff, and curriculum. This has stratified private schools, some of which are very costly by domestic standards, while others are more accessible. Some private universities offered students scholarships, loans or part-time jobs. The leading private universities have begun tapping their alumni – many now émigrés – to raise funds for scholarship programmes and basic operating costs, but the situation is grim.

Law schools differ in whether they belong to public autonomous universities, government-controlled universities, or private universities. Figure 1 presents the distribution of the 19,532 graduates in 2015.

The differences can be explained partly by selectivity and other policies. The public autonomous universities, the oldest, house research institutes and have the highest proportion of full-time professors, robust administrative infrastructures, law reviews, and academic presses. Because they enjoy academic prestige and tuition is free, competition for entry is very intense. Admission to a fixed number of spots used to depend on a test, but the government recently ordered the universities to eliminate it and other selection criteria and accept students based on a government lottery, letting universities decide only the number of students admitted.

The oldest public autonomous law school is part of Universidad Central de Venezuela (UCV). Established in the eighteenth century, it educated the political elites until the mid-twentieth century (Pérez-Perdomo 1981). Most judges, especially Supreme Court Justices, traditionally were UCV graduates. The law school still has the largest graduate programme, with an array of masters, specialisations, and doctoral degrees. Its law

Figure 1 Distribution of Law Graduates by Law School Type (2015)

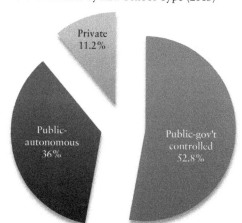

journal, *Revista de la Facultad de Ciencias Jurídicas y Políticas*, is the oldest and its publishing house one of the most important and prestigious. The curriculum is very traditional, having changed little since the mid-twentieth century.

Law schools were among the first departments established by the private universities authorised in the mid-twentieth century. The restriction on creating law schools in the 1960s and 1970s was lifted during in the next two decades, with the result that private universities enrolled more than 70 per cent of students by the end of the twentieth century. They differ greatly in prestige, academic quality, admission policies, class size, library holdings and technological facilities. Most of their faculty is paid by the course or hour. The most prestigious have full-time professors. The top private law schools house legal research centres, clinics, and academic publications and emphasise high quality scholarship. UCAB (founded in 1953) has a very solid reputation. Until the 1980s, its curriculum resembled UCV's, but it has since introduced important innovations while preserving the traditional lectures and placing little emphasis on law practice. Unimet, though younger, is increasingly prestigious. Its curriculum, perhaps the most innovative, emphasises skills, problem-based learning, and interactive discussions and is oriented toward entrepreneurship and business. It also offers joint degrees with liberal arts and other disciplines. Like UCAB's graduates, many of Unimet's have joined the private sector, but the current crisis has prompted more to migrate to foreign countries (Capriles and Pérez-Perdomo 2019).[1]

Public government-controlled law schools resulted from the government's aggressive efforts to expand higher education and advance its political agenda. Although only three have been created since 2000, they enrol the vast majority of law students. The most visible one belongs to the UBV, which has branches throughout the country. Its curriculum emphasises project-based learning but offers very little law-related content. Admission is easy, although the criteria are obscure. Because UBV does not publish faculty names

---

[1] Rogelio Pérez-Perdomo, co-author of this chapter, was the founding dean of this law school.

or the content of its programmes, it is difficult to assess the quality, scholarly activity, and student-faculty student ratio – an important datum because project-based learning requires a low ratio of students to creative full-time faculty. Its website declares that UBV's mission is to serve as 'one of the engines of the revolution', which sounds more like grooming political loyalists than training legal professionals. UBV graduates are favoured for government positions and judgeships, which may be the main attraction of these government-controlled law schools.

Besides the Inpreabogado data, which represent only who is *eligible* to practise law, the country lacks a census of how many lawyers are active and what they do. Table 2 offers an estimate.

Table 2 Lawyers and Population per Lawyer (1981–2015)

Year	Number of lawyers	Population per lawyer
1981	16,045	901
1990	31,350	629
2000	66,263	370
2010	122,636	237
2015	224,074	139

Sources: For general population and for lawyers in 1981, Instituto Nacional de Estadística: Censo Nacional 1981. Other figures are estimates based on Inpreabogado's registry.

Beginning in 2000, growth increased exponentially because of the greater number of law schools and their geographical dispersion and relatively low cost. In other Latin American countries, the legal profession also experienced significant growth between 2000 and 2013: from 112,000 to 225,000 in Colombia, 200,000 to 321,000 in Mexico, and 420,000 to 840,000 in Brazil (Gómez and Pérez-Perdomo 2018: 8; Pérez-Perdomo 2014). But Venezuela is distinctive in two ways. First, the number of Venezuelan lawyers grew threefold, whereas the number in other countries only doubled. Second, whereas the other countries generally respect democracy and the rule of law, the Venezuelan government has become increasingly authoritarian. Clark (1999) observed that the number of lawyers tends to be low in socialist regimes. One reason is that lawyers lose their salience when the number of conflicts regarding property and other rights declines and when claims against the government are systematically rejected (Markovits 1996; 2010). But though both of these are true in Venezuela, the Chavista regimes have viewed the government-controlled law schools as training centres for its political operatives. Pérez-Perdomo (2018) showed that the curriculum of the government-controlled law schools focuses on Chávez's ideas and political activism to the virtual exclusion of law. These law schools graduate the vast majority of Venezuelan lawyers (138,919 between 2010 and 2017), more than half the total population.

The legal profession also experienced early feminisation. Women were 27 per cent of UCV law students in 1960, slightly outnumbered men in 1980, and were 60 per cent from 1990 (Roche 2003: 212). The proportions were similar in other universities. A study of judges at the end of twentieth century also showed that a majority were women (IESA 1998). We believe the opposite is true in the corporate legal sector.

A more diversified stratified legal education also means a more segmented legal profession. For example, most of the corporate legal sector is drawn from graduates of UCAB, Unimet, and to a lesser degree Universidad Monteávila (UM), another elite private law school founded in the late 1990s. Judges and public officials traditionally were UCV graduates, but that privilege is now reserved to UBV alumni. In the western state of Zulia, we believe that most public and private lawyers come from La Universidad del Zulia (LUZ); and the same could be said about those in the state of Mérida and the Universidad de Los Andes (ULA).

VI. PROFESSIONAL LEGAL CAREERS, LAWYERS, AND LITIGATION

By the end of the twentieth century the Venezuelan legal profession resembled that of other civil law countries. Lawyers in their late twenties or early thirties could choose to become a judge, prosecutor, public lawyer for the protection of children and adolescents, or civil servant. The stability of the political system made a public sector career possible. A 1997 study found that about 80 per cent of judges had spent more than 20 years in the judiciary, where some had started working as law students (IESA 1998). The Chavista revolution abolished the professionalisation of public sector lawyers, breaking with the past.

The twentieth century also saw the consolidation of a generation of legal scholars. Universities hired full-time law professors, who were expected to conduct research and publish, as well as teach. Law graduates who had pursued graduate studies in foreign universities, originally in Europe and later in the US, constituted the nucleus of this group. Other law graduates practised law most of their careers, some combining this with law teaching, gaining recognition for intellectual prowess within the legal profession and in society at large. The current government's hostility towards universities and academic activities has substantially shrunk this already small group (Pérez-Perdomo 2016), and the exodus of legal professionals contributed.

Litigation is the most visible aspect of legal practice, representing what most people think lawyers do, and popular culture disseminates this imagery. In Venezuela, however, the politicisation of the judiciary and its subjection to influence by both the government and the private sector deters litigation, a situation seized upon by promoters of alternative dispute resolution during the recent wave of judicial reform throughout Latin American and elsewhere (Gómez 2007). Their hypothesis was that disputants wanted transparency, efficiency and fairness, which the dysfunctional courts of many Latin American countries did not offer. Nevertheless, the importance of social networks in the operation of the legal system and a culture valuing know-who much more than know-how has meant that those with the proper connections continued to prefer the courts, which offered greater certainty than the newly-minted arbitration centers (ibid).

In a study of litigation and lawyers in Venezuela, Pérez-Perdomo (1996) found four types of litigants, whose differences explained the specialisation and stratification of lawyers. The first was the involuntary litigant: defendants in criminal or civil cases. Criminal defendants also differed. White-collar defendants tended to be high-income individuals, who were represented by prominent attorneys, some of whom enjoyed celebrity status. The advent of the Chavista revolution and its prosecution of political enemies created another category of criminal defendants: victims of human rights violations represented by their corporate lawyers (Gómez 2010). The unfortunate explosion of human rights abuses has inspired an increasing number of lawyers to join the ranks of activists and defenders of political prisoners and other victims of government repression. Some non-governmental organisations (NGOs) like PROVEA and COFAVIC, which predate the Chavista regime, were staffed by a small number of lawyers; but the recent decade has seen them grow and be supplemented by other groups, including *Foro Penal Venezolano*, *Paz Activa*, *Observatorio Venezolano de la Justicia*, and a number of university-affiliated human rights centres. Foreign donors from the US, Canada and Germany frequently finance NGOs, but the government has greatly restricted them.

A second type was instrumental litigants who sought to take advantage of the judicial system's weakness. Although their lawyers achieved short-term gains from an injunction or emergency ruling, they did not enjoy professional prestige and were often shunned by peers, suffered retaliation, and sometimes were sanctioned by the court.

The third category was the functional litigants: banks, insurance companies and other corporate actors. Their lawyers were repeat players, who became efficient users of the legal system. Because their clients often had no choice but to use the court in a wholesale manner (eg to collect debts from or enforce judgments against hundreds or thousands) the lawyers needed to foster good relations with judges, clerks and bailiffs and learn how to navigate the judicial system efficiently. Some of these lawyers were acting in family cases (ie divorce, custody, or alimony) or labour and employment matters but still used the courts in a quasi-notarial manner, such as when a couple had decided to part amicably but still needed a divorce from a judge.

The fourth type of litigant was the expressive, seeking to uphold a reputation or send a message to an opponent or society about values or prestige, even if trying a case did not make financial sense because it would cost more than the amount at stake.

Although these categories illuminate the role of courts in society, most lawyers do not litigate but rather serve as advisers. This is especially true of those in the corporate legal sector, whose most common organisational form is the law firm. The earliest Venezuelan firms, dating back more than a century, emerged to serve foreign investors. In the early twentieth century foreign lawyers established professional partnerships with local law firms, for example the Travieso Evans firm in 1920 (Mészaros and Pérez Perdomo 2017). From 1950 to 1980, Venezuela received a flow of immigrants, first from Europe and later from other Latin American countries, as well as significant international investment. Foreign lawyers only had to take exams on Venezuelan law at the public autonomous universities in order to practise and could act as legal consultants on foreign law without taking any exam. Nevertheless, few took advantage of these benefits.

Elite local firms competing with their foreign counterparts in terms of expertise, quality, and price increasingly populated the legal market. The leading members were social and economic elites, who had access to high quality education, local and international connections, fluency in foreign languages, and familiarity with foreign legal cultures (Gómez and Pérez-Perdomo 2018; Meszaros and Pérez Perdomo 2017). In 1955 Baker McKenzie opened a Caracas office, its first outside Chicago, thereby initiating the globalisation of American law firms. The expansion of business law firms fluctuated with the economic and political climate, peaking during the 1990s (Gómez and Pérez-Perdomo, 2018).

Table 3 Business Law Firms by Number of Lawyers (1990–2017)

Firm (year established)	1990	1999	2009	2017
Hoet, Peláez, Castillo & Duque (1942)[2]	27	59	48	56
Baker McKenzie (1955)	46	76	84	49
D'Empaire Reyna (1972)	21	35	38	44
Travieso Evans Arria Rengel & Paz (1920)	24	45	43	38
Mendoza Palacios Acedo Borjas (1945)	30	34	31	34
Rodríguez & Mendoza (1910)	23	44	35	33
Araque Reyna Sosa & Brito (1986)	25	25	35	33
Norton Rose Fulbright (1997)[3]	–	12	48	31
Tinoco Travieso Planchart & Núñez (1914)	23	44	35	22
Torres Plaz & Araujo (1972)	10	33	28	22
Average	22.9	40.6	42.5	36.2

Sources: Gómez and Pérez Perdomo (2017) and Latin Lawyer 250.

Table 3 shows the rapid growth of business law firms during the 1990s, coinciding with the last decade of democracy and the 'oil opening'. The effects of this boom lasted until 2009, even though most business opportunities had long disappeared, because the dissolution of companies, bankruptcies, legal claims, and restructuring also required a great deal of legal work. The table also shows that after 2009 the number and size of law firms declined significantly, although some were affected more than others. Torres Plaz & Araujo, for example, had 37 lawyers in 2006 and shrank precipitously. Mendoza Palacios Acedo Borjas, one of the emblematic elite Venezuelan firms, had 43 lawyers in 2006 and also declined. Baumeister & Brewer, perhaps the most prominent administrative law firm for several decades, had 24 lawyers in 1999 but has since disappeared from Latin Lawyer 250 and other guides. But a few firms took advantage of opportunities during the early 2000s. Hogan Lovells, McLeod Dixon (later Norton Rose Fulbright and now Dentons) and Littler Mendelson established branches in Caracas during the last two decades and, at least until a couple of years ago, were faring reasonably well. Nevertheless, in early 2018 Hogan Lovells closed its Caracas office, and the other firms are suffering like the rest of the Venezuelan lawyers.

Interestingly, in 1999 the average Venezuelan law firm was larger than its counterparts in Chile, Colombia, Peru, and several Central American countries. By 2015, the opposite was true (Gómez and Pérez-Perdomo 2018: 15). This might reveal a connection between the size of business law firms and the openness of national markets to investments.

VII. LAWYERS AND THE RULE OF LAW

There is a *Colegio de Abogados* (Bar Association) in Caracas and each state capital, as well as a national *Federación de Colegios de Abogados*. The members of each Bar

---
[2] Previously, Bentata Hoet & Asociados; now Lega.
[3] Originally named Macleod Dixon, now Dentons.

Association elect their governing boards, who choose the federation's board. Since 2000, the Bar Associations became increasingly active in protesting government actions and policies. Pro-Chavista groups have lost these elections, allowing the opposition to dominate most Bar Associations, most importantly that in Caracas. The Supreme Justice Tribunal retaliated by suspending the elections, provoking an institutional crisis. Other groups of lawyers have defended the rule of law and human rights, including the Venezuelan Association of Administrative Law (*Asociación Venezolana de Derecho Administrativo, AVEDA*) and the Group of Public Law Professors (*Grupo de Profesores de Derecho Público*). Law deans, jointly and individually, have condemned the numerous violations and publicly supported the fight against rampant illegality. Other groups at the forefront of the fight for human rights are law school clinics and human rights centres and NGOs like *Paz Activa*, PROVEA, *Foro Penal Venezolano, Acceso a la Justicia, Observatorio Venezolano de la Violencia, Observatorio Venezolano de Prisiones*, and the Venezuelan chapter of Transparency International.

During the early twentieth-century, Venezuelan dictators Juan Vicente Gómez (1909–35) and Marcos Pérez Jiménez (1952–58) enjoyed the services of many distinguished lawyers and legal scholars who justified their actions through books and articles. The present regime also attracted lawyers eager to serve as judges, prosecutors, and public officials, but professional and academic organisations have become dissidents. A recent study of more than 1,000 articles published in the main Venezuelan law journals could not find a single article favorable to the government, although there were many critical works, especially after 2006 (Pérez-Perdomo 2015).

By several criteria, the Chavista and Maduro regimes are dictatorships, but they differ from earlier dictatorial governments. Previous dictators did not seek to change the economic foundations or basic political tenets of Venezuelan society. They viewed their role as maintaining order and organising society but respected property and preserved the appearance of an independent judiciary. In fact, there was a dual justice system: repressive and tyrannical toward dissidents but routine for apolitical matters. Law schools and courts operated normally without interference by the regime. Most law professors and lawyers were legal formalists who did not investigate the repressive part of the system or publicly criticise it, thereby sustaining the illusion of independence.

The current regime is very different. Since its earliest days, the Chavista revolution has defined its political project as a struggle to create a new state based on socialist ideas. The government became anti-business and contemptuous of property rights, although it actually promoted the businesses and respected the property of its self-appointed revolutionary elite. The judiciary was purged to ensure the unconditional loyalty of judges and prosecutors, and all dissidents were persecuted and banished. Since 2006, the Justices of the Supreme Justice Tribunal have publicly declared their allegiance to the Chavista revolution (Arias Castillo, 2012).

The ideological basis for the actions of many Chavista lawyers and judges can be found in the writings of José Manuel Delgado Ocando, a well-known Venezuelan legal scholar who argued that the legal system should serve revolutionary political power (Delgado Ocando 1978). This notion seems to resonate with many lawyers supporting the Maduro regime, who claim to embrace the old positivist-legalist ideology, according to which law is a neutral instrument, subservient to state power. Nevertheless, the Maduro regime's constant abuses of ordinary citizens and political opponents and its complete disdain for the rule of law and the most fundamental tenets of a democratic society are impossible to justify under any conception of law that respects individual liberties, property and human rights. Lawyers may also be motivated to swear fealty to the Maduro regime for selfish reasons: friends of the revolution enjoy favours, such as political appointments and help with business ventures. By contrast, lawyers seen as political enemies are called 'radioactive' and barred from participating in lucrative hydrocarbon contracts and deals. To stay in Venezuela today requires enormous patience and courage.

REFERENCES

Alguíndigue, C and Pérez-Perdomo, R (2008) 'The inquisitor strikes back: obstacles to the reform of criminal procedure in revolutionary Venezuela' 15(1) *Southwestern Journal of Law and Trade in the Americas*.

—— (2013) 'Revolución y proceso penal en Venezuela 1999–2012' 13(2) *Anales de la Universidad Metropolitana* 119.

Arias Castillo, T (2012) 'Los actos de apertura del año judicial en Venezuela, 1999–2012' in S Aranguren, L Kiriakidis and A Castillo *Crisis de la función judicial* (Caracas, Academia de Ciencias Políticas y Sociales, Acceso a la Justicia y Universidad Metropolitana).

Canova, G, Orellana, H, Ortega, R and Graterol, S (2014) *El TSJ al servicio de la revolución* (Caracas, Galipán).

Capriles, V, Fernandez, I and Pérez-Perdomo, R (2018) 'Los abogados graduados en la Universidad Metropolitana 2006–2016: Estudio de una cohorte profesional en tiempos de revolución' 6(23) *Pedaogía Universitaria y Didáctica del Derecho*.

Carroll, R (2009) 'Hugo Chávez demands jailing of judge who freed banker' (*The Guardian* 15 December) www.theguardian.com/world/2009/dec/15/chavez-venezuela-judge-cedeno.

Casey, N (2018) 'Venezuela Inflation Could Reach One Million by Year's End' (*New York Times* 23 July).

Chavero Gazdik, R (2011) *La justicia revolucionaria: una década de reestructuración (o involución) judicial en Venezuela* (Caracas, Aequitas).

Delgado Ocando, JM (1978) 'Hipótesis para una filosofía antihegemónica del Derecho y del estado' (IFD Universidad del Zulia, Maracaibo).

Faiola, A (2018) 'From Riches to Rags: Venezuelans become Latin America's new underclass' (*Washington Post* 27 July) www.washingtonpost.com/news/world/wp/2018/07/27/feature/as-venezuela-crumbles-its-fleeing-citizens-are-becoming-latin-americas-new-underclass/?utm_term=.73edd8bc62d3.

Forero, J (2018) 'Venezuela's Misery Fuels Migration on Epic Scale' (*Wall Street Journal* 3 February) www.wsj.com/articles/venezuelas-misery-fuels-migration-on-epic-scale-1518517800.

Foro Penal Venezolano (2018) *Reporte sobre la represión del Estado venezolano* (March) foropenal.com/wp-content/uploads/2018/04/INFORME-REPRESION-MARZO-2018.pdf.

Gillespie, P (2017) 'Venezuela brain drain: I miss mom, but don't want to go back' (*CNN Money* 4 April) money.cnn.com/2017/04/04/news/economy/venezuela-crisis-brain-drain/.

Gómez, M (2007) All in the Family: The Influence of Social Networks on Dispute Processing. JSD dissertation, Stanford University.

—— (2010) 'Political Activism and the Practice of Law in Venezuela' in J Couso, A Huneeus and R Sieder (eds), *Cultures of Legality: Judicialization and Political Activism in Latin America* (Cambridge, Cambridge University Press).

—— (2011) 'Greasing the Squeaky Wheel of Justice: Lawyers, Social Networks and Dispute Processing' in Y Dezalay and B Garth (eds), *Lawyers and the Rule of Law in an Era of Globalization* (New York, Routledge).

—— (2015) 'The manipulation of law through the social agenda: The case of two Bolivarian misiones' in M Gómez and R Pérez-Perdomo (eds), *Legal and Political Culture in Revolutionary Venezuela 1999–2013* (FIU Law).

—— (2017) 'The South American Way: Sub-Regional Integration under ALBA and UNASUR and International Dispute Resolution' 58(4) Hungarian Journal of Legal Studies 449–57.

Gómez, M and Perez-Perdomo, R (2018) 'Big law in Venezuela: From globalization to revolution' in M Gómez and R Pérez-Perdomo (eds), *Big Law in Latin America: Globalization and Adjustments in the Provision of High End Legal Services* (London, Palgrave McMillan).

Gómez, M, Pérez-Perdomo, R and Guerrero-Rocca, G (2020) 'Venezuelan Expatriate Lawyers' unpublished manuscript.

Human Rights Center, Universidad Católica Andrés Bello (2011) 'Maria Lourdes Afiuni, Urgent Appeal, Deterioration of her health conditions' (January) w2.ucab.edu.ve/tl_files/CDH/Maria%20Lourdes%20Afiuni/Update_on_the_health_conditions_of_Judge_Afiuni.pdf.

IESA (1998) *Informe sobre las necesidades de formación de los jueces de Venezuela*. Presentado ante el Consejo de la Judicatura (Caracas, IESA).

Jatar-Hausman, AJ (2006) *Apartheid del siglo XXI: la informática al servicio de la discriminación política* (Caracas, Sumate).

Karl, T (1986) 'Petroleum and political pacts: the transition to democracy in Venezuela' in G O'Donnell, P Schmitter and L Whitehead (eds), *Transitions from Authoritarian Rule/ Latin America* (Baltimore, John Hopkins University Press).

Kornblith, M (1998) *Venezuela en los 90. Las crisis de la democracia* (Caracas, Universidad Central de Venezuela y Ediciones IESA).

Londoño, E (2018) '"Their Country is Being Invaded": Exodus of Venezuelans Overwhelms Northern Brazil' (*The New York Times* 28 April) www.nytimes.com/2018/04/28/world/americas/venezuela-brazil-migrants.html.

Long, G and Schipani, A (2018) 'Venezuela's imploding economy sparks refugee crisis' (*Financial Times* 16 April) www.ft.com/content/a62038a4-3bdc-11e8-b9f9-de94fa33a81e.

López Maya, M (2005) *Del viernes negro al referendo revocatorio* (Caracas, Alfadil).

—— (2016) *El ocaso del chavismo* (Caracas, Alfa).

Louza Sconamiglio, L (2011) *La revolución judicial en Venezuela* (Caracas, FUNEDA).

Markovits, I (1996) 'Children of a Lesser God: GDR Lawyers in Post-Socialist Germany' 94(7) *Michigan Law Review* 2270–2308.

—— (2010) *Justice in Lüritz: Experiencing Socialist Law in East Germany* (Princeton University Press).

Mészaros, M and Pérez-Perdomo, R (2017) 'La internacionalización de los abogados venezolanos' (Caracas, Universidad Metropolitana) unpublished manuscript.

Moreno Losada, V (2017) 'Sentencias de la Sala Constitucional son firmadas por jueces que incumplen los requisitos para el cargo' (*Efecto Cocuyo* 5 April) www.efectococuyo.com.

Neuman, W and Díaz, ME (2013) 'Court in Venezuela Orders Release of a Judge Once Scorned and Jailed by Chávez' (*New York Times* 14 June) www.nytimes.com/2013/06/15/world/americas/court-in-venezuela-orders-release-of-a-judge-once-scorned-and-jailed-by-chavez.html.

Observatorio Venezolano de la Justicia (2017) 'Magistrados exprés en el ojo del huracán' (20 June) www.accesoalajusticia.org/magistrados-expres-en-el-ojo-del-huracan/.

Olivares, F (2014) 'Best and brightest for export' (13 September) web.archive.org/web/20171019152840/http://www.eluniversal.com/nacional-y-politica/140913/best-and-brightest-for-export.

Pérez Perdomo, R (1981) *Los abogados en Venezuela* (Caracas, Monte Avila).

—— (2003) 'Venezuela, 1958–1999: The legal system in an impaired democracy' in L Friedman and R Pérez-Perdomo (eds), *Legal Cultures in the Age of Globalization (Latin Europe and Latin America)* (Stanford, Stanford University Press).

—— (2004) 'Reforma judicial, estado de derecho y revolución en Venezuela' in L Pásara (ed) *En búsqueda de una justicia distinta. Experiencias de reforma en América Latina* (Lima, Consorcio Justicia Viva) 335–74.

—— (2005) 'Judicialization and regime change: the Venezuelan Supreme Court' in Sieder, R Schjolden, L, and Angell, A (eds), *The Judicialization of Politics in Latin America* (London, Palgrave Macmillan).

—— (2006) 'La educación jurídica en Venezuela, 1960–2005. Expansión y diferenciación' in R Pérez Perdomo and J Rodríguez Torres (eds) *La educación jurídica en América Latina. Tensiones e innovaciones en tiempos de globalización* (Universidad Externado de Colombia, Bogota).

—— (2006b) 'Corrupción, instituciones y contexto político. El caso de Venezuela' in A Azuela (ed), *La corrupción en América. Un continente, muchos frentes* (México, Instituto de Investigaciones Sociales, UNAM).

—— (2009) *Derecho y cultura jurídica en Venezuela en tiempos de revolución (1999–2009)* (Caracas, Fundación Manuel García Pelayo).

—— (2011) *Justicia e injusticias en Venezuela* (Caracas, Universidad Metropolitana y Academia Nacional de la Historia).

—— (2014) 'Represión y justicia en Venezuela en tiempo de protesta' *Debates, Revista de Ciência Política* 8.

—— (2014a): 'Advogados e a educação jurídica na América Latina. Algumas tendências, conjecturas e questões' 10 *Cadernos FGV Direito Rio*.

—— (2015) 'Las revistas jurídicas venezolanas en tiempo de revolución' *Boletín Mexicano de Derecho Comparado* 142.

—— (2018) 'Educación jurídica y política en Venezuela revolucionaria' in G González Mantilla (ed) *La educación jurídica como política pública en América Latina* (Lima, Palestra Editores).

Pérez Perdomo, R and Gómez, M (2006) *Justicias Alternativas en Venezuela,* 7 *Revista Mexicana de Justicia*, 161–90.

Pérez Perdomo, R and Santacruz, A (2016) 'La legitimidad de jueces y legisladores en el estado constitucional de derecho: la Asamblea Nacional y el Tribunal Supremo venezolano en 2016' *Doxa. Cuadernos de Filosofía del Derecho* 39.

—— (2017): 'The Chavist revolution and the justice system' 8(2) *Latin American Policy* 189.

Pimentel, O and Herrera, I (2017) '88% de jóvenes venezolanos se quieren ir del país' (*Venezuela al día* 12 February) www.venezuelaaldia.com/2017/02/12/88-de-jovenes-venezolanos-se-quieren-ir-del-pais-infografia/.

Sánchez Uribarri, R (2011) 'Courts between democracy and hybrid authoritarianism. Evidence from the Venezuelan Supreme Court' 36 *Law and Social Inquiry* 36.

Silva Franco, M (2014) *El rostro de los presos politicos en Venezuela* (*La Vanguardia* 11 June) www.lavanguardia.com/internacional/20140611/54409796076/presos-politicos-venezuela.html.

UN News Centre (2008) 'Venezuelan leader violates independence of judiciary-UN rights experts' www.un.org/apps/news/story.asp?NewsID=33273&Cr=judges&Cr1.

US Department of the Treasury, 'Treasury Sanctions Prominent Venezuelan Drug Trafficker Tareck El Aissami and His Primary Frontman Samark Lopez Bello' (13 February) www.treasury.gov/press-center/press-releases/Pages/as0005.aspx.

Wyss, J (2017) 'As Venezuela faces critical week, Colombia prepares for a wave of migrants' (*Miami Herald* 25 July) www.miamiherald.com/news/nation-world/world/americas/colombia/article163600573.html.

Zubillaga Gabaldón, MT (2007) 'La justicia de paz y su evolución' *Derecho y democracia* 1 (Caracas, Universidad Metropolitana).

Part V

Africa

23

Burundi

Middlemen and Opponents in the Shadow of the Ethno-state

SARA DEZALAY*

I. INTRODUCTION: A RESEARCH AGENDA ON LEGAL INTERMEDIARIES IN BURUNDI

A. Legal Professions in Burundi: Knowledge *Chiaroscuro* and the Puzzle of the Colonial Legacy

'OUTLINING THE LEGAL framework in the Congo, Rwanda and Burundi could appear to be at best a futile exercise, at worst an insult to the inhabitants of these countries, considering their state of lawlessness since the early 1990s' (Vanderlinden 1997: 551).[1] This statement by a prominent historian of Belgium's former African colonies echoes a common image of Burundi: a tiny, densely populated, landlocked Central African country, one of the five poorest in the world,[2] whose postcolonial history has been punctuated by massacres, wars and now another dictatorship.[3] These characteristics make it, at first blush, an unlikely place to study the transformation of legal professions.

Yet this image of lawlessness is contradicted by the core role law played in Burundi. To take just one recent example: the formidable investment of international non-governmental organisations (INGOs), diplomats, and European donors in Burundi from the mid-1990s focused on reforming a justice sector thought to be a root cause of the 1993 massacres but also a potential vector of peace and development. But identifying

---

* This chapter is based on fieldwork funded by the French national research agency (IRENE programme on international peace professionals, ISP/CNRS) and the Cluster of Excellence 'The Formation of normative orders', Goethe Universität. I am extremely grateful to Yves Dezalay for his invaluable comments and suggestions on earlier drafts.

[1] I have translated all French quotes.

[2] With a 40% official development aid to GDP ratio.

[3] At least five major waves of violence have marked Burundi's post-colonial history, in 1965, 1972, 1988, 1991 and 1993–2003/8. UNHCR reported about 400,000 Burundian refugees as of 2018.

and mapping the role, organisation and evolution of legal professions in Burundi pose significant difficulties for the canonic literature on legal professions, which starts from the premise that they constitute a relatively homogenous group governed either by internal competition or common universals.

The first challenge is the lack of primary sources. Studies of the 'colonial question' have undergone a relative boom in the past 15 years in Belgium, emulating the rich literature on the former French and British Empires (eg Renucci 2011; Dorsett and McLaren 2014). However, knowledge about legal professions in the Belgian Congo and Burundi-Rwanda is still in its infancy because of the ongoing ideological battles over the violence of Belgian colonisation (Ngongo et al 2017).[4] The relative neglect of Burundi, overshadowed by Cold War politics in 1962–93, was compounded by a dearth of research on the country, except for historical studies by Burundian, French and Belgian scholars (eg Gahama 2001; Deslaurier 2002; Chrétien and Dupaquier 2007). The vast volume of policy publications on rule of law reforms in post-conflict Burundi since 1993 overwhelmingly denounces the colonial legacy, including the legal transplants inherited from the mandate period. It therefore reads like a succession of abortive fixes to the perennial problem of justice in the country (Kolhagen 2012).

Legal professionals remain a blind-spot in this literature – as they do in many former African colonies (S Dezalay 2015; S Dezalay forthcoming). The resulting *chiaroscuro* of available knowledge is connected to a wider problem. Like other post-colonial settings, Burundi requires the researcher to remember Pierre Bourdieu's warning (1993) about the pitfall of being subjected to knowledge forged *for* and *by* the state.

What George Steinmetz (2013) termed 'imperial entanglements' help to account for the volume of doctrine on 'customary justice' produced by Belgian magistrates in colonial Congo, and later Burundi-Rwanda, and the contradictions of their position. The policy of 'indirect rule' aimed both to foster social order and to promote their own position as buffers against the extreme violence of Belgian colonialism. Political entanglement also explains knowledge production in the shadow of Cold War politics in Francophone Africa. With the repeated massacres in Burundi and neighbouring Rwanda either ignored or left to the policing role of France in its wide 'pré-carré'[5] throughout the Cold War, historical accounts continue to be permeated by intense political battles across Paris, Brussels, Bujumbura and Kigali. By the same token, the enormous volume of publications on post-conflict justice in Burundi since 1993 cannot be understood without considering the position of their producers as consultants for Belgian and other European NGOs and international development agencies, which, due to their own dependence on institutional funding, contribute actively – albeit unwittingly – to the ebb and flow of international policies in the region (see S Dezalay 2016).

The effect is a double bias when the focus turns to legal professions in Burundi. The tendency is both for historical short-cuts and a reduction of the country's trajectory to cycles of violence from the colonial administrator or the post-colonial state. Legal

---

[4] The files of the 400 Belgian magistrates who operated in Belgian colonies and protectorates after 1908 are still classified.

[5] 'Pré-carré' – or preserve – refers to the 'privileged relations' (primarily in economic and military terms) that France maintained with its former colonial Empire and beyond, in Francophone Africa through the Cold War as the 'Gendarme of Africa'.

professions are seen as either corrupted or antidotes to violence. This criticism could be generalised to studies of the British empire, which also tend to reify the opposition between the 'promise of civilisation' endorsed by European empires and the exceptionality of colonialism's violence (Halliday et al 2012).

B. From Legal *Professions* to Legal *Intermediaries* in the Trajectory of the State and Globalisation

This chapter responds to these studies in two ways, integrating the specificities of the Burundi case study into a wider reflection on the articulation between law, politics and globalisation in African (post)colonies (S Dezalay forthcoming). First, it espouses a political sociology of law and the state in switching the focus from *institutionalised occupations* to *structural positions*. This emphasises the position of lawyers as 'intermediary elites' or 'double agents' who juggle contradictory social, political, and economic interests (Y Dezalay and Garth 2010; Vauchez 2008). Focusing on *intermediaries of the law* – rather than legal professionals – is all the more imperative in Burundi in order to embrace those agents who were not lawyers, such as chiefs in colonial Burundi, but who operated as the 'middlemen' of colonisation (Benton and Ford 2016).

This shifts the focus towards the structuration over time of the *space* carved out for and by these intermediaries in relation to the state and external actors. Looking at the legal 'field' in Burundi as a relatively autonomous social microcosm – to borrow Bourdieu's conceptual tool (Bourdieu and Wacquant 1992) – transcends oppositions that have been reified in the literature, such as that between formal and informal law. The focus, rather, is on the strategies and types of resources (educational and political but also social and family capital) that produce and reproduce hierarchies within that space.

One prominent resource in Burundi has been ethnic affiliation. Paired with race in colonial Burundi, ethnicity was used to justify the promotion of certain groups – foremost the princely *Baganwa* and Tutsi elites – as middlemen between the colonial ruler and the population. As in Rwanda, ethnicity has continuously been instrumentalised as a political tool to justify violence through the post-independence period. Predominantly targeting the Hutu in Burundi,[6] this ethnic violence has shaped the organisation of the legal system and the distribution of positions within the legal field. Another core resource has been what Bayart (2000) terms 'extraversion': the *rent* derived from material and symbolic links with the international and deployed at the domestic level.

Rather than simply underlining the *dependence* of the Burundian legal field on external resources, this chapter examines the structuration of this space over time as a *globalised* history, underscoring the need to go beyond Burundi as the frame for analysis. The wealth of research on the history of empires and 'world-history' in the past 20 years has amply documented the need to trace what circulates rather than what partitions (Boucheron 2009): inter(national) connections that influence social, political, and legal change at the national level (see Subrahmanyam 2004). While the trajectory of Burundi must be understood in relation to that of its neighbours – foremost the

---

[6] It targeted the Tutsi minority in neighbouring Rwanda. This is an overly generalised account.

Democratic Republic of the Congo and Rwanda – this also suggests that the history of the legal field in colonial Burundi was primarily an *imperial* story, shaped by intra-imperial circulations across the Belgian empire, inter-imperial competition in the shadow of the British hegemon, and local struggles. This also foregrounds the question of legacy not as rupture but as 'revival' of earlier struggles and contradictions (Y Dezalay and Garth 2010). To trace the history of the Burundian legal field it is necessary, therefore, to relate it not only to the transformation of the national field of state power but also to the multi-scalar interconnections that have shaped the nationalised trajectory of Burundi over time (Steinmetz 2014; Bourdieu 2012).

This chapter identifies a defining thread in the relationship between the legal field and state power in Burundi, originating in Belgian colonial policies from the mid-1910s. What Mamdani (1996) describes as the 'decentralized despotism' fostered by 'indirect rule' was revived by each post-colonial regime. Each created its own despotism through fluid forms of legal pluralism enabling distinctions of race and/or ethnicity, urban and rural areas, and sometimes exacerbated by violence or ossified by post-conflict reforms and subjected to a regionalised 'politics of the belly'.[7] Shaped by a combination of ethnic identity and violence, virtue and economic extraction, as well as extraversion, the structure of the legal field has thus favoured successive systems of opposition in which lawyers have been positioned in relation to the state and external actors as middlemen of colonisation (be they White or racially and ethnically (re)defined 'customary chiefs'), ethnically co-opted into the state bureaucracy in the first decades of independence under a succession of military Republics, co-opted or 'NGOised' and politicised against the state in the post-1993 period, and, since 2005, co-opted as agents of an authoritarian state redeemed as 'developmental' following the transition from war.

The second section focuses on the positions and roles of legal intermediaries in colonial Burundi in 1916–62, a period that marked the beginning of globalisation in the country. Due to the limited first-hand data, it builds on secondary sources and interviews with agents (lawyers and historians), born during the mandate period, who witnessed and navigated Burundi's post-colonial history. It seeks to draw hypotheses about the impact of this early period on the structuration of the legal field in Burundi. Though the chronology is somewhat arbitrary, the sections are demarcated by events that have shaped Burundi's contemporary history. These sections are based on fieldwork in 2011–14 asking respondents about their educational, professional and social characteristics to reveal changes in the structuration of the legal field.[8] Section III, focusing on the first decades of independence, traces the structure of the legal field in the context of the military dictatorships in power between 1965 and 1993. Section IV recounts the effects on the structure of the legal field of the massive international investments responding to the 1993 massacres and the war that lasted until 2005. Section V concludes briefly with later developments, beyond the increasing violence of the current regime, pointing to a new wave of globalisation.

---

[7] 'Politics of the belly', a translation of the French 'politiques du ventre', refers to a Cameroonian expression popularised by Bayart (2009) to highlight the significance of idioms of eating and the belly to African conceptions of power and the importance of clientelism and corruption in power relations.

[8] I conducted about 70 interviews with practising lawyers (Burundians but also Europeans and North Americans in Burundi) as well as agents (nationals and internationals) working for NGOs and international organisations in Burundi. Except for well-known figures, all interviews have been anonymised to protect respondents

II. 1916–1962: UNRAVELLING THE LEGACY OF THE DEVIL'S 'PROMISE OF PROTECTION'

A. The Belgian Empire: A lawless realm?

It is suggestive of law's centrality to the colonial enterprise that victors' histories of independence in the post-colonial world were written by indigenous lawyers: Elias in Nigeria, Nehru in India, Mandela in South Africa. That lawyers could be 'freedom fighters' in the British and French empires but *not* in the Belgian would reinforce the common portrayal of Belgian colonialism as a lawless realm. The exceptional violence of Leopold II's colonial enterprise in the ill-named 'État indépendant du Congo' (ÉIC) pervades the image of a colonialism based on the 'colonial trinity' of state, missionary and private company interests (Turner 2007: 28): a 'paternalistic' model implemented by ruthless administrators, awash with rivalries among missionaries and lacking a social vision. The colonial history of the Congo's ill-fated neighbours, the Kingdoms of Rwanda and Burundi, commonly embraces this narrative. Those Kingdoms had been relatively protected from external intrusions until the nineteenth century: while there were slave raids from the Swahili of the coast, there was little Islamisation; the first European settlements were by Christian missionaries – officially to combat slavery – at the end of that century (Chrétien 2013).

Both countries were allocated to Germany at the Berlin conference in 1886 and, in 1903, effectively incorporated into the German empire, which relied on their hierarchical power structures to manage the two Kingdoms, under the name Ruanda-Urundi. Burundi had consolidated as a unified kingdom in the first half of the nineteenth century, with a society headed by a *mwami* (King) and organised along social categories, with the princely *Baganwa* at the apex (a specificity of the Burundian social structure, while the King's dynasty was drawn from the Tutsi in Rwanda), Tutsi and Hutu elites controlling hundreds of small fiefdoms consisting of a predominantly Hutu peasantry, and a group of outcasts, the Twa. World War I marked the second intrusion of globalisation: occupied by Congolese troops under the Belgian flag from 1916, the two Kingdoms were formally entrusted to Belgium by the new League of Nations as mandate territories in 1922 and administratively annexed – transformed into *de facto* colonies – to the Congo in 1923.

The violence of the racial and ethnic discrimination by the Belgians looms large in the rejection of the legacy of colonialism. Singling out the Tutsi in Rwanda as an intermediary race (Chrétien and Kabanda 2013) between Europeans and natives has commonly been seen as a root cause of the 1994 genocide. Racial discrimination and ethnic hierarchies also dominated the organisation of justice in Burundi and determined the promotion (or demotion) of categories of middlemen in the colonial enterprise.

B. Middlemen of the Empire: Collaborators and Rebels

To make sense of the revival of this legacy, it is essential to trace how Belgian colonial strategies were reflected in the habitus of those designated as middlemen by the colonial administrator – whether White Europeans or indigenous chiefs – as well as in the *structure* of the legal field. Historiography has done much to dislodge the contradictory positions and dynamics inherent in the Belgian colonial strategy. For instance, the new Burundian state negotiated its independence through Prince Rwagasore, the son of the *mwami*, Mwambutsa IV, along with a team of Belgian lawyers, whose nickname, the 'clan of the lawyers', undermines a historiography concerned with constructing Rwagasore as a national hero (Deslaurier 2013). There is very little information on these lawyers, who were decried by the colonial administration as sympathisers of the nationalist cause while being uneasily woven into the nationalist narrative as legal advisers, whose sole role was to assuage the distrust of the colonial administration and the distress of European traders based in Bujumbura (Deslaurier 2002). The message of their role for Europeans was clear: independence would not greatly affect the operations of indirect rule.

A couple of weeks into these negotiations a Greek national and two pro-Belgian Burundians, who were themselves middle-men of the Empire as chiefs and princes, assassinated Rwagasore. This triggered inter-ethnic rivalries among Tutsi and Hutu within the Union for National Progress (UPRONA), a political party created by Rwagasore as an interethnic group, but which dominated political life until 1993 as a Tutsi-dominated party. Rwagasore's murder certainly helped make him a hero of the nation, the personification of a golden age of inter-ethnic harmony despite colonial rule. Yet the contradictions of colonialism were embedded in his own trajectory.

As the son of the *mwami*, Rwagasore epitomised a nationalist movement heralding the return of the King at the apex of Burundian society while simultaneously obscuring how the King's position had been simultaneously reinforced by collaboration with the Belgian administration and weakened by six decades of colonisation. Rwagasore himself was very much a product of 'indirect rule'. As a member of the princely elite of the *Baganwa*, he was educated at the École d'Astrida, founded by missionaries in the early 1920s with the endorsement of the Belgian administration to (re)create a class of 'chiefs' charged with dispensing 'customary' justice in rural Burundi and Rwanda. Although the Belgian project of creating a 'non-hereditary aristocracy' (Gahama 2001: 247) never succeeded, chiefs were handpicked by the colonial administration for their legitimacy as members of the *Baganwa* or Tutsi elites (considered racially superior by the Belgian rulers) and their subservience to the colonial administration. Reflecting the ambiguous role played by indigenous lawyers at independence in other colonial settings (Oguamanam and Pue 2006), Rwagasore was simultaneously collaborator and rebel, a necessary kingpin of the Empire while also – as the 'fighting brigade of the people' – a central factor in its demise.

C. The Belgian Colonial Model: Capitalist Extraction and Legal Pluralism

Recent research, most of it focused on the ÉIC and Belgian Congo, is tracing a story much more complex than the common dialectic between the *mission civilisatrice* advocated by King Leopold II and the *raubwirtschaft* (plunder economy) practised by the Belgian colonial ruler in Congo, Burundi and Rwanda (eg Plasman 2014). This scholarship suggests the need to analyse inter-imperial confrontations, intra-imperial circulations and struggles between (and within) the 'colonial state' and the *métropole* (see more generally Steinmetz 2014).

At the time of the Berlin conference, Belgium was a young nation, the product of European wars and inter-imperial confrontations shaped by the 'empire of the free trade' imposed by the British hegemon, including the partition of Africa and the allocation of the Congo to Belgium. The position of colonial magistrates in the ÉIC, created as Leopold II's private domain, is emblematic. Law became a central terrain. Among other scandals, the Stokes-Lothaire incident in 1895, in which a Belgian administrator summarily executed an Irish missionary turned trader, epitomised ideological struggles – the right to a fair trial championed by the British, the fight against slavery invoked by the Belgians – which also expressed imperial confrontations.

Establishing a colonial legal system in the Congo was essential to resisting the power of European merchants, ie to evade the cost of free trade in the Congo imposed by merchants' justice. Seeking to counter the British imperial hegemon, Leopold II devised a Belgian variant: chartered companies, rule implemented through the military and missionaries, enabling a symbiosis between state and capital and using custom reinvented as law to achieve social order and present a civilising mission to the international audience.

In the face of a Belgian population opposed to the colonial enterprise, the handful of magistrates first sent to the ÉIC were from 'small' European countries (especially Italy and Norway). When the ÉIC was returned to the Belgian state in 1908, this colonial judiciary was gradually 'Belgianised' though very poorly staffed with about 400 magistrates sent to the Congo between 1908 and independence. A prosopography of these magistrates (Ngongo et al 2017) suggests they constituted a relatively homogeneous milieu, the majority originating from humanist legal networks in Liège. But the doctrine they produced reflected the ambiguity of their position. Developing a doctrinal body of customary law, these magistrates sought to position themselves in both the Belgian-style system of justice created for Europeans and the 'customary' judicial system designed for the indigenous population. Yet while the magistrates promoted a model of 'indirect rule' in contrast to the 'direct rule' implemented by Belgian administrators, their flagship journals[9] were funded by Belgian mining companies operating in Katanga, which considered the codification of customary law indispensable for the management of colonial Congo (Plasman 2014).

The rubber boom at the turn of the twentieth century profoundly shaped the colony, but the dominant role of the mining industry also contributed to the specificity of the Belgian colonial model (Etemad 2005). Called the 'Empire of the Générale' after the Société Générale, the first European bank established in Brussels in the early 1920s, Belgian colonialism built on the symbiosis of finance, corporate interests and the state, which (a uniquely Belgian feature) directly participated in mining corporations. This political economy is essential to understanding the position of Burundi and Rwanda in the Belgian empire. As in the Congo, the bulk of the metropole's colonial budget was devoted solely to the *Force publique* (police). Designed to fund the cost of administration themselves, the colonies were also shaped by a logic of extraction, producing primary goods for international markets, the profits of which could be infused into the Belgium economy. Although Burundi had experienced a mining boom in nickel, this was so overshadowed by the mineral resources of Katanga in the Congo that Belgium opted

---

[9] Notably the *Bulletin des juridictions indigènes et du droit coutumier congolais*, created in 1933 with the collaboration of missionaries to provide guidelines for the hundreds of 'indigenous' jurisdictions established in 1926 in the Congo and Burundi-Rwanda.

to maintain subsistence agriculture for the bulk of the Burundian population (who had to pay heavy tributes to the colonial administrator), settling on coffee (introduced by the Germans) and cotton as primary products intended for an export market and using the two territories as a reservoir of workers for the sparsely populated Katanga.

D. Indirect Rule in Burundi: Divide and Rule in the Shadow of Colonial Congo

Gahama's (2001) account of the mandate administration, which remains the most exhaustive source, suggests that the colonial legal and judicial strategy in Burundi and Rwanda emulated that in the Congo, with the racial/ethnic discrimination built on the social hierarchies of the two Kingdoms a local specificity. He is solely concerned with the co-optation (and eradication) of these hierarchies – what Mamdani (1996) has described as the elevation of 'custom' to a form of governmentality by the colonial state. But Gahama does not provide any information about the forms of government and justice devised in the new urban centres – especially Bujumbura, the capital – and among European merchants.

His account also overlooks the processual and conflicted nature of the colonisers' legal and judicial strategy. When Burundi and Rwanda were annexed to the Congo – an event that generated almost no debate at the League of Nations, despite these territories' protected status as mandates[10] – the dual judicial structure devised by Belgian magistrates for the Congo was extended to them. Until then the Congo's judicial system was totally separated from the Belgian. From the mid-1920s, the dual structure of civil law and customary justice was formally integrated into the hierarchy of Belgian courts, with the *Cour de Cassation* in Brussels at its apex. In practice, however, justice in the Congo remained an object of intense struggles between administrators and magistrates and mining corporations, which continued to invoke social disorder as an excuse for their private policing.

Similarly, governance in Burundi and Rwanda was contested by the Minister of the Colonies in Brussels, who favoured retaining the policy of indirect rule introduced by the Germans, and the *Commissaire général* of Belgian Congo, who advocated the application of direct rule. The indirect rule instituted in 1926 relied on chiefs as justices and administrators but also made the Belgian administrator the ultimate arbiter of justice. Socially, the system was more akin to direct rule: 'Belgium instituted an administrative apparatus devoid of "customary" agents considered to be uncooperative, thereby asserting full administrative powers' (Gahama 2001: 36). There were very few colonial administrators (just 56 in 1936), but the intense administrative reorganisation of the country (which reduced hundreds of fiefdoms to a few dozen administrative territories) ensured there were only 'chiefs who were either willing or resigned' (ibid: 62). The legal and judicial system in Burundi was both racialised and ethnicised, restricting some crimes to the indigenous population. The princely *Baganwa* and Tutsi elites, even when unruly, were made chiefs and sub-chiefs charged with dispensing customary justice.

---

[10] Only Germany protested. Belgium's position was strengthened by the fact that Britain was doing the same with Tanganyika.

Table 1 Judicial Organisation at the Beginning of (German) Colonisation

Family arbitration	among members of the family
'Hill' arbitration	through palavers, instruction and sentencing by the *bashingantahe*
Tribunals of the chief and sub-chiefs	appeals of hill arbitration sentences, before princes or local notabilities, with the *bashingantahe*
Tribunal of the King	tribunal of last resort, with the *bashingantahe* (royal advisers, mostly *Baganwa*)

Source: Gahama 2001.

Table 2 Judicial Organisation under the Belgian Mandate

Customary jurisdictions (indigenous populations)[11]	Criminal jurisdictions (racial segregation; specific crimes by Africans)[12]	Civil jurisdictions (Europeans)[13]
Tribunal de chefferie Chiefs, *bashingantahe* with only consultative role	*Tribunal de police* Territorial administrator Petty crimes by Africans	*Tribunal de district* Magistrates
Tribunal de territoire Presiding judge (Territorial administrator) and chiefs as assessors	*Tribunal de district* Magistrates All crimes by Africans Petty crimes by Europeans	*Tribunal de 1ère instance* Magistrates
Tribunal du mwami (King) Mwami presiding with Baganwa as assessors	*Tribunal de 1ère instance* Magistrates Some appeals for Africans *Cour d'Appel (Bujumbura)* Magistrates *Cour de Cassation (Brussels)* Magistrates	*Cour d'Appel (Bujumbura)* Magistrates *Cour de Cassation (Brussels)* Magistrates

Source: Gahama 2001; Cornet 2009.

III. 1965–93: IN THE SHADOW OF MILITARY REPUBLICS AND ETHNIC ULTRA-VIOLENCE: THE CHOICE BETWEEN CO-OPTATION AND MARGINALISATION

A. Ethnic Ultra-Violence: A Misleading Lens

Nous avons reçu un entraînement à la souplesse. Un prévenu m'a dit que voir un avocat tutsi c'est comme si on était mordu par une vipère et qu'on allait se plaindre chez un python.[14]

---

[11] Non-customary jurisdictions (for Africans in the new urban centres) not included here: while they contributed to a further segregation (between urban and non-urban 'natives') they concerned very few people.
[12] Racial segregation was the primary criterion (with acute difficulties, notably for 'métis' individuals); repressive jurisdiction was progressively taken away from customary jurisdictions.
[13] Special jurisdictions for Europeans (Conseil de guerre; Conseil de guerre d'Appel) not included here.
[14] Author's interview with DN, a lawyer at the Burundi Bar, Bujumbura, 7 May 2013.

[We were trained to be flexible. A defendant told me that to be assisted by a Tutsi lawyer was like complaining to a python about having been bitten by a viper.]

Talking about *ethnies* (ethnic groups) is taboo in Bujumbura, where all elites – administrative, legal, political, and commercial – are still concentrated. In rural areas, a euphemism is used for the waves of massacres that have plagued the country since independence – 'ikiza' in Kirundi ('great calamity') – a word that also invokes the collective memory of the persistent famines of the mandate era.

That a Bujumbura lawyer in 2013 should explicitly use the ethnic word to explain his position as a Tutsi lawyer for Hutu defendants was undoubtedly the result of the *juridical* process operating in the country since 2000. That year, the Arusha peace agreement officially ended the conflict that had begun in 1993. It was signed by all political parties and armed groups – except the National Council for the Defence of Democracy-Forces for the Defence of Democracy (CNDD-FDD), in control since 2005 – and redistributed power in the administrative, political, judicial and military spheres according to ethnic affiliation – a recipe known as 'consociational democracy' (Vandeginste 2010).

In 1996, the International Commission of Inquiry for Burundi had submitted a report to the UN Security Council[15] officially designating as 'genocides' two mass killings: the 1972 massacres of Hutu by the Tutsi-dominated army and the 1993 mass killings of both Tutsi and Hutu, perpetrated by the population, the Tutsi-dominated army, and Hutu-dominated armed groups. The 1972 events stayed under the radar of Cold War politics, whereas the response to the 1993 massacres was intensely internationalised. In 2003, the puzzle for the UN High Commissioner for Human Rights (which established its first local office in Bujumbura that year) and for the dozens of Belgian, French and US NGOs arriving in the country at the turn of the 2000s became how to deal with the thousands of Hutu who had been imprisoned since 1993 given that there were only a dozen lawyers called to the Burundi Bar, including just one Hutu.

The country's troubled past has had important consequences for the structure of the legal field since the early 2000s, as well as for other sectors of the public sphere where ethnicity has been ossified as an institutional resource. Contemporary scholarship, and the international policies implemented in the country over the past two decades, have been concerned primarily with countering the effects of the colonial legacy on a judicial system deemed either to have exacerbated ethnic violence or to be disconnected from local realities, notably the acute pressure on arable land by a population still depending on subsistence agriculture (Kolhagen 2009). Yet the violence of debates among historians and politicians about the 1994 genocide of Tutsi in Rwanda and the genocides in Burundi testifies to the fact that the politics of ethnic affiliation are also inter/national, part and parcel of a political controversy that was continuously waged in Kigali and Paris, Bujumbura and Brussels in the post-colonial period. It also exposes the pitfall of casually adopting a narrative that reduces collective violence, and with it legal politics, to ethnic *identity*.

---

[15] United Nations, 22 August 1996, pp 19, 75, S/1996/682.

The genocide in Rwanda in 1994 – and the massacres unfolding at the same time in neighbouring Burundi (which were less visible in the Western media) – sent a shock wave through the small world of historians (most located in Belgium and France) specialising in the Great Lakes region of Africa. Jean-Pierre Chrétien (eg 2012) argued against two persistent images of collective violence in that region and Africa generally. Like the first US intervention in Iraq, the 1994 genocide in Rwanda symbolised the 'CNN effect', displaying images of massacred bodies to Western viewers, almost in real time. These reinforced a persistent vision, embedded in decades of ignorance and Western racism, of 'machete violence' in Africa: an atavistic outburst devoid of political meaning. Criticism of this vision sought not only to integrate African massacres into the horrific litany of Western genocides but also to produce a historicised and political explanation emancipated from the legacy of colonial anthropology, which had been used to justify colonial racial and ethnic discrimination. Singling out the Tutsi as a superior, intermediary race – epitomised by the ethnic identity cards imposed by Belgian administrators in 1932 (Chrétien and Kabanda 2013) – had lasting effects, as did commingling the social fabrics of Rwanda and Burundi. The Hutu-led 'social revolution' in Rwanda in 1959, which brought a Hutu majority to power until 1994, had ripple effects in Burundi, where the persistent fear of a Hutu rebellion was used repeatedly to justify violent repression by the Tutsi-dominated army; and each violent episode had echoes in both countries.

Yet, Chrétien and Dupaquier (2007) underline how these flows and counter-flows of ethnic politics across both countries were also deeply connected to the structuration of the field of state power in Rwanda and Burundi. They start with the puzzle noted by a 1959 study of rural areas commissioned by the Belgian administration to prepare Burundi for independence: the 'problem' of relations between Tutsi and Hutu was not the same in Rwanda as it was in Burundi, where both groups seemed to enjoy the same social and economic rights. Rather, in Burundi it originated in abuses by the dominant class, the princely *Baganwa*, which had no equivalent in Rwanda (Deslaurier 2002: 15).

B. Reviving Colonial Legacies in the Structuration of the Field of State Power: Rent, Patrimonialism, Regionalism and Ethnicity

The 1972 massacres played a crucial role in crystallising ethnicity as a vehicle of violence and ethnic discrimination by operationalising it as a defining vector for the allocation of social, political, economic and symbolic power. Hutu elites were eradicated: either killed or forced to flee. These massacres, together with fears of a Hutu uprising fuelled by the military Republics that acceded to power from 1965, contributed to a process of conscientising ethnic divisions through violence. Indeed, ethnic violence justified the emergence of each military Republic through a coup d'état and the violent repression each orchestrated by means of military trials and summary executions in 1972, 1988 and 1991. Ethnic violence thus consolidated the despotic political system while reinforcing the dominance of a very small Tutsi urban elite over the field of state power: 'promoting tribalism as politics, members of the state apparatus endeavoured, unwittingly or consciously, to prevent the peasantry from building consciousness as a social class aware of its exploitation by the bourgeoisie connected to the state' (Chrétien and Dupaquier 2007: 39).

To trace the reciprocal effects of these dynamics between the fields of state power and law during this period it is necessary to look more closely at the structure of elites at independence. They exhibited the patrimonialisation of the state – what Bayart (2009) has termed the 'politics of the belly' – built on ethnic affiliation and extraversion. The colonial administration had initially resisted the emergence of elites (Gahama 2001: 247). Only in 1959 did the Belgians attempt to reverse this trend. However, efforts to 'Africanise' the administrative *cadres* abruptly ended with independence. The elites that competed for power at independence came from two main groups of secondary school graduates: the 'Astridiens' from the École d'Astrida for chiefs and the 'Séminaristes' from the Mugere seminary, originally designed to train local clergy but from which many school teachers and public servants also emerged.

Devolving education to missionaries had already been the practice in colonial Congo: the 1906 agreement between the Vatican and Brussels prioritised Catholic missions, which also held a prominent position in Burundi (while Protestant missions predominated in Rwanda). Conceived as a modality of social control,[16] education in colonial Burundi focused on the formation of the middlemen of the colonial administration:

> [G]enerally, [the missionaries] attempted to provide the bulk of the population with a limited education. [The colonial administration] tolerated the emergence of a small elite, but exclusively among the so-called customary leading class, who had to be trained in a separate school where they were to be educated to be subservient. (Gahama 2001: 245)

The dozen university graduates at independence (who did not include any lawyers) had been handpicked by the missions to receive their secondary education at the Collège du Saint Esprit, created in the 1940s for the best primary school graduates in Burundi and Rwanda. This Collège was conceived as a 'laboratory of inter-racial relations',[17] enrolling sons of Tutsi and Hutu from both Rwanda and Burundi, as well as Europeans. These endeavours contributed to the formation of a small 'bureaucratic-meritocratic elite' of 'semi-diploma' holders, most of whom served in the administration and army, often at high levels (Chrétien and Dupaquier 2007: 24).

The structure of this independence elite also exhibited the colonial administration's divide and rule strategy. General Michel Micombero, who took power through a coup d'état in 1966, was part of the small meritocratic elite formed by the Collège du Saint Esprit. Trained as an officer at the Royal Military Academy in Brussels, he also was the product of the Belgians' attempt to create an army from 1958 and pit a Tutsi elite against the princely *Baganwa* in order to weaken anti-Belgian factions within the nationalist movement. In so doing, the colonial administration built on the patrimonial competition among chiefs fostered by coffee production. Promoted as an export crop, coffee culture also relied on control of the population by chiefs motivated by their ability to extort rent through tributes. The 'Groupe de Bururi', which took power with Micombero and retained it under Colonel Bagaza in 1976 and Major Buyoya in 1987, came from the Bururi region, which had been sidelined by colonial strategies favouring the Muramvya region of the princely *Baganwa*.

---

[16] Based on the model devised for African-American pupils in the 1920s by the Phelps-Stokes Foundation in the US.
[17] Author's interview with EN, a lawyer at the Burundi Bar, Bujumbura, 21 December 2011.

Belgian colonial policies also extended the power of this small urban elite into the rural sphere. Between 1945 and 1952, colonial administrators introduced several reforms. The chiefs were replaced by elected mayors, while the institution of the '*bashingantahe*' (literally 'wise men'), which traditionally had played the role of countervailing power in administration and justice, was rendered impotent (Kolhagen 2012). Throughout the post-colonial history of the country until 1993, this ensured the monopoly of the country's single party, UPRONA, as the sole point of contact between the people and the state (Deslaurier 2003).

Thus, in Burundi, 'politics provide the opportunity and the means to *eat*' (Chrétien and Dupaquier 2007: 51, emphasis in the original). The state that emerged in the 1970s was intensely bureaucratic, dependent on rents from coffee as the country's primary export crop (Hatungimana 2008) but even more on development aid. Still provided mainly by the former *métropole*, the latter represented 30 per cent of the GDP in the early 1970s and ensured a tight Belgo-Burundian operational system in all public sectors. The fluid transition of the colonial administration into 'cooperation' ensured the lasting presence of *coopérants*, consultants, and religious missions.

C. Co-optation and Extraversion in the Structure of the Legal Field

The legal field was structured in the shadow of these dynamics. In 1962, the legal framework was officially 'de-racialised'. The law of 1962 on the organisation of justice dismantled customary law jurisdictions and universalised the colonial civil law system, previously reserved for Europeans. Since then there has been only one legal system, modelled on the Belgian and regulated by procedural rules inherited from the Germans in 1886. However, legal and judicial decolonisation was a slow process: the first codifications were undertaken only in the 1970s by Belgian consultants seconded to the Burundi Ministry of Justice. Belgian professors, judges and barristers continued to practise in Burundi after independence: 'the transition was soft'.[18] A law professor at the Université du Burundi recalled:

> The first elites were not lawyers. The colonial administrative authority did not favour the law. It was, rather, agronomy .... Law was considered a luxury. When I started there were, in fact, very few trained judges: only the presidents of tribunals had some legal background.[19]

Although nationalised, the post-colonial legal institutions reproduced the urban/rural divide constructed by the colonial regime, with professional judges sitting in higher courts in the urban centres and a mostly untrained staff in the lower courts, the 'Tribunaux d'instance', in the rural areas.

The Université du Burundi was created in 1964 as an extension of the Faculté Notre-Dame de la Paix in Namur, Belgium. The first cohort obtained their diplomas in 1974. As explained by a law professor at the Université: 'the first generation of Burundian lawyers, it was us in 1969. When I started studying law most of the classes were taught by Belgian

---

[18] Author's interview with GG, Professor at the Université du Burundi, Bujumbura, 3 May 2013.
[19] ibid.

professors .... It was clear that we were there to ensure the succession'.[20] This university, which monopolised legal education until the early 2000s and produced an average of 30 law diplomas a year, was also quickly affected by the ethnic and factionalist politics of the Micombero regime. From the 1972 massacres until the 2000s, over 90 per cent of law students were Tutsi, according to some reports (Vandeginste 2010: 97).

These dynamics of extraversion, clientelism and exclusion have heavily affected the structuration of the legal field, which was segmented between a small elite of law professors and a mass of magistrates distributed according to hierarchies determined by political, economic and ethnic resources. Law professors continue to construct their status by obtaining a PhD at a Belgian faculty. Mostly originating from the same region, Mwaro, they were suspected of bias against students from Bururi, the stronghold of the military elite, creating uneasy relations with the Micombero and Bagaza military juntas. Before the emergence of this academic legal elite, the Micombero regime had appealed to ideologically extremist lawyers, such as Artémon Simbananye, accused of orchestrating the 1972 purge against the Hutu. It is only in the Third Republic, following the 1987 coup d'état by Major Buyoya and some liberalisation, that law professors served as legal advisers on constitutional reforms.

The intensely bureaucratic nature of the state until the 2000s contributed to the rising demand for lawyers. A former judge, who entered the judiciary in 1998, explained: 'there was work for everybody, there weren't enough law professionals. We were not necessarily assigned where we wanted, but there was work for everybody'.[21] Executive control over the judiciary through a form of 'diffuse interference'[22] (selective promotions and demotions) was facilitated by the absence of an 'École de la magistrature', which made it easier to remove judges.

The political economy of a country whose people depend on subsistence agriculture limited the private market for legal services. As explained by a magistrate: 'the possibility that was offered to me was the judiciary. Because to be a barrister you needed to have economic resources'.[23] The repressive politics of the Micombero military regime, reproduced by the Bagaza junta, also made private practice a dangerous form of political opposition. Etienne Ntyiyankundiye was the first Burundian lawyer to be called to the Bar in 1966, after graduating from the Université of Namur in Belgium. His trajectory illustrates the Bar's relationship to the military juntas until the end of the 1980s. A friend of Micombero, with whom he had attended the Collège du Saint Esprit, Ntyiyankundiye was appointed Minister of Justice in 1969 before being disgraced. He was arrested in 1971 along with his clients – Tutsi military from the Muramvya region accused of having fomented a coup.

During the 1970s–80s, dozens of military trials were conducted to reinforce the military regimes, but defendants were assisted exclusively by foreign lawyers, mostly Belgian. Ntyiyankundiye explained: 'My choice was to stay out of politics .... My legal practice focused on businesses. Personally, I had hardly any income, I cultivated a plot

---

[20] ibid.
[21] Interview with AB, a lawyer at the Gitega Bar, Bujumbura, 7 May 2013.
[22] Interview with FN, a lawyer at the Burundi Bar, Bujumbura, 24 April 2014.
[23] ibid.

of land .... The avenue of justice was completely blocked'.[24] 'The monopoly of foreign lawyers'[25] – the Burundi Bar – had been founded around 1950, presumably to cater for European traders based in Bujumbura. Some of the Belgian lawyers associated with the 'clan of the lawyers' who assisted UPRONA in the negotiations for independence – such as Willy Vanderplancken – seem to have represented political defendants in the military trials conducted by the junta in the 1970s. This mobilisation of the Bar as a political platform through foreign lawyers later became a defining feature. Eric Gillet and Bernard Maingain, of the Brussels Bar, for example, often represented defendants in Rwanda and Burundi in political cases.

IV. 1993–2015: NAVIGATING THE (INTERNATIONAL) RULES OF ETHNIC REDISTRIBUTION

A. Burundi's Third Wave: Human Rights and Ethnicity as Mediums of Political Opposition

Major Buyoya, who installed himself as president in 1987 after a military coup, embodies the ambiguity of what has commonly been dubbed the 'Third Wave' of global democratisation. A native of the Bururi region like his predecessors, Buyoya continued to deploy the repressive toolkit of previous military juntas, suppressing a 1988 attempted Hutu uprising with extreme violence. But Buyoya also announced an agenda of political liberalisation and better Hutu-Tutsi relations. Indeed, he justified his coup d'état against Bagaza in the name of civil liberties. At a French-African summit in 1990 in La Baule, French President Mitterrand had announced that aid would flow 'more enthusiastically' to African countries taking steps towards democracy, effectively introducing conditionality in the disbursement of development funds. Belgium did not follow suit. Nonetheless, as Buyoya recalled: 'we were not subjected to the France-Africa summit at La Baule but we adapted ourselves to the political context' (Ngabire 2015).

This liberalisation policy had important domestic effects. The legalisation of opposition parties in 1991 fostered a rapprochement between Hutu and Tutsi. The creation of the Front for Democracy in Burundi (FRODEBU) by Melchior Ndadaye encouraged the return of the Hutu diaspora, who had fled the country after 1972. Exiled in Rwanda, Ndadaye epitomised the new political generation formed by an educated Hutu elite organised into resistance movements. Buyoya also appointed a commission tasked with drafting a new constitution, adopted by referendum in 1992, which called for a non-ethnic government with a president and a parliament.

In practice, however, the coupling of structural adjustment policies and political liberalisation echoed the contradictory dimensions of the impact of neo-liberal globalisation found elsewhere in the world during this period. While opening the possibility of a domestic space for human rights activism attuned to the international market for human rights, liberal reforms in Burundi also deepened the capacity of the state to shape and

---

[24] ibid.
[25] Interview with E Ntyiyankundiye, a lawyer at the Burundi Bar, Bujumbura, 21 December 2011.

neutralise political opposition. The practice of political interference in civil society even bears its own term in Kirundi: 'nyakurisation'. The Ligue Iteka, the country's first human rights organisation, is emblematic of this contradiction. It was created in 1994 as a sister organisation of the International League of Human Rights and became both a platform of political opposition and a site of professionalisation for new generations of human rights activists. Yet, it was rumoured to be a stronghold of FRODEBU. Thus, the very year of its creation, a concurrent organisation, the Ligue Sonera, was launched to compete for the same pool of international resources and funding as the preserve of close affiliates of UPRONA and members of the old Tutsi legal elite at the Université du Burundi.

Similarly, these liberalisation policies had a limited though symbolic impact on the social structure of the legal field. Buyoya's politics of inter-ethnic appeasement sought to transform the ethnic fabric of the judiciary by nominating Hutu judges. But that had little effect on the Burundi Bar, which remained the preserve of a dozen Tutsi lawyers in the early 1990s. Fabien Segatwa, the first Hutu lawyer called to the Burundi Bar in 1993, had lived in exile in the Democratic Republic of the Congo since 1972. He recalled: 'to encourage the return of the elite Hutu diaspora, the government and the UN High Commissioner for Refugees organised a visit of Hutu elites to campaign for their return from neighbouring countries'.[26] His own swearing in as a barrister was actively resisted by the Bar, which defended its monopoly over the very restricted market for private legal practice.

B. The Post-1993 Crisis: A Legal Boom in the Shadow of the Geopolitics of the 'Bottom-up' State

Democratic elections in June 1993 were won by Melchior Ndadaye, the first Hutu president. But this radical change in Burundi's political landscape was abruptly terminated by his assassination just months later by segments of the Tutsi-dominated army. Ndadaye's murder triggered large scale massacres and the country's descent into civil war.

The 1993 crisis in Burundi bulked large in the formidable expansion of international markets for conflict resolution. Burundi became the testing ground for novel forms of external intervention, involving INGOs seeking to promote rule of law reforms 'from the bottom up', sidestepping domestic state authorities and operating outside official diplomatic and military channels (S Dezalay 2016). These internationalised policies were shaped by post-Cold War politics and the opening of new non-governmental markets from the early 1990s, encouraged by transformations in international development politics, notably the emphasis on preventing violent conflict (S Dezalay 2011).

International reaction to the 1993 crisis was deeply shaped by the parallel disaster of US intervention in Somalia and the months-long hesitation of the US and other Western powers in reacting to the Rwanda genocide. The ad hoc solution was to involve NGOs, such as the US-based Search for Common Ground and the British International Alert, which specialised in 'conflict resolution', to rebuild the rule of law and reform judicial institutions outside official channels of intervention. Decentralised and non-governmental,

---

[26] Interview with Fabien Segatwa, lawyer at the Burundi Bar, Bujumbura, 16 April 2014.

these were a cheaper option than creating an international criminal tribunal, as in the case of Rwanda. They also enabled the disbursement of development monies outside official state channels in a war zone and in the face of the embargo imposed on Burundi following Buyoya's second coup in 1996.

These international endeavours were also integrated into a revival of colonial and autocratic politics. Indeed, Burundi's domestic response to the 1993 crisis was judicial. Following the second coup d'état by Major Buyoya in 1996, judicial proceedings were begun against those suspected of assassinating Ndadaye (before the Judicial Chamber of the Supreme Court) and those suspected of participating in the subsequent massacres (before the Criminal Chambers of the Court of Appeal) (Vandeginste 2010: 87ff). Previous attempted coups and uprisings had been prosecuted before military courts, usually on sedition and rebellion charges. The novelty here was the imprimatur of a genocidal wording in the judicial response to the 1993 crisis. This reflected pressure at the domestic level from victims' associations, including the extremist Tutsi defence organisation AC-Génocide. Thousands of suspects, predominantly Hutu, were arrested in a wartime context immediately after the massacres.

A prominent actor in the internationalisation of these post-1993 trials (commonly known as the *contentieux de 1993*), the Belgian NGO Avocats Sans Frontières (ASF), had been created in 1992 in collaboration with the International League of Human Rights. Its initial objective was to send lawyers – following the *sans frontières* approach of Médecins Sans Frontières (MSF) – to observe trials in autocratic contexts, especially in Africa. Following the Rwanda genocide, ASF shifted focus to criminal defence in the context of the ad hoc International Tribunal for Rwanda and the defence of Hutu defendants in the *contentieux de 1993*. According to a former director of the Belgian section of ASF, access to Burundi was eased by a 'good conjuncture': the crisis of Belgian development aid caused by the suspension of Belgium's development programmes in the context of the wars in the Democratic Republic of Congo, Rwanda and Burundi. This was coupled with the desire of then Development Minister Réginald Moreels, former director of MSF-Belgium, to reengage in the Great Lakes region through informal efforts to implement justice reforms.[27]

Another core organisation in these efforts, the UN High Commissioner for Human Rights, established its first office in Burundi to assemble a team of lawyers, international and local, to represent the Hutu defendants of the *contentieux de 1993*. In the wake of these initiatives, ASF appealed to international lawyers to intervene in the prosecutions and created rosters of domestic lawyers, whom they trained and assisted.

These endeavours had an enormous impact on the legal field in Burundi. There were only ten lawyers called to the Burundi Bar in 1993. There were over 400 in Bujumbura by 2000–01 and several hundred more in the competing Gitega Bar created in the mid-2010s. As expressed by a lawyer at the Burundi Bar: 'ultimately, Avocats Sans Frontières has created the market for barristers'.[28] The salary international organisations paid to lawyers involved in the *contentieux de 1993* – 1 million FBU per month as opposed to roughly 58,000 FBU for a higher court magistrate – played a large role in making private

---

[27] Interview with Luc Walleyn, former president of ASF, Brussels, 13 December 2012.
[28] Interview with WR, a lawyer at the Burundi Bar, Bujumbura, 3 May 2013.

law practice an attractive market and fostering what one lawyer described as the 'mental gymnastics'[29] necessary to overcome the resistance of Tutsi lawyers to defending Hutu. The expansion of the pool of private legal practitioners is also attributable to the devaluation of justice institutions. The judiciary and its infrastructure had been relatively unscathed by the 1993 crisis and resulting war, compared to those in Rwanda, but they were totally discredited by the peace process and the legacy of political subservience and corruption. As encapsulated ironically by a former magistrate called to the Burundi Bar at the end of the 1990s: 'the cow speaks better French than the barrister'.[30]

The 2005 general elections organised by the Arusha peace process enabled the ascendance of the CNDD-FDD (a former Hutu-dominated rebel group transformed into a political party). Its victory signalled the entry into the political field of 'bush elites', whose symbolic capital is derived mostly from fighting as members of Hutu-dominated rebel groups during the 1993–2003 war, thereby constituting a break with established elites, including those of the Catholic Church, symbolised by the fact that the current ruler, Pierre Nkurunziza, is a self-proclaimed 'born again' Christian. The change of regime also meant that 'a whole market for training new elites was opened'.[31] The long-standing negotiations between the government and the UN over the transitional justice mechanisms planned by the Arusha agreement (Lima and S Dezalay 2015), together with the expansion of the market for legal education, also contributed to the legal boom, reflected in the creation of dozens of domestic law-oriented NGOs.

C. The Private Market for (Inter)national Legal Practice: A Buffer between Foreign Diplomacy and Despotic Rule

These dynamics have fostered the emergence of a new generation of Burundian lawyers who are now called to the Bar right after graduating, rather than starting their careers in the judiciary. However, this legal boom has not been accompanied by an expansion of the private legal services market. This younger generation usually combines solo private practice as barristers with positions as human rights advocates within domestic NGOs and contracts as consultants for INGOs and international organisations. This domestic market therefore suffers from a double bind: dependent on and vulnerable to the volatile demand from international donors and organisations and weakened as a buffer between international diplomacy and a repressive government.

This contradictory position affects INGOs within the Burundian market. A former ASF director recalled the 'war of position' among INGOs competing for the same EU sources of funding and the difficulty of adapting to donors' short-time horizon and changing priorities.[32] Vulnerable to shifting donor demands, INGOs also occupy an insecure position in relation to local authorities. To explain the lack of international reaction when the CNDD-FDD abruptly terminated the post-1993 trials and amnestied

---

[29] Interview with DN, a lawyer at the Burundi Bar, Bujumbura, 7 May 2013.
[30] Interview with AN, a lawyer at the Burundi Bar, Bujumbura, 2 May 2013.
[31] Author's interview with JM, Thematic Expert, ASF, Brussels, 13 June 2013.
[32] Interview with LdC, Coopération technique belge, Bujumbura, 22 April 2014.

former Hutu rebel groups, another Belgian ASF employee explained: 'the problem is that political advocacy has been left to NGOs, while donors embrace a technical approach [to development aid] without any political capacity'.[33]

The result of these international rule of law efforts has been a haphazard, decentralised web of small-scale projects, vulnerable to international policy change and domestic political transformation. International initiatives did not seek to modify the framework of the *contentieux de 1993*, which primarily targeted the Hutu. The increasingly repressive politics of the CNDD-FDD government since 2005 have further accentuated a kind of 'tango dance' among international diplomats intent on maintaining the appearance of good relations with Burundian authorities in the face of an increasingly violent regime. In order to bypass a judicial system that is hard to reform because of political resistance and continuous diffuse interference by the executive, international donors, ironically, are now turning to 'informal' justice, notably by seeking to revive the *bashingantahe* (Deslaurier 2003).

These dynamics are also accentuating the role of the Bar and law-oriented NGOs as platforms of political opposition. The current regime is reviving the long tradition of political interference in civil society. The Burundi Bar, still seen as a stronghold of the Tutsi elite, has been paired with the Gitega Bar, allegedly infiltrated by CNDD-FDD. This contest within civil society conceals a professional competition: efforts by the Bar to preserve its monopoly over the very limited domestic market for private legal services. It also underscores the persistent legacy of the repressive practices of the military juntas, notwithstanding the outsider and Hutu identity of CNDD-FDD. Yet the Bar's position as an opposition platform is experiencing transformation under the impetus of regional dynamics. Since the integration of Burundi into the East African Community in 2007, the East African Court of Human Rights has regularly been used by prominent political lawyers at the Burundi Bar, in association with Kenyan and Tanzanian law societies. Integration into the East African Community may also mark the gradual opening of a business hemisphere within the Burundi Bar, evidenced by the emergence of firms with several associates (still a rarity in Bujumbura) catering to East African and Asian clients.

V. CONCLUSION 2015–

Since Nkurunziza's bid for a third presidential term in 2015 and his reelection in 2015, Burundi has again descended into a cycle of violence. But a quiet transformation is unfolding in parallel: viewed as a pariah by the diplomatic and development aid community, Nkurunziza's regime is being reinstated as a 'developmental' partner by mining corporations and European states, especially Germany, intent on exploiting Burundi's mineral resources (S Dezalay 2018), making the country once more a 'petri dish' where 'mobile, globally competitive capital … finds minimally regulated zones in which to vest its operations' (Comaroff and Comaroff 2012: 13).

---

[33] Interview with RC, Senior Justice Advisor, ISSAT-DCAF, Brussels, 13 June 2013.

REFERENCES

Bayart, J-F (2009) *The State in Africa. The Politics of the Belly*, 2nd edn (Hoboken, NJ).
—— (2000) 'Africa in the world: a history of extraversion' 99 *African Affairs* 217–67.
Benton, L and Ford, L (2016) *Rage for Order. The British Empire and the Origins of International Law, 1800–1850* (Cambridge, Mass, Harvard University Press).
Boucheron, P (ed) (2009) *Histoire du monde au XVè siècle* (Paris, Fayard).
Bourdieu, P (1993) 'Esprits d'Etat [Genèse et structure du champ bureaucratique] Genèse et structure du champ bureaucratique' 96–97 *Actes de la recherche en sciences sociales* 49–62.
—— (2012) *Sur l'État. Cours au Collège de France (1989–1992)* (Paris, Le Seuil).
Bourdieu, P and Wacquant LJD (1992) *An Invitation to Reflexive Sociology* (Chicago, University of Chicago Press).
Chrétien, J-P (ed) (2012) *Le défi de l'ethnisme. Rwanda et Burundi* (Paris, Karthala).
—— (2013) 'La question de la traite au Burundi et au Rwanda au début de la colonisation allemande (1890–1906)' in H Médard, M-L Derat, T Vernet and M-P Ballarin, *Traites et esclavages en Afrique orientale et dans l'océan Indien* (Paris, Editions Karthala) 339–56.
Chrétien, J-P and Dupaquier, J-F (2007) *Burundi 1972. Au bord des génocides* (Paris, Karthala).
Chrétien, J-P and Kabanda, M (2013) *Rwanda, Racisme et Génocide. L'idéologie hamitique* (Paris, Belin).
Comaroff, J and Comaroff, JL (2012) *Theory from the South. Or, How Euro-America is evolving toward Africa* (Boulder, Paradigm Publishers).
Deslaurier, C (2002) 'Un monde politique en mutation: le Burundi à la veille de l'indépendance (circa 1956–1961)' PhD thesis in History, Université Paris I, unpublished.
—— (2003) 'Le "bushingantahe" peut-il réconcilier le Burundi ?' 92 *Politique africaine* 76–96.
—— (2013) 'Rwagasore for ever? Des usages contemporains d'un héros consensuel au Burundi' 118(2) *Vingtième Siècle. Revue d'histoire* 15–30.
Dezalay, S (2011) 'Revamping Law by Circumventing the State. Non-governmental organizations in the international management of social violence on the African continent' PhD of Laws, European University Institute.
—— (2015) 'Les juristes en Afrique: entre trajectoires d'État, sillons d'empire et mondialisation' 138 *Politique africaine* 5–23.
—— (2016) 'Répondre aux crises? Dynamiques de "gestion des crises" par l'instrument: de la Commission européenne aux réformes de la justice au Burundi' 5(2) *Gouvernement & action publique* 31–50.
—— (2018) 'Lawyers in Africa: Brokers of the State, Intermediaries of Globalization. A Case Study of the "Africa" Bar in Paris' 25(2) *International Journal of Global Legal Studies* 639–69.
—— (forthcoming) 'Africa's lawyers: between imperial legacies and transformations in global capitalism' in R Abel, H Sommerlad, O Hammerslev and U Schultz (eds), *Lawyers in 21st Century Societies. Vol II: Comparisons and Theories* (Oxford, Hart Publishing).
Dezalay, Y and Garth, BG (2010) *Asian Legal Revivals. Lawyers in the Shadow of Empire* (London, University of Chicago Press).
Dorsett, S and McLaren, J (eds) (2014) *Legal Histories of the British Empire. Laws, Engagement and Legacies* (Abingdon, Routledge).
Etemad, B, (2005) *De l'utilité des Empires: colonisation et prospérité de l'Europe* (Paris, Armand Collin).
Gahama, J (2001) *Le Burundi sous administration belge*, 2nd edn (Paris, Karthala).
Halliday, TC, Karpik, L and Feeley, MM (eds) (2012) *Fates of Political Liberalism in the British Post-Colony. The Politics of the Legal Complex* (Cambridge, Cambridge University Press).
Hatungimana, A (2008) 'Le café et les pouvoirs au Burundi' *Les Cahiers d'Outre-Mer* 243 journals. openedition.org/com/5298.

Kohlhagen, D (2009) *Burundi: la justice en milieu rural* (Brussels, RCN Justice & Démocratie).

—— (2012) 'Oser une refondation de la Justice en Afrique. Attentes citoyennes et alternatives au Burundi' in C Eberhard (ed), *Le courage des alternatives* (Cahiers d'anthropologie du droit. Hors-série, Paris, Karthala) 177–95.

Lima, J and Dezalay, S (2015) 'La "cause" de la justice de transition dans le Burundi de l'après-conflit" 67 *Critique internationale* 51–66.

Mamdani, M (1996) *Citizen and Subject: Contemporary Africa and the Legacy of Late Colonialism* (Princeton, Princeton University Press).

Ngabire, E (2015) 'La politique de l'unité nationale, socle de Buyoya 1er' (Iwacu, 23 November).

Ngongo, E, Piret, B, Montel, L and le Polain de Waroux, P (2017) 'Prosopographie et biographie: regards croisés sur la magistrature coloniale belge' 40 *C@hiers du CRHIDI* popups.uliege.be/1370-2262/index.php?id=356.

Oguamanam, C and Pue, W (2006) 'Lawyers' Professionalism, Colonialism, State Formation and National Life in Nigeria, 1900–1960: "the Fighting Brigade of the People"' ssrn.com/abstract=953313.

Plasman, P-L (2014) 'Un État de non-droit? L'établissement du pouvoir judiciaire au Congo léopoldien 1885–1889' in C Braillon, L Montel, B Piret and P-L Plasman, *Droit et justice en Afrique coloniale: tradition, production et réformes* (Brussels, Université Saint-Louis) 27–28.

Renucci, F (2011) 'Les chantiers de l'histoire du droit colonial. Introduction' *Clio@Themis* www.cliothemis.com/Clio-Themis-numero-4.

Steinmetz, G (2013) *Sociology and Empire. The imperial entanglements of a discipline* (Durham, NC, Duke University Press).

—— (2014) 'Etat-mort, Etat-fort, Etat-empire' 201–202 *Actes de la recherche en sciences sociales* 112–19.

Subrahmanyam, S (2004) *Explorations in Connected History: From the Tagus to the Ganges* (Oxford India Paperbacks).

Turner, T (2007) *The Congo Wars: Conflict, Myth, and Reality*, 2nd edn (London, Zed Books).

Vandeginste, S (2010) *Stones Left Unturned. Law and Transitional Justice in Burundi* (Antwerp, Intersentia).

Vanderlinden, J (19997) 'Law: Burundi, Congo, and Rwanda' in J Middleton and J Calder Miller (eds), *Encyclopedia of Africa, Vol II* (New York, Charles Scribner's Sons).

Vauchez, A (2008) 'The Force of a Weak Field: Law and Lawyers in the Government of the European Union (For a Renewed Research Agenda)' 2(2) *International Political Sociology* 128–44.

24

Kenya
Between Globalisation and Constitutionalism

WINIFRED KAMAU

I. INTRODUCTION

THE LEGAL PROFESSION has grown from a mere 300 advocates in 1961 to over 15,000 in 2018 and undergone significant changes. Ghai and MacAuslan (1970) traced the origin and development of the legal profession from the colonial period to the early years after independence. Subsequent writing analysed the professionalisation of Kenyan lawyers within the political economy of the post-colonial state, highlighting the struggles leading to Africanisation of the bar (Odenyo 1979; Ghai 1981). Later works focused on the structure of legal education (Ojwang and Salter 1989) and the legal profession (Ojwang and Salter 1990). Since then, the legal profession has seen demographic shifts (especially the increasing number of women and the dominance of younger lawyers), changes in legal education, and the effects of market liberalisation, globalisation and regional integration. However, there has been little scholarly attention to these changes, aside from their impact on legal ethics (Ojienda and Juma 2013). Ghai and Ghai (2014) explore the consequences of the 2010 Constitution, including legal education (Kameri-Mbote 2014), lawyer discipline (Kegoro et al 2014) and globalisation (Mboya 2014).

This chapter tracks the major developments in the legal profession over the last 30 years, including demographics, legal education, emerging patterns of practice, internal tensions and fissures, and the changing relations between the Bar and the state. It considers the challenges and opportunities introduced by the 2010 Constitution and examines how the profession negotiates the tensions between championing justice and the rule of law on one hand and the 'bread and butter issues' that require lawyers to respond to the market forces of liberalisation and globalisation on the other.

II. HISTORICAL DEVELOPMENT

A. Colonial Period

Prior to colonialism, indigenous legal structures had no formalised category of lawyer. Ghai and McAuslan (1970) trace the development of the nascent legal profession in Kenya during British colonial rule (1895–1963) in the context of a racially stratified legal system, with native tribunals applying customary law to indigenous Africans (the vast majority of the population) and English legal institutions for British settlers and the Asian business community.

The heterogeneous collection of English barristers and solicitors, Indian pleaders and lay *vakeels* (local persons knowledgeable about basic court procedures but possessing no legal qualifications) developed into an organised profession enjoying substantial autonomy and self-regulation after the 1949 Advocates Ordinance and Law Society of Kenya Ordinance transferred authority from the Chief Justice and gave the profession a monopoly over legal services, prohibiting practice by unqualified persons. By 1961, all practising advocates had to belong to the Law Society. Most private practitioners were Asian, and the entire colonial legal service was English. Because lawyers could not appear in native tribunals there was no scheme for training Africans in law, with the result that Argwings Kodhek was the first to qualify in 1958, and only five more had done so by independence.

B. Post-Independence Period

i. The Early Years: Africanisation (1960s–mid-1980s)

After the opening of legal education to Africans following independence, the number entering the profession began to increase. Initially most went into public service because they found it difficult to penetrate the closed world of the Bar (although SN Waruhiu became the first African Chairman of the Law Society of Kenya (LSK) in 1970). By the mid-1980s, African lawyers outnumbered British and Asian.

ii. The Middle Years: Professionalisation (1980s to Early 2000s)

This period saw the domination of the profession by Africans. Ever since Amos Wako was elected Law Society Chairman (now called President) in 1979, all successors have been African. It was a time of consolidating professionalism, with an increase in self-regulation in the form of professional indemnity insurance, continuing professional development, and revised codes of etiquette and ethics.

iii. Current Period: A Profession in Flux (2010 to the Present)

This period has been characterised by significant changes in the profession, including the entry of more women and the increasing dominance of young lawyers. There have been internal wrangles between 'Young Turks' and the old guard, fuelled by ideological differences concerning discipline and governance. Market forces have driven the emergence of large law firms and the formation of regional and global alliances.

The promulgation of the 2010 Constitution ushered in a new era of governance based on values of democracy, rule of law, equity, transparency and accountability.

III. CONSTITUTION OF KENYA 2010

A. Opportunities for the Legal Profession

Ghai (2014) emphasises the importance of the legal profession for promoting constitutionalism and the rule of law. Article 10 of the Constitution enumerates the values of human dignity and human rights, good governance, integrity, transparency and accountability, which underlie the Republic, binding both the state and the populace.

The Constitution contains an expansive Bill of Rights, including socio-economic rights to housing, education, food, water and access to justice. Articles 21–23 ease access to courts by dismantling rigid *locus standi* rules and allowing *amici curiae* and interested parties to participate in lawsuits, encouraging the rise of public interest litigation spearheaded by civil society organisations. The intense civic education preceding the 2010 referendum heightened public awareness of rights. The common law tradition, which depends on the presentation of arguments by advocates, emphasises their role as partners of the judiciary.

The Judicial Service Commission includes two representatives of LSK, guaranteeing its role in influencing decisions on the appointment and removal of judges and management of the judiciary. Furthermore, all judges and magistrates are required to be qualified lawyers. The Constitution also creates new law jobs, notably the constitutional Commissions staffed and often led by lawyers. Many government bodies and tribunals allocate positions to advocates as either individuals or representatives of the LSK. Schedule Five to the Constitution required promulgation of a great deal of legislation, creating unique opportunities for the legal profession.

B. Challenges for the Legal Profession

The Constitution also presents challenges for the legal profession, especially in Chapter Six on Leadership and Integrity. It demands transparency and accountability as well as effective and efficient delivery of service. Its guarantees of consumer rights and access to justice create high expectations for lawyers' competence and integrity. The Constitution recognises alternative dispute resolution mechanisms, opening the possibility of dispute resolution by non-lawyers, such as arbitrators, mediators and traditional justice structures. Accreditation and licensing of mediators under the Marriage Act 2014 has already begun.

IV. DEMOGRAPHICS OF THE LEGAL PROFESSION

A. Numbers

There has been a vast increase in the number of advocates, largely due to the expansion of legal education, particularly in the last two decades. The number of admissions tripled between 2008 and 2013 (Mboya 2014), and the number of registered lawyers grew 69 per cent between 2009 and 2016 (see Table 1 and Figure 1), jumping from 12,046 in 2017 to 15,095 in 2018. Growth is expected to accelerate in the future as more advocates graduate from law schools.

Table 1 Number of Advocates in Kenya (2009–16)

Year	Total
2009	6,938
2010	7,246
2011	7,660
2012	8,328
2013	8,981
2014	9,818
2015	10,662
2016	11,753

Source: Law Society of Kenya.

Figure 1 Number of Advocates in Kenya (Total, Male, Female, Unknown) (2009–16)

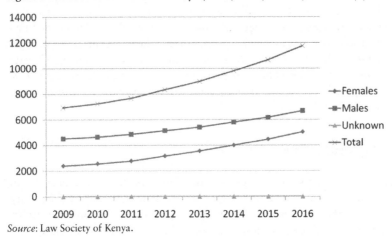

Source: Law Society of Kenya.

B. Gender

The participation of women in the legal profession should be viewed in the context of colonial policy concerning African education as well as prevailing attitudes towards women. While all Africans were disadvantaged in terms of legal education, the position of women was even worse. Because men were regarded as the main source of labour there were very few secondary schools for girls (Kamau 2013), and their low enrolment and retention rates limited the number eligible to enter university and study law. Kalpana Rawal, the first woman to enter practice in 1978, later became Deputy Chief Justice.

In 1980 only 35 women were admitted. But affirmative action policies aimed at increasing women's enrolment and retention led to their becoming 51.8 per cent of students at the Kenya School of Law (KSL – the only port of entry to the profession) in 2008 and 60.8 per cent in 2011. Women rose from 34.6 per cent of advocates in 2006 to 43 per cent in 2016, consistent with the global trend towards the 'feminisation' of legal education and the profession (Menkel-Meadow 1986; Sommerlad 1994; Schultz and Shaw 2013).

Despite their impressive numbers in the profession, women have been grossly underrepresented in leadership positions. For example, there has been only one woman Chairperson or President of LSK since its inception, Raychelle Omamo, who served in 2001–03. Furthermore, only four out of 26 Senior Counsel are women.[1] Women's representation in the LSK Council and Committees has been low. However, there has been a notable improvement in recent years. The last three LSK Vice-Presidents have been women, and the current Council has a majority of women (8/13). This may be attributable to the increased proportion of women in the profession as well as the influence of the constitutional value of gender equity in elective and appointive positions, which has been adopted by LSK.[2]

Wambua (2013) found that women lawyers in Kenya face multiple challenges, including work-life balance, discrimination, negative gender stereotypes and informal social mechanisms. Only 37.9 per cent of women lawyers were in private practice, the others having chosen positions in government or corporations, which have more stable working hours and terms of service. In law firms, 64 per cent of women were associates with little decision-making power. Women were generally allocated less remunerative and prestigious work, mostly in family law, probate and general practice rather than corporate law.

C. Age

The legal profession has experienced a dramatic change in the age profile of advocates (Mboya 2014). Kegoro et al (2014) report that those admitted between 2008 and 2013 constituted more than a third of the total. Younger advocates have displaced the older generation as members of the LSK Council and Committees. Mboya (2013) notes that this trend began in 2003 when Ahmednasir Abdullahi, an advocate of only ten years' standing, was elected LSK Chair. All subsequent elections brought an increasing number of young lawyers into the leadership, replacing the older members. Recognising this, LSK now has programmes tailored for young lawyers (defined as those with less than five years of practice).

D. Race and Ethnicity

The colonial policy of excluding Africans from legal education meant that the profession was long dominated by British and Asian advocates, many not citizens. However, with

---

[1] Senior Counsel refers to a title conferred on advocates who have rendered exemplary service to the law and the public (see VII.B below).
[2] See Law Society of Kenya Act 2014, § 4.

the independent government's policy of Africanisation and expansion of legal education to the indigenous African population, the profession is now dominated by Africans. Amendments to the Advocates Act in 1989 provided that only Kenyan citizens (extended in 2002 to Ugandans and Tanzanians) could be admitted as advocates.[3] The few remaining English and Asian lawyers have little influence in the LSK (Mboya 2014).

V. STRUCTURES OF PRACTICE

A. Law Firms

Under the Advocates (Practice) Rules a firm name must consist of current or former partners' names. Because there is no requirement to register law firms unless using '& Company' or '& Associates' in addition to the partners' names it is difficult to estimate the number of law firms, although the 2016 LSK Directory of Advocates included 500 firms.

Most advocates practise in sole proprietorships or firms of less than three partners, in the capital city of Nairobi and the larger cities or towns, such as Mombasa, Kisumu and Eldoret. Some Nairobi firms have branches outside the capital (Mwaluma 2014). Firms recently have merged or acquired smaller firms in order to bid for big assignments and achieve economies of scale (Mboya 2014). The Partnership Act of 2012 repealed the ceiling of 20 partners, opening the way for larger firms, many consisting of relatively young advocates (see Table 2). Many firms have associations with regional and global networks of lawyers.

Table 2 Top 10 Law Firms Ranked by Number of Advocates

No	Name of Law Firm	Total Advocates	Total Partners	Female Partners	Male Partners	Total Associates	Female Associates	Male Associates
1	Bowmans (Coulson Harney)	400 (Regional) 71 (Kenya)	170 (Regional) 18 (Kenya)	6	12	48	37	11
2	Anjarwalla & Khanna	91	15	6	9	54	29	25
3	Kaplan & Stratton Advocates	47	22	9	13	25	16	9
4	Iseme, Kamau & Maema	39	10	5	5	29	16	13
5	Hamilton, Harrison & Mathews	37	9	3	6	28	14	14

(continued)

---

[3] Further extension to Rwanda and Burundi nationals was granted after the expansion of the East African Community.

Table 2 (Continued)

No	Name of Law Firm	Total Advocates	Total Partners	Female Partners	Male Partners	Total Associates	Female Associates	Male Associates
6	MMC Africa Law Advocates	29	12	4	8	17	–	–
7	Daly & Inamdar	27	12	4	8	15	8	7
8	Triple OK Law Advocates	25	9	2	7	16	9	7
10	Oraro & Co	25	13	7	6	12	8	4
9	Walker Kontos Advocates	20	9	3	6	11	–	–
10	Mboya Wangong'u & Waiyaki	18	6	2	4	12	8	4

Source: Law firms' websites.

An emerging phenomenon is the classification of Kenyan law firms into tiers and bands by international groups such as Chambers Global or Legal 500, which are usually relied on by foreign companies seeking legal services. Certain kinds of corporate work, such as mergers and acquisitions, oil and gas contracts, and public/private partnerships, are often the preserve of the law firms that are globally indexed and ranked.

B. Limited Liability Partnerships

The Limited Liability Partnerships Act, 2011 introduced a new form of business association allowing partners to enjoy the limited liability available in corporations. Several firms have registered as LLPs, mostly those competing in the global legal market and belonging to regional or global legal networks (ibid). LSK has not yet amended its practice rules, which envisage personal liability, to cover LLPs.

C. Practice Areas

LSK requires all advocates holding practising certificates to indicate the kind of legal work they undertake. Most solo practitioners and small firms are generalists. The most common types of work include general commercial law, property and conveyancing, family law and succession and employment law (see Table 3). The least common are maritime law, mining law, intellectual property law and pro bono work. Although there is only a rudimentary form of legal aid, the Legal Aid Act 2015 launched a national legal aid scheme.

Table 3 Areas of Practice by Number of Advocates (2016)

Area of practice	Number
Alternative dispute resolution	913
Commercial law – general	2,677
Construction and engineering	210
Corporate law	1,281
Defamation and media law	146
General practice	1,403
Intellectual property law	464
Maritime, carriage of goods and personal law	5
Occupational and environmental health law	122
Planning, environment, local government and land court	863
Property, conveyancing, landlord and tenant law	2,651
Taxation and revenue	233
Banking, finance and securities law	1,604
Constitutional and human rights law	1,097
Consumer protection	127
Criminal law – general	949
Family law and succession matters	1,583
Industrial relations, unions and employment law	1,293
Legislative drafting	334
Mining law	64
Personal injuries and insurance law	1,285
Pro bono legal services	603
Regional and international law	206

Source: Law Society of Kenya.

The larger law firms specialise in litigation, conveyancing and corporate/commercial work (Mwaluma 2014). The fields least practised were debt collection, media and information communication technology. Other emerging areas include cyber law, media and entertainment law, mergers and acquisitions, international arbitration, public/private partnerships, international criminal law and public interest litigation. Following the recent discovery of oil and natural gas in Kenya, legal practice related to the extractive industries is developing.

Historically, there was a divide between public and private legal practice in British colonies (Ghai and McAuslan 1970: 18), but this is diminishing. Advocates today may practise in diverse settings, including international and national non-governmental organisations (NGOs), civil society and human rights organisations, multinational corporations, banks and insurance companies, real estate, and other sectors of commerce and industry (Ojienda and Juma 2013). Civil society NGOs such as Kituo cha Sheria

(Legal Aid Centre), Kenya Human Rights Commission, Federation of Women Lawyers (FIDA-K), ICJ-Kenya and Katiba Institute (sometimes referred to as the 'third sector') are well known for their commitment to access to justice and protection of fundamental human rights and often spearhead public interest litigation.

D. Globalisation of Legal Practice

According to Mboya (2014), 'it is estimated that 80–90% of legal fees spent on matters related to Africa [is] spent outside of Africa. These include big-ticket litigation and arbitration, project finance work and private equity work'. The current legal framework is restrictive, forbidding Kenyan lawyers to practise abroad and foreign lawyers to practise in Kenya except in limited circumstances.[4]

To surmount these barriers, law firms in Kenya and across Africa have adopted innovative arrangements enabling them to participate in the global legal market. These typically involve networks and alliances of independent law firms (Mboya 2013). An example is Lex Africa, the largest pan-African legal alliance, founded in 1993, with leading law firms in 24 African countries, comprising over 600 lawyers.[5] Another is Africa Legal Network (ALN), with members in 16 African countries, an associate firm in South Africa, and a regional office in the United Arab Emirates. Kenyan firms also belong to SNR Denton and DLA Piper Group. Such arrangements provide member firms knowledgeable about local laws and the local business environment and offer the size and competence to bid for large assignments. The most common practice areas include mining, insolvency and business rescue, dispute resolution, corporate mergers and acquisitions, competition, banking and finance.

An interesting arrangement is Bowmans, which calls itself 'a leading Pan-African law firm providing integrated legal services in four countries (Kenya, Tanzania, Uganda, South Africa) with over 400 lawyers and having offices in Cape Town, Dar-es-Salaam, Durban, Johannesburg, Kampala and Nairobi'. Their Nairobi office is Coulson Harney, LLP. They are also representatives of *Lex Mundi*, a global association, with more than 160 independent law firms in all the major world centres.[6]

Some foreign lawyers practise as consultants in Kenya on behalf of corporations. Such arrangements constitute a grey area not covered by the relevant practice rules. Lawyers are increasingly facing competition from other professional groups, such as realty firms, arbitrators and mediators and company secretarial service providers.

VI. LEGAL EDUCATION AND TRAINING

Legal education in Kenya has been a site of contestation between the government, the legal profession and other stakeholders over whether to emphasise theory or practice

---

[4] See Advocates Act (Cap 16), §11.
[5] Kenyan members include Kaplan & Stratton and Mboya, Wangong'u & Waiyaki. See www.lexafrica.com/.
[6] See www.bowmanslaw.com/our-firm/company-profile/.

(cf Kameri-Mbote 2014 and Mboya 2013). I focus on undergraduate university legal education and post-graduate professional training at KSL.[7]

A. Development of Legal Education

Ojwang and Salter (1980) and Kameri-Mbote (2014) have documented the development of legal education from the colonial policy of excluding Africans for fear they would agitate for independence. Following the recommendations of the Denning Committee (1961), a faculty of law was established in University College, Dar-es-Salaam (part of the University of East Africa) in 1961. However, due to LSK opposition to university legal education, a system of articled clerkship was instituted under KSL in 1963. Kenya thus adopted a dual track for legal training, which was only dismantled in 1989 through amendments to the Advocates Act, making a university degree the sole means of entry to the profession. KSL became a post-graduate institution offering practical training for university law graduates.

In 1970, the newly established University of Nairobi launched the first Faculty of Law (now School of Law) in Kenya. This remained the only LLB programme until Moi University opened the second law school in 1994. At first, university education was fully funded by the government (except for a small loan component), but access was severely restricted by the small number of places available.

The World Bank/IMF-led structural adjustment programmes (SAPS) in the late 1980s reduced government funding of education (Sifuna 2010), requiring students and their families to pay fees. Government policy also favoured the creation of private universities, enhancing access to university education. The Catholic University of East Africa established the first private law school in 2004. Public universities also began to accept students paying full fees. There are currently 76 universities and university colleges.[8] Demand for legal education is high because law is considered a lucrative and prestigious profession. Universities are also eager to offer legal education, which involves minimal cost and produces a high rate of return on investment (Kameri-Mbote 2014). The demand for education is bolstered by the constitutional guarantee of the right to education. In December 2017 there were 11 legal education providers, two more pending renewal of certificate, and four new applications.[9]

B. Regulation of Legal Education

Kenya first regulated legal education in 1961 when the Council of Legal Education (CLE) was established under the Advocates Ordinance with the limited function of vetting candidates for admission to the bar. The Council of Legal Education Act followed the 1995

---

[7] Continuing judicial education provided by the Judicial Service Commission through the Judiciary Training Institute pursuant to Art 172 of the Constitution is beyond the scope of this chapter.
[8] Commission for University Education website: www.cue.or.ke.
[9] Council of Legal Education website: www.cle.or.ke.

Akiwumi Report recommendation to transform CLE into an independent body vested with responsibility to regulate legal education. However, KSL remained an appendage of CLE, which acted as its Board. This conflict of interest severely compromised CLE's regulatory function. In 2009, the Muigai Task Force Report made far-reaching recommendations, including delinking CLE from KSL and revising the curriculum for the Advocates Training Programme (ATP) at KSL to provide practical clinical training. The curriculum reforms were effected immediately, but the two institutions were only decoupled by the 2012 Universities Act, Legal Education Act and Kenya School of Law Act. KSL became a statutory body responsible for postgraduate professional legal education but without any regulatory functions, which were allocated to CLE, which has the power to accredit other institutions to offer the ATP. Thus, it may be only a matter of time before KSL's monopoly is broken. The Universities Act gives the Commission of University Education (CUE) oversight of public and private universities, including accreditation and approval of curricula, setting the stage for conflict with CLE.

C. Form and Structure of Legal Education

Admission to the four-year LLB course requires a mean C+ score in the Kenya Certificate of Secondary Education (high school national examinations) or equivalent and a B Plain in English or Kiswahili.[10] Individual universities may impose higher requirements. The 12-month ATP consists of nine mandatory courses[11] followed by six months of pupillage with an advocate of not less than five years' standing. Applicants must have an LLB from a Kenyan university or a foreign university recognised by CLE. After the prescribed instruction, candidates sit Bar examinations administered by CLE, which took over this function from KSL in 2015.

D. Accreditation of Institutions

CLE has imposed a rigorous application process for accreditation aimed at ensuring the quality of law programmes. The regulations specify curriculum content, core texts, minimum lecture/contact hours, lecturer-student ratios, and student numbers. All law schools, including individual campuses, must have a niche area distinguishing them from other law schools. Failure to adhere to CLE standards may lead to non-accreditation, non-renewal of licence or closure.[12] The CLE website publishes a list of accredited schools; students

---

[10] Legal Education (Accreditation and Quality Assurance) Regulations 2016, reg 5. Under the previous regulations, only English was accepted as a qualifying language. There is now a controversy among law schools about whether to admit candidates with a B in Kiswahili, which, despite being an official language under the 2010 Constitution, is not a language of instruction at university and is not the language of the courts.

[11] These are: Civil Litigation, Criminal Litigation, Probate and Administration, Legal Writing and Drafting, Trial Advocacy (including a clinical programme), Professional Ethics, Legal Practice Management, Conveyancing, and Commercial Transactions.

[12] See Legal Education (Accreditation) Regulations, Legal Notice No 170 of 2009. In 2016 CLE ordered the closure of Moi University and Mount Kenya law schools for failing to comply with the Council's standards. However, the orders were rescinded by the High Court, which held that CLE had no power to close institutions.

trained in non-accredited institutions are ineligible for admission to KSL and cannot be admitted as advocates. While the majority of law schools have striven to comply with these requirements, a few like Moi University have challenged CLE's mandate. Accreditation seems to favour new law schools, which are more likely to meet CLE requirements of a 1:15 lecturer-student ratio and the teaching of core texts (Kameri-Mbote 2014).

CLE requires 16 core courses.[13] Students who have not completed them must take a bridging course at an accredited institution,[14] increasing the time and cost of qualifying. However, CLE has not stipulated the minimum content of the mandatory courses or the criteria for equivalence, creating uncertainty, particularly over nomenclature of the courses. The rule mostly affects those with foreign degrees, because local universities have complied with the CLE curriculum.[15] Doing so has required local law schools to restrict electives,[16] which conflicts with the requirement that they identify a niche area, producing an overloaded curriculum and contrived efforts at uniqueness (Kameri-Mbote 2014).

The 2009 regulations provided for pre-Bar examinations for KSL applicants without the minimum score of B in English. KSL later sought to require pre-Bar examinations for all applicants. After a successful class action[17] challenging the regulations as retrospective, a moratorium was placed on the pre-Bar examinations.

E. Conflicting Mandates of CLE and CUE

Because both the Universities Act §5A and the Legal Education Act §8 claim priority in the event of a conflict with another law it is not clear which takes precedence. In *Moi University v Council of Legal Education*[18] the High Court held that, under the principle of complementarity, CUE has general oversight over all universities, while CLE has a specific oversight over legal education. The Court stressed that specific oversight is restricted to setting and enforcing standards relating to the accreditation of legal education providers for the purposes of licensing and does not include the power to accredit universities or institutions offering legal education.[19] Issues have also arisen regarding recognition of degrees from foreign universities.[20]

Under the regulations, CLE also has authority to regulate postgraduate law degrees. Only the University of Nairobi has been offering post-graduate studies, but in 2018 Strathmore University began an LLM programme. It is questionable whether CLE has

---

[13] The mandatory courses are: Legal Research, Tort, Contract, Legal System and Method, Criminal Law, Family Law and Succession, Evidence, Commercial Law (including sale of goods, hire purchase and agency), Law of Business Association, Administrative Law, Constitutional Law, Jurisprudence, Equity and Trusts, Property Law, Public International Law and Labour Law.
[14] The only accredited institution for that purpose is Riara University Law School, a private university.
[15] See eg *Eunice Maema v CLE* [2013] eKLR.
[16] For example, at the University of Nairobi, electives are only offered during the fourth year of the LLB.
[17] *Kevin K Mwiti & Others v Kenya School of Law & Others* [2015] eKLR.
[18] [2016] eKLR.
[19] However, despite the Court's order, CLE issued a public notice in 2017 excluding Moi University from its list of licensed legal education providers.
[20] See eg *Jonnah Tusasirwe & 10 Others v Council of Legal Education & 3 Others* [2017] eKLR, a case involving Ugandan students.

the ability to regulate postgraduate legal education since its Board is composed mostly of government representatives and legal practitioners, with only two academics. It is arguable that such regulation would be an unjustified encroachment on the academic freedom of universities guaranteed by Article 33 of the Constitution and section 29 of the Universities Act (Kameri-Mbote 2014).[21]

F. Quality of Legal Education

Due to the increased number of law schools and law students, KSL enrolment has grown tremendously. Large class sizes at many law schools make effective teaching difficult, and it is nearly impossible for KSL to deliver the practical training envisaged by the Muigai Report or impart the knowledge, skills and attitudes required by lawyers in a globalising world. Legal educational institutions lack adequate facilities and qualified lecturers, relying on part-time faculty and inappropriate teaching methodologies. The failure rate on the Bar examination has been high, with only 22 per cent of candidates in the 2017 examinations passing all nine subjects at the first attempt.[22] LSK created an ad hoc committee to investigate the issue in 2017 following a directive by the High Court, which took notice of the 'worrying trend' of declining pass rates.[23] A national task force was also established to review legal education.

VII. REGULATION OF THE LEGAL PROFESSION

The Advocates Act, 1989 specifies qualifications for admission, remuneration, and discipline. The Law Society of Kenya Act, 2014 provides for the internal governance of the profession, such as membership in LSK and professional ethics and etiquette. Although the legal profession is largely autonomous and self-regulating, the state has retained a limited regulatory role (Odenyo 1979; Ghai 2014).

A. Qualifications for Practice as an Advocate

The academic qualifications for Kenyan advocates consist of a four-year law degree from a recognised Kenyan university or a foreign university approved by CLE. This is followed by 18 months' post-graduate professional training at the Kenya School of Law (which includes six months of pupillage) and Bar examinations administered by CLE. The Advocates Act allows a right of practice to foreign advocates but at the absolute discretion

---

[21] Strathmore University's LLM programme started in 2017 as the second after the University of Nairobi's. It appears that Strathmore's application is still pending approval by CLE: see www.cle.ke.
[22] Council of Legal Education website, see www.cle.or.ke/barexaminations/. See also 'Shock as Law graduates fail crucial bar exams again', *The Standard* (Nairobi, 3 February 2018) www.standardmedia.co.ke/article/2001268272/88-percent-of-kenyan-law-graduates-fail-crucial-bar-exams.
[23] See judgment by Justice Mativo in *Daniel Ingida Aluvaala & Another v Council of Legal Education & Another* [2017] eKLR.

of the Attorney General and restricted to a specific suit or matter.[24] An exemption is made for advocates from the East African Community (Uganda, Tanzania, Rwanda and Burundi) provided they hold a law degree from an approved university. A 2017 amendment made the failure to renew the annual practising certificate professional misconduct. Under the Advocates (Continuing Professional Development) Regulations, 2014 advocates must earn at least five CPD credits in order to renew their practising certificates. CPD is offered primarily by LSK, but it may accredit other institutions.

B. Senior Counsel

In 2009, the Advocates Act created the title of Senior Counsel, conferred by the President of Kenya (following the recommendation of the Committee of Senior Counsel) on advocates or designated public officers with 15 years' experience and irreproachable conduct, who have rendered exemplary professional and public service. Senior Counsel have a special Roll and rank high in precedence, just after the Attorney General, DPP and Solicitor General. At first this rank was automatically conferred on former LSK Chairpersons, but the Advocates (Senior Counsel Conferment and Privileges) Rules, 2011 provided a framework for the appointments. Some sectors of the profession have argued that the title introduces unnecessary hierarchy into the profession.[25]

C. Unqualified Persons

The Advocates Act, 1989 prohibited non-lawyers from representing clients in court and drafting documents (including property conveyances, formation of limited liability companies, partnership agreements, and grants of probate). Amendments in 2017 extended the prohibition to advocates who fail to obtain a practising certificate; violators may be charged with contempt of court and a criminal offence. These provisions seem unduly restrictive; other countries allow laypersons to incorporate companies, manage probate, and transfer property. The restrictions may also violate the constitutional guarantee of access to justice, which allows representation in court by non-legal intermediaries (Ojienda and Juma 2013).

D. In-house Counsel

There has been an increase in the number of in-house counsel employed by banks, insurance companies, and real estate firms who advise on corporate governance and regulatory compliance, provide company secretarial services, draft legal documents, and appear in

---

[24] For example, in December 2018 the Attorney General approved a foreign lawyer, Khawar Qureshi QC, to prosecute a corruption case against Deputy Chief Justice Philomena Mwilu.

[25] See *Jacqueline Okeyo Manani v AG & LSK* [2018] eKLR, a constitutional petition challenging the requirement that a candidate for senior counsel must have argued a substantive matter before a superior, regional or international court on the ground that it discriminated against non-litigation advocates. The petition was dismissed in August 2018 as lacking in merit.

court on behalf of their employers (ibid). The 2012 amendments to the Advocates Act require an in-house advocate to be an independent professional legal adviser and not charge less than the minimum prescribed fees. The Advocates (Practice) Rules and LSK Code of Ethics and Conduct prohibit in-house counsel from sharing profits, commissions and bonuses with unqualified persons.

E. Remuneration of Advocates

Advocates are prohibited from charging less than the scale fees prescribed by the Chief Justice, sharing profits with unqualified persons, touting, or acting as an agent for an unqualified person. They may not charge contingency fees or contract out of liability for professional negligence. In 2013 the Competition Authority of Kenya (CAK) attempted to block LSK's plan to increase legal fees on the ground that this violated competition law. However, LSK went ahead and issued the Advocates Remuneration Order 2014, insisting CAK lacked jurisdiction over the matter.[26] The younger generation of lawyers is resisting traditional patterns of practice and remuneration, such as the rules against undercutting and fee sharing with non-lawyers (Mboya 2014).

F. Marketing and Advertising

Practice rules prohibiting all forms of advertising by advocates were challenged in *Okenyo Omwansa George & Another v Attorney General & 2 Others*[27] as an unreasonable restriction and violation of the constitutional right to information and access to justice. The Court held that a complete ban on advertising was inconsistent with the Constitution. LSK responded by promulgating the Advocates (Marketing and Advertising) Rules 2014, allowing advertising that is objective, truthful, dignified and not calculated to attract business unfairly and specifying the content and modes of advertising. Advocates may participate in conferences and seminars and publish papers, circulars, periodicals and articles provided they do not use media appearances as a means of professional advertisement. In 2014 the LSK Council publicised the International Bar Association (IBA) International Principles on Social Media Conduct for the Legal Profession to offer guidance to the Society on issues arising from online advertising, websites and social media platforms like Facebook and Twitter.[28]

VIII. LAW SOCIETY OF KENYA

The 1949 Law Society of Kenya Act was primarily concerned with safeguarding the profession's interests. The Law Society of Kenya Act, 2014 was enacted to align

---

[26] M Mutegi, 'Watchdog stops lawyers' bid to increase legal fees' *Business Daily* (Nairobi, 28 October 2013) www.businessdailyafrica.com/news/Watchdog-stops-lawyers--bid-to-increase-legal-fees/539546-2051072-hliv8l/index.html.
[27] [2012] eKLR.
[28] As a corporate member of IBA, LSK is expected to uphold the IBA guidance and principles.

the Society with the spirit and purposes of the Constitution of Kenya, 2010 by expanding the Society's objects beyond traditional 'bread and butter' issues to include protection of legal services consumers, mechanisms for resolving complaints against legal practitioners, assisting government and the courts with legislation and the administration of justice, upholding the Constitution and advancing the rule of law, and assisting members of the public.

A. Governance of the Law Society

The LSK is governed by a Council consisting of the President, Vice-President, three representatives of the general membership (one with at least 15 years' standing), three representatives from Nairobi, one from the Coast, and four from the rest of Kenya. 'Upcountry' members had resented what they saw as Nairobi advocates' domination of the Society. Reflecting the principle of devolution in the 2010 Constitution, the Society was divided into eight branches (Nairobi, the Coast, and six others). But these branches only advise the Council and lack executive authority. In recent years, Society elections have been conducted by the Independent Electoral and Boundaries Commission because previous LSK elections had been characterised by rigging and electoral misconduct. The rift between the older and younger generations of lawyers escalated during the 2016 LSK elections when a faction of young lawyers began a campaign dubbed 'Okoa LSK' (translated 'Save LSK') aimed at toppling 'establishment' lawyers from the LSK Council.[29] The campaign succeeded in securing the presidency of the LSK and three slots in the Council and halted construction of a proposed Arbitration Centre.

B. Discipline of Advocates

Many commentators have decried the falling standard of professional ethics and the growth of professional misconduct (Mutunga 2014; Lumumba 2014; Kegoro et al 2014). There is a two-step disciplinary process. The Complaints Commission (which is appointed by the President of Kenya and must include one person qualified to serve on the High Court)[30] investigates public complaints against advocates or their employees and refers those that constitute a disciplinary offence to the Disciplinary Tribunal, disposing of the others through reconciliation, compensation or reimbursement, or referral to court. However, disciplinary offences are not defined. Regional Disciplinary Committees composed entirely of advocates were established in 2007 in the seven regions other than Nairobi. The Disciplinary Tribunal, consisting of the Attorney General, Solicitor-General or nominee, and six advocates elected by the Society, hears complaints of disgraceful or dishonourable conduct incompatible with the status of an advocate and may admonish, suspend from practice, strike off the roll, or order payment of a fine or compensation.

---

[29] 'Okoa LSK won battle, but has yet to win war' *Daily Nation* (Nairobi, 28 February 2016) www.nation.co.ke/news/Okoa-LSK-won-battle-but-has-yet-to-win-war/1056-3095378-nfa4hu/index.html.
[30] Advocates Act, §53.

Because the Complaints Commission was established in 1989 at a time when relations between government and the Law Society were acrimonious, LSK is seen as an extension of government control (Kegoro et al 2014). There are also differences about discipline between Nairobi and upcountry members and older and younger members. Upcountry members view disciplinary mechanisms as a means of repression by their urban counterparts, and the exclusion of Nairobi from the Regional Disciplinary Committees compounds their feeling of marginalisation. Similarly, younger lawyers perceive discipline as a mechanism by which the old guard preserves its power, while older lawyers claim that their younger brethren fail to respect ethical standards. The state's lack of commitment to the disciplinary system is shown by the fact that the Attorney General has never sat in the Committee and the Solicitor-General has not sent a nominee (ibid).

The Commission and the Tribunal deal with similar types of complaints, causing confusion among the public about which body is appropriate. Lacking a secretariat, the Tribunal relies on the LSK, whose members also dominate it. The Tribunal therefore lacks independent mechanisms to investigate complaints, and its activities (or inactivity) are opaque. Complaints to the Tribunal have been declining just when the number of advocates has been increasing, suggesting a lack of confidence in the system. The Advocates (Professional Indemnity) Regulations 2014 require advocates to have professional indemnity insurance. Although one object of the Advocates Act was to establish a Client Compensation Fund, the idea provoked so much opposition within the Bar that the text of the Act never mentions the Fund.

IX. BAR AND STATE RELATIONS

During colonial rule the legal profession, dominated by Europeans and Asians, was mainly concerned with securing from the government a large measure of autonomy and self-regulation. European lawyers served government interests and those of the white settlers, while Asian lawyers catered to the small but growing commercial class among their community. Lawyers were an elite group, who allied themselves with the government particularly in order to preserve their independence (Ghai and McAuslan 1970). The period 1952–61 witnessed the Mau Mau insurrection, with the clamour for return of lands taken by white settlers and agitation for political independence. The colonial government responded with massive detention without trial, imprisonment, and seizure of property facilitated by emergency laws and regulations. The legal profession was passive in the face of these violations of the rule of law, and few lawyers were willing to defend the victims. Some notable exceptions included AR Kapila, the prominent Asian lawyer who defended Jomo Kenyatta (later first Prime Minister and President of Kenya) in the infamous Kapenguria Trial (Nowrojee 2014), and Argwings Kodhek, the first Kenyan African lawyer, who actively represented people charged with Mau Mau-related offences (Kuria 1991).

The first two decades after independence were characterised by consolidation of executive power. The state used legal measures to do this, including constitutional changes that stripped judges and the Attorney General of security of tenure and made Kenya a *de jure* one party state. The Law Society together with the clergy emerged as the *de facto* opposition to KANU, the ruling party. The *Nairobi Law Monthly* published by

Gitobu Imanyara, a leading human rights lawyer, became a popular forum for discussing pertinent political issues. The state had a deep suspicion of the legal profession and strongly resisted lawyers' calls for political pluralism. Lawyers who opposed the state were subjected to harassment, trumped up charges, imprisonment and detention without trial.[31]

In the late-1990s lawyers took an active role in the democratisation process, starting with the Inter Party Parliamentary Group (IPPG) constitutional reforms, which resulted in dismantling one party KANU rule and set the stage for the transition to multiparty democracy. From the early 2000s, lawyers' groups, notably the Law Society, Kenya Human Rights Commission and ICJ-Kenya, played a leading role in the constitutional review process. The Constitution of Kenya Review Committees, which drafted the constitutional documents, and the Committee of Experts, which was mandated to finalise the draft Constitution, were composed of lawyers.

Despite this stellar record, members of the legal profession have regrettably also been involved in state patronage, corruption and negative ethnicity, featuring at the heart of major corruption scandals, such Goldenberg in 2000 and Anglo Leasing in 2003. Lawyers have been implicated as abettors of corruption within the judiciary (Mutunga 2014). Nevertheless, the Law Society played a key role in the purge of judicial corruption, which led to the sacking and resignation of many judges and magistrates in 2003.

Following the post-2010 constitutional dispensation, which ushered in an era of expanded democratic space and respect for the rule of law, relations between the legal profession and the state have changed substantially. Lawyers are no longer seen as threats by government. This is reflected in the increased representation of lawyers in state offices, such as the National Assembly and County Assemblies, and independent commissions. However, as Nowrojee urges (2014), there is need for continued vigilance on the part of lawyers to safeguard the democratic gains.

More recently, relations between the Bar and the state have been problematised by the rising number of incidents of state interference in court cases. For example, the tragic extrajudicial killing of human rights lawyer Willie Kimani (and his client and driver) in 2016 sparked a week-long 'purple ribbon' protest by lawyers condemning the killings.[32] Lawyers have continued to work actively with civil society organisations in addressing public issues, such as spearheading mediation talks between the government and doctors in a bid to end the nationwide doctors' strike in 2017.[33]

X. CONCLUSION

The last 30 years have seen dramatic change in the legal profession. Internal pressures have been generated by the entry of women and younger lawyers displacing older more

---

[31] These included Gibson Kamau Kuria, Gitobu Imanyara, Beatrice Nduta, Pheroze Nowrojee and Willy Mutunga.

[32] C Ombati and J Ngetich, 'Lawyers and civil society groups protest against extra-judicial killings', *Standard Digital* (Nairobi, 5 July2016) www.standardmedia.co.ke/article/2000207544/lawyers-and-civil-society-groups-protest-against-extra-judicial-killings.

[33] A Mukuru, 'Law society appoints members to mediate doctors' strike' *Citizen Digital* (Nairobi, 16 February 2017) citizentv.co.ke/news/law-society-appoints-members-to-mediate-doctors-strike-157969/.

conservative lawyers in the Law Society leadership and generating struggles over its governance. External pressures come from liberalisation and globalisation, prompting new forms of practice, while the profession has continued to defend its monopoly. The Constitution of 2010 brought opportunities as well as challenges for the legal profession and raised the standards of integrity and service. It is vital for the profession to reflect on its relationship to the values and aspirations enshrined in the Constitution.

REFERENCES

Ghai, YP (2014) 'The Attorneys-General: Upholders or Destroyers of Constitutionalism?' in YP Ghai and JC Ghai (eds), *The Legal Profession and the New Constitutional Order in Kenya* (Strathmore University Press) 139.

Ghai, YP and Ghai, JC (eds) (2014) *The Legal Profession and the New Constitutional Order in Kenya* (Nairobi, Strathmore University Press).

Ghai, YP and McAuslan, JPWB (1970) *Public Law and Political Change in Kenya* (Oxford, Oxford University Press).

Kamau, W (2013) 'Women Judges and Magistrates in Kenya: Challenges, Opportunities and Contributions' in U Schultz and G Shaw (eds), *Gender and Judging* (Oxford, Hart Publishing) 167.

Kameri-Mbote, P (2014) 'Legal Education and Lawyers' in YP Ghai and JC Ghai (eds), *The Legal Profession and the New Constitutional Order in Kenya* (Nairobi, Strathmore University Press) 121.

Kegoro, G et al (2014) 'Professional Integrity and Disciplining of Advocates: Room for Improvement' in YP Ghai and JC Ghai (eds), *The Legal Profession and the New Constitutional Order in Kenya* (Nairobi, Strathmore University Press) 101.

Kuria, GK, 'The Rule of Law in Kenya and the Status of Human Rights' (1991) 16 *Yale Journal of International Law* 217.

Lumumba, PLO (2014) 'The Legal Profession and Crisis of Ethics' in YP Ghai and JC Ghai (eds), *The Legal Profession and the New Constitutional Order in Kenya* (Nairobi, Strathmore University Press) 77.

Mboya, A (2014) 'The Bar: Challenges and Opportunities' in YP Ghai and JC Ghai (eds), *The Legal Profession and the New Constitutional Order in Kenya* (Nairobi, Strathmore University Press) 241.

Menkel-Meadow, C (1986) 'The Comparative Sociology of Women Lawyers: The "Feminization" of the Legal Profession' 24 *Osgoode Hall Law Journal* 897.

Mutunga, W (2014) 'The 2010 Constitution of Kenya: Its Vision of a New Bench-Bar Relationship' in YP Ghai and JC Ghai (eds), *The Legal Profession and the New Constitutional Order in Kenya* (Nairobi, Strathmore University Press) 59.

Mwaluma, J (2014) 'Strategies Adopted by Law Firms in Kenya in Response to Changes in the External Environment' (MBA Project, University of Nairobi, unpublished).

Mwangi, P (2001) *The Black Bar: Corruption and Political Intrigue within Kenya's Legal Fraternity* (Nairobi, Oakland Media Services).

Nowrojee, P (2014) 'The Legal Profession 1963–2013: All This Can Happen Again – Soon' in YP Ghai and JC Ghai (eds), *The Legal Profession and the New Constitutional Order in Kenya* (Nairobi, Strathmore University Press) 33.

Odenyo, A (1979) 'Professionalization amidst Change: The Case of the Emerging Legal Profession in Kenya' 22 *African Studies Review* 33.

Ojienda, T (ed) (2002) *The Legal Profession and Constitutional Change in Kenya, Laying Foundations for Reform* (Nairobi, Law Society of Kenya).

Ojienda, T and Juma, K (2013) *Professional Ethics: A Kenyan Perspective* (Nairobi, Law Africa).

Ojwang, JB and Salter, DR (1989) 'Legal Education in Kenya' 33 *Journal of African Law* 9.
—— (1990) 'Legal Profession in Kenya' 34 *Journal of African Law* 78.
Schultz, U (2003) 'Introduction: Women in the World's Legal Professions – Overview and Synthesis' in U Schultz and G Shaw (eds), *Women in the World's Legal Professions* (Oxford, Hart Publishing).
Sifuna, DN (2010) 'Some Reflections on the Expansion and Quality of Higher Education in Public Universities in Kenya' 15 *Research in Post-Compulsory Education* 415.
Sommerlad, H (1994) 'The Myth of Feminisation: Women and Cultural Change in the Legal Profession' 1 *International Journal of the Legal Profession* 31.
Vyas, Y et al (eds) (1994) *Law and Development in the Third World* (Faculty of Law, University of Nairobi).
Wambua, M (2013) 'Challenges Facing Women Legal Practitioners in Kenya' MA project, University of Nairobi, unpublished.

25

Nigeria
An Account of Adaptation

ENIBOKUN UZEBU-IMARHIAGBE

I. INTRODUCTION

When Richard Abel and Philip Lewis published their seminal three-volume collection, *Lawyers in Society*, the western-style legal profession in Nigeria was just over 100 years old. Prior to its introduction, precolonial Nigerian societies had their own indigenous systems of law and adjudicatory processes for the administration of justice, designed not only to ensure peace but also to maintain order and promote the welfare of the community. For this reason, those responsible for administering justice were usually the elders, who combined judicial and executive functions (Elias 1962: 212–14; Adewoye 1977a: 3; Emiola 2005: 51).

The objective of adjudication was to seek a settlement that dissolved rancour and restored social harmony (Adewoye 1977b: 4–5). As precolonial Nigerian societies experienced social and economic upheaval from increased interaction with Europeans, indigenous judicial structures became inadequate to resolve the disputes that naturally arose (Uzebu 2018: 42). This led to many experiments in adjudicating disputes between Nigerians and Europeans (Adewoye 1977a).

The English legal system imposed by colonial administrators emphasised the parties' strict legal rights. Nevertheless, the application of English law, the establishment of English-type courts and the practice of law as a profession developed slowly (Adewoye 1977b: 16), primarily because of the severe dearth of qualified personnel (Toby 1992: 8). In 1876, the qualification for practice in the new courts was admission to the English, Scottish or Irish Bar or having 'served five years continuously in the office of a practicing barrister or solicitor residing within the jurisdiction of the [Supreme] court'.[1] In addition, the Chief Justice of the Supreme Court could admit fit and proper persons with a basic education and some knowledge of English law for a renewable six-month term.[2]

---

[1] Supreme Court Ordinance, No 4, 1876, ss 71, 73.
[2] ibid, s 74.

It was under this provision that the precursors of the modern legal profession – variously known as 'local-made solicitors', 'self-taught attorneys', or just 'attorneys' – were enrolled to practise in Lagos courts (Adewoye 1969a: 50). Until the end of the first decade of the twentieth century they fulfilled a need, not only giving the Lagos indigenous population a foretaste of the English approach to justice but also helping to construct English legal institutions in Nigeria (Adewoye 1969b).

By 1913, when the Chief Judge stopped issuing practising licences to non-lawyers, nine local attorneys were enrolled (Adewoye 1969a: 62). Because all those admitted later had legal qualifications, that year marked the inception of the legal profession properly so-called (Adewoye 1969b: 115). Until Nigeria gained independence in 1960, many Nigerian lawyers qualified by becoming English barristers (often through Call to the Bar without a law degree) or solicitors (Geary 1965: 11).

II. THE LEGAL PROFESSION IN COLONIAL NIGERIA

Law was one of several professions open to the educated elite in colonial Nigeria. Law offered brighter career prospects than most other professions. Compared with medicine or engineering, for instance, legal training was shorter and a practice was easier to establish. Moreover, a practising lawyer could earn a living independently of the colonial government, that is, without having to be a civil servant. Lawyers enjoyed a measure of personal freedom denied to most other professionals. Indeed, under colonial rule, law was virtually the only profession where educated Africans could feel themselves the equals of the colonialists (Adewoye 1977b: 67).

Prior to 1933, opportunities to practise law in colonial Nigeria were severely circumscribed (ibid: 66–90). The judicial system was hierarchical. The Supreme Court was at the top, but its power was limited to criminal cases, and its jurisdiction did not extend to all areas in the South because of the Provincial Courts operating there. The Provincial Courts did not admit legal practitioners. Procedures in the Provincial Courts resembled those in the Supreme Court except that all types of cases could be heard summarily and barristers were excluded. At the bottom of the ladder was the Native Court system staffed by persons who had traditionally exercised judicial powers and District Officers (Nicholson 1970: 202).

It took the judicial reform of 1933, initiated by Sir Donald Cameron, the Governor of Nigeria, to infuse a liberal spirit into the system of judicial administration (Committee on the Future of the Nigerian Legal Profession 1959). The jurisdiction of the Supreme Court was extended into the Protectorate,[3] allowing it to hear appeals from all inferior courts, including Native Courts. In place of the Provincial Courts, Magistrates' Courts

---

[3] For easy and effective administration, Nigeria was divided into three parts; the Colony and Protectorate of Lagos (including the Yoruba protectorate), the Protectorate of Northern Nigeria, and the Protectorate of Southern Nigeria. The North was administered as a separate political unit. In 1906, the Colony and Protectorate of Lagos and the Protectorate of Southern Nigeria were merged into the Colony and Protectorate of Southern Nigeria. The Protectorates were further divided into Central, Western, and Eastern Provinces and Lagos. A Protectorate implies that jurisdiction is exercised primarily over external affairs, while a Colony wields unlimited powers over both the territory and its inhabitants (Nicholson 1970; Nwabueze 1982).

and a High Court were established in the Protectorate. Appeals from the Supreme Court were heard by the West African Court of Appeal until 1954.[4]

Five ordinances enacted in 1943 extended the liberal spirit of Cameron's judicial reform, allowing lawyers to participate in all litigation (Adewoye 1977b: 99–100). The regionalisation of the judicial system in 1954 (in accordance with the country's Federal constitutional development) created a High Court in the Western, Eastern and Northern Regions and Lagos (now a Federal territory). High Court decisions could be appealed to the Federal Supreme Court and ultimately the Judicial Committee of the Privy Council (ibid).

In 1958, an experienced barrister was required to preside over Grade A and some Grade B Customary Courts (the former Native Courts) in the Western and Eastern Regions (but not Grades C or D), and lawyers were entitled to appear in these Courts (Committee on the Future of the Nigerian Legal Profession 1959: 100). However, it took a long time for lawyers to begin practising outside Lagos. Indeed, until the early 1940s, practising in the interior was often viewed as a sign of professional incompetence. However, the creation of more English-type courts – the High Court and Magistrates' Courts – ultimately encouraged young lawyers to move to the provinces. By 1954, lawyers had established practices in Ibadan, Ijebu-Ode, Ife, Warri, Benin, Enugu, Port-Harcourt, Jos, Kano, and a few other towns. In the 1960s lawyers ventured to even more remote towns, usually administrative centres of Divisional or District Local Government Councils. The North, however, was served mostly by lawyers based elsewhere (Adewoye 1977b: 10–02).

Practice in the Eastern and Central Provinces was not as lucrative as it was in Lagos Colony and the Southern Provinces. Until 1914, the only manifestation of a modern legal profession east of the Niger was the Attorney General of the Southern Nigeria Protectorate, who drafted agreements and simple deeds for private individuals (ibid: 46). In the absence of a well-organised traditional chieftaincy system, the Supreme Court and the legal profession had more scope to operate in the Eastern and Central Provinces. There were no judicial agreements to hamper the operations of the court or curb the professional activities of lawyers. This, however, ultimately prompted the colonial administration to take the drastic measure of curtailing the jurisdiction of the Supreme Court in the provinces and subsequently throughout the country (ibid: 55).

The legal profession was virtually unknown in Northern Nigeria in the early decades of the twentieth century. Judicial and administrative duties devolved on British political officers. The Supreme Court, Provincial Courts, Cantonment Courts and Native Courts barely functioned there. Before 1914, the Supreme Court heard no criminal cases and just one civil action (ibid: 61). Sir William Geary, who travelled from Lagos to represent an expatriate company, Messrs L and K (Kano), in that case, wrote: 'the existence of the Supreme Court in Northern Nigeria in the period 1900–1914 was one of a long vacation and the judicial machinery was a legal and practical joke' (ibid).

The only legal practitioner in the Northern provinces before February 1914 was Joshua John Peele, an English solicitor based in Kano, who was enrolled to practise law in Nigeria in December 1912 (ibid: 62). The first lawyer of Northern origin, Abdul Ganiyu Razaq, was called to the Bar in 1955 (Fawehinmi 1988: 316). This reflects the

[4] Protectorate Courts Ordinance (1933) s 5.

educational gap between Northern and Southern Nigeria, explicable partly in terms of the different pace at which they assimilated Western culture. The Muslim North believed their Islamic culture and practices and the Emirs' authority would be undermined if their children were exposed to western influence. Even Abdul Razaq was educated in Southern Nigeria. In October 1913 the colonial administration of Northern Nigeria sought legislation to prevent lawyers and other foreigners from the South from settling in predominantly 'native' towns, including Kano and Zaria (Adewoye 1977b: 62–63).

Throughout the colonial period, administrators regarded lawyers as a threat to the stability and smooth operation of the state. Nevertheless, the legal profession remained attractive to Nigerians who could afford the cost of overseas training. The popular notion that a lawyer could easily make a fortune at the Bar and the conspicuous roles lawyers played in public life, particularly in challenging the colonial status quo, enhanced the attraction of the profession (ibid: 40). On 16 November, 1935, Stella James Thomas was enrolled at the Supreme Court as the first female lawyer in West Africa. By the eve of political independence, almost 30 women had followed in her footsteps (Fawehinmi 1988: 374–410).

After World War II, there was a phenomenal increase in the number of enrolled legal practitioners. Even greater interest was expressed in law as national consciousness intensified during the decolonisation struggles. Nigerian nationalists saw a judiciary dominated and controlled by colonialists as a stronghold of oppression. The agitations of educated Nigerians ultimately elicited a change in official attitudes, leading to the appointment of Olumuyiwa Jibowu on 13 February, 1931 as the first indigenous Police Magistrate in Lagos.

Seven years later, other legal and judicial appointments were made: RA Doherty as Nigerian Crown Counsel on 1 April 1938 and Adebiyi Desalu, Adetokunbo Ademola, and FEO Euba as Magistrates on 1 November 1938, 1 April 1939 and 1 August 1940 respectively. As a result of the acute staff shortage in the judiciary during World War II, 14 more indigenous magistrates were appointed between 1941 and 1945. By the end of 1945, two Nigerian lawyers, Olumuyiwa Jibowu and Steven Bankole Rhodes, were puisne Judges of the Supreme Court. Rhodes became the first Nigerian lawyer be appointed to the Supreme Court straight from the Bar (Adewoye 1977b: 104–105).

The constitutional developments of the late 1950s, coupled with the regionalisation of the judiciary, created even more opportunities for judicial and legal appointments at the Federal and regional levels. On 1 April 1955, Adetokunbo Ademola was appointed Chief Justice of the Western Region, becoming the first indigenous Chief Justice. In 1959, Sir LN Mbanefo became Chief Justice of the Eastern Region. At the same time, Nigerians held top appointments in the Ministries of Justice in both Regions.[5]

The picture in the North was different because of the growing regional consciousness and rivalry in the period immediately before independence and the scarcity of legally qualified northerners. Its judiciary, dominated by expatriates, had only three indigenous lawyers in its lower echelon as late as 1962 (Adewoye 1977b: 106). But elsewhere, the judiciary was one of the first government departments to be 'Nigerianised'. As though

---

[5] National Archives Ibadan (herein after referred to as NAI), Western Region of Nigeria, Staff List, 1956–1963; Eastern Region of Nigeria, Staff List, 1956–1963.

in preparation for the country's independence in 1960, Sir Adetokunbo Ademola was appointed Chief Justice of the Federal Supreme Court on 28 April 1958. About five months later GKJ Amachree was appointed Federal Solicitor General. At independence on 1 October 1960, Dr Taslim Olawale Elias, a renowned legal scholar, was appointed Federal Attorney General and Minister of Justice. At independence Nigeria had 963 lawyers, 540 of them indigenous (Fawehinmi 1988: 833–52). After independence, most foreign barristers gradually left, and the legal profession progressively became more representative of the population.

III. DEVELOPMENTS SINCE INDEPENDENCE

Shortly before independence it became apparent that the training received by Nigerian lawyers at the English Inns of Court was inadequate. While Nigerian legal practitioners were expected to practise as both barristers and solicitors, they received no training for the latter role. The training they did receive was designed for those intending to practise in the United Kingdom (ibid: 39). Moreover, the vast majority of Nigerian students who trained at the Inns had no previous higher education. Unlike their English counterparts, they did not complete a pupillage in the chambers of an English barrister (Ghai 1987). Also, they had no knowledge of Nigerian law, particularly customary and Islamic law. Consequently, it was not easy for them to combine both aspects of the profession and render efficient service as legal practitioners on their return to Nigeria.

It was against this background that the colonial government created the Committee on the Future of the Nigerian Legal Profession, headed by EIG Unsworth, Attorney General of Nigeria.[6] The Committee, composed of the Federal and Regional Legal Officers and five prominent members of the Nigerian Bar Association (NBA), was charged with making recommendations about legal education, admission to practice and rights of audience (Doherty 1998: 270). Those recommendations formed the bulk of the provisions enacted by the Nigerian parliament as the Legal Education Act of 1962 and the Legal Practitioners Act of 1962, which have become the Legal Education (Consolidation, etc) Act, Cap 206, Laws of the Federation of Nigeria 1990, and the Legal Practitioners Act, Cap 207 Laws of the Federation of Nigeria 1990 (as amended) (Oolujinmi 2011: 4–5).

The Legal Education Act established the Council of Legal Education, composed of the Attorney General of the Federation as Chairman, the States Attorneys-General, two persons appointed by the President, the President and two members of the NBA, two persons who held or had held high judicial office (appointed by the Chief Justice of the Federation), the Principal of any Law School[7] maintained by the Council, and the head of each Faculty of Law in the country. The Council issues qualifying certificates

---

[6] Federal Government of Nigeria, *Official Gazette* 30 April 1959, Government Notice No 915.
[7] The Council of Legal Education, which was authorised to operate a school for the practical training of lawyers, established the Nigerian Law School in 1962. Thereafter, all foreign-trained lawyers had to undergo a compulsory period of practical training at the Nigerian Law School. When Nigerian universities established law faculties offering a first degree in law, Nigerian-trained lawyers were also required to undergo practical training at the Nigerian Law School before being granted a licence to practise in Nigeria.

to Nigerian law graduates who have completed the mandatory Law School programme. A non-Nigerian who has passed the Bar exams may also be issued a qualifying certificate (The Legal Education Act 1975, s 5(2)). Consequently, all entrants to the profession since January 1963 (when the Law School admitted its first eight students) must undertake courses at the Nigerian Law School and pass their examinations before being eligible to practise in Nigeria.

The Legal Practitioners Act established the Body of Benchers, charged with the responsibility for the formal call to the Bar of Nigerian citizens who possess a qualifying certificate and demonstrate good character (The Legal Education Act 1975, s 3(1)). The Body may withdraw the certificate of call for misconduct or fraud (The Legal Education Act 1975, s 5(1)). The Chief Registrar of the Supreme Court of Nigeria maintains a similar Roll of Legal Practitioners (The Legal Education Act 1975, s 10(1)). However, the Attorney-General of the Federation may, after consultation with the General Council of the Bar, make regulations for the enrolment of those authorised to practise in any other country offering reciprocity to Nigerian lawyers. The legal profession is also regulated by Rules of Courts, the Nigerian Constitution and other laws (Fawehinmi 1988: 477–518; Oko 2007).

A. Professional Associations

There have been three phases in the evolution of the professional associations of lawyers in Nigeria. In 1897, a group of fewer than 20 lawyers established the Lagos Bar Association to promote their professional interests, meeting only when needed or to project a professional image.[8] Because of the inhospitable political environment, the association soon became moribund. In 1911, *The Nigerian Handbook* referred to a Local Bar. By statute all practitioners were members, the most senior being regarded as the leader. The Attorney General, Solicitor General and Crown Prosecutor were ex-officio members, and the Attorney General was the President.[9] Having been created by statute, the Local Bar was effectively an appendage of the colonial judiciary (Adewoye 1977b: 88–89).

The Lagos Law Society, a voluntary association, was established in 1924 to promote the interests of members and acquire information on subjects connected with the study and practice of law. A year later the Nigerian Provincial Bar association was launched in Calabar, open to lawyers, law officers and other persons officially connected with the administration of justice in the Province. It was independent of the Lagos Bar Association, but the two organisations worked together on matters of common interest (Adewoye 1977b: 88). Radical young lawyers were eager to establish a national Bar independent of official control. Adebesin Folarin, who had a lucrative practice in Abeokuta, was a prolific pamphleteer and instrumental in launching the *Nigerian Law Journal* in 1921. In 1925 he made elaborate proposals for an independent national Bar Association, which 'would suppress or fight the incidences of dishonourable conducts or practices among

---

[8] NAI Letter Book: 18 August–3 September 1896, CAS Williams and six others to Smalman Smith, 12 January 1897.
[9] *The Nigerian Handbook* 1911 p 247.

members, set up and maintain a law library and adequate reading rooms, revise existing laws and monitor the promulgation of new ones' (Adewoye 1977b: 90). But the realisation of this ambitious project had to await independence.

However, the NBA formally received legislative recognition in 1933.[10] There was no office of the President since, by law, the Attorney General as leader of the Bar was the President; the Association only 'elected' a Chairman (but actually always chose the most senior member) (Thompson 1991: 182). This showed that the Association was firmly under British colonial control. The colonial administration restricted lawyers to the Supreme Court centres, barring them from appearing before the lower courts. Poor transport and communication made it difficult for lawyers to organise nationally (Adewoye 1970: 55).

Another major impediment to the emergence of a national Bar Association was the paucity of publications by Nigerian lawyers during the colonial period. Only Folarin and a few others like JC Zizer were thinking about the future of the profession (Adewoye 1977b: 90). Folarin was convinced that the *Nigerian Law Journal* would compel 'counsels to be more alive to his sense of responsibilities to his clients and arouse him from his state of lethargy to the domain of legal acuteness and literacy culture'.[11] But in fact, the *Nigerian Law Journal* was more of a Law Report, noting important local and foreign (mainly British) cases. And due to the lukewarm response and lack of support from members of the Nigerian Bar, it ceased publication in October 1926. Lawyers also showed little interest in indigenous laws and institutions since all were foreign trained and had been called to the Bar in England, Scotland, Ireland or a Commonwealth country and tended to regard the legal profession as merely a money-making occupation (Adewoye 1977b: 89–90).

In 1952 the younger members of the Bar renewed their demand that the NBA be independent and elect its president (rather than accept the Attorney General).[12] This was resisted by the older more conservative members. Harrison Obafemi, SA Ogunkeye and Omotola Adegunwa, young radical lawyers practising in Ibadan, responded by establishing the first independent professional association of lawyers, the Western Bar Association, in Ibadan in December 1954 (Ogbogbo and Ajayi 2012). They also intensified their demand that the Local Bar, to which they belonged by law, be freed from colonial control.

The August 1960 NBA Conference, which drew the largest attendance to date, resolved it would henceforth elect its president (Thompson 1991:184). The NBA is funded by the annual practising fees paid by lawyers to secure rights of audience in court, as well as member donations and grants from the MacArthur Foundation, Open Society Foundation, United States Agency for International Development, and UNICEF. The NBA has observer status with the African Commission on Human and Peoples Rights and a working partnership with many national and international non-governmental organisations concerned with human rights, the rule of law and good governance in Nigeria and in Africa.[13]

---

[10] Legal Practitioners Ordinance No 57 of 1933, ss 2(a) and (b) and 4.
[11] (1922) I(1) *Nigerian Law Journal* editorial comments.
[12] (1952) *Nigerian Bar Journal* 1, Letter to the Editor by 'Res Ipsa'.
[13] Nigerian Bar Association (NBA) Committee on Professionalisation of the NBA Secretariat: *Final Report* (hereinafter referred to as the NBA Report) p 8.

From 1960 to the mid-1980s, the NBA was run by part-time volunteers who could combine those activities with their professional duties. Until 1998, the administrative structure consisted of the President, Vice-President, Secretary, Treasurer, Financial Secretary and Assistant Secretary. Because NBA membership increased to over 100,000 in 88 branches in the 36 states and the Federal Capital Territory, the Association was restructured in 2001.[14] NBA instituted an informal convention of rotating its presidency among the three ethnic forums that had emerged in the three historic regions of Nigeria at independence – *Arewa* Lawyers Forum in the North, Eastern Bar Forum in the East, and *Egbe Amofin Oodua* in the West – each of which is also allocated a Vice-President.[15]

As was the case in national politics, this 'gentleman's accord' to rotate the presidency has intensified regional and ethnic sentiments. This arrangement is problematic because the three NBA zones do not coincide with Nigeria's six geopolitical zones. It has engendered opposition from lawyers belonging to minority ethnic groups. For example, the Midwest is not included in the NBA zoning arrangement. The Midwest Lawyers Forum, consisting of lawyers from Edo and Delta States in Nigeria's South-South geopolitical zone, is not part of NBA's Eastern zone, like their other South-South neighbours. This politics of regional cleavages is creating disputes that threaten to compromise the integrity of the NBA as a national organisation (Nwokoro 2018; Uka 2014; Unachukwu and Jibueze 2014).

B. Military Rule

Military rule greatly affected the legal profession in Nigeria. The military ruled Nigeria for 28 of the first 33 years of independence. This placed the legal profession in a precarious position. Lawyers sought to reinstate the rule of law and restore democratic institutions in the face of military dictatorships demanding unrestricted powers to advance national security and their own economic interests. The military harassed and detained lawyers while recognising that the legal profession could help to legitimise military rule (Olanrewaju 1992; Oko 2007: 217–29).

Military rulers used political manipulation and patronage to control and destabilise the NBA, by giving key government positions to influential senior members as well as human rights activists. This weakened the NBA, causing intense internal friction and reducing its credibility in the eyes of lawyers and the general public (ibid: 228). The NBA was rendered effectively comatose after its 1991 Annual Conference, which tried to elect new leadership (Human Rights Watch 1991). The military government of Ibrahim Babangida wanted to install a Bar leadership it could manipulate. The conference ended in chaos as a result of police interference and court orders. NBA had no leadership at the national level until military rule ended eight years later (Odinkalu 2012). Military administrations also created military tribunals to try civilian offences, limiting the jurisdiction

---

[14] The Constitution of the Nigerian Bar Association 2001, Art 14(a).
[15] The Constitution of the Nigerian Bar Association 2015, s 2(2), Sch 2.

of civilian courts, and enacted retroactive legislation, all in a bid to destabilise the legal profession (Olanrewaju 1992).

C. Legal Aid in Nigeria

During the military era, some Nigerian lawyers and judges began to agitate for free legal assistance and advice to indigent Nigerians. Their activities led to the enactment of the Legal Aid Decree No 56 of 1976 by the Federal Military Government, establishing the Legal Aid Council which operated a scheme similar to that created by the Legal Aid and Advice Act 1949 of England and Wales (Njoku 2005: 73).

In 1979, the scheme was amended to include criminal offences in the Penal Code (Legal Aid (Amendment) Decree No 18 of 1979). In 1986, it was also extended to personal accidents and some criminal offences previously excluded (Legal Aid (Amendment) Decree No 10 of 1986). It was further amended in 1994 to include damages for breach of fundamental human rights guaranteed under the 1979 Constitution (Legal Aid (Amendment) Decree No 22 of 1994). The Legal Aid Council Act 2011 brought the scheme in line with international standards, expanded its civil mandate and extended the criminal jurisdiction to include armed robbery.

The Act requires the Council to maintain a panel of legal practitioners willing to take cases and forbids them from taking any form of remuneration from legally-aided clients. However, the low fee discourages private lawyers from offering their services. The Legal Aid Council of Nigeria has been unable to achieve its mandate of providing quality service to the teeming millions of poor and vulnerable for many reasons: too few lawyers to meet the increasing need for free legal services, inadequate funding, lack of publicity, inadequate information on access to justice, delays in investigating crime by the police, prison congestion, delays in the administration of justice, the exclusion of certain categories of recipients and legal matters, and the limited scope of eligibility. Fee levels are so low that some lawyers have done legal aid work free of charge because it was not worthwhile claiming the nominal fee. In order to complement the efforts of the Legal Aid Council, NBA declared in 2009 that members should provide 200 hours or three days of pro bono legal services annually.[16] In 2015, it expanded this to pro bono services to at least five indigent individuals, groups of persons or communities annually.[17]

IV. CHANGES IN THE LEGAL PROFESSION IN THE LAST 30 YEARS

When the legal profession marked its first 100 years in 1986 there was no reference book a judge could use to determine whether a litigant's representative was a qualified lawyer. Because it was relatively easy to impersonate a lawyer, Gani Fawehinmi, the leading human rights lawyer, published a book in 1988 listing all the judges and lawyers.

---

[16] Pro bono Declaration for members of the Nigerian Bar Association (Office of the President of the NBA) p 2; www.internationalprobono.com/resources/attachment163155.
[17] See the May 2015 Pro bono Declaration of the Nigerian Bar Association www.nigeriabar.com/2015/05/probono-declaration-for-members-of-the-nigerian-bar-association.

A. Growth in Numbers

The legal profession has witnessed substantial growth since the establishment in 1962 of the Nigerian Law School, whose pioneering class had eight students. Its original campus in Lagos has been supplemented by those in Abuja, Enugu, Kano, Yenegoa and Yola. In 2018, 5,846 students sat for the final Bar examinations, and 4,779 passed and were called to the Nigerian Bar (Nnochiri 2018). This exponential growth not only made the Nigerian legal profession the largest in Africa but also changed its composition.

B. Changes in the Socio-Economic Background of Lawyers

For most of the colonial period, the legal profession was dominated by foreigners (Adewoye 1977b: 135). The relatively few Nigerians admitted were men, mostly from affluent Yoruba families, educated abroad and admitted to one of the English Inns of Court (Adewoye 1977b: 137; Fawehinmi 1988: 833–49; Oko 2007: 90). The proliferation of law faculties in Nigerian universities made the profession accessible to other socio-economic strata. Nevertheless, more than 50 per cent of lawyers still come from middle class families, 18 per cent from upper class families, and only 23 per cent from families of modest means (Oko 2007: 90). By the end of 2018, the Council of Legal Education had accredited 55 law faculties: 16 owned by the Federal Government, 20 by the State Government, and 19 by private individuals and establishments.

Table 1 Approved Law Faculties[18]

University	Year Law Faculty was established	Ownership	Approved Student Quota
University of Nigeria	1961	Federal	220
University of Lagos	1962	Federal	270
Obafemi Awolowo University	1962	Federal	250
Ahmadu Bello University	1962	Federal	280
Bayero University, Kano	1978	Federal	220
University of Maiduguri	1978	Federal	200
University of Calabar	1980	Federal	170
University of Jos	1980	Federal	170
Usmanu Dan Fodio University	1980	Federal	80
University of Benin	1981	Federal	180
Bendel State University (now Ambrose Alli University)	1981	State	120

(continued)

---

[18] Compiled from G Fawehinmi (1988) and www.myschoolgist.com/ng/approved-faculties-of-law/.

Table 1 (Continued)

University	Year Law Faculty was established	Ownership	Approved Student Quota
Rivers State University of Science And Technology	1981	State	250
Imo State University	1981	State	100
University of Ilorin	1983	Federal	150
Ogun State University (now Olabisi Onabanjo University)	1983	State	170
University of Ibadan	1984	Federal	150
University of Cross River State (now University of Uyo)	1985	Federal	150
Anambra State University of Technology (now Nnamdi Azikwe University)	1985	Federal	180
Lagos State University	1985	State	Nil
University of Abuja	1990	Federal	Nil
Enugu State University of Science And Technology	1991	State	100
Abia State University	1991	State	130
Ekiti State University	1992	State	60
Benue State University	1993	State	Nil
Delta State University	1995	State	120
Adekunle Ajasin University	1999	State	50
Ebonyi State University	1999	State	150
Madonna University	1999	Private	50
Igbinedion University	1999	Private	100
Chukwuemeka Odumegwu University (formerly Anambra State University)	2000	State	100
Kogi State University	2000	State	60
Niger Delta University	2000	State	80
Babcock University	2000	Private	100
Nasarawa State University	2002	State	40
Benson Idahosa University	2002	Private	60
Osun State University	2010	State	50
Bowen University	2013	Private	50
Bauchi State University	2018	State	50

(continued)

Table 1 *(Continued)*

University	Year Law Faculty was established	Ownership	Approved Student Quota
Bukar Abba Ibrahim University	2018	State	50
Musa Yar'adua Univesity	2018	State	50
University of Port Harcourt	2018	Federal	50
Afe Babalola University	2018	Private	180
American University of Nigeria	2018	Private	50
Crescent University Abeokuta	2018	Private	50
Baze University Abuja	2018	Private	50
Al-Hikman University	2018	Private	50
Leadcity University	2018	Private	50
Ajayi Crowther University	2018	Private	50
Edwin Clark University	2018	Private	50
Nigerian Turkish Nile University	2018	Private	50
Joseph Ayo Babalola University	2018	Private	50
Elizade University	2018	Private	50
Salem University	2018	Private	50
Gregory University	2018	Private	50
Edo University	2018	Private	50

C. Pedagogy, Duration and Cost of Legal Education in Nigeria

In Nigeria, possession of a law degree does not, of itself, enable the holder to practise as a lawyer. An intending practitioner may attend a Nigerian university or an accredited foreign university to study for a law degree. A uniform curriculum designed by the Nigerian Universities Commission and approved by the Council of Legal Education is taught by all Nigerian universities in order to maintain minimum academic standards. There are 12 compulsory core law courses: Legal Methods, Nigerian Legal System, Contract Law, Constitutional Law, Company Law, Law of Torts, Commercial Law, Law of Equity and Trusts, Criminal Law, Land Law, Law of Evidence, and Jurisprudence (Mamman 2009: 9–11).

The optional law courses include: Administrative Law, Revenue Law and Taxation, Industrial Law, Labour Law, Oil and Gas Law, Public and International Law, Conveyancing, Islamic Law, Banking and Insurance Law. The compulsory non-law courses are: The Use of English, History and Philosophy of Science, Logic and Philosophic Thought, Nigerian Peoples and Culture, Introduction to Computer and Application, Social Science and English Literature. Optional non-law courses include: Economics, Element of Business Management, Philosophy, Social Relations, and Psychology (Mamman 2009: 9–11; Onolaja 2003: 8).

Following the NUC report on the minimum standard of academic legal education from 1990/91, the length of academic legal education has been five years for those possessing Senior Secondary School Certificates and four years for direct entry students who hold a Higher National Diploma or a First Degree. During the first and part of the second year, students may study non-law courses; the remaining three-and-half years are devoted to law courses. Most universities in common law countries are accredited by the Council of Legal Education, and their graduates are admitted to the Nigerian Law School (Onolaja 2003: 9).

However, foreign-trained graduates study at the Nigerian Law School for two years. The first year, they take the Bar Part I course, which teaches four core subjects: Constitutional Law, Legal System, Criminal Law and Nigerian Land Law. They then join Nigerian university graduates for the Bar Part II programme. All of the Bar Part II courses – Criminal Litigation, Civil Litigation, Corporate Law and Practice, Property Law and Law in Practice (Ethics and Skills) – are compulsory, and students must obtain a pass in each (Onolaja 2003: 9).

Clinical Legal Education (CLE) was introduced into the curriculum in 2004, shifting the emphasis from classroom work to obtaining practical skills in other venues, including courts. The report of the Council of Legal Education Committee on the Review of Legal Education in Nigeria, submitted on 29 July 2004, mandated that law faculties and the Nigerian Law School 'as a matter of "urgency" ... provide appropriate facilities, such as clinical consultation rooms ... for purposes of achieving interactive teaching, proper training will have to be given to lecturers at the various law faculties and the Nigerian Law School'. The National Universities Commission required new faculties to have law clinics which have been established in over 18 law faculties (Ojukwu 2004).

Funds for the public university system in Nigeria come almost entirely from the government. Whereas federal universities are supported by the federal government, state universities receive financial support from state governments and are usually more expensive (Oko 2007: 103). Federal universities receive 84 per cent of their income from the government, 7 per cent from internal income-generating activities, and 9 per cent from student fees (even though undergraduates pay no tuition) (Agboola and Adeyemi 2012: 283).

The National Universities Commission (NUC) approved unit cost for the undergraduate university education in law is 192,897.30 naira. However, the cost to the students averages 104,702.71 naira per annum (just under $300, at 2019 exchange rates) (Agboola and Adeyemi 2012: 288), which is financed mostly by the students or their families. The cost of legal education in private universities is much higher because they are financed mainly by tuition and other student fees (Ajadi 2010: 23).

The cost of tuition and other fees for Nigerians for one year at the Nigerian Law School for the 2018/19 session was 295,000 naira (excluding books, and other living expenses). This is beyond the reach of many law students, given that the average pay of workers in Nigeria is less than 40,000 naira per month. Less privileged students who have struggled to pay for their undergraduate law degree programme find it difficult to complete their training in the Nigerian Law School (Okere 2018). This generated concern in the House of Representatives, which directed its Committees on Justice, Tertiary Education and Service, and Finance to meet with the Director-General of the Nigerian Law School and other stakeholders to find ways to lower the cost (Daniel 2017).

D. Changes in the Age Structure

There has also been a radical transformation of the age structure of the legal profession since the 1980s. My survey[19] confirms Oko's (2007: 92) ten years earlier: students were admitted into law faculties directly from secondary schools at 17 or 18 and graduated at 21–23. Before the 1980s, by contrast, secondary school graduates had worked for some time before entering law faculties.

E. Changes in the Gender Structure

The number of women qualifying to practise began increasing in the 1970s, reaching a quarter of entrants in the 1980s, a third by the mid-1990s, and half by the end of the 2000s (see Table 2). In the 2018 final Bar examinations, women were 113 of the 161 receiving a first-class degree (Nnochiri 2018).

Table 2 Number of New Legal Practitioners Enrolled by Gender, 1931–2010

Year	Women	Men	Total
1931	0	3	3
1932	0	2	2
1933	0	1	1
1934	0	3	3
1935	1	2	3
1936	0	3	3
1937	0	2	2
1938	0	2	2
1939	0	4	4
1940	0	4	4
1941	0	4	4
1942	0	5	5
1943	0	6	6
1944	0	3	3
1945	0	6	6
1946	0	7	7
1947	1	28	29
1948	0	32	32
1949	1	19	20

(continued)

---

[19] The survey was conducted in Kaduna (Northern Nigeria) 7–10 October, 2018; Enugu (Eastern Nigeria) 30 October, 4 November, 2018; Lagos and Ibadan (Western Nigeria) 5–15 September, 2018.

Table 2 (Continued)

Year	Women	Men	Total
1950	1	29	30
1951	1	30	31
1952	1	48	49
1953	4	37	41
1954	1	40	41
1955	0	55	55
1956	3	54	57
1957	1	68	69
1958	2	83	85
1959	8	98	116
1960	5	132	137
1961	11	132	143
1962	4	187	191
1963	11	122	133
1964	17	219	238
1965	7	223	230
1966	11	263	276
1967	6	87	93
1968	8	99	117
1969	9	111	120
1970	11	140	151
1971	18	246	264
1972	11	217	228
1973	26	212	238
1974	29	181	210
1975	40	211	251
1976	56	195	251
1977	60	235	295
1978	88	274	362
1979	92	350	442
1980	120	403	523
1981	146	359	505
1982	169	504	673
1983	168	578	746
1984	209	663	872

(continued)

Table 2 *(Continued)*

Year	Women	Men	Total
1985	307	928	1,235
1986	381	1,150	1,531
1987	202	658	860
1988	426	1,324	1,750
1989	552	1,349	1,901
1990	591	1,569	2,160
1991	742	1,697	2,439
1992	772	1,633	2,405
1993	885	1,667	2,552
1994	86	139	266
1995	734	1,217	1,951
1996	456	728	1,184
1997	94	61	155
1998	493	794	1,287
1999	689	1,094	1,783
2000	982	2,453	3,435
2001	407	762	1,169
2002	822	1,387	2,209
2003	1,510	2,787	4,297
2004	1,931	2,315	4,246
2005	1,960	2,344	4,304
2006	1,503	1,884	3,387
2007	2,985	3,987	6,972
2008	1,628	1,779	3,407
2009	2,200	2,189	4,389
2010	2,136	2,219	4,355

Source: Fawehinmi (1988: 837, 1029); Oputa (2014).

F. Changes in Legal Practice

The legal profession is still 'paper based': few offices are connected to the Internet, research is done manually, and even judges take handwritten notes of evidence. Because clients are often ahead of lawyers in adopting new technologies and have increased access to legal information, much of it available on the Internet. They demand efficiency and responsiveness at lower cost (Ali 2017). The persistent economic recession in Nigeria has adversely affected law practice. Lawyer unemployment, unheard of 20 years ago, is increasing. However, technology has also allowed innovative solo and small-firm practitioners to compete with larger firms (Ali 2017).

Technological advances have also benefited professional associations. Previously, the NBA elected its officers through a system of delegates drawn from the 100 branches of the Bar. Each branch was entitled to one delegate and additional delegates for every 100 members above the first 100. All lawyer members of the Body of Benchers (except judges), Senior Advocates of Nigeria (SAN) and members of the expanded NBA National Executive Committee (NEC) were also entitled to vote as delegates. This electorate at its largest contained fewer than 2,000 voters (Odinkalu 2012).

On 1 August 2016, for the first time in a quarter of a century, the NBA held its leadership elections based on universal suffrage, having amended its constitution in 2015 to abolish the delegate electoral system and deploying technological advances to conduct its elections. By introducing One-Lawyer-One-Vote (OLOV) and remote voting through an online platform, the NBA addressed three problems: insulating the electoral process from external, political influence; reducing costs; and making the leadership transition more efficient and transparent (Odinkalu 2016).

The voting platform should improve revenues by linking access to voting to the payment of practising fees and membership dues. This additional revenue will enable the NBA to defend its independence and ward off political predators. Digital literacy at the Bar will improve, making Nigerian lawyers more competitive and accountable. Young lawyers will have a bigger voice in the affairs of the Bar because they have the votes, energy and technological knowledge. Digital voting will also put the legal profession and legal practice on the path to data-driven and effective service delivery (Odinkalu 2016).

The globalisation of legal practice and the impact of the Internet have also wrought a huge transformation in legal practices. Large law firms are growing in number and size, although small firms continue to predominate (Ali 2017). Large corporations now import legal services from big international law firms, without regard to Nigeria's municipal licensing laws. The NBA has sought to tighten the regulatory guidelines to control this foreign invasion (Mahmoud 2017). Nigerian law firms adapt by subcontracting work dealing with unfamiliar subject matters to overseas law firms and then rubber-stamping the documents to appear to comply with the Local Content Law requirement (Eimunjeze 2015: 201). But only the big law firms have the resources and capacity to outsource their business. Most lawyers are still contending with the economic recession and the mega firms.

V. CONCLUSION

The story of the legal profession in Nigeria has been one of adaptation. The dearth of qualified attorneys led to the admission of fit and proper persons with a basic education and some knowledge of English Law. This led to the development of a fused profession, with no distinction between barristers and solicitors. Lawyers have responded to the challenge of globalisation by contracting work to foreign firms but this has provoked the NBA to seek to prevent the loss of revenue to Nigerian lawyers. The legal profession must develop the capacity not only to adapt but also to overcome the challenges it is facing in the twenty-first century.

REFERENCES

Adewoye, O (1969) 'Self-Taught Attorneys in Lagos, 1865–1913' *Journal of the Historical Society of Nigeria* 47–65.

—— (1970) 'Prelude to the Legal Profession in Lagos 1861–1880' 14(2) *Journal of African Law* 98–114.

—— (1977a) *The Judicial System in Southern Nigeria 1854–1954: Law and Justice in a Dependency* (London, Longman).

—— (1977b) *The Legal Profession in Nigeria 1865–1962* (Lagos, Longman Nigeria Ltd).

—— (1982) 'Legal Practice in Ibadan, 1904–1960' 11(1/2) *Journal of the Historical Society of Nigeria* 52–66.

Agboola, BM and Adeyemi, JK (2012) 'Analysis of Private Cost of Education in A Selected Nigerian University' 10(3) *Journal of Research in National Development* 281–92.

Ajadi, TA (2010) 'Private Universities in Nigeria- the Challenges Ahead' 7 *American Journal of Scientific Research* 5–24.

Ali, Y (2017) 'Liberalization Of Legal Services: Perspective Of Nigerian Legal Practitioners And Law Firms' Being A Paper Delivered At The Annual General Conference Of The Nigerian Bar Association (NBA) held in Lagos 23 August.

Committee on the Future of the Nigerian Legal Profession. (1959) *Report* (Lagos: Government Printers).

Daniel, J (2017) 'Reps Decry Exorbitant Fee Charged by Nigerian Law School' *Information Nigeria* (3 March).

Doherty, O (1998) *Legal Practice and Management in Nigeria* (London, Cavendish).

Eimunjeze, F (2015) 'Achieving Excellence in the Legal Profession in a Globalized World: Imperatives for Developing Economies' 5(1) *Afe Babalola University Journal of Sustainable Development Law and Policy* 198–218.

Elias, TO (1962) *The Nature of African Customary Law* (Manchester, Manchester University Press).

Emiola, A (2005) *The Principles of African Customary Law* (Ogbomosho, Emiola Publishers).

Fawehinmi, G (1988) *Bench and Bar* (Lagos, Nigerian Law Publications Ltd).

Federal Government of Nigeria (1959) *Official Gazette* 30 April (Lagos, Government Printing Press).

Geary, WN (1965) *Nigeria Under British Rule* (London, Longman).

Ghai, Y (1987) 'Law, Development and African Scholarship' 50(6) *The Modern Law Review* 752.

Human Rights Watch (1991) On the Eve of 'Change' Transition to What? (New York, Human Rights Watch).

Mahmoud, AB (2017) 'Speech given at the Inauguration of the NBA Legal Profession Regulation Review Committee' by Abubakar Balarabe Mahmoud (SAN) the President of the Nigerian Bar Association, at the Conference Room of the NBA, NBA House, Abuja, on 24 January.

Mamman, T (2009) 'The Globalisation of Legal Practice: The Challenges for Legal Education in Nigeria' Paper Delivered by Dr Tahir Mamman – Director General, Nigerian Law School at the 2nd Annual Business Luncheon of SPA Ajibade & Co – Legal Practitioners on 19 November.

National Archives Ibadan NAI Letter Book: 18 August–3 September 1896, CAS Williams and six others to Smalman Smith, 12 January 1897.

National Archives Ibadan NAI, Chief Secretary Office CSO 1/32, CXVI, Officer Administering the Government to Colonial Office, 4 January 1933. *Enclosure.*

National Archives Ibadan NAI Eastern Region of Nigeria, Staff List, 1956–1963.

National Archives Ibadan NAI Western Region of Nigeria; Staff List, 1956–1963.

Nicolson, IF (1970) *The Administration of Nigeria, 1900–1960: Men, Methods And Myths* (Oxford, Clarendon Press).

Nigerian Bar Association (2001) *The Constitution of the Nigerian Bar Association* (Abuja, NBA).

—— (2014) *Committee on Professionalisation of the NBA Secretariat: Final Report* (Lagos, NBA Secretariat).
Njoku, A (2005) *History of the Legal Profession in Nigeria* (Lagos, Lisbon Investment Ltd).
Nnochiri, I (2018) '113 female First Class Law graduates, 4,666 others admitted into the Nigerian Bar' *Vanguard News Nigeria* (27 November).
Nwokoro, S (2018) 'Lawyer threatens to sue bar association over zoning' *The Guardian* 18 January, guardian.ng/features/law/lawyer-threatens-to-sue-bar-association-over-zoning/amp/.
Odinkalu, C (2016) '#ABraveNewBar: How A.B. Mahmoud Emerged As NBA President' *Premium Times* 9 August, opinion.premiumtimesng.com/2016/08/09/174278/.
—— (2012) 'Reforming the Bar' *Premium Times*.
Ogbogbo, CBN and Ajayi, DO (2012) 'Ibadan and the Beginnings of the Nigerian Bar Association' 5 *Journal of Intra-African Studies* 55–72.
Ojukwu, E (2004) 'The Development of Clinical Legal Education' NULAI Nigeria at the 1st Clinical Legal Education Colloquium 12th–14th February, Abuja www.nulai.org/index.php/blog/83-cle.
Okere, A (2018) 'Lawyer Advocates Review of Law School Fees' *Punch* 17 May punchng.com/lawyer-advocates-review-of-law-school-fees/.
Oko, O (2007) *Problems and Challenges of Lawyers in Africa: Lessons from Nigeria* (New York, Edwin Mellen Press).
Olanrewaju, A (1992) *The Bar and the Bench in Defence of the Rule of Law in Nigeria* (Lagos, Nigeria Law Publications Ltd).
Olujinmi, A (2011) 'The State of the Legal Profession in Nigeria' *Public Lecture Series* (Nigeria, Nigeria institute of Advanced Legal Studies).
Onolaja, MO (2003) 'Problem of Legal Education in Nigeria' www.alimiandco.com/publications/ACCREDITATION%20AND%20LEGAL%20EDUCATION%20IN%20NIGERIA.pdf.
Oputa, GU (2014) *The Roll of Legal Practitioners, 1886 to 2013* (Abuja, Justice Watch).
Thompson, T (1991) *Reminiscences at the Bar* (Ibadan, Verity Publishers).
Toby, N (1992) *The Nigerian Judges* (Lagos, A & T Publishers).
Uka, O (2014) 'How the NBA chooses its president and why the lawyers are fighting this time' *The Scoop* 16 May www.thescoopng.com/2014/05/16/scoop-explains-nba-chooses-president-lawyers-fighting-time/
Unachukwu, JA and Jibueze, J (2014) 'NBA presidency: Row over zoning' *The Nation* 16 May thenationonlineng.net/nba-presidency-row-zoning/.
Uzebu, E (2018) *Women Judges in the Judiciary of Mid-Western Nigeria, 1960–2010* PhD thesis, Department of History, University of Ibadan, unpublished.

26

South Africa
A Profession in Transformation

JONATHAN KLAAREN

I. INTRODUCTION

THE DYNAMICS OF the contemporary South African legal profession have many roots in the events of the last 30 years. These were momentous times – from the 1980s state of emergency through the transition from apartheid to the constitutional democracy of the 1990s and then to the decidedly more uncertain present. To a large extent, the last three decades are a story of what has *not* happened. The legal profession has not transformed to the extent many imagined, hoped, or feared. One example is the relative proportions of advocates and attorneys. Attorneys are the equivalent of English solicitors, taking instructions from clients. While they may, and sometimes do, perform courtroom work themselves, most brief the much less numerous advocates, the equivalent of English barristers, who engage in specialised litigation and high-level opinion work. When dealing with title deeds, attorneys may also work as conveyancers, a separate professional status gained through a specialist examination, usually taken at the same time as the attorneys' admission exams.

In the mid-1980s, blacks (persons classified under apartheid as Indian, Coloured or African) were about 10 per cent of the 6,500 attorneys and about 7 per cent of the 650 advocates recognised by the General Council of the Bar (GCB) (Abel 1995: 19). The ratio of attorneys to advocates was about 10:1. 30 years later, little has changed. The 2017 ratio between these two sub-professions is effectively the same – 25,283 attorneys to 2,915 advocates (see Figure 1). More troubling, the racial composition of the profession has changed much less than one might have expected in a country where Africans were about 80 per cent and whites about 9 per cent of the population in the latest census. In 2017, whites were still 58 per cent of practising attorneys and 63 per cent of advocates.[1]

---

[1] Law Society of South Africa (2017a) www.lssa.org.za/upload/LSSA%20LEAD%20STATISTICS%20JULY%202017.pdf.

Figure 1 Practising Attorneys and Advocates 1999–2017

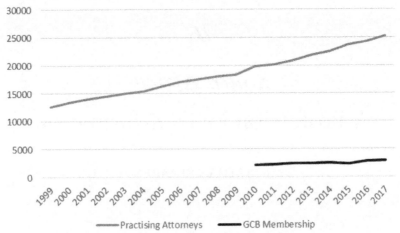

Source: author's compilation using data from LEAD, Law Society of South Africa.

The slow pace of demographic change has been matched by that of other transformations – educational, pro-competitive, and regulatory – all of which affect the legal profession. After sketching the current structure of the legal profession, this chapter investigates these four processes as well as other significant developments. It concludes after briefly touching on access to justice and public interest law.

To qualify as an attorney one must be an LLB graduate of a South African law school, complete an apprenticeship (articles of clerkship) with an admitted attorney, and pass an examination administered by the Law Society of South Africa. Since 1993, another requirement is a practical legal training (PLT) course of at least 25 days.

The statutory period for articles of clerkship is two years. However, many entrants reduce this to one by taking additional PLT at a post-graduate training centre (the School for Legal Practice) established by the Law Society in the mid-1990s. These schools, organisationally separate from university law schools, were supported by the judiciary and eventually recognised in legislation (Davis et al 2000: 889–90). A candidate attorney who successfully completes the School for Legal Practice can reduce the length of articles by six months; and those who attend the 'night' School and serve their articles simultaneously may complete just one year of articles.[2]

It is significantly easier for a law graduate to complete the formal requirements to become an advocate by simply presenting oneself before a court. This is no longer the formidable experience it was for blacks under apartheid (Moseneke 2016). The real barrier is the dominant position of the private associations of advocates (most of them organised in cities), which are joined together in the GCB. The GCB built its dominance in part through a closed-shop rule – it was an excludable offence for a member to work with a non-member advocate – as well as through the referral rule (advocates could accept briefs only from attorneys).

---

[2] Law Society of South Africa, 'History of LEAD' www.lssalead.org.za/about-lead/history.

Under pressure from the competition authorities, the closed-shop rule was invalidated in 2002, but the referral rule has survived. This has allowed the constituent associations of the GCB to dominate the market for specialised litigation services. By far the largest of these advocates' associations is the Johannesburg Bar, which contains about half of all GCB advocates (Klaaren and Brown 2013). Admission to a Bar requires a one-year pupillage (increased from six months in the early 2000s) and passage of a Bar-administered examination. Pupillage plus the start-up period for a practice mean that junior advocates earn little or nothing for 2–3 years, a significant entry barrier (ibid). There is a small but steady exchange between the two sub-professions as some attorneys (usually the younger) step up to the advocates profession and some advocates (usually the less successful) drop down into practice as attorneys.

Prefiguring the unification process of the Legal Practice Act (discussed below), a significant post-apartheid change involved the core professional issue of appearance rights. A 1995 law allowed attorneys (with three years' experience or an LLB) to enjoy most of the appearance rights of advocates after completing an administrative procedure. Because attorneys are more numerous and more representative of the population, it was no longer tenable to argue that advocates should have exclusive rights of appearance in the first-instance High Courts of South Africa. Advocates unsurprisingly objected to this change, arguing for a judicially supervised process of obtaining appearance rights and a more extensive definition of the ethical duties of attorneys appearing in the Supreme Court. The implementation of this measure was complicated by issues of civil procedure and the transition from four apartheid provinces and ten homelands to nine post-apartheid provinces (Davis et al 1999: 784–85; Davis et al 1995: 739; Law Society of South Africa, 'Legal Practice Act Latest').

II. THE DEMOGRAPHIC TRANSFORMATION

The legal profession faces an urgent challenge to transform its race and gender composition. In April 2017, attorneys were 61 per cent male and 58 per cent white, 25 per cent African, 9 per cent Asian, and 5 per cent Coloured (2 per cent unknown). Advocates were 63 per cent white and 37 per cent black (Law Society of South Africa 2017a). Noting that the profession was 77 per cent white, one 2007 study asked whether 'the problem lies with weak demand for African attorneys or is it a case of insufficient supply?' (Godfrey 2009: 119–20). Having found that 'a significant number of Africans [are] graduating with an LLB' and 'the number of African attorneys being admitted is increasing steadily', the study concluded that demand for African attorneys in the private sector was 'relatively weak', although this was mitigated by 'employment of African law professionals in the public sector'.

The picture ten years later is marginally more encouraging. Attorneys are 35 per cent white men, 26 per cent black men, 23 per cent white women, and 16 per cent black women (Law Society of South Africa 2017b). At this rate of change, white male attorneys will be displaced by black male attorneys as the largest sub-group in a few years.

A study of the demographics of large corporate law firms in 2013 found this most lucrative category still dominated by white men, especially in its upper echelons. Nearly half the African women employed professionally by these firms (48.1 per cent) were candidate attorneys (Klaaren 2014). A later study of the entire profession found that gender discrimination was generally accepted – particularly with respect to pregnancy – and sexual harassment was widespread (Centre for Applied Legal Studies 2014). Black women experienced racial as well as gender discrimination. Many respondents expressed pessimism about the possibilities of meaningful change in the near term.

The current drive for transformation must be seen in relation to the profession's history (Ngcukaitobi 2018). There is a long tradition of black lawyering in South Africa, much of it the legacy of the Black Lawyers' Association (BLA). Former Deputy Chief Justice Moseneke has pointed to the paradox that even in the 1970s there was 'a sturdy trickle of black legal practitioners despite apartheid odds' (Moseneke 2016: 220). Now, 'virtually every member of the BLA of my generation has risen to become a judge of our superior courts at all three levels – the High Court, the Supreme Court of Appeal, and the Constitutional Court'. Black lawyers no longer practise solely before white judges (Broun 2000). As of April 2017, whites were only 35 per cent of permanent judges, and black men were the single largest race-gender category in the judiciary (28 per cent), while men were 64 per cent of judges.

There is a widening disparity between the two hemispheres of the profession. The past 30 years have seen the emergence of a large corporate law firm sector. As of 2013, 51 firms employed more than 20 lawyers. The six largest (in the Johannesburg suburb of Sandton, with branch offices around the country and in the rest of Africa) each employed 250–600 lawyers (Klaaren 2015: 226). At the other end of the scale, nearly 40 per cent of attorneys practise as sole practitioners. The small law firms, few advocates' groups and solo practitioners that remain in the central business district near the High Court in Johannesburg focus on criminal and road accident fund work and have largely black staff.

III. LAW GRADUATES AND EDUCATIONAL TRANSFORMATION

The size and shape of law schools have remained relatively constant over the past three decades. In mid-2018, there were 16 public universities accredited and offering the LLB law degree, as well as law majors in other undergraduate degrees. The public institutions have recently been joined by five law programmes at private universities. While there are few reliable statistics on staff demographics, there is great concern that the legal academy is too white (Madlingozi 2006; Modiri 2013).

A high proportion of those who begin law degrees do not become lawyers. Using cohort (not longitudinal) data for 2000–06 from the public universities, Godfrey found that less than half (49 per cent) of those entering law school and less than a third (32 per cent) of black students graduated four years later (Godfrey 2009: 113). Among graduates, 92 per cent obtained articles and 82 per cent were admitted as attorneys. As a result, just 37 per cent of those registering for the first year of an LLB in 2000 were admitted six years later. This study concluded that '[t]he four-year LLB degree therefore appears to be a problem for many students that wish to become attorneys, while articles and the attorneys' admission examination seem to be less of an obstacle'. Similar data for 2010–17 show a slightly different picture. After another decade of efforts at educational transformation, 53 per cent of students who registered in 2010 graduated in 2013. This means that the university drop-out rate over the period 2010–16 is 47 per cent, a slight improvement from the 51 per cent drop-out rate found in the earlier study (Law Society of South Africa 2017).

Figure 2 Law Graduates, Articles and Admissions

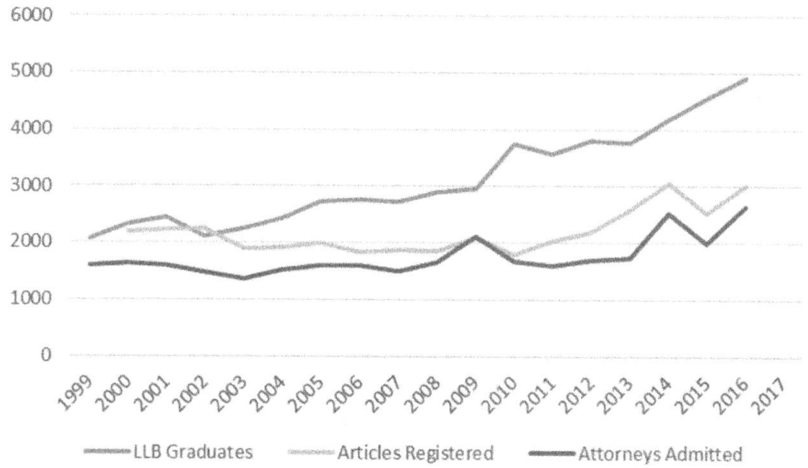

Source: author's compilation using data from LEAD, Law Society of South Africa.

In 2017, blacks were nearly two-thirds (63 per cent) of candidate attorneys (law graduates who are serving articles), and women were a majority (57 per cent). In a significant inversion of the historical demographics, black women were the largest category (35 per cent), followed by black men (28 per cent), white women (22 per cent), and finally white men (15 per cent). In the most recent pupillage intake, black men were the largest group (44 per cent), then black women (25 per cent), white women (16 per cent), and lastly white men (15 per cent). Among final year LLB students in 2017, women were 57 per cent and blacks 78 per cent (61 per cent African) (ibid).

The law curriculum has been a site of significant contestation in the past 30 years (Whitear-Nel and Freedman 2015). Before the 1990s, students could choose among three law degrees: BJuris, BProc, and LLB. The first two (taken mostly by black students) were four-year undergraduate degrees; the third (taken mostly by white students) was postgraduate (generally two years following a three-year undergraduate degree with some law subjects).

In the two years around 1996, this structure changed radically. The first two degrees were abolished, and the third became an undergraduate degree. Responding to the democratic transformation, law schools accepted the change with varying degrees of compliance and enthusiasm. However, some judges and other leaders of the profession felt the move to an undergraduate degree was hasty and ill-informed (Dibetle 2007). Concern about falling standards led to a May 2013 conference organised by the Law Society of South Africa and the South African Law Dean's conference. While that meeting expressed a desire to return to a 'five-year degree', it did not recommend an implementation process and remained unclear about whether a 'five-year degree' meant a two-year postgraduate degree following a three-year undergraduate degree or an extended five-year undergraduate degree. As of 2017, there seemed little prospect of substantial change. Indeed, the University of the Witwatersrand, which had unilaterally announced its intention to resume admitting only postgraduates to the law degree, has now complied with a recommendation from the higher education regulator to offer admission to students entering the university system for the first time.

There is some evidence that the law degree functions as a general commercial studies first degree. A 2016 survey found that 59.3 per cent of law students chose 'attorney' as their short-term goal, but only 22 per cent called it their long-term goal, whereas 26 per cent hoped to become advocates and 9.9 per cent commercial advisers (Law Society of South Africa 2016).

IV. COMPETITION POLICY AND THE SLOW PACE OF INSTITUTIONAL CHANGE

After its transition from apartheid, South Africa embarked upon significant social and economic policy changes, including adoption of a competition regime with sophisticated enabling legislation and a well-resourced enforcement agency (Lewis 2012). Unlike some other jurisdictions, South Africa has yet to experience much change as a result of this policy.[3]

South African competition authorities first addressed the legal profession in 1999–2002. Although most advocates belong to the GCB, membership is not compulsory. Many advocates practising in labour or criminal courts prefer to join the Independent Association of Advocates (IAA); advocates providing legal opinions (chambers work) are divided between the two organisations. The constituent Bars of the GCB require compliance with the referral rule in almost all cases, although the IAA does not. When the IAA complained to the Competition Commission about the anti-competitive effect of the GCB's professional rules, it responded by seeking an exemption from the competition regime. On 8 November 2000, the Commissioner informed the GCB that the application was partially granted and partially denied.

The GCB then sought High Court review on two grounds: the Commission lacked legal authority for its decision, and the Commission had followed a policy memorandum (the Meyer report) from the Minister of Justice without affording the GCB an opportunity to respond, violating procedural fairness. The High Court found that the Commission had been biased and substituted its own decision, which upheld the Bar's three foundational rules (the referral and closed-shop rules and the rule generally prohibiting contingent fees) but declined to exempt six others: the two-counsel rule (requiring a junior to be briefed with a senior counsel), the prohibition of partnerships, the defaulters' list (collecting and publishing the names of solicitors who failed to pay barristers' fees), advertising, fee tariffs, and limitations on the location of chambers. The Supreme Court of Appeal upheld the Commission's appeal with respect to the last two foundational rules but exempted the referral rule, calling it 'the law of the land' after the Constitutional Court's decision in *De Freitas* (see below). This was a partial substantive victory for the competition authorities but an overall procedural defeat: some anti-competitive practices remained operative, and at least one foundational practice, the referral rule, was exempted.

In part through the referral rule, the GCB's position would survive for at least another 15 years. The only other judicial challenge was rejected in separate litigation. The Supreme Court of Appeal upheld a decision striking from the roll an advocate belonging to the

---

[3] See Chapter 2 on Australia.

IAA, who had accepted instructions from clients without the intervention of an attorney.[4] The majority held that the referral rule clearly served the best interests of the professions and the public by fostering the specialised legal skills of a divided profession and the independence of advocates. It also offered clients the protection of the attorneys' trust fund. The majority saw no reason to abandon the referral rule just because attorneys had obtained a right of appearance in the High Court (Davis et al 2001). Concurring, Cameron JA would have upheld the referral rule on the narrow ground that the intermediary role of an attorney with a mandatory trust fund offers clients protection they would not receive from advocates, who are not required to have such a fund.

The Constitutional Court found it inappropriate to decide the constitutionality of the referral rule because 'both the narrower and the broader issues are currently being canvassed and debated in a number of forums, more particularly within and amongst all the branches of the legal profession'.[5] This course of action may have been influenced by the submissions made at the time by the Minister of Justice and Constitutional Development regarding the Legal Practice Bill (see below) (Davis et al 2002: 1003–05; Davis et al 1998: 885–86).

V. REGULATORY CHANGE AND THE LEGAL PROFESSION

South African regulation of the legal profession mirrors the regimes in other jurisdictions: formally recognising two sub-sectors without covering practising lawyers not enrolled as either attorneys or advocates or the estimated 3,500 paralegals (Maqubela and Mnguni). Legal advisers (law graduates who offer legal services either 'in-house' for an organisation or as self-employed consultants or independent contractors) are much less tightly organised than advocates or attorneys. Neither legal advisers nor paralegals have statutory recognition.

To address the effects of apartheid, the Recognition of Foreign Legal Qualifications and Practice Act 114 of 1993 recognised the foreign legal qualifications of South African citizens returning from exile and some others, thereby granting the right to practise. Although this was intended to benefit those who had fled for political reasons, it soon became a broader loophole for nearly any South African returning with foreign legal credentials. It ended without replacement in April 1998 (Davis et al 1998: 883). The more significant regulatory change has been the passage of new legislation governing the profession. After a nearly two-decade gestation, the Legal Practice Act 2014 (LPA) replaced the legislation governing advocates and attorneys, creating a single category of legal practitioner and 'a consolidated database of all legal practitioners – attorneys and advocates' (Whittle 2015). The statute provides authority to establish a single South African Legal Practice Council with regulatory and disciplinary powers, as well as a Legal Services Ombudsman. Discussions began in 1995, but progress was so slow that this author entitled one commentary on the drafting 'Waiting for Godot' – and then stopped waiting. Prominent advocates for access to justice, such as Geoff Budlender, the

---

[4] *De Freitas v Society of Advocates of Natal* 2001 (3) SA 750 (SCA).
[5] *Van der Spuy v General Council of the Bar of South Africa* (CCT48/01) [2002] ZACC 17; 2002 (5) SA 392; 2002 (10) BCLR 1092.

former director the Legal Resources Centre, also disengaged from the apparently blocked process.

Three factors were significant in breaking the logjam. First, a Black Economic Empowerment charter for lawyers, the Legal Services Charter, was enacted as part of the campaign for economic empowerment of disadvantaged persons in post-apartheid South Africa. The Charter was debated at length and seemed to have secured support from all significant participants in the legal services sector. But it failed to achieve its goal (Centre for Applied Legal Studies 2014).

Second, after its procedural defeat, the Competition Commission continued to press competitiveness on the profession, denying in significant part applications for exemption from attorneys and advocates. The Law Society rules concerned professional fees, reserved work, organisational forms and multi-disciplinary practices, and advertising, marketing and touting. The GCB application covered 11 rules relating to fees, organisational forms and multi-disciplinary practices, and advertising and marketing. The Commission recommended that the Legal Practice Act be amended to make fair competition an objective. Because the Commission depended on legal professionals to advocate for and enforce competition policy in other sectors of the economy, however, it ended most litigation against their associations, adopting an advocacy and engagement approach.

Third, government scaled back its ambitions to regulate the legal profession, opting for an approach that was less command and control and more co-regulatory and gradual. The Legal Practice Act directed that an interim council first discuss for 18 months a final regulatory body and regime. Although the advocates resisted, attorneys agreed to be represented on an equal basis, even though they outnumbered advocates at least 6:1. Advocates were represented by the GCB, Advocates for Transformation (a largely black group), and the National Bar Council of South Africa (independent advocates) ('History of the NBCSA' 2019). Nevertheless, there was deep mistrust about the legislation, particularly among advocates (Gauntlett 2010).

The LPA's long title declares that its purpose is 'to provide a legislative framework for the transformation and restructuring of the legal profession in line with constitutional imperatives so as to facilitate and enhance an independent legal profession that broadly reflects the diversity and demographics of the Republic'. The preamble explicitly notes that 'the legal profession is not broadly representative of the demographics of South Africa'.

One focus of resistance was lawyer discipline. Disciplinary hearings within the profession had remained closed even after the Constitution came into effect. However, the LPA mandated open hearings and public participation. Only in 2014 did the advocates' profession agree it was 'simply wrong' to close disciplinary hearings automatically. The attorneys' profession took even longer to concede: unless members were struck from the roll in open court, provincial law societies would not reveal their names (Saunderson-Meyer 2013 Saunderson-Meyer 2014). There was significant evidence of misconduct. In 2012, the Law Society of the Northern Provinces (the largest) 'held 203 inquiries involving 603 attorneys. Some 425 complaints were upheld, leading to 25 warnings and 23 suspensions'. Nationwide, 78 attorneys were struck from the roll. In 2016–17 the Law Society of the Northern Provinces held 161 inquiries involving 724 attorneys and 2 candidate attorneys. The High Court struck 33 from the roll, suspended 29, and interdicted four from practising on their own account (The President's Report 2017).

The National Forum on the Legal Profession, created as the interim structure to implement the Act, finalised its recommendations to the Justice Minister in July 2018. Three issues remained for resolution through processes of consultation and regulation-drafting after the LPA came into effect on 1 November 2018: the admission and enrolment of foreign legal practitioners, community service, and prescribed fees (LPA, ss 24(3), 29(1), and 35(4)).

Recently the profession has studied ways to transform briefing patterns. A Summit, convened by the Law Society of South Africa on 31 March 2016, established an Action Group of representatives of the attorneys' and advocates' professions, the big law firms and the Department of Justice and Constitutional Development to study the distribution of legal services work from government departments and state-owned entities. A year later the Group reported 'a lack of cooperation from certain Government departments, state-owned entities and the business sector' and was 'exploring alternatives including the use of the Promotion of Access to Information Act 2 of 2000 to have access to the information required'.

VI. ACCESS TO JUSTICE AND THE ESTABLISHMENT OF LEGAL AID SA

Although apartheid was the epitome of unequal justice, initiatives to promote access to justice began to gain traction during that period. In the 1970s the legal profession permitted clinics operated by universities and non-governmental organisations (NGOs) like the Legal Resources Centre to offer free services in certain areas of practice (Holness 2014). These clinics continue to seek rules authorising student practice and pupillages at public interest organisations.

In the post-apartheid era access to justice has become the dominant discourse (Klaaren 2015). In the 1990s, Legal Aid SA, established in 1969, was transformed from a judicare model to an organisation based on salaried lawyers. It now operates 64 Justice Centres and is the largest legal services provider in South Africa, with 2,070 professional legal positions and 174 paralegals in March 2017.[6] It offers criminal and (to a lesser extent) civil legal services to indigent people (with monthly incomes less than approximately US$500). Nearly 70 per cent of clients require only advice, provided by paralegals. A telephone Legal Aid Advice Line has operated since 2010. Significant budget cuts due to the economic recession are being implemented for three years starting in 2017/18 (ibid).

Paralegals remain on the margins of the profession, although there was a concerted push to regulate them within the Legal Practice Bill process. The third draft of the LPA at the end of 2000 envisaged separate rolls for legal practitioners, paralegal practitioners and conveyancers (Whittle 2001). However, it was later decided to address paralegals in future legislation. In the early 2000s, there were an estimated 750 paralegals 'working in 250 advice offices located mainly in communities, rural areas, and townships that are not accessible to the legal aid system'. By 2013, the number of these organisations had grown to about 350. In terms of access to justice, it is encouraging that the ratio of population per lawyer fell from 4,377 in the 1980s to 2,176 in 2017 (Klaaren 2018).

---

[6] Legal Aid South Africa, 'South Africa Country Report' (International Legal Aid Group, Johannesburg South Africa, 2017) 1–26, available at www.internationallegalaidgroup.org/images/miscdocs/SA_Country_report_-April_2017.pdf.

Attention is now beginning to turn to government lawyers, who serve in either the Offices of the State Legal Adviser (typically advocates) or the Chief Litigation Officer (CLO) (typically attorneys) (Klaaren 2015). The CLO has 299 lawyers (about one quarter the size of Legal Aid South Africa), established in 12 major cities since 1925. Spending on legal services provided by outside counsel is more than twice that on civil government lawyers (ibid: 421) There is official and judicial concern regarding the quality of government legal services and the demographic profile of government lawyers (ibid: 422).

VII. PUBLIC INTEREST LAW

Drawing inspiration from the Constitution that facilitated South Africa's transition from apartheid, public interest law in the country is healthy and diverse (Socio-Economic Rights Institute 2015). It includes NGOs such as the Legal Resources Centre, Lawyers for Human Rights, the Centre for Applied Legal Studies, and the Black Lawyers Association, all of which played important roles in legal campaigns against apartheid policies. This sector has achieved a number of significant litigation victories, including the provision of anti-retroviral medicines in response to the HIV/AIDS crisis (Brickhill 2018). Public interest lawyers have addressed issues such as poverty, inequality, unemployment, access to healthcare and education, housing and evictions, and gender-based violence and have represented vulnerable groups such as foreign nationals, LGBT and intersex persons, and those living in rural communities. These NGOs played significant roles in making South Africa the first African country to legalise same-sex marriage and civil unions. There is significant collaboration with community advice offices through referral networks and information sharing, including an annual Public Interest Law Gathering.

VIII. CONCLUSION: THE LEGAL PROFESSION AND POLITICAL SPACE

The legal profession has often been at the centre of South African politics, as illustrated by its role in the struggle against apartheid (Abel 1995). Since the early 2000s, South Africa has seen the emergence of a new form of litigation for political purposes among factions and organisations in the public sphere, suggesting the limited ability of the South African state to respond to social challenges. As the post-apartheid Constitution's promise of social democracy has disappointed and been displaced by a focus on decoloniality (Modiri 2014; Sibanda 2017), a new focus on the legal profession and social change is warranted.

REFERENCES

Abel, RL (1995) *Politics by Other Means: Law in the Struggle against Apartheid, 1980–1994* (New York, Routledge)
Brickhill, J (2018) *Public Interest Litigation in South Africa* (Cape Town, Juta).
Broun, KS (2000) *Black Lawyers, White Courts: The Soul of South African Law* (Athens, Ohio University Press).

Centre for Applied Legal Studies (2014) 'Transformation of the Legal Profession' (Johannesburg, Centre for Applied Legal Studies and Foundation for Human Rights).
Davis, D, Marcus, G and Klaaren, J (1995) 'Administration of Justice, Law Reform, and Jurisprudence' *Annual Survey of South African Law 1995*.
—— (1998) 'Administration of Justice' *Annual Survey of South African Law 1998*.
—— (1999) 'Administration of Justice' *Annual Survey of South African Law 1999*.
—— (2000) 'Administration of Justice' *Annual Survey of South African Law 2000*.
—— (2001) 'Administration of Justice' *Annual Survey of South African Law 2001*.
—— (2002) 'Administration of Justice' *Annual Survey of South African Law 2002*.
Dibetle, M (2007) 'Quality of Law Degrees Questioned' *The M&G Online* (14 November) mg.co.za/article/2007-11-14-quality-of-law-degrees-questioned/.
Dugard, J and Drage, K (2013) 'To Whom Do The People Take Their Issues? The Contribution of Community-Based Paralegals to Access to Justice in South Africa' (World Bank).
Gauntlett, J (2010) 'The Rule of Law and an Independent Legal Profession: A South African Perspective' 23 *The Advocate* 55.
Godfrey, S (2009) 'The Legal Profession: Transformation and Skills' 126 *South African Law Journal* 91.
'History of the NBCSA' (National Bar Council of South Africa 2019) nationalbarcouncil.co.za/history_of_the_nbcsa/.
Holness, D (2014) 'Coordinating Free Legal Services in Civil Matters for Improved Access to Justice for Indigent People in South Africa' *New York Law School Law Review* www.nylslawreview.com/wp-content/uploads/sites/16/2014/11/Holness.pdf.
Klaaren, J (2014) 'Current Demographics in Large Corporate Law Firms in South Africa' 7 *African Journal of Legal Studies* 587.
—— (2015a) 'African Corporate Lawyering and Globalization' 22 *International Journal of the Legal Profession* 226.
—— (2015b) 'Civil Government Lawyers in South Africa' 60 *New York Law School Law Review* 365.
—— (2015c) 'Transformation of the Judicial System in South Africa, 2012–2013' 47 *George Washington International Law Review* 481.
—— (2018) 'Towards Affordable Legal Services: Legal Costs in South Africa and a Comparison with Other Professional Sectors' in South African Law Reform Commission International Conference (Access to Justice, Legal Costs, and Other Interventions, Durban, South Africa, 2018).
Klaaren, J and Brown, A (2013) 'Transformation, Groups and Johannesburg Bar' unpublished conference paper, Annual Meeting of the Law & Society Association.
Law Society of South Africa (2016) 'Preferred Law Occupation: Overall Summary'.
—— (2017a) 'LEAD Statistics for the Legal Profession 2016/2017' www.lssa.org.za/upload/LSSA%20LEAD%20STATISTICS%20JULY%202017.pdf.
—— (2017b) 'Statistics for the Attorneys' Profession' (*Statistics for the attorneys' profession*, October 2017).
—— (2018) 'Legal Practice Act Latest – Law Society of South Africa' (16 August).
—— 'History of LEAD' www.lssalead.org.za/about-lead/history.
Legal Aid South Africa (2017) 'South Africa Country Report' www.internationallegalaidgroup.org/images/miscdocs/SA_Country_report_-April_2017.pdf.
Lewis, D (2012) *Thieves at the Dinner Table: Enforcing the Competition Act, a Personal Account* (Johannesburg, Jacana Media).
Madlingozi, T (2006) 'Legal Academics, Progressive Politics and Transformation in South African Law Schools' (Pretoria, Pretoria University Law Press, PULP Fictions).
Maisel, P (2006) 'Expanding and Sustaining Clinical Legal Education in Developing Countries: What We Can Learn from South Africa Symposium: Global Alliance for Justice Education (GAJE) North American Regional Conference' 30 *Fordham International Law Journal* 374.

Maqubela, N and Mnguni, S, 'Joint Submission to the South African Parliamentary Portfolio Committee on Justice and Constitutional Development on the Legal Practice Bill [B20-2012]'.

McQuoid-Mason, D (2017) 'Challenges When Drafting Legal Aid Legislation to Ensure Access to Justice in Developing Countries with Small Numbers of Lawyers: Thinking Outside the Box' www.internationallegalaidgroup.org/images/miscdocs/Conference_Papers/David_McQuoid-Mason_-_Session_1.pdf.

Modiri, J (2013) 'Transformation, Tension and Transgression : Reflections on the Culture and Ideology of South African Legal Education' 24 *Stellenbosch Law Review* 455.

—— (2014) 'The Crises in Legal Education' 46 *Acta Academica* 1.

Moseneke, D (2016) *My Own Liberator: A Memoir* (London, Pan Macmillan South Africa).

Ngcukaitobi, T (2018) *The Land Is Ours: Black Lawyers and the Birth of Constitutionalism in South Africa* (Cape Town, Penguin).

Saunderson-Meyer, W (2013) 'Just Trust Me, I'm a Lawyer …' (*Thought Leader Mail & Guardian*, 13 April) thoughtleader.co.za/williamsaundersonmeyer/2013/04/13/just-trust-me-im-a-lawyer/.

—— (2014) 'South Africa's Lawyers Should Be Desperately Ashamed' (*Thought Leader Mail & Guardian*, 8 March) thoughtleader.co.za/williamsaundersonmeyer/2014/03/08/south-africas-lawyers-should-be-desperately-ashamed/.

Sibanda, S (forthcoming) 'When Do You Call Time on a Compromise? The Future of Transformative Constitutionalism in South Africa' in B de Sousa Santos, S Araújo and O Arágon Andrade (eds), *Decolonising the State: Beyond False or Impossible Promises*.

Socio-Economic Rights Institute (2015) 'Public Interest Legal Services in South Africa' www.raith.org.za/docs/Seri_Pils_report_Final.pdf.

'The President's Report: The Law Society of the Northern Provinces, 2016–2017' (2017).

Thornton, M and Wood, A (2019) 'The Australian Legal Profession: Globalised and Magnified' in RL Abel, O Hammerslev, H Sommerlad and U Schultz (eds), *Lawyers in 21st-Century Societies, Vol 1: National Reports* (Oxford, Hart Publishing).

Whitear-Nel, N and Freedman, W (2015) 'A Historical Review of the Development of the Post-Apartheid South African LLB Degree – with Particular Reference to Legal Ethics' 21 *Fundamina* 234.

Whittle, B (2001) 'Three Rolls in Third Draft Legal Practice Bill' 14 *De Rebus* 6.

—— (2015) 'National Forum Starts Shaping the New Dispensation' 18 *De Rebus* 155.

27

Zimbabwe

Legal Practitioners, Politics and Transformation Since 1980

GEORGE H KAREKWAIVANANE*

I. INTRODUCTION

THIS CHAPTER EXAMINES some key changes in the Zimbabwean legal profession since 1980, when the country gained its independence from British rule. I explore how national, continental and global factors played a role in shaping the nature of the profession, the training it offered law students, and its relationship to the state. Although global processes such as the end of the Cold War played an important role, the late independence of Zimbabwe (compared to other colonies) and domestic politics were more influential. The chapter is divided chronologically into four sections. The first provides a brief history of the legal system and legal profession from the early days of colonial occupation. The next section deals with the ambiguous transformation of the 1980s, when important reforms in the legal arena and profession went hand in hand with the continued use of repressive laws in the political sphere. In the third section I examine the central developments within the legal profession during the 1990s, especially the emergence of lawyer-led civil society organisations focusing on human rights and constitutional reform. The last section examines the responses of the legal profession, led by the Law Society of Zimbabwe (LSZ), to the deepening national crisis from 2000.

II. HISTORICAL BACKGROUND

An early step in the establishment of a colonial legal system in Southern Rhodesia (Zimbabwe's colonial name) was the British South Africa Company (BSAC) Administrator's decision in 1890 to apply the Roman-Dutch law of the Cape Colony to the new

---

* I am grateful to the Leverhulme Trust for funding the research for this chapter through their Early Career Fellowship scheme.

protectorate (Karekwaivanane 2017: 25). This was followed in 1891 by the appointment in Mashonaland of magistrates who exercised criminal and civil jurisdiction over Europeans but could hear cases involving Africans only in very limited circumstances (Palley 1966: 513). The 1894 Matabeleland Order in Council extended magistrates' jurisdiction to all residents in the colony regardless of race and established the Matabeleland High Court, which also had jurisdiction over all residents (Government of Rhodesia 1971: 26–27). The 1898 Order in Council reconstituted the Matabeleland High Court as the Southern Rhodesia High Court, appeals from which were heard in the Cape Supreme Court in South Africa, later renamed the Appellate Division of the Union of South Africa. The final court of appeal for Southern Rhodesia was the Judicial Committee of the Privy Council in Britain, until the Rhodesian Front government unilaterally declared independence in 1965 (Government of Rhodesia 1971: 9).

The establishment of the legal system was accompanied by the emergence of a legal profession, which responded to the demand for legal services from the colony's growing mining, agriculture and commercial sectors. Because many Southern Rhodesian lawyers had migrated from South Africa they sought to preserve the characteristics of that country's legal profession, especially its structure, commitment to formalism, and efforts to restrict entry on the grounds of gender and race (Karekwaivanane 2017: 28–29). As in South Africa, the Southern Rhodesian legal profession was divided between advocates and attorneys. Although attorneys could appear in the lower courts and be retained directly by clients, they could not appear before the High Court. By contrast, advocates could appear in the High Court but had to be briefed by an attorney. However, there was little justification for such specialisation given how few clients could afford lawyers' services in the colony. This 'division of juridical labour' was partly a reflection of South African legal traditions. It also helped lawyers control supply and thereby increase the cost of legal services.

The legal fraternity also actively policed entry into the profession. The process of becoming an attorney involved an apprenticeship in a law firm as an 'articled clerk'; its length depended on whether one had a law degree or prior legal experience as an advocate (Currie 1982: 39). This was followed by a three-part Attorney's Admission Exam; those wanting to work as a notary public or conveyancer had to take additional exams. Admission to the Southern Rhodesian Bar as an advocate was based on having qualified as a barrister or obtained a law degree in Britain or South Africa. After a pupillage, aspiring advocates had to sit exams in local statute law; those who had studied in Britain also took an exam in Roman-Dutch law.

In theory, the legal profession was open to all inhabitants of the colony regardless of race, ethnicity or gender; however, the reality was different. Both colonial officials and European lawyers opposed the entry of Africans into the profession. The racial prejudices underpinning colonial rule were shared by most European lawyers in Southern Rhodesia, who also wanted to control the supply of legal services. The government and European law firms thus worked together to restrict African entry, an effort facilitated by the existence of a large settler population. The limited financial resources and poor education of most Africans meant that few were able to attain the necessary qualifications to train as a lawyer (Karekwaivanane 2017: 142). Although the government provided some scholarships for Africans to study education or medicine at university, there was no such provision for the study of law.[1] The few Africans who managed to acquire the necessary financial resources and educational qualifications to pursue a legal career were soon confronted with the reality that law firms were generally unwilling to take them on as articled clerks.

As a result, while colonies like the Gold Coast and Nigeria had indigenous lawyers by the late nineteenth century, it was only in 1953 that the first African, Herbert Chitepo, joined the Southern Rhodesian legal profession (Mlambo 1972: 305). By 1960 there were only three African lawyers in Southern Rhodesia, compared to approximately 540 in Nigeria. There was very little improvement even after the University College of Rhodesia and Nyasaland began offering a law degree in 1965. On the eve of independence, just five of the 175 attorneys, seven of the 40 articled clerks and seven of the 56 advocates were Africans.[2]

III. TRANSFORMATION AND CONTINUITY: THE 1980S

The new ZANU PF government that took office in 1980, therefore, faced the huge task of transforming the legacies of the colonial period, including the legal profession. This was led by Simbi Mubako, the country's first Minister of Justice, Legal and Parliamentary Affairs.[3] Two factors shaped the post-independence re-organisation of the legal profession. The first was the effort by black lawyers in the 1980s to eliminate the discriminatory practices that had become entrenched in the profession during the colonial period. Members of the first generation of black lawyers who now held senior positions in government, such as Mubako and his deputy, Godfrey Chidyausiku, worked with colleagues in private practice like Simplisius Chihambakwe and Kennedy Sibanda. Many of these lawyers had long-standing relationships forged during the anti-colonial struggle and had advised the nationalist leaders during the constitutional negotiations leading to independence in 1980. These relationships fostered close ties between Law Society officials and the new government during the 1980s and 1990s – what Ethan Michelson (2011: 41) has described as 'political embeddedness'.

A case in point was Chihambakwe, who had been part of ZANU's legal team during the constitutional negotiations in Geneva.[4] In 1979, he opened the first black-owned law firm with his then partner, Amos Chirunda. Soon after independence Chihambakwe was appointed the government's representative on the LSZ Council and later served as its President for much of the 1980s. He was also appointed by the government to chair the Detainees Review Tribunal (which presided over the cases of hundreds of political detainees in the 1980s) and the 1983 Commission of Enquiry into Matabeleland (which investigated the allegations of state-directed massacres in that region). As I show below,

---

[1] Interview with S Mubako, Harare, 26 April 2011.
[2] National Archives of Zimbabwe RG4, Committee of Enquiry into the Legal Profession, Provisional Report, April 1978.
[3] Interview with Mubako.
[4] Interviews with Simplisius Chihambakwe, Harare, 15 March 2009 and 16 March 2011.

this political embeddedness remained an enduring feature of the legal profession, shaping its relations with the government for more than three decades.

One of Mubako's central objectives was the 'Africanisation' of the legal profession. However, his efforts were hindered by the scarcity of African legal professionals, the structure of the profession, and the governing legislation. The white-dominated law firms and advocates' chambers continued to exercise substantial control over entry to the profession. In addition, the constitutional stipulations regarding judges' qualifications restricted the new government's ability to appoint black lawyers to the bench. For example, judicial nominees had to have been practising *advocates* for at least seven years, which excluded all the black lawyers who had qualified as *attorneys* in the 1970s. To eliminate these obstacles, Mubako had Parliament pass the Legal Practitioners Act in 1981,[5] fusing the legal profession and ending the privileges reserved to advocates, such as exclusive rights of audience in the High Court and eligibility for judicial appointment. In addition, the length of pupillage was shortened from three years to one, enabling newly-trained lawyers to establish their practices earlier.

Another legal provision stipulated that until February 1985 all lawyers qualified in countries where English or Roman-Dutch law prevailed or English was the official language could register to practise in Zimbabwe without taking further examinations (Austin 1987). At the University of Zimbabwe, increased efforts were made to enrol more black law students, and the Legal Resources Foundation opened a library for new lawyers to conduct their research.[6] A fast-track training programme for prosecutors and magistrates was also launched to staff the courts which had been hit by the mass exodus of white legal professionals after independence. The cumulative effect of these changes was to undercut the power of established law firms to control entry into the profession and transfer it to the newly created Council for Legal Education. By March 1986 there were 86 firms containing 261 lawyers, 210 of them in the two largest cities, Harare and Bulawayo, and the rest in seven smaller towns and cities (Austin 1987: 175).

The second factor shaping the reorganisation of the legal profession was the fact that it coincided with the corporatist bargains the new government was striking with key interest groups, such as organised labour, which were reflected in the regulatory framework governing the legal profession. On one hand, LSZ was granted substantial autonomy, control over the provision of legal services, and privileged access to government officials. On the other, the government introduced new mechanisms to monitor and control the profession. The Legal Practitioners Act of 1981 empowered the Minister of Justice to appoint two representatives to the LSZ Council and authorised the Minister or a designated representative to attend Council meetings. In addition, tariffs for legal services could be raised only with the Minister's approval. Crucially, LSZ itself was created by statute and therefore vulnerable to interference through legislative amendments if it ever displeased the government.

The erosion of the gatekeeping power of the established law firms and the elimination of the racial and gender barriers to entry they had created allowed new currents of legal thinking to challenge the *status quo*. This was most evident at the University of Zimbabwe Law School. Reginald Austin, who became its head in 1982, had been a member

---

[5] Interview with Mubako.
[6] Interview with Reginald Austin, Harare, 29 April 2011.

of the nationalist Zimbabwe African People's Union (ZAPU) in the 1970s and had led its legal team at the Lancaster House negotiations.[7] During his deanship the composition of the student body changed substantially in terms of race, gender and class. Prior to 1980 it had been common for an entering class of about 30 students to have just one to five black students. After 1980 the class size tripled, with 90 students being admitted in 1980, and black students soon constituted more than 90 per cent of the student body (Austin 1987: 182). The number of black women, who had been even more underrepresented in the legal profession, also began to rise gradually to about 25 per cent in 1988. However, by the 2000s it was commonplace for there to be equal numbers of men and women entering law school. This rise in the number of black law students in the 1980s was made possible by the government's undertaking to finance university education through the provision of student grants. Because of Austin's connections with regional liberation movements, SWAPO and the ANC also began sending their members to study law in Zimbabwe.

New expatriate members of staff were hired to teach in the Law School, including Doris Galen (who had studied law at Yale) and Shadrach Gutto (a leftist Kenyan academic who had fled after criticising the government). A staff development programme was also established, and promising young law graduates were sent to study abroad and return to teach, including Mary Maboreke and Welshman Ncube (University of Oslo), Pearson Nherere and Arthur Manase (University of Cambridge), and Shepherd Nzombe and Lawrence Tshuma (University of London). These new members of staff brought novel pedagogical and ideological approaches to teaching law, enhancing the intellectual environment. Whereas 'black letter' law had been the dominant approach since the establishment of the Law School, the 1980s saw the introduction of the 'law in context' approach and Marxist pedagogy.

Feminist legal scholarship also flourished during this period. Law lecturers like Julie Stewart became closely involved in drafting important laws, such as the 1984 Legal Age of Majority Act, which enshrined the equal status of women in law.[8] The law school was involved in important litigation, such as the 1984 test case *Katekwe v Muchabaiwa* (SC 87/84), which affirmed 18 as the age of majority for women. In addition, the Women in Law Southern Africa initiative fostered research on the gap between women's new legal rights and their lived reality.[9] This research also increasingly paid attention to the intersections of race, class, and gender. Owing to all these efforts, by the early 1990s Women's Law had emerged as a distinct legal field, complete with its own Centre offering graduate degrees to a student body drawn from Southern and Eastern Africa.

Although the new government had introduced important progressive changes to laws governing the society and economy, in politics it emulated the previous settler governments by deploying a discourse of law and order to criminalise opponents. Every six months between 1980 and 1990 the government renewed the nationwide state of emergency, which had been declared by the settler government in 1965. Between 1982 and 1987 thousands of citizens were abducted, tortured, maimed and killed as the ZANU PF government sought to crush its major opponent, PF ZAPU.

---

[7] ZAPU was one of the two main nationalist parties participating in the anti-colonial struggle.
[8] Interview with Julie Stewart, Harare, 12 April 2011.
[9] Interview with Amy Tsanga, Harare, 15 May 2014.

Given that the new government was actively using the repressive laws inherited from the era of settler rule to neutralise political opponents, it was not long before members of the Law School began to scrutinise it. Journals such as the *Zimbabwe Law Review* and the *Legal Forum* became venues for criticising the government's legal practices. This was not confined to academic scholarship. Many lecturers and students remember the Law School of the 1980s and 1990s as deeply engaged in the political debates exercising the country.[10] It is no surprise, therefore, that lawyers were at the forefront of the influential civil society organisations and coalitions that played an important role in Zimbabwean politics during the 1990s and after.

LSZ's engagement with the state in the 1980s was shaped by the 'political embeddedness' of many senior African lawyers, whose long-standing relationships with the nationalist movements made them reluctant to publicly criticise the government. This approach was exemplified by the Council's response to the behaviour of the Minister Home Affairs, Herbert Ushewokunze, who had openly criticised judges who quashed his detention orders and had ordered the re-detention of individuals acquitted by the courts. After a lengthy debate about Ushewokunze during their September 1983 meeting, the Council agreed:

> it was the duty of the Law Society to uphold the rule of law and that even if there were differing views as to how this should be applied, the Council was obliged to uphold the authority of the courts and criticise action which tended to abrogate the rule of law.[11]

They resolved to raise these matters privately with the Minister of Justice. At the November meeting the Council discussed a High Court ruling which found that the police were obtaining statements through torture; but the Council decided against issuing a press statement. Instead, David Zamchiya, a Council member and senior ZANU PF official, was asked to raise the Council's concerns privately with Ministers Mubako and Zvobgo (who was the Minister of Labour and a lawyer) during a conference trip to Australia. In a candid but amicable meeting in December 1983, the Council voiced its concerns to Mubako.[12]

The most public clash between the legal profession and the government was occasioned by a series of judicial rulings during the late 1980s exposing the incompatibility between punishments prescribed by law (such as corporal punishment, solitary confinement and spare diet) and Section 15(1) of the Bill of Rights stipulating that 'No person shall be subjected to torture or to inhuman or degrading punishment or other such treatment'. The issue came to a head in the 1990 Supreme Court challenge to the constitutionality of hanging. The new Chief Justice, Antony Gubbay, duly instructed lawyers on both sides to prepare arguments on the matter (Karekwaivanane 2017: 211). However, the executive pre-empted the hearing by commuting the sentences of several death row prisoners to life imprisonment and then had Parliament pass Constitutional Amendment 11, which declared that male corporal punishment for juveniles and execution by hanging were not inhuman or degrading punishments. The Amendment also empowered the government to

---

[10] Interview with Welshman Ncube, Bulawayo, 1 August 2013.
[11] Sibanda Private Archives File: Law Society 1983, Law Society Minutes, 5 September 1983.
[12] Sibanda Private Archives File: Law Society Minutes, 12 December 1983.

compulsorily acquire land and withdrew the courts' authority to determine the quantity and timing of payments for expropriated land.

Justice Gubbay made his disapproval clear when he reaffirmed the role of judges in defending the Constitution in his speech to mark the opening of the 1991 Legal Year (Gubbay 1991: 7). This provoked a stern response from the executive. The Attorney General assailed the remarks as 'unwarranted', pointing out that 'the issue of validity or otherwise of the Constitutional Amendment Bill (No 11) was not before the courts and yet one is left with no doubt that a judgement has already been delivered'.[13] President Mugabe condemned the Chief Justice's comments as 'political', asserting that 'the work of judges is to interpret the law and not to make it' and ending with an indirect invitation to Gubbay to resign.[14]

These actions and subsequent government statements sparked an outcry from the legal fraternity. Among the first to defend judicial independence and human rights were former Chief Justice Enoch Dumbutshena (1991) and the Catholic Commission for Justice and Peace (1991). LSZ (1991) also published a strongly worded press release criticising the government's actions, as did the Law Faculty. Although many of the speakers supported judicial independence in principle, there were different opinions about human rights and judicial activism. The Law Faculty (1991) took a much more nuanced position. On one hand, it underscored the need to 'safeguard internationally recognised rights of the individual' and criticised the amendments seeking to reinstate punishments the courts had found violated the Bill of Rights. On the other, it took issue with the Constitution's articles on land ownership, arguing that they 'safeguard individual rights at the expense of the broader interests of the community as a whole'. Reflecting the leftist influences in the law school, the statement expressed support for the amendment allowing the government to compulsorily acquire land, contending that the previous constitutional provisions 'sought to perpetuate the grossly inequitable pattern of land distribution which existed before independence'.

The editorial in the *Legal Forum* also defended human rights and judicial independence but questioned the wisdom of Justice Gubbay's public remarks, which put his impartiality in doubt should the matter come before the courts. Ben Hlatshwayo (1991–92), a Law School lecturer, felt that in making an argument for the role of the judiciary in development, the Chief Justice had transgressed the acceptable boundaries of judicial activism, which should be limited to defending constitutional rights. This coalescence of voices was not necessarily a conscious effort to build alliances across the legal profession and mobilise against the amendment. Rather, the government's actions had provoked an important debate within the profession about judicial independence, human rights and judicial activism.

IV. THE 1990S AND THE BROADENING OF CIVIC SPACE

Although the 1990s began with a near constitutional crisis, much of the decade was characterised by relative political stability, especially when compared to the 1980s, which

---

[13] *The Herald*, 16 January 1991.
[14] *The Herald*, 18 January 1991.

had witnessed state-directed massacres in Matabeleland, or indeed the post-2000 period, which saw the country sink into deep intractable political, economic and social crises. This stability had two important consequences for the legal profession. First, it allowed legal practitioners to maintain an inward focus. Second, it facilitated the broadening of civic space and the entry of lawyers into human rights work.

Private practitioners, represented by LSZ, were largely inward looking, concerned with managing the profession's own affairs and liaising with the government on matters affecting them, such as the administration of the law. The growth of the profession led to a corresponding increase in LSZ's administrative work and the expansion of its secretariat. In the early 1990s LSZ had about 200 members, but this number quickly rose to 350 in 1994 and 550 by 1998.[15] With a total of about 1,200 lawyers under its disciplinary oversight by 1998, LSZ faced a significant challenge in handling cases of misconduct. 'Domestic business' (ie disciplinary matters) routinely occupied more than half the space in Council minutes. While this partly reflected the need to closely document the Council's deliberations in these matters, it also attested to the rising number of cases, such as misappropriation of trust funds. Interviews with former LSZ officials from this period also suggested that disciplinary problems had multiplied faster than the number of lawyers.[16] The sensitivity of these cases was compounded by the fact that several were covered by the national media, bringing the profession into disrepute. Many senior legal professionals blamed the problem on the shortening of apprenticeship from three years to one, maintaining that, while this eased access for previously disadvantaged groups, it compromised the standard of service offered by some legal practitioners. These concerns ultimately led to the gazetting of Statutory Instrument 137 of 1999, which restored the length of pupillage to three years.[17]

Where relations with the government were concerned, LSZ continued to prefer private meetings with government officials to public confrontations. For much of the 1980s and 1990s, LSZ carefully cultivated its relationship with the government, as shown by the fact that one of the Council's permanent sub-committees was the Ministry Liaison Committee, whose members met regularly with officials from the Ministry of Justice, Legal and Parliamentary Affairs. These meetings discussed matters relating to the operations of the legal system, from High Court staffing problems to government requests for lawyers to serve as presiding officers on the newly-established Small Claims Courts. The Council also held luncheons and dinners with senior officials, such as the Chief Justice, Minister of Justice, and Permanent Secretary, which often became occasions to raise the legal profession's concerns in a relaxed atmosphere. The Council also organised cocktail parties when judges were appointed to or retired from the bench. Examination of the Council's activities during the 1990s reveals its skill at cultivating social capital, which could later be used to obtain favourable government policies.

Despite its cautious approach, LSZ confronted a government that tolerated no challenge to its authority. This emerged very clearly in the exchanges between LSZ

---

[15] LSZ Archives FILE – Society Signed Minutes 1994–2002, LSZ Minutes of a Special General Meeting held in Harare on 12 November 1998.
[16] Interview with Chihambakwe, Harare 15 March 2009
[17] *Sunday Mail*, 21 June 1998.

and the government over the gazetting of the Presidential Powers Regulations (Sales in Execution) in 1994. These empowered the government to intervene in legal proceedings between creditors and debtors 'to ensure that owners/occupiers of residential properties are not rendered homeless' if judgment were entered against them. The LSZ Council took the view that such government intervention would violate due process of law, potentially undermining the authority of the courts and the interests of creditors. The Council thus wrote to the then Minister of Justice, Emmerson Mnangagwa, who was tasked with administering the regulations. His acerbic response revealed the limits of LSZ's quiet diplomacy. After emphatically rejecting its concerns point by point, Mnangagwa concluded:

> You have been afforded that courtesy of a detailed reply so that the record can be set straight with regard to baseless accusations firstly as to government's intentions and secondly as to the consequences of the regulations. It is my considered view that nothing of substance, from either a factual or legal viewpoint, has been raised which merits considerations.[18]

When the Council discussed the letter in September, it appeared to have been suitably chastised, agreeing that its President and Canaan Dube (a Council member related to Mnangagwa) should arrange to meet Mnangagwa in order to 'convey the message the Law Society is not trying to seek confrontation with him or the Ministry, but that the aim is to point out areas where the Law Society has some concern'.[19]

Perhaps the most significant development during the 1990s was the strengthening of a human rights ethos, which led to the formation of lawyers' organisations devoted to promoting and defending human rights. These included the Zimbabwe Women Lawyers Association (ZWLA 1992), Zimbabwe Lawyers for Human Rights (ZLHR 1996), and Zimbabwe Human Rights NGO Forum (established to provide legal counsel to victims of state torture in the aftermath of the 1998 food riots, in which well over 2,500 people were arrested). These organisations supplemented their predecessors: the Legal Resources Foundation (LRF, 1984) and the Catholic Commission for Justice and Peace (CCJP, 1972). Aside from their championing of human rights, the importance of these organisations also lay in the fact that they provided legal aid, which was otherwise poorly funded and extremely limited. In the 1980s legal aid was primarily offered by the Legal Aid Clinic of the Law Faculty and the Citizens Advice Bureau (Austin 1987: 173). This was later complemented by the LRF's paralegal programme, which began in the mid-1980s. In addition to these services, private practitioners were required to provide compulsory *Pro Deo* and *in forma pauperis* services.

The formation of these human rights organisations is explained, in part, by the Marxist pedagogy that became prominent during the 1980s. Although it was ultimately disavowed, it had an enduring impact and equipped lawyers to critique the ZANU PF government's repressive uses of the law. Another important factor contributing to the emergence of human rights organisations was the relative political calm during much of the 1990s. Whereas the 1980s had witnessed ZANU PF's brutal and

---

[18] LSZ Archives FILE – Society Signed Minutes 1994–2002, Letter from the Minister of Justice ED Mnangangwa to LSZ Secretary BD Brighton, 21 August 1994.
[19] LSZ Archives FILE – Society Signed Minutes 1994–2002, LSZ Council Minutes, 12 September 1994.

sustained crackdown on PF ZAPU, the early to mid-1990s were much more stable, due partly to the 1987 unity accord, which effectively led to the absorption of PF ZAPU into ZANU PF, creating a *de facto* one-party state. This, in turn, reduced the political insecurity of ZANU PF, which had been a significant stimulus for the 1980s repression, leading to greater tolerance of civic organisations. This period also saw the emergence of civil society coalitions, such as the National Constitutional Assembly (NCA) in 1997, and the formation of the opposition party Movement for Democratic Change (MDC) in 1999.

The local political context was complemented by external influences. The entire African continent was witnessing what scholars have called a 'democratic wave', which supplanted military regimes, personal dictatorships, and one-party states (Bratton and Van de Valle 1994). In neighbouring Zambia, for example, pressure from labour and religious organisations led to multi-party elections in 1991, ending the rule of Kenneth Kaunda, who had been in office since independence in 1964 (Bayliss and Szeftel 1992). These developments in Zambia and other African countries had a 'demonstration effect' in Zimbabwe, helping to fuel the growing assertiveness of civil society organisations. One example was the NCA, a coalition of civil society organisations seeking a new constitution to replace the one that had been negotiated on the eve of independence (Dorman 2003). They maintained that because this 'ceasefire document' no longer expressed the people's aspirations, a consultative process was required to write a new constitution. The government sought to seize the initiative by establishing a Constitutional Commission, whose draft constitution was submitted to a referendum in February 2000. Because this preserved the executive president, which the public had explicitly rejected during the consultations, the NCA successfully campaigned against it. This first significant political defeat in a plebiscite since independence provoked ZANU PF to resume its repressive politics.

At the global level, the end of the Cold War and the increased legitimacy and currency of human rights discourse was conducive to the rise of lawyers' organisations focused on human rights. This helps explain the growing prominence of human rights within Zimbabwean civil society and the increased frequency of high-profile events such as the 1991 Commonwealth Africa Human Rights Conference, the 1994 Human Rights Conference in Victoria Falls convened by the LRF and CCJP, and the 1997 public march on International Human Rights Day by 100 ZLHR members who defied police repression to exercise their freedoms of assembly and expression.

The formation of ZWLA was the result of this confluence of factors, along with others specific to women and law. These included the increasing numbers of women who were studying or practising law, the growth of research and teaching about women's law, the networks established with feminist organisations around the world through the International Federation for Women Lawyers, and the pressing need to implement the progressive legal changes in women's status, which had been effected in the 1980s.

Because the transformation of the legal profession during the 1980s had focused on removing racial entry barriers, it became clear by the 1990s that more had to be done to dismantle formal and informal gender barriers, both within the profession and in the larger society. One of these was the common perception among lawyers that private practice was too demanding for women, who were better suited for work in the civil service as prosecutors or magistrates.[20] A second obstacle was clients' gendered stereotypes. Whereas prior to independence black lawyers struggled to get white clients, who believed them to be less competent than white lawyers, after independence it was primarily black women lawyers who had to fight the perception that they were less competent than their male counterparts. As a result, many black women who entered private practice in the 1980s and early 1990s found themselves serving mainly female clients, whose concerns dealt mostly with family law issues such as child custody, divorce, and abusive partners.

It was this environment that prompted a group of lawyers, including Virginia Mudimu, Elizabeth Gwaunza, Sara Moyo and Catherine Msipa, to discuss creating what would become ZWLA. Their efforts were supported by two organisations interested in women's law: Women in Law and Development Africa and Women in Law Southern Africa. The invitation to the first meeting on 7 November 1992 highlighted both the inward and outward foci of the proposed organisation: 'Because of their training and knowledge of the law, women lawyers have great potential to help not only themselves as women, but many of their less privileged sisters as well'.[21] Over the next three years this two-pronged focus was elaborated and finally incorporated in the Notarial Deed of Trust registered on 27 June 1996. Section 6 listed ZWLA main objectives:

(a) To promote and enhance the legal status and rights of women and children in Zimbabwe
(b) To provide legal advice and assistance to women and children
(c) To contribute to legal research and legal publications:
(d) To promote public legal education
(e) To initiate law reform and to propose, promote or oppose legislation
(f) To any projects [sic] and to support any organisations or institutions, which promote and enhance the legal status and rights of women and children in Zimbabwe.
(g) To promote the professional interests of women lawyers in Zimbabwe
(h) To engage in or provide assistance for any related activities which in the opinion of the trustees are likely to further the interests of law and justice in Zimbabwe.[22]

ZWLA opened its office in a building occupied by the Feminist Study Centre in the affluent suburb of Milton Park and began providing legal aid to women, including giving advice, drafting court papers, and providing representation in court. However, a 1997 evaluation of the association's work resulted in a move to the less affluent suburb of Highfield, where the need for legal aid was greater and the office more accessible to indigent women.[23] Soon thereafter ZWLA established an advocacy unit focused on lobbying for changes to constitutional provisions that impaired women's rights. A central objective was the repeal of parts of section 23 dealing with protection against discrimination. Although subsection 1(a) clearly stated that 'no law shall make any provision that is discriminatory either of itself or in its effect', this was undermined by subsection 3(b) exempting the application of African customary law. Women activists found this especially troubling because much discrimination against women was justified on the grounds of custom.

---

[20] Interview with Rita Makarau, Harare, 11 June 2014.
[21] Zimbabwean Women Lawyers Association (ZWLA) Archives, FILE – ZWLA Launch Trust and Constitution, Letter from E Gwaunza and P Maramba to Women lawyers, 22 October 1992.
[22] ZWLA Archives FILE – ZWLA Launch Trust and Constitution, Notarial Deed of Trust 27 June 1996.
[23] ZWLA Archives FILE – ZWLA Launch Trust and Constitution, ZWLA Strategic Plan 2002.

ZWLA therefore worked to establish a coalition of women's organisations to encourage women to participate in the constitution-making process of the late 1990s and press for changes in those provisions.

V. FROM CONFRONTATION TO RAPPROCHEMENT: THE POST-2000 PERIOD

If the 1990s were a period of relative political stability, the post-2000 years were marked by crisis. In the months leading up to the February 2000 constitutional referendum, the Movement for Democratic Change joined forces with the NCA and successfully campaigned for the rejection of the government's draft constitution. In June 2000 the MDC proceeded to win 57 out of the 120 Parliamentary seats and challenged the results in another 37. Within a year of its formation the MDC had not only achieved what no other opposition party had been able to do since independence but also was poised to relegate ZANU PF to the status of an opposition party. This very real political threat led to a determined effort by ZANU PF to retain power at all costs, aggressively violating human rights, the rule of law, and judicial independence.

As lawyers inevitably became involved in litigating against these blatant abuses, LSZ was drawn into the political struggles convulsing the body politic and progressively became more active in championing the rule of law, human rights and judicial independence. It used four main strategies: issuing public statements criticising the government's actions, mounting legal challenges to specific laws or actions, defying government directives, and engaging in street protests. Media accounts of LSZ actions portray it as a fearless and assertive advocate for the rule of law, judicial independence, and human rights. The Council's minutes, however, reveal considerable apprehensiveness about confronting the state. LSZ, which had been more accustomed to leading charm offensives, agonised over assuming the new role of publicly holding the government to account and chose to tread carefully. As a result, the Council rejected several proposals to hold protests or issue public statements. The Law Society's caution was also evident in its 2001 decision not to pursue a disciplinary case against the former Attorney General, Patrick Chinamasa, then serving as Minister of Justice.[24] Indeed, in September 2006 the Council resolved: 'LSZ will from now on have greater engagement with the Ministry of Justice before naming and shaming any in respect of any undesirable public policy issue that affects human rights'.[25] While I do not want to deprecate LSZ's efforts to hold the government accountable, it is illuminating to contrast the greater assertiveness of Bar Associations in other African countries, such as Zambia and Tunisia.

Part of the reason for LSZ's caution was government pushback. In December 2000, the Law Society had issued a public statement criticising President Mugabe's executive order nullifying all legal challenges to the results of the June 2000 Parliamentary election. In response, Information Minister Jonathan Moyo indicated the government would consider taking steps to amend the Legal Practitioner's Act to prevent lawyers from using the professional association as a political platform. This allegation – that LSZ leaders were making the organisation an instrument for opposition politics – became the

---

[24] LSZ Archives FILE – Law Society Signed Minutes April 01 – Aug 04, LSZ Council Minutes, 25 June 2001.
[25] LSZ Archives FILE – Council Meetings Dec 06 – April 08, LSZ Council Minutes, 25 September 2006.

government's constant refrain, underlying at least 30 articles attacking LSZ published by government-controlled newspapers between 2006 and 2008.

Matters came to a head in August 2007, when the Law Society responded to hyperinflation by raising its tariffs in direct defiance of a government directive mandating a national price freeze. The government seriously considered amending the Legal Practitioners Act in order to clip the Law Society's wings. At the same time a group of 'senior lawyers' sympathetic to the ZANU PF government began making moves to change the Society's direction. After a private discussion at the offices of Simplicius Chihambakwe, the group secured a meeting with the Law Society President, Beatrice Mtetwa, which had two important outcomes.[26] First, the lawyers emphasised that the government was prepared to undermine the independence of the legal profession if the Law Society continued on what the government viewed as a 'confrontational' path. Second, the lawyers distinguished between what they called LSZ's legally mandated regulatory functions and its inappropriate human rights advocacy. This distinction would establish the terms of subsequent debates within the profession about the Law Society's role.

After this episode the Society became deeply concerned about protecting its independence from the government. It was also clear that the legal profession had not been spared the deep political polarisation dividing the country. The Society ultimately decided to focus on the regulatory function and leave human rights advocacy to organisations like ZLHR. LSZ also sought rapprochement with the government by actively participating in the constitutional drafting process and organising a forum in which judges and senior lawyers could interact and defuse the tensions between them. These efforts were initiated by the next LSZ President, Josphat Tshuma, and continued by his successor, Tinoziva Bere, who declared at the end of his term in December 2012:

> Law Society of Zimbabwe is now back to its traditional role. It has not been easy but we are pleased that the improving environment has released us from over commitment to human rights and rule of law. It has made it possible for us to strengthen the profession from its centre ....[27]

This rapprochement was facilitated by the fact that the political environment became less charged during the national unity government from late 2008 to mid-2013. But though there was some relief among lawyers, even those who strongly defended human rights, it would be inaccurate to suggest that the Law Society had simply capitulated to pressure. In fact, in 2009 lawyers staged a public demonstration against the government's harassment of colleagues who were just doing their job.

Aside from the clashes between LSZ and the state, the post-2000 years also witnessed important struggles to define the boundaries of the profession, in terms of who could enter the profession and who could provide legal services. Efforts to establish a second law school at the Great Zimbabwe University in 2004 were abortive. The Council for Legal Education refused to grant official recognition to the law degree after its fact-finding mission discovered that the university had enrolled 320 students despite lacking sufficient textbooks, lecturers, law reports and lecture rooms.[28] In the meantime Midlands State

---

[26] LSZ Archives FILE – Council Meetings Dec 06- April 08, Minutes of the Meeting between the LSZ President and Senior Lawyers on 25 August 2007.
[27] T Bere, LSZ President's Report, December 2012.
[28] LSZ Archives FILE – Law Society Signed Minutes April 01 – Aug 04, LSZ Council Minutes, 3 May 2004.

University introduced a law degree in 2007, ending the dominance of the University of Zimbabwe as the sole provider of legal training in the country. The Great Zimbabwe University law school was re-opened in 2014. However, efforts by a disbarred lawyer to establish a college awarding paralegal qualifications were blocked by LSZ, as were moves to launch legal aid societies offering legal services for a fixed monthly payment.

A persistent challenge for the profession has been the difficult economic environment since 2000, a period characterised by high inflation, company closures throughout the economy and high unemployment. All but the largest law firms have struggled to attract business. It is not uncommon for law firms to struggle to pay salaries on time. One important consequence has been the emergence of the 'rent a chair' practice, which has altered the traditional partnership structure of law firms. The LSZ Secretary forcefully addressed this in the Society's February 2012 newsletter:

> The rent a chair craze, whilst a viable and acceptable business form for hair salons, is certainly unlawful and not an acceptable business structure for law firms. We are disturbed to note that a number of emerging law firms are adopting the rent a chair business form. A law firm is a legal partnership. It is not a loose association of lawyers where every lawyer eats what he kills.[29]

Notwithstanding LSZ's firm stance, the practice has persisted due to the tough economic environment.

VI. CONCLUSION

Since 1980 the Zimbabwean legal profession has undergone substantial changes shaped by the interplay between local, continental and global processes. Although local political processes were the primary drivers, the transnational movement of people and legal ideas also played a role, as attested by the rise of human rights organisations and the constitutional reform movement in the 1990s. The manifold dimensions of transformation documented in this chapter, from the content of legal education to the composition of the profession, and the nature of its engagement with the state, were often characterised by ambiguity. For example, although the Legal Practitioners Act of 1981 granted the profession a significant degree of autonomy, it also gave the state mechanisms with which to rein in lawyers should it choose to do so. In addition, while racial entry barriers were progressively dismantled in the 1980s, gender barriers stubbornly persist. The process of change has sometimes been cyclical, as the profession revisited matters it had previously debated, such as the divided profession. Some senior lawyers who had favoured fusion in the 1980s now advocate for greater specialisation.[30] Whereas the fault-lines on this question during the 1980s often were racial, recently they have been generational, with junior lawyers objecting to re-introducing a divided profession on the ground that it would unfairly privilege senior lawyers. Although much has changed in the legal profession, some things have stayed the same. This is particularly the case for the geographical distribution and gender composition of private practitioners. Of the 1,160 lawyers in private practice in 2013, only 160 were women. And of the 415 law firms that year, 263 were

---

[29] Law Society of Zimbabwe Newsletter, February 2012.
[30] Interview with Mordecai Mahlangu, Harare, 8 August 2014.

based in Harare and 41 in Bulawayo, with the other 111 firms spread among 26 towns and cities.[31] Looking ahead, the coming years will see a stronger inward focus as LSZ continues its drive to revise legal education at local universities, and strengthen continuous professional development. Despite the increased overt and covert involvement of the military in national politics, the legal profession is unlikely to return to its vocal stance of the early 2000s. Instead, private representations to the relevant government authorities are likely to be the strategy of choice. The difficult economic environment in the country will remain an important challenge for the legal profession, which will influence the career choices of individual lawyers, the viability of law firms, and efforts by LSZ to protect lawyers' turf against organisations such as debt-collectors and legal aid societies.

REFERENCES

Adewoye, O (1982) *The Legal Profession in Nigeria 1865–1962* (Lagos, Longman).
Austin, R (1987) 'Access to Legal Education and the Profession in Zimbabwe' 5 *Zimbabwe Law Review* 172.
Bayliss, C and Szeftel, M (1992) 'The Fall and Rise of Multi-party Politics in Zambia' 19 *Review of African Political Economy* 54.
Bratton, M and Van de Valle, N (1994) 'Neopatrimonial Regimes and Political Transitions in Africa' 4 *World Politics* 453.
Catholic Commission for Justice and Peace (1991) 'Statement by the Catholic Commission for Justice and Peace in Zimbabwe on The Proposed Constitutional Amendment 9 November 1990' 3 *Legal Forum* 14.
Chanock, M (1999) 'The Lawyer's Self: Sketches on Establishing a Professional Identity in South Africa, 1900–1925' 1 *Law in Context* 59.
Currie, ME (1982) *The History of Gill, Godlonton and Gerrans, 1912–1980* (Harare).
Dorman, SR (2003) 'NGOs and the Constitutional Debate in Zimbabwe: From Inclusion to Exclusion' 29 *Journal of Southern African Studies* 845.
Dumbutshena, E (1991) 'Remarks made by the Honourable Dr E. Dumbutshena in his speech at the opening of the Dumbutshena Library and the Bulawayo Legal Projects Centre on 3 December 1990' 3 *Legal Forum* 12–13.
Faculty of Law, University of Zimbabwe (1991) 'Statement from the Faculty of Law of the University of Zimbabwe on the Constitution of Zimbabwe Amendment (No 11) Bill', 3 *Legal Forum* 16.
Feltoe, G (1978) 'Law, Ideology and Coercion in Southern Rhodesia' MPhil dissertation, University of Kent.
Government of Rhodesia (1971) *Report of the Courts of Inquiry Commission* (Salisbury, Government Printer).
Gubbay AR (1991) 'Speech delivered by the Chief Justice, The Honourable Mr Justice AR Gubbay at the Opening of the 1991 Legal year' 3 *Legal Forum* 7.
Hlatshwayo, B (1991–92) 'Judicial Activism and Development–Warning Signs from Zimbabwe' 9–10 *Zimbabwe Law Review* 11.
Karekwaivanane, GH (2017) *The Struggle over State Power in Zimbabwe: Law and Politics since 1950* (Cambridge, Cambridge University Press).
Law Society of Zimbabwe (1991) 'Press Statement by the Law Society of Zimbabwe' 3 *Legal Forum* 16.

---

[31] LSZ Annual Report 2013.

Legal Forum (1991) 'Editorial: The Role of the Government and the Courts in Relation to the Safeguarding of Fundamental Human Rights' 3 *Legal Forum* 2–4.

Michelson, E (2011) 'Lawyers, political embeddedness and institutional continuity in China's transition from Socialism' in Y Dezalay and B Garth (eds), *Lawyers and the Rule of Law in an Era of Globalization* (Abingdon, Routledge).

Mlambo, E (1972) *Rhodesia: Struggle for a Birthright* (London, C Hurst).

Palley, C (1966) *The Constitutional History and Law of Southern Rhodesia, 1888–1965* (London, Oxford University Press).

Part VI

North Africa and Middle East

28

Egypt
The Long Decline of the Legal Profession

NATHALIE BERNARD-MAUGIRON AND MENNA OMAR

I. INTRODUCTION

UNTIL THE END of the nineteenth century Egypt had no legal profession. According to Islamic jurisprudence (*fiqh*), the judge (*qadi*) questioned the parties and applied the law with the help of professional witnesses and specialists in *fiqh*.[1] Lawyers first appeared following the introduction of Western-style civil courts. A Bar Association was created by the European lawyers (French, Belgian, Italian and Swiss) practising before the Mixed Courts[2] in 1876, and an 1888 law established a register of qualified advocates (Hoyle 1985). In 1893, new advocates were required to have a diploma from an Egyptian or foreign law school (Hill 1979). In 1912 lawyers practising before the National Courts (created in 1883) established a Bar.[3] Their numbers had grown to 512 from 144 in 1888 (El-Tawil 2007). In 1916, lawyers practising before the traditional Sharia courts (with jurisdiction in matters of personal status among Muslims) also decided to create their own Bar Association (Reid 1974a).

In the first half of the twentieth century, law was the most prestigious profession and the first choice of middle and upper class Egyptians (Reid 1974b). Lawyers held high positions in government and Parliament and fought for national independence and the rule of law.[4] Many belonged to political parties, especially the Wafd Party.[5] Some believe that the 'legal elite' governed from 1882 to March 1954 (Al-Shalakany 2013).

---

[1] As early as 1845, however, a plaintiff could be represented by a proxy before the Alexandria Commercial Council (El-Tawil 2007).

[2] The Mixed Courts, modelled on French civil law, were created in 1875 to replace multiple consular jurisdictions. They handled civil and criminal litigation between Europeans of different nationalities or between Europeans and Egyptians, applying French-inspired codes and operating in French, Italian, Arabic, and (after 1905) English. They were abolished in 1949 and their cases transferred to the National Courts.

[3] National Courts had jurisdiction over civil and criminal litigation between Egyptians, except family law disputes.

[4] For instance, Saad Zaghloul, a lawyer, became Minister of Education and then Prime Minister and founded the Wafd Party. He was at the head of Egypt's delegation to the Paris Peace conference (1919), which demanded independence. The British government's decision to exile him triggered the Revolution of 1919, leading to independence in 1923.

[5] This nationalist and liberal party, then in the majority, struggled against British occupation and accused King Farouk of abusing his powers and violating the Constitution.

After the Revolution of 1952, however, the new regime was hostile to lawyers, judges and law professors. The Bar Association opposed most government decisions. Suffering from a decline in the quality of legal education, an increase in the number of practitioners, and political divisions within the Bar, the legal profession lost its prominent position within society.

The relationship between lawyers and judges has always been very tense: lawyers complain that judges despise and disrespect them and consider the judiciary a privileged profession appropriate only for middle class law graduates,[6] while judges complain that lawyers offend them. Judges view lawyers as 'assistants' rather than partners in the litigation process. Lawyers often demonstrate and strike when colleagues are imprisoned for offending the judiciary. The attack on a judge by a group of lawyers in Alexandria in 2005 was one cause of the revolt of the judiciary in 2005/06 (Ghamroun and Saghieh 2006; Bernard-Maugiron 2008). In 2010, lawyers went on strike when two of them trying to enter a prosecution office were charged with assault and sentenced to five years' imprisonment.

Successive authoritarian governments tried to control the Bar Association through legislation. Under Nasser, a new Advocates Law was adopted in 1958 (Law No 61). Sadat adopted Law No 125 of 1981, which was declared unconstitutional and replaced under Mubarak by the Advocates Law No 17 of 1983 (still in force), which regulates access to the profession, lawyers' rights and duties, and the Bar Association.

This chapter is divided into four parts: the evolution of legal practice; how legal education contributed to the decline of the profession; the Bar Association; and the role and status of lawyers under the different political regimes.

II. LEGAL PRACTICE

A. Historical Background

Before the establishment of the Bar Association in 1912, an 1888 regulation required those seeking to practise in the National Courts to pass an exam before a special admissions committee, which was criticised for its biased judgments (Ziadeh 1968: 41–42). In 1893, a new law required candidates to have a law degree in order to be inscribed in the register of advocates (now called 'lawyers' or *avocados, muhamum* in Arabic)[7] and prescribed their rights and duties. The 1912 Law (No 26) established the Bar Association and required a two-year training period before lawyers could appear in first instance courts and two years of practice there before they could plead in courts of appeal. It prohibited lawyers from engaging in other specified professions, created a disciplinary procedure, and allowed lawyers to be registered on a 'non-practising' list, while retaining their seniority, and resume practising law when they wished.

---

[6] Although judges are ostensibly recruited by competition, candidates do not have equal opportunities. Judicial appointments discriminate against the underprivileged, women and political opponents and favour judges' sons and relatives. Underprivileged law graduates have no alternative but to become lawyers.

[7] Because lawyers appearing before the Mixed Courts refused to let those in the National Courts be called 'lawyers', they had been called 'mandatories' (*ukala*').

Law No 135 of 1939 created rolls of trainee lawyers, first instance lawyers, appellate lawyers, and lawyers before the Court of Cassation, in addition to non-practitioners. Trainee lawyers with a PhD had to spend only one year training. To plead before first instance courts, lawyers had to attend two hearings a week at a summary court and lectures organised by the Bar and submit a certificate from the law firms where they had been trained, an official statement of the number of cases they had pleaded, and an official statement from the clerk of the court listing the hearings they attended. To register on the appeal roll they had to practise for three years as a first instance lawyer.[8] And to appear before the Court of Cassation they had to practise seven years before appeal courts.[9]

In 1944, Law No 98 empowered the Board of the Bar to place lawyers on the list of non-practitioners if they exercised a prohibited profession, and it regulated the activities trainee lawyers could and could not undertake. The number of registered lawyers needed to organise the General Assembly of the Bar increased from 100 in 1939 to 200 in 1944.[10]

After the 1952 Revolution Nasser adopted a new law in 1957 to organise the practice of law before the newly established State Council.[11] The quorum for a General Assembly of the Bar Association was 300, which shows that the number of lawyers was increasing.[12]

Law No 61 of 1968 allowed lawyers registered on the first instance roll to run for the Bar Association Board, but half its members had to be lawyers pleading before appeal and supreme courts, and only members of the Arab Socialist Union, the sole party, could run for the Board or presidency. In 1955, Sharia courts were abolished by Law No 462, their work was assigned to the National Courts, and Sharia lawyers were allowed to register at the Bar Association and plead in all matters before the National Courts.

B. Lawyers in the 1983 Advocate Law

The 1983 Advocates Law broadened the concept of 'lawyer', whose functions are not restricted to appearing before courts and investigative bodies but include 'providing opinions and legal advice' and 'formulating contracts and taking the necessary measures to declare and notarise them'. Anyone with a law degree who works as a private lawyer or for a public sector company can be registered. Lawyers in legal departments of banks and cooperative societies are also eligible for membership in the Bar Association. Only registered lawyers can practise. Non-lawyers cannot provide legal advice or draft contracts. Lawyers do not have to complete a training programme or pass an examination. Graduates from an Egyptian law school or equivalent foreign university who produce a letter from a lawyer accepting them as a trainee for two years may get a licence. Lawyers may not hold ministerial positions, engage in commerce, serve on the Board of a commercial company, or occupy any public office except in legal departments or universities and may not belong to other professional associations.

---

[8] Art 17 of Law No 135 of 1939.
[9] Art 19 of Law No 135 of 1939.
[10] Art 72 of Law No 135 of 1939 and Art 71 of Law No 98 of 1944.
[11] The State Council, created by Law No 112 of 1946, adjudicates suits and claims against administrative authorities. It includes the Court of Administrative Justice and the Supreme Administrative Court.
[12] Art 72 of Law No 96 of 1957.

Applications for registration are submitted to an admissions committee chaired by the dean of the Bar Association or secretary general and composed of four lawyers chosen by the Board; decisions may be appealed to the Cairo Court of Appeals.[13] The committee reviews the rolls annually to see if anyone should be transferred to the roll of non-practitioners.

Lawyers from middle- or upper-class backgrounds with good connections can be trained in large law firms or the legal department of a foreign company. Some trainee lawyers will be paid, usually in well-known firms, but ordinary law firms may not pay or will cover only transportation costs. Trainees working in a corporate firm will assist in drafting contracts and registering companies. Those in a litigation firm will assist in preparing cases, drafting memos, or doing paperwork in court. Only a few senior lawyers have the ability, time and patience to engage in serious training. Every lawyer admitted to plead before courts of appeal or supreme courts should accept at least one trainee.

In 2017, the bar association Board decided that trainees who had not served their full two years would complete training in the newly created 'Advocates Institute' and pass exams in order to practise before first instance courts. This new requirement sought to reduce the number of practitioners.

After five years of practice, a lawyer may appear before courts of appeal and the Court of Administrative Justice and after ten years may plead before the Court of Cassation, the Supreme Administrative Court and the Supreme Constitutional Court. Judges can be members of the Bar Association on the 'non-practising list', but only practising lawyers can vote in Bar Association elections.

C. Rights and Duties of Lawyers

The Advocates Law guarantees the citizen's right to defence, including lawyers' right not to be responsible for matters contained in their pleadings. Bar Association branches are directed to create legal assistance committees and assign lawyers to defend indigents without cost, though this has not happened, and there is no culture of pro bono work.

Lawyers should be treated respectfully and investigated only by the public prosecutor, with notice to the branch Bar Association. Lawyers may not be arrested or detained because of written or oral statements made during their practice or for performing their professional duties.

Lawyers must pursue the best interests of their clients, to whom they owe a duty of confidentiality. A lawyer who violates the duties of the profession or commits acts affecting the integrity of the profession or damaging its reputation is liable to be disciplined. Such a lawyer is entitled to be defended by another lawyer. Disciplinary proceedings are confidential, and decisions may not be published. Penalties range from a warning to permanent disbarment. Decisions may be appealed to the Boards of the branch and central Bar Associations. The public prosecutor and the convicted lawyer may challenge decisions of the disciplinary council within 15 days before a Board composed of four counsellors of the Court of Cassation appointed annually by its General Assembly and the Bar Association's dean or secretary-general and two Board members.

---

[13] The committee is not known to have denied an application that fulfilled the required conditions.

D. Lawyers in Practice

Many law graduates belong to the Bar Association, even though they do not practise, in order to benefit from its health insurance and pension (Omar 2017).[14] Because of the heavy costs of these schemes, the Bar Association has debated eliminating non-practising lawyers from its membership.

The number of lawyers grew slowly from 582 when the Bar Association was established in 1912 to 1,959 in 1930 and 4,433 in 1949 (Tawil 2007). In 2013, more than 700,000 lawyers were registered with the Bar Association (Omar 2017). Although a small minority work for large law firms and are well-paid, most are generalists in small law offices, who earn little (IBAHRI 2011). In the 1980s, lawyers benefited from the regime's economic reform as privatisation opened the door for commercial legal services. In addition, Egyptian law firms collaborated with American and British firms for international transactions (Mostafa 2007).

The increase in the number of law students has led to a decline in the quality of their education, which already was low because of the lack of a training institute. Furthermore, graduates from the Faculty of Law and Sharia at the al-Azhar University[15] can enroll in the Bar Association or become prosecutors and judges even though they have not completed a comprehensive course in Egyptian state law (Al-Shalakany 2013).

The social and professional diversity among lawyers prevents cohesion and engenders struggles between groups defending their interests, such as public and private sector lawyers or large and small firm lawyers. Men outnumber women, most of whom perform office work and avoid litigation, prosecution offices and government departments (Tawil 2007).

In 1969, the State Council's Fatwa and Legislation Department declared:

> [P]ractising law is not a condition for registration in the rolls of practitioners. Rather, registration in this roll is the condition for practising law; it is a precondition for practising the profession and necessary before beginning practice.[16]

Therefore, lawyers' registrations remain valid as long as they pay their contributions, do not violate their professional duties, and do not practise an incompatible profession (Omar 2017).

For years, calls have been multiplying to reduce the number of lawyers and 'clean' the Bar Association's roll. Starting in 2008, candidates for the Board have complained that members who died or emigrated were still registered and non-practising lawyers participated in the elections (Omar 2017). Finally, in 2012, the Board decided to raise the fees for first-time memberships from EGP 1,200 to EGP 3,500 (then US$200 to US$600) in order to improve the Bar's finances and reduce the number of applications. However, some lawyers sued in the Court of Administrative Justice, which stayed the decision because it was issued by the Board rather than the General Assembly, violating the association's

---

[14] The numbers registered in the health care programme were 160,224 in 2017 and 153,036 in 2018 (see the Bar Association website at www.egyls.com).
[15] Al-Azhar is a Sunni Islam mosque and university to which a national network of schools (Azhari schools) is attached.
[16] See legal opinion No 1184, 30 December 1969, session of 24 December 1969.

bye-laws.[17] The Board then decided to close the door to registration, but the Court of Administrative Justice stayed that decision as well (Omar 2017).

In 2015, despite the decision of the State Council's Fatwa and Legislation Department, the Bar Association Board required lawyers to submit evidence of their engagement in the profession (such as powers of attorneys, minutes of hearings, etc) in order to benefit from health services. In November 2016, lawyers were required to submit evidence of engagement[18] from 2013 to 2016 to renew their membership for 2017 or change their level of registration (eg from first instance to appellate lawyer) (Omar 2017). Several lawyers condemned this decision, arguing that many practise in firms where only the names of senior lawyers appear on powers of attorneys, many do legal work for companies or individuals, and some could not work in a given year. The Bar Association agreed to exempt lawyers on the general roll (trainee lawyers) from having to submit evidence of engagement to renew their membership, allowed the submission of other documents as evidence, and permitted lawyers who could not find a document for one year to present two for another (Omar 2017). When a group of lawyers decided to challenge the decision, the Court of Administrative Justice stayed execution and referred the case to its Board of State Commissioners.[19] The Court emphasised that the concept of lawyering work varied with the level of registration, the law did not require attorneys to demonstrate actual work, and the five-year requirement applied only to the appellate roll. It held that the Bar's decision deprived lawyers of the right to practise without a legal basis or disciplinary decision and violated the right to work guaranteed by the 2014 Constitution (Omar 2017).

When the Bar Association appealed the ruling, the Supreme Administrative Court confirmed the ruling of the Court of Administrative Justice, holding that only the dean was empowered to make the decision, not the Board or the admission committee.[20] It also held that the new requirements were not authorised by the Advocates Law, which allowed lawyers to be deprived of their licences only if they engaged in an incompatible profession or committed an offence. Claiming that this judgment contradicted previous State Council decisions, the Bar challenged it in another State Council circuit. Meanwhile, the Bar cancelled its 2017 decision and issued a new one requiring lawyers to submit a certificate of all their travels during the previous 10 years (to make sure they did not live abroad), a certificate that they did not have medical insurance from a public or private sector job, a copy of their tax file, and proof they had performed at least four of the legal acts listed in Article 3 of the Advocates Law (or two and two powers of attorney). The number of registrations dropped from 350,000 in 2016 to 146,409 in 2017 and 123,340 as of April 2018, indicating that the new requirements had succeeded in reducing the number of registered lawyers.[21]

---

[17] Court of Administrative Justice, case No 59787, year 66, 30 September 2012.
[18] Such as an official copy of an administrative record, an expert report, a prosecution interrogation the lawyer attended, a statement of claim, an official court attestation of the number of cases filed in the lawyer's name each year, an official copy of a contract, or the minutes of a hearing (see Guide to Bar's Membership and Medical Insurance for 2017, published on the Egyptian Bar Association's website, 4 January 2017).
[19] Court of Administrative Justice, Second Circuit, case No 15264, year 71q.
[20] Supreme Administrative Court, First Circuit, Case No 42623, year 63.
[21] See the Bar website. Lawyers pursuing graduate study abroad find it difficult to meet the new requirements.

E. Human Rights Lawyers

Both individual lawyers and human rights non-governmental organisations (NGOs) help citizens defend their rights against governmental bodies and officials (Mostafa 2008). The Center for Human Rights Legal Aid (CHRLA), founded in 1994, had filed 1,616 cases by 1997. Like all human rights groups in Egypt, CHRLA depends mainly on foreign funding. Because of legal restrictions, most human rights NGOs are registered as non-profit law firms, which can file lawsuits and conduct regular legal work. Their lawyers, both young and experienced, handle cases involving labour and social and economic rights in civil courts and appear in criminal court on behalf of demonstrators charged with 'demonstrating without a permit', 'disturbing the public order', or 'being part of an illegal group' (Omar 2016c). Some specialise exclusively in human rights, while others draft contracts or handle other civil or criminal cases to generate income for the firm.

Some human rights lawyers filed 'strategic litigation' cases in the State Council or Supreme Constitutional Court to invalidate administrative regulations and laws. The Egyptian Center for Economic and Social Rights, established in 2009 to empower the poor and advance economic and social rights, worked on cases seeking to annul contracts selling state lands or privatising public companies. The Hisham Mubarak Law Center, established in 1999, challenges human rights violations and laws incompatible with the Constitution, including cases concerning genital mutilation and the right of Egyptians living abroad to vote in elections after the Revolution. Other organisations are the Egyptian Initiative for Personal Rights and the Association for Freedom of Thought and Expression.

The fact that there are no other legal or political avenues for reform increases the importance of these cases, especially challenges before the Supreme Constitutional Court. But human rights lawyers also are subject to harassment, stigma and restrictions on their freedoms of expression and association (IBAHRI 2011). Some have been physically attacked and arrested. Many are accused by colleagues of engaging in political activities and seeking fame, and are blamed for the failure of police to respect lawyers. The Bar Association has not defended them, or fought to protect human rights or change laws.

III. LEGAL EDUCATION IN EGYPT[22]

Like other professions in Egypt, law was influenced by France. A School of Law and Administration, opened in 1868, was operated for more than 20 years by a Frenchman. It initially accepted students from public and Azhari high schools as well as from missionary schools, but after 1893 it admitted only public high school graduates.[23] The fact that they came from secular schools and studied foreign laws and languages at the School under the supervision of foreigners contributed to lawyers' prestige in the first half of the twentieth century (El-Tawil 2007). For the first two years students studied French,

---

[22] This section is based on unpublished research by Nathalie Bernard-Maugiron and Karim El-Chazli.
[23] Western missionaries opened Protestant and Catholic schools in Egypt in the mid-nineteenth century. About 200 of them still serve about 100,000 pupils, 55–60 per cent of whom are Muslim (Sidarouss 2011).

Arabic, history, geography, the judicial system and an introduction to procedural law; in the last three years they learned how to practise law. In 1925, the School became part of Cairo University. Law courses were introduced at the University of Alexandria in 1938, which opened a School of Law in 1942. The School of Law at Ain Shams University was established in 1950. Until 1960, law students had to pay fees, which only middle- and upper-class students could afford.[24]

In 1890, the Free School of Law was established by the French Government to train Egyptians for the newly created Mixed and National Courts. Students graduated with a 'licence' after three years but could not practise in the National Courts unless they obtained a degree in Sharia and Arabic. This school, which consolidated the influence of French law on the Egyptian legal and judicial systems, was abolished in 1931.

There are now 14 law schools in public universities.[25] Admission depends on the applicant's baccalaureate grade and place of residence. The Faculty of Law of Cairo University is the flagship institution. About 15 per cent of entrants complete the four-year degree.[26]

Egyptian law is also taught at the Faculty of Police and (in addition to Islamic law) at the Faculty of Sharia and Law of the University of al-Azhar. Law courses are also taught at the Sadat Academy and Faculties of Polytechnic, Commerce and Teacher Training. Since 2006, all faculties offer a human rights course in the first year.

Since 1961, the Egyptian government has committed itself to providing free higher education, but the rising population and low registration fees have led to growing university enrolment and overcrowded classrooms and auditoriums. The reduced fees increased access by poorer students to universities, especially law schools. The Faculty of Economics and Political Sciences was established in 1960 to train for the civil service, Parliament and the diplomatic corps, attracting students from middle and upper classes who could attain the necessary high grades at their baccalaureate level. By contrast, law schools (like faculties of literature or languages) are open to students with average results. Law faculties, therefore, have lost their prestige and produce too many lawyers from poorer backgrounds.

The quality of university students also is influenced by the dominant pedagogy, which demands rote learning and memorisation. Many teachers require students to purchase their course packs, which gives them additional financial resources. The number of students enrolled in law faculties, which had been the most selective, increased from nearly 180,000 in 1970 to over 550,000 in 1980. Professors often teach in an amphitheatre containing more than a thousand students, who generate an incessant hubbub, making lecture halls more a meeting place for men and women than a site of learning. Tutorial classes, when they exist, serve primarily to revise (or acquire) the lecture material. Law students are not trained to analyse cases. The exams only deal with previously announced questions, which require a good memory rather than a capacity for analysis and reflection. There is little use of practitioners.

---

[24] The School of Law and Administration, initially free, imposed a fee of EGP 15 in 1892, which rose to EGP 40 in the late 1940s, a large amount at the time (El-Tawil 2007).

[25] Cairo, Ain Shams, Alexandria, Assiut, Banha, Beni Suef, Helwan, Kafr al-Sheikh, Mansoura, Menoufiyya, South-Valley, Al-Sadat, Tanta, Zagazig.

[26] For instance, 237,458 students started law school in public universities in the academic year 2011/12 and only 36,153 graduated in 2015. The number graduating in earlier years was 44,811 in 2011, 44,308 in 2012, 50,991 in 2013, and 21,539 in 2014: *The Statistical Yearbook Book* (2017 edn) Education section, available online at www.capmas.gov.eg.

Advancement within the faculty positions is closely linked to the university hierarchy, which subordinates assistants to professors.[27] Some assistants work in their professor's law office, which both increases subordination and obstructs their ability to conduct academic work. Some assistants adopt a low profile, seeking to hide their ability so as not to be seen as competitors by their teachers, who could delay their advancement. Assistant positions are even left vacant to avoid competition in the distribution of courses.

Whereas law had long been offered only in public institutions, the private sector is starting to play a role. Since 2004, the American University of Cairo has had a Department of Law offering two graduate diplomas: an MA in International Human Rights Law and an LLM in Business Law and Comparative Law. At the end of 2006 a new private university, Pharos International University, was inaugurated in Alexandria with a Faculty of Law and International Legal Relations. Since 2016, the British University of Egypt has also had a Faculty of Law. Two of these teach the common law. All are very expensive, accessible only to the wealthy. Their graduates, trained in common law, will have a better chance of working for prestigious foreign law firms in Egypt or will travel and study abroad in American or British universities.

In 1995–96, Cairo University created an English section of courses on Egyptian law taught by Egyptians, leading to a diploma. In 1998, it created a French law degree programme in collaboration with the Universités of Paris I Panthéon-Sorbonne, Paris II Panthéon-Assas and Paris IX Dauphine, letting students study French and Egyptian Law and obtain 'licence' diplomas from both Université Paris I Pantheon-Sorbonne and Cairo University. This French law section is also preparing an LLM and since 2007, it has offered a master's degree in French law, funded by the French Ministry of Foreign Affairs and coordinated by a French law professor, leading to a degree in French law. A Francophone section of law was created in 2002 at the University of Ain Shams (the capital's second university) in partnership with Université Lyon 3 in France. About 50 French teachers make short visits each year. The French-language section of Alexandria, created in 2000, merged with Pierre Mendès France Université in Grenoble. Mansoura University also has English and French sections. These Anglophone and Francophone streams provide a higher quality of education, attracting students who had fled public law schools for more prestigious faculties like medicine or political science. Having mastered foreign languages and learned through different pedagogies, these students have greater opportunities to continue their studies abroad, after which many work for foreign law firms.

IV. THE BAR ASSOCIATION

The Bar Association, with headquarters in Cairo and 21 regional branches, is the largest in the Arab world and the largest professional association in Egypt. It monitors lawyers' competence and defends both their independence and interests. Because it guarantees the right to defence it has an obligation to provide legal aid for the needy and a lawyer for those

---

[27] At the bottom of the ladder is the assistant (*mu'id*), who must have an honours law degree, followed by the lecturer (*mudarris musa'id*), who must have a master's degree. Assistants and lecturers cannot be charged with teaching hours outside tutorial classes. A senior lecturer (*mudarris*) must have a PhD. A senior lecturer can be appointed assistant professor (*ustaz musa'id*) after teaching for five years and publishing three pieces of research, and professor (*ustaz*) after another five years of teaching and five more publications.

who do not have one. Although the Bar is charged with 'drafting project laws aimed at developing and modernising legislation in order to strengthen public liberties, justice, human rights and the rule of law for citizens', it has played no role in law reform. In an authoritarian state like Egypt, Parliament rarely invites civil society to comment on proposed laws. Nevertheless, the Bar Association always speaks when Parliament discusses provisions concerning lawyers. In the first quarter of 2018, during the debates over amending the criminal procedure law, the Bar wrote to Parliament about the provision for trying lawyers accused of offending judges during hearings. However, only human rights lawyers and NGOs issued statements about legislation concerning human rights violations, the rule of law, public liberties and justice. And the Bar did nothing when lawyers were excluded from the State Security Court prosecution building, although this violated the right to defence and offended lawyers, or when prison visits were shortened or denied (Omar 2016b).

A. The General Assembly

The General Assembly consists of all members who have registered and paid their fees. It convenes annually at the Bar Association headquarters. A quorum is the lesser of a third of the members or 3,000. If the first meeting does not secure a quorum, further attempts must be made fortnightly until a quorum of 1,500 is present.

B. The Board

The Board consists of the Dean of the Bar, a member representing each first instance court, elected by the General Assembly of each branch association, and 15 members registered before courts of appeal (Article 131). Three seats are reserved for lawyers employed in the public sector. Only lawyers who have practised for at least seven years (and therefore can plead in appellate courts) are eligible for the Board, thus excluding first-instance lawyers. The Egyptian Center for Economic and Social Rights has challenged this provision in a case pending before the Supreme Constitutional Court (Omar 2016b).

The Dean of the Board (*naqib*), elected by the General Assembly, must be able to plead in the supreme courts, have practised law at least 20 years, and have his own firm. He can serve for two consecutive four-year terms. He represents Egyptian lawyers, preserves the dignity of the Bar Association and its members, ensures that traditions are respected, and supervises all Bar activities. Although lawyers are subject to a fine for not voting in Board elections, none has ever been imposed.

In practice, especially under Mubarak, the dean made all decisions without the General Assembly's participation (Fahmy 1998). One held office in 1966–71 and 1982–95, while the present incumbent was dean 2001–08 and 2011–19.

V. LAWYERS VERSUS SUCCESSIVE EGYPTIAN AUTHORITARIAN REGIMES

The Bar Association has a long history of confrontation with the government. The state has responded by dissolving its Boards, endorsing candidates or postponing elections.

The Bar Association has also suffered from internal divisions and power struggles, with one faction suing another.

A. A Bastion of Liberalism and Nationalism under the Monarchy

The Bar Association played a major role in defending the rule of law and liberal reform against violations by the King, who banned freedom of assembly and of the press (El-Tawil 2007). For example, during the 1919 Revolution, the Bar went on strike: lawyers boycotted the courts and refused to defend their clients, making it impossible for courts to function. Lawyers took a similar position when Saad Zaghloul was arrested in 1921. The Bar defended those, especially students, who protested foreign occupation (Salem 2010) and played an active role during the many constitutional and political crises in this era (El-Tawil 2007).

In 1929, three lawyers were fined for having 'offended judges during the hearings', provoking an extraordinary General Assembly and requests to amend the Advocates Law to grant lawyers immunity. In 1946, after a judge refused to include all the lawyer's arguments in the hearing minutes, the Bar organised an extraordinary general meeting, which declared that the judge's actions violated the right to defence, leading him to join a delegation of the Court of Appeal and apologise for having 'offended the legal profession' (Al-Shalakany 2013).

The government was cautious not to provoke Bar leaders, who enjoyed national stature (Reid 1974b). In 1920, the Bar launched its own Journal, *Al-Muhamah*, which published research papers analysing and commenting on legal decisions. The Bar Association defended the independence of the legal system and sided with the Wafd Party in its battle to abolish the Mixed Courts. In 1937, they succeeded in eliminating the right of foreigners to be judged by the Mixed Courts, and in 1949 these courts were abolished and their jurisdiction transferred to the National Courts (Al-Shalakany 2013). Lawyers also played a prominent role in eliminating the Sharia courts in 1955.

The Bar Association was dominated by the Wafd Party and functioned as a political organisation. In response to the Bar's opposition, the government dissolved its Board several times and amended the Advocates Law (Reid 1974b). This was the Golden Age for lawyers and the Bar Association, which were forces for modernisation, challenging the King's attempts to preserve his privileges and leading the nationalist movement and the struggle for independence (Ziadeh 1968: 62–76).

B. Loss of Prestige and Independence Under Nasser (1952–70)

In its first General Assembly after the 1952 Revolution led by the 'Free Officers', the Bar sent a 'congratulatory note' to their leader, Mohammad Naguib, welcoming this step and wishing them success. Many lawyers initially supported the coup, hoping it would end the Wafd Party's privileges and domination of the Board. Although divisions within the Wafd Party led to the resignation of Board members, the dean retained his seat in the new elections after making an alliance with the Free Officers. Until March 1954, the Bar Association concentrated on professional rather than political issues, although some lawyers expressed concern about the establishment of exceptional courts to try opponents (Omar 2017), the trial of Wafd Party leaders, the adoption of a new law on political parties and the arrest of lawyers (El-Tawil 2007).

In 1954, the Bar sided with Mohammad Naguib, Nasser's rival, and advocated political liberalisation and the revival of Parliament. Many lawyers called on the military to quit politics and urged an end to martial law, respect for human rights and a return to constitutional governance. Other professions and social groups such as journalists, teachers and students followed suit, demonstrating that the Bar Association had regained its leadership role. Nasser responded by stripping many lawyers of their political rights and dissolving the Bar's Board (Rutherford 1999). The military government appointed a new dean. This was the beginning of the fall of the Bar Association (Al-Shalakany 2013).

From 1954 to 1958, the Bar Association was suspended and its affairs managed by government-appointed committees. In 1968, only members of the state's sole party, the Arab Socialist Union, were allowed to stand for the Board.[28] Under Nasser, the number of lawyers working for the public sector and the legal departments of public sector firms increased, even surpassing the number of private practitioners in the Bar Association. They were law school graduates from lower socio-economic backgrounds than the members of the Wafd Party, who supported Nasser's politics and were grateful for the opportunity to study at university and become Bar members.

Liberal lawyers lost their majority to public sector lawyers, allowing the government to exercise influence over the Bar Association (Rutherford 1999). Nasser's widespread nationalisation measures reduced the number of commercial cases, leaving private practitioners with the choice of handling only civil and criminal cases, which paid less well (Mostafa 2007), or working for public sector companies and supporting the government (Rutherford 1999). This transformed the legal profession from one of most attractive and lucrative careers into one of the least attractive.[29]

The increase in the membership of the Bar Association as a result of its opening to public sector lawyers and free access to university transformed it from a bastion of liberal constitutionalism into a social service organisation without a clear ideological character (Rutherford 1999). The legal profession lost its earlier prestige. The government implemented socialist policies directly affecting investment and business. Lawyers lost their clients, wealth and role in politics, which became the exclusive domain of the military. Only after the 1967 war inflicted heavy losses on Egypt and Israel occupied the Sinai did the Bar Association begin a comeback by calling for prosecution of the officers responsible for that debacle.

C. Conflictual Relations between the Bar and President Sadat (1970–81)

Although prominent members of the Bar helped draft the 1971 Constitution (IBAHRI 2011), Sadat dissolved its Board the same year. The Bar called for greater civil and political rights (Rutherford 1999) and denounced Sadat's repressive security laws, offering free

---

[28] Art 13 of Law No 61 of 1968.

[29] Nasser also tried to control the judiciary by pressuring judges to join the Arab Socialist Union, but they refused, declaring that party membership compromised their independence. In 1969, Nasser adopted several laws undermining judicial independence, dubbed 'laws on the massacre of the judiciary'.

legal representation to anyone charged under them. It also launched a forum about major policy issues and used its journal, *Al-Muhamah*, to discuss political as well as legal issues. A new conflict emerged when the bar opposed the Camp David Peace Agreement, claiming it betrayed the Egyptian people, abandoned Palestinians and strengthened Israel.[30] On 22 July 1981, Parliament dissolved the Board, replacing it with a steering committee. After the disbanded Bar challenged the constitutionality of that action before the Supreme Constitutional Court, Parliament adopted a new law in 1983.[31]

D. Internal Divisions within the Bar Association under Mubarak (1981–2011)

Both the Sadat and Mubarak regimes used police to prevent the Bar from organising conferences promoting anti-government views (Fahmy 1998). In addition, the state used police to support candidates in Bar elections. The Bar was divided between Islamists (including the Muslim Brotherhood) and pro-regime Nasserites. In the late 1980s, because of the weakness of political parties, associations were very active politically and internally divided. In 1986, a conflict between the Cairo branch and the national Bar Association led to the formation of two factions, one supporting secession and the other standing firmly for unity. The conflict mainly involved Wafdist members, giving the impression it was an internal party struggle. In anticipation of the 1989 Board elections, divisions deepened between public and private sector lawyers, between those who wanted the Bar to play a professional or a political role, and between the Muslim Brotherhood, Marxists, Nasserites, and the Wafdists. Between 1986 and 1990, the association could not hold a General Assembly because of these constant internal battles.

In 1992, although the government-endorsed candidate retained the Bar Association presidency, Brotherhood-backed candidates won nearly two-thirds of the Board seats,[32] partly because of the failure of the previous Board either to address lawyers' deteriorating economic and professional situation or to support lawyers who clashed with the security forces. Besides, 'the new leadership focused on making the bar a social service agency, rather than an advocate of political and social change' (Rutherford 1999); these social services were very important for lawyers, most of whom could barely live on their incomes.

The arrival of the Muslim Brotherhood on the Board transformed its activities. A Sharia committee established in all branches to offer social and cultural services to lawyers and their families began to draft legislation to conform laws to Sharia (Mostafa 2007a). The Bar's legal aid department offered free legal representation in cases against the government until the government suspended the Bar in 1996 (Mustafa 2007b). The Law on Democratic Trade Union Organisations was amended in 1993 to prevent or delay

---

[30] After the 1973 War the majority of Egyptians opposed peace with Israel and Sadat's visit to Jerusalem. Students, workers and members of several associations (including the Bar) organised demonstrations against the treaty.

[31] The Supreme Constitutional Court found that the dissolution violated Art 56 of the 1971 Constitution, which required that trade unions and associations be governed democratically, whereas Parliament had denied Bar members the right to choose their leaders and representatives (SCC, 21 June 1983).

[32] For an explanation of the factors that facilitated the Muslim Brotherhood's takeover of the Bar Association and other associations see Fahmy (1998). The Muslim Brotherhood had already gained control of the Boards of the professional associations of medical doctors (1986), engineers (1987) and pharmacists (1990).

future Bar Association elections by requiring a quorum of half the members. After a group of lawyers sued to challenge financial irregularities and the misuse of funds to finance Muslim Brotherhood activities, the Bar was placed under judicial custodianship in 1996. In response, a woman lawyer, probably encouraged by the Muslim Brotherhood, sued to challenge this ruling, and the custodianship was lifted in 2000. In the February 2001 elections the Muslim Brotherhood again won a majority of seats, engendering constant disputes between Board members. This was repeated after the 2005 elections (El-Hafeez 2015). The regime took advantage of these internal conflicts. All this weakened the association, reducing its ability to protect members and diminishing the number participating in Board elections (Fahmy 1998).

In 2007, the State Council invalidated the 2005 election. In 2008 and 2009, it postponed the elections on the ground of procedural irregularities in the voting lists. The elections finally held in June 2009 were won by an independent candidate thought to be close to the Muslim Brotherhood. Islamists also won almost half the Board seats. But these elections were invalidated by the State Council after the Supreme Constitutional Court overturned Law No 100 of 1993 on trade unions, on which the elections had been based. In the 2011 elections lawyers affiliated to the Muslim Brotherhood won more than half the Board seats, but the Nasserist Sameh Achour was elected dean.

In 2009, lawyers had opposed a law drafted by the Justice Minister, which would have increased plaintiffs' litigation fees to improve the courts' performance, on the ground that this would reduce low-income citizens' access to the courts and put lawyers out of work. Courts in several cities were paralysed by lawyer boycotts. In May 2009, however, Parliament approved a fee increase for filing lawsuits and drafting legal documents.

E. The Crackdown on Lawyers after 2011

After 2011, lawyers who worked for NGOs critical of the regime and defended political detainees were subject to attacks, as were ordinary lawyers in interactions with police officers. For example, lawyers from the Hisham Mubarak Law Centre and the Egyptian Centre for Economic and Social Rights were arrested by military police in February 2011 while documenting violence against civilians and providing legal advice to demonstrators. After 2013, there was increasing abuse of lawyers by the police, who saw them as an obstacle to their ability to inflict arbitrary punishment. For example, a lawyer who defended several Islamist detainees was arrested and tortured to death in Al-Matariyya police station (Omar 2016b). In June 2015, the Bar Association declared a general strike after a senior police officer in a police station attacked a lawyer with a shoe – a profound insult. Many lawyers who defended regime opponents were arrested and charged without a warrant, in violation of Article 51 of the Advocates Law.

The crisis worsened when judges and prosecutors refused to meet with lawyers, referring many for investigation for contempt of court (Omar 2016b). The right to defence was often violated by judges and prosecutors, for example when investigations and trials were conducted inside police stations. Lawyers complained of mistreatment by judicial bodies in violation of Article 49 of the Advocates Law, which gives them the right to be treated with respect by courts and all bodies in which they appear. This mistreatment led the Bar to forbid lawyers to appear or plead in certain courts or chambers. In addition, lawyers were banned from entering state security courts, and the public prosecution office was relocated from its historical premises in downtown Cairo to the suburbs, increasing lawyers' costs. After 2013, the government launched a campaign against human rights NGOs, depriving many lawyers of their jobs.

The Bar Association organised human rights conferences, and its liberties committee issued statements on human rights issues, including opposition to military trials (IBAHRI 2011). During the drafting of the 2014 Constitution, the dean of the Bar demanded the inclusion of an article guaranteeing lawyers' independence and prohibiting their imprisonment for crimes related to or committed in the course of their professional activities. But judges refused, arguing this would grant them special immunities. Therefore lawyers, unlike judges and police, have no protection in the performance of their duties. In addition, the Bar plays no significant role in protecting lawyers against the government's violation of their rights (Omar 2016b).

VI. CONCLUSION

The last 30 years have witnessed a decline in the status of Egyptian lawyers, who now come from a wider variety of socio-economic backgrounds and thus have lost the class homogeneity they enjoyed in the first half of the twentieth century. It is difficult indeed to organise a general strike or advocate for a cause when the interests of lawyers are so divergent and they do not constitute a coherent unit. The poor quality of legal education, the overproduction of lawyers, the government's economic policies and its desire to control the Bar Association are the principal causes. Because the quality of legal education is low and few lawyers care about continuous learning and legal culture, most are narrow-minded and unimaginative in handling cases and cannot participate in public or political life or influence legislation. Every day police officers attack lawyers with impunity, and relations between lawyers, judges and prosecutors have deteriorated continuously.

The Bar Association has also been weakened. The large number of badly trained lawyers has tarnished its reputation. The 700,000 lawyers are far too many. The Bar's success in reducing the number of registered lawyers may be meaningless, since unregistered lawyers can still function outside the courts. The Bar should focus on creating an effective screening procedure, for example through an exam followed by a training session, before giving law graduates a licence to practise. And to regain its former status, the Bar should allow young lawyers to serve on its Board, since first-instance lawyers are currently ineligible.

REFERENCES

Abd al-Hafiz, A (2015) 'Egyptian Parties and Syndicates vis-à-vis Judicial Decisions' in N Bernard-Maugiron (ed), *Judges and Political Reform in Egypt* (Cairo, American University in Cairo Press) 213–25.

Al-Shalakany, A (2013) 'The Rise and Fall of Egypt's Legal Elite: 1805–2005' (Dar El-Shorouk) (in Arabic).

Bernard-Maugiron, N (2008) *Judges and Politics in Egypt* (Cairo, American University in Cairo Press).

El-Tawil, A (2007) *Lawyers between the Profession and the Politics: Study in the History of Egypt's Elite* (Cairo, Dar El-Shorouk) (in Arabic).

Fahmy, NS (1998) 'The Performance of the Muslim Brotherhood in the Egyptian Syndicates: An Alternative Formula for Reform?' 52 *Middle East Journal* 551–62.

—— (2002) *The Politics of Egypt: The State-Society Relationship* (Abingdon, Routledge).

Hill, E (1979) *Mahkama! Studies in the Egyptian Legal System. Courts and Crimes. Law and Society* (London, Ithaca Press).

International Bar Association's Human Rights Institute (IBAHRI) (November 2011) *Justice at a Crossroads, The Legal Profession and the Rule of Law in the New Egypt* (London, IBAHRI).

Mostafa, T (2007a) *The Struggle for Constitutional Power: Law, Politics, and Economic Development in Egypt* (Cambridge, Cambridge University Press).

—— (2007b) 'Mobilizing the Law in an Authoritarian State: the Legal Complex in Contemporary Egypt' in TC Halliday, L Karpik and MM Feeley, *Fighting for Political Freedom: Comparative Studies of the Legal Complex and Political Liberalism* (Oxford, Hart Publishing).

Omar, M (2016a) 'Who Protects Egyptian Lawyers' (I) (July) *Legal Agenda*.

—— (2016b) 'Who Protects Egyptian Lawyers (II)' (July) *Legal Agenda*.

—— (2016c) 'Human Rights Non-Governmental Organizations in Egypt' in N Erakat and N Saghieh, *NGOs in the Arab World Post-Arab Uprisings: Domestic and International Politics of Funding and Regulation* (Tadween Publishing).

—— (2017a) 'Lawyering in Egypt: Regulation and Reform' (May) *Legal Agenda*.

—— (2017b) 'The Rise of Egypt's Exceptional Courts' (December) *Legal Agenda*.

Reid, DM (1974a) 'The Rise of Professions and Professional Organizations in Modern Egypt' (January) 1 *Comparative Studies in Society and History* XVI 24–57.

—— (1974b) 'The National Bar Association and Egyptian Politics, 1912–1054' 7 *The International Journal of African Historical Studies* 608–46.

Rutherford, BK (1999) *The Struggle for Constitutionalism in Egypt: Understanding the obstacles to Democratic Transition in the Arab World* PhD thesis, Yale University.

Salem, ML (2010) *The Egyptian Judicial System 1914–1952* (Dar El-Shorouk) (in Arabic).

Sidarouss, FSJ (2011) 'Catholic Schools in Egypt: an Educational Mission in Difficult Conditions' 1 *International Studies in Catholic Education*, Volume 3.

Ziadeh, FJ (1968) *Lawyers, the Rule of Law and Liberalism* (Stanford, Hoover Institution).

29
Iran
A Clash of Two Legal Cultures?

REZA BANAKAR AND KEYVAN ZIAEE

I. INTRODUCTION

SINCE THE 1979 Revolution, the clerical regime in Iran has been limiting the legal profession's autonomy by preventing members of the Iranian Bar Association (IBA) from freely electing their Board of Directors and, by establishing a new body of lawyers – the Legal Advisers of the Judiciary – to contest the IBA's professional monopoly. Clerics have even attempted to bring the legal profession under the control of the Ministry of Justice and merge it with the legal advisers. The IBA's struggle to remain a civil society organisation independent of the judiciary offers a vantage point from which to explore the role of the legal profession in Iranian society and the legal system of the Islamic Republic. Why does the Iranian judiciary oppose an independent legal profession, and why does the profession refuse to capitulate? What are the implications of this ongoing conflict for the legal order of the Islamic Republic, whose political elite consists mainly of Islamic jurists? What are the socio-cultural consequences of undermining the integrity and autonomy of the legal profession? These questions will guide our inquiry.

After discussing the IBA's development before and after the 1979 Revolution, we describe how practising attorneys view the IBA, advocacy, legal practice, legal services and their troubled relationship with the judiciary. They recount the obstacles they encounter within a politicised judicial order and explain how they preserve professional integrity within a legal system that lacks the public's confidence. We conclude by arguing that the Islamic Republic's attempt to subordinate the legal profession to administrative and ideological control by the judiciary reflects the clash of two legal cultures. Iranian judges reconstruct and apply Islamic jurisprudence (*fiqh*) as part of their efforts to deliver substantive justice within a codified legal system, while IBA attorneys understand and seek to practise law consistent with the ideals of due process, certainty and uniformity in legal decision-making.

This study is based on semi-structured approximately hour-long interviews with 23 men and 18 women conducted in Farsi in Tehran between 2012 and 2016: 32 IBA members, four Legal Advisers of the Judiciary, four judges (three retired), and one managing director of a law firm. A number of shorter interviews (26 in total) asked ordinary Iranians about their knowledge of lawyers' work and views on and experience of legal services.

II. THE EVOLUTION OF THE LEGAL PROFESSION IN IRAN

A. The Legal Profession's Early Years

The contours of a legal profession began to take shape when a modern judicial system gradually emerged following the 1906 Constitutional Revolution. The 1911 Law of Judiciary Organisation laid the foundation for a secular judicial hierarchy inspired by the European civil law tradition, especially the French legal system. It defined the function of judges (distinguishing them from prosecutors[1]) and introduced the First Charter of Attorneyship, which required lawyers to pass a Bar examination before entering legal practice (Nayyeri 2012: 3). The first Bar Association, established in 1921, enjoyed neither financial nor legal independence, operating under the Ministry of Justice, which also issued, renewed and revoked attorneys' licences.[2] The new judiciary, wary of an organised body of attorneys, neither tolerated an independent Bar Association nor encouraged the growth of the legal profession (Mohammadi 2008: 71). The Minister of Justice, Ali Akbar Dāvar, a Swiss-educated lawyer and influential statesman during Reza Shah's reign (1925–41), was an exception. He appointed a committee that drafted new laws, compiled legal codes, established courts and selected judges from qualified Islamic jurists and government officials.[3] He not only regarded advocacy favourably but also considered a Bar Association, capable of organising and training competent lawyers, to be essential to the effective operation of a modern legal system. He thus actively encouraged 'the formation of the association of lawyers, albeit under the auspices of the Ministry of Justice' in 1930 (Enayat 2011: 133). Dāvar is widely considered the architect of the modern Iranian legal system.

The Law of Attorneyship, adopted in 1937, granted legal personality to the Bar Association for the first time. Although it was now considered financially independent, some organisational arrangements, such as the appointment of its Board of Directors, remained under Ministry of Justice control. Another 15 years had to elapse before the IBA was granted full independence. Dr Mohammad Mosaddeq, the Prime Minister of Iran at the time and himself a lawyer, signed the 'Bill of Independence of the Iranian Bar Association' in 1953, terminating the judiciary's administration of the IBA. The Law of Independence stipulated that the IBA was an independent body with a legal personality, to be established in the jurisdiction of every Provincial Court. The IBA consisted of a General Assembly, a Board of Directors elected by attorneys through ballots, and 'Attorneys' Disciplinary Prosecutor Office and Disciplinary Courts' (Nayyeri 2012: 4). Initially, there were only three Bar Associations: the Central Bar Association in Tehran and the Tabriz and Shiraz Bar Associations.[4] These operated as independent professional bodies for the next 25 years, electing their own Board members, granting and revoking licences,

---

[1] Prior to 1906, Iran had a dual court system consisting of secular *urf* (or *orfi*) courts, dealing with matters of public order, and Sharia courts, largely concerned with religious matters and private law disputes. Neither distinguished between judge and prosecutor. For a discussion see Banakar 2018.

[2] Iranian Bar Association Union (2003) 'Complete *History of Law Practice in Iran*' (Tārikhcheye Kāmele Vekālat dar Iran) www.iranbar.com/pe191.php.

[3] 'Dāvar, Ali-Akbar' *Encyclopaedia Iranica* at www.iranicaonline.org/articles/davar-ali-akbar.

[4] According to the Iranian Bar Associations Union (2016), created in 2003 to coordinate local Bar Associations, the number has increased to 20.

and processing complaints of lawyer misconduct without the interference of the judiciary until the 1979 Revolution.

B. After the 1979 Revolution

At the top of the political agenda of the Islamic groups that took power after the revolution was Islamisation of laws and legal institutions. A new Constitution was drafted requiring that all laws be consistent with 'Islamic criteria', after which the judiciary was dismantled and its members replaced by Islamic jurists and clerics.[5] At the same time, 'all female judges were dismissed or assigned to clerical and administrative positions' (Tavassolian 2012: 2), many attorneys disbarred, and the majority of the IBA Board of Directors arrested and imprisoned (LCHR 1993).[6] An attorney during this time recalled:

> Many courts refused to allow attorneys to present cases and had put up a notice on their doors saying: 'We are unable to receive lawyers'. This went on until the Constitution was amended in 1989, and article 35 stated that those appearing before any court had the right to be represented by attorneys.

The Supreme Council of the Judiciary reopened the IBA in 1984, although it revoked the right of members to elect its director.[7] Instead, a new director was appointed directly by the judiciary to supervise the association (Nayyeri 2012: 5–6). The decade following the 1979 Revolution, which coincided with the eight-year war of attrition between Iran and Iraq, was the hardest period for lawyers in Iran: many attorneys were purged, some were executed, and others fled the country or went into hiding. The courts denied defendants legal counsel and made arbitrary judgments, systematically violating the principles of Islamic law as well as the human rights of the political opponents of the regime. During this time, lawyers were too intimidated to appear before the courts. As the Iran-Iraq war ended and the internal political situation stabilised, a Bill was submitted to Parliament in 1990 declaring that parties to a lawsuit had the right to appoint 'an attorney at law', and all courts were obliged to receive them. This provoked an objection from the powerful Council of Guardians, which is responsible for ensuring the compatibility of all new legislation with the principles of Islam. Eventually, a compromise was reached by deleting 'at law' after 'attorney'. By replacing 'attorney at law' (*vakīl-e dādgūstarī*) with 'attorney' (*vakīl*), Parliament established that legal representation did not need to be conducted by a qualified lawyer, or legal counsel, who had passed the Bar: anyone could represent any

---

[5] Before the 1979 Revolution, Iran was a mixed jurisdiction whose private law melded ideas from the French Civil Code 1804 and Islamic law. Although the criminal law appeared Islamic, it had largely abandoned Sharia principles in favour of civil law institutions and procedures. Those areas of law, regarded as 'un-Islamic', such as criminal and family law, were fundamentally revised after the 1979 Revolution to conform to Sharia. Nevertheless, the legal system of the Islamic Republic continues to bear the hallmarks of its precursor, combining elements from Islamic and civil law traditions.

[6] There were no female judges in Iran until 1970, when five women were appointed to the bench. Only 45 of the 2,053 district judges in 1976 were female (Butler and Levasseur 1976: 18, 30). We have no statistics on the number of attorneys at that time, but only 28 were women.

[7] 'Iranian bar association seeks greater independence' (7 March) www.al-monitor.com/pulse/originals/2014/03/iran-bar-association-lawyer-independence.html.

case in court. This view, which is consistent with Sharia, continues to inform the attitudes of many judges towards legal counsel.

With the victory of Mahmoud Ahmadinejad in the 2005 presidential elections, hardline conservatives dominated the political scene once again and started to curtail the limited freedoms some civil society organisations, like the IBA, had enjoyed under President Khatami's reformist government (1997–2005). The new government approved 'the draft Bill of Formal Attorneyship, which [increased] Government supervision over the Iranian Bar Association' (SRRI 2013: 7). An open letter signed by 35 Iranian human rights lawyers criticised the Bill for replacing the title 'Bar Association' with 'Organisation of Attorneys', demonstrating 'the determination of the authorities to downgrade the position of the Bar from an independent body to a subordinate governmental organisation' (IHRCC 2013). Moreover, the new Bill prescribed a 'Supervisory Commission', created by the Head of the Judiciary to administer 'confirmation of the elections, suspension and revocation of the licences of all attorneys, including even the directors of the bar, appointment of the members of the Examining Committees, among other tasks (arts. 25–30)'. The Bill sought to increase governmental control over the IBA by allowing the judiciary to decide 'who can become a lawyer, how they should be disciplined and whether or not they should be able to continue their practices'. This Bill was suspended before the 2013 presidential elections, but 'several amended versions of the draft Bill were submitted to Parliament in September 2014', reasserting the Islamic Republic's commitment to curtail the IBA's independence (SRRI 2015: 7–8).

Although this occurred during Ahmadinezhad's term, the idea of the Bill originated in the judiciary, which often disagreed with him (Hujjati 2014). During his last days in office, he ordered his Cabinet to shelve the Bill in what appeared to be an attack on the judiciary, producing a strong reaction. Sadeq Larijani, head of the judiciary, condemned Ahmadinezhad for acting on a 'childish grudge' rather than displaying statesmanship (ICHRI 2013). But this was not the end of the story. Immediately after Larijani's retort, a member of the parliamentary commission reviewing the Bill declared it was still being considered. He explained that 'the President's viewpoint is not for the Bill to be completely removed from the review agenda of the Cabinet commissions [but to eliminate] certain articles in the Bill that allow the judiciary to interfere in the civil organisation of the legal profession' (ICHRI 2013). In short, a revised version of this Bill was submitted to Parliament in 2015. The Legal and Judicial Commission of Parliament considered and rejected the Bill in July 2017 since it found no reason for amending the existing law (IRINN 2017). Thus, the status quo of the existing restrictions on the IBA's independence was restored.

C. The Legal Advisers of the Judiciary (Article 187)

One attorney told us that when the Islamic Republic confronts civil society organisations and associations like the IBA, which persist in questioning the legitimacy of the clerical regime, it resorts to a strategy of duplicating the defiant organisation. Given time and state support, the replica will assimilate the nonconformist organisation. This was how the clerical regime sought to neutralise the IBA. A new body of lawyers was created by the judiciary in 2001 and 'authorised to present cases in court' under Article 187 of the Law of Third Economic, Social and Cultural Development Plan of 2000 (International Bar

Association 2007: 9). This group is officially known as the Legal Advisers of the Judiciary. The Centre for Legal Advisers and Experts of the Judiciary trains and examines its own members and issues and renews their licences to practise.

IBA members referred to legal advisers somewhat disparagingly as 'the 187s', who had entered by the back door because their training and examinations were not as rigorous as those of the IBA. Legal advisers must pass one qualifying examination and complete a six-month pupillage, whereas IBA attorneys must pass several examinations and complete an 18-month traineeship under the supervision of a lawyer with more than 10 years' experience. (As we shall see, the attorneys are also very critical of their own pupillage.) Some of our attorneys questioned the competence of the 187 legal advisers, calling their training insufficient to instil the skills to manage complex cases. Others felt that though advisers initially lacked skill, they improved over time and could perform as well as IBA attorneys. But all our IBA attorneys were concerned about legal advisers' subordination to the judiciary, which according to them impeded the advisers' professional autonomy. Many also wondered how legal advisers' connection with the judiciary influenced clients' choice of counsel:

> Some clients opt for 187-advisors rather than for IBA attorneys, because they believe that their case will benefit from the advisors' connections with the judiciary. This belief channels certain cases in the direction of advisors.

The Iranian government defended its decision to establish the legal advisers' body, arguing that the IBA had used its monopoly on issuing licences to restrict the number of new entrants into legal practice. The IBA rejected this allegation, explaining that, under the Law of Conditions for Obtaining Attorney's Licence Article 1, it was obliged to hold the Bar exam at least once a year (Nayyeri 2012: 13). Moreover, the number of trainees admitted annually was set by 'a special Commission with only one member representing the Bar's interests'. Had the judiciary been concerned about the shortage of lawyers, they could have raised the number of IBA trainees 'instead of creating a new breed of dependent lawyers'.

Unlike the IBA, which has an independent procedure for renewing licences, legal advisers' permits are renewed with the approval of the judiciary. This was regarded as highly problematic by most of our interviewees. One attorney reported that 'IBA members don't fear their licences would be revoked at the end of the year because they might have defended a dissident or given interviews, but the judiciary can revoke legal advisers' licences at will'.[8] It is possible that some of the objections voiced by attorneys were partly motivated by the fact that legal advisers were perceived as competitors in a tight market for legal services. However, the attorneys were also genuinely concerned about legal advisers' professional autonomy and political independence from the judiciary. The International Bar Association (2007: 10–11) voiced similar unease about legal advisers operating under the control and scrutiny of the judiciary. According to them,

---

[8] See the case of *Nematollahi Gonabadi* Order of *Sufi Dervishes*. Two 187-legal advisers who had represented sufi dervishes had their licences 'revoked by the Legal Advisors' Centre, in September 2008' (Nayyeri 2012). Although *Nematollahi Gonabadi* dervishes are Shi'a Muslims, the clerical regime does not approve their practices, which are inspired by Sufi philosophy. Their members are persecuted and their houses of worship destroyed by the Islamic Republic.

it represented an encroachment on the independence of lawyers and the legal profession as well as an impairment of the autonomy and impartiality of the judicial system, ultimately, undermining 'public confidence in the law and in the work of lawyers'.

III. WORKING AS AN ATTORNEY

Very few Iranian lawyers specialise in one area of law, and most take any case that comes along. This reflects the underdeveloped state of the market, which generates insufficient legal work in different areas to ensure a steady demand for specialised services. Nevertheless, the number of lawyers has tripled over the last decade, from 20,000 to about 60,000 (over 20,000 legal advisers and 40,000 IBA members).[9] In addition, there are about 10,000 IBA trainees. In 2016, Iran's population was just over 80 million, which means that the ratio of population per lawyer (not including the judiciary and notaries) was 1,133:1. According to an attorney who used to work for the IBA's public relations arm, only 12,000 of the 20,000 registered lawyers were in good standing and regularly paid their dues; 4–5,000 of those were women.[10]

Several interviewees reported a mismatch between the conditions affecting lawyering and the requirements of Iranian society: 'It is true that the number of lawyers might be small considering the size of the population, but we must also remember that not many people use lawyers'. The attorneys argued that the quality of lawyering had deteriorated and lawyers were no longer respected because of a few 'bad apples'. While most lawyers exhibited professional integrity, some acted as 'chic brokers' or classy agents, whose primary task was to negotiate and 'fix' deals – even at the expense undermining the law. Neither the public nor the authorities, and at times not even other IBA attorneys, trusted lawyers' professionalism.

Attorneys also complained about the negative image of lawyers as fraudsters disseminated through soap operas produced by *Sedā va Simā*, the state-run television network, over the last decade.[11] True, one attorney said, there were fraudulent practitioners in the IBA, but they were a very small group compared to the overwhelming majority of attorneys who diligently served their clients and the law. He also pointed out that some judges violated their code of conduct, but 'you would never find a TV series in which the judge breaks the law'.

A. Attorneys' View of the IBA

The IBA is responsible for issuing and renewing licences, investigating allegations of misconduct against members, disciplining violations of its code of conduct, and

---

[9] The figures are interviewees' estimates for Tehran (which has the highest density of lawyers); they tally with those provided by other interviews regarding the Central IBA, covering Tehran and a few neighbouring provinces.
[10] A retired judge told us there were about 10,000 judges in 2016.
[11] We are dubious about the causal connection because not all Iranians watch soap operas, and not all watchers form a negative view of lawyers or even agree that they are shown in a poor light. For a discussion see Banakar and Ziaee 2018.

providing workshops, courses and lectures for trainee lawyers. According to an IBA manager, in December 2016 the Central IBA (representing Tehran and a few other provinces in the north of Iran) had 28,694 members, 5,537 of them trainees. IBA statistics do not include gender, but all those we interviewed said the number of female lawyers has increased noticeably over the last two decades. Fewer than 20 per cent of members ever participate in the election of Directors which are arranged once every two years. One explanation is that attorneys feel alienated from their association, which they visit only to renew their licences or on the rare occasions when they are summoned to a disciplinary hearing. Otherwise, they have no idea about the IBA's policy debates, concerns or plans. More importantly, they felt it avoided confrontation with the judiciary in order to ensure its survival and failed to oppose state officials who violated the rights of attorneys.

Some attorneys acknowledged that the IBA was constantly under political scrutiny and could not challenge the judiciary without jeopardising its limited independence. Others admitted that since the IBA was devoting all its resources to surviving, it had little time or energy to promote members' welfare. Nevertheless, even those sympathising with the IBA's predicament and the political constraints under which it operated argued it should do much more to protect the legal rights of its members and ensure their general welfare.

Understandably, the IBA sees these problems differently. Amir Hussain-Abady explained that during his two terms on the Board of Directors, it had taken 'every possible step available to it to uphold the IBA's independence and safeguard the rights of its members' (*Vekālat* 2011: 44). But since the IBA had to act discreetly in seeking the release of detained attorneys, and the authorities often denied it a fair hearing or simply refused to grant any hearing, the Board appeared to do nothing to protect its members. This former Board member was admitting the IBA had very little symbolic capital to deploy in the field of power and had to work behind the scenes and through sympathetic political agents.

B. The Hostile Judiciary

'The lawyer steps into the court', said a younger attorney in his early 30s, 'and the judge thinks to himself: "here comes the enemy"'. An experienced female attorney agreed that 'judges and attorneys [were] always set against each other'; both assumed a defensive posture, 'raising their shields' as soon as they faced each other in court, turning it 'into a battle ground where a bizarre moral confrontation is played out between these two groups'. Attorneys were the underdog in this setting because they were 'more vulnerable to the abuse of power'. Another attorney complained that not only the judges but also the entire court staff treated lawyers disrespectfully, something he had resisted:

> I wrote a formal complaint last year and had it signed by 550 attorneys and submitted it to the Head of the Judiciary, which issued a directive urging the judges and court clerks to conduct themselves towards attorneys with due respect. But in practice, nothing happened. I can only guess that behind the scenes the judiciary approves of humiliating lawyers.

We were told repeatedly that the judiciary viewed IBA attorneys' representations on behalf of defendants as obstructing the legal process. This negative view varied from court to court: although some judges would trust attorneys they knew, others would 'call in your client, close the door behind them and tell them in confidence that they should get rid of you'. Several attorneys reported that the judge had either told their clients they did not need a lawyer or advised them to dismiss their legal representative in order to get a favourable judgment.

Our attorneys attributed judges' animosity to either economic rivalry or legal and ideological training. Lawyers competed against each other and struggled collectively against 187-legal advisers in the market for legal services. Judges, by contrast, received a fixed salary.

> Judges work very hard and have demanding duties, but they are paid less than some attorneys. Some judges joke about it openly, but others bottle it up and use it in court to make your life hell.

The retired judges we interviewed admitted the judiciary was hostile to lawyers, who they believed 'fed parasitically on court decisions', often earning considerably more than judges. However, they also claimed that hostility did not always have economic roots but could be provoked by what they perceived as attorneys' 'abuse of the law' and 'misrepresentations of right and wrong'.

Attorneys also attributed the tensions with judges to their different attitudes toward *fiqh* (Islamic jurisprudence). They argued that judges construed the law substantively, in light of social conditions and their understanding of justice and fairness, whereas attorneys were driven instrumentally to win their cases. The more experienced attorneys emphasised the ideological nature of legal interpretation and decision-making in Iranian courts, best revealed in authorities' violations of defendants' rights. They criticised judges' attempts to construe the law in terms of *fiqh*, which precluded legal certainty about the outcome of cases. One senior lawyer argued that whereas defence attorneys had studied law, 'most judges [had] studied *fiqh*' and decided cases through *fiqh* 'because of the conceptual training they [had] received at *howzah* [theological seminaries]'.[12] Judges regarded the procedural requirements of decision-making as 'presentational' (*tashrifātī*) and thus 'superficial'. Their training encouraged them to make substantive decisions about what they believed to be right, preventing them from giving sufficient weight to the formal aspects of law. 'If you object to them pointing out that correct legal decisions require following the correct legal procedures, they accuse you of looking for excuses to delay the proceeding'. Lawyers saw this as a form of '*qadi*- justice', a Weberian ideal-type of legal decision-making, which 'knows no rational "rules of decision"' (Weber 1978: 976). Notwithstanding our attorneys' critique of the judiciary, it would be misleading to describe Iranian judges as Weberian *qadis* because they operate within a civil law system. In cases where they find themselves restricted by codified law, they turn to *fiqh* to safeguard the ideological framework that shapes their legal culture. The problem is that this methodology – employing *fiqh* within codified law – contains an ideological core not shared by the IBA attorneys we interviewed.

---

[12] Immediately after the 1979 Revolution, some Iranian judges were recruited from theological schools. But the new generation of judges have studied at law schools.

C. Fiqh

Sharia consists of primary sources, including the Qur'an and *Sunnah*,[13] and secondary sources based on the consensus among Islamic jurists (*ijma*), analogy (*qiyas*) and reason (*aql*). The application of *ijtihād*[14] enables Islamic jurists to employ independent reasoning to establish the secondary rulings of Sharia in accordance with the Quran and *Sunnah*. By contrast, *fiqh* reasoning makes interpretations consistent with what judges consider to be the requirements of time and place.[15] In the context of Iranian law, however, the doctrine of *maslahat-e nezam*, ie expediency of the state, overrides all doctrinal considerations and effectively paves the way for secularisation of the Islamic Republic.[16]

The notion of *fiqh* arose in many interviews when attorneys reflected on how judges decided civil and criminal cases or talked about the judiciary's negative attitude toward lawyers and lawyering. One interviewee blamed the harsh sentencing practices of Iranian judges on their tendency to reason through '*fiqh*'. Another argued that 'most of our judges have studied *fiqh*' and 'expect to hear arguments based on *fiqh*'. Because defence lawyers had 'studied law and made their case in a *legal* language … we fail to communicate, and I fail to convince [the judge] of the validity of my argument'. One judge expressed this somewhat differently, arguing that the Iranian legal system was a hybrid of Sharia and civil law institutions and procedures:

> Iranian legal order is a civil law system, structurally speaking. [It is] based on codified law. But when it comes to Islamic processing of cases … it becomes a common law system. I mean, the judge has the same approach, method and leeway as a common law judge. … We have the foundations of common law in Shari'a.

It is questionable whether Iranian law has a common law core. Moreover, the judge's analogy ignores the fact that criminal law in common law jurisdictions is statutory, not judge-made. Nevertheless, he draws attention to an important aspect of judicial work: Iranian judges, a few of whom have reached the stage of *ijtihād* (ie are recognised as Islamic jurists who may develop the law) are expected to manoeuvre between codified law and *fiqh*.

Part of Iranian law, such as family law, is linked to *fiqh*, whose application in other areas such as criminal law (which is directly formed by Sharia) is the subject of ongoing deliberation (Mousavian 2005). The new penal code, which became effective in 2013, draws its evidentiary requirements for the proof of crime from *fiqh*, including 'judge's knowledge' in addition to confession, witness testimony and sworn oath. The knowledge

---

[13] *Sunnah* is the system of customary rules and practices of the Islamic community based on the teachings and practices of the Prophet Muhammad.

[14] *Ijtihād* refers to independent reasoning of jurists in cases where a legal issue cannot be satisfactorily resolved by applying existing rules and precedents (Burns 2014: 31). *Ijtihād* requires a command of Arabic (which most Iranians lack) and a mastery of Islamic theology and jurisprudence. For an Iranian judge to reach the stage of *ijtihād*, he must become a recognised theologian and expert in exegesis of the sources of Islamic law.

[15] Iranian law consists of 'a mixture of pre-Revolutionary sources, regulations laid down by new organs of State and materials drawn from Shi'a law, generating certain contradictions and confusion' (Owsia 1991: 37–38).

[16] Ayatollah Khomeini (2006: 217) introduced the concept of *fiqh-ul maslahe* (expediency of *fiqhi*) into Shi'a jurisprudence in an attempt to address internal conflicts between Islamic jurists and the elected government. For a discussion of *maslahat-e nezam* and the secularisation of the sacred, see Ghobadzadeh (2013).

of the judge is the insight or intuition he gains as he considers the evidence. The judge can disregard evidence submitted on oath because he believes it to be unreliable and instead base his judgment on his knowledge of the case. He can disregard codified law in search of the substantively correct decision. One of our attorneys described a divorce case in which the wife had claimed a substantial *mehrieh* (dowry), an amount specified in the marriage contract, payable by the husband to the wife on her request, typically in the event of divorce. Searching for a way to avoid paying *mehrieh*, the husband turned to an Ayatollah, a senior cleric and *mujtahid* well known for his hardline politics, requesting a religious ruling (*fatwa*) on *mehrieh*.

> In contravention of the codified family law, which recognises *mehrieh* without restricting its amount, [the Ayatollah] issued a *fatwa* declaring payment of *this* [substantial] amount of *mehrieh* to be prohibited and treated as sinful (*harām*). The judge ... disregarded the codified valid family law and, instead, made a ruling based on [the Ayatollah's] *fatwa*.[17]

Whereas Iranian judges might explain this as the leeway permitted by *fiqh*, the attorney representing the wife saw it as an arbitrary decision violating codified law. He felt it was unjust because he had no way of anticipating that a *fatwa* would restrict *mehrieh* and a judge would adopt this religious ruling to override codified law.[18]

D. The Selection and Training of Judges

To explore the roots of this hostility, we need to consider how Iranian judges are selected and expected to behave. According to the 1982 Law on the Qualifications for the Appointment of Judges, only a man who has faith, is just, and possesses 'a practical commitment to Islamic principles and loyalty to the system of the Islamic Republic' may be considered for appointment as a judge or prosecutor (Official Gazette 1982). The candidate also must be recognised as *mujtahid* by the judiciary.[19] If not enough applicants have reached *ijtihād*, the judiciary may select judges from law school graduates, religious seminaries (*howzah*) and theological faculties (Tavassolian 2012: 2–3). In the early 1980s, when the judiciary was purged, some clerics were appointed to the bench even though they had been trained at religious seminaries, where they were taught to construe Sharia through the ideological lens of the Islamic regime.[20] Today, however, most judges have been trained at law schools, although one attorney noted important differences between the outlooks of lawyers and judges.

> When discussing judges with colleagues, we wonder where they studied law; obviously not in the same schools as we did. Their overall understanding of the law and the way they construe it

---

[17] A *fatwa*, issued by an Islamic jurist (a *mufti*, a Grand Ayatollah or a so-called *Maraj'e-Taghlid*), normally consists of a verdict on a question or a response to a specific circumstance that has not previously been subjected to legal scrutiny. It is not binding 'on the person or persons to whom [it is] addressed, unless it is issued by a court in a case under its consideration, in which case the decision would carry a binding force' (Kamali 2012: 162).

[18] The overwhelming majority of attorneys we interviewed were critical of family law and claimed that they avoided family law disputes. For a discussion on Iranian family law see Banakar and Ziaee 2018.

[19] A *mujtahid* is an Islamic scholar who has reached the stage of *ijtihād*.

[20] The Iranian government recruited 1,000 judges from graduates and students of theological seminaries in 1980, a number that had risen to 2,000 by 1989 (LCHR 1993).

is strikingly different from our understanding and interpretations of it, but you must consider one thing: in Iran, a judge's interpretation in certain cases may be guided by his personal inclination. ... Some legal decisions appear to have been made in an arbitrary way. The judge can always say that it is *his* interpretation of the law. And you can't argue with the judge.

Several attorneys made similar statements about the judges' tendency to base their decisions on 'personal opinion'. What they perceive as arbitrary decision-making, however, is one of the consequences of the application of *fiqh*.

Candidates for judgeships are carefully vetted by the Supreme Selection Council and Ministry of Intelligence through the *gozinesh* (selection) process (IHRDC 2015: 37). Moreover, to ensure judges' adherence to the ideologically correct interpretation of Islamic jurisprudence, the judiciary has been operating a special school for training judges since 1982. The recruitment procedure through *gozinesh* and subsequent training create a socio-politically homogeneous body of men, which contrasts sharply with the more diverse group of attorneys. A female lawyer explained that although she could not 'claim that membership of the IBA [was] socially and politically homogeneous', she was certain 'that all judges belong to one group. The IBA attorneys might be religious or secular, republican or royalist and so on, but judges share the same basic ideological and religious views'. Several attorneys maintained that judges come from the 'lower classes' or social groups without influence before the revolution, which was why they had a chip on their shoulder. A female attorney described judges as 'a very conservative group of people', who 'were brought up in very traditional and religious environments or [had] moved from small villages to cities and become judges', in contrast with IBA attorneys, who were mainly from middle-class backgrounds.[21]

Another interviewee offered a different view of judges, arguing that the IBA attorneys' training was 'scientific', whereas judges' training involved 'a lot of ideological, political and theological instruction'. Although this instruction had been moderated over time, judges' training continued to differ from the IBA attorneys' scientific approach to law. This attorney added that judges also were distinguished by their religiosity: 'they have to be religious to get into the system'. Another attorney, who teaches law school part time, claimed she could 'spot' potential judges among her students by a 'mindset' that disposed them to joining the judiciary. According to her, however, not all judges came from a religious background. Some 'had failed the bar exam and couldn't become attorneys', which tainted their attitude towards attorneys.

Our interviews with IBA attorneys reflect only *their* views of a dysfunctional relationship with judges. It is reasonable to assume the judiciary experiences the daily functioning of courts differently. Only four of our interviewees had served on the bench, and two of them were practising as attorneys when interviewed. One pointed to the caseloads, explaining that the number of cases judges must decide every month had increased perhaps tenfold compared to when he presided in pre-revolutionary courts (Banakar 2016: 67). Judges who agreed to speak to us insisted there were no differences between IBA attorneys and legal advisers, who were treated equally and with due respect. However, one expressed frustration with 'some defence lawyers who come up with irrelevant arguments which take the court's time and delay proceedings'. His court processed

---

[21] For a more comprehensive description of female attorneys see Banakar and Ziaee 2018.

120 cases per month; on the day he was interviewed he was hearing six, not a heavy caseload compared to some family courts, which can hear up to double that number, according to the Attorney General (ISNA 2017). But when asked about the nature of his caseload, this judge said only about 10 per cent were straightforward cases, while 90 per cent were complicated and time-consuming.

> Most of our cases are voluminous, and since we are inundated with work, we don't get the time to study them carefully before the hearing. We go through them summarily when we set the date for hearing cases, but otherwise we use our general overview of cases together with the details which are discussed when they are heard in court, to make a judgment.

The IBA attorneys were critical of judges for not reading cases before a hearing, blaming this lack of careful consideration for many strange and incorrect legal decisions.

E. Corruption

Many attorneys we interviewed talked openly about corruption, suggesting it was widely discussed both within and outside the legal system. A young attorney saw corruption as an inescapable part of legal practice, saying in a matter-of-fact tone that 'in a lawsuit which is worth billions of Toman,[22] you won't get anywhere without lubricating the wheels of justice' by paying off officials and judges. 'As soon as the value of your case exceeds an amount, you have to pay'. Another attorney claimed that she had had 'a few cases where the judge directly asks for money to deliver his judgment'. The senior judges were often not involved in this type of bribery, but the others were all corrupt, especially court experts (*karshenas-e dadgah*). A few attorneys refrained from accusing all judges of corruption, stressing that some could not be bribed while adding that corrupt judges severely undermined the public's confidence in the entire system. Others insisted the entire legal system was 'corrupt through and through' and the judiciary responsible for corrupting the legal profession.

> If there are corrupt attorneys, it is because they are forced into corruption. If our judges decided cases on the basis of the law, you couldn't resort to bribery. But that's not the case and when litigating a lawsuit, you are afraid that the other party might have paid off the judge.

A female attorney explained that upholding the code of professional conduct in an environment where corrupt practices are the norm exerts enormous social and psychological pressure on attorneys: 'Everyone thinks there is something wrong with you if you insist on working with integrity and refuse to lie or take bribes'.

One attorney argued that officers of the courts and those who run the judicial system were poorly paid. Because judges 'know that some clients pay large legal fees for some of the private lawsuits they process' they often ask how much attorneys are charging, expecting to receive 'their share of legal fees'. Corruption can take more subtle forms, mediated by informal networks. Cronyism is endemic. One interviewee explained: 'even attorneys can get their work done more quickly if their cousin happens to work in the

---

[22] In December 2017 a billion Toman (10 billion riyal) was worth approximately US$277,000.

courts'. Corruption had reached such proportions that the legal system could no longer feign ignorance. Recently, a few judges have been accused and fired and a few others transferred. The Attorney General acknowledged the scale of the problem by publicly admitting that some judges 'become corrupt after serving a few years on the bench' (ISNA 2017).

F. Clients and their Attitudes Towards Legal Services

Our attorneys all mentioned that many Iranians who retained their services had little understanding of what a lawyer could reasonably achieve in their cases. Most were 'convinced that their claim was right and the other party was in the wrong, so they would get very upset if you told them that they should pay back an amount of money or pay compensation to the other side'. Clients often expected a lawyer to 'perform a miracle', and 'if you failed, they would turn on you, accusing you of all sorts of things, and saying that you haven't done a thing for them, that you are incompetent or have colluded with the other side and so on and so forth. Then they would refuse to pay their remaining fees', forcing many lawyers to get as much of their fees upfront as possible.

Our interviews suggested several explanations for the negative attitudes towards legal services. The idea of retaining legal counsel is unfamiliar to Iranians, most of whom do not seek lawyers' advice when they encounter a legal problem but rather turn to friends and family.[23] We found repeated references to *farhang* (culture) and assertions that 'Iranians have not developed a culture of law'. One interviewee argued that people had not internalised 'the culture of using lawyers' and would not approach them for advice, even when they knew they might lose property or business. However, interviews with members of the public revealed that some had become highly sceptical of lawyers, holding them in low esteem because of past experiences. This is consistent with studies from other countries finding that clients became disappointed when lawyers failed to meet their expectations (Hengstler 1993; Galanter 1998).

There is a broader cultural explanation for this collective behaviour: Iranians do not readily trust people they do not know (Banakar 2016). According to one legal adviser, official statistics show that only 7 per cent of those who appear in court are represented by a lawyer; and there was general agreement among those we interviewed that relatively few people retain legal representation when appearing in court. To avoid paying fees and entrusting business or private matters to a stranger, people turn to family and acquaintances, most of whom do not know the law well enough to resolve legal problems. An attorney said people consult anyone they think can draft a petition, and 'sometimes they come to me with a complete package full of advice – advice from people who don't know the law – and … it is very difficult to convince them of what needs to be done in their case'. Another attorney said 'clients aren't likely to trust lawyers they don't already know, and if they turn to a lawyer they don't know, they keep secrets from him/her, [thereby] jeopardising their own case'.

---

[23] This point was raised by almost all the lawyers we interviewed, eg interview 2:1:18 in Banakar (2016: 92).

G. Female Lawyers

Four main observations based on our interviews may help to understand the gendered dimensions of the Iranian legal system: (1) a number of female assistant judges (*dādyār*) serve in some courts, especially those dealing with custody cases, but all presiding judges are male, whereas lawyers are both male and female; (2) Iranian law is seen by most attorneys as biased against women, although it does not differentiate between lawyers by gender; (3) male lawyers are more easily accepted by the judiciary (although not necessarily more respected); (4) female attorneys, especially younger ones, are treated badly by police officers and court officials.

Within the legal system, we were told, no one openly objected to female lawyers.

> No, it is subtler than that. In a lawsuit I had recently, my opposite was a female lawyer. I didn't really have a case and expected to lose, especially since she submitted a convincing argument. Then, something happened which I couldn't make sense of and still wonder about. The presiding judge – and he is a very decent and respected judge – suddenly turned against the female lawyer and decided in my favour. It was almost as if he just wanted to make a point to the female attorney that in his court *he* decided.

Another male attorney saw little subtlety in the treatment of female lawyers, claiming that 'the all-male judiciary' saw them not as lawyers but as 'sexual objects'. A young female attorney, who combined practising and teaching law, did not see the discriminatory treatment of female lawyers as specific to the legal system:

> Even when I teach at the university, I see students taking male lecturers more seriously. ... Also, clients think that male lawyers are more capable and can do things that women lawyers can't, [which is why clients] trust female attorneys less. You find the same thing in courts. Judges hear male lawyers differently.

A female 187-legal adviser, who also argued categorically that judges treated male and female attorneys differently, claimed she had often heard from female colleagues that:

> The judge had interrupted their presentation during the hearing and told them, for example, 'Be quiet! Your voice wrecks my nerves', or 'First, go out and fix your *hijab*, then come and speak'. I saw this myself in a hearing when the judge made a gesture with his hand telling a woman lawyer to be quiet.

She added that although judges verbally abused both male and female attorneys, abuse directed at female lawyers targeted their gender.

Women lawyers also face cultural obstacles external to the legal system. According to one interviewee, social attitudes to women in public life have improved, but many – both men and women – continue to hold traditional views of gender roles:

> [Iranian] men don't like to see their wives succeed in their careers. They believe that a woman who earns a living and is publicly successful in her work must fail in her private life. A very traditional view of gender roles prevails, and a lot of people believe that the man is the breadwinner in the family. That is why a lot of women don't take their careers seriously and why many female lawyers discontinue their practice as soon as they get married and have children.

Although the numbers of female law students, trainees and lawyers aged 25–35 years old have increased, few women remain in practice. The prevailing gendered social attitudes to women in the public sphere hinder many female lawyers from pursuing a successful public career, whilst simultaneously undermining the public's confidence in their competence. One of our male attorneys said: 'society doesn't normally believe enough in female lawyers' ability to put its trust in them'. Several attorneys reported that many clients were wary of entrusting their cases to female lawyers. 'Even women trust male lawyers more than female lawyers'. The public believed that 'women can't successfully handle a case which needs a show of aggression, confronting the other party and the judge, making connections and paying bribes and so on'.

H. Law Firms

Most 'law firms' do not have a corporate structure or partners and associates but are groups of sole practitioners working side by side. A few corporate law firms are operated by small groups of international lawyers, often educated and trained abroad, associated with foreign international law firms, dealing exclusively with shipping and international trade law.

Iranian attorneys are reluctant to work collectively. One international lawyer explained: 'lawyers who have worked as sole practitioners and have been their own boss and managed their business as it suits them throughout their career, find it very difficult to work in a law firm which runs like an office and where you have to prove your worth'. What appear to outsiders as law firms often are just a handful of lawyers who have come together 'either because they are friends and know and respect each other, or because they have a common interest'.

There are two types of organisation. The first, officially called a 'legal bureau' (*moassess-e hūghūghī*), is a recent innovation created by managers who may not be lawyers. These act primarily as middlemen, providing 'lawyer-on-demand' services by allocating cases to a loose network of freelance lawyers. The IBA attorneys we interviewed were very critical of these forms, claiming no self-respecting lawyer would work for them. Our respondents said legal bureaus were managed unprofessionally, exploited trainee lawyers or new entrants desperate for work, and allowed unethical practices, such as giving potential clients misleading information. Managers, who often were not experienced lawyers and thus neither understood law practice nor were constrained by lawyers' professional codes of conduct, would promise anything to attract clients. The IBA attorneys saw the rise of legal bureaus as yet another effort by the judiciary to undermine their legal work. The second category of law firm is operated collectively by younger lawyers to strengthen their network of business contacts, improve access to the legal market, create a higher profile that attracts clients and, most importantly, share expenses. The IBA attorneys viewed this type of law firm positively, and many thought the IBA should help them overcome obstacles. But they generally agreed that as long as Iranian lawyers did not specialise (partly a function of the underdeveloped market) there would be little incentive to create law firms.

I. Legal Education and Training

Legal education leading to an LLB involves four years of intensive study of some 70 subjects. Because the curriculum 'reflects the religious nature of its legal system', it includes not only municipal and international law (organised along lines similar to Western curricula) but also subjects like Islamic education, Islamic morality, Islamic revolution, the history of Islam and even Arabic (Talaie 2004–05: 120, 127).

All our interviewees criticised the curriculum for devoting too much time to theory instead of helping students acquire legal skills. We heard repeatedly that they 'learn the academic basis of the law but not the practical reality of working as a lawyer', and 'anyone who studies law at university in Iran leaves without knowing the first thing about legal practice'. Some of the IBA attorneys were also critical of Islamic jurisprudence and Arabic,[24] feeling that neither was relevant to legal practice. This is surprising since mastering Islamic jurisprudence, which requires familiarity with Arabic texts, is essential for grasping how judges employ *fiqh* in forming a judgment and passing sentence. One attorney who teaches part time explained that law schools were aware of their failings, which could be addressed by introducing clinical programmes; but the volume and number of subjects in the required curriculum left no time for teaching practical skills. Since 2007, Mofid University in Qom has been offering clinical programmes, but they remain embryonic. Some respondents contrasted the limited training of attorneys to the systematic training of judges, who regularly attend court hearings during their pupillage and continue their training on the bench by attending special courses and workshops.

After obtaining a law degree, those intending to practise must complete an 18-month pupillage and pass a qualifying examination. The pupillage must be served under an established practitioner with at least ten years' experience. Each month pupils must attend a lecture organised by the IBA as well as two court hearings, which they must report in writing; they must also write a research-based dissertation.

In practice, a senior member of the IBA said, this training scheme left much to be desired.

> The training period consists basically of attending certain courts a number of times. ... If I am not mistaken, one month is family courts, then it is juvenile courts, then revolutionary courts, three months in the court of appeal, several months in private law courts and so on. ... I have seen very few courts which allow pupils to attend and observe and discuss matters with judges. Instead, courts send trainees off to the archives and give them a case to read and write a report. ... This doesn't provide sufficient training. The IBA ... helps with teaching specialised skills to lawyers. There are also lectures and mooting workshops, but these revolve around academic themes and don't help much with developing your practical skills.

The negative attitude of judges was seen as an obstacle to teaching legal skills to IBA trainees. Some judges show their reluctance to have IBA pupils attend their hearings by instructing the court clerk to send them to the archives to read cases. By contrast, trainee judges enjoy the total support of presiding judges, who encourage them to observe court sessions and discuss legal issues. IBA trainees are dependent on their supervisors' willingness and ability to show them the ropes, but supervisors differ in how they mentor

---

[24] Farsi (or Persian) is an Indo-European language, whereas Arabic is Semitic. Although they have borrowed vocabulary from each other, and Farsi uses a variant of the Arabic alphabet, they differ radically in grammar, syntax and morphology.

pupils. To make matters worse, there are no standards for mentoring and no assessment of pupils' progress.

> Your supervisor might tell you that you may not attend client consultation sessions and you should not expect to have your own clients. I have come across supervisors who charged their pupils for a consultation. ... And no one would know if you have learnt anything during your pupillage. What counts is to pass your qualifying Bar exam, which is also more theoretical and does not contain questions on legal practice. They might ask you to define, for example, various types of crime, but not how you would go about, say, winning a forfeiture case if your clients' property has been seized.

Attorneys were very critical of the IBA's pupillage programme, calling it a 'formality' that required 'going through the motions' rather than acquiring the skills needed to practise law. As a result, lawyers begin their professional careers with very different experiences of advocacy and other legal work.

J. Codes of Professional Responsibility

While discussing the shortcomings of legal education, an international lawyer said:

> There are Iranian lawyers who don't know what is meant by 'code of conduct'. ... When I was a student, we spent one whole term discussing the Islamic jurisprudence of the validity of family contracts, but no one even mentioned the code of conduct to us.

Interviewees admitted their sense of professionalism was weak, and few lawyers took the code of conduct seriously. Many attorneys disregarded the code for economic reasons. Many had entered the profession in the previous 10–12 years 'only to make money'. One respondent argued that in a legal system where judges do not perform their duties properly, lawyers will also fail in their professional duties. The obligation of zealous advocacy was not understood by the public, or even some lawyers and judges.

> One thing which upsets me most is the attitude of my colleagues [the other attorneys] and the court staff. The judge in a way sees you as his opponent – you are up against him. Colleagues refuse to talk to you outside the court, because you have argued against them legally. They seem not to understand that you are *representing* your client and it's not a personal thing. ... In these situations, I think they violate our code of professional conduct.

This interviewee argued it was difficult to serve the interests of one's client and conduct oneself professionally within a legal system that did not recognise the lawyer's professional integrity. Confrontations could not be confined to clashes between the judiciary and IBA attorneys and spilled into the professional relationship between attorneys. 'Many colleagues think that the case they represent is their own dispute and get very personal. They lose their temper in the court and treat each other with disrespect'.

When asked about their professional code of conduct, none of our interviewees discussed the importance of due diligence, providing professional services of the highest standards, refusing to undertake work the lawyer was not competent to handle, confidentiality, or conflicts of interest. Instead, they talked about professional conduct in a politicised and morally corrupt legal system and in 'the context of the wider society, which has become morally uncertain and socially unstable'.

IV. CONCLUSION: THE CLASH OF TWO LEGAL CULTURES

Concealed behind descriptions of a hostile judiciary lies a clash between two legal cultures over the most valuable symbolic capital of the juridical field – the authority to determine the law – grounded in political conflicts between reformist political groups seeking the separation of state and religion and supporters of the hierocracy. What is at stake is no less than the future of Iranian modernity played out as a confrontation between the judiciary and the legal profession. This clash is intensified by judges' bitterness over being deprived of the economic opportunities available to practitioners. The economic competition turns many judges against lawyers and corrupts the entire legal system. This is to be expected. A judicial system designed to embody an ideology to which it requires total commitment cannot avoid widespread cronyism. Corrupt practices have multiple causes, including judges' and attorneys' lack of autonomy, direct and indirect political interference in the enforcement of laws, private financial gain or bribery, and cultural practices promoting cronyism and informal networks of personal and family contacts.

One legal culture is created by carefully selecting judges from a socially homogeneous group of men and imbuing them with the political values of the Islamic Republic. This training includes understanding and enforcing the law in terms of *fiqh*, or Islamic jurisprudence, as developed by Shi'a jurists. The other legal culture is based on the jurisprudence of modern law schools, which see the law as a rule-based rational construct for decision-making. In the context of codified law and due process, Iranian judges' application of *fiqh* introduces an element of legal uncertainty and arbitrariness that many defence attorneys find difficult to anticipate and react to.

Our IBA attorneys are agents in the juridical field, competing with the judiciary for the 'monopoly of the right to determine the law' and access to legal resources (Bourdieu 1987: 817). But they are also members of the middle class and the intellectual elite in Iranian civil society – a segment that continues to argue for the rule of law in a country organised under clerical rule in accordance with Islamic ideology. This suggests a deep-rooted ideological schism between the IBA rank and file and the judiciary, reflecting the ideological division defining Iranian society at large. To describe this rupture in terms of modern/traditionalist or secular/religious dichotomies would overlook two points. The jurisprudence of the Iranian judiciary – however politicised, illiberal and repressive it may be – contains many innovative ideas challenging a traditional understanding of Sharia. Moreover, Sharia has always contained secular practices and a secularisation of the divine has been occurring since Khomeini introduced the principle of *maslahat-e nezam* (expediency of the state), which overrides all religious doctrine.

In the ongoing contest for Iranian modernity, the legal profession has played, and will continue to play, a key role. Its struggle for autonomy questions the ideological hegemony of the clerical establishment, and its recent feminisation challenges the internal and external cultures of Iranian law. The socio-cultural and political obstacles confronting the legal profession may appear insurmountable. Independent lawyers are undermined by the Islamic Republic's judicial system and forced to pay the price for public distrust of the law and legal institutions, which is paradoxically related to the clerical regime's lack of legitimacy. Nonetheless, the IBA's continued insistence on, and fight for, independence, and the professional courage displayed by the generation of lawyers born after the 1979

Revolution, who refuse to surrender their fidelity to a broadly conceived notion of law and due process, offer grounds for optimism against all odds.

REFERENCES

Amnesty International (2015) 'Iran: Draconian Amendment further Erodes Fair Trial Rights' www.amnesty.org/en/documents/mde13/1943/2015/en/.
Banakar, R (2016) *Driving Culture in Iran: Law and Society on the Roads of the Islamic Republic* (London, IB Tauris).
—— (2018) 'Double-Thinking and Contradictory Arrangements in Iranian Law and Society' 27(1) *Digest of Middle Eastern Studies* 6–33.
Banakar, R and Ziaee, K (2018) 'The Life of Law in the Islamic Republic of Iran' 51(5) *Iranian Studies Journal* 717–46.
Bourdieu, P (1987) 'The Force of Law: Toward a Sociology of the Juridical Field' 38(5) *Hastings Law Journal* 814–53.
Burns, JG (2014) *Introduction to Islamic Law: Principles of Civil, Criminal, and International Law under the Shari'a* (TellerBooks, JuraLaw).
Butler, WJ and Levasseur, G (1976) *Human Rights and the Legal System in Iran* (Geneva, International Commission of Jurists).
Enayat, H (2013) *Law, State, and Society in Modern Iran* (London, Palgrave Macmillan).
Entessar, N (1988) 'Criminal Law and the Legal System in Revolutionary Iran' 8(1) *Boston College Third World Law Journal* 91–102.
Galanter, M (1998) 'The Faces of Mistrust: The Image of Lawyers in Public Opinion, Jokes, and Political Discourse' 66 *University of Cincinnati Law Review* 805–45.
Ghobadzadeh (2013) 'Religious Secularity: A vision for Religious Political Islam' *Philosophy and Social Criticism* 1005–27.
Hengstler, GA (1993) 'The Public Perception of Lawyers: ABA Poll' *ABA Journal* 60–66.
HRDI (2016) 'Iran's Grand Ayatollah Makarem Shirazi Blasts Due Process of Law' (Human Rights and Democracy for Iran) www.iranrights.org/fa/library/document/2701.
Hujjati, M (2014) *Didgahay-e Senfi-e Yak Vakil-e Dadgostary* [*The Professional Viewpoints of an Attorney at Law*] (Tehran, Āvā).
Human Rights Watch (2010) 'Iran: Lawyer's Defence Work is Repaid with Loss of Freedom' www.hrw.org/news/2010/10/01/iran-lawyers-defence-work-repaid-loss-freedom.
ICHRI (2011) 'Lacking Independence: Bar Association Remains Silent as Lawyers are Prosecuted' (International Campaign for Human Rights in Iran) www.iranhumanrights.org/2011/08/bar-association-under-attack/.
—— (2013) 'Lawyers Say Bill on Legal Profession Destroys Lawyer Independence' www.iranhumanrights.org/2013/07/lawyers_independence/.
—— (2015) 'Parliamentary Bills Further Threaten Autonomy of Legal Profession in Iran' www.iranhumanrights.org/2015/07/parliamentary-threaten-legal-profession/.
—— (2016) 'Prominent Lawyers Disqualified from Iran's Bar Association Elec' www.iranhumanrights.org/2016/02/top-lawyers-disqualified-for-bar-association-elections/.
IHRDC (2015) 'Iranian Judiciary: A Complex and Dysfunctional System' (Iran Human Rights Documentation Center) iranhrdc.org/the-iranian-judiciary-a-complex-and-dysfunctional-system.
International Bar Association (2007) 'Balancing Independence and Access to Justice: A background report on the justice system in Iran' www.ibanet.org/Document/Default.aspx?DocumentUid=ecbef5ba-b42d-4b53-b0f4-51a5975a8d65.
Iranian Bar Association Union (2016) www.iranbar.com/ltrenuni1.php#4.

IRINN (2017) 'The Comprehensive General Bill of the Bar Association Rejected' www.irinn.ir/fa/news/510111/دش-در-تل‌اکو-عماج-هحی‌ال-تای‌لک.

ISNA (2017) 'Ghoveh Ghazaeieh Niazmandeh Ghozateh Salem Ast' (Iranian Students' News Agency) 4 January www.isna.ir.

Khomeini, RM (2006) *Sahifeh Noor [The Book of Light: Collection of Ayatollah Khomeini's Speeches, Messages, Letters and Statements]* Vol 20 (Tehran, Moasseseh Tanzim va Nashre Asare Imam).

LCHR (1993) 'The Justice System of the Islamic Republic of Iran' (Lawyers Committee for Human Rights) iranrights.org/library/document/93/the-justice-system-of-the-islamic-republic-of-iran#sthash.p6Ql90S8.agkom0xx.dpbs.

Mohammadi, M (2008) *Judicial Reform and Reorganization in 20th Century Iran: State Building, Modernisation and Islamization* (London, Routledge).

Mousavian, SA (2005) 'The Scope of Probative Judge's Knowledge Judgement in Fiqh' 38(3) *Maqalat wa Barrasiha* 93–119.

Nayyeri, MH (2012) 'Iranian Bar Association: Struggle for Independence' (Iran Human Rights Documentation Centre) www.iranhrdc.org.

Official Gazette (1982) 'Ghānūn-e Sharayet-e Entekhābāt-e Ghozzat-e Dādgūstarī' (Law on the Qualifications for the Appointment of Judges), approved on 14 May 1982, Code Collection, rc. majlis.ir/fa/law/show/90547.

Owsia, P (1991) 'Sources of Law Under English, French, Islamic and Iranian Law: A Comparative Review of Legal Techniques' 6(1) *Arab Law Quarterly* 33–67.

SRRI (2013) *Report of the Special Rapporteur on the Situation of Human Rights in the Islamic Republic of Iran* (United Nations) A/67/369 www.ohchr.org/Documents/Countries/IR/A-HRC-22-56_en.pdf.

—— (2015) *Report of the Special Rapporteur on the Situation of Human Rights in the Islamic Republic of Iran* (United Nations) A/HRC/28/70, digitallibrary.un.org/record/795162.

Talaie, F (2004–2005) 'A Description of the Law Curricula in the Iranian Colleges of Law' 8 *Newcastle Law Review* 117–40.

Tavassolian, N (2012) 'Reform within the Judiciary of Iran' *Legatum Institute* lif.blob.core.windows.net/lif/docs/default-source/future-of-iran/2012-future-of-iran-by-nargess-tavassolian-reform-within-the-judiciary-of-iran.pdf?sfvrsn=0.

Weber, M (1978) *Economy and Society: An Outline of Interpretive Sociology* Vol II (Berkeley, University of California Press).

Vekālat (2011) 'Kanone-h vokala che-h mytavand bekonad'['What Could the Iranian Bar Association do?'] *Esfand* 44–45.

30

Israel

Numbers, Make-Up and Modes of Practice

EYAL KATVAN, LIMOR ZER-GUTMAN AND NETA ZIV

I. INTRODUCTION

THE ISRAELI LEGAL system derives from Ottoman and English law – the two empires that governed Israel before independence in 1948. Israeli jurisprudence strongly resembles the common law, given the British mandate. English law most conspicuously influenced the judiciary, reflected in its hierarchical structure and the status of its judges.

The Israeli legal profession is also rooted in English law and preceded the State of Israel. From the beginning, it was a 'free profession', whose members demanded individual freedom and institutional autonomy. After enactment of the Israeli Bar Association Act in 1961, the profession gained exclusive and autonomous self-regulatory powers, which it has enjoyed ever since. The Israel Bar Association (IBA) was established as an autonomous entity with compulsory membership. The IBA has a dual identity. On one hand, it considers itself a representative body, advancing the professional interests of its members. On the other, it has claimed a special responsibility in the public debate surrounding the rule of law, human rights and democracy. The IBA Act was amended to include an obligation 'to protect the rule of law, human rights and the basic values of the State of Israel'.

This chapter reviews the evolution of the IBA's regulatory regime, focusing on two recent amendments to the IBA Act in 2008 and 2016. We conclude that though the IBA is facing challenges to its monolithic regulatory regime, including pressure for decentralisation, the basic regulatory structure has not fundamentally altered since it was first established, despite vast changes within Israeli society, economy and polity, belief systems and demography, as well the role of law in political and everyday life. We attribute this continuity to the long-standing alliance between the legal profession and the judiciary and between the IBA and the state, especially the Ministry of Justice and the Parliament.

In recent decades the legal profession has played an increasing role in improving access to justice. State-supported civil legal aid was instituted in 1973 and criminal defence two decades later in 1996. Public interest lawyering in civil society emerged in the mid-1980s and has grown rapidly, today including a wide-range of non-governmental organisations (NGOs). All law schools in Israel operate legal clinics, which have become an integral part of legal education. Pro bono services, however, remain quite limited.

In 1949, a year after the State of Israel was established, there were 765 registered lawyers (IBA Jubilee Book 2011). In 2018 there were over 65,000. Since 2000, Israel has consistently had the highest number of lawyers per capita, significantly more than its nearest competitor. The most striking characteristic of the Israeli legal profession in recent decades is the dramatic increase in the number of lawyers and the changes in the demographic profile and status of lawyers. The genesis of these changes was the opening of new law schools since the 1990s, most of them private law colleges. What had been three law schools with 2,000 students each year became 14 law schools with 16,000 students. The diversification of legal education also contributed to the emergence of two hemispheres in the Israeli legal profession.

II. FORMATION OF THE LEGAL PROFESSION AND ESTABLISHMENT OF THE ISRAEL BAR ASSOCIATION

The territory that became the state of Israel was ruled as a Mandate by Britain after 1917, following the conquest of the Ottoman empire. In the first two decades of the twentieth century there were fewer than ten active lawyers (Brun 2008). Under the Ottoman Code of Civil Procedure people were entitled to be represented by a lawyer, but most legal services were provided by other professional groups: petition writers (scriveners) without formal legal education, or religious pleaders in the various religious courts.

From the beginning of the Mandate to the IBA Act in 1961 lawyers were governed by two kinds of organisations. The first was the Legal Board (*Mo'atsa Mishpatit*, later named the Legal Council), an agency of the Mandate government, which initially operated under the 1922 Advocates Ordinance and then under the 1938 Legal Council Ordinance. The Legal Council was responsible for licensing lawyers and supervising their professional conduct (Likhovsky 2006: 26). The other organisations were ethnic: the Jewish and the Arab Lawyers Associations. Of the 49 registered lawyers in Palestine in 1921, four were Jewish and the rest Arab (Brun 2008). In 1948, just before the state of Israel was established, the Jewish Lawyers Association included around 800 members and the Arab Lawyers Association approximately 500. Because membership in both organisations was voluntary, their legitimacy and power depended on their numbers. This weakness was explicitly addressed in the parliamentary debates leading to enactment of the IBA Act. As in other common law countries, disciplinary authority over lawyers initially was vested in the courts, under the Chief Justice, and transferred to the Legal Council in 1938.

In 1949, a year after the establishment of the State of Israel, its lawyers moved to create a new regulatory regime, which would differ from those of both the Mandate and its English motherland. Within an emerging liberal democracy, in a strongly statist era, lawyers' main goal·was to create a system granting the profession more autonomy from the state through enactment of a comprehensive law consolidating all the powers of the organised Bar in a single entity. To that end, lawyers sought enactment of the IBA Act, giving their organisation broad powers of self-governance and ensuring themselves a broad exclusive jurisdiction through strict unauthorised practice of law (UPL) rules. Because the early years of Israeli statehood were saturated with notions of nationalism and collectivism (Ziv 2002–2003; Ziv 2015; Rosen-Zvi 2001), it took lawyers more than a decade to reach this goal. Their claim to professional independence as a means to protect the rule of law (as well as their private interests) encountered suspicion and some hostility from members of Parliament. Nevertheless, in 1961 Parliament enacted the IBA Act, granting lawyers an unprecedented autonomous professional status (Salzberger 2002).

The IBA Act established a single body to govern the legal profession. Membership became mandatory, yearly fees obligatory, and both were (and are) conditions for practising law. Through its various committees and bodies, the IBA oversees the apprenticeship requirement (a prerequisite for taking the Bar exams), administers Bar exams, and controls licensing. The IBA is authorised to promulgate disciplinary rules (which must be approved by the Ministry of Justice), issues ethical pre-ruling opinions to members, prosecutes lawyers for disciplinary misconduct, operates the regional and national internal disciplinary boards (from which there is an appeal to the civil court), sets dress codes, enforces advertising restrictions, and is very active in defending jurisdictional exclusivity against unauthorised practice of law.

Several amendments have been introduced, most significantly those relating to the disciplinary system in 2008 and IBA internal institutions in 2016. Public pressure led to the establishment of public commissions that recommended implementation of these amendments. But an analysis of the legislative process reveals that both amendments largely ratified the Bar's position, which had never accepted any dilution of self-regulation. Thus, 55 years since the law was passed, the IBA retains its original form and exercises vast policing powers over its members (Zer-Gutman 2010; Ziv 2015).

The IBA performs dual functions that are often in conflict. It represents the collective interests of the profession and is highly proactive in resisting any real or perceived threat to the profession's symbolic status or material concerns. At the same time, it enjoys vast powers to oversee and police its members through a centralised disciplinary system in which it wields legislative, executive and semi-judicial powers (Zer-Gutman 2013b). As described below, there has been some encroachment on this centralised self-regulatory regime, but the IBA's basic structure and broad control over the profession have remained almost intact.

A prominent example (albeit not an exclusive one) of the quest to maintain control over entry into the profession is the IBA's incessant preoccupation with the length of the mandatory apprenticeship. When the IBA was enacted, apprenticeship lasted two years and partially overlapped with the legal studies. Subsequent changes required Parliamentary action. In 1985, the apprenticeship was shortened to 18 months but separated from academic legal studies. In 1994, the apprenticeship was again shortened – this time to one year – apparently to help the growing number of law graduates find a position and in the belief that legal training (unlike that in medicine) does not require specialisation in a particular area of law (IBA Jubilee Book 2011). Another justification for this decision was the fact that most Israelis begin their legal studies after three years of mandatory army services, having 'lost' a period of professional development.

The continuing exponential growth in the number of lawyers in Israel since 1995 revived the public debate about the length of the apprenticeship. In 2002, a public committee chaired by a District Court Judge recommended extending the apprenticeship period to 18 months. The IBA lobbied strongly with the Ministry of Justice and Parliament to implement the proposed changes (IBA Jubilee Book, 2011) but succeeded only in 2017. The IBA argued that this change was necessary to ensure quality of service and professional competence, but other groups (including associations of law students and interns) claimed the motive was to restrict entry. In 2017, the IBA Act was amended and the apprenticeship is now 18 months. There is no official data on the number of law graduates unable find internships or the salaries paid to interns. The Bar does not report the number of internships it disqualifies or its reasons for doing so.

III. THE REGULATORY REGIME

Until the mid-1990s, disciplinary rules limiting internal and external competition included the prohibition of solicitation and advertising, mandatory minimum fees, and a ban on practising vocations other than lawyering (such as certified public accountant, real estate broker, or any other occupation unbecoming to the profession). Those restrictions have been relaxed in the last two decades following challenges, mostly from lawyers claiming economic harms (Zer-Gutman 2008; Ziv 2015). In 2003, the Israeli Supreme Court rejected a petition to end the IBA's monopoly.[1] In 2008, legislative attempts to effect significant reductions in IBA control over the disciplinary process ended in minor changes to the existing law (Amendment No 32). In 2016, another legislative attempt to bring about the most extensive transformation ever ended with many new sections added to the Act but no change to the profession's self-regulation, autonomy or monopoly (Amendment No 38).

The profession has a very broad monopoly of legal representation, placing Israel among the 12 of 46 European countries enjoying a full monopoly (CEPEJ 2016). The IBA has been highly proactive in seeking to prevent competition from outsiders, mainly private companies offering services to the public in the areas of disability and medical entitlement, debt collection and land registration. Because discretion is limited by the relatively technical nature of these bodies of law, they are more easily infiltrated by competing professions (Abbott 1988). Even though UPL has been the most salient issue on the IBA's agenda for the last two decades, an estimated 16 per cent of the legal services market has been 'lost' to non-lawyer activity of this sort (Zalmanovitsh 2017). In a series of cases initiated by the IBA, courts have interpreted UPL law in a way that slightly narrows lawyers' monopoly by allowing private service providers to assist clients in filing claims for social insurance and disability allowance (Ziv 2015). In other areas, such as civil writ execution, family disputes and debt collection, the IBA succeeded in blocking private entrepreneurs from encroaching upon lawyers' exclusive jurisdiction. But some of the small firms threatened by such competition have eagerly cooperated with such companies. There are few online semi-legal providers in Israel because the IBA has been very assertive in obtaining restraining orders, intimidating others from entering the field (Ziv 2016).

In other areas of law, courts have taken the lead in establishing standards for lawyers' conduct. In several cases (mainly involving real estate transactions), courts held that lawyers, as guardians of the civil justice system, were liable in negligence for engaging in

---

[1] HCJ 2334/02 *Attorney Stanger v Chair, the Knesset et al*, IsrSC 58(1) 786 (2003) (Hebrew).

overzealous representation of their clients at the expense of an adversary or unrepresented third party (Zer-Gutman 2005; Ziv 2005). For example, a lawyer drafted a contract allowing the lender-client to seize the borrower's apartment after any delay in payment even though it was worth much more than the debt. The lender, using his lawyer's services, enforced the contract, with the result that the family was evicted, the borrower lost his job, and social services placed his children away from their nonfunctioning home.[2] In contrast to the jurisprudence developed by the civil courts, the IBA's ethics committees (at the first stage of the disciplinary process) as well as the disciplinary tribunals (at the second stage) stress lawyers' primary obligation to clients and seldom regard being 'overzealous' as unethical behaviour (Zer-Gutman 2016).

In addition, courts have been exercising their authority to determine the scope of the lawyer-client privilege (as well as duties of confidentiality), thereby challenging the IBA's exclusive power to set standards on a matter at the core of the profession's governance (Ziv 2015). In the last two decades, for example, the Supreme Court narrowed the type of information covered by the privilege, excluding the client's identity, fee contract, and billing information.[3]

Another site of jurisdictional and regulatory struggle is the standards governing lawyers in the context of the global campaign against money laundering (Alef 2014). The IBA vehemently objected when the Ministries of Finance and Justice (pressured by global actors such as the Financial Action Task Force and the Committee of Experts on the Evaluation of Anti-Money Laundering Measures and the Financing of Terrorism) sought to impose heightened requirements on lawyers as gatekeepers against money laundering (with obligations to monitor, document and report suspicious client activity). The parties reached a compromise imposing elevated standards on lawyers but leaving the IBA with partial control over enforcement (Alef 2014). Similarly, in 2009, following pressure from the Organisation for Economic Co-operation and Development, Parliament amended the IBA Act to allow 'foreign' (non-Israeli) lawyers to work in Israel under certain conditions. The IBA objected to this amendment but failed to block it, settling for control over the registrar of the foreign lawyers section and a mandatory exam in English on Israeli legal ethics (Ziv 2015). Under this amendment, foreign lawyers may only provide legal services on 'foreign law', are bound by Israeli ethical rules, must have insurance, and cannot form a partnership with Israeli lawyers. As of 2016, 55 lawyers from the US, China, Belgium, France and Australia are registered in Israel and operate eight law firms. In sum, we are witnessing a gradual process by which the IBA – although still wielding broad powers over lawyers – is facing challenges to its monolithic regulatory regime, leading to more decentralised regulation.

IV. RELATIONS BETWEEN THE PROFESSION, THE JUDICIARY AND THE STATE

Until the 1990s, the Bar and bench (mainly the Israeli Supreme Court) maintained a united 'front' vis-à-vis the state and its political apparatus (Salzberger 2001; Rosen-Zvi 2001; Ziv 2015). The court rarely intervened in matters concerning the legal profession and

---

[2] CA 2625/02 *Attorney Silvio v Dorenbaum* (2004) IsrSC 48(3) 385 (Hebrew).
[3] RCA 751/15 *Abargil v The State of Israel* (2016) (Hebrew).

endorsed most IBA policies and decisions, accepting the claim that broad autonomy and self-regulation were legitimate and necessary to ensure the quality of legal services. This relationship was forged during the first era of Israeli statehood, when the Supreme Court needed to establish the judiciary's independence from politics in an emerging nation. The legal profession was a cohesive network: judges and lawyers were socially proximate – belonging to similar social circles – and shared an ethos of collegiality (Rosen-Zvi 2001). Since the 1990s, there has been a notable rift between bench and bar, a shifting, ad hoc positioning replacing the earlier stable alliance. The Supreme Court has been supportive of the Bar's fundamental structure, dismissing challenges to its monopoly, mandatory IBA membership and fees, and UPL rules. But on issues with narrower implications, the Court has imposed normative standards that sharply differ from those of the Bar, as when the Supreme Court invalidated an ethical rule limiting the ability of clients to switch lawyers during a fee dispute, imposed heightened fiduciary duties towards third parties, rejected IBA challenges to a ceiling on lawyers' fees, and restricted the scope of UPL rules by allowing private companies to provide services over which the IBA claimed a monopoly (Ziv 2015).

Parliament displayed little interest in lawyers' affairs during the first three decades after the IBA was established, a period when the private market was less developed and state regulation (as opposed to direct provision of services) was rare (Barzilai 2007). In the mid-1980s the shift from a strong state-centered economy to a privatised, globalised liberalised economy threatened the status of the IBA and the profession. Because the new economic policies favoured competition, the IBA's monopoly has come under constant contestation. Government officials and members of Parliament from both libertarian and social democratic parties expressed a growing distrust of the old arrangement, claiming that it served the interests of lawyers, not those of the general public (Ziv 2015).

But despite this more hostile climate, the IBA has succeeded in maintaining most of its institutional advantages and privileges. Broad legislative initiatives to limit the Bar's monopoly have not been successful, as shown by the 2008 revision of the disciplinary system (Amendment No 32). The IBA managed to control the legislative process (which took over five years) and preserve its authority over the disciplinary system, with only few modest changes. A legislative amendment aimed at addressing two major flaws – the extreme politicisation of disciplinary hearings and the lack of transparency – produced only minor changes, leaving most of the problems unresolved (Zer-Gutman 2010; 2017).

In 2016, the IBA Act underwent the most comprehensive amendment since its enactment. Amendment No 38 was the outcome of a detailed report by a public committee appointed by the Minister of Justice after the IBA was paralysed by a dispute between its president and other elected officials. But despite this rare opportunity to make major changes in the IBA Act and other laws, parliamentary deliberations revealed an intimate alliance with the Bar, which ended in a compromise agreed by the new Bar president, the Ministry of Justice and the chair of the relevant parliamentary committee. The amendments the IBA had opposed were either deleted or remanded to the parliamentary committee. Amendments that the Bar approved were ratified. Amendment no 38 reflects effective lobbying by the IBA and the strong alliance it had formed with Parliament and the Minister of Justice (Zer-Gutman 2017).

V. THE IBA AS A CIVIC ACTOR

Perhaps because of changes in its public image and relation to the state, since the early 2000s the IBA has become more engaged in issues that do not directly affect lawyers or the profession (Barzilai 2007; Ziv 2015). It took a stand regarding the status of the Israeli Supreme Court and the controversy about judicial activism (Salzberger, 2001). It could be argued that because anything concerning the judicial system affects lawyers, this action does not represent a significant repositioning. However, starting in the early 2000s, IBA president Shlomo Cohen, who entered office with a left-liberal agenda, demanded that the organisation take a position on human rights violations in Israel and the Occupied Territories (Ziv 2009). Despite deep controversies within the Bar about the legitimacy of this demand, the IBA has broadened its involvement in public affairs and become an important civic actor, regardless of the political affiliation of its president, engaging numerous public issues, such as prison conditions, civil procedure and debt collection, financial reforms, employment rights, and social and minority rights (IBA Jubilee Book 2011).

The organisation also proposed an amendment to the IBA Act in 2010 to make the provision of legal services to the needy a mandatory institutional obligation, instead of the discretionary responsibility it had been. A formal pro bono program instituted by the IBA in 2003 initially provoked resistance from lawyers concerned about competition from colleagues working for no fee. Nevertheless, the IBA's pro bono program expanded to become an integral part of its activities. In 2014, 4,499 of the 56,750 active lawyers dealt with 1,109 cases (out of 25,389 applications for assistance) (IBA Annual Report 2014).

The IBA keeps seeking to enhance its reputation for serving interests broader than those of its membership. In 2016, the IBA Act amended its original mandate – to 'incorporate the advocates in Israel' and 'take good care to observe, supervise and ensure the standards and ethics of the legal profession' – to add a commitment 'to protect the rule of law, human rights and the basic values of the State of Israel' (Amendment No 38). Whether this represents a genuine shift in its identity or just a way to reposition itself as a legitimate public institution, the IBA today fuses extensive public activity with vigorous advocacy for the interests of the profession.

VI. PUBLIC SERVICE AND PUBLIC INTEREST LAWYERING

During the first four decades of Israeli statehood, lawyering was considered mainly a private means to make a living. The IBA was little occupied with questions of access to justice or the rule of law, and there were few public interest organisations operating independent of the state. Elite lawyers from the Mandate period took positions within the newly established state, while the rank and file of the lawyers were busy representing individual clients, with no inclination to assume a public role. The notion that lawyers, individually or collectively, can or should utilise their professional skills to promote the public interest emerged in Israel only in the 1980s. Since then, public interest lawyering has expanded rapidly and now constitutes an important part of the legal profession. Public service lawyers work in the state apparatus, NGOs and law school legal clinics. There are also a small number of private law firms staffed by 'ideological lawyers' who represent indigent clients for little or no fee or take law reform cases on a pro bono or low bono basis (Ziv 2015). Some are also active in social movements or political parties.

A. State Support: Civil Legal Aid

Legal aid, introduced in 1973 in response to public demand as part of Israel's socialist polity and welfare economy, was not rights-based but conditioned on need. It still employs a means test (income and wealth, except for certain areas like welfare benefits) and requires applicants to show that their claims or defences have a legal basis. Legal aid is delivered by about 50 staff lawyers and a pool of over 1200 private practitioners who take cases on assignment for a fee. Lawyers can apply to be included in the pool and are screened by the legal aid office; fees vary with the type of case and the actions required for representation.

For many years, the civil legal aid budget was low and did not come close to meeting the needs of those who could not afford private legal services. In the early 2000s it was 40 million shekels a year, compared to about 70 million for criminal defence in 2001. The under-budgeting of civil legal aid triggered the appointment of a public committee to examine unmet legal needs, which found a grave shortage in state-funded legal aid (Ziv 2015). Although the office of legal aid did not undergo a comprehensive reform, the government has gradually been expanding its budget: 58 million shekels in 2005, 62 million in 2008, 100 million in 2013. The caseload also increased, if not proportionally: 48,000 applications in 2005, 61,000 in 2009, and 71,000 in 2011. The office handles about 150,000 cases a year, and has been expanding the groups entitled to assistance to include people with mental disabilities and victims of human trafficking. In addition, the office now sees itself not only as a service organisation for needy individuals but also as the advocate for the rights and interests of the poor and disadvantaged.

B. State Support: Criminal Defence

Criminal defence was established in 1996, two decades after civil legal aid. Before then, because eligibility for publicly-funded criminal defence rested on extremely narrow grounds, most defendants were represented by the private bar. That year the Office of the Public Defense at the Ministry of Justice was established following extensive efforts by Professor Kenneth Mann (who originally operated from the criminal justice clinic at Tel Aviv University Faculty of Law) and a small group of dedicated activists (Ogletree and Sapir 2004). Mann became the first Chief Public Defender (PD) and performed this role for seven years. The mid-1990s was the peak of the 'rights era' in Israeli jurisprudence, and the establishment of a public defence system was seen as an expression of the duty to protect individual liberty and due process.

Since then, criminal defence in Israel has undergone a major reform, manifested in increased budgets, broader eligibility criteria applying to all criminal proceedings (arrest through all appeals) and a growing caseload. The PD budget was 20 million shekels in 1998, 50 million in 2000, 70 million in 2001, 107 million in 2007, 136 million in 2009, 178.5 million in 2013 and 249 million in 2016. In 2016, the PD office employed 120 lawyers and outsourced cases to another 850. Employment in the PD Office is considered prestigious. The latest report indicates that 57 per cent of defendants in the magistrate courts and 33 per cent in the district courts were represented by the PD. The PD also plays a significant role in legislation and policy-making in criminal law (PD Annual Reports).

C. Public Interest Lawyering in Civil Society: NGOs and Law School Legal Clinics

Public interest lawyering did not exist in Israel until the mid-1980s because civil society was under-developed. True, a handful of lawyers – Arabs and Jews – represented minority causes during the first era of Israeli statehood, including cases relating to land expropriation and restrictions on the civil liberties of the Arab citizens justified in the name of national security. But lawyering for these causes was rare and unorganised, limited to lawyers affiliated with the Israeli left (Langer 1988). The 1980s saw a rapid process of 'NGO-isation' in which many the newly established NGOs hired lawyers to advance their objectives. Lawyers began working in civil liberties and civil rights organisations advocating for women, religious and national minorities, lesbian, gay, bisexual, and transgender (LGBT) people, those with disabilities or in receipt of welfare benefits, environmental groups, and organisations devoted to the rule of law, anti-corruption, distributive justice, and consumers rights. Public interest litigation on human rights issues in the context of the Israeli-Palestinian conflict forms a significant part of the caseload of a number of organisations, such as the Association for Civil Rights in Israel, Yesh-Din, the Committee Against Torture, Hamoked – Center for the Defense of the Individual, and Adalah – the Legal Center for Arab Minority Rights in Israel (Kretzmer 2002). Most lawyers working on the rights of Palestinians enjoy the protection of professionalism and rarely suffer political harassment.

Lawyers in public interest organisations have utilised diverse methods, including individual representation, impact litigation and legislative reform, and community lawyering and organising (Feit and Aharoni 2008; Ziv 2008). The emergence of this form of legal practice can be attributed to an innovative programme jointly established by the New Israel Fund and the Washington College of Law at American University in Washington, DC. Starting in 1984, the programme sent two or three Israeli lawyers a year to the US to study for an LLM degree and serve an internship in a public interest legal organisation. Upon their return, the lawyers were committed to working in an Israeli NGO for at least one year. This programme launched the first generation of Israeli public interest lawyers and offered a platform on which lawyers for minority groups – Arabs, women, Mizrachi, LGBT, Ethiopian-Israelis, and people with disabilities – established their practice.

Since the early 2000s, lawyers in civil society were joined by legal clinics that had begun to emerge in Israeli law schools and now operate in all law schools and law colleges in Israel, providing legal assistance in diverse areas of law through the activities of law faculty, clinical lawyers and hundreds of law students a year (Wizner 2001). For two decades lawyers in civil society – within NGOs and law clinics – operated with little attention or interference from the IBA. As long as the practice remained marginal, the Bar tended to contain or ignore public interest lawyers, who generally were accorded enjoyed broad legitimacy by courts and the state. As their practice gained in salience and recognition and broadened its services, however, the IBA began restricting their work, demanding that they adhere to certain forms of practice (for example, not charge any fee or collect court-ordered fees), and prohibited them from conducting certain activities by applying narrowly interpreted UPL rules (Zer-Gutman 2013a). Despite such opposition, public interest lawyers in Israel, though few in number, are effective advocates, whose impact is greater than their numbers.

VII. A CHANGING PROFESSION: BROADENING LEGAL EDUCATION, GROWTH AND DIVERSIFICATION OF THE LEGAL PROFESSION

The number of lawyers began to rise considerably in the mid-1990s, following the opening of non-university law schools (also called law colleges). The 7,254 lawyers registered in 1980 had increased to 10,697 in 1990, which used to be the growth rate before the opening of the law colleges (an average of 337 law graduates were admitted annually between 1948 and 1994, see Figure 1). But in the decade 1990–2000, the number of lawyers doubled to 23,127, and in the next decade it doubled again to 46,515. The average number of lawyers annually admitted soared to 2,583 by 2011, a record increase of 7,670 per cent from the earlier period (Zer-Gutman 2012).

Figure 1 Growth in the Number of Lawyers and Population in Israel, 1950–2015

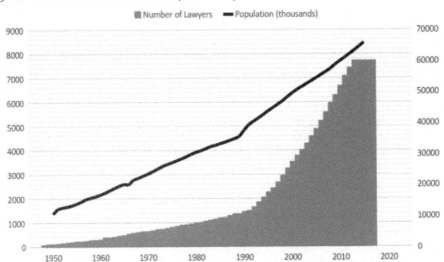

The rate of growth in the number of lawyers was significantly greater than that of the population (Zer-Gutman 2012). Several factors caused this acceleration. A lax regulatory framework led to the opening of many new colleges, including law colleges (Ben-Yaakov 2000). Until the early 1990s, there were three law schools in Israel, all at research universities (Jerusalem, Tel-Aviv and Bar-Ilan). Since then another university has opened a law school (Haifa, 1991) and ten law colleges (two public, eight private) were established in response to the rising demand for legal education and the ample supply of qualified law teachers (Katvan 2012). The number of law students grew from 2000 in 1990 to 16,000 in 2010 (13,000 in law colleges, 3000 in universities), an eightfold increase (see Figure 2) (Katvan 2012).

Figure 2 Total Number of LLB Students, 1970–2015

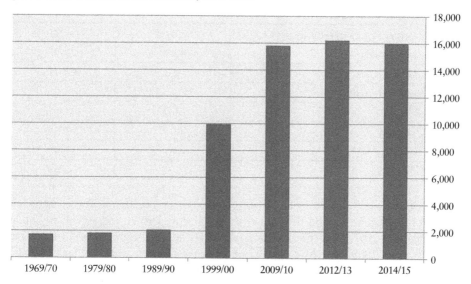

The expansion of law schools is explained by the fact that the largest number of students are in private law schools, which are funded solely by student tuition and do not require huge investments (no laboratories or expensive equipment are needed) (see Table 1). Demand for legal education was rising and tuition fees are high (three times those of the universities and publicly-funded law schools). Therefore, when the regulatory framework changed, some existing colleges added a law school while in other cases the law school triggered the opening of the college; in two cases the college has only a law school. Almost all law schools have classes only 2–3 days a week to allow students to work; a couple of private colleges offer at least one evening of classes.

The IBA and some university law faculty deans objected to the new law colleges, accusing them of overcrowding the profession and lowering the standard of legal practice. Other opponents argued that the law colleges did not realise the objectives for which they were established: to give excluded groups access to legal education (given their high tuition fees). That was the reason why two state-funded colleges were founded in the periphery: Safed (in the North) and Sapir (in the South).

Table 1 Law Schools in Israel, 2018/19: Categories, Enrolment Figures and Year of Establishment

Name of the Law School	Number of first-degree students	Established
Publicly Funded Law Colleges		
Sapir Academic College	557	2009
Zefat Academic College	237	2008
Non-Funded/Private Law Colleges		
College of Management – Academic Studies	806	1990
Netanya Academic College	910	1994
Interdisciplinary Center, Herzliya	1,289	1994
Sha'arei Mishpat – The College of Legal Studies	798	1995
Academic Center of Law and Business	refused	1995
Ono Academic College	4,400	1995
Peres Academic Center	373	2011
Law School in Universities		
Haifa University	470	1992
Hebrew University	1,020	1949
Tel-Aviv University	941	1965
Bar-Ilan University	503	1969

Other factors contributing to the rise in the number of lawyers were the changes in Israel's political economy and the shift from a collectivist to an individualistic, liberal society (Barzilai 2007). The proliferation of 'legalism' and 'rights talk' in the Israeli polity (Mautner 2008; Ziv 2012) led to an increase in the number of cases filed in courts after the mid-1990s (Zer-Gutman 2012). And the restrictive UPL rules compelled anyone who wanted to work in the legal services market to become a licensed lawyer (Ziv 2012).

Opening law colleges increased diversity since entrants came from social groups that had been excluded from the research university law schools. Even though state subsidies kept tuition at university law faculties and subsidised public law colleges at about a third that of private law colleges, the latter allowed minority groups to become lawyers: the ultra-Orthodox as well as new immigrants from the former Soviet Union and Ethiopia and people from the periphery (Katvan 2012; Zer-Gutman 2012).

Two hemispheres in legal education and the profession have emerged in Israel, analogous to those in the US. Compared with students at university faculties, those at the law colleges are older, and a higher percentage are married with children; some study law while working to support their families and maintaining their careers; a lower percentage of their parents have an academic education (implying a lower socio-economic status); and more have 'Sephardi' orgins (Katvan 2012)

The overall Bar exam pass rate remained quite steady until 2015, at more than 80 per cent; it has since declined dramatically to 45 per cent. Graduates also differ in pass rates on the Bar exam. In recent years, 90 per cent or more of graduates of university faculties have passed, compared with 60–40 percent of graduates of private law colleges (Israel Bar Association 2013, 2014, 2015, 2016). The IBA has some control over the design of the entry exam and has been accused of seeking to curb entry by making it harder to pass. The IBA vehemently rebuts these allegations, claiming that the exam is a tool to screen for merit and quality of service, rather than an entry barrier to reduce internal competition. The Bar's efforts succeeded and, since the end of 2017, there has been a new and more complex Bar exam that requires, for the first time, legal writing skills.

The two hemispheres of legal education are reproduced in the profession. Large commercial firms located in Tel Aviv target the top university graduates and pay them 80 per cent more than those hired by small offices in the periphery primarily representing households. The salary gap has increased, reaching hundreds of percent in a decade (Zalmanovitsh 2010).

The rapid expansion of the profession has also rejuvenated it: in 2017, 70 per cent of lawyers listed with the IBA were under 40 (Zalmanovitsh 2017), whereas in 1970, 40 per cent of lawyers were under 40 and 21 per cent over 60 (Yogev 1971).

The increase in the number of lawyers intensified competition, driving down prices, especially in small and medium-sized firms serving small households (while big firms are often charging twice as much for the same work) (Zer-Gutman 2012). Despite the decline in fees, the legal needs of the poor are not met and access to justice has not improved (Ziv 2012).

The increased number of lawyers has had little or no impact on ethical behaviour and discipline. The number of complaints filed against lawyers has remained constant, meaning that the ratio of complaints per lawyer has declined dramatically (Zer-Gutman 2012). This may be due in part to public distrust of the Bar's disciplinary system and the fact that an estimated 30 per cent of registered lawyers do not practise (Zer-Gutman 2012). Contrary to common opinion, lawyers who joined the Bar after 1995 are less likely to commit disciplinary offenses, and veteran lawyers commit disciplinary infractions at almost twice the average rate (Zer-Gutman 2012).

VIII. WOMEN IN THE LEGAL PROFESSION

Women entered the legal profession only after a 10-year battle against British Mandate authorities. In 1930, the High Court of Justice ruled that women are 'persons' and therefore allowed to practise law (Katvan and Halperin-Kaddari 2009; 2010). Before the foundation of the State of Israel in 1948, only 42 women were admitted to the Bar (in comparison to 1,300 men) (Katvan and Halperin-Kaddari 2009; Katvan 2011). Most were upper-middle class. Until the 1970s, the increase in the number of women was moderate (Yogev 1971). Since then, the profession has rapidly feminised: 13.4 per cent in the 1970s, 35 per cent in the 1980s, 40 per cent in the 1990s, and 47 per cent in 2016.

Although women have achieved numerical equality with men, there are still significant gender gaps in the patterns of employment. Explanations include the perceived conflict between family and career and the socialisation process that lowers women's occupational expectations (Elias and Starei 1998). Women are 71 per cent of jurists in the public sectors, 66 per cent of the lawyers in the district and state attorney's office, and 50 per cent of judges (four of the 15 Supreme Court justices). They are 57 per cent of the lawyers in the legal departments in the top 100 commercial companies. But women are senior partners in only 30 of the top 100 law firms and heads of only seven (Zalmanovitsh 2017).

IX. MODES OF PRACTICE

Three-quarters of active lawyers work in law firms, 18 per cent as legal consultants in public or private bodies, and 7 per cent are paying dues to the Bar but not practising law (most of them working in management) (Zalmanovitsh 2017). The proportion of lawyers listed with the Bar but not paying membership dues because they are inactive has remained relatively constant from 1971 to the present (ranging from 11 to 14 per cent) (Zer-Gutman 2012). In recent years, lawyers have been leaving firms to start their own offices, and firms of all sizes have been merging. The average size of the ten largest firms grew from 47 lawyers in 2000 to 185 in 2016, an increase of almost 400 per cent. The largest firm in 2000 had just 75 lawyers; 16 years later the largest had 276.

Figure 3 Average Number of Lawyers in Top 10 Firms, 2000–2016

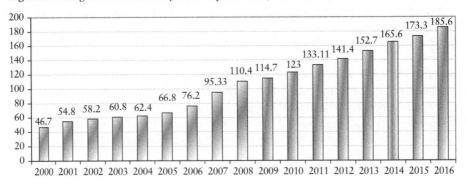

X. CONCLUSION

The Israeli legal profession has sought to maintain its independence in an era dominated by neoliberal ideologies of free competition and global cooperation. Through its governing institution – the IBA – the profession has succeeded in maintaining a broad degree of institutional independence despite constant challenges from market actors, administrative regulators and Parliament to the Bar's broad monopoly over the provision of legal services and its gatekeeping control over entry into the profession.

Since 2000, Israel has had the largest number of lawyers per capita in the world: 1:130. That was a consequence of the reform of legal education, which began in the 1990s, allowing the number of law schools to jump from three to 14 While this enlarged opportunities for formerly excluded groups, it led to the 'flooding' of the profession and intense competition among lawyers and between them and new non-lawyer providers of legal services. In response, the IBA sought to tighten entry, with partial success. Our analysis depicts the tension between the profession's determination to promote the self-interest of its members and its need to present itself as a social institution furthering the public interest.

REFERENCES

Abbott, A (1988) *The System of Professions: An Essay on the Division of Expert Labor* (Chicago, University of Chicago Press).

Aharoni, M and Feit, G (2008) 'From Rights Struggles to Economic Empowerment, Legal Aid for Community Economic Development as a New Form of Social Lawyering' in G Mundlak and M Ajzenstadt (eds), *Empowerment in Law* (Nevo Publishing) 545, 547 (Hebrew).

Alef, A (2014) 'Is the Israeli lawyer a "Gatekeeper" or a Policeman. "Know your Customer" under the Anti Money-Laundering Act – an earthquake in Principles of Ethics' 20 *HaMishpat Law Review* 269 (Hebrew).

Barzilai, G (2007) 'The Ambivalent Language of Lawyers in Israel: Liberal Politics, Economic Liberalism, Silence and Dissent' in TC Halliday et al (eds), *Fighting for Political Freedom: Comparative Studies of the Legal Complex and Political Liberalism* (Oxford, Hart Publishing) 247, 250–51, 256–57.

Ben-Yaakov, A (2000) 'About the Beginning of the Colleges' in D Landau (ed), *The Book About Colleges* (Hebrew).

Brun, N (2008) *Judges and Lawyers in Eretz Israel: Between Constantinople and Jerusalem, 1900–1930* (Jerusalem, The Hebrew University Magnes Press) (Hebrew).

CEPEJ (2016) 'European Judicial Systems Efficiency and Quality of Justice' CEPEJ Studies No 26 (Edition 2016 (2014 Data)).

Elias, N and Shitrai, M (1998) *Women Lawyers are Worth Less: Patterns of Segregation and Inequality in the Legal Profession in Israel* Discussion Paper No 95 (Golda Meir Institute for Social and Labour Research, Tel Aviv University) (Hebrew).

Israel Bar Association (2011) *Jubilee Book – The Israeli Bar's 50th Anniversary, 1961–2011* (The Israel Bar Publishing House) 154 (Hebrew).

—— (2013) *Statistical Data*, 69% of those who took written bar exam tests passed the test on November 3, 2013. IBA Spokesperson, 11 November 2103 (Hebrew) www.israelbar.org.il/article_inner.asp?pgId=154401&catId=7.

—— (2014) *Statistical Data*, 70% of those who took written bar exam tests passed the test on October 29, 2014. IBA Spokesperson, 28 December 2014 (Hebrew) www.israelbar.org.il/article_inner.asp?pgId=201306&catId=7.

—— (2014) *Annual Report* (Hebrew) www.israelbar.org.il/UpLoadFiles/activity_report_2014_site.pdf.

—— (2015), Statistical Data, 59.6% of those who took written bar exam tests passed the test on October 29, 2015. IBA Spokesperson, November 30, 2015 (Hebrew) www.israelbar.org.il/article_inner.asp?pgId=223116&catId=7.

Katvan, E (2011) '"Women in a Male Toga": Women's Integration into the Legal Profession in the Yishuv and Israel' in M Shilo and G Katz (eds), *Gender in Israel: New Studies on Gender in the Yishuv and State* vol 1 (Sede Boker, The Ben-Gurion Research Institute) 263–305 (Hebrew).

—— (2012) 'The "Overcrowding the Profession" Argument and the Professional Melting Pot' 19 *International Journal of the Legal Profession* 301–19.

Katvan, E, Halperin-Kaddari, R and Trau-Zitnitski, T (2009) *The First Women Lawyers in Mandatory Palestine, 1930–1948* (Tel Aviv) (Hebrew).

Katvan, E and Halperin-Kaddari, R (2009) 'The Feminist Proposal is Really Ridiculous: The Battle over Women's Right to Practice Law in Pre-State Palestine' 25(1) *Bar-Ilan Law Studies* 237–84 (Hebrew).

—— (2010) '"When a Woman Becomes a Lawyer": Rosa Ginzberg and Her Battle to Become a Lawyer in pre-State Israel' in E Katvan, M Shilo and R Halperin-Kadari (eds), *One Law for Man and Woman: Women, Rights and Law in Mandatory Palestine* (Ramat-Gan, Bar-Ilan University Press) 253–92 (Hebrew).

Kretzmer, D (2002) *The Occupation of Justice – The Supreme Court of Israel and the Occupied Territories* (Albany, SUNY Press).

Langer, F (1988) *An Age of Stone* (Quartet Books Ltd).

Likhovski, A (2006) *Law and Identity in Mandate Palestine* (Chapel Hill, University of North Carolina Press).

Mautner, M (2008) *Law and the Culture of Israel at the Threshold of the Twenty-First Century* (Tel Aviv University Press and Am-Oved) (Hebrew).

Ogletree, CJ and Sapir, Y (2004) 'Keeping Gideon's Promise, A Comparison of the American and Israeli Public Defender Experiences' 29 *New York University Review of Law and Social Change* 203.

PD Annual Reports, Public Defender Annual Reports www.justice.gov.il/Units/SanegoriaZiborit/DohotRishmi/Pages/dohot.aspx.

Rosen-Zvi, I (2001) 'Constructing Professionalism: The Professional Project of the Israeli Judiciary' 31 *Seton Hall Law Review* 760, 786.

Salzberger, E (2002) 'The Israeli Lawyers' Connection: On the Israel Bar Association and its Allies' 32 *Mishpatim Law Review* 43 (Hebrew).

Wizner, S (2001) 'The Legal Clinic: Legal Education in the Name of Public Interest' 25 *Tel Aviv University Law Review* 369 (Hebrew).

Yogev, Z (1971) *Survey, The Population of Lawyers in Israel, 1970/71* (Tel Aviv, Israel Bar Association) (Hebrew).

Zalmanovitsh, D (2010) 'The legal labor market and stresses on the assessment and employment lawyers' (Hebrew) www.glawbal.com/upload/Year%202010%20-%20Short%20Summarize.pdf.

—— (2017) 'The Legal Sector in the World and in Israel' (Hebrew) www.glawbal.com/upload/GLawBAL%202017.pdf.

Zer-Gutman, L (2005) 'Legal Representation towards Unrepresented Party: Lawyers' Cavent' 1 *Haifa University Law Review* 153 (Hebrew).

—— (2008) 'Preserving the Legal Profession's Image and Lawyers' Advertising' 24 *Bar Ilan University Law Review* 491 (Hebrew).

—— (2010) 'The Reform in Lawyers' Disciplinary System: Were the Deficiencies Corrected?' 15 *HaMishpat Law Review* 27 (Hebrew).

—— (2012) 'Effects of the Acceleration in the Number of Lawyers in Israel' 19 *International Journal of the Legal Profession* 247.

—— (2013a) 'The Israeli Bar and the Legal Clinics: Anatomy of a Struggle' 17 *HaMishpat Law Review* 59 (Hebrew).

—— (2013b) Minority opinion, Public Committee Report regarding the Israel Bar Association (Hebrew).

—— (2016) 'The loyalties of a Lawyer' in R Plato-Shinar and J Segev (eds), *Fiduciary Duties in the Israeli Law* (Nevo Publishing) 245 (Hebrew).

—— (2017) 'Israel: Regulation of Lawyers and the Legal Services in Israel' in A Boon (ed), *International Perspectives on the Regulation of Lawyers and Legal Services* (Oxford, Hart Publishing) 139–59.

Ziv, N (2002–2003) 'Combining Professionalism, Nation Building and Public Service: The Professional Project of the Israeli Bar 1928–2002' 4 *Fordham Law Review* 1621.

—— (2005) 'Lawyers' Accountability for the Ends of Representation: From a Moral to a Legal Responsibility, a Response to Limor Zer Gutman' 1 *Haifa Law Review* 201 (Hebrew).
—— (2008) 'Who Moved my Gown? On Unauthorized Practice of Law in Israel' *Bar Ilan Law Studies* 439–89 (Hebrew).
—— (2009) 'Regulation of Israeli Lawyers: from Professional Autonomy to Multi Institutional Regulation' 77 *Fordham Law Review* 1763–94.
—— (2012) 'Unauthorized Practice of Law and the Production of Lawyers in Israel' 19 *International Journal of the Legal Profession* 175–92.
—— (2015) *Who Will Guard the Guardians of Law? Lawyers in Israel between the State, Market and Civil Society* (Bar Ilan University Press and Hakibbutz Hameuchad Publishing) (Hebrew).
—— (2016) 'Who Moved My Mouse? Technology, Online Legal Services and Professional Ethics' 39 *Tel Aviv University Law Review* 189 (Hebrew).

31

Libya

Lawyers between Ideology and the Market

JESSICA CARLISLE*

THE ARREST OF a lawyer and human rights defender, Fathi Terbil, is regarded by many Libyans as a pivotal event in bringing down Muammar Gaddafi's regime. Many factors fed the subsequent demonstrations and stoked the popular resistance that rapidly became Libya's 'Arab Spring'. However, Terbil's arrest in Benghazi on 15 February 2011, and the spontaneous demonstration that gathered in front of the city's main courthouse to demand his release, became emblematic of the 2011 revolution. Terbil was well-known for representing families of many victims of Libya's most notorious post-colonial human rights abuse: the massacre of 1,270 political prisoners at Abu Selim prison on 19 June 1996. The regime had gradually acknowledged these deaths throughout the 2000s, publicly denying responsibility while privately reaching financial settlements with some of the victims' families. During his work on these cases, Terbil had been forced out of his position in a law firm, detained several times and tortured. When he was arrested in February 2011, it was relatives of the Abu Selim victims who first called for his release.

Terbil's arrest (and speedy release) is a useful starting point for analysing the fluctuating fortunes of lawyers in post-Ottoman Libya, which have been shaped by the oscillating relationship between the legal profession and the government. Although lawyers at times have been able to function as an independent profession, they have frequently been constrained, co-opted or subjected to ideologically driven state attacks. Lawyers have responded with different strategies of allegiance or resistance, resulting in diverse attitudes among legal professionals towards the state following the overthrow of Gaddafi's regime and tensions between professional bodies.

The other main force shaping the standing and structure of lawyering has been domestic or international demand for their services. Since the end of Italian occupation, Libyan lawyers have benefited from opportunities afforded by national independence,

---

* In 2012–13 I was hired by the Dutch-based Institute for Global Justice to work on a collaboration between the Van Vollenhoven Institute in the Netherlands and Libyan social scientists coordinated by the School of Law at the University of Benghazi for a study of knowledge transfer and the rule of law in post-conflict Libya. See Otto et al (2013).

the discovery of oil, the class and gender mobility produced by Gaddafi's 'revolution', the creation of a universal legal aid service, economic liberalisation and economic boom in the 2000s, and the rise of a human rights discourse and movement (to which Terbil belonged), ostensibly geared towards the transition from authoritarian dictatorship to multi-party democracy, good governance and truth-telling.

This analysis of the emergence, position and professional activity of Libyan lawyers examines the influence of state policies towards legal education and accreditation, the regulation of professional associations and interventions in lawyers' access to the wider global legal professions, and ebbs and flows in the demand for their services. As will become clear, ideology has both contracted and expanded the market, and commitment to the market is itself ideological.

I. LAWYERS IN MODERN LIBYA: FROM THE ITALIAN OCCUPATION TO THE COUP

The modern state of Libya united three regions, which have preserved distinct political and social identities into the twenty-first century: Tripolitana in the coastal north-west, containing Tripoli; Cyrenaica in the coastal north-east, containing Benghazi; and the southern Fezzan. Most Libyans are descendants of Amazigh (Berber) and Arab populations, with the notable exception of the Tawerghan, Tebu and Tuareg communities, which are of sub-Saharan descent. Five Amazigh languages are still spoken, but the dominant language is Libyan Arabic. Almost all the population is *Sunni* Muslim, and most identify with one of an estimated 140 tribes (Varvelli 2013). Tribal Councils of Wisemen (*majalis al-hukama wa al-shura*) have traditionally settled disputes and offered financial and social support to the needy. Libya's small cities, towns and rural regions include majority and minority tribal populations. The politics of tribal identity were intensified and exploited during the Gaddafi dictatorship and have been an aggravating factor in post-Gaddafi militia violence and an organising structure in attempts to negotiate peace (through tribal councils) during the civil war.

Libya began the twentieth century as part of the Ottoman Empire before being occupied by Italy in 1911 and enduring domination by Mussolini's fascist government from 1922. Following its 'liberation' by Allied forces, Libya was ruled by the French and British from 1943, achieving independence under the Senussi monarchy in 1951. In 1969, Muammar Gaddafi seized power in a bloodless coup and remained in power, often through violence and terror, until the revolution and subsequent war of 2011.

A. Italian Occupation and the Mandate Period: The Suppression of Libyan Professions

Although there had been incremental developments in administration under Ottoman occupation from 1835, Italian colonisation of Libya in 1911 deliberately excluded Libyans from government. Ottoman *Majelle* legislation was replaced by Italian criminal, civil and commercial legislation and frequently martial law; only the Sharia courts dealing with family and inheritance law remaining unchanged. Italy's colonial policies stifled cultural and literary expression, limited Libyans' education to primary schools, and 'actively discouraged indigenous political activity' (St John 2011). Because the Italian occupation viewed Libyans as 'little more than a pool of labour' (Pargeter 2012), it left the country with a meagre legacy of skilled, informed, and politically active citizens (St John 2011). A small number of people in coastal cities amassed significant wealth by collaborating with the regime.

Libyan resistance to Italian rule was met with brutality, particularly under the fascist government after 1922. The Italian regime reacted to guerrilla fighters (based primarily in Cyrenaica) with 'savage campaigns of repression, killing fighters (as well as suspected rebels and civilians) with what can only be described as detached abandon' (Pargeter 2012). During the height of Libyan resistance in the early 1930s under the leadership of Omar al-Mukhtar, Italy forced about two-thirds of the population of eastern Libya into concentration camps, blocked wells and slaughtered livestock (St John 2011: 17). The 'gallows became a regular feature of life'; some historians suggest that in 1930 alone 12,000 Cyrenaicans were executed (Pargeter 2012). By the mid-1930s the Libyan population had been halved through famine, war, disease and emigration, recovering its pre-colonial numbers only in 1950, at the dawn of independence.

Following the Italian defeat by the French in the Fezzan (in the south) in 1943 and the British in Cyrenaica (in the east) in 1942 and Tripoli (in the west) in 1943, the country was governed by British Military Administration in Cyrenaica and Tripolitania and French Military Administration in the Fezzan and central Libya. Most existing legislation was retained, and courts were staffed predominantly by Italian, English, Tunisian and Egyptian judges. However, flouting the 1907 Hague Convention governing the conduct of war, both administrations modified Libyan law and administration, which they should have preserved on a care and maintenance basis.

Development of the country was significantly impeded by World War II and a subsequent period of political uncertainty (Anderson 1986: Khadduri 1963; St John 2011; Wright 1982). In 1948, a Commission appointed by the Four Powers (UK, France, US and USSR) reported that while there was widespread support for independence, 'the country was politically, economically and socially unprepared for such a step' (Pargeter 2012).

After Britain and France failed to extend their governance and, following complicated wrangling within the UN, a National Assembly was appointed under the auspices of the UN, which passed a resolution on 2 December 1950 that Libya should be a federal monarchy under Sayyid Mohammed Idris al-Mahdi al-Senussi of Cyrenaica. Libya, consequently, emerged as 'an accident of history ... born of the machinations of the victorious Allied powers', principally to secure pro-Western leadership (Pargeter 2012). Sayyid Idris was chosen because he was considered the head of the religious Senussi order, which had significant political and religious authority in the east and had included the hero of the independence struggle, Omar Al-Mukhtar, among its important figures.

B. Independence: Oil and the Emergence of a Plutocratic Elite

It has been argued that the lack of effective local government, the resurgence of monarchical politics, and a general hostility to bureaucracy meant that post-colonial Libya was governed by leaders whose legitimacy depended entirely on external patronage or military might (Anderson 1986; St John 2011). The infrastructure in Cyrenaica had been largely destroyed by Allied bombing. In 1951 Libya was the poorest independent country in the world, with an annual per capita income of about US$50, few post-primary school graduates, and an illiteracy rate of about 90 per cent.

The 1951 Constitution enshrined al-Senussi and his male descendants as the ruling family. The parliament consisted of a senate of 24 members, eight each from Tripolitania, Cyrenaica and Fezzan (half appointed by the king and half chosen by provincial legislative councils) and a house of representatives elected by adult men (St John 2011). The capital rotated between Tripoli and Benghazi every two years, resulting in a 'complex and cumbersome political system' (Pargeter 2012).

The economy was dependent on an unproductive agricultural sector and lacked basic raw materials, skilled manpower, capital, and a banking sector (St John 2011). The salvage of scrap metal from World War II combat was an important source of income. Mortality was high; just 537 were attending secondary and technical schools in a country of about a million (St John 2011). Libyans had no experience in administration and almost no technical training (Pargeter 2012).

The choice of Sayyid Idris as monarch had been supported by both Cyrenaica and Tripolitania. The Constitution empowered him to issue decrees, appoint and remove senior officials, and legislate in conjunction with parliament (St John 2011). In practice, the king withdrew from daily political involvement, governing through a system of patronage, whose key institutions were the royal household (handling the king's personal and family affairs) and a palace cabinet (managing affairs of the kingdom) (El Fathaly 1977; Pargeter 2012; St John 2011; Sury 1982). In this 'benign despotism' (St John 2011) elections were rigged, political parties and demonstrations banned, and newspapers censored. Politics 'became an assertion of family, factional, tribal and parochial interests' (Pargeter 2012).

Libya's post-independence legal system was principally staffed by Egyptian judges, and its laws were modelled on Egypt's, which had absorbed much of the European legal tradition inherited from Ottoman rule followed by French and British colonialism. The main exception was Libya's retention of Sharia courts applying uncodified Islamic law (specifically Maliki *fiqh*) until the Gaddafi regime integrated the family courts into the civil court system (Law 87/1973 on Unifying the Judiciary) and partially codified Muslim family law (Law 76/1972 Protecting Some Rights of Women in Marriage, Divorce for Harm, and Consensual Divorce).

The lack of constitutional checks on the executive and the embryonic state of the legal system were compounded by a federal system in which co-ordination between the central and provincial governments was weak, producing contradictory policies and duplication of services (St John 2011). This was highlighted following the discovery of oil in neighbouring Algeria in 1955. Libya responded by passing Petroleum Law (1955) to encourage oil exploration and development, granting geographically limited, short-term concessions to foreign companies. By 1957, there were about a dozen oil companies working on about 60 concessions. By the mid-1960s foreign oil companies had built an extensive infrastructure of pipelines and coastal export terminals. The booming oil industry massively increased the country's revenue because foreign companies paid a 12.5 per cent royalty on their revenues and a 50 per cent tax on their profits. In 1967, oil contributed £170 million to GDP and constituted 95 per cent of Libya's exports (Blake 1969).

However, this burgeoning industry exposed tensions produced by the different jurisdictions and policy-making powers situated at the levels of federal and provincial governments. Provincial government was subordinated to the federal government in 1962–63 (Pargeter 2012). The renamed Kingdom of Libya was divided into ten administrative units (St John 2011; Sury 2003; Vandewalle 2006; Wright 1982). This centralisation increased the power exercised by a small coterie surrounding the king: patronage and the distribution of subsidies such as interest-free loans became embedded political practices, and bureaucracy mushroomed (St John 2011). Corruption and nepotism were rampant as the benefits of oil flowed to an elite, widening the gap between them and most Libyans and between regions. Securing a government position became a 'byword for lining one's pockets' (Pargeter 2012). A small number of skilled individuals became rich very quickly, while the major cities were surrounded by shanty towns, whose inhabitants struggled to survive (Pargeter 2012).

C. The Rise of the Legal Profession and University Law Faculties

The demand for lawyers during the later monarchy was largely driven by foreign companies working in the growing oil sector (Abdelmoula 1992). The domestic need for lawyers to assist Libyans in civil, criminal and family (Sharia) cases was limited, since many legal issues were settled by traditional fora presided over by tribal authority figures or Sharia courts (Abdelmoula 1992). Lawyers did not participate in the Sharia courts, where the judges directed proceedings, questioned litigants and witnesses before passing their rulings. In 1954 the monarchy attempted to merge the Sharia and secular legal systems and subordinate Islamic law to secular law. In 1958, however, popular opposition forced the restoration of separate religious and secular jurisdictions.

The secular legal professions did, however, benefit from the establishment of the University of Libya in 1955. It initially had a Faculty of Arts in Benghazi and a Faculty of Science in Tripoli, but in 1973 it was divided into what have become the two largest public universities: Al Fateh in Tripoli and Gar Younis in Benghazi. The first Faculty of Law was opened at Gar Younis University in 1962, the same year as the founding of the Libyan Bar Association (ILAC 2013). Law faculties or departments have since opened in Tripoli (Al Fateh University in 1994), Sebha University, Al-Beyda (Omar al-Mukhtar University), Al-Khuma (El-Merghib University), University of Gharyan, Beni Walid (Azzaytuna University), Misrata University, Sabratha University, and Al-Zawiya University. The larger law faculties are sub-divided into Departments of Public, Private, Criminal and Islamic Law. These faculties and departments, combined with Libya's policy of fully funding university education for Libyan nationals and rapid population growth, have fuelled a steady increase in the number of law graduates. There are no open access figures for the number of law students. However, by 2014, there were over half a million students enrolled in higher education, most in overstretched public universities; Al-Fateh and Gar Younis each had over 100,000. As a result of economic development and social change throughout the second half of the twentieth century, law graduates have entered an expanding job market to work in commercial, family, administrative and criminal law or as a government lawyer, public prosecutor or judge.

II. GADDAFI'S 'REVOLUTION': LAWYERS AS AGENTS OF THE STATE

Some commentators have argued that heightened expectations engendered by oil wealth fostered five years of demonstrations and frequently violent unrest that began in 1964 and ended with Gaddafi's ascent in 1969 (St John 2011). Resistance to, and dissatisfaction with, the monarchy was expressed mostly through Arab nationalism, influenced by events in neighbouring Egypt under Gamal Abdel Nasser, and calls for Libyan solidarity with regional struggles, notably the 1967 Arab/Israeli War (Pargeter 2012). The coup, although perpetrated by previously unknown junior army officers with luck on their side, is seen by many as having been inevitable (Hilsum 2012; St John 2011). The monarchy's failure to establish 'a real sense of unity of nationhood … left [Gaddafi] an empty playing field upon which to impose his own unorthodox brand of nationhood' (Pargeter 2012). Libya 'was well and truly ripe for change' (Pargeter 2012). The overthrow of the monarchy enjoyed widespread popular support reflecting the desire for change (Hilsum 2012; St John 2011; Pargeter 2012), and Gaddafi's regime was welcomed by many members of the educated middle-class, including lawyers, for whom the appeal to nationalism and the promise of respect for fundamental rights was perhaps particularly attractive (Abdelmoula 1992).

A. Gaddafi's Ideology and the Regime's Political Control

The new regime took power on 1 September 1969 after a largely bloodless coup. The 12 leading perpetrators became the Revolutionary Command Council (RCC). But it soon became clear that Muammar Gaddafi was its most influential member (Pargeter 2012), and by 1975 the RCC had been reduced to five following an unsuccessful attempt to oust Gaddafi (St John 2011). From then until the 2011 uprising Gaddafi dominated the regime (St John 1987), pursuing an ideology combining socialism (which he regularly associated with Islam), Arab nationalism and anti-imperialism effected through the distribution of Libya's immense oil wealth, co-optation, repression, and state-sanctioned violence (St John 2011). Although Gaddafi's initial inspiration was Nasser's Arab nationalist socialism and a commitment to nationalising oil production, his ideology became increasingly quixotic and his political methods more brutal during his four decades in power.

On 11 September 1969, the RCC annulled the 1951 Constitution and issued a Provisional Constitutional Declaration under which it assumed all legislative, judicial and executive powers, promulgating laws through decrees that took effect as soon as they were published in the Official Gazette (St John 2011). The preamble proclaimed the revolution's goals of freedom, socialism and unity. Eight of the 15 articles in the first chapter addressed aspects of the economy and social rights, including a commitment to economic self-sufficiency and independence from foreign investment (St John 2011), the sanctity of homes (Article 12) and the right of all citizens to education and medical care (Articles 14 and 15).

The 15 articles in the second chapter outlined the structure of the government, making the RCC the highest authority. Article 19 empowered the RCC to appoint and dismiss a cabinet consisting of a President and Council of Ministers with responsibility to execute the policies issued by the RCC. Articles 21, 23, 24 and 25 gave the RCC powers to declare war, martial law and a state of national emergency and control over the national budget (St John 2011). Article 28 declared that the judiciary was independent, while Article 18 immunised RCC legislation from judicial review.

Although a mixed military and civilian cabinet was appointed within a week of the coup, the RCC was reluctant to delegate tasks to it, and Gaddafi emphasised that the RCC would have to approve all policy decisions (Pargeter 2012). Consequently, the drive towards modernisation through the appointment of forward-thinking administrators failed. This period was characterised by tensions between the RCC's determination to control policy and its attempts to engage the administration and the Libyan people in its revolutionary project. Following the failure to resolve these two aims, Gaddafi increasingly asserted all decision-making power. The confusion was compounded by the promulgation of a bewildering number of laws and regulations with no clear hierarchy or order and the expectation that Gaddafi's rambling speeches should have legal force (Chaplin Metz 1987; ILAC 2013).

This centralisation of power was intensified by the regime's hostility to political opposition. Following the overthrow of the monarchy, the RCC attempted to outmanoeuvre popular resistance to its ideology and consolidate its power by reducing regional and tribal authority and creating a new leadership supportive of revolutionary change (Pargeter 2012; St John 2011). One strategy was to associate traditional leadership with former colonial powers and the corrupt monarchy (El Fathaly and Abusedra 1977; St John 2011). The RCC created new administrative zones, dividing and combining tribal areas and renaming the sheikh a zone administrator (Pargeter 2012; St John 2011).

The regime initially sought to 'mobilize, motivate and politicize' the population by channelling political activity though the Arab Socialist Union (ASU), which was supposed to 'become the primary link between the people and the central government, filling the void left by the abolition of the tribal system' (St John 2011). But this effort was stillborn because of the RCC's rigid central leadership, the ASU's complex structure, resistance from existing state institutions, and unresponsiveness to local needs. The regime subsequently banned political parties and independent organisations, which Gaddafi accused of seeking the domination of an entire population by a small number of voters. Law No 71/1972 made engaging in party politics punishable by death (Pargeter 2012).

Political opposition was further undermined by the 'Decision on the Protection of the Revolution', issued on 11 December 1969, defining crimes against the state as any forcible attempt to overthrow the regime or rally opposition to it. In 1971, a People's Court was established to try members of the royal family, former prime ministers and other officials of the monarchy, people accused of rigging elections on behalf of the previous government, and journalists and editors accused of corrupting public opinion before the revolution. An RCC member presided over the court, which included one representative each from the armed forces, the Islamic University, the Supreme Court, and the police. Trials and retrials continued until at least 1975, when former King Idris was sentenced to death in absentia. Several People's Courts were still hearing cases in the late 1970s to suppress perceived threats to the regime. In January 1977, a new people's court was formed to try political detainees.

B. Reorganisation of the Court System

During this initial period, the regime also modernised the ordinary court system. Law 87/1973 on Unifying the Judiciary integrated the civil and Sharia judiciary (Article 1), reallocating Sharia judges and folding the work of the Islamic courts into the civil legal system at three levels: district courts (also called misdemeanour or partial courts), primary courts of first instance, and appeals courts. These constitute Libya's contemporary judicial system together with the Supreme Court (whose powers are set out in Law 6/1982 on the Reregulation of the Supreme Court) (Algheita and Ibrahim 2014).

The district court (*al-mahkamat al-juz'iya*) is presided over by a single judge with jurisdiction in civil and commercial cases worth no more than 1,000 Libyan dinars, and other cases regardless of their value (eg compensation for damage resulting from misdemeanours); personal status (family law) claims regarding separation and divorce, maintenance, child custody, and inheritance and divorce; and misdemeanours and contraventions (Algheita and Ibrahim 2014). The primary court (*al-mahkamat al-ibtida'iya*) has jurisdiction over all civil and personal status matters outside the district court's jurisdiction and hears appeals against district court rulings (ibid). At the outbreak of the 2011 revolution there was an extensive network of district and primary courts (Law 55/1971 on the Justice System for Remote Areas). The appeals court (*al-mahkamat al-isti'naaf*), comprised of a president and senior judges sitting in seven locations, reviews disputed primary court rulings in civil and family cases, hears first instance administrative claims, and has jurisdiction over felonies (ibid).

The authority of the Supreme Court (*al-mahkamat al-'alya*) has ebbed and flowed since it was established under al-Senussi's monarchy. The Court sits in Tripoli and has five chambers: civil and commercial, criminal, administrative, constitutional, and Sharia. In addition to divesting it of the power to review legislation, the Gaddafi regime controlled it by appointing its justices and president. Law 6/1982 on the Reregulation of the Supreme Court (later amended by Law 17/1994 and Law 8/2004) reinstated some of its authority by directing all courts to abide by the legal principles flowing from its rulings. Currently, the court has jurisdiction over petitions claiming a law is unconstitutional, which can be brought by anyone with a direct, personal interest. It also has authority to opine on any 'legally essential matter concerning the constitution or its interpretation, which arises during any case being heard by any court', resolve jurisdictional conflicts between courts and any 'exceptional judicial authority', settle any dispute concerning the execution of two conflicting final rulings issued by a court and an exceptional judicial authority, modify the Supreme Court's principles, and deal with any challenge against lower court rulings concerning civil, commercial, personal status, administrative, and criminal matters (ibid).

C. 'Revolutionary' Policies and Initial Relations between the Regime and the Bar

In an apparently unilateral decision in April 1973, Gaddafi announced a cultural or 'Popular Revolution' under the rubric of his 'Third Universal Theory', outlined in full in his 'Green Book' (Hilsum 2012). His five-point programme advocated

> a) the repeal of all existing laws and their replacement with revolutionary enactments; b) the weeding out of all anti-revolutionary elements by taking appropriate action against 'perverts and deviators'; c) the staging of an administrative revolution to destroy all forms of bourgeoisie and bureaucracy; d) the arming of the people to create a people's militia to protect the revolution; and e) the staging of a cultural revolution to get rid of all imported poisonous ideas that were contrary to the Qu'ran (Pargeter 2012).

Throughout his rule, Gaddafi regularly interfered with the make-up and responsibilities of the branches of government: renaming, merging or dismantling them every couple of years (Pargeter 2011) or issuing unwritten orders that contradicted his ministers (Hilsum 2012).

The impact of these policies was to undermine democratic accountability and eliminate the possibility of challenging the executive. Throughout the 1970s Gaddafi 'continued to tinker with what was increasingly becoming a very novel form of political innovation' (St John 2011), establishing a 'mind-bogglingly complex' system of 'direct democracy' (Pargeter 2012). The policy was based on the formation of Popular Committees by 'every village, town, college factory and school', which would be elected directly by the people and run everything from universities to companies and government offices (Pargeter 2012). This announcement resulted in the purging of the former administration, including local mayors and municipal councils. By August 1973, the more than 2,000 popular committees had become vehicles for arresting political opponents.

In addition to the popular committees tasked with operating the institutions, 'Basic People's Congresses' were established as a vehicle for political participation. These Congresses were charged with debating local and national issues and transmitting their decisions to the General People's Congress (a kind of parliament), which would formulate policies regarding agriculture, health, housing, and industry for implementation by the General People's Secretariat (a kind of cabinet) (Pargeter 2012; St John 2011).

The newly formed Congresses were less committed to modernisation than the administrators they replaced, but they were more willing to challenge traditional elites (St John 2011). From their inception, the Basic People's Congresses were poorly attended, ineptly managed by careless or absent officials, and corrupt (Pargeter 2012). However, the system 'provided for widespread participation in the selection of leadership and allowed popular involvement in the local policy-making process' (St John 2011). The bureaucracy mushroomed, becoming an avenue for social advancement and an instrument by which the regime could control society (Pargeter 2012). Simultaneously, the regime enacted legislation increasing its capacity to move or sack members of the judiciary and removing certain crimes from the jurisdiction of the normal courts (Law 51/1976 Promulgating the Legal System).

In 1977, Gaddafi launched the culmination of this system with a 'Declaration of the Establishment of the Authority of the People', renaming Libya the 'Socialist People's Libyan Arab Jamahiriyah' and appointing himself head of the 970-member General People's Congress. He ostensibly resigned from the GPC in 1978, but no one doubted that power remained vested in him and his inner circle (his relatives, tribal allies, and RCC members). Refinements introduced in 1975–77 reduced competition between the Popular Committees, Basic People's Congresses and ASU. Revolutionary control was strengthened by requiring everyone to become politically involved but restricting participation to sanctioned organisations (St John 2011). In the same period, Gaddafi announced that 'people's authority' would be separated from 'revolutionary authority', allowing him to build an alternative power base with which to 'create a truly populist force that would enable him to rally the masses in support of his vision' (Pargeter 2012).

The resulting body was the 'Revolutionary Committees Movement', a paramilitary movement operating in co-ordination with the Popular Committees in schools, universities, unions, the police force and the army. Because the Revolutionary Committees had more power than the People's Congresses and 'were not in any way regulated by legal statutes' (St John 2011) they became 'one of the most feared institutions of Gaddafi's long rule' (Pargeter 2012), ultimately accountable only to Gaddafi himself. Responsible for encouraging revolutionary fervour, the Revolutionary Committees were composed of young men 'eager to seize the opportunity to better themselves', who undertook ideological surveillance, later assuming a significant security role, making arrests and trying people according to the 'law of the revolution' (*qanun al-thawra*) (Pargeter 2012). From March 1979, the Committees were tasked with eliminating regime opponents both inside and outside Libya (Pargeter 2012; St John 2011).

In principle, Law 6/1982 provided several guarantees for those accused of crimes, including the prohibition of retroactive legislation, the principle of personal liability, the presumption of innocence, the right to all means of defence including legal counsel, and a ban on torture and bodily or mental injury (Abdelmoula 1992). The regime avoided these restraints by erecting complex networks of military, security, and revolutionary courts and resorting to illegal detentions and denials.

In the early 1980s, a separate 'judicial' system emerged, abrogating the procedures and rights ensured by the traditional court system. Encouraged by the regime, Revolutionary Committee members established ad hoc revolutionary courts empowered to pass death sentences, which held public trials of those charged with crimes against the revolution. Some show trials and hangings were televised. Court personnel were not legally trained, there was no legal procedure, those accused were not legally represented, and there was no right of appeal (Abdelmoula 1992).

The Revolutionary Committees, with the backing of the affiliated revolutionary courts, effectively rendered 'formal political institutions impotent, turning them into little more than a facade' by penetrating them from top to bottom (Pargeter 2012: 96). The only institution spared was the National Oil Company, which was always professionally managed (Hilsum 2012). In 1979, Revolutionary Committees were charged with co-ordinating elections to the Basic People's Congresses and could veto any candidate they disliked (Pargeter 2012). They were also tasked with ensuring that the media were ideologically loyal to the regime. The Committees themselves were controlled through the Revolutionary Committees Liaison Office staffed by some of Gaddafi's key allies (Pargeter 2012). After 1979 the Libyan state was effectively divided into two parallel systems: the 'revolutionary' sector consisting of Gaddafi, his close allies and the Revolutionary Committees; and the 'ruling' sector containing the system of Basic People's Congresses and the General People's Congress (St John 2011: 64).

D. The Nationalisation of the Legal Profession

The impact of these dramatic political events on the legal profession seems to have been gradual. Despite the rapid development of a political class opposed to 'bourgeois' institutions associated with the monarchy, both the Bar Association and individual lawyers were initially involved in advising the Gaddafi regime (Abdelmoula 1992). Moreover, members of the Bar represented pro bono those accused of political crimes, and the Bar Association retained its independence for the first 11 years of the regime, remaining a member of international networks such as the Arab Lawyers' Union and the International Association of Democratic Lawyers (Abdelmoula 1992). As the regime increasingly violated the law, however, lawyers inevitably came under attack as political opponents.

The rise of revolutionary ideology and institutions during the late 1970s and early 1980s had a profound impact on the functioning of legal institutions and the independence of the legal profession as the regime enacted legislation and established a parallel system to neutralise actual or perceived political opposition.

On 7 January 1981 Gaddafi repealed the Libyan Advocacy Law 82/1975, accusing 'lawyers of seeking to further their private interests and the accumulation of money' in opposition to 'the socialist transformation of the country' (Abdelmoula 1992). Law 4/1981 Establishing the Department of People's Legal Defence effectively nationalised the profession by requiring all lawyers to stop practising or join the 'Directorate of People's Legal Defence' (popularly known in 2014 as the people's lawyers), working on a fee scale fixed by the state.

The directorate had its own administration, which operated 'without prejudice to the powers of the People's Committees for Justice in municipalities' (Article 16, Law 4/1981). The law allowed only Arab nationals to plead before the courts (Article 27, Law 4/1981) and replaced the Bar Association with a General Professional Conference modelled on a People's Congress, with a membership of appointees and a secretariat answerable to the Secretariat of the General People's Committee for Justice (Article 28, Law 4/1981; Abdelmoula 1992). Law 4/1981 promulgated professional standards of confidentiality, commitment to the client, regular inspection and disciplinary procedures (Articles 21–24).

Lawyers agreeing to join this nationalising project received the pay and working conditions of members of the judiciary and the public prosecution (Article 7, Law 4/1981). The legislation opened an alternative route into legal practice by allowing court clerks and other administrative employees to take exams after several years of work in order to qualify as a (people's) lawyer and authorised the transfer of staff between the people's lawyers, the judiciary and the public prosecution (Article 15 Law 4/1981), which became annual event. The fee schedule and disciplinary procedures were administered by political institutions allied to the regime, which also obtained unspecified powers to 'interrogate' lawyers suspected of malpractice (Abdelmoula 1992). This reorganisation ruptured relationships between lawyers and clients and collaborations among private firms. Lawyers experienced difficulty adjusting to the new system, some leaving the profession and many feeling its reputation had been seriously damaged (Abdelmoula 1992).

Despite the reorganisation's explicit political motives, the offer of legal representation to all sectors of the Libyan population (except those charged in the parallel legal system or illegally detained in prison) radically increased access to justice. In principle, litigants must apply for a fee waiver (Article 8, Law 4/1981), but while I was conducting fieldwork in 2013 in Tripoli, state employed legal professionals reported that free legal representation was standard practice.

The effect was a massive expansion of lawyers' potential market. In 2013, despite the escalating violence and political insecurity, the Tripoli branch was busy dealing with cases. Branches of the people's lawyers located in every appeal court allocate representation to litigants from a staff of lawyers specialising in all areas of law (Articles 3, 7, Law 4/1981). The service is also available to foreign companies and individuals for an agreed fee (Articles 9 and 10, Law 4/1981). The legal aid service is obliged to 'guide citizens and make them aware of the various provisions of laws and regulations that relate to their rights, duties, and interests', but it also directs lawyers to encourage litigants to end their disputes amicably (Article 5, Law 4/1981). I observed female people's lawyers representing women and the poor in family courts and defending state employees who had been dismissed during the widespread, post-2011 revolution lustration campaign (Carlisle 2014).

E. The Return of Private Practice and Tensions between the Bar and the Regime

In 1990, after a decade of economic recession, violent conflict with an armed Islamist opposition, and increasing marginalisation by the international community, the regime made a 180-degree turn and allowed lawyers to resume private practice while retaining the Directorate of People's Legal Defence (Law 10/1990 on the Reorganisation of Legal Practice). Lawyers have since been required to choose between employment as people's lawyers or private practice, and litigants can use either service (Articles 2–3, Law 10/1990). Lawyers in private practice are allowed to practise in individual or collective offices and to charge fees that are not 'exploitative' (Article 4, Law 10/1990).

The Gaddafi regime retained the right to issue secondary legislation (in the form of executive regulations passed by the General People's Committee) determining 'the rights, obligations, and rules of discipline pertaining to' lawyers, the procedure for evaluating and registering lawyers as private practitioners, the cost of registration, and the content and location of the oath taken by entrants (Article 5, Law 10/1990). The resulting Decree from the General People's Committee (Decree 885/1990) called lawyers protectors of rights and freedoms, who provided a 'sacred right to defence' (Article 1, Decree 885/1990). Lawyers had to be Arab residents of Libya, have capacity, good character, and no criminal convictions or disciplinary measures, and possess either a qualification in law or the Sharia or experience working in judicial institutions (Article 2 a–f, Decree 885/1990). Lawyers must be respectful of their clients, honourable, and careful not to involve unqualified persons in their cases and must preserve client confidentiality (Articles 24–27, Decree 885/1990). The regulations also reaffirmed ethical rules, such as giving sufficient notice when terminating a relationship with a client (Article 30, Decree 885/1990).

After a two-year apprenticeship with a registered lawyer licensed to appear before the Supreme Court or Courts of Appeal (Article 10, Decree 885/1990), trainees could apply to the Committee for Admission of Lawyers at the Ministry of Justice for a licence to practise in the primary courts (Algheitta 2013). The Committee's decision should be based on the supervising lawyer's report (Article 10, Decree 885/1990). Judges, public prosecutors, law professors and anyone who had practised law for more than two years (presumably meaning people's lawyers) could apply directly to the Admission Committee for registration (Article 13, Decree 885/1990). Control of this process was vested in the General People's Committee for Justice, which annually appointed the Admission Committee, principally from the judicial institutions (Article 4:a, Decree 885/1990).

The regime undermined the independence of private practitioners by empowering the General People's Committee to appoint the Admission Committee's secretary (Article 3:c, Decree 885/1990), mandating that a list of active lawyers should be provided to the Ministry of Justice (Article 3:e), giving the General People's Committee authority to set a ceiling on lawyers' fees (Article 19, Decree 885/1990), and directing lawyers to notify the General People's Committee if they worked for a foreign government or international organisation (Article 31, Decree 885/1990).

Neither primary nor secondary legislation mentioned the Bar Association, and the regime persisted in denigrating private lawyers as 'profit seekers' lacking revolutionary commitment (Abdelmoula 1992). The right of Libyan professionals – including lawyers – to organise collectively was formally established in Law 23/2007 on Syndicates, Unions, and Professional Associations, which gave the General People's Congress control of the Bar Association's bylaws and committed the Association to the regime's ideology (Articles 3, 5, Law 23/2007). The Lawyers Syndicate's responsibilities included registering active and inactive lawyers, settling fee disputes and supervising disputes between lawyers (Articles 3, 20a:a, 29, Decree 885/1990).

The co-existence of private practice and the people's lawyers has become embedded in the legal system. In June 2013, the state employed 1,139 people's lawyers, 773 of them women. However, by the 2011 uprising private practice had become a desirable option, attracting many former judges and public prosecutors eager to discard government control or to earn more money (Algheita 2013).

The regime's decision to lift the prohibition on private practice was part of a raft of policies meant to signal a move away from authoritarianism. In June 1989, the General People's Conference issued the 'Green Charter of Human Rights in the Era of the Masses', the first of several false starts towards a real commitment to human rights and access to justice throughout the 1990s and 2000s (increasingly under the direction of the political heir apparent, Saif Al-Gaddafi). This included Law 20/1991 on the Promotion of Freedom, purporting to protect the fundamental rights of men, women and children.

The lack of genuine political commitment to improving human rights was demonstrated by legislation (issued shortly before the Green Charter) formalising the People's Court (Law 5/1988 Creating the People's Court) and giving it jurisdiction over a vast range of criminal offences (including those defined by 'revolutionary' legislation such as the RCC's 'Decree for the Protection of the Revolution'). It had the overtly political mandate of 'promoting freedom and justice for the oppressed' and should have been presided over by a President of the Court with a legal qualification who was regarded as 'a well-known, well-respected and committed revolutionary' (Articles 1, 3.2, 3.4, Law 5/1988).

In practice, loyalty to the regime was more important than legal expertise because the court was often staffed by laypersons from the Revolutionary Committees. As final arbiter of fundamental rights, it served as an instrument of state oppression with powers equivalent to 'the court of last resort in most judicial systems' (Abdelmoula 1992). The court, which had its own Prosecutors Office, could hear cases in private and impose the death penalty (Articles 11, 16, Law 5/1988). Prosecutors regularly violated due process, denying the right to legal representation and access to evidence, and security agents prevented lawyers from accompanying clients to interrogations or seeing case files (HRW 2006).

Although these kinds of abuses also occurred in the regular criminal courts, their frequency and severity in the People's Court meant that some private practitioners refused to appear there (HRW 2006).[1] Consequently, the reputation of the People's Lawyers was

---

[1] In 2005, the General People's Congress passed a resolution abolishing the People's Court (Law 7/2005), although it created a State Security Court in 2008 (for offences against state security and unauthorised political activity), which was not abolished until after the fall of the Gaddafi regime.

tainted by their association with the People's Court, where they were expected to represent those accused of political and other crimes (Article 13, Law 5/1988).

In 2005, the regime reportedly ordered a raid on the Benghazi Bar Association and appointed its leaders in defiance of the members' wishes. More than 100 lawyers protested, demanding legislation to regulate the legal profession and give lawyers control over the Bar Association (HRW 2006). That year the regime proposed a revised Penal Code and Code of Criminal Procedure (based on the Great Green Charter of Human Rights), which was openly criticised at a public meeting of the Tripoli Bar Association (HRW 2009b).

Despite these constraints, the market for private lawyers grew during the final decade and a half of the Gaddafi regime after UN and then US economic sanctions were lifted in 2003–04 and the regime encouraged international investment while tightly controlling the exploitation of oil resources. Prime jobs were offered by law firms serving the oil industry and overseas investors as Tripoli experienced a property and consumer boom. It was estimated in 2007 that 2,500 lawyers were working in Libya (Freedom House 2007). In 2014, the Bar Association nominally represented some 9,000 lawyers (4,000 of them in Tripoli), 3,500–4,000 of whom actually practised (ILAC 2014). However, all but the best connected elite practitioners were hampered by poor language skills (as a result of Gaddafi's policy of isolation) and had 'a weak and inaccurate understanding of international and comparative law, and the legal systems of even neighbouring countries' (ILAC 2014). Most private practitioners do not specialise, although they can gain a good reputation in a specific field of law and their fees can be substantial (I was told a minimum of €500–€2,500 depending on the complexity of a case).

III. POST-CONFLICT PRESSURES ON LEGAL PRACTICE

The Gaddafi regime's eventual collapse was swift and brutal. Several lawyers (including Terbil) were leading members of the National Transitional Council, the revolutionary proto-government that emerged out of the opposition movement in Benghazi. However, the void left by the destruction of Gaddafi's political and security institutions towards the end of 2011 was swiftly filled by a proliferation of armed militia claiming legitimacy as liberators of Libya from dictatorship. Although the former government's administrative and bureaucratic infrastructure remained intact under the first post-revolution government (the National Transitional Council), its staffing was weakened by a succession of lustration laws (which sacked many former employees) passed by the subsequently elected parliament of the General National Congress.

These two post-Gaddafi, Tripoli-based governments were unable to prevent the proliferation of armed factions. Some militias asserted a continuing political role as 'guardians of the revolution', using violent protest and their roles in national policing and security to force the GNC to enact 'anti-loyalist' policies. Other (mostly non-Libyan) jihadi factions sought to dismantle the Libyan state altogether by attacking political authorities in Tripoli and Benghazi.

By late summer 2014 legislative authority was disputed between the Tripoli-based GNC in the west and the more recently elected House of Representatives (HoR) in Cyrenaica in the east. In November 2014, a Supreme Court ruling that the HoR was unconstitutional increased the violence between loose coalitions in support of the rival parliaments, with the Benghazi-based General Khalifa Haftar, Egypt and the UAE backing the HoR and the Islamist coalition 'Libya Dawn' and other militias, Qatar, Turkey and Sudan backing the GNC.[2] To further complicate the situation, in December 2015 the UN Security Council oversaw the signing of the Libyan Political Accord in Morocco, establishing a Government of National Accord, adding a third entity claiming legitimate authority.

A. Debates about Reform of the Legal Professions

The overthrow of the Gaddafi regime during the 'Arab Spring' cleared the way for major reforms of the legal system and legislation, heightening tensions between the two branches of the legal profession. The politicisation of lawyering under the former regime (underpinned by very real control mechanisms) was still keenly felt during discussions in 2013 about post-conflict reconstruction of the legal profession. The hostility of many private practitioners towards the Directorate of People's Legal Defence was rooted in their perception that its lawyers had colluded with Gaddafi's repressive ideology by providing a mask of legality for the persecution of opponents. By contrast, people's lawyers and some leftist and feminist private practitioners pointed to the fact that people's lawyers provided an effective legal aid service accessible to all.

In 2012–13, Libya hosted many foreign funded UN-to-government, government-to-government, government-to-domestic NGO, and INGO-to-domestic NGO programmes offering technical assistance to the legal system and support for the rule of law (Carlisle 2014: 35). Many of these (except for those of the UNDP and UN Special Mission in Libya) were based on recommendations from non-Libyan consultants, who relied heavily on private practitioners when assessing the legal system. As a result, some of the private practitioners' hostility towards people's lawyers was replicated in international donors' reports authored by consultants with an ideological commitment to pro bono or other partial forms of legal aid provision and against universal, non-means tested, state funded legal assistance (Carlisle 2014).

Internal political pressure to scrap the people's lawyers was evident immediately after the regime's collapse. Under Gaddafi, the legal aid service had been embedded in the state's judicial institutions by the inclusion of the head of the Directorate of the People's Lawyers in the Supreme Council for Judicial Institutions, which also included the Minister of Justice and representatives of the Mufti's Office (*dar al-ifta'*) and other judicial institutions. However, Law 4/2011 appeared to marginalise the Directorate by transferring management of the judiciary to a newly formed Supreme Council for the Judiciary,

---

[2] This ruling was justified on the ground that a May 2014 vote to amend the transitional roadmap had lacked a quorum, rendering the June 2014 election of the HoR invalid. In summer of 2015, the HoR was recognised by the US and EU states, while the GNC continued to claim political legitimacy. See 'Report of the Secretary-General on the United Nations Support Mission in Libya', UN Security Council, 5 September 2014, available at reliefweb.int/sites/reliefweb.int/files/resources/N1451232.pdf.

whose membership was restricted to the president of the Supreme Court, the presidents of the seven appeals courts, and the public prosecutor general. This change was seen by many state legal professionals as demoting the people's lawyers and signalling future changes to the profession. The impact of this amendment, however, was reversed by a Minister of Justice who supported the Directorate. Law 4/2013 concerning the Amendment of the Judiciary not only referred to the institution as 'public lawyers' – thereby distancing the former *people's* lawyers from Gaddafi's ideology – but also reintegrated the head of the Directorate into the Supreme Council for the Judiciary.

Although lobbying to abolish the Directorate failed during 2012–13, the Bar Association succeed in raising its profile, opening professional opportunities, and drafting new legislation governing the profession. The Association was organised in seven regional offices under a new, unelected, national and regional caretaker leadership, headed by a provisional Executive Council of eight members (consisting of a president and representatives from each region), which was formed in early 2012 (ILAC 2014). Some of the small number of globally connected private lawyers became active in debates about post-conflict reconstruction of the legal system.

In 2012, the government passed Decree 340/2012 Authorising Non-Arab Lawyers to Practise before Libyan Courts. The Bar Association's inaugural post-Revolution national conference in 2012 endorsed draft legislation to govern the profession and initiated the development of a professional ethics code and communication strategy (ILAC 2014). However, in the absence of enacted legislation, there were tensions between the (Tripoli-based) national executive and regional offices over the allocation of limited resources and authority to make decisions about the Bar's future (ILAC 2014).

In 2014, the General National Congress in Tripoli finally passed Law 3/2014 on Legal Practice. Although the Bar Association had limited input into most legislative drafting in the post-revolution years, it significantly shaped this law (ILAC 2013). The new law requires all lawyers in private practice to pay an annual fee to belong to the Bar, which has regional offices and headquarters in Tripoli (Articles 51, 52, 55). The Bar is made responsible for professional admissions and promotions, instructed to distinguish between practising and inactive lawyers (including those suspended or dismissed), expected to register legal practices and tasked with authorising non-Libyan lawyers to work in Libya (Articles 13, 14, 22, 25). It also has broader authority to defend lawyers' professional interests and independence, develop legal thought and protect the separation of powers, encourage academic research, contribute to university law curricula, and organise training, seminars and conferences (Article 59).

Law 3/2014 definitively breaks from Decree 88/1990 in asserting lawyers' freedom from state control, declaring that the legal profession is 'free and independent' and committed to 'justice' and 'safeguarding liberties' (Article 1). Lawyers enjoy the same immunities as members of the judiciary and can set their own fees; perhaps reflecting increasing lawlessness from mid-2013, their offices cannot be raided without a judicial ruling (Articles 27–30). They are also entitled to a state pension (Article 60).

Echoing Decree 885/1990, they are prohibited from working in government or business, required to protect client confidentiality, forbidden to tout their services or work on cases with non-lawyers, prevented from taking power of attorney over former clients, and required to give clients reasonable notice if they decide to withdraw their services (Articles 30–36). The Bar has extensive powers to discipline lawyers for unspecified offences without any involvement by state bodies (Article 41).

B. Security Risks and the Breakdown of the Rule of Law

The impact of this new legislation is difficult to assess. Law 3/2014 was passed by a government whose political authority was increasingly contested. Furthermore, the security situation, including the violent physical occupation of the Ministry of Justice and the General National Congress, made operating the legal system difficult. In 2013, the courts, especially criminal courts, were handling few cases in Tripoli. In Derna, Benghazi and Sirte courts were largely suspended from March 2014, and the last working Court of First Instance in Benghazi closed in May 2014, forcing those seeking justice to go to Al-Marj. Courts in Tripoli effectively stopped working in mid-July 2014 because of violent attacks and heavy shelling of courts and judicial offices.[3]

Legal professionals themselves were attacked. By April 2014, at least seven judges and public prosecutors had been assassinated, prompting judges in the east (notably in Benghazi and Derna) and south (around Sebha) to refuse to work.[4] Lawyers also were targeted. In June 2014, the women's rights lawyer Salwa Bugaighis was murdered by gunmen in her home. This followed the assassination of the human rights lawyer Abdulsalam Al-Mesmari in the street in July 2013. Both had been actively involved in the Benghazi uprising in February 2011 and are presumed to have been singled out for criticising the influence and ideologies of Islamist groups. As militia violence spiralled into civil war, many professionals – including lawyers – fled the country. Those staying – particularly minority rights activists, journalists and human rights defenders – remained at risk from factions jostling for supremacy. In 2018, there were reports that the Fezzan lawyer Mokhtar Bin Rajab had died in a Tripoli prison following his arrest at the direction of Tripoli's Public Prosecutor.[5]

IV. CONCLUSION

The threats facing lawyers in the post-Gaddafi period are symptomatic of the profession's continuing vulnerability to fluctuations in the politics of the Libyan state. The influence of government policy on lawyers is perhaps not that extraordinary, but there have been dramatic shifts in the fortunes of Libya's lawyers during their country's short, traumatic history.

The post-Ottoman evolution of the profession was impeded by the Italian occupation's scorched earth policy. The profession emerged slowly under the monarchy, supported by colleagues from other Arab states. Although the Senussi government engaged in state building and limited institutional development, it was the discovery of oil that significantly increased the need for legal services. This demand for globally connected lawyers persisted under Gaddafi, despite greater state control of the oil industry. The regime

---

[3] *Libya: Judiciary and Security Sector* Land Info at www.landinfo.no/asset/3026/1/3026_1.pdf.
[4] Army and police personnel have been the main targets of assassinations, especially in and around Benghazi. However, legal professionals, journalists and civil society activists have also been targeted. See Human Rights Watch, 'Libya: Government Institutions at Risk of Collapse' *Human Rights Watch*, 7 March 2014, www.hrw.org/news/2014/03/07/libya-government-institutions-risk-collapse; H Salah, 'Libya's Justice Pandemonium' *Jurist* 12 April 2014, jurist.org/hotline/2014/04/hanan-salah-libyan-government.php.
[5] See www.libyaobserver.ly/inbrief/sabha-lawyer-died-tripoli-prison-days-after-arrest.

additionally helped increase demand for lawyers by integrating the Sharia courts into the ordinary court system and creating free legal aid (in the form of the people's lawyers).

However, the tension in Gaddafi's Libya between the need for lawyers to service the economy and the regime's determination to control the profession has left a problematic legacy. Successive policies designed to co-opt, nationalise and then undermine the independence of lawyers split the profession into private and state-salaried practitioners, with a small number of private practitioners in elite legal firms serving corporate and international clients while the majority work for individuals or local businesses. The large number of state-salaried public (formerly people's) lawyers have not been able to escape their association with the abuses perpetrated by the former regime and their seeming lack of independence.

The profession is fragmented by an ideological dispute about the allocation of resources to ensure access to justice and the enormous gulf between elite lawyers working in the oil industry and the mass of lawyers serving domestic clients. Following the 2011 uprising, these schisms have been exacerbated by the ignorance of lawyers' professional bodies about their membership, activities, pay and conditions of work. The debate about the future of the profession during the influx of international donor aid in 2012–13 tended to be driven by the Bar Association and well-connected elite lawyers. However, their recommendations (such as the dissolution of the public lawyers' legal aid service) were not based on deep research or knowledge of the profession, nor did they evaluate the gender, ethnic or class composition of the profession.

This lack of knowledge exacerbated the problematic issue of the politicisation of lawyering as foreign donors and internal lobbies argued for rejecting the ideological legacy of state-salaried legal aid and opening legal services to market forces. During this debate the professional and political hostility of private practitioners toward public lawyers complemented international donors' neo-liberal critique of direct, state funded legal aid. Reformers emphasised strengthening the capacity of criminal lawyers to challenge the state (during a period of anticipated transitional justice) rather than engaging the more mundane fields of family, public and administrative law. The proponents of these reforms saw their proposals as non-ideological, confident of the market's capacity to motivate lawyers to defend the rule of law. There was no research into the impact of these reforms on equality of opportunity within the profession or access to justice.

The Ministry of Justice response to demands for reform during the transitional (February 2011–July 2012) and subsequent GNC (August 2012–August 2014) governments was cautious and largely maintained the status quo, aside from increasing protections for lawyers' independence in Law 3/2014 on Legal Practice. The civil war that has dominated Libya's politics, economy and society since 2014 has prevented the restructuring of the profession. This war has once again isolated Libya's lawyers: the Libyan Bar Association is no longer a member of the International Bar Association, many lawyers have fled the violence, and the oil industry has been massively disrupted as rival armed groups fight to seize fields and control revenues. Once again the profession is enmeshed in struggles for the control of the state. The future of lawyering in Libya will depend on the ideology of the victorious military factions and the post-conflict recovery of a market for their services.

REFERENCES

Abdelmoula, A (1992) 'Libya: The Control of Lawyers by the State' 17 *Journal of the Legal Profession* 55.

Algheita, N (2014) 'The Role of Criminal Defence Lawyers in the Administration of Justice in Libya: Challenges and Prospects' in JM Otto, J Carlisle and S Ibrahim (eds), *Searching for Justice in Post-Gaddafi Libya: A Socio-Legal Exploration of People's Concerns and Institutional Responses at Home and from Abroad* (Leiden, Van Vollenhoven Institute)

Algheita, N and Ibrahim, S (2014) 'Additional Report: Libya's Court Structure' in JM Otto, J Carlisle and S Ibrahim (eds), *Searching for Justice in Post-Gaddafi Libya: A Socio-Legal Exploration of People's Concerns and Institutional Responses at Home and from Abroad* (Leiden, Van Vollenhoven Institute)

Anderson, L (1986) *The State and Social Transformation in Tunisia and Libya, 1830–1980* (Princeton, Princeton University Press).

Blake, GH (1969) 'Oil Production in Libya' 54(2) *Geography* 221.

Carlisle, J (2014) 'Perspectives on Justice in Libya: A Review of International Reports' in JM Otto, J Carlisle and S Ibrahim (eds), *Searching for Justice in Post-Gaddafi Libya: A Socio-Legal Exploration of People's Concerns and Institutional Responses at Home and From Abroad* (Leiden, Van Vollenhoven Institute).

—— (2014) 'Access to Justice and Legal Aid in Libya: The Future of the People's Lawyers' in JM Otto, J Carlisle and S Ibrahim (eds), *Searching for Justice in Post-Gaddafi Libya: A Socio-Legal Exploration of People's Concerns and Institutional Responses at Home and From Abroad* (Leiden, Van Vollenhoven Institute).

Chaplin Metz, H (1987) *Libya – A Country Study* (Washington DC, Library of Congress).

El Fathaly, OI (1977) 'Libya: The Social, Economic and Historical Milieus' in OI El Fathaly, M Palmer and R Chackerian (eds), *Political Development and Bureaucracy in Libya* (Lexington MA, DC Heath).

El Fathaly, OI and Abusedra, FS (1980) 'The Impact of Socio-Political Change on Economic Development in Libya' 16(3) *Middle Eastern Studies* 225.

First, R (1974) *Libya: The Elusive Revolution* (London, Penguin).

Freedom House (2007) *Countries at the Crossroads 2007* (Washington DC, Freedom House).

Hilsum, L (2012) *Sandstorm: Libya in the Time of Revolution* (London, Faber & Faber).

Human Rights Watch (2006) *Libya: Words to Deeds: The Urgent Need for Human Rights Reform* (New York, Human Rights Watch).

—— (2009) *Truth and Justice Can't Wait: Human Rights Developments in Libya Amid Institutional Obstacles* (New York, Human Rights Watch).

—— (2009) *Libya: In Repressive Atmosphere, Pockets of Improvement* (New York, Human Rights Watch).

International Legal Assistance Consortium (2013) *Rule of Law Assessment Report: Libya 2013* (Stockholm, ILAC).

Khadduri, M (1963) *Modern Libya: A Study in Political Development* (Baltimore, John Hopkins Press).

Mayer, E (1995) 'In Search of Sacred Law: The Meandering Course of Gadaffi's Legal Policy' in D Vandewalle (ed), *Gadaffi's 1969–1994* (New York: St Martin's Press).

Otto, JM, Carlisle, J and Ibrahim, S (2013) *Searching for Justice in Post-Gaddafi Libya: A Socio-Legal Exploration of People's Concerns and Institutional Responses at Home and From Abroad* (Leiden, Van Vollenhoven Institute).

Pargeter, A (2012) *Libya: The Rise and Fall of Qaddafi* (New Haven, Yale University Press).

St John, RB (2011) *Libya: Continuity and Change* (New York, Routledge).

Sury, SH (2003) 'A New System for a New State: The Libyan Experiment in Statehood, 1951–69' in A Badinetti (ed), *Modern and Contemporary Libya: Sources and Histriographies* (Rome, Instituto Italianoper L'Africa e L'Oriente).

Varvelli, A (2013) 'The Role of Tribal Dynamics in the Libyan Future', *Instituto per gli Studi di Politica Internazionale (ISPI)* www.ispionline.it/sites/default/files/pubblicazioni/analysis_172_2013.pdf.

Wright, J (1982) *Libya: A Modern History* (London, Croom Helm).

32

Palestine
Lawyering between Colonisation and the Struggle for Professional Independence

MUTAZ M QAFISHEH

I. INTRODUCTION

REGULATION OF THE Palestinian legal profession dates from the arrival of British forces during World War I and is an amalgam of the legal systems that have governed Palestine since its detachment from the Ottoman Empire (British, Jordanian, Egyptian, Israeli and Palestinian) (Qafisheh 2013). Under the Ottoman Empire, the profession was codified by the Case Agents (Advocates) Law of 14 January 1876 (Ramadan 1928: vol 5, 346), enacted during efforts to modernise the legal system, chiefly by importing legislation from Europe (Milhem 2014: 17–51). In 1871, a law school was opened in Istanbul (Bisharat 1989: 20), from which a number of Palestinians graduated (Likhovski 2016: 178).

This chapter analyses the current Palestinian legal profession in historical perspective. Part II discusses its emergence under British rule (1917–48), in the West Bank after its annexation by Jordan and in Gaza under Egyptian administration (1948–67), and under Israeli occupation (1967–93). Part III deals with the profession under Palestinian rule from 1994 to the adoption of the first Palestinian Advocates Law in 1999 and the formation of the Palestinian Bar Association (PBA), until now. Parts IV and V explore the qualifications to practise law and legal ethics in Palestine today.

II. DEVELOPMENT OF THE LEGAL PROFESSION IN PALESTINE

Because different regimes ruled Palestine, its law is a mixture of various systems. While Ottoman legislation was based on Islamic and European civil law, legislation enacted by Britain prior to May 1948 reflected the common law. The West Bank and Gaza were subjected to civil law from 1948 and 1967: when the West Bank was annexed by Jordan, Jordanian law, largely derived from the Egyptian/French legal system, was imposed. In Gaza, Egypt retained British law but enacted some legislation influenced by Egyptian law.

After it occupied the West Bank and Gaza in June 1967, Israel did not extend its law (except in East Jerusalem) but instead issued military orders (different for Gaza and the West Bank) amending or replacing existing law (Qafisheh 2013).

Even before setting foot in Palestinian territory, Palestinian Authority President Yasser Arafat issued Decree No 1 of 20 May 1994,[1] declaring that all laws passed before the Israeli occupation would remain in force. Arafat continued to rule by decrees until the election of the first Palestinian Legislative Council (PLC) on 16 December 1996.[2] The PLC lasted until June 2007, when the Islamic Resistance Movement (Hamas), which opposes PA rule, took over the Gaza Strip by force. The Palestinian split led to the creation of two de facto governments centred in the cities of Gaza and Ramallah (Muwatin 2016).

A. Palestinian Lawyers in the British Era

Towards the end of Ottoman rule, its laws had little if any influence on the legal profession in Palestine. Norman Bentwich reported that in 1918 the number of lawyers at the time 'could be counted on the fingers of two hands' (Likhovski 2006: 25). Others said there were 83 (Bisharat 1989: 24). In the early years of the British occupation, the legal profession was supervised by the British-appointed Attorney General, who granted licences to lawyers (Bisharat 1989: 25). As early as 1918, the British regulated lawyers' fees.[3] They enacted the first law governing the legal profession in Palestine, Advocates Ordinance No 13, on 22 July 1922 (Drayton 1934), by which time there were 123 lawyers (Likhovski 2006: 26). This instrument, along with its Rules, established the Legal Board to administer the legal profession,[4] including lawyers' admission, training, examinations, fees, and professional responsibility.[5] Because the number of lawyers had increased to an estimated 358 in 1937 (Likhovski 2006: 26), the 1922 Ordinance was replaced by Advocates Ordinance No 32 of 21 November 1938,[6] which governed the legal profession (with minor amendments in 1939, 1941, 1945 and 1946) until the end of British rule.

The 1938 Ordinance assigned the administration of the legal profession to a governmental Law Council[7] headed by the Attorney General acting *ex officio*, with a minimum of six members, including four practising lawyers appointed by the British High Commissioner for a three-year renewable term.[8] The Council accredited the academic degrees required by lawyers,[9] administered professional examinations, supervised apprentice lawyers,[10] and licensed lawyers.[11]

---

[1] Palestine Gazette (PG), No 1, 20 November 1994, 10.
[2] Election of Local Government Law No 5 of 1996, PG, No 16, 20 January 1997, 6.
[3] Advocates' Fees Rules of 7 November 1918.
[4] Advocates Ordinance of 1922, Art 6.
[5] Law Examinations (Payment of Expenses) Rules of 1934, PG (Supplement 2) No 448, 21 June 1934, 503.
[6] PG (Supplement 1) No 843, 24 November 1938, 113.
[7] PG (Supplement 1) No 843, 24 November 1938, 24, 130.
[8] ibid, Art 3.
[9] ibid, Art 2.
[10] Law Council Rules of 23 November 1938. PG No 843 (Supplement 2), 24 November 1938, 1779, Arts 10–12.
[11] Law Council Ordinance, Art 4.

Because Palestine was divided along ethno-national lines – Arabs (Muslims and Christians) and Jews (Qafisheh 2008: 195–207) – there was no unified or official Bar association. Instead, Jews and Arab Palestinians created separate ones, both informally recognised by the British authorities (Likhovski 2006: 26; Bisharat 1989: 26). Although these bodies were not empowered to license lawyers or formally administer law practice, they planted the seeds for the later Israeli and Palestinian Bar associations.

At the end of British rule in 1948 there were over 1,000 practising lawyers in Palestine, about half of whom were Arab Palestinians (Bisharat 1989: 26). The latter, most of whom found themselves in the West Bank, Gaza, or Jordan (as refugees from the parts of Palestine that became Israel), constituted the founders of the profession. Indeed, 'the [British-run] Mandate period would seem to have marked the apogee of the social and political power of lawyers in Palestinian Arab society' (Bisharat 1989: 28).

After the withdrawal of British forces on 14 May 1948, Palestine was divided into three parts: the State of Israel was established on 78 per cent, the West Bank consisted of the 20 per cent annexed by Jordan, and the 2 per cent in the Gaza Strip came under Egyptian administration (Harris et al 2002: 13–20).

B. The Legal Profession in Gaza under Egyptian Administration

Ever since 1948, Gaza has developed a separate political, social and legal character (Feldman 2008). After the end of British rule, Egypt exercised military rule but retained the laws of the British Mandate,[12] and Gaza lawyers continued practising before local courts (Wahiedi 1992: 333 ff). Because there was no Bar association, the Law Council performed its previous functions (Abuhannoud 2000: nn 23–24).

New law graduates, most of whom studied in Egypt, could become lawyers after acquiring a licence to practise from the Law Council, whose members were appointed by the Egyptian-run government of Gaza.[13] In one of the rare modifications of the 1938 Ordinance, the Egyptian Governor decided in 1955 to let those who had performed any judicial function for a year become lawyers if they held a law degree and were approved by the Gaza Chief Justice and Governor (Abuhannoud 2000: n 23). At the same time, the Governor reduced apprenticeship to a year.[14] Lawyers founded a de facto Bar association (called 'Lawyers Society'), which participated in the regional Arab Lawyers Union in Cairo (Abuhannoud 2000: n 24).

C. West Bank Lawyers under Jordanian Rule

During the 1948–49 war, the Jordanian army occupied parts of eastern Palestine designated for the Arab State in the UN Partition Plan of 29 November 1947.[15] Jordan annexed

---

[12] Israel and Egypt General Armistice Agreement, 42 UNTS 252 (1949).
[13] Interview with Dr Abdelkarim Shami, a lawyer and an official of the Palestinian Ministry of Justice (Gaza, 25 May 2016).
[14] Interview with Dr Abdelrahman Abunaser, the 1996 elected head of the Gaza Lawyers Society (Gaza, 6 June 2016).
[15] UN Doc A/RES/181(II), 29 November 1947.

the West Bank shortly after signing the armistice agreement with Israel on 3 April 1949.[16] For the next two years chaos prevailed (Katz 2018). Courts were virtually locked, and the legal profession ceased to function.[17] Because lawyers were not required to have offices, many gathered in coffee shops to meet clients. After formal annexation of the West Bank by Jordan on 24 April 1950, however, the legal profession was gradually restructured. Palestinian lawyers who found themselves in the West and East Banks could practise after being licensed by the Jordanian Minister of Justice.[18]

Yet recognition of Palestinian lawyers by Jordanian courts did not always proceed smoothly. On one occasion, a Jordanian magistrate required all Palestinian lawyers to produce copies of their law degrees before appearing in his court.[19] Shortly after adoption of the Civil Bar Association Law, No 31 of 16 September 1950, the legal profession was strengthened by the formation of the Jordanian Bar Association, whose first president was a West Bank Palestinian lawyer, Mr Abdelatif Salah (Bisharat 1989: 28). Five years later, the Bar Association Law was replaced by the Civil Bar Association Law No 5 of 6 February 1955.[20]

The 1955 law, like its predecessor, prescribed the formation of the Bar, rights and obligations of lawyers, apprenticeship, and legal ethics. Bye-laws adopted on 6 April 1951[21] and 8 July 1955[22] regulated the elections to and functions of the Bar association, its staff and budget, committees and branches, disciplinary actions against unethical lawyers, and lawyers' fees. Civil lawyers in Jordan, including the West Bank, could appear before all civil courts, including magistrates, courts of first instance, courts of appeal, High Court of Justice (the administrative court), and Court of Cassation. This is still the case in the West Bank (and Gaza) today.

The Bar took over the profession's affairs. Bar membership became a requirement for anyone practising law. After the first election of its seven-member council in 1951,[23] Bar elections were held annually.[24] Three to four members came from the East Bank and the rest from the West Bank.[25] Except for one year, Palestinian lawyers headed the Jordanian Bar throughout the 1950s (Bisharat 1989: 28). Although the Bar was headquartered in Amman, a branch was opened in Jerusalem in 1964.[26]

One year before the end of Jordan's control of the West Bank, its parliament passed the Civil Bar Association Law No 11 of 2 February 1966,[27] and the Jordanian Bar adopted its bye-law on 17 June 1966,[28] both of which applied throughout the Israeli occupation of the West Bank until enactment of the Palestinian Advocates Law in 1999. Jordanian law

---

[16] Jordanian-Israeli General Armistice Agreement, 42 UNTS 304 (1949).
[17] Interview with Mr Fuad Shihadeh, one of the graduates of the Jerusalem Law Classes and currently the oldest practising lawyer in Palestine (Ramallah, 23 May 2016).
[18] ibid.
[19] ibid.
[20] Jordanian Official Gazette (JOG) No 1214, 16 February 1955, 152.
[21] JOG No 1063, 5 July 1951, 64.
[22] This bye-law was confirmed by the Minister of Justice on 16 August 1955 (JOG No 1237, 16 December 1955, 815).
[23] The 1966 Bar Association Law increased the number of Bar council members to 11 (Art 80).
[24] Bar Association Law 1955, Art 30.
[25] Shihadeh, n 17.
[26] Interview with Professor Othman Takrouri, a lawyer under Jordanian rule (Hebron, 22 May 2016).
[27] JOG No 1905, 5 March 1966, 315.
[28] JOG No 1978, 16 January 1967, 105.

continues to influence Palestinian lawyers.[29] Just 121 lawyers voted in the 1964 Bar council elections, which chose four members from the West Bank and three from the East Bank and named Mr Fuad Shihadeh of Ramallah as president. On the eve of Israeli occupation in 1967, there were about 100 lawyers in the West Bank.[30]

D. Palestinian Lawyers under Israeli Occupation

When Israel occupied the West Bank and Gaza in June 1967, the legal profession entered a dark period lasting three decades. Palestinians were ruled by the Israeli army under two military commanders (one in Gaza and another in the West Bank), who issued separate but similar military orders modifying pre-existing law (Shehadeh 1990). Legal affairs fell under the authority of the military 'justice officer', who replaced the Bar in the West Bank and the Law Council in Gaza[31] in licensing lawyers,[32] recognising law schools, and managing apprenticeship, lawyers' daily work[33] and relations with clients.[34] Israel banned politically active lawyers from practice[35] and deported some of them.[36]

By abolishing the elected Bar in the West Bank, Israel reasserted government control over the profession (which had existed throughout Palestine before 1948) and maintained the status quo that had existed under the Egyptian administration of Gaza (1948–67). Lawyers from the West Bank and Gaza were allowed to appear in the courts of both territories[37] and practise before Israeli military tribunals,[38] as well as the Israeli High Court of Justice.[39] By defending prisoners before Israeli tribunals and in detention, West Bank lawyers reconnected with their colleagues in Gaza after two decades of isolation, giving them an opportunity to discuss and think about national and professional issues as 'Palestinians' rather than Gazans or West Bankers.[40]

In response to Israel's annexation of East Jerusalem on 28 June 1967[41] and its decision to move the headquarters of the West Bank Court of Appeal from Jerusalem to Ramallah,[42] over 50 West Bank lawyers met in Jerusalem and signed a petition declaring a

---

[29] Interview with Mr Fawzi Maswadi, a practising lawyer since 1966 (Hebron, 19 May 2016).
[30] Shihadeh, n 17.
[31] Order Concerning Local Courts No 412 of 5 October 1970, *Proclamations, Orders and Appointments (West Bank)*, 1 March 1971, 954, Art 2.
[32] High Court of Justice, Case No 16/2000 (Ramallah, 18 December 2002).
[33] Order on the Operation of Imprisonment Installation No 29 of 23 June 1967, *Proclamations, Orders and Appointments (West Bank)*, 15 September 1967, 57, Arts 11 and 13.
[34] Order on Lawyer Licenses No 260 of 23 June 1968, *Proclamations, Orders and Appointments (West Bank)*, 22 July 1968, 516; Order on Lawyers (Gaza Strip and Northern Sinai) No 63 of 24 August 1967, *Proclamations, Orders and Appointments (Gaza)*, 31 December 1967, 195.
[35] Shihadeh, n 17.
[36] Interview with Mr Morsi Hujier, Head of Jerusalem/West Bank branch of the Jordanian Bar Association 1981-93 (Ramallah, 13 June 2016).
[37] Shihadeh, n 17.
[38] Order Concerning Defense in Military Tribunals No 400 of 13 July 1970, *Proclamations, Orders and Appointments (West Bank)*, 1 March 1971, 933.
[39] Shihadeh, n 17. See Order on Security Instructions No 378 of 1970, *Proclamations, Orders and Appointments (West Bank)*, 22 April 1970, Arts 8, 19, 29, 32, and 34.
[40] Hujier, n 36; Abunaser, n 14.
[41] Takrouri, n 26.
[42] Order No 412, n 31, Art 6.

boycott of Israeli courts.[43] On 22 August 1967, the Jordanian Bar Association instructed all West Bank lawyers to join the strike (Abuhannoud 2000: n 40). Initially, 'almost all [lawyers] declined to resume working, to honour the strike' (Bisharat 1989: 74). Those who did so were paid salaries by the Jordanians and allowed to practise in Jordan[44] and before West Bank religious courts.[45] The Jordanian Bar expelled those who refused to strike (an action upheld by the Jordanian High Court of Justice in 1981, when a lawyer who had defied the strike challenged his expulsion) (Abuhannoud 2000: nn 41–42).[46] The boycott contributed to the 'deterioration of the formal courts system' (Bisharat 1989: 125). In Gaza, Palestinian lawyers continued pleading before Israeli-run civil and military courts.[47]

Israel responded by permitting its lawyers to appear in West Bank courts and defend Palestinian clients.[48] In 1969, 14 prominent West Bank lawyers met in Ramallah and decided to terminate the strike 'based on the belief that Palestinian lawyers are better equipped to defend their fellow citizens, determining that the strike is useless'.[49] In 1971, over 70 lawyers resumed practice in those courts (Abuhannoud 2000: n 40). The split among West Bank lawyers produced two factions: by the late 1980s, 320 lawyers were striking and 188 were practising (Bisharat 1989: 73). Years later a consensus emerged that the strike had been a mistake. One lawyer reported that although he was expelled from the Jordanian Bar after resuming practice, he was later praised as a hero for defending Palestinian rights.[50]

The practising West Bank lawyers were prevented from forming a Bar association. In 1984, six lawyers asked the Israeli military commander to establish a Bar based on the 1966 Jordanian Bar Association Law and challenged his refusal in the Israeli High Court of Justice. The commander then agreed to set up a law council subordinate to the military, which would appoint the members and could veto their decisions. The lawyers refused to participate (Abuhannoud 2000: n 36), instead, creating the Arab Lawyers Union,[51] whose membership was voluntary (Abuhannoud 2000: n 43). Nine lawyers formed the Union Council, but Israel did not recognise the Union.[52] In Gaza, advocates formed the Lawyers Society based on the still-valid Ottoman Association Law and adopted a bye-law.[53] In 1977, the Gaza Society had 364 lawyers (Abuhannoud 2000: n 42). Despite their informal nature, both associations managed to organise the legal profession, adopt unified positions on national questions,[54] issue membership cards, train new lawyers,

---

[43] Hujier, n 36.
[44] Takrouri, n 26.
[45] ibid.
[46] Shihadeh, n 17.
[47] Abunaser, n 14. See Order on the Appearance of Israeli Lawyers in the Courts No 958 of 7 July 1988, *Proclamations, Orders and Appointments (Gaza)*, 25 September 1989, 9029.
[48] Order on the Appearance of Israeli Lawyers in the Courts No 145 of 23 October 1967, *Proclamations, Orders and Appointments (West Bank)*, 29 December 1967, 306.
[49] Shihadeh, n 17.
[50] ibid.
[51] Maswadi, n 29.
[52] Interview with Mr Adnan Abulaila, one of Arab Lawyers Union's founders (Nablus, 13 June 2016).
[53] Shami, n 13.
[54] Interview with Mr Ishaq Maswadi, a practising lawyer in the West Bank since 1975 (Hebron, 18 May 2016); Hujier, n 36; Abulaila, n 52; Abunaser, n 14.

offer legal aid to needy persons, defend lawyers' interests, and hold elections.[55] Members of these three bodies (Gaza Society, Arab Lawyers Union, and Jordanian Bar) served on the committee that drafted the 1999 Palestinian Advocates Law, paving the way for the *de jure* establishment of the current Palestinian Bar Association.[56]

III. THE LEGAL PROFESSION UNDER PALESTINIAN RULE

A. The Transitional Phase

In 1994, the Palestinian Authority (PA) was established in Gaza and the West Bank after the signing of the Israeli-Palestinian Declaration of Principles on Interim Self-Government Arrangement of 13 September 1993, which was followed by the Israeli-Palestinian Interim Agreement on the West Bank and the Gaza Strip of 28 September 1995.[57] The latter agreement's Protocol Concerning Legal Affairs transferred jurisdiction over the judicial system to the PA.

For a few years, Palestinian lawyers operated as they had under Israeli occupation, while a consensus emerged on the need to form a unified Bar (Abuhannoud 2000: nn 43–45). Lawyers were represented by three informal bodies: the Arab Lawyers Union, including some 750 practising members in the West Bank,[58] the Palestinian branch of the Jordanian Bar, including over 250 striking West Bank lawyers,[59] and the Lawyers Society of Gaza, with about 300 members.[60] The Union and the Society continued to operate, while the Palestinian Minister of Justice assumed the functions of the Israeli military justice officer concerning the legal profession (Abuhannoud 2000: n 43). The absence of a unified law for the West Bank and Gaza, disagreement among lawyers in the three factions, and physical separation between the two regions delayed the emergence of a unified Bar,[61] but consultations among the three bodies intensified.[62]

On 9 July 1997, President Yasser Arafat, following a recommendation of the three bodies (Abuhannoud 2000: nn 46–47), issued Decree No 78 of 1997, establishing a nine-member transitional council for the Palestinian Bar Association (PBA), headed by Abdelrahman Abunaser, former head of the Gaza Lawyers Society.[63] Article 2 empowered the council to perform its functions based on existing legislation and draft a proposed law for the PBA. The nine-member council consisted of three members from each association.[64] This breakthrough unified Palestinian lawyers into a single body for the first time. Because Gaza law did not authorise an elected bar, the council was instructed to follow the West Bank's 1966 Jordanian Bar law.[65]

---

[55] Abunaser, n 14.
[56] Shami, n 13.
[57] (1997) 36 *International Legal Materials* 551.
[58] Abulaila, n 52.
[59] Hujier, n 36.
[60] Abunaser, n 14.
[61] Abulaila, n 52.
[62] Abunaser, n 14.
[63] PG No 19, 15 October 1997, 10, Art 1.
[64] Hujier, n 36.
[65] Decree No 120 of 17 December 1997, PG No 23, 8 June 1998, 44.

This transitional Bar council, initially expected to last only a year,[66] was formally extended by Presidential Decree No 2 of 12 January 1999 'until the enactment and enforcement of the Palestinian Bar Association Law and holding of the [bar] elections'.[67] Some lawyers questioned the legitimacy of this appointed council, believing it should have been dissolved and an election conducted after adoption of the Advocates Law in June 1999. On 16 May 2000, a lawyer sued in the Palestinian High Court of Justice, claiming that the Bar council's term had ended. The Court rejected the contention, allowing the council to continue administering the legal profession until the Bar election.[68] However, such objections helped produce the first bar association's election on 11 July 2003 (Mehanna 2007).

Most of the subsequent Palestinian Bars (2005–18) built on the practices adopted by the first appointed Bar council (Mehanna 2007). This council supervised the legal profession, registered eligible lawyers (who initially numbered 890), set membership fees, admitted new lawyers, supervised apprenticeship, appointed a secretariat, opened branches in major cities, formed specialised committees, and sanctioned lawyers who violated professional ethics. On 1 January 1998, the founding council adopted the Lawyers Retirement Bye-law based on the 1966 Bar law, the first social security scheme protecting lawyers.[69]

The key achievement of the transitional bar council was drafting the Legal Profession Law No 3 of 24 June 1999,[70] which repealed the 1938 Advocates Ordinance applicable in Gaza as well as the 1966 Bar Association Law enforced in the West Bank (Qafisheh 2013: 26). A few months later, the name was changed to the Civil Advocates Law.[71] On 22 September 2000, the general assembly of the PBA adopted a bye-law.[72] The law and its bye-laws regulated the Bar's structure, elections, financial resources, qualifications for law practice, apprenticeship, lawyers' rights and obligations, and discipline of unethical lawyers.

Following the 2003 election establishing the Bar, there were two more in April 2005 and April 2007. But two months after the latter, Hamas took over Gaza, and elections were delayed several times because of the political split between Fatah in the West Bank and the ruling regime of Gaza. Hamas was unable to control the Gaza Bar, since most lawyers were Fatah affiliates, but it could prevent Gaza lawyers from participating in subsequent elections.[73] That led President Abbas to amend the Advocates Law by Decree-Law No 14 of 5 November 2011.[74] A month later, members of the West Bank Bar council, including the president, resigned, and the general assembly elected a transitional council pending a new election.[75]

---

[66] Decree No 78 of 1997, n 63, Art 3.
[67] PG No 28, 13 March 1999, 52.
[68] Case No 90/2000 (Gaza, 2 July 2000); Case No 15/2003 (Gaza, 8 February 2003).
[69] PG No 25, 24 September 1998, 58.
[70] PG No 30, 10 October 1999, 5.
[71] Law No 5 of 28 December 1999 Concerning the Amendment of Legal Profession Law No 3 of 1999, PG No 32, 29 February 2000, 5.
[72] PG No 34, 30 September 2000, 117.
[73] Interview with Mr Riyad Sulaiman, member of the training and legal committees of the Gaza centre of PBA (Gaza, 6 June 2016).
[74] PG No 92, 25 December 2011, 44.
[75] Maan News, *The Election of Transitional Committee for Lawyers in the Jerusalem [i.e. West Bank] Center* (Bethlehem, 4 December 2011).

The main feature of the decree is its recognition that the political split effectively created two Bars, one for the West Bank and another for Gaza, with separate general assemblies, financial assets, secretariats, headquarters, vice-presidents, and even websites.[76] Yet the Palestinian Bar still has a single set of laws and bye-laws, president, election day, and external representative.[77] A 'unified' Bar council was scheduled to be elected in the West Bank and Gaza on 7 April 2012. But when it became apparent that Fatah would win, Hamas obtained a court order banning the Gaza vote.[78] Thus, only West Bank lawyers voted for the Bar council on 6 April 2015.[79] Due to internal conflicts, the West Bank branch of the council resigned and a transitional Bar was elected for a one-year term on 6 May 2017.[80] On 5 April 2018, a unified Palestinian bar council was elected for both Gaza and the West Bank.[81] Given the separation of the two regions by the Israeli occupation blockade, the Bar council's Gaza members cannot physically meet their West Bank counterparts except on rare occasions. In a sense, therefore, the PBA is actually a 'federation' of two Bars.

B. Structure of the Palestinian Bar Association

The current PBA is composed of a general assembly, council, specialised committees, and geographic/district committees. The PBA's general assembly includes all practising lawyers who pay the annual membership fee and register on the lawyers roll. The assembly elects the council, adopts bye-laws, endorses the budget, and governs 'all legal profession affairs'.[82] In 2018 there were more than 6,000 members: 4,459 in the West Bank[83] and 1,700 in Gaza.[84] Most lawyers practise alone, although some belong to firms, groups or companies. Only 12 law offices are formally registered under the companies law, although collaborative practice is increasing.[85] Women are about 28 per cent of lawyers in the West Bank and a little under 13 per cent in Gaza.[86]

Elected by secret ballot every three years,[87] the council has 15 members, nine from the West Bank and six from Gaza.[88] It registers lawyers, grants licences to practise, sets membership fees, drafts bye-laws for general assembly approval, appoints and supervises the Bar's staff, monitors the budget, carries out projects, disciplines lawyers

---

[76] The West Bank website is: palestinebar.ps; the Gaza website is: pbaps.ps.
[77] Art 4(3).
[78] Noqta, *What Happens in the Elections of Palestinian Bar Association between the West Bank and Gaza?!* (Abu Dhabi, 22 April 2012).
[79] PBA, *Electing Husain Shabanah as President of the Bar Association* (Ramallah, 13 April 2015).
[80] PBA, *Electing Members for the Transitional Bar Association* (Ramallah, 7 May 2017).
[81] PBA, *The Bar Council Elects Advocate Mr. Jawad Obayat as a President of the Palestinian Bar Association for the Period 2018–2021* (Ramallah, 10 April 2018).
[82] The Law, Art 36(2)(b).
[83] PBA, *Administrative and Financial Report* (Ramallah 2018) 10.
[84] Interview with Mr Ala Farra, Manager of the Gaza Bar (Gaza, 30 June 2018).
[85] Interview with Mr Dawoud Fouda, Manager of the West Bank Bar (Ramallah, 28 June 2018).
[86] The number of female lawyers in the West Bank is 1,232; Administrative and Financial Report 2018, n 83, 10. In Gaza there are only 220 female lawyers; Farra, n 84.
[87] Decree-Law No 14 of 2011, Art 5(2).
[88] Bye-law, Art 23.

who violate professional ethics, regulates lawyers' fees, and resolves conflicts among lawyers.[89] In practice, the council far exceeds its statutory mandate, using its powers to represent lawyers and defend their interests. It advocates the rights of lawyers vis-à-vis the government.[90] It protects lawyers from attack, particularly by security forces.[91] It provides legal aid for needy people.[92] It holds symposia on the legal profession and human rights,[93] cooperates with others in the legal system, including the judiciary, prosecution, police, and networks with other Bars, regionally and globally.[94] The council elects a member as its president.

The PBA has 15 specialised committees (each headed by a council member and collectively involving 150 lawyers) on topics including apprenticeship, women, social benefits, lawyers' fees, complaints, discipline, legal aid, and public freedoms.[95] It also has committees (of 3–7 lawyers) for each of the 16 Palestinian districts. The PBA is contemplating institutionalising committees by adopting their bye-laws and choosing them by elections rather than council appointment.[96]

IV. QUALIFICATIONS FOR LAW PRACTICE

In order to qualify as a lawyer in Palestine and be admitted by the Bar (which is compulsory), the applicant must: (1) be a Palestinian citizen; (2) have an LLB; (3) be a resident of Palestine; (4) be of good character (no convictions for a felony or misdemeanour affecting one's honour);[97] (5) enjoy full civil capacity (eg not be bankrupt); and (6) complete an apprenticeship. Lawyers must pay annual fees, including those for retirement.[98] Applicants also sit a series of examinations.

A. Legal Education

Anyone wishing to practise law in Palestine must hold a law degree from a Palestinian university or its equivalent (Qafisheh 2016). After the end of British rule there were no law schools in the West Bank or Gaza (Likhovski 2016). Palestinian universities were prevented from initiating law programmes under Israeli occupation (Bisharat 1989: 76). In 1986, Hebron University started teaching law but stopped when Israel threatened to

---

[89] Advocates Law 1999, Art 42.
[90] PBA, *President of the Bar Sends a Letter to the Tax Department* (Ramallah, 10 March 2016).
[91] MUSAWA, 'Ongoing Attacks on Human Rights Defenders: Lawyers and Journalists', 18 *Eye on Justice* (Ramallah, December 2015) 2.
[92] PBA, *Launching the National Strategic Plan for Legal Aid* (Ramallah, 31 December 2015).
[93] PBA, *Concluding the International Conference on Palestinian Political Prisoners in Israeli Custody* (Amman, 17 September 2015).
[94] PBA, *Meeting with Florence Bar* (Ramallah, 28 February 2016).
[95] PBA, *Administrative and Financial Report* (Ramallah 2016) 9–65.
[96] Meeting with Mr Fadi Abbas, Member of the Bar Council (Ramallah, 28 June 2018).
[97] High Court of Justice, Case No 27/2000 (Ramallah, 12 March 2003).
[98] High Court of Justice, Case No 60/2003 (Gaza, 7 July 2003); High Court of Justice, Case No 353/2008 (Ramallah, 9 May 2011).

shut down the university.[99] The Israeli occupation apparently feared that Palestinian lawyers would use the courts to resist military rule.[100] In 1994, a year after the establishment of the PA, Al-Quds became the first university to establish a law school. There are now 11 university law schools (Takrouri 2013) with over 9,000 students.[101] The course of study for the LLB normally lasts four years.

A law graduate who applies for Bar membership must present a copy of a law degree certified by the Ministry of Higher Education.[102] The PBA does not accredit law schools or control their curricula, despite some initial attempts to do so,[103] but merely 'recognises' the academic institution issuing the degree.[104] Like legal education in other Middle Eastern countries, legal education in Palestine is largely theoretical (Mahasneh and Critchlow 2016), following the French model introduced under the Ottomans (Rosenbaum 2016).

Nonetheless, Palestine is not isolated from educational trends prevalent across the globe. Most universities now host legal clinics in which students practise law and contribute to social justice by providing pro bono legal advice, community education, and representation (Ghannam et al 2016). Clients are sometimes referred by the clinics to relevant government offices, civil society institutions, international organisations, or private lawyers. To ensure that clinical students are equipped with the necessary skills, they can only take clinics in their final year (Al-Markaz for Development and Marketing Consultations 2018). Each student must focus on one legal area, such as criminal, family, or labour law. Students research legislation, executive orders, and court judgments and draft 'legal opinions' consisting of the facts, relevant law, and conclusions. At Hebron University Legal Clinics, for example, 40 per cent of the student's grade is based on the merits of the advice offered: background research, citation of relevant sources, legal reasoning, writing style, consistency and clarity (Qafisheh 2016).

B. Apprenticeship

Apprenticeship builds on the system the British introduced in the 1920s. Any law graduate who wishes to become a lawyer must spend two years in the office of a lawyer with more than five years in practice.[105] Because training should be full time, apprentices (though unpaid) cannot have any paid employment.[106] With the ever-increasing flow of

---

[99] A copy of the Department of Law and Jurisprudence profile is in Hebron University archives.
[100] Interview with Professor Othman Takrouri, former President of Hebron University (Ramallah, 29 March 2012).
[101] Project on the Development of the Capacity of Legal Education in Palestine, *Legal Professions and the Work Market: Where is the Problem and What Can be Done?* (Nablus, Center for International Legal Cooperation, 15 March 2018) 3.
[102] Lawyers Apprenticeship Bylaw No 1 of 8 October 2004, as amended on 24 May 2013, Art 3.
[103] In March 2018, representatives of the PBA, including its president, and deans of six Palestinian law schools met in Amman to discuss the relationship between the PBA and Palestinian universities. They agreed that the PBA would ask law schools to require a set of unified core courses essential to the practice of law. PBA, *The Palestinian Bar Association and Law Schools Signed a Declaration of Principles* (Amman, 27 March 2018).
[104] Lawyers Apprenticeship Bylaw, Art 5.
[105] ibid, Arts 8(a) and 9.
[106] ibid, Art 7(b). The Bar may expel an apprentice lawyer for working as a police officer: High Court of Justice, Case No 25/2004 (Ramallah, 26 October 2005).

law graduates, the number of apprentices in the West Bank rose from 540 in 2006 to 3,068 by April 2018 (with another 1,200 in Gaza, making a total of over 4,200).[107] In 2017 alone, 1,372 law graduates were admitted as apprentices in the West Bank. Women are 46 per cent of apprentices in the West Bank and 15 per cent in Gaza.[108]

The apprenticeship has several problems. Some practitioners do not have enough cases or experience to train new graduates.[109] Others lack interest in training newcomers, fearing competition. Some lawyers take advantage of apprentices, using them for administrative tasks or personal chores.[110] Because apprentices are unpaid, many must take other jobs,[111] violating the ban on paid work.[112] It is not unusual to find apprentices who never attend court hearings or even report to the lawyer's offices. It is not surprising, therefore, that 72 per cent of apprentice lawyers distrust the apprenticeship.[113] The growing number law graduates interested in becoming lawyers far exceeds the number of lawyers able or willing to offer training (Halaika 2015: 50–54). Exacerbating this situation, the PBA decided in April 2018 that lawyers with 5–10 years of experience could train only one apprentice and only those lawyers with 10 years or more could train two.[114]

To overcome that problem, this author urged the PBA council to replace the two-year apprenticeship with a year at a university legal clinic (Qafisheh 2014).[115] Students would be trained exclusively by experienced lawyers, judges, prosecutors, and experts. Apprentices could give legal advice, represent clients in court, conduct moot courts, analyse cases, undertake field research or placements, and be trained in legal writing and ethics. Those completing the year would receive a 'lawyering diploma' qualifying them to take the Bar examination and then be eligible to practise law.[116] The proposed system would ensure that new lawyers receive uniform high-quality training, preserve the Bar's supervisory role over training, and reduce the burden on unpaid apprentice lawyers. In March 2018, the bar was considering this proposal.[117]

C. Bar Examinations

By amending the Lawyers Apprenticeship Bye-law of 2004 on 24 May 2013,[118] the Palestinian Bar's general assembly required apprentice lawyers to sit for a pre-admission written test

---

[107] *Administrative and Financial Report 2018*, n 83, 7.
[108] ibid, 8; Farra, n 84.
[109] MUSAWA, *Third Legal Monitor: The Stable and Changeable in the Status of Justice in Palestine* (Ramallah 2014) 136.
[110] 49 per cent of apprentices believe they work as 'servants' for their trainers; ibid, 144.
[111] ibid, 139.
[112] Lawyers Apprenticeship Bylaw, Art 7(b).
[113] *Third Legal Monitor*, n 109, 138.
[114] PBA, *Amendments of the Lawyers Apprenticeship Bylaw of 2004*, adopted by the PBA General Assembly (Ramallah, 4 April 2018), Art 10(b) amendment.
[115] According to the MUSAWA's *Third Legal Monitor* (n 109, 143), 53 per cent of apprentices believe the two-year apprenticeship is too long.
[116] 53 per cent of apprentices preferred a 'lawyering diploma' over the apprenticeship; ibid.
[117] Amman Declaration (n 103) endorsed the proposal to set up 'lawyers training institute'.
[118] See n 114.

and oral interview (Article 7),[119] attend a series of training sessions,[120] write a research paper,[121] and take final written and oral examinations.[122] In addition to limiting the flow of new entrants, these measures were introduced to ensure the quality of young lawyers and their familiarity with domestic law and procedure (*cf* Maranlou 2016). The pre-admission examination was abolished by the High Court of Justice on 30 June 2015 (Sulaiman 2015),[123] but revived in April 2018.[124] The semi-annual post-apprenticeship examination, introduced in 2004 for the first time since the end of British rule, has a pass rate of 60–70 per cent.[125] In 2017, 865 of 1,335 West Bank apprentices passed (64 per cent).[126]

V. LEGAL ETHICS

Lawyers in Palestine are bound by three kinds of ethical obligations (stipulated in the 1999 Advocates Law) concerning the honour of the profession, the lawyer-client relationship, and lawyers' relations with fellow lawyers and the bar. Other ethical standards are derived from earlier statutes and obligations accepted worldwide (Ramadan 2017). All these were finally codified in the Legal Profession Code of Ethics adopted by the PBA Council on 3 April 2016.[127]

To preserve the profession's honour, lawyers should have an appropriate law office, wear suitable attire when pleading in court, and receive clients at their offices rather than pursuing them directly or through brokers or advertisements.[128] Lawyers may not engage in other businesses or professions or accept employment in private sector institutions, international organisations, or government (except teaching law at universities).[129] Lawyers who want to do other work may register as 'non-practising lawyers'[130] (4,551: 2,912 in the West Bank,[131] and 1,639 in Gaza).[132] Non-practitioners can be readmitted to the lawyers' roll if they relinquish positions outside the legal profession.[133]

---

[119] The entry test was first conducted on 7 September 2013. It included 259 graduates. PBA, *The Bar Conducts First Entry Examination* (15 Ramallah, September 2013).
[120] Lawyers Apprenticeship Bylaw (2013 amendment), Arts 24–25.
[121] ibid, Arts 26–28.
[122] Lawyers Apprenticeship Bylaw (2013 amendment), Arts 8(e) and 30–31.
[123] Case No 89/2015 (Ramallah).
[124] Amendments of the Lawyers Training Bylaw 2018, Art 3 (amendment/addition). On 14 June 2018, the High Court of Justice rejected a new challenge to the pre-admission exam (interview with Mr Tawfik Qafisheh, lawyer, Hebron, 29 June 2018). However, there are several other pending challenges to the legality of this exam: Abbas, n 97.
[125] Interview with Ms Nour Maddah, Director of PBA Training Department (Ramallah, 28 June 2018). According to Farra (n 85), the success rate in the Bar exam in Gaza is about 75 per cent.
[126] *Administrative and Financial Report 2018*, n 83, 6.
[127] PG No 127, 4 December 2016, 208.
[128] Advocates Law 1999, Art 26(1)–(2) and 4); Art 28(1); the Code, Arts 7, 9 and 16.
[129] Advocates Law 1999, Arts 6, 7(3); Code, Art 18.
[130] Advocates Law 1999, Art 8(1).
[131] *Administrative and Financial Report 2016*, n 95, 23.
[132] Sulaiman, n 73.
[133] Advocates Law 1999, Art 8(2). In 2017, 144 non-practising lawyers were re-admitted by the bar as practitioners; *Administrative and Financial Report 2018*, n 83, 9.

Lawyers should represent their clients honestly and work under the client's direction.[134] A lawyer may not assign representation to another lawyer without the client's approval.[135] Lawyers may not bring cases against institutions for which they work[136] or represent a client in a case in which they acted as judge, investigator or arbitrator.[137] Lawyers may not abandon a case at an inappropriate time[138] and must pursue it if the client's interest so requires.[139] Lawyers may not represent two parties in the same case[140] or act against a client who gave the lawyer a general power of attorney or in case about which the lawyer expressed an opinion.[141]

Lawyers must preserve client confidentiality and privacy.[142] They may not testify against clients based on information obtained during representation or give an opinion to the opposing party during or after the lawsuit.[143] Lawyers may not buy assets or rights arising out of a case in which they have acted.[144] After representation ends, the lawyer should return the case documents to the client.[145]

Cooperation with other lawyers and the Bar Association is a fundamental obligation. Lawyers may not sue each other or the Bar without permission from the PBA's council.[146] Lawyers from the same law firm may not plead against each other.[147]

The 2016 Code of Ethics added other requirements. Lawyers must respect and cooperate with courts in good faith[148] and not corrupt judges, talk to them ex parte,[149] or waste judicial time by seeking unjustified delays.[150] Lawyers may not betray clients by wasting their time, making false promises, or accepting money from an adversary and not giving it to the client.[151] A lawyer may not cite private conversations with another lawyer in a case without the latter's permission.[152]

Some of these unethical behaviours are unfortunately common and reported to, and processed by, the Bar council.[153] From September 2014 to September 2015, for instance, 199 complaints were filed against lawyers, involving 53 types of misconduct, which can be grouped in four categories: negligence, client betrayal, attacking other lawyers or the Bar,

---

[134] ibid, Art 26(3).
[135] If the power of attorney is silent on that delegation, lawyers may ask another to act on their behalf without client's approval: Law No 5 of 1999, n 126, Art 2(4)(b).
[136] High Court of Justice, Case No 15/2005 (Ramallah, 12 April 2006); the Code, Art 40(5).
[137] Advocates Law 1999, Art 9; the Code, Art 40(7).
[138] Advocates Law 1999, Art 24; the Code, Art 39.
[139] Court of Cassation, Case No 251/2009 (Ramallah, 14 September 2009).
[140] Court of Cassation, Case No 179/2004 (Ramallah, 5 February 2005); the Code, Art 40(1).
[141] Advocates Law 1999, Art 27(3); the Code, Art 40(2)–(6).
[142] The Code, Arts 13–14 (the latter article deals specifically with the lawyer obligation of confidentially in cases involving women subjected to violence).
[143] Advocates Law 1999, Art 28 (4)–(5); the Code, Arts 17 and 45.
[144] Advocates Law 1999, Art 28(2); the Code, Art 16(2).
[145] Advocates Law 1999, Art 22(2); the Code, Art 47(2).
[146] Advocates Law 1999, Art 26(5); the Code, Art 30.
[147] Advocates Law 1999, Art 27(2); the Code, Art 35.
[148] The Code, Art 50.
[149] ibid, Arts 19 and 52.
[150] ibid, Art 54.
[151] ibid, Arts 36–38.
[152] ibid, Art 29.
[153] PBA Disciplinary Council, Case No 207/2011 (Ramallah, 13 September 2015).

and ordinary crimes.[154] Examples of negligence were failure to appeal a case in time or to initiate a lawsuit after beginning representation, confiscating a client's assets received from the other party, dropping a case without the client's permission, settling without the client's approval, delay in registering land, procrastination, claiming fees without performing the required task, and failing to prosecute perpetrators in criminal cases.

Client betrayal included accepting representation to appeal after the time to do so had expired, taking advantage of a power of attorney to sell land, conspiring with opposing counsel, revoking a power of attorney at an inappropriate time, destroying contract papers, failing to return documents to a client, seeking imprisonment of a debtor who has paid the debt, continuing representation after termination of a power of attorney, and charging excessive fees (Ramadan 2017). Lawyers and the Bar have filed complaints against lawyers for suing fellow lawyers without the Bar's permission, conflict with or mistreatment of apprentice lawyers, representing a client who has another lawyer, insulting another lawyer or the Bar, and using non-practising lawyers to draft contracts. People also file complaints against lawyers for committing crimes like slander, forgery, fraud, carrying weapons, threatening to kill, illegal restriction of liberty, and non-payment of debt, but the Bar generally denies it has jurisdiction on ordinary crimes committed by lawyers outside the practice of law.[155]

Before adopting the Code, the Bar punished lawyers by invoking the general obligations of lawyers in the 1999 Advocates Law. Some were convicted under Article 20, authorising punishment of any lawyer who:

> breaches his obligations as set forth in this law or its bylaws or the legal ethics bylaw that the [Bar] council may adopt, or who exceeds or neglects the professional obligations or misleads the justice or carries out any conduct that affects the honour or morals of the profession or who behaves in his private life in a way that degrades the profession.

Aware of the inadequacies of such an approach, the BPA commissioned a lawyer to draft a code and formed a committee to revise the draft and propose a comprehensive Bill, which yielded the 2016 code of ethics (Nasra 2011). The PBA adopted procedures for investigation,[156] proportional penalties for each offence, and the formation of complaint committees. It developed a complaint form,[157] fixed the fees for complainants,[158] drafted a form for declaring that the complaint is true, and provided a process for notifying the parties and rules for the hearings.[159]

Unethical conduct is investigated through disciplinary councils consisting of three lawyers who have practised 10 years or more (Ramadan 2017). Complaints may be reported to the Bar council by the Attorney General, a lawyer, or a party. After a preliminary examination, the Bar may refer the complaint to a disciplinary council, which investigates according to criminal procedure law.[160] The lawyer may be instructed to stop

---

[154] MUSAWA, 'The Bar Association Complaints Department Handles 199 Complaints in the Judicial Year from 1 September 2014 to 1 September 2015', in *Eye on Justice*, n 91, 49.
[155] Interview with Ms Alaa Abusafieh, Complaints Officer at PBA (Ramallah, 1 May 2016).
[156] ibid.
[157] A copy of the form is on file with the author.
[158] A receipt of paying fees by a complainant is on file with the author (2013).
[159] PBA, *Bar Association Organizes a Workshop on the Legal Ethics Bylaw* (Jericho, 4 October 2015).
[160] High Court of Justice, Case No 851/2009 (Ramallah, 12 September 2011).

practising during the investigation. Acting as a quasi-judicial body,[161] the disciplinary council reviews written documents, notifies parties, conducts pleading sessions, hears witnesses, discusses evidence, and records the proceeding.[162] After reaching its conclusion, the disciplinary council reports its findings to the Bar council, which acts as an appellate court and may confirm, modify, or ignore the recommendation.[163]

The Bar Council may declare the lawyer innocent or impose four types of penalties:[164] (1) notification;[165] (2) admonition; (3) suspension of licence for up to five years;[166] or (4) expulsion from the Bar. When the Council suspends a lawyer, it informs the relevant official institutions, including the High Judicial Council (courts), Attorney General, Lands Authority, and Companies Registry.[167] A convicted lawyer can appeal within 30 days to the High Court of Justice.[168] In 2015/2016, nine did so.[169]

The Bar Council recently formed three 'complaint committees' to conduct preliminary examinations before referring cases to disciplinary councils.[170] The PBA has started to take complaints more seriously. In 2014/15, for example, it received 343 complaints, referred 16 to disciplinary councils and convicted only three. By contrast, the following year (until April 2016), it received 273 complaints, referred 53 to disciplinary councils, and convicted 43, notifying four, admonishing one, and suspending (usually for 3–6 months) or expelling 38.[171] In 2017/18, however, it convicted just 20 of the 321 lawyers subject to complaints.[172]

The public has a low opinion of lawyers (Bisharat 1989: 74–75), partly because of ethical misconduct (Malah 2013: 16; *cf* Nicolson 2016). Popular culture portrays the best lawyer as a liar. Honest lawyers are considered weak, and most remain obscure. Hence, it is important to teach legal ethics and professional responsibility at law schools and during apprenticeship (*cf* Chavkin 2011; Tarr 2009; Vagts 2000). Hebron University, for instance, has introduced a course on legal ethics[173] and made ethics an integral part of its legal clinic syllabi, exposing students to relevant rules of professional responsibility and having them analyse cases of lawyer misconduct (Qafisheh 2016: 231; Ghannam et al 2016: 248).

---

[161] The term 'court of discipline' was used for such bodies under the British rule; they were composed of judges and lawyers: Advocates Ordinance of 1922, Art 18.
[162] In one disciplinary case (2015), for instance, the file comprised 47 pages; in another, the file was 48 pages (copies of these cases are on file with the author).
[163] A copy of a disciplinary report (recommendation) on Case No 252/2013 (Ramallah, 12 March 2016) is on file with the author. The Bar Council confirmed the recommendation on 2 April 2016.
[164] Advocates Law 1999, Art 29.
[165] High Court of Justice, Case No 204/2010 (Ramallah, 6 June 2011).
[166] High Court of Justice, Case No 303/2010 (Ramallah, 28 March 2011).
[167] Abusafieh, n 155. Copies of such letters on Case No 252/2013 (n 163) are in the author's file. Such letters are normally sent also to the court in which convicted lawyer often appears.
[168] Advocates Law 1999, Arts 33(3) and 34(3).
[169] *Administrative and Financial Report 2016*, n 95, 33.
[170] Investigated cases obtained from the PBA (May 2016–December 2017) are on file with the author. The author was requested not to report their details as they are confidential.
[171] *Administrative and Financial Report 2016*, n 95, 32–33.
[172] ibid, 12.
[173] Curricula of Hebron University College of Law and Political Science (2015); on file with the author.

VI. CONCLUSION

Despite their colonial history, Palestinian lawyers managed to establish an elected Bar association comparable to those in independent states. However, the heritage of Ottoman, British, Jordanian and Egyptian rule is still visible in the profession. Under Israeli occupation after 1967, Palestinian lawyers managed to create three representative bodies: one for Gaza lawyers, one for practising West Bank lawyers, and a third for striking West Bank lawyers affiliated with the Jordanian Bar Association. Palestinians had to wait half a century to resume discussions about forming a unified Palestinian Bar Association in 1994. That dream came true in 2003, when the first Palestine Bar was elected. It has administered and advanced the profession's affairs and has become well-established and influential.

Yet challenges remain. The involvement of women in leadership positions is still in its infancy, notwithstanding the increasing number of women lawyers (Husnieh 2015). The apprenticeship system for young lawyers should be reformed to provide meaningful training and to control the quality of entrants. Continuing education programmes should be adopted. The PBA should lead an adequate legal aid system (Qafisheh 2018).

REFERENCES

Abuhannoud, H (2000) *Report on the Palestinian Bar Association* (Ramallah, Palestinian Independent Commission for Citizens' Rights).

Al-Markaz for Development and Marketing Consultations (2018) *Final Evaluation Report: 'Legal Clinics Inside Law Schools in Palestinian Universities'* (Ramallah, UNDP).

Bisharat, G (1989) *Palestinian Lawyers and Israeli Rule: Law and Disorder in the West Bank* (Austin, University of Texas Press).

Chavkin, D (2011) 'Experience is the Only Teacher: Bringing Practice to the Teaching of Ethics' in M Robertson, L Corbin, K Tranter and F Bartlett (eds), *The Ethics Project in Legal Education* (London, Routledge) 52–78.

Drayton, R (ed) (1934) *The Laws of Palestine in Force on the 31st Day of December 1933* (London, Waterlow and Sons).

Feldman, I (2008) *Governing Gaza: Bureaucracy, Authority, and the Work of Rule, 1917–1967* (Durham, NC, Duke University Press).

Ghannam, N, Rea, N and Taylor, N (2016) 'Criminal Defense Law Clinics: A Path to Better Lawyering in Palestine' in M Qafisheh and S Rosenbaum (eds), *Experimental Legal Education in a Globalized World: The Middle East & Beyond* (Newcastle, Cambridge Scholars) 236–53.

Halaika, H (2015) 'Apprentice Lawyers: Present and Prospects' in MUSAW, *The Fourth Conference on the Independence of Lawyers* (Ramallah) 50–54.

Harris, R, Kedar, A, Lahav P and Likhovski, A (eds) (2002) *The History of Law in a Multi-Cultural Society: Israel 1917–1967* (Farnham, Ashgate) 13–20.

Husnieh, I (2015) 'Vision of the Female Lawyer on Its Role in the Bar Association' in MUSAWA, *The Fourth Conference on the Independence of Lawyers* (Ramallah) 29–31.

Katz, K (2018), 'Hebron between Jordan and Egypt: an uncertain transition resulting from the 1948 Palestine war' *Urban History* 1, doi:10.1017/S0963926818000032.

Likhovski, A (2006) *Law and Identity in Mandate Palestine* (Chapel Hill, University of North Carolina Press).

—— (2016) 'History of British Legal Education in Mandatory Palestine' in M Qafisheh and S Rosenbaum (eds), *Experimental Legal Education in a Globalized World: The Middle East & Beyond* (Newcastle, Cambridge Scholars).

Mahasneh, N and Critchlow, G (2016) 'A Dialogue on Jordanian Legal Education' in M Qafisheh and S Rosenbaum (eds), *Experimental Legal Education in a Globalized World: The Middle East & Beyond* (Newcastle, Cambridge Scholars) 57–84.

Malah, B (2013) 'The Stereotyping Image of Lawyers in the Palestinian Society: Effects on the Rule of Law', paper presented at the *International Conference on Global Legal Education Approaches: Experiences for Palestine* (Hebron, 1–3 October).

Maranlou, S (2016) 'Modernization Prospects for Legal Education in Iran' in M Qafisheh and S Rosenbaum (eds), *Experimental Legal Education in a Globalized World: The Middle East & Beyond* (Newcastle, Cambridge Scholars) 144–50.

Milhem, F (2014), *The Origins and Evolution of the Palestinian Sources of Law* (Brussels, Vrije Universiteit Faculty of Law).

Muhanna, A (2007) *Lecture on Law Profession and Bar Association: Current Situation and Future Prospects* (Birzeit, 23 June).

Muwatin (Palestinian Institute for the Study of Democracy) (2016) *Legislation at the Time of Internal Division: Studies on the Legislation Enacted Since 2007* (Ramallah).

Nasra, A (2011) *Draft Law Profession Ethics Bylaws* (Ramallah, PBA).

Nicolson, D (2016) 'Teaching Ethics Clinically without Breaking the Bank' in M Qafisheh and S Rosenbaum (eds), *Experimental Legal Education in a Globalized World: The Middle East & Beyond* (Newcastle, Cambridge Scholars) 450–71.

Qafisheh, M (2008) *The International Law Foundations of Palestinian Nationality: A Legal Examination of Palestinian Nationality under Britain's Rule* (The Hague, Nijhoff).

—— (2013) 'Legislative Drafting in Transitional States: The Case of Palestine' 2 *International Journal of Legislative Drafting and Law Reform* 266.

—— (2014) 'An Open Letter to Palestinian Bar Association' *Maan News* (Bethlehem, 23 March).

—— (2016) 'Modern Legal Education in Palestine: The Clinical Programs of Hebron University' in M Qafisheh and S Rosenbaum (eds), *Experimental Legal Education in a Globalized World: The Middle East & Beyond* (Newcastle, Cambridge Scholars) 198–235.

—— (2018) 'A Century of the Legal Profession in Palestine: Quo Vadis?' 25 *International Journal of the Legal Profession* 175–212.

Ramadan, A (ed) (1928) *Completion of Laws: Ottoman Legislation Applicable in Arab States Detached from the Ottoman Government* (Beirut, Science Press).

Ramadan, S (2017) *The Disciplinary Responsibility of Lawyers in Palestine* (Jerusalem, Al-Quds University Faculty of Law).

Rosenbaum, S (2016), 'After the Revolution: Laying a Foundation for Experiential Education in Egypt' in M Qafisheh and S Rosenbaum (eds), *Experimental Legal Education in a Globalized World: The Middle East & Beyond* (Newcastle, Cambridge Scholars) 85–114.

Shehadeh, R (1990) *Occupier's Law: Israel and the West Bank* (Beirut, Institute for Palestine Studies).

Sulaiman, A (2015) *Legal Evaluation Concerning the Enforcement of the High Court of Justice's Judgment No 89/2015 Dated June 30, 20115* (Ramallah, 8 July).

Takrouri, O (2013) 'Past, Present, and Future of Legal Education in Palestine: Evaluation of the Programs of Eleven Palestinian Law Schools', paper presented at the *International Conference on Global Legal Education Approaches: Experiences for Palestine* (Hebron, 1–3 October).

Tarr, N (2009) 'Ethics, Internal Law School Clinics, and Training the Next Generation of Poverty Lawyers' 35 *William Mitchell Law Review* 1011.

Vagts, D (2000) 'Professional Responsibility in Transborder Practice: Conflict and Resolution' 13 *Georgetown Journal of Legal Ethics* 677.

Wahiedi, F (1992) *Constitutional Developments in Palestine: 1917–1989* (Gaza, Salam Publishing).

33

Tunisia

A Political Profession?

ERIC GOBE

On 14 January 2011, after 23 years in power and a month of popular protest demanding his resignation, President Ben Ali fled Tunisia. Images of Tunisian lawyers demonstrating in their robes in front of the Ministry of the Interior, broadcast around the world on television and the web, made people think these lawyers had played a fundamental role in the protest movements that led to the fall of the authoritarian regime, which had ruled the country since Independence (1956). Although such a brief causal account does not tell the whole story, the fact remains that, due to their right of defence in judicial procedures, lawyers, more than any other profession, enjoy a close relationship between their function and politics. The socio-historical approach taken in this chapter demonstrates the extent to which professional facts may assume a political dimension. The profession had already shown a greater ability than other social groups to resist the regimes of Ben Ali and Habib Bourguiba ('the father of independence'), allowing it to benefit symbolically and materially from the fall of the Ben Ali regime.

Tunisia's colonisation has been the matrix of the constitution of its liberal professions based on the French model: shortly after the country's independence, the Tunisian rulers (for the most part lawyers trained at French universities) reproduced the organisational model of the protectorate's legal profession by conferring public powers on Tunisian Bar associations. Furthermore, by ensuring the profession's autonomy, the new Tunisian state adopted the liberal inheritance of the French legal profession, elements of which contended with future regimes' logic of authoritarianism.

I. THE LEGAL PROFESSION BETWEEN TUTELAGE AND EMANCIPATION

The law of 15 March 1958 governing the legal profession, though adapted to the Tunisian situation, did not differ from earlier laws regulating the profession under the protectorate. It 'Tunisified' and unified the profession by merging the Tunisian proxies exclusively practising within the local judiciary (*oukils*) and lawyers attached to the French judiciary, while reproducing the decentralised French model of allocating lawyers to the local Bar Associations practising within the Tunisian courts of appeal (Tunis, Sousse, Sfax).

Local Bar associations were endowed by the state with delegated public powers. Each was represented before all political and administrative authorities by its *bâtonnier* (president), charged with disciplinary and conciliatory functions. He was responsible for investigating complaints directed at members of the Bar, convening and chairing membership meetings as well as meetings of the *Conseil de l'ordre* (roughly equivalent to board of governors), which had comprehensive regulatory and disciplinary powers mirroring those enjoyed by French Bar associations.

Furthermore, the law of 1958 (as amended) required applicants for admission to the Bar to show a certificate of aptitude for the profession of advocate (*certificat d'aptitude à la profession d'avocat*, CAPA) issued by the Tunisian state after applicants passed an examination organised by the Ministry of Justice. By exempting from the CAPA requirement judges with at least three years' experience as well as holders of a third cycle legal qualification, the 1958 law intended to open the examination to students enrolled in their final year for their *licence* (master's in law) (Quentin 1972).

The prerogatives of public power and the autonomy granted to local Bar associations at independence soon irritated the new authoritarian state. President Bourguiba, who studied law in France and briefly practised, likened lawyers to judicial assistants who should content themselves with helping judges 'in the search for truth and the establishment of justice amongst men' (Youssef 2004).

In the late 1950s and early 1960s local Bar associations, dominated by the regime's opponents, resisted Bourguiba's authoritarian project. The nationalist and repressive atmosphere following the July 1961 confrontation between French and Tunisian troops at the Bizerte military air base offered the head of state the chance to neutralise the associations. The restrictions following that episode caused nearly two-thirds of Jewish Tunisian lawyers to leave for France or Israel, reducing the number of lawyers from about 400 to 277 in 1962–63 (Débats parlementaires 1989: 437; Hélin 1994: 66–67). This trend was reinforced during the early years of independence by integrating Neo-Destour activists (Bourguiba's party) into the government and judiciary. This served to introduce jurists trained in modern branches of the law, such as private international and commercial law, into a judiciary trained during the French protectorate in indigenous justice with religious and secular dimensions (Hélin 1997: 42–43).

The implementation of economic policies prioritizing the public sector encouraged legal studies strongly oriented towards careers within it (Larif-Béatrix 1988: 232). The 1960s saw only a slow increase in the number of Bar registrations, an average of five a year (including trainees). In this context of declining Bar membership, it became relatively easy to abolish the profession's elected bodies. In 1961, after arresting the *bâtonniers*, Bourguiba dissolved the governing councils of Tunis, Sfax and Sousse and replaced them with administrative committees.[1] Although these operated for four years, Bourguiba still was unable to control the profession entirely. Some lawyers from the Neo-Destour party wanted the profession to exercise normal functions through its elected representatives (Gobe and Salaymeh 2016: 325–29).

Negotiations between Bourguiba and the Bar led to a 1963 law creating the national *Ordre National des Avocats de Tunisie* (Tunisian Bar Association, TBA), intended to

---

[1] *Journal officiel de la République tunisienne* (JORT), 'Décret n° 61-266 du 8 août 1961 portant dissolution des conseils de l'ordre des avocats près les cours d'appel de Tunis, de Sfax et de Sousse', 8 August 1961, p 1042.

'strengthen the influence of the president over the bar and the authorities'.[2] The Bourguiba regime, reflecting an authoritarian state's logic of corporatism (Schmitter 1974: 93–94), viewed this as an opportunity to coopt the TBA president, while accepting 'normal' elections for the Bar's governing council. By contrast, lawyers viewed the unified Bar as as a unique interlocutor with the government, allowing the profession to represent its interests more effectively (Cherif 1990: 175). In fact, the TBA could not be entirely co-opted, and the Bar's autonomy gave it political leverage.

But though lawyers regained the ability to elect their own representatives, most TBA presidents were members of the Neo-Destour party or aligned with the regime. The TBA's first president was a party member who had served as Minister of Social Affairs in Bourguiba's first government, and subsequent presidents in the 1970s were also more or less connected to the authoritarian regime or the Neo-Destour party.

Only during the late 1970s and early 1980s – a short interval of liberalisation in the Tunisian government – did the TBA elect presidents who were not close to Bourguiba or his political allies. The first was Lazhar Karoui Chebbi, who had been the personal secretary of Salah Ben Youssef, Bourguiba's political adversary at the beginning of Tunisia's independence. The next was Mansour Cheffi, president four times in the 1980s and early 1990s, who was a leftist with ties to Habib Achour – the General Secretary of the *Union Générale Tunisienne du Travail* (UGTT), which had tense relations with the regime (Tabib 2006: 83).

The 1970s and 1980s saw a rapid increase in the number of Bar registrations: from 309 in 1971–72 to 466 in 1974–75, 707 in 1979–80, 981 in 1985–86, and 1,429 in 1991–92.[3] In the 1980s the economic situation of young lawyers became a recurrent topic in annual Bar reports. The TBA complained about the lack of training for young lawyers and the growth of the profession, while new entrants demanded that the state pay lawyers-in-training to serve as court-appointed lawyers, claiming that the 'democratisation' of the Bar meant that fewer lawyers could be supported by their families while they waited to earn enough to live on. During the final years of the Bourguiba regime, the profession proposed legislation strengthening entry barriers: making CAPA a requirement for lawyers and judges and reducing from 50 to 40 the maximum age for inscription in the Bar register in order to prevent retired public servants from qualifying as lawyers to increase their old age pension.

During the nearly two years of political liberalisation following Ben Ali's successful 1987 coup d'état, the profession hoped the TBA proposals might be adopted. Instead, however, Ben Ali pushed parliament to vote in 1989, during the tenure of TBA President Cheffi, on a Bill limiting the profession's autonomy. The TBA's governing bodies challenged two provisions of the law. Article 46 authorised a judge, after notifying a regional TBA representative, to charge an attorney with 'bad faith' in arguments or statements in court.[4] The second disputed provision permitted judges to become lawyers after serving on the bench for ten years, even if they had retired. As a result, retired judges increased

---

[2] Débats de l'assemblée nationale, *Rapport sur le projet de loi modifiant la loi n° 37 de l'année 1958, daté du 15 mars 1958 et réglementant la profession d'avocat* (in Arabic), 1963, p 233.
[3] TBA tables, the judicial years: 1971–72; 1974–75; 1979–80; 1985–86; 1991–92.
[4] *JORT*, 'Loi n° 89-87 du 7 septembre 1989, portant l'organisation de la profession d'avocat', 12 September 1989, pp 1385–92.

from 10 per cent of the Bar in the mid-1970s to a peak of 22 per cent in the early 1990s before beginning to decline as new graduates entered the profession.

The TBA wanted to add a clause requiring judges to pass an exam to become members of the Bar. The secretary of its governing council argued it was inconceivable that someone who spent many years 'as a magistrate could be authorised by the provision to join the bar, while young lawyers, recently graduated, cannot even find the money to pay their electricity bills' (Tabib, 1988). The TBA also distrusted judges it saw as aligned with the authoritarian regime. Because of TBA's opposition, its president, Cheffi, was denied access to a military court.[5]

In response, the TBA's governing council convened a general meeting, which called on Tunisian lawyers to strike for two hours on 1 November 1990 to protest the repeated violations of lawyers' rights (Ben M'barek 2003: 409). This collective action, the first of its kind in post-independence Tunisia, had little effect. The TBA was unable either to amend the 1989 law or prevent government harassment of its members. Indeed, the 1990s was a dark decade for the TBA. In 1992, thousands of Ennahadha party members, including lawyers, were arrested, tortured, and sentenced for 'conspiracy against state security' or membership in an illegal organisation. In addition, the Ben Ali regime gradually tightened its grip on all autonomous public bodies, including the TBA, which elected two presidents close to the Ben Ali regime, hoping their professional and economic demands would be considered by the regime. However, the Ben Ali regime simply denied the TBA's requests, intensifying tensions between government and professional bodies (Gobe 2010).

II. THE SOCIAL STRUCTURE OF THE BAR UNDER BEN ALI: FROM MASS PRODUCTION OF LAWYERS TO THE EMERGENCE OF A 'REVOLUTIONARY' LAWYER

From the mid-1990s the Tunisian state, believing in the emergence of a 'knowledge economy', embarked on a policy of massification of higher education even though the labour market could not absorb the influx of new graduates. Between 2000 and 2011 the proportion of the relevant age group enrolled in higher education rose from 19 to 36 per cent.[6] The World Bank study of 2008 found that the number of unemployed with a higher education diploma almost doubled in 10 years, from 121,800 in 1996–97 to 336,000 in 2006–07. Management, finance and law accounted for over 60 per cent of diplomas awarded in the mid-2000s at a time when unemployment was at its peak, reaching 68 per cent 18 months after graduation among those with an LLM (World Bank & Ministry for Employment and Professional Insertion 2008).

During Ben Ali's reign, the legal profession experienced continuous exponential growth, a trend the regime hoped would disguise the joblessness among recent graduates (Gobe 2017). From 1991 to 2011, Bar membership increased nearly sixfold, from approximately 1,400 to 7,759 members (1,500 lawyers entered the profession between

---

[5] Mohamed Abdelkefi (Interview), 'Abdelwaheb el Béhi: la grève est une tentative pour que l'on prenne en considération l'avocat (in Arabic)', *al-Sabâh al-usbû'î*, 5 November 1990.

[6] Organisation internationale du travail, *Analyse du système éducatif Tunisien* (2013), available at adapt.it/adapt-indice-a-z/wp-content/uploads/2014/09/oit_analyse_syst%C3%A9me_%C3%A9ducatif_tunisien_2013.pdf.

June 2008 and June 2011). During the same two decades, the total labour force grew only 1.6 times (from about 2.3 million people to just over 3.7 million). In 2011, trainees represented almost 40 per cent of the legal profession, with the result that new entrants found themselves surrounded by trainers and internship supervisors little older than themselves.

This coincided with rapid feminisation of the profession: women increased from 5 per cent of the profession in 1980 to 25 per cent in 2001 and 43 per cent in 2015.[7] The class backgrounds of lawyers also changed: those whose fathers operated or worked at small farms increased from 8 per cent in 1945–79 to 25 per cent in 2000–09, while those whose fathers operated medium-sized or large farms decreased from 16 to 3 per cent; those whose fathers were middle managers, senior technicians or elementary school teachers increased from 25 to 32 per cent, while those whose fathers were professionals or senior executives decreased from 31 to 25 per cent.

Until 2008 entrants could qualify either via CAPA or with a Master of Advanced Studies in Law. Two-thirds qualified by the first method beween 1985 and 1994 and 70 per cent between 1995 and 2009. But the latter path became more accessible with the multiplication of postgraduate law courses in Tunisia from 30 in 2004–05 to 61 in 2012–13.[8]

After 2000, the search for internship (lasting at least two years) constituted an important obstacle for newly registered lawyers, who had to present a certificate of internship issued by a lawyer who had been registered before the Bar of either the Supreme Court (Cour de Cassation) or an Appeals Court for at least three years. Those unable to find a supervisor could ask the President of one of the regional TBA branches for help. Because lawyers with the required experience sometimes refused to accept trainees (20 per cent of those interviewed in 2008–10), citing a lack of office space, there was a waiting list, and the search could last a year. Some trainees had a professional address with their training supervisor but no space in the office. In 2010, this led the TBA's governing council to appeal to lawyers qualified to receive trainees 'to make their offices available to young lawyers and so help them train under appropriate conditions' and avoid the issuance of sub-standard certificates (*attestations de complaisance*).[9]

The Bar adopted a dual policy toward the stream of new entrants. First, it sought to prevent certain categories of law graduates from registering. Second, it asked the Ministry of Justice to implement reforms limiting access to the profession. Both initiatives were blocked by the authorities. During the early 2000s the governing council refused to register certain categories of diplomas, particularly Algerian CAPAs and LLMs. As early as 1996, the Tunisian Bar had begun disqualifying Algerian lawyers who lacked a Tunisian CAPA. This provoked the Algerian Bar to disqualify 28 Tunisian lawyers; but though most wanted to return to practise in Tunisia, the TBA refused to reintegrate them because their CAPA was Algerian. Following intervention by President Ben Ali, the TBA's governing council was forced to register the 28 lawyers.[10] Even if the number of lawyers involved was small, the episode revealed the feeling of TBA members that the Bar's subordination

---

[7] TBA, *Rapport moral de l'année judiciaire 2014–2015, assemblée générale ordinaire* (in Arabic), 2015.
[8] Statistical volumes consulted on site at the Tunisian Ministry of Higher Education, November 2016.
[9] TBA, *Rapport moral pour l'année judiciaire 2009–2010. Assemblée générale élective* (in Arabic), 19 June 2010.
[10] 'Sur décision du conseil de l'ordre: une dizaine d'avocats privés d'exercer leur métier' *Tunis Hebdo*, 19 May 2003.

was unacceptable. The creation of a higher authority within the TBA to monitor and control admission to the profession generated further confrontations between it and the government, which firmly refused to delegate recruitment of lawyers to the TBA.

After 2000, the Bar argued for uniform access to the profession through a Bar Institute, qualified to award the CAPA and controlled by the TBA. In May 2006, the Ben Ali regime seemed to respond positively by passing a law establishing a Higher Bar Institute, which became the obligatory portal into the profession except for magistrates and teachers in higher education.[11] But the TBA found itself marginalised within the Higher Bar Institute, a public institution supervised by the Ministries of Justice and Higher Education. The Institute's Scientific Council consists of 12 members: four lawyers, four political appointees of the two ministries, and two each from the judiciary and the university faculty.

By authorising holders of a law degree to join the Bar directly (during the four years beginning with the effective date of the 2006 law), provisional arrangements laid out in the law of May 2006 allowed the Bar to grow 25 per cent between 2008 and 2010.[12] The TBA criticised these 'unjustified transitional measures' as a means of 'submerging the profession'. Since the fall of the Ben Ali regime the requirement of qualifying via the Institute has limited entry to the 150–200 a year to whom it awards the CAPA, with the result that the number of practising lawyers increased just 10 per cent between 2011 and 2016.[13]

The Tunisian legal profession functions along liberal, individualist lines: salaried work is almost unknown, and almost 90 per cent of lawyers are self-employed. Almost 80 per cent have just a secretary and a clerk who attends court proceedings, or a single person performing both roles. The few law firms (about 100 in 2010) containing 5 per cent of the Bar were often composed of just two or three lawyers, sometimes belonging to the same family, three-quarters of them with 1–4 employees. Partnerships were permitted only in 1998. Tunisian lawyers attribute the paucity and small size of firms to the modest legal market and the professional culture.

Most lawyers are generalists representing individual clients and to a lesser degree enterprises; only a fifth specialise, half in commercial law. The four largest firms have annual revenues of $500,000–2,500,000; another eight solo commercial practitioners have revenues of $50-500,000. Generalists had revenues of $5–35,000. (A Tunisian earning the minimum wage would have an income of about $1,800.)

The profession continued to be attractive, despite its economic problems: 42 per cent of lawyers worked before joining the Bar, about evenly divided between the public and private sectors. Becoming lawyers often allowed them to increase their independence and earnings. Civil servants also could convert their social capital into a client base, although some were excluded from cases involving state companies and institutions after expressing criticism of the Ben Ali regime (Gobe 2013b).

---

[11] Parliamentary debates, *Projet de loi modifiant et complétant la loi n° 87 de l'année 1989, daté du 7 septembre 1989 et portant organisation de la profession d'avocat* (in Arabic), 9 May 2006, n° 22, p 928.

[12] *JORT*, 'Loi n° 2006-30 du 15 mai 2006, modifiant et complétant la loi 98-87 du 7 septembre 1989 portant l'organisation de la profession d'avocat', n° 41, 23 May 2006, p 1364. The end in 2010 of the transitional period pushed nearly 1,000 law graduates to apply for registration with the Bar. TBA, *Rapport moral de l'année judiciaire 2009–2010*, assemblée générale élective (in Arabic), 19 June 2010.

[13] TBA, *Rapport moral de l'année judiciaire 2015–2016* (in Arabic), 9 July 2016.

The authorities rewarded and penalised each group according to a patronage-based logic. The 'Bar of the State Party' (*le Barreau du parti-État*) – lawyers belonging to the RCD (*rassemblement constitutionnel démocratique*) – reaped many material and symbolic advantages. During the 'revolutionary' phase (December 2010–January 2011), this 'Bar of the State Party' tried in vain to prevent lawyers from organising strikes.

III. BAR OF THE STATE PARTY AND COMMERCIAL LAWYERS: DEFENDERS OF THE AUTHORITARIAN STATUS QUO

Under the patronage of the Ben Ali regime, politically connected lawyers (about 500 or 7 per cent of the profession) enjoyed a virtual monopoly of litigation work from the public administration and state-owned companies. In exchange for these financial advantages, the governing elites expected those lawyers to expose and counter collective action by their colleagues. The lower rung of the Bar strongly resented these privileges. Belonging to the RCD, however, could not guarantee work representing public institutions; over 40 per cent of party members had briefs only from individuals or private companies. Some young RCD lawyers complained that public work was monopolised by others.[14]

A committee of RCD party bosses charged with examining the files of lawyers representing administrative and public institutions regularly compiled lists of lawyers who were and were not eligible for such work, distinguishing between strong supporters (*mutahammisin*) who participated in party activities and 'ordinary lawyers'.[15] There was ferocious competition among young RCD members seeking public sector clients. Those who could claim a connection to a senior party figure or, better yet, the President of the Republic or his family circle, would see their public client rolls grow.

If the militant RCD lawyers engaged in counter-mobilisation during the protest movement of December 2010–January 2011, the youngest party members, who joined in the hope of gaining access to public litigation, at least did not try to thwart their colleagues' mobilisation, notably during the profession's general strike on 6 January 2011. This apathy among the young RCD lawyers is largely explained by the collapse of the party's patronage resources. Because the RCD could not distribute enough business to its supporters it was unable to mobilise the young RCD lawyers, whose sociological profile resembled that of their colleagues on the 'lower rung' of the Tunisian Bar.

Another segment of the profession that failed to mobilise against the Ben Ali regime was specialised lawyers at the top of the income hierarchy (fewer than 10 per cent of the total), especially commercial lawyers too preoccupied with money making or concerned that political involvement might negatively affect their incomes. Some of these instead compromised with the authoritarian regime. Prospering as a commercial lawyer required at least the appearance of support for the governing power. Some lawyers in large firms

---

[14] Interview by the author with A, a young member of the RCD and Appeal Court lawyer of less than a year's standing, October 2009.

[15] Secrétariat général, présidence de la République, *Mémorandum adressé par le secrétaire général de la présidence à la haute attention de son Excellence le président de la République, Objet: la liste des avocats traitant avec les établissements publics* (in Arabic), Carthage, 30 May 2000. Archives of the National Commission of Inquiry into the facts of corruption and embezzlement.

also belonged to the RCD, not necessarily in anticipation of getting business from public institutions but rather as a form of insurance against unwarranted state intrusion into private legal affairs and a way of facilitating contacts with a potentially lucrative international clientele. (These lawyers were often involved with foreign direct investment, privatisations, international calls for tender, and arbitrage.) A 1998 law also allowed lawyers who were retired or not practising (including RCD members holding high state positions) to have an equity interest in law firms.[16] Symbolically, Tunisian commercial lawyers became the equals of American and European professionals operating in the international market of legal services (partly because foreign law firms and lawyers could not settle in Tunisia or plead before Tunisian courts). 'Large' law firms (more than 10 employees) represent only a small segment of the Bar but make the greatest contribution to business volume. Their decision to organise as a limited liability company or joint-stock corporation indicated their 'modern' character. Furthermore, this legal structure allowed them to establish branches throughout Tunisia.

In a majority of the larger firms structured around a strong family network, the older generation occupied the position of managing partner and rainmaker. The FAR[17] firm is one the largest legal practices in Tunisia. It was established in the early 2000s by EGO[18], who retained 60 per cent of the shares and was joined by an RCD oligarch and a firm controlled by two Sfaxian associates (holding the other 40 per cent). EGO, who had practised commercial law since the mid-1980s, came from a Monastir family (in the Sahel) close to Bourguiba. In the late 2000s, the two Sfaxian associates sold their shares to EGO, who transferred a stake to his son.

In 2008/09 the firm had a staff of 60, including 25 lawyers, four accountants and ten graduates of the *Institut supérieur des hautes études commerciales*, the most important Tunisian higher education institution for management and accountancy. The legal trainees, collaborators and degree-holding managers had to be fluent in French and English. The firm was divided into two main departments, legal advice and litigation; clients that sought legal advice often then retained the firm for litigation. The latter, however, was only marginally profitable because of the human resources required: litigation produced no more than 5 per cent of the firm's turnover but requireed five full-time trainee lawyers and support staff.

Other firms have diversified geographically while remaining dominated by one family. MED[19] was founded by commercial lawyers from Médenine, in Southern Tunisia, to represent emigrants from Ghomrassen (in France, Germany, Italy and the Middle East) who invested their savings in property in Tunis or Ghomrassen. In order to be better represented in Tunis, the founding partner (a former judge) and his older brother joined forces with two Tunisian lawyers, one a former examining magistrate (*juge d'instruction*) able to develop a sizable clientele. The firm primarily handles property matters (mainly in Médenine and Ghomrassen) and investment law, a specialty of the elder of the brothers and a Tunisian partner, while the other two partners focus on insurance law, working

---

[16] JORT, 'Loi n° 98-65 du 20 juillet 1998, relative aux sociétés professionnelles d'avocats', 28 July 1998, pp 1640–42.
[17] Fictitious name for a law firm.
[18] Fictitious name for a commercial lawyer.
[19] Fictitious name for a law firm.

with the country's two principal insurers. The company has 14 employees (10 in Tunis and four in Médenine) and four trainees who work in accounts while also serving an embryonic clientele. More than three quarters of the clients come from the south of the country. Some firms systematically try to include partners from a variety of regions in order to reach larger segments of the legal services market (Gobe 2013a).

None of the law firms studied sought to integrate trainees and collaborators into the firm's capital structure. Neither they nor salaried lawyers have much chance of becoming partners. The family-based structure and the limited workload combine to give trainees and collaborators little choice but to leave the organisation, thereby ensuring high and often rapid turnover in these firms. In addition to these legal entrepreneurs, some commercial lawyers practise alone, with up to five employees and one or two trainees.

This prosperous Bar has little to do with the segment of the profession that mobilised against the Ben Ali regime: lawyers of the 'lower rung', inspired by opposition lawyers who went into the streets to support the popular manifestations demanding the resignation of President Ben Ali.

IV. THE SOCIAL FRUSTRATIONS OF THE 'LOWER ECHELON' OF THE TUNISIAN BAR

The qualitative interviews I conducted before the fall of the Ben Ali regime with 'young lawyers' (the largest segment of the Bar) provide valuable insights into how political and professional variables influenced lawyers' mobilisation. Feeling harassed by an authoritarian regime determined to serve them, these lawyers were unable to realise their socio-professional expectations. Their discontent provided a strong leaven for mobilisation among the lower-echelons of the legal profession during the popular uprising of December 2010–January 2011.

These lawyers serve an almost exclusively individual clientele, usually from the working-class neighbourhoods where they themselves were raised. They work primarily in the areas of family law (divorce, alimony, etc), real estate (writing sales contracts for inexpensive properties), petty crimes (primarily misdemeanours), and neighbourhood disputes. Their incomes are very low, especially during the first ten years of practice, because they compete with non-lawyers to perform functions that do not strictly require a lawyer's assistance.

Competition to establish a client base has led to large-scale soliciting of clients, an illegal practice lawyers call 'lesser samsara' (*al-samsara al-sughra* in Arabic). The difficulty of finding work in Tunisia's main cities – Tunis, Sfax and Sousse – encouraged lawyers to resort to third party intermediaries paid to 'hustle' clients. This phenomenon developed extensively in Tunisia where, unlike most Western countries, potential litigants did not have access to legal aid. For lawyers with little social capital, *samsars* are an important resource, especially in market sectors that are particularly competitive and volatile, where 'price is the only distinguishing feature' (Karpik 1995: 273). Similar institutional arrangements exist in India (Gandhi 1982) and in the US, where some lawyers developed networks of police and hospital employees to gain access to traffic accident victims and persuade them to sign retainers (Carlin 1962: 87; Abel 2011: 67–120).

Samsars mediate between two parties, one seeking to sell legal services and the other to purchase them. But unlike simple brokers, *samsars* tout. They receive a commission from the service provider (ie the lawyer). Clients do not remunerate them and do not always recognise them as touts because *samsars* try to create a relationship of trust, presenting themselves as disinterested parties desiring only to lend a friendly helping hand and offer the client 'good advice'.

Touting could occur either through direct interaction independent of any institutional relationship (in the course of a more or less coercive transaction) or within an institutional context. The first type normally occurred in the Palace of Justice and frequently involved clients with limited education, who had come to court either to attend a hearing for which a lawyer was not required (eg to collect a copy of a judgment) or to find somebody (eg a public writer) to draft a petition.[20] They would be approached within or near the court by a clerk,[21] a lawyer's assistant,[22] or a policeman who offered to help them find their way around and, in so doing, suggested the right lawyer for the job. A similar thing could happen to a relative who attended court to discover a detainee's situation and was approached by a *samsara*, who introduced the client to a lawyer who had an office nearby or was a 'roaming' lawyer active in the cafés around the Palace of Justice.[23]

The second type of *samsara* operated in an institutional setting such as a prison, hospital, or police station, where the intermediary held an office that allowed him to 'lean' on the client (sometimes literally). Informants described policemen and members of the National Guard (a rural equivalent of the police, which is officially part of the military) directing detainees to a lawyer who paid a commission, which the intermediary shared with police colleagues. Detainees were at the mercy of police officers, who could harass them in many ways. Road accidents were a particularly fertile ground for the development of *samsara*. These incidents normally involved four or five different actors: the lawyer, a police or National Guard officer, a paramedic, and a doctor or nurse. The last three suggested to hospitalised victims that the police officer or mandated expert might be able to write a favourable report.

During the 1990s and 2000s, the TBA disciplinary council sometimes severely sanctioned lawyers involved in *samsara*, but the appeals court systematically reduced or eliminated the punishment. Given the systemic corruption within the Ben Ali regime, the *samsara* allowed certain members of the security forces to be the main beneficiaries of payments by the *samsara*.

Young generalist lawyers at the bottom of the hierarchies of income and status were especially sensitive to the divergence between their difficult material situation and their idealised image of the profession, rendering them receptive to the actions of militant lawyers and political opponents of the regime well before the December 2010 outbreak of violence in Sidi Bouzid. Throughout the 1990s and even more during the 2000s, these lawyers 'in search of a cause' (Siméant 1998: 394) systematically sought to highlight acts of government repression in order to mobilise protests against the Ben Ali regime.

---

[20] A public scribe offers his services to those who lack the writing skills to produce legal, administrative, or private documents.
[21] A clerk (*greffier*) registers documents submitted to court, compiles the files, informs parties of hearing dates, drafts reports and decisions, and assists the judge at hearings.
[22] The lawyer's clerk (*clerc d'avocat*) runs errands at the court.
[23] In 2008/09 I found that 6 per cent of lawyers had no employees. Some had no office. Others registered their private address as their professional one but did not receive clients there, working instead in cafés near the courts either by using *samsars* to attract clients or by touting themselves.

V. THE OPPOSITION BAR UNDER BEN ALI: LAWYERING FOR DEFENSIVE CAUSES

Tunisian cause lawyers engaged in defensive cause lawyering focused on specific demands, such as ending torture, defending human rights, or protecting the rights of labourers. Many employed their professional skills to challenge the status quo (rather than simply serve client interests) (Hajjar 2001: 68). Although marginalised and attacked by the authoritarian regime, Tunisian cause lawyers persevered and eventually shaped how other Tunisian lawyers viewed the legal profession.

Political activist lawyers fall into two groups in terms their age and activist socialisation. The first includes opposition lawyers born in the 1950s, who engaged in highly transgressive activism as part of the mobilisation during Bourguiba's era. A few (about 15) concentrated in Tunis were affiliated with the far left (Marxist-Leninists and Maoists, sometimes associated with Arab nationalism) and to a lesser extent with political Islam. All were arrested and beaten by police and most were imprisoned, a biographical rupture that constituted a fertile period for redefining their activist identity and professional vocation. Their lifelong involvement as opposition lawyers was a continuation of their past political involvement. Defending human rights and defendants' rights conferred a 'moral dimension' (Agrikoliansky 2010) on both their previous political activism and their later professional work: in activist groups and the courts and as elected officials of professional organisations. Harassed by the state's repressive machinery (beatings, car tampering, telephone wiretapping, tax inspections, etc), these lawyers shared the difficult financial situation of their younger colleagues in the lower level of the profession.

The second group of opposition lawyers (about 60) were younger professionals, born in the 1970s, involved in less transgressive political activities because they confronted the repressive apparatus that had suppressed the Ennahdha Islamist party in the early 1990s. Arab nationalists, affiliated with radical left fringe groups, Islamists or human rights advocates, they represented labour leaders and political activists and mobilised against the RCD lawyers in TBA elections. As members of the lower level of the profession, they became spokespersons for young lawyers' financial demands while also championing the profession's values (human rights, criminal defence). Opposition lawyers acted collectively during the 2000s, urging TBA officials to condemn the oppressive policies of the Ben Ali regime, staging a courtroom strike, and instigating the sit-in protest against the arrest, incarceration and sentencing of their colleague Mohamed Abbou in 2005.[24]

Mobilisation of 'lower rung' lawyers was facilitated by the growing gap between the profession's self-image and the reality of the hand-to-mouth existence during the 1990s, especially among the more vulnerable young lawyers who experienced frustration and material difficulties from the start of their careers. Lawyers were one of the few groups to protest in the early 2000s. But until the eruption of the protest movement leading to President Ben Ali's ouster, their collective actions had been limited to legal professional concerns. The popular uprising of 2010–11 transformed lawyer mobilisations into an important part of the global opposition to the Ben Ali regime.

---

[24] A politically active lawyer and member of the Congress for the Republic (CPR) Party, which was not recognised under Ben Ali, Abbou was arrested and imprisoned in 2005 during the World Summit on the Information Society (SMSI) for publishing an article comparing President Ali with Israeli Prime Minister Ariel Sharon. Abbou was appointed Minister for Administrative Reform in the first government of the troïka.

VI. LAWYERS IN POST-BEN-ALI TUNISIA: COLLECTIVE ACTORS OF THE REVOLUTION AND POLITICAL TRANSITION IN TUNISIA (2011–16)

The collective action of lawyers between December 2010 and January 2011 began in courthouses in the capital and provinces. Activist lawyers encouraged their colleagues to express solidarity with the protesters by joining marches, rallies and sit-ins. Lawyers could appear in political protests as a collective body, identified by wearing black robes. Courthouses, as topographical embodiments of justice situated at the core of urban life and the protest movements, became the sites where the lawyers' mobilisation crystallised.

The popular uprisings at the end of December 2010 were not the result of organisations representing the legal profession. Having remained inactive at the beginning of the protest movement, the TBA's governing bodies acted more to restrain the uprising than to foment it. In fact, from his election as TBA President in June 2010, Abderrazak Kilani was intent on negotiating with the Ben Ali regime to forge a compromise that would satisfy the professional demands of the 'lower rung' of the Bar in exchange for conceding professional demands the regime saw as explicitly political (defence of human rights, respect for the rule of law, protection of public and private freedoms). In the end, it was the scope of the protests, as well as decisions by the regional UGTT federations to call general strikes starting 12 January, that finally drove the TBA to join the protest movement and call for a lawyers' strike on 14 January (Gobe and Salaymeh 2016: 325–39). The TBA representatives thereby reduced the risks of their opposition and acted as free riders on collective actions led by others, letting the Association profit from the fall of the Ben Ali regime, at least symbolically, until the election of the National Constituent Assembly on 23 October 2011.

The mobilisation of lawyers between December 2010 and January 2011 endowed the TBA with a 'revolutionary legitimacy' on which it could draw, after Ben Ali's departure, to play an important political role and consolidate corporatist gains. Its moral capital allowed the TBA to participate in February 2011 in creating the National Council for Safeguarding the Revolution, which became a rival to the provisional governments headed by Mohammed Ghanouchi and subsequently let the TBA advance professional demands it had formulated under the Ben Ali regime.

The disappearance of the old regime disqualified the lawyers of the (now dissolved) RCD party, who no longer enjoyed easy access to government following the discrediting of the Ben Ali faction. These 'party lawyers' officially lost their monopoly of state litigation, a development confirmed when the transitional government issued a circular authorising corporations and public institutions to choose their legal representation. The Prime Minister's text instructed the heads of public institutions to apply objective criteria of competence and transparency when engaging the services of a lawyer, independent of any list of names compiled earlier.[25]

Even so, a number of lawyers reported that some RCD members had renewed relations with their portfolio of public clients, changing their political colours while remaining close to state power.[26] In response, the TBA asked the transitional governments to ensure

---

[25] *Prime Ministerial Circular No 4, Addressed to Heads of State Companies and Establishments* (in Arabic), 9 February 2011, Prime Minister's Office.

[26] Interview with Mokhtar Jallali, lawyer at the Supreme Court, 24 April 2013 and Mohamed Ali Gherib, lawyer at the Supreme Court, 18 June 2016.

the transparent allocation of litigation by public institutions.[27] In January 2014, the transitional government of Ali Laarayedh issued a decree establishing an administrative protocol for assigning public litigation contracts in response to invitations to tender.

The *bâtonnier* clearly benefited from the collapse of the Ben Ali regime. He constructed, even fabricated, a revolutionary image by presenting the involvement of lawyers in the 2010–11 mobilisations as the concerted action of a profession united behind its President. Legislation authorising the Tunisian President to promulgate certain statutory decrees during the interim period prompted the *bâtonnier* to accelerate a Bill reorganising the legal profession.

The proposed Bill sought to transform the profession by making lawyers more than mere agents of the law. Previously, the Bar had been 'a liberal and independent profession whose purpose was understood as assisting with the enactment of justice'.[28] The first article of the 2011 Bill committed the TBA to fostering the 'establishment of justice and the defence of human rights and freedoms'.[29] By raising the profession's status, the Bill sought to enhance lawyers' professional power. 'Political lawyering' was part of the Bar's 'professionalisation plan' (Abbott 2003: 30), a means of legitimating its professional demands.

Lawyers invoked their support for the protest movements to justify an enlarged monopoly over legal services. The TBA accused competing professions of having received special treatment under the previous authoritarian regime, as evidenced by their failure to participate in the protests. It then used this accusation to claim a broader professional jurisdiction at the expense of notaries, tax specialists, real estate agents, and certified public accountants. The statute declared that only lawyers are 'qualified to represent and act as counsel to clients… and to defend them in courts of law, in any other judicial, administrative or disciplinary hearings, and against an investigating officer'.[30] Competing professions feared that the wording of this article would prevent them from providing legal, tax, or accounting advice to clients, as well as from carrying out certain administrative procedures. Professional bodies representing accountants, notaries, and tax specialists viewed the statute as an attempt 'by one profession to appropriate for itself the attributes and sphere of professional activity of other professions'.[31] The statutory language provocatively endowed lawyers with the exclusive right to 'draw up company statutes and administer certain forms of increase and reduction in the company's capital' and gave lawyers exclusive rights 'to draft contracts, real estate deeds of transfer, and certificates of capital investment in a company in the form of real estate, excepting those expressly attributed to notaries and draftsmen from the Land Registry Agency'.[32]

---

[27] TBA, *Rapport moral de l'année judiciaire 2014–2015*, n 7.
[28] *JORT*, 'Loi n° 89-87 du 7 septembre 1989, portant l'organisation de la profession d'avocat', 12 September 1989, pp 1385–92.
[29] *JORT*, 'Décret-loi n° 2011-79 du 20 août 2011 portant l'organisation de la profession d'avocat', 23 August 2011, p 1595.
[30] An investigating officer (*officier de police judiciaire*) is a representative of the legal system mandated to carry out investigations and perform arrests: *JORT*, 'Décret-loi n° 79 en date du 20 août 2011 portant sur l'organisation de la profession d'avocat', n 26, p 1596.
[31] *Le Temps*, 13 March 2011.
[32] This agency is a French colonial institution established throughout North Africa and designed to levy stamp duty on property transactions.

This last claim, however, showed that the text finally promulgated by the Executive gave lawyers fewer advantages than had been sought by the Bar President. The Bill as drafted by the profession would have eliminated the recording function of the Land Registry. This body of civil servants had been created under President Ben Ali as a means of facilitating access to justice. For the new government, it was a means of reducing the cost of property transactions for Tunisia's poorest property owners. In the difficult economic climate of the transition, the government of Beji Caïd Essebsi feared the Bar's demand would increase property transfer costs, and it blocked that reform.[33]

The gains effected by statutory reforms regulating the legal profession proved more modest than anticipated. The transition governments that followed either did not wish to or could not implement the measures of the new law. By questioning some of the prerogatives granted to judges under the Ben Ali regime, the TBA proposals provoked strong opposition among magistrates' associations. Unlike lawyers, judges and magistrates did not participate in the popular uprising of December 2010–January 2011. They did, however, organise themselves to influence the political process after the Ben Ali regime fell. As a central agent within the judicial system, judges and magistrates knew how to mobilise the resources to limit the TBA's aspirations to equality.

VII. THE JUDICIARY BEFORE THE BAR: PRESERVING STATUS AND MAINTAINING INDEPENDENCE

The highly controversial Article 46 of the law of 1989, which subordinated lawyers to judges, was replaced by Article 47 of the law passed in 2011, which specified that 'transactions, pleas, and submissions made by a lawyer in the exercise of her duties' could not be the basis for a prosecution, nor could lawyers 'be subject to disciplinary measures undertaken by anybody other than those instances, authorities, and establishments before which she exercises her practice'.[34] Lawyers were granted this immunity to let them freely exercise 'their natural role as defenders of rights and freedoms and to contribute to the accomplishments resulting from the revolution'.[35]

Because judges resented this loss of power as well as the fact that the law excluded retired judges and anyone over 40 from entering the legal profession, the two professional organisations representing judges strongly opposed the draft Bill initially adopted by the government. The *Syndicat des magistrats tunisiens* (SMT)[36] denounced the text as opportunist, attributed its drafting to a pro-lawyer 'lobby'[37] embedded in the heart of the

---

[33] Interview with Samir al-Annabi, lawyer at the Supreme Court and former President of the National Authority Fighting Corruption, April 2012.

[34] *JORT*, 'Décret-loi n° 2011-79 du 20 août 2011 portant l'organisation de la profession d'avocat', n 26, p 1596.

[35] ibid.

[36] The SMT (founded in 2011) have many members linked to the Ben Ali regime. In the middle of the 2000s, some of his current leaders forced out the leaders of the historical Association of Tunisian Magistrates (AMT, *Association des magistrats tunisiens*), who were then sanctioned by the regime by being transferred to minor or regional positions.

[37] Lotfi Ben Saleh, "Le lobby des avocats monopolisent l'Exécutif et le Législatif " (in Arabic), *al-Sarih*, 30 June 2011.

government, called a three-day strike, and urged the interim president and prime minister not to sign the law. When the SMT assailed the immunity as a form of 'impunity', lawyers responded that it protected them only when exercising their duties – in other words, when defending their clients' rights.[38]

But more important to judges than lawyers' immunity were the efforts to purge the judiciary of members of the old regime as well as to limit access to the Bar by retired judges. The SMT opposed the TBA's attempts to purge the judiciary. And pointing to inadequate retirement pensions and the difficult material conditions in Tunisia, judges and magistrates demanded the right to register with the Bar after retirement, winning a change in the law declaring that candidates who had practised as judges for ten years were not affected by the 40-year age limit.

After this first confrontation between the two organisations, disputes between them became a regular feature in Tunisian courts. The TBA President and Bar Council were relentless in denouncing magistrates' systematic violations of lawyers' immunity: investigating magistrates (*juges d'instruction*) continued to charge lawyers with contempt of court. Conflict between the TBA and magistrates reached a peak at the beginning of 2014, when lawyers used a debate over a constitutional amendment to assert their status vis-à-vis the judiciary.

The strong representation of lawyers in the Asemblée Nationale Constituante allowed the TBA to benefit from the initiative of two deputies to propose, in plenary session, adding an article on the profession and its social role. Adopted by a large majority, Article 105 reaffirmed Article 1 of the law of August 2011 declaring the equality of lawyers with judges.[39]

Lawyers and judges continued to struggle over mobility between the two branches. In the half century after independence, the executive had elevated only a single lawyer to the bench: Bourguiba's niece, Saïda Sassi. But on 18 January 2014, the Minister of Justice appointed 533 lawyers and academics to be judges under Article 32 of Law 67-29.[40] The government's stated objective was to reduce the backlog of cases. The TBA praised this decision for reestablishing reciprocal circulation between lawyers and magistrates, alleviating congestion within the Bar, and filling judicial vacancies.[41] But the two magistrates' organisations (Association des magistrats tunisiens and SMT) denounced the action for abridging equal opportunities, capitulating to political expediency, and challenging the authority to nominate judges exercised by the Provisional Judicial Organisation (the temporary High Council of the Judiciary). After intense lobbying, the 'technocratic government' (led by Mehdi Jomaa) suspended the measure.[42] Disputes between the two professions intensified, resulting in strikes by both in 2014 and 2015, paralysing the courts. Although judges sought to expel lawyers from the new High Council of the Judiciary (HCJ), lawyers secured legislative support for their presence in all HCJ organs.[43]

---

[38] ibid.
[39] Interview with Samir Al-Annabi, 10 May 2015.
[40] *JORT*, 'Loi n° 67-29 du 14 juillet 1967, Relative à l'oranisation judiciaire, au conseil supérieur de la magistrature et au statut de la magistrature' 1967, p 934.
[41] Interview by the author with Chawki Tabib former *bâtonnier*, 28 February 2014.
[42] SMT, *Announcement* (in Arabic), 4 February 2014.
[43] TBA, *Rapport moral de l'année judiciaire 2015–2016* (in Arabic).

These conflicts expressed the efforts by lawyers and judges to shape the restructuring of the judiciary.

Apparent gains by lawyers vis-à-vis the judiciary have not significantly improved the material condition of the 'lower rung' of the Bar, even if its jurisdiction has grown. Every year the TBA's policy report maintains that the persistent economic crisis engulfing the country since the fall of the Ben Ali regime has negatively affected lawyers' activities and incomes. This has motivated the TBA to seek to expand the lawyers' domain, making their presence compulsory in all matters dealt with by a court.[44] The TBA has also sought to require that companies with a minimum turnover (not yet specified) obtain legal advice, just as they must be audited by a certified public accountant. A 2016 amendment to the criminal procedure code, offering legal assistance to persons in police custody, has been represented by the TBA *bâtonnier* as not only affirmating the rule of law but also extending lawyers' field of action, thereby offering further evidence of the high esteem enjoyed by lawyers and the sympathy for their professional project.[45]

The constant aim of the TBA since 2011 has been to make the new rulers accept an enlargement of lawyers' market based on their expertise, which they regard as having been unjustly disparaged by supporters of the Ben Ali regime. They have legitimated that demand by pointing to the mass of lawyers who took to the streets to support the movement against the Ben Ali regime, the censorship suffered by lawyers, and the democratic character of the appointment of Bar officers.

REFERENCES

Abel, R (2011) *Lawyers on Trial: Understanding Ethical Misconduct* (Oxford, Oxford University Press).

Abbott, A (2003) 'Écologies liées: à propos du système des professions' in P-M Menger (ed), *Les professions et leurs sociologues. Modèles théoriques, catégorisations, évolutions* (Paris, Éditions de la Maison des sciences de l'homme) 29–50.

Agrikoliansky E (2010) 'Les usages protestataires du droit' in E Agrikoliansky, O Filleule, and I Sommier (eds), *Penser les mouvements sociaux* (Paris, La Découverte) 225–43.

Ben M'barek, K (2003) 'L'élan brisé du mouvement démocratique' *Annuaire de l'Afrique du Nord 2000–2001* 39, 401–34.

Ben Youssef, A (2004) 'Les relations entre Bourguiba, les avocats et les instances ordinales au début de l'indépendance (in Arabic)' Proceedings of the Fourth Congress on *Justice and Legislation in Bourguiba's Tunisia and the Arab Countries* (Tunis, Temimi and Konrad Adenauer Stifung Foundation) 19–54.

Carlin, JE (1962) *Lawyers on their Own. A Study of Individual Practitioners in Chicago* (New Brunswick, NJ, Rutgers University Press).

Cherif, E (1990) *Mémoire d'un beldi* (Tunis, Ceres productions).

Gandhi, JS (1982) *Lawyers and Touts. A Study of the Legal Profession* (Delhi, Hindustan Publishing Corporation).

Gobe, E (2010) 'The Tunisian Bar to the test of authoritarianism: professional and political movements in Ben Ali's Tunisia (1990–2007)' 15(3) *Journal of North African Studies* 333–47.

---

[44] Interview with former *bâtonnier* (President of the Bar) Mohamed Fadhel Mahfoudh.
[45] ibid.

—— (2013a) *Les avocats en Tunisie de la colonisation à la révolution (1883–2011). Sociohistoire d'une profession politique* (Paris, IRMC-Karthala).

—— (2013b) 'Of Lawyers and *Samsars*: the Legal Services Market and the Authoritarian State in Ben Ali's Tunisia (1987-2011)' 67(1) *The Middle East Journal* 44–62.

—— (2017) 'Lawyers mobilizing in the Tunisian uprising: A matter of 'generations' in MM Ayyash and R Hadj-Moussa (eds), *Protests and Generations: Legacies and Emergencies in the Middle East, North Africa and the Mediterranean* (Leiden, Brill) 73–95.

Gobe, E and Salaymeh, L (2016) 'Tunisia's 'Revolutionary' Lawyers: From Professional Autonomy to Political Mobilization' 41(2) *Law & Social Inquiry* 311–45.

Hajjar, L (2001) 'From the Fight for Legal Rights to the Promotion of Human Rights. Israeli and Palestinian Cause Lawyers in the Trenches of Globalization' in S Austin and SA Scheingold (eds), *Cause Lawyering and the State in a Global Era* (New York, Oxford University Press) 68–95.

Hélin, E (1994) *La profession d'avocat en Tunisie*, (Aix-en-Provence, Master's thesis in Political Science, Institute of Political Studies).

Karpik, L (1995) *Les avocats entre l'État, le public et le marché XIIIe-XXe siècle* (Paris, Gallimard).

Larif-Béatrix, A (1988), *Édification étatique et environnement culturel. Le personnel politico-administratif dans la Tunisie contemporaine* (Paris, Publisud).

Quentin, J (1972) *Quelques réflexions sur le statut de la profession d'avocat en Tunisie* (Tunis, ENA Publication).

Schmitter, P (1974) 'Still the Century of Corporatism?' 36(1) *The Review of Politics* 85–131.

Siméant, J (1998) *La cause des sans-papiers* (Paris, Presse de Sciences po).

Tabib, C (1988) 'Prochaine réforme dans le Barreau tunisien. Avocats: la mutation désirée' *Info-Soir*, 24 November.

—— (2006) *Avocats et politique en Tunisie. Étude empirique* (Tunis, Master's thesis in Political Science, Faculty of Law and Political Science).

World Bank and the Ministry for Employment and Professional Insertion (2008), *Dynamiques de l'emploi et adéquation de la formation parmi les diplômés universitaires. Volume I: rapport sur l'insertion des diplômés de l'année 2004*.

34

Turkey

Emergence and Development of the Legal Profession

SEDA KALEM*

I. EARLY DAYS OF THE REPUBLIC (1923–45)

THE PROJECT OF modernisation in Turkey, which took off with the establishment of the Republic in 1923, considered educational reform the primary axis of social change through which a new generation could be shaped (Erozan 2005: 64; Söğütlü 2004: 122).[1] Law was the second axis. Although significant legal reforms were achieved before the Republic, especially during the Tanzimat Period (1839–76), the legal system of the late Ottoman era still had a dualist corpus juris, judiciary, and legal cadres. After the founding of the Republic, however, driven by the modernisation aspirations and reformist ideals of the new regime, the entire legal apparatus was restructured. In 1926, significant changes were made in the legal corpus, such as replacement of Mecelle (the Ottoman Civil Code) by the new Civil Code and adoption of the Code of Obligations (both modelled after their Swiss counterparts), the German Commercial Code, and part of the Italian Criminal Code. These were accompanied by the transformation of the judiciary, including replacement of Sharia courts by secular courts in 1924. Judicial reform required a new staff of legal professionals who would not only interpret and apply this new legal corpus but also guide the thought and behaviour of the people according to Republican principles.[2] Hence, training new legal cadres was an extension of the regime's aspiration to create its own national intellectuals, who would be mobilised as agents of this modernisation process (Erozan 2005: 67; Özman 2000). While a new generation

---

* I would like to express my gratitude to Kadir Eryılmaz for his contribution to data collection.

[1] Modernisation was actually an Ottoman-Turkish state project initially launched in late nineteenth century, which was particularly effective in restructuring state administration in the last decades of the Empire. It was however, the underlying paradigm of the new nation state founded by Mustafa Kemal, known as Atatürk.

[2] The term 'legal professional', which is primarily associated with practising lawyers in Anglo-Saxon countries, has a much wider ambit in Turkey, where it includes judges, prosecutors, practising lawyers and notaries. It is in this sense closer to concept of *jurist* employed by some scholars. In this chapter, however, I follow the Anglo-Saxon usage.

of legal professionals were to be trained at new law faculties, old cadres also were to be imbued with the ideals of the Republic and principles of the secular legal system.

Modern legal education, therefore, emerged as a politically-oriented training with a strongly Kemalist orientation.[3] It was monopolised by two faculties in Istanbul and Ankara until 1978, when a third was opened in Izmir.[4] Istanbul University Law Faculty had been established in the late nineteenth-century but was renamed and redesigned in 1933 to conform to the Republic's ideological aspirations. Following World War I, the shortage of legal professionals and the fact that Istanbul University had too few students to meet the needs of the new regime and was indifferent to the political excitement engendered by the revolution led to the creation of a new faculty in Ankara in 1925 (Mumcu 1995; Özman 2000: 171). It was charged with producing 'well educated legal professionals who will protect, teach and improve the law of the Republic'.[5] Symbolic acts – locating the new university in the capital of the Republic, which was politically controlled by the regime, or holding the inauguration ceremony at the General Headquarters of *Cumhuriyet Halk Partisi* (Republican People's Party – CHP), Ataturk's party – demonstrated the school's mission to disseminate the regime's values and train a generation of legal professionals to undertake this ideological mission (Erozan 2005: 72; Özman 1995: 96).

The emergence of the new profession was also consolidated through legislation and professional associations. The 1924 Muhamat Kanunu (Legal Professional Code No 460) was the first law institutionalising the profession by regulating entry (including a mandatory internship) and professional competence and establishing bar associations. The Code replaced the term *dava vekili* (trial lawyer) with *muhâmî* (derived from *muhamat*, meaning protection), thereby recognising a much more inclusive profession (Karabulut 2013: 85; Toprak 2014: 40). It limited the profession to Turkish citizens, effecting a 'nationalisation of bar associations' reflecting the new state's aspiration to create a political community freed from all non-national elements (Özman 1995: 103). Making 'betrayal of the nation' a ground for disqualification exposed lawyers to discipline on arbitrary and highly ideological criteria (Karabulut 2013: 89; Özkent 1940: 114). Because the Ministry of Justice exercised ultimate authority in disciplinary proceedings, the Code was used by the executive to neutralise lawyers it viewed as a threat to the regime. 374 of the 805 lawyers registered at Istanbul Bar were dismissed, although we do not know how many dismissals were based on moral reasons (Özman 2000: 173). Even stronger measures were authorised by the 1938 *Avukatlık Kanunu* (Legal Professional Code No 3499), which defined the profession as an independent practice with a 'public service quality', subordinating it to the executive in order to guard the 'public interest'. Paradoxically, lawyers were the principal supporters of state supervision of the profession, arguing this would allow monitoring of a profession that had been 'set loose' (Toprak 2014: 185).

---

[3] The founding ideology of the Republic, following the principles of Atatürk.
[4] Faculty is used in the British sense to denote a branch of teaching or a department of study at a university, not a teaching staff.
[5] Ankara Üniversitesi Hukuk Fakültesi, see www.law.ankara.edu.tr/tarihce/. Unofficial sources report that throughout the period 1925–39, 13,979 students were enrolled at Istanbul Law Faculty. In its first year, Ankara Law Faculty had 301 students, all men (Oğuzoğlu 1966, cited in Mumcu 1977: 117).

II. MULTI-PARTY PERIOD AND MILITARY INTERVENTIONS (1945–80)

From the beginning of World War II until the 1980 coup d'état, developments in the legal profession occurred against a backdrop of growing political, economic and social flux. In 1946, transition to a multi-party system was triggered by post-war pressures for fundamental change, leading to the founding of the *Demokrat Parti* (Democrat Party – DP) under Adnan Menderes, representing the opposition within the existing single party Parliament. DP achieved a historical victory in the 1950 elections, ending the 27-year rule of the CHP. In the mid-1950s, however, increasing economic distress and the DP's authoritarian measures raised serious doubts about its alleged liberalism and support for popular democracy, setting the stage for military intervention on 27 May 1960 and the execution of Menderes and two cabinet members. Against a backdrop of civil rights movements, anti-war rallies and socialist resurgence in the West, Turkey entered a period of growing discontent, with political instability and injustice. As elsewhere, economic stagnation, workers' protests, and secular reactions to religious conservatism led to political opposition by organised youth, which began peacefully but eventually turned into violent demonstrations at universities, paving the way for another military intervention. On 12 March 1971, only 11 years after the previous junta, a group of military leaders read a memorandum on public television, accusing the government of failing to cope with anarchy and declaring the military's responsibility to take over the administration to protect the Republic. A period of martial law, extrajudicial arrests and trials of students, intellectuals, journalists and workers followed the memorandum and the fall of the government. Instability continued throughout the 1970s, with 11 different prime ministers, an increasingly stagnant economy, and the spread of violence between left- and right-wing groups, leaving the way open for the 1980 military intervention, the most violent of all.

The legal profession's alliance with the state seems to have continued with limited setbacks until the 1950s because the profession considered itself the guardian of the Kemalist regime. The transition to a multi-party system, however, not only terminated the CHP's privileged role in state administration but also introduced ideological conflict between the State and the DP government. The hostility of Prime Minister Menderes toward judges who acted as servants of the regime was one manifestation of this widening gap between the establishment and the new government. When many judges were forced to retire in 1957 and replaced by the ruling party's political appointees, legal professionals declared their solidarity with the judiciary. Özman argues that though this resistance failed, it demonstrated the Kemalist regime's success in creating a legal field whose members were unanimously dedicated to protecting the regime (1995: 132). Hence, in the face of the government's repressive measures and promotion of political Islam as an anti-communist strategy, legal professionals maintained their ideological position as protectors of the regime. This was manifested again in the profession's support for the 1960 coup, which the legal community played a major role in legitimating, not only by remaining silent in the face of trials and executions but also by prohibiting lawyers from defending members of the ruling party. In the 1960s and 1970s, however, paralleling the global ideological shift to the left, the legal profession started to move from its role as guardian of the Kemalist regime to a more diverse political engagement. This shift, most visible among lawyers who were politically active in the 1960s and 1970s, followed larger political alignments. One indicator of such polarisation within the Istanbul Bar Association was the emergence of *Çağdaş Avukatlar Grubu* (the Modern Lawyers Group, ÇAG), a 'loose politically oriented platform' with a leftist constitution, and *Meslek Birlik Grubu* (the Professional Unity Group), right-wing group (Öngün and Hassan 2013: 143). Although the latter won the 1974 Bar elections ÇAG defeated it two years later, retaining power until now with brief interruptions, despite internal divisions. Particularly in the first couple of presidential terms, the ÇAG-led Istanbul Bar was actively involved in everyday politics through a series of protests against unconstitutional, extrajudicial and illegal practices by the state and the military.

Professional developments also reflected these shifting alliances and political complexities. The most significant was the 1969 *Avukatlık Kanunu* (Legal Profession Code No 1136), which remains the principal legislation regulating the profession despite many changes. Against a backdrop of increasing demands for freedom worldwide and enactment of the 1961 Constitution (considered the most progressive in the history of the Republic), the 1969 Code was drafted in response to the legal profession's quest for greater autonomy from the executive. One of its primary achievements was establishing the *Türkiye Barolar Birliği* (Union of Turkish Bar Associations, TBB) as the umbrella professional organisation located in Ankara and transferring responsibility to it (from the Ministry of Justice) for supervising and monitoring individual Bar associations. This had significant implications for the relationship between the state and the profession as the TBB resisted the repressive policies of an executive confronting an increasingly violent socio-political environment.

Although the Turkish population grew rapidly during this period, reaching almost 40 million, there were only 18,000 registered lawyers, just 14,000 of them active (Ayiter). Similarly, the 31 Bar associations established during the one-party period were supplemented by only eight founded after it ended, although all these were located in the less developed eastern and northern provinces. The relatively small number of lawyers was also related to the limited capacity of legal education. A third law faculty founded in 1978 under the aegis of Ege University enrolled just 200 students and graduated 76 in 1982, compared with the 550 and 400 graduating from Istanbul and Ankara law faculties that year.[6]

III. GLOBALISATION, LIBERALISATION, POLARISATION (1980–2002)

The malicious military coup on 12 September 1980 in the face of increasing political instability and violence shaped the succeeding decades. During the junta period, all political parties were banned, Parliament was dissolved, and the 1961 Constitution was replaced by the highly authoritarian and repressive 1982 Constitution, which remained in force in 2017. In the 1983 elections, the victory of the centre-right *Anavatan Partisi* (Motherland Party – ANAP) initiated a period of rapid economic liberalisation together with 'reorganisation as well as further centralisation of the state apparatus' (Öniş 1992: 19). This period also saw the growth of civil society in response to new

---

[6] The faculty was transferred to Dokuz Eylül University in 1982.

political demands, mainly by Kurdish nationalism, political Islam and the feminist movement (Tekeli 1991; Ertürk 2006: 93). State repression of the first two led to an escalation in political mobilisation by both groups. Following the 1995 elections, the *Refah Partisi* (Welfare Party – RP) with an Islamist pedigree took power as head of a coalition government, which stayed in office until the 1997 intervention – also known as the 28 February post-modern coup – when the military issued an ultimatum to the Government in the name of the Republic and 'democratic values'. In the 1999 elections, the centre-left party *Demokratik Sol Parti* (Democratic Left Party – DSP) took the lead after two decades of right-wing rule. However, the political and economic repercussions of two major earthquakes and the 2001 financial crisis were never fully overcome; and several months of political turmoil within Parliament and the accompanying social exhaustion ultimately compelled the Government to hold early elections, leading to the historic victory of the *Adalet ve Kalkınma Partisi* (Justice and Development Party – AKP).

The early 1980s were characterised by burnout among lawyers confronting the reactionary politics. In the 1983 Istanbul Bar elections, the association's political involvement caused ÇAG to lose the presidency after three terms, replaced by *Birleşmiş Avukatlar Grubu* (United Lawyers Group), representing the more conservative wing, whose campaign discourse focused on 'saving the Bar' from political struggles by shifting attention to purely professional matters (İnanıcı 2008: 177). This transfer of power from ÇAG was interpreted as indicating lawyers' desire for 'peace and stability' and a return to a narrower political involvement limited to 'preserving the State and its Kemalist values' (Silverman 2017). When ÇAG regained power toward the end of the 1980s, however, the Bar again assumed an active role in politics. The 1990s saw further divisions among coalitions within the Istanbul Bar Association, especially the rise of a Kemalist group among ÇAG lawyers. The founding of *Önce İlke- Çağdaş Avukatlar Grubu* (Principles First-Modern Lawyers Group, Öİ-ÇAG) was the first official split within ÇAG as a reaction to its egalitarian approach to Islamic revivalism. Starting in the early 2000s, Öİ-ÇAG gained power by mobilising older lawyers, thereby managing to shape the politics of the Istanbul Bar Association in the following two decades (Öngün and Hassan 2013: 150). Political sectarianism was not limited to the Istanbul Bar. The Izmir Bar Association, infamous for its unanimous commitment to a secular Kemalist leftism, has never had a right-wing president. However, its unity was shattered in 2002 when Izmir ÇAG also split into two groups over the 1997 postmodern coup and the headscarf debate it sparked. The new fraction, called *Cumhuriyetçi Avukatlar* (Republican Lawyers), focused on the primacy of a Kemalist secularism with respect to the political visibility of Islam. ÇAG, by contrast, was increasingly identified as pro-Kurdish and accused of being a PKK supporter.

A. Professional Developments

Reflecting the authoritarian character of the junta and its 1982 Constitution, the 1969 Legal Profession Code was amended seven times by 1988 to include ever more repressive provisions. Amendments in 1984 introduced greater executive supervision of the legal profession through provisions regulating Bar association activities and defining sanctions for violating professional boundaries. For instance, Article 76, which had prohibited

Bar associations from engaging in any activity (including politics) other than those outlined by law, was amended to include more specific limitations, such as 'organising meetings and demonstrations, acting with political parties, trade unions and associations, entering political collaborations, or supporting candidates in general or local elections'. The new regulation also allowed provincial governors to dismiss elected Bar administrators in urgent cases where the 'existence, independence and integrity of the state and nation are threatened'. In addition, the Ministry of Justice was empowered to monitor the administrative and financial affairs of professional organisations. This increasing authoritarianism also stimulated Kurdish legal activism deploying the individual petition mechanism of the European Court of Human Rights. The Kurdish Human Rights Project (KHRP) was initiated in 1992 as a transnational network of human rights defenders, lawyers and academics, becoming the central mechanism through which lawyers transformed complaints of human rights violations into 'well documented and legally compelling rights claims' (Anagnostou 2014: 171).

The early-twenty-first century was marked by political pressures for democratisation and a wave of legal changes constituting the most comprehensive reform after the early Republican period. Following Turkey's recognition as a candidate for EU membership in 1999, accession negotiations started in 2005 after the European Commission concluded that the Copenhagen political criteria had been met. Because the negotiation process depended largely on harmonisation efforts through rule transfers, juridical reform was central (Müftüler-Baç 2016: 8). The 2001 amendments to the 1969 Code sought to align existing laws with European legislation, introducing revolutionary changes. One novelty was official recognition of the profession as a tier of the judiciary, thereby increasing lawyers' public and professional credibility and identifying advocacy as a prestigious profession deserving protection by the state, not monitoring. This change was also meaningful in the context of provisions replacing the Ministry of Justice with the TBB as final authority on professional issues, like registering lawyers in or removing them from the Bar, prohibiting them from working, or disciplining them. Such transfers of power, although not comprehensive, were appreciated by the legal community as reducing military tutelage over the profession.

Increasing the quality of legal services was another concern addressed by provisions regarding entry, professional boundaries and rules of conduct. The new regulations required joint stock companies with a capital of more than 250,000 Turkish Lira to hire a lawyer.[7] The 2001 amendments also introduced a compulsory Bar exam to harmonise differences in legal education stemming from rapid increase in the number of law faculties. In 2006, that provision was annulled by Parliament just before the first exam was to occur. In 2009, however, the Constitutional Court overturned that action, declaring that the public demanded qualified lawyers. The Court reasoned that minimal legal training was insufficient to practise law, and professional competence could be achieved only through special training and selective entry. Nevertheless, by 2019 the examination still had not been administered.

The 2001 amendments also introduced new practice arrangements. Previously, lawyers registered at the same Bar could enter partnerships in the form of a 'joint law office',

---

[7] US $41,000 as of 31 July 2019.

sharing revenues and expenses and deciding managerial issues collectively. A 1999 study of 1099 members of Istanbul Bar Association found that a large majority of lawyers (78 per cent) were self-employed, and most of these either had other lawyers working for them (38 per cent) or worked on their own (32 per cent). Among the 22 per cent reporting they were not self-employed, 34 per cent were working as a salaried employee of a lawyer (Istanbul Bar Association 1999). The 2001 amendments, however, allowed lawyers to offer specialised legal services under 'lawyer partnerships', separate legal entities recognised by Bar associations. This type of practice is subject to taxation rules and regulations regarding private companies. In line with regulations promoting foreign investment, foreign lawyer partnerships are also allowed on condition that they only offer advice on foreign law. In such entities, Turkish partners do not become a branch of the global law firm but continue to practise in independent firms providing services on Turkish law as part of a global network of legal capital and business (Emre 2015). However, these foreign partnerships have raised suspicions concerning the limits of their consultancy services (TBB 2009).

B. Legal Education

Developments in legal education in the 1980s followed that decade's overall economic growth. The 1983 amendments to the 1981 *Yükseköğretim Kanunu* (Code on Higher Education No 2547) allowed foundations to establish non-profit institutions of higher education, promoting a sharp increase in the number of universities: 56 were established between 1980 and 2002. Law was one of the most profitable faculties because the promise of a solid professional training and a relatively secure financial future, together with the steadily expanding global market for legal services, increased the demand for legal education.[8] By 2001, there were 23 law faculties, 11 at privately funded universities and eight of these outside of Istanbul, Ankara and Izmir, helping to diversify the profession.[9]

All these developments forced professional organisations to track the rapid changes in the legal field.

Table 1 Number of Lawyers (1999–2001)

Year	Women	Men	Total
1999	11,004	27,982	38,986
2000	11,857	29,570	41,427
2001	No info	No info	44,221

Source: TBB, www.barobirlik.org.tr/Barolar.

---

[8] In 2009, 70 per cent of students taking the university entrance exam gave law as their first choice. A majority of these students did so because of their interest in the field and their desire to be useful to the community (Öztoprak-Sağır 2010: 129).

[9] For a discussion of the power of the Bar Associations in these three cities, see Elveriş (2014: 150–51).

Table 2 Number of Lawyers in the Istanbul, Ankara, and Izmir Bar Associations (1999–2001)

Year	Istanbul	Ankara	Izmir	Total	% of all lawyers
1999	14,011	5,940	3,841	23,792	61
2000	15,050	6,200	3,963	25,213	61
2001	16,234	6,402	4,317	26,953	61

Source: TBB, www.barobirlik.org.tr/Barolar.

IV. AKP PERIOD (2002–17)

In the 2002 elections, all political parties except the CHP and the newly established pro-Islamist AKP led by Recep Tayyip Erdoğan failed to get Parliamentary seats. AKP got 34 per cent of the votes and initiated a period of single-party rule after a decade of coalitions characterised by economic fluctuations and political uncertainties. The party not only benefited from the collapse of centre-right parties but also managed to appeal to an ideologically and geographically more diverse electorate than its predecessors, which had usually limited their constituencies to conservative Islamists and central Anatolia (Çarkoğlu 2002: 149). AKP's initial attraction derived from its combination of a moderate version of political Islam, economic liberalism, and the promise of EU membership. In 2004, AKP consolidated its power in local elections, increasing its share to 42 per cent and winning in 12 of the country's 16 major municipalities. Hence, in its first couple of terms, in addition to promoting economic growth benefiting long-neglected segments of the population, AKP won support for tackling chronic political and social issues, such as limiting the military's role in public affairs, amending the authoritarian 1982 Constitution and major codes, recognising minority rights, normalising the wearing of headscarves in public life, and negotiating with the Kurdish movement to resolve decades of strife. Political leaders and commentators celebrated Erdoğan as a modern democratic pro-Western Muslim leader, an example for the Middle East of the compatibility of Islam and democracy, a 'shining success story, both economically and politically' (eg Sontag 2003; Falk 2012; Kanani 2014; Letsch 2014).

Nevertheless, the Government's Islamist pedigree raised serious anxieties among Kemalist segments of the population. 2007 began with controversies around the upcoming presidential election, triggered by the possibility of Erdoğan winning. In April 2007, mass demonstrations called 'republican meetings', organised primarily by Kemalist civil society, mobilised thousands of people concerned about the visibility of the Islamist lifestyle in public life and especially about the nomination of a pro-Islamist politician as head of the State. AKP nominated Foreign Affairs Minister Abdullah Gül instead of Erdoğan. But his candidacy was sabotaged by a series of 'constitutional battles' over the number of seats required for an absolute majority (Özbudun 2012). In the evening of 27 April 2007, the military intervened again, publishing an e-memorandum on its official website declaring its determination to guard the foundational principles of the Republic, pre-eminently secularism. Political deadlock led to early elections in July 2007, in which AKP increased its share to 46 per cent; and Gül was ultimately elected President on 28 August. AKP introduced a series of constitutional amendments, including a provision for popular election of the President for a maximum of two five-year terms, which were approved by the people in October 2007, enhancing AKP's legitimacy. In 2008, however, the constitutional crisis was intensified by a so-called judicial coup in the form of a closure case against AKP for becoming 'the focus of anti-secular activities'.[10] The case was overruled by a close vote, and AKP was merely deprived of state funding. In December 2009, however, the Court affirmed the closure of the *Demokratik Toplum Partisi* (Democratic Society Party – DTP), representing Kurdish voters, because of its alleged activities 'against unity of the State with its nation'. Ironically, that was the year of the 'democratic opening', a government-led initiative bringing together a diverse group of actors from politics, academia, journalism and civil society to resolve the Kurdish issue (Çakır 2010). In the next two years, democratic opening talks first were replaced by a discourse of 'resolution process' which would be suspended in March 2015 and never mentioned again in political debates (Yeğen 2015).

This period also saw a fundamental change in the relationship between the State and the armed forces. For the first time in its history, the military faced judicial investigations based on alleged anti-government plots in the *Ergenekon* and *Balyoz* trials. Along with politicians, bureaucrats, academics and journalists, high ranking military officers, including the former Chief of Staff, were tried and sentenced for being members of an organised criminal conspiracy against the democratically elected government.[11] Meanwhile, the AKP's 2010 constitutional amendments, framed as a means of 'getting rid of the legacy of 1980 coup', were approved by 58 per cent of the electorate. The constitutional package was promoted as an opportunity to liquidate the 'authoritarian, statist, and tutelary features of the 1982 Constitution', thereby garnering support from the intelligentsia and further enhancing the legitimacy of AKP's populist programme (Özbudun 2012). Hence, when the Government won the largest share of the vote for the third time in a row in the 2011 elections, AKP's continuing success was seen as demonstrating its increasing appeal to a diverse constituency and its potential contribution to a 'consolidation and stabilization of electoral preferences' (Çarkoğlu 2011: 50). In summer 2013, amid social and political tensions provoked by controversies around the role of the headscarf in public life, allegations of illegal wiretapping of the judiciary, intensifying police violence, devastating earthquakes, and violations of rights and freedoms, Turkey witnessed a nationwide uprising commonly referred to as the 'Gezi events', in which thousands demonstrated against the Government's repressive policies.

The dust never quite settled after Gezi and the succeeding corruption accusations against AKP. When the *Halkların Demokratik Partisi* (Peoples' Democratic Party, HDP), which championed Kurdish rights, managed to pass the 10 per cent threshold, entering Parliament as the second largest minority group in the June 2015 elections, AKP lost its

---

[10] About 30 parties, mostly pro-Islamist or pro-Kurdish, have been closed down by the Constitutional Court since its establishment in 1961, most in 1990s. In the closure case, filed with an overwhelming parliamentary majority, AKP was primarily accused of unconstitutional statements and activities undermining the secular character of the Republic. For more on party closures in Turkey, see Belge (2006); Koğacıoğlu (2004).

[11] Although most of the accused received lengthy prison sentences, the convictions were overturned in 2016 following the failed coup attempt against the AKP Government, allegedly organised by the exiled cleric Fethullah Gülen and his outlawed movement.

majority for the first time. Its lack of an authentic political platform frustrated negotiations for a coalition government, leading to early elections in November 2015. AKP again formed a single-party government by wrapping a promise of stability (in the face of increasing violence) in an appeal to nationalism. However, economic, social, and political stability were unattainable: 2016 was one of the most violent years in Turkish history, with numerous suicide bombings, a constant increase in attacks on women and children, greater use of force by the police, and arrests of journalists, academics, politicians and civilians on terror charges. A Petition of Academics for Peace Initiative signed by 2,000 scholars intensified the Government's hostility towards the opposition, leading to arrests of and administrative sanctions against academics, such as forced resignations, suspensions, and travel bans. The situation became even more critical when the 15 July 2016 failed coup attempt shattered the already unstable political and social environment. The state of emergency that followed was lifted in July 2018. Statutory decrees became the means by which the government legitimised the dismissal and arrest of hundreds of thousands of state employees, journalists, academics and politicians. The constitutional referendum of April 2017 proposing to expand presidential powers was held in this tense atmosphere, with yes votes barely exceeding the opposition (51 per cent). The July 2017 March for Justice, a three-week demonstration organised by the CHP, whose leader, Kemal Kılıçdaroğlu, marched from Ankara to Istanbul with hundreds of thousands of protestors, was a response to the government's increasing authoritarianism after the coup attempt.

After 2007, Bar associations and the TBB adopted a critical attitude toward the government. In December 2007, a rally for an independent judiciary was organised by TBB and joined by representatives of civil society organisations and bar associations, as well as members of the judiciary, academia, and military. After 2009, the legal profession reacted more frequently and forcibly to the increasing politicisation of legal issues and threats against judicial independence. Politically motivated actions by the Ministry of Justice, such as requesting the dismissal of judges based on unconstitutionally gathered information, were particularly troubling. The Istanbul Bar Association condemned these developments as clear evidence of the Government's determination to control the judiciary and replace existing judges with its own loyalists. Professional organisations also criticised the 2010 constitutional package. The Istanbul Bar Association and TBB warned that the proposed changes would violate separation of powers and benefit the executive. TBB was also concerned about the arrest of judicial staff, high ranking military officers, and lawyers in the *Ergenekon*, *Balyoz*, and *KCK* cases and rising police violence against journalists and lawyers. Until 2013, however, TBB maintained a serious, professional and legalistic tone in its public statements, prompting CHP to criticise the TBB Head for being too reticent in addressing the emerging legal and political crises. With the election of Metin Feyzioğlu as TBB Head, however, its administration assumed a much more defiant stance, with a very explicit Kemalist and Republican outlook. This administration often has admonished the government, and its Head has made more frequent, confrontational public appearances. On 10 May 2014, during Feyzioğlu's speech at the 146th anniversary of the Council of State, Prime Minister Erdoğan stalked out of the auditorium, accusing Feyzioğlu of 'being shameless' in commenting on political matters about which he knew nothing. The September 2014 Judicial Year Opening Ceremony was boycotted by many cabinet members, including then President Erdoğan, who were protesting the inclusion of Feyzioğlu in the programme.[12] In November 2014, the Government annulled the legislative basis of this ceremony, accusing it of becoming a political occasion to attack the Prime Minister (Hürriyet 2014). In 2015, the ceremony was split in two, one organised by the Court of Appeals and attended by the President and another 'alternative opening' organised by TBB with the participation of Bar associations and the CHP Head.[13] In 2016, when the Judicial Year Opening Ceremony was held at the presidential complex with a talk by the President for the first time, TBB refused to participate.

Meanwhile, Erdoğan and the AKP Government continued accusing TBB, and especially Feyzioğlu, of improper involvement in political issues, asking him to 'take off his robe and do politics'. His engagement with politics was most vividly epitomised by his participation in the campaign on the April 2017 referendum. Travelling around the country and abroad, Feyzioğlu claimed that he had 'hit the road' to let people know that the proposed amendments would expand the President's power, propelling Turkey towards a more authoritarian system. TBB was 'enlightening everyone on a vital issue that was above politics', a responsibility vested in it by the 1969 Code. Although these meetings were entitled 'we are discussing the Constitution', they were more about why people should say no to proposed amendments than how they could make an informed choice. Feyzioğlu was usually accompanied by several influential figures from the Kemalist establishment during these gatherings, which were organised by popular Kemalist civil society organisations and supported by local Bar associations. These events deeply disturbed the President, who openly warned Feyzioğlu about the possible consequences. When Feyzioğlu was invited to the 2017 Judicial Year Opening ceremony as a guest, not as a speaker, TBB announced it would not attend 'just to applaud', escalating tensions between the executive and the profession.

A. Professional Developments

As the legal profession struggled to respond to these political developments it also faced other pressing issues. A 2003 bye-law prohibiting advertising was liberalised in 2010 to allow lawyers to launch websites promoting their services (TBB/2003/25296). Such legislative responses to the demands of an increasingly global market, together with the proliferation of law schools and steady increase in lawyer numbers, raised concerns about quality. In the absence of a Bar exam, differences between faculties in the number and credentials of academic staff generated questions about the uniformity of law degrees. At the same time, the creation of specialised jurisdictions like consumer courts or criminal courts for intellectual and industrial property rights also increased the demand for specialisation, which had been discouraged by the prevailing generalist legal education and practice. The emergence of neoliberal regulatory regimes challenged the role of legal

---

[12] Each year the anniversaries of high courts like the Council of State and Court of Appeals are celebrated with ceremonies including members of the judiciary and high state and government officials. The Judicial Year Opening Ceremony, held at the Court of Appeals in early September, is another symbolically significant gathering for the judiciary. Traditionally, the TBB Head is expected to deliver a speech at all these gatherings as a sign of the indispensability of defence for the judiciary. These speeches are usually full of references to major contemporary political and social issues (Elveriş 2014).

[13] This cooperation between TBB and CHP has also been criticised by lawyers (Elveriş 2014: 91–92).

professionals in dispute resolution processes and introduced a more 'complex system of rules whose legality is more often than not assessed in terms of its technicality and only secondarily in terms of metaphysical legal concerns such as justice and legitimacy' (Türem and Ballestero 2014: 7). The Competition Council, empowered to regulate, monitor and impose sanctions, is seen as a quasi-legislative and judicial institution (Tekinsoy 2007: 121). Similar points have been made in the context of new practice settings and fields of practice, such as mediation (Kalem 2010). All these challenges have prompted debates on the meaning and ideology of lawyering (İnanıcı 2008: 75–87; Kalem 2010).

The profession continues to grow younger and more feminised, raising questions about professional hierarchies and inequalities. Younger lawyers are increasingly insecure and dissatisfied with their practice (Akbaş 2011; Tavşancıl et al 2007).[14] Women were 43 per cent of lawyers in 2016 but continue to be much less represented in leadership positions.

i. Growth

The growth of the profession accelerated, with the total at the end of 2016 reaching 100,461 lawyers registered at 79 Bar associations. As in previous years, lawyers from Istanbul (38 per cent), Ankara (14) and Izmir (8) constituted 60 per cent of the profession. Since 1999, when TBB started sharing official data, the profession has been growing about 30 per cent every five years.

Figure 1 Growth of the Profession (2002–16)

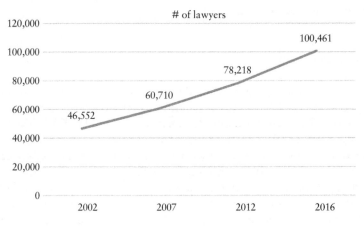

Source: TBB, www.barobirlik.org.tr/Barolar.

ii. Feminisation

In line with global trends, the number of women has grown rapidly, now constituting 43 per cent of the profession.

---

[14] Data from the Istanbul Bar Association, which contains more than 30 per cent of all lawyers, reveal that in 2016, 42 per cent of Istanbul lawyers were younger than 35 and 69 per cent were younger than 45.

Figure 2 Gender Demographics of the Profession (2002–16)

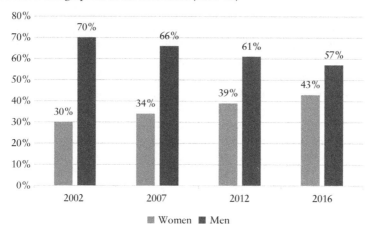

Source: TBB, www.barobirlik.org.tr/Barolar.

But they are still underrepresented in executive positions, eg just six of the 79 Bar Association presidents. The Istanbul Bar Association, one of the oldest and largest in the world, has never been headed by a woman, nor has TBB had a woman president during its nearly half century. These results are consistent with other comparisons in the legal field (Kalem 2013).

iii. Practice Settings

Lawyers traditionally worked either alone or in joint law offices; since 2001, they have been able to form partnerships. A 2011 study found that 69 per cent of Istanbul lawyers were self-employed; almost half the respondents had salaried lawyers in their offices. Among the self-employed lawyers, 62 per cent were solo practitioners, 29 per cent worked in a joint office, and only 9 per cent were in a partnership (Akbaş 2011: 234). The 24 per cent of lawyers who were salaried represented the gradual proletarianisation of what had been a middle-class profession.[15] The expansion of legal education (some of dubious quality) and a legal market responding to the demands of global capital seem to have engendered an army of junior professionals with uneven qualifications forced to seek work in an increasingly competitive field. Rather than establishing their own practices, young lawyers find they have to work as salaried employees in large law offices. Those earning above-average salaries practising business law in firms with international connections are called plaza attorneys in reference to the skyscrapers where they work (Şeref 2013). Salaried employment in a firm or business is not considered a professional practice because Article 1 of the 1969 Code defines advocacy as an independent profession (İnanıcı 2008: 227–28). Instead, it is a 'practice compatible with advocacy'. Indeed, almost half the salaried lawyers surveyed felt they were doing clerical work, and another 17 per cent saw themselves as blue-collar workers (Akbaş 2011: 243).

---

[15] For an earlier analysis of the phenomenon, see İnanıcı (2008: 225–39).

Dissatisfaction with salaried employment is most often voiced by lawyers with five years of professional experience or less.[16] In 2006, TBB responded by setting a minimum monthly wage for salaried lawyers working next to a lawyer in firms or businesses. But this was annulled by the Council of State on the ground that the relationship between the employer and salaried lawyer was purely contractual and therefore subject to regulations under the Labour Law. This decision recognised that treating a salaried lawyer as a 'worker' was incompatible with the definition of the profession as an independent practice. At the end of a lengthy procedural battle with the Council, TBB issued a bye-law in December 2015 regulating the working conditions of salaried lawyers by introducing professional liability insurance and holding the employer liable for a salaried lawyer's actions (TBB/2015/29574). But in September 2016 the Ministry of Justice persuaded the Council of State to annul this as well, on the ground that many of the provisions concerned rights and freedoms, which had to be regulated by law.

B. Legal Education

In the period 2003–11, AKP's first two terms in office, 50 state universities and 39 private universities were established, greatly expanding the number of law faculties (much faster, interestingly, than the number of lawyers, compare Figure 1). After the number of law faculties increased 110 per cent between 2007 and 2012, it increased only marginally (from 63 to 67 in 2014 and 2015) and then returned to the 2012 figure, the first time it had declined (because some private universities were closed by statute following the 15 July 2016 coup attempt).

Figure 3 Growth in Number of Law Faculties (1978–2017)

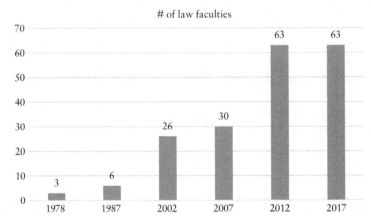

This expansion also increased geographic accessibility: 58 per cent of faculties were in Istanbul in 2009 but just 41 per cent in 2017 (Öztoprak-Sağır 2010: 48). Still, almost

---

[16] Reports by *Genç Avukatlar Kurultayı* (Young Lawyers Congress) since 2013 have repeatedly focused on issues of employment, such as minimum wages, hours, and working conditions.

58 per cent of students were in Istanbul, Ankara and Izmir, which had just 31 per cent of the population. Istanbul alone has 36 per cent of all law students (nearly 20 per cent of these at Istanbul University Law Faculty). Yet the fact that graduates of Istanbul University and Marmara Law Faculties were 88 per cent of practising lawyers in Istanbul in 1999 but just 55 per cent in 2017 shows the declining primacy of those two faculties.[17] The rapid establishment of new faculties around the country, often with little or no academic staff and insufficient infrastructure, is more an expression of populist policies (in the case of state universities) and beneficial relations between the state and private capital (in the case of privately funded universities) than a response to market forces. Yet the belief that a law degree opens career opportunities continues to fuel the demand for legal education (Emre 2015).

This unregulated increase in law faculties, however, has generated serious debates between law schools, professional organisations and political authorities concerning the quality, uniformity and adequacy of legal education. A 2012 survey of 1,066 lawyers, legal academics, judges, and law students identified legal education as the third most significant problem in the Turkish legal system; and the lawyers were most likely to cite legal education as one of the three most troublesome issues (Kalem 2012). At the beginning of 2015, *Yüksek Öğretim Kurumu* (Higher Education Council – YÖK), the highest authority regulating higher education, announced its decision to increase the quality of legal education by allowing law faculties to enrol students only ranked among the top 150,000.[18] Many critics believe that the proliferation of law schools has introduced wide differences in the professional competence of their graduates, leading to a deterioration in quality of legal services (Öztoprak-Sağır 2010: 103). Differences between faculties were particularly dramatic in a comparison of 'pioneer schools' (Istanbul, Ankara, and other older, more established state schools, such as Dokuz Eylül and Marmara) with newly founded, predominantly privately funded institutions.[19] The academic staff of Istanbul and Ankara Law Faculties believe there is a gap between graduates of different law faculties (Öztoprak-Sağır 2010: 102). Many of the new faculties lack sufficient full-time staff, and some rely entirely on visiting staff or practitioners (Emre 2015; Öztoprak-Sağır 2010: 97). Professors were 15 per cent of legal academics in 2009, assistant professors 23 per cent, and research assistants 42 per cent, revealing the dominance of junior staff (Öztoprak-Sağır 2010: 91). In a recent study, TBB compared the education and research capacity of 53 law faculties to ascertain the quality of legal education in Turkey and help prospective students make informed decisions (2017). Indicators included the number of full-time academic staff; the presence of law libraries, research centres, and mock courtrooms; courses offered; the faculty's national and international affiliations; exchange programs; academic events; and foreign language competence. The study found that eight of the top ten faculties were at public universities. Although pioneer schools seem to be losing their market share, Istanbul, Ankara, Dokuz Eylül and Marmara law faculties are still regarded as the best qualified.

---

[17] Istanbul Bar Association's official response to author's inquiry.
[18] This would ultimately mean an increase in the minimum number of points that a student needs to score in the university entrance exam.
[19] The Anglo-Saxon literature refers to 'elite schools', which implies top-tier expensive schools. I use the term 'pioneer schools' to refer to faculties preferred for their long history, classical education with a traditional curriculum, and the prestige of their academic staff.

Differences in the academic capacity of faculties, however, do not imply similar differences in their admission processes or curricula. Like all secondary school graduates seeking a bachelor's degree, students wanting to study law must pass a state exam. Law is a four-year undergraduate degree. All law faculties follow the same curriculum of compulsory courses determined mostly by YÖK (with minor differences in how and when they are taught). Elective offerings depend on the resources available. TBB has very little impact, if any, on the curriculum. This standardisation of legal education is considered particularly important in the absence of qualifying exams. Modelled on continental Europe, legal education in Turkey is highly positivistic and doctrinal, with almost no practical work. Particularly until late 1980s when there were only the two law faculties at Istanbul and Ankara Universities, the traditional lecture style was the only possible teaching method given their large enrolments. Lectures remain the most prominent method of teaching, especially among senior staff (Öztoprak-Sağır 2010: 113). Nevertheless, the new private law faculties with fewer students and more elective courses have tried alternative pedagogy. Clinical legal education was introduced at the beginning of this century and became more popular following a 2016 protocol between Ministry of Justice and the Rectors of 13 universities.

Modes of qualification for the profession also do not differ among law schools. All law graduates need to complete a one-year internship: half in a court (supervised by Justice Commissions)[20] and half with a private practitioner with at least five years' experience (supervised by the local Bar association). Interns are responsible for 'attending hearings with the lawyer, going to relevant conferences, carrying out tasks assigned by the lawyer and the Bar management, organising case files and fulfilling other duties to be regulated by a bye-law'. Since 2001, they also conduct cases in civil courts of peace, criminal courts of peace and courts of enforcement with the written permission of the supervising lawyer. During this year-long internship, TBB provides trainees with financial support derived mainly from stamps attached to proxy statements submitted to authorities. Graduates wishing to become judges or prosecutors take written and oral exams. After successfully completing both, candidates follow a two-year professional training course offered by the Justice Academy of the Ministry of Justice (which trains judges, prosecutors, lawyers, notaries and other judicial staff).

V. CONCLUSION

This chapter has sought to historicise legislative and professional developments concerning the Turkish legal profession within the larger socio-political context – a necessity because the professional field has always been shaped by political debates and ideological struggles (Bourdieu 1987). The historical overview of the mobilisation of law as a crucial instrument of Kemalist modernisation revealed the fundamental ideological alliance between the profession and the Republic. This was the key determinant of the profession's positions with respect to social and political issues, especially in the early decades

---

[20] Administrative units responsible for the work of courthouse personnel not appointed by the Ministry of Justice, such as clerks and bailiffs.

of the new state. The relationship, however, has always been influenced by the changing national and international political context. Whereas the profession seemed content to subordinate itself to the executive until the 1950s, the transition to a multi-party system intensified political polarisation, generating controversies about the profession's relationship with the state. In the following decades, the global leftward movement encouraged many lawyers to actively challenge illegalities. The increasing authoritarianism and widening social and political cleavages of 1980s and 1990s, by contrast, led to a resurgence of the Kemalist constituency within professional associations. Bar associations and the TBB took increasingly ideological positions towards the growing political tensions. In recent years, efforts by the Government to assert absolute control over the state apparatus have provoked the profession to assume a major role in the political opposition.

Elveriş (2014) argues that TBB has never functioned as a true corporatist structure cooperating with the government to pursue its own economic and professional interests. Turkish lawyers have always been advocates of political and ideological values and principles (Kalem 2010). This can be seen in TBB's resistance to cooperating with judicial, executive, administrative and legislative authorities in policymaking. The latest example is the drafting of a new legal professional code. In 2014, the Ministry of Justice presented its draft to TBB, which rejected it and prepared a counter-proposal. In April 2017, the Minister of Justice promised to give Parliament a radically different draft (including a mandatory Bar exam) by the end of the year. In February 2019, the Minister of Justice gave a press statement about the planned judicial reform package that would include a Bar exam. The exam, however, is planned to be prepared and delivered by *Ölçme, Seçme ve Yerleştirme Merkezi* (Centre for Assessment, Selection and Placement, ÖSYM), which is the central state organ responsible for delivering university entrance exams and some other professional qualification exams.

Interestingly, in June 2019 the President of TBB declared that he applauded the new reform package and that he trusted that ÖSYM would deliver the Bar exam safely. Given that the same Feyzioğlu was only recently removed from judicial ceremonies, travelling around the country campaigning against constitutional amendments that would increase executive powers, this new positive turn is yet to be tested against political developments.

REFERENCES

Akbaş, K (2011) *Avukatlık mesleğinin ekonomi politiği: Avukatların sınıfsal konumlarındaki değişim, Istanbul örneği* (Istanbul, NotaBene Yayınları).

Anagnostou, D (2014) 'From Belfast to Diyarbakir and Grozny via Strasbourg: Transnational legal mobilisation against state violations in contexts of armed conflict' in D Anagnostou (ed), *Rights and Courts in Pursuit of Social Change: Legal Mobilisation in the Multi-level European System* (Oxford, Hart Publishing).

Anderson, S (2001) 'The hunger warriors' *NY Times*, 21 October www.nytimes.com/2001/10/21/magazine/the-hunger-warriors.html.

Ayıter, K, hukuk.deu.edu.tr/fakultemiz/tarihce/.

Belge, C (2006) 'Friends of the Court: The republican alliance and selective activism of the Constitutional Court of Turkey' 40(3) *Law & Society Review* 653–92.

Bourdieu, P (1987) 'The force of law: Toward a sociology of the juridical field' 38 *Hastings Law Journal* 805–53.

Bowcott, O (2002) 'Hope dies in Turkish prison hunger strike' *The Guardian*, 19 January www.theguardian.com/world/2002/jan/19/owenbowcott.

Çakır, R (2010) 'Kurdish political movement and the "Democratic Opening"' 12(2) *Insight Turkey* 179–92 www.insightturkey.com/articles/kurdish-political-movement-and-the-democratic-opening.

Çarkoğlu, A (2002) 'The rise of the new generation pro-Islamists in Turkey: The Justice and Development Party phenomenon in the November 2002 elections in Turkey' 7(3) *South European Society & Politics* 123–56.

—— (2011) 'Turkey's 2011 General elections: Towards a dominant party system?' 13(3) *Insight Turkey* 43–62.

Elveriş, İ (2014) *Barolar ve siyaset* (Istanbul, Istanbul Bilgi Üniversitesi Yayınları).

Emre, A (2015) 'Türkiye'de avukatlık: 80 bin avukatın dünyası' *HaberTürk*, 27 April www.haberturk.com/yazi-dizisi/haber/1070820-turkiyede-avukatlik.

Erozan, HB (2005) 'Producing obedience: Law professors and the Turkish state' PhD thesis, University of Minnesota.

Ertürk, Y (2006) 'Turkey's modern paradoxes: Identity politics, women's agency and universal rights' in MM Ferree and AM Tripp (eds), *Global Feminism: Transnational Women's Activism, Organizing and Human Rights* (NY, NYU Press) 79–109.

Falk, R (2012) 'Ten years of AKP leadership in Turkey' richardfalk.wordpress.com/2012/08/.

Genç Avukatlar Kurultayı (2013) 'Genç avukatlar kurultayı sonuç bildirgesi' www.barobirlik.org.tr/dosyalar/duyurular/sonucbildirgesi.pdf.

Hürriyet (2014) 'Adli yıl açılış töreni kalktı' www.hurriyet.com.tr/adli-yil-acilis-toreni-kalkti-27566137.

İnanıcı, H (2008) *21 yüzyılda avukatlık ve baro* (Istanbul, Legal Yayınevi).

Istanbul Bar Association (1999) 'İstanbul Barosu üyeleri araştırması' unpublished.

Kalem, S (2010) 'Contested meanings-imagined practices: Law at the intersection of mediation and legal profession; a socio-legal study of the juridical field in Turkey' PhD thesis, The New School for Social Research.

—— (2012) 'Türkiye'de hukuk sisteminin en önemli sorunları ve değerlendirme' 5 *Güncel Hukuk* 15–23.

—— (2013) 'Toplumsal cinsiyet ve profesyonelleşme: Hukuk mesleğinde kadın örneği' 16(1) *Sosyoloji Araştırmaları Dergisi* 75–103 dergipark.ulakbim.gov.tr/sosars/article/view/5000093012/5000086489.

Kanani, R (2014) 'The rise of Turkey: The twenty-first century's first Muslim power' *Forbes* 5 March www.forbes.com/sites/rahimkanani/2014/03/05/the-rise-of-turkey-the-twenty-first-centurys-first-muslim-power/#49d474ee6507.

Karabulut, U (2013) 'Muhâmât Kanunu: Türkiye'de avukatlık kurumunun düzenlenmesi ve Istanbul Barosunda yaşanan tasfiyeler' XIII(27) *Çağdaş Türkiye Tarihi Araştırmaları Dergisi* 79–104.

Koğacıoğlu, D (2004) 'Progress, unity and democracy: dissolving political parties in Turkey' 38(3) *Law & Society Review* 433–61.

Letsch, C (2014) 'Turkey's economic success threatened by political instability' *The Guardian*, 9 January www.theguardian.com/world/2014/jan/09/turkey-instability-threatens-economic-success-erdogan.

Mumcu, A (1977) *Ankara Adliye Hukuk Mektebi'nden Ankara Üniversitesi Hukuk Fakültesine (1925–1975)* (Ankara, Ankara Üniversitesi Hukuk Fakültesi Yayınları).

—— (1995) 'Ankara üniversitesi hukuk fakültesi neden ve nasıl kuruldu?' 44(1–4) *Ankara Üniversitesi Hukuk Fakültesi Dergisi* 540–52.

Müftüler-Baç (2016) 'Judicial reform in Turkey and the EU's political conditionality: (Mis)fit between domestic preferences and EU demands' userpage.fu-berlin.de/kfgeu/maxcap/system/files/maxcap_wp_18.pdf.

Öngün, E and Hassan, M (2013) 'How political dynamics work in professional organizations: The radical left and the Istanbul Bar Association' in É Massicard and NF Watts (eds), *Negotiating Political Power in Turkey: Breaking up the Party* (New York, Routledge) 140–56.

Öniş, Z (1992) 'Redemocratization and economic liberalization in Turkey: The limits of state autonomy' 27(2) *Studies in Comparative International Development* 3–23.

Özbudun, E (2012) 'Turkey's search for a new constitution' 14(1) *Insight Turkey* 39–50.

Özkent, AH (1940) *Avukatın kitabı* (İstanbul, Arkadaş Basımevi).

Özman, A (1995) 'The state and bar associations in Turkey: a study in interest-group politics' PhD thesis, Bilkent University.

—— (2000/01) 'Hukuk, siyaset, ideoloji ekseninde hukukçu kimliğinin yeniden tanımlanması: Erken cumhuriyet dönemi üzerine bir inceleme' 87 *Toplum ve Bilim* 164–76.

Öztoprak-Sağır, M (2010) *Güncel gelişmeler ışığında Türkiye'de hukuk eğitimi* (Ankara, TBB Yayınları).

Silverman, R (2017) 'Who's left: Filiz Kerestecioğlu and the struggle for rights in Turkey' 22 February reubensilverman.wordpress.com/2017/02/22/whos-left-filiz-kerestecioglu-and-the-struggle-for-rights-in-turkey/#_ednref48.

Sontag, D (2003) 'The Erdoğan experiment' NY Times Magazine, 11 May www.nytimes.com/2003/05/11/magazine/the-erdogan-experiment.html.

Söğütlü, İ (2004) 'Darülfünun'dan üniversite'ye: Cumhuriyet Türkiyesi'nde ilk üniversite reformu (1933)' 34 *Liberal Düşünce* 121–28.

Şeref, E (2013/14) 'Emergent distinctions in the juridical field: The case of "plaza attorneys" in Turkey' MA thesis, Sabancı University.

Tavşancıl, İ, Demirel, D and Koç, E (2007) Interview with young lawyers (17 November Ankara).

Tekeli, Ş (1991) *Women in Modern Turkish Society* (London, Zed Books.)

Tekinsoy, MA (2007) 'Bağımsız idari otoriteler ve regülasyon anlayışı – Tartışmalar, sorunlar' 65(2) *Ankara Barosu Dergisi* 119–34.

Toprak, M (2014) *Geçmişten günümüze avukatlık kanunları* (Ankara, TBB yayınları).

Türem, U and Ballestero, A (2014) 'Regulatory translations: expertise and affect in global legal fields' 21(1) *Indiana Journal of Global Legal Studies* 1–25.

Türkiye Barolar Birliği (2003/25296) 'Reklam yasağı yönetmeliği' www.barobirlik.org.tr/mevzuat/avukata_ozel/yonetmelikler/belgeler/Reklam_Yasagi_Yonetmeligi.pdf.

—— (2009) 'Yabancı hukuk bürolarıyla ilgili çalışmalar'.

—— (2015/29574) 'Bir avukatın yanında, avukatlık ortaklığında veya avukatlık bürosunda ücret karşılığı birlikte çalışan avukatların çalışma esaslarına ilişkin yönetmelik' www.resmigazete.gov.tr/eskiler/2015/12/20151226-6.htm.

—— (2017) 'Türkiye'nin en iyi hukuk fakülteleri belli oldu' www.barobirlik.org.tr/Detay.aspx?ID=77841.

Yeğen, M (2015) 'The Kurdish peace process in Turkey: genesis, evolution and prospects' Global Turkey in Europe Working Paper 11 www.iai.it/sites/default/files/gte_wp_11.pdf.

Part VII

Asia

35

China

A Tale of Four Decades

SIDA LIU

I. INTRODUCTION

Despite its long history, China has one of the youngest legal professions in the world. In Imperial China, litigation masters (*songshi*) practised informally without establishing an organised occupational group (Macauley 1998). Lawyers as an organised profession emerged in the Republican era in the early twentieth century (Xu 2000), but they were labelled 'rightists' in 1957 after the communists took power, and it was not until after the end of the Cultural Revolution that China revived its legal profession in 1980. Over the next four decades, the Chinese legal profession has grown at a stunning speed, and by November 2017 the number of lawyers exceeded 340,000, working in more than 26,000 law firms across the country (People's Daily 2017). Only a handful of countries (eg India, the US, and Brazil) have more lawyers than China today. And if we include judges, procurators, and alternative legal service providers (eg basic-level legal workers, enterprise legal advisers, etc), China has nearly a million law practitioners.

Like those in many other countries, the legal profession in China is stratified, and the geographic distribution of lawyers is highly unequal. While corporate law firms in Beijing and Shanghai have grown into megafirms with hundreds of lawyers and a complex division of labour, many rural counties in western China still have no lawyers, and most legal services are provided by non-lawyers (Liu and Wu 2016; Li 2016). Furthermore, China's rapidly globalising economy and its resilient authoritarian regime present unique challenges and opportunities for its legal system and profession (Gallagher 2017). To present a relatively comprehensive profile of this rapidly changing profession I discuss four major features: (1) growth in size; (2) stratification and inequality; (3) political activism; and (4) globalisation.

II. GROWTH IN SIZE

To a large extent, the massive growth in the number of Chinese lawyers since 1980 echoes that of the economy. As China started its market reform in the late 1970s, the 1980 Interim Regulation on Lawyers re-established the legal profession. Although the number of lawyers increased steadily in the 1980s, by 1988 there were still only 21,051 full-time and 10,359 part-time lawyers in 3,473 law firms in a country with over a billion people (Liu 2011: 282). Following the Soviet model, all law firms were affiliated with various state agencies or work units, and all lawyers were state employees, just like judges and procurators. A majority of lawyers engaged in criminal defence and ordinary civil litigation, whereas corporate legal work was mostly restricted to transactions involving foreign investors. The shortage of lawyers in the 1980s led the Chinese Ministry of Justice to create a secondary legal profession – township legal workers (*xiangzhen falü gongzuozhe*) – to provide legal services in grassroots communities, where few lawyers practised (Liu 2011; Li 2016).

Two significant reforms were initiated in 1988. First, a new organisational structure, the 'cooperative law firm' (*hezuo lüshi shiwusuo*), was piloted in a few major cities, such as Beijing and Shenzhen. Unlike state-owned law firms, these were collectively owned by the firm's lawyers and received no financial support from the government. They served as a transitional organisational form before partnership law firms were permitted in the 1990s. For instance, Jun He, the first major corporate law firm in Beijing, was established as a cooperative law firm in 1989 and converted into a partnership in 1994 (Liu and Wu 2016: 806). This was the first step in Chinese lawyers' march from the state to the market.

Second, following an internal Bar exam conducted in 1986, the Ministry of Justice organised the first national Bar exam open to the general public in 1988. All Chinese citizens with at least a junior college degree were eligible to take the exam, which became the only path to the legal profession with the adoption of the unified national judicial exam for judges, procurators, and lawyers in 2001 (Stern 2016). The lack of any legal education requirement echoed the practice of other East Asian countries such as Japan and South Korea (Alford 2007), but it also reflected the Chinese government's desire to rapidly expand the number of lawyers in order to meet the needs of the economic reform. The national Bar exam was held biennially until 1993, when it became annual. Many of today's leading lawyers passed the Bar exam in the late 1980s or early 1990s, becoming the first generation of market-oriented lawyers.

The 1990s were a booming decade for the Chinese legal profession. As China's economic reform proceeded, many new areas of practice emerged, especially in eastern cities. In addition to criminal and civil litigation, which remained the primary activity for most lawyers, real estate, securities, foreign direct investment (FDI), mergers and acquisitions (M&A), intellectual property, commercial arbitration and other areas of corporate work also grew, leading to the rise of the first generation of corporate law firms in business centres such as Beijing, Shanghai, and Shenzhen. By the turn of the twenty-first century, the number of lawyers in China had increased to 117,260 in 9,541 law firms (Liu 2016: 186). After a massive 'unhooking and restructuring' (*tuogou gaizhi*) campaign in 2000–01 (Michelson 2003), a majority of Chinese law firms had been privatised into partnership firms, officially permitted by the 1997 Lawyers Law. State-owned law firms survived only in less developed regions and rural areas. Cooperative law firms had also become less popular and were eventually abolished in the 2008 Lawyers Law revision.

In 2001, the national Bar exam for lawyers was merged with the qualifying exams for judges and procurators to create the national judicial exam for all the three legal professions. Except for a few politicised questions concerning the legitimacy and policies of the party-state (Stern 2016), most of the exam tested technical legal knowledge.

Although only a university degree (not necessarily a law degree) was required to take this closed-book exam, over the next two decades the unification of licensing exams for lawyers, judges, and procurators significantly enhanced both the quality of legal professionals and collegiality among the three professions. The pass rate for the first national judicial exam in 2002 was as low as 6.94 per cent, increasing dramatically to about 20 per cent in the late 2000s thanks to a government policy that sought to qualify more legal professionals in rural and western areas, and then declining to less than 15 per cent in the early 2010s (Stern 2016: 512). The number of test-takers, however, kept increasing from fewer than 200,000 in 2003 to more than 400,000 in 2013.

As the numbers of judges and procurators in China have remained relatively stable since 2001, the legal profession absorbed the majority of those passing the national judicial exam and seeking a legal career. In January 2017, it was reported that the number of Chinese lawyers had exceeded 300,000 for the first time (Xinhua News 2017); and by November 2017, the number had increased to more than 340,000 (People's Daily 2017). The nearly threefold increase in the lawyer population from 2000 to 2017 was a result not only of the increasing demand for legal services stemming from China's stunning economic growth but also of the growing supply of law graduates resulting from the proliferation of law schools (Minzner 2013). With the Ministry of Education's national policy of developing 'comprehensive research universities' in the early twenty-first century, the number of Chinese law schools increased from fewer than 200 in the 1990s to more than 600 in 2006, and the number of enrolled law students in China grew from 25,075 in 1991 to 449,295 in 2005 and 613,752 in 2012 (Wang et al 2017: 237, 241). These include law students in four-year undergraduate and research-oriented graduate programmes, both of which follow the civil law tradition, as well as those in the new three-year Juris Master's (JM) programmes modelled on common law institutions, which do not require an undergraduate law degree. The strong supply of law graduates is the primary force driving the dramatic increase in the numbers of national judicial exam test-takers and licensed lawyers in this period.

After nearly four decades of development, the Chinese Bar has become one of the largest in the world. Furthermore, it is important to note that lawyers are only one of several types of legal service providers. Since the 1980s, township legal workers (renamed 'basic-level legal service workers' in 2001) have coexisted with lawyers in providing legal services in urban and rural areas (Alford 1995; Liu 2011). Although the educational and licensing requirements for township legal workers are significantly lower than those for lawyers, the scope of their services includes most of lawyers' work, with the notable exception of criminal defence. Until the turn of the twenty-first century, township legal workers outnumbered lawyers in China and conducted most ordinary litigation, whereas lawyers were both more expensive and less well-connected to local courts and justice bureaux. Although the number of township legal workers declined from a peak of 121,904 in 1999 to 77,408 in 2006 (Liu 2011: 284), and some became lawyers after passing the national judicial exam, this occupation still plays a significant role in providing affordable legal services to ordinary citizens, particularly in less developed and rural areas (Li 2015, 2016; Liu 2017).

In addition to lawyers and township legal workers, enterprise legal advisers (*qiye falü guwen*) in state-owned enterprises (Liu 2012), lawyers in foreign law offices, patent agents, and trademark agents were also separately licensed by the Ministry of Justice and other state ministries. The jurisdictional boundaries between them are often poorly defined due to regulatory fragmentation, and interprofessional competition is prevalent (Abbott 1988; Liu 2015). This kaleidoscopic array of legal professions is very different from the Anglo-American situation, where most legal service providers belong to one or two major legal professions (Abel 1988, 1989; Hagan and Kay 1995). In recent years, with its rapid growth, lawyers have consolidated their status as the primary legal profession in China, but they have not achieved a durable market monopoly (Larson 1977; Abel 1989) and still face serious competition from alternative legal service providers.

III. STRATIFICATION AND INEQUALITY

The rapid growth of Chinese lawyers in the post-Mao era has been accompanied by increasing internal stratification. For any legal profession, there are two main sources of stratification: geography and specialisation. Like the stratification between City solicitors in London and provincial solicitors in the rest of England (Hanlon 1997; Flood 2011), the Chinese Bar is also highly stratified between major cities of the east coast (Beijing, Shanghai, Shenzhen, Guangzhou, Hangzhou, etc) and the rest of China. Within any major city, there is a growing gap between lawyers handling corporate transactions and those conducting ordinary litigation, as the Heinz and Laumann's (1982) 'two-hemisphere thesis' suggests. Gender inequality is evident, though stratification by race and ethnicity is not as notable in China as it is in many other countries (eg Wilkins and Gulati 1996; Headworth et al 2016) because Han are 92 per cent of the Chinese population. Furthermore, another source of stratification – political embeddedness – is more pronounced in China than elsewhere (Michelson 2007; Liu and Halliday 2011). Lawyers with connections to the state's judicial and law enforcement agencies enjoy significant advantages over those without previous work experience or personal ties to the state.

The geographic distribution of Chinese lawyers has experienced two diametrically opposed waves of decentralisation and concentration since the late 1980s. The privatisation of the legal profession in the 1990s vastly improved the availability of lawyers throughout China, decentralising the Chinese Bar. In 2000, no province had more than 10 per cent of full-time Chinese lawyers, and only 4.6 per cent of full-time lawyers (3,159 out of 68,381) practised in Beijing (Liu et al 2014: 194). This decentralisation was not a result of lawyers moving from larger to smaller cities or across provinces, however, but mostly reflected the nationwide proliferation of lawyers and private law firms caused by the rising demand for legal services and the relaxation of state regulatory policies in the reform era.

From the early to mid-2000s, there was a reverse process of concentration in major east coast cities. Whereas the growth in the number of lawyers in the 1990s had been widely dispersed, in the 2000s the redistribution of lawyers was primarily driven by migration from western and inland provinces to major cities such as Beijing, Shanghai, and Shenzhen. This spatial mobility of Chinese lawyers was greatly facilitated by the promulgation of the Administrative License Law in 2003, which abolished most provincial and local restrictions on the registration and practice of out-of-town lawyers. As a result, many migrant lawyers swarmed into Beijing and Shanghai, as well as other major business centres along the east coast. Even though many had to downgrade their practices to lower-end riskier areas such as criminal defence, the prices for legal services, which were much higher in those cities than in their hometowns, constituted a strong incentive for lawyer migration. By 2007, the proportion of full-time lawyers in Beijing had increased to 11.3 per cent (14,522 out of 127,995), and their numbers grew at an average annual rate of 24.4 per cent from 2000 to 2007 (Liu et al 2014: 194). Shanghai and Guangdong Province, two other major destinations for lawyer migration, also had average annual growth rates of approximately 12–13 per cent during this period.

Lawyer migration had two notable consequences. On one hand, it aggravated the shortage of lawyers in western and rural areas, as more capable lawyers often chose to 'fly southeast' (*dong nan fei*) to metropolitan areas with abundant business opportunities and higher billing rates. On the other, it greatly increased market competition in major cities such as Beijing and Shanghai, especially at the low end of the legal services market. To strengthen their market positions, many migrant lawyers began to specialise in less profitable areas of practice, such as divorce, urban demolition, or criminal defence. Some lucky ones were able to carve out a niche for themselves over time, while most migrant lawyers struggled to survive, and many were forced out of the Beijing or Shanghai Bar in less than a year. Nevertheless, the success stories of the few continued to draw newcomers from all over the country.

Triggered by large-scale lawyer migration, specialisation has greatly changed the social structure of the urban Chinese Bar. Although general practitioners are still widespread across China, the two hemispheres of the legal profession (Heinz and Laumann 1982) are more evident today than they were in the early 2000s, when most Chinese lawyers resembled individual entrepreneurs (*getihu*) (Michelson 2007). In the personal sector, lawyers and firms specialising in just one or two areas of practice have become quite common, even in risky fields like criminal defence or labour law (Liu and Halliday 2016; Gallagher 2017). In the corporate sector, a number of Chinese law firms have grown into megafirms of hundreds or even thousands of lawyers, and their organisational structure and management model increasingly resemble those of large, multinational Anglo-American law firms (Liu and Wu 2016; see the 'Globalisation' section below). The gap in income and status between the two hemispheres of the Chinese Bar is increasingly evident.

Yet the stratification of the Chinese legal profession by no means replicates what happened elsewhere, such as the transformation of the American legal profession in the late twentieth century (Heinz and Laumann 1982; Abel 1989). A few notable characteristics distinguish the Chinese case. First, whereas most other legal professions began as solo and small-firm practices (Carlin 1962; Abel and Lewis 1989; Seron 1996), in China the 'individual law firm' (*geren lüshi shiwusuo*), which resembles solo practice, was not permitted until a revised Lawyers Law came into effect in 2008. In other words, for nearly three decades after the legal profession's revival in 1980, most Chinese lawyers had no choice but to join a state-owned, cooperative, or partnership law firm in order to practise. However, except for collecting a commission fee of a fixed percentage of lawyers' billings to cover administrative expenses, many firms provided very little support for their lawyers' daily work (Michelson 2006). This unique history of 'compulsory partnership' not only constrained collegiality in Chinese law firms but also aggravated the inequality of income and status between the 'haves' (eg the firm director and other senior partners) and 'have-nots' (other lawyers). This commission-fee model of law firm management remains popular, even in some of the largest firms (Liu and Wu 2016).

Second, as Michelson (2007) shows in his pioneering study, there is a fundamental division between politically embedded lawyers and others. Politically embedded lawyers have 'ongoing structural relations to the state and its actors' (Michelson 2007: 356): previous work experience in the state sector (eg the police, procuracy, or court) or ongoing personal ties to judicial and other bureaucratic actors in the state through the symbiotic exchange of resources and power (Liu 2011). Political embeddedness not only significantly reduces obstacles in professional practice but also generates business opportunities and improves the lawyer's income and status. From the most profitable areas, such as securities and foreign investments, to the riskiest, such as criminal defence and administrative litigation, politically embedded lawyers enjoy notable advantages over other practitioners (Liu 2006; Liu and Halliday 2011; Stern 2013). And there is no sign that their advantages are declining even after nearly two decades of privatisation.

Third, unlike most other countries where one or two cities (London, Tokyo, Moscow, Paris, etc) dominate the corporate legal market and drive the stratification between the 'city Bar' and the rest of the profession, at least four or five cities belong to the first tier of the Chinese Bar. In this respect, it resembles the US Bar more closely than the legal professions in Europe or other Asian countries. Although Beijing firms have a clear edge in both size and national presence thanks to their proximity to the central ministries and corporate headquarters, Shanghai, Shenzhen, Guangzhou, and Hangzhou are all major markets with large, sophisticated full-service corporate law firms reflecting their vibrant regional and local economies. Even outside China's affluent east coast, many provinces have developed their own ecologies of law firms. While several large Beijing firms (eg Dacheng, DeHeng, and Yingke) have built a national network by expanding to the provinces (Liu and Wu 2016), some law firms in provincial capitals (Hangzhou, Chengdu, Kunming, etc) are also actively expanding to smaller cities within the province and becoming large law firms with multiple offices. The fundamental geographic divide in the Chinese Bar is not so much 'Beijing and Shanghai versus the rest of China' as between major and smaller cities.

The discussion thus far has emphasised the stratification and inequality in geography, areas of practice, and political embeddedness. Yet like most other legal professions, the Chinese is also highly stratified in terms of gender (Kay and Gorman 2008; Michelson 2013). One important difference is that, whereas many other legal professions were entirely male for decades or centuries before feminising, the Chinese profession emerged so recently that women entered at about the same time it expanded. Unfortunately, the issue of gender inequality has not been given enough attention in the Chinese Bar, and even basic statistics on the number and percentage of female lawyers are not published regularly. According to the *Chinese Yearbook of Lawyers*, the *Chinese Women Development Outline (2011–2020)*, and the official statistics of the All China Lawyers Association (ACLA), the percentage of women among Chinese lawyers increased from 13.3 per cent (15,610) in 2000 to 15.8 per cent (24,361) in 2005 and then to 26.6 per cent (61,717) in 2012 and 27.8 per cent (approximately 69,000) in 2013. Although the percentage seems low compared to most legal professions in Europe and the Americas, Michelson's (2013: 1082) study of the global supply of lawyers suggests that the percentages of women in other Asian legal professions (eg Japan, Korea, and India) were significantly lower than that in China. Assuming the growth rate continues, China will soon cross what Michelson (2013: 1083) calls 'an important threshold' in the feminisation of legal professions: 30 per cent.

According to the Shanghai Lawyers Association's official statistics, the percentage was 37.3 per cent (7,751 out of 13,040) in April 2017 (Shanghai Lawyers Association 2017).

Despite the rising percentage of women in the Chinese legal profession, however, they still encounter an enduring 'glass ceiling'. Although there are no reliable national statistics on the percentage of law firm partners who are women, it is common knowledge that most senior partners in major law firms are men. Women in Chinese law firms face the same disadvantages in compensation, promotion, and retention they encounter elsewhere (Kay and Gorman 2008). Sexual harassment by male colleagues is also prevalent in some law offices. If there is anything special in the Chinese case, it is that foreign law offices in China employ a significantly larger proportion of women as associates than Chinese law firms do. It is not unusual to find a foreign law office in Beijing or Shanghai with all female employees except for one or two male partners, a phenomenon that parallels the Indian case (Ballakrishnen 2017). This is partly because women's superior foreign language skills give them an advantage over men when competing for these jobs (Liu 2008: 791). Nevertheless, female associates in foreign law offices still face high barriers to promotion, and many choose to leave and pursue other career options (eg in-house counsel) after a few years. As a recent study shows, a similar 'elastic ceiling' confronts women judges in China (Zheng et al 2017).

The Chinese legal profession is still rapidly evolving. New patterns of stratification and inequality are likely to emerge in the near future, as social forces like feminisation, urbanisation, and globalisation reshape both the supply and demand sides of the profession. In the meantime, the relationship between lawyers and the state remains a key issue for understanding the social structure of the Chinese legal profession. While the discussion in this section has focused on lawyers' political embeddedness, the next section examines the rising political activism among Chinese lawyers in the early twenty-first century.

IV. POLITICAL ACTIVISM

Politics has always been an important dimension for understanding the legal profession (Rueschemeyer 1986; Halliday 1987; Halliday and Karpik 1997; Sarat and Scheingold 1998). In the case of China, however, lawyers' political mobilisation is a recent phenomenon. Until Chinese lawyers were privatised in the 1990s, it was not possible for lawyers working in state-owned law firms to act collectively and challenge the abuse of power by government agencies or law enforcement officials. Even in criminal defence work, which is often considered a highly political area of practice, Chinese lawyers were given no more than seven days to prepare for trial until the 1996 revision of the Criminal Procedure Law (Liu and Halliday 2009).

From the early 2000s, as most law firms were privatised (Michelson 2003), political mobilisation began to emerge. The first wave of lawyer activism was led by the 'progressive elites' (Liu and Halliday 2011) in Beijing and Shanghai. For instance, Xu Zhiyong, Teng Biao, and Yu Jiang, three activist legal scholars in Beijing, filed a petition to the National People's Congress in 2003 regarding Sun Zhigang, a college graduate who migrated to Guangzhou and was beaten to death by the local police (Hand 2006). The petition generated wide public attention and soon led to the abolition of China's notorious 'custody and repatriation' (*shourong qiansong*) system. Xu and Teng continued to pursue constitutional reform and suffered harsh state repression in later years (Teng 2009; Xu 2017). Also in 2003, Zheng Enchong, a Shanghai lawyer, organised a collective lawsuit on behalf of residents illegally evicted by a district government and a wealthy businessman. Yet Zheng was soon arrested and sentenced to three years for leaking state secrets to Human Rights in China, a non-governmental organisation in New York (Fu and Cullen 2008: 114; Biddulph 2015: 201). Another prominent example of this early wave of activism is Gao Zhisheng, who once received a 'Ten Best Lawyers' award from the Ministry of Justice and then started to defend Falun Gong practitioners. In 2006, he was disbarred and sentenced to three years in prison for subverting state power (Gao 2007).

During this first wave of political activism most participants were isolated and collective action was sporadic. However, this began to change dramatically in the late 2000s. In 2008, a group of activist lawyers in Beijing organised a campaign calling for direct election of the Beijing Lawyers Association (BLA) leaders (Cohen 2009). Although the campaign provoked a harsh response from the Beijing Bureau of Justice, which controls BLA's finances and personnel, and many key participants were disbarred or forced out of their law firms (Fu and Cullen 2011; Pils 2015), it generated strong support among Beijing lawyers and led to a reduction of the BLA's annual membership fees. Soon after the end of the BLA direct election campaign, Li Zhuang, a criminal defence lawyer in an elite law firm in Beijing, was arrested in Chongqing in December 2009 and charged with perjury. His trial prompted thousands of lawyers across China to mobilise against the Chongqing authorities and their populist contempt for legal proceduralism (Liu et al 2014). Greatly facilitated by the rise of social media, the Li Zhuang case became a watershed event in the history of lawyer activism in China, leading to the rise of a unique form of lawyer mobilisation, which Chinese lawyers call 'diehard lawyering' (*sike lüshi*).

Participants in the diehard lawyering movement included progressive elites, notable activists, and grassroots activists (Liu and Halliday 2016). Many of these lawyers began to pursue activism locally before the Li Zhuang case, engaging in a variety of practice areas, such as public interest law, environmental law, labour rights, and women's rights. With the increasing popularity of social media in China, particularly Weibo and WeChat, a critical mass of activist lawyers began to organise 'lawyer groups' (*lüshi tuan*) and mobilise collectively. In a series of conspicuous cases, these diehard lawyers used a combination of courtroom drama, street theatre, and online 'surrounding gaze' (Teng 2012) to fight the abuse of power by judges and law enforcement officials. Their online and offline activities generated wide public attention and often led to concessions by the judicial authorities in the early stage of the diehard lawyer movement (eg the Beihai case in 2011 and the Xiaohe case in 2012).

Political mobilisation in an authoritarian context is very risky, however, and some diehard lawyers soon paid a heavy price. On 9 July 2015, the Chinese government initiated a large-scale crackdown on diehard lawyers across the country, in which over 200 were detained by the police and state security. Although most were released after a short period of questioning, several human rights lawyers were held for more than six months and criminally charged (Liu and Halliday 2016; Fu 2018). This so-called '709 Crackdown' (ie crackdown on 9 July) dealt a heavy blow to the diehard lawyering movement, nearly eviscerating its human rights core. High-profile human rights lawyers such as Li Heping, Wang Quanzhang, Wang Yu, Zhang Kai, and Zhou Shifeng were either convicted or released on bail after a televised confession. It was also a dire warning to all lawyers who participated in or supported the diehard lawyering movement that the party-state would not tolerate collective action against it.

After this massive crackdown, the Chinese government continued to intensify the regulation of lawyers' behaviour inside and outside the courtroom, including online speeches. In 2017, two lawyers in Zhejiang Province and Shandong Province, respectively, were sanctioned by the local justice bureaux and Bar associations for inappropriate social media posts against the regime. The licence of the Zhejiang lawyer, Wu Youshui, was suspended for nine months for unethical comments against the Bar association and the justice bureau (Hangzhou Lawyers Association 2017); and the Shandong lawyer Zhu Shengwu was disbarred for 'anti-Communist Party, anti-socialist' comments (Cao 2017). In August 2017 the Minister of Justice, Zhang Jun, personally conducted a two-day training session for criminal defence lawyers, including some participants of the diehard lawyering movement. This was widely perceived as an effort to persuade activist lawyers to bow to the state's interests.

With both sticks and carrots, therefore, the Chinese state seeks to limit lawyers to the courtroom and the economy. Yet the momentum of Chinese lawyers' political activism did not cease after July 2015. Instead, it has spilled over from criminal defence and human rights to other areas of law practice, such as labour rights, women's rights, LGBT rights, and environmental protection. Activist lawyers were working in those areas before 2015, but their numbers were small, and many were supported by foreign donors (Stern 2013; Wang 2013; Halegua 2016). After the 709 Crackdown, however, some diehard lawyers who had focused on criminal cases began to shift their attention to these less sensitive areas. Some filed environmental lawsuits against local governments for air pollution, while others represented LGBT activists in their struggles against employment discrimination and marriage inequality. Because the Chinese government does not see these issues as being as subversive as human rights, and lawyers mostly use civil or administrative litigation to hold the relevant authorities accountable, such challenges are more difficult for the state to repress. Activism in those grey zones of legal practice deserves more attention.

The future of lawyer activism in China is highly uncertain. Unlike lawyers who fight for basic legal freedoms in many other social contexts (Halliday and Karpik 1997; Halliday et al Feeley 2007, 2012; Marshall and Hale 2014), Chinese lawyers work in a repressive and unpredictable political environment. The capacity for political mobilisation depends on where the state sets the boundaries of acceptable practice (Stern and O'Brien 2012). In this context, lawyers have no choice but to try different areas of practice and adopt creative strategies like diehard lawyering in order to survive and pursue their political goals. It is 'a deadly serious cat-and-mouse game' (Liu and Halliday 2016: 181), which occurs daily.

V. GLOBALISATION

While activist lawyers in China engage the state, corporate lawyers are fighting another battle: to make their firms as large and competitive as the so-called 'global law firms' from Western countries. Although China is arguably a latecomer to the global market for legal services, ever since the founding of the first generation of corporate law firms in the early 1990s elite Chinese lawyers have modelled their firms on global law firms from Britain and the United States. In their early years, most Chinese corporate law firms merely helped with the FDI, M&A and related corporate transactional work of foreign law offices, which were permitted by the Ministry of Justice to enter China in 1992. By the turn of the twenty-first century, however, a few Chinese law firms (eg Jun He, Haiwen, and King & Wood) had developed strong expertise in high-end corporate law by recruiting Chinese lawyers who studied and worked abroad (Liu 2006). Accordingly, the relationship between domestic and foreign law offices in China gradually changed from collaboration to competition, especially in inbound FDI (Liu 2008).

Competition between foreign and domestic law firms in China has always been unequal because foreign law offices may not handle 'Chinese legal affairs' or employ licensed PRC lawyers. Although these restrictions are often compromised in practice, and many foreign law offices routinely employ Chinese lawyers willing to suspend their Bar registrations (Liu 2008), the rules still constitute a significant legal obstacle to the expansion of foreign law firms in China. However, for elite Chinese law firms, the threat of future mergers by large Anglo-American law firms was the real concern. To prevent this from happening and get ahead of their domestic competition, a few major Chinese firms began to expand domestically and internationally in the mid-2000s. While most foreign law offices in China remain small 'outpost offices' (Stern and Li 2016), by the mid-2010s the largest Chinese law firms had grown into megafirms with thousands of lawyers (Liu and Wu 2016).

The speed and magnitude of law firm growth in China in the early twenty-first century were unprecedented anywhere in the world. In 2002, the largest Chinese law firm, King & Wood, had five offices and fewer than 200 lawyers. By 2015, the largest firm was Dacheng, with over 4,000 lawyers in 51 offices, eight outside mainland China. The fastest-growing firm, Yingke, expanded from fewer than 30 lawyers in 2008 to over 3,000 in 2015. The growth of these large Chinese law firms followed different models. Whereas King & Wood adopted an 'assimilation' model, recruiting lateral partners from other firms, Dacheng expanded by an 'accommodation' model, merging local firms across China into its franchise, and Yingke's miraculous growth was based on an innovative 'space-rental' model, securing office space first and then recruiting lawyers to fill it (Liu and Wu 2016). The three paths led to the same outcome, however: by the mid-2010s, China had some of the world's largest law firms.

The massive domestic expansion was followed by a wave of globalisation. Although Chinese law firms started to establish offices abroad as early as Jun He's New York office in 1993, international expansion was slow and steady until 2008. Most overseas offices remained small satellite operations with only one or two partners and limited business. Even in Hong Kong, which was returned to China by Britain in 1997 but remains a separate legal jurisdiction, only Jun He and Grandall had officially opened offices through alliances with two local law firms as late as 2008. However, the global financial crisis that year was a turning point for the globalisation of Chinese law firms, most of which survived it without much damage (Li and Liu 2012). While Western law firms struggled to recover from the crisis, the global footprint of Chinese law firms has vastly expanded, with locations ranging from global cities such as New York, London, Tokyo, and Singapore to less obvious places such as Detroit, Istanbul, Mexico City, and São Paulo.

In March 2012, King & Wood, an elite Chinese law firm with more than a thousand lawyers, announced a merger with Mallesons Stephen Jaques, a large Australian law firm with 800 lawyers, creating King & Wood Mallesons (KWM) using the Swiss verein structure, which allowed the two firms to share the same brand yet retain financial independence. In November 2013, KWM merged with the British firm SJ Berwin using the same structure, adding 900 lawyers and more offices in Europe and the Middle East. The two KWM mergers made international headlines by creating the first global law firm dominated by the Chinese. In 2015, Dacheng, the largest Chinese law firm, made a similar alliance with the global law firm Dentons, creating the largest law firm in the world with over 7,000 lawyers and more than a hundred offices around the globe. In just three years, two Chinese law firms had transformed themselves into global firms.

The Swiss verein structure allows both King & Wood and Dacheng to maintain their legal status as domestic Chinese firms while seeking alliances with foreign law firms abroad. Nevertheless, the structure has not been widely appropriated by other Chinese law firms. For example, Jun He and Zhong Lun, both of which are widely regarded as the peers of King & Wood within the Chinese corporate bar, decided to remain domestic law firms and limit their overseas offices to a few key global cities, such as New York, London, and Tokyo. In the meantime, they have maintained a good cooperative relationship with a large number of elite Anglo-American law firms, including the Magic Circle firms in Britain and Wall Street firms in the United States. In comparison to the aggressive expansion of King & Wood and Dacheng, this more cautious approach enables the Chinese firms to maintain their autonomy while working with more prestigious firms and clients abroad. A similar strategy has been adopted by a few elite boutique firms, such as Haiwen, Fangda, and Han Kun. Instead of seeking rapid growth, they chose to specialise in a few high-end areas of practice, such as securities, private equity, and commercial arbitration, to maintain their expertise and elite status – a process Liu and Wu (2016) call 'purification' (as opposed to King & Wood's 'assimilation').

Just when many expected the globalisation of Chinese law firms to accelerate, its pioneer, King & Wood, suffered a major setback. In January 2017, the European arm of KWM, which had merged with the legacy firm SJ Berwin in 2013, went into administration after the defection of many lawyers, including several high-profile London partners. This constituted the largest law firm failure in the history of the UK legal services market. Although the collapse of KWM in Europe had no direct financial impact on its Chinese and Australian arms thanks to the verein structure, it damaged the reputation of the entire firm. To rescue the firm, KWM China took over some of KWM Europe's offices and sent a senior partner to London to manage them. However, the global reputation of the KWM brand will take years to recover.

The failure of KWM Europe lowered not only its global ambitions but also those of other major Chinese law firms. It made many partners realise that international expansion is a long winding road, and a highly aggressive approach could be counterproductive. Nevertheless, with the launch of China's 'Belt & Road Initiative' in the mid-2010s, which aims to expand China's economic influence on adjacent Asian and Eurasian countries, more Chinese law firms are expected to help their clients navigate the world. It is also possible that the geographic focus of new overseas offices will gradually shift from conspicuous global cities such as New York and London to China's neighbours. After all, we are only witnessing the beginning of Chinese law firms' global expansion.

VI. CONCLUSION

For nearly four decades, the Chinese legal profession has developed in the belief that China had a shortage of lawyers and Chinese law firms needed to grow bigger and stronger to catch up with their Western counterparts. By the late 2010s, however, those assumptions seem increasingly outdated. China already has one of the largest number of lawyers in the world, and the population/lawyer ratio has decreased to less than 5,000, lower than those of most of China's East Asian neighbours and many other countries. It is no longer possible to call Chinese law a system of 'law without lawyers' (Li 1978). Meanwhile, Chinese law firms have successfully made the transition from Soviet-style state-owned firms to Western-style partnerships, and some of the leading firms have grown into megafirms with a global presence (Liu and Wu 2016).

Yet the story of Chinese lawyers is not just a happy one of growth and modernisation. Beneath the veneer of a rapidly expanding and specialising profession, lawyers still face significant competition from a variety of alternative legal service providers in China, including basic-level legal services, enterprise legal advisers, foreign law offices, patent agents, and unauthorised practitioners (Liu 2011, 2015). Furthermore, the most serious threats to lawyers' practice still come from the state, as activist lawyers continue to suffer harsh repression (Pils 2015; Liu and Halliday 2016; Fu 2018) and the Communist Party's control over the legal profession strengthens under Xi Jinping's leadership (Minzner 2018). It is no exaggeration to say that the Chinese legal profession is one of the most vibrant but also most precarious professions in history, and its future remains unclear.

REFERENCES

Abbott, A (1988) *The System of Professions: An Essay on the Division of Expert Labor* (Chicago, University of Chicago Press).
Abel, RL (1988) *The Legal Profession in England and Wales* (Oxford, Blackwell).
—— (1989) *American Lawyers* (Oxford: Oxford University Press).
Abel, RL and Lewis, PSC (eds) (1989) *Lawyers in Society: Vol III Comparative Theories* (Berkeley, University of California Press).
Alford, WP (1995) 'Tasselled Loafers for Barefoot Lawyers: Transformations and Tensions in the World of Chinese Lawyers' 141 *China Quarterly* 22–38.
Alford, WP (ed) (2007) *Raising the Bar: The Emerging Legal Profession in East Asia* (Cambridge, Ma, Harvard University Press).
Ballakrishnen, SS (2017) '"She Gets the Job Done": Entrenched Gender Meanings and New Returns to Essentialism in India's Elite Professional Firms' 4 *Journal of Professions and Organization* 324–42.
Biddulph, S (2015) *The Stability Imperative: Human Rights and Law in China* (Vancouver, University of British Columbia Press).
Cao, Y (2017) 'Little-Known Chinese Lawyer Disbarred for Defending Freedom of Speech' *China Change*, 3 October chinachange.org/2017/10/03/little-known-chinese-lawyer-disbarred-for-defending-freedom-of-speech/.
Carlin, JE (1962) *Lawyers on Their Own: A Study of Individual Practitioners in Chicago* (New Brunswick, NJ, Rutgers University Press).
Cohen, JA (2009) 'The Struggle for Autonomy of Beijing's Public Interest Lawyers' (Human Rights in China) 1 April www.hrichina.org/en/content/3692.

Flood, J (2011) 'The Re-landscaping of the Legal Profession: Large Law Firms and Professional Re-regulation' 59 *Current Sociology* 507–29.

Fu, H (2018) 'The July 9th (709) Crackdown on Human Rights Lawyers: Legal Advocacy in an Authoritarian State' *Journal of Contemporary China* 15 February 2018 doi.org/10.1080/10670 564.2018.1433491.

Fu, H and Cullen, R (2008) 'Weiquan (rights protection) Lawyering in an Authoritarian State: Building a Culture of Public-Interest Lawyering' 59 *China Journal* 111–27.

—— (2011) 'Climbing the Weiquan Ladder: A Radicalizing Process for Rights-Protection Lawyers' 205 *China Quarterly* 40–59.

Gallagher, ME (2017) *Authoritarian Legality in China: Law, Workers, and the State* (Cambridge, Cambridge University Press).

Gao, Z (2007) *A China More Just: My Fight as a Rights Lawyer in the World's Largest Communist State* (Los Angeles, Broad Press).

Hagan, J and Kay, F (1995) *Gender in Practice, A Study of Lawyers' Lives* (Oxford, Oxford University Press).

Halegua, A (2016) 'Who Will Represent China's Workers? Lawyers, Legal Aid, and the Enforcement of Labor Rights' Report of the US-Asia Law Institute, New York University School of Law, October 2016 www.aaronhalegua.com/chinasworkers.

Halliday, TC (1987) *Beyond Monopoly: Lawyers, State Crises, and Professional Empowerment* (Chicago, University of Chicago Press).

Halliday, TC and Karpik, L (eds) (1997) *Lawyers and the Rise of Western Political Liberalism: Europe and North American from the Eighteenth to Twentieth Centuries* (Oxford, Clarendon Press).

Halliday, TC, Karpik, L and Feeley, MM (eds) (2007) *Fighting for Political Freedom: Comparative Studies of the Legal Complex and Political Liberalism* (Oxford, Hart Publishing).

—— (2012) *Fates of Political Liberalism in the British Post-Colony: The Politics of the Legal Complex* (Cambridge, Cambridge University Press).

Hand, KJ (2006) 'Using Law for a Righteous Purpose: The Sun Zhigang Incident and Evolving Forms of Citizen Action in the People's Republic of China' 45 *Columbia Journal of Transnational Law* 114–95.

Hangzhou Lawyers Association (2017) 'Hangzhou Lawyers Association's Decision Letter on the Sanction of Lawyer Wu Youshui' 18 August weibo.com/ttarticle/p/show?id=23094041421664390 11681&ssl_rnd=1510492240.158.

Hanlon, G (1997) 'A Profession in Transition? Lawyers, the Market and Significant Others' 60 *Modern Law Review* 798–822.

Headworth, S, Nelson, RL, Dinovitzer, R and Wilkins, DB (eds) (2016) *Diversity in Practice: Race, Gender, and Class in Legal and Professional Careers* (Cambridge, Cambridge University Press).

Heinz, JP and Laumann, EO (1982) *Chicago Lawyers: The Social Structure of the Bar* (New York, Russell Sage Foundation and Chicago: American Bar Foundation).

Kay, F and Gorman, E (2008) 'Women in the Legal Profession' 4 *Annual Review of Law & Social Science* 299–332.

Larson, MS (1977) *The Rise of Professionalism: A Sociological Analysis* (Berkeley, University of California Press).

Li, K (2015) '"What He Did Was Lawful": Divorce Litigation and Gender Inequality in China' 37 *Law & Policy* 153–79.

—— (2016) 'Relational Embeddedness and Socially Motivated Case Screening in the Practice of Law in Rural China' 50 *Law & Society Review* 920–52.

Li, VH (1978) *Law without Lawyers: A Comparative View of Law in China and the United States* (Boulder, Westview Press).

Li, X and Liu, S (2012) 'The Learning Process of Globalization: How Chinese Law Firms Survived the Financial Crisis' 80 *Fordham Law Review* 2847–66.

Liu, S (2006) 'Client Influence and the Contingency of Professionalism: The Work of Elite Corporate Lawyers in China' 40 *Law & Society Review* 751–82.

—— (2008) 'Globalization as Boundary-Blurring: International and Local Law Firms in China's Corporate Law Market' 42 *Law & Society Review* 771–84.

—— (2011) 'Lawyers, State Officials, and Significant Others: Symbiotic Exchange in the Chinese Legal Services Market' 206 *China Quarterly* 276–93.

—— (2012) 'Palace Wars over Professional Regulation: In-House Counsel in Chinese State-owned Enterprises' *Wisconsin Law Review* 549–71.

—— (2015) 'Boundary Work and Exchange: The Formation of a Professional Service Market' 38 *Symbolic Interaction* 1–21.

—— (2016) 'The Changing Roles of Lawyers in China: State Bureaucrats, Market Brokers, and Political Activists' in H Klug and SE Merry (eds), *The New Legal Realism: Studying Law Globally* (Cambridge, Cambridge University Press) 180–97.

Liu, S and Halliday, TC (2009) 'Recursivity in Legal Change: Lawyers and Reforms of China's Criminal Procedure Law' 34 *Law & Social Inquiry* 911–50.

—— (2011) 'Political Liberalism and Political Embeddedness: Understanding Politics in the Work of Chinese Criminal Defense Lawyers' 45 *Law & Society Review* 831–65.

—— (2016) *Criminal Defense in China: The Politics of Lawyers at Work* (Cambridge, Cambridge University Press).

Liu, S, Liang, L and Halliday, TC (2014) 'The Trial of Li Zhuang: Chinese Lawyers' Collective Action against Populism' 1 *Asian Journal of Law and Society* 79–97.

Liu, S, Liang, L and Michelson, H (2014) 'Migration and Social Structure: The Spatial Mobility of Chinese Lawyers' 36 *Law & Policy* 165–94.

Liu, S and Wu, H (2016) 'The Ecology of Organizational Growth: Chinese Law Firms in the Age of Globalization' 122 *American Journal of Sociology* 798–837.

Macauley, M (1998) *Social Power and Legal Culture: Litigation Masters in Late Imperial China* (Stanford, Stanford University Press).

Marshall, A-M and Crocker Hale, D (2014) 'Cause Lawyering' 10 *Annual Review of Law and Social Science* 301–20.

Michelson, E (2003) 'Unhooking from the State: Chinese Lawyers in Transition' PhD thesis, Department of Sociology, University of Chicago.

—— (2006) 'The Practice of Law as an Obstacle to Justice: Chinese Lawyers at Work' 40 *Law & Society Review* 1–38.

—— (2007) 'Lawyers, Political Embeddedness, and Institutional Continuity in China's Transition from Socialism' 113 *American Journal of Sociology* 352–414.

—— (2013) 'Women in the Legal Profession, 1970–2010: A Study of the Global Supply of Lawyers' 20 *Indiana Journal of Global Legal Studies* 1071–137.

Minzner, CF (2013) 'The Rise and Fall of Chinese Legal Education' 36 *Fordham International Law Journal* 334–95.

—— (2018) *End of an Era: How China's Authoritarian Revival Is Undermining Its Rise* (Oxford, Oxford University Press).

People's Daily (2017) 'The Party Committee for the National Legal Profession was Founded' 1 November 1 legal.people.com.cn/n1/2017/1101/c42510-29619220.html.

Pils, E (2015) *China's Human Rights Lawyers: Advocacy and Resistance* (London, Routledge).

Rueschemeyer, D (1986) 'Comparing Legal Professions Cross-Nationally: From a Profession-Centered to a State-Centered Approach' 11 *American Bar Foundation Research Journal* 415–46.

Sarat, A and Scheingold, S (eds) (1998) *Cause Lawyering: Political Commitments and Professional Responsibilities* (Oxford, Oxford University Press).

Seron, C (1996) *The Business of Practicing Law: The Work Lives of Solo and Small-Firm Attorneys* (Philadelphia, Temple University Press).

Shanghai Lawyers Association (2017) 'Shanghai has a Total of over 20,000 Lawyers' 27 April mp.weixin.qq.com/s/LRwY_H6u8IBQz1u-iF2sTQ.

Stern, RE (2013) *Environmental Litigation in China: A Study in Political Ambivalence* (Cambridge, Cambridge University Press).

—— (2016) 'Political Reliability and the Chinese Bar Exam; 43 *Journal of Law and Society* 506–33.

Stern, RE and Li, S (2016) 'The Outpost Office: How International Law Firms Approach the China Market' 41 *Law & Social Inquiry* 184–211.

Stern, RE and O'Brien, KJ (2012) 'Politics at the Boundary: Mixed Signals and the Chinese State' 38 *Modern China* 174–98.

Teng, B (2009) 'I Cannot Give Up: Record of a Kidnapping' (1) *China Rights Forum* 30–41.

—— (2012) 'Rights Defense (weiquan), Microblogs (weibo), and the Surrounding Gaze (weiguan)' (3) *China Perspectives* 29–41.

Wang, AL (2013) 'The Search for Sustainable Legitimacy: Environmental Law and Bureaucracy in China' 37 *Harvard Environmental Law Review* 365–440.

Wang, Z, Liu, S and Li, X (2017) 'Internationalizing Chinese Legal Education in the Early Twenty-First Century' 66 *Journal of Legal Education* 237–66.

Wilkins, DB and Mitu Gulati, G (1996) '"Why Are There So Few Black Lawyers in Corporate Law Firms? An Institutional Analysis' 84 *California Law Review* 493–625.

Xinhua News (2017) 'The Number of Lawyers in Our Country Has Exceeded 300,000' 9 January news.xinhuanet.com/politics/2017-01/09/c_1120275319.htm.

Xu, X (2000) *Chinese Professionals and the Republican State: The Rise of Professional Associations in Shanghai, 1912–1937* (Cambridge, Cambridge University Press).

Xu, Z (2017) *To Build a Free China: A Citizen's Journey* (Boulder, Lynne Rienner Publishers).

Zheng, C, Ai, J and Liu, S (2017) 'The Elastic Ceiling: Gender and Professional Career in Chinese Courts' 51 *Law & Society Review* 168–99.

36

India

Present and Future: A Revised Sociological Portrait

SWETHAA S BALLAKRISHNEN*

I. INTRODUCTION

Accounts of the Indian legal profession generally concur that its state at independence was cause for grave concern. The elements of this historic 'pathology' (Mendelsohn 1981) or 'crisis' (Baxi 1982) reinforced each other: India had ill-developed feeder institutions to train lawyers (Von Mehren 1965); the profession had little formal organisation and depended excessively on kinship (Morrison 1972); and corrupt 'tout' networks (Gandhi 1982) perpetuated inequalities. Averting a bleak future, as Gandhi warned (1989: 379), would require a 'radical change'. By contrast with these doomsayers, other observers pointed to systemic triumphs such as public interest or 'social action' litigation (PIL),[1] and these micro-institutional accounts, though not representative of the profession, contributed to a more nuanced portrait. However, as Galanter's early 'incomplete bibliography' (1969a) indicates, both sweeping characterisations (of the profession as doomed) and accounts of specific deficiencies (and triumphs) pointed to the challenges of offering a comprehensive picture of India's large, multi-faceted legal system.

Galanter's note about the difficulties of surveying comprehensively a very heterogeneous professional system remains true, as does his lament about inadequate and unreliable data. In the half-century since he wrote, accounts of the profession remain either too broad or too narrow. Most research is historical (Paul 1991) or confined to specific facets: for

---

* Alongside the gratitude I owe to the editorial team for their comprehensive revisions, I wish to thank Aparna Asokan, Rabiya Imran and Rupali Samuel for research assistance at various stages of this project, as well as Marc Galanter, Bryon Fong, Bryant Garth, Aniruddha Jairam, Kalpana Kannabiran, Rahela Khorakiwala, Jay Krishnan, Sida Liu, Nick Robinson, Suryapratim Roy, Carol Silver, and David Wilkins for invaluable comments and reviews of earlier drafts and presentations of this chapter.

[1] PIL benefited from the relaxation of formal rules by socially progressive judges starting in the late 1970s (Baxi 1985; Mendelsohn 1991; Sathe 2002; Galanter and Krishnan 2003). Catapulted to national significance following the Emergency years (1975–77), the PIL movement appeared to demonstrate the capacity of the legal profession to respond to social change. PIL scholarship has since become more conflicted about its success and political implications (Gauri and Brinks 2008; Bhuwania 2016); but most agree that PIL forced a rethinking of judicial capacities.

example, the Amritsar litigating Bar (Gandhi 1982), women lawyers in the Punjab High Court (Sethi 1987), Lok Adalats in Uttar Pradesh (Moog 1998), gender in the Delhi courts (Sharma 2002) or the Uttar Pradesh district courts (Mishra 2015). Even the most ambitious recent study (Wilkins et al 2017) addresses only the corporate sector of the profession. Primary data are even harder to find. As discussed below, the *Access to Justice* survey by the non-governmental organisation (NGO) Daksh contains one of the few large-scale data sets. The Law Commission of India periodically publishes reports on lawyers and the legal process but usually focused on litigants and lawsuits. The Bar Council of India no longer publishes the number and gender of enrolled advocates by state.[2] Data requests to individual Bar associations proved largely fruitless,[3] and despite efforts to collect more comprehensive data through a new verification processes, they remain scarce and unreliable.[4]

As a result, this review cannot present broad demographics or systematic categorical analysis. It also does not duplicate the excellent existing reviews of existing scholarship (Garth 2016; Krishnan and Thomas 2015; Sharafi 2015). Instead, I focus on three institutional changes that complicate earlier understandings of the Indian legal profession: (a) legal education, especially the five-year National Law Schools; (b) the new organisational forms employing their graduates; and (c) the regulation of legal practice, especially the distinction between local and foreign lawyers. To ground this inquiry theoretically, I ask which actors are embedded within which institutions and how that affects closure mechanisms.

II. PROFESSIONAL PORTRAIT: PERSISTENT PATTERNS IN A (MOSTLY) UNCHANGING PROFESSION

The widely touted number of 'over a million' lawyers in India is a close approximation to the truth. The estimate offered by the Bar Council of India (BCI) has varied between 1.7 and 1.2 million (Legally India 2013). In 2011, it reported that 'approximately' 400–500,000 were studying law and 60–70,000 graduating annually (Ganz 2011). These numbers are both small in comparison to the population and large given the GDP. The ratio of one lawyer for every thousand people is comparable to that in many other countries, if far less than in the US and UK. Similarly, the GDP per lawyer in India is about $1.4 million – a strikingly small amount, especially when compared to other lawyer-heavy countries (Ganz 2011).[5]

Although there is deep stratification within the profession, the bar to entry remains relatively low. Lawyers are governed by the Advocate Act, 1961, which stipulates that lawyers must have a law degree, be at least 21, and pay a stamp duty and a modest fee to

---

[2] In 2010 the Legal Education Committee and Bar Council of India introduced new rules for admission to the bar, including passing the All India Bar Exam (AIBE): allindiabarexamination.com/.

[3] Responses to applications under the Right to Information Act for lawyer demographics revealed that this information has not been collected systematically.

[4] The Bar Council of India Certificate and Place of Practice (Verification) Rules, 2015 required State Bar Councils to collect and verify data about enrolled lawyers. A challenge before the Supreme Court is pending (*Ajayinder Sangwan v Bar Council of Delhi*, Transfer Case (Civil) No 126 of 2015).

[5] According to these data, Israel, a country with a low ratio of population per lawyer, has about $5.4 million GDP per lawyer. Countries like the US and UK have GDPs of $12.1 million/lawyer and $18.9 million/lawyer respectively. Japan is at the other extreme on both indices: $236 million GDP per lawyer and 5,534 people per lawyer.

enrol in a Bar council. Admission to one Bar allows advocates to practise in every court. An estimated 50–80,000 students graduate annually from over 900 law schools, but the BCI's efforts to require a national qualifying examination have generated controversy and legal challenges (Venkatesan 2011).[6]

A BCI response to a 2013 Right to Information request from Kush Karla, a Delhi advocate, revealed more comprehensive data (see Table 1). The estimate of 1.3 million lawyers is considerably less than the 1.7 million lawyers cited by the BCI Chairman a few months before these data became public (Vyawahare 2013). The state data further reveal a fragmented localised profession: lawyers in Uttar Pradesh (with the most lawyers) or Punjab and Haryana and Delhi (with high lawyer densities) are fundamentally different from those in states like Jharkhand or Jammu and Kashmir (which have small but faster-growing legal professions). And though the national ratio of 886 people per lawyer is lower than the thousand estimated by Ganz two years earlier, there is huge regional variation, from Delhi (309) and Punjab and Haryana (391) to Jharkhand (3,369) and remote regions with serious problems of political integration (Assam, Nagaland etc 1,436).

The reliability of these numbers was questioned when a 2015 BCI verification drive reportedly found that almost half the profession was not practising (Garg 2017), even in the capital, Delhi (Azeem 2016). Here, too, numbers are speculative – news reports claim that anywhere between 45 per cent (Garg 2017) and 60 per cent (Sarda 2017) of lawyers are 'false', illustrating the difficulty of distinguishing licensed lawyers who practise from licensed lawyers who do not and unlicensed lawyers who do.

These phantom lawyers – and the BCI's characterisation of them as threats to the health of the profession[7] – are important reminders about the state of legal education. A law degree is still seen as easy to obtain, especially since many talented students choose other subjects (Dhru 2010). As in other countries a law degree in India confers status, whether or not the holder practises (Rosalio 1970), and this is especially important for those seeking political office (Arora 1972). But the benefits may be diminishing. For example, while almost a third (15) of Narendra Modi's 44-member ministry cabinet held a law degree (the most common professional degree) in 2014, only 4 per cent of current Lok Sabha members are lawyers (compared with 36 per cent of the first Lok Sabha in 1952 and 31.8 and 29.1 per cent of the Seventh and Eighth Lok Sabhas).[8]

A. Gender

Gandhi (1989) does not mention women in his study except to note their absence (1989: 373), and there are only a few more women in the profession now than there

---

[6] Whether BCI can require such an examination as a condition for admission to a state Bar is before a constitutional bench of the Supreme Court. Meanwhile, examinations under the AIBE are still being conducted. For a case in favour of the AIBE, see thewire.in/25073/in-defence-of-the-all-india-bar-exam/ (Utkarsh Srivastava, 17 March 2016). Shamnad Basheer, a prominent legal education activist, has argued that the AIBE requirement is unconstitutional without an amendment of the Advocates Act. See www.livelaw.in/right-to-practice-law-is-a-fundamental-right-and-aibe-negates-the-very-right-sc/. Srivastava and Basheer are alumni of the 5-year national law schools described below. See also Basheer and Mukherjee (2010).

[7] BCI Chairman Manan Kumar Mishra said about the verification drive: 'The number of practicing lawyers is about to come down to 55–60% after the completion of the verification process. This will certainly improve the quality of our legal profession' (Garg 2017).

[8] Gandhi (1989: 381).

Table 1 Number of Lawyers

Area	Total Advocates	Advocates enrolled in last 5 years	5-year growth %	Annual Growth rate last 5 years %	State GDP (US$bn)	GDP / lawyer (US$)	State population (m)	Population per lawyer
Uttar Pradesh	288,297	51,335	17.8	3.6	122.9	426,366	200	692
Bihar	113,298	13,394	11.8	2.4	47.7	420,749	104	916
Maharashtra & Goa	112,706	28,547	25.3	5.1	222.8	1,976,470	114	1,010
Andhra Pradesh	80,225	12,922	16.1	3.2	124.8	1,555,126	85	1,055
Karnataka	74,032	15,615	21.1	4.2	84.6	1,143,289	61	826
Tamil Nadu	67,000	15,924	23.8	4.8	115.5	1,723,284	72	1,077
Punjab & Haryana	64,826	16,831	26.0	5.2	103.4	1,595,039	25	391
Madhya Pradesh	64,562	15,704	24.3	4.9	52.7	816,579	33	517
Gujarat	64,261	7,071	11.0	2.2	105.4	1,640,186	60	940
Rajasthan	63,370	15,454	24.4	4.9	67.2	1,060,439	69	1,083
West Bengal	59,535	n/a			100.0	1,679,180	91	1,534
Delhi	54,258	15,709	29.0	5.8	57.0	1,050,536	17	309
Orissa	44,625	5,831	13.1	2.6	41.1	921,681	42	940
Kerala	43,339	5,656	13.1	2.6	59.4	1,370,359	33	770
Assam, Nagaland, etc	23,077	7,074	30.7	6.1	23.2	1,004,030	33	1,436
Chhatisgarh	22,940	4,409	19.2	3.8	24.6	1,072,363	26	1,113
Jharkhand	9,789	4,378	44.7	8.9	21.7	2,216,774	33	3,368
Uttarakhand	9,277	2,821	30.4	6.1	15.8	1,703,137	10	1,091
Himachal Pradesh	7,921	1,770	22.3	4.5	11.4	1,439,212	7	866
Jammu & Kashsmir	5,951	2,080	35.0	7.0	12.1	2,028,231	13	2,109
TOTAL	1,273,289	242,525	19.0	3.8	1413.2	1,109,850	1,128	886

Source: Legally India (2013).

were in the 1981 census (his data point). Although India enacted the Legal Practitioners (Women) Act of 1923 in response to the Allahabad Bar's admission of Cornelia Sorabji as the first woman lawyer, the number of women lawyers remained very low until 1991 (Table 2). Furthermore, although it was predicted (based on their representation among law students) that women would be 40 per cent of the profession before 2005

Table 2 Gender of Legal Professionals (Per Cent)

	1961		1971		1981		1991	
Category	Male	Female	Male	Female	Male	Female	Male	Female
Judges and Magistrates	98.4	1.6	98.9	1.1	97.8	2.2	97.1	2.9
Legal Practitioners and Advisers	99.3	0.7	99.0	1.0	95.4	4.6	93.2	6.8
Legal Assistants	99.2	0.8	99.9	0.04	98.8	1.2	98.9	1.1
Jurists and Legal Technicians	99.0	1.0	99.9	1.0	98.9	1.1	98.3	1.7

Sources: Nagla (2001: 77) Sharma (2002: 96).

(Sharma 2002: 97), they remain a mere 10 per cent (approximately) of lawyers registered with the BCI (Ballakrishnen 2017: Table 3).

Ethan Michelson's comparative demography of the legal profession (2013) reports census data indicating that women are just 5 per cent of lawyers, about half the number in Bar council admission records for a similar time period (Table 3). Case studies of the barriers to entry in smaller courts (eg Nagla 2001; Sethi 1987; Sharma 2002) are consistent with findings by the literature on work in India that most women professionals are young, unmarried and from forward caste communities. Mishra (2015) found that women formed a much larger proportion of lawyers enrolled in the Lucknow High Court in 1998–2005 (12.3 per cent) than they did in 1962–97 (3 per cent).

Table 3 Male and Female Advocates Enrolled With State Bar Councils (31 March 2007)

State Bar Council	Men	Women	Total	% Women
Andhra Pradesh	58,147	9,605	67,752	14
Assam, Nagaland, etc**	9,703	2,022	11,725	17
Bihar**	89,594	3,043	92,637	3
Chhatisgarh	10,000	4,949	14,949	33
Delhi	30,000	8,549	38,549	18
Gujrat	38,586	9,208	47,794	19
Himachal Pradesh	4,680	741	5,421	14
Jammu and Kashmir	2,832	597	3,429	17
Jharkhand	5,407	485	5,892	8
Karntaka**	37,861	6,756	44,617	15
Kerlala	30,000	6,437	36,437	18
Madhya Pradesh	60,000	9,208	69,208	13
Maharashtra and Goa	78,522	5,636	84,158	7
Orissa	31,000	6,993	37,993	18

(*continued*)

Table 3 *(Continued)*

State Bar Council	Men	Women	Total	% Women
Punjab and Haryana	42,411	4,265	46,676	9
Rajasthan	35,000	5,823	40,823	14
Tamil Nadu	46,575	5,902	52,477	11
Uttarakhand***	359	76	435	17
Uttar Pradesh*	195,780	6,000	201,780	3
West Bengal	50,000	2,261	52,261	4
Totals	856,457	98,556	955,013	10

Source: Bar Council of India (no longer publicly available on website, last accessed 2009).
* 31 March 2006.
** 31 December 2006.
*** 31 March 2007.

Women are even less well represented at the higher levels of the professional hierarchy: judges (Table 4), senior counsel (see Figure 1) or bar council officers (see Figure 2). For example, only five of the 397 senior advocates in the Supreme Court of India between 1962 and 2011 were women (Makhija and Raha 2011). And these few women encounter ongoing obstacles. Indira Jaisingh, the first woman senior advocate in the Bombay High

Table 4 Men and Women Judges by Court (2018, Historic)

Court	Current (2018)			Historic*		
	Total	Men	Women	Total	Men	Women
Supreme Court of India	24	22	2	205	200	5
Delhi High Court	35	27	8°	162	147	15
Calcutta High Court	37	31	6	41**	39**	2**
Madras High Court	62	50	12°	38**	37**	1**
Bombay High Court	69	59	10°	398	391	7

Source: Court Websites of the Supreme Court and High Courts.
* Note that all historic totals include judges appointed in a given court (who were not sitting judges in 2018). The historic timelines of appointment vary by court and start at the year the first judge was appointed: ie Supreme Court (1950), Delhi High Court (1966), Bombay High Court (1862), Calcutta High Court (1862), Madras High Court (1862). Note that Bombay, Calcutta, and Madras High Courts were pre-independence courts whereas the Delhi High Courts and Supreme Court were post-Independence courts formed after 1947. Housed in presidency towns, the Bombay, Calcutta, and Madras High Courts were established by Queen Victoria's letters patent under the Indian High Courts Act 1861.
° In 2018 the current sitting chief justices in Bombay (Acting Chief Justice Tahilramani), Delhi (Acting Chief Justice Mittal), and Madras (Chief Justice Banerjee) High Courts were all women.
** Official court websites give data only about past Chief Justices.

Figure 1 Unequal Distribution

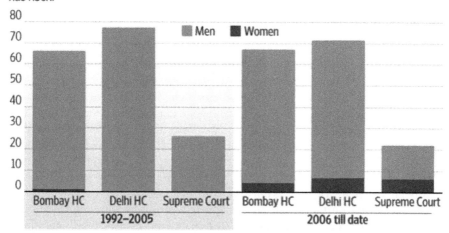

Source: K Ganz, *Legally India* 15 July 2015, available at www.legallyindia.com/the-bench-and-the-bar/senior-counsel-system-borked-20150714-6283.

Figure 2 Bar Council Officers

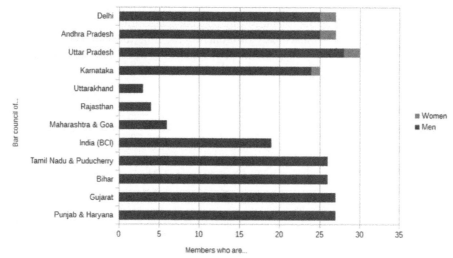

Source: *Legally India*, 12 July 2016, available at www.legallyindia.com/the-bench-and-the-bar/thought-senior-counsel-had-an-old-boys-club-try-bar-councils-where-only-3-of-members-are-women-and-most-have-none-20160712-7820.

Court (which bestowed this distinction on only four others in the last three decades), has described a culture of profound sexism in the courtroom,[9] which she is challenging in the Supreme Court. Despite their growing representation in law faculties, women still occupy few positions of power in academia, even (indeed especially) in new elite law schools (Ballakrishnen and Samuel 2018).[10]

B. Caste

Empirical research across various sites indicates that caste continues to matter for the litigating Bar (Mishra 2015; Nagla 2001; Sharma 2002). As earlier studies found (eg Gadbois 1969; Morrison 1972), forward caste Hindus and local elites continue to reap unequal rewards (Dezalay and Garth 2010; Galanter and Robinson 2017); and caste, kinship and communal ties matter even in newer corporate ecosystems (Krishnan 2013; Nanda et al 2017; Wilkins and Khanna 2017). Gadbois's recent book on the Supreme Court (2011), for example, shows much the same patterns he found 50 years earlier: 40 per cent of Supreme Court judges were Brahmin, and another 50 per cent were from other forward castes. Yet caste plays out differently in other contexts. For example, in 2014 in the Madras High Court in Tamil Nadu, a state with strong anti-Brahmin politics,[11] less than 15 per cent of judges came from forward castes, and the possible appointment of more forward caste judges generated unprecedented controversy.[12]

C. Economic Stratification and Income

Theories of stratification in Indian courts (Berti 2011; Galanter and Krishnan 2003, Kapur and Mehta 2007; Moog 1998; Robinson 2009) also illuminate the structure of the legal profession. The winner-takes-all model of the litigating Bar, especially in the higher courts, is symptomatic: 10 per cent of the Bar do about 90 per cent of the work.

---

[9] See S Mishra, 'I was sexually harassed in the corridors of the Supreme Court' *The Week* (13 November 2016), available at www.theweek.in/theweek/cover/interview-indira-jaising-senior-lawyer.html.

[10] Numbers do not do justice to the important work of eminent women legal and socio-legal academics in these schools – notably Amita Dhanda, VS Elizabeth, Sarasu Esther and Kalpana Kannabiran. Even so, only 10 of 102 members of Academic Councils in what are commonly considered the 'top 6' national law schools in the country are women. By contrast, each of the three law departments at Delhi University is headed by a woman (Ballakrishnen and Samuel 2018).

[11] For commentary on courts and caste in the Madras High Court more generally, see Chandru 2015, Vijayakumar 2015. In her recent ethnography of the judicial iconography in the Madras High Court, Khorakiwala (2018) suggests that 'the issue of dalit (lowest caste) politics today engulfs the Madras High Court', as is evident in the Karnan case (see below), but extends beyond it to politics around public statues of noted Dalit legal icon (and drafter of the Indian Constitution) Dr BR Ambedkar.

[12] In 2014, close to 15,000 advocates stayed home from work and Justice CS Karnan, a dalit sitting judge of the High Court, impeded a courtroom in session denouncing 'unfairness' when three upper caste names were included on a list of 12 recommended for judicial appointment by the high court collegium (Deccan Herald 2014, Legally India 2014). The Karnan court disruption has been controversial (Ramasubramanian 2015, Hindu 2016) as has his career trajectory following it. In May 2017, Justice Karnan (who, in 2011, had alleged victimisation and discrimination by fellow judges before the National Commission for Scheduled Castes) was sent to prison for contempt of court (Yamunan 2017); and upon release, in May 2018, he floated a pro-women, anti-corruption political party from the BR Ambedkar Memorial House (India Today 2018).

Globalisation of the corporate transactional Bar has had little impact on the prestige or earning capacity of elite litigators (Galanter and Robinson 2017). India's leading advocates are some of the best paid lawyers in the world (Saghal and Bamzai, 2010), earning as much as business tycoons (Dhawan 2011). The most successful advocates earn US$2–10 million a year and charge US$10–12,000 per court appearance (Galanter and Robinson 2017), often appearing on behalf of corporate clients whose transactions are handled by elite law firms. Engaging senior counsel can influence outcomes (Kumar 2015), and the structure of the litigating Bar intensifies this stratification. Senior advocates may only appear in cases referred by advocates-on-record (briefing counsel), who in turn often work for senior counsel in smaller matters. These strong recursive ties ensure that a small group of lawyers, firms and senior counsel exclude the rest (Dam 2017).

Kanan Dhru's national survey (2010) of 280 lawyers and judges confirms the role of kinship: 92 per cent agreed that family background facilitated entry to and success within the legal system (2010: 22–25). And her law graduate respondents agreed: almost half (46 per cent) gave 'lack of family background' as the reason for not becoming litigators, second only to 'no financial incentive' (85 per cent). 85 per cent of her graduate respondents who became litigators had a family connection, and all those who did *not* become litigators had none. Although there are no national data on the income of non-elite lawyers, the few case studies reveal widespread poverty. About half the lawyers in *Tiz Hazari* (district) court in Delhi earned 1,000–5,000 Rupees a month (about US$17–86 at the average foreign exchange rate in 2000), and the highest incomes were 10–20,000 Rupees (US$172–344); many lawyers worked for nothing, viewing themselves as apprentices (Nagla 2001). In Mishra's (2015) study of 101 women lawyers in the Lucknow High Court, only 8 of the 73 respondents earned enough to be in a tax-paying bracket.

D. Pro Bono, Legal Aid and Political Activism

Income and social networks matter as much for litigants as they do for lawyers. Daksh (2015) conducted a representative survey of 9,329 litigants from 305 locations in 24 states. Most were first-time offenders (95 per cent) and male (84.3 per cent), and most civil disputes involved land or property (66 per cent). Because advertising is illegal[13] and connections matter, these data suggest that most people still use family and friendship networks to find legal help (82 per cent for criminal cases, 85 per cent for civil). Most litigants are not well-off. A little over 90 per cent earned less than 300,000 Rupees per year (US$4,500), and half earned less than 100,000 Rupees per year (US$1,500). These figures put the costs of litigation in perspective: between 497 Rupees (US$7.6) and 844 Rupees (US$13) in lost earnings for each day of civil court hearings and about US$23 for criminal court hearings. Most litigants believe their cases will take a long time; only

---

[13] Part VI, Chapter II, Section IV, Rule 36 of the Bar Council of India Rules of the Advocates Act, 1961 forbids the solicitation of work under 'duty to colleagues'. In 2008, this was slightly modified to allow limited, pre-approved websites (Resolution No 50/2008, 24 March 2008). Large firms and elite lawyers are ranked by independent authorities like the UK-based legal strategy and consulting firm RSG India and Chambers and Partners Rankings for the region. However, most of these lawyers obtain work through word of mouth and long-standing associations with repeat clients (Wilkins and Khanna 2017: 142, 151; Varottil 2017: 195).

32 per cent of civil and 42 per cent of criminal litigants expect their cases to be resolved within a year.

Most local lawyers are case omnivores, accepting all clients (but geographic proximity is relevant – 85 per cent of litigants travel less than 30 miles to find a lawyer) (Daksh 2015). Although the 44th Amendment to the Constitution mandates free legal aid,[14] implementation has been incomplete (Dhavan 1994). Moog (1998: 413) comments that 'while governments have gone through the motions of establishing legal aid structures on paper, to a great extent the program has been a failure'. Corporate lawyers have begun offering pro bono services (Gupta 2017), particularly following efforts by online lawyer networks like iProbono,[15] which connect organisations with lawyers wishing to provide assistance. And many law schools have established legal aid clinics (though without any official rule from the BCI). A third of the Daksh respondents (almost all earning less than 300,000 Rupees or US$4,500 a year) used alternate dispute resolution (ADR) mechanisms. The actual number using ADR would likely be much higher if we took into account mechanisms like the women's courts (Vatuk 2013), local customary ADR like 'Shiv Sena courts'[16] (Eckert 2003, 2004; Bedi 2016) or the popular illegal (and problematic) *Khap Panchayats* or 'kangaroo courts',[17] which have displaced official judicial systems across the country (Iyer 2016; John 2013; Kaur 2010).

Although a portrait of the profession limited to the data above would not be structurally different from Gandhi's account in 1989, the changes following market liberalisation in 1991 are potentially momentous.

---

[14] In addition to national and state legal aid services like National Legal Services Authority and Delhi Legal Services Authority, the Department of Justice launched in April 2017 'tele law services' and 'nyaya mitra schemes'. The Nyaya Mitra scheme, launched in 227 districts across India, is aimed at reducing pendency of cases across selected districts, with special focus on those pending for more than 10 years. Operating through a retired judicial or executive officer (with legal experience) designated as the 'Nyaya Mitra' ('Justice Friend' in Hindi), the project aims to assist litigants suffering delays in investigations or trial, by actively identifying such cases through the National Judicial Data Grid, providing legal advice and connecting litigants to government agencies and civil society organisations. Tele Law services facilitate delivery of legal advice through an expert panel of lawyers, stationed at the State Legal Services Authorities (SLSA), who are connected with clients through video conferencing facilities operated by paralegal volunteers. See pib.nic.in/newsite/PrintRelease.aspx?relid=161179.

[15] iProbono was co-founded by an alumnus of the National Law School, Swathi Sukumar, and is increasingly recognised for its social justice work. It defines itself as a 'platform for civic engagement, to amplify the voices of civil society and defend human rights'. See a list of case studies at www.i-probono.com/case-study.

[16] In her ethnography of the far-right regional political party Shiv Sena, Eckert (2003, 2004) offers a nuanced portrait of the authority yielded by the Sena through their local party offices (*shakhas*) which act as court alternatives to help bypass the otherwise inaccessible and ineffective state agencies. The courts, legitimised by the Sena as 'close to the people' or appealing to the 'common man's sense of justice', operate as an alternative people's court, presided over by local leaders untrained in the law and delivering oral judgements with no written record. Fees are typically non-monetary, 'orders' are enforced through threats of violence, and the local police typically collude with the process. Eckert uses the popularity of these institutions as a foil to explain the 'charismatic militancy' and violence of the autocratic party: the local community fears the Sena but also seek its protection and trust its 'cult of direct action'.

[17] *Khap Panchayats* are self-proclaimed courts of village 'caste lords', who offer a parallel system of justice in all-male forums that reinforce notions of caste-based 'honour' and hierarchy. Judgments are unilateral, often barbaric and regressive (eg mutilation of body parts, testing a woman's 'purity' by making her fry food in hot oil and finding her guilty if her hands burn) (Kachhwaha 2011). Courts have consistently declared these rulings unconstitutional, but they remain very popular, especially in parts of North India.

III. NEW SCHOOLS, NEW FIRMS: ORGANISATIONAL TRANSFORMATION OVER THE LAST 30 YEARS

To understand the Indian transformation as the outcome of 'specific historical, political or professional conditions' (Cotterell 1998: 177) it is imperative to focus on the 1991 economic market reforms, which were central to making the Indian economy one of the fastest growing in the world and have profoundly reshaped the legal profession. The dramatic expansion of international trade and transactions, an essential by-product of this liberalisation, required new laws and regulations and, consequently, lawyers to implement them (Flood 2017; Wilkins et al 2017). And over the last three decades, India has seen the burgeoning of both new kinds of legal practice (eg cross-border mergers and acquisitions) (Varottil 2017) and new kinds of lawyers who could perform such transactions (Ballakrishnen 2017; Gingerich et al 2017; Krishnan 2010; Papa and Wilkins 2011). These reforms have been accompanied by the emergence of two new kinds of institutions (law schools and organisations to employ their graduates), requiring a renegotiation of both the regulations governing practice and the broader links between the local and the global.

A. Education: Domestic Credentialing via National Law Schools

Save for a few 'islands of excellence',[18] the state of Indian legal education is not that different from the 'indifferent to deplorable' condition (1989: 375) Gandhi described in the 1980s. The country remains overpopulated with law schools – 1,390 as of 2013 (Gingerich and Robinson 2017: 521, 543) – only a small fraction of which are 'elite'. Yet these elite schools (and their several hundred annual graduates), while not representative of the country's estimated 60,000 annual graduates, offer insight into an institutional shift that is reshaping the Indian legal profession.

Historical accounts of legal education in India (eg Ballakrishnen 2009; Gupta 2006; Krishnan 2004; Menon 2009) agree that the National Law Schools were created in the late 1980s in response to the need for a 'model' law school – a 'Harvard of the East'– which could provide quality legal education (Menon 2009: 40). India had similar specialised schools in engineering (Indian Institutes of Technology) and business (Indian Institutes of Management), which were highly selective and seen as globally competitive. The goal was to create an equally rigorous and competitive domestic law school. The first such school – National Law School of India University (NLSIU) – was established in Bangalore in 1986 after years of deliberation (Mathur 2017), with tangible and symbolic investments from the BCI, judiciary, local government and external actors like the Ford Foundation (Krishnan 2004). Madhava Menon, widely regarded as the godfather of this innovation, was committed to creating an institutional model distinct from traditional Indian law schools.[19]

---

[18] A term used by Prime Minister Dr Manmohan Singh to distinguish the national law schools from the 'sea of institutionalized mediocrity'. See Prime Minister's Inaugural Address at the Conference of National Consultation for Second Generation Reforms in Legal Education (1 May 2010) archivepmo.nic.in/drmanmohansingh/speech-details.php?nodeid=889.

[19] Although Menon deserves credit for realising his vision, momentum had already been generated by Upendra Baxi (a prominent jurist co-opted by the BCI for this task) and Justice Hidayatullah (Mathur 2017). Baxi described himself as 'heavily pregnant for 13 years', only to 'allow a caesarian surgery, after all, by Madhava Menon' (Baxi 2007: 19 n 39).

Following the recommendation of the Ahmadi Committee at the Chief Justices' Conference (1993), a consortium of government and judicial stakeholders established four more schools based on the NLSIU model within the decade, in Hyderabad (NALSAR), Bhopal (NLIU), Kolkata (NUJS), and Jodhpur (NLU). In 2017 there were 17 schools based on the model, with more planned in each state. The quality and reputation of these schools vary; but based on independent law school rankings (eg India Today, IMS India), student preferences (Gingerich and Robinson 2017), and employer mentions (Gingerich et al 2017), NLSIU, NALSAR occupy the highest tier (often joined by NUJS, see Ganz 2010). These schools provided five-year multi-disciplinary undergraduate programmes rather than the traditional three-year graduate programme. Entry occurred through a highly competitive exam (no similar barriers existed for other law schools). And students were evaluated on a range of criteria, including research papers, class participation and internships (whereas rote memorisation and lectures were the norm in traditional law colleges). In addition, there are elite private law schools like the Jindal Global Law School, which use a modified LSAT for admissions and have international institutional collaborators and a young, globally-trained faculty. In contrast, older 'legacy schools' (eg Delhi Law Faculty) pride themselves on their low cost (about US$100 a year compared to about US$2,000 at the national law schools and about US$8,500 at Jindal Global Law School) and commitment to the litigating bar (Gingerich and Robinson 2017: 534).

There have been other changes in access to international legal education. Foreign legal training, especially in England, was a status symbol for India's old legal elite, but some of their successors have preferred US LLM programmes (Ballakrishnen 2011). Although students agree that the latter enhance their professional toolkit and offer 'exposure and multicultural diversity' (Ganz 2012), the impact on the profession has varied (Ballakrishnen 2011). While those seeking an LLM degree are increasingly strategic about preparing for successful admission into these programmes (eg by investing in judicial clerkships, Chandrachud 2014), the degree's value in domestic and international job markets remains uncertain (Legally India 2012). Entry barriers at elite schools also engendered other new institutional actors: prep schools like the Law School Tutorials (started by three NLSIU alumni) to prepare students for the increasingly competitive entrance exams;[20] and online platforms like MyLaw.net (again, spearheaded by an NLSIU alumnus), which seek to democratise legal education through online course videos and learning apps.[21]

B. Organisations: New Firms for New Lawyers

Pedagogic innovations were crucial in shaping these new law schools (Gingerich and Robinson 2017; Schukoske 2009), whose success was ensured by their competitive entry requirements. While exams previously were administered by individual schools, all national law schools now use the Common Law Admission Test (CLAT). In 2017,

---

[20] Preparatory courses for law schools cost between US$100 for online mock tests and about US$750 a year for more extensive training.

[21] In the first year since its launch in January 2017, MyLaw.net had 12,000 unique learners, almost half of whom were from non-metropolitan Indian cities, reflecting a possible democratic expansion of quality legal education, which law schools have been unable to offer. See mylaw.net/.

about 45,000 students took this test (compared to about 11,000 in 2008, when it was first administered). These numbers are significant because each school admits only 80–120 students a year. Beyond raising the quality of legal education, this selective recruitment has aided graduates in signalling their competitiveness in the emerging corporate legal market (Gingerich et al 2017; Nanda et al 2017). Although these schools did not initially intend to be feeders for these law firms (Gingerich and Robinson 2017: 528), a majority of their graduates populate organisations that did not exist three decades ago: global-style corporate law firms, legal departments of large multinational corporations, banks, and legal process outsourcing firms.

Some of this symbiosis reflects disenchantment with the possibilities in litigation. Only 12 per cent of senior lawyers and judges believed that 'bright youngsters' with law degrees were becoming litigators; a mere 6.5 per cent of students wanted to practise in the Supreme Court and just 4.92 per cent in the High Courts (Dhru 2010). Whereas litigation recruitment relied on informal networks (Galanter and Robinson 2017) and 'godfathers' in the industry (Dhru 2010), these new organisations spoke the language of meritocracy, which students from these schools found appealing. As Gingerich and colleagues (2017) show, the structure of the new recruitment system – a formal recruitment committee, faculty advisers, official recruitment days – dovetailed well with that of the law firms. The difference between these schools and the traditional failing system ensured that students who entered and graduated from them believed the market would perceive and reward their value accurately. What they could not demand from a stable, entrenched litigation system they had a better chance of finding within these new firms, which were sensitive to global ideals of meritocracy (Ballakrishnen 2017). For those unwilling or unable to strive for the brass rings of litigation victories, or uninterested in doing so, these firms offered financially rewarding careers and a sense of being valued.

Furthermore, these schools have not just passively accepted a symbiotic relationship with the emerging market. Rather, they have actively jettisoned the original ideal of the 'moral law school' (Dezalay and Garth 2010: 235), aimed at producing liberal, socially-relevant lawyers (Ballakrishnen 2009; Krishnan 2004; Menon 2006),[22] and instead invested in the institutional apparatus that could make their students attractive to the country's emerging elite corporate law sector. Gingerich and Robinson (2017) suggest that schools have introduced curriculum changes, elective choices and extracurricular activities to help students appear interested in law firms. These organisational decisions have reinforced students' own preferences for 'secure placement in a corporate desk job'. These developments represent the biggest structural change within the legal profession in the last 30 years: the rise of a corporate legal elite whose members are chosen not by ascription but on the basis of achievement and merit.

---

[22] In addition to critics disappointed by the failure of these schools to produce social advocacy lawyers, others fear that the schools are graduating an elite that will undo earlier progressive achievements. See eg Kannabiran's (*The Hindu*, 12 October 2015) response to Anup Surendranath's comment that constitutional rights had been historically – and incrementally – compromised in India (*The Hindu*, 9 October 2015): www.thehindu.com/opinion/letters/upholding-pluralism/article7750330.ece.

C. In or Out? The Complicated Relationship with Liberalisation

As discussed above, the new kinds of lawyers and organisations emerged within the context of India's participation in the global political economy following the 1991 market reforms. Increased foreign direct investment (and transactional work for lawyers) (Nanda et al 2017; Varottil 2017; Wilkins and Fong 2017) co-existed with a protectionist legal profession prohibiting the entry of foreign lawyers and law firms. The Advocates Act, 1961 sections 24 and 37 restrict the right to practise to Indian citizens and practitioners from countries offering reciprocity.[23] And while the Bar Council has allowed a few individual foreign lawyers (all of Indian origin) from recognised universities[24] to practise in Indian Courts,[25] foreign law firms are still excluded. The meaning of 'practice of law' in the Advocates Act 1961 has been hotly debated since the first foreign law firms attempted to establish liaison offices in India in the early 1990s (Singh 2017: 371). The Bombay High Court ruled in *Lawyers Collective v Bar Council of India Chadbourne, Ashurst, White & Case, and Others* (2009) that the 'practice of law' is limited to Indian citizens. But in 2012 the Madras High Court held that nothing in the Advocates Act prohibited foreign lawyers from visiting India on a temporary 'fly-in/fly-out' basis or subcontracting legal work to outsourcing firms. In March 2018, the Supreme Court ruled that foreign lawyers could visit on a 'casual basis' and advise on foreign laws and international commercial arbitration, so long as such visiting and advising was within the rules of the BCI.

These decisions only confirm a well-established practice. Many foreign law firms have dedicated India desks either in London or elsewhere in Asia, usually Singapore or Hong Kong (Singh 2017a: 384). At various times over the last decade, Clifford Chance, Linklaters and Allen & Overy have had 'best friend' agreements with Indian law firms (AZB & Partners, Talware Thakore & Associates, and Trilegal, respectively). Similarly, Indian legal process outsourcing firms (LPOs), which do everything from document support and back office work to drafting and negotiating contacts for global firms and corporations, have not been found to have contravened the 'unauthorised practice' restrictions of either the US or India.[26] India does not have an institutionalised paralegal system. However, even though data on the industry is hard to collect, non-lawyers are often employed in these LPOs because, technically, they do not constitute the 'unauthorized practice of law' (Khanna 2017). Thus, although the broad provisions of the Advocates Act prohibit entry, India continues to offer a range of hybrid professional spaces that circumvent this blanket barrier.

Yet, as Krishnan argues (2009: 4), the situation is neither unambiguous nor easily explained by monolithic logics like 'large firms want a monopoly' or 'real lawyers don't

---

[23] Proposals to expand the scope of this reciprocity have met resistance within and outside the country: see economictimes.indiatimes.com/News/International_Business/NRI_lawyers_demand_removal_of_restrictions_on_working_in_UK/articleshow/3536849.cms.

[24] See www.lawentrance.com/recognisedunivs.htm for a list of recognised universities.

[25] See www.barcouncilofindia.org/about/legal-education for a list of relevant resolutions on acceptable reciprocal standards.

[26] As long as the outsourcing entity (ie the foreign lawyer) can ensure the quality of the work and client confidentiality, the ABA is unlikely to view this as unauthorised practice. In India, the *AK Balaji v Union of India and Others* (2010) decision held that LPOs were outside the purview of the Advocates Act because they were not engaged in 'legal practice' (Khanna 2017; Singh 2017a, 2017b).

care'. Corporate law firms have fiercely guarded their monopoly against foreign firms, claiming they are under-prepared for global competition while simultaneously preparing for and hedging against a future that might include these foreign firms (Singh 2017a; 2017b). Smaller law firms and litigators have been ideologically opposed to foreign firms for 'nationalist' reasons (Krishnan 2010; Singh 2017b). Competitive threats come not just from foreign firms that have found ways around regulatory barriers but also from a new generation of 'peel off' law firms tired of restrictive practices (Krishnan 2013). By contrast, the 'creamy layer' of litigators who should be unconcerned about the entry of foreign firms (which will still need them to appear in court) nevertheless have strong views about liberalisation, which fluctuate with the political climate (Ganz 2015). Although the future of liberalisation is uncertain, there is consensus that a further opening will yield healthier market conditions for many actors (Galanter and Robinson 2017; Krishnan 2013; Khanna 2017; Singh 2017a; 2017b). Furthermore, despite what may seem like a transformation, the creamy layer in question is still only a small sliver of the population: Krishnan (2013: 25–31) suggests there are only 200 corporate law firms in the country. And although commentary on the legal profession through legal blogs and websites remains focused on these elite law schools and firms, the majority of Indian lawyers are still trained in local colleges and practise in environments shaped by communal networks.

IV. NEW ACTORS, OLD INEQUALITIES: THE REPRODUCTION OF HIERARCHY

Despite changes at the periphery, the bulk of the profession has remained relatively unaltered over the last 30 years. Ascription continues to shape entry and success for most lawyers. Nevertheless, the new organisations emerging after liberalisation in the early 1990s have valorised, and even demanded, entrants who made claims based on merit. This new cohort of law graduates, and the parallel elite of commercial lawyers, feel empowered to assert themselves in a profession historically hostile to them. The changes of the last 30 years have had another, less predictable, consequence for the middle-class law graduate without contacts: they have provided a chance to renegotiate gender hierarchies (Ballakrishnen 2017). Although women remain a small minority of the profession, they are well represented in large law firms at both entry and the more senior levels of partnership; and many feel that gender is 'not an issue' (Ballakrishnen 2017). Yet this is hardly an uncomplicated success. While women partners in elite firms perceive less discrimination, their reference points are the experiences of other kinds of professionals, and indeed women litigators, who confront major obstacles and more blatantly hostile work environments.[27] And although they are not always traditionally

---

[27] In 2013, a spate of complaints against members of the litigating Bar began to surface, following public outrage at the December 2012 *Nirbhaya* rape case (where a young paramedic student was severely assaulted and gang-raped by six men inside a moving bus in South Delhi before being thrown out on the road naked, dying a few days later from her injuries). Some were concerned about sexual harassment (see timesofindia.indiatimes.com/india/Another-lawyer-opens-up-says-she-too-was-sexually-harassed/articleshow/26060769.cms). Others were public statements about how the Bar was gendered, oppressive and hostile to women generally. For example, members of the Calicut Bar Association (literally) threw chairs at a woman for writing a Facebook post about gender inequalities in her professional environments ('Violence at bar association meeting over woman lawyer's Facebook post' *Times of India*, 10 January 2014: timesofindia.indiatimes.com/city/kozhikode/Violence-at-bar-association-meeting-over-woman-lawyers-Facebook-post/articleshow/28656823.cms). For a statement about the gender

elite (ie from 'legal families'), successful women professionals also enjoy the intersectional advantage of other kinds of cosmopolitan cultural capital: their parents are often professionals themselves, and they are socialised in urban city schools and proficient in English. Simply put, these are women whose presence in the profession, while novel, does not threaten other entrenched inequalities of caste and class (Ballakrishnen 2017). Furthermore, this might be a short-lived advantage given the institutional youth of these organisations. In light of what we know about persistent gender inequality (Ridgeway 2011) and the fact that women in similar sites often qualify their understandings of success over time (Hunter 2002), the future of this advantage is uncertain.

Despite these qualifications, when juxtaposed against the nepotistic patterns of reproduction in the rest of the profession, elite law firms might appear to offer young lawyers greater ease of entry and upward mobility. However, a handful of elite firms dominate most transactional work. And given their process of recruitment (ie mostly from elite law schools), these firms still breed an unequal – albeit novel – homophily. Different accounts confirm this meritocratic inequality. Data from IDIA (an organisation committed to increasing diversity in law schools) reveal that most law schools are predominantly Hindu and forward caste,[28] and recent empirical research on students in these law schools confirms long-standing suspicions that caste and socio-economic status significantly influence success in these schools (Jain et al 2016: 150–53). English remains the dominant language (Jain et al 2016: 37). Few students come from rural areas, such as the northeast and Kashmir (Basheer et al 2017: 578), and their educational experiences are significantly different from those of the majority. Although there are not enough data over time to confirm this, one could hypothesise that these variations affect careers. Even when networks are not directly useful to obtain permanent jobs in new law firms, they can help to obtain internships, which can lead to jobs (Gingerich et al 2017: 558). As Basheer and his colleagues argue (2017: 578), the new national law schools have been good at teaching 'lofty ideals of social justice and equality, but have a serious issue of manifest injustice in their face'.[29]

---

disparities and hostile environment confronting female advocates trying to find a voice, see K Kannabiran *The Hindu*, 18 January 2014: www.thehindu.com/opinion/op-ed/lawyer-judge-and-aam-aadmi/article5587057.ece.

[28] The IDIA Diversity Survey 2013–14 found that 69.11 per cent belonged to the general category, 11.65 per cent to the Scheduled Caste (SC) category and 5.06 per cent to the Scheduled Tribes (ST) category. About 59 per cent of NLS students were upper caste, 2.3 per cent Other Backward Classes (OBC), 14.9 per cent SC, and 7.1 per cent ST. 10.7 per cent reported not having a caste, while 6 per cent reported being unaware of their caste. Similarly, NLSIU data reveal that Muslims are underrepresented in these schools (Jain et al 2016: 30–32). SC, ST, and OBC are official classifications of the population of India. SC/ST are historically disadvantaged groups with special constitutional sanction (under Arts 341, 342). OBC is a collective category used by the Government of India to classify castes that are economically and socially disadvantaged but *not* by caste (there are forward caste OBCs, for example, as well as Muslim and Christian OBCs). According to constitutional orders in 1950, there are 1,108 SCs in 29 states and 744 STs in 22 states. SCs and STs comprise about 16.6 per cent and 8.6 per cent respectively of the total population (according to the 2011 census). In 2006, the National Commission for Backward Classes (NCBC) estimated that 5013 castes were OBC, amounting to 41.1 per cent of the population according to the National Sample Survey Organization (which took place the same year). In 2015, the NCBC proposed further classifications and an income ceiling (US$2,222 dollars/year) within the category to ensure that its privileges were not being abused.

[29] Sanjeev Gumpenapalli, a dalit queer feminist paints a rich portrait of these dissonances and the 'liberal façade' that hides these inequalities, especially for lower caste and sexual minority students in these schools. See 'NALSAR University of Law: Sexism and Casteism Behind a Liberal Façade', available at feminisminindia.com/2017/12/11/nalsar-university-law-casteism-within-liberal-facade/ (11 December 2017).

V. CONCLUSION: A REVISED AND RECURSIVE PORTRAIT

In many ways, not much has changed since the early portraits of the Indian legal profession. A majority of the country still practises law in ways that are unperturbed by globalisation and its implications. Prestige and networks are still central: litigation, in particular, still depends on relationships with government, and many 'grand advocates' are closely and publicly linked to political parties (Galanter and Robinson 2017). And, as discussed above, inequalities are rampant even in new kinds of workspaces. A common refrain about the change in the legal profession is the decline in political commitment among lawyers, given their history. Indian lawyers played significant political roles, both during and after the independence struggle and in the 1970s and 1980s, the heyday of many social movements. But though their engagement might seem less obvious now, it would be misleading to call them apolitical.[30] A new intellectual and political legal elite – many trained in the national law schools – have played crucial roles in setting up law-related NGOs (eg Alternative Law Forum, Centre for Law and Policy Research, Center for Social Justice, Indian Institute of Paralegal Studies) and legal education initiatives (eg IDIA, Rainmaker, MyLaw.Net). Legal scholars trained in these schools are also active in research think tanks focused on the intersections between law and public policy (eg Centre for Policy and Research). Legal activists have similarly been key players in and commentators on socio-legal political movements concerning sexual harassment, queer rights, the death penalty, pro bono legal services, Internet governance and intellectual property. Still others are part of a new wave of legal academics in India (Ballakrishnen and Samuel 2018) and abroad (Sharafi 2015).

Alongside this recursive similarity with its predecessor, much has changed in other ways since early portraits of India's legal profession (Galanter 1969b; Gandhi 1989). First, as this chapter reviews, the profession is no longer understudied, and new kinds of actors (eg online blogs) have become integral to its archiving. Second, while Gandhi's snapshot revealed a profession still reacting to and reproducing the colonial experience, recent decades have produced accounts in response to a globalising world order, which both view and appraise this change. While the profession depicted by Gandhi sought legitimacy from tradition, the contemporary profession – at least the parts that are changing – looks forward, often dictated by new and nuanced market logics (Ballakrishnen 2018). Third, the profession is also anticipating a future peopled by other novel actors (eg tax law firms and multidisciplinary firms), and online legal education might democratise the field in unanticipated ways.

In describing the task facing post-independence Indian courts, scholarly commentary identified a tension between 'being independent' and 'being affected by independence' (Baxi 1982). The 1991 liberalisation posed a similar challenge to the legal profession, and it is the negotiation of this tension that will determine its future.

---

[30] Narrain and Thiruvengadam (2013) refute the claim by Charles Epp (1998) that India has had only a 'weak rights revolution' despite being endowed with a vibrant Constitution and Supreme Court. Pointing to the Alternate Law Forum, they argue that this does not 'appreciate the radiating effects and achievements of the activism initiated by PIL campaigns seeking to develop a culture of respect for constitutionalism and human rights' (2013: 564).

REFERENCES

Arora, S (1972) 'Social Background of the Indian Cabinet' 7(31/33) *Economic and Political Weekly* 1523.

Azeem, A (2016) 'Delhi Has Maximum Number of Munnabhai Lawyers, Verification Process Reveals' *Times of India* 2 June.

Ballakrishnen, SS (2009) 'Where Do We Come From, Where Do We Go: An Enquiry into the Students and Systems of Legal Education in India' 7(2) *Journal of Commonwealth Law and Legal Education* 133–54.

—— (2011) 'Homeward bound: What does a Global Legal Education Offer the Indian Returnees' 80 *Fordham Law Review* 2441.

—— (2017) 'Women in India's 'Global' Law Firms: Comparative Gender Frames and the Advantage of New Organizations' in DB Wilkins, VS Khanna and DM Trubek (eds), *The Indian Legal Profession in the Age of Globalization* (Cambridge, Cambridge University Press).

—— (2018) 'Just Like Global Firms: Unintended Gender Parity and Speculative Isomorphism in India's Elite Professions' 53(1) *Law & Society Review* 108.

Ballakrishnen, SS and Samuel, R (2018) 'India's Legal Academics: Who They Are and Where You Might Find Them' in U Schultz (ed), *Gender and Careers in the Legal Academy* (London, Hart Publishing).

Basheer, S and Mukherjee, S (2010) 'Regulating Indian Legal Education: Some Thoughts for Reform' available at papers.ssrn.com/sol3/papers.cfm?abstract_id=1584037.

Basheer, S, Krishnaprasad, KV, Mitra, S and Mohapatra, P (2017) 'The Making of Legal Elites and the IDIA of Justice' in DB Wilkins, VS Khanna and DM Trubek (eds), *The Indian Legal Profession in the Age of Globalization* (Cambridge, Cambridge University Press).

Baxi, U (1982) *The Crisis of the Indian Legal System* (New Delhi, Vikas).

—— (1985) 'Taking suffering seriously: social action litigation in the Supreme Court of India' in R Dhavan et al (eds), *Judges and the Judicial Power: Essays in Honour of Justice VR Krishna Iyer* (London, Sweet & Maxwell).

—— (2007) 'Enculturing Law: Some Unphilosophical Remarks' in M John and S Kakarala (eds), *Enculturing Law: New Agendas for Legal Pedagogy* (Delhi, Tulika Books).

Bedi, T (2016) *The Dashing Ladies of Shiv Sena: Political Matronage in Urbanizing India* (Albany, SUNY Press).

Berti, D (2011) 'Courts of Law and Legal Practice' *A Companion to the Anthropology of India* (Wiley) 353–70.

Bhuwania, A (2016) *Public Interest Litigation and Political Society in Post-Emergency India* (Cambridge, Cambridge University Press).

Chandrachud, A (2014) 'From Hyderabad to Harvard: How US Law Schools Make it Worthwhile to Clerk on India's Supreme Court' 21(1) *International Journal of the Legal Profession* 73–101.

Chandru, K (2015) 'Judges, Castes and Social Justice' *The Hindu* 16 March www.thehindu.com/opinion/op-ed/judges-castes-and-social-justice/article6996279.ece.

Cotterell, R (1998) 'Why must legal ideas be interpreted sociologically?' 25(2) *Journal of Law & Society* 171–92.

Dam, S (2017) 'A Super Elite Club of Lawyers Dominates India's Justice System. How Long Will It Rule?' *Quartz India* (5 November 5) qz.com/1119667/a-super-elite-club-of-senior-advocates-dominates-indias-courts-how-long-will-it-rule/.

Daksh (2015) *Access to Justice Survey* dakshindia.org/access-to-justice-survey/.

Deccan Herald (2014) 'HC Judges create flutter in court' 8 January www.deccanherald.com/content/379389/hc-judge-creates-flutter-court.html.

Dezalay, Y and Garth, BG (2002) *The Internationalization of Palace Wars: Lawyers, Economists, and the Contest to Transform Latin American States* (Chicago, University of Chicago Press).

—— (2010) *Asian Legal Revivals: Lawyers in the Shadow of Empire* (Chicago, University of Chicago Press).

Dhavan, R (1994) 'Law as struggle: Public Interest Law in India' 36 *Journal of the Indian Law Institute* 325.

Dhawan, H (2011) 'Abhishek Manu Singhvi, Vijay Mallya are Top Earners in Rajya Sabha' *Times of India* 18 November.

Dhru, K (2010) *Entry Barriers to the Litigation Profession in India* (Ahmedbad, Research Foundation for Governance in India) www.rfgindia.org/publications/Entry%20Barriers%20to%20Litigation.pdf.

Eckert, J (2003) *The Charisma of Direct Action: Power, Politics and the Shiv Sena* (Oxford, Oxford University Press).

—— (2004) 'Urban Governance and Emergent Forms of Legal Pluralism in Mumbai' 36(50) *The Journal of Legal Pluralism and Unofficial Law* 29–60.

Epp, CR (1998) *The Rights Revolution: Lawyers, Activists, and Supreme Courts in Comparative Perspective* (Chicago, University of Chicago Press).

Flood, J (2017) 'Theories of Law Firm Globalization in the Shadow of Colonialism: A Cultural and Institutional Analysis of English and Indian Corporate Law Firms in the Twentieth and Twenty-First Centuries' in DB Wilkins, VS Khanna and DM Trubek (eds), *The Indian Legal Profession in the Age of Globalization* (Cambridge, Cambridge University Press).

Gadbois, GH (1969) 'Selection, Background Characteristics, and Voting Behavior of Indian Supreme Court Judges, 1950–1959' *Comparative Judicial Behavior* 221–56.

—— (2011) *Judges of the Supreme Court of India: 1950–1989* (Oxford, Oxford University Press).

Galanter, M (1969a) 'An Incomplete Bibliography of the Indian Legal Profession' 3(3) *Law & Society Review* 445–62.

—— (1969b) 'Introduction: the Study of the Indian Legal Profession' 3(2) *Law & Society Review* 201–18.

Galanter, M and Krishnan, JK (2003) 'Debased Informalism' in T Heller and E Jensen (eds), *Beyond Common Knowledge Empirical Approaches to the Rule of Law* (Palo Alto, Stanford University Press).

Galanter, M and Robinson, N (2017) 'India's Grand Advocates: a Legal Elite Flourishing in the Era of Globalization' in DB Wilkins, VS Khanna and DM Trubek (eds), *The Indian Legal Profession in the Age of Globalization* (Cambridge, Cambridge University Press).

Gandhi, JS (1982) *Lawyers and Touts. A Study in the Sociology of Legal Profession* (New Delhi, Hindustan Publishing Corp).

—— (1989) 'A Sociological Portrait of the Indian Legal Profession' in RL Abel and PSC Lewis (eds), *Lawyers in Society: Vol I The Common Law World* (Berkeley, University of California Press).

Ganz, K (2010) 'NUJS-ers Threaten Outlook & India Today Law School Rankings with Press Council Complaint' *Legally India* 20 August www.legallyindia.com/lawschools/nujs-ers-threaten-outlook-a-india-today-law-school-rankings-with-press-council-complaint-20100820-1213.

—— (2011) 'Demystifying India's Legal Market' *Livemint* 25 November www.livemint.com/Opinion/7wgxY0tcuLyw2yG2G0HcvL/Demystifying-India8217s-legal-market.html.

—— (2012) 'Fascination with LLMs in India' *Livemint* 19 January www.livemint.com/Opinion/H8pipHDB9aVr9fRZJ6PrQO/Fascination-with-LLMs-in-India.html.

—— (2015) 'Can Foreign Law Firms Enter Now' *Livemint* 3 March www.livemint.com/Politics/Y1W6WftQGES2pGatn2SKaO/Can-foreign-law-firms-enter-India-now.html.

Garg, A (2017) 'Almost Half of All Indian Lawyers Are Fake, Bar Council Claims' *IndiaTimes* 23 January.

Garth, BG (2016) 'Corporate Lawyers in Emerging Markets' 12 *Annual Review of Law and Social Science* 441–57.

Gauri, V and Brinks, D (eds) (2008) *Courting Social Justice: Judicial Enforcement of Social and Economic Rights in the Developing World* (Cambridge, Cambridge University Press).

Gingerich, J, Khanna, VS and Singh, A (2017) 'The Anatomy of Legal Recruitment in India: Tracing the Tracks of Globalization' in DB Wilkins, VS Khanna and DM Trubek (eds), *The Indian Legal Profession in the Age of Globalization* (Cambridge, Cambridge University Press).

Gingerich, J and Robinson, N (2017) 'Responding to the Market: the Impact of the Rise of Corporate Law Firms on Elite Legal Education in India' in DB Wilkins, VS Khanna and DM Trubek (eds), *The Indian Legal Profession in the Age of Globalization* (Cambridge, Cambridge University Press).

Gupta, A (2017) 'Probono and Corporate Legal Sector in India' in DB Wilkins, VS Khanna and DM Trubek (eds), *The Indian Legal Profession in the Age of Globalization* (Cambridge, Cambridge University Press).

Gupta, S (2006) *History of Legal Education* (Delhi, Deep and Deep Publications).

Hindu Editorial (2016) 'The curious case of Justice Karnan' 17 February www.thehindu.com/opinion/editorial/the-curious-case-of-justice-karnan/article8245394.ece.

Hunter, R (2002) 'Taking up equality: Women barristers and the denial of discrimination' 10(2) *Feminist Legal Studies* 113–30.

Iyer, S (2016) 'Kangaroo Court in Bengal Punishes Woman who had Extra-Marital Affair, Orders Husband to Cut off her Hair' *India News* 13 October www.india.com/news/india/kangaroo-court-in-bengal-punishes-woman-who-had-extra-marital-affair-orders-husband-to-cut-off-her-hair-1554266/.

Jain, C, Jayaraj, S, Muraleedharan, S, Singh, H and Galanter, M (2016) 'The Elusive Island of Excellence: A Study on Student Demographics, Accessibility and Inclusivity at National Law School 2015–16' barandbench.com/wp-content/uploads/2016/06/SSRN-id2788311.pdf.

Jensen, EG and Heller, TC (eds) (2003) *Beyond Common Knowledge: Empirical Approaches to the Rule of Law* (Palo Alto, Stanford University Press).

John, S (2013) 'Kangaroo Courts Rise and Thrive in India' *The Times of India* 15 March timesofindia.indiatimes.com/india/Kangaroo-courts-rise-and-thrive-in-India/articleshow/18981684.cms.

Kachhwaha, K (2011) 'Khap Adjudication in India: Honouring the culture with crimes' 6(1/2) *International Journal of Criminal Justice Sciences* 297.

Kaur, R (2010) 'Khap Panchayats, Sex Ratio and Female Agency' XLV(23) *Economic and Political Weekly* 14.

Khanna, VS (2017) 'The Evolving Global Supply Chain for Legal Services: India's Role as a Critical Link' in DB Wilkins, VS Khanna and DM Trubek (eds), *The Indian Legal Profession in the Age of Globalization* (Cambridge, Cambridge University Press).

Khorakiwala, R (2018) 'Legal Consciousness as Viewed through the Judicial Iconography of the Madras High Court' *Asian Journal of Law and Society* 1–23.

Krishnan, JK (2004) 'Professor Kingsfield Goes to Delhi: American Academics, the Ford Foundation, and the Development of Legal Education in India' 46(4) *The American Journal of Legal History* 447–99.

—— (2009) '(Un)Wanted Outsiders: The Debate Over Excluding American and British Law Firms from a Thriving Capital Market' *Draft Conference Paper* on file with author.

—— (2010) 'Globetrotting Law Firms' 23 *Georgetown Journal of Legal Ethics* 57–114.

—— (2013) 'Peel-Off Lawyers: Legal Professionals in India's Corporate Law Firm Sector' 9(1) *Socio-Legal Review*.

Krishnan, JK and Thomas, PW (2015) 'Surveying Key Aspects of Sociolegal Scholarship on India: an Overview' 11(1) *Annual Review of Law and Social Science* 337–52.

Kumar, AP (2015) 'Does a senior counsel double your chances of success in the supreme court? Research suggests it might' *Legally India* 15 September www.legallyindia.com/the-bench-and-the-bar/does-a-senior-counsel-double-your-chances-of-success-in-the-sc-research-suggests-it-might-20150915-6602.

Legally India (2012) 'US Job Market Remains in Dumps; 92% of Indian LLM grads come home empty handed?' 19 January www.legallyindia.com/analysis/li-mint-us-job-market-remains-in-dumps-92-of-indian-llm-grads-come-home-empty-handed-20120119-2506.

—— (2013) 'RTI Reveals: 1.3 Million Advocates' 18 February www.legallyindia.com/the-bench-and-the-bar/rti-reveals-number-of-lawyers-india-20130218-3448.

—— (2014) 'Untangling the Madras HC turmoil: A bar at war, a question of caste, or business as usual?' 17 January www.legallyindia.com/analysis/madras-hc-turmoil-a-bar-at-war-20140117-4250.

Makhija, S and Raha, S (2011) 'Challenges Faced by Indian Women Legal Professionals' *Rainmaker India*, www.scribd.com/document/101516872/Challenges-Faced-by-Indian-Women-Legal-Professionals-Executive-Summary.

Mathur, NN (2017) 'National Law Universities, Original Intent & Real Founders' *Law.In* 24 July www.livelaw.in/national-law-universities-original-intent-real-founders/.

Mehren, Von, AT (1965) 'Law and Legal Education in India: Some Observations' 78(6) *Harvard Law Review* 1180–89.

Mehta, PB (2007) 'India's Judiciary: The Promise of Uncertainty' in D Kapur and PB Mehta (eds), *Public Institutions in India: Performance and Design* (Oxford: Oxford University Press).

Mendelsohn, O (1981) 'The Pathology of the Indian Legal System' 15(4) *Modern Asian Studies* 823–63.

Menon, NRM (2009) *Turning Point: Memoirs of Padmashree Professor. NR Madhava Menon* (Delhi, Universal Law Publishing Company).

Michelson, E (2013) 'Women in the Legal Profession, 1970–2010: A Study of the Global Supply of Lawyers' 20(1) *Indiana Journal of Global Legal Studies* 1071.

Mishra, S (2015) 'Women in Indian Courts of Law: A Study of Women Legal Professionals in the District Court of Lucknow, Uttar Pradesh, India' *e-cadernos* 24 October journals.openedition.org/eces/1976.

Moog, RS (1998) 'Elite-Court Relations in India: An Unsatisfactory Arrangement' 38(4) *Asian Survey* 410–23.

Morrison, C (1972) 'Kinship in Professional Relations' 14(1) *Comparative Studies in Society and History* 100–25.

Nagla, BK (2001) 'Sociology of Legal Profession: A Study of Women Lawyers in India' 1 *MDU Law Journal* 73–94.

Nanda, A, Wilkins, DB and Fong, B (2017) 'Mapping India's Corporate Law Firm Sector' in DB Wilkins, VS Khanna and DM Trubek (eds), *The Indian Legal Profession in the Age of Globalization* (Cambridge, Cambridge University Press).

Narrain, A and Thiruvengadam, AK (2013) 'Social Justice Lawyering and the Meaning of Indian Constitutionalism: A Case Study of the Alternative Law Forum' 31(3) *Wisconsin International Law Journal* 525.

Papa, M and Wilkins, DB (2011) 'Globalization, Lawyers and India: Toward a Theoretical Synthesis of Globalization Studies and the Sociology of the Legal Profession' 18(3) *International Journal of the Legal Profession* 175–209.

Paul, JJ (1991) *The Legal Profession in Colonial South India* (Bombay, Oxford University Press).

Ramasubramanian, R (2015) 'Madras High Court: "Never before has it fallen to such low levels," said the CJI' *Scroll India* 29 September scroll.in/article/758584/madras-high-court-never-before-has-it-fallen-to-such-low-levels-said-the-cji.

Ridgeway, C (2011) *Framed By Gender: How Inequalities Persist In The Modern World* (New York, Oxford University Press).

Robinson, N (2009) 'Expanding judiciaries: India and the rise of the good governance court' 8(1) *Washington University Global Studies Law Review* 1.

Rosalio, W (1970) 'Electoral Participation and the Occupational Composition of Cabinets and Parliaments' 75 *American Journal of Sociology* 185.

Sahgal, P and Bamzai, K (2010) 'Rich Lawyers: The New Nawabs' *India Today* 4 December.

Sarda, K (2017) '12 Lakh Lawyers Plague India's Courts' *The New Indian Express* 5 February www.newindianexpress.com/thesundaystandard/2017/feb/05/12-lakh-fake-lawyers-plague-indias-courts-1567019.html.

Sathe SP (2002) *Judicial Activism in India: Transgressing Borders and Enforcing Limits* (New Delhi, Oxford University Press).

Schukoske, JE (2009) 'Legal Education: Legal Education Reform in India: Dialogue Among Indian Law Teachers' 1 *Jindal Global Law Review* 251.

Sethi, R (1987) 'Women Lawyers: A Study in Professionalisation' 29(1) *Journal of the Indian Law* 29–47.

Sharma, S (2002) 'Women Lawyers Practicing at Delhi courts: A Sociological Study' dissertation, Jawaharlal Nehru University, unpublished.

Sharafi, M (2015) 'South Asian Legal History' 11(1) *Annual Review of Law and Social Science* 309–36.

Singh, A (2017) 'Globalization of the Legal Profession and Regulation of Law Practice in India: The 'Foreign Entry' Debate' in DB Wilkins, VS Khanna and DM Trubek (eds), *The Indian Legal Profession in the Age of Globalization* (Cambridge, Cambridge University Press).

Singh, R (2017) 'Festina Lente or Disguised protectionism: Monopoly and Competition in the Indian Legal Profession' in DB Wilkins, VS Khanna and DM Trubek (eds), *The Indian Legal Profession in the Age of Globalization* (Cambridge, Cambridge University Press).

Varottil, U (2017) 'The Impact of Globalization and Cross-Border Mergers and Acquisitions on the Legal Profession in India' in DB Wilkins, VS Khanna and DM Trubek (eds), *The Indian Legal Profession in the Age of Globalization* (Cambridge, Cambridge University Press).

Vatuk, S (2013) 'The "women's court" in India: an alternative dispute resolution body for women in distress' 45(1) *The Journal of Legal Pluralism and Unofficial Law* 76–103.

Venkatesan, J (2011) 'Former BCI Vice-Chief Gets Bail in Corruption Case' *The Hindu* 20 April.

Vijayakumar, C (2015) 'Judges and Castes: a Counterview' *The Hindu* 19 March www.thehindu.com/opinion/op-ed/judges-and-castes-a-counterview/article7008156.ece.

Vyawahare, M (2013) 'A Conversation With: Bar Council Chairman Manan Kumar Mishra' *New York Times Blog* 24 January india.blogs.nytimes.com/2013/01/24/a-conversation-with-bar-council-of-india-chairman-manan-kumar-mishra/.

Wilkins, DB and Khanna, VS (2017) 'Globalization and the Rise of the In-House Counsel Movement in India' in DB Wilkins, VS Khanna and DM Trubek (eds), *The Indian Legal Profession in the Age of Globalization* (Cambridge, Cambridge University Press).

Wilkins, DB, Khanna, VS and Trubek, DM (eds) (2017) *The Indian Legal Profession in the Age of Globalization* (Cambridge, Cambridge University Press).

Yamunan, S (2017) 'Justice Karnan is a Standing Momentum to the Failure of the Collegium System, Claims Former Judge' *Scroll.In* 12 March scroll.in/article/831587/justice-karnan-is-a-standing-monument-to-the-failure-of-the-collegium-system-claims-former-judge.

37

Indonesia
Professionals, Brokers and Fixers[1]

SANTY KOUWAGAM AND ADRIAAN BEDNER

I. INTRODUCTION

As in virtually all countries, globalisation has redefined the organisation and role of lawyers in Indonesia. Foreign investment and international commerce have promoted an increase in the number and size of modern corporate law firms, growing specialisation within the legal profession, more foreign lawyers, and a rise in commercial arbitration and litigation. The promotion of human rights has stimulated public interest litigation and the related growth of legal departments in civil society organisations (Lindsey and Crouch 2013; Crouch 2011; Lev 2011). This development has been supported by the transition from the authoritarian New Order of President Suharto to a liberal democracy, which produced, among other things, a new activist Constitutional Court (Butt 2012; Mietzner 2010). The objectives of these corporate and public interest lawyers – whom we will refer to as 'professionals' – are very different, but they are united in subscribing to the ideal of the rule of law and having legal expertise as their primary capital.

However, a large group of lawyers has a different orientation and capital. They are 'fixers' or 'problem-solvers', who use the law as a means to an end or even break it to achieve their goals. The rise of fixers during the New Order years was the result not of globalisation but of domestic conditions. A key issue was the corruption that infected the entire bureaucracy, police, prosecutor's service and judiciary. Fixers operate in the grey areas of law, business and politics, presenting themselves as experts not in law but in manipulating the justice system in order to 'get things done'. They enjoy considerable autonomy from clients and have different views about professional ideals and ethics.

Most lawyers find themselves somewhere between the 'professionals' and the fixers, resembling the 'brokers' of routine civil litigation in the US (Kritzer 1990). Like the fixers, they are primarily motivated to achieve their clients' goals but retain a professional attachment to rule of law ideals. Many brokers operate within the law's boundaries in

---

[1] We use the term 'lawyers' and 'legal profession' for those in private practice. The common term in Indonesia is *pengacara* or *advokat* or *penasehat hukum* (literally legal adviser).

some cases but transgress them in others, depending on the circumstances. Furthermore, the roles of professional and fixer need not be united in one person. Some firms have both on their payrolls, and some firms of professionals refer clients to a fixer.

Despite their differences, all lawyers share an interest in erecting entry barriers, which enhance their status and limit internal and external competition (Abel 1989; 2011). But the profound heterogeneity of Indonesia's legal profession produces unusually deep fault lines, reflected in constant infighting within the Bar and the proliferation of competing Bar associations. Heterogeneity also undermines the profession's claim to self-regulation and legitimises government efforts to assert control, even if these have not yet succeeded.

The current problems in the legal profession are closely intertwined with those confronting the legal system. The difficult transition from colonialism to independence, lengthy periods of authoritarian rule and economic problems fostered the spread of corruption throughout all legal institutions and a decline in the quality of legal education and of legal reasoning and the use of precedent in developing the law. This has contributed to the indeterminacy of law, skewing the system in favour of fixers.

The focus of this chapter is on commercial lawyers. We begin with a historical overview of the roots and development of the profession, with particular attention to its organisation. We then move to the education and training of lawyers before discussing the organisation of law firms: how they relate to the formation of professional ideologies and perform different functions. Next, we discuss the different types of lawyers and how they operate, as well as their relationships within the firm and with lawyers from other firms and clients.[2] We conclude that despite the profession's problems there is hope for improvement.

II. A SHORT HISTORY OF THE INDONESIAN LEGAL PROFESSION AND ITS ORGANISATION

In the colonial era, Indonesian lawyers were a small group of accomplished and independent professionals, mostly Javanese aristocrats trained in the Netherlands and devoted to Dutch legal institutions and codes.[3] Together with a much larger number of Dutch lawyers they organised a Bar association called the *Balie van Advocaten*.[4] Possessing skill and status, many relinquished private practice for positions in government or the judiciary after independence in 1945, further reducing the small number of private practitioners.[5]

During the 1950s and early 1960s, Indonesia moved from a democratic to an authoritarian political system, seriously jeopardising the independence of the judiciary. All

---

[2] Data in this study have been gathered through participant observation by Santy Kouwagam, who worked for the firm of a 'family' lawyer for four years and conducted in-depth interviews with 48 lawyers across the professional spectrum.

[3] The first law school in the Netherlands Indies educating lawyers to the level of *mr* (Master) was the *Rechtshogeschool* in Batavia (now Jakarta) established in 1924.

[4] The informal Indonesian *pokrol bambu* or bush-lawyers organised themselves into *Persatuan Pengacara Indonesia* in 1927. University-educated lawyers were contemptuous of their limited legal education, but they played an important role in providing legal assistance to the poorer segments of the population.

[5] Lev (1976: 134) estimates that 75 per cent of ethnic Indonesian lawyers (around 300) were involved in the nationalist movement.

jurists suffered from the decline in the rule of law, while those in commercial practice also had to struggle with a lack of work due to the national economy's collapse. This situation improved during the early years of Suharto's New Order (1965–70), which began to restore the rule of law (Lev 1978; Pompe 2005). The number of lawyers grew as the economy rapidly expanded because of increased foreign and domestic investment. The profession also gained respect from the Indonesian Bar association's role in defending civil rights, including lobbying for the right of citizens to seek legal assistance, which was formally recognised in Law 14/1970.

PERADIN (*Persatuan Advokat Indonesia* or United Indonesian Lawyers) was established in 1963 and recognised as the official representative of Indonesian lawyers three years later. When PERADIN openly challenged the regime's increasingly authoritarian ways, however, the government encouraged members with personal ambitions to leave and set up a competing association, though this failed to impair PERADIN's influence. In 1985, therefore, the government forced lawyers into a new association – IKADIN (*Ikatan Advokat Indonesia* or Indonesian Lawyers League) – which it tried to subject to state supervision (Lev 1987). The autonomy of the profession declined further when Law 2/1986 exposed lawyers' daily activities to supervision by district court chairmen. But despite these measures, the government never managed to gain full control of either PERADIN or IKADIN, and its leaders continued to resist government interference with the rule of law (Lev 1992: 30).

Other organisational changes followed from the specialisation that began in response to rapid economic development and the need to master complex legal forms. Specialist lawyers established IPHI (*Ikatan Penasehat Hukum Indonesia* or Association of Indonesian Legal Counsellors) in 1987, AKHI (*Asosiasi Konsultan Hukum Indonesia* or Association of Indonesian Legal Consultants) in 1988, and HKHPM (*Himpunan Konsultan Hukum Pasar Modal* or Association of Capital Market Legal Consultants) in 1989. In 1990, the government sponsored another split in IKADIN by supporting a number of lawyers in establishing AAI (*Asosiasi Advokat Indonesia* or Indonesian Lawyers' Association); and in 1993 HAPI (*Himpunan Advokat/Pengacara Indonesia* or Indonesian Congregation of Indonesian Solicitors/Barristers) split off from IPHI. These divisions made it more difficult for lawyers to form a united front against the government, but they also showed that lawyers could not be brought under its full control.

Despite the promise of a return to the rule of law at the start of the New Order, the legal system soon suffered as much from Suharto's authoritarian rule as it had from Sukarno's. The appointment of Suharto favorite, Oemar Seno Adji, as Chief Justice in 1974 opened the floodgates to an unprecedented degree of corruption in the judiciary. Judgments had ceased regular publication long before, and judicial development of the law almost came to a standstill (Pompe 2005: 413–16). This change had a profound influence on the practice of litigation lawyers, who confronted the need to engage in corruption rather than legal argument in order to win cases. Many adapted to the new dispensation, while others tried to keep practising as they had.

Until then, legislation on lawyers had created only two types of litigation licences.[6] This changed with Law 8/1995, which introduced an important division among corporate

---

[6] One permitted practice in a single province whereas the other allowed practice anywhere in Indonesia (see Point 8 of Supreme Court Circular Letter 8/1987).

lawyers between litigators and 'legal consultants', who could provide legal opinions but not appear in court (unless they held a separate licence). The latter had less contact with judges but also avoided the taint of corrupt practices in court.

After Suharto stepped down in 1998, reformers pushed through major legislative and organisational changes to guarantee the independence of the judiciary. By then, however, problems in the courts ran so deep that a return to the rule of law had become extremely difficult. Almost 20 years later some things have changed for the better, but the problems are still far from resolved. Although judgments are theoretically accessible, few have been made workable sources of law, limiting their role in legal debate and their influence on legal development (Bedner 2013: 257). Legal certainty thus remains unattainable, and corruption has continued unabated.

In 2003 Indonesia enacted its first Law on Lawyers (18/2003, henceforth LL), as part of a whole package of reforms to the legal system sponsored by the IMF. It required the adoption of a code of ethics, establishment of a Lawyers Council to enforce the code, and creation of a new Bar Association. It addressed issues of registration and discipline, supervision, rights and responsibilities, remuneration, duty to provide legal aid, and admission of foreign lawyers.

The registration of *all* practising lawyers was an important innovation. Lawyers who represented clients in court always had to register, but the practice of law was otherwise unregulated, allowing so-called *pokrol bambu* or bush-lawyers to offer their services in resolving legal problems, despite opposition by professional lawyers (Lev 2000: 147). The new Law even criminalised practising law without being registered, but the Constitutional Court declared this unconstitutional.[7] The LL also requires all lawyers to take an oath at the court of appeal before practising. Since only Bar Association members can take the oath, it has become the gatekeeper for legal practice. Such changes meant that for the first time in the 58 years since independence the government recognised the autonomy of the legal profession, allowing it to regulate access and behaviour.

This raised the question of how to establish the Bar Association prescribed by the LL, given the patchwork of lawyers' associations. After a task force of eight associations discussed this for two years, PERADI (*Persatuan Advokat Indonesia* or Indonesian Lawyers Union) was established in 2005.[8] However, even without political pressure from an authoritarian state, internal conflict soon erupted, leading to the creation of a second association, KAI (*Kongres Advokat Indonesia* or Indonesian Lawyers Congress).

The split had nothing to do with different visions of lawyers' role in a democracy but rather expressed competition over who would administer the Bar exam. The Supreme Court got involved as well because it had to decide who could take the oath at the court of appeal. At first it supported PERADI, allowing only its members to be registered.[9] However, this led to vehement protests and even lawsuits by KAI.[10] After the incumbent Chief Justice retired, his successor allowed courts of appeal to accept lawyers from both organisations.[11]

---

[7] No 006/PUU-II/2004.
[8] See www.peradi.or.id/index.php/profil/detail/1; peradi.org/2015/12/05/sejarah/.
[9] Circular Letters 089/KMA/VI/2010 and 052/KMA/HK.01/III/2011.
[10] See eg Constitutional Court Decision No 40/PUU-XII/2014 and Central Jakarta District Court Decision No 394/Pdt.G/2011/PN.JKT.PST.
[11] Head of Supreme Court letter No 73/KMA/HK.01/IX/2015.

The tendency of Indonesian lawyers to get embroiled in disputes has also marred PERADI's internal organisation. When members had to elect a new chairperson in 2015, they could not even agree on the procedure. The police had to intervene to ensure that the arguments did not turn into a brawl after three candidates claimed to have won. The dispute then moved from the meeting room to the media, without much prospect for a solution. In the end, PERADI split into three parts, all claiming to be the legitimate representative.[12]

Before this turmoil, President Yudhoyono sent Parliament the draft for a new Law on Lawyers, which would introduce a new mechanism to deal with lawyers involved in corruption, a National Lawyers Board with members selected by Parliament, thereby curtailing self-regulation. More emphatically than the LL, the Bill mandated a single Bar Association. A few respected senior lawyers supported the proposed Board but rejected unification of the Bar.[13] Others disagreed with both proposals. Demonstrating under the banner of PERADI and wearing their robes, hundreds of lawyers took to the streets to protest the draft law.[14] Parliament responded by terminating its debates, thereby upholding the autonomy of the profession but leaving the Bar divided into multiple associations with separate disciplinary boards.[15]

III. TRAINING OF LAWYERS

A. Law Schools

To join a Bar association one must hold a *Sarjana Hukum* (LLB) degree from an Indonesian university. Law is not a prestigious field of study, requiring minimal scores on entrance exams compared to other fields (Arnold 2008: 16).[16] There are enormous status differences among the more than 300 law faculties. Students seeking to enter a corporate law firm must attend one of the two most prestigious state universities or a few expensive private universities.[17]

Studying law is neither challenging nor exciting at any university. Teaching consists mostly of lectures to classes of 100 students or more; materials are usually limited to statutory law and codes; precedents are seldom mentioned, let alone studied; and few

---

[12] news.detik.com/berita/2872158/munas-peradi-pecah-menjadi-3-kubu; nasional.tempo.co/read/653488/munas-ricuh-peradi-pecah-jadi-tiga-kubu.

[13] They even filed a case at the Constitutional Court, but it was rejected on procedural grounds (Constitutional Court Decision No 66/PUU-VIII/2010).

[14] Kompas 24 September 2014 Tolak RUU Advokat, Peradi Unjuk Rasa di Bundaran HI (Refusing the Draft Law on Lawyers PERADI stages a demonstration at the HI roundabout).

[15] Older 'Bar associations' such as IKADIN and AAI also survive. Lawyers' inability to unify is likely to persist, given the more than 20 petitions against the LL filed with the Constitutional Court, mostly about the constitutionality of the oath-taking requirements and whether to have one or more Bar associations.

[16] The national entrance exam is divided into two main subjects: science-technology and social-humaniora. Law is part of social-humaniora. Within social-humaniora, law is among the highest but lower than international relations. In 2016–17 Universitas Indonesia required a 53 per cent score in order to be accepted on an international relations course, compared to 50 per cent for law. Still, both are much lower than the 62 per cent for medicine.

[17] Universitas Indonesia, Universitas Gadjah Mada, and Universitas Pelita Harapan (private) are at the top of the official ranking system; some graduates of Universitas Padjadjaran and Universitas Parahyangan (private) also enter those firms.

students see the inside of a court. At the end of their studies law students are familiar with the main concepts and categories of black letter law but have obtained little insight into its operation and moral underpinnings or training in skills like legal reasoning and writing (ABNR 1999: 50–51).

Few law graduates seek master's degrees.[18] An increasing but still relatively small number take an LLM abroad, mainly lawyers in the corporate law firms. Most pay for this by themselves, though a few obtain a government grant or foreign scholarship or are supported by their law firms. This is usually their first encounter with other legal systems and methods of legal interpretation. Such a degree is important for those who wish to advance in the prestigious Jakarta law firms because of the status it confers as well as the skills it conveys. Proficiency in English is particularly important because many of those firms' clients are foreigners (ABNR 1999: 56).

B. On the Job Training and Certification

In order to become a member of a Bar association a law graduate needs to pass the Bar exam. To prepare for the Bar exam one must follow a professional course administered by PERADI, KAI or IKADIN involving lectures by practitioners on the role and function of lawyers, the judicial system, professional ethics, and civil, criminal, administrative, religious and labour court procedure. At the end, participants take a mock exam. The Bar exam consists of about 200 multiple-choice questions on formal aspects of legal procedure, such as how to refer to the parties or which kind of stamp to attach to documents. Candidates also draft a power of attorney and a court claim for a case, which is the same every year. The quality of legal argument does not significantly affect the exam grade.

Candidate lawyers also must provide verification criteria determined by the Bar association, which are quite arbitrary and frequently changed.[19] Candidates can then register to be sworn in at the high court of their domicile; but because of disputes between Bar associations, those associations must negotiate with the chair of the court of appeal to arrange the ceremony. There are not many opportunities to do so, and they are announced on the Bar association websites shortly before the ceremony takes place, causing candidates more stress than the Bar exam itself.[20]

IV. LAW FIRMS

There are three legal models for law firms: (1) a single lawyer or a collective without any formal establishment; (2) a firm based on a deed of establishment containing articles of

---

[18] Interview 6 October 2015 with PERADI administrator Anthony Siburian, who said that no more than 10 per cent of registered lawyers have master's degrees.

[19] The requirements fluctuate with the interest of Bar associations in recruiting new members. From 2010 to 2014, when the status of PERADI was quite secure, candidates had to intern at a law firm for at least two years and then submit reports to PERADI describing at least three civil and three criminal cases they had witnessed. KAI did not require this.

[20] Some candidates even obtain false identification cards to participate in the ceremony at a court of appeal outside their domicile. However, this has become more difficult with the new digital identity registration system.

association; and (3) a partnership based on a contract between partners without limited liability. Most lawyers now work in firms that resemble corporations, requiring a notarial deed of establishment and an article of association. Because they are so dominant we will focus on them.

In 1999, 75 per cent of corporate firms had only one or two partners and fewer than 15 associates (ABNR 1999: 43). Now the largest firms have about 15 partners and more than 100 associates.[21] They started to develop after the Suharto regime enacted a new law on foreign investment in 1967.[22] The first firm was Ali Budiardjo, Nugroho, Reksodiputro, which had the mining giant Freeport-McMoRan as its first client.[23] In 1971, the first Indonesian law firm based on the American model was founded by Mochtar Kusumaatmadja, who graduated from a US university (Dezalay and Garth 2010: 221). Most of the lawyers do transactional work, but modern corporate firms also have a litigation department.

What makes law firms 'modern' is a hierarchy of partners, associates and paralegals or legal assistants. Modern firms deploy information technology and data management to facilitate internal collaboration. Most modern firms cooperate with foreign or transnational law firms as well as tax consultants and accountants. They hire graduates with good grades from well-known universities, who display a cooperative rather than a competitive attitude.[24] Modern firms employ foreign lawyers for transactional work, but their number may not exceed one for every three Indonesian lawyers, with a maximum of five per firm.[25]

Traditional firms are usually directed by a single person, who may work with up to 40 lawyers. These firms are organised much more loosely; even when there is a distinction between partners and associates it does not significantly affect the power structure. Most firms do not enforce office hours, especially for litigators, who need to spend a lot of time in courthouses and police stations. Unlike modern firms, which use their websites as promotional and informational tools, traditional firms rarely publish lists of their members.

Traditional firms differ greatly in whom they hire. Those established by lawyers with a background in legal aid and cause lawyering tend to look for similar candidates. Traditional firms operating in the grey areas of the legal system look for candidates who either have or can cultivate connections with police officers, prosecutors, judges, politicians, and even court registrars. They are usually hired on the spot without an employment agreement.[26]

---

[21] They follow the Cravath model, hiring graduates from top universities and assigning associates to a partner and/or specialised practice area.
[22] See www.hukumonline.com/berita/baca/lt59db6406dab3a/menelusuri-jejak-kantor-advokat-modern-generasi-pertama.
[23] See www.hukumonline.com/berita/baca/lt59dcb8fc81263/abnr-pendobrak-standar-praktik-firma-hukum-di-indonesia.
[24] Interviews with six partners from five modern firms: ABNR, Ginting & Reksodiputro / Allen & Overy, Hadiputranto Hadinoto & Partners / Baker McKenzie, Oentoeng Suria & Partners / Ashurst and Dermawan & Co.
[25] Art 6 of Decision Letter No M.11-HT.04.02 of the Ministry of Law and Human Rights.
[26] The same method is followed by many non-governmental organisations, including the well-known legal aid institution YLBHI (Pangaribuan 2016: 186–87).

Traditional firms also draft contracts, even if this seldom is their main occupation. These are relatively short documents based on civil law models dating from colonial times, by contrast with the contracts modern corporate firms prepare for their clientele of foreign investors and large Indonesian companies, which are hundreds of pages long, following the Anglo-American model. There is little competition between modern and traditional firms. Modern law firms seldom handle land disputes, practise criminal law,[27] or appear in the administrative court – functions that are the exclusive domain of traditional firms. By contrast, competition between traditional firms can be fierce.

A few traditional firm owners have opened multiple offices, which are permitted as long as they are reported to the Bar association.[28] Such satellite firms appear to be separate entities but actually are controlled by the central firm. Their offices usually are an empty room or mailbox, while the actual workplace is the central firm. Fixers (see below) use this system to assume complete control over litigation, because it enables them to represent opposing parties in a case, thereby evading discipline for conflict of interest. They may also seek to deflect attacks on the central firm by assigning satellite firms the controversial aspects of cases, which might generate risks of defamation actions or criminal prosecution.

V. SIZE, DEMOGRAPHICS, AND SUB-DIVISIONS OF THE PROFESSION

It is difficult to ascertain the number of lawyers in the absence of published data. During the 1970s the number rose from a few hundred to approximately 3,000 (Lev 1992: 5). In 2014, PERADI claimed 26,000 members, with 6,000 more aspiring lawyers waiting to take their oaths. Its 2015 annual report listed 27,912 members. KAI has never published membership information. Even if inconclusive, these numbers indicate a sharp rise in the number of lawyers. However, relative to its population of 260 million, Indonesia still has far fewer private lawyers than neighbouring countries with better developed economies.[29] This is not because there are too few candidates. The World Bank reported in 1999 that approximately 13,000 Indonesian law students graduate annually (ABNR 1999: 19), a number that must have risen over the past two decades, and many of these graduates wish to become lawyers. Instead, we speculate that the reason for the relatively high ratio of population per lawyer is the preference to resolve disputes outside of court because of the many uncertainties of formal litigation.[30]

---

[27] They do assist foreign clients involved in US Foreign Corrupt Practices Act procedures and antitrust allegations.

[28] Elucidation of Article 5(2) Law 18/2003 on Advocates. We know of at least three that operate 2–5 satellite firms.

[29] Neighbouring Malaysia, for instance, has more than 20,000 lawyers for a population of 31 million (1:1,550), www.malaysianbar.org.my/statistics_no_of_lawyers_and_law_firms.html, while Thailand in 2008 had 54,000 for a population of 60 million (1:115) (Munger 2008: 747). In 2016, Indonesia had a GDP per capita of US$11,612, compared with US$16,917 in Thailand and US$27,681 in Malaysia (World Bank, data.worldbank.org/indicator/NY.GDP.PCAP.PP.CD?view=chart).

[30] By way of example, between 2013 and 2016 fewer than 1,000 bankruptcy cases were filed in commercial courts in Indonesia. This seems an absurdly low number when we consider that the Ministry of Industry lists around 3 million industrial companies registered in Indonesia (excluding non-industrial companies).

The profession is not free from gender imbalances, biases and discrimination. While women formed 50.9 per cent of Indonesia's workforce in 2015,[31] they were just 16 per cent of PERADI members. At the higher echelons of both modern and traditional firms men far outnumber women. By contrast, a large majority of junior associates in modern corporate firms are women,[32] allegedly because middle-aged male partners see young women as 'cooperative and not competitive'. A few corporate firms are led by women, who manage to break the glass ceiling through cooperation with foreign firms or by serving long-term foreign clients or partners. In most traditional firms, women are a small minority, usually relegated to drafting lawsuits or taking notes in closed meetings with clients and representing firms in the visual media.

Ethnic alliances are found throughout law firms and even play a role in relations with the judiciary. The first law firms in Indonesia were established by Javanese, but 'Sumatran' firms soon followed (Lev 1976: 154–55). Kinship and patronage are still important in the legal profession. Ethnic Batak (from North Sumatra), often stereotyped as vociferous, remain overrepresented, particularly among litigators. When Batak and Chinese brokers/fixers collaborate, the former take care of practical matters in public, while the latter remain in the background because of their ethnicity. Brokers and fixers hire darker skinned Muslims who look more Indonesian and can 'level' with the predominantly Muslim male policemen, prosecutors, judges and court officials. Modern firms increasingly hire Indonesian-Chinese lawyers who perform well in university. Virtually all modern firms were established by lawyers from elite backgrounds, whereas traditional firms are often led by those who have fought their way up (Hendriyanto: 15–16). This will not change unless modern firms hire lawyers from lower class backgrounds, which is unlikely given the developments in legal education discussed above.

Originally, Indonesian lawyers were engaged almost exclusively in litigation; drafting articles of incorporation and contracts was traditionally managed by notaries (Lev 2000: 245). Today, the growing complexity of commercial transactions has meant that corporate lawyers draft complex legal documents or review those drafted by in-house counsel or foreign law firms for conformity with Indonesian law. Litigation is still the central activity of other lawyers, who obtained a monopoly on representation in court from the 2003 Law on Lawyers.

As already mentioned, Indonesia's commercial lawyers can be divided into three categories: professionals, brokers, and fixers. The professionals include all transactional lawyers and litigators working in modern corporate firms for foreign investors and large Indonesian companies. This category also includes a number of transactional lawyers and litigators working for smaller Indonesian companies, in both modern and traditional firms. Brokers focus more on dealing with the justice system than on legal expertise and rule of law. The majority are found in traditional firms, but some modern firms also employ this type of lawyer. Fixers' only concern is to resolve their client's problem. They focus on litigation and work only in traditional firms. Fixers are used to wallowing in the

---

[31] UNDP Human Development Report 2016, Table 5 (see hdr.undp.org/en/composite/GII).
[32] The proportions of partners who are women in the five largest firms in August 2019 are: Ali Budiardjo, Nugroho, Reksodiputro (7/22), Assegaf, Hamzah & Partners (6/22), Hadiputranto, Hadinoto & Partners (5/16), and Lubis Ganie Surowidjojo (1/7).

mire. The litigation they practise is messy, forcing them to compromise the principles of justice underlying the legal system. A subtype is the 'family lawyer'.

A. Professionals: Transactional Lawyers

Corporate transactional lawyers in modern firms epitomise the professional lawyer. They belong to a global legal profession, are organised in efficient law firms in a 'comfortable commercial stratosphere', and enjoy a high income (Lev 2000: 308). They do not go to court. Their practice is highly specialised, determined by the needs of capital-intensive enterprises, such as natural resource exploitation, plantation agriculture, manufacturing, and project development. They give legal advice about mergers, acquisitions and other commercial activities, draft contracts, and perform due diligence.[33] Most of their clients are foreign investors and large Indonesian companies.

Corporate transactional lawyers expect clients to know their objectives and discuss the details of legal documents. Their legal knowledge and skills involve mastery of detailed rules and regulations related to particular business areas. Their principal attribute is meticulousness. They draft contracts as though the legal system offered the guarantees found in jurisdictions with a high degree of legal certainty. They seek such predictability by choosing arbitration outside Indonesia as their main dispute resolution mechanism. When this does not work, contracts are exposed to the often unpredictable interpretations of the Indonesian judiciary. Several respondents mentioned that not all clients understand how problematic enforcement of contracts can be; for them, due diligence is merely whether the paperwork has been done well and all the boxes have been ticked.[34]

Corporate lawyers are paid in Indonesian rupiahs (because salaries cannot legally be paid in foreign currencies), but a US dollar equivalent is mentioned in their employment contracts. Salaries for associates are US$800–10,000 per month (excluding an annual bonus of at least two months' salary and a performance bonus based on hours billed). Clients pay an hourly rate: US$70–500 for associates, US$425–1,000 for partners. Before accepting an assignment, lawyers usually offer an estimate, propose a fee and draft an engagement letter. Clients rarely pay for all the hours billed, generally getting a discount of 20–50 per cent.

In order to demonstrate their prominence in law and promote themselves, many corporate lawyers give guest lectures and conduct training at universities and government agencies.[35] They also publish in legal journals that are partly commercial and partly academic, more to advertise their knowledge than to advance legal debates.[36] They have few other encounters with jurists outside their firms.

---

[33] Most of these lawyers are members of AKHI or HKHPM, a requirement for issuing legal opinions on capital market matters for publicly listed companies.

[34] Personal communication from a corporate lawyer, observation of corporate lawyers doing due diligence and personal communication from the client of an international bank.

[35] Foreign lawyers must teach in order to obtain a recommendation for a work permit issued by the Ministry of Law and Human Rights.

[36] Firms need to pay high fees for this, ranging from US$2,500 for a paragraph to US$25,000 for a full article in journals like the *International Financial Law Review* or the *International Comparative Legal Guide*.

Transactional lawyers in traditional firms serve smaller companies and cannot avoid the Indonesian legal system as easily as their corporate counterparts. When disputes arise, they or their litigator colleagues must appear before Indonesian courts instead of international arbitrators. The probability of such disputes is increased by reliance on Indonesian statutes, which present many uncertainties because interpretations are not regularly updated by Supreme Court case law, especially concerning the Civil and Commercial Codes, which date from colonial times. But what distinguishes all these professional transactional lawyers from brokers is that they conduct their business in conformity with the law rather than looking for loopholes.

B. Professionals: Litigators

Most modern corporate law firms also have departments with specialised litigators. Some of their cases concern contracts drafted by colleagues, but clients also come to them directly. These litigators prefer arbitration to litigation and foreign arbitration (in Singapore and Hong Kong, for instance) to arbitration in Indonesia. But because adversaries manage to circumvent arbitration, and some disputes (such as those involving land) cannot be resolved through arbitration, litigators still have to deal with the realities of Indonesian courts. Professional litigators in traditional firms do this daily, since they are seldom involved in arbitration. Furthermore, they do not handle criminal cases, which they refer to brokers or fixers.

All professional litigators prepare their cases with scrupulous care to reduce judges' room for manoeuvre because Indonesian law offers little certainty. Many statutory provisions are vague or conflicting. The neglect of precedent is justified by the specious argument that judgments are not a source of law in civil law systems (Bedner 2016: 27). By studying judgments published on the Supreme Court's website, professional litigators try to find support for their arguments. However, this is time consuming because judgments often appear years after being issued, are not organised into categories, and lack 'added value'.[37] Lawyers from corporate law firms said they told clients they would not use extra-legal means to win cases and advised clients to choose another firm if they wanted to use a broker or a fixer.[38]

C. Brokers

The majority of Indonesian lawyers fall into this category. They are not committed to the rule of law, legal expertise or legal development. Though they prefer to observe the law, some push the legal system's boundaries. They examine the character and weaknesses of judges in order to manipulate judicial opinions. They also actively solicit clients, loitering

---

[37] For some legal aid and public interest lawyers, building a better system is an extra incentive to start litigation.
[38] The legal obligation to avoid corrupt practices (because of the US Foreign Corrupt Practices Act) is an important incentive for foreign corporations to work with professional litigators.

around the courthouse and police station to hear when claims or complaints are filed. A litigator who finds an interesting case will offer his services to the accused or justice seeker. Because brokers cannot advertise like modern corporate law firms and lack repeat-player clients, such unconventional methods are necessary to ensure their 'operational stock'. Litigators' engagement letters are usually vague and broad; a power of attorney will list their professional responsibilities in greater detail. Until they are retained they are free to talk to the opposing party and test the waters.

Most brokers would like to enjoy the prestige and income of professionals or the power of fixers, but the messy reality of Indonesian business, bureaucracy, police, prosecutors and judiciary forces them to play by the informal rules. As a result, their practices sometimes resemble those of professionals and sometimes those of fixers.

D. Fixers

Fixers are the mirror image of transactional lawyers. Their main practice is criminal law. Successful ones seek the limelight, voicing opinions in the media whenever they get the chance. They have been socialised to compete with other lawyers. At the same time, they are secretive about what they do. Fixers we interviewed tended to speak of the law in exalted terms but became very cautious when asked about ethical issues. They insisted their job was just to defend clients to the best of their ability but then added, as an afterthought: 'as long as it is in accordance with the law'. According to a renowned senior public interest lawyer, this actually means they 'blindly' defend clients, using any means to achieve a positive outcome.[39] Indeed, many will approach judges, play golf with prosecutors and police, and engage in other suspicious activities to realise their objectives, unafraid of sanctions because of the weak disciplinary system. In court, some test the limits of the system and have to be reprimanded for insulting opponents.[40]

Good fixers are the most knowledgeable about the nuts and bolts of legal procedure. They resort to illicit means to enforce judgments, using *preman* (thugs), bribery and threats. Their capital consists mostly of their networks. They exploit every opportunity to speak to the media about law and justice in order to promote a client's cause, hoping to influence judges, who will read about cases they are adjudicating.[41] Well-known fixers (and brokers) appear in a weekly television talk show, 'Indonesian Lawyers Club', where they argue about cases and current legal issues.

Most fixers earn US$200–2,800 per month as well as an annual bonus and sometimes a percentage of a money judgment but still far less than corporate lawyers. They also charge most clients a discretionary 'professional fee' for the purpose of bribing public officials, part of which may end up in their own pockets. It is to no surprise that fixers are called *makelar kasus* (case brokers) and are considered part of the 'judicial mafia' (see eg Butt and Lindsey 2011).

---

[39] Interview with Frans Hendra Winarta 6 March 2014.
[40] For example, the notorious litigator Hotman Paris called opposing counsel ugly, bald, corrupt and lacking self-esteem (hearing at Jakarta Administrative Court, 14 November 2013).
[41] They strategically time these announcements, paying newspapers to publish them and cultivating contacts with journalists.

E. Premier League Fixers: 'Family' Lawyers

One select group of fixers constitute a class of their own. The firms they lead are fully dependent on their personal image and networks and offer a 'boutique, one-stop service'. Their main practice areas are land disputes, tax, antitrust, securities, and real estate development. They delegate work like drafting contracts to employees and rarely go to court. Instead, they 'fix' licences, design complex, sometimes shady, financial transactions, and 'resolve problems'. They see their clients as business partners, often taking a financial stake. These lawyers often refer to themselves as 'the lawyer of [a client's] family'.

Their clients are not corporations but individual heads of family corporate groups, mostly Chinese-Indonesian businessmen active in construction and natural resource exploitation. For anything that concerns law, these businessmen will contact their 'family lawyers'. Some family lawyers operate satellite firms and can mobilise an army of lawyers in other countries where their clients are active, such as Singapore and Hong Kong. For family lawyers, the end justifies (almost) any means. In this respect they are no different from common fixers, but their means are more powerful and complex.

VI. SUPERVISION, SELF-REGULATION AND DISCIPLINE

Bar associations are supposed to supervise and discipline lawyers. Since 2003 the Lawyers Ethics Council of the Bar association has had the power to impose disciplinary sanctions for ethical violations. They hear about a case a week, but because these never result in serious sanctions professional liability is a minimal risk.

Nevertheless, few unhappy clients sue their lawyers. In 1999, the modern firm Dermawan and Co was sued for conflict of interest in the South Jakarta District Court.[42] In 2001 that court dismissed for insufficient evidence another lawsuit accusing a modern firm, Hadiputranto, Hadinoto & Partners, of unlawfully settling a case without the client's consent. In 2013, Ali Budiardjo, Nugroho, Reksodiputro was sued for malpractice when an allegedly incomplete legal opinion caused client losses, but the South Jakarta District Court found for the law firm and was affirmed by the Jakarta Court of Appeal and the Supreme Court.[43] The situation of brokers and fixers is different. A number have been prosecuted for bribing judges,[44] court staff,[45] and police officers,[46] and several of them have been found guilty. The Corruption Eradication Commission (KPK) has played an important role in some of these cases.

This reveals the clear difference between modern and traditional firms. The former may be civilly liable to pay damages to disappointed clients; individual lawyers in the latter may be criminally prosecuted. An aggrieved client can file a case before the ethical committee of the Bar association has acted. Thus, the failure of the profession to regulate

---

[42] Although we could not determine the outcome, it is unlikely the firm was held liable.
[43] In July 2017 ABNR was sued for an alleged conflict of interest. This proceeding is ongoing.
[44] Lawyers Harini Wijoso, Adner Sirait, Yagari Bhastara, and OC Kaligis.
[45] Lawyers Tengku Syaifuddin Popon, Mario Bernardo, and Yagari Bhastara.
[46] Lawyers Haposan Hutagalung and Lambertus Palang Ana.

itself, because of its inability to act collectively, has exposed lawyers to a harsher liability regime outside their control.

VII. PROFESSIONAL RELATIONSHIPS

A. Lawyers and Clients

Lawyers need to decide whether to impose their methods and ideals on clients or explain the risks and consequences of alternative strategies and let clients choose. The first approach places more responsibility on the lawyer for the final outcome. The second runs the risk that lawyers will be blamed for clients' decisions. To minimise both disadvantages, lawyers keep clients at a distance. Professional lawyers do so by carefully drafting engagement letters and powers of attorney, disclosing all relevant information, and keeping matters confidential.

Brokers and fixers prefer to keep information to themselves. They need to determine what clients want, which is seldom transparent, especially when emotions run high. Initial interviews with their clients, therefore, often sound more like interrogations than conversations. Otherwise, these lawyers are very cautious in dealing with clients. Especially in criminal cases some even record the information gathered from clients in a formal document, which they can later cite to justify their decisions if clients change their stories. Lawyers are also reluctant to share information about their networks and how they can use them, a trade secret that is their primary capital.

Good communication and full disclosure by professional lawyers are also ways to avoid the taint of corruption. These lawyers conduct conflict checks and sometimes use 'Chinese walls' when acting for and against the same client. However, most professionals do not do 'Know Your Client' checks.[47] Because professional lawyers are cautious about ethical boundaries, some of their clients choose a broker/fixer to ensure that every possible strategy is deployed to achieve their ends.

B. Lawyers and Lawyers

Relations between professionals differ greatly from those among brokers and fixers. The latter interact little and rarely about work. They call and instant-message each other rather than using email. The loose structure of the traditional firms in which they work fosters competition, since staff can change rapidly and in informal ways. In modern, corporate firms, lawyers work closely together, especially when engaging in due diligence or drafting legal documents.

With a few exceptions there is little contact between lawyers in modern and traditional firms. Broker and fixer litigators will seek the assistance of professionals in drafting contracts in enforcement matters.[48] And professionals refer clients to brokers/fixers for

---

[47] Personal communication from Gustaaf Reerink, lawyer at ABNR, 3 December 2017.
[48] See www.iflr.com/Article/2633920/The-only-way-to-enforce.html.

criminal law cases (in the context of commercial disputes) or litigation potentially involving illicit means; but generally speaking, they feel contempt for each other.[49] Professionals allege that brokers and fixers are corrupt, while the latter claim that professionals exploit clients by overcharging and wasting time.[50]

C. 'What is a Good Lawyer?'

Most lawyers we interviewed answered this question by referring to ethical rules concerning corrupt practices, revealing that lawyers are aware their profession is associated with corruption and they operate in a corrupt *field*. They protest that *they* do not engage in such practices. At the same time, professionals are accused of just talking about rules without really caring about their clients.[51] The rules governing lawyers are inadequate. There are no rules of professional conduct; and the Code of Ethics is too abstract to regulate behaviour. Kronman (1999) defined good lawyers as those who are really skilled at their jobs and possess the full range of emotional, perceptual and intellectual equipment to exercise good judgement. From the perspective of many Indonesian clients, however, a good lawyer is 'someone who can get things done'. Lawyers are seen as service providers. Clients demand that they be zealous. Brokers and fixers should be relational rather than rational agents. For the brokers and fixers themselves, winning cases in court, not problem-solving, is the hallmark of a good lawyer.

VIII. CONCLUSION

Indonesian lawyers reflect the social divide characteristic of developing countries. On one hand, they serve the globalised world of investment, business and finance; on the other, they deal with corrupt bureaucracies, incomplete registers, and inconsistent laws. This has caused a split in the profession, more profound than that found in most other jurisdictions.[52] One extreme is the modern corporate law firm, in an air-conditioned skyscraper along Jalan Jenderal Sudirman in South Jakarta, whose professionals deal mainly with foreign and large firms and operate according to international standards. The other is the fixer who cares little about law and uses any means, including bribes and thugs, to resolve a client's problem. In between are two groups: professionals who have to deal with the Indonesian legal system but reject the illicit rules governing much of the police, prosecutors and judiciary; and brokers who observe the law when they can but who do not hesitate to break it when they feel they must.

As we have seen, the current situation is the product of a long decline in the rule of law, caused by neglect and repression during authoritarian regimes as well as the rise of pervasive corruption. Together with courts and universities, lawyers form a largely

---

[49] See www.nytimes.com/2010/04/24/world/asia/24hotman.html.
[50] Mentioned during interviews by five brokers and three fixers.
[51] Mentioned during interviews by a broker, four clients and two in-house counsel.
[52] They are different from and more profound than the two hemispheres discussed by Heinz and Laumann (1982).

dysfunctional system, which fails to produce the careful interpretation and application of laws that promote justice and legal certainty.

The divisions within Indonesia's legal profession have led to persistent problems in self-regulation. Ironically, lawyers' lack of formal regulatory powers under the authoritarian regimes of Sukarno's Old and Suharto's New Orders allowed their associations to avoid government control. After lawyers obtained the right of self-regulation under the 2003 LL they almost lost it because of the endless fights between and within the competing Bar associations. This is analogous to (if different from) the way specialisation prevents lawyers from collectively pursuing common interests (Rostain 2004: 150) or enforcing professional ideals (Nelson and Trubek 1992: 13).

Just as brokers and fixers compete to win cases by any means, so the focus on short-term interests has impeded the formation of a single Bar association. But this risks long-term costs, such as loss of control over disciplinary sanctions. Having to deal with the Corruption Eradication Commission is a foretaste of what may happen.

The behaviour of fixers reflects poorly on the image of lawyers and the legal system to which they belong. Media coverage of the controversies and unethical behaviour of the most notorious litigators breeds deep public distrust of the legal system. A joint study by USAID, the Asia Foundation and PSHK found that most respondents considered the main task of lawyers to be handing out money to judges. While this is an exaggeration, it accurately reflects the profound disillusion.

This situation is unlikely to change soon given the complex linkages among the various problems. Still, the presence of professional litigators and the fact that their clientele is expanding gives reason for long-term optimism. Because foreign investment in Indonesia keeps growing and foreign firms are constrained by international and transnational obligations, the ethical climate may eventually improve.

But there is a long road ahead. In 2011, Sebastiaan Pompe, one of the foremost experts on Indonesian law and practice, wrote an op-ed in the *Jakarta Post* blaming lawyers for the persistence of legal uncertainty in Indonesia because they failed to use the judgments on the Supreme Court website.[53] Professional litigators seem to have taken up this challenge, meeting one of the preconditions for legal development. A legal information service as Hukumonline has done the same, providing legal digests, commenting on legal developments and establishing a web-based forum for debate. But if other lawyers and university lecturers do not start categorising and analysing court judgments and fail to engage in debates about what the law is and should become, this effort may be wasted.

REFERENCES

Abel, R (1989) *American Lawyers* (New York, Oxford University Press).
—— (2011) 'Just Law' in S Cummings (ed), *The Paradox of Professionalism: Lawyers and the Possibility of Justice* (Cambridge, Cambridge University Press).

---

[53] 'Legal uncertainty is caused by advocates' *The Jakarta Post* 29 March 2011.

ABNR (1999) 'Reformasi Hukum di Indonesia Diagnostic Assessment of Legal Development in Indonesia' World Bank Project IDF Grant No 28557 (Jakarta, Cyberconsult).

Arnold, L (2008) 'How to promote bad governance: the reputational failure of formal legal education in Indonesia' LLM dissertation, SOAS, University of London, unpublished.

Bedner, AW (2013) 'Indonesian Legal Scholarship and Jurisprudence as an Obstacle for Transplanting Legal Institutions' 5(2) *Hague Journal on the Rule of Law* 253–73.

— (2016) 'Autonomy of law in Indonesia' 37 *Recht der Werkelijkheid* 27.

Butt, S (2012) 'Indonesia's Constitutional Court: Conservative activist or strategic operator?' in B Dressel (ed), *The Judicialisation of Politics in Asia* (Abingdon, Routledge).

Butt, S and Lindsey, T (2011) 'Judicial mafia: the courts and state illegality in Indonesia' in E Aspinall and G van Klinken (eds), *The State and Illegality in Indonesia* (Brill Open E-book Collection).

Crouch, M (2011) 'Cause Lawyers, the Legal Profession and the Courts in Indonesia: The Bar Association Controversy' 63 *Lawasia Journal* 86.

Dezalay, Y and Garth, BG (2010) *Asian Legal Revivals: Lawyers in the Shadow of Empire* (Chicago, University of Chicago Press).

Flood, J (1991) 'Doing Business: Managing Uncertainty in Lawyer's Work' 25 *Law & Society Review* 1.

Gilson, RJ and Mnookin, RH (1994) 'Disputing through Agents: Cooperation and Conflict between Lawyers in Litigation' 94(2) *Columbia Law Review* 509–66.

Hendriyanto '(Nothing Can) Stop The Course of History: Reflection on the Evolution of Indonesian Advocacy', unpublished paper.

Kadafi, B (2002) *Advokat Indonesia mencari legitimasi: Studi tentang tanggung jawab profesi hukum di Indonesia* (Jakarta, Pusat Studi Hukum & Kebijakan Indonesia).

Kritzer, HM (1990) *The Justice Broker: Lawyers and Ordinary Litigation* (Oxford, Oxford University Press on Demand).

Kronman, AT (1999) 'Professionalism' 2 *Journal of the Institute for the Study of Legal Ethics* 89.

Lev, DS (1976) 'Origins of the Indonesian Advocacy' 21 *Indonesia* 134.

— (1978) 'Judicial authority and the struggle for an Indonesian Rechtsstaat' *Law and Society Review* 37–71.

— (1992) *Lawyers as Outsiders: Advocacy versus the State in Indonesia* (London, School of Oriental and African Studies, University of London, Working Paper No. 2).

— (2000) *Legal Evolution and Political Authority in Indonesia: Selected Essays* (The Hague, Kluwer Law International).

— (2011) *No Concessions The Life of Yap Thiam Hien, Indonesian Human Rights Lawyer* (Seattle, University of Washington Press).

Lindsey, T (2008) *Indonesia: Law and Society* (Leichhardt, NSW: Federation Press).

Lindsey, T and Crouch, M (2013) 'Cause Lawyers in Indonesia: A House Divided' 31 *Wisconsin International Law Journal* 620, 645.

Liu, S (2013) 'The Legal Profession as a Social Process: A Theory on Lawyers and Globalisation' 38 *Law & Social Inquiry* 670–93.

Masson, A and Shariff, MJ (eds) (2009) *Legal Strategies: How Corporations use Law to Improve Performance* (Secaucus, NJ, Springer Science & Business Media).

Menkel-Meadow, C (2000) 'When Winning Isn't Everything: The Lawyer as Problem Solver' 28 *Hofstra Law Review* 905.

Mietzner, M (2010) 'Political conflict resolution and democratic consolidation in Indonesia: The role of the constitutional court' 10(3) *Journal of East Asian Studies* 397–424.

Munger, F (2008) 'Globalisation, Investing in Law, and the Careers of Lawyers for Social Cause: Taking on Rights in Thailand' 53 *New York Law School Law Review* 745–47.

Nelson, RL and Trubek, DM (1992) 'New Problems and New Paradigms in Studies of the Legal Profession' in RL Nelson, DM Trubek and RL Solomon (eds), *Lawyers' Ideals/lawyers' Practices: Transformations in the American Legal Profession* (Ithaca, NY, Cornell University Press).

Pangaribuan, MP (2016) *Pengadilan, Hakim dan Advokat* (Jakarta, Pustaka Kemang).

Pompe, S (2005) *The Indonesian Supreme Court: A Study of Institutional Collapse* (Ithaca, Cornell University Press).

Rostain, T (2004) 'Professional Power: Lawyers and the Constitution of Professional Authority' in A Sarat (ed), *The Blackwell Companion to Law and Society* (Oxford, Blackwell).

38

Japan
Towards Stratification, Diversification and Specialisation

MASAYUKI MURAYAMA

I. INTRODUCTION

SINCE 1980, THE Japanese legal profession has changed significantly as a result of anticipated and real increases in the lawyer population. The number of practising attorneys grew from 11,441 in 1980 to 37,680 in 2016, when almost 40 per cent of those practising had passed the new Bar examination, which began in 2006 (see Table 1). The Bar examination is a part of the new professional legal education system under the Justice System Reform, which sought to change the governance structure of Japan in order to establish the rule of law throughout Japanese society. The Justice System Reform was the culmination of a national policy of deregulation and structural change beginning around 1990. But an early impetus to increase the number of lawyers came from the United States, which demanded that Japan open its legal services market to American lawyers in the early 1980s.

I will discuss the changes by dividing the period into three stages: 1980–95, 1996–2005, and 2006–17. In the first, law practice showed little significant change, though political pressure for deregulation gradually intensified. In the second, deregulation became a national policy, and the economy, especially finance, was deregulated, increasing the demand for business lawyers. In the third, Justice System Reform policies were implemented, and a sharp increase in the number of lawyers resulted in diversification and stratification.

II. STABLE LEGAL PRACTICE DURING THE BUBBLE ECONOMY AND ITS COLLAPSE: 1980–95

The number passing the Bar examination was tightly controlled by the so-called 'judicial three': Japan Federation of Bar Associations (JFBA), Supreme Court (SC) and Ministry of Justice (MOJ). During most of the period, only about 500 passed the examination

Table 1 Number of Registered Private Attorneys and Annual Change (1950–2017)

Year	Number	Annual Increase	Year	Number	Annual Increase
1950	5,827	0	1984	12,377	245
1951	5,804	−23	1985	12,604	227
1952	5,822	18	1986	12,830	226
1953	5,836	14	1987	13,074	244
1954	5,837	1	1988	13,288	214
1955	5,899	62	1989	13,541	253
1956	5,967	68	1990	13,800	259
1957	6,009	42	1991	14,080	280
1958	6,100	91	1992	14,329	249
1959	6,217	117	1993	14,596	267
1960	6,321	105	1994	14,809	213
1961	6,439	118	1995	15,108	299
1962	6,604	165	1996	15,456	348
1963	6,732	128	1997	15,866	410
1964	6,849	117	1998	16,305	439
1965	7,082	233	1999	16,731	426
1966	7,343	261	2000	17,126	395
1967	7,645	302	2001	18,243	1,117
1968	7,918	273	2002	18,838	595
1969	8,198	280	2003	19,508	670
1970	8,478	280	2004	20,224	716
1971	8,797	319	2005	21,185	961
1972	9,106	309	2006	22,021	836
1973	9,541	435	2007	23,119	1,098
1974	9,830	289	2008	25,041	1,922
1975	10,115	285	2009	26,930	1,889
1976	10,421	306	2010	28,789	1,859
1977	10,689	268	2011	30,485	1,696
1978	10,977	288	2012	32,088	1,603
1979	11,206	229	2013	33,624	1,536
1980	11,441	235	2014	35,045	1,421
1981	11,624	183	2015	36,415	1,370
1982	11,888	264	2016	37,680	1,265
1983	12,132	244	2017	38,980	1,300

Source: Nihon Bengoshi Rengokai (JFBA) 2017: 30.

every year; about 250–300 became practising attorneys, and the rest judges or prosecutors. The number of attorneys grew slowly from 11,441 in 1980 to 13,800 in 1990 and 15,108 in 1995, very few for the Japanese population of 117 million, 124 million, and 126 million respectively.

A. General Practice in Small Offices as the Dominant Style

Half the lawyers were solo practitioners, generalists who represented 'small and middle size business enterprises and propertied individuals' in court; a few specialised in 'patent law, international trade, or labor union matters' (Rokumoto 1988: 172–73). This did not change during the 1980s. Cost sharing was much more common than income sharing.

B. US Pressure to Open the Japanese Legal Market and Its Consequences

The initial impetus to increase the number of lawyers came from the US in 1982, when its government demanded that Japan allow US lawyers to practise. In 1986, the Foreign Lawyers Act (No 66) was enacted, allowing lawyers licensed to practise in a foreign country to practise in Japan but not litigate. Because the Japanese economy was expanding rapidly, large Anglo-American law firms began to open offices in Tokyo. Most international transactions were out-bound as Japanese companies invested in the US and Europe.

Facing competition from foreign law firms, Japanese law offices specialising in international transaction began actively to recruit graduates of the Legal Training and Research Institute (LTRI), where those passing the Bar examination received professional legal training for two years before choosing to be a judge, prosecutor or attorney. Although those Japanese law offices were relatively small, with 30–40 lawyers, they tried to recruit the best graduates by offering a high starting salary. As a result, the SC and in particular the MOJ began to have problems recruiting enough judges and prosecutors and sought to increase the number passing the Bar examination.

The judicial three began discussing the reform of the Bar examination in 1988. Because the number of lawyers was small, most were guaranteed a high income for life. The examination was extremely competitive, with just 2–5 per cent passing each year (see Table 2). As a result, applicants tended to be preoccupied with passing the Bar exam and had little other knowledge or social experience. Applicants took a long time to pass the exam (Rokumoto 1988: 165). Therefore, reformers also sought to increase the number of those passing who had diversified academic and social backgrounds.[1]

The judicial three agreed to increase the number passing from 500 to 700 in 1990 and to 1,000 in 1997. In 1996, in order to let young applicants pass the examination, 30 per cent of successful examinees were chosen from those who had taken the examination less than four times, though the JFBA called this unfair.

---

[1] Lawyers who had passed the Bar exam after years of effort opposed this and later criticised the new law schools.

C. Underdeveloped System of Legal Aid and Public Defence

Horitsu Hujo Kyokai (The Legal Aid Association, LAA) was established in 1952 by the JFBA to provide civil legal aid to the indigent. State subsidies were minimal: $740,000 ($1=100 Yen) in 1980 and $1.16 million in 1990 (Horitsu Hujo Kyokai (LAA) 2004: 70). Legal aid handled 2,423 cases in 1980 (LAA 1982: 783) and 4,072 in 1990, which were only 3.8 per cent of those filed in the district courts (LAA 1992: 436). Recipients had to repay what the LAA had paid the lawyer. Because of this, legal aid was given only to those highly likely to win. Legal advice to the indigent was free of charge, but the numbers were not significant: 20,720 cases in 1980 (LAA 1982: 783) and 22,480 in 1990 (LAA 1992: 440–41). Because advice was limited to half an hour, recipients often obtained little more than general information.

In contrast, criminal defence grew rapidly from 1980 to 1995. In 1980, 97 per cent of defendants tried in district courts were represented by lawyers, 51 per cent of whom were appointed by the courts (Saiko Saibansho 1980: 150). In 1995, the latter proportion had increased to 67 per cent (Saiko Saibansho 1995: 146). However, the quality of representation was mixed. Because the fee for such work was low compared to those charged by privately retained counsel, court appointed lawyers tended to be young and inexperienced.

As the courts appointed defence lawyers only after indictment, a majority of suspects did not have lawyers. Oita Bar Association, a small Bar association in Kyushu, created a scheme of free legal advice for those arrested in 1990.[2] LAA also established a small fund to help those arrested retain lawyers. Although the practical significance of this scheme was limited, it led to the creation of a nationwide system of public defence for suspects as a part of the Justice System Reform.

III. DEREGULATION, EMERGENCE OF THE BIG FOUR AND JUSTICE SYSTEM REFORM: 1996–2005

In 1990 the JFBA announced its declaration of judicial reform at the general meeting emphasising that the reforms were a response to public expectations and lawyers had to reconsider their numbers and qualifications. In 1994, Keizaidoyukai (Japan Association of Corporate Executives) issued its report on the ills of Japanese society, recommending a judiciary close to the people, drastic expansion of the legal profession, more legal aid, and establishment of council to draft reforms (Keizaidoyukai 1994).[3] In 1997 Diet members from the Liberal Democratic Party (LDP) began to promote judicial reform (Yasuoka 2008). These initiatives led to the establishment of the Justice System Reform Council (JSRC) inside the Cabinet in 1999 (Act No 68). It submitted its final report in

---

[2] Free legal advice was given only for the first meeting.
[3] The business sector had been opposed to expanding the judicial system or increasing the number of lawyers because companies were often sued over labour, pollution and consumer issues. But compared with Keidanren, the other business association, Keizaidoyukai was more innovative because its members were more involved in international trade and eager for deregulation. Keizaidoyukai proposed to restructure the entire post-war governing system, while Keidanren just wanted to increase the efficiency of the judicial system for business, as well as the number of lawyers (Keidanren 1998).

2001, declaring that the rule of law was a fundamental principle of Japanese society. It proposed a comprehensive reform of the legal system, which was implemented, though its real impact is yet to be felt.

A. Deregulation and the Emergence of Large Law Firms

In the first half of the 1990s, the Japanese economy did not perform well, and foreign and Japanese law firms did not grow. But this trend was reversed when large financial institutions and manufacturers went bankrupt. From the latter half of the 1990s, business law firms steadily expanded as the domestic legal market began to grow under deregulation.

Because deregulation allowed foreign investors to buy Japanese companies more easily, in-bound transactions increased sometime around 1996. Unlike out-bound investment, in-bound capital required Japanese lawyers. Responding to increasing demand for corporate and cross-border legal work and, especially, the ability to handle M&A, Japanese firms specialising in corporate law and finance began to merge, growing to more than 100 lawyers. The Big Four were created by such mergers between 2000 and 2007. A gradual increase in the number passing the Bar exam in the late 1990s also helped them expand (Nagashima 2011: 51–52, 103–05, 143–45).

B. The Establishment of Law Schools and the Increase in the Number Passing the Bar Examination

Among the JSRC reform proposals, the policy of increasing the number passing the Bar examination had the most significant impact on subsequent changes in the legal profession, especially those concerning practising attorneys. To increase the number passing, the Council proposed to establish law schools at the graduate level offering a broad professional education. At the time, legal education was an undergraduate programme, followed not only by future lawyers but also by public officials and white collar employees.[4] Therefore, undergraduate legal education has its own value, beyond educating future lawyers. Professional legal training was given only at LTRI.[5]

In the new system not only academics but also judges, prosecutors and practising attorneys were appointed to teach at law schools, which were expected to admit applicants with diverse educational backgrounds and social experiences. The pass rate of the bar examination was expected to be about 80 per cent. Only graduates of the new law schools could take the Bar exam and could do so no more than three times in five years. In this way, the JSRC proposed to increase the annual number passing to 3,000 persons by 2010, thereby increasing the number of practising attorneys to 50,000 by 2018, producing a population:lawyer ratio similar to that in France (JSRC 2001). This proposal was

---

[4] Graduate programmes in law existed but mainly to train future academics.
[5] An LLB was not required to take the Bar exam, and anybody who passed the Bar exam could become a lawyer after completing the training at LTRI.

widely welcomed, and in 2004 the new law schools began teaching competent students from diverse backgrounds. However, there were serious problems with the design of legal education.

The first was that undergraduate legal education was not abolished. Those faculties are a significant component of universities and employ many law professors. Therefore, new law schools offer a two-year programme for those with an LLB and a three-year programme for the rest. The second problem was that the 74 new law schools were too many. It was obvious that the Bar examination pass rate would be far lower than 80 per cent if there were 9,400 first-year law students. Yet the convention survived that the number passing the Bar examination was fixed.

C. Deregulation of Legal Practice

Because the policy of increasing access to lawyers anticipated a growing lawyer population, the JFBA adopted significant changes in how lawyers were regulated.

i. Deregulation of Advertising

Lawyer advertising was prohibited by the JFBA in 1955. But the prohibition was partially lifted in 1987 and abolished in 2000 in order to increase access to lawyers and expand business opportunities for lawyers.

ii. Legal Professional Corporation

In 2002, the Attorney Act was amended to allow legal professional corporations organised by member lawyers, each of whom would represent the corporation and assume unlimited liability (Law No 41, 2001). A legal professional corporation can employ lawyers and set up branch offices. Four years later, 157 legal professional corporations had been established, but only 40 had branches (only two of them more than one), and 76 per cent had fewer than four lawyers, while the largest had 63 (Nihon Bengoshi Rengokai (JFBA) 2005: 95).

iii. Deregulation on Concurrent Position

In 2004 a law abolished the prohibition on lawyers serving as public officials and required those engaging in profit-making activities only to report it to their Bar associations rather than seeking permission (Act No 128 of 2003).

D. Development of Public-Interest Law Practice and the Establishment of the Japanese Legal Support Center

i. JFBA Sunflower Fund Law Office

When the need to increase the number of lawyers was discussed, it was often pointed out that many court jurisdictions had none. The JFBA responded by establishing the

Sunflower Fund, to help young lawyers launch law offices in such places. The first opened in 2000, and by July 2005 there were 50.

ii. The Development of Legal Aid and the Establishment of the Japanese Legal Support Center

Anticipating a drastic expansion of civil legal aid, the Civil Legal Aid Act was enacted in 2000 (No 55). The legal character of LAA was changed from an incorporated foundation, which heavily relied on the JFBA, to one designated by the MOJ. Even among lawyers working for legal aid, there was uneasiness about being subjected to MOJ supervision. But it was obvious that legal aid had to be expanded and the JFBA could not bear the financial responsibility. State subsidies for civil legal aid more than quadrupled from 405 million Yen in 1998 to 1.7 billion Yen in 2000 (LAA 2004: 17).

Another significant reform was the establishment of the Japan Legal Support Center (JLSC) in 2006 as an incorporated administrative agency under the MOJ (Comprehensive Legal Support Act, No 53 of 2004). The lawyers and staff working for the LAA moved to the JLSC, and the MOJ and SC also sent personnel there. Some lawyers were sceptical about the influence of the MOJ, but there were no strong objections to the JLSC.

IV. IMPACT OF THE JUSTICE SYSTEM REFORM: 2006–17

Graduates of the new law schools began to take the Bar examination in 2006 and the annual number passing exceeded 2,000 in 2007 (Table 2). During this third stage, a series of reforms recommended by the JSRC were implemented, with significant effects on the practice of private attorneys: further stratification and diversification and the emergence of mass legal service providers for individual clients. Although more than 2,000 passed the Bar examination annually for just seven years, and the number never reached 3,000, those who passed during those nine years constituted 38 per cent of practising attorneys in 2016. This rapid increase during a short period provoked a strong reaction against further increases, and the new law school system began to disintegrate under lawyers' harsh criticism.

A. Backlash against the Lawyer Population Increase

i. Mounting Demand by Bar Associations to Reduce the Number Passing the Examination

While the JSRC discussed a drastic increase in the number of lawyers, the JFBA held an extraordinary general meeting in 2000, which agreed on an increase in the number passing the Bar exam to 3,000 (Nihon Bengoshi Rengokai 2000).[6] This meeting was said to have been the most turbulent in decades, because some lawyers vehemently opposed the

---

[6] 3,000 was not mentioned in the agenda, but that number was understood because it had been proposed at a JSRC meeting.

Table 2 Number Passing the Bar Exam and Pass Rates (per cent) (1949–2017)

Year	Number Passing	Pass Rate Old Exam	Year	Number Passing	Pass Rate Old Exam	New Exam	Preliminary
1949	265	10.31	1984	453	1.89		
1950	269	9.59	1985	486	2.04		
1951	272	7.42	1986	486	2.03		
1952	253	5.31	1987	489	1.98		
1953	224	4.36	1988	512	2.19		
1954	250	4.76	1989	506	2.18		
1955	264	4.16	1990	499	2.18		
1956	297	4.41	1991	605	2.68		
1957	286	4.13	1992	630	2.69		
1958	346	4.87	1993	712	3.42		
1959	319	4.06	1994	740	3.28		
1960	345	4.13	1995	738	3.01		
1961	380	3.48	1996	734	2.88		
1962	459	4.27	1997	746	2.75		
1963	496	4.24	1998	812	2.66		
1964	508	4	1999	1,000	2.94		
1965	526	3.86	2000	994	2.75		
1966	554	3.73	2001	990	2.54		
1967	537	3.26	2002	1,183	2.59		
1968	525	2.96	2003	1,170	2.33		
1969	501	2.72	2004	1,483	2.97		
1970	507	2.51	2005	1,464	3.19		
1971	533	2.39	2006	1,558	1.53	48.3	
1972	537	2.29	2007	2,099	0.89	40.2	
1973	537	2.12	2008	2,065	0.8	33	
1974	491	1.84	2009	2,043	0.6	27.6	
1975	472	1.7	2010	2,074	0.6	25.4	
1976	465	1.6	2011	2,063	0.4	23.5	
1977	465	1.59	2012	2,102		24.6	68.2
1978	485	1.65	2013	2,049		25.8	71.9
1979	503	1.76	2014	1,810		21.2	66.8
1980	486	1.7	2015	1,850		21.6	61.8
1981	446	1.6	2016	1,583		20.7	61.5
1982	457	1.74	2017	1,543		22.5	72.5
1983	448	1.78					

Source: Homusho (MOJ); Nihon Bengoshi Rengokai (JFBA) 2010: 76; 2011: 92; 2017: 45, 46.

Table 3 Exposure to Competition

	Percentage of Lawyers Feeling They Are Exposed to Competition		
Year	Every Day	Sometimes	Never
1980	8.9	38.4	52.7
1990	9.6	38.4	51.7
2000	15.0	41.4	43.2
2010*	44.4	25.4	30.2

Sources: Nihon Bengoshi Rengokai (JFBA) (1988: 150); JFBA (1991: 98; 2002: 188; 2011: 204).
*This survey asked: 'Compared to 10 years ago, do you think that competition with other lawyers has become severe?' Responses were: (1) I think so, (2) I cannot say either, (3) I do not think so.

proposal. When the number passing exceeded 2,000 in 2007, lawyers began to complain that some LTRI graduates could not find positions. Although this was disputed, it seemed clear that the increasing number of young lawyers intensified competition among them, jeopardising their financial prospects. Table 3 shows changes in lawyers' beliefs about competition.

In 2007 some LDP members, including the Minister of Justice, declared they would reconsider the lawyer population policy.[7] In 2008, JFBA issued an emergency proposal to slow the increase in the lawyer population, though it did not abandon the official policy of expansion. In 2009, a group of Diet members across party lines also demanded a drastic reduction in the number of law schools and students. In 2010 a lawyer who opposed increasing the lawyer population was elected as JFBA president. At the end of his term in 2012, the JFBA proposed reducing the number passing the Bar exam to 1,500. That year the Ministry of Internal Affairs and Communications (MIC) officially endorsed the opposition to increasing the number of lawyers by publishing its evaluation and recommendations to the MOJ and the Ministry of Education (MEXT). It bitterly criticised the quality of professional education at the new law schools and argued that allowing 2,000 to pass the Bar examination had created an oversupply of practising attorneys (Somusho (MIC) 2012).[8]

ii. The Failing System of New Law Schools

Because there were too many law schools to sustain an 80 per cent pass rate, the actual rate turned out to be far lower: 48 per cent in 2006, 24 per cent in 2011 and 23 per cent in 2016 (Table 4).

The new law schools suffered their fatal blow in 2011, when a preliminary examination was instituted as an alternative for those who, the MOJ claimed, could not pay the

---

[7] The political alignments over the Justice System Reform, including the issue of the lawyer population, were complex and transcended party divisions. Generally speaking, privatisation and deregulation have been supported by the business sector and LDP and opposed by labour, social democrats and the Communist Party. But LDP Diet members were divided over the lawyer population policy because some of those qualified as lawyers believed in the old Bar exam system.

[8] There is no systematic evidence that the quality of law school graduates passing the new Bar exam was lower than that of those passing the old exam.

Table 4 Law School Applicants and Bar Exam Pass Rate (per cent) (2004–17)

Year	Law School Applicants	Bar Exam Takers	Bar Exam Pass Rate	Pass Rate Among LLBs	Pass Rate Among Non-LLBs
2004	72,800				
2005	41,756				
2006	40,341	2,091	48.3	48.8	44.6
2007	45,207	4,607	40.2	41.9	35.2
2008	39,555	6,261	33.0	35.0	27.3
2009	29,714	7,392	27.6	29.4	22.6
2010	24,014	8,163	25.4	27.5	19.2
2011	22,927	8,765	23.5	25.9	16.7
2012	18,446	8,387	25.1	26.8	17.7
2013	13,924	7,653	26.8	27.7	19.6
2014	11,450	8,015	22.6	23.1	14.4
2015	10,370	8,016	23.1	23.2	16.1
2016	8,274	6,899	22.9	22.3	14.7
2017	8,159	5,967	25.9	24.2	15.5

Source: JFBA, 2017: 43–45.

high tuition fees.[9] Although anyone can take the preliminary examination, which tests whether the examinee has learned as much as a law school graduate, most examinees have been undergraduate law students. Those passing the preliminary examination can take the new Bar exam without attending a new law school. This alternative resembled the old Bar exam, which did not require any formal legal education, and revived the old system of postponing professional training to the LTRI (after the applicant passed the Bar exam).

In 2013, Conference of Ministers concerned with legal professional education decided to withdraw the 3,000 target for those passing the Bar examination. In 2015, MEXT set that number at 1,500 and penalised law schools whose graduates' pass rates fell below the average by withholding their subsidies. As a result, 40 of the 74 law schools were abolished or stopped admitting students by April 2019. The number of students who applied to law schools decreased from 72,800 in 2004 to 8,159 in 2017 (Table 4).

The declining pass rate had profound impacts on the law schools. Externally, it cut the number of applicants to both the new graduate law schools and the undergraduate programmes.[10] Internally, law students have become preoccupied with passing the

---

[9] Among the 74 new law schools, 25 were public (23 national and 2 prefectural and city) and 49 private. The average annual tuition was 800,000 Yen for public law schools and 1,000,000–1,500,000 Yen for private. But most law schools, especially the private ones, offered scholarships.

[10] Because undergraduate legal education endows future white-collar employees with basic legal knowledge, law has been a popular subject. Therefore, the number of first-year undergraduate law students increased from

Bar examination, and undergraduate law students began to cram at prep-schools for the preliminary examination. Even some new law school students now go to prep-schools, which had been very popular during the old Bar examination from the 1980s to the early 2000s and are reviving.

MEXT had required law schools to admit at least 30 per cent of the admitted students from among applicants without LLBs in order to keep diversity among law students, but because the pass rate was worse for those without an undergraduate law degree, MEXT decided at the end of 2017 to eliminate the requirement (Monbukagakusho (MEXT) 2017).

B. Stratification and Diversification of Practising Attorneys

i. The Growth of Big Law Firms

After the merger, the Big Four kept expanding by actively recruiting LTRI graduates as the number passing the Bar examination increased. In 2017, the five largest law firms, called the Big Five, each had more than 300 lawyers (Table 5). These firms offered the highest starting salaries, around 12 million Yen (about $110,000) per year, the best fringe benefits, and opportunities to study abroad, often in the US. Most associates have been graduates of top law schools.

Table 5 Ten Largest Law Firms in 2017 and Growth from 2010

Rank in 2017	Law Firm	Number of Lawyers							
		2010	2011	2012	2013	2014	2015	2016	2017
1	Nishimura Asahi	471	481	465	452	473	499	508	525
2	Anderson Mohri	290	310	316	308	296	313	396	414
3	Nagashima Ohno	338	347	334	333	317	319	353	379
4	Mori Hamada	299	312	304	319	336	347	360	374
5	TMI	224	234	242	261	292	313	350	361
6	Adire			88	124	127	144	162	193
7	City Yuwa	110	113	114	123	126	128	136	139
8	Very Best							105	134
9	Ohebashi	94	93	101	108	110	116	122	132
10	Baker McKenzie	118	119	122	109	106	104	111	113

Source: Nihon Bengoshi Rengokai (JFBA), White Paper 2010: 96; 2011: 103; 2012: 122; 2013: 99; 2014: 89; 2015: 73; 2016: 56; 2017: 56.

412,437 in 1980 to 568,576 in 1995, and they remained 9 per cent of all the first-year undergraduates (Monbukagakusho (MEXT) 1980, 1985, 1990, 1995). Both the number and the proportion have since decreased, the latter to 6 per cent in 2015 (MEXT 2000, 2005, 2010, 2015). This may be partly attributable to the growth of new faculties for undergraduates. A more serious problem is that the quality of undergraduate law students has been declining at top universities, whose graduates join the legal profession or the national ministries.

ii. Foreign Lawyers

When the Foreign Lawyers Act allowed foreigners to practise foreign law in 1987, they were not permitted to employ or enter into a partnership with Japanese lawyers. In 1995 partnership was allowed in some situations, and in 2005 foreign lawyers could employ or partner with Japanese lawyers (Act No 128 of 2003). As soon as the Japanese legal services market was opened, foreign lawyers began to practise in Japan, but the numbers increased more rapidly after 2000 (see Table 6).

The number of partnership offices gradually increased, and the number of Japanese partners and associates had more than doubled by 2017 (Table 7). Large Anglo-American law firms entered into partnerships with Japanese firms, but the Big Four (with the exception of TMI) did not do so with foreign firms.

The Foreign Lawyers Act was amended in 2014 to let foreign lawyers organise a legal professional corporation (Act No 29 of 2014). In 2017, there were only five, each of which had a single partner.

iii. The Decrease of Solo-Practitioners and Increase in Specialisation

The growth of large business law firms represents the emergence of a small upper stratum of practising attorneys. But the other practising attorneys have also been changing. The distribution of lawyers by office size did not change significantly between 1980

Table 6 Number of Foreign Lawyers (1988–2017)

Year	Number	Year	Number
1988	31	2003	189
1989	47	2004	213
1990	58	2005	236
1991	78	2006	241
1992	79	2007	252
1993	78	2008	267
1994	79	2009	290
1995	77	2010	344
1996	77	2011	359
1997	80	2012	357
1998	87	2013	360
1999	97	2014	386
2000	125	2015	380
2001	150	2016	391
2002	186	2017	411

Source: JFBA White Paper 2011: 112; 2012: 131; 2013: 110; 2014: 100; 2015: 80; 2016: 62; 2017: 62.

Table 7 Collaboration between Japanese and Foreign Lawyers (2005–17)

Year	Partnership Office	Japanese Partner	Japanese Associate	Foreign Partner	Foreign Associate
2005	19	77	235	67	32
2006	23	137	399	74	35
2007	28	688		116	
2008	30	755		116	
2009	30	175	664	81	43
2010	34	195	627	93	55
2011	37	199	531	91	64
2012	40	215	513	94	60
2013	36	183	494	77	48
2014	38	194	533	87	46
2015	40	176	591	81	56
2016	39	168	549	73	63
2017	41	169	570	74	62

Source: JFBA, White Paper, 2005: 88; 2006: 53; 2007: 98; 2008: 103; 2009: 75; 2010: 91; 2011: 114–15; 2012: 132–33; 2013: 111–12; 2014: 101–02; 2015: 81–82; 2016: 63–64; 2017: 63–64.

and 2000.[11] But the proportion practising alone decreased from 50 per cent in 2000 to 34 per cent in 2010 (JFBA, 1981: 54; 1991: 16; 2002: 20; 2011: 32) and 25 per cent in 2017. By contrast, the proportion of those working at offices with more than 100 lawyers increased from 1 per cent in 2002 to 7 per cent in 2017 (JFBA, White Paper, 2002: 41; 2017: 56.).

The decline of solo practice has resulted from the increase in those passing the Bar exam and the changing aspirations of LTRI graduates. Those graduates have traditionally been employed by practising lawyers, called 'boss' lawyers. Therefore, more people passing the Bar exam led to an increase in the number of law offices with more than one lawyer. Although many lawyers wanted to and did become independent practitioners after several years, the percentage practising alone decreased from 2002 to 2017, indicating that lawyers prefer to continue practising with others. Solo practices remain the majority of law offices, 60 per cent in 2017, down from 76 per cent in 2002. And 95 per cent of law offices had five lawyers or fewer in 2017 (JFBA White Paper 2002: 41, 2008: 108; 2014: 89; 2017: 56).

Law offices can be classified into four main categories: (1) a lawyer working alone; (2) a single management lawyer employing other lawyers; (3) management lawyers

---

[11] The JFBA conducted nationwide surveys of practising lawyers in 1980, 1990, 2000 and 2010. The first was directed by Kahei Rokumoto, who wrote the 1988 Japanese national report. The later surveys have suffered from low response rates: 41 per cent in 1980, 26 per cent in 1990, 17 per cent in 2000 and 18 per cent in 2010. The JFBA began to publish White Papers in 2002. We rely on those data when they are based on JFBA registrations.

sharing costs; and (4) management lawyers sharing income. Solo practitioners cannot choose clients and, therefore, tend to be generalists. But if the office expands to four or five lawyers, they can begin to specialise.[12] Compared to cost-sharing offices, those that share income tend to be larger and more specialised (Rokumoto, 1988: 167–68). The proportions of both have decreased since 1980. Nevertheless, 18 per cent of lawyers belonged to legal professional corporations or income-sharing offices in 2010, indicating a movement toward specialisation (JFBA 2002: 23; 2011: 260).

iv. Legal Adviser

Most lawyers work as legal advisers for private companies, public organisations or affluent individuals. Small companies[13] have been the main clients of legal advisers for three decades (JFBA 1991: 52; 2002: 91; 2011: 74). Fees for legal advice are a stable source of income for lawyers, on average about 20 per cent of the pre-tax total in 1980, 1990 and 2000 (JFBA 1991: 54, 2002: 86). The role also helps lawyers to obtain new clients through introductions by the individuals and companies they advise. The proportion of lawyers serving as legal advisers has decreased from 86 per cent in 1990 to 81 per cent in 2000 and 64 per cent in 2010 (JFBA, 1991: 182; 2002: 296; 2011: 71). The increase in the number of associates explains at least part of the declining proportion of lawyers working as legal advisers after 2000. There also seems to be more competition among lawyers for such work.

v. Gender Disparities

The legal profession was long a male occupation. The first woman began to practise in 1940. As Table 8 shows, the proportion of lawyers who are women exceeded 10 per cent only in 2001. The new Bar exam helped to increase the number of women lawyers, but their proportion has stagnated at 18 per cent in recent years.

Women lawyers are much less likely than men to practice alone. Although women were 14 per cent of lawyers in 2008, they were only 7 per cent of solo practitioners. Women lawyers tended to practise in larger offices than men in 2008 and 2010, but that pattern reversed in later years (JFBA White Paper 2008: 109; 2009: 81; 2010: 97; 2011: 104; 2012: 122; 2013: 100; 2014: 90; 2015: 74; 2016: 56; 2017: 56).

Women lawyers are more likely than men to handle divorce and other family cases and less likely to negotiate for business clients because of the stereotype that they are weak negotiators in the male-dominated business world. Such a situation began to change as the number of women in management positions increased.

The mean income of male lawyers was US$178,443 (US$1=100 Yen) in 2000 and US$155,200 in 2010 compared with US$80,395 and US$98,900 for females (JFBA 2002: 225; 2011: 115).

---

[12] Large business law firms have three main divisions: corporate law, finance, and litigation and bankruptcy. Associates tend to work in one of these, often specialising even further. They can move to another of these fields but rarely go outside them. *Adire* and legal boutiques adopt another strategy: compartmentalising legal practice into particular areas, such as overpayment of debt, traffic accidents, criminal defence. Lawyers working at these law offices are not generalists. Finally, although most lawyers in general practice are not specialised, they spend more time on particular kinds of cases because they prefer that field or want to increase their income.

[13] Companies with 50 employees or fewer in the commercial and service industries or 300 employees or fewer in other industries.

Table 8 Proportion of Lawyers Who Are Women (1950–2017)

Year	Number of Lawyers	Number of Women Lawyers	Per cent Women	Year	Number of Lawyers	Number of Women	Per cent Women
1950	5,827	6	0	1984	12,377	554	4
1951	5,804	6	0	1985	12,604	590	5
1952	5,822	9	0	1986	12,830	620	5
1953	5,836	9	0	1987	13,074	654	5
1954	5,837	10	0	1988	13,288	694	5
1955	5,899	11	0	1989	13,541	721	5
1956	5,967	14	0	1990	13,800	766	6
1957	6,009	17	0	1991	14,080	811	6
1958	6,100	24	0	1992	14,329	846	6
1959	6,217	31	0	1993	14,596	894	6
1960	6,321	42	1	1994	14,809	938	6
1961	6,439	46	1	1995	15,108	996	7
1962	6,604	54	1	1996	15,456	1070	7
1963	6,732	60	1	1997	15,866	1176	7
1964	6,849	69	1	1998	16,305	1295	8
1965	7,082	86	1	1999	16,731	1398	8
1966	7,343	105	1	2000	17,126	1530	9
1967	7,645	128	2	2001	18,243	1849	10
1968	7,918	149	2	2002	18,838	2063	11
1969	8,198	166	2	2003	19,508	2273	12
1970	8,478	180	2	2004	20,224	2448	12
1971	8,797	197	2	2005	21,185	2648	12
1972	9,106	224	2	2006	22,021	2859	13
1973	9,541	254	3	2007	23,119	3152	14
1974	9,830	279	3	2008	25,041	3599	14
1975	10,115	303	3	2009	26,930	4127	15
1976	10,421	330	3	2010	28,789	4660	16
1977	10,689	344	3	2011	30,485	5115	17
1978	10,977	362	3	2012	32,088	5595	17
1979	11,206	384	3	2013	33,624	5936	18
1980	11,441	420	4	2014	35,045	6336	18
1981	11,624	446	4	2015	36,415	6618	18
1982	11,888	477	4	2016	37,680	6896	18
1983	12,132	514	4	2017	38,980	7179	18

Source: JFBA White Paper 2017: 30.

Women lawyers are less likely than men to work as legal advisers – 43 per cent versus 67 per cent in 2010; and women legal advisers had fewer clients on average: 6 versus 15 (JFBA 2002: 296; 2011: 74). But women lawyers were much more likely to be employed as in-house counsel for business and public bureaucracies.

vi. Income

The economic boom doubled the average income of lawyers from US$70,300 in 1980 to US$154,400 in 1990. After 1990, despite of the bursting of the bubble economy, the average income further increased to US$170,100 in 2000. But in 2010, it decreased to US$147,100 (JFBA, 1988: 127; 2002: 128; 2011: 114–15).[14]

Starting salaries tended to decrease. But we saw that Big Five law firms offered much higher starting salaries. In 2000 and 2010 the median income was US$139,000 and US$95,900 while the mean was US$179,500 and US$147,100. The fact that the difference between mean and median was larger in 2010 (US$51,200) than in 2000 (US$40,500) indicates that the income differences among lawyers increased (JFBA 2002: 129; 2011: 113).

vii. Disciplinary Action

When the number passing the Bar exam increased under the new law school system, newspapers reported that the number of disciplined lawyers reached record highs in 2009 and 2010 (Nihon Keizai Shinbun, 2010, 2011). This was misleading. The number of disciplined lawyers did increase from eight in 1980 to 45 in 2000 and 93 in 2015, but this mainly reflected the larger number of lawyers. The percentage of lawyers disciplined rose sharply before 2000, from 0.07 per cent in 1980 to 0.26 per cent in 2000. Thereafter, the rate of disciplinary action tended to be stable: 0.28 per cent in 2010 and 0.26 per cent in 2015.[15] Despite the large increase in the number of lawyers with the least experience, more experienced lawyers were more likely to be disciplined (Ishida 2017).

viii. The Emergence of Large Law Firms and Legal Boutiques for Individual Clients

The deregulation of advertising, the creation of legal professional corporations and the increase in the number of LTRI graduates all contributed to the emergence of law firms specialising in particular legal fields and providing mass legal services for individual clients. A typical example is Adire, a firm that began with three attorneys in 2004 representing clients seeking to recover alleged overpayments to credit companies.[16] Adire advertised on television and the Internet, quickly establishing branches nationwide.

---

[14] The consumer price index for all items increased from 1 in 1980 to 1.2 in 1990, but since 1991 it has been stable as 1.3. See Table zni2015s at www.e-stat.go.jp/stat-search/files?page=1&layout=datalist&toukei=0020 0573&tstat=000001084976&cycle=0&tclass1=000001085995&tclass2=000001085936&tclass3=000001085996&tclass4=000001085997. The average income adjusted by the consumer price index is US$70,300 in 1980, US$128,667 in 1990, US$130,846 in 2000 and US$113,154 in 2010.

[15] The numbers and percentages are calculated by counting public announcements of disciplinary actions by JFBA published in *Jiyu to Seigi* in 1980, 1990, 2000, 2010 and 2015.

[16] Very Best is another. See Table 5.

In March 2017, it was the sixth largest firm, with 193 lawyers in more than 80 offices, and had expanded its practice to traffic accidents, family, labour law, criminal defence, and compensation claims for Hepatitis B. The firm offers clients clear criteria to calculate the fee that will be charged.[17]

Japanese lawyers long relied on personal networks to obtain clients. Most lawyers have been reluctant to accept clients without a personal introduction, though this is changing.[18] Most laypeople see lawyers as elites and fear how much lawyers would ask them to pay (Murayama et al 2010: 444). Adire may not be able to eliminate this concern, but its television and radio commercials as well as its websites create a sense of familiarity.

In February 2016, the Consumer Affairs Agency issued an administrative order to Adire to stop advertising (Consumer Affairs Agency 2016). Following this order, more than 30 Bar Associations received demands for disciplinary action against Adire; and in October 2017 the Tokyo Bar Association suspended it for two months and its top partner for three (Tokyo Bar Association, 2017). When the disciplinary sanction was imposed, Adire had about 90,000 clients. It resumed practice in January 2018 and two months later had about 160 lawyers in 75 offices.

Other legal boutiques in Tokyo, Osaka and Nagoya specialise in family law, criminal defence, and Hepatitis B compensation. Many law offices have created websites, which will increase the number of clients they obtain without personal introduction.[19]

ix. The Increasing Number of In-House Lawyers

(a) In-House Lawyers in Private Corporations

The size and status of law departments differ significantly among corporations. They emerged in the 1960s when Japanese export companies began to face litigation in the US. But as late as 1980 there were few legally-qualified employees in corporate law departments. Rather than employing registered lawyers, large corporations sent young employees to US law schools to qualify there and then work as intermediaries with US law firms after returning to Japan. In the 1990s US companies in Japan began to employ registered Japanese lawyers, and the Japanese In-House Lawyers Association was established in 2001, when 66 lawyers were employed by business corporations and other entities. The number of in-house lawyers increased to 428 in 2010 and 1,931 in 2017, when they were 5 per cent of all the registered lawyers (*Nihon Soshikinai Bengoshi Kyokai* (Japan In-House Lawyer Association, JILA) 2017a). Although women were 18 per cent of all lawyers in 2017, they were 40 per cent of in-house lawyers (JILA 2017a). And 75 per cent of in-house lawyers had entered LTRI since 2006, when law school graduates began doing so (JILA 2017b).

---

[17] In a debt overpayment case, for instance, if the client had paid the debt completely, there was no initial fee and the success fee was a 21,600 Yen handling charge, plus 21.6 per cent of the amount obtained by negotiation or 27 per cent by litigation: www.adire.jp/fee/debt.html.

[18] Clients without an introduction were just 3 per cent of new business in 1980, 4 per cent in 1990, 3 per cent in 2000 and 18 per cent in 2010 (JFBA 1988: 74; 1991: 45; 2002: 77; 2011: 101).

[19] 37 per cent of respondents said that they had created home pages or blogs (JFBA 2011: 53).

(b) Temporary Employment of Lawyers in National and Local Government

The four-year undergraduate LLB has been the main source of national and local government officials since the 1950s. National ministries employ university graduates who passed the National Civil Service Examination (NCSE).[20] Routine law-related work could be handled by such law graduates at ministries. But as ministries began to face complex demands, they began to employ people with special skills or experience for fixed terms in 2000.

The 2004 repeal of the ban on practising lawyers holding other positions prompted an increase in the number of lawyers working in national and local government. In 2005, national ministries and agencies employed 60 lawyers (JFBA White Paper 2005: 119), and local governments began to employ them in 2009 (JFBA White Paper 2009: 6–7). By 2017, there were 109 lawyers in the national government and 89 in local governments (JFBA White Paper 2017: 128–32).

Women have always been significantly overrepresented in national and local government (27 and 38 per cent), compared to their numbers in the profession, but this has been decreasing (JFBA White Paper 2008: 173–74; 2010: 163–64; 2015: 150–53; 2017: 128–32). They may prefer such positions, as well as work as judges and prosecutors, because of the superior work-life balance (JFBA White Paper 2017: 47).

C. Expansion of Legal Aid and Public Defence and Continued Efforts to Keep Public Interest Law Offices

i. Increase in the Budget for Civil Legal Aid and Court-Appointed Criminal Defence Lawyers

(a) Legal Aid for Civil Cases

The JLSC has established 112 offices throughout Japan employing 199 lawyers, 66 of them women, most working for a fixed term of 2–3 years (JFBA White Paper 2017: 218, 224). It provides comprehensive legal services, including a telephone information service for the general public and civil (advice and representation) and criminal legal aid for the indigent.

The establishment of the JLSC greatly increased state subsidies for civil legal aid from $21.6 million ($1=100 Yen) for LAA in 2000 to $155.4 in 2010, though the budget has stagnated recently (Nihon Shiho Shien Sentar (JLSC) 2016: 15). This has resulted in a sharp increase in the number of representation cases handled, from 20,261 in 2000 to 110,217 in 2010 and 107,358 in 2015, and in the number of advice cases from 35,505 in 2000 to 256,719 in 2010 and 286,602 in 2015 (LAA 2004: 71; JLSC 2016: 45). As the number of lawyers increased, the number enrolling to offer legal aid also increased, both absolutely (from 8,523 in 2006 to 21,885 in 2016) and proportionately (from 37 per cent

---

[20] Not only law graduates but also those in political science and economics pass the NCSE and become national government officials, although law graduates tend to dominate ministry positions. Local governments, such as prefectures and cities, employ people who passed examinations designed by those entities.

of lawyers in 2006 to 56 per cent in 2016). Tokyo has the lowest sign-up rate (33 per cent), while Osaka's is much higher (71 per cent) (JLSC 2015: 46; 2017: 46).

(b) Public Criminal Defence

The number of lawyers who signed up to offer public criminal defence increased from 10,783 in 2007 to 27,667 in 2017 and the proportion from 47 per cent to 71 per cent. Larger Bar associations tend to have low sign-up rates: compare Tokyo (15 per cent) with Osaka (34 per cent) in 2017 (JLSC 2015: 84; 2017: 82).

Indigent suspects in detention charged with crimes whose minimum punishment was imprisonment for a year or more were entitled to counsel appointed by the court from 2006. In 2009, when the lay judge system was introduced, the scope of public defence for suspects was expanded, increasing the number of publicly defended suspects from 7,415 in 2008 to 61,857 in 2009 (JLSC White Paper 2016: 86). Public defence was extended to all detained indigent suspects in 2018 (Act No 54 of 2016). Defendants had court-appointed counsel in 84 per cent of district court criminal trials and 92 per cent of Summary Court hearings in 2015 (Saiko Saibansho 2015: 26–27).

ii. The Creation of Staff Lawyers at JLSC Offices

The Tokyo local offices had 22 staff lawyers, but most others had just one or two in 2017. State subsidies have stagnated in recent years, and the number of staff lawyers has decreased for the last four. JLSC has to find ways to cooperate with practising lawyers in local areas.

iii. JFBA Sunflower Fund Law Offices

JFBA has opened 117 Sunflower Fund law offices since 2000, 67 of them between October 2005 and October 2017 (JFBA, 2017: 191–93). Because lawyers at 66 offices continued to practise in the region, while two offices were closed, 49 Sunflower Fund offices were open in 2017. That year no district court jurisdiction lacked a lawyer and just one had a single lawyer. The Fund has effectively achieved its purpose of eliminating court-jurisdictions without lawyers. It now fulfils a role of providing young public-interest lawyers with opportunities to gain practice experience close to local residents.

V. CONCLUSION

The world of practising attorneys has changed since 1980. The Justice System Reform introduced a set of institutional changes; and though some did not achieve their initial aims, most had significant impacts on the practice of private attorneys. Retrospectively, the increase in the lawyer population was the most significant factor. Even the modest rise in the number of lawyers at the end of 1990s stimulated the growth of big business law firms, starting the process of professional stratification. The dramatic increase in the number of lawyers under the new law school system and the deregulation of legal practice in the 2000s resulted in further diversification and stratification. Attorneys in large business law firms enjoy the highest incomes. Mass processing firms and legal boutiques advertised widely for individual clients on TV, radio and the Internet. Another dimension of diversification is the increasing number of in-house lawyers, particularly after 2010, at both private companies and national ministries (where they draft legislation as well as handle disputes).

The increasing number of lawyers envisaged by JSRC was frustrated by strong resistance from the JFBA and local Bar Associations, and the new system of law schools did not develop as planned. But those who qualified under the new law school system constitute more than 40 per cent of practising lawyers.

Now that the number passing the Bar exam has been cut to 1,500 anually, the pace of change may slacken, but the stratification and diversification of legal practice will continue. Large business law firms continue to recruit a substantial number of LTRI graduates. As competition intensifies among practising lawyers, they tend to share offices to reduce costs; this, together with the increasing number of associates, tends to reduce the number practising alone. Most practising attorneys are generalists, but younger lawyers try to distinguish themselves by identifying their fields of practice on the Internet.

At this point, it is not clear whether mass legal service providers like Adire will multiply. But lawyers will be more inclined to advertise their practices on the Internet, if not through TV or radio commercials. This will increase the possibility that lawyers may try to create regional or national practices, intensifying competition for individual clients.

The establishment of the JLSC greatly increased state subsidies for legal aid, but the system still operates by lending money to indigent clients. On the other hand, unless the JLSC restricts its practice to the indigent, it will be difficult to improve its relationship with local lawyers. There is still much to do to improve public access to lawyers.

REFERENCES

Homusho (MOJ) 'Kyu Shiho Shiken Dainiji Shiken Shutsugansu/Gokakusha Su nadono Suii' [Changes of the Numbers of Applicants and Passers of the Second Bar Examination] www.moj.go.jp/content/000054973.pdf.

Horitsu Hujo Kyokai [Legal Aid Association (LAA)] (1982) *Horitsu Hujo no Rekishi to Tenbo [History and Prospect of Legal Aid]* (Tokyo, Horitsu Hujo Kyokai).

—— (1992) *Legal Aid no Kihon Mondai [Fundamental Problems of Legal Aid]* (Tokyo, Horitsu Hujo Kyokai).

—— (2004) *Heisei 15 Nendo Jigyo Hokokusho [Activity Report for 2003 Fiscal Year]*.

Ishida, K (2017) 'Deterioration or refinement? Impacts of an increasing number of lawyers on the lawyer discipline system in Japan; 24(3) *International Journal of the Legal Profession* 243–57 www.tandfonline.com/doi/abs/10.1080/09695958.2017.1324557.

Justice System Reform Council (JSRC) (2001) *Recommendations of the Justice System Reform Council – For a Just System to Support Japan in the 21st Century* 12 June japan.kantei.go.jp/judiciary/2001/0612report.html.

Keidanren (1998) 'Shiho Seido Kaikaku ni tusiteno Iken' [Opinion about Justice System Reform] 19 May www.keidanren.or.jp/japanese/policy/pol173.html.

Keizaidoyukai (1994) 'Gendai Nihon Shakai no Byori to Shoho – Kojin wo Ikasu Shakai no Jitsugen ni Mukete' [The Illness and Its Prescription of Contemporary Japanese Society – Toward Building a Society That Values Individuals] June www.doyukai.or.jp/policyproposals/articles/past/940630a.html.

Monbukagakusho (MEXT) (1980, 1985, 1990, 1995, 2000, 2005, 2010) *Gakko Kihon Chosa [Basic Research on Schools]* (Koto Kyoiku Kikan, Gakko Chosa, Daigaku/Daigakuin, Hyo 18 [Higher Education Institutions, School Survey, Universities/Graduate Schools, Table 18]).

—— (2015) *Gakko Kihon Chosa [Basic Research on Schools]* Koto Kyoiku Kikan, Gakko Chosa, Daigaku/Daigakuin, Hyo 15 [Higher Education Institutions, School Survey, Universities/Graduate Schools, Table 15].

—— (2017) 'Hoka Daigakuin kankei no Shorei no Kaisei ni tsuite (An)' [On the Change of the Ministerial Ordinances Concerned with Law Schools (Draft)], Distributed as Fourth Material, at the 83rd Meeting of the Special Committee on Law Schools 22 November 2017. www.mext.go.jp/b_menu/shingi/chukyo/chukyo4/041/siryo/__icsFiles/afieldfile/2017/11/27/1398626_013.pdf.

Murayama, M, Moriya, A, Ishida, K, Maeda, T, Niki, T and Ono, R (2010) 'Wagakuni ni okeru Horitsu Sodan Riyo no Jittai' [Realities of the Use of Legal Consultation in Our Country 83(1) *Horitsu Ronso* 411–58.

Nagashima, Yasuharu (ed) (2011) *Nihon no Rofarmu no Tanjo to Hatten: Wagakuni Keizai no Hukko/Seicho wo Sasaeta Bijinesu Bengoshitachi no Shogen [The Birth and Development of Law Firms in Japan: Testimonies of Business Lawyers Who Supported the Recovery/Growth of the Economy of Our Country]* (Tokyo, Shoji Homu).

Nihon Bengoshi Rengokai (JFBA) (1981) 'Bengoshi Gyomu no Keizaiteki Kiban ni kansuru Jittai Chosa Hokokusho' [Preliminary Report on the Survey of the Economic Basis of the Japanese Legal Practice] 32(10) *Jiyu to Seigi*.

—— (1988) *Nihon no Horitsu Jimusho: Bengoshi Gyomu no Keizaiteki Kiban ni kansuru Jittai Chosa Hokokusho [Law Offices in Japan: Report on the Survey of the Economic Basis of the Japanese Legal Practice]* (Tokyo, Gyosei).

—— (1991) 'Bengoshi Gyomu no Keizaiteki Kiban ni kansuru Jittai Chosa Hokokusho' [Law Offices in Japan: Report on the Survey of the Economic Basis of the Japanese Legal Practice] 42(13) *Jiyu to Seigi*.

—— (2000) 'Rinji Sokai: Hoso Jinko, Hoso Yosei Seido narabini Shingikai heno Yobo ni kansuru Ketsugi' [Extraordinary General Meeting: Decision concerning the Population of the Legal Profession, the Professional Legal Education and Requests to the Justice System Council] 1 November 1 www.nichibenren.or.jp/activity/document/assembly_resolution/year/2000/2000_4.html.

—— (2002) 'Bengoshi Gyomu no Keizaiteki Kiban ni kansuru Jittai Chosa Hokokusho' [Law Offices in Japan: Report on the Survey of the Economic Basis of the Japanese Legal Practice] 53(13) *Jiyu to Seigi*.

—— (2002–2017) *Bengoshi Hakusho [White Paper of Practicing Lawyers]*.

—— (2011) 'Bengoshi Gyomu no Keizaiteki Kiban ni kansuru Jittai Chosa Hokokusho' [Law Offices in Japan: Report on the Survey of the Economic Basis of the Japanese Legal Practice] 62(6) *Jiyu to Seigi*.

Nihon Keizai Shinbun (2010) 'Bengoshi Chokai Shobun, Kako Saita no 76 Ken, Sakunen, Nichibenren Matome' [Disciplinary Actions Taken Against Lawyers, 76 Cases, Record High, Last Year, Presented by JFBA] 4 March 2010 Morning Edition p 42.

—— (2011) 'Bengoshi Chokai Shobun, Sakunen Saita no 80 Ken' [Disciplinary Actions Taken Against Lawyers, 80 Cases, Record High, Last Year] 3 March 2011 Evening Edition, p 14.

Nihon Shiho Shien Sentar [Japan Legal Support Centre (JLSC)] (2015, 2016, 2017) *Ho Terasu Hakusho [White Paper of JLSC]*.

Nihon Soshikinai Bengoshi Kyokai [Japan In-House Lawyers Association] (2017a) 'Kigyonai Bengoshi no Danjobetsu Ninzu (2001–2017)' [Number of In-House Corporate Lawyers by Gender (2001–2017)] jila.jp/wp/wp-content/themes/jila/pdf/analysis.pdf.

—— (2017b) 'Kigyonai Bengoshisu no Suii (2001–2017)' [Changes of the Number of In-House Corporate Lawyers (2001–2017)] jila.jp/wp/wp-content/themes/jila/pdf/transition.pdf.

Rokumoto, K (1988) 'The Present State of Japanese Practicing Attorneys: On the Way to Full Professionalization?' in RL Abel and PSC Lewis (eds), *Lawyers in Society: Vol II The Civil Law World* (Berkeley, University of California Press) 160–99.

Saiko Saibansho, Jimusokyoku [Supreme Court (SC), General Secretariat] (1980, 1995, 2015) *Shiho Tokei Nenpo, 2 Keiji Hen [Judicial Annual Statistics, 2 Criminal Cases]*.

Shohishacho [Consumer Affairs Agency] (2016) 'Huto Keihinrui oyobi Huto Hyoji Boshi Ho dai 6 jo no Kitei ni motozuku Sochi Meirei' [Administrative Order based on Article 6 of Act against Unjustifiable Premiums and Misleading Representations] 16 February www.caa.go.jp/policies/policy/representation/fair_labeling/pdf/160216premiums_1.pdf.

Somusho [Ministrty of Internal Affairs and Communications (MIC)] (2012) *Hoso Jinko no Kakudai oyobi Hoso Yosei Seido no Kaikaku ni kansuru Seisaku Hyokasho [Policy Evaluation Paper on the Expansion of the Lawyer Population and the Reform of Professional Legal Education System]* April 2012 www.soumu.go.jp/main_content/000158230.pdf.

Tokyo Bengoshikai [Tokyo Bar Association] (2017) 'Chokai Shobun no Kohyo' [Public Statement on Disciplinary Action] 11 October www.toben.or.jp/message/pdf/171011adire.pdf.

Yasuoka, O (2008) *Seiji Shudo no Jidai – Tochi Kozo Kaikaku ni Torikunda 30 Nen [Age of Political Initiative – 30 Years of Struggle for Reforms of the Governance Structure]* (Tokyo, Chuokoron Shinsha).

39
Myanmar
Law as a Desirable and Dangerous Profession

MELISSA CROUCH

I. INTRODUCTION

THE LEGAL PROFESSION is paradoxically a lucrative and potentially dangerous profession in Myanmar today. On one hand, the opening of Myanmar to the outside world and the shift to a market economy since 2011 has led to the establishment and growth of the first generation of commercial lawyers, many earning an enviable salary. On the other, lawyers who choose to advocate for the rule of law and social reforms risk danger, imprisonment, physical harm and death. This was illustrated in January 2017 with the brutal assassination of U Ko Ni, a lawyer who was outspoken as an advocate for constitutional reform (Crouch 2017c). To understand the role of the legal profession in Myanmar today, it is necessary to trace its historical roots and the symbiotic relationship between the state/politics and the legal profession. That is, under what conditions have lawyers influenced the state and how have lawyers been influenced by politics? The chapter explores the present and future direction of the legal profession by identifying the possible career paths for law graduates.

This chapter provides an overview of the history of the legal profession in Myanmar, with a particular focus on the last 70 years from the post-independence period in 1948 to 2018. It takes a broad view of the legal profession, because those who study or practise law may go into a range of careers – from high-level politics, to the judiciary, the civil service, the public prosecution and academia. There are no reliable statistics on lawyers in Myanmar today. The rough figure of 40,000 is often cited, but this is likely to be inaccurate, outdated, and this list may include deceased and non-practising lawyers. The legal profession is undergoing rapid change and this turbulence is likely to continue over the next few decades.

Unlike many other countries covered in this volume, there have not been any comprehensive studies of the legal profession in Myanmar, either past or present. This chapter primarily offers an original empirical account based on archival and field research, and where relevant it reflects on the academic contributions of the late Professor Andrew Huxley, Christian Lammerts, Maung Maung, Myint Zan, Nick Cheesman and Melissa Crouch.

II. BUDDHISM AND THE PRE-COLONIAL LEGAL PROFESSION

During the time of the Burmese kings, there was a well-established legal profession as early at the thirteenth century (Huxley 2014; 1996).[1] The first kingdom to be established by the Burmans was known as the Kingdom of Bagan. Over several kingdoms, historical records bear testimony to a distinct legal culture practised by lawyers and judges that developed from the Burmese Buddhist tradition. The body of written law known in Burmese as *dhammathat* was used in the adjudication of cases.[2] The *dhammathats* have been described as a 'manual of instruction' for judges, whose legal authority was derived from their 'moral and educational' credentials (Lammerts 2010: 434, 492). The *dhammathats* were the primary legal reference at this time.

The *dhammathats* are generally structured around 18 major titles of law. These titles comprise criminal, personal and economic matters; *dhammathats* also contain extensive rules on legal procedure, kingship and monastic law. The history of their reception is complex but until the eighteenth century *dhammathat* was generally regarded as a form of law that originated in Buddhist tradition and was preserved and passed down by the legal profession and the kings. Up until the colonial era, the *dhammathat* was regarded as authoritative Buddhist literature, on a par with, and even included in, the Buddhist canon (Lammerts 2013).

This source of law was developed over successive kingdoms. The first main king was Anawratha (1044–77); King Bayinnaung (1551–81) achieved an unrivalled expansion of power; and King Alaungpaya (1752–60) was the first to sign an agreement with a foreign power, England. The king was known as the head of the Hluttaw, the Supreme Council of State. The Hluttaw fulfilled numerous roles, including as a legislative chamber, a ministerial cabinet, and a court that had civil and criminal jurisdiction, and could hear appeals from lower courts. Some kings have been noted for the significant legal reforms they undertook, such as King Mindon (1853–78), who initiated changes to the court system of administration and improved social infrastructure.

The development of this distinct legal tradition coincided with the emergence of a unique legal profession. Law advocates were known by the term *she-ne*, which captures the role of lawyers as advocating on behalf of their clients because it literally means 'those who stand in front' (Huxley 1994: 219). This rich legal tradition and the professional lawyers who serviced it met their demise in the 1800s with the onset of British colonialism from 1825. The social, political and legal customs and traditions established and developed during the period of the kings was profoundly disrupted and displaced by the Anglo-Burmese Wars (1824–26, 1852–53 and 1885), which were the result of both internal

---

[1] In many respects, this chapter on Myanmar deserves to be in the 'old/established' legal profession volume of this series on *Lawyers in Society*, rather than the 'new' legal profession volume.
[2] For an analysis of the significance of *dhammathat* to Burmese legal culture, see Huxley (1997). For a more extensive explanation of its Pali etymology, see Lammerts (2010).

factors and external developments in the region. The First Anglo-Burmese War (1824–26) led to the signing of the Treaty of Yandabo, ceding parts of southern and western Burma to the British, and the annexation of the Rakhine and Tenasserim regions. The responsibility for establishing a new judicial system was given to the first Commissioner of Tenasserim. The Second Anglo-Burmese War (1852–53) led to the British takeover of Rangoon and other parts of Lower Burma. British authorities began to take more concrete steps to establish a legal system to consolidate territorial rule. In 1866, the Chief Commissioner was given power to enforce the laws of India in Burma, although did not have power to promulgate laws. In 1872, the first Judicial Commissioner of Burma, Douglas Sandford, was appointed and took over judicial powers from the Chief Commissioner.

The ultimate demise and displacement of the monarchy, its system of law and its professional lawyers occurred in 1885 as a result of the Third Anglo-Burmese War. The last king of the Konbaung dynasty, King Thibaw (1752–1885), and his family were captured by the British and shipped off to India. Burma was annexed to British India and made subordinate to the British Indian common law tradition.

III. A COMMON LAW PROFESSION FOR THE COLONIAL STATE

The experience of British colonial rule in Burma was the shortest in Southeast Asia. This meant that the colonial legal system and the corresponding legal profession did not evolve over a long period of time but was largely imported wholesale from British India. The legal profession first emerged in key colonial outposts, like Moulemein, Sittwe and then Rangoon in 1885. The legal profession was initially imported from India, and legal personnel at first were either English or Indian. Over several years, a Burmese legal profession emerged as they trained as lawyers in London and then returned to Burma, or apprenticed themselves to a senior lawyer in Burma.

The legal profession was to advise clients according to the common law and to the Indian Codes that came to apply to all of Burma as a province of British India. Staple bodies of law, from criminal law to property to contracts, were copied from India, and most remain in force today. A hierarchy of courts and administrative control extended across Upper and Lower Burma. The Burma Laws Act 1898 allows for the recognition of customary law in matters of family personal law and remains valid today. Some legal professionals specialised in the practice of customary law, for Muslims (Anglo-Muhammadan law), Hindus (Hindu Law) and Buddhists (Burmese Buddhist law) in family law matters (Crouch 2016a; 2016c).

In 1897, a Legislative Council was established in Rangoon and its members were responsible for assisting the Lieutenant Governor in drafting legislation for Burma. In the early 1900s the judiciary was separated from the executive, although it remained common in some areas for government civil servants (the executive) to also act as judges. In 1921, after pressure from nationalists, the British Parliament passed legislation granting Burma dyarchy, that is, the opportunity to elect Burmese locals to government departments. This legislative reform was followed by further judicial reforms. In 1922 a High Court was established as the highest court of appeal in Burma, replacing the Chief Court of Lower Burma and the Judicial Commissioner of Upper Burma. In 1926, the local legal profession was regulated with the creation of a 15-member Bar Council, similar to that in India (under the Bar Council Act 1926). The Bar Council included the Attorney General as chairperson, four members nominated by the High Court, and 10 elected by advocates of the High Court. The Bar Council was responsible for regulating admission to practice and inquiring into cases of misconduct.

In the late 1930s, pressure from the nationalist movement led to changes in Burma's relations with British India. In April 1937, the Government of Burma Act 1935 came into force, and from then on Burma was considered to be a separate colony, no longer under British India administration. Similar to the Government of India Act 1935, the Act provided for the first bicameral legislature. In the nationalist politics of the 1900s–1940s, lawyers had a significant influence on legal and political developments in Burma.

The early modern legal system of Burma was disproportionately shaped by a handful of prominent Burmese legal professionals. For example, E Maung (1889–1972) was a Burmese lawyer, and later became an academic at the University of Rangoon (1926–32). He went on to serve as judge of the High Court and then the Supreme Court, before being appointed to the role of Minister of Foreign Affairs (1949), Minister for Judicial Affairs (1958) and Minister for Home Affairs (1961). Throughout his life and work, he argued for the retention of the common law legal system, and also published in areas such as Burmese Buddhist law and constitutional law.

In the 1940s, the legal institutions and the practise of law of Burma were disrupted by World War II and the invasion by the Japanese. In 1942, the Governor of Burma suspended the jurisdiction of the High Court in Rangoon and later declared the courts closed. It was only with the end of the war in 1945 that the common law legal system recommenced, and some lawyers began to throw themselves into the work of preparing for independence.

IV. THE LEGAL PROFESSION IN AN ERA OF PARLIAMENTARY DEMOCRACY

The legal profession enjoyed significant autonomy in the post-independence era from 1948 to 1962, and benefited from the more democratic political environment. This was an era when an increasing percentage of legal roles were taken over by Burmese people from foreign (English/Indian) legal experts. In independent Burma, those already trained as lawyers now had new career opportunities to become prominent legal and political figures and influence the new democratic political system. Many lawyers, judges and political figures were involved in the Constituent Assembly to draft the 1947 Constitution. At independence, the members of the Constituent Assembly became the Provisional Parliament until the first elections were held in 1955. The new Supreme Court in Burma became powerful as the final court of appeal, with appeals to the Privy Council ending at independence. This era of parliamentary democracy, although fragile, provided an unprecedented environment in which lawyers could advocate for rights and petition the court for the writ of habeas corpus at a time when the new government was abusing its powers to arrest and detain those perceived to be causing social unrest.

For students beginning their legal studies and embarking on a career in law, the path to becoming a lawyer now lay in Rangoon, rather than beginning in London. Chambers students began their training under Advocates in Rangoon and other major towns as opportunities to train in London declined, in part because Burma chose not to join the British Commonwealth after independence. The primary model of a lawyer was the traditional common law model of a legal practitioner who is licensed as an Advocate. An Advocate is also a Chambers Master who supervises chambers students, who are law graduates seeking to complete their chambers apprenticeship. Junior lawyers are known as Higher Grade Pleaders and can only appear in the lower courts. After several years' work experience in the courts, they can apply to the Supreme Court to become Advocates. Advocates are essentially senior litigation lawyers or barrister, and the bulk of their work is in criminal law, with some also dealing with civil cases. This traditional model of legal practice remains prevalent in Myanmar today.

The lawyers trained in this era were affected by the dramatic political changes that began in the 1960s. This is evident in the career of one of Myanmar's most prominent lawyers. Dr Maung Maung (1924–1994) began his career in 1953 as a law officer in the Attorney General's office. He studied at Utrecht University and was later a visiting fellow at Yale University. Once the socialist coup took place in 1962, he became a judge and was appointed to the position of Chief Justice in 1965. From 1971 to 1974, under the socialist regime, he held the position of Minister for Judicial Affairs and was a member of General Ne Win's Revolutionary Council. Dr Maung Maung was responsible for the devastating restructuring of the legal system in the 1960s and 1970s, and played a role in the drafting of the 1974 socialist Constitution. While his initial writings contain exhortations about the rule of law and constitutionalism (see Taylor 2008), by the time he ended his public career – with his role as President in 1988 lasting for less than a few weeks – he had discarded those ideas. Instead, he left behind much of the common law tradition and embodied the socialist-military concept of legality that prevailed for 50 years since the 1960s. The degeneration of the legal system, including its legal profession, can be attributed to the concrete steps taken by figures such as Dr Maung Maung away from the common law and towards a more socialist-military form of legal rule.

V. SUBORDINATING THE LEGAL PROFESSION UNDER SOCIALIST-MILITARY RULE

The legal profession, along with the entire legal system was rendered subordinate and docile to the unbridled administrative power of the socialist state. On 2 March 1962, the military – under the leadership of General Ne Win – arrested a wide range of members of the democratically elected government, the Chief Justice Myint Thein and other individuals perceived as a threat to its takeover. They remained in jail for many years without trial. The democratically elected government was replaced by a 17-member Revolutionary Council, and a hierarchy of councils that permeated down to the village level, all overseen by military officers. The Burmese Way to Socialism was introduced and the Burma Socialist Programme Party (BSPP) was established, which by 1964 was the only political party permitted. Its membership remained small until the 1970s when Ne Win sought to make the BSPP a mass-based organisation. The state ultimately came to control all economic activity of any significance through a process of mass nationalisation of everything from schools to companies. This negated any need for a commercial legal profession.

In 1962, a new Chief Court was established as the apex of the judicial system. The coup spelled the end of judicial independence and judicial activism. The role of the general courts and their independence was undercut by the creation of Special Criminal Courts (see Cheesman 2012). On 7 August 1972, the People's Judicial System was introduced under the guidance of Dr Maung Maung. Professional judges were removed from their posts and replaced by members of the BSPP, loyal to the socialist state and ready to put socialist policy above law.

The qualifications of judicial members varied. For example, the first chair of the Council of People's Justice, U Aung Pe (1974–81), was a former colonel, while his replacement, U Maung Maung Kyaw Win (1981–83), was a former brigadier and barrister. It was only the third chair, U Tin Aung Hein (1983–88), who actually had a law degree. The Council of People's Justices had a limited mandate: it was responsible to the unicameral parliament and was required to uphold the socialist system. Burmese language was mandated as the language of law, rejecting the previous use of English as the primary language of the courts. This further cut off the legal profession from its prior common law, English influence.

This affected the role of lawyers, not least because they could no longer aspire to a career at the bench. The prestige of the legal profession as a whole suffered, and lawyering became heavily influenced by socialist ideas of legality. The socialist era also had a profound effect on legal education, as universities were sporadically closed due to student protests, particularly after the major student protests of 1974. When universities opened again their curriculum was tightly controlled. Subjects such as company law were, for example, no longer taught as part of a law degree during the socialist era. Civil servants during this period who studied abroad no longer went to common law jurisdictions, but instead went to socialist regimes such as East Germany.

The fortunes of the legal profession were also affected by the country's plunge into full-scale poverty in 1987, with Burma officially listed as a 'Least Developed Country' by the United Nations. There was growing discontent with the BSPP government, particularly because of gross economic mismanagement. A brawl in a tea shop led to growing student unrest, aggravated when several hundred protestors were killed at the White Bridge, near Inya Lake in Yangon, now known as the Red Bridge. This led to major student protests demanding democracy, and was followed by a brutal military crackdown. On 18 September 1988, the State Law and Order Restoration Council (SLORC) took over, co-opting the 'law' in its title as a means of justifying its rule by force. Many lawyers and Bar associations participated in the 1988 democracy uprising. As a consequence, the military regime imposed significant restrictions on the ability of professional Bar associations to mobilise. For example, U Ko Yu was a Central Executive Committee member of the National League for Democracy and contributed to the Bar Council statement supporting the 1988 pro-democracy uprisings and denouncing the socialist regime. He was later imprisoned for his support of the pro-democracy movement. The period of 1990s-2000s was extremely difficult and offered almost no space for the activism of cause lawyers (Cheesman and Kyaw Min San 2013).

VI. A NEW ERA FOR THE LEGAL PROFESSION

A. Mass Legal Education

The career options for law graduates have increased, although the prospects for many students are limited by the low quality of legal education they receive. To become a lawyer in Myanmar today first requires completing an LLB degree at university. The military coup had a major impact on universities, including on legal education. In 1988 the universities were closed due to student demonstrations and the University of Yangon did not reopen until 1993. The military then introduced a strategy of mass expansion of tertiary education, including of law. Up until this time, there was only one law department in the entire country at the University of Yangon. Then 17 new law departments were established across the country. Some were located in major towns such as Mandalay, Taunggyi and Myitkyina, but others were located on the outskirts of Yangon, such as Dagon University and East Yangon University, to draw students away from the city centre and reduce the risks of student political activism. Out of the 14 states and regions in Myanmar, there is no law department in Chin State, Karen State or Kayah State.

The two most prominent universities in Myanmar – the University of Yangon and the University of Mandalay – were closed to undergraduate law students until 2012. Instead, from the 1990s, two new departments – the University of Yangon Distance Education and the University of Mandalay Distance Education – offered undergraduate courses in law. However, learning in these courses is reduced to ten-days per year of face-to-face teaching and minimal online content consisting of basic written materials and audio files.

Law students who studied during the 1990s and 2000s became one among thousands of new graduates. The very low entrance score devalued the worth of a law degree and reduced both the perceived and actual quality of law graduates. The majority of graduates were female (in part because degrees such as medicine or engineering had a higher entrance score for women than for men). The feminisation of the legal profession has been part of the military's strategy to pacify the profession and reduce its status, which presents a future challenge for gender equality. Women *already* make up a majority of the legal profession, a majority of judges and law professors. This is a stark contrast from the colonial and post-independence period, when the vast majority of legal professionals were men. This shift may have begun during the socialist era, as the legal profession began to diminish in political importance and influence. The high numbers of women today in the legal profession in Myanmar is in contrast to many parts of Asia, such as Japan, South Korea and India, where the small numbers of women in the legal profession have been documented. This overrepresentation of women in the legal profession does not, however, translate into women occupying the highest positions. For example, all judges on the Union Supreme Court are men.

There have been some significant changes in legal education since the 2011 transition. In 2013, the on-campus LLB degree recommenced at the Law Department of the University of Yangon and Mandalay University. Students in this program were chosen through a new selection process from among the top performing high school students. The future opportunities for these law graduates are significant, as law is once again a path of ambition and success in Myanmar. The challenge, however, remains to reconnect legal education to legal practice, and to increase the quality of legal education to ensure graduates are equipped to respond to the demand for legal skills in Myanmar and the pressures of globalisation. University education is required to be in English, although the quality of instruction depends on many factors, such as accessibility of English textbooks and the English proficiency of professors. The dominant model of legal education is focused on memorising content and rote learning.

In other respects, the reform environment has brought very limited freedoms for law students. On one hand, student unions are still banned in Myanmar, despite unions for other sectors now being legalised and permitted to organise. There are exceptional groups of talented law students outside of Yangon, such as the Dagon University Law Student Association (known as DULSA). This highly motivated, articulate and intelligent group of law students have made a remarkable effort to organise professional career opportunities for students. This is despite the fact they are often misunderstood by their university and faculty, and have faced pressures to cease their activities. This has included training initiatives, moot courts and other engagements supported by international non-governmental organisations (NGOs) as well as with foreign law firms. Some of these law students have undertaken internships with commercial firms, which is highly unusual for law students in Myanmar but is becoming more common.

B. Legal Career Paths in Myanmar

The career paths for law graduates in Myanmar remains highly stratified, specialised and fragmented, although some new opportunities are emerging. The basic distinction in career paths is the choice of whether to go into the civil service (either as an academic, judge or public prosecutor) or into private practice (either as a litigator or commercial lawyer).

On the first path, law graduates may choose to become a law tutor, undertake an LLM degree and then a PhD in order to pursue a career as an academic. The role of academics is largely understood in terms of their teaching and administration; there is no emphasis on research or publications, and many have never practised law. Law graduates may alternatively choose to take the test to become a career prosecutor in the Union Attorney General's Office, or take the exam to become a career judge. The fact that most judges are career judges in Myanmar is at variance with its common law roots (Crouch 2017c). In the early stages of their career, civil servants will receive training by the Central Institute of Civil Service, and then for judges the Judicial Training Institute or for prosecutors from the training division of the Attorney Generals' Office. All three of these career paths are part of the civil service and the most important factor in career advancement is years of service. The civil service in Myanmar remains highly regulated and is constrained by certain features such as being posted to several different locations around the country during the course of their career.

The second career path for law graduates is to find a chambers master and begin an apprenticeship in their law chambers. Some of the most famous and experienced lawyers may require chambers students to pay them for the privilege of being their student. Other students may rely on family connections to secure a chambers master. For less well-known lawyers, chambers students may simply work for free or, if they are fortunate, may receive a small allowance. It can therefore be difficult for those without family connections, status or wealth to enter the profession. In order to be registered as a Higher Grade Pleader, students must demonstrate to the Supreme Court that they have represented clients in a number of different courts and matters. Most chambers are located close to the vicinity of local courts. However, the move of the highest court, the Union Supreme Court, to the capital city Naypyidaw, has created particular challenges due to the isolated location of the court. After several more years' experience, a Higher Grade Pleader can apply to be recognised as an Advocate. Advocates are generalists and do not usually specialise in a particular area of law. The main role of Advocates is to meet with clients and represent clients in court.

Many senior legal professionals, such as retired judges or prosecutors who worked as part of the socialist/military legal regime, are now reinventing themselves by working in or advising on rule of law programs of local organisations or international NGOs. There has been a growth in paralegals, the emergence of legal aid, and the expansion of political space to advocate for a wide range of legal reforms – from women's rights to environmental law, land rights, migrant workers, children's rights, the regulation of hate speech, labour rights, constitutional reform, and other social justice causes. In this respect, there has been an expansion of space for cause lawyers in Myanmar. The work of Nick Cheesman has identified the challenges in criminal legal practice and the ways that cause lawyers have sought to advocate for the idea of law itself (Cheesman 2015; Cheesman and Kyaw Min San 2013). Some areas of advocacy are not without significant risks. The assassination of U Ko Ni, a prominent Burmese Muslim lawyer and legal adviser to the NLD who was vocal on the need for constitutional reform, was taken as a personal assault on the legal profession (Crouch 2017a). His death has dampened efforts at more radical constitutional change, and for now the military remains entrenched in its role in governance and as unelected members of parliament. The careers of cause lawyers remain risky, controversial and may court danger, prison, torture or death.

A separate and more comfortable area of growing interest is commercial law, a career path that I discuss in the next section in some detail due to its newness in the context of Myanmar.

C. The First Generation of Commercial Lawyers

One trend since the 1990s has been the emergence of a small but growing pool of local commercial lawyers, as well as foreign law firms. In the mid-1990s, a handful of commercial law firms were established during the military turn to a market economy (Crouch 2017a). After 1988, the military regime made an effort to shift from a socialist economy to a market-based economy, although the economy remained under the control of the military and its cronies. From the early to mid-1990s, new legislation was introduced to implement this shift from a socialist to a market-based system. A range of new commercial legislation was passed for the first time, including the Central Bank of Myanmar Law; the Financial Institutions of Myanmar Law; the Commercial Tax Law and the Private Industrial Enterprise Law. A new Myanmar Tourism Law was introduced in an attempt to encourage tourism. This was combined with a desperate effort to attract significant foreign investment and tourism by designating 1996 the year of 'Visit Myanmar'. Due to heavy Western sanctions it was not a successful campaign. The military also introduced the Myanmar Citizens Investment Law and the Mines Law, in anticipation of new investment.

At around the same time, in the 1990s, a handful of commercial law firms were established in Yangon. In 1995–96, this included Kelvin Chia, DFDL and Lucy Wayne & Associates, with other firms such as Myanmar Legal Services being established in 1998. A handful of Burmese lawyers also set up practice in Singapore, servicing Burmese companies abroad and facilitating the regime's business interests. The 2000s were a period when tight Western sanctions remained, and so the hoped-for foreign investment from Western sources did not eventuate and the handful of commercial law firms remained small outfits, while some closed altogether.

It was not until 2012, after the political shift under President Thein Sein, that commercial law firms once again began to establish offices in Yangon. In 2015, the commercial and corporate law market was said to be the most crowded legal market in Southeast Asia. This market includes a wide range of Korean, Japanese, German, American, Thai, Singaporean, Malaysian, UK, regional and global law firms. Since the NLD government came to power in 2016, there has been a decline in demand for legal services due to the uncertainties of a new government and the instabilities provoked by mass displacement and allegations of genocide in Rakhine State.

There is no regulation of foreign lawyers or foreign law firms. This has caused some tensions between local litigators and foreign commercial lawyers and consultants, and may lead to some form of specific government regulation of foreign lawyers and foreign law firms in the future. Most foreign law firms seek to mitigate the possibility of this happening by maintaining close ties with the Attorney General, and providing pro bono legal training to the Attorney General's Office and to university students.

Foreign law firms are one forum where a new generation of Burmese commercial lawyers are being trained. Members of this new generation generally have less than six years' experience in legal practice. The profession in many respects is similar to the state of the commercial legal profession of Thailand or Vietnam in the 1980s and 1990s. Some Burmese lawyers are now working as in-house counsel for local companies, regional companies or international firms. This number will continue to grow in the immediate future. The number of lawyers in government institutions and departments remains extremely small, and again this is likely to be an area in need of significant growth in the future.

There also remain tensions and misunderstandings within the local legal profession between litigators and commercial lawyers. This is because to qualify as a Higher Grade Pleader, a chambers student must go before the court and declare that they do not have any commercial or business interests and solely work as a litigation lawyer. This has been interpreted to mean that a person cannot work in a commercial law firm while also training to become registered as a Higher Grade Pleader. Essentially, law graduates can become commercial lawyers only after training and qualifying as litigation lawyers. Some students have taken a different path, first getting a job as a paralegal in a commercial law firm, then deciding to undertake a law degree and then work as a chambers student in order to enter the profession.

There is currently no process for Burmese citizens or diaspora who obtain legal qualifications overseas to be recognised or able to convert their qualifications to practise law in Myanmar. This is an impediment to improving the cadre of the legal profession in Myanmar, and remains a disincentive for highly qualified Burmese citizens who have returned to Myanmar since 2011.

There are other real barriers to entry into the legal profession. In more recent years the process to become a qualified Higher Grade Pleader has become more discriminatory. The Supreme Court will now only grant licences to applicants who can prove that both of their parents have full citizenship. Even if a person has a law degree and has the requisite experience as a chambers student, they will not be granted a practising licence if one of their parents holds a partial or temporary form of citizenship, which may be the case for those who are of part-Chinese heritage or Rohingya.

The young commercial legal profession is highly mobile and there is very high turnover among law firms. Local lawyers in foreign law firms are often given tasks that are local in nature rather than related to global legal practice, such as translation, filing of documents with government agencies, and research tasks. Moving between law firms is partly driven by the desire of local lawyers to continue to improve their skills, gain the best work experience and, more importantly, be recognised as lawyers who can take on more difficult legal tasks and have the opportunity to deal with clients.

There is currently no existing professional legal education provider in Myanmar and therefore no formal ongoing continuing legal education for the profession. This is a significant gap, given the importance of continuing legal education programmes to the development of the skills and knowledge of practising lawyers in many other countries.

Finally, it is worth noting that commercial lawyers are not usually members of either the official Bar Association, nor of the newer independent association, the Independent Lawyers' Association of Myanmar (ILAM). The government-run 11-member Bar Association is under the control of the Attorney General's Office and there are likely to be reforms to the regulation of lawyers in the future. The profession is currently regulated under the Legal Profession Act and the Bar Council Act. Because of concerns about its lack of independence, in 2016, a new independent Bar association, ILAM, was established. This initiative was heavily sponsored and driven by the International Bar Association, and supported by Aung San Suu Kyi. ILAM, however, it is still in its early stages. For commercial lawyers, there are a range of new and emerging networks such as the Arbitration Association, the IP Lawyers Network, and the Myanmar Commercial Law Network. These new networks suggest a growing professionalisation and specialisation of commercial lawyers in Myanmar.

VII. CONCLUSION

The history and development of the legal profession in Myanmar, and the career opportunities for law graduates, has been impacted by the political regime of the day. Legal practise contains traces of the pre-colonial legal regime with the ongoing use of Burmese Buddhist law for family law matters. The legal profession was also shaped by the British colonial regime, and then later subordinated by decades of socialist and military rule. There have always been lawyers who sought to influence the political system, but it is only now, post-2011, that lawyers and legal professionals have new opportunities and space to influence political, economic and legal reforms in Myanmar in ways that potentially challenge the political status quo.

From this brief mapping of the development of the legal profession in Myanmar, we can identify new opportunities for research on the legal profession in Myanmar. First, there is now greater opportunity to build on the legacy of Andrew Huxley's research on the history of the Burmese legal profession prior to colonialism, as scholars such as Christian Lammerts have begun to do. Second, there has never been a thorough examination of the legal profession during 1825–1947 and its influence on and implications in the colonial project. Third, there are new opportunities to study how the legal profession changed and was impacted by the socialist and military regimes from the 1960s onwards, as access to documentation from this period increases. Finally, the emergence of new areas of growth in the legal profession – paralegals, cause lawyering and space for advocacy, commercial lawyers, foreign lawyers, the role of women lawyers, and shifts in legal education – represents a field ripe for research. This corresponds with renewed scholarly interest in areas such as corporate lawyers in emerging markets (Garth 2016).

Finally, one of the key questions in comparative research on the legal profession over the past few decades has been the impact of globalisation on legal practice. This question is of growing relevance to Myanmar, given the dramatic political opening since 2011 and major economic reforms and foreign investment initiatives. In the future, understanding the impact of globalisation on the legal profession in Myanmar will be vital. However, as Galanter and Robinson (2013) have observed in the context of India, the potentially homogenising forces of globalisation may not necessarily lead to convergence in the structure of the legal profession in Myanmar. Instead, the future is likely to see greater bifurcation, with the persistence of traditional litigation practice in Myanmar alongside the burgeoning commercial law industry and the growth of legal non-government advocacy organisations. This will continue to provide new and diverse career opportunities for law graduates. The political environment also opens up new opportunities for lawyers to influence legal reforms, although this potential requires a choice between the benefits of safe career in areas such as commercial law against the risks associated with advocating for more fundamental political and legal change.

REFERENCES

Cheesman, N (2012) 'How an Authoritarian Regime in Burma Used Special Courts to Defeat Judicial Independence' 45 *Law & Society Review* 801.
—— (2015) *Opposing the Rule of Law: How Myanmar's Courts Make Law and Order* (Cambridge, Cambridge University Press).
Cheesman, N and Kyaw Min San (2013) 'Not Just Defending: Advocating for Rule of Law' 31 *Wisconsin Journal of International Law* 702.
Crouch, M (2014) 'The Layers of Legal Development in Myanmar' in M Crouch and T Lindsey (eds), *Law, Society and Transition in Myanmar* (Oxford, Hart Publishing) 33–58.
—— (2016a) 'Promiscuity, Polygyny and the Power of Revenge: Burmese Buddhist Law in an Era of Law Reform in Myanmar' 3 *Asian Journal of Law and Society* 85.
—— (2016b) 'Personal Law & Colonial Legacy' in M Crouch (ed), *Islam & the State in Myanmar: Muslim-Buddhist Relations & the Politics of Belonging* (Oxford, Oxford University Press) 69–97.
—— (2017a) *The Business of Transition: Law Reform, Development and Economics in Myanmar* (Cambridge, Cambridge University Press).
—— (2017b) 'Judicial Power in Myanmar and the challenge of judicial independence' in HP Lee and M Pittard (eds), *Asia-Pacific Judiciaries: Independence, Impartiality and Integrity* (Cambridge, Cambridge University Press) 264–83.
—— (2017c) 'Myanmar's Advocate for Constitutional Reform: A Tribute to Saya U Ko Ni' 14(1) *Australian Journal of Asian Law* 1.
Dezalay, Y and Garth, B (2002) *The Internationalisation of Palace Wars: Lawyers, Economists and the Contest to Transform Latin American States* (Chicago, University of Chicago Press).
Galanter, M and Robinson, N (2013) 'India's Grand Advocates: A Legal Elite Flourishing in an Era of Globalisation' 20(3) *International Journal of the Legal Profession* 241–65.

Garth, B (2016) 'Corporate Lawyers in Emerging Markets' 12 *Annual Review of Law and Social Science* 441.

Huxley, A (1994) 'The Reception of Buddhist Law in Southeast Asia 200 BC–1860 CE' in M Doucet and J Vanderlinden (eds), *La Reception Des Systemes Juridiques: Implantation Et Destin* (Bruylant, Universite Libre De Bruxelles, and Universite De Moncton) 139–247.

—— (1996) 'The Legal Profession of Burma 1200–1880' in *Receuils de la Société Jean Bodin* (Brussels, De Boeck Universite) 155–87.

—— (1997) 'The Importance of the Dhammathats in Burmese Law and Culture' 1 *Journal of Burma Studies* 1–17.

—— (1998) 'The Last Fifty Years of Burmese Law: E Maung and Maung Maung' *LAWASIA: Journal of the Law Association of Asia and West Pacific* 9.

—— (2014) 'Is Burmese Law Buddhist? Transition and Tradition' in M Crouch and T Lindsey (eds), *Law, Society and Transition in Myanmar* (Oxford, Hart Publishing) 59–75.

Lammerts, DC (2010) 'Buddhism and Written Law: Dhammasattha Manuscripts and Texts in Premodern Burma' PhD thesis, Cornell University.

—— (2013) 'Narratives of Buddhist Legislation: Textual Authority and Legal Heterodoxy in 17th–19th Century Burma' 44(1) *Journal of Southeast Asian Studies* 118.

Myint Zan (2008a) 'Legal Education in Burma Since the Mid-1960s' 12 *Journal of Burma Studies* 63.

Taylor, R (2008) *Dr Maung Maung: Gentleman, Scholar, Patriot* (Singapore, Institute of Southeast Asian Studies).

40

South Korea[1]
Reshaping the Legal Profession

JAEWON KIM

I. HISTORICAL INTRODUCTION

THE VARIOUS KINGDOMS on the Korean peninsula were united by the Koryo dynasty in 936 AD, and the Chosun dynasty ruled the peninsula from the late fourteenth century. These kingdoms had sophisticated customary laws as well as codified laws strongly influenced by China, particularly the Tang and Great Ming Codes. This legal tradition, however, was ruptured by Japanese colonialism in the early twentieth century. Suppressing Korea's law and legal system, Japan introduced its Westernised code and legal system (modelled on those of Prussia). Through this colonial implantation, Korea involuntarily joined the civil law family.

After disarming Japanese imperial forces in 1945, the US and USSR occupied the Korean peninsula until 1948. North Korea adopted a socialist legal system under the influence of the Soviet Union. However, the influence of the US legal system was also noticeable in many areas of South Korean law, including constitutional law, criminal procedure, commercial law and labour law. Reflecting the growing military, diplomatic and economic ties with the US, South Korean law adopted more American features over the next five decades.

The Korean War (1950–53) was one of the most tragic events in Korean history. In addition to enormous combatant and civilian casualties, it destroyed almost all housing, public buildings, roads and industries in both South and North Korea. And it had two enduring consequences for South Korean society: a strong military and use of the National Security Act to suppress democratic demands. After 1961, when General Park Chung-hee seized power through a militry coup, two more generals became heads of state. Only after the 1987 'June Revolution' and the Constitution it adopted did South Korea

---

[1] The Korean Peninsula lies between China and Japan. After World War II it was divided into the Republic of Korea (South Korea) and the Democratic People's Republic of Korea (North Korea). The peninsula is about the same size as Great Britain, and its population is approximately 77 million. North Korea covers slightly more than half the peninsula, but its population is less than half that of South Korea's 51.3 million. In this chapter, 'Korea' is used interchangeably with 'South Korea' unless otherwise indicated.

fully embrace democracy and the rule of law. In most countries over the last 30 years, legal professions have experienced significant change, growing in size and diversifying demographically. Legal practice has been transformed, often significantly internationalising. Many of these trends are particularly pronounced in South Korea.

II. RAPID GROWTH OF THE PROFESSION

It took about 100 years for the number of lawyers to reach 10,000 but just eight to add another 10,000. There were 9,240 lawyers registered with the Korean Bar Association in 2007 but 23,154 on 1 August 2017, including 19,640 active members.[2] Because of the recent rapid growth, more than half of active lawyers (approximately 11,000) have less than ten years' experience. The annual quota for new lawyers under the old Bar exam scheme had been gradually increased to one thousand. However, the recent expansion was a consequence of the new law school system, which has produced over 1,500 new lawyers annually since 2012. Like the US system, this is a post-graduate three-year JD degree programme, which was approved by the Ministry of Education in 2008 and began to operate in 2009.

This development needs to be placed in historical perspective. The Roh Moo-hyun administration (2003–08) worked very hard for its judicial reform campaign, whose central element was the Law School Act, which barely passed in July 2007 after a long fierce fight. The Roh administration was not the first to attempt such a reform. As early as the 1970s, some law professors, and later their national association, proposed reforms to improve the quality of legal education and produce the larger number of lawyers needed by a democratic society. Civic organisations agitated for more lawyers to increase access to justice. The Kim Young-sam administration (1993–98) announced a 'globalisation plan'. To improve the quality of legal services so that Korean lawyers could compete with foreign lawyers (including American), the Presidential Commission for Globalisation, led by the Prime Minister, proposed the establishment of American-style law schools. During the Kim Dae-jung administration (1998–2003) a presidential committee proposed detailed standards for new postgraduate law schools. Despite strenuous efforts over 10 years, these administrations failed to achieve their goal, primarily because of opposition by the Supreme Court.

Following the Japanese model, the only path to becoming a licensed lawyer was through the Judicial Research and Training Institute (JRTI), directly controlled by the Supreme Court, which did not respect or trust law professors and did not want to surrender control over the production of lawyers. Eager to preserve the high entry barriers, the Korean Bar Association also opposed the new law school plan. After a 14-year struggle by three administrations, the reform of legal education finally succeeded in 2007. The ultimate reason was that the Supreme Court changed its position, though it is not known why Choi Jong-young, Chief Justice of the Supreme Court (1999–2005), agreed with President Roh Moo-hyun to establish the Judicial Reform Committee. Unlike previous committees subordinate to the President, this one was created by the Chief Justice.

---

[2] *The Korean Bar Association News*, 4 September 2017, 1.

After protracted and heated debates, the committee voted 13-2 for the plan proposed by the Supreme Court, defeating the Korean Bar Association's plan to preserve undergraduate law departments with some modifications. The representatives of liberal non-governmental organisations (NGOs), which actively supported President Roh's election,[3] endorsed the Supreme Court's plan during the committee vote. It is widely understood that Chief Justice Choi could not resist the determination of President Roh. He was the first Korean president with a lawyer's licence but was very different from the mainstream Bar. He was a vocational high school graduate from a poor family who had never gone to university but studied by himself to pass the extraordinarily difficult judicial exam. Because of that experience, he was determined to eliminate the cartel of the elite Korean legal profession by adopting a new educational and examination system.

Chief Justice Lee Yong-hoon (2005–11), Choi's successor, played a decisive role in realising the plan. As an outspoken supporter of law reform, the new Chief Justice, appointed by President Roh, was eager to curb prosecutorial power. Ever since General Park Chung-hee, all Korean presidents had used prosecutorial powers to suppress the opposition and decide many important socio-economic issues without democratic processes. This longstanding practice had made prosecutors the most powerful elite group, barely controlled even by presidents. To rectify prosecutors' abnormal superiority to judges, the Chief Justice wanted a new legal education system. The Supreme Court also wanted to introduce jury trials in criminal cases and adopt a new system for recruiting judges based on the American one. These reform efforts were supported by young elite judges who had earned an LLM in prestigious US law schools,[4] exposing them to American law and legal culture.

For many decades, all Korean judges and prosecutors had been classmates at JRTI, starting their careers at a very young age but going in different directions. The location and architecture of prosecutors' offices reveal the relationship between the Korean judiciary and prosecution. All prosecutors' buildings are as big as those of courts and located next to them (Kim JW 2007: 57).[5] Under the new system, a judge must have served at least ten years as prosecutor, practising lawyer, or law professor. Hoping to gain superiority to prosecutors in this way, the Supreme Court agreed to abolish the JRTI, allowing universities to operate the new law schools. Chief Justice Lee also introduced a paradigm shift in the trial process. The traditional Korean trial was a 'document trial', heavily dependent on the submission and exchange of documents. Lee proposed and enacted a series of rules to change this practice, which had made it very difficult for judges, especially those who were young and inexperienced, to rebut documents submitted by powerful prosecutors or well-known senior lawyers. Having promulgated rules making oral argument central to trials, Lee wanted the new law schools to prepare lawyers for this novel procedure.

---

[3] As a former labour lawyer, Roh Moo-hyun was able to win the presidential election with the strong support from labour unions and NGOs, whose leadership was former student activists, notably, People's Solidarity for Participatory Democracy.

[4] Recognising the importance of American law and legal system, the Supreme Court has long sponsored one-year expense-paid sabbaticals for selected judges after five years of service (Song 2007: 27).

[5] It is not a matter of style or efficiency: the law dictates the position. Article 3 of the Prosecutors' Office Act provides that each prosecutor's office building shall be located alongside the corresponding courthouse.

Traditionally, a position as judge or prosecutor had been treated as temporary, a form of practical training financed by the government. Most judges and prosecutors left for private practice before reaching their mid-forties. But growing competition in legal markets forced many judges to treat the position as permanent. Many could marry spouses from rich families, thanks to their cultural capital; and some were children of prestigious lawyers (Lee 2015: 405). Because these judges were relatively free from economic pressure to leave the judiciary, they supported the judicial reform, including the American-style law school, hoping it would enhance their authority. Under the circumstances, it was no surprise that prosecutors opposed the plan.

Political democratisation in Korea has demanded a more responsive legal system (Kim JW 2007: 74). The globalisation and expansion of the Korean economy obviously required more and better lawyers who could handle sophisticated and often transnational legal problems. Big business had demanded this for decades, without success. The change in the Supreme Court's position removed one obstacle. But the question remained: how many more lawyers should be produced?

III. A SEA-CHANGE IN THE PRODUCTION OF LAWYERS

In both Korea and Japan, proposals to make legal education more like that in the US began to attract public attention in the mid-1990s. Although Korea initiated such proposals earlier, Japan made the change in 2004 and Korea only in 2009. The old legal education system faced similar challenges and criticisms in both countries (Kim CR 2013: 434). Students entering an undergraduate law department received a liberal arts education for the first year and took courses on legal subjects as well as economics and political science for the next three. Some graduates took the government's civil service examinations, the successful becoming high-ranking civil servants or diplomats. Few could pass the Bar examination – always less than 5 per cent and, for a long time, less than 3 per cent. Those who did could enter the JRTI and, when they graduated, qualify as lawyers.

There was a huge disconnect between university legal education and qualification as a lawyer (Song 2007: 31). About 70 of the 100 law departments never produced a single graduate who passed the Bar examination. The vast majority sought jobs in business, while some became central or local government employees. Some who never attempted or failed the Bar exam work as paralegals in law offices or law firms. A few take different government exams, to be hired as administrative staff for courts or prosecutors' offices.

In the 1990s, facing internal and external challenges, reformers in both Japan and Korea believed American-style law school would better prepare their students for an increasingly globalised law practice. Japanese universities added postgraduate JD programmes to existing undergraduate law departments, whereas Korean universities had to choose between the two. Since all Korean secondary and post-secondary schools, public or private, are tightly regulated and supervised by the national government, the Korean universities interested in establishing the new law schools needed the government's new regulations and legislation.

There is a widespread belief in Korea that every leading university must have a medical school (and university-run hospital) and a law school. Because of this, over

40 universities applied to establish the new law schools, complicating the approval process. The judicial reform committee, which had proposed the new law school system, failed to reach a consensus on the number of new law schools or the annual quota of new lawyers. It was believed that a majority of the committee wanted approximately 1,200 new law students each year because the annual quota of new lawyer licences was 1,000, and they anticipated a 75–80 per cent pass rate on the new Bar exam. Since they could not agree on the numbers, they proposed that the Minister of Education decide (Kim SS: 99).

After the Law School Act passed in July 2007, the Minister appointed a Legal Education Committee including a judge, a prosecutor and two practising attorneys; but the majority (nine) were law professors and others from government agencies or NGOs. The Committee announced in October 2007 that there would be 25 new law schools accepting a total of 2,000 students a year. It also published a 100-page document specifying 132 criteria for law school approval (Kim CR 2013: 127). The decision to authorise 25 new law schools was a political compromise to allocate one to each major province. While the 25 universities selected stopped recruiting students to their undergraduate law programmes, those universities that failed to have new law schools approved (or never applied) could continue to operate their undergraduate college of law or law department. This, however, turned out to be wishful thinking. Because they had difficulty recruiting qualified students, many closed their law departments or consolidated them into departments of political science, public administration, or business administration.

When the government invited applications for the new law schools it imposed very strict standards, including at least 20 full-time faculty (20 per cent of whom had practised more than five years) and a student-faculty ratio of 15:1. It anticipated that not many applicants could meet these requirements, rendering the approval process less competitive and troublesome. The government could not have been more wrong. Forty-one universities satisfied the requirements to submit applications, and the 16 rejected fiercely protested the government's decision, some challenging it by lawsuits. Even after protests and litigation failed, some kept hoping the government would approve more law schools in the future. This has not happened, and it would be very difficult to increase the number of law schools when the job market for graduates is unpromising.

Anyone who completes a four-year undergraduate degree can apply for a three-year postgraduate JD programme. All applicants must take the Legal Education Eligibility Test (LEET) administered by the Korean Association of Law Schools. Over 8,000 do so every year, 10,206 in 2017. All law schools also consider the applicant's undergraduate Grade Point Average and English proficiency as well as outstanding work experiences or other foreign language skills (usually Chinese or Japanese). Some schools, notably SNU, are known to prefer young applicants over older ones with significant work or academic experience.

All law schools must use a separate admission process for disadvantaged applicants[6] – including those with physical or mental disabilities or from low-income families or socially disadvantaged backgrounds, such as North Korean refugees – who constitute about 10 per cent of each school's entering class. Almost all those from very low-income

---

[6] The Law School Act, Art 23, para 4.

families receive full scholarships. According to the Korean Association of Law Schools,[7] approximately 15 per cent of all law students receive a full tuition waiver and another 30 per cent a half-waiver. About 40 per cent of tuition revenues go back to students in the form of scholarships or tuition waivers. This is a very heavy burden on law schools, particularly private ones, and represents an unsustainable financial structure for the long term.[8] Most students receive some support from family members, and some finance their tuition and living expenses by borrowing from commercial banks or the government.

The prevailing mode of instruction is lectures on legal principles and the interpretation of codes and leading cases, though some professors occasionally use the Socratic method, student presentations, and problem-based learning. All law schools offer role-playing in moot courts, which are required by the Law School Act. Incumbent judges and prosecutors teach trial advocacy and prosecutorial practice, and all law students extern in a court, prosecutor's office, law firm or government agency. In 2011, the Korean Association of Law Schools, fearing the Bar exam pass rate might be set too low by the Ministry of Justice, proposed a very strict mandatory grading system, which was eventually accepted by most law schools. This not only sets the scale for A, B, or C grades but also requires a D for 4 per cent of students in classes with over 10 students. This grading system has introduced many problems, limiting a student's choice of courses (Song 2011: 106).

Following a three-year JD, students must take the Ministry of Justice Bar examination to qualify as a lawyer after first passing the national legal ethics examination (which few fail). For first-takers, the average pass rate on the bar examination is about 75 per cent. Those who fail can retake it four more times in five years. Because of the growing number of re-takers, the overall pass rate in 2018 dropped to less than 50 per cent. Those who pass must join a local Bar association and then are licensed as lawyers. In order to represent clients, they must apprentice for six months with an organisation approved by the Korean Bar Association, including law firms and government agencies.

Public opinion about the new law schools has been generally unfavourable. They have been ridiculed as 'money schools' for the rich, a label the mass media constantly repeat. Reluctantly responding to the bad publicity and criticism, the Ministry of Education asked all private law schools to lower tuition fees by about 15 per cent in exchange for a relaxation of the accreditation standards, such as raising the student-faculty ratio to 20:1. Some critics introduced a Bill for a two-track system, which would retain the old Bar examination and JRTI as an alternative to the new law school and Bar exam. Opponents pointed to the failure of the similar Japanese reform. In any case, it would be difficult to revive the old bar exam, which was terminated in 2017 by the Law School Act. On 28 December 2017, the Constitutional Court upheld the constitutionality of the Act terminating the old Bar exam. Since the new law schools are very elite institutions, the system has been strongly criticised. In order to widen the access to legal education, the Ministry of Education, as well as the Korean Association of Law Schools, began to consider introducing evening and online law programmes (Kim JW 2016: 211).

---

[7] See info.leet.or.kr/introduce/present.htm.
[8] While in the process of approving new law schools, most universities submitted an overreaching financial plan to win the government approval, without due consideration of their financial capability.

From their inception, there was a hierarchy among the new schools. The top four are Seoul National University (SNU), Korea, Sungkyunkwan (SKKU) and Yonsei; all but SNU are private. Just below them are major private universities in Seoul (eg Hanyang, Ewha, and KyungHee) and a few big national universities in other major cities; 14 are affiliated with major private research universities, and the rest are part of public universities run by national or local governments. Allocation of students was linked to this hierarchy: 150 for SNU, 120 for Korea, SKKU, Yonsei and some national universities in the major provinces, 100 for Hanynag and Ewha and 40–80 for the rest. Unlike all other schools, Ewha admits only women, a practice unsuccessfully challenged in the Constitutional Court. The most prestigious Korean law firm, Kim & Chang (often called the best in Asia), has recruited new associates mostly from SNU. After strong criticism, it began to hire a few from the top three private law schools.

IV. NEW FACETS OF THE LEGAL PRACTICE

Of the 19,640 active members of the Korean Bar Association in 2017, 10,045 were solo practitioners, a substantial majority of whom share office space and support staff. Another 1,460 lawyers operate law offices with other lawyers under various partnership agreements, and 113 lawyers operate a special form of law office with the power of a notary public, granted very selectively by the Ministry of Justice. Most law firms are composed of managing partners, of counsel, associates, foreign attorneys (Foreign Legal Consultant or FLC under South Korean law), and other expert advisers, such as certified public accountants and patent attorneys. Although the Ministry of Justice and some scholars supported by corporate interests have studied and proposed multi-disciplinary partnerships, these are still prohibited.

According to a recent survey, most Korean lawyers still engage in a general practice of civil and criminal litigation, which represents 26.8 per cent of all lawyers' work. Other categories include corporate or commercial (13.2 per cent), real estate (10.8 per cent), banking and security (9.3 per cent), divorce and domestic relation (6.5 per cent), fair trade (6.4 per cent), government affairs (6.2 per cent), intellectual property (6 per cent), and labour (5 per cent) (Choe 2015: 407). Lawyers are geographically highly concentrated. Although the capital city, Seoul, contains only a fifth of the population, it has nearly three-quarters of all lawyers (73 per cent) and two-thirds of all law firms (682 out of 1,037), including all top firms.[9] As of 2017, 11 Korean firms had more than 100 lawyers: Kim & Chang (654), Lee & Ko (454) Bae, Kim & Lee (414), Shin & Kim (325), Yoon & Yang (272), Yulchon (257), Barun Law (192), DR & AJU (146), Dongin Law (135). Jipyong (125) and Logos (111).[10]

Tension among law-related professions has recently intensified. The official organisation of patent attorneys has asserted members' right to represent clients in the courtroom, provoking resistance by lawyers' organisations. The existence of judicial and administrative scriveners, tax attorneys, and certified labour advisers has made it very difficult

---

[9] Seoul accounts for 22 per cent of GDP and houses half the financial corporations and most big companies, including SAMSUNG, LG, and Hyundai.
[10] *The Law Times* 27 December 2017.

for lawyers to expand their market beyond their traditional litigation work. In 2015, the Korean Bar Association successfully lobbied the National Assembly to require large companies to hire lawyers as mandatory compliance officers. Some young lawyers move to small towns with few or no competitors. Others choose public interest law offices, although salaries are low. A few explore new substantive areas, such as digital game law and animal law; others try to compete with real estate brokers to handle land transactions and title registration. Law firms and law offices employ paralegals with a college law degree but no law licence. Legal information from do-it-yourself legal services available through major Internet search engines and social network service blogs poses a serious competitive threat to lawyers.

The number of in-house counsel has recently increased substantially, to an estimated 3,000, and the Korea In-House Counsel Association membership doubled between 2014 and 2017.[11] Big companies have been hiring graduates of the new law schools. Because the Korean Bar Association Code allows corporate legal departments to handle only 10 cases a year, regardless of the number of lawyers they employ, in-house counsel outsource most litigation work. Since the number of in-house counsel is growing rapidly, and retaining outside lawyers for litigation is expensive, the association of in-house counsel has sought to increase the annual limit to 50 cases per corporation.

Foreign lawyers seeking to practise in Korea must obtain authorisation from the Minster of Justice and register with the Korean Bar Association under the Foreign Legal Consultant Act, passed in March 2009 and since revised twice. By November 2017, the Minister had authorised 145 FLCs: 109 from the US, 23 from the UK, eight from Australia, and one each from other countries like France, Scotland, New Zealand, Singapore and China. Two US firms (Ropes & Gray and Sheppard Mullin) and one UK mega firm (Clifford Chance) established their FLC offices in Seoul the first day this was possible in July 2012. Clifford Chance had been actively working with Korean companies and foreign investors for over 30 years through its Hong Kong office (Kim Jin 2016: 253). Top US firms have followed these pioneers: Baker McKenzie (2013), Skadden Arps (2014), White & Case (2015), and Latham & Watkins (2016).

Like those in many other countries, the Korean legal profession had long been a man's world. But that is no longer true. Over 40 per cent of new law students and 28 per cent of all Korean lawyers are women. Nevertheless, full gender equality is a long way off. The average income of female lawyers is about 70 per cent that of men. Many female lawyers complain of sexual harassment at work (Choe 2015: 410, 417) Because of a glass ceiling in major law firms, some of the best women law graduates prefer to be judges or prosecutors, believing there is less gender-discrimination in public jobs.

Since licensed lawyers must belong to the Korean Bar Association, whose leadership tended to be conservative, some progressive lawyers organised the Lawyers' Association for a Democratic Society (Minbyun) in 1988, which now has over a thousand members on its roll. In 2000, Minbyun almost succeeded in changing the Lawyer's Act to abolish compulsory membership in the Korean Bar Association. Even though the effort failed, the amended Act mandated 30 hours of pro bono work a year. Responding to the public outcry, permanent disqualification was then also added to the list of lawyer discipline.

---

[11] *The Law Journal* 19 November 2017.

NGOs have long demanded an end to the notorious practice called 'predecessor's privilege' in which retiring judges and prosecutors, practising as attorneys in their former worksite, enjoyed special treatment from their incumbent former colleagues. This practice has caused serious conflicts of interest and spawned a deep distrust in courts in general and the criminal justice system in particular.

Lawyer licensing, competence and ethical behaviour were regulated by the Ministry of Justice until 2000. The revision of the Lawyer's Act that year allowed self-regulation by the Korean Bar Association, although the Ministry can review its disciplinary actions. For a long time the public has been calling for lower legal fees and costs. Outrageously high retainer fees received by attorneys who retired as high ranking judges or prosecutors raise particular ire. The legislature is currently trying to draft a law to restrict such unethical practices. The Korean Bar Association recently asked all former Supreme Court justices not to represent cases before the Supreme Court.[12]

The growing number of lawyers has reduced fees and increased access to justice but has also affected the income of lawyers, especially recent entrants. Many of those who worked for big corporations before entering law school have to accept a legal job paying less than their previous salary. The average fee for a criminal case in Seoul has fallen 40 per cent, from about US$4,500 ten years ago to US$2,700 in 2017. Since this comparison does not take account of inflation, the actual decline has been over 50 per cent. Court filing fees, which are proportioned to the value of the lawsuit, have been criticised by many civic organisations for restricting access to justice. The doubling of filing fees for appellate cases makes it very difficult for the parties to appeal to the highest court. This filing fee system has long been justified as necessary to prevent frivolous litigation. But the system has denied the poor and socially disadvantaged groups access to justice (Kim JC: 17). In 2017 the Korean Bar Association proposed legislation to lower fees substantially.

V. LAWYERS FOR SOCIAL CHANGE

Since the adoption of the 1987 Constitution, which was the outcome of citizen struggles against the authoritarian regime of former generals, lawyers have become major players in South Korean society (Yoon: 22). The Constitutional Court and the National Human Rights Commission, among other institutions, have helped make society freer and more egalitarian. On 1 September 1988, the day the Constitutional Court Act became effective, the Court had no judges, building, budget or personnel. That the new institution generated little interest among lawyers, politicians or the public was unsurprising since its predecessor, the Constitutional Commission, had not handled a single case in its 15 years under the 1972 Constitution, which authorised General Park Chung Hee to rule as long as he wanted. Expectations for the new Constitutional Court were low. Three of its nine judges were merely honorary members (like all but one member of the Constitutional Commission), although three years after the Court's creation all nine members were given standing to hear cases because of the rising caseload.

---

[12] *The Korean Bar Association News*, 18 July 2016, 1.

The Constitutional Court began to take an active role, embarrassing both the government and its rival institution, the Supreme Court (Yang 2000: 36). Two years after the Court was established it declared unconstitutional parts of the Protecting Society Act, which had allowed those convicted to be isolated for the purpose of 'preventing crimes', even after they had served their terms (88 Hun-Ka 5). It created unenumerated constitutional rights, such as 'right to know' (89 HunMa 113), which has been effectively utilised in subsequent cases where the government claimed 'national security' interests (Ahn 1997: 90). The Court also declared that the common practice of National Information Agency (formerly the Korean CIA) agents eavesdropping on lawyer-client conversations under the National Security Act violated the constitutionally guaranteed right to counsel (91 Hun-Ma 111). It held that the system of pre-screening and distribution-restraint of movies was unconstitutional (93 HunKa 13). The Court's invalidation of the family head system and the marriage ban between those with the same surname (2004 HunKa 5) was praised as a monumental decision for gender equality in a patriarchal Korean culture. It also struck down mandatory self-identification by Internet service users as a violation of freedom of expression (2010 HunMa 47). The Court invalidated a provision of the Criminal Act punishing adultery (2014 Hun-Ka 4). As of February 2019, the Court had received over 36,000 petitions and found constitutional violations in 1,683. Ever since its 2004 decision, the Court had repeatedly upheld the law penalising conscientious objection to mandatory military service (2002 HunGa 1). In June 2018, however, the Court announced its new position, holding that the law was inconsistent with the constitutional protection of conscience (2015 HunGa 5). One of its best-known recent decisions was the impeachment of President Park Geun-Hye on 10 March 2017 (2016 Hun-Na 1). By rendering numerous decisions significantly affecting Korean society over the last 30 years, the Court has become a 'battlefield for justice' (Ahn 1997: 75).

Established in November 2001, the National Human Rights Commission has helped to protect minorities. It prohibited longstanding discrimination against persons with disabilities and has been quite active in preventing forced institutionalisation of people with mental disabilities (Yoon 2000: 212). The Commission has worked to protect the fundamental rights of students and prisoners. Since Korea has compulsory military service, the Commission has been vigilant to protect servicemen and women from degrading treatment and civil rights violations. It also reinforced the duty of the police to observe the Miranda principles and vigorously supported the rights to assembly and petition for those who protested government policies. But its efforts to protect LGBTs from discrimination often faced strong opposition from conservative and religious groups.

Under the regimes of Presidents Lee and Park (2008–16), South Korean society tended to move backwards, as neoliberal economic policies abrogated many social welfare rights granted by previous administrations. Freedom of speech and labour and other fundamental rights were also substantially suppressed or restricted. But this eight-year conservative and anti-democratic period provoked a strong protest, known as the 'candlelight revolution', which led to the impeachment of President Park and the opposition party's presidential victory. Lawyers played pivotal roles throughout this dramatic process. On the last Saturday of October 2016, over 50,000 people holding candles gathered in Seoul's central park to criticise the government of Park Geun-hye and call for her impeachment. By 11 March 2017 over 16.5 million people had participated in the weekly protests.

Because the main issues were her unconstitutional actions, many lawyers were involved, helping citizens understand the constitution and the impeachment process.

The Korean Legal Aid Corporation, a government organisation with an annual budget of US$38 million, employs more than 200 lawyers in 120 offices offering free or inexpensive legal services to the poor and minorities. Courts may also exempt the indigent from legal fees in civil actions. The concept of public interest or pro bono lawyering only fully entered public discourse after the mid-1990s with the advent of new NGOs such as People's Solidarity for Participatory Democracy, and the number of lawyers working full-time in public interest lawyers' groups and nonprofit organisations remains small. The first public interest lawyer's group, Gonggam (literally 'empathy'), was established in the mid-2000s and has inspired other public interest lawyers' groups, which have represented social minorities. Nonprofit organisations are increasingly hiring lawyers as well. A 2000 amendment to the Lawyers Act requires all lawyers to perform 20 or 30 hours of 'public interest activities' a year (although they may substitute a payment to the Bar's pro bono fund). The requirement has several limitations, including the broad, vague definition of what constitutes 'pro bono activity', no vetting of lawyers' reports of pro bono hours or significant penalties for violations, and growing lawyer dissatisfaction with the requirement. Nevertheless, it has persuaded lawyers, especially those in major law firms, to devote time to pro bono activities. In a few firms, pro bono coordinators have attempted to leverage this requirement to promote pro bono work by previously uninterested lawyers. The Korean Bar Association and the legal clinics of the 25 law schools also provide legal aid.

VI. CONCLUSION

For the last 30 years, South Korean lawyers have experienced major changes, both inside their profession (its substantial growth) and outside (deregulation, globalisation, economic growth, and public demands for rights and access to justice). A new system of producing lawyers based on US law schools replaced the old Japanese model. This represented a big shift from a state-run profession to greater competition. The introduction of American-style law schools was accompanied by the adoption of other American legal institutions. For the last three decades, Korean lawyers have been key players in changing Korean society, which has travelled a long way from the rule of men to the rule of law, democratising politics and increasing transparency in socio-economic activities. During this period, two lawyers with substantial reputations as human rights champions became President. The role of Korean lawyers today is more crucial and vital than ever before.

REFERENCES

Abel, RL and Lewis, PSC (eds) (1995) *Lawyers in Society: An Overview* (Berkeley, University of California Press).

Ahn, Kyong Whan (1997) 'The Influence of American Constitutionalism on South Korea' 22 *Southern Illinois University Law Journal* 71.

Alford, WP (ed) (2007) *Raising the Bar: the Emerging Legal Profession in East Asia* (Cambridge, MA, Harvard University Press).
Choe, Yukyong (2015) 'Gender Stratification of the Legal Profession Under the Post-Reform Law School System in Korea' 50 *Korean Journal of Law and Society* 383.
Dezalay Y and Garth BG (2010) *Asian Legal Revivals* (Chicago, University of Chicago Press).
Ginsburg, T (ed) (2004) *Legal Reform in Korea* (London, RoutledgeCurzon).
Kim, Chang Rok (2006) 'The National Bar Examination in Korea' 24 *Wisconsin International Law Journal* 234.
—— (2013) *Advocating the Law School System* (Seoul, Unistory).
Kim, JaeWon (2007) 'Legal Profession and Legal Culture during Korea's Transition to Democracy and a Market Economy' in WP Alford (ed), *Raising the Bar: the Emerging Legal Profession in East Asia* (Cambridge, MA, Harvard University Press) 47–80.
—— (2016) 'Widening Access to Legal Education and Introducing Evening and Online Law Programs' 714 *Korean Lawyers Association Journal* 183–214.
Kim, Jin Won (2016) *Law Firms in Korea* (Seoul, Legal Times).
Kim, Jong Cheol (2015) 'The Unconstitutionality of the Filing Fee System: With Focus on the Right to Access to Justice and Constitutional Principles' 50 *Korean Journal of Law and Society* 1–24.
Kim, Sun Soo (2008) *A Report on the Judicial Reform* (Seoul, Pakyoungsa).
Lee, Jae-Hyup et al (2015) 'Law School Lawyers in Korea, Who Are They?' 56 *Seoul Law Journal* 367–411.
Lim, Jibong (2004) 'The Korean Constitutional Court, judicial activism, and social change' in T Ginsburg (ed), *Legal Reform in Korea* 20–35.
Song, Ki-Choon (2011) 'Objection to the New Grading System in Law Schools' 40 *Korean Journal of Law & Society* 93–115.
Song, Sang Hyun (2007) 'The Education and Training of the Legal Profession in Korea: Problems and Prospects for Reform' in WP Alford (ed), *Raising the Bar: the Emerging Legal Profession in East Asia* (Cambridge, MA, Harvard University Press) 21–45.
Yang, Kun (2000) 'The Constitutional Court and Democratization' in Dae-Kyu Yoon (2000) *Recent Transformations in Korean Law and Society* (Seoul, Seoul National University Press) 33–46.
Yoon, Dae-Kyu (2010) *Law and Democracy in South Korea: Democratic Development since 1987* (Kyungnam University Press).

41

Taiwan and Hong Kong
Localisation and Politicisation

CHING-FANG HSU

I. INTRODUCTION

Lawyers are practitioners grounded in local contexts and, inescapably, political advocates. Juxtaposing two fundamentally different jurisdictions, Taiwan and Hong Kong, this chapter aims to show that their lawyers are experiencing localisation and politicisation despite the waxing and waning of liberal politics and different degrees of globalisation. Although both Asian jurisdictions began drastic economic and political transformations in the 1980s, they present stark contrasts, offering analytical leverage to understand the two trends. Taiwan, a civil law system, witnessed democratisation and systematic political liberalisation, but its economy as a multi-national trade hub has stagnated recently, and the legal profession finds itself in a closed market structured mainly by domestic factors. Hong Kong, a common law jurisdiction, enjoyed some civil liberties under British colonial rule, but its political space gradually contracted after retrocession to authoritarian Chinese rule. At the same time, Hong Kong has continued to grow as an international financial centre, which supports a global legal services market. The institutional structures of the two legal professions are also critically different: while Hong Kong has preserved the colonial categories of barristers and solicitors, the Taiwanese legal profession has three principal divisions: lawyers, judges and prosecutors. The fact that the two jurisdictions share few characteristics offers a natural research design to expose the trends of localisation and politicisation.

A brief overview of the political history and evolution of the two legal professions is a necessary preliminary. In Taiwan, democratisation is essentially localisation of a Mainland Chinese government in exile. In 1949, the Chinese Nationalists (Kuomintang or KMT) lost the mainland to the Chinese Communist Party in the civil war and retreated to Taiwan. The island state and China have been effectively separated as political entities ever since. In the 1970s, however, the KMT regime began to face pressure from the growing Taiwanese population, which never had officially approved the ethnic minority government. It experienced a major legitimacy crisis in 1979 when the US terminated official diplomatic relations with Republic of China, which the KMT claimed to represent. Social and political change induced the KMT to open up governance, instituting local elections, loosening social control, and recruiting Taiwanese as party cadres. As part of this trend, more locally born and educated lawyers were admitted, leading to an ideological transformation in the profession. The localised bar leadership assertively joined the intense contemporary political movements, using their expertise as people's advocates to encourage democratisation.

In Hong Kong, glocalisation of the legal profession is a distinctive social phenomenon. Not all Hong Kong lawyers are locally born, raised or educated, yet most are locally qualified and pursue careers focused on domestic law. First established by the British colonial administration, the Hong Kong legal profession was initially composed mostly of English expatriates. As the economy expanded, however, Hong Kong consciously took steps to liberalise the profession to meet market demand in the 1990s. The growth of the Chinese economy contributed to further expansion, attracting many international practitioners offering services for Chinese enterprises available only in Hong Kong. Trained in different jurisdictions and coming from diverse backgrounds, these lawyers either practise foreign law or are admitted to the local profession through a variety of qualification schemes. Politically, Hong Kong's transition from a British colony to a special administrative region of the authoritarian, idiosyncratic Chinese regime was unique and unprecedented. Yet the principle guiding the transformation, oddly, was continuity – the expectation that Hong Kong would remain 'unchanged for fifty years'. Stakeholders in the transfer negotiations shared the consensus that the city should continue to serve as an economic and financial hub; because political stability was a prerequisite, legal autonomy was preserved. The Hong Kong Basic Law, the jurisdiction's constitution, defined the power structure after 1997. Inscribing a fundamental disparity between the political authority of the central government in Beijing and local citizens in Hong Kong, the Basic Law became a crucial arena for political mobilisation against the constraints of arbitrary authoritarian power. Lawyers, fluent in the language of law, inevitably became involved in political turmoil.

As its title indicates, this chapter addresses two major issues of the legal professions in Hong Kong and Taiwan, localisation and politicisation, followed by a brief note on feminisation. In each section, the two jurisdictions are compared. Data come from archival research, including newspapers, government gazettes, professional association reports, and other published records, as well as field observations and interviews with legal practitioners during the author's visits between 2016 and 2018.

II. LOCALISATION AND *GLOCALISATION*: LEGAL PROFESSIONS GROWING IN A GLOBAL LEGAL SERVICES MARKET

In the second half of the twentieth century the legal professions in Taiwan and Hong Kong were small, comprised mostly of 'foreign' or expatriate lawyers, and then grew locally in response to market demand. In Hong Kong, the profession was established by and composed of British expatriates. In Taiwan, most lawyers were Mainland Chinese migrants or Taiwanese with strong connections to the KMT regime. The foreign character of the legal profession began to change in the 1970s. In Taiwan, although local education was institutionalised and the population grew rapidly, the authoritarian KMT government still controlled the legal profession through admission policies, ensuring that lawyers supported the regime. In Hong Kong, the establishment of a local law school also reflected the increasing market demand and the professional associations' determination to continue dominating the local market. While Mainland lawyers in Taiwan lost their dominance, the Hong Kong profession began putting on a 'Chinese face' as the influence of British expatriates declined. More accurately, the Taiwanese profession outgrew its foreign Mainland Chinese character, while the Hong Kong profession *glocalised* as lawyers around the world came to serve the expanding Chinese market.

A. Taiwan

i. A Contained Bar after World War II

In the second half of the twentieth century, the Taipei Bar remained small and dominated by the state, which kept the number passing the Bar exam very low, often in the single digits and never more than 50 before 1987 (see Figure 1; Chang 2007: 49–50). The slow rate of expansion is striking, especially comparing the number registering for and passing the exam (Chang 2007: 49–50; see Figure 2). This limited growth is puzzling, since Taiwan experienced dramatic industrialisation and rapid development in international trade during the 1970s.

Figure 1 Number Qualifying via Taiwan National Bar Exam 1950–2011

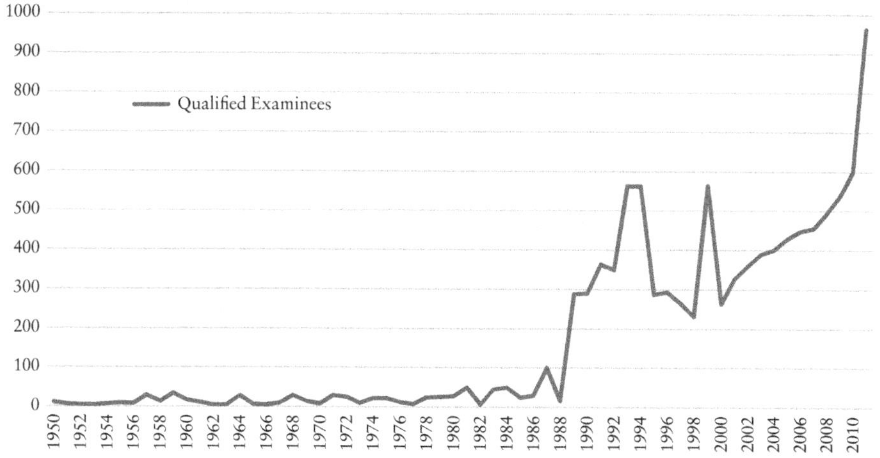

Source: Chang (2007).

Figure 2 Number Registering for and Qualifying by the Taiwan National Bar Exam 1950–2011

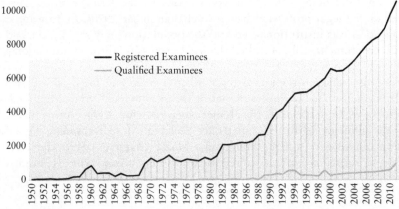

Source: Chang (2007).

Instead of raising the pass rate, the state sought to fill the profession through another route – accreditation – preferring legal practitioners who had prior relationships with the bureaucracy. Accreditation allowed judges (including military judges), prosecutors, legislators, law clerks, law professors and those with a doctorate to qualify as a lawyer. The two main sources have been military judges and, to a lesser extent, judges and prosecutors (Taipei Bar Association 2005: 179–80). The number of admissions via accreditation exceeded the number passing the Bar as late as 1987 (the year martial law was lifted) (see Figure 3; Chang 2007: 51). A comparison of the national exams for lawyers and judicial officers (judge and prosecutor) confirms the state's preference for former bureaucrats (see Figure 4). For the two decades 1969–89 it was easier to become a judge or prosecutor than a lawyer (Chang 2007: 49–50; Liu 2007: 235). As the party-state developed mechanisms to supervise career judges and prosecutors, their numbers grew, allowing many to become lawyers through accreditation.

Figure 3 Number of Taiwanese Lawyers Qualified by Exam and Accreditation, 1942–2010

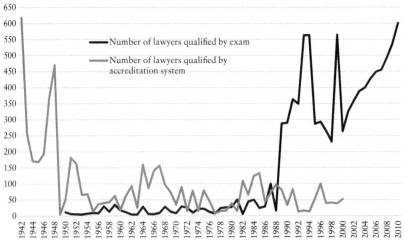

Source: The original data source is the Ministry of Examination in Taiwan. Numbers were first compiled by Chang (2007: 51–53), and data before 1998 were compiled by Liu (2005: 241–42).

Figure 4 Comparison of Passing Rate on Exams for Lawyers and Judicial Officers (Judges and Prosecutors) 1960–2011

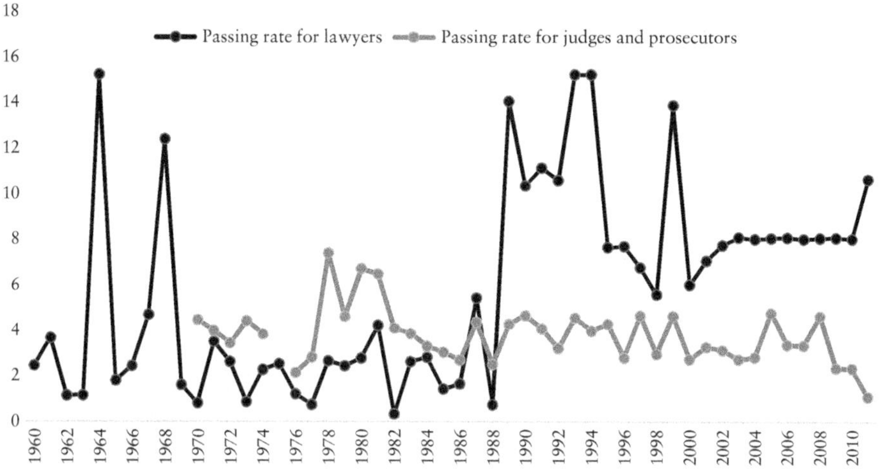

Note: the scale on the left is per cent.
Source: Chang (2007); Liu (2007).

ii. Dominance and Decline of Mainland Lawyers

The social divisions within the Taipei Bar also reflected the policy of authoritarian containment in Taiwan. Fleeing the Chinese civil war between 1945 and 1950, approximately two million mainland Chinese civilians and military personnel settled in Taiwan at a time when the island had only 6.27 million people. Taiwanese refer to mainlanders as *wai-sheng-ren* (people from other provinces) and themselves as *ben-sheng-ren* (people from this province). Minority mainlanders continue to wield power, and their informal influence transcends politics. They are the core of the KMT party-state because of its origin as a Chinese mainland government; and their hegemony is reproduced by a 'province-based' recruitment of civil servants. In addition, mainlanders had a linguistic advantage because the Taiwanese people used Japanese as the official and intellectual language before war (reflecting the Japanese occupation), and the transition to Mandarin Chinese took at least a half generation. This transition was particularly difficult for professionals and intellectuals, rendering them uncompetive for, and distant from, leadership positions in both the state and civil society.

The ethnic composition of the Taipei Bar reflected this mainlander dominance until the 1980s (see Figure 5). Immediately after World War II, the number of registered members was in two digits. In 1949, however, following with the retreat of the KMT government to the island, the number of mainland lawyers in Taipei rose suddenly from 45 to 160, making them 90 per cent of the Bar. Mainlanders maintained their dominance as the local Taiwanese membership slowly grew, only exceeding the number of mainlanders in 1985 (Taipei Bar Association 2005: 167). Mainlanders dominated not only numbers but also leadership. Cheng Benji, who became a Taipei Bar member in 1958, said: 'bar associations were all led by old lawyers from the Mainland, and the National Bar Association didn't even hold elections for the directors and supervisors' (Taipei Bar Association 2005: 294).

Figure 5 Taipei Bar Association: Members' Ethnicity

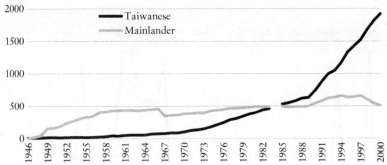

Source: Taipei Bar Association (2005).

Another indicator, the educational background of Taipei lawyers, displays similar trends. Comparing the two groups with different educational background in the Taipei Bar, it is clear that the local-civilian Taiwanese lawyers outnumbered the Mainland-military Chinese lawyers in 1980s, just as democratisation was about to take off (see Figure 6).

Figure 6 Comparison of Mainland-military Lawyers and Local-civilian Lawyers in Taipei

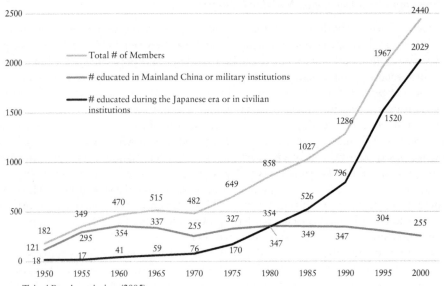

Source: Taipei Bar Association (2005).

Mainland lawyers multiplied quickly from 1948, dominated the Bar in the 1960s, and then gradually declined in influence during the 1970s and 1980s (Taipei Bar Association 2005: 182). The 1970s witnessed the rise of two groups: 'civilian lawyers' educated in post-war Taiwanese universities and 'military lawyers' educated in the military and accredited after serving on the military bench. A senior Bar member recalled that the increase in military lawyers in the early 1970s reflected state policy (Taipei Bar Association 2005: 340).

> The military judge recruitment started in 1961, and they have to serve 10 years to get honourary discharge. Afterwards they get accreditation for sure. So, starting from 1973, every year the Taipei Bar saw dozens of retired military judges becoming lawyers, but at the time, the national bar exam only takes several civilian school educated lawyers.

Archival data show that the accreditation of military judges as lawyers started earlier: in 1964–68 only 76 lawyers were admitted after passing the bar exam, whereas 405 former military judges were admitted. The increasing number of military lawyers was critical because they were ideologically and organisationally aligned with the pre-war Mainland lawyers.

> [The Taipei Bar] was dominated by the old lawyers from Mainland China. When these old lawyers started to fade away, the military judges emerged to connect with them, taking over. Regarding ethnicity, some of the military-judge-lawyers are *wai-sheng-ren*, and some of them are *ben-sheng-ren*, but they are closely united ideationally and ideologically. They are very much inclined to cooperate with the Mainlander seniors. (Taipei Bar Association 2005: 349)

Nevertheless, by 1980, the number of lawyers educated in post-war civilian institutions exceeded the number educated in pre-war Mainland China, breaking the latter's decades-long dominance of the Taipei Bar. In retrospect, this seems inevitable, given that the pre-war educated Mainlanders dominated because of a one-time event (retreat from China), and local population growth resulted in locally educated lawyers becoming a majority of the legal profession.

iii. Localisation in Action: Civilian versus Military Lawyers

The demographic change in the Taipei Bar later contributed to a fundamental transformation in the character of the legal profession (Hsu 2018). In 1990, the Alliance of Civilian-School Lawyers (ACL) defeated the military-background lawyers, winning an overwhelming electoral victory for the Boards of Advisors and Supervisors and changing the ideology and character of the Bar. First started as a lawyers' alumni club of National Taiwan University, this liberal group was unhappy with the Taipei Bar, whose leadership did not seem to reflect the interests of most lawyers (Taipei Bar Association 2005: 323). A senior member identified the Bar's character as 'static, never-ever changing', because 'the directors and supervisors are always the same batch of people' (ibid: 321). The association's connection with the ruling party was also an important aspect of the Taipei Bar in the early days. In fact, the KMT's City Party Office used to send letters to all members soliciting votes for certain candidates in the board elections and offering financial and organisational support (ibid: 341).

With the number of civilian-educated lawyers growing, a small group of young practitioners backed Lin Ming-sheng, a prominent international patent lawyer, to lead the election team. In the 1990 election, the ACL ran candidates for the Boards of Advisors and Supervisors, winning all 38 seats.

> Using his law firm computer, lawyer Lin Ming-sheng categorised all members into different sections by school, ethnicity (*wai-sheng-ren* or *ben-sheng-ren*), age, and gender. And each

candidate took part of the list to solicit votes. In fact, there were a lot of civilian lawyers at that time already, but they were not united and did not care about the Taipei Bar. (ibid: 340)

The groundwork was effective, boosting participation, as another lawyer remembered.

> I went to vote very early in the morning, but the meeting hall was packed. All old lawyers! In front of me! The serious mobilisation ... some people even stayed in the hotel across the street the night before (Huang 2009).

Under new leadership, the Taipei Bar completely changed its character, shifting its focus to advocating for human rights, democratisation, and professionalisation. First, the Bar quickly assumed responsibility for regulating lawyers, issuing a guide to professional ethics, developing a standard operating procedure to investigate ethical complaints, and actively pursuing cases. Another indicator of the new civilian Bar's support and legitimacy were the resources the leadership could mobilise. In 1996, the Taipei Bar moved from a small room in the courthouse to a spacious office of 10,675 square feet in the culture-business district, costing approximately 4.36 million (in 2017 US dollars). Second, the Bar developed a vocal and proactive political outlet. It not only issued public statements supporting major political reforms and demonstrated in the streets to end criminal persecution of dissidents but also conducted organisational reforms, establishing human rights committees and creating a chair for the Board of Advisors. Although the last might seem trivial, it actually demonstrated how the Taipei Bar challenged authoritarian control. Chairmanship had been illegal during the martial law era; the Civil Association Act allowed only rotating chairs 'because Kuomintang wanted the bar associations to be headless' (Taipei Bar Association 2005: 342). Inspired by this small but critical organisational reform, other Bar associations began to institute board chairs.

The civilian takeover of the Taipei Bar and its continuing influence nicely reflects the localisation of the legal profession in Taiwan, a transformation in both demography and character. The displacement of the Mainland component of the legal profession accurately mirrors the broader societal localisation and political democratisation throughout Taiwan.

B. Hong Kong

In Hong Kong, by contrast, the relationship with China has shaped the evolution of the legal profession. The booming Chinese market induces the glocalisation of the profession, attracting a large diverse group of global legal practitioners to Hong Kong for a unique career embedded in the local context. In Hong Kong, everyone is from somewhere else, yet they are here nonetheless.

i. Glocalisation: Numbers and Institutional Structure

The legal profession in Hong Kong has expanded exponentially. In 1951, the Bar was so small 'there was a charming custom whereby the newest member of the Bar would call on all those more senior to him' (Hong Kong Bar Association 2000: 5). There were only about 30 solicitors in 1953 (Chan 1997: 15) and 24 barristers in 1965 (ibid: 8). The numbers grew steadily in the 1970s and 1980s, accelerating since the 1990s (see Figure 7).

In 2015, there were 8,647 solicitors and 1,331 barristers in Hong Kong, not including foreign practitioners.

Figure 7 Growth of Barristers and Solicitors in Hong Kong 1980–2015

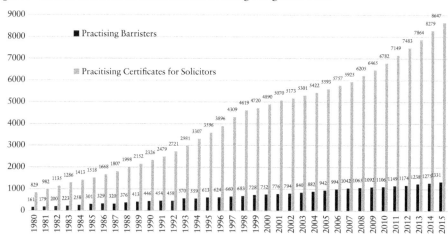

Source: Hong Kong Law Society; Hong Kong Bar Association.[1]

Local law schools were an essential factor in localisation. The Department of Law at the University of Hong Kong (HKU) was founded in 1969; three years later it graduated its first class, whose members were warmly received by the profession. When the first HKU trained barrister, Kenneth Kwok, was called to the Bar in 1974, a full court heard his application to commemorate the occasion (Hong Kong Bar Association 2000). The City University of Hong Kong established the second law school in 1987 and the Chinese University of Hong Kong the third in 2004.

The 1970s and 1980s also witnessed another institutional development important for the profession. Both the Bar and the Law Society increased their regulatory activities, revising several rules in the 1970s. Later they addressed their relationship with the UK legal profession. The Hong Kong Bar took a proactive move, successfully lobbying the General Council of the Bar of England and Wales to let Hong Kong barristers with three years' experience practise in the UK. By contrast, the Hong Kong Law Society took the opposite approach, protecting its turf by declaring in 1987 that 'there should no longer be a complete waiver by the Council [...] in favor of UK solicitors who have acquired substantial experience in law in the UK' and instead requiring them to practise in Hong Kong for a year before obtaining an unconditional practising certificate (Hong Kong Law Society 1987: 7).

These moves reflected market pressures. In 1984, the Law Society noted that 'rapid increases in the number of overseas lawyers arriving in Hong Kong to seek China-related work have led to some of the fundamental practice rules governing the solicitors' profession being questioned' (Hong Kong Law Society 1984: 4). In 1986, seven American

---

[1] Data first compiled by the author and confirmed by staff in later correspondence.

law firms sought to register and practise in Hong Kong. In 1988, under pressure from the US government, the Hong Kong government allowed foreign law firms to hire or partner with Hong Kong lawyers. The Hong Kong Law Society was strongly opposed: in an extraordinary meeting 97 per cent of members voted against this policy.

In the early 1990s, the government finalised the official policies regarding foreign legal practitioners in the Hong Kong market. The Law Society issued a report in 1991, on which these were based:

a) Foreign lawyers must register and advise only on the law of jurisdictions other than Hong Kong.
b) They cannot hire or partner with Hong Kong solicitors.
c) Foreign law firms can align with local law firms, but the personnel ratio must be 1:1.
d) After practising in Hong Kong for three years, foreign lawyers can be qualified as Hong Kong lawyers.
e) The Law Society would regulate the qualification of overseas lawyers.

The Legal Practitioners Bill was amended in 1994, regulating the registration and operation of foreign law practices in Hong Kong and establishing 'an inspectorate within the Law Society aimed at dealing with malpractice' (Hong Kong Law Society 1994). The following year 135 foreign lawyers from 12 jurisdictions sat for the first Overseas Lawyers Qualification Examination.

ii. A Diverse and Global Legal Profession

The Hong Kong legal services market has been open to competition ever since. Two indicators show its intensity. First, the number of foreign lawyers has steadily grown, especially in the late 2000s (see Figure 8). Foreign lawyers have consistently been 18 per cent of Hong Kong solicitors since late 1990s, numbering 1,200 in 2008 and 1,400 in 2014.

Figure 8 Number of Foreign Lawyers in Hong Kong 1996–2016

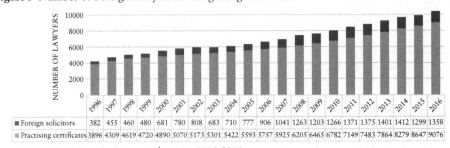

Source: Hong Kong Law Society annual reports 1996–2016.

Competition is strongly international. Four jurisdictions accounted for most foreign lawyers: the US, UK, Australia and China (see Table 1). Both American and British lawyers have consistently been dominant. US lawyers represented 70 per cent of the total in 1996 but, because of the growth of other foreign lawyers, declined to 40 per cent in the late

2000s and even less in the late 2010s. British solicitors rose to approximately 20 per cent in the late 2000s. Australian lawyers experienced a quick but brief increase in the early 2000s, jumping from 6.7 per cent in 1999 to 15 per cent in 2002, but soon dropped to 10 per cent in 2006. Chinese lawyers, by contrast, grew rapidly from 7 per cent in the late 1990s to 15 per cent in 2016, and the trend is continuing.

Table 1 Top 10 Origins of Foreign Lawyers in Hong Kong 1996–2016

	Total foreign solicitors	USA	England & Wales	China	Australia	Bermuda	Singapore	British Virgin Islands	New Zealand	Canada	France
1996	382	269	17	18	13	5	11	0	3	22	6
1997	455	315	18	26	26	5	11		4	19	8
1998	460	300	23	42	27	5	8	0	5	14	7
1999	480	291	45	37	32	7	14	0	4	13	6
2000	681	379	92	41	59	11	28		14	21	6
2001	780	398	122	55	100	16	23	0	11	22	6
2002	808	406	114	65	127	15	18	0	11	20	6
2003	683	335	103	74	94	17	9	0	8	10	6
2004	710	348	128	70	80	16	15	2	6	8	7
2005	777	373	143	77	74	17	28	4	8	7	8
2006	906	398	174	94	97	20	43	5	8	6	13
2007	1,041	445	198	97	123	27	52	5	11	8	14
2008	1,263	560	260	107	131	30	51	10	14	16	13
2009	1,203	559	254	107	103	27	31	12	13	13	13
2010	1,266	565	285	121	106	28	28	9	12	16	11
2011	1,371	592	333	139	118	29	25	11	22	12	15
2012	1,375	584	332	148	117	28	23	14	21	14	11
2013	1,401	568	328	174	125	28	23	19	22	18	11
2014	1,412	534	332	201	124	27	26	22	23	17	13
2015	1,299	477	301	193	119	29	26	22	17	16	13
2016	1,358	491	306	202	126	28	35	27	17	14	14

Source: Hong Kong Law Society annual reports 1996–2016.

Second, foreign law firms display the same trend. The number of international law firms in Hong Kong remained about 50 in late 1990s, gradually dropped to 34 in 2003 and 2004, and then steadily grew to over 80 in 2016. American, Chinese and British firms are the major players (Figure 9). The US showed a strong interest in entering the market in the late 1990s, but this weakened in the second half of the 2000s. 2006 marked another wave of growth and competition, when seven Chinese firms registered in Hong Kong, becoming a quarter of the foreign firms. The Chinese presence grew steadily, and many associated with local firms in preparation for full localisation. Because the Law Society records the year a foreign law firm first registers in Hong Kong, this figure only captures the date the firm entered the territory but not the continuing competition. Nevertheless, this figure clearly shows shifts in the representation of the three principal countries in the Hong Kong market.

Figure 9 Number of Major Foreign Law Firms 1994–2016

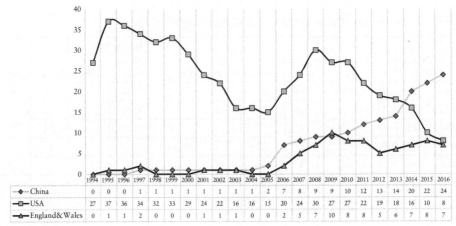

Source: Hong Kong Law Society annual reports 1994–2016.

Interestingly, despite continuous globalisation, the Hong Kong legal profession is undoubtedly putting on a 'Chinese face' (see Figure 10). In the 1950s, fewer than 10 of the approximately 30 solicitors were ethnic Chinese, and the proportion of the Bar was even smaller. Yet ethnic Chinese solicitors quickly grew from 53.4 per cent of the profession in 1983 to 82 per cent in 2004. In spite of their diverse educational and professional backgrounds, Hong Kong lawyers are now predominantly Chinese, an enormous change from the small original Bar of British expatriates.

Figure 10 Ethnicity of Hong Kong Solicitors

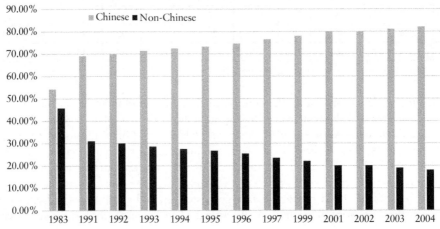

Source: Hong Kong Law Society annual reports 1983, 1991–2004.

III. POLITICISATION OF THE LEGAL PROFESSION: PROACTIVE AND DEFENSIVE MOBILISATION IN THE RETREAT AND ADVANCE OF AUTHORITARIANISM

At the turn of the twenty-first century, the Taiwan and Hong Kong legal professions displayed strong political mobilisation concerning both issues affecting them as lawyers and broader debates. This raises two questions: (a) Why did such different legal systems and professions witness intensifying political engagement within and beyond the Bar? (b) Given the divergent political trajectories of the two jurisdictions, how did the constriction or expansion of political space hinder or facilitate lawyers' political mobilisation?

This section argues that power reconfigurations explain the timing, character and path of Bar politicisation: whether the direction of political transition is away from or towards authoritarian rule. Because the legal profession can and does reframe political cleavages in legal language, fundamental power reconfigurations give lawyers an opportunity to represent political possibilities as alternatives to the extant political authority. In the 1990s, both Taiwan and Hong Kong initiated a transformation that continues today. It is the break with political stability that creates the conditions under which lawyers mobilise, whatever the direction of the shift. The nature of the regime at the time of a power reconfiguration determines the character of the political alternative lawyers offer. As the following analysis demonstrates, in response to a declining KMT regime, Taiwanese lawyers mobilised proactively to advance democracy; by contrast, Hong Kong lawyers reacted to preserve the status quo against a wave of Chinese Mainlandisation.

This explains the different political strategies: Hong Kong lawyers defended judicial autonomy, whereas Taiwanese lawyers advocated for judicial reform. While both pursued a liberal agenda, Taiwanese lawyers soon moved from professional to national politics, creating and occupying authority positions and utilising various institutional platforms to advance their agenda. Conversely, Hong Kong lawyers acted collectively only when they felt threatened by change, although they became more sensitive as those threats multiplied and intensified.

A. Taiwan

After martial law was lifted in 1987, the Taipei Bar soon witnessed a leadership turnover in 1990, when a group of 'civilian lawyers' unseated the 'military lawyers', as discussed in the previous section. This event marked a paradigm shift for Taiwanese lawyers, from subordinates of the party-state apparatus to an autonomous and politically active group, self-identified as 'the legal profession in opposition'. Two developments demonstrate this political proactivity: in the 1990s, lawyers' collective actions forcefully targeted national political reform; in the early 2000s, lawyers quite successfully led the judicial reform agenda. Several key statutes were negotiated and passed, reshaping the judicial infrastructure.

i. Collective Action in the 1990s

The political assertiveness lawyers exhibited can best be captured by their collective statements on constitutional reform. In the 1990s, Taiwan went through seven rounds of constitutional revision, democratised the state organs, and transformed itself from a multi-provincial continental nation to a unitary island state. The Taipei Bar forcefully joined the debate: in June 1990, just before the National Forum was to be held by the then President Lee Deng Hui, the Bar bought a half-page advertisement in the national press entitled 'Ten Requests for Constitutional Reform', expressly making the legal profession's political stance clear:

(1) Abolish the Provisional Division of the Constitution [...]
(2) Abolish the National Assembly and the Control Yuan,[2] unify the legislative structure
(3) Abolish special quotas for professional organisations, diaspora [Taiwanese] and women, so the legislators are truly representative of the population
(4) On electoral design: set up a party proportional system, and we oppose a representation system based on Mainland China
(5) Clarify the role of the highest executive official, and clarify the relationship between the legislature and administration
(6) Abolish the Judicial Yuan: legislate the principle of judicial self-governance, and confer judicial review power on all levels of the judiciary
(7) Abolish the Examination Yuan: bring it under the administrative structure to be supervised by the legislature
(8) Legislation regarding local governments should be regulated in accordance with political reality in Taiwan and the spirit of local autonomy
(9) The Constitution should clearly acknowledge the reality of territorial division between Mainland China and Taiwan
(10) We request that the two major parties take the above advice and hold a referendum on the reform proposal no later than the year of 1992.

Framed more like a proclamation than a press release, each request clearly focused on a foundational issue that Taiwan, as a transitional democracy, had to address, making this statement a clear diagnosis and prescription about the constitutional issues and their solutions. The lawyers' collective statement confidently proposed a normative framework for the constitutional republic, transmuting technical legal expertise into moral authority. The call for a referendum most clearly expressed the lawyers' claim to political authority.

In the subsequent years, the Taipei Bar continuously engaged in national politics, making their liberal presence the default situation in major political events. In 1996, when Taiwan's elected vice-president was also nominated as the premier, the Taipei Bar authoritatively joined the debate on the constitutionality of the nomination. In 1997, the Taipei Bar publicly called for radical reform of the national government structure: first, to centralise power in a single national legislature, the Bar advocated abolishing the National Assembly and vesting its constitutional making power in the Legislative Yuan. Second, to simplify the organisation of the executive department, the Bar called for abolition of the provincial government. Because Taiwan was the only province[3] that the

---

[2] Yuan means 'institution'. The five major constitutional organs in Taiwan are the president, Legislative Yuan (the national legislature), Judicial Yuan (the judiciary), Control Yuan (the ombudsman's office) and Examination Yuan (the institution that manages civil servants).

[3] To be accurate, the Taiwan Province is the only *full* province that ROC effectively rules. There are other small islands also effectively ruled by ROC, such as Kinmen and Matsu, which are administered under Fujian Province. These territories are mostly military bases.

Republic of China (ROC) effectively ruled, the range of ROC national government rule was almost identical to that of Taiwanese Provincial government rule. This political claim was radical because, by recognising Taiwan as an island state, it directly challenged the Mainland perspective and the KMT-ROC regime claims to represent Mainland China as well. More radically, the Taipei Bar also advocated a constitutional amendment authorising a referendum declaring independence. Indeed, the Bar did not sidestep the core political cleavage in Taiwan; on the issue of unification with China, the Bar issued a statement: 'Insist on Self-determination, Remove the National Unification Guidelines'.

The lawyers' involvement in political liberalisation converged with a large-scale societal transformation. Lawyers were deeply connected with the vibrant civil movements. They were in the streets, protesting against the Criminal Code's notorious Article 100, which criminalised much political action as potentially treasonous. They were also in parliament, petitioning for repeal of the Gangster Prevention Act, which gave police excessive discretion to detain suspects. Lawyers aligned with journalists to oppose the government and the military holding shares in major television stations. After the catastrophic 1999 earthquake, lawyers collaborated with social workers to provide legal aid and represent victims in class actions.

ii. Lobbying in the 2000s

Another aspect of Taiwanese lawyers' politicisation is their leadership in legal reform. As the democratic system opened up and civil society strengthened, liberal-minded lawyers extended their political influence by creating new institutions, including a non-governmental organization (NGO) and a state agency, in order to realise their normative commitments to accountability and access to justice.

In 1994, the Alliance of Civilian-school Lawyers (ACL) decided to create a foundation to advocate for judicial and legal reform. Disappointed by the official agenda, lawyers believed that the Judicial Yuan lacked the commitment and ability to transform the judiciary. The leadership network wanted an independent organisation outside the Bar associations, whose members could not achieve the consensus necessary to take specific positions.

With a collective donation of US$420,000,[4] the Judicial Reform Foundation (JRF) successfully registered in 1997 and began operation, focusing on research and legislative lobbying, policy analysis, innocent case rescue, legal education, and outreach and legal support. It works on a wide variety of policy proposals, organises volunteers to visit and write to prisoners challenging their convictions, observes court proceedings to identify incompetent judges and prosecutors, and recruits volunteer lawyers to represent dissidents and social movement participants. The JRF developed such strong networks that it founded a branch office in Taichung (the second largest city) to deepen grassroots mobilisation and spawned two more independent NGOs.

It successfully persuaded politicians to address vital policy issues. In 1999, the Judicial Yuan held the first National Judicial Reform Forum, in which hundreds of judges, prosecutors, lawyers, legal scholars and community leaders debated 54 proposals, making

---

[4] At the time, Taiwan's per capita GDP was approximately US$13,500.

a comprehensive attempt to transform the judicial infrastructure. More than half the policy objectives discussed directly concerned lawyers, such as legal aid, lay participation, the adversarial system, cross-examination, evidentiary rules, and the quality of judges and prosecutor. Lawyers in the ACL-JRF network were not only invited to the Forum but also served on the preparatory committee:

> The real scenes are the preparatory committee meetings, six months before the National Forum. Participants were worked to death communicating and negotiating. The representatives from the Bar, Ministry of Justice, and the Judicial Yuan met almost every night at the National Taiwan University law school. (TW201715)

The 1999 National Judicial Reform Forum made dozens of proposals, some requiring legislation, others administrative support. In the 2000s, the arena of judicial reform shifted to the legislature. JRF became a key player in structuring the debate, exercising an informal veto power other lobbyists could not circumvent. Especially in the mid-2000s, when the incumbent Democratic Progressive Party appointed Fan Kuang-chun, a lawyer in the civilian-school lawyer network, as secretary general of the Judicial Yuan, the JRF enjoyed such easy communication with the administration that it could even act as spokesman legislators on behalf of the Judicial Yuan. Two JRF lawyers working at the management level in the 2000s expressed strong confidence in their lobbying ability:

> We had smooth communication with the Judicial Yuan with KC Fan as secretary general. We got results immediately. During the whole year of negotiations for the Judges Act, JRF sometime conceded, mainly because Fan is one of us it didn't want to give him a hard time. (TW201715)

Another JRF lawyer explained its soft veto power, using legislation creating a special prosecutor as an example:

> In 2007, the Organic Judicial Law was on the floor. The reformist prosecutors proposed to establish a special investigation unit. If the JRF had opposed it, the legislation wouldn't have passed because we had lobbying capacity and DPP [Director of Public Prosecutions] would listen to us. If the DPP opposed the legislation it wouldn't pass. You know that, in the legislature, if one party stalls the legislation dies. (TWL201612)

The Legal Aid Foundation Act (LAF) exemplifies the capacity of the ACL-JRF network to shape judicial infrastructure. LAF is a state-subsidised but independent agency administering public funds to offer legal advice, formal representation and other legal services. Its institutionalisation is clearly a product of the ACL-JRF network, as the Bill's foreword demonstrates:

> [T]he Taipei Bar Association, Judicial Reform Foundation and the Taiwan Association for Human Rights collaborated to form an action group in 1998, calling monthly meetings to convene scholars and lawyers to study comparative institutions. In July 1999, the National Judicial Reform Forum also resolved to 'institute a legal aid institution' with similar goals, reaffirming our resolution (Legislative Yuan 2003: 485).

With a mandate from the National Judicial Reform Forum, the judiciary agreed to take responsibility and draft a Bill in 2002. The Judicial Yuan faced a crisis in legal aid: there were only 51 public defenders, each handling an average of 26.4 cases a month, while courts throughout Taiwan heard 11,750 cases a year. Without a new legal aid institution, these defendants could not receive adequate legal representation, especially when the Yuan was also introducing a new cross-examination procedure in 2003. Because the Bar and bench were on the same page, the LAF Bill was seen as non-partisan and soon signed into law. The Foundation started operation in 2004 with an executive team of lawyers appointed by the Judicial Yuan. Its budget, personnel and capacity grew exponentially in the next decade: the LAF now has 22 branch offices with 3,722 lawyers registered to offer services; by 2016 it had provided assistance in approximately 50,000 cases. In addition, in several recent public interest lawsuits, the LAF became a hub, coordinating volunteer lawyers, civic organisations, and class action clients. As the LAF has become the infrastructure for access to justice in Taiwan, both as an official agency a civil society actor, it offers a striking example of the political capacity of Taiwanese lawyers to manoeuvre in the political arena to institutionalise their normative commitments.

Since the late 1980s, Taiwan has dramatically illustrated the politicisation of the legal profession. The paradigm shift was marked by a Bar leadership election in 1990, through which Taiwanese lawyers transformed themselves from a silent subservient group to an eloquent critical political actor. Politicisation can be observed first in lawyers' vocal assertive participation in constitutional and other major political reforms in the 1990s and then in their effective engagement in policy making, both shaping the agenda and lobbying for legislation. The institutionalisation of their political influence is striking: while some became national politicians, others created a state agency, entered the judicial administration and led important reform initiatives from within (although not always successfully), or remained active in civil society, whose agenda expanded to cover a wide range of social justice issues.

B. Hong Kong

Lawyer politicisation in Hong Kong resembles that in Taiwan in timing and political orientation but differs critically in proactivity: while Taiwanese lawyers were able to implement their ideals in the political arena, Hong Kong lawyers adopted a defensive stance, resisting political intervention from Beijing. This was evident in both institutionalised elections within the legal domain and sporadic collective actions on political-legal issues. More Bar members became active in these events, and the legal community was increasingly connected to the broader political turmoil. Bar politics reflected Hong Kong politics as the legal profession radicalised in electoral debates framed by political controversies concerning Beijing. Since 1997, each incident seen as a political threat to judicial autonomy – whether a policy paper or a Basic Law interpretation from Beijing or a bar leader's statement or action – triggered a response by the Hong Kong legal profession. The scale of mobilisation increased, contestation intensified, and the middle ground contracted.

i. Lawyers' Elections: Bar Leadership, Legislative Council Members, and other Official Representatives

> I don't think there's much legal profession politics that is not connected in some way to Hong Kong politics. (HK201718)

Electoral politics within the Hong Kong legal profession has always mirrored that in the larger society. However, connections between the two political streams have strengthened: professional elections were publicised, intra-professional fractions diverged politically, and member participation increased, in both regular elections and extraordinary meetings.

The Hong Kong legal profession participates as an independent constituency in four major elections. The legal sector (barristers, solicitors, and judicial officers) elects a member of the Legislative Council (LegCo); and 30 Electoral Committee members who vote for the chief executive. Private practitioners and government lawyers also vote as citizens. Barristers vote for the chairman and Executive Council of the Hong Kong Bar Association. Solicitors vote for Council members (but not the president) of the Law Society of Hong Kong.

Voter growth is the first indicator of greater lawyer participation in politics. Since 1997, the proportion of lawyers voting in LegCo elections increased 7 per cent. Because the profession itself grew, the number of lawyers participating in LegCo elections doubled, from 2,320 in 1998 to 4,901 in 2016.

Figure 11 Voter Turnout in the Legal Functional Constituency 1998–2016

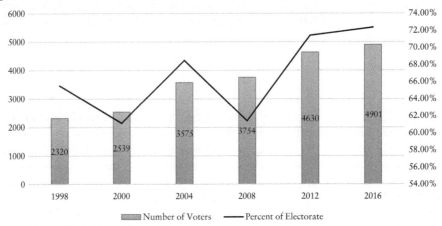

Source: Electoral Affairs Commission of Hong Kong.
Note: left axis is the number of votes; right axis is voter turnout rate in per cent.

A closer look at the vote indicates that support for the pro-democracy camp also grew as participation expanded. While pro-democracy candidates enjoyed roughly the same share of votes over the past 20 years (70 per cent), the number voting for those candidates doubled from 1,741 in 1998 to 3,405 in 2016.

Figure 12 Distribution of LegCo Votes between Pro-Democracy Candidate (Pro-D) and Other Candidates (Non-PD), 1998–2016

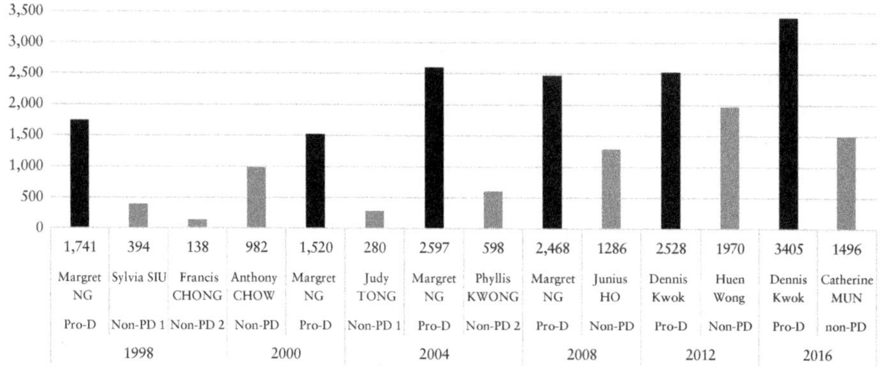

Year	1998			2000		2004			2008		2012		2016	
Votes	1,741	394	138	982	1,520	280	2597	598	2,468	1286	2528	1970	3405	1496
Candidate	Margret NG	Sylvia SIU	Francis CHONG	Anthony CHOW	Margret NG	Judy TONG	Margret NG	Phyllis KWONG	Margret NG	Junius HO	Dennis Kwok	Huen Wong	Dennis Kwok	Catherine MUN
Type	Pro-D	Non-PD 1	Non-PD 2	Non-PD	Pro-D	Non-PD 1	Pro-D	Non-PD 2	Pro-D	Non-PD	Pro-D	Non-PD	Pro-D	non-PD

Source: Electoral Affairs Commission of Hong Kong.

Voter numbers capture only one aspect of growing participation. Hong Kong lawyers are not just passive voters; they have also become activists who use professional institutions in both the barrister and solicitor communities to advance their causes. Hong Kong solicitors, long seen as mostly pro-government or pro-Beijing because their clients are Chinese businesses, took a revolutionary step in removing their Law Society President, Ambrose Lam, after his controversial speech supporting the Chinese Communist Party and the 2014 White Paper. The White Paper, an official document of the Chinese State Council, declared that Hong Kong enjoyed only as much autonomy as China allowed, and government officials must be patriots who 'love the country and love Hong Kong'. Read as a riposte to the universal suffrage movement in Hong Kong, the White Paper ignited grave discontent among Hong Kong people. Less than a week after its publication, however, Law Society President Ambrose Lam openly defended the Paper, insisting there was 'no judicial independence issue in asking judges to be patriots'. A day later he added that 'I think the Communist Party is great because it brought the country to a new era'. These statements quickly provoked strong opposition from the solicitor community: in just five days, 240 signatures were collected calling for a no-confidence vote, demanding that he retract his comment on the White Paper, and appealing to the Law Society to issue an official statement in support of the rule of law and judicial independence. Forty-nine days later, an extraordinary meeting of more than 3,000 passed three motions, voting 1,827-1,323 that they lacked confidence in Lam, who later resigned. The voter turnout represented a historic peak, and Kevin Yam, one of the three organisers, was moved to tears in front of the press, saying 'the result is comforting [...] Hong Kong still has strong-willed lawyers willing to step up, and solicitors can finally feel proud of our profession'. This membership challenge to Law Society leadership was unprecedented in its 108-year history.

Hong Kong barristers also witnessed growing contestation, if not radicalisation, in their leadership elections. Long a small elite club, the Hong Kong Bar still had fewer than 1,000 members in the 2000s, and leadership elections did not attract much public attention.

The first internal split erupted in 2008, when then Chairman Rimsky Yuen took a seat on the People's Political Consultative Committee of Guangdong Province without consulting the general membership (Ming Pao Daily News 2008: A2). Senior barristers suspected Yuen of capitalising on the chairmanship to advance his political career, arguing that a seat in Chinese local government compromised his integrity and even violated the Bar's long tradition of resisting political intervention by mainland China (Lee 2008; Ng 2008). The timing of his political appointment was particularly controversial because the deadline for nominations to challenge his chairmanship had passed, resulting in Yuen's automatic re-election for another term. Ten former Bar Association chairmen, many of them pro-democracy lawyer-politicians, issued an open letter to Yuen asserting that 'the two positions are contradictory in character' and urging him to resign his chairmanship or reject the appointment (Sing Tao Daily 2008). As Ronny Tong, Bar Chairman 1999–2000 and Yuen's senior colleague, asked in an interview: 'will he be a voice for human rights in Hong Kong in the future? Will he keep his head down to avoid offending Beijing?' (Ciao 2008). The central government's political influence was a matter of grave concern. Nevertheless, the Bar Association's executive committee supported Yuen (Hong Kong Bar Association 2008), declaring that

> the People's Political Consultative Committee is an institution for consultation and members [...] provide opinions freely. We believe there is no contradiction between being a member of the Consultative Committee in Guangdong and being the Hong Kong Bar Association Chairman [...] The Bar sees this appointment as a positive recognition of the Chairman and the Bar, an organisation well-known for its support of human rights and the rule of law in Hong Kong and other regions. The Bar has never changed its stance on these issues, and never will. [...] The Bar unanimously supports and welcomes this appointment.

The internal division deepened in a general meeting attended by 200 members but then ended in a deadlock. Some younger barristers made an unsuccessful attempt to call an emergency meeting to impeach Yuen (Apple Daily 2008: A02). The pro-democracy lawyer-politicians conceded, fearing that, 'an emergency meeting splits the Bar, which might be exactly the purpose of Beijing' (Hong Kong Economic Journal 2008). Yuen remained Bar chairman until the end of his 2008 term.

A decade later, the 2018 Bar leadership election again became contentious. Philip Dykes, a leading human rights lawyer, unseated the incumbent chairman Paul Lam 'after the most heated and politically charged contest in years' (Lam 2018a). Dykes's challenge itself was controversial because it is very rare for the incumbent to face competition, given the Bar's shared understanding that the chair holds the post for two years, as Yuen had done in 2007–08 and Dykes himself in 2005–06. His action was prompted by a disagreement with the bar leadership on a political issue. A young barrister explained how Dykes, representing a segment of the bar, intended to radicalise it:

> The remote cause was that the Bar refused to comment on the joint checkpoint arrangement in the future Kowloon high speed rail station. The co-location arrangement is very likely to violate the Basic Law, and in fact the Bar had a standing committee that wrote a report on this. But the Bar didn't release the report. Barristers went indignant: how can the Bar restrain itself on such a critical issue! So Phil ran [for chair] out of the concern that Paul will continue to hold the

spot but say nothing, especially since in the next couple of years Hong Kong will have a lot of constitutional issues. (HKB201701)

Indeed, the timing of opposition to Chinese dominance was at the centre of the debate. The Bar's delay in taking a political stance was read as acquiescence to Beijing, not just prudence. Dykes publicly declared: 'it was regrettable that the Bar association had not issued a strong statement until December, after Beijing officially endorsed the joint checkpoint proposal' (Lam 2018b). And the Bar's passivity directly contributed to Dykes challenging the incumbent, as the South China Morning Post reported: 'Dykes' six-person team [...] have slammed the Bar under Lam's leadership for failing to issue a timely response over the legality of [the] joint checkpoint proposal' (Lau and Lam 2018).

This reveals the precise nature of the split: the two candidates differed not about what stance the Bar should take but about how proactive it should be. That is, the disagreement igniting an unconventional Bar election concerned the priority and interpretation of a political issue. While this is not politicisation in the instrumental sense of transforming a professional body into a political instrument, as some critics of Dykes have said, the connection between a territorial issue and a professional election is a form of politicisation.

Barristers and solicitors in Hong Kong have developed a mechanism to resist Beijing's interventions, perceived or actual. Recent disputes follow a similar pattern:

(a) the leadership displays an affinity towards Beijing or at least a lack of resistance;
(b) the general membership reacts, either through regularly scheduled elections or extraordinary meetings;
(c) new leadership reaffirms the profession's commitment to judicial autonomy in Hong Kong.

Lawyers see their professional associations not only as interest groups but also as collectivities with a normative obligation to resist potential threats to Hong Kong's judicial autonomy, an institutional foundation of the rule of law.

There is a common perception in Hong Kong that only barristers are liberal-minded, while solicitors – the majority of the profession – are conservative (Sing Tao Daily, 2008). But two kinds of evidence contradict this. First, from 1986 to 2016 the legal functional constituency of the Hong Kong LegCo has consistently elected a pro-democracy barrister, who would not have succeeded without the support of solicitors, who constitute a majority of this electorate. An unlikely case demonstrates this. In the 2012 LegCo election, the most heated contest pitted Daniel Kwok, a young pro-democracy barrister, against a former Law Society president. Kwok won by a 12 per cent margin, securing 2,528 votes from an electorate of 1,174 barristers and 7,483 solicitors. Without substantial support from solicitors, Kwok's victory would not have been possible. This was also clear in 1998, when barrister Margret Ng won a landslide victory with 1,741 votes (75 per cent) from an electorate of 683 barristers and 4,619 solicitors.

Table 2 Comparisons of Two Major LegCo Elections

LegCo Election Year	Historical Setting	Voter Turnout (per cent)	Winning share (per cent)	Elected Candidate (votes)	Number of Practising Barristers	Number of Practising Solicitors
1998	First election after sovereignty change, also **highest** vote share for pro-democracy candidate	65.56	75	Margret Ng (1,741)	683	4,619
2012	Most contested year, **lowest** vote share of pro-democracy candidate	72.36	54.6	Dennis Kwok (2,528)	1,174	7,483

Source: Electoral Affairs Commission of Hong Kong.

The second piece of evidence against the common misperception is that the legal sector has consistently chosen pro-democracy candidates for 20–30 of the Electoral Committee members who vote on their behalf in the chief executive election. In fact, from 2011 to 2016, the pro-democratic camp has won *all* the Electoral Committee seats, during a decade when the median number of votes for an individual Electoral Committee member grew dramatically from 913 in 2006 to 2,191 in 2016.

The gap between public perceptions of Hong Kong solicitors and their actual voting records indicates that, though solicitors are much less likely than barristers to proclaim their politics in public, their votes in the privacy of the ballot box align with those of barristers. This behavioural pattern may be attributable to both solicitors' clientele and the structure of their law firms. A politically active barrister explained:

> [W]hen people can vote, and they don't all have to publicly take a stance, most of them would vote Democrats in a liberal way. But if they have to come out publicly and say 'no I'm against this guy', then it's much more difficult to persuade solicitors to come out. There are two reasons. Because solicitors are employees within a law firm, if a young junior solicitor comes out and says 'I hate the Chinese Communist Party' then he would probably get a phone call from the managing partner, 'hey shut up, we're doing a lot of business in China'. Secondly, a lot of them depend on business related to China, so if a managing partner comes out and says 'I hate the CCP' then they're not going to get any of the China related business. (HK201718)

Three law firm mechanisms silence solicitors: informal pressure in daily practice, proxy votes in elections, and self-censorship in inter-firm competition. A junior solicitor recalled that when asked in his first job interview whether he participated in the Umbrella Movement,[5] he replied, 'well, perhaps I passed by'. The interviewer sensed his politics

---

[5] The Umbrella Movement refers to a series of sit-in street protests that occurred in Hong Kong from 26 September to 15 December 2014. Protesters urged the central government in Beijing to institute universal suffrage in Hong Kong to elect its Chief Executive.

and gave him a long face. Although he was hired, 'she kept picking on me since then' (HK201706). Afterwards, he used a pen name when publishing political commentaries and changed it whenever he thought someone was about to recognise him.

The second mechanism operates during Law Society elections, when law firm partners collect proxy votes from their junior associates (HK201825; HK201834; HK201845). A mid-career solicitor explained the success of the 2014 non-confidence vote removing the Law Society president to young solicitors. There were:

> two reasons: first, many young solicitors used all kinds of ridiculous excuses not to render their proxies to their partners. Second, the rule says if you present yourself at the meeting, your vote invalidates your prior proxy vote. And so, so many people attended the meeting that day. (HK201704)

A senior expatriate solicitor who had been a partner in a major American law firm claimed that international firms were different.

> [T]he local firm partners [are] not afraid of telling their associates what they think and how to vote or asking them to hand in proxies. But in international firms, partners would never tell associates what they should do, although they might not participate actively either. (HK201711)

Nevertheless, he acknowledged there was self-censorship of political speech:

> Even the international law firms are concerned. This is a competitive market, there's always some other firm willing to take up the work, and the political speech worries the clients. But I have heard no real story [that clients leave a firm because of political attitudes], just self-censuring. (HK201711)

Self-censuring is itself an effective mechanism for silencing people. This informant, who sometimes wrote for English-language newspapers, was changing careers and had been asked by a human resources interviewer if he would 'turn down the tone' in the future (HK201711). Evidently, political pressure was experienced by junior and senior solicitors, locals and expatriates.

ii. Lawyers March against Beijing

Lawyers organised four 'dress in black, march in silence' demonstrations to defend judicial independence and protest Beijing's political interference in Hong Kong's legal system. That the number of protesters tripled from hundreds to thousands indicates the growing politicisation of legal issues. Lawyers were motivated to march by the fear that Beijing intended to undermine the 'one country, two systems' design in the Basic Law by limiting judicial autonomy and redefining the role of courts. Demonstrations in 1999, 2005 and 2016 were direct responses to the Basic Law interpretations by the Standing Committee of the National People's Congress (NPCSC) in Beijing, while the 2014 protest was sparked by the contention in the Chinese State Council White Paper that judges, as part of the Hong Kong government, should be patriotic. The following table summarises the date, size, cause and rationale of the four demonstrations.

Table 3 Size, Stimuli and Rationales of Lawyers' Demonstrations, 1999–2016

Date	Number of Participants	Triggering Event	Protesters' Rationale
1999	circa 600	The SCNPC issued its first Basic Law interpretation of the right of abode	Violating judicial autonomy: (a) the Hong Kong government requested Beijing to interpret the law to change a Court of Final Appeal decision; (b) the SCNPC struck down the Court's decision
2005	850–900	The SCNPC made its third Basic Law interpretation, determining the length of the Interim Chief Executive's remaining term after the incumbent CE resigned	Limiting Hong Kong autonomy: instead of filing a case in court, the Hong Kong government asked Beijing to interpret the Basic Law
2014	circa 1,600	The State Council in Beijing issued a White Paper contending that the 'Hong Kong ruling team' should properly understand and execute the Basic Law, and patriotism was demanded of all government employees, including judges.	Violating judicial independence: the Hong Kong judiciary should be independent, applying the law and only the law.
2016	circa 2,000	The SCNPC made its fifth Basic Law interpretation, contending that Hong Kong legislators should solemnly take their oaths of office, thereby targeting several newly elected legislators who expressed anti-China sentiments.	Violating judicial autonomy: the SCNPC proactively issued the interpretation, without any request from Hong Kong.

The common theme of these collective actions is the defence of judicial autonomy, which includes the claims that the judiciary and legal practice in Hong Kong must remain immune from political interference, especially by Beijing, and that the judiciary must be the supreme authority in Hong Kong, adjudicating the constitutionality of legislation and resolving value conflicts. Analytically, the former is a more legalistic point, while the latter takes a position that is unavoidably political in the Hong Kong context. Defending the Court of Final Appeal's exclusive power to say what the law is necessarily challenges Beijing's 'complete state authority over the Hong Kong Special Administrative Region'. By demonstrating, lawyers declared that the Hong Kong judiciary, not Beijing, was the appropriate authority to decide how Hong Kong should be governed. Although this might seem a legal nicety, it presupposes a fundamentally different normative understanding: the judiciary enjoys independent power, not one delegated by the central government.

To conclude: since 1997 the Hong Kong legal profession has been politicised in several ways, including greater participation, synchronisation of professional and Hong Kong politics, and radicalisation of electoral competition. A liberal tendency is evident in the legal profession's choice of representatives in both LegCo and the Electoral Committee that chooses the Chief Executive. Based on field interviews and historical voting data, I argued that although the majority of the legal profession (solicitors) are restrained by their clientele and organisational structures from openly voicing their political concerns, both branches of the profession consistently support the pro-democracy wing of Hong Kong politics. But legal professionals act defensively to preserve the architecture and operation of the judiciary from external political influence, especially by Beijing. A defence of 'unchanging practice' is, by default, conservative, and the rule of law banner under which Hong Kong lawyers march reflects this limitation. The profession's actions are reactive, triggered by challenges to local autonomy, and lack proactive agenda-setting power.

IV. FEMINISATION OF THE LEGAL PROFESSION

The Hong Kong and Taiwan legal professions were predominantly, if not exclusively, male in the post-war era. Only in the late 1970s and early 1980s did the number of women lawyers begin to increase, reaching 20 per cent of entrants in the 1990s and 20 per cent of members a decade later (Figures 13 and 14; Taipei Bar Association 2005: 160, 166).[6]

Figure 13 Gender Distribution of Taipei Bar Association Members 1946–2000

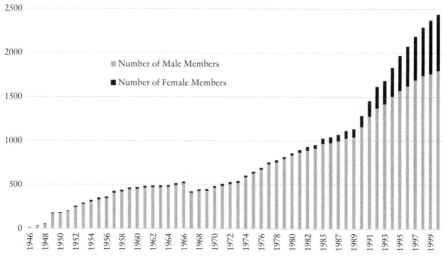

Source: Taipei Bar Association (2005).

---

[6] There are two justifications for using Taipei Bar data as a proxy for Taiwan. First, Taipei is the only Bar association that publishes data for the time span of this research project. Second, Taipei has been the largest, and arguably the most influential, Bar association, because Taipei has been Taiwan's economic and political centre since World War II. In 2017, the Taipei Bar had over 7,000 members, approximately 70 per cent of the profession.

Historically, almost all Hong Kong solicitors also were men; but in 2000 more women solicitors than men were admitted, and the disproportion has persisted in admissions and among trainee solicitors, with the result that women solicitors are on course to reach parity with men in the next few years (see Figure 14). However, women are still underrepresented at the management level, having remained roughly a quarter of partners in solicitors' firms throughout the decade 2005–16 (compare Figures 14, 15, 16).

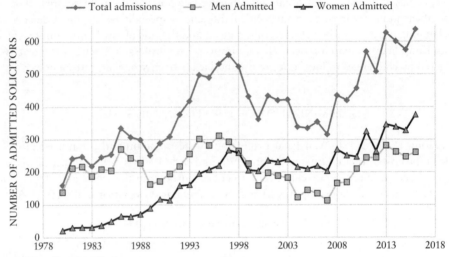

Figure 14 Gender Distribution of Hong Kong Solicitor Admissions

Source: Hong Kong Law Society.

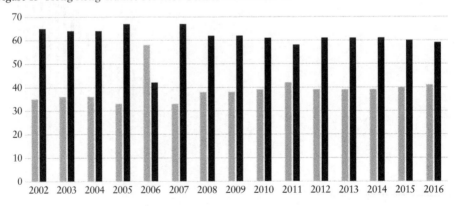

Figure 15 Hong Kong Trainee Solicitor Gender Ratio 2002–16

Source: Hong Kong Law Society annual reports 2002–16.

Figure 16 Hong Kong Partner Solicitor Gender Ratio 2005–16

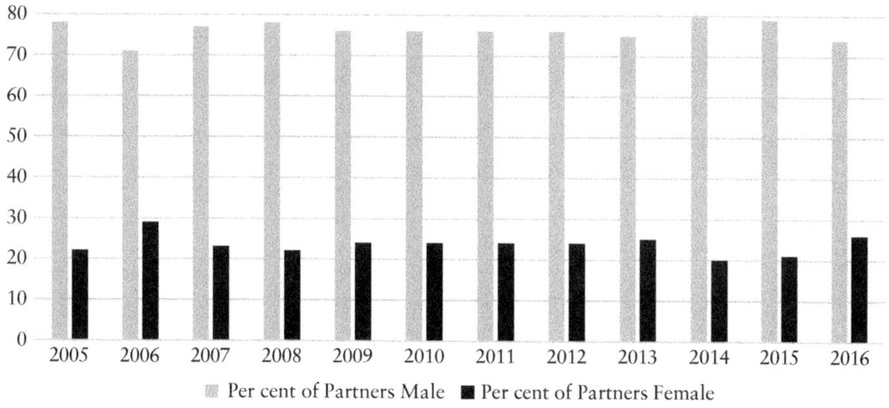

[Bar chart showing Per cent of Partners Male and Per cent of Partners Female from 2005 to 2016]

Source: Hong Kong Law Society annual reports 2002–16.

V. CONCLUSION

This chapter juxtaposes two different Asian jurisdictions to demonstrate two consistent trends: localisation and politicisation. Despite differences in social stratification and economic globalisation, both Hong Kong and Taiwan developed strong local characters, which are fundamentally different from the 'foreign' or expatriate legal professions of the post-war era. In addition, despite divergent interactions with authoritarian rule, in which Taiwan democratised but Hong Kong's political space fragmented, both legal professions displayed strong political mobilisation. The political changes, however, meant that the Taiwanese Bar proactively advanced a reform agenda, while the Hong Kong legal profession could only play defence, resisting Beijing's influence.

These preliminary findings generate several important questions. For Hong Kong: how does the internationalisation of the market transform competition and collaboration between law firms? What is the impact on the legal profession in terms of prestige, careers and education? How is China's regional economic integration affecting the legal sector? For Taiwan: what was the impact of democratisation on the legal profession? How did the judiciary and procuracy become independent? How does the legal profession cope with China's growing economic power and aggressive political agenda? Addressing these questions may provide a starting point for future research to help us better understand legal professions during fundamental power transitions in East Asia, both in the past and the future.

APPENDIX

I conducted 77 interviews in Hong Kong and 168 interviews in Taiwan between 2016 and 2018. They are coded by location and timing: for example, TW201738 refers to the 38th interview I conducted in 2017 in Taiwan and HK201812 to the 12th interview I conducted in 2018 in Hong Kong. Because some were group interviews and included respondents from different professional backgrounds, I also specified their vocation. In Hong Kong, 'B' refers to barrister and 'S' to solicitor. In Taiwan, 'L' refers to lawyer, 'P' to prosecutor, and 'J' to judge. In both jurisdictions, 'O' refers to other specialists, such as journalists, academics, policy makers or NGO staff. For example, HKB2017-01 refers to the first barrister I interviewed in 2017, and TWL2017-26 to the 26th Taiwanese lawyer I interviewed in 2017. The table below lists interviews and interviewees quoted in this paper, following the order they appear in the chapter.

Interview #	Interviewee	Vocation	Gender	Years of practice	Region	Notes
TW201715	TWL2017-07	Lawyer	Male	20	Northern Taiwan	Small law firm
TW201612	TWL2016-03	Lawyer	Male	27	Northern Taiwan	Political Adviser
HK201718	HKB2017-04	Barrister	Male	10	Hong Kong	Large Chambers
HK201801	HKB2018-01	Barrister	Male	2	Hong Kong	Mid-size Chambers
HK201706	HKS2017-03	Solicitor	Male	Less than 5	Hong Kong	Mid-size local law firm
HK201825	HKS2018-08	Solicitor	Male	Less than 5	Hong Kong	Large local law firm
HK201834	HKS2018-11	Solicitor	Female	6–10 years	Hong Kong	Large local law firm
HK201845	HKS2018-15	Solicitor	Male	Less than 5	Hong Kong	Large Chinese law firm
HK201704	HKS2017-01	Solicitor	Male	16–20 years	Hong Kong	Large International law firm
HK201711	HKS2017-06	Solicitor	Male	16–20 years	Hong Kong	Large International law firm

REFERENCES

Apple Daily (2008) 'Young Members Attempt to Impeach Yuen' 18 January.
Chan, P (1997) Report *Hong Kong Youth Legal Profession Association Review*.
Chang F-C (2007) *Taiwan Lawyers after World War II – in Support of Human Rights from Individual Action to Collective Action* (National Taiwan University, Taipei, Taiwan).
Ciao, X (2008) 'Why Ronny Tang is Grudging' Ta Kung Pao 大公報 25 January.
Electoral Affairs Commission of Hong Kong Special Administrative Region www.eac.hk/en/legco/lce.htm.
Hong Kong Bar Association (2000) *Hong Kong Bar Association: 50th Anniversary* (Hong Kong, Sweet & Maxwell Asia).

—— (2008) 'Bar Association's Statement on Chairman Rimsky Yuen's Appointment to the People's Political Consultative Committee of Guangdong Province'.
Hong Kong Economic Journal (2008) 'Yuen Automatically Re-elects Chairman, Former Chairpersons Concern for a Split' 15 January.
Hong Kong Law Society (1983) *Hong Kong Law Society Annual Report 1983*.
—— (1984) *Hong Kong Law Society Annual Report 1984*.
—— (1987) *Hong Kong Law Society Annual Report 1987*.
—— (1994) *Hong Kong Law Society Annual Report 1994*.
—— (1995) *Hong Kong Law Society Annual Report 1995*.
—— (1996) *Hong Kong Law Society Annual Report 1996*.
—— (1997) *Hong Kong Law Society Annual Report 1997*.
—— (1998) *Hong Kong Law Society Annual Report 1998*.
—— (1999) *Hong Kong Law Society Annual Report 1999*.
—— (2000) *Hong Kong Law Society Annual Report 2000*.
—— (2001) *Hong Kong Law Society Annual Report 2001*.
—— (2002) *Hong Kong Law Society Annual Report 2002*.
—— (2003) *Hong Kong Law Society Annual Report 2003*.
—— (2004) *Hong Kong Law Society Annual Report 2004*.
—— (2005) *Hong Kong Law Society Annual Report 2005*.
—— (2006) *Hong Kong Law Society Annual Report 2006*.
Hsu, C (2018) 'The Political Origins of Professional Identity: Lawyers, Judges, and Prosecutors in Taiwan's State Transformation' *Asian Journal of Law and Society* 1–26, doi:10.1017/als.2018.35.
Huang, J-Y (2009) 'A Page of Judicial Reform History in Taiwan, Written by Lawyers' *Read Mag* 22 October.
Lam, J (2018a) 'Philip Dykes Elected New Head of Hong Kong Bar Association in Upset Win' *South China Morning Post* 19 January.
Lam, J (2018b) 'Hong Kong's Barristers Go to the Polls for Tightest Contest in Years' *South China Morning Post* 18 January.
Lau, C and Jeffie Lam (2018) 'Hong Kong Bar Association Must Steer Clear of Politics, Top Lawyer Warns, as Poll Contest Heats Up' *South China Morning Post* 10 January.
Lee, M (2008) 'Deterioration' *Next Mag* A144 24 April.
Liu, H (2007) 'Transformation of Taiwanese Legal Education: A Perspective of Knowledge Succession and Discipline Locating' PhD thesis, National Taiwan University, Taipei, Taiwan, unpublished.
Ming Pao Daily News (2008) 'Bar Chair to Be Appointed to Political Consultative Committee of Guangdong Province, Alan Leung Urges Rimsky Yuen to Choose One Role' 16 January.
Ng, M (2008) 'To Sustain the Rule of law, Stand out; the Glorious Tradition of Hong Kong Bar' *Hong Kong Econ J* 25 January.
Sing Tao Daily (2008) 'Chairman's Concurrent Appointment Stimulates Controversies; the Bar Splits' 22 January.
Taipei Bar Association (2005) *Taipei Bar Association: The 20th Century History* (Taipei, Interminds Publishing Inc).

42

Thailand

The Evolution of Law, the Legal Profession and Political Authority

FRANK W MUNGER*

I. A 'QUASI-COLONIAL' MODERNISATION

EUROPEAN LEGAL SYSTEMS were introduced by colonial governments throughout Southeast Asia during the nineteenth and early twentieth centuries. Siam alone (later Thailand[1]) escaped colonisation, but territorial concessions and extraterritorial jurisdiction under treaties between 1850 and 1900 protected many foreign enterprises from Siam's feudal law, elevating the legal privileges of foreigners, including other Asians. In part to end the indignities of subordination, progressive monarchs began modernising government administration and the legal system along European lines to face world powers on equal terms (Loos 2006). The monarchs' eventual success might be measured by the elimination of extraterritorial jurisdiction a half century later, but by then the path of legal development had been influenced by nearly a century of entanglement with other legal cultures, foreign legal advisers, and the rulers' own choices.

Adaptation of European bureaucratic administration, centralised courts, and civil codes has been characterised as a 'quasi-colonial modernity' (Loos 2006). The country's rulers were also pursuing their own colonisation project: consolidation of culturally distinct regions with little historical allegiance to Bangkok, including a northern region that recently belonged to a Burmese empire and three southern Muslim provinces detached from Malaysia by the British. The monarchs believed that adaptation of European statecraft and assimilation of Western knowledge were necessary not only to consolidate their authority over feudal lords and diverse, sometimes resistant, regional cultures but also to improve the well-being and productive participation of their subjects. Through dual

---

*I want to thank my dedicated Bangkok-based assistants and collaborators, Peerawich Thoviriyavej and Vorapitchaya Rabiablok, for their research as well as invaluable insights and suggestions. This research has been made possible, in part, through generous support from the Law School Admissions Council and New York Law School.

[1] Siam was not permanently renamed Thailand until 1949 (Baker and Phongpaichit 2005). For convenience, I use the modern name throughout this chapter.

projects of external resistance and internal consolidation, law became the skeleton of the modern Thai state.

Interest in the emergence of legal professions in developing countries grew initially from the assumption that lawyers strengthened liberal legalism – the rule of law ideal in developed democracies. Case studies quickly provided counterexamples requiring a different entry point to explain the profession's development. Lawyers are specialists in mobilising the power of modern states (Rueschmeyer 1989). In Asia, as in Europe, a legal profession typically emerged to serve state power (Dezalay and Garth 2010); and recent studies of the rule of law in new states emphasise politics and the power of the state as key determinants of the evolution of law and the legal profession.

Legal evolution in Southeast Asian states, like Thailand, Malaysia, Indonesia, and their neighbours to the east and north, has followed paths different from those in the colonising nations of Old Europe or North America. Jayasuria (1999) compares law's authority in developed liberal democracies with law's role in a typical Asian state, which resembles Max Weber's Prussia, dominated by a powerful executive branch and massive bureaucracy. In many such states, sponsored market capitalism developed along with a rule of law limited to market relations, maintained by a technically skilled judiciary and legal profession, while the state exercised strict, and often illiberal, political control.

With economic takeoff, many Asian bureaucratic states experienced exponential growth in the number of technically skilled lawyers needed to transact business, negotiate relationships in the global marketplace, and facilitate increasingly complex regulatory systems (Ginsburg 2009a). At the same time, state investment and clientelism bound emerging power centres in the economy and civil society to high-level bureaucrats and state leaders, eliminating opportunities for lawyers to mediate between power holders and establish their own independence. Potentially influential members of the legal profession, like other emerging power holders including the judiciary, remained bound to the interests of the state, and political control limited the mobilisation of civil society to oppose state authority.

Legal evolution in Thailand is distinctive because, until very recently, alliance with the monarchy determined the legitimacy of modern governments. When the absolute monarchy ended in 1932, successors cultivated the king's charisma as a powerful source of popular legitimacy. Well into the twenty-first century, political power has remained concentrated in networks of bureaucrats, military leaders, major banking and business enterprises and other elites allied with the monarchy. Without divisive occupation by a foreign power or a popular revolution to open space for opposition to the state (Slater 2010), elite factions have engaged in internecine fights but survived as a class through a pervasive network of patron-client relationships and support for the monarchy. Even as the values of many elites and the educated middle class liberalise, the limited opportunities to mobilise law against state power have weakened the identities of both judges and the legal profession as guarantors of the rule of law. The judiciary has seldom broken with its history as servant of the king.

Rapid and successful development at the end of the twentieth century accelerated economic and social change, potentially weakening this legacy. Educated middle classes populated urban centres, and growing numbers of 'urbanised peasants' carried new perceptions of their position in Thai society back to the countryside (Naruemon and McCargo 2011). New political players have altered the frequency and nature of political conflict. A popular uprising in 1973 overthrew a military dictator who lacked the support of the monarchy; bloody middle-class resistance to another overreaching dictator in 1991 ended military rule; and after liberal constitutional reform following the Asian Financial Crisis, 'colour' politics pitted groups supporting (Red Shirt) or opposing (Yellow Shirt) Thaksin Shinawatra, the corrupt populist prime minister, at times flooding the streets of central Bangkok, bringing government to a standstill. Impasse invited a return to Thailand's long history of military coups (two occurred in 2006 and 2014). Popular participation in politics after 1973 also opened space for law and the legal profession: the emergence of a self-sustaining community of non-governmental organisation (NGO) lawyers; leadership of the movement for constitutional reform after 1991; and consolidation of a network of working groups to use new courts and constitutional rights. After a military coup ended Thaksin's administration in 2006, these lawyers played more overtly political roles using the language of constitutionalism and human rights (Munger 2015).

Opportunities for courts and lawyers to achieve greater independence are still limited by three factors: long-standing ambiguity about law's role in modernisation; a divide between judges and practitioners (characteristic of civil law systems but augmented by Thailand's traditional social hierarchy and the judiciary's close connection with the monarchy); and finally political influence flowing from the centres of political power – the 'network monarchy' and military. Today, new forms of political contention are creating opportunities to expand the profession's role, increasing its power and altering history's trajectory.

II. FROM SERVANTS OF THE KING TO A COMMON CALLING

A. Training the Nobility

In 1888, the monarch Rama V (1868–1910) announced his plan for a European-style bureaucratic state with ministries managed by members of his family and the inner circle of collaborators (Baker and Phongpaichit 2009). Centralisation of power in state ministries converted a landed royalty into powerful bureaucrats answerable directly to the monarch and his council of advisers (ibid). A centralised system of Royal Courts of Justice superseded 30-odd feudal courts under regional lords. Supervised by the king's youngest brother, work began on a comprehensive legal code. Rama V and his advisers chose European civil codes as a model because they were established in the countries with extraterritorial jurisdiction and more likely to impress them (Loos 2006; Kittisak 1991). A law school founded in 1897 trained members of the nobility for service as judges and ministers, guaranteeing a growing core of Thai elites in key posts committed to modernising Thailand while retaining its distinctive character.[2] Elite bureaucrats of noble origin, judges and prosecutors dominated the profession, controlling the Thai Bar Association established in 1914. By contrast, relatively few domestically trained lawyers practised until well after World War II, and practising lawyers were not authorised to establish an independent Bar association until 1985.

---

[2] To fill new offices, Rama V also employed foreigners, some with long colonial experience elsewhere, calling them 'readymade textbooks' (Baker and Phongpaichit 2009: 68; see generally Thai Bar Association 2008).

Drafting a comprehensive legal code between 1900 and 1935 initiated consequential changes in Thailand's legal culture. Traditional courts applied the received wisdom of Thai jurisprudence, principles contained in a document known as the Three Seals Law.[3] Far from a modern code (only a few official copies existed), its broad precepts were used by judges (who were nobles themselves) to guide their moral sensibilities. Appeals, while not unknown, required impugning the integrity of the judge, who was punished if a judgment was overturned (Loos 2006; Lingat 1950). The Royal Courts of Justice established the authority of a new, comprehensive legal code, which required careful textual application. Appeals necessitated a further exercise in statutory interpretation rather than an accusation of judicial malfeasance.[4]

The legal code, completed in 1935, ended extraterritoriality but also embodied the internal colonisation project as an instrument of both centralisation and hierarchy. The monarchy's 'juridical conquest' of the large Muslim minority in Thailand's southernmost provinces subjected them to the uniform Thai law in all matters except Islamic family law, administered by a separate system of local Muslim courts, a bifurcation that still exists (Loos 2006). Many Code provisions are literal translations of European statutes, reproducing phrases and concepts familiar to Western lawyers but alien to Thai jurisprudence and culture. Some provisions embodied liberal ideals the monarchs admired in Western political life, including freedom and equality; but, as Loos notes (2006: 68–69), the word 'liberty' was translated by a term expressing liberty to enjoy the privileges of status within a hierarchy, ie freedom from the arbitrary authority of superiors but not equal liberty for all.[5] As Siffin (1966: 162–63) said about Thai bureaucratic behaviour at mid-century:

> Individuals are protected and authority is restrained, not in response to recognition of any principle of the political rights of individuals per se, but on the basis of religion-centered values which in subtle ways limit the scope of the social system's control over the individuals.

Rules became relevant, but rules and their interpretations often reflected traditional Thai understandings of relationships and values.

i. The 1932 Revolution and a Law School for Commoners

Even before World War II, the growth of commercial centres, an emerging urban middle class, and expanding government administration created opportunities for lawyers in private practice. Lawyers who lacked a Thai law degree were limited to practising within a designed urban district (see below). A few Thai commoners of modest means obtained legal training by working for a small firm or, perhaps, a judge. Children of wealthier non-noble families studied law in England or Europe, hoping for government employment on their return. The Chinese immigrant community, whose leading entrepreneurs were increasingly wealthy, powerful and independent of Thai patronage (Baker and Phongpaichit 2005), mainly employed lawyers from their own community.

---

[3] The earliest extant version dates from 1805, the reign of Rama I (1782–1908) (Loos 2006).
[4] English philosopher John Austin's legal positivism dominated law school instruction (Prokati 2009; Lingat 1950).
[5] Family law was carefully adapted to preserve Thailand's patriarchal practices, including polygyny (Loos 2006).

Pridi Banomyong is an important example of the influence of a growing class of Western-educated commoners occupying significant bureaucratic and military posts. Pridi's[6] upper-middle-class family used its connections to secure his admission to the royal law school. After continuing his law studies in France and frustrated, like many other well-educated commoners, by the absence of meritocracy and a monarchy that talked of democracy and constitutionalism but initiated few changes, Pridi led a group of Western-educated commoners in overthrowing the absolute monarchy in 1932. Calling itself the People's Party, Pridi's group announced sweeping liberal goals, including universal equality and an end to royal privilege. The Party's lack of strong popular roots together with the monarchy's de facto power were reflected in the group's petition for the king's approval of their reform proposals. Nevertheless, the uprising marked the end of absolute monarchy and the beginning of constitutional government, creating new possibilities for law. Over the next 15 years, struggles between Pridi's liberal faction and authoritarian factions led by military officers resulted in Pridi's permanent expulsion from Thailand in 1949. Before departing, he completed the final sections of the legal code, drafted a liberal constitution, and initiated legal reforms, including an end to polygamy (Loos 2006).

In 1934, Pridi established Thammasat University[7] to prepare a new generation of public servants who were not only knowledgeable in law and government administration but also trained in values associated with public service.[8] The new university absorbed what had been the royal law school, provided low-cost legal education to commoners, and remained Thailand's only law school until 1972 (Thai Bar Association 2008). Most students aspired to a secure, respected job in government service rather than private law practice, and relatively few became licensed attorneys. Even though the end of extraterritoriality probably intensified demand for domestically trained attorneys, there were fewer than 2,000 as late as 1960 (National Statistical Office 1970: 159).

Thongbai Thongbao[9]

Thongbai Thongbao's career contrasts sharply with Pridi's. He was born in 1926 to poor rice farmers in Mahasarakham, in Northeast Thailand. In primary school, he was inspired to enter public service by a young teacher who had studied at Thammasat University. As the youngest of six, he was not expected to assume responsibility for his family's farm or to support his siblings, and Thongbai's pleas and prospects for upward mobility persuaded his family to support his ambition to attend Thammasat. With little money, Thongbai lived without cost at a temple. After graduation, finding no opportunities to make a living helping the people he knew best – those like himself, with little means – Thongbai became a journalist, a profession he greatly enjoyed. (Later, as an experienced legal practitioner, poor clients paid him with food, lodging or small gifts.) In 1969, he travelled to China with a group of journalists to view an exciting Asian revolution. On return home he was charged with treason by the virulently anti-communist

---

[6] It is customary for Thai to use the given name of a person familiar to the reader in contrast to European and North American practice of using a family name. Throughout this chapter I follow the Thai practice after the initial reference, where I give the full name.

[7] Originally named the University of Moral and Political Sciences [มหาวิทยาลัยวิชาธรรมศาสตร์และการเมือง] [list of universities established in Thailand], it was later renamed Thammasat University.

[8] Pridi's own lectures on the legal system conveyed the importance of rights held by the people, evidence that Thailand already recognised many rights and the fundamental importance of the Western rule of law (2000).

[9] This vignette and others in this chapter are based on my interviews between 2006 and 2014 unless otherwise indicated.

military government. His career took a sharp turn back towards law when he chose to defend himself before a military tribunal and successfully sued for release of fellow political prisoners. Thongbai's account of this experience in his autobiography made him an icon among student leaders of the 1973 popular uprising that toppled a military dictator. After the military's return to power in 1976, Thongbai defended the students, winning international acclaim from human rights advocates and a prestigious international human rights award in 1984.

B. Law and Development under the 'Bureaucratic Polity'

Two factors contributed to the profession's slow expansion. Although constitutional in form, Thailand's government continued to be animated by values other than Pridi's rule of law ideals. Anticipating challenges to the monarchy's legitimacy from modernisation and eventual democratisation, Rama VI (1910–25), third in the line of modernising monarchs, had promulgated a state ideology built upon Thai traditions and modern democratic ideals. His influential formulation of a 'civic religion' with deep roots in Thailand's history embodied his understanding of the spiritual and moral fabric of modern Thailand's communities and citizens and the monarch's importance as caretaker of the people. The 1932 coup leaders who overthrew his successor, far from breaking with the principles of this 'civic religion' – Nation, Religion, Monarchy – embraced its terms to legitimate their constitutional government, adding constitutionalism as the embodiment of its democratic elements (Connors 2001). The judiciary's predisposition to reject challenges to the constitutional legitimacy of governments supported by the monarchy has been reinforced by careful cultivation of the Thai monarch as a unifying symbol (Reynolds 1978; Baker and Phongpaichit 2009).

After Pridi's exile in 1949, military governments became authoritarian and nationalist. Thailand was ruled by its 'bureaucratic polity' (Riggs 1966), a network of powerful bureaucrats, military leaders, and the monarchy linked to heads of dominant business clans by mutually beneficial, sometimes fractious, patron-client relationships. Constitutions were abrogated and rewritten to reflect winners in their power struggles, and parliaments had limited independence.

Many have judged the rule of law in Thailand from the tumultuous course of its politics, but it should be no surprise that the country's dominating state administration has been an important factor in determining the power of law and the role of the legal profession in mediating the relationship between citizens and state. The value orientation of Thailand's bureaucratic system at mid-century was not productivity, rationality and efficiency. Rather, as Siffin argued (1966: 161–62), the bureaucracy is 'a social system, or at least as a major subsystem of Thai society ... [that] reflects and supports basic social values', including hierarchy, personalism, and security, because being a bureaucrat was a way of life and a social status.[10]

---

[10] Among other qualities that diverge from Western liberal values, there was no sense of equality, due process or individual rights. Siffin noted a special feature of the system, which he called 'the override'. A high-ranking official 'can often sweep aside rules which impede his immediate aims; political officials at the very top of the system can sometimes do this almost without specific limitations of their power' (1966: 163).

Following World War II, Thailand became the Asian showcase for free market capitalism. Guided by World Bank plans and fuelled by foreign investment, the bureaucratic polity implemented policies that facilitated development while profiting from banks and businesses owned in partnership with Sino-Thai business leaders. As in other Asian bureaucratic states (but with more equal partnerships because of the relative power and independence of leading Sino-Thai business conglomerates), control of the economy was maintained through continuing patron-client relationships between government and favoured entrepreneurs, retarding development of a meaningful rule-based regulatory system and reducing the importance of courts and lawyers in power struggles. Nevertheless, regulatory infrastructure was added, including the establishment of special labour and intellectual property courts, not only to improve the performance of banks and the management of trade policy but also to protect foreign private investors (Vichai 2001).

The Asian Financial Crisis of 1997, triggered in part by missteps of Thai administrators, prompted another round of intervention by the World Bank, IMF, and foreign advisers counselling constitutional reform to create more effective oversight of government. The liberal constitutional reform that year established not only a democratic government but also independent institutions for law-based oversight: a Constitutional Court, administrative courts, and other oversight agencies. As the private sector has become stronger and more independent, courts and lawyers have grown more important as technicians and litigators, but the profession's identity as overseer of government compliance with law has shallow roots.

C. Practice of Law as a Common Calling

By the middle of the twentieth century, expansion of higher education was among the first investments by American and Thai funders seeking to staff expanding ministries to serve and manage a developing economy and civil society and to establish a private sector and middle class. Prior to 1960, five universities existed, only one of which offered a law degree to a limited number of students. The university system expanded rapidly through the mid-1990s, tracking expansion of the Thai economy and taking off again after enactment of the 1997 Constitution (see Table 1).[11] An increasingly popular route for upward mobility, by 2014 an LLB approved by the Lawyers Council could be earned at 14 of Thailand's 26 'closed' (selective admission) public universities, its two 'open' (unrestricted admission) public universities, and 27 private universities.[12]

---

[11] Between 1990 and 1998 alone, 11 new universities opened, many offering a law degree (see summary of university web page sources at th.wikipedia.org/wiki/รายชื่อมหาวิทยาลัยของรัฐในประเทศไทยเรียงตามการสถาปนา).

[12] See www.lawyerscouncil.or.th/news/. In addition, 29 former teachers colleges have upgraded programmes offering law degrees on the approved list (see Rajabat University Act B.E.2547 available at www.ratchakitcha.soc.go.th/DATA/PDF/0AA/00141755.PDF). Graduates from programmes not on the list, including graduates from foreign law schools, are limited to work as a legal clerk unless they earn a second law degree, typically at one of the open universities. Graduates of foreign law schools are often hired by global firms (see text) to work as advisers to foreign businesses even though they cannot litigate in Thai courts. The Thai Bar Association publishes a separate list of approved Thai and foreign universities offering LLB degrees required to take the Thai Bar Exam, a prerequisite for prosecutorial, judicial and more prestigious government offices (Thai Bar Association Institute of Legal Education at www.thethaibar.or.th/thaibarweb/files/Data_web/3_%20Kong_Borikan/thabian_naksueksa/un_thethabar122018.pdf).

Table 1 University Graduates and Law Graduates by Gender 1991–2016

Year	University graduates Total	% female	Law graduates Total	% female
1991	59,654	n/a	5,239	n/a
1992	61,658	n/a	5,260	n/a
1993	63,749	n/a	4,941	n/a
1994	68,503	n/a	5,266	n/a
1995	71,048	n/a	4,997	n/a
1996	61,009	54	4,861	19
1997	65,892	54	6,214	19
1998	69,532	56	4,048	24
1999	73,647	56	4,934	24
2000	80,671	57	5,171	28
2001	93,764	58	5,849	31
2002	82,158	55	5,932	31
2003	220,142	59	6639	37
2004	257,881	n/a	n/a	–
2005	272,886	62	n/a	–
2006	259,089	62	11,059	40
2007	268,508	61	9,747	41
2008	289,413	61	7,841	43
2009	274,473	60	9,634	43
2010	231,733	61	9,833	45
2011	248,871	61	8,129	45
2012	182,216	61	7,246	43
2013	140,653	64	7,867	43
2014	245,566	62	8,311	47
2015	262,807	63	6,888	51
2016	220,768	65	4,063	52

Sources: Bureau of Policy and Planning (1998; 1997–2004); Information Center Bureau of Administration (2005–06); Office of Higher Education Commission data for 2006–16 available at www.info.mua.go.th/information.

The trend suggests that law practice has become well-established among the middle class. Notwithstanding low-cost state schools and attempts to introduce a nationwide admissions test,[13] increasing economic stratification has meant that the most prestigious

---

[13] Versions of this state-administered test have been in place since the 1970s (see Association of the Council of University Presidents of Thailand found at a.cupt.net/aboutadm.php).

'closed' universities are increasingly the preserve of students from upper middle-class families and recruiting stations for elite Bangkok law firms.

Historically, women were all but excluded from legal education and barred from government jobs and the judiciary.[14] Legal barriers to government employment have been removed, and enrolment of women in universities, and LLB programmes in particular, increased steadily from the 1970s. The number of female graduates now exceeds that of male graduates in higher education generally and law schools in particular (see Table 1). Somewhat lower percentages of women pass the Thai Bar or Attorneys Bar Examinations each year, qualifying them to become a prosecutor or judge or to law practise law, respectively (Table 2).

Table 2 Bar Passage by Gender, 2011–16

Year	Thai Bar Pass		Attorneys Bar Pass	
	Total	% female	Total	% female
2011	n/a	–	1,918	46
2012	1,231	44	3,087	46
2013	1,227	46	3,182	55
2014	1,485	46	2,599	46
2015	1,302	49	2,420	45
2016	928	48	1,630	42

Source: Thai Bar data courtesy of Thai Bar Association; Attorneys Bar data from Lawyers Council (2011–15) and unpublished 2016 data courtesy of the Lawyers Council.

Women have benefited from the expansion of middle class professions, and law flexibly offers opportunities for both independence and family. Many women have established law practices of their own or in small firms with men, but few Thai women lawyers work for larger, more prominent local[15] or international firms.[16] Women are comparatively well represented among leaders of NGOs and their attorneys and as staff lawyers in government service, and they are regularly appointed to offices and commissions concerned with human rights and gender-related policy issues (Vichit-Vadakan 2008). Few have held high government office.[17]

---

[14] The first woman law graduate was admitted as a barrister in 1930: Library of Congress, Women in History: Lawyers and Judges, available at blogs.loc.gov/law/2015/03/women-in-history-lawyers-and-judges/. The first woman was appointed a judge of the Royal Thai Courts in 1965: National Statistical Office of Thailand web. nso.go.th/gender/estatus.htm.

[15] See subsection E below.

[16] During a year of interviewing lawyers at half a dozen large Bangkok firms, I met English and Italian women but few Thai women. One female lawyer, a prominent member of the National Human Rights Commission in 2007, confirmed that women encounter barriers to career advancement.

[17] The recently deposed female Prime Minister, Yingluck Shinawatra, may be the exception that proves the rule, since she served as the surrogate for her brother, Thaksin Shinawatra, removed from the same office in 2006 by a military coup.

D. Licensing and Oversight of Practitioners, Judges, Prosecutors

Regulation of the profession is divided between two statutory entities. The Thai Bar Association, established in 1914, primarily represents the interests of elite professionals – judges and prosecutors. The Lawyers Council, established in 1985, licenses and oversees the practising bar. Judges and prosecutors, although no longer recruited predominantly from a particular social class, comprise a highly select group who typically enter bureaucratic careers shortly after law school. Candidates complete a course of study with the Thai Bar Association and must pass the difficult Thai Bar Exam.

Graduates of the royal law school were permitted to appear in court if they passed an exam at the end of their studies. Other attorneys could be admitted to practise within designated commercial centres. Both forms of admission were acknowledged in the 1914 Attorneys Act, which created two kinds of licences, a First Class licence for applicants with an LLB and a Second Class licence awarded at the discretion of the Director General of Judges for Bangkok for practice only in that jurisdiction. The express purpose of the 1914 Attorneys Act was to prevent fraud and incompetence. More specifically, licensing served the monarchy's goal of modernising Thai law by ensuring that attorneys who appeared before government administrators or judges were knowledgeable about the new system of government administration and the legal code modelled on Western practices unfamiliar to most Thai.[18]

Thailand's current legislation, the 1985 Lawyers Act, creates a single class of practitioner licences required for all activities related to representing a client in court (including counselling and drafting documents) (Institute for Developing Economies 2001: 50). Licensing does not apply to the much larger number of law graduates who advise clients about legal matters without representing them in court, including 'legal advisers' working in businesses or government.[19] Trainees and associates working for other lawyers and lawyers on the staff of an NGO or other organisation may also be unlicensed. The Lawyers Council, established by the Lawyers Act, enforces licensing requirements, oversees and regulates practitioners, and occasionally provides expert opinions to Parliamentary committees. To obtain a licence, an applicant must be a Thai citizen with an LLB or related law degree, pass a practitioner's Bar exam and complete a training course run by the Lawyers Council, and practise for a period under supervision in a law office. Until 2017, foreign lawyers were not permitted to practise in Thailand, but plans to remove this limitation are under consideration by the Thai Parliament following recent ASEAN Economic Council free trade requirements.

The Lawyers Council estimates that there are more than 83,000 licensed practitioners in Thailand, but its officials believe that only about 20,000 actively engage in

---

[18] Although maintenance of professional monopolies dominates much Western scholarship about professions, this probably was not the motive for early forms of regulation in Thailand. In 1914, lawyers in private practice were few. Subsequent regulation of the profession made a licence mandatory for court appearances but not for giving legal advice, leaving a vast unregulated terrain of unlicensed competition, which the Lawyers Council has never challenged.

[19] The Lawyers Council estimates that fewer than 25 per cent of licensed practitioners are actively practising, which may indicate a glut of law graduates.

private practice.[20] Through 2016, the Lawyers Council had registered 9,530 law firms, 8,265 notaries (mostly attorneys), and 1,479 debt collection firms.[21]

The Lawyers Council is also charged with establishing a committee to oversee lawyers' ethics by hearing complaints from the judiciary and members of the public about lawyers' conduct.[22] While the Lawyers Council recently adopted regulations for licensing notaries, a service typically performed by practising lawyers, there is little evidence of any interest in defending a professional monopoly by extending licensing to legal advisers.

E. Global Law and Bangkok's Largest Firms[23]

The role of lawyers and law firms in Thailand's distinctive form of capitalist development must be left to future research,[24] but there is no disputing that commercial centres like Bangkok are well-supplied with lawyers who thrive on Thailand's businesses. Although many of the 60 firms advertising in Martindale.com list personal injury and domestic relations among their services, most focus on international commercial transactions, intellectual property, and finance. These firms average ten or more lawyers, the largest five listing 25–75.[25] Back office needs of businesses, such as collections and employee relations, domestic relations, property and criminal cases are bread and butter for a much larger number of smaller firms and individual practitioners who do not subscribe to Martindale.com.

This discussion will be limited to Thailand's ten largest firms, all located in Bangkok and dominated by international business interests. The oldest global firms, founded by foreign lawyers trained in England or Europe, have roots in Thailand's early economic

---

[20] Data courtesy of the Lawyers Council. The Lawyers Council makes 'some adjustment' for mortality but does not update its registry of permanent members, requiring no periodic renewal of membership.

[21] Data courtesy of the Lawyers Council. In 2016, the Thailand Department of Business Development reported more than 3,000 businesses registered to supply legal services, a figure that excludes NGOs, foundations and other not-for-profits offering legal representation. Notaries are similar in function to common law counterparts, and most are attorneys in practice. Debt collection firms are required to register with the Lawyers Council under the Debt Collection Act of 2015.

[22] In 2015, the Lawyers Council reported new 280 complaints, terminated the licences of 76 attorneys, and suspended or reprimanded 135 (Lawyers Council 2016).

[23] The frequently used terms 'global' and 'local' are imprecise, referring sometimes to the proportion of international clientele and sometimes to the location of the firm's principal office and its ownership. Neither term adequately captures the complex story of firm origins or the fact that 'international' business matters drive many practices at all levels and in firms of all sizes.

[24] Hewison (1989) argues that long-standing personal networks linking powerful bureaucrats and wealthy Thai bankers rendered economic modernisation and development relatively independent of control by international counterparts and global financial institutions. His extraordinarily rich findings demonstrating the lasting power of networks centred on Sino-Thai banking families, among others, raise important questions about the applicability of Western theories predicting the influence of democratic constitutionalism, rule of law, and neoliberalism, forces that have shaped the legal profession in Europe and the US.

[25] Information about the size of firms is contradictory. For example, while some internet sources claim that Baker McKenzie Bangkok has over 50 partners and 200 associates, Martindale.com suggests the number of lawyers working in the Bangkok office was considerably smaller. Interviews with firm partners in 2008 suggested that Baker McKenzie had 7 partners and 55 associates (in close agreement with Martindale.com), while Allen & Overy had five partners and 25 associates. I have relied on Martindale.com and, where possible, interviews to estimate size.

development. Tillike & Gibbons, currently Thailand's second largest firm by revenues,[26] was founded by a Sri Lankan solicitor in 1894. Domnern, Somgiat & Boonma Law Office, the eighth largest and an early offshoot of Tilleke, was founded by a Danish lawyer. Recent additions to the top ten are also Thai owned. KTB Law Ltd, third largest, is a subsidiary of Krung Thai Bank, a major banking conglomerate and political powerhouse. Weerawon, Chinnavat & Partners, Ltd, fourth largest, is an independent firm spun off by White & Case in 2009 as the New York firm downsized in the wake of the 2008 financial crisis. Siam Premier International Law Office, tenth largest, established by Thai lawyers in 1990, is representative of later generations who graduated from elite law schools (Thammasat, Chulalongkorn or Ramkamhaeng) and earned a further degree in the US. Five of the top ten have no affiliation with a global firm but instead have filled a gap by expanding regionally.

Baker McKenzie remains by far the largest firm, measured by revenues. The Chicago-based firm established itself in Bangkok in the 1980s by absorbing a Thai firm, and the office's managing partner has remained a Thai. UK Magic Circle firms Allen & Overy and Linklaters are among the other global firms with Bangkok offices and, like Baker McKenzie, are managed by Thai lawyers. One of Bangkok's large indigenous firms, Chandler & Thong-ek, established in 1971 by a Harvard graduate, was acquired in 2016 by the Japanese global firm MHM to become Chandler MHM. Its 54 lawyers make it one of Bangkok's largest.[27] It is especially interesting that as firm revenues have steadily risen, tracking the GDP,[28] ownership of Thailand's international legal services continues to shift from the US and Europe toward Thailand and Asia.

Firms servicing international businesses generally require that new lawyers have training outside Thailand and know other languages. Graduates of Bangkok's elite law schools are rarely employed without study abroad or extensive retraining by the firm. Partners, both Thai and non-Thai, viewed those graduates as inadequately prepared for practice. Dissatisfaction with Thai law graduates arises from two sources: first, the mismatch between legal education based on rigid statutory construction and international law practice dominated by aggressive common law advocacy; and second, what Western-trained lawyers perceive as an embedded system of social deference unsuited to client representation. Some Thai lawyers saw deference as potentially the most effective way of obtaining agreement; but others viewed it as a problem deriving from the broad discretion wielded by Thai bureaucrats unchecked by rules a lawyer can invoke.

Bangkok's largest firms do little pro bono work as that concept is understood by Western legal professions. While the firms have given money to causes such as a fund for women's health or tsunami relief, several partners expressed the view that the Lawyers Council (described further below) is responsible for doing legal work on behalf of the public. In other ways, Bangkok's largest firms reflect the influence of global norms, for example, by offering more opportunities for women. One female Baker McKenzie partner said she had experienced no discrimination in the Bangkok office, noting that the

---

[26] Based on law firm gross income 2013–16, reported online by the Thailand Ministry of Commerce, Thailand Department of Business Development found at datawarehouse.dbd.go.th/.
[27] See chandlermhm.com/news-3-august-2016.
[28] See data.worldbank.org/country/thailand.

managing partner at the time was a Thai woman. She estimated that about 30 per cent of the lawyers in the Bangkok office were female, but a smaller percentage were partners because they had begun their careers much more recently than their male partners.

F. Lawyers in Civic Life: Legal Aid, Public Office and Politics

In 1985, the Lawyers Act charged the Lawyers Council with responsibility for providing legal assistance to the poor, supported by an annual Parliamentary appropriation. Both the Office of the Public Prosecutor and the Thai Bar Association also have a statutory duty to provide legal assistance through voluntary efforts of staff members (prosecutors) or paid staff and volunteer private attorneys (Thai Bar Association).[29] Lawyers Council funds give volunteer lawyers a small per diem to cover travel, room and board, while the Thai Bar Association pays fees to volunteer lawyers.[30] All three organisations annually report significant numbers of persons advised or represented in legal matters (Department of Civil Rights Protection and Legal Aid 2002–16; Jaiharn et al 2004; Lawyers Council 2012–16).[31] However, in 2014 the US State Department concluded that legal aid in Thailand has been carried out 'on an intermittent, voluntary and public-service basis' and was 'of low standard'.[32]

Thailand's legal profession, especially its global elite, stays out of politics.[33] Lawyers have run for office and served in appointed positions, especially those requiring legal expertise, such as the Ministry of Justice or the National Human Rights Commission; but a law degree has not been a vehicle for entering politics, as it has in Europe or the US.[34] While lawyers are becoming indispensable for managing the technical requirements of business and government, and business litigation is increasing, lawyers have not become political power brokers, nor is the profession identified with defending legal

---

[29] The 2007 Thai Constitution Art 40(7) and (8) guaranteed state subsidised legal representation in both civil and criminal cases. The new, military-drafted constitution ratified by popular referendum in 2016 has no similar provisions.

[30] The Lawyers Council has a number of programmes for advice and litigation assistance under which lawyers receive a small per diem for expenses, limiting the attorneys willing to take cases to the relatively inexperienced or unusually dedicated.

[31] In the most recent year for which reports are available, the Prosecutors Office provided legal advice in 43,009 cases, the Thai Bar Association in 205, and the Lawyers Council in 2,656. The Lawyers Council alone has the resources to engage in extensive, complex litigation. Additional data courtesy of these organisations and interviews by the author.

[32] US Department of State, Bureau of Democracy, Human Rights and Labor (2014) *Country Report on Human Rights Practices for 2014* (Thailand), at www.state.gov/j/drl/rls/hrrpt/humanrightsreport/index.htm?year=2014&dlid=236480.

[33] Elite global lawyers, both Thai and non-Thai, may exercise considerable influence on economic regulation using the leverage of international business and finance. For example, in 2010 a Cabinet proposal to bar international contract arbitration agreements, prompted by the Ministry of Justice's belief that too many international arbitrations favoured foreign businesses, was dropped in part because of the threatened loss of international business.

[34] The 1997 Constitution required first-time Parliamentary candidates to have a bachelor's degree (exempting those previously elected). The proportion of representatives with an LLB rose to about 20 per cent (compared to about 40 per cent in the US Congress in 2016, an all-time low): Const 2540 BE Sec 107(3). The 1997 Constitution was abrogated after a military coup in 2006, and later constitutions (2007 and 2017) dropped the requirement: Const 2550 BE Sec 101. Const 2560 Art 97.

or political rights. Nevertheless, Thailand's strife over democracy, political authority, and commitment to constitutionalism has enhanced the salience of law and created new opportunities to mobilise it for social change.

III. SEEDS OF INDEPENDENCE

This Part describes four interrelated sources of change in the political importance of the rule of law and the role of practitioners: (1) the rise of the revolutionary 'October Generation'; (2) the emergence of a self-sustaining community of social justice advocates; (3) women lawyers sponsoring reform; and (4) adoption of the 1997 'Peoples Constitution' and its aftermath.

A. The October Generation

Marut Bunnag

Marut's family descended from famous advisers to the monarchy in the nineteenth century. He attended Thammasat University in 1947, distinguishing himself as a student by speaking out against the military and, after graduation, rejecting a secure government post to work for a small law firm. Soon after graduating, Marut established his own firm to handle local cases, representing political dissidents, accused criminals and unpopular causes, and later a family firm representing business clients. After the 1973 uprising, he connected with advocates for groups of workers, farmers, and others newly mobilised to contest injustices long ignored by the government. Both firms mentored and credentialed October Generation law graduates and later generations drawn to activism. Marut's activism coloured his relationship with the Thai Bar Association. Objecting to its elitism, reflected in licensing regulations granting only graduates of Chulalongkorn University (successor to several royal schools) a diploma privilege to enter the profession, in 1957 he helped organise a voluntary association to protect the rights of lawyers and provide free legal aid. The Lawyers Association took public stands against the legality of orders issued by the military government under martial law or by military courts. Taking advantage of the 1973 opening, he won a position on the Thai Bar Association council, where he and his colleagues achieved limited reforms. Appointed Minister of Justice following amnesty in 1979, Marut sponsored the 1985 Lawyers Act establishing the Lawyers Council with independent authority to license practitioners and public funding to provide legal aid.

On 14 October 1973, a student-led uprising toppled an oppressive military dictator, a turning point in modern Thai history. The uprising and subsequent three years of vibrant democracy have long been remembered by the so-called October Generation as a moment of shared hopes and a reminder of the value of constitutionalism and political liberalisation. But that ended with a brutal crackdown on 6 October 1976, which slaughtered students, led to arrest and trial for many, and forced thousands to flee, some seeking sanctuary with communist cadres on Thailand's borders. Benedict Anderson's (1998) seminal essay on the October uprising suggests that its importance lay not only in the participants' ideals but also, more importantly, in successful participation by non-elites in a political system historically dominated by elite insiders. Anderson concluded that the two events, uprising and crushing reprisal, are keys to understanding the contemporary political situation, in which entrenched, traditional elites struggle to adapt to the emergence of new, potentially powerful social groups.

In the 1960s, an expanding university system opened higher education to students whose families had previously been unable to access it. The students quickly discovered that they knew little about their country's politics or people. New ideas about society and government flowed not only from Western-educated faculty but also from neighbouring China and Vietnam, where popular revolutions and confrontations with Western powers offered alternatives. The first NGOs were created with faculty guidance to assist long-neglected communities – projects that became models for continuing 'Thai-style' NGOs and activism by October Generation lawyers. The military dictator's failure to adopt a constitution violated the 'civic religion' underlying the legitimacy of elite-dominated governments, but the demand for a constitution from below was unprecedented. A new vision of the rule of law was introduced, if not fully realised or universally appreciated, animating efforts to use law to advance social causes and effect change (Lertchoosakul 2016).

B. Lawyers for Social Causes

Even before graduation, October Generation students pursued projects for social change, supplementing the government's deficient health or educational programmes, documenting poverty, and supporting farmers mobilising in the countryside, unions seeking better treatment from employers, and residents of neglected slums. Graduates worked with lawyers like Marut and Thongbai, who were prepared to embrace these causes. Others joined newly formed NGOs offering legal assistance to the poor, such as the faculty-organised Thammasat Legal Services Center. A particularly influential NGO, the Union for Civil Liberties (UCL), was established by two European-educated university academics in 1973 to raise popular consciousness about the rule of law and human rights. Disappointed with the results, the founders turned to 'campaigns' for rights awareness in targeted communities and legal support for collective action, providing training and social capital and disseminating a discourse of human rights and government accountability among lawyers and NGO leaders, which unified subsequent generations (Connors 2001; Munger 2015). During the brief window for democracy between 1973 and 1976, lawyers working with social causes discovered that law could become a weapon of the weak (Haberkorn 2011).

In 1976, projects for change that had nurtured professional and political independence were suppressed; UCL was specifically targeted and its staff arrested. Thousands of activists were forced to flee to the jungle, where many joined communist cadres on the Thai border. After amnesty in 1979, semi-democratic governments under military supervision, more responsive to international criticism of Thailand's human rights violations, permitted moderate NGOs and community-based organisations to pursue reform. Returning October Generation lawyers founded NGOs and small firms to aid these projects, recruiting new generations of lawyers to their cause.

Two broadly defined strategies employed law as an instrument of change, each requiring consequential commitments (Munger 2014; 2015). First, networks of personal influence could connect October Generation NGO activists with foreign funders, sympathetic government collaborators, and even less activist officials who viewed collaboration as advantageous for their work. Second, social movement and local community mobilisation provided alternative resources for change. As a network of anti-development NGOs emerged in the 1980s to resist government-sponsored projects that displaced communities, polluted landscapes, or destroyed means of livelihood, lawyers became community advisers, legal strategists, and popular educators (Connors 2001: 262). With the support of government, anti-development NGOs formed a peak bargaining council to discuss broader issues of development and change with government officials. In 1991, leading social justice lawyers joined a bloody rebellion led by Bangkok's middle class against a dictator who broke his commitment to restore civilian control, becoming leaders of a movement for constitutional reform. Lawyers from the network became spokespersons and intermediaries, informing broad segments of the public about the progress of constitutional reform and, in turn, communicating demands for change to the drafting the 1997 liberal Constitution.

C. Elite Women and Gender Advocacy

Tamara Loos argues that failure to fully implement constitutional and statutory mandates for equality revealed the determination of elite rulers to preserve Thailand's male-dominated social hierarchy and Buddhist heritage (2006: 11). Women fought to implement full legal equality, using their positions as lawyers and wives of powerful men. Thammasat University's open admissions allowed women to enter the legal profession in significant numbers for the first time in 1933. In 1947, 80 female graduates established a legal aid programme, focusing on gender inequality.[35] In 1955, the same group founded the Women Lawyers Association of Thailand under the Queen's patronage and soon launched a campaign for women's equality, joining other women's organisations to draft legislation permitting the appointment of women as civil servants and judges (Doneys 2002). In 1961, the Queen provided funding for a National Women's Council, which has grown into an influential source of support for women leaders and programmes for women and families.

The basis of women's advocacy for change has shifted over time, especially after the democratic opening in 1973. A broader and more effective women's movement was one important outcome. Women lawyers elected to the National Legislative Assembly in 1974 succeeded in adding the first gender equality clause to Thailand's constitution (Pruekpongsawalee 2004). In the 1970s and 1980s, women founded many of the first and most influential 'Thai-style' NGOs to address issues of family, poverty, and human trafficking, among others. These NGOs employed an innovative strategy that deployed the force of law for change through a network of relationships extending inside government. In the 1990s, the Women Lawyers Association used its far-reaching local network and relationships with other women's reform groups to create a cohesive women's movement and mobilise popular support for constitutional reform (Doneys 2002). Since the late 1990s,

---

[35] In 1943, the newly created Ministry of Culture established an Office of Culture on Women's Affairs to promote the traditional role of women; but under the direction of the Prime Minister's wife, it sought to improve the status and treatment of women

more women than men have enrolled in law at universities, and women lawyers continue to lead NGOs and foundations challenging government authority.[36]

D. Constitutionalism and New Courts

Somchai Homla-or

Somchai is an October Generation lawyer activist with a distinguished legal career. After the 1973 uprising, he worked on farmers' land rights but was also a leader in his generation of activists. In 1976 he was arrested but escaped to live with communist cadres until amnesty was declared. Identified by the military as a communist sympathiser, he was driven from his post as UCL director in 1985 and forced to flee again, this time to the Asian Human Rights Centre in Hong Kong and eventually the US, where he studied human rights practices. On his return, he became a leading voice for human rights and the rule of law, taking to the streets in 1992 to resist an overreaching military dictator and becoming a leader of the popular movement for constitutional reform. After constitutional reform in 1997, he was appointed chair of the Human Rights Committee of the Lawyers Council, where he organised a national network of social cause lawyers to make use of the new courts and rights. Specialised working groups selected problems brought by social movements and NGOs, devising litigation strategies to shape legal principles. A lasting effect of Somchai's Committee has been the development of expertise and innovative litigation, absent among conventional lawyers. Lawyers working with the Committee were among the first to use the new administrative courts to push ministries for more responsive policies, an example followed by lawyers less interested in community welfare than fees and reputation.

By 1997, a critical mass of support existed for meaningful constitutional accountability, but constituencies for reform were deeply divided about the principles of limited government. Liberal royalists who controlled the drafting process promoted an impressive Bill of Rights, an independent Constitutional Court, administrative courts, independent watchdog agencies to manage elections and control corruption, and full democracy, responding to critics and following the prescriptions of Western advisers.[37] In the draft they prepared, Thailand was described as a democracy 'with the King as head of state', linking national identity and the government's legitimacy to the monarchy's moral authority. Far from rejecting Nation–Religion–Monarchy, these framers intended to translate the civic religion into the language of the new Constitution (Connors 2001). Although clauses of this celebrated constitution appear to retain legitimacy even after the 2006 military coup abrogated it (Ginsburg 2009b), its original meaning is deeply contested by different interpretations of the 1997 political settlement.

The Human Rights Committee of the Lawyers Council, organised by October Generation activist Somchai Homla-or, has won notable legal victories. Attorneys in the network have blocked government plans to privatise important public services, closed an important

---

[36] Prominent NGOs and public interest law firms established by women include: Community Resource Centre, Human Rights Lawyers Association, SR Law and iLaw (established by a non-lawyer in collaboration with lawyers), Friends of Women, FACE International, and ECPAT (now ECPAT Thailand) and the legal arm of the Center for Protection of Child Rights, and TRAFCORD.

[37] Thailand is not alone in Asia in placing its faith in constitutional and administrative courts or seeking to preserve elite hegemony (Ginsberg 2009a; Hirschl 2004).

industrial park because of environmental violations, initiated 'SLAPP-back'[38] litigation, and expanded compensable litigation costs, enabling poor communities to participate in lengthy court battles. Lawyers Council attorneys brought the first class-action test case in 2015 under newly enacted legislation, while major businesses and global firms watched from the sidelines.[39]

Few of these victories were won in the Constitutional Court, which has done little to develop the promising bill of rights introduced by the 1997 Constitution (and strengthened by the 2007 constitution) (Klein 2003). Furthermore, following the 2006 military coup and revision of the procedures for selecting judges of the Constitutional Court, it has been accused of politicisation for favouring policies advocated by elites allied with the monarchy and failing to place constitutional limits on the military's power (McCargo 2014). Lawyers for social causes have litigated successfully in either the administrative courts or Royal Courts of Justice, which have been more willing to impose the rule of law on Thai bureaucrats; but none of Thailand's high courts has challenged the political order represented by the monarchy and its network.

E. A Politically Divided Profession

While the Human Rights Committee was gathering momentum, political conditions rapidly changed. After abandoning politics in the 1990s, the military has stepped in twice, in 2006 and 2014, ending elected Red Shirt governments and suspending constitutions enacted by Parliament. Unexpectedly, the military's return in 2006 divided the lawyers who had advocated for rights and accountability under law, not only by political 'colour' but also by differences about the legitimacy of the two military coups. Although voluntary associations of lawyers were part of the evolution of the profession (eg the Women Lawyers Association and Marut's voluntary Lawyers Association), they have become far more overtly political. In 2010, the elected President of the Lawyers Council issued a statement supporting the 2006 coup. A group of young critics openly challenged the Lawyers Council's failure to uphold the rule of law; and in 2014, following the second coup, the same group formed the Human Rights Lawyers Association to defend political prisoners and document government abuses. The Lawyers Association organised by Marut in the 1950s remained moribund until lawyers supporting the Red Shirt cause revived it, making it their platform.

The conflict among lawyers is deeper than partisan politics. Two groups of elite legal academics hold opposing views about the legitimacy of military invention and the meaning of the 1997 Constitution. Their debates over the legality of actions taken by Red Shirt and coup governments have so far avoided the suppression that silenced the press and intimidated ordinary Thais. Persecution of lawyers for victims of state violence under Thaksin and the military is further evidence of law's growing political salience.

---

[38] SLAPP is an acronym for 'strategic litigation against public participation', typically brought against public interest organisations as a preemptive strategy to discourage opposition to a corporation's development plans.
[39] *Royal Gazette* (8 April 2015); see also www.tilleke.com/resources/class-action-legal-proceedings-now-available-thailand) and litigation described in Bangkok Post (28 May 2016) at www.bangkokpost.com/print/991641/.

Most spectacularly, the leader of the Muslim Lawyers Association, formed with Somchai Homla-or's support to represent victims of Thaksin's brutal military occupation of the Muslim provinces in the south, was assassinated in 2004 by members of the Thai police, a murder never fully investigated. Members of the Human Rights Lawyers Association have been harassed and arrested for representing protesters and student dissidents, and the military has employed defamation law to suppress reports of its human rights violations and invoked the country's anachronistic *lèse majesté* laws to punish anything deemed critical of government authority on the theory that it is an attack on the King.[40]

Thailand's first exposure to mass party politics, followed by the rapid rise of a powerful and autocratic prime minister, exposed lawyers' political disarray and deep disagreements about the military's extra-constitutional authority. The coups might easily be dismissed as a familiar failure of liberal government in a Global South state, backsliding on the path to modern democracy, or evidence of traditional elites' refusal to yield power. But unexpected conflict among the most committed advocates for the rule of law shows that, in Thailand (and perhaps elsewhere), there is a more complex story about constitutional reform, the meaning of the rule of law, and the role of the legal profession in social change.

IV. CONCLUSION: LEGACIES AND PROSPECTS FOR CHANGE

Sor Rattanamanee Pokla

Sor's life weaves through Thailand's political upheavals. The eldest of five from a family of farmers in Thailand's south, she was fortunate to attend university. Educating daughters is now more common (though not for an eldest child who could work to support her poor family). Her parents were retired government workers who bought a farm, placing them among the middle class in their community. Sor entered Thammasat Law School, graduating in 1986 under a stable semi-democracy supervised by the military. A decade after the uprising, students continued to visit the countryside, volunteering to help communities. Sor was deeply influenced by a fourth-year student she met at the Rule of Law Club, Surachai Trong-ngam, already well-known as an activist. Guided by faculty to a small firm, she became a business lawyer first, learned her trade, and (to her surprise) liked litigation. Still moved by Thammasat's activist tradition and the October uprising, she reconnected with Surachai in 2000, quickly becoming his partner in litigation. In the mid-1990s, Surachai had joined four other lawyers to form a firm devoted to social causes. When administrative courts opened for business in 2001, Surachai filed a case challenging inadequate oversight of waste disposal, winning a new standard for reasonableness and, eventually, damages against the polluter. Sor and Surachai worked on the first cases demonstrating the willingness of administrative and civil courts to hold private companies and Thai bureaucrats accountable for policies and practices causing widespread injury. In 2007, she was awarded an Asian Human Rights Commission internship, followed by an invitation to join the staff of the Asian Legal Research Centre. International contacts, knowledge of human rights conventions and practical experience working with the Centre informed her litigation strategies when she returned to launch her own law office in 2010. The Open Society Institute

---

[40] In 2014, the leader of the legal scholars who challenged the constitutional legitimacy of the coup government was ordered by the military to enter its reeducation program (*Thailand News*, 18 June 2014, at www.thailandnews.co/tag/worajet-pakeerat/).

funded her proposal to open a public interest law firm, the Community Resource Centre, to defend the land tenure and environmental rights of poor communities. Sor does not consider herself a partisan in Thailand's political conflict, nor does she concern herself with the Constitutional Court's seeming indifference to constitutionalism. Her string of victories for local government accountability and remedies against corporations have been won in administrative and civil courts. Her command of English has enabled her to develop a growing network of international contacts who provide professional support. She is neither Red nor Yellow, but 'sa-lim' [สลิ่ม] (a multi-coloured Indian dessert – slang for politically undecided). Her work in the courts and out of the spotlight attracts judicial allies and finds openings for law created by the shifting balance of power underlying Thailand's political upheavals.

This chapter views the role of Thailand's legal profession through a broader lens, taking into account evolving institutions and politics that go far towards explaining the profession's changing demography, organisation, and status. Pressures for change as well as opportunities for adaptation arose from multiple sources at many different levels. Dezalay and Garth (2010) argue that the rule of law can be institutionalised by lawyer entrepreneurs who find openings to convert political or social capital – conferred by an independent judiciary, strong popular movements, or individual lawyers' elite standing – into the force of law. Notwithstanding the fact that in Thailand each of these sources of lawyer independence appear to be relatively weak, law has become an increasingly effective 'weapon of the weak', inspiring new strategies by NGOs and social movements. Important opportunities were created by the 1973 uprising and the 1997 Constitution and its 'afterlife' following two military coups (Ginsburg 2009b). Constitutionalism and rule of law are potent legacies, but they are legacies that continue to evolve under pressures from the loss of political standing by liberal elites, the determination of military leaders to retain power, and a consequent closing of political space.

The judiciary is a prime example of subtle, incremental change that will influence the role of both the courts and the legal profession. The new courts created in 1997 with a mandate to secure constitutional and statutory accountability of private and government actors have shown signs of internalising the novel political expectations in complex ways. Even the Constitutional Court has not always bowed to politics (McCargo 2014). The new administrative courts have displayed greater independence from the executive branch and its politics (Leyland 2009), which may be explained in part by the courts' mandate to hold government officials to the letter of the law, something Thai judges can do very effectively. Independent interpretation may also have progressed incrementally for a related reason: effective advocacy by lawyers inspired to advance new visions of law by exposure to leaders of popular mobilisation and increasing familiarity with advocacy for human rights and the rule of law outside Thailand. And finally, judges, like lawyers, have identities shaped by the cross-currents in Thai society, immersing them in an international discourse about the role of law (Ginsburg 2009a). Thus, the efficacy of separation of powers and a more liberal rule of law may rely not only on the influence of popular mobilisation on lawyers but also on subtle changes in the role of judges with quite conventional professional identities.[41]

---

[41] The relative independence of the administrative courts may, in turn, be driving change in the Royal Courts of Justice through parallel litigation to implement legal remedies. See Munger (forthcoming).

REFERENCES

Andersen, B (1998) 'Withdrawal Symptoms' in B Anderson (ed), *The Spectre of Comparisons: Nationalism, Southeast Asia and the World* (London, Verso).

Baker, C and Phongpaichit, P (2009) *A History of Thailand*, 2nd edn (Cambridge, Cambridge University Press).

Banomyong, P (2000) trans by Baker, C and Phonpaichit, P, *Pridi by Pridi: Selected Writings on Life, Politics, and Economy* (Chiang Mai, Silkworm Books).

Bureau of Policy and Planning (1998) *Five-Year Summary Report on Higher Education Statistics 1992–1996* (Bangkok, Minister of University Affairs).

—— (1997–2004) *Report of Public Higher Education* (Bangkok, Minister of University Affairs).

Connors, MK (2001) *Democracy and National Identity in Thailand* (London, Routledge/Curzon).

Department of Civil Rights Protection and Legal Aid (2002–2016) *Annual Report* (Bangkok, Office of the Attorney General).

Dezalay, Y and Garth, B (2010) *Asian Legal Revivals: Lawyers in the Shadow of Empire* (Chicago, University of Chicago Press).

Doneys, P (2002) 'Political Reform Thorough the Public Sphere: Women's Groups and the Fabric of Governance' in D McCargo (ed), *Reforming Thai Politics* (Copenhagen, Nordic Institute of Asian Studies).

Engel, D (1975) *Law and Kingship in Thailand During the Reign of King Chulalongkorn* Michigan Papers on South and Southeast Asian No 9 (Ann Arbor, University of Michigan, Center for South and Southeast Asian Studies).

Ginsburg, T (2009a) 'The judicialization of administrative governance: causes, consequences and limits' in T Ginsburg and AHY Chen (eds), *Administrative Law and Governance in Asia: Comparative Perspectives* (New York, Routledge).

—— (2009b) 'Constitutional Afterlife: The Continuing Impact of Thailand's Post-Political Constitution' 7 *International Journal of Constitutional Law* 83.

Haberkorn, T (2011) *Revolution Interrupted: Farmers, Student, Law, and Violence in Northern Thailand* (Madison, WI, University of Wisconsin Press).

Hewison, K (1989) *Bankers and Bureaucrats: Capital and the Role of the State in Thailand*, Yale University Southeast Asia Studies Yale Center for International and Area Studies Monograph Series No 34 (New Haven, Yale University Southeast Asian Studies).

Hirschl, R (2004) *Towards Juristocracy: The Origins and Consequences of the New Constitutionalism* (Cambridge, Harvard University Press).

Information Center Bureau of Administration (2005–2006) *Higher Education Data and Information* (Bangkok, Office of Higher Education Commission).

Institute for Developing Economies (2001) *The Judicial System in Thailand: An Outlook for a New Century* (Tokyo, Japan External Trade Organization) www.ide-jetro.jp/English/Publish/Download/Als/pdf/06.pdf.

Jaiharn, N et al (2004) *Project to Study and Develop a Public Defender System* (Thammasat University Faculty of Law, Bangkok) (in Thai).

Jayasuriya, K (1999) 'Introduction: A Framework for the Analysis of Legal Institutional in East Asia' in K Jayasuriya (ed), *Law, Capitalism and Power in Asia, The Rule of Law and Legal Institutions* (London, Routledge).

Klein, JR (2003) 'The Battle for the Rule of Law in Thailand: The Constitutional Court of Thailand' in A Raksasataya and JR Klein (eds), *The Constitutional Court of Thailand: The Provisions and the Working of the Court* (Bangkok, The Asia Foundation).

Lawyers Council (2011–2016) *Annual Reports* (Bangkok, Lawyers Council Under Royal Patronage) (in Thai).

Lev, D (1998) 'Lawyers' Causes in Indonesia and Malaysia' in A Sarat and S Scheingold (eds), *Cause Lawyering: Political Commitments and Professional Responsibilities* (New York, Oxford University Press).

Lertchoosakul, K (2016) *The Rise of the Octobrists in Contemporary Thailand* (New Haven, Yale University Press).

Leyland P (2009) 'The emergence of administrative justice in Thailand under the 1997 Constitution' in T Ginsburg and AHY Chen (eds), *Administrative Law and Governance in Asia: Comparative Perspectives* (New York, Routledge).

Lingat, R (1950) 'Evolution of the Conception of Law in Burma and Siam' 39 *Journal of the Siam Society* 9.

Loos, T (2006) *Subject Siam: Family, Law and Colonial Modernity in Thailand* (Ithaca, Cornell University Press).

McCargo, D (2005) 'Network monarchy and legitimacy crises in Thailand' 18 *The Pacific Review* 499.

—— (2014) 'Competing Notions of Judicialization in Thailand' 36 *Journal of Contemporary Asia* 417.

McCargo, D and Tanruangporn, P (2015) 'Branding Dissent: Nitirat, Thailand's Enlightened Jurists' 45 *Journal of Contemporary Asia* 419.

Munger, F (2014) 'Revolution Imagined: Cause Advocacy, Consumer Rights, and the Evolving Role of NGOs in Thailand' 9 *Asian Journal of Comparative Law* 29.

—— (2015) 'Thailand's Cause Lawyers and Twenty-First Century Military Coups: Nation, Identity, and Conflicting Visions of the Rule of Law' 2 *Asian Journal of Law and Society* 301.

—— (2019) 'Thailand 21st Century Administrative Court: Judicialization and the Special Role of Lawyers for Social Causes in Asia, 25 *Indiana Journal of Global Legal Studies* (forthcoming).

Naruemon, T and McCargo, D (2011) 'Urbanized Villagers in the 2010 Redshirt Protests: Not Just Poor Farmers?' 51 *Asian Survey* 993.

National Statistical Office (1970) *Thailand Yearbook 1967–1969* (Bangkok, National Statistical Office).

Prokati, K (2009) 'General Principles of Application and Interpretation' in *Academic Proceedings in Memory of Professor Jitti Tingsabot* (Bangkok, Thammasat University Faculty of Law) (in Thai).

Pruekpongsawalee, M (2004) 'The Constitutions and the Legal Status of Women in Family Related Law in Thailand: A Historical Perspective' in S Satha-Anand (ed), *Women's Studies in Thailand: Power, Knowledge and Justice* (Seoul, Ewha Womans University Press).

Rueschemeyer, D (1989) 'Comparing Legal Professions: A State-Centered Approach' in RL Abel and PSC Lewis (eds), *Lawyers in Society: Vol III Comparative Theories* (Berkeley, University of California Press).

Reynolds, F (1978) 'Religion and Rebellion: Thailand's Civic Religion and the Student Uprising of October 1973' in BL Smith (ed), *Legitimation of Power in Thailand, Laos, and Burma* (Chambersburg, PA, Anima).

Riggs, FW (1966) *Thailand: The Modernization of a Bureaucratic Polity* (Honolulu, East-West Center Press).

Siffin, WJ (1966) *The Thai Bureaucracy: Institutional Change and Development* (Honolulu, East-West Center Press).

Slater, D (2010) *Ordering Power: Contentious Politics and Authoritarian Leviathans in Southeast Asia* (New York, Cambridge University Press).

Thai Bar Association (2008) *100th Anniversary of Law Schools* (Bangkok, Institute of Legal Education, Thai Bar Association) (in Thai).

—— (1997) *80th Anniversary of the Thai Bar Association on January 1 2538 B.E.* (Bangkok, Institute of Legal Education, Thai Bar Association) (in Thai).

Vichai, A (2001) 'The Judicial System in Thailand: An outlook for a new century' in Institute for Developing Economies (ed) *Proceedings of the Roundtable Meeting Law, Development and Socio-Economic Changes in Asia* (Tokyo, Japan External Trade Organization) www.ide.go.jp/English/Publish/Download/Als/01.html.

Vichit-Vadakan, J (2008) 'Women in Politics and Women and Politics: A Socio-Cultural Analysis of the Thai Context' in K Iwanga (ed) *Women and Politics in Thailand: Continuity and Change* (Copenhagen, NIAS Press).

43

Vietnam
From Cadres to a 'Managed' Profession

PIP NICHOLSON AND DO HAI HA

In 1986, 11 years after the country's reunification, the Vietnamese Party-state announced its policy of '*Đổi mới*', or renovation, heralding an opening to foreign investment and a transition from a planned economy to a socialist-oriented market economy. Simultaneously, the Communist Party of Vietnam (CPV or Party) has sought to maintain strong leadership of economic, political and legal institutions. While relying on repressive measures to maintain political stability and Party paramountcy, the CPV has become increasingly responsive to public concerns, criticism and demands, whether communicated through sanctioned or unsanctioned channels (Kerkvliet 2010), opening space for civil society activities and state-society interactions.

Economic, political and social change have resulted in remarkable legal reform. The CPV officially introduced the doctrine of 'socialist law-based state' (which calls for a greater role for law in state governance) in 1994, although the term had been increasingly used unofficially since 1989. This doctrine has slowly reshaped the existing doctrine of 'socialist legality' (Pham and Do 2018: 123–24), introducing ambiguity and allowing debate about and incremental influence of Western legal principles and institutions (Pham and Do 2018: 124–25). This has generated major legislative change and some institutional reform, including constitutional reform and commitments to human rights (Bui 2013; Vu and Tran 2016), substantial court-related reforms (Nicholson 2015; 2007b; Quinn 2003), and wide-ranging procedural reforms (Pham and Do 2018: 126).

This chapter chronicles the evolution of lawyers and lawyering since the introduction of *Đổi mới*, focusing on the contemporary period and the ways in which the Party-state manages the profession. We rely on incomplete fragmentary statistics provided by Party-state institutions, eleven interviews with legal practitioners, scholars and an official from the Ministry of Justice (MOJ) between October 2017 and November 2018,[1] and organisational websites, online newspapers and Vietnamese lawyers' Facebook sites.

---

[1] The interviews took place as follows: Lawyer A (22 October 2017); Lawyer B (24 October 2017); Lawyer C (1 November 2017); Lawyer D (3 November 2017); Lawyer E (4 November 2017); Lawyer F (5 November 2017); Lawyer G (30 October 2018); Lawyer H (1 November 2018); Lawyer-Scholar I (24 April 2018); Scholar J (3 November 2017); Official K (5 May 2018).

We highlight lawyers' increasing numbers, growing professionalism, and significant, if not free, interaction with the Party-state. These changes, however, should not be misunderstood as a shift towards a Western-style legal profession, independent of politics. Drawing on Kerkvliet's (2003) explanation of post-*Đổi mới* state-society relations, we argue that the Vietnamese legal profession is currently characterised by three divergent features. First, it remains heavily constrained by the Party-state, including politically oriented and ambiguous ethical standards, the co-optation of lawyers' organisations (Sidel 2008: 175–83, 188–91; Nguyen and Steiner 2005: 196–97), Party control of judges, police and procurators, moderating how lawyers operate (Lindsey and Nicholson 2016: 239–42; Nicholson and Pham 2018), institutional limits on legal advocacy (Sidel 2008: 175–83; Lindsey and Nicholson 2016: 252–58; Nicholson 2010: 188–216), and government control of legal education. Second, despite this, lawyers increasingly seek to and do influence Party-state organisations through authorised channels, such as CPV-controlled lawyers' organisations and consultation on law reform, ironically legitimising the Party-state. Third, limited autonomy from the Party-state enables activist lawyers to mobilise social pressure. We suggest, therefore, that ultimately Vietnam's legal field is populated by advocates, reformers and state functionaries who concurrently conform to and contest the regulation of lawyers. The Party retains the power to determine when a lawyer has moved from reformer to activist and to constrain such behaviour by alleging breaches of Party discipline (CPV Statute 2011; Nicholson 2010: 188–216), the Criminal Code and ethical rules.

Following a brief history of lawyers in Vietnam, Part II describes legal education, the regulation of lawyers since *Đổi mới*, the demographics of the profession, and the incidence of firms and private lawyering. Part III focuses on the role of lawyers as activists, working within and beyond state boundaries. We conclude that the parameters constraining lawyers operate differently in different spaces and jurisdictions. Private commercial lawyers working for non-state clients in matters not involving the state are relatively immune from interference. The more lawyers' work challenges the Party-state's power or interests, the more vulnerable they are to state interference.

I. HISTORICAL BACKGROUND

A. Pre-*Đổi mới* Legal Profession

The Vietnamese legal profession was created in 1876 by the French colonial regime (Ngô 2014). Joining the profession became more attractive after 1930, when the colonial government opened bar associations to Vietnamese nationals, recognised the right to counsel of local Vietnamese people and permitted lawyers to appear in locally run courts (Ngô 2014). Following its declaration of independence in 1945, the Democratic Republic of Vietnam (DRV) selectively preserved the colonial legal system (Ginsburg 1979: 191–92), including the legal profession. The new government recognised the role of lawyers and retained the colonial legal and institutional frameworks of the legal profession (Decree 46/SL 1945), working with French-trained lawyers in establishing the Vietnamese state (Sidel 1994: 163–74).

The war conditions and the DRV's increasing turn to the Soviet legal model significantly affected the legal system and profession. From the early 1950s, and particularly after 1959–60, the socialist transition accelerated, marked by the promulgation of a Soviet-style constitution in 1959, recognition of the Soviet doctrine of socialist legality at the 1960 Party Congress, and introduction of a central system of socialist courts and procuracies (Nicholson 2007a: 63–67, 103–39; Pham and Do 2018: 103–104). Law became a political instrument, subordinate to Party policy (Pham and Do 2018: 104–105). Legal institutions – including courts, procuracies and the legal profession – promoted socialist legality under the leadership of the CPV (Ginsburg 1979; Nicholson 2007a: 196–97). As French-trained lawyers were gradually marginalised, if not purged, and replaced by Soviet-trained, politically oriented legal cadres (Gillespie 2007: 144; Nguyen and Steiner 2005: 193–94), the private profession and practise of law ceased (Nguyen and Steiner 2005: 194–95), and French colonial influence was essentially eliminated from the DRV legal system by the 1960s (Ginsburg 1979; Gillespie 2006: 58–62).

From the 1960s, legal offices did not require legal training, and legal education was abolished (Sidel 1993: 224). The MOJ was closed in 1960 (Nicholson 2007a: 108–09). Courts were staffed not by legal professionals but by politically-oriented cadres, accountable to the CPV (Nicholson 2007a: 37–137). From 1949, technically qualified lawyers were gradually replaced by people's advocates, who were managed and paid by state authorities, usually worked part-time, and were not subject to professional requirements (Nguyen and Steiner 2005: 193–95). Lawyers and advocates were considered inferior to the procuracy and all other state agencies (Nguyen 2007: 162–77).

In 1955, the Vietnam Lawyers Association (VLA) was established in the North under Party direction and leadership (VLA 2015: 11–12). Despite its name, the members of this association – *luật gia* – included not only lawyers (*luật sư*) but also Party-state officials working in a legal capacity (Nguyen and Steiner 2005: 194). The VLA was not a professional but a socio-political organisation. From its establishment to the 1980s, its main function was to assist the Party-state with international relations, such as criticising the US government for violating international law and rebutting international criticism of socialist Vietnam for human right abuses (VLA 2015: 18–24).

In contrast, the legal profession persisted in the southern capitalist state, the Republic of Vietnam (RVN), from 1954 to 1975. Compared with the DRV, RVN legal services were much more developed (Nguyen and Steiner 2005: 195). By 1974–75 the Bar associations in Saigon and Hue had approximately 1,030 members (Phan and Trương 2015: 145). In addition, lawyers played an active role in the RVN's government and political life (Phan and Trương 2015: 144–80). And, despite the oppression of dissident lawyers, RVN lawyers generally enjoyed much greater autonomy from the government than their northern colleagues (Phan and Trương 2015: 77–104, 144–80).

South Vietnamese Bar associations were dissolved immediately after national reunification in 1975 (Phan and Trương 2015: 189–93), and numerous lawyers were sent to re-education camps or escaped to foreign countries (Gillespie 2006: 62). As had happened earlier in the North, private professional lawyers were replaced by people's advocates, of whom there were less than 400 throughout Vietnam by the end of 1987 (Nguyễn 2012: 95).

B. Post-*Đổi mới* Legal Profession

The post-*Đổi mới* era saw the incremental revival of the legal profession in socialist Vietnam (Ordinance on Lawyers' Organisations 1987; Ordinance on Lawyers 2001; Law on Lawyers (LOL) 2006; LOL (Revised) 2012). State restrictions on the practice of law were relaxed, especially concerning the admission to and operation of bar associations and the incorporation of legal businesses (Phan and Trương 2015: 193–211). Simultaneously, lawyers' professional qualifications and organisations became increasingly standardised and aligned with international practice (Nguyễn 2012: 95–124).

The revival of lawyers in post-reform Vietnam resembles that in post-reform China (Liu 2002: 1058–71). The Vietnamese Party-state – especially the MOJ and its local subsidiaries – played a critical role in establishing lawyers' organisations (Phan and Trương 2015: 192–203; Nguyễn 2012: 95–114). As in China (Liu 2002: 1059; Michelson 2011: 44–49), lawyers with political ties dominated the professional revival. The new Bar associations established in Hanoi and Ho Chi Minh City (HCMC) were populated mostly by former legal officials or incumbent Party-state officials practising law part-time (Ngô and Anh 2014; Phan and Trương 2015: 192–201). The emerging Chinese and Vietnamese legal professions were closely connected with, rather than independent from, Party-state organisations.

Nevertheless, the reconstruction of the Vietnamese legal profession has distinct features. Lawyers with Western-style (French/RVN) legal education played a significant role in this process, especially in southern regions (Phan and Trương 2015: 192–96). All three Presidents of the HCMC Bar Association[2] have been graduates of the Saigon law schools that predated 1975 (Lawyer G 2018). Unlike China (Michelson 2011: 47–49), Vietnam did not have state-owned law firms. Furthermore, Vietnamese public servants, including legal academics, have been prevented from acting as part-time lawyers since 2001 (Ordinance on Lawyers 2001, Article 8). Unlike China, this ordinance also required newly admitted lawyers to have an LLB (Articles 8, 42), effectively excluding from the legal profession former legal officials without tertiary legal education. Vietnam has fostered a more technically expert legal profession and a clearer division between the profession and the Party-state. As in China (Michelson 2011), however, political connections are relevant to the work of Vietnamese lawyers in many ways, facilitating rent seeking, making communication with state officials more effective, and reducing 'practical difficulties' (Lawyers E and F 2017).

The re-emergence of Vietnamese lawyers arguably reflects the Party-state's changing view about the need for expertise and education post-unification, including the role of law and the legal profession. This transformation is exemplified by the re-opening of tertiary legal education in 1976–79, the re-establishment of the MOJ in 1981, and the increasing emphasis on legal regulation in policy discourse from 1982 (Gillespie 2007: 146; Sidel 1993: 224). Furthermore, the Party-state acknowledged the role of lawyers' organisations in the 1980 Constitution (Article 133), established the Hanoi Bar Association in 1984,[3] and allowed the HCMC Lawyers Association to provide legal services on a pilot basis in 1986 (Phan and Trương 2015: 192–99).

Đổi mới played a crucial role in the revival of Vietnamese lawyers. Vietnam's expanding market economy and increasing integration into the global economy generated rising demand for legal services (Lawyers B, C, E and F 2017). Liberalisation of state-society

---

[2] See www.hcmcbar.org.
[3] See www.luatsuhanoi.vn.

relations, including the Party-state's increasing tolerance of public criticism and associational activities, has also fostered the development of private lawyers. Re-establishing and reforming the legal profession is a part of a broader effort to strengthen legal institutions in response to the changing economy and society after Đổi mới (Nicholson 2005: 160–70; 2007a: 247–51).

II. VIETNAMESE LAWYERS AND THE PROFESSION

The reform of legal institutions intensified in the 2000s with the CPV's announcement of bold judicial reforms (CPV 2002, 2005) and the enactment of new laws requiring that legal professionals, including judges, procurators and lawyers, hold an LLB and complete professional training (Ordinance on Lawyers 2001; Ordinance on Judges and People's Jurors 2002; Ordinance on Procurators 2002). The commitment to legal credentialism should not, however, be confused with making the legal system independent of politics. It remains fundamentally socialist, requiring officials (including academics, judges and procurators) and private practitioners to demonstrate loyalty to the Party-state.

A. Legal Education

i. The Revival of Legal Education after Đổi mới

The re-emergence of legal education in socialist Vietnam began soon after national reunification with the establishment of a law faculty inside Hanoi University in 1976, followed by the foundation of Hanoi University of Law (HAUL) three years later (Sidel 1993: 224). After the adoption of economic reforms in the late 1980s, the expansion of law colleges and faculties accelerated, including the opening of several law colleges and faculties in Hanoi, HCMC and subsequently elsewhere.

The government managed the growth of legal education cautiously. At least until 2008, private institutions were not supposed to offer law degrees, although this prohibition was not formal. There were just over 20 state-managed law colleges and faculties (Scholar J 2017; Bui 2010: 299, 301). Since then, the Ministry of Education and Training (MOET) has relaxed its opposition, prompting public and private universities to open law programmes (Scholar J 2017; Official K 2018). By doing so, the government sought to produce more technically trained experts to promote economic integration and trade and enable public universities to generate new sources of income. Today, there are 40 public and 24 private universities offering four-year LLB programmes across the country (Duy Tân University 2019). Postgraduate legal education has also grown significantly, with at least 18 institutions offering masters degrees and 11 offering doctorates in law in 2019. Private universities, however, remain informally restricted to offering law programmes only in business, international and international trade law (Lawyer-Scholar I 2018; Official K 2018); instruction in public law is restricted to public universities to ensure the political orientation of the curriculum and pedagogy (Official K 2018).

More than half the law faculties are located in Hanoi and HCMC. In 2019, MOET capped the number of students allowed to enrol in these institutions for a 'regular' (*chính quy*) LLB at more than 15,860,[4] although many universities routinely over-enrol (Lawyer-Scholar I 2018; Scholar J 2017). The biggest and best-known institutions are HAUL and HCMC University of Law (HCMCUL), each of which has enrolled more than 1,000 regular undergraduate students annually since the 1990s (Lawyer-Scholar I 2018; Scholar J 2017).[5] Other law schools have also increased enrolments and improved their reputations (Lawyer-Scholar I 2018; Scholar J 2017).

Apart from regular courses, several law schools concurrently offer irregular (*không chính quy*) or in-service (*tại chức/vừa học, vừa làm*) courses, which permit students to work full-time and complete their courses in the same timeframe as a full-time student (Lawyer-Scholar I 2018; Scholar J 2017). Introduced in the early 1990s, irregular LLB programmes primarily allowed state officials, including judges, procurators, investigators and administrative officials, to obtain newly introduced professional credentials (Nicholson and Nguyen 2005; Lawyer-Scholar I 2018), while also increasingly attracting students from the private sector (Lawyer-Scholar I 2018; Scholar J 2017). Today most, if not all, postgraduate courses take this form (Lawyer-Scholar I 2018; Scholar J 2017). HAUL and HCMCUL have also enrolled large numbers of irregular undergraduates (Lawyer-Scholar I 2018; Scholar J 2017). Between 1996 and mid-2016, the latter awarded LLBs to 22,803 irregular students and 22,012 regular students (HCMCUL 2018). During the last decade, 85–98 per cent of LLB students at the five leading law schools completed their degrees (LawNet 2018). Interviews suggest that newly established law schools also have very high completion rates (Lawyer-Scholar I 2018; Scholar J 2017).

The expansion of Vietnamese legal education over the past 30 years had several causes. The government's insistence that employees working in its legal and administrative institutions have bachelor's degrees generated the need for tertiary credentials (Lawyer-Scholar I 2018).[6] Interviews indicate that the expanding state absorbed a large number of law graduates, (Lawyer-Scholar I 2018; Scholar J 2017). Concurrently, the private market for legal services expanded, reflecting Vietnam's growing foreign trade and the development of strong internal markets. Finally, the transfer of control of higher education policy from individual ministries, such as the MOJ, to the MOET, the marketisation of tertiary education, and the growing space for private education have enabled higher education institutions to build markets of their own (Lawyer-Scholar I 2018; Scholar J 2017; Official K).

ii. The Transformation of Legal Teaching and Continual Challenges

Post-*Đổi mới* legal education not only grew but also changed (Bui 2005; 2010: 304–305). Law schools have modernised their curricula by restructuring conventional subjects and introducing new ones more relevant to legal practice and development (Bui 2010: 304–305;

---

[4] This number excludes three institutions due to the unavailability of data. In 1993 there were just 2,800 students enrolled in the HAUL, including its HCMC branch (HCMCUL's predecessor), supplemented by several hundred LLB students in two other nascent institutions (Sidel 1994: 165–66).

[5] The enrolment quotas of HAUL and HCMCUL in 2019 were 2,215 and 1,850 regular LLB students respectively (Duy Tân University 2019).

[6] Professionalisation of state employees was an important aspect of public administration reform from the mid-1990s (Buhmann 2007: 241).

Scholar J 2017). For example, civil law has been divided into: an introductory subject, general issues of civil law; followed by property, ownership and succession; contract; and tort. Civil law has also been supplemented by new subjects, like intellectual property, negotiation and drafting of civil contracts and housing transactions (Scholar J 2017). Leading institutions have also updated their textbooks (Bui 2010: 304–305; Scholar J 2017) and begun to develop casebooks (Lawyer-Scholar I 2018).

Nearly ten years ago, Vietnam introduced five-year double degree programmes at HCMCUL and more recently at HAUL and the School of Economics and Law within the National University, HCMC (Scholar J 2017). Beginning in the 1990s with sponsorship by the Swedish International Development Agency, HAUL and HCMCUL maintained a joint LLM/PhD programme with Lund University for nearly 15 years (Scholar J 2017). HAUL and HCMCUL also launched joint Masters' programmes with the University of West England (UWE) about ten years ago (Scholar J 2017). The joint HAUL-UWE programme has ended, but the HCMCUL-UWE programme continues, and a joint LLM programme with the University of Montesquieu Bordeaux IV has been initiated (Scholar J 2017).

In the past ten years, pedagogy has been reformed, especially in established law schools (Lawyer-Scholar I 2018; Scholar J 2017), although most radical innovation is undertaken by individuals on a small scale (Lawyer-Scholar I 2018; Scholar J 2017). Changes include a shift from lectures to increasing student participation through class presentations, group assignments, discussion and debate, role play and competitions (Lawyer B 2017; Lawyer-Scholar I 2018; Scholar J 2017). In leading law schools, reform-minded teachers have increasingly used court judgments and real problems in teaching and assessment, while students have begun to participate in national and international mooting competitions, and some law clinics have been established (Lawyer B 2017; Lawyer-Scholar I 2018; Scholar J 2017). Judges and practising lawyers are increasingly involved in teaching and other activities in law colleges (Lawyers B and C 2017; Lawyer-Scholar I 2018; Scholar J 2017). More recently, several universities have experimented with teaching in foreign languages (English, French or Japanese), exchanging students with foreign universities, and using foreign materials (Lawyer-Scholar I 2018; Scholar J 2017).

While curriculum reform has been undertaken in various places, southern institutions appear to be the pioneers (Bui 2010: 305; Lawyer-Scholar I 2018; Scholar J 2017). This may be explained by RVN's historically strong profession and the impact of market forces (Bui 2010: 305), given that HCMC is the most economically dynamic city. Furthermore, southern institutions, like the HCMCUL, seem to be less dominated by scholars formerly trained in the Eastern bloc than are northern institutions like the HAUL (Lawyer-Scholar I 2018; Scholar J 2017).

Notwithstanding remarkable change in the last 30 years, quality legal education remains elusive (Bui 2005: 135; Lawyer B 2017; Lawyer-Scholar I 2018; Scholar J 2017; Ho 2016: 82–91). Many claim that legal curricula and syllabi fail to reflect post-*Đổi mới* economic, political and legal developments and pay insufficient attention to private law, legal practice and legal skills training (Bui 2010, 305; Ho 2016: 82–88; Lawyer B 2017; Lawyer-Scholar I 2018; Scholar J 2017). Curricula still reflect Soviet legal education, where students must take political-ideological subjects, such as Fundamental Principles of Marxism-Leninism, Ho Chi Minh Thought, CPV History, CPV Revolutionary Strategy and Theory of State and Law, as well as the major 'branches of law', such as constitutional, administrative, criminal and civil law (Bui 2005: 139; Lawyer-Scholar I 2018; Scholar J 2017). Most of the newly introduced subjects are optional and constitute only 10–15 per cent of the curriculum (Scholar J 2017). Despite the introduction of the new doctrine of the 'law-based state' and the enactment of numerous market-based/Western-style laws, the Theory of State and Law essentially teaches Marxist-Leninist concepts popularised during the Soviet era and remains the theoretical foundation for all legal subjects (Lawyer-Scholar I 2018; Scholar J 2017). Legal textbooks simply summarise newly introduced legal texts with little reference to legal doctrine or practice, including court decisions (Lawyer-Scholar I 2018; Scholar J 2017).

The weakness of Vietnamese legal education, compared with its Chinese counterpart (Bui 2010: 307–308), can be understood from political, historical and institutional perspectives. Strict governmental control has restricted curricular innovation (Ho 2016: 85; Lawyer-Scholar I 2018; Scholar J 2017). While direct control has been relaxed since 2010 (Ho 2016: 78–79), the authoritarian state's continued commitment to Marxism-Leninism operates as an 'invisible constraint' on radical reforms in the teaching of legal theory and the use of foreign curricula (Lawyer-Scholar I 2018; Scholar J 2017).

Legal education in socialist Vietnam has developed in a near vacuum, with limited support from the government and foreign donors, including the former Soviet Union, capitalist states and international organisations (Bui 2010: 307–308; Lawyer-Scholar I 2018). Personnel, expertise and resources are scarce (Lawyer-Scholar I 2018; Scholar J 2017). Most, if not all, newly established law schools rely mainly on visiting and part-time lecturers and have small libraries (Lawyer-Scholar I 2018; Scholar J 2017). One faculty with nearly 2,000 students had only five or six full-time lecturers; the library of another with about 450 students has virtually no legal resources other than HCMCUL textbooks (Scholar J 2017).

Legal education reform is led by Party-state scholars, most of whom were educated in the Eastern bloc and have little experience of other legal systems or contact with the legal services market (Lawyer-Scholar I 2018; Scholar J 2017; Sidel 1994: 167–68). The growing number of scholars trained in Western or East Asian capitalist states remain a minority with little influence because of the constraints on curricular reform (Bui 2010: 307; Lawyer-Scholar I 2018; Scholar J 2017). Furthermore, there is no demand from international law graduates for master's programmes in Vietnamese law. Many lawyers trained in Western states seek to emigrate.

iii. Finance and Tuition Fees

Most public universities rely on state sponsorship (for land, buildings, facility maintenance and operating expenditures) and tuition fees, which have become increasingly important (Lawyer-Scholar I 2018; Scholar J 2017). Many institutions, like HAUL and HCMCUL, have also periodically received foreign aid (Scholar J 2017). HAUL, HCMCUL and some other public universities are piloting 'financial autonomy', depending largely on tuition fees to cover the investment in facilities and operating costs (Scholar J 2017).

The Government imposes limits on public university tuition fees, capping those for regular LLB programmes at VN$7,400,000 (US$326) per year (Decree 86/2015/ND-CP 2015, Article 5.2). Financially autonomous institutions cannot charge more than VN$17,500,000 per year (US$771) (Decree 86/2015/ND-CP 2015, Article 5.1). The caps applicable to master's and doctoral programmes are 1.5 and 2.5 times higher (Decree 86/2015/ND-CP 2015, Article 5.3). Tuition fees for irregular LLB courses must not exceed 150 per cent of those for regular courses (Decree 86/2015/ND-CP 2015, Article 5.8). These limits, however, do not apply to 'high-quality' (*chất lượng cao*) programmes, although ministerial approval is required for their tuition fees (Decree 86/2015/ND-CP 2015, Article 5.10), which were VN$40,000,000 (US$1,778) per year at HCMCUL in 2017 (Scholar J 2017).

The term 'high-quality' indicates better lecturers, modernised curricula, new teaching methods, and better learning facilities (Lawyer-Scholar I 2018; Scholar J 2017). However, the actual difference between these and normal courses is not as significant as advertised (except in relation to facilities), especially in new law schools (Lawyer-Scholar I 2018; Scholar J 2017). Some universities offer high-quality programmes, more to avoid tuition fee restrictions and raise revenue than to innovate pedagogically (Lawyer-Scholar I 2018; Scholar J 2017). Private universities are financed almost entirely by tuition fees (Scholar J 2017; Law on Education (revised) 2009, Article 66), which can reach VN$80,000,000 (US$3,555) a year (Lawyer-Scholar I 2018; Scholar J 2017).

Given Vietnam's modest per capita GDP (US$2,385 in 2017 (GSO 2017)), the rise of tuition fees in both private and public institutions has threatened educational opportunity and equality, especially for students from rural areas (about 65 per cent of the national population), where per capita GDP is less than 80 per cent of the national figure (GSO 2018). Since 2007, the Government has experimented with a capped loan scheme, but it only offers small loans (VN$1,000,000 (US$44) per month) at a high rate of interest (7.2 per cent per year) to a limited range of students (*Decision 157/2007/QD-TTg* 2007). Unsurprisingly, almost all students in high-quality programmes and private schools are from high-income families (Lawyer-Scholar I 2018; Scholar J 2017).

B. The Regulation of Lawyers

i. Licensing

Regulators have raised the professional qualifications for public office, requiring judges and prosecutors to have an LLB, thereby allowing the profession to make technical arguments and engage with state functionaries not only as their CPV-led masters but also as fellow professionals (Nicholson and Nguyen 2017). Interactions between state and private lawyers remain strained, however, because the former have significantly more power (Lindsey and Nicholson 2016: 239–42, 252–58).

The 2006 LOL, revised in 2012 and 2015 (LOL 2015), states that a Vietnamese citizen must generally satisfy four requirements to be a lawyer: hold an LLB (LOL 2015, Article 9); successfully complete the MOJ Judicial Academy's one-year training course and final examination (LOL 2015, Articles 10, 12);[7] apprentice for a year at a law firm; and pass the VBF bar examination (LOL 2015, Articles 10, 14–15). The trainee lawyer must then obtain a lawyers' certificate from the MOJ, be admitted to a provincial bar, and receive a

---

[7] Although the Government conditionally authorised the Vietnam Bar Federation (VBF) to establish its own institution for lawyer training (Decree 123/2013/ND-CP), it continues to rely on the Judicial Academy.

lawyers' card from the VBF (LOL 2015, Articles 17, 20). Foreign citizens may also practise law in Vietnam if they are admitted to practice in another jurisdiction, have been transferred to or are employed by a foreign or domestic law firm based in Vietnam, and have received a licence to practise law from the MOJ (LOL 2015, Article 74).

ii. Ethical Standards

Legal practitioners in Vietnam must maintain their independence, honesty, integrity and fairness; avoid conflicts of interest; act in the best interest of clients; honour clients' freedom and confidentiality; exercise competence and care; and duly discharge their undertakings (LOL 2015, Article 9.1; Code of Conduct and Ethics for Vietnamese Lawyers (COC) 2011). In Vietnam's political-legal context, legal ethics also demand that lawyers promote socio-economic development and state management (including, but not limited to, legal propaganda and crime prevention) (LOL 2015, Article 3; COC 2011, rr 25.3–25.4, 26.1).

Ethical rules are a 'tool' to ensure the loyalty of lawyers to the Party-state. Article 3 of the LOL 2015 requires that the 'legal profession contributes to ... the construction of a *socialist* law-based state' (emphasis added). More explicitly, lawyers are prohibited from:

> exploiting their practice of law [and] their capacity as a lawyer to cause a negative impact on national security [or] public order and safety, [or] infringe upon the interests of the state, public interests [or] lawful rights and interests of other agencies, organisations or individuals. (LOL 2015, Article 9(1)(g))

According to the COC 2011 (r 24.5), lawyers are not allowed:

> to make statements that infringe upon national interest, social interest, national solidarity [or] religious solidarity, or to propagandise [and] disseminate viewpoints contrary to the law or social morality.

These regulations impose broad ambiguous moral obligations on legal professionals, affecting relationships with clients, other lawyers, the courts, and other state agencies, including the police, procuracies and administrative organs (COC 2011, chs IV–V). Legal professionals also are obliged to co-operate with the media, which is often tightly controlled by the Party-state (COC 2011, r 26.1).

The ambiguity of these obligations renders legal practitioners in Vietnam vulnerable to political interference (LOL 2015, Article 9(1)(g); COC 2011, r 24.5). Lawyers are also prohibited from making 'critical [or] offensive statements' or 'taking action offending other individuals, organisations and state agencies' during legal proceedings (LOL 2015, Article 9.1(i); COC 2011, r 24.4). Lawyers must ensure their clients do 'not waste public resources' or 'impede state management of public order and safety' (COC 2011, r 25.3).

Finally, lawyers who resist cooperating with the state may be prosecuted (Criminal Code (Revised) 2017, Articles 19, 390). For decades, lawyers were subject to criminal liability if they failed to denounce their clients' offences, although the 2015 Criminal Code now offers lawyers limited protection (Criminal Code 1985, Articles 19, 247; Criminal Code 1999, Articles 22, 313) if the lawyer became aware of the offence while representing the client and the offence is not one of the 84 that endanger national security or is not particularly serious (Criminal Code (Revised) 2017, Article 19.3).

In short, lawyers are, in most cases, obliged to disclose their clients' planned and past offences. Additionally, they appear to be generally excluded from the limited protection of the attorney-client privilege arising in criminal matters. Accordingly, Article 19.3 has arguably weakened not only the ethical standards regarding confidentiality, but also diminished lawyers' ability to maintain independence and act in the best interest of their clients. This regulatory framework illustrates how the CPV uses legal ethics to shape lawyers' duties and behaviours.

iii. Liability and Ethics

Violating Vietnamese legal professional ethical standards can result in disciplinary action, administrative sanctions, or civil liability to a client. Discipline ranges from a reprimand to a provincial Bar association's removal of a lawyer from its list of practitioners (LOL 2015, Article 85). A disciplined lawyer may appeal that decision to the VBF and then the Minister of Justice (LOL 2015, Article 86). The limited statistics reveal that 94 lawyers were disciplined for ethical violations between 2009 and 2014, 22 of whom were removed from the Bar roll (VBF 2015a: 16). Recently, there has been a marked increase in the numbers of lawyers disbarred: 17 in 2016 and 8 and the first quarter of 2017 (Thục 2017). Given the frequent acknowledgement of lawyers' involvement in rent-seeking practices (Bui 2010: 313; Hoàng and Vân 2014; Lawyers E and F 2017), these low rates indicate lax enforcement of ethical standards rather than scrupulous compliance. Many factors have contributed to this laxity, including tolerance by Bar associations, practical difficulties in proving misconduct, and lawyers' attempts to resolve clients' complaints by early negotiation (Lawyers B, E and F 2017; Hoàng and Vân 2014).

Lawyers appear to know little about disciplinary cases (Lawyers A, B, C, D, E and F 2017). The Hanoi and HCMC Bars publish accounts of discipline on their websites, but the HCMC Bar does not disclose the nature of these cases, and the Hanoi Bar merely states which rules have been violated. According to a member of the VBF's Committee of Discipline and Reward, lawyers have regularly been disciplined for dishonesty, failure to respect clients' interests and property, failure to discharge undertakings, and improperly collecting service fees (Huệ 2017). Some lawyers, such as Lê Công Định and Lê Trần Luật, were disbarred for infringing national security (Dung 2009; Mặc 2009). State-supervised newspapers have reported two cases where local state agencies pressed Bar associations to discipline lawyers for making critical or offensive statements against the police, procuracies or courts but the local Bar associations successfully resisted (Hồng 2015b; Nguyễn 2014).

When lawyers violate ethical principles embodied in laws rather than the COC, they are technically subject to administrative sanctions, usually a fine (LOL 2015, Article 89). These sanctions are imposed not by professional associations but by state agencies, including the MOJ and local administrations (Decree 110/2013/ND-CP 2013, Ch VII). In very serious cases, the MOJ can cancel lawyers' professional certificates (LOL 2015, Article 18).

Finally, lawyers can be sued by their clients for breach of service contracts (LOL 2015, Articles 26, 59). Provincial Bars must mediate such disputes (LOL 2015, Article 88). While few cases have been submitted to courts or arbitration (Lawyers A,B, C, D, E and F 2017), 443 complaints were handled by the VBF between 2009 and 2014 (VBF 2015a: 16). There is little arbitration or litigation since lawyers usually settle with their clients (Lawyers E and F 2017). In addition, provincial Bars often resolve contractual claims during disciplinary proceedings, though this is not clearly mandated by either law or VBF regulations (Lawyer B 2017; VBF Regulation on Disciplining Lawyers 2012).

iv. Competitive Restrictions

The legal profession in Vietnam is subject to several restrictive practices. First, 'legal services' must be performed by qualified lawyers (LOL 2015, Article 11). Lay people, including legal experts without appropriate certificates or licences, and other professional consultants and firms cannot render legal services (LOL 2015, Articles 11, 23, 32; Decree 110/2013/ND-CP 2013, Articles 6.5, 7.6). The Supreme People's Court (SPC) has declared null and void a contract in which a consulting company rather than a law firm was engaged to represent and assist the client in arbitration (SPC Economic Court 2008: 4–5).

The Ministry of Planning and Investment (MPI) has recently contested the above restriction. Arguing that the LOL does not prescribe lawyers and law firms as the only lawful providers of 'legal services', the MPI has directed local administrations to license non-law firms to provide such services. This has prompted a robust debate between this ministry and the MOJ and lawyers' associations. All parties are awaiting the Prime Minister's decision to resolve the debate (Nghĩa 2019).

The exclusive privilege of lawyers in providing legal services has also been undermined by the fact that lay people can participate in civil proceedings as authorised representatives of parties (Lawyers E and F 2017; Civil Procedure Code 2015, Article 85; Hoàng 2013; Phiên 2012). This has enabled people with legal expertise, experience or connection with legal institutions, but no practising certificate, to perform litigation services (Hoàng 2013; Lawyers E and F 2017; Phiên 2012). Further, while the LOL defines 'legal services' to include 'participation in legal proceedings, legal consultancy, representation of clients (other than in legal proceedings) and provision of other legal services' (LOL 2015, Article 4), courts have not yet decided to what extent consultancy services, like accounting or administrative services, are different from legal consultancy (Lawyers E and F 2017).

There are also restrictions on competition between lawyers. Under Article 23 of the 2015 LOL, lawyers must practise either through a law firm or as 'a lawyer practising on an individual basis'. In the latter case, lawyers must be hired by an employer other than a law firm and restrict their services to that employer (LOL 2015, Article 49), but this restriction has not been effectively enforced (Lawyer E 2017).

Foreign lawyers (who can only obtain a renewable five-year licence) and foreign law firms are restricted to offering legal advice (LOL 2015, Articles 70, 76, 82.2). Foreign practitioners are not permitted to advise on Vietnamese law unless they have completed an LLB and the required one-year professional training in Vietnam (LOL 2015, Article 76), although law firms have not strictly observed this requirement (Lawyer A 2017).

Finally, the COC prohibits certain competitive practices, such as approaching potential clients in front of the offices of law enforcement agencies, encouraging potential clients to refuse other lawyers or law firms, making comparative statements to influence client choice, and damaging the reputation of other lawyers or firms (COC 2011, r 20). Disputes between lawyers must be resolved by negotiation and conciliation (COC 2011, r 19). Interviews suggest that the competition among law firms is moderate, possibly due to an expanding market (Lawyers A, B, C, E and F 2017), and lawyers in domestic law firms share knowledge and collaborate in providing services (Lawyers A, B, C, E and F 2017). There is increasing competition, however, among top-tier, internationally-oriented law firms, which are growing in number, size, and skills (Lawyers A, B, and D 2017).

C. Professional Associations of Lawyers

i. Vietnam Lawyers Association

With 46,000 members, the VLA is the biggest association of Vietnamese legal professionals (VLA 2015: 85). Because the 11,000 lawyers are a minority, VLA is commonly led by incumbent and retired Party-state leaders, such as members of central party committees and officials in the MOJ, SPC and Supreme People's Procuracy (ibid: 13–90; VLA Statute 2009, Preamble). Following the introduction of Đổi mới, the Party redirected the VLA's focus to domestic affairs (ibid: 29–31), such as law making, legal aid, propaganda and research (ibid: 32–81); but the VLA remained active on international legal issues, echoing the 'officially' sanctioned line (ibid: 71–75). The VLA is largely silent on issues relating to lawyers' interests, such as access to clients and attorney-client privilege. Lawyers generally do not 'identify' with the VLA even though they are members (Lawyers A, B, C, D, E and F 2017). The VLA rarely cooperates with the VBF and provincial bars, except in legal aid and activities mandated by the Party-state (Lawyers A, B, C, D, E and F 2017).

ii. Vietnam Bar Federation

Formed in 2009 through a process orchestrated by the MOJ and the central government (Bui 2010: 310–11), the VBF is the national socio-professional organisation of legal practitioners. By law, all lawyers and provincial Bar associations are VBF members (LOL 2015, Article 64.1). The National Representative Congress, its highest body, convenes every five years (VBF Statute 2009, Article 6) to elect the National Lawyers' Council, which in turn elects the Executive Committee, President and Deputy Presidents (VBF Statute 2009, Articles 7–9). The VBF leadership has been dominated by Hanoi and HCMC lawyers.

The VBF has a regulatory function, which includes organising Bar examinations, issuing lawyers' cards, enacting professional rules, supervising the implementation of legal and professional regulations (including involvement in disciplinary proceedings), and directing congresses of provincial Bars (LOL 2015, Article 65). The VBF also has a representative function, which it has exercised more effectively than the VLA. In the consultations preceding the 2015 Criminal Procedure Code (CPC), the VBF advocated for reforms to enhance the position of lawyers, including reducing the procedural barriers to their participation in criminal proceedings, recognising defence lawyers' right to collect evidence, and extending the right to counsel (VBF 2015b; Trực 2015). The VBF's opposition to Circular 28/2014/TT-BCA of the Ministry of Public Security (MPS) exemplifies its advocacy. Under this Circular, police investigators were authorised to act against defence lawyers who allegedly challenged the investigative process, even recording their acts or statements (Circular 28/2014/TT-BCA 2014, Article 38). Because of objections from the legal community, including the VBF, the MPS substantially amended this provision before it came into effect (Phan 2014).

Nevertheless, the VBF remains a relatively weak voice in governmental fora. For example, it failed to persuade the National Assembly to recognise attorney-client privilege in the 2015 Criminal Code or to secure more radical procedural changes, including equality between procurators and defence lawyers. Faced with strong opposition from Party-state officials (Hoàng 2017; Đức and Chân 2017), the VBF failed to take a strong position on 2015 Criminal Code Article 19.3 limiting protection for lawyers, despite extensive calls from members to do so (Lawyers D and E 2017; Lawyer H 2018; LS Lê Ngọc Luân 2017). VBF leaders also effectively restrained lawyers from expressing their dissatisfaction with Article 19.3 by delaying a workshop at which individual lawyers hoped to influence the debate (Lawyer E 2017; Lawyer H 2018).

Periodically the VBF has sided with the Party-state rather than its own members. VBF leaders remained silent when members called for a demonstration to support lawyers Lê Luân and Trần Thu Nam, who were targeted by the Party-state (Lawyer E 2017; Tran 2015b), and when lawyers like Lê Công Định and Lê Trần Luật were convicted for 'infringing national security'. Recently, the VBF asked members to 'strictly comply with the line [and] policy of the Party [and] the State', warning them to 'be cautious in making statements, observations [and] comments in the media in complicated issues where the authorities have not made conclusions' (VBF 2017).

The role of the VBF must be related to its close supervision by the Party-state. It must report its activities to the MOJ (LOL 2015, Article 65.18; Lawyer B 2017). The VBF Party Committee is under the direct supervision of the CPV's Central Commission for Internal Affairs (CCIA). The Party has maintained tight control over the VBF leadership, ensuring that Party members have leadership roles and retaining a decisive voice in nominations (Lawyers B and D 2017).

However, there are indications that lawyers are increasingly resisting CPV control. In 2009, the Party directed that Lê Thúc Anh, a former leader of the CCIA and the SPC, be elected as President at the First VBF Congress (Lawyers D and F 2017). Senior lawyers from the HCMC Bar, such as Nguyễn Đăng Trừng, opposed this, arguing that Anh was not an 'actual' lawyer (Lawyers D and F 2017; Bui 2010: 310–11). Nevertheless, Anh was elected VBF President and held this position until 2015. At the Second VBF Congress in 2015, the Party nominated Anh for another term (Lawyers B, D and F 2017) but, anticipating resistance, prepared a second candidate, Phạm Quý Ty, a retired Deputy Minister of Justice (Tran 2015a). During the Congress some delegates criticised the VBF leadership and the Party's intervention, although their microphones were muted (Lawyer D 2017). Several Hanoi lawyers joined their HCMC colleagues to block Anh's bid for a seat on the National Lawyers' Council, rendering him ineligible to be President (Lawyer D 2017; Tran 2015a). Because Ty was just barely elected to the Council, Đỗ Ngọc Thịnh, a former CCIA official with practical legal experience, was made Acting President (Lawyer D 2017; Tran 2015a), becoming President a year later. But though these events suggest that some lawyers seek a leader who understands and represents them (Lawyer D 2017), others, especially those from small provincial Bars which depend significantly on state funding, do not support independence for lawyers' organisations (Bui 2010: 310; Lawyer B 2017).

iii. Bar Associations

Provincial Bar associations are the primary socio-professional groupings of lawyers. Like the VBF, they regulate training and apprenticeship, assess applications for lawyers' certificates (before forwarding them to the authorities), enforce professional rules (and take disciplinary action), and handle complaints and disputes relating to lawyers (LOL 2015, Article 61).

Although Bar associations are required to defend the interests of legal practitioners (LOL 2015, Article 61.1), provincial Bars traditionally have not done so (Lawyers B, D, E and F 2017). Recently, however, the Hanoi and HCMC Bar Associations have become increasingly active. The Hanoi Bar played an important role in opposing Circular 28/2014/TT-BCA, marshalling public opinion against the regulation (Nghĩa 2014), and attempted to assist lawyers facing state pressure (Hanoi Bar 2015). Concurrently, leaders of the HCMC Bar sought to resist party control of their associations. Most recently, the HCMC Bar publicly called on the National Assembly to recognise legal professional privilege (HCMC Bar 2017). Nevertheless, members still criticise these associations for failing to represent lawyers (Lawyers B, E and F 2017).

Provincial Bars are closely controlled by both the VBF and provincial authorities. This was particularly evident in the 2014 Congress of the HCMC Bar, when the VBF and the HCMC authorities managed to oust the high-profile lawyer Nguyễn Đăng Trừng from the Presidency he had held since 1995. Despite being a veteran party member, he was known for conflicts with the VBF and Party-state authorities, including resistance to Lê Thúc Anh as VBF President in 2009 (Lawyers B, D, E and F 2017). In the lead-up to the 2014 Congress, therefore, the VBF and the HCMC authorities required that Presidents be no older than 70 and serve no more than two terms (Lawyers B, E and F 2017; VBF 2014; HCMC People's Committee 2014), thereby excluding Trừng.

Trừng fought back (with strong support from lawyers), arguing that this directive was unauthorised by the *LOL*, contrary to the practice of other provincial bars, and inconsistent with an earlier HCMC poll (HCMC Bar 2014a; HCMC Bar 2014b). He also publicly criticised the local Party-state authorities for violating the autonomy of legal professional associations (HCMC Bar 2014c). The HCMC authorities responded by ordering the police to seize his seal and prevented him from attending the Congress, which elected a new president (Lawyers D, E and F 2017). The Party expelled Trừng, but he retained a lawyer's certificate (Lawyers D, E and F 2017). Trừng received considerable support from younger colleagues (Lawyers A, D, E and F 2017), possibly reflecting their weaker connection to the Party-state and stronger attachment to professional independence. By contrast, several senior lawyers endorsed Trừng's disqualification, citing his failure to develop the organisation (Lawyers B, C, E and F 2017). Some did not support him personally but endorsed his resistance to Party intervention (Lawyer D 2017).

D. Demographics: Lawyers and Firms

i. Lawyers

Lawyers have grown in number while remaining concentrated in major cities. There are 10,914 lawyers, a third of them women (VBF 2016a),[8] or about 8,500 people per lawyer.[9] When Bar associations were re-established in Hanoi (1984) and HCMC (1989), they only had 16 and 28 lawyers respectively (Phan and Trương 2015: 193–201). In 2016, they had

---

[8] These figures do not include procurators, who are considered legal officials rather than lawyers.
[9] Vietnam's population in 2016 was 92.7 million (GSO 2016).

2,959 and 4,584 members respectively, accounting for over 69 per cent of lawyers (VBF 2016a). Only five of the other 61 Bar associations (all based in economically developed regions) had more than 100 members, while five in mountainous and rural provinces had less than ten (MOJ 2016a). In 2011, only 104 of 7,072 lawyers (1.47 per cent) reported practising outside law firms (MOJ 2012: 4), indicating the immaturity of in-house counsel. There were also 165 foreigners licensed to practise law in 2016 (MOJ 2016b).

ii. Firms

Law firms must be registered as either a law office (an unlimited company wholly owned by one lawyer) or a law company (a partnership or proprietary limited company) (LOL 2015, Articles 32.1, 33.1, 34.1). There were 3,711 domestic and 68 foreign-owned law firms by the end of 2016; 62.6 per cent were law offices, and 67 per cent were in Hanoi and HCMC (MOJ 2016a; 2016b). Vietnamese law firms average less than three lawyers. A typical HCMC firm includes 5–10 legal and support staff (Lawyers E and F 2017). Bigger domestic or foreign-owned firms have approximately 60–80 staff, including paralegals, who are usually new law graduates but can also be law students or others familiar with legal processes and state institutions (Lawyers A, B, D, E and F 2017).

iii. Working Practices

Except for foreign firms, which are legally restricted to legal advice, most law firms also perform litigation and other legal services (Lawyers B, D, E and F 2017). Despite their small size, domestic firms are usually prepared to assist clients in most substantive areas, although there is increasing specialisation (Lawyers D, E and F 2017). Foreign-owned firms and top-tier internationally-oriented domestic firms tend to focus on business law (Lawyers A, B, C, D, E and F 2017). Foreign-owned and top domestic law firms regularly receive outsourced projects from global law firms (Lawyers A, B and C 2017), and foreign-owned firms must refer litigation to domestic firms (LOL 2015, Article 70), although they often continue to liaise between clients and the domestic firms (Lawyers A and C 2017). Outsourcing also occurs between domestic firms because of lack of expertise or geographical distance (Lawyers B, E and F 2017).

E. Publicly Funded and Pro Bono Work

Lawyers in Vietnam must participate in publicly funded work in two ways. First, as paid contractors they help state-sponsored legal aid centres provide free legal services for the poor and vulnerable (LOL 2015, Article 21; Law on Legal Aid 2017, Article 17). In 2015, 10.7 per cent of law firms and 12.1 per cent of lawyers were registered to work with legal aid centres (MOJ 2015). Between 2007 and 2014, lawyers offered legal services through these centres in 126,426 matters, including 37,999 litigated cases (MOJ 2015). But because legal aid services are poorly paid, they fail to attract competent lawyers (MOJ 2015; Lawyer E 2017).

Second, lawyers are publicly funded to assist certain criminal defendants, including juveniles, the physically or mentally disabled, and defendants potentially subject to jail terms of 20-years or more or the death penalty (CPC (Revised) 2017, Article 76). The relevant provincial Bar must assign a law firm to provide such services when requested by the State (CPC (Revised) 2017, Article 76). Firms often choose junior inexperienced lawyers to perform them because of the low pay rates (Lawyers E and F 2017).

Article 27.2 of the VBF Statute requires lawyers to provide pro bono services. Bar associations often cooperate with legal aid centres to organise free legal consultancy and education for poor people, for example through briefing or Q&A sessions (Lawyers B and F 2017). The impact is insignificant, however, because of insufficient time and poor organisation (Lawyers B and F 2017).

F. Legal Services Market

Demand for lawyers appears to have grown rapidly in the past 30 years. The remarkable supply-side expansion, including lawyers, law firms and colleges, is a strong indicator. A lawyer from a leading commercial firm said large Vietnamese corporations had replaced foreign companies as half of his clients (Lawyer B 2017). Smaller firms also have benefited from greater use of lawyers by individuals and small and medium enterprises, not just for dispute resolution, as in the past, but also for important transactions, administrative procedures and daily corporate operations (Lawyers E and F 2017). The government has also begun to engage lawyers in big investment projects (Lawyer D 2017).

The increasing involvement of lawyers in civil and commercial transactions has gradually reinforced the importance of law in the eyes of their clients, further increasing demand (Lawyers E and F 2017). Online newspapers and social media have extensively covered cases in which lawyers successfully assisted their clients. Judges increasingly seem to appreciate the role of lawyers in encouraging parties to seek legal advice (Lawyers E and F 2017).

Litigation fees are often structured as a base fee and an incentive fee varying by outcome (Lawyers B, E and F 2017). Hourly fees for criminal defence case are capped at 30 per cent of the government's monthly base wage rate, currently VN$390,000 (US$17.20) (Decree 123/2013/ND-CP 2013, Article 18.1).

III. LAWYERING

A. Statism, Party Control and Activism

Lawyers have resisted the Party-state and actively defended their clients, often at great personal risk. Lawyers also support their clients in extra-legal ways, using social networks.[10] The following case illustrates these interactions. In 2014–15, lawyer Võ An Đôn represented a family in a criminal case, in which five police officers were prosecuted for torturing their relative to death. State-sponsored newspapers reported serious concerns about the abuse of police power and local authorities' lenient response (Lawyers D

---

[10] For example, lawyer Lê Luân posted legal arguments used at trial and the final comments of Mother Mushroom (a Vietnamese blogger activist) on Facebook (Wallace 2017).

and C 2014). After the trial, the Police, Procuracy and Court of Tuy Hoà (a district of Phú Yên Province) sent an official letter to the Department of Justice (DOJ) and the Phú Yên Bar Association urging revocation of Đôn's lawyer's certificate (Tấn 2014). They alleged that Đôn had 'made uncultured statements which were offensive to those participating in the case and many incumbent leaders of law enforcement agencies' and criticised him for 'creating a negative hot spot in public opinion' through his 'statements, writing, interviews [and] commentary in social media [and] local and international [media] fora' (Tấn 2014). The DOJ announced it would inspect Đôn's law office as part of an 'annual plan', although his was the only law office investigated in 2015 (Hồng 2015a).

The threat of disciplinary action against Đôn was widely reported in state-sponsored newspapers and social media, eliciting broad support for him from other lawyers and the public (Tấn 2014; Lawyer H 2018). VBF leaders sent a taskforce to meet with provincial Party-state authorities, who acknowledged failing to provide sufficient evidence or follow proper procedures (ibid). Nevertheless, the VBF publicly advised Đôn to be more cautious in his speech and behaviour (ibid). Đôn subsequently successfully pressed the authorities to prosecute another police officer, but failed to secure a conviction for murder rather than torture (Ngọc 2016).[11] Intensifying his criticism of the Party-state in the media and his participation in political dissident cases and mass conflicts with the government, Đôn continued to be targeted by local authorities and was removed from the Bar roll in November 2017 (Võ 2015; Hùng 2016 and 2017; Tấn 2017). The VBF upheld this removal (Trung 2018), and the state media was less supportive.

This case reveals how state and social media may help activist lawyers gain support from the public and the legal community, thereby reducing the power disparity between individual lawyers and the Party-state. But it also indicates the risks of such a strategy, given the Party-state's tight control over lawyers.

B. Lawyers as Reform Agents: Pro Bono and Constitutional Change

i. Pro Bono Assistance – Novel Resistance?

Individual lawyers have increasingly volunteered to assist the poor and vulnerable in criminal cases and large-scale environmental and land conflicts with the state or corporate actors (Lawyers E and F 2017). Recently, pro bono lawyers have either incorporated as social enterprises like the Nine Lawyers' Channel (Kênh 9 Luật sư)[12] or formed loosely connected groups like the For-Justice Project (Dự án Phục vụ Công lý)[13] and the Defence Panel (Hội đồng Bào chữa) (Lawyer E 2017). While the impact of pro bono assistance in large-scale conflicts remains uncertain, there is considerable evidence that such lawyers have successfully helped wrongfully convicted or powerless plaintiffs in criminal proceedings (Lawyer E and F 2017).

---

[11] See also Tuổi trẻ online, 'Tag: Ngô Thanh Kiều' www.tuoitre.vn/ngo-thanh-kieu.html containing 28 articles reporting on this case from 24 August 2012 to 23 August 2016.
[12] Kênh 9 Luật sư [Nine Lawyers' Channel] www.facebook.com/9lawyerschannel/.
[13] Phục vụ Công lý [For Justice] www.facebook.com/PH%E1%BB%A4C-V%E1%BB%A4-C%C3%94NGL%C3%9D-449052351965796/.

Whereas some interviewees appreciate the work of pro bono lawyers (Lawyers E and F 2017), others portray them as self-promoting or otherwise 'unusual' (LawyersB and D 2017; Lawyer-Scholar I 2018). Pro bono lawyers receive little support from their organisations. The VBF, for instance, refused to endorse the For-Justice Project and directed provincial Bars to adopt the same position (VBF 2016b). And Party-state authorities have not welcomed the involvement of pro bono lawyers in large-scale conflicts or criminal proceedings involving political offences (Mai et al 2017; Giáo 2017).

ii. Constitutional Activism

During the last constitutional amendment process in 2011–12, the Party-state called for an open dialogue about constitutional change on any matter. In response, 72 high-profile retired officials and intellectuals, including a former Minister of Justice, submitted Petition 72 calling for wide-ranging reforms, including multi-Party democracy (Bui 2013). Others proposed their own agendas (Vo 2016; Bui 2016: 224–30). Those involved in these events demonstrated strategic acumen by choosing the Party-state sanctioned debate on constitutional reform to push the boundaries of acceptable discourse and deploying sophisticated linguistic strategies by using ambiguous terms, hoping to see their language incorporated into the 2013 Constitution so as to permit ongoing contestation (Bui 2016: 224–230; Vo 2016; Nicholson 2017). But the Party-state retaliated by discrediting some of the main actors, particularly those involved in Petition 72 (Bui and Nicholson 2016). The Party continues to rely on the enduring socialist principle, democratic centralism, which allows policies to be debated (the democratic element) until the State reaches a decision, which must be implemented without further criticism (Bui 2016, Nicholson and Pham 2018).

IV. CONCLUSION

The constraints on lawyers vary across jurisdictions. Private commercial lawyers working for non-state clients in matters unconnected with the state are relatively immune from interference. But lawyers who contest the Party-state's power or interests (particularly in criminal cases) are more vulnerable to state pressures. The opacity of the limits on acceptable activism elevates the risks for reformist lawyers. Lawyers have increasingly sought to protect each other, often through social media. While individual actors probe the boundaries of permissible activism, institutions, particularly the VLA and VBF, are more constrained. This reflects their co-optation through supervision by the Party-state, whose members belong to and often lead professional associations. Nevertheless, the Hanoi and HCMC Bars have increasingly resisted Party-state pressures by criticising legal system dysfunction – actions that are facilitated by the fact that these Bars include influential Party-state figures. Their location in cities, where lawyers are better educated and the Party-state is more open to debate, may also help. Whatever the explanation, Vietnamese lawyers are testing boundaries and contesting laws and practices in the name of 'justice' in diverse jurisdictions and seeking to embolden their professional organisations.

REFERENCES

(Vietnamese names are set out reflecting Vietnamese custom: surname, middle name and then first name)

Buhman, K (2007) 'Building Blocks for the Rule of Law? Legal Reforms and Public Administration in Vietnam' in M Sidel and S Balme (eds), *Vietnam's New Order: International Perspectives on the State and Reform in Vietnam* (New York, Palgrave Macmillan).

Bui, Hai Thiem (2016) 'Constitutionalizing Single Party Leadership in Vietnam: Dilemmas of Reform' 11 *Asian Journal of Comparative Law* 224.

Bui, Ngoc Son (2013) 'Petition 72: The Struggle for Constitutional Reforms in Vietnam', *I-CONnect: Blog of the International Journal of Constitutional Law and ConstitutionMaking.org*, www.iconnectblog.com/2013/03/petition-72-the-struggle-for-constitutional-reforms-in-vietnam/.

Bui, Ngoc Son and Nicholson, P (2016) 'Activism and Popular Constitutionalism in Vietnam' 42 *Law & Social Inquiry* 677.

Bui, Thi Bich Lien (2005) 'Legal Education in Transitional Vietnam' in John Gillespie and Pip Nicholson, *Asian Socialism and Legal Change The Dynamics of Vietnamese and Chinese Reform* (Canberra, ANU E Press).

Bui, Thi Bich Lien (2010) 'Legal Education and the Legal Profession in Contemporary Vietnam' in J Gillespie and A Chen (eds), *Legal Reforms in China and Vietnam: A Comparison of Asian Communist Regimes* (Abingdon, Routledge).

Communist Party of Vietnam (CPV) (2002) *Resolution 08-NQ/TW on Major Tasks of the Judicial Work in the Forthcoming Period* 2 January.

—— (2005) *Resolution 49-NQ/TW on Strategies for Judicial Reforms until 2020* 2 June.

D, Thanh and C, Mai (2014) 'The Case of Five Policemen Using Torture: Awaiting for a Lawful Judgment' *Tuổi trẻ* 3 April www.tuoitre.vn/vu-5-cong-an-dung-nhuc-hinh-cho-mot-phan-quyet-dung-phap-luat-601191.htm.

Đức, Minh and Chân, Luận (2017) 'Debate regarding Lawyers Denunciating Clients' *Pháp luật TPHCM* 26 May www.plo.vn/phap-luat/nong-chuyen-luat-su-to-giac-than-chu-704549.html.

Dung, Ngọc (2009), 'Excluding Le Cong Dinh from the Bar Association' *Tiền phong* 23 June www.tienphong.vn/phap-luat/khai-tru-le-cong-dinh-khoi-doan-luat-sunbsp-164304.tpo.

Duy Tân University (2019) *Essential Information on University and College Enrolment in 2019* www.nhungdieucanbiet.edu.vn/Pages/Clients/Default.aspx.

General Statistics Office (GSO) (2016) *Press Release on the Socioeconomic Situation of 2016* 28 December.

—— (2017) *Press Release on the Socioeconomic Situation of 2017* 27 December.

—— (2018) *Health, Monthly Average Income Per Capita at Current Prices by Residence and Region*.

Giáo, Luật (2017) 'About Lawyers Who Always Lose' *Văn nghệ TPHCM* 13 July www.tuanbaovannghetphcm.vn/ve-doi-ngu-luat-su-toan-thua.

Gillespie, J (2006) *Transplanting Commercial Law Reform: Developing a 'Rule of Law' in Vietnam* (Aldershot, Ashgate).

—— (2007) 'Understanding Legality in Vietnam' in M Sidel and S Balme (eds), *Vietnam's New Order: International Perspectives on the State and Reform in Vietnam* (New York, Palgrave Macmillan).

Ginsburg, G (1979) 'The Genesis of the People's Procuracy in the Democratic Republic of Vietnam' 5 *Review of Socialist Law* 187.

Hanoi Bar (2015) *Official Letter 298/DLSHN-BCN Requesting the Initiation of Criminal Proceedings against the Infringement upon the Life, Health and Properties of Lawyers* 3 November.

HCMC Bar (2014a) *Official Letter 135/DLS Responding to Official Letter 140/LDLSVN of the VBF President dated 10 April 2014* 20 May.

—— (2014b) *Official Letter 135A/DLS Responding to Official Letter 2495/UBND-PCNC dated 3 June 2014* 9 June.

—— (2014c) *Notice 135B/DLS on Recent Development regarding the HCMC Bar Congress for the 4th (2013–2018) Tenure* 16 June.

—— (2017), *Official Letter 103/CV-DLS regarding Comments on Article 19.3 of the 2015 Criminal Code* 12 June.

HCMC People's Committee (2014) *Official Letter 2495/UBND-PCNC Declining to Approve the Organisation Plan for the Next HCMC Bar Congress Enclosed with Document No. 18B/DLSTPHCM* 3 June.

HCMCUL (2018) *Strengths of the HCMCUL* 10 March ts.hcmulaw.edu.vn/vi/tong-quan-ulaw/cac-the-manh-cua-truong-dai-hoc-luat-tp-ho-chi-minh.

Ho, Ai Nhan (2016) 'Legal Education in Vietnam: The History, Current Situation and Challenges' 26 *Legal Education Review* 69.

Hoàng, Điệp and Vân, Trường (2014) 'How to Enforce Legal Ethics?' *Tuổi trẻ* 23 October www.tuoitre.vn/giam-sat-dao-duc-luat-su-bang-cach-nao-661741.htm.

Hồng, Ánh (2015a) 'Lawyer Vo An Don Is under the Radar Again' *Người Lao động* 9 January www.nld.com.vn/thoi-su-trong-nuoc/luat-su-vo-an-don-lai-bi-soi-20150109231731918.htm.

—— (2015b) 'The Case of Lawyer Vo An Don Has Gone Too Far?' *Người Lao động* 22 January www.nld.com.vn/thoi-su-trong-nuoc/vu-luat-su-vo-an-don-bi-day-qua-xa-20150122221141054.htm.

Hoàng, Thuỳ (2017) 'National Assembly Chairperson: "Lawyers Must Not Only Protect Clients, But Also Protect Justice"' *VnExpress* 30 May www.vnexpress.net/tin-tuc/phap-luat/chu-tich-quoc-hoi-luat-su-bao-ve-than-chu-nhung-cung-phai-bao-ve-cong-ly-3592549.html.

Hoàng, Yến (2013) 'Does a Legal Expert Have the Right to Enter a Contract for Legal Services?' *Người Đưa tin* 8 May www.nguoiduatin.vn/luat-gia-co-quyen-ky-hop-dong-thuc-hien-dich-vu-phap-ly-a79769.html.

Huệ, Linh (2017) 'When Lawyers Are Removed from the Bar Roll' *An ninh Thủ đô* 7 May www.anninhthudo.vn/chinh-tri-xa-hoi/khi-luat-su-bi-xoa-ten-do-vi-pham-dao-duc-nghe-nghiep/727112.antd.

Hùng, Phiên (2016) 'The Police Invited Lawyer Vo An Don to Work about Facebook' *Dân Việt* 7 March www.danviet.vn/phap-luat/cong-an-moi-luat-su-vo-an-don-lam-viec-ve-facebook-665507.html.

—— (2017) 'Phu Yen: Lawyer Vo An Don is Proposed to Be Disciplined for … Criticising the Profession' *Dân Việt* 20 August www.danviet.vn/tin-tuc/phu-yen-luat-su-vo-an-don-bi-de-nghi-ky-luat-vi-noi-xau-nghe-797766.html.

Kerkvliet, Benedict J Tria (2003) 'Authorities and the People: An Analysis of State-Society Relations in Vietnam' in Hy Van Luong (ed), *Postwar Vietnam: Dynamics of a Transforming Society* (Singapore, Institute of Southeast Asian Studies).

—— (2010) 'Governance, Development, and the Responsive-Repressive State in Vietnam' 37 *Forum for Development Studies* 33.

LawNet (2018) '89.9% of Law Graduates Have Jobs' lawnet.thukyluat.vn/posts/t7262-89-9-sinh-vien-luat-ra-truong-co-viec-lam-sau-12-thang.

Lindsey, T and Nicholson, P (2016) *Drugs Law and Legal Practice in Southeast Asia* (Oxford, Hart Publishing).

Liu, Charles Chao (2002) 'China's Lawyer System: Dawning upon the World through a Tortuous Process' 23 *Whittier Law Review* 1037.

LS Lê Ngọc Luân (2017), 'I Officially Submit a Letter to the NA' [Facebook post] 30 May www.www.facebook.com/permalink.php?story_fbid=497662050565168&id=100009641314161.

M, Quang (2014) 'Five Police Officers Using Torture: More Offences Prosecuted' *Tuổi trẻ* (7 September) www.tuoitre.vn/5-cong-an-dung-nhuc-hinh-khoi-to-them-toi-646756.htm.

Mặc, Lâm (2009) 'Lawyer Le Tran Luat Is Removed from the Bar Roll' *RFA Vietnamese* 1 November www.rfa.org/vietnamese/in_depth/The-bar-association-of-ninh-thuan-province-deleted-the-name-of-lawyer-le-tran-luat-from-its-list-mlam-11012009120520.html.

Mai, Hà, Lê, Quân and Minh, Sang (2017), 'Releasing the Draft Conclusion on Inspecting the Dong Tam Land Dispute' *Thanh niên* 7 July www.thanhnien.vn/thoi-su/cong-bo-du-thao-ket-luan-thanh-tra-dat-dong-tam-852902.html.

Michelson, E (2011) 'Lawyers, Political Embeddedness, and Institutional Continuity in China's Transition from Socialism' in Y Dezalay and B Garth (eds), *Lawyers and the Rule of Law in an Era of Globalization* (New York, Routledge).

MOJ (2012) *Report No 46/BC-TP on the Five Years' Implementation of the LOL* 6 March.

—— (2015) *The Role of Lawyers in Renovating Legal Aid Work* 17 December www.moj.gov.vn/qt/tintuc/Pages/nghien-cuu-trao-doi.aspx?ItemID=1891.

—— (2016a) *National Statistics on the Organisation and Operation of Lawyers* (unpublished).

—— (2016b) *Twenty Years of Foreign Lawyers Practising in Vietnam* 11 March www.moj.gov.vn/qt/tintuc/Pages/hoat-dong-cua-lanh-dao-bo.aspx?ItemID=2580.

Nghĩa, Nhân (2014) 'Circular 28 of the Ministry of Public Security' *Pháp luật TPHCM* 17 August www.plo.vn/thoi-su/chinh-tri/thong-tu-28-cua-bo-cong-an-bo-cong-an-hua-tiep-thu-y-kien-cua-lien-doan-luat-su-490141.html.

—— (2019) 'Two Ministries Debate regarding the Legal Services Profession: Awaiting the Prime Minister's Conclusion' *Pháp luật TPHCM* 26 July www.plo.vn/phap-luat/2-bo-tranh-cai-nghe-tu-van-luat-cho-thu-tuong-phan-xu-848198.html.

Ngô, Tất Hữu and Anh, Tú (2014) 'Hanoi Bar Association: 30 Years of Construction and Growth' *Dân trí* 20 November www.dantri.com.vn/phap-luat/doan-luat-su-thanh-pho-ha-noi-30-nam-xay-dung-va-truong-thanh-1417088542.htm.

Ngô, Văn Hiệp (2014) 'The Historical Emergence and Evolution of the Legal Profession in Vietnam' 7 *Tạp chí Nghề luật* 17.

Ngọc, Trường (2016) 'Reducing Penalties for the Policemen Using Torture to Death' *VnExpress* 13 September www.vnexpress.net/tin-tuc/phap-luat/cong-an-dung-nhuc-hinh-gay-chet-nguoi-duoc-giam-an-3467115.html.

Nguyễn, Cường (2014) 'What Did the Lawyer Condemned as "Offending State Agencies Carrying out Legal Proceedings on Facebook" Say?' *Infonet* 21 April www.infonet.vn/luat-su-bi-to-xuc-pham-co-quan-to-tung-tren-facebook-noi-gi-post126958.info.

Nguyen, Hung Quang (2007) 'Lawyers and Prosecutors under Legal reform in Vietnam: The Problem of Equality' in M Sidel and S Balme (eds), *Vietnam's New Order: International Perspectives on the State and Reform in Vietnam* (New York, Palgrave Macmillan).

Nguyen, Hung Quang and Steiner, Kerstin (2005) 'Ideology and professionalism: the resurgence of the Vietnamese bar in Vietnam' in J Gillespie and P Nicholson (eds), *Asian Socialism and Legal Change: The Dynamics of Vietnamese and Chinese Reform* (Canberra, ANU E Press).

Nguyen, Nhu Phat (1997) 'The Role of Law during the Formation of a Market-Driven Mechanism in Vietnam' in J Gillespie (ed), *Commercial Legal Development in Vietnam: Vietnamese and Foreign Commentaries* (Sydney, Butterworths).

Nguyễn, Văn Tuân (2012) *Some Issues regarding Lawyers and the Legal Profession* (Hanoi, Tư pháp Publishing House).

Nicholson, P (2005) 'Vietnamese Jurisprudence: Informing Court Reform' in J Gillespie and P Nicholson (eds), *Asian Socialism & Legal Change: The Dynamics of Vietnamese and Chinese Reform* (Canberra ACT, Australian National University Press).

—— (2007a) *Borrowing Court Systems: The Experience of Socialist Vietnam* (Leiden, Martinus Nijhoff).

—— (2007b) 'Vietnamese Courts: Contemporary Interactions Between Party-State and Law' in M Sidel and S Balme (eds), *Vietnam's New Order: International Perspectives on the State and Reform in Vietnam* (New York, Palgrave Macmillan).

—— (2010) 'Access to Justice in Vietnam: State Supply – Private Distrust' in J Gillespie and A Chen (eds), *Legal Reforms in China and Vietnam: A Comparison of Asian Communist Regimes* (Abingdon, Routledge).

—— (2015) 'Renovating Courts: The Role of Courts in Contemporary Vietnam' in Jiunn-Rong Yeh and Wen-Chen Chang (eds), *Asian Courts in Context* (Cambridge, Cambridge University Press).

—— (2017) 'Rule of Law with Socialist Characteristics and Democratic Centralism: Vietnam Considered' Paper presented at 'Troubling the Rule of Law' Kiola, NSW, unpublished.

Nicholson, P and Nguyen, Hung Quang (2005) 'The Vietnamese Judiciary: The Politics of Appointment and Promotion' 14 *Pacific Rim Law and Policy Journal* 1.

—— (2017) 'Asia-Pacific Judiciaries: Independence, Impartiality and Integrity in Vietnam' in HP Lee (ed), *Asia Pacific Judiciaries* (Cambridge, Cambridge University Press).

Nicholson, P and Pham, Lan Phuong (2018) 'Roots and Routes: Adapting the Soviet-inspired Vietnamese Court and Procuracy Systems' in Fu Hualing, J Gillespie, P Nicholson and W Partlett (eds), *Socialist Law in Socialist East Asia* (Cambridge, Cambridge University Press).

Pham, Duy Nghia and Do, Hai Ha (2018) 'The Soviet Legacy and Its Impact on Contemporary Vietnam' in Fu Hualing, J Gillespie, P Nicholson and W Partlett (eds), *Socialist Law in Socialist East Asia* (Cambridge, Cambridge University Press).

Phan, Đăng Thanh and Trương, Thị Hoà (2015) *History of the Legal Profession in Vietnam* (HCMC, HCMC Publishing House).

Phan, Trung Hoài (2014) 'Good Signals from the Decision of the Ministry of Public Security' *Lao động* 1 September www.laodong.vn/lao-dong-cuoi-tuan/tin-hieu-vui-tu-quyet-dinh-cua-bo-cong-an-239607.bld.

Phiên, Giang (2012) 'The Lawyer Has Won the "Lawyer-Is-Not-a-Lawyer" Case' *Người Đưa tin* 27 December www.nguoiduatin.vn/luat-su-thang-kien-vu-luat-su-khong-phai-la-luat-su-a36531.html.

Quinn, BJM (2003) 'Vietnam's Continuing Legal Reforms: Gaining Control Over the Courts' 4 *Asian-Pacific Law & Policy Journal* 432.

Sidel, M (1993) 'Law Reform in Vietnam: The Complex Transition from Socialism and Soviet Models in Legal Scholarship and Training' 11 *UCLA Pacific Basin Law Journal* 221.

—— (1994) 'The Re-emergence of Legal Discourse in Vietnam' 43 *International and Comparative Law Quarterly* 163.

—— (2008) *Law and Society in Vietnam* (Cambridge, Cambridge University Press).

SPC Economic Court (2008) *Judgment No 10/2008/KDTM-GDT* 30 December 2008.

Tấn, Lộc (2014) 'The Case of Five Policemen Beating a Person to Death in Phu Yen: the Police, Court and Procuracy Requested that the Lawyer Be "Punished"' *Pháp luật TPHCM* 5 December www.plo.vn/thoi-su/vu-nam-ca-danh-chet-nguoi-o-phu-yen-ca-toa-vien-doi-xu-luat-su-513796.html.

—— (2017) 'Removing Lawyer Vo An Don from the Phu Yen Bar Roll' *Pháp luật TPHCM* 26 November www.plo.vn/phap-luat/xoa-ten-luat-su-vo-an-don-khoi-doan-luat-su-phu-yen-741766.html.

Thục, Quyên (2017) 'Tightening Conditions for Becoming a Lawyer' *Pháp luật Việt Nam Plus* 5 June www.phapluatplus.vn/siet-chat-tieu-chuan-tro-thanh-luat-su-d44998.html.

Tran, Thu Nam (2015a) 'VBF Congress' [Facebook post] 19 April www.facebook.com/luatsutrannam/posts/933452106694610.

—— (2015b) 'Event' [Facebook post] 11 November www.facebook.com/luatsutrannam/posts/1035053026534517.

Trực, Ngôn (2015) 'More Rights for Lawyers' *Người Lao động* 27 May www.nld.com.vn/phap-luat/them-quyen-cho-luat-su-20150527223257662.htm.

Trung, Thi (2018) 'Revocation of the Lawyer's Card of Võ An Đôn' *Dân trí* 25 May dantri.com.vn/phap-luat/thu-hoi-the-luat-su-doi-voi-ong-vo-an-don-20180525085627732.htm.

VBF (2014) *Official Letter 140/LDLSVN regarding Organising HCMC Bar Congress* 10 April.

—— (2015a) *Report on the Work of the First Tenure (2009–2014) and Orientation for the Work of the Second Tenure (2014–2019)*.

—— (2015b) *VBF Representatives Participated in the Conference of Full-time National Assembly Delegates that Discussed Some Draft Bills* 28 August 2015 www.liendoanluatsu.org.vn/web/Dai-dien-Lien-doan-Luat-su-Viet-Nam-tham-du-Hoi-nghi-dai-bieu-Quoc-hoi-chuyen-trach-thao-luan-mot-so-du-an-Luat-187.html.
—— (2016a) Statistics sent to authors by VBF official, unpublished.
—— (2016b) *Official Letter 139/LDLS Providing the Opinion about the For-Justice Project* 12 April.
—— (2017) *Official Letter 173/BTV-LDLS Reminding Individual Lawyers in Their Practice and Statements on the Media* 31 May.
VLA (2015) *60 Years of Constructing and Developing the VLA (4/4/1955 – 4/4/2015)* (Hanoi, Hồng Đức Publishing House).
Võ, An Đôn (2015) 'I am Going to Be Disciplined and Revoked the Lawyer's Certificate' [Facebook post] 19 June www.www.facebook.com/100008231020747/videos/1612568255694193/.
Vo, Tri Hao (2016) 'Integration of the Principle of Separation of Power into the Constitution Amendment 2013 within the "Keeping Face" Cultural Context' paper presented at 'Constitutional Debate in Vietnam' Conference, National University of Singapore 19–20 March unpublished.
Vu, Cong Giao and Tran, Kien (2016) 'Constitutional Debate and Developments on Human Rights in Vietnam' 11 *Asian Journal of Comparative Law* 235.
Wallace, J (2017) 'With Social Media, Vietnam's Dissidents Grow Bolder Despite Crackdown' *The New York Times* 2 July www.nytimes.com/2017/07/02/world/asia/vietnam-mother-mushroom-social-media-dissidents.html.

44

Comparative Sociology of Lawyers, 1988–2018

The Professional Project

RICHARD L ABEL[1]

THE NATIONAL REPORTS offer thick descriptions and interpretations of the ways in which legal professions have been shaped by history, economics, politics, social context and outside influences (colonialism, emulation, regional groupings, globalisation). This chapter seeks to identify, understand, assess, and extrapolate the differences that emerge through comparisons among countries (the 19 in the 1988/89 volumes and the 46 in this volume), within them (between professional fractions), and over time.[2] Only comparison can generate and test hypotheses about why a legal profession possesses its distinctive characteristics and how it might change. But comparison faces many challenges. What is to be compared? The original books soon discovered that their core concepts were problematic: taken-for-granted English words like 'legal profession' and 'lawyer' were not easily translated and meant different things – or nothing at all – in other societies. It is easier to compare similar phenomena (eg the US and UK) but also less revealing. Common law professions oriented toward markets and civil law professions structured by the state required different theorisations (see Konttinen 2003; Siegrist 2003; Modéer 2003). Quantification facilitates comparison across countries, but it necessarily simplifies and may distort by positing false equivalences; and data in one country often are unavailable in others. Numbers may be ambiguous: 9,000 lawyers belonged to the Libyan Bar Association in 2014, but only 3,500–4,000 actually practised (because, as in other countries such as Egypt, many belonged for the health care and pension benefits).[3] Qualitative comparison of entire legal professions confronts

---

[1] I am grateful to Ole Hammerslev, Hilary Sommerlad and Ulrike Schultz for their close reading of this chapter, which helped me avoid errors, clarify my meaning, and deepen the analysis.

[2] Unless otherwise indicated, all data come from this volume. Chapters in the 1988/89 volumes will be cited only when data from them appear for the first time.

[3] The Egyptian Bar Association sought to discourage non-practising lawyers from registering by tripling its fees, closing new registrations, and requiring registrants to prove they were practising. Although lawyers successfully sued to block each rule, the number of registrations more than halved, from 350,000 in 2016 to 123,340 in 2018.

the complexity of numerous confounding variables. This chapter, therefore, poses more questions than it answers (in the hope of stimulating others to explore them).

My understanding of the legal profession has been powerfully shaped by Magali Sarfatti Larson's theory of the professional project (1977; see Abel 1979a; 1995), which reflected Max Weber's views about professions (1954; 1978), perhaps shaped by his own legal training. Professions construct themselves by controlling the production *of* producers: erecting entry barriers that influence how many aspirants qualify and which ones do. Professions also seek to control production *by* producers: who may offer services and how they may practise. This 'project' – the term embodies the contingent nature of professionalism, always a process, never an uncontested achievement (Bucher and Strauss 1961) – affects both the profession's economic well-being (by suppressing external and internal competition) and its social status (a function of entrants' ascribed characteristics and a gentlemanly disdain for 'trade', exemplified by Weber's *honoratiores*). No theory can explain everything about a complex social phenomenon like a profession. (I discuss the relationship between lawyers and the state in the conclusion to the companion volume.) But because occupations that exercise no market control are not professions – like American lawyers during the Jacksonian era, when any adult white male could call himself a lawyer – I believe relations with the market are an appropriate starting point.[4] This theorisation suggests several comparative inquiries.

I. HOW MANY LAWYERS?

Conceptualising the legal profession as a project of supply control focuses attention on how its size fluctuates and how it responds (Abel 2017a). The number of lawyers (relative to the larger population) may affect access to justice, the cost of legal services, social mobility, the social status of members, and the profession's political influence. When the Working Group for Comparative Study of Legal Professions examined this question in 1988, some legal professions had recently entered a post-war growth spurt, following a long period of relative stasis, during which its numbers had failed to keep up with population increase and economic growth. That mismatch had been produced by the conjunction of entry barriers the profession had erected or accepted (apprenticeship, examinations, limited university places) and the effects of two World Wars and the Great Depression. Even though the number of US law school places increased nearly tenfold from 4,486 in 1889 to 44,341 in 1927 (as entry shifted from apprenticeship to formal education), the ratio of population per lawyer in 1950 was exactly what it had been in 1900 (Abel 1988a). This changed dramatically in the 1960s: 37 law schools opened between 1966 and 1981, the number of law students tripled between 1961 and 1980, and the annual number of Bar admissions rose from the 10,000s in the 1960s to the 40,000s in the 1980s. As a result, the number of lawyers tripled between 1950 and 1980, and the ratio of population to lawyers halved (Abel 1989: Table 22). In the UK,[5] the number of practising solicitors was

---

[4] I replied to criticisms of market theory in Abel (1995).
[5] All references to the UK pertain to England and Wales.

almost the same in 1948 as it had been in 1890; after World War I tragically reduced the practising strength of the Bar by about a fourth it remained at that depressed level until well after World War II (Abel 1988b). Then the number of law students increased from under 3,200 in 1961/62 to over 8,500 in 1981/82; the number of new barristers grew from the 100s in the 1950s/60s to the 200s in the 1980s, with the result that the total number of barristers increased 2.5 times; and the number of new solicitors grew from under 1,000 before 1965 to the low 2,000s in the 1980s, with the result that among privately practising solicitors the number of principals doubled while the number of assistant solicitors increased sixfold (Abel 1988c: Table 3.2). Germany had *fewer Anwälte* in 1959 (18,214) than it had in 1933 (19,200) and almost the same population:lawyer ratio (3,014 and 3,438), partly because of the Nazi expulsion of Jewish lawyers and murder of those who did not flee and German deaths during the war (Reifner 1986).

Other countries experienced similar post-war expansions. Despite a 4 per cent population decline, the number of new Scottish solicitors rose from under 100 to 400 (although the number of new advocates remained constant). In Canada, both law students and lawyers tripled (while the population grew by just a third) (Arthurs et al 1988). In Germany the number passing the second state jurists examination doubled from the 1950s to the 1980s (while the population grew only 15 per cent) (Blankenburg and Schultz 1988). The number of lawyers admitted annually in Geneva increased from under ten to more than 60 (Bastard and Cardia-Vonèche 1988). The number of law students tripled in Spain in just seven years (1971/72 to 1978/79) (Viladás Jene 1988), quadrupled in Norway (Johnsen 1988), and increased sixfold in the Netherlands (Schuyt 1988) and Australia (Weisbrot 1988) and nearly tenfold in Italy (Olgiati and Pocar 1988). In France, the number of law degrees awarded increased from below 2,000 in the 1960s to 7,000 in the 1980s, and the number passing CAPA (the professional entry exam) rose from the 200s to 1,000 (while the population grew just 18 per cent) (Boigeol 1988). In Belgium, the number of law degrees rose from the 300s to 1,200, and the number of lawyers doubled (while the population grew less than seven per cent) (Huyse 1988). In Israel the number of lawyers grew from 765 in 1949 to 10,687 in 1990 (while the population increased little more than threefold). In 1940, Colombia had ten law faculties; 32 more were established by 1967, more than half of them after 1960 (Lynch 1981: 34). The number of law students more than tripled in Egypt, from 180,000 in 1970 to over 550,000 in 1980. Whereas an average of 45 lawyers qualified in Nigeria annually in 1947–58, 238 did so in 1964 (four years after independence), 523 by 1980, 1,235 by 1985, over 2,000 a year starting in 1990, and more than 4,000 after 2003. The number of lawyers increased 1.5 times in the Netherlands, just under twofold in Japan, and twofold in France. In some countries, the ratio of law students to private practitioners portended rapid future growth: it was 1:1 in Venezuela (Pérez Perdomo 1988), 1.5:1 in Brazil (Falcão 1988), 2:1 in India in 1971 (Gandhi 1988), 2–3:1 in Spain (Viladás Jene 1988), and 3:1 in Italy in 1978 (Olgiati and Pocar 1988). Elsewhere, however, the ratio suggested future stasis or even decline: 1:6 in Scotland, 1:5 in the US, 1:4 in Canada, 1:3 in the UK, 2:5 in Australia, and 3.5:5 in Norway.

These figures must be interpreted with caution. Although almost all law students graduate and become lawyers in the US and Canada, that is much less true elsewhere. Attrition is high in other countries: just 10 per cent of Spanish law students ultimately graduated, 15 per cent in Egypt, 20 per cent in Venezuela, 30 per cent in Argentina, 33–50 per cent in Norway, 38 per cent in Germany, and 50 per cent in Belgium. India is an extreme case: just 2–5 per cent of law school entrants ended up practising; 200,000 students entered law faculties in 1978/79, but only 10,000 new lawyers registered with their Bars. Today, about half of Germans who begin studying law drop out; 70 per cent of those taking the first state exam pass; 10 per cent of those passing do not take the second, and another 12–18 per cent of those taking the second exam fail (for an overall attrition of nearly 75 per cent). Because of inadequate secondary education, only 21 per cent of those entering Chilean law schools complete their degrees. In Australia, less than 40 per cent of law graduates enter private practice. In Russia, *most* of those who earn a law degree do not practise.

This post-War burst of growth – explosive in some instances – had multiple causes. Some common law countries saw an erosion of supply control as apprenticeship (which the profession controlled) was displaced by formal education (which it did not). In England and Wales, articles for solicitors (even after premiums were abolished) and pupillage for barristers represented significant obstacles: finding a place and – for barristers who are not salaried – enough briefs to earn a living. Aspiring lawyers in Myanmar have difficulty obtaining a one-year apprenticeship with a chambers master. In Germany, by contrast, all those passing the first state examination get a two-year apprenticeship as a salaried civil servant. Zimbabwe shortened pupillage from three years to one to accelerate the entry of black lawyers.

Other factors were beyond the profession's control. Women, who had been almost entirely excluded, entered in numbers gradually approaching and even exceeding those of men (discussed below). The state expanded public education in response to pressure for equal opportunity among those disadvantaged by class or ethnicity; for the same reasons, as well as the influence of neoliberalism, the state began to tolerate private universities. And the post-war economic boom, the increasing prominence of human rights discourse, and the rise of the welfare state spurred demand for lawyers' services.

But if the first four decades after World War II displayed a widespread pattern of professional growth, the last three have seen dramatic differences in national rates (see Tables 1–3; Katvan et al 2017). The *annual* increase ranged from a staggering 568 per cent in Vietnam (where the number of lawyers in Hanoi and Ho Chi Minh City grew from 44 in 1984/89 to 7,543 in 2016 and the number of law schools increased from 20 in 2008 to 53 in 2017, while the national population increased just 1–3 per cent a year) to just 2.9 per cent in the US between 1990 and 2015 (not much faster than the population growth of 0.71–1.4 per cent). Countries that had almost no legal profession under colonialism saw it expand dramatically after independence: in Egypt from 4,433 lawyers in 1949 to 700,000 in 2013, in Nigeria from fewer than a thousand at independence in 1960 to over 100,000 today.

National legal professions can be grouped into several categories by growth rate. First, countries that have (or had) communist planned economies have seen their professions expand rapidly in response to the privatisation of state enterprises, emergence of a domestic market, and increasing international trade and investment, eg Czech Republic, China, and Russia.[6] The DDR (including East Berlin) had just 592 *Anwälte* for 17 million

---

[6] For Georgia, see Waters (2004).

people in 1989; the former Eastern states of the unified Germany (excluding Berlin) had 12,311 for 12.6 million in 2017. In Poland, the number of business enterprises multiplied more than 2.5 times between 1990 and 2016. Although the number of advocates increased only 17 per cent and the number of attorneys at law barely changed in the first seven years after the end of communism, the number of trainees for both categories doubled over the next seven. In Czechoslovakia the number of lawyers declined drastically from 3,845 in 1938 to 570 in 1951 as a result of the Nazi occupation (and the expulsion or murder of Jews), World War II, and the communist takeover. Following the end of communism, the number in the Czech Republic rose from 826 in 1989 to 6,554 in 1999 and 11,310 in 2016. In Bosnia and Herzegovina, the number nearly quadrupled, while the population declined, with the result that the ratio of population per lawyer fell to nearly a fifth of what it had been; in Serbia the number of lawyers nearly quadrupled between 1990 and 2018 while the population per advocate fell from 3,834 to 761. When China decided to revive its legal profession after the depredations of the Cultural Revolution, the number of law students *doubled every year* from 1991 to 2012: from 25,075 in 200 law schools in 1991 to 613,752 in more than 600 law schools in 2012 (see Table 1). In 1988 there were just 21,051 full-time and 10,359 part-time lawyers; by 2017 there were over a million. In Russia, the number of law schools increased from 30 in the 1980s to over a thousand in 2012, granting 150,000 degrees a year, with the result that the annual increase in the number of lawyers rose from 3.1 per cent in 1939–59 to 13.4 per cent in 1959–2015.

Second, several countries deliberately expanded and diversified their legal professions for a variety of political reasons. In Egypt, Nasser abolished university tuition in 1961. Under Chávez and Maduro, Venezuela aggressively sought to democratise its profession – increasing the annual number of law graduates more than fivefold (from an average of 3,599 in 1986/89 to 19,532 in 2015) and more than tripling the size of the legal profession (from 66,263 in 2000 to 224,074 in 2015) – in order to open it to the poorer classes, increase access to justice, and perhaps dilute the power of the legal establishment, which was critical of the regime. In post-apartheid South Africa, the profession felt an urgent need to recruit from the 85 per cent of the population who had been virtually excluded because they were Black, with the result that since the 1980s the number of attorneys increased from 6,500 to 25,383 and the number of advocates from 650 to 2,915. (But because the Black majority had been subjected to 'Bantu education' under apartheid and continue to suffer from inadequate schooling and other disadvantages, half of those who entered law school in 2000–06 failed to graduate in four years.) In the 1960s, Dutch law schools dropped the requirement that applicants know Latin and Greek, thereby opening the door to those who had not attended elite gymnasia. Israel's newer private law schools have opened the profession to an increasing number of Sephardim and orthodox religious Jews. In Burundi, the number of lawyers increased tenfold following the 1993 massacre of Tutsi because of the nation's determination to redress past injustices.

Iran's mullahs created a new category of lawyer – advisers to the judiciary – who entered the profession through the easier route of religious study. As a result, the profession tripled between 2005 and 2015. Because advisers' licences must be renewed annually, they are subject to political control and more subservient to the theocratic regime. Several countries facilitated entry to private practice by those who had served the state, thereby demonstrating their loyalty. Under Gaddafi, Libya allowed court clerks and other judicial employees with several years' experience to qualify by examination; and others could do so by studying Sharia. In Egypt, graduates of al-Azhar University Faculty of Law and Sharia may become lawyers even though they do not complete a comprehensive course on state law. Countries as diverse as Tunisia and Taiwan allowed judges (including military judges) to retire to private practice, again bolstering support for the regime.

East Asian countries like Japan, South Korea and Taiwan, which had drastically limited entry through an extraordinarily difficult professional examination, decided that economic growth and globalisation required more (and perhaps different) lawyers. The contortions of Japan's educational reforms expose the complex politics of supply control. The Japanese Federal Bar Association (JFBA), Supreme Court and Ministry of Justice decided to increase the number admitted to the Institute of Legal Training and Research (the sole path to becoming a *bengoshi*) from 500 in 1988 to 1,000 in 1997 and 3,000 in 2010.[7] It planned to do so by supplementing the existing entrance exam (with a pass rate of 2–5 per cent) for those with an undergraduate law degree with a new exam (with a pass rate of 80 per cent) for those graduating from the newly established post-graduate law schools. But the reformers were stunned that 72,800 enrolled in 74 new graduate law schools in 2004. When the first graduates took the new exam in 2006, 1,558 passed (48 per cent of takers), and more than 2,000 did so each of the next six years (even though the pass rate was cut to 25 per cent in 2010 and remained at or below that level). The rapid growth in the number of new entrants provoked the JFBA to demand that the total number passing be reduced to 1,500. Although it took a hundred years for the number of South Korean lawyers to reach 10,000 in 2009, it took less than ten for the number to more than double, reaching 23,557 in 2017. Although Hong Kong's earliest lawyers were expatriates or trained abroad, its first law school graduated its first class in 1972, and its third school did so in 2004.

Third, some countries with just a few public law schools allowed private schools to proliferate (see Kritzer 2012). Serbia added a sixth public law faculty in 1976 and a seventh in 2006; but it now also has five private faculties enrolling 16 per cent of law students. In Chile the number of law schools rose from five in 1980 to 49 by 2014, some with multiple campuses, with the result that the number of entrants more than quadrupled, from 815 in 1997 to 3,487 in 2015. Most Latin American countries admit any secondary school graduate to law school and have no Bar exam (eg Argentina, Chile, Mexico). In Mexico the number of law schools increased from 93 to a staggering 1,715 in the last 30 years (though many new schools are very small). Brazil had 130 law schools with 135,026 students in 1988 but 1,158 law schools with 737,000 students in 2012 (increases of nearly ninefold and more than fivefold, respectively), with the result that the number of law graduates rose from 20,599 to 97,900 (nearly fivefold); and the number of lawyers increased 8.5 per cent annually between 1981 and 2012. Although the military in Myanmar closed all universities in 1988, the first law school reopened in 1993, and 17 have since been established. Palestine opened its first law school in 1994 (following the Oslo Peace Accords); by 2017 its 11 law schools enrolled over 8,000 students. Nigeria established four public law schools immediately after independence in 1960 and 23 more between 1978 and 1999; the years

---

[7] It also sought to favour younger examinees by requiring that at least 30 per cent of those passing had taken the exam less than four times. Because of its difficulty (and the investment of years of study), some older aspirants repeated the exam indefinitely.

2000–18 saw the establishment of nine more public and 17 private law faculties. In Turkey it took almost a century for the number of law schools to increase from one to three in 1978; after private foundations were permitted to establish law schools in 1983 the total exploded to 63 in 2012, and the number of lawyers increased from 39,000 in 1990 to 100,461 in 2016. In Israel the number of law schools jumped from 3 to 14, with the result that the annual growth of the legal profession doubled, from 4.7 per cent in 1980–90 to over 10 per cent in 1990–2010. In Tunisia the number of law schools offering an LLM doubled from 30 in 2004/05 to 61 in 2012/13. Australia had just 12 law schools in 1988 but 40 in 2016. Before 1960, Thailand had just two public law schools; by 2014, it had law schools at 14 selective public universities, two public universities with unrestricted admissions, and 27 private universities; the annual number of law graduates increased from 5,000 in the 1990s to nearly 10,000 in 2010.

Finally, countries whose legal professions had experienced significant expansion before 1988 have seen much slower growth since then (about 5 per cent a year) or even declines in new entrants (Canada, France, Netherlands, Italy, UK, Switzerland, US). Applications to and enrolment in US law schools fell in response to the 2008 recession and the upward spiral of tuition fees (increases of 46 per cent at private and 132 per cent at public law schools between 1999 and 2014) and of the consequent educational debt burden; and they have only partly recovered (Abel 2015; 2017b).

The growth patterns described above affected the ratio of population per lawyer, which has declined everywhere but at different rates; the greatest drops are 90 per cent in Serbia since the 1940s, 85 per cent in the Netherlands since the 1960s, and 83 per cent in Venezuela since 1981 (see Table 4). Even more revealing is the fact that some national ratios are more than 60 times higher than others.[8] The highest today are found in present or former communist countries (eg Vietnam, Russia, Bosnia and Herzegovina), less developed countries (eg South Africa, Tunisia, Iran), and East Asian countries that historically restricted entry to the profession (eg South Korea, Japan). But within those categories, the ratio is lower in countries that allowed or encouraged the number of law students to increase: developing countries like Chile, Mexico, Brazil, and Venezuela; and former communist countries like Serbia and Poland. And though the ratio is generally lower in developed countries, there are marked differences among them: France is almost four times and Switzerland three times as high as Italy. Israel is the most extreme case, with a ratio less than half that of other developed countries. There are also large internal differences. In India in 1981, there were 747 people per lawyer in Delhi compared with 8,373 in the outlying states of Assam and Nagaland; in 2017, the difference was less than half as great but still substantial: 309 and 1,436. The ways in which individuals and organisations relate to their legal systems cannot help but be shaped by whether there is one lawyer for every 139 people (Venezuela) or every 8,500 (Vietnam) (countries whose per capita GDP differs by less than 2:1); similarly, what it means to be a lawyer is influenced by the number competing for business. Further insight might be found by examining the GDP per lawyer, which ranges from US$5.4 million in Israel to US$236 million in Japan.

---

[8] Barzilai (2007: Table 8.1) gives 2005 figures for 39 countries, ranging from 211 for Israel to 6,357 for South Korea.

What explains these differences and changes? There is ample evidence that professions have tried to limit entry, with varying degrees of success. Some have been protected by a *numerus clausus*: French *notaires* (Shaw 2006) and *officiers ministériels*[9] as well as *avocats* at the Conseil d'État and Cour de Cassation; *Anwälte* in the German Supreme Court; Dutch notaries; Czech notaries and private bailiffs. In the England and Wales, Queen's Counsel have consistently been limited to 10 per cent of barristers. Starting in the nineteenth century, the English Law Society required aspiring solicitors to take a growing number of increasingly difficult examinations, whose pass rates fluctuated, rising after the two World Wars (during which many died and few qualified) and falling during the Great Depression (as demand for legal services contracted) (Abel 1988b). In the US, state Bar associations and supreme courts steadily raised the educational requirements for lawyers; and Bar examination pass rates varied with the state's attractiveness to entrants: as high as 100 per cent in poor rural jurisdictions like Vermont, Montana, New Mexico, and North Dakota but much lower in rich urban states like New Jersey (37 per cent) and Massachusetts (46 per cent) (Abel 1989: Tables 15–16, 18). When universities displaced apprenticeship as the initial gateway as well as the locus of post-graduate practical training, the number of places they offered continued to limit entry. In the 1980s, four times as many took the Law School Aptitude Test (LSAT) as obtained a place in a US law school (ibid: Table 4); there were 17 applicants per place in UK law faculties (Abel 1988c: Table 3.6), 5–10 in Canada (Arthurs et al 1988). Similarly, professional associations limited the number of places in their mandatory post-graduate training courses (Abel 2003: ch 3).

As discussed above, professional examinations in some East Asian countries had exceptionally low pass rates (even though examinees crammed for years after completing a law degree): Japan (2 per cent), South Korea (3–5 per cent), and Taiwan (under 9 per cent). Indeed, not a single graduate from 70 of South Korea's 100 law schools *ever* passed the exam. But because the number of examinees in Taiwan rapidly increased, the annual number of new lawyers rose from less than 30 before 1989 to over 1,000 today. And when South Korea replaced undergraduate legal education with graduate law schools (which had selective admissions based on a test like the LSAT), it also replaced the Bar exam with a final examination whose pass rate was 75 per cent (and which could be retaken four times). China required only a junior college degree when it first decided to expand its legal profession, moving to a university degree (not necessarily in law) only in 2001 (by which time there were many more university places). When it merged the Bar exam for private practitioners with those for prosecutors and judges, the pass rate on the first administration in 2002 was just 7 per cent. That was raised to 20 per cent later that decade in order to increase the number of lawyers in rural and western areas and then cut to under 15 per cent in the 2010s as the number of examinees doubled from 200,000 in 2003 to over 400,000 in 2013. In Indonesia, by contrast, the Bar examination consists of answering 200 multiple choice questions (from a list that can be studied in advance) and drafting legal papers (which can be memorised). The real obstacle to entry is discovering when and where Bar associations are administering the mandatory oath!

---

[9] On their resistance to neoliberal reforms, see Mathieu-Fritz and Quemin (2009).

When legal education expanded (usually because private law schools were permitted and had a market incentive to increase enrolment), some legal professions sought to stem the tide by introducing a professional examination. Although this campaign failed in Mexico, the Brazilian Bar Association required an examination whose average pass rate in 2010–14 was just 17.5 per cent. In Turkey, the issue was hotly contested. In response to the proliferation of private law schools, an exam was introduced in 2001; this was annulled by Parliament; but though that decision was overturned by the Constitutional Court the exam still had not been administered in 2017. In 2015, the Higher Education Council took another tack, requiring minimum secondary school grades to enter law faculties. Israel responded to concern about rising numbers by cutting the Bar exam pass rate from 70 per cent in October 2014 to below 50 per cent in 2016 and 2017 and restoring the mandatory apprenticeship to 18 months (after it had been reduced to 12 to facilitate entry) (Kricheli-Katz et al 2018: 444–45). But the Bar exam has been criticised for excluding a higher proportion of private law school graduates (often from Sephardic families with less education and fewer resources). A Palestinian Bar association instituted a pre-apprenticeship examination, which was blocked by the High Court and then revived. An effort to institute a national Bar exam in India (where graduation from law school qualifies for practice) is being litigated. By contrast, Spain, Mexico and Venezuela have no requirements beyond a university law degree; Scotland, England and Wales, and Australia exempted most university law graduates from professional exams; and almost all law school graduates in Canada, New Zealand (Murray 1988) and France pass the professional exams.

Apprenticeship requirements also fluctuate. The Czech Republic requires a three-year apprenticeship. Although trainers traditionally had a close relationship with trainees, supervising just one at a time, some trainers began taking as many trainees as possible in order to maximise the number of clients they could serve (and their own profits) while doing little actual training. In 2017 the profession responded by limiting trainers to five trainees. Palestine limited supervisors with five years' experience to one apprentice and those with ten or more to two. These variations in entry barriers – between countries and within them over time – are unsupported by systematic evidence (as opposed to anecdote) demonstrating any relationship to the quality of practice, strongly suggesting that professions manipulate barriers to control their numbers (a strategy whose success depends on politics).[10]

Just as US states vary in their receptiveness to out-of-state lawyers, so countries differ greatly in their response to globalisation. Foreign lawyers had just begun to practise across national borders in significant numbers in 1988 (Abel 1994; see also Godwin 2015). Their numbers, dispersion, and influence have greatly increased in the last three decades. India has totally excluded them (Singh 2017). Israel, Tunisia and Serbia are protectionist, whereas Mexico is hospitable. In China, foreign lawyers cannot practise Chinese law or employ Chinese lawyers (unless the latter suspend their Bar registrations), but Chinese firms have merged with foreign firms to offer clients multinational competence. Japan allowed foreign lawyers to practise foreign law in 1987, become partners with Japanese

---

[10] In the US, the National Conference of Bar Examiners and the Institute for the Advancement of the American Legal System are launching two of the first empirical studies into whether the Bar exams measure lawyer competence (Sloan 2019).

lawyers in 1995, and employ them in 2005. Large Anglo-American firms have merged with Japanese firms, and the number of foreign lawyers practising in the country grew from under 100 in 2000 to 411 in 2017. Hong Kong has been so hospitable (UK lawyers effectively can waive in) that 3.3 per cent of all private practitioners and 18 per cent of the profession were foreign in 2014 (although those not admitted cannot practise Hong Kong law). In Paris in 1987, the 400 foreign lawyers earned as much as the 7,000 French lawyers; in 2017, the 50 international firms earned twice as much as the 100 large French firms doing similar work. A thousand EU lawyers have qualified to practise in Germany, and another 300 practise foreign law. (Nevertheless, an average of just 0.5 per cent of lawyers in EU countries are foreign trained.) Foreign firms have merged or formed relationships with local firms in the Netherlands and Australia but not in Italy. Although US firms outsource work to cheaper foreign lawyers (eg in India), the US also exported an estimated $20 billion worth of legal services in 2004. The foreign offices of US firms contain more local lawyers practising local law than US lawyers practising US law (especially in the UK). Despite protectionism and the vagaries of trade negotiations and regional unions, globalisation will clearly continue to increase. (More than a quarter of US medical doctors have trained abroad, see American Immigration Council 2018).

Those seeking to enter the legal profession find ways around the barriers. Chilean law students who fail at more rigorous universities may transfer to less demanding ones (and graduate to become lawyers). Some US law graduates take an easier state Bar examination and then claim reciprocity from a state whose exam is more difficult; Italians qualify in Spain or Romania (both EU members) before returning home to practise. Because there are many more applicants than places in Canadian law schools, some Canadians qualify in the US before returning home (just as US citizens attend medical schools abroad). In response to protectionism, foreign lawyers fly into India for the day from Singapore and Hong Kong. Although foreign law and accountancy firms failed to establish beachheads in Denmark, lawyers commute from neighbouring countries (primarily Sweden and Finland). In Tunisia, the relative percentages qualifying via the easier *troisième étage* (LLM) and the more difficult CAPA examination inverted from 26/64 in 1985/86 to 70/28 in 1995–2009; but Tunisia refused to admit its citizens who qualified in Algeria. Some countries deliberately create alternative routes. Tunisia and Taiwan facilitate entry to private practice by retired judges and prosecutors in order to ensure a cadre favourably inclined toward the state. Palestinian judges who have served as little as a year can become lawyers without an apprenticeship. In Thailand, by contrast, the Bar exam for judges and prosecutors was more difficult than that for attorneys.

Although I have focused on supply factors, the size of the profession is also influenced by demand (Abel and Lewis 1989). But establishing that relationship confronts the difficulty of measuring demand independent of the number of lawyers (Sander and Williams 1989). Population and GNP are sometimes used, but the variation documented above suggests they are poor indices. Nor can litigation be disentangled from the number of lawyers. The fact that Russians filed more than three times as many civil and administrative cases in 2015 as they did in 2000 cannot demonstrate a tripling of demand. Some of this stunning increase may rather be attributable to the guesstimated one million non-lawyers offering legal services, who can appear in civil and administrative courts without any formal qualifications; but since their activities are wholly unregulated, we do not know if their numbers increased and, if so, how much.

There is evidence that legal professions seek to generate demand (Abel 2003: 26–67; 2003: chs 7–8; Bevan et al 1994).[11] I have argued that lawyers seek to preserve and expand legal aid out of self-interest as well as a commitment to access to justice. Some legal professions did campaign to generate demand during the last 30 years. In Turkey, a regulation mandated that joint stock companies with a capital of more than 250,000 Turkish Lira employ a lawyer. South Korea required large companies to hire lawyers as compliance officers. Exogenous factors can affect demand: the foreign (primarily US) crackdown on Swiss bank secrecy may have reduced the demand for Swiss lawyers to conceal funds, but it simultaneously increased the demand for criminal lawyers to defend those accused of money laundering. Brexit may reduce demand in the UK (by shrinking the financial sector); but it also will limit competition from foreign lawyers no longer able to practise there. Professions that rely heavily on performing a single function – such as English solicitors, who once derived half their income from conveyancing (Abel 1988c: 219) or Libyan lawyers representing the petroleum industry – may suffer a decline in demand when they lose their monopoly. Divorce mediation may curtail demand for lawyers in marriage dissolutions. Self-driving cars may lower the number of road accidents, and social insurance may lower the incentive to sue. More potential clients may resort to do-it-yourself methods, especially as artificial intelligence continues to develop.

Lawyer incomes seem to be correlated with the ratio of population to lawyers, one reason professional associations seek to control entry. The limited data (not directly comparable across countries) tend to confirm the relationship. Japanese lawyers, serving 3,370 people, enjoyed extraordinary average pre-tax incomes of $353,600 for men and $196,600 for women. Lawyers in Switzerland (840:1) earned an average of $147,000 in 2012; full-time partners averaged more than $600,000. By contrast, Belgian lawyers (599:1) averaged just $54,740; and German lawyers (503:1) earned an average hourly pre-tax profit of €53 in the former western states and €41 in the former eastern states, while employed advocates earned an annual average of €66,000. But there are numerous confounding variables, including the nature of the economy, the distribution of wealth, the range of services lawyers perform, and the existence of fee schedules. And French lawyers (1,075:1) averaged only $89,250. Lawyers complain that growing numbers have intensified competition and depressed fees, which fell 50 per cent in South Korea as entry rose dramatically. In many countries, recent law graduates cannot find employment. In the Netherlands, some work as paralegals in large firms. In Brazil, those who fail the Bar exam become paralegals and legal assistants. More than two-thirds of recently qualified Tunisian lawyers were unemployed 18 months after graduation. India has always had many underemployed lawyers. We lack evidence about the relationship between the population:lawyer ratio and access to justice.

Qualified lawyers face other competitors. In Thailand, law graduates who do not take (or pass) the Bar exam may still counsel clients (though they cannot represent them in court). In India 40–60 per cent of practitioners are not qualified. In Russia, lawyers compete with an estimated one million unqualified practitioners in everything but criminal defence; clients may not know or care whether their lawyer is qualified. To enhance

---

[11] An early precursor of the argument that third-party payment encourages demand to meet supply (rather than vice versa, as conventional economics predicts) is Roemer's Law: 'in an insured population a hospital bed built is a filled bed' (Shain and Roemer 1959).

access to justice in rural areas in the 1980s, China created township legal workers (renamed basic level legal service workers), who could do everything but criminal defence. (Their numbers declined from 121,904 in 1999 to 77,408 in 2006, but some became lawyers.) Clerics in Iran allowed non-lawyers to appear in court, ostensibly to increase access to justice but actually to dilute the influence of private practitioners, who were less loyal to the regime. The potential effect of letting unlicensed lawyers perform some legal functions is suggested by the impact of Uber, Lyft and other ride-sharing services on the cost and availability of transportation (and the wages of taxi drivers) and of AirBnB, VRBO, HomeAway and other short-term housing services on hotel prices.

When private practitioners multiply more rapidly than judges (because neoliberal regimes starve the public sector), judicial caseloads tend to rise, leading to speed-ups, quotas, and other new public management practices, as well as the delegation of judicial work to special masters, magistrate judges, administrative law judges, arbitrators and mediators, and clerical staff. That phenomenon may accelerate convergence between civil and common law countries (since the latter historically had a much higher ratio of lawyers to judges), including a shift from an inquisitorial procedure (which relies more on judges) to an adversarial system (which relies more on lawyers). In Poland between 1990 and 2016, the number of cases filed increased more than sevenfold, while the number of judges only doubled. In Germany the ratio of judges to *Anwälte* inverted from 1.6:1 in 1883 through equality in 1909 to 1:7.9 in 2017. Paradoxically, the same phenomenon may increase pressure to move some kinds of cases out of court – such as divorces and accidental injuries – reducing demand for lawyers just when their numbers are growing.

II. WHO ARE LAWYERS?

Larson (1977) conceptualised the professional project as seeking not just economic rewards (though market control) but also collective status enhancement by associating lawyers with privileged ascribed characteristics.[12] In the UK, entry barriers excluded and sorted by class (Abel 1988c: chs 4, 11; Francis 2011: ch 3); in the US they did so by race and ethnoreligious background (Abel 1989: ch 4); in civil law countries, universities admitted only graduates of gymnasia or their equivalents, excluding the lower class. And all countries excluded women. In recent decades, however, some legal professions have redefined their warrants of social status, replacing exclusivity with representativeness (Abel 2003: ch 4).[13]

The growth of legal professions since the 1970s coincides with their feminisation (see Table 5; Menkel-Meadow 1989; Schultz and Shaw 2003; Michelson 2013). In many

---

[12] Among professional projects, those of lawyers may be particularly concerned about status because the lawyer's role tends to elicit popular suspicion, as shown in Marc Galanter's masterful analysis of lawyer jokes (2005; see also Abel 2007). Frederick the Great is said to have demanded that lawyers wear gowns so the scoundrels could be spotted from a distance. (I am grateful to Ulrike Schultz for this anecdote.)

[13] When Paul, Weiss, a leading US corporate firm, announced its next class of partners – 11 white men and one white woman – criticism was immediate and harsh. More than 170 General Counsels and Chief Legal Officers wrote an open letter urging law firm partners to 'join us in a shared and authentic commitment to diversity and inclusion': Scheiber and Eligon, 'Elite Law Firm's All-White Partner Class Stirs Debate on Diversity', *New York Times* (27 January 2019); www.linkedin.com/feed/update/urn:li:activity:6495355575147335680/.

countries, indeed, *all* growth is attributable to the entry of women. Every country exhibits an increase in women as a proportion of law students and graduates, new lawyers and all lawyers, but the timing and rate of change vary.[14] Feminisation began earlier in some countries: women were half of private practitioners in Yugoslavia by the 1970s and over 70 per cent of Serbian law students in 2006 (and 35 per cent of practising lawyers and 71 per cent of judges in 2018); they were 58 per cent of advocate trainees in Bosnia and Herzegovina in 2018. They were high proportions in other communist countries, such as Bulgaria and Romania, and 60 per cent of law students and 62.5 per cent of law graduates in Poland in 2016. Significant numbers of women entered some West European legal professions relatively early: 14 per cent of Belgian law students in 1951, 54 per cent of Norwegian law students in 1988 and 65 per cent in 2012, half of Danish law students by the late 1980s and nearly two-thirds by 2015 (although they were still just 32 per cent of private practitioners in 2015), and more than half of new lawyers and a third of all lawyers in France in 1988. In Germany in 2017, women were 55 per cent of law students, 43 per cent of new *Anwälte*, and 35 per cent of all *Anwälte*.

There is greater variation outside of Europe. Although there had been few women law students in Zimbabwe immediately after it gained independence in 1980, they were a quarter of students by 1988 and about half by the 2000s (but still only 14 per cent of private practitioners in 2013). Women were a less than a tenth of new Nigerian lawyers until the 1970s, a quarter in the 1980s, a third by the mid-1990s and half by the end of the 2000s. Although women are underrepresented in tertiary education in many Muslim countries (McClendon et al 2018), they are 33–42 per cent of lawyers in theocratic Iran and 43 per cent in Turkey (a secular nation even though almost all its population is Muslim). Nevertheless, they were just 28 per cent of Palestinian lawyers in the West Bank and less than half that in Gaza (dominated by fundamentalist Hamas); and though they were half the Indonesian workforce, they were just 16 per cent of one prominent Bar association. Professions in some Asian countries also have been significantly slower to feminise: women were 18 per cent of lawyers in Japan (a proportion that had not increased since 2013), 28 per cent in South Korea in 2017 (but 40 per cent of law students), and 28 per cent in China in 2013 (but 37 per cent in Shanghai in 2017). Although the first woman qualified as a lawyer in India in the 1920s, as late as 2007 women were just 10 per cent of registered lawyers (ranging from 19 per cent in urbanised Gujarat to 3 per cent in rural Bihar). It is striking, therefore, that they are well represented in the new elite Indian national law schools and large commercial firms (Ballakrishnen 2017), as they are in large firms in China and Indonesia. Other Asian countries resemble Europe and North America. Women were nearly half of solicitors in Hong Kong by 2016, 52 per cent of law graduates in Thailand, and a majority of private practitioners, judges and law professors in Myanmar (which deliberately feminised the profession in the hope of depoliticising it).

At the same time, the distribution of women across professional sectors and roles tends to vary inversely with material rewards, status and power. They are better represented among solicitors compared with barristers (England and Wales, Scotland, Australia,

---

[14] Michelson (2013) explains the sequencing of feminisation in terms of lawyer density; but since the increase in lawyer density is attributable largely to the entry of women, the explanation runs the risk of tautology.

South Africa), judges and prosecutors compared with private practitioners (Netherlands, Czech Republic, Canada), lower court judges compared with those in higher courts (Australia), law firm associates compared with partners (US,[15] UK, Brazil, Hong Kong, Switzerland) (Sommerlad and Sanderson 1998; Rachman-Moore et al 2006; Melville and Stephens 2011; da Gloria Bonelli and de Pieri Benedito 2018). In Germany they are overrepresented among probationary prosecutors and judges (59 and 58 per cent respectively) and underrepresented among partners in the 200 largest law firms (just 11 per cent) and notaries. Among private practitioners, they tend to specialise in less remunerative fields (family and social law and medical malpractice) and earn less than men (averages of €64,000 and €80,000 in 2016). (The same is true in Belgium and Switzerland; and Japanese women lawyers earn little more than half as much as men.) Even after German women law students had outnumbered men for almost two decades, they remained less than 15 per cent of partners in all but three of the 20 largest law firms (and just 7 per cent in the three largest) and held just 16 per cent of chairs in law departments, though they were almost half of assistants. In Poland, women were 62.5 per cent of judges in administrative courts but 45.5 per cent in the Supreme Administrative Court; and they were 65 per cent in the regional courts, 61 per cent in District Courts, and 58 per cent in the appellate courts but just 29 per cent in the Supreme Court and 13.5 per cent in the Constitutional Tribunal. In Serbia, women are less well represented in the higher ranks of legal academia (30 per cent of full professors, 40 per cent of lecturers and 52 per cent of teaching assistants), though this may change as younger women ascend the ranks.

This dramatic global transformation has significant implications. First, it suggests that the rapid growth experienced by many legal professions in recent decades is likely to taper off as women are equally represented. Indeed, growth has already slowed in some countries. In Germany, the number of Referendare passing the second state examination *halved* from the early 2000s to 2013, and the number of high school graduates is declining as a result of falling birth rates.[16] The cohort of 19–24-year-olds shrank 31 per cent in Poland between 2005 and 2016. The number of law students in Denmark was 3.5 times as great in 1978 as it had been in 1958 but only 1.25 times as great in 1997 as it had been in 1978; although the number of jurists increased from 9,324 to 15,384 between 1985 and 2000 it barely rose (to 15,730) in 2014.

Second, if the profession (or a sector of it) 'tips', becoming majority female, its prestige and income may decline. (This happened to other professions in the past – school teachers and clerical staff in the US and doctors in the USSR; but the powerful contemporary movement for gender equality and the centrality of lawyers to the polity and economy make a repetition less likely.) Third, we need to study how the profession continues to reproduce internal gender inequalities in terms of income, status and power

---

[15] Wave III of the American Bar Foundation's 'After the JD' study of US lawyers admitted to the bar in 2000 reported in 2013 that fewer were in private practice than 10 years earlier (down from 68.8 to 44.1 per cent) and more were in business, where hours are more predictable (up from 8.4 to 20 per cent). Women working full time in law firms still earned just 80 per cent as much as men, and women were less likely to be partners (52.3 versus 68.8 per cent) and, if partners, less likely to be equity partners (53 versus 65.5 per cent) (American Bar Foundation 2018: 14).

[16] In 2018, Japan had the lowest number of births since 1899, when its population was a third as large (Josuka, 'Japan suffers biggest natural population decline ever in 2018', CNN 23 December 2018).

and how it distributes work demands and family responsibilities across gender lines. Fourth, if women and men relate to and practise law differently (as some have argued, eg Menkel-Meadow 1989), then the entry, equality, and perhaps dominance of women may transform notions of legality.

In the 1988 volumes, the few national reports dealing with race described the underrepresentation of religious minorities (Muslims in India), racial minorities (in the US and UK), and indigenous peoples (in Canada, Australia and New Zealand). In the present volume, more chapters address diversity, documenting the underrepresentation of immigrants in the Netherlands (12 per cent of the population in 2014 but just 8 per cent of new law students in 1997–2001), Asians in Australia, and blacks in Brazil (more than half the population but just 20 per cent of law students in 2012 and 5 per cent of lawyers in 2016). At Nigeria's independence in 1960, slightly more than half of its lawyers (540 out of 963) were indigenous, but most expatriates soon left. Under South African apartheid, there were few black attorneys and hardly any black advocates. Today blacks (91 per cent of the population) are still only 42 per cent of attorneys and 37 per cent of advocates; but this will continue to change since blacks are 78 per cent of final year LLB students, 63 per cent of candidate attorneys, and 69 per cent of advocate pupils. Southern Rhodesia emulated South Africa by excluding blacks (who were only five of the 175 attorneys and seven of the 56 advocates in 1980); but after Zimbabwe became independent that year, blacks quickly dominated the profession, and most white lawyers emigrated. Before independence, blacks had been just 1–5 of the 30 entering law students; but in 1980 they were more than 90 per cent of the 90 new students. Zimbabwe fused the divided profession in part to increase the entry of blacks and qualify them for appointment to the bench. In the US, blacks, Latinos, American Indians and Alaskan Natives were a static 9 per cent of lawyers in both 2000 and 2010 (barely more than the 8.2 per cent they had been in 1985/86), although they were more than 30 per cent of the population. Asian Americans, by contrast, who are 5.6 per cent of the population, increased from 1 to 3 per cent of the profession during this period. Visible minorities in Canada (a category that includes Asians but not Indigenous people) were 4.7 per cent of the population and 2.4 per cent of the profession in 1981; 30 years later both categories had increased (to 20 and 11.3 per cent), but the profession was no more racially representative. In some countries, the racial composition of the profession now reflects that of the society. The category Black, Asian or Minority Ethnic was 12.8 per cent of the British population but 15 per cent of solicitors in 2014 and 33 per cent of law students. (However, Asians are overrepresented). In Indonesia, ethnic subgroups cluster in different roles: Javanese elite in large firms, Sumatrans as litigators, Chinese as fixers and in large firms, and Muslims in dealing with police and lower courts.

As these fragmentary data reveal, countries differ greatly in the extent to which they address minority representation (or even keep statistics), how they categorise minorities, and what measures (if any) they take to redress underrepresentation. In India, 'forward castes' (the 7–8 per cent of the population who do not qualify for affirmative action) were 90 per cent of federal Supreme Court judges but just 15 per cent of Supreme Court judges in Madras, which has engaged in affirmative action. Like law schools in other countries, those in India reproduce social inequalities (Basheer et al 2017; Kumar 2017). Myanmar requires entrants to the profession to prove that both parents are citizens, discriminating against Chinese and Muslims. Given the ways in which African colonial administrators constructed and manipulated 'tribal' identities to divide and rule, exacerbating tensions that have persisted and intensified since independence, it is unsurprising that there are few data on the ethnic composition of African legal professions. The historical experiences of minorities and oppressed majorities differ greatly across countries (ethnicity versus religion, slavery versus migration, who migrates, and public attitudes towards migrants); and so do their relative successes in achieving proportional representation in both the profession as a whole and particular segments and strata (especially the heights of private practice and the judiciary). The extent to which the profession is representative of racial minorities has profound implications for their upward mobility, access to law, and the administration of justice.

As the profession expands, it also grows younger. The earlier volumes documented this in national professions that began growing in the 1960s: in 1988, half of US lawyers had practised less than ten years; in 1981, half of New Zealand lawyers were under 35. The professions experiencing steep growth curves over the last three decades also became more youthful. A number of consequences may follow: younger cohorts may have difficulty establishing themselves in practice (suffering un- and under-employment) and be less (or more) compliant with ethical precepts; they may revolt against gerontocratic rule; and the professions they increasingly dominate may display different attitudes towards issues of gender, race, work-life balance, access to justice, restrictive practices, and politics. And because the dramatic growth of recent decades was attributable in part to the fact that the entering cohorts were much larger than the aging cohorts who were retiring or dying, growth will decline or even reverse as this difference diminishes or reverses.

III. MAKING LAWYERS

Education is not just an entry barrier; it also shapes which entrants become what kinds of lawyers, what they know, how they practise, and how they relate to each other. In most countries, all law graduates attend similar institutions; in some, judges and prosecutors then undergo further training; but Russia has special law schools for prosecutors and police investigators. Until the last few decades, legal education was a post-graduate course only in the US and Canada. At about the same time that Australia, Japan[17] and South Korea were moving in that direction, South Africa took the opposite route (to reduce differences in training, and therefore careers, between white and black lawyers). More countries are introducing clinical legal education, emulating the US, which pioneered 'experiential learning' and increasingly requires it (for instance, in California). Paradoxically, however, the proportion of new US law faculty members with PhDs in non-legal subjects increased from 13 per cent in 1996–2000 to a stunning 48 per cent in 2011–15, with the result that fewer have significant practice experience (LoPucki 2016). Alternatively, some countries have acknowledged the limited pedagogic value of apprenticeship (since practitioner mentors prioritise service to clients) by replacing it (in whole or part) with professional training institutes (whose limited number of places can also be used to

---

[17] When Japan introduced a new examination as an *alternative* to post-graduate legal education, so many undergraduate degree holders chose to cram for it (as they had been accustomed to do for other exams) rather than attend the new post-graduate law schools that 35 of the 74 closed for lack of enrolment.

control entry, eg in Egypt, or the UK, Abel 2003: 105–14). In most countries (eg Mexico, Israel, Turkey), legal education expanded at the bottom of the prestige hierarchy, often in small schools that were private (and hence expensive), possessed few resources, and relied on practitioners teaching part-time. (In Russia, 72 per cent of all law students take correspondence courses while working full time.) Private legal education allows the market to respond to rising demand (especially when institutions are profit-making, see Tejani 2017); but it also leaves students burdened by debt, which may influence their career choices. India, by contrast, created new public national law schools, which generated intense competition for admission; although these were intended to educate public interest lawyers, most graduates were seduced by the high salaries and prestige offered by the new large globally-oriented firms (Gingerich and Robinson 2017). Legal education tends to be homogeneous within countries (sometimes because of compulsory national curricula or in order to qualify for exemption from professional examinations); but new law schools in Chile are differentiated by research agenda, subject-matter specialisation, and political orientation. Post-graduate legal education (beyond whatever degree is required for practice) is proliferating (eg Tunisia and Latin America), often pursued abroad by those aspiring to work in global firms. Legal professions increasingly require continuing legal education. Denmark did so in part to protect lawyers' turf from accountants, imposing an expense resented by those unthreatened by such competitors. All these phenomena – making law a post-graduate degree, hiring law faculty with PhDs in non-law subjects, and the increasing number of law graduates who earn an LLM or JSD, often in another country – may represent credential inflation (Collins 1979; 2002). Unfortunately, we know almost nothing about relationships between the content or quality of education and lawyer performance.

IV. CONTROLLING COMPETITION

Following Larson and Weber, I have argued that professions seek not only to control entry but also to dampen competition among entrants and with others through a variety of restrictive practices (eg Abel 1988c: chs 5, 12; 1989: ch 5; 2003: ch 6). From its inception, the California State Bar Association was preoccupied with ambulance chasing and 'unauthorised practice of law' by non-lawyers (Abel 2011: 3–5). The US, some Canadian provinces and Vietnam are unique in extending lawyers' monopoly to legal advice (although Belgium did this in response to the emergence of law shops in the 1970s, designed to increase access to justice; and Germany and Norway did so during the Depression). Some countries (eg Brazil, Germany, Italy, Spain, and Venezuela) prohibit pro se representation in higher courts; Argentina does so in all courts.[18] Russia and Vietnam occupy the other end of this spectrum, allowing non-lawyers to represent clients in court in all matters except criminal defence. And newly established specialist courts may encourage representation by non-lawyers (eg for labour disputes in Brazil, Belgium and Spain). In Poland, legal advisers have sought formal recognition (and rights of audience), as have debt collectors and personal injury claims agents (some of whom obtained law

---

[18] The US Supreme Court constitutionalised the right to self-representation in criminal cases, *Faretta v California*, 422 US 806 (1975).

degrees but did not qualify via apprenticeship). In Indonesia, *pokrol bamboo* (bush lawyers) practise law without formal training. In 2003, under pressure from the IMF, Indonesia required all lawyers to register with a new national Bar association; but the Constitutional Court held that practising without having registered was not a criminal offence. In 1995 Indonesia also introduced a division between litigators and transactional lawyers (partly to immunise the latter from the taint of association with corrupt courts). Lawyers may lose functions to competitors: accountants replaced English solicitors in giving tax advice (Abel 1988c: 187); scriveners took over patent and copyright work from Japanese *bengoshi*. Australian solicitors lost the conveyancing monopoly in 1995.[19] When English solicitors lost their monopoly over land transactions to licensed conveyancers (and feared competition from the much larger estate agents and building societies), they successfully challenged the Bar's monopoly over audience rights in the higher courts (Abel 2003: chs 5–6).

Since 1988, competition has further intensified. Countries (sometimes under EU pressure) have repealed rules limiting practice to geographic subdivisions within federal polities (eg regional and appeal courts in German *Länder*, French *départements*, Swiss *cantons*, Danish regions). Functional divisions have been abolished: German syndic attorneys have been incorporated into *Anwälte*; French *conseils juridiques* became *avocats* in 1991, Czech commercial counsel joined advocates in 1996. In the UK, barristers may now offer direct access to clients and be employed by or partners in solicitors' firms, and solicitors may appear in higher courts. Although some Australian states preserve a de jure or de facto divided profession, similar divisions have been abolished elsewhere. In 1995, South Africa allowed attorneys to appear in most courts because they were more racially representative of the population than advocates (who had enjoyed exclusive rights of audience); and it merged the two branches in 2014. German house counsel can represent their employers in court and, if they are *Anwälte*, represent others. German courts have invalidated rules limiting lawyers to practice in a single office in one state. Although the Nazi regime had expanded the lawyers' monopoly in response to the Depression, a German court recently allowed non-lawyers to offer some legal services. Employed lawyers in several countries now can engage in advocacy (eg Netherlands, UK). Denmark repealed the Pettifogger Act, which prohibited non-lawyers from offering legal advice, and it regulated commercial legal counselling by non-lawyers, allowing them to represent clients in cases involving relatively small amounts. In Sweden, non-lawyers can offer legal advice and represent parties in civil cases. Polish tax advisers compete with advocates. Hundreds of German lawyers have dual qualifications as auditors, tax advisers and certified accountants. Yet notaries remain a distinct, prestigious, highly remunerative profession in some civil law jurisdictions (even protected by a *numerus clausus*, eg in Germany).

Although legal professions in other countries mocked US lawyers as cowboys and ambulance chasers after the Supreme Court annulled the advertising ban (Abel 2002),[20] many of those professions have since followed suit (eg England and Wales, France, South Africa, Turkey). Similarly, the US Supreme Court's nullification of minimum fees[21]

---

[19] On interprofessional competition for trusts and estates work in England and Wales, see Francis (2011: ch 6).
[20] *Bates v State Bar of Arizona*, 433 US 350 (1977).
[21] *Goldfarb v Virginia State Bar*, 421 US 773 (1975).

anticipated the abolition of price fixing elsewhere (eg Belgium, South Africa). Germany relaxed the ban on advertising and made scale fees more flexible. Some countries tolerate traditional practices of touting, eg *samsara* in Tunisia (who are paid out of the lawyer's fee). Japan allowed lawyers to advertise in 2000 and form professional corporations in 2002 and let private practitioners serve as public officials and engage in profit-making activities. Nevertheless, lawyers who advertise cheap mass-produced legal services often experience hostility from small firm competitors, eg in France, Canada, Israel and Brazil. Japan prohibited the mass processing law firm Adire from advertising and suspended its operations for two months. Several countries now permit conditional or contingent fees, especially in personal injury cases (partly to reduce legal aid costs) (eg England and Wales, Abel 2002; 2003: ch 8). Some countries allow lawyers to join multi-disciplinary partnerships (MDPs) – with notaries in the Netherlands, generally in Australia, which also lets lawyers incorporate and list their firms on the stock exchange to sell equity interests to non-lawyers; Denmark allows non-lawyers to own a ten per cent share.

Lateral movement across professional divisions has increased (eg between *avocats*, house counsel, *notaires*, and employment in business, government, and accountancy firms in France). Non-lawyers continue to make inroads into lawyers' monopolies, eg UK claims agents and Dutch legal advisers handling personal injury cases; paralegals in Ontario, notaries public there and in other Canadian provinces, and paralegals in Washington State and California performing various legal functions. The Polish Constitutional Court declared that law graduates who had not completed their traineeships (whose numbers were limited by local Bar associations) could nevertheless provide legal services in simpler civil cases, debt collection, and personal injury claims.

Some countries, however, successfully resisted these trends. Italy rejected legislation eliminating minimum fees and allowing advertising, MDPs, specialisation, and corporate structures. South Africa required that advocates be briefed by attorneys (until the branches were merged in 2014, in part to redress the underrepresentation of blacks among advocates); and it still prohibits contingent fees. South Korea limits house counsel to advocating ten cases a year. Polish advocates (who may not be employed) have successfully resisted fusion with the much larger number of attorneys at law (who may); but the latter have obtained audience rights in everything except criminal defence. And there has been push-back elsewhere. When Serbia granted notaries (a profession revived in 2013) a monopoly over real estate transactions, the Serbian Bar Association called a strike (enforced with threats and penalties), compelling the legislature to back down and let advocates perform those transactions (a similar struggle occurred in Bosnia and Herzegovina). The Serbian Bar Association also successfully resisted proposals to let civil society organisations offer free legal aid. Russian advocates still cannot be employed or engage in commercial activity. In 2015, Russia required a law degree (though not a lawyer's licence) to practise in administrative courts. Serbian law firms may not incorporate or establish branch offices, and advertising is restricted. Kenya still limits firms to 20 partners (a ceiling England and Wales abolished in 1967). In Egypt and Palestine, lawyers cannot engage in some kinds of non-legal work. Egypt and Myanmar reserve practice in the higher courts to more experienced (ie older) lawyers. In India, Senior Advocates can appear only if they have been briefed by advocates-on-record. (All these practices mimic the UK's divided profession and distinction between Queen's Counsel and juniors.)

The 1988 national reports documented the different ways nations distribute law graduates among the professions' sectors. Private practice dominates common law professions, typically comprising nearly 90 per cent of all lawyers and offering the greatest prestige and highest incomes. Furthermore, there is considerable movement between sectors. Most US judges have spent decades as private practitioners or prosecutors (more rarely academics) before being appointed to the bench; some retire from it to practice (usually for financial reasons); and there is a highly lucrative revolving door between private practice and government service (especially in regulatory agencies). In civil law professions, by contrast, the categories of private practice, house counsel, and government (judges, prosecutors and civil servants) were relatively equal in size and usually represented lifetime careers (with no movement within government). Government employees often enjoy incomes and status equal to or greater than those of private practitioners. The growth of the regulatory/welfare state in the mid-twentieth century increased the number, power, and prestige of legally-trained civil servants (if not their incomes). But the movement toward neoliberalism in recent decades elevated the private sector over public service, increasing the demand for and rewards of private practitioners while worsening the relative pay and working conditions of civil servants (compared with elite practitioners). At the same time, traditional legal identities have been supplanted by new ones. In Belgium, the percentages of law graduates in traditional roles (attorney, notary, bailiff and magistrate) compared to those in non-traditional roles (civil servant and house counsel) inverted from 69:31 in the 1960s to 45:55 in the 1990s. Between 2004 and 2014, the annual increase in number of attorneys was just 2.3 per cent while that of house counsel was 9.2 per cent. After the end of communism, Poland privatised bailiffs, prompting their numbers to triple from 459 in 1990 to 1,574 in 2016. (The Czech Republic did something similar.) Because they could practise throughout Poland (not just within the jurisdiction of the appellate court in which they were admitted), some quickly concentrated in large firms serving mass creditors (in 2013, 11 firms handled nearly a quarter of all debt collection cases). The legislature responded by restricting the number of cases bailiffs could handle outside their appellate court jurisdiction. (The number of notaries also increased from 862 in 1990 to 3,293 in 2015.) Some fear that the shift from independent practice to employment threatens professional ideals; others deplore the privatisation of formerly public roles.

V. STRUCTURES OF PRACTICE

Private practice has its own de facto internal divisions. In many countries (both civil and common law), advocates must be sole independent practitioners, neither in partnership nor employed by or employing other lawyers. This creates a simulacrum of equality – a traditional claim of professions. But there always is a status hierarchy. This is formalised in England and Wales (and its former colonies) by a division between 'juniors' (who may be older) and Queen's or Senior Counsel, who often sport a distinctive court dress (hence the name 'silk'), charge higher fees, must be assisted by juniors, and may monopolise judicial appointments. In divided professions (preeminently in England and Wales and its former colonies), barristers (or advocates) traditionally were the social superiors of solicitors (or attorneys), who 'attended on' advocates (never vice versa). This relationship has been equalised, indeed reversed, in some common law countries as large firm transactional lawyers surpassed litigators in income, prestige, and influence. In most communist countries all lawyers were state employees. In 1988, China required them to belong to a 'cooperative law firm' – an inversion of the requirement in capitalist countries that lawyers practise alone to ensure their 'independence'. (Chinese lawyers were later permitted to form partnerships, which became the preferred structure after 2000, and to practise alone after the cooperative law firm was abolished in 2008.)

The 1988 national reports documented several dramatic changes in practice structures. Despite the idealisation of solo practice as the epitome of the independent professional, their proportions of private practitioners have declined: from 64 per cent of all US lawyers in 1948 to 33 per cent in 1980 (though they remained half of private practitioners); from 25 per cent of UK solicitors in 1939 to 8 per cent in 1982; from 63 per cent in Auckland, New Zealand in 1940 to 33 per cent in 1985. Nevertheless, solo practice still dominated professions in many countries: 63 per cent in Australia (1985), 59 per cent in Japan (1980), 61 per cent in Rio de Janeiro (1980), 51 per cent in Milan (1978), more than 80 per cent in France (1988), 50 per cent in Geneva (1988), and 67 per cent in Germany (1980). Furthermore, most other firms in those countries were small: 62 per cent of firms in both Scotland and England and Wales in 1984 had 2–9 partners; in 1980, only nine of a sample of 227 Japanese law firms had ten or more lawyers; in 1985, only 42 of the 6,879 German firms had ten or more lawyers; in 1979, only 4 per cent of Dutch lawyers practised in firms of ten or more; even in the US in 1985, only 20 per cent of lawyers practised in firms of 11 or more.

The most significant change, however, was the increase in the number of US firms with more than 100 lawyers, from 90 in 1979 to 250 in 1986. Large firms had only begun to emerge elsewhere. England and Wales (which first permitted partnerships over 20 in 1967) had just one firm with more than 60 partners in 1983; in Scotland the largest was 32, in Australia it was 240; Canada had ten firms with more than 100 lawyers. The civil law world lagged far behind. Brazil, atypically, had several firms with over 50 lawyers. But the largest firm had 30 lawyers in Venezuela and 20 in Geneva; and France, Italy and Spain had few large firms.

Thirty years later, both trends have intensified (see Table 6). Solo practice declined dramatically in Brazil (from 61 per cent nationwide in 1980 to 1.6 per cent in São Paulo in 2017) and the Netherlands (to 16 per cent). But it remained significant or even dominant in many other countries: 87 per cent in the Czech Republic, growing from 32 per cent of French firms in 1997 to 36 per cent in 2014, remaining about a third of private practitioners in Canada and 40 per cent in South Africa and about half of all lawyers in South Korea, and rising from more than half of private practitioners in the US. Even though a 2001 law allowed Turkish lawyers to create a new form of partnership, 62 per cent of Istanbul lawyers still practised alone in 2011. Although the proportion of Japanese *bengoshi* practising alone halved (from 50 per cent to 25 per cent) between 2000 and 2017 (because the large cohort of newly qualified lawyers sought the security of salaried employment), 95 per cent of law firms had five or fewer lawyers. The proportion of German *Anwälte* practising alone declined from 2000 to 2016 because litigation dropped 32 per cent while the number of lawyers grew 57 per cent (intensifying competition). Still, 45 per cent of firms have just two partners, 18 per cent three, 12 per cent four, and only 8 per cent ten or more. Most Russian lawyers practise alone (even those formally members of collectives); most Iranian firms do not share profits. Most other firms remain small: 31 per cent of Dutch lawyers are in firms of 2–5; 40 per cent of Dutch-speaking Belgian lawyers in firms are in those with 2–10; the average number of partners per firm in France declined from 3.1 in 1997 to 2.3 in 2014; 92 per cent of lawyers in São Paulo firms are in firms of 2–5; Vietnamese firms average less than three lawyers. The number of solo practitioners in Denmark increased from 654 in 1998 to 969 in 2004 (while the number of firms with 2–19 lawyers dropped by half and the number with 20–49 lawyers by two-thirds).

Why is the legal profession so impervious to pressures for rationalisation and concentration – compared, for instance, to medicine (where solo and even group practices in the US have been absorbed by huge corporations) – especially when market forces have been so powerful at the other end of the private practice spectrum (which will be described below)? The reason is unlikely to be the need to avoid conflicts of interest, which are rare when the clientele is mostly individuals, especially since the largest firms have found ways to deal with much more complicated conflicts (Shapiro 2002). Perhaps those attracted to law also prefer to be individual entrepreneurs, reluctant to share profits. (Many of the solo practitioners Jerome Carlin (1962) studied in Chicago in the 1950s were sons of small business owners.) Others may have been forced into self-employment by the 2008 recession. And restrictive practices may moderate the market forces that otherwise might drive lawyers to seek economies of scale (since there is little price competition). Some insight into this conundrum might be found in the experiences of firms mass processing clients for reduced fees (in the US, UK, Japan, France, Brazil and Israel).

But at the same time that solo and small firm practices have survived (and even thrived), the number and size of the largest firms have grown rapidly (with a resultant decline of mid-size firms). This is most dramatic in the US, where the median size of the 200 largest firms more than doubled, from 205 in 1987 to 445 in 2015; 44 firms have more than a thousand lawyers, and Baker McKenzie grew nearly eightfold, from 755 in 1985 to over 6,000 in 2015 (then the world's largest). Eight Canadian firms have more than 500 lawyers, and two merged with large UK firms. The largest UK firm in 1999 was Clifford Chance, with 2,000 lawyers; the largest in 2015 was DLA Piper, with 4,000. Each of the six largest South African firms has 250–600 lawyers. There are now 38 firms with more than 100 partners in Brazil, 33 in Canada, 13 in the Netherlands (the largest with 300 lawyers), and 10 in South Korea. In Germany, the tenth largest firm had 278 lawyers and the largest 655 (although only 4.5 per cent of lawyers worked at the 30 largest firms). The average size of the ten largest firms in Israel grew from 47 lawyers in 2000 to 185 in 2016. Between 1992 and 2016, the number of Hong Kong firms with 11–20 lawyers rose from 7 to 35, while the number of larger firms rose from 2 to 13. The largest Chinese firm in 2002 had five offices and fewer than 200 lawyers, but firms began to expand in the mid-2000s in anticipation of foreign competition. By 2015, Dacheng, the largest, had 51 offices (eight outside the mainland) and over 4,000 lawyers. It then allied with Dentons, creating the largest firm in the world (with over 7,000 lawyers in more than 100 offices). Yingke grew from 30 lawyers in 2008 to over 3,000 in 2015. King & Wood surpassed 1,000 lawyers in 2012 and then merged with Mallesons Stephen Jacques (an Australian firm with 800 lawyers) and SJ Berwin (a UK firm with 900) (KWM Europe subsequently collapsed). The five largest Thai firms have 25–75 lawyers. Although no Chilean firm had more than 20 lawyers in 1985, four had more than 100 in 2013, the largest with 152. Ten South Korean firms had more than 100. By 2017, Japan had ten firms with more than 100 lawyers, five of which had over 350. (Two of the ten served a mass clientele rather than corporations.) The ten largest firms in Venezuela grew from an average of 23 lawyers in 1990 to 42.5 in 2009 (though they declined to 36.2 in 2017, following the country's economic devastation). Geneva, which had no firms larger than 20 in 1986, had five mid-sized firms (31–80 lawyers) in 2017 and four larger firms (140–160 lawyers). Italy, which had *no* large firms 30 years ago, now has three, each with about 300 lawyers. Denmark had no firms with over 100 lawyers in 1998 but eight by 2017 (and the ten largest firms earned two-thirds of their revenue from foreign clients). Large firms, especially global megafirms, raise important questions. Do their lawyers practise differently from those in smaller firms? Are they less autonomous? Are there limits to expansion and concentration? Why have US and UK firms dominated the global market, and will they continue to do so?

These changes – the persistence of solo and small firms (if in diminished numbers) and the growth of large firms – have produced what Heinz and Laumann (1982) called the two hemispheres of the US legal profession – a phenomenon observed earlier (see Reed 1921; Carlin 1962; Smigel 1964). Heinz and Laumann found that students from different socio-economic backgrounds entered law schools situated in different strata of the educational hierarchy, which distributed them across the professional hierarchy of solo practitioners and small firms, large firms, and government, where they performed different functions for different clients. A replication 20 years later found that the amount of time Chicago lawyers devoted to the two client categories (corporations versus individuals and small businesses) had changed from approximate equality in 1975 to approximately 2:1 (Heinz et al 2005: 46–47). Other countries (such as China, India and Brazil) increasingly display a variety of divisions (Wilkins et al 2017; Cunha et al 2018). In Indonesia, lawyers are categorised as professionals (who use law to achieve their ends) and fixers (who resort to corrupt practices), with brokers acting as intermediaries. In all countries, lawyers are overrepresented in cities (compared to population). In Zimbabwe in 2013, 263 law firms were located in Harare and 41 in Bulawayo, with just 111 in the remaining 26 towns and cities. China had deliberately distributed lawyers to rural areas. As late as 2000, no province had more than 20 per cent of full-time lawyers, and only 4.6 per cent of lawyers practised in Beijing. But after a 2003 law eased migration to cities, 11.3 per cent of full-time lawyers were found in Beijing in 2007, and the profession grew rapidly in Shanghai and Guangzhou. When Denmark merged 82 jurisdictions into 24, lawyers moved to the cities that retained district courts; in 2000, two-thirds of firms were in the two largest cities, and by 2006, half of all lawyers were in Copenhagen. Whereas German law faculties traditionally enjoyed roughly equal status (Klausa 1981), legal education in many countries is increasingly hierarchical: more and less selective law faculties in Germany, public and private law schools in Israel, Russell Group universities in the UK, the Group of Eight in Australia, older and newer universities in Chile, the US News ranking in the US (Espeland and Sauder 2016; Abel 2017b). Ambitious French law graduates take a second degree or gain business experience. The various educational tracks lead to radically different rewards: US graduates start at an average of $135,000 in large firms compared with $43,000 in legal services; UK trainee solicitors start at £40,000 in large firms compared with £18,000 in small, and Bar pupils start at £72,500 in commercial chambers compared to £12,000 in legal aid chambers; Canadian law graduates start at Can$105,000 in firms with over 250 lawyers compared with Can$60,000 in solo practice. In Switzerland in 2012, partners in incorporated law firms earned an average of 546,000CHF compared with

234,000CHF for solo practitioners. In India, a small number of elite litigators monopolise almost all important litigation, earning $2–10 million a year, whereas most lawyers earn only $17–86 a month (Galanter and Robinson 2017). Revenues of the top five and next five Danish firms grew 166 and 251 per cent respectively between 2000 and 2014, while those of smaller firms grew much more slowly or not at all. These divisions, which are likely to emerge in other countries and intensify everywhere, represent another challenge to the concept of a legal profession.

VI. A RESEARCH AGENDA

Comparative research – like encountering any new environment – has the salutary effect of disorienting travellers, forcing them to see that what they had taken for granted is actually contingent, a product of history, society, politics, economics, and culture. Comparison, therefore, suggests a variety of questions about why legal professions take the forms they do and how they might change.

There is wide variation in the ratio of population (or GNP) per lawyer, both between countries and within them over relatively short time periods. The number of lawyers can fluctuate rapidly: down, following revolutions or wars; up, following changes in regime or ideology (colonialism to independence, communism to capitalism, protectionism to neoliberalism). Recessions and trade wars can dampen demand for lawyers. (The 2008 recession provoked a host of doomsayers to predict radical changes in US legal education, eg Tamanaha 2012, but these have not occurred, see Abel 2015.) The welfare state greatly expanded legal aid, boosting demand (Abel 1985); neoliberalism has drastically curtailed state budgets and therefore legal aid (relegating those seeking legal representation to legal expenses insurance, contingent or conditional fees, and litigation finance lenders, see Abel 2002; 2003: chs 7–8; 2006–07). Legal changes can increase demand (new complex laws and regulations) or reduce it (no-fault divorce and mediation; no-fault compensation for accidental injuries; decriminalisation, eg of drugs; simplification of land transactions and wills, see Abel 1979b). Demographic shifts can expand or constrict both supply and demand (birth rates are falling in wealthier countries).[22] Migration can increase them, though it may take a generation until the children of immigrants enter higher education. Technology can reduce the need for lawyers and the cost of lawyering. And all these influences may pale in comparison with the potential of artificial intelligence to replace head work (including some forms of lawyering, see Susskind 2010), just as the new energy sources harnessed by the industrial revolution (water, steam, electricity) replaced human muscle in hand work. (Consider how ATMs have substituted for bank tellers, the Internet has largely eliminated travel agents, and Amazon is devastating brick and mortar stores.) Both the frequent complaint that there are 'too many lawyers' (Katvan et al 2017) and the

---

[22] Many West European countries fall below the replacement rate of 2.1 children per woman: Germany (1.4), Spain (1.4), Italy (1.4), UK (1.7), Netherlands (1.8). That is also true in wealthier Asian countries – Chinese (1.08) and Indians (1.09) in Singapore, South Korea (1.2), Japan (1.3), China (1.6) – and former communist countries: Poland (1.3), Bosnia and Herzegovina (1.3), Russia (1.7). See Yew, 'Warning Bell for Developed Countries: Declining Birth Rates', *Forbes* (16 October 2012); Gallagher, '"Remarkable" decline in fertility rates', *BBC News* (1 November 2018).

less common concern that there are too few (in some East Asian countries) lack empirical foundation (Abel 2017). Although Weber theorised about the law and the economy (1954; 1978), and the World Bank advocates for a western legal system and legal profession as a precondition for development (2001), we have little data about the relationship. Nor is there any evidence for the claims that a rapidly expanding legal profession erodes quality or ethics or has caused a 'litigation crisis' (Galanter 1986). As Milton Friedman noted in arguing against medical licensure 50 years ago, care by a less highly trained provider often is better than no care at all.[23] Many functions lawyers perform can be, and are being, performed by others (Kritzer 1998). We also lack evidence that producing more lawyers lowers the price of legal services or improves access to justice. And we need to know more about the costs of overproduction: waste (out-of-pocket and opportunity costs of education that is never used); educational debt burdens; un- and under-employment. (In the US, the cost of higher education, which is rising faster than inflation and imposing a growing debt burden, has intensified pressure to abbreviate courses and switch to much cheaper distance learning, Abel 2015.) Even if we had a better understanding of the costs and benefits of more or fewer lawyers, the question remains: who should regulate their numbers? The interests of the state, the profession, aspirants to entry, and the legal academy diverge. The experience of planned economies offers no ground for optimism that the government would get it right (and may be motivated to seek a complaisant profession). Legal professions have their own vested interests – usually to dampen competition (though some practitioners may wish to increase their profits by exploiting apprentices). Professions justify self-regulation by the claim that only they have the expertise to evaluate the quality of entrants and ensure it meets minimum standards. But there are virtually no data validating any of the entrance requirements – formal education, apprenticeship, examinations (set by universities, professions, or the state) – in terms of lawyer performance. Nor do we have an adequate understanding of how each of those barriers affects the gender, class and race composition of the profession and how they distribute entrants to places in the professional hierarchy. (There may be trade-offs between waste and access: early barriers, eg limiting entry to university, avoid pointless investments by those who will drop out; but they also exclude some who might succeed.)

The national reports offer compelling evidence that the expansion of legal professions in recent decades has been driven by legal education. There were demands for entry by previously excluded groups: women, those from poorer families, racial and ethnic minorities. (Some of these have sparked a backlash in the name of 'meritocracy', eg Kronman 2019.) Our knowledge economy views education as an unqualified good. For the government, education is far less expensive than other social services, such as health care or housing; and legal education is much cheaper than other subjects because it requires no laboratories, and lectures can be offered to virtually unlimited numbers of students (especially when relatively few attend). Students view law as a soft option compared to the sciences. Neoliberal reforms encourage private universities to open law faculties, rapidly increasing the number of places at no cost to the government. And loans let students finance their own education.

---

[23] Perry, 'Milton Friedman Told Us The Answer Decades Ago – Now It'll Probably Be IBM's Watson', *Forbes* (4 June 2017).

Legal professions control production by producers through a variety of anti-competitive rules (Abel 1981). In recent years, however, many of these have been eliminated. We need to understand how that happened: pressure from clients (eg to end solicitors' monopoly over conveyancing, Abel 2003: ch 6); rivalry among professional fractions (solicitors responding by challenging barristers' exclusive rights of audience in the higher courts (ibid: ch 5)); actions by legislatures or courts. What explains why nations differ in repealing or retaining rules: historical traditions, ideology (neoliberalism), lawyer density (intensity of competition), the power of the profession, its internal unity or divisions? We have no evidence about whether the remaining restrictive practices foster the effects they claim. What have been the consequences of eliminating or reducing internal divisions (eg between advocates and transactional lawyers, employed and independent practitioners)? What difference does it make whether a legal functionary (such as bailiff) is a state employee or an independent practitioner? What is the justification for compelling advocates to practise alone? Does that ensure 'independence'? What does the concept mean, and why is it important? Do price controls enhance quality; does price competition reduce it (below acceptable levels)? When should consumers be able to trade off price for quality? (Should it matter that the ideal of equal justice under law may be compromised when adversaries have unequal resources?) Does competition erode trust between lawyers and their ability to act collectively to enforce professional norms? Does advertising invite frivolous legal claims? (Or is justice frustrated by the failure to assert meritorious claims, ie false negatives rather than false positives, see Abel 1987). Does advertising mislead consumers? Do they have less or worse information than they would if advertising were banned? How does mass processing of claims compare with representation by solo and small firm practitioners in terms of price and quality (Van Hoy 1997)? Which functions reserved to lawyers could be performed by others? How would that affect price and quality? How would those others be educated and regulated? How do lawyers delegate tasks to their non-lawyer employees? Could the latter perform those functions competently without lawyer supervision? Could lawyers and independent non-lawyer practitioners collaborate by dividing tasks between them ('unbundling' legal services, see Mosten 2000)? Where have non-lawyers, individually or collectively, claimed a share of the lawyers' market, and with what results? What have been the consequences of allowing multi-disciplinary partnerships? Have accountants and management consultants displaced lawyers (as the latter feared)? If so, how has this affected consumers? What justifies the restrictions on foreign lawyers? Are the sophisticated corporate consumers of their services unable to evaluate quality (Abel 1994)? How has the presence of foreign law firms affected large domestic firms?

Legal professions historically were divided into distinct families. Many non-western legal systems did not possess a differentiated category of lawyer (Abel 1973). Each of the world's major religions sometimes dominated legal systems and performed the functions of the legal profession. Common and civil law countries differed along multiple dimensions: the locus of legal authority (codes or case law); roles of judges, lawyers and legal academics; and distribution of law graduates across the sectors of private practice, judiciary, business, and civil service (and their relative rewards). Communist countries sought to eliminate or drastically shrink their legal professions and subordinate them to the state. Are we witnessing a convergence of these different traditions? Are private practitioners increasing their numbers (and status) compared to judges? How has this affected adjudication? Collective action by legal professionals? Have employed lawyers gained in status (as they have acquired rights of audience)? Are legal educational systems becoming more similar? Is convergence a function of globalisation? American hegemony?

To what extent have legal professions moved from enforcing exclusivity (to enhance their collective status) to becoming demographically representative of the societies they serve? How do formerly excluded groups compare in their proportions of the profession and allocation to roles within it? What explains cross-national differences, eg between former communist and capitalist countries; northern and southern Europe; India, China and Japan compared with other Asian countries? What could we learn from comparing the different experiences of racial minorities in the global North with racial majorities in the global South who had been oppressed under colonialism or apartheid? Will the backlash against affirmative action in the US find echoes in 'populist' anti-immigrant agitation in other countries? What forms of inequality persist, and what might correct them? Will childrearing responsibility be equally divided by gender? If not, can the income and status rewards of full- and part-time work be equalised?

The private practice sector also is undergoing transformation. It historically was quite homogeneous, either mandated by professional rules (advocates had to be sole practitioners) or shaped by market forces (few large consumers with complex problems requiring teams of lawyers). Now, however, every national report describes the emergence of a large firm sector, differentiated from the majority of solo or small firm practitioners by location (major cities rather than suburbs or rural areas), function (transactional work rather than litigation), size, internal organisation (multiple strata, with relatively few equity partners), specialisation, education (elite domestic law faculties and foreign post-graduate degrees), income and status. Are there limits to the size of megafirms? Will they be dominated by a few countries (US, UK, perhaps China)? (Each of the Big Four accounting firms has 207–280,000 employees; each of the Big Three management consulting firms has 8–25,000 employees; all are US-UK dominated.) Unlike historical divisions, these two spheres are not inscribed in law or regulations. Will the gap between them widen? If so, does it foreshadow a new formal division?

Comparison may help to answer these questions – and inevitably generate new ones.

TABLES

Table 1 Increase in Law Students

Country	Period	Total increase (per cent)	Annual increase (per cent)
China	1991–2012	2,348	111.8
Brazil	1988–2012	446	18.6
UK	1980–2014	456	13.4
Canada	2002–2014	32	2.7

Table 2 Increase in New Lawyers

Country	Period	Total increase (per cent)	Annual increase (per cent)
Chile	1977–2015	1,670	43.9
Mexico	1988–2018 (?)	748	24.9
Brazil[24]	1988–2012	375	15.6
Venezuela[25]	1986/89–2015	443	15.8
Switzerland	1984–2016	94	2.9

Table 3 Increase in Number of Lawyers

Country	Period	Annual increase (per cent)	Period	Annual increase (per cent)	Period	Annual increase (per cent)	Period	Annual increase (per cent)
Vietnam							1984/89–2016[26]	568.2
Czech Republic							1989–2016	47
China					1988–2000	28.9[27]	2000–17	44.3
Iran							2005–15	20
South Korea							2009–17	17
Venezuela	1981–90	10.6	1990–2000	11.1	2000–2010	8.5	2010–15	16.6
India							1981–2017	10.7–16.3[28]
Russia	1939–59	3.1					1959–2015	13.4
South Africa: advocates							1980s–2017[29]	11.6
South Africa: attorneys							1980s–2017[30]	9.6
Israel	1980–90	4.7	1990–2000	11.6			2000–10	10.1
Turkey	1960s–1999[31]	5.9					1999–2016	9.3
Canada	1931–81	5.6	1971–82	12.9			1982–2014	6.9
France	1973–90	5.3					1991–2014	6
Bosnia and Herzegovina	1945–75	37	1975–90	8.8			1990–2018	6.0
Netherlands	1960–86	6.3	1986–94	6.8			1994–2016	5.4
Italy	1965–82	1.0	1982–97	6.2	1997–2006	10.8	2006–12	4.4
Brazil	1981–2012	8.5					2012–16	3.8
UK solicitors	1984–94	4.2	1994–2004	5.2			2005–16	3.3
Switzerland					1984–2006	5.6	2006–16	3.2
US							1990–2015	2.9
Tunisia					1991–2011	23	2011–16	1.6

[24] Law graduates.
[25] Law graduates (annualised for 1986/89).
[26] Hanoi and Ho Chi Minh City; calculated as 30 years.
[27] Treating part-time lawyers as half a full-time.
[28] Estimates for the present size of the profession vary between 1.2 and 1.7 million.
[29] Calculated as 30 years.
[30] Calculated as 30 years.
[31] Calculated as 30 years.

Table 4 Decline in Ratio of Population per Lawyer

Nation	Year	Ratio	Year	Ratio	Year	Ratio	Year	Ratio	Year	Ratio
Vietnam									2017	8,500
Japan	1980	10,226	1990	8,986	1995	8,340				3,370
South Korea									2017	2,609
Bosnia and Herzegovina	1945	10,017	1975	10,493	1983	10,059	1987	7,196		2,220
South Africa	1980s	4,377							2016	2,176
Russia[32]									2015	2,000
Tunisia	1991	5,941	2,011	1,375					2016	1,333
Iran									2015	1,333
France	1983	3,546	2007	1,471	2014	1,104			2017	1,075
India	1981–83	2,770							2017	1,000
Netherlands	1960s	6,520	1985	2,941					2016	971
Switzerland	2006	1,000							2016	840
Serbia	1947	7,875	1978	6,441	1990	4,184			2018	761
Poland	1989	2,128	1997	2,083					2018	758
Belgium									2013	599
Germany	1981	1,651	2001	708			2013	524	2017	503
Chile	1982	1,724							2014	435
UK[33]									2017	432
Italy									2013	370
Mexico									2017	348
Argentina									2006/10	327
Australia									2017	325
Canada	1971	1,337							2011	273
Italy									2017	272
Brazil	1988	681	2012	245					2016	219
Israel									2010	164
Venezuela	1981	801	1990	629	2000	370	2010	237	2015	139

---

[32] This figure is based on advocates; Russia also has a large number of unlicensed lawyers, with estimates ranging from 172,000 to 1 million.

[33] Solicitors and barristers but not legal executives or licensed conveyancers.

Table 5 Feminisation of the Legal Profession (per cent Women)

Country	Category	Year(s)	Per cent	Year(s)	Per cent	Year	Per cent
Belgium	Law students	1951	14	1983	34		
	Law graduates	1940s	4			2005	62
	Private practitioners	1961	8	1983	24		
US	Law students	1950	3	1984	39		
	New lawyers	1960s	5	1988	34		
	Lawyers	1952	2	1984	13	2015	35
UK	Law graduates	1967	14	1984	43		
	Law students	1967	17	1978	39	2017	60
	Barristers	1954	4	1985	13		
	Bar admissions	1958	5	1980	41		
	New solicitors	1958	5	1985	41	2017	60
	Solicitors	1950	3	1983	20		
Scotland	Law students	1970	20	1980	40		
	Advocates	1975	3	1975–81[34]	13		
	Solicitors	1972	4	1982[35]	36		
Netherlands	Law students	1969	21	1980	41	2017	65
	Private practitioners	1970	10	1979	15	2015	25
	Judges			1990	20	2015	50+
Brazil	Law graduates	1950	3	1980	25		
	Law students					2012	46
	Lawyers					2016	47
	Magistrates			1988	8	2016	38
Germany	Lawyers	1962	2.5	1985[36]	36		
New Zealand	Lawyers	1971	2	1983[37]	50+		
France	Lawyers	1988	33			2014	54
	New lawyers	1988	50+				
Norway	Law students	1983	54				
India	Lawyers	1988	1				
Japan	Law students	1988	10				
	New lawyers[38]	1988	5				

(continued)

[34] New advocates.
[35] New solicitors.
[36] Admissions.
[37] New lawyers.
[38] Institute for Legal Training and Research graduates.

Table 5 (Continued)

Country	Category	Year(s)	Per cent	Year(s)	Per cent	Year	Per cent
Israel	Lawyers	1970s	13			2017	47
Australia	Law students					2017	63
	Barristers					2017	23
	Senior Counsel					2017	11
	High Court Judges					2017	34
Italy	Lawyers			1985	9	2014	47
Iran						2017	33–42
Hong Kong	New solicitors					2000	50+
	Solicitors					2016	48
Canada	Lawyers			1981	12	2014	42
South Africa	Attorneys					2017	39
	Candidate Attorneys					2017	57
	Pupils (Bar)					2017	41
Thailand	Law graduates			1996	19	2016	52
Turkey	Lawyers			2000	29	2016	43
Chile	Lawyers	1970	27			2010	53
South Korea	Lawyers					2017	28
	Law students					2017	40
China	Lawyers			2000	13	2013	28
Czech Republic	Prosecutors					2017	54
	Notaries					2017	74
	Advocates					2017	39
	Judges					2017	61
Switzerland	Lawyers			2002	17	2016	28
	Law students (Lausanne)					2016	61
Argentina	Buenos Aires					2018	50

Table 6 Structures of Private Practice

Table 6A Per cent in Solo Practice

Country	Year	Per cent	Year	Per cent
US	1948	64	1980	33
UK	1939	25	1982	8
Australia[39]	1985	63	2017[40]	76
New Zealand	1940	63	1985	33
Japan	1985	59		
Brazil	1980	61	2017[41]	1.6
Italy	1978	51		
France	1988	50	2014	36
Germany	1967	75	1980	67
Canada			2017	c.33
Netherlands			2016	16
Belgium[42]			2012/13	30
Tunisia			2017	90
South Africa			2013	40
Turkey			1999	78
South Korea			2017	c.50
Czech Republic			2017	87
Kenya			2017	37

Table 6B Number of Firms with 100+ Partners

Country	Year	Number	Year	Number
US	1979	90	1986	250
UK	1983[43]	1		
Brazil			2017[44]	38
Canada	1980	1	2016	33
Netherlands			2016	13
South Korea			2017	10

[39] Suburban.
[40] Solo.
[41] São Paulo.
[42] Dutch-speaking.
[43] 60+ partners.
[44] São Paulo.

REFERENCES

Abel, RL (1973) 'A Comparative Theory of Dispute Institutions in Society' 8 *Law & Society Review* 217.
—— (1979a) 'The Rise of Professionalism' 6 *British Journal of Law and Society* 82.
—— (1979b) 'Delegalization: A Critical Review of Its Ideology, Manifestations, and Social Consequences' in E Blankenburg, E Klausa and H Rottleuthner (eds), *Alternative Rechtsformen und Alternativen zum Recht 27* (Jahrbuch für Rechtssoziologie und Rechtstheorie, Band VI) (Opladen, Westdeutscher Verlag).
—— (1981) 'Why Does the American Bar Association Promulgate Ethical Rules?' 59 *Texas Law Review* 639.
—— (1985) 'Law Without Politics: Legal Aid under Advanced Capitalism' 32 *UCLA Law Review* 474.
—— (1987) 'The Real Tort Crisis – Too *Few* Claims' 48 *Ohio State Law Journal* 443.
—— (1988a) 'United States: The Contradictions of Professionalism' in RL Abel and PSC Lewis (eds), *Lawyers in Society: Vol I The Common Law World* (Berkeley, University of California Press) ch 5.
—— (1988b) 'England and Wales: A Comparison of the Professional Projects of Barristers and Solicitors' in RL Abel and PSC Lewis (eds), *Lawyers in Society: Vol I The Common Law World* (Berkeley, University of California Press) ch 2.
—— (1988c) *The Legal Profession in England and Wales* (Oxford, Basil Blackwell).
—— (1989) *American Lawyers* (New York, Oxford University Press).
—— (1994) 'Transnational Law Practice' 44 *Case Western Reserve Law Review* 737.
—— (1995) 'Revisioning Lawyers' in RL Abel and PSC Lewis (eds), *Lawyers in Society: An Overview* (Berkeley, University of California Press) ch 1.
—— (2002) 'An American Hamburger Stand in St Paul's Cathedral: Replacing Legal Aid with Conditional Fees in English Personal Injury Litigation' 51 *DePaul Law Review* 253.
—— (2003) *English Lawyers between Market and State: The Politics of Professionalism* (Oxford, Oxford University Press).
—— (2006–07) 'How the Plaintiffs' Bar Bars Plaintiffs' 51 *New York Law School Law Review* 345.
—— (2011) *Lawyers on Trial: Understanding Ethical Misconduct* (New York, Oxford University Press).
—— (2015) '"You Never Want a Serious Crisis to Go to Waste": Reflections on the Reform of Legal Education in the US, UK and Australia' 22 *International Journal of the Legal Profession* 3.
—— (2017a) 'What *does* and *should* influence the number of lawyers?' in E Katvan, C Silver, N Ziv and A Sherr (eds), *Too Many Lawyers? The Future of the Legal Profession* (New York, Routledge) 9–24.
—— (2017b) 'Crunched by the Numbers' 66 *Journal of Legal Education* 961.
Abel, RL and Lewis, PSC (1989) 'Putting Law Back into the Sociology of Lawyers' in RL Abel and PSC Lewis (eds), *Lawyers in Society: Vol III Comparative Theories* (Berkeley, University of California Press) ch 11.
American Bar Foundation (2018) *2017 Annual Report* (Chicago, ABF).
Arthurs, HW, Weisman, R and Zemans, FH (1988) 'Canadian Lawyers: A Peculiar Profession' in RL Abel and PSC Lewis (eds), *Lawyers in Society: Vol I The Common Law World* (Berkeley, University of California Press) ch 4.
American Immigration Council (2018) 'Foreign-Trained Doctors are Critical to Serving Many US Communities' (Washington, DC, AIC).
Ballakrishnen, SS (2017) 'Women in India's "Global" Law Firms: Comparative Gender Frames and the Advantage of New Organizations' in DB Wilkins, VS Khanna and DM Trubek (eds), *The Indian Legal Profession in the Age of Globalization* (New York, Cambridge University Press) ch 7.

Barzilai, G (2007) 'The Ambivalent Language of Lawyers in Israel: Liberal Politics, Economic Liberalism, Silence and Dissent' in TC Halliday, L Karpik and MM Feeley (eds), *Fighting for Political Freedom: Comparative Studies of the Legal Complex and Political Liberalism* (Oxford, Hart Publishing) ch 8.

Basheer, S, Krishnaprasad, KV, Mitra, S and Mohapatra, P (2017) 'The Making of Legal Elites and the IDIA of Justice' in DB Wilkins, VS Khanna and DM Trubek (eds), *The Indian Legal Profession in the Age of Globalization* (New York, Cambridge University Press) ch 18.

Bastard, B and Cardia-Vonèche, L (1988) 'The Lawyers of Geneva: An Analysis of Change in the Legal Profession' in RL Abel and PSC Lewis (eds), *Lawyers in Society: Vol II The Civil Law World* (Berkeley, University of California Press) ch 8.

Bevan, G, Holland, T and Partington, M (1994) 'Organising Cost-Effective Access to Justice (Memorandum No 7)' (London, Social Market Foundation).

Blankenburg, E and Schultz, U (1988) 'German Advocates: A Highly Regulated Profession' in RL Abel and PSC Lewis (eds), *Lawyers in Society: Vol II The Civil Law World* (Berkeley, University of California Press) ch 3.

Boigeol, A (1988) 'The French Bar: The Difficulties of Unifying a Divided Profession' in RL Abel and PSC Lewis (eds), *Lawyers in Society: Vol II The Civil Law World* (Berkeley, University of California Press) ch 7.

Bucher, R and Strauss, A (1961) 'Professions in Process' 66 *American Journal of Sociology* 325.

Carlin, JE (1962) *Lawyers on Their Own* (New Brunswick, NJ, Rutgers University Press).

Collins, R (1979) *The Credential Society: An Historical Sociology of Education and Stratification* (New York, Academic Press).

—— (2002) 'Credential inflation and the Future of Universities' in S Brint (ed), *The Future of the City of Intellect: The Changing American University* (Palo Alto, Stanford University Press).

Cunha, LG, Monteiro-Gabbay, D, Ghirardi, JG, Trubek, DM and Wilkins, DB (eds) (2018) *The Brazilian Legal Profession in the Age of Globalization: The Rise of the Corporate Legal Sector and Its Impact on Lawyers and Society* (New York, Cambridge University Press).

Da Gloria Bonelli, M and de Pieri Benedito, C (2018) 'Globalizing Processes for São Paulo Attorneys: Gender Stratification in Law Firms and Law-Related Businesses' in LG Cunha, D Monteiro-Gabbay, JG Ghirardi, DM Trubek and DB Wilkins (eds) (2018) *The Brazilian Legal Profession in the Age of Globalization: The Rise of the Corporate Legal Sector and Its Impact on Lawyers and Society* (New York, Cambridge University Press) ch 5.

Dawuni, JJ (2017) 'Lawyers in Ghana' presented at the International Meeting on Law and Society, Mexico City.

Espeland, WN and Sauder, M (2016) *Engines of Anxiety: Academic Rankings, Reputation, and Accountability* (New York, Russell Sage Foundation).

Falcão, J (1988) 'Lawyers in Brazil' in RL Abel and PSC Lewis (eds), *Lawyers in Society: Vol II The Civil Law World* (Berkeley, University of California Press) ch 12.

Francis, A (2011) *At the Edge of the Law: Emergent and Divergent Models of Legal Professionalism* (Farnham, Ashgate).

Galanter, M (1986) 'The Day After the Litigation Explosion' 46 *Maryland Law Review* 3.

—— (2005) *Lowering the Bar: Lawyer Jokes and Legal Culture* (Madison, University of Wisconsin Press).

Galanter, M and Robinson, N (2017) 'Grand Advocates: The Traditional Elite Lawyers' in DB Wilkins, VS Khanna and DM Trubek (eds), *The Indian Legal Profession in the Age of Globalization* (New York, Cambridge University Press) ch 14.

Gandhi, JS (1988) 'Past and Present: A Sociological Portrait of the Indian Legal Profession' in RL Abel and PSC Lewis (eds), *Lawyers in Society: Vol I The Common Law World* (Berkeley, University of California Press) ch 8.

Gingerich, J and Robinson, N (2017) 'Responding to the Market: The Impact of the Rise of Corporate Law Firms on Elite Legal Education in India' in DB Wilkins, VS Khanna and DM Trubek (eds), *The Indian Legal Profession in the Age of Globalization* (New York, Cambridge University Press) ch 16.
Godwin, A (2015) 'Barriers to practice by foreign lawyers in Asia – exploring the role of lawyers in society' 22 *International Journal of the Legal Profession* 299.
Heinz, JP and Laumann, EO (1982) *Chicago Lawyers: The Social Structure of the Bar* (New York, Russell Sage Foundation and Chicago: American Bar Foundation).
Heinz, JP, Nelson, RL, Sandefur, RL and Laumann, EO (2005) *Urban Lawyers: The New Social Structure of the Bar* (Chicago, University of Chicago Press).
Huyse, L (1988) 'Legal Experts in Belgium' in RL Abel and PSC Lewis (eds), *Lawyers in Society: Vol II The Civil Law World* (Berkeley, University of California Press) ch 6.
Johnsen, JT (1988) 'The Professionalization of Legal Counseling in Norway' in RL Abel and PSC Lewis (eds), *Lawyers in Society: Vol II The Civil Law World* (Berkeley, University of California Press) ch 2.
Katvan, E, Silver, C, Ziv, N and Sherr, A (eds) (2017) *Too Many Lawyers? The Future of the Legal Profession* (New York, Routledge).
Klausa, E (1981) *Deutsche und amerikanische Rechtslehrer* (Baden-Baden, Nomos-Verfagsgesselschaft).
Kricheli-Katz, T, Rosen-Zvi, I and Ziv, N (2018) 'Hierarchy and Stratification in the Israel Legal Profession' 52 *Law & Society Review* 436.
Konttinen, E (2003) '"Finland's Route" of Professionalisation and Lawyer-Officials' in WW Pue and D Sugarman (eds), *Lawyers and Vampires: Cultural Histories of Legal Professions* (Oxford, Hart Publishing) ch 4.
Kritzer, HM (1998) *Legal Advocacy: Lawyers and Nonlawyers at Work* (Ann Arbor, MI, University of Michigan Press).
—— (2012) 'It's the law schools stupid! Explaining the continuing increase in the number of lawyers' 19 *International Journal of the Legal Profession* 209.
Kronman, A (2019) *The Assault on American Excellence* (New York, Free Press).
Kumar, CR (2017) 'Experiments in Legal Education in India: Jindal Global Law School and Private Nonprofit Legal Education' in DB Wilkins, VS Khanna and DM Trubek (eds), *The Indian Legal Profession in the Age of Globalization* (New York, Cambridge University Press) ch 19.
Larson, MS (1977) *The Rise of Professionalism: A Sociological Analysis* (Berkeley, University of California Press).
LoPucki, LM (2016) 'Dawn of the Discipline-Based Law Faculty' 65 *Journal of Legal Education* 506.
Lynch, DO (1981) 'Legal Roles in Colombia: Some Social, Economic, and Political Perspectives' in CJ Dias, R Luckham, DO Lynch and JCN Paul (eds), *Lawyers in the Third World: Comparative and Developmental Perspectives* (Uppsala: Scandinavian Institute of African Studies) ch 2.
Mathieu-Fritz, A and Quemin, A (2009) 'French "*officiers ministériels*": autonomy of the legal professions, protection of their market and an ambivalent relationship with the state' 16 *International Journal of the Legal Profession* 167.
McClendon, D, Hackett, C, Potančoková, M, Stonawski, M and Skirbekk, V (2018) 'Women's Education in the Muslim World' 44 *Population and Development Review* 1.
Melville, AL and Stephens, FH (2011) 'The more things change, the more they stay the same: explaining stratification within the Faculty of Advocates, Scotland' 18 *International Journal of the Legal Profession* 2011.
Menkel-Meadow, C (1989) 'Feminization of the Legal Profession: The Comparative Sociology of Women Lawyers' in RL Abel and PSC Lewis (eds), *Lawyers in Society: Vol III Comparative Theories* (Berkeley, University of California Press) ch 5.

Michelson, E (2013) 'Women in the Legal Profession, 1970–2010: A Study of the Global Supply of Lawyers' 20 *International Journal of Global Legal Studies* 1071.

Modéer, K (2003) 'From "Rechtsstaat" to "Welfare-State": Swedish Judicial Culture in Transition 1870–1970' in WW Pue and D Sugarman (eds), *Lawyers and Vampires: Cultural Histories of Legal Professions* (Oxford, Hart Publishing) ch 6.

Mosten, FS (2000) *Unbundling Legal Services: A Guide to Delivering Legal Services à la Carte* (Chicago, American Bar Association).

Murray, G (1988) 'New Zealand Lawyers: From Colonial GPs to the Servants of Capital' in RL Abel and PSC Lewis (eds), *Lawyers in Society: Vol I The Common Law World* (Berkeley, University of California Press) ch 7.

Olgiati, V and Pocar, V (1988) 'The Italian Legal Profession: An Institutional Dilemma' in RL Abel and PSC Lewis (eds), *Lawyers in Society: Vol II The Civil Law World* (Berkeley, University of California Press) ch 9.

Paterson, AA (1988) 'The Legal Profession in Scotland – An Endangered Species or a Problem Case for Market Theory?' in RL Abel and PSC Lewis (eds), *Lawyers in Society: Vol I The Common Law World* (Berkeley, University of California Press) ch 3.

Pérez Perdomo, R (1988) 'The Venezuelan Legal Profession: Lawyers in an Inegalitarian Society' in RL Abel and PSC Lewis (eds), *Lawyers in Society: Vol II The Civil Law World* (Berkeley, University of California Press) ch 11.

Rachman-Moore, D, Almore, T and Kogman, M (2006) 'Equal investments, different rewards: gender inequalities among Israeli lawyers' 13 *International Journal of the Legal Profession* 189.

Reed, AZ (1921) *Training for the Public Profession of Law* (New York, Carnegie Foundation).

Reifner, U (1986) 'The Bar in the Third Reich: Anti-Semitism and the Decline of Liberal Advocacy' 32 *McGill Law Review* 96.

Rokumoto. K (1988) 'The Present State of Japanese Practicing Attorneys: On the Way to Full Professionalization?' in RL Abel and PSC Lewis (eds), *Lawyers in Society: Vol II The Civil Law World* (Berkeley, University of California Press) ch 4.

Sander, R and William, R (1989) 'Why Are There so Many Lawyers? Perspectives on a Turbulent Market' 14 *Law & Social Inquiry* 431.

Schultz, U and Shaw, G (eds) (2003) *Women in the World's Legal Professions* (Oxford, Hart Publishing).

Schuyt, K (1988) 'The Rise of Lawyers in the Dutch Welfare State' in RL Abel and PSC Lewis (eds), *Lawyers in Society: Vol II The Civil Law World* (Berkeley, University of California Press) ch 5.

Shain, M and Roemer, M (1959) 'Hospital Costs Related to the Supply of Beds' 92 *Modern Hospital* 71.

Shapiro, SP (2002) *Tangled Loyalties: Conflict of Interest in Legal Practice* (Ann Arbor, University of Michigan Press).

Shaw, G (2006) '*Notaires* in France – an unassailable profession. Or are they?' 13 *International Journal of the Legal Profession* 243.

Siegrist, H (2003) 'Juridicalisation, Professionalisation and the Occupational Culture of the Advocate in the Nineteenth and the early Twenieth centuries: A Comparison of Germany, Italy and Switzerland' in WW Pue and D Sugarman (eds), *Lawyers and Vampires: Cultural Histories of Legal Professions* (Oxford, Hart Publishing) ch 5.

Singh, A (2017) 'Globalization and the Legal Profession and Regulation of Law Practice in India: The "Foreign Entry" Debate' in in DB Wilkins, VS Khanna and DM Trubek (eds), *The Indian Legal Profession in the Age of Globalization* (New York, Cambridge University Press) ch 11.

Sloan, K (2019) 'Overhaul the Bar Exam? Two Major Studies Focus on the Test's Future', *National Law Journal* (31 July).

Smigel, EO (1964) *The Wall Street Lawyer* (Bloomington, Indiana University Press).

Sommerlad, H and Sanderson, P (1998) *Gender, Choice and Commitment: Women Solicitors in England and Wales and the Struggle for Equality* (Aldershot, Ashgate).

Susskind, R (2010) *The End of Lawyers? Rethinking the Nature of Legal Services* (Oxford, Oxford University Press).

Tamanaha, BZ (2012) *Failing Law Schools* (New York, Oxford University Press).

Tejani, R (2017) *Law Mart: Justice, Access, and For-Profit Law Schools* (Palo Alto, Stanford University Press).

Van Hoy, J (1997) *Franchise Law Firms and the Transformation of Personal Legal Service* (Westport, Conn, Quorum Books).

Viladás Jene, C (1988) 'The Legal Profession in Spain: An Understudied but Blooming Occupation' in RL Abel and PSC Lewis (eds), *Lawyers in Society: Vol II The Civil Law World* (Berkeley, University of California Press) ch 10.

Waters, CPM (2004) *Counsel in the Caucasus: Professionalization and Law in Georgia* (Leiden, Martinus Nijhoff).

Weber, M (1954) *Law in Economy and Society* (transl E Shils and M Rheinstein; ed M Rheinstein) (Cambridge, Harvard University Press).

—— (1978) *Economy and Society* (eds G Roth and C Wittich) (Berkeley, University of California Press).

Weisbrot, D (1988) 'The Australian Legal Profession: From Provincial Family Firms to Multinationals' in RL Abel and PSC Lewis (eds), *Lawyers in Society: Vol I The Common Law World* (Berkeley, University of California Press) ch 6.

Wilkins, DB, Khanna, VS and Trubek, DM (eds) (2017) *The Indian Legal Profession in the Age of Globalization* (New York, Cambridge University Press).

World Bank (2001) 'Legal and judicial reform: strategic directions' (Working Paper 26916) (Washington, DC, World Bank).

Index

Please note that references to Tables are followed by the letter 't', whereas those for Figures by the letter 'f'

Abel, R 3–5, 7, 21, 22, 90, 103, 117, 289, 515
access to justice
  Belgium 162–3
  Canada 79
  England and Wales 105–107
  Netherlands 264–5
  South Africa 543–4
  United States 143–5
  see also legal aid
Achour, H 659
Ademola, A 518
advocates
  Bosnia and Herzegovina (BiH) 358
  Czech Republic 292–5
  Egypt 567–8
  Germany 210–11, 217–24
    in 2030 230
    Act on Advocates 209, 215
    Chambers of Advocates 210–11, 215, 225, 226
    changing scope of practice 217–18
    data 218–19
    declining importance of court work 218
    female 221–4
    German Advocates Association 211, 215, 225, 226, 227
    liability, fees and income 219–20
    specialisation 220–1
    women 221–4
  Kenya
    discipline of 510–11
    qualifications to practise as 507–508
    remuneration 509
  Myanmar 776
  Poland 316–26
    advocates 323–4
    attorneys at law 323–4
    from 1989 to 1997 316–17
    deregulation on basis of 2013 Act 322–3
    efforts to open up legal profession (1997–2005) 318–21
    evident weaknesses of statutory aims 324–6
    implementing of changes and 2009 Act (2005–11) 321–2
    legal services market, situation of 323–4
    realisation of statutory aims 324–6
    transformation, consequences 326–8
  Russia
    contemporary, professional hallmarks 341–3
    current position 349–50
    elite 343
    exclusive jurisdiction 332
    Federal Chamber of Advocates 341
    following Perestroika 339–45
    Guild of Russian Advocates 340
    officers of the court 338
    rise of competition/failure to unify 339–41
    in Russian Empire 335–7
    in the Soviet Union 337–9
  Scotland 120
  Serbia
    contemporary 361–4
    historical background 357–9
    strikes 363
Afiuni, ML 457, 458
Africa/African states
  colonialism
    Burundi 478–80, 481t, 483–5
    Kenya 496
    Nigeria 516–19
  Congo, divide and rule in 480
  military rule
    Burundi 481–7
    Nigeria 522–3
  see also Burundi; ethnicity; Kenya; Nigeria; Rwanda; South Africa; Zimbabwe
age factors, in legal profession
  Australia 59
  Kenya 499
  Nigeria 528
agency lawyers, United States 139–40
Ahmadinejad, M 584
Alternative Business Structures (ABSs)
  Canada 82
  England and Wales 90, 95
  Scotland 121, 123, 124
American Bar Association (ABA) 24, 77, 129, 140, 146, 726
  Model Rules of Professional Conduct 145
Anderson, B 844
Arafat, Y 640, 645

Argentina 377–90
  Association for Civil Rights 386
  Bars and Bar associations 379–81
  Centre for Legal and Social Studies 385
  Civil Association for Equality and Justice 386
  Constitution 378, 387
  constitutionalisation 384
  corruption 388
  Council of Magistrates (CM) 389
  de-codification 384
  globalisation 385, 386
  human rights 383, 386
  immigrants 378
  independence 377
  judiciary/judges 381–2, 389
    judicialisation of politics 384
    politicisation of judiciary 384
  legal education and training 379, 385, 387, 388
  legal profession 379–81, 387–9
    fragmentation 384
    and politics 377, 382–90
  National Supreme Court of Justice (CSJN) 389
  Public Bar of the City of Buenos Aires 380
  Public Interest Law Clinic of University of Palermo Law School 385
  rule of law 388
  solo practitioners 379
  transition to democracy and reconfiguration of law 382–7
  violence 384
Argersinger v Hamlin judgment, US 139
Asian countries *see* China; Hong Kong; India; Indonesia; Japan; Myanmar; South Korea; Taiwan; Thailand; Vietnam
Asian Financial Crisis 1997 833, 837
Ataturk, MK 676
attorneys
  Iran 586–97
    clash of legal cultures 598–9
    clients, attitudes towards legal services 593
    codes of professional responsibility 597
    corruption 592–3
    female lawyers 594–5
    fiqh (Islamic jurisprudence) 589–90
    hostile judiciary 587–8
    on Iranian Bar Association (IBA) 586–7
    law firms 595
    legal education and training 595–7
    selection and training of judges 590–2
  Netherlands 262–3
  Poland 316–26
    attorneys at law 323–4
    from 1989 to 1997 316–17
    deregulation on basis of 2013 Act 322–3
    efforts to open up legal profession (1997–2005) 318–21
    evident weaknesses of statutory aims 324–6
    expanding scope of professional rights (1997) 317–18
    implementing of changes and 2009 Act (2005–11) 321–2
    legal services market, situation of 323–4
    realisation of statutory aims 324–6
    transformation, consequences 326–8
Aung San Suu Kyi 785
Austin, R 550–1
Australia 45–64
  attrition of female associates from law firms 48
  Bar associations 49, 51
  Brisbane 50
  and China 47
  Commission for Uniform Legal Services Regulation 52
  Commonwealth
    Commonwealth Tertiary Education Commission (CTEC) 54
    Native Title Act 1993 57
  community legal centres (CLCs) 53
  competition, legal services market 46–9
  Competition and Consumer Commission 46
  competition policy 45, 46
  Council of Australian Governments 52
  cyber law 48–9
  demographics, legal profession 49–51
  diversity issues in legal profession 57–60
    age 59
    class 59–60
    Diversity and Equality Charter 57
    gender 58–9
    lawyers born overseas 58
    National Attrition and Re-engagement Study (NARS) Report 57
    Native Title Act 1993 57
    racial/ethnic minorities 57–8
  export of legal services 47
  female lawyers 51, 58–9
  fit and proper person requirement 49
  Gender Equitable Briefing Policy 51
  gender structure, legal profession 58–9
  and global financial crisis 46, 47
  Group of Eight (Go8) 54, 55
  High Court 51, 57–8
  Indigenous lawyers 45
  internationalisation of economy 47
  Law Apps 49
  Law Council of Australia 48, 51
    Federal Election Policy Platform (2016) 60

law firms
  boutique 50
  large 47, 48, 60
  small 47, 48, 60
lawyers
  born overseas 58
  and contemporary politics 60
  proliferation 55
legal aid 53
legal education and training 49, 53–7
  Australian Tertiary Admission Rank 55
  clinical programmes 56
  Dawkins reforms 53
  FEE-HELP 53, 54, 56
  Higher Education Contribution Scheme (HECS) 53, 60
  Indigenous Tutorial Assistance Scheme 58
  Juris Doctor (JD) 55
  law schools 54, 55–7
  LLB (Bachelor of Law) programmes 55, 56
  practical legal training (PLT) 49, 56, 58
  Priestley Eleven 56
  Tertiary Education Quality and Standards Agency 55
legal profession 57–60
  barristers 51
  female lawyers 48, 51, 58–9
  judges 51
  law firms 47, 50, 60
  regulation of 52–3
  solicitors 49–50, 52
  transformation of 46–9
  'two hemispheres' thesis 47
Legal Profession Uniform Law (LPUL) 50, 52
Legal Services Council 52
liberalism 45, 53, 60
National Legal Profession Reform Taskforce 52
neoliberalism 45, 57
New South Wales (NSW)
  fragmentation 49
  Law Admission Test 55
  law schools 56
  Law Society Indigenous Reconciliation Strategic Plan 2016 58
  Legal Profession Act 2004 52
  Legal Profession Admission Board 50, 54
  Legal Profession Uniform Law (LPUL) 52
  Office of the Legal Services Commissioner (OLSC) 46
NewLaw 48–9
pricing structures 48
qualified lawyers 56
Queensland
  Attorney-General 51
  fragmentation of profession 49
  law schools 54
  resources industry 50
  Supreme Court 51
regional, rural and remote (RRR) firms 47, 50, 60
Senior Counsel 50
South Australia 57
Supreme Courts 49, 51
Victoria
  Attorney-General 51
  fragmentation of profession 49
  Legal Profession Uniform Law (LPUL) 52
  Supreme Court 51
Western Australia 50
regulation of legal profession 52

Bachelor of Law (LLB) programmes
  Australia 55, 56
  Belgium 157
  Brazil 394–5
  Canada 78
  England and Wales 99
  Germany 215–16
  Mexico 429, 434, 436–7, 440, 442
  Norway 188
  Scotland 118
bailiffs
  candidate 170
  court 297, 313–14
  incumbent 170
  private 292, 297–8, 886, 898
Baker McKenzie (major law firm) 23, 900
  Mexico 430–1
  Russia 345
  South Korea 796
  Switzerland 275, 282
  Thailand 841, 842
  United States 133
  Venezuela 452, 464
Balzer, HD 335
bank secrecy, Switzerland 277–9
barristers
  Australia 51
  England and Wales 90, 92–3
  Hong Kong 819, 821
Bars and Bar associations
  Argentina 379–81
  Australia 49, 51
  Belgium 161–7
    alternative dispute resolution (ADR) 164–5
    Association of the French-speaking and German-speaking Bars (OBFG) 161, 163, 166
    Bar associations 162, 163
    feminisation 165

Flemish Bar Association (OVB)   161, 163–4, 166
  institutional independence   161–2
  legislative amendments   164–5
  mediation   164–5
  organisation   161–2
  profession, lawyering as   167
Bosnia and Herzegovina (BiH)   359, 360
Brazil   392, 393–7, 405, 887
Burundi   488, 489
Canada   82
CBA (Chicago Bar Association)   411
Chicago Bar   200, 258
Chile   411, 415, 416–19, 422, 423
  governance   417
  legal aid   418
  organisation   416–19
  traditional Bar   418–19
China   699, 700
Danish Bar and Law Society (DBLS)   176, 179, 181, 185
Egypt   565, 566, 569, 570
  Bar Association   573–4
  Board   567, 568, 574
  General Assembly   574
  internal divisions, under Mubarak (1981–2011)   577–8
  Sadat, conflictual relations with (1970–81)   576–7
England and Wales   92–3
  Bar Council   92, 95, 107, 809
  Bar Professional Training Course (BPTC)   88, 94, 99, 100
  Bar Standards Board   92, 95, 96
  class structure   105
examinations   650–1, 757–8
France   193, 194
  Bar associations   193
  governing bodies   204
  National Bar Council (CNB)   193, 195, 197, 204
  Paris   204
Hong Kong   809, 812, 817, 820
India   714, 715
Indonesia   737
Iran   581, 582, 586–7
Israel   601, 602–604, 612–13, 887
  as a civic actor   607
  establishment   602–604
Japan   757–8, 884
  Bar Association demand to reduce numbers passing examination   759, 761
  Japan Federal Bar Association (JFBA)   716, 753, 758–9, 771, 772, 884
Jordan   644

Kenya   495
Libya   628, 629, 631, 632, 634, 636
  initial relations with regime   626–8
  tensions with regime   630–2
Mexico   443, 444–5
Myanmar   785
Netherlands   258–64
  Dutch Bar Association   254, 259, 262, 263
  entry to   258
  gender/ethnic background   260–1
  general developments within the legal profession   261
  internationalisation of law firms   260
  office size   258–9
Nigeria   519, 520, 521, 522
Palestine   639, 642, 645, 647–8, 650–1
  examinations   650–1
  split in   647
  structure   647–8
  transitional Bar council   646
Poland   317, 318
Rhodesia   548
Russia
  alternative Bars   344
  Federal Bar Act 2002   332, 344, 345
  qualifications   342
  Soviet Union, former   340
Scotland   120, 123
Serbia   363, 364, 897
South Africa   535, 536, 537, 540–1
South Korea   794, 795, 796
Sweden   189, 190
Switzerland   272, 273, 274, 282
Taiwan   803–804, 805, 807, 808, 813, 814, 817
Thailand   833
Tunisia   658–9
  Bar of the State Party and commercial lawyers (RCD)   663–5, 667
  Ben Ali, under   660–3, 667
  judiciary   670–2
  local associations   658
  'lower echelon' of Bar   665–6
  Opposition Bar, under Ben Ali   667
  samsars   665–6
  social structure   660–3
Turkey   676, 679, 684, 685, 691
United States
  Bar associations   127
  disaggregated   145–6
  entry practices   143
  private practice   129
Venezuela   452, 465–6
Vietnam   857, 858, 865, 868–9
Yugoslavia, former   358–9

Bastard, B   271
Bayart, J-F   475, 484
Belgium   157–73
   Appointments Committee for the Notarial
      Profession   168
   Bars and Bar associations   161–7
     alternative dispute resolution (ADR)   164–5
     Association of the French-speaking and
       German-speaking Bars (OBFG)   161,
       163, 166
     feminisation   165
     Flemish Bar Association (OVB)   161, 163–4, 166
     institutional independence   161–2
     legislative amendments   164–5
     mediation   164–5
     organisation   161–2
     profession, lawyering as   167
   Code of Economic Law   164
   colonialism   474, 478–80, 481t, 484, 485
   Commission for Legal Aid   160
   Constitutional Court   165, 170
   Cour de Cassation   162, 164, 480
   Court of Assizes   170
   diversification of lawyers   160
   diversity issues in legal profession   160, 168
   Empire
     and Burundi   477–80
     colonial model   478–80
     middlemen of   477–8
   judiciary/judges
     Burundi, organisation under Belgian
       mandates   481t
     Judicial Code   164, 165, 166
     lay judges   170
   legal aid   160–1
   Legal Aid Act 1998   160
   legal education and training
     democratisation of the educational
       system   159
     growth in number of law school
       graduates   157–9
     law degree programmes   157
     LLB (Bachelor of Law) programmes   157
   legal profession   161–71
     access to profession   162–3
     consultations, numbers of   161
     corporate lawyers   170–1
     earnings of lawyers   889
     ethics, codification   163–7
     female lawyers   168, 892
     feminisation   273–5
     judges   170
     lawyering in Belgium as a profession   167
     numerus clausus   167, 168, 171
     partnership and specialisation   165–7
     local Bar associations   162
     magistracy   169–70
     mandates, judicial organisation under   481t
     National Bar Association   162
     NGOs (non-governmental organisations)   489
     notarial practice   167–8
     regional Bar associations   162, 163
     Supreme Court   169
     violence   165
   see also Burundi
Bellini, A   237
Ben Ali, ZEA   657, 672
   Bar of the State Party   663
   coup d'état   659–60
   legal profession following rule of   668–70
   Opposition Bars under   667
   social structure of Tunisian Bar under   660–3
   see also Tunisia
BigLaw   22–3
BiH *see* Bosnia and Herzegovina (BiH)
Boigeol, A   193
Bolívar, S   453
Bourdieu, P.   11
Bosnia and Herzegovina (BiH)   353–73
   advocates   358, 359–60
   Bars and Bar associations   359, 360
   corruption   367, 368, 370
   Council of Bars and Law Societies in Europe
     (CCBE)   359, 360
   diversity issues in legal profession   360
   FBiH Bar Association   359, 360
   High Judicial and Prosecutorial Council
     (HJPC)   357, 367, 368
   independence   359
   Independent Judicial Commission   367
   judiciary/judges   364–5, 367–9
   Law on Attorney Order 1883   358
   Law on Providers of Free Legal Aid 2016   360
   legal academics   369
   legal education and training   356–7, 369
   legal profession   360, 367–9
     female lawyers   360, 891
   Office of the High Representative (OHR)   360
   RS Bar Association   359, 360
   Serbia contrasted   370
   see also Serbia; Yugoslavia, former
Bourdieu, P   11, 475, 476
Bourguiba, H   657, 658, 659
boutique firms
   Australia   50
   Brazil   401–403, 405
   Chile   419, 707
   Germany   24, 25, 228
   Indonesia   747
   Italy   243

Japan 768–9
Netherlands 259
specialised 24, 25, 403
United States 133, 136
Venezuela 454
Brazil 391–409
 alternative dispute resolution (ADR) 403
 arbitration 402
 Bars and Bar associations 392, 393–7, 405, 887
 Brazilian Institute for Research and Education of Paralegals 395
 Centre for Studies on Law Firms (CESA) 402
 Commission for Defence of Consumers 401
 Constitution 392
 corruption 400
 defence of society and the poor 400
 democratisation 393
 development of profession 393, 394
 diversity issues in legal profession 404–405
  class 393, 405
  gender 396–9, 404–405
  racial/ethnic minorities 396–8, 405
 Federal Attorney General's Office (AGO) 399–401, 405, 406
 globalisation 393–4, 403–404
 Guidelines for Education Act 1996 393
 historical transformations 392–5
 Institute of Brazilian Lawyers (IAB) 394
 Institute Pro Bono (IPB) 402
 JBM (law firm) 405
 law firms
  boutique 401, 403, 405
  large 403
  private practice 402–405
  small 402, 403
 legal education and training 395–9
  failed LLBs 394
  post-graduate programmes 398–9
  professionalisation of legal academia 397–9
  quality 395–7
  unlicensed law graduates 394–5
 legal profession
  alternative dispute resolution (ADR) 391
  Bachelors of Law 394–5
  careers 399–402
  class 405
  defence of society and the poor 400
  earnings of lawyers 889
  female lawyers 396–9, 404–405
  fragmentation 404
  General Counsel 402
  hierarchy, status and competition 403–404
  historical background 392
  judges 399
  National Council of Justice (CNT) 399
  Office of Public Defender (IPD) 391
  old hierarchical duality 392–3, 403
  private lawyering 402–405
  prosecutors, new roles 400
  public careers of legal professionals 399–402
  public defenders 400
  racial/ethnic minorities 405
  regulation 395–7
  sexual orientation 405
  social inclusion challenge 404–405
  solo practitioners 402, 403, 899
  'two hemispheres' thesis 391
  unlicensed practitioners 405
  unqualified practitioners 394
 liberalism 392, 406
 mass litigation 403
 Ministry of Education (MEC) 396, 397, 405
 National Association of Bachelors of Laws (NABL) 394
 National Council of Justice (CNJ) 399
 OAB (Brazilian Bar Association) 392, 393–4, 405
  regulatory efforts 395–7
 Office of Public Defender (OPD) 391, 392, 400, 405
 pro bono services 401–402
 public interest litigation 400–402
 qualified lawyers 394, 395
 Quotas Act 2012 393
Brexit 91, 107, 109
Bugaighis, S 635
Burma *see* **Myanmar**
Burundi 473–93
 Bar 488, 489
 Belgian colonialism 474, 477–80, 481t, 484, 485
  'middlemen' 475–8
 colonialism
  capitalism and legal pluralism 478–80
  colonial legacies, reviving 483–5
  German colonisation and judicial organisation 481t
 Congo, annexed to 480
 Congo, divide and rule in 480
 co-optation and marginalisation, legal field 485–7
 corruption 476, 490
 ethnic affiliation and violence 474–8, 480, 483, 484, 487–90
  ethnic ultra-violence 481–3
  geopolitics of the 'bottom-up' state 488–90
  and human rights/political opposition 487–8
  International Commission of Inquiry 482
  massacres 473, 474, 483
  post-1993 crisis 488–90
  third wave of global democratisation 487–8

extraversion 475, 484, 485–7
foreign diplomacy and despotic rule 490–1
Front for Democracy (FRODEBU) 487, 488
human rights 487–8, 489
indirect rule in 480
INGOs (international NGOs) 473, 488, 490
intermediaries of the law 475, 476
lawlessness 473, 477
legal profession
    double bias 474–5
    foreign diplomacy and despotic rule 490–1
    intermediaries 473–6
    knowledge *chiaroscuru* and colonial legacy 474
    post-2015 491
    private market for international legal practice 490–1
    research agenda 473–6
    solo practitioners 490
    state and globalisation 475–6
    types 473–5
liberalisation of market 487
Ligue Iteka (human rights organisation) 488
military republics 481–7
Ministry of Justice 485
National Council for the Defence of Democracy- Forces for the Defence of Democracy (CNDD-FDD) 482, 490, 491
patrimonialism 484
'politics of the belly' 476, 484
'promise of protection' (1916–62) 477–80
rent 484, 485
Search for Common Ground and the British International Alert 488
state power 483–5
Union for National Progress (UPRONA) 478
Buyoya, P (Major) 487, 488, 489

Caballero, J 430
Caldera, R 452
Cameron, D 516
Canada 65–88
    Alberta 65
    Alternative Business Structures (ABSs) 82
    background to legal profession 65
    'Big Four' accounting firms 82
    British Columbia 65, 78
    Canadian Bar Association (CBA) 82
    Charter of Rights and Freedoms 79
    competition, legal services market 79–82
    complaints 83–4
    Counsel Network 70
    demographics 71–3
    discipline 83–4
    distribution of lawyers 65, 66t
    diversity issues in legal profession 71–3
    ethnicity and immigration 72–3
    Federation of Law Societies of Canada (FLSC) 69, 71t, 72t, 77
        Model Code of Professional Conduct 83
        National Discipline Standards 83
    law firms
        large 69
        public sector 69–70
        small 67–8
    Law Societies 67t, 76
        Law Societies of Nova Scotia and BC 80–1
        Law Society of BC 78
        Law Society of Upper Canada (LSUC) 78, 82
    legal aid 79
    legal education and training 76–9
        articling 78–9
        Bora Laskin Faculty of Law 76
        curriculum 77–8
        demographics 76–7
        diploma in notarial law (DDN) 81
        entry to profession 78–9
        Law School Aptitude Test (LSAT) 76, 77
        law schools 76, 77, 78
        LLB (Bachelor of Law) programmes 78
        McGill degrees 78
        National Committee on Accreditation (NCA) 77
    legal profession
        access to justice 79
        Alternative Business Structures (ABSs) 82
        changes in the regulation of paralegals 80–1
        corporate counsel 70
        earnings of lawyers 74, 75f, 76
        entry barriers, addressing 888
        female lawyers 71, 72
        future of 79–82
        large firms 69
        multi-disciplinary practices (MDPs) 81–2
        notaries 79, 81
        pro bono services 79
        public sector 69–70
        rise of legal alternatives 82
        small firms 67–8
    Montreal, ethnicity and immigration 73
    multi-disciplinary practices (MDPs) 81–2
    National Household Survey (NHS) 69
    non-practising lawyers 70, 71t
    Ontario 68t
        complaints and discipline 83–4
        ethnicity and immigration 73
        multi-disciplinary practices (MDPs) 81–2
    population and distribution 65–7
    Quebec
        Chambre des Notaires du Québec (CNQ) 81

female lawyers 71
  legal education and training 76, 78
  notaries 79, 81
  population and distribution 65
Toronto
  ethnicity and immigration 73
  population and distribution 65
  'Seven Sisters' (law firms) 69
Vancouver, ethnicity and immigration 72
capitalism, and legal pluralism (Burundi) 478–80
Carbon Law Partners, England and Wales 95
Cardia-Vonèche, L 271
Carr, J 271, 280
caste system, India 720
Cedeño, E 457
changes in legal profession *see* transformation, legal profession
Chappuis, B 272, 282, 283
Chávez, H 450, 452–5, 457, 462, 883
Chebbi, LK 659
Cheesman, N 783
Cheng Benji 805
Chihambakwe, S 549
Chile 411–27
  Antitrust Prosecution Office 420–1
  Association of Labour Lawyers 419
  Bars and Bar associations 411, 415, 416–19, 422, 423
    governance 417
    legal aid 418
    organisation 416–19
    traditional Bar 418–19
  CBA (Bar Association) 411, 415, 416–19, 422, 423
    complaints resolved by 417–18
  Code of Ethics 417
  Constitutional Court 412, 418
  diversity issues in legal profession 422
  Family Lawyers Guild 419
  human rights 423, 424
  law firms
    boutique 419, 707
    large 419, 420
  legal aid 418
  legal education and training 413–16, 419, 420
    law schools 415, 416
    LLM (Master of Law) Programmes 416, 420
    mass higher education 413–16
    shortcomings 415–16
  legal profession
    female lawyers 422
    law firms 419, 420, 707
    litigation 421
    market economy, effect on 412–19

  solo practitioners 701
  specialisation 419–22
  unlicensed practitioners 418
  LGBTI issues 423, 424
  National Criminal Defence Office 418
  new politics of rights 422–4
  NGOs (non-governmental organisations) 423, 424
  Regional Agencies of Legal Aid 418
  Superintendence of Insurance and Securities 421
  Supreme Court 412, 415, 416, 421
  think tanks 423
  Wall Street model, law firms organised on 419
China 697–711
  Administrative License Law 2003 700
  All China Lawyers Association 702
  and Australia 47
  Bar 699, 700
  Beijing Lawyers Association (BLA) 703
  Chinese Communist Party 819
  civil war 805
  Dacheng firm 707
  diversity issues in legal profession 703
  globalisation 705–707
  growth of international corporate firm 23
  and Hong Kong 812
  Hong Kong lawyers' march against Beijing 823–5
  Interim Regulation on Lawyers 1980 697–8
  King & Wood law firm 707
  KWM Europe 707
  law firms 705–707
  legal education and training 698, 699, 886
  legal profession
    in 1990s 698
    evolving 703
    female lawyers 703
    growth in size of profession 697–700
    lawyer migration 701
    post-Mao era 700
    stratification and inequality 700–703
    'two hemispheres' thesis 700, 701
  LGBTI issues 703
  liberalism 17
  Mainland China 815
  National People's Congress (NPCSC), Standing Committee 823
  political activism 703–705
  Republic of China (ROC) 802, 815
  separation from Taiwan 801
  Shanghai Lawyers Association 703
  State Council, White Paper 823
  Vietnam contrasted 858
  White Paper 2014 819

Chinamasa, P 558
Chitepo, H 549
Chrétien, J-P 483
class
 Australia 59–60
 Belgium 159
 Brazil 393, 405
 Egypt 568
 Thailand 832, 834, 835, 842
Claude, M 423
Codes of Conduct *see* regulation of legal profession
colonialism
 Burundi 478–80, 481t
 judicial organisation at beginning of German colonialisation 481t
 Kenya 496
 Myanmar
  common law legal profession 777–8
  pre-colonial legal profession 776–7
 Nigeria 516–19
 Thailand, 'quasi-colonial' modernisation 831–3
comparative sociology (1988–2018) 880–915
 competition, controlling 895–8
 defining role of lawyer 890–4
 making lawyers 894–5
 numbers of lawyers 880–90
 research agenda 902–904, 905–910t
 structures of practice 898–902
Comparative Studies of Legal Profession, Working Group (WG) vii
competition, legal services market 896
 Australia 45, 46–9
 Canada 79–82
 controlling 895–8
 Denmark 179–80, 183
 England and Wales 96–8
 Scotland 122
 South Africa 540–1
 Switzerland 279–83
 Vietnam 866–7
Competition and Markets Authority (CMA)
 and England and Wales 96, 98
 and Scotland 122, 123
competitors, qualified lawyers 889–90
complaints, Canada 83–4
Congo
 Belgian colonial model 478, 479
 customary justice 474
 divide and rule in 480
 education 484
corporate lawyers
 Belgium 170–1
 Canada 70
 Czech Republic 298–9

corruption
 Argentina 388
 Bosnia and Herzegovina (BiH) 367, 368, 370
 Brazil 400
 Burundi 476, 490
 Indonesia 735–9, 748, 749
 Iran 592–3
 Kenya 508, 512
 Libya 623
 Mexico 435
 Netherlands 253
 Serbia 366
 Thailand 847
 Tunisia 663, 666
 Turkey 683
 Venezuela 451, 453, 457, 458
courts
 access to 265
 court bailiffs 297, 313–14
 management 263–4
 reorganisation of system 625–6
cross-pressures, lawyers under 183–4
curriculum, legal
 Canada 77–8
 Netherlands
  content 257–8
  unification 256–7
cyber law, Australia 48–9
Czech Republic 289–307
 Action Committees 291
 Advocacy Acts 293, 294
 Advocacy Advisory Bureaus (AABs) 293, 301
 Chamber of Advocacy (CCA) 293, 294, 298
 Chamber of Bailiffs 298
 Chamber of Commercial Counsel (CCC) 294
 Communist Party (CP) 291, 292
 court system 295–6
 diversity issues in legal profession 294, 301–302
 faculties of law 299–301
  common problems 300–301
  legal research facilities 300
 General Prosecutor 296
 High Courts (HC) 295
 Institute of State and Law (ISL) 300
 intersections 301–304
 language 290
 legal education and training 302–303
  apprenticeship 887
  law schools 291
  law teachers and scholars 303–304
  professional legal training 304
  Second World War, following 291
 legal profession
  advocates 292–5
  bailiffs 297–8

corporate counsel 298–9
female lawyers 294, 301–302
historical transitions 290–2
judges 295–6
and lawyers 289–90
notaries 296–7
numbers of professions 289–90
present professions 292
privatisation 297
prosecutors 296
solo practitioners 294, 295
State Service counsel 299
and Nazism 291
numerus clausus 292–3, 296, 297
Pro Bono Alliance (NGO) 303
Regional Associations of Advocacy (RAAs) 293, 301
Regional Courts (RC) 295
State Prosecutor's Office (SPO) 296
Supreme Administrative Court (SAC) 295–6
Supreme Association of Advocacy (SAA) 293
work contracts, legal academia 300–301

data 14–22
De la Maza, I 419–20
Delgado Ocando, JM 466
democracy/democratisation
Argentina 382–7
Belgium 159
Brazil 393
Mexico 431–2
Myanmar 778–9
Venezuela 450–3
Zimbabwe 556
demographics
Australia 49–51
Canada 71–3
legal education and training 76–7
Switzerland 273
de-nationalisation 6–7
Denmark 175–92
Administration of Justice Act 1990 179
Association of Danish Law Firms 185
Association of Lawyers and Economists 177
cross-pressures, lawyers under 183–4
Danish Bar and Law Society (DBLS) 176, 179, 185
Advokaten magazine 181, 183, 184
diversity issues in legal profession 184
law firms 176, 181, 189
lawyers 190
legal aid 186–7, 188, 190
legal education and training 178–9, 185–6
legal profession 178–85
changes in demography/structure 176–8

competition from foreign firms and lawyers 183
cross-pressures, lawyers under 183–4
developments 180–3
external changes 180–3
female lawyers 184, 891
'fly-in-fly-out' counsel 183
jurists, 'replacement' 177–8
Kammeradvokaten (Junior Counsel to the Treasury) 184–5
liberalisation of market 179–80
new competitive structures 179–80
prior to the 1980s 180
solo practitioners 900
neoliberalism 181
Pettifogger Act, repeal (2006) 179
qualified lawyers 185
welfare state 175, 176
see also Scandinavian countries
Dezalay, Y 431
Dhru, K 721
disciplinary measures
Canada 83–4
Indonesia 747–8
Japan 768
Kenya 510–11
Mexico 442
Thailand 841
Tunisia 666
Vietnam 872
see also regulation of legal profession
diversity issues in legal profession
addressing 883
age factors
Australia 59
Kenya 499
Nigeria 528
Australia 57–60
Diversity and Equality Charter 57
gender 48, 51, 58–9
lawyers born overseas 58
National Attrition and Re-engagement Study (NARS) Report 57
Native Title Act 1993 57
Belgium 160, 168
Bosnia and Herzegovina (BiH) 360
Brazil 396–9, 404–405
Burundi 481–4, 487–90
ethnic ultra-violence *see* Burundi
geopolitics of the 'bottom-up' state 488–90
and human rights/political opposition 487–8
post-1993 crisis 488–90
racial/ethnic minorities 481–4, 487–90
third wave of global democratisation 487–8

Canada 71–3, 72t
  gender 71, 72
Chile 422
China, gender 703
class 59–60, 405
Czech Republic 294, 301–302
Denmark 184
Egypt, class 568
England and Wales 103–105
  Black, Asian and Minority Ethnic (BAME) law students 99, 104, 893
  class 104–105
  gender 104
entry to legal profession
  Belgium 162–3
  Canada 78–9
  England and Wales 95
  Scotland 118
  United States 141
France, gender 195–6, 200
gender *see* gender structure, legal profession; women lawyers
Germany 221–4
Hong Kong 825–6, 827f
India 715–21, 719f
Israel 613–14
Japan 766, 767t, 768
Kenya 498–9
Mexico 433
Myanmar 781, 891
Netherlands 260–1, 883
Nigeria 524, 525–6t
  age structure 528
  gender 528, 529–30t
  socio-economic backgrounds 525–6t
Palestine 650
Poland 310–11
racial/ethnic minorities
  Australia 57–8
  Brazil 405
  Burundi 481–4, 487–90
  Kenya 499–500
  Netherlands 261
Scotland 119
Serbia 355
sexual orientation 405
South Africa 883
  gender 537–8
  racial/ethnic minorities 538, 542
Switzerland 273–5, 283
Taiwan 825–6, 827f
Thailand
  class 832, 835, 838, 839, 842
  gender 839, 842–3
Tunisia 661

Turkey 686–7
United States 128, 141–6
Venezuela 462
Zimbabwe 551, 555
see also class; gender structure, legal profession; racial/ethnic minorities
Doherty, RA 518
Dumbutshena, E 553

earnings of lawyers
  Brazil 889
  Canada 74, 75t, 76
  France 276, 889
  gender pay differences 223–4
  Germany 210, 219–20, 889
  Poland 325
  ratio of population to lawyers 889
  Russia 338
  South Korea 889
  Switzerland 271–2, 276, 889
  United States 132–3, 143
economic liberalism 118, 682
Egypt 565–80
  Bars and Bar associations 565, 566, 569, 570, 573–4, 579
    Board 567, 568, 574, 577
    General Assembly 574
    internal divisions, under Mubarak (1981–2011) 577–8
    Sadat, conflictual relations with (1970–81) 576–7
  Centre for Economic and Social Rights 574
  Centre for Human Rights Legal Aid (CHRLA) 571
  conflictual relations between Bars and President Sadat (1970–81) 576–7
  Court of Administrative Justice 568
  Court of Cassation 568
  fiqh (Islamic jurisprudence) 565
  Hisham Mubarak Law Centre 571
  human rights 571
  legal education and training 569, 571–3
  legal profession
    Advocates Law 1983 567–8, 578
    Bar Association 573–4, 577–8
    crackdown on lawyers following 2011 578–9
    historical background 566–7
    human rights lawyers 571
    lawyers in practice 569–70
    rights and duties of lawyers 568
  monarchy, liberalism and nationalism under 575
  Mubarak, internal divisions within Bars Association under (1981–2011) 577–8
  Muslim Brotherhood 577

Nasser, loss of prestige and independence under (1952–70)   575–6
NGOs (non-governmental organisations)   571
    qualified lawyers   565
Sadat, conflictual relations with Bar (1970–81)   576–7
Sharia courts   565, 567
State Council   569, 570, 578
successive Egyptian authoritarian regimes   574–9
Supreme Administrative Court   568
Supreme Constitutional Court   571
Elveriş, İ   691
England and Wales   89–115
    access to justice   105–107
    Access to Justice Act 1999   106
    Alternative Business Structures (ABSs)   90, 95, 166
    Bars and Bar associations   92–3
        Bar Council   92, 95, 107, 809
        Bar Professional Training Course (BPTC)   88, 94, 99, 100
        Bar Standards Board   92, 95, 96
        class structure   105
    and Brexit   91, 107, 109
    Chartered Institute of Legal Executives (CILEX)   93, 99
    City of London Law Society   101
    civil legal aid   106
    Community Legal Service (CLS)   106
    competition, legal services market   96–8
    contemporary politics and lawyers   107–108
    Council of Licensed Conveyancers (CLC)   93
    Criminal Defence Service (CDS)   106–107
    Crown Prosecution Service (CPS)   92
    disintegration of traditional professional model   90
    diversity issues in legal profession   103–105
        Black, Asian and Minority Ethnic (BAME) law students   99, 104, 893
        class   104–105
        gender   104
    EU (Withdrawal) Act 2018   109
    globalisation   89, 92
    Government Legal Department (GLD)   92, 94
    Human Rights Act 1998   106
    Judicial Appointments Commission (JAC)   94
    law firm insurers   96
    law firms   101, 122
    Law Society   95, 101, 105, 107, 109, 886
    legal aid   105–107
    Legal Aid Agency (LAA)   106
    Legal Aid Board (LAB)   105, 106
    Legal Aid, Sentencing and Punishment of Offenders Act (LASPO) 2012   90, 106, 107
    Legal Disciplinary Partnerships (LDPs)   90
    legal education and training   98–103
        Bar Professional Training Course (BPTC)   88, 94, 99, 100
        College of Law   99
        Common Professional Exam   99
        contracts, competition for   100
        Inns of Court   100
        Institute of Advanced Legal Studies   102
        Legal Education and Training Review (LETR)   100–101
        Legal Practice Course (LPC)   94, 99, 100
        LLB (Bachelor of Law) programmes   99
        qualifying law degree (QLD)   99
        'Russell Group' university   104
        Solicitors Qualifying Examination (SQE)   101
        Teaching Excellence Framework (TEF)   101
    Legal Ombudsman   96
    legal profession   91–103
        Alternative Business Structures (ABSs)   90, 95, 166
        barristers   90, 92–3, 164
        'cab rank' rule, barristers   164
        changing work patterns   103
        female lawyers   104
        government lawyers   94
        key developments   103–108
        Legal Disciplinary Partnerships (LDPs)   90, 95
        Legal Executives   93, 99
        licensed conveyancers   93
        new entrants to the market   95
        paralegals   93–4
        regulation   95–8
        solicitors   90, 91–3, 95–7, 101
        split   118
        unqualified practitioners   90
    Legal Services Act 2007   146, 166
    Legal Services Board (LSB)   95–6
    Legal Services Commission (LSC)   106
    Magic Circle firms   92, 707, 842
    neoliberalism   90
    New Labour   102, 106
    New Public Management   102, 105, 108
    Northern Italy and England contrasted   7–8
    Palestinian lawyers in British era   640–1
    Professional Service Firms (PSFs)   92, 93
    qualified lawyers   90, 94, 99, 101, 104
    Queen's Counsel (QC)   92, 886, 898
    regulation of legal profession
        architecture   95–6
        Codes of Conduct   96
        competition, legal services market   96–8
        Competition and Markets Authority (CMA)   96, 98
        developments   96–8

fragmentation 96
legal education and training and
    academy 98–103
    new entrants to the market 95
    private forms 96
    professional associations 98
Research Excellence Framework (REF) 102
Senior Counsel 898
solicitors 90, 91–2
    Solicitors Managing Clerks Association
        (SMCA) 93
    Solicitors Qualifying Examination (SQE) 101
    Solicitors Regulation Authority (SRA) 95, 96,
        97, 101, 163
see also Scotland
entry to legal profession
    accountancy firms 189
    barriers, addressing 888
    Belgium 162–3
    Canada 78–9
    England and Wales 95
    Russia 342
    Scotland 118
    Tunisia 661–2
    United States 141
    see also legal education and training; legal
        profession
epistemological turns, new 10–11
Erdoğan, RT 682
ethics, legal
    Belgium 163–4
    Germany 225–6
    Palestine 651–4
    standards 864–5
    Vietnam 865–6
ethnicity see racial/ethnic minorities
European Court of Justice (ECJ), and England
    and Wales 89
European Union
    Charter of Fundamental Rights 109
    UK withdrawal (Brexit) 91, 107, 109

faculties of law
    Czech Republic 299–301
    Libya 623
    Mexico 433–4
    Netherlands 255–6
Falcão, J 392–3
Fan Kuang Yuan 816
Fawehinmi, G 523
female lawyers see gender structure, legal
    profession; women lawyers
feminisation of legal profession 890–1
    Belgium 165
    Germany 221, 222

Hong Kong 825–6, 827f
Myanmar 781
Netherlands 260
Serbia 356
Switzerland 273–5
Tunisia 661
Turkey 686–7
Venezuela 462
see also gender structure, legal profession;
    women lawyers
field theory (Bourdieu) 11, 475, 476
Finland 189
fit and proper person requirement 49, 515, 531
Fix-Fierro, H 431
Folarin, A 520, 521
fragmentation of legal profession
    Australia 52
    Brazil 404
    England and Wales 96
    Libya 636
    Russia 331–2, 349
    Scotland 122
France
    Bars and Bar associations 193, 194
        governing bodies 204
        National Bar Council (CNB) 193, 195, 197,
            204
        Paris 204
    diversity issues in legal profession, gender
        195–6, 200
    in-house counsel 195
    intellectual property, legal advisers 195
    law firms
        gap between business law and traditional bars,
            widening 200–201
        growth strategies 201
        large 200, 204, 206
        organised as independent professional
            companies, rise of 198–200
        proliferation of interlocking
            organisations 201–202
        publicly funded work 203
        sharp contrasts among 198–203
        small 194, 201
    legal education and training 196–7
    legal profession 193–208
        business law and traditional bars, gap
            between 200–201
        careers 196–7
        changes in demography/structure 194–203
        earnings of lawyers 276, 889
        female lawyers 195–6, 200
        geographical polarisation 197–8
        governing bodies 204
        independent professionals (SELs) 198

interlocking organisations, proliferation of   201–202
law firms, sharp contrasts among   198–203
legal advisers, 1991 admission   194–6
numbers of lawyers   194–6
preservation of façade   205
publicly funded work   203
reconfigured   203–205
segmentation and dissolution   203–204
specialisation   197
unity, affirmations of   205
qualified lawyers   196
Rapport Darrois   195
SELARL (independent limited professional company)   199
France, P   197
Fuensalida, C   422

Gaddafi, Muammar   619, 623–32, 636
collapse of regime   632
demand for globally connected lawyers   635
'revolution'   620, 883–4
  ideology and political control   624–5, 634
  nationalisation of legal profession   628–30
  reorganisation of court system   625–6
  'revolutionary' policies   626–8
seizure of power   620, 624
speeches   625
see also Libya
Galanter, M   48, 713–14, 786
Galen, D   551
Gandhi, JS   713, 715–16
Garth, BG   431
Gaza
Bar Council   647
British law   639
Israeli occupation   640, 643
Lawyers Society   644, 645
legal profession   641
see also Palestine; West Bank
Geary, W   517
gender structure, legal profession
Australia   48, 51, 58–9
Belgium   168, 892
Bosnia and Herzegovina (BiH)   360, 891
Brazil   396–9, 404–405
Canada   71, 72
Chile   422
China   703, 891
Czech Republic   301–302
Denmark   184, 891
England and Wales   104
France   195–6, 200
Germany   221–4, 891, 892
Hong Kong   825–6, 827f

India   715–20, 719f
Iran   594–5
Israel   613–14
Japan   766, 767t, 768, 891
Kenya   498–9
Mexico   433
Myanmar   781, 891
Netherlands   260–1
Nigeria   528, 529–30t, 891
Norway   891
Palestine   650
Poland   310–11, 891, 892
Scotland   119
Serbia   355, 364, 891
South Africa   537–8
South Korea   891
Switzerland   273–5, 283, 892
Taiwan   825–6, 827f
Thailand   839, 842–3, 846–7, 891
Turkey   686–7, 891
United States   141
Venezuela   462
Zimbabwe   551, 555, 891
see also women lawyers
General Agreement on Tariffs and Trade (GATT)   430
genocide   474, 477, 482–3, 488–9, 784
Germany   209–233
advocates   210–11
  in 2030   230
  Act on Advocates   209, 215
  Chambers of Advocates   210–11, 215, 225, 226
  changing scope of practice   217–18
  data   218–19
  declining importance of court work   218
  German Advocates Association   211, 215, 225, 226, 227
  liability, fees and income   219–20
  specialisation   220–1
  women   221–4
Basic Law   210, 225, 227
civil law inquisitorial system   212
diversity issues in legal profession   221–4
Federal Advocates' Act   210, 217
Federal Advocates Fees Act   218
Federal Constitutional Court   210, 225, 226, 228
Federal Ministry of Justice   210
Federal Republic   210
Federal Social Court   215
German Democratic Republic (GDR)   211
German Empire   209, 212
judiciary/judges   212, 222, 481t
law firms
  boutique   24, 25, 228
  general partnerships   219

large   219
small   217, 224, 225
legal education and training   882
  Bachelor's and Master's in Law   215–16
  dual education system   217
  non-academic legal advisers
    (*Rechtsbeistände*)   216
  para-professionals
    (*Rechtsanwaltsfachangestellte*)   217
  registered legal service providers (*Registrierte Rechtsdienstleister*)   216
  uniform, for traditional legal
    professionals   213–15
legal profession
  advocates   210–11, 217–24
  earnings of lawyers   210, 219–20, 223, 889
  female lawyers   221–4, 891, 892
  in-house counsel
    (*Syndikusrechtsanwalte*)   215, 216
  judges   212, 222
  notaries (*Anwaltsnotare*)   211
  numerus clausus   209, 211
  professionalisation from above   209–210
  traditional legal professions   210–12
  unlicensed practitioners   227
Legal Services Act 2008   216, 227
LGBTI issues   224
qualified lawyers   227, 888
regulatory reform
  authorised and unauthorised practice
    of law   226–7
  end of self-limited self-regulation   225–6
  Federal Advocates' Act   225, 226
  parochialism and transregional/international
    lawyering   228–9
  practice rules and legal ethics   225–6
  Rules of Professional Conduct   225
reunification (1990)   211
and Roman law tradition   211, 213
State Ministry of Justice   210
state regulation   209–210
statistics   229–30
Supreme Court   210, 211, 225
Ghai, YP   495, 497
Gideon v Wainright judgment, US   139
Gingerich, J   725
global financial crisis (GFC), Australia   46, 47
globalisation   887–8
  Argentina   385, 386
  Australia   47
  Brazil   393–4, 403–404
  China   705–707
  England and Wales   89, 92
  Hong Kong   801
  and internationalisation   47, 130, 260, 266

and neoliberalism   45
new world order, lawyers in   7, 8–9
states and legal intermediaries (Burundi)
    475–6
Taiwan   801
Turkey   678–81, 682t
United States   127, 128, 130, 133–5, 146
variations in impact   14–22
see also states
glocalisation of legal profession, Asia   802–812
Godfrey, S   538
Gómez, JV   466
government lawyers/sector
  England and Wales   94
  Netherlands   262–4
  United States   137–40
Great Recession   135
Gubbay, A   552, 553
Gül, A   682
Gutto, S   551
Gwauna, E   557

Heinz, JP   258, 283
Hlatshwayo, B   553
Hong Kong   801–803, 817–25
  authoritarianism   813
  Bars and Bar associations   809, 812, 817, 820
  Basic Law   802, 817, 823
  and China   812
  diversity issues in legal profession   825–6, 827f
  elections   818–23
  Electoral Committee   822, 825
  globalisation   801
  glocalisation   808–810
  law firms   810, 811, 823, 827
  Law Society   809, 810, 811–12
  legal profession   802–803
    barristers   819, 821
    composition   802–803
    diverse and global   810–12
    elections   818–23
    female lawyers   825–6, 827f
    feminisation   825–6, 827f
    glocalisation   802
    lawyers' march against Beijing   823–5
    numbers and institutional structure   808–810
    politicisation of profession   813–25
    solicitors   819, 821, 826
  Legislative Council (LegCo)   818, 819f, 821, 822t, 825
  mobilisation   813
  qualified lawyers   802, 810
  Special Administrative Region   824
  see also China; Taiwan
Hughes, E   334

human rights
  Argentina   383, 386
  Burundi   487–8
  Chile   423–4
  Egypt   571
  England and Wales   106
  Libya   631
  Mexico   443
  South Korea   798
  Venezuela   455, 464
  Zimbabwe   553, 555, 556
  see also genocide; Inter-American Commission on Human Rights; Inter-American Convention on Human Rights; Inter-American Court of Human Rights
Hussain-Abady, A   587
Huxley, A   785

Idris, S   622
India   713–34
  Advocate Act 1961   714
  Bar Council of India (BCI)   714, 715
  caste system   720
  Chief Justices' Conference, Ahmadi Committee   724
  Common Law Admission Test (CLAT)   724
  diversity issues in legal profession   715–20, 719f
  economic stratification and income   720–1
  Law Commission of India   714
  law firms   725, 726
    corporate   727
    elite   721, 728
    foreign   726
    large   727
    small   727
    tax   729
  legal aid   721–2
  legal education and training   714–15, 723–4
  legal process outsourcing firms (LPOs)   726
  legal profession   715–20, 719f
    alternative dispute resolution (ADR)   722
    entry barriers, addressing   888
    hierarchy, reproduction of   727–8
    organisational transformation   723–7
    persistent patterns   714–22
    pro bono services   721–2
    professional portrait   714–22
    revised/recursive portrait   729
    unlicensed practitioners   715
  liberalisation   726–7
  National Law Schools   714
    National Law School of India University (NLSIU)   723
  NGOs (non-governmental organisations)   714
  political activism   721–2

  public interest or social action litigation (PIL)   713
  qualified lawyers   891
  Supreme Court   718, 725
  violence   722
Indonesia   735–52
  AAI (Indonesian Lawyers' Association)   737
  AKHI (Association of Indonesian Legal Consultants)   737
  Bar Association   737
  corruption   735–9, 748, 749
  HAPI (Indonesian Congregation of Indonesian Solicitors/Barristers)   737
  HKHPM (Association of Capital Market Legal Consultants)   737
  IKADIN (Indonesian Lawyers League)   737
  IPHI (Association of Indonesian Legal Counsellors   737
  KAI (Indonesian Lawyers Congress)   738
  law firms   740–2, 747, 749
    traditional   741, 742
  Law on Lawyers (LL)   738
  legal education and training   739–40, 886
  legal evolution   832
  legal profession
    brokers   745–6
    discipline   747–8
    'family' lawyers   747
    fixers   746–7
    history of profession   736–9
    law firms   740–2
    lawyers and clients   748
    lawyers, interaction between   748–9
    licensing   737–8
    litigators   745
    premier league fixers   747
    professional relationships   748–9
    quality lawyer, defining   749
    self-regulation   747–8
    size, demographics and sub-divisions   742–7
    supervision   747–8
    transactional lawyers   744–5
    'two hemispheres' thesis   749
  New Order   735, 737
  PERADI (Indonesian Lawyers Union)   738, 739, 742, 743
  PERADIN (United Indonesian Lawyers)   737
inequality
  Switzerland   274–5
  United States   141–6
  see also diversity issues in legal profession; gender structure, legal profession
INGOs (international NGOs), Burundi   473, 488, 490

in-house counsel
  France   195
  Germany   215
  Italy   246
  Kenya   508–509
  United States   135
innovation, United States   127, 128, 130–1
Inter-American Commission on Human
    Rights   130, 383, 424
Inter-American Convention on Human Rights   20,
    412, 423
Inter-American Court of Human Rights   383, 423,
    424, 458
internationalisation
  Australia   47
  Netherlands   260, 266
  United States   130
  see also globalisation
Iran   581–600
  attorneys   586–97
    clash of legal cultures   598–9
    clients, attitudes towards legal services   593
    codes of professional responsibility   597
    corruption   592–3
    female lawyers   594–5
    fiqh (Islamic jurisprudence)   589–90
    hostile judiciary   587–8
    law firms   595
    legal education and training   595–7
    selection and training of judges   590–2
  Bars and Bar associations   581, 582, 586–7
  corruption   592–3
  fiqh (Islamic jurisprudence)   588, 589
  First Charter of Attorneyship   582
  Iranian Bar Association (IBA)   581, 585,
      586–7
    attorneys on   586–7
    Board of Directors   583
  judiciary/judges   584–6
    legal advisers   587–8
    selection and training   590–2
  Law of Attorneyship   582
  legal education and training   590–2, 595–7, 883
  legal profession
    attorney, working as   586–97
    codes of professional responsibility   597
    corruption   592–3
    early years   582–3
    evolution   582–6
    following the 1979 Revolution   583–4
    judiciary/judges   584–6, 590–2
    legal advisers of the judiciary   584–6
  qualified lawyers   582, 583
  Revolution of 1979   583–4
Islamic Resistance Movement (Hamas)   640, 646

Israel   601–617
  civil legal aid   608
  criminal defence support   608–609
  diversity issues in legal profession   613–14
  East Jerusalem, annexation (1967)   643–4
  formation of State of Israel (1948)   602, 641
  Gaza, occupation of   640
  Israel Bar Association (IBA)   601, 887
    as a civic actor   607
    establishment   602–604
    examinations   612–13
    functions   603
    IBA Act 1961   602, 607
    regulatory regime   604, 605
  Jewish Lawyers Association   602
  judiciary/judges   605–606
  law firms   604, 605, 607–608, 614
  legal education and training   611–13, 883
    law school legal clinics   609–610
    'two hemispheres' thesis in legal
        profession   602, 612, 613
  legal profession
    changes in   610–13
    female lawyers   613–14
    formation   602–604
    modes of practice   614
    public service and public interest
        lawyering   607–610
    regulatory regime   604–605
    relations with the judiciary and state   605–606
    'two hemispheres' thesis   602, 612, 613
    women in   613–14
  money laundering legislation   605
  NGOs (non-governmental organisations)   602,
      609–610
  Ottoman Code of Civil Procedure   602
  Palestinian lawyers under occupation
      of   643–5
  qualified lawyers   611
  state support   608–609
  Supreme Court   606
  unauthorised practice of law (UPL)   603, 604,
      606
  West Bank, occupation of   640
Italy   235–52
  Association of In-House Counsel (AIGI)   246
  Authority for Competition and the Market   245
  changes in legal profession
    balance between maintenance and
        change   248–9
    determining what change is possible
        249–51
    instigators of change   249–51
    institutional, professional resistance
        to   247–51

elite schools 241
law firms
  boutique 243
  large 243, 244t, 245
  small 243, 245
legal education and training 241–2
legal profession
  balance between maintenance and change 248–9
  Code of Conduct 243, 247, 250
  cognitive pillar 248
  determining what change is possible 249–51
  employment of lawyers 243–6, 247t
  entry barriers, addressing 888
  Franzo Grande Stevens (law firm) 243
  historical organisation 243
  in-house counsel 246
  instigators of change 249–51
  normative pillar 247–8
  persistence of national institutional features 247–51
  professional resistance to institutional change 247–51
  regulatory pillar 247
  size and demographics 236–8, 239f, 240, 241f
Libya, occupation of 620–1
Northern Italy and England contrasted 7–8

Japan 753–74, 754t
  Bars and Bar associations 757–8, 884
    Bar Association demand to reduce numbers passing examination 759, 761
    Japan Federal Bar Association (JFBA) 716, 753, 758–9, 771, 772, 884
  Big Four, emergence of 756–9
  boutique firms 768–9
  bubble economy and collapse (1980–95) 753, 754t, 755, 756
  Conference of Ministers 762
  deregulation 756–9
    advertising 758
    on concurrent position 758
    and emergence of large law firms 757
    of legal practice 758
    legal professional corporations 758
  diversity issues in legal profession 766, 767t, 768
  Japan Federal Bar Association (JFBA) 753, 761, 772, 884
    Sunflower Fund Law Office 758–9, 771
  Japan Legal Support Centre (JLSC) 759, 770–2
    creation of staff lawyers at 771

  JILA (Japan In-House Lawyer Association) 769
  justice system reform (1996–2005) 753, 756–9
    deregulation 757, 758
    Justice System Reform Council (JSRC) 756
    law schools 757–8
  justice system reform (2006–17) 759–71, 760t, 761
  LAA (Legal Aid Association) 756
  legal aid 756, 759, 770–1
  legal education and training 757–8, 886
    new law schools, failing system 761–3
  legal profession 766, 767t, 768
    Bar Association 759, 761
    'boss' lawyers 765
    court-appointed criminal defence lawyers 770–1
    deregulation 758
    disciplinary measures 768
    female lawyers 891
    foreign lawyers 764
    general practice in small offices 755
    in-house lawyers 769–70
    income 768
    law firms 763, 768–9
    lawyer population increase, backlash against 759–63
    legal advisers 766
    legal support centres 758–9
    private corporations, in-house lawyers in 769
    public criminal defence 771
    public interest law offices, efforts to keep 770–1
    public interest law practice, development 758–9
    solo practitioners 755, 764–6
    specialisation 764–6
    stable legal practice, in bubble economy 753, 754t, 755, 756
    stratification and diversification of practising attorneys 763–70
    temporary employment in national and local government 770
    US pressure to open up market, consequences 755
  legal professional corporations 758
  legal support centres, establishment 758–9
  Legal Training and Research Institute 755
  Liberal Democratic Party (LDP) 756
  Ministry of Justice (MOJ) 753
  National Civil Service Examination (NCSE) 770
  qualified lawyers 769, 772, 899
  Supreme Court (SC) 753
Jayasuria, K 832
Jibowu, O 518
Jiménez, MP 466

Johnsen, Jon J 175
Jordan
　Bar Association 644
　recognition of Palestinian lawyers 642
　rule of West Bank 639, 641–3
judiciary/judges
　Argentina 381–2, 389
　Australia 51
　Belgium
　　Burundi, organisation under Belgian mandates 481t
　　Judicial Code 164, 165, 166
　　lay judges 170
　Bosnia and Herzegovina (BiH) 364–5, 367–9
　Brazil 399
　Czech Republic 295–6
　Egypt 565, 567
　Germany 212, 222, 481t
　hybrid systems 458
　Iran 584–6, 587–8, 590–2
　Israel 605–606
　Libya 622, 623, 625, 628
　Mexico 439–40
　Poland 311–12
　Serbia 364–7
　　contemporary position 365–7
　　historical background 364–5
　　Judicial Academy 366
　　Judicial Centre for Training and Professional Development (*later* Judicial Academy) 354–5
　Thailand 840–1
　Tunisia 670–2
　United States 138

Kameri-Mbote, P 504
Kaminskaya, D 338
Karpik, L 193, 203
Kaunda, K 556
Keating, Paul 46, 47
Kenya 495–514
　advocates
　　discipline of 510–11
　　qualifications to practise as 507–508
　　remuneration 509
　Advocates Ordinance 496
　Bar and state relations 511–12
　Bars and Bar associations 495
　colonial period 496
　Commission of University Education (CUE) 505–507
　Competition Authority of Kenya (CAK) 509
　Complaints Commission 510, 511
　Constitution (2010) 497
　Constitution of Kenya Review Committees 512

　corruption 508, 512
　Council of Legal Education (CLE) 504–507
　current period (2010 to the present) 496–7
　diversity issues in legal profession 498–9
　early years (Africanisation, 1960s–mid 1980s) 496
　historical background 496–7
　Independent Electoral and Boundaries Commission 510
　Inter Party Parliamentary Group (IPPG) 512
　Judicial Service Commission 497
　KANU party 511, 512
　Kenya School of Law 499
　law firms 500–501
　Law Society of Kenya 496, 509–511
　Law Society of Kenya Act 1949 509
　Law Society of Kenya Act 2014 509–510
　Law Society of Kenya Ordinance 496
　Legal Aid Act 2015 501
　legal education 503–507
　　accreditation of institutions 505–506
　　Commission of University Education (CUE) 505–507
　　conflicting mandates of CLE and CUE 506–507
　　Council of Legal Education (CLE) 504–507
　　development of profession 504
　　form and structure 505
　　quality 507
　　regulation 504–505
　legal profession 498–9
　　age factors 499
　　challenges for 497
　　demographics 497–500
　　female lawyers 498–9
　　globalisation of legal practice 503
　　in-house counsel 508–509
　　law firms 500–501
　　limited liability partnerships 501
　　marketing and advertising 509
　　opportunities for 497
　　practice areas 501–503
　　qualifications to practise as an advocate 507–508
　　racial/ethnic minorities and ethnicity 499–500
　　regulation 507–509
　　remuneration of advocates 509
　　Senior Counsel 508
　　solo practitioners 501
　　statistics 497–8
　　structures of practice 500–503
　　unqualified practitioners 496, 508, 509
　Mau Mau insurrection 511
　middle years (professionalisation, 1980s–early 2000s) 496

NGOs (non-governmental
        organisations)   502–503
    Partnership Act 2012   500
    post-independence period   496–7
    qualified lawyers   497, 507, 510
    regulation of legal profession   507–509
Kerkvliet, BJT   856
Kim Young-sam   790
Kimani, W   512
Klaus, V   294
Kwok, D   821

Lam, A   819, 821
Lammerts, C   785
Larijani, S   584
Larson, MS   880, 890, 895
Latin America *see* Argentina; Brazil; Chile; Mexico;
        Venezuela
Laumann, EO   258, 283
Law and Society Association (LSA)   vii, viii
law firms *see* legal profession
law graduates
    Brazil   394–5
    Mexico   437–8
    South Africa   538–40
    unlicensed   394–5
    see also legal education and training; legal
        profession
law schools
    Australia   54, 55–7
    Belgium
        democratisation of the educational system   159
        growth in number of law school
            graduates   157–9
        law degree programmes   157
    Canada   76, 77, 78
    Chile   413–16
    Czech Republic   291
    graduates *see* graduates of law
    India   714, 723–4
    Indonesia   739–40
    Israel   609–610
    Japan   757–8, 761–3
    Mexico   432–3
        increase in   434–6
    Thailand   834–6
    see also legal education and training
Law Societies
    Canada   67t, 76
        Law Societies of Nova Scotia and BC   80–1
        Law Society of BC   78
        Law Society of Upper Canada (LSUC)   78, 82
    Denmark   185
    England and Wales   95, 101, 105, 107, 109, 122,
        886

Hong Kong   809, 810, 811–12
Kenya   509–511
Scotland (LSS)   118
    Alternative Business Structures (ABSs)   124
    Code of Conduct   122
    Committees   121
    Council   121
    Fair Access to the Legal Profession
        Initiative   120
    reform   122–3
    structure   121–2
South Africa   539, 543
Zimbabwe   547, 550, 552–5, 558–9
Law Society, Denmark   185
Lawyers in Society project (1988–89)
    new world order   12–14
    origins   vii
    revisiting (2014)   12
    volumes, production of   vii
Lee Deng Hui, President of Taiwan   814
Lee Yong-hoon   791
legal academies
    Bosnia and Herzegovina (BiH)   369
    Brazil   397–9
    Scotland   121
    Serbia   369
    United States   140–1
legal aid
    Australia   53
    Belgium   160–1
    Canada   79
    Chile   418
    Denmark   186–7, 188, 190
    England and Wales   105–107
    India   721–2
    Israel   608
    Japan   756, 759, 770–1
    Libya   629, 633
    Netherlands   253, 264, 265t, 267
    Nigeria   523
    Norway   188, 190
    Palestine   645, 648, 655
    Poland   325
    Scotland   118
    South Africa   543–4
    South Korea   799
    Sweden   190
    Taiwan   816
    United States   144–5
    see also access to justice
Legal Disciplinary Partnerships (LDPs), England
        and Wales   90, 95
legal education and training
    accreditation of institutions   505–506
    Australia *see* Australia

Bachelor of Laws (LLB) programmes
   Australia 55, 56
   Belgium 157
   Brazil 394–5
   Canada 78
   England and Wales 99
   Germany 215–16
   Indonesia 740
   Mexico 429, 434, 436–7, 440, 442
   Myanmar 781
   Norway 188
   Scotland 118
   South Africa 538, 539
   Thailand 837, 839
   Vietnam 860, 862, 863
Belgium *see* Belgium
Bosnia and Herzegovina (BiH) *see* Bosnia and Herzegovina (BiH)
Brazil *see* Brazil
Burundi *see* Burundi
Canada *see* Canada
Chile *see* Chile
China *see* China
costs 526–7
curriculum
   Canada 77–8
   content 257–8
   Netherlands 256–7
   unification 256–7
   Vietnam 861–2
Czech Republic *see* Czech Republic
Denmark *see* Denmark
duration 526–7
Egypt *see* Egypt
England and Wales *see* England and Wales
European Higher Education Area (EHEA) 256
faculties of law
   Czech Republic 299–301
   Mexico 433–4
   Netherlands 255–6
France *see* France
Germany *see* Germany
growth in number of law school graduates
   Belgium 157–9
   Nigeria 524
Hong Kong *see* Hong Kong
India *see* India
Indonesia *see* Indonesia
Iran *see* Iran
Israel *see* Israel
Italy *see* Italy
Japan *see* Japan
on the job training and certification 740
Kenya *see* Kenya

law faculties, staff and student numbers, Netherlands 255–6
Law School Aptitude Test (LSAT)
   Canada 76, 77
   United States 141
Libya *see* Libya
Master of Laws (LLM) programmes
   Belgium 157, 167, 170
   Chile 416, 420
   Germany 215–16
   India 724
   Norway 188
   South Korea 791
   Tunisia 660, 661
   United States 140, 143
   Venezuela 453
   Vietnam 861
Mexico *see* Mexico
Myanmar *see* Myanmar
Netherlands *see* Netherlands
Nigeria *see* Nigeria
Norway 188
Palestine *see* Palestine
pedagogy 526–7
Poland *see* Poland
Russia *see* Russia
Scotland *see* Scotland
Serbia *see* Serbia
South Africa *see* South Africa
South Korea *see* South Korea
Switzerland *see* Switzerland
Taiwan *see* Taiwan
Thailand *see* Thailand
Tunisia *see* Tunisia
Turkey *see* Turkey
United States *see* United States
Venezuela *see* Venezuela
Vietnam *see* Vietnam
Zimbabwe *see* Zimbabwe
see also entry to legal profession; law schools
Legal Executives
   England and Wales 93, 99
   Scotland 121
legal intermediaries, Burundi 473–6
legal pluralism and capitalism, Burundi 478–80
legal profession
   advocates *see* advocates
   agency lawyers, United States 139–40
   Alternative Business Structures (ABSs)
      Canada 82
      England and Wales 90, 95, 166
      Scotland 121, 123, 124
   alternative dispute resolution (ADR) 164–5, 391, 403, 722
   Anglo-Saxon models 250

apprenticeship 649–50, 887
Argentina *see* Argentina
Association of European Lawyers 260
attitudes towards legal services 593
attorney, role of 262–3
Australia *see* Australia
bailiffs
  Belgium 170
  Bosnia and Herzegovina (BiH) 369
  Czech Republic 297–8
  Poland 313–14
  Serbia 369
the Bar *see* Bars and Bar associations
barristers
  Australia 51
  England and Wales 90, 92–3, 164
  Hong Kong 819, 821
Belgium *see* Belgium
Bosnia and Herzegovina *see* Bosnia and Herzegovina (BiH)
boutique firms
  Australia 50
  Brazil 401–403, 405
  Chile 419, 707
  Germany 24, 25, 228
  Indonesia 747
  Italy 243
  Japan 768–9
  Netherlands 259
  specialised 24, 25, 403
  United States 133, 136
  Venezuela 454
Brazil *see* Brazil
Burundi *see* Burundi
Canada *see* Canada
changes in demography/structure
  France 194–203
  Scandinavian countries 176–8
changing work patterns, England and Wales 103
Chile *see* Chile
China *see* China
clients and lawyers 593, 748
concentration of firms 280–2
conservatism 48
cooperative firms 698
corporate lawyers 170–1
corruption, Iran 592–3
Czech Republic *see* Czech Republic
defining a good lawyer 749
Denmark *see* Denmark
disaggregated, United States 143, 145–6
distribution of legal services, United States 143–5
diversity in *see* diversity issues in legal profession
earnings of lawyers *see* earnings of lawyers

Egypt *see* Egypt
England and Wales *see* England and Wales
entry
  Belgium 162–3
  Canada 78–9
  Netherlands 258–64
  United States 141
ethics, codification, Belgium 163–4
female lawyers *see* women lawyers
feminisation
  Belgium 165
  Germany 221, 222
  Hong Kong 825–6, 827f
  Myanmar 781
  Netherlands 260
  Switzerland 273–5
  Turkey 686–7
  see also gender structure, legal profession; women lawyers
France *see* France
future of, Canada 79–82
Germany *see* Germany
global law firms 703
globalisation
  Australia 47
  Brazil 393–4
  Burundi 475–6
  Kenya 503
  United States 130
glocalisation 802–812
government lawyers/sector
  England and Wales 94
  Netherlands 262–4
  United States 137–40
Hong Kong *see* Hong Kong
impact on structure, logics and coherence 24–8
India *see* India
Indonesia *see* Indonesia
institutional independence, Belgium 161–2
internationalisation of law firms *see* internationalisation
Iran *see* Iran
Israel *see* Israel
Japan *see* Japan
judiciary/judges
  Argentina 381–2
  Australia 51
  Bosnia and Herzegovina (BiH) 367–9
  Brazil 399
  Czech Republic 295–6
  jurists, 'replacement' 177–8
  Poland 311–12
  Serbia 364–5
  Thailand 840–1
  United States 138

Index   939

Kenya *see* Kenya
large firms   20, 889, 891, 893, 898, 899, 901
   Australia   47, 48, 60
   Brazil   403
   Canada   69
   Chile   419, 420
   Czech Republic   295
   Denmark   176
   England and Wales   122
   France   200, 204, 206
   Germany   219
   India   726
   Indonesia   749
   Italy   244t, 245
   Mexico   430–1
   Netherlands   259
   Norway   188
   Scotland   119
   Serbia   362
   South Africa   537–8
   Sweden   189
   Switzerland   282, 283
   Thailand   841–3
   Tunisia   663
   United States   133–5
legal process outsourcing (LPO)   130, 726
Libya *see* Libya
licensed conveyancers, England and Wales   93
licensing
   Mexico   437–8
   Thailand   840–1
   Vietnam   863–4
limited liability partnerships
   Kenya   501
   Scotland   122
litigation   421
   Brazil   400–402, 403
   Chile   421
   Indonesia   745
   Venezuela   463–5
mega-law firms   23
mergers of firms
   Scandinavian countries   181, 189
   Switzerland   280
Mexico *see* Mexico
multi-disciplinary practices (MDPs)
   Canada   81–2
   Germany   219
   United States   146
Myanmar *see* Myanmar
nationalisation, in Libya   628–30
Netherlands *see* Netherlands
new entrants to the market, England and
      Wales   95
Nigeria *see* Nigeria

nonprofit sector, United States   136–7
notaries/notaries public
   Belgium   167–8
   Bosnia and Herzegovina (BiH)   369
   Canada   81
   Czech Republic   296–7
   Germany   211
   Poland   314–15
   Serbia   369
numbers of legal professionals, expansion
   Belgium   157–9
   China   699
   comparative sociology (1988–2018)
      880–90
   France   194–6
   Hong Kong   808–810
   Israel   610
   Japan   759, 761
   Mexico   440–2
   Netherlands   255–6
   Nigeria   524
   South Korea   790–2
   Tunisia   660–1
   Turkey   686
Palestine *see* Palestine
paralegals
   Canada   80–1
   England and Wales   93–4
   Scotland   118, 121
partnership and specialisation   165–7
Poland *see* Poland
polarisation
   France   197–8
   in Switzerland   282–3
   Turkey   678–81, 682t
private practice, United States   131–5
pro bono services
   Brazil   401–402
   Canada   79
   India   721–2
professional associations
   England and Wales   98
   Nigeria   520–2
   Vietnam   867–9
professional relationships   748–9
professionalisation from above
   Germany   209–210
   Russia   335–9
promotion within, US   141–3
prosecutors
   Brazil   400
   Czech Republic   296
   Poland   312–13
   Thailand   840–1
   United States   138–9

public defenders
  Brazil 400
  United States 138–9, 144
public interest law organisations, United States 136–7
public sector, Canada 69–70
qualitative comparison 880–1
reform debates, Libya 633–4
regulation *see* regulation of legal profession
rise of legal alternatives, Canada 82
Russia *see* Russia
Scotland *see* Scotland
Senior Counsel 50, 508, 898
Serbia *see* Serbia
small firms 15, 26, 901
  Australia 47, 48, 60
  Brazil 402, 403
  Canada 67–8
  England and Wales 101
  France 194, 201
  Germany 217, 224, 225
  Israel 604
  Italy 243, 245
  Kenya 501
  Netherlands 258, 259, 266
  Nigeria 531
  Norway 188
  Switzerland 283, 284
  Thailand 839, 845
  United States 128, 131–3, 143
socio-legal questions 353
solicitors
  Australia 49–50
  England and Wales 91–2
  Scotland 49–50
solo practitioners *see* solo practitioners
South Africa *see* South Africa
and state re-configurations 28–33
Switzerland *see* Switzerland
Taiwan *see* Taiwan
Thailand *see* Thailand
transformation *see* transformation, legal profession
Tunisia *see* Tunisia
Turkey *see* Turkey
'two hemispheres' thesis *see* 'two hemispheres' thesis in legal profession
United States *see* United States
unlicensed practitioners 16, 890
  Brazil 405
  Chile 418
  Germany 227
  India 715
  Russia 331–5, 340, 341, 343–5, 347, 349, 350
  Thailand 840
  Venezuela *see* Venezuela

Vietnam *see* Vietnam
see also law firms; legal practice
legal research facilities, Czech Republic 300
legal services market
  competition *see* competition, legal services market
  England and Wales 96–8
  liberalisation 262
  Netherlands 262
  Poland 323–4
  Scotland 118–21
  United States 136
LegalZoom (web-based consumer-oriented platform) 130, 146
Lenz, R 280
Leopold II 478, 479
Levin-Stankevich, BL 349
Lewis, P 3, 4, 12, 117, 289, 515
Lex Africa 503
Li Zhuang 703
liberalisation
  Denmark 179–80
  India 726–7
  Mexico 430–1
  Netherlands 262
  Tunisia 659–60
  Turkey 678–81, 682t
  Vietnam 858–9
liberalism
  Australia 45, 53, 60
  Brazil 392, 406
  China 17
  economic 118, 682
  Egypt 575
  neoliberalism 102, 187
  Norway 187
  political 392, 406
  social 45, 53, 60
  Turkey 677, 682
Libya 619–38
  Abu Selim prison 619
  Arab Socialist Union (ASU) 625
  Bar Association 628, 629, 631, 632, 634, 636
    initial relations with regime 626–8
    tensions with regime 630–2
  Basic People's Congresses 627, 628
  collapse of Gaddafi regime 632
  Constitution 622
  corruption 623
  court system, reorganisation 625–6
  Courts of Appeal 630
  Directorate of People's Defence 629, 630
  Directorate of People's Lawyers in the Supreme Council for Judicial Institutions 633
  fiqh (Islamic jurisprudence) 622

Gaddafi's 'revolution'   620, 623–32, 635, 636, 883–4
  'Green Book'   626
  ideology and political control   624–5, 634
  nationalisation of legal profession   628–30
  reorganisation of court system   625–6
  Revolutionary Command Council (RCC)   624, 625, 631
  'Revolutionary Committees Movement'   627–8
  'revolutionary' policies   626–8
General People's Committee   630
General People's Conference   631
General People's Congress   627
human rights   631
independence   621–3
Italian occupation and mandate period   620–1
judiciary/judges   622, 623, 625, 628
Kingdom of   622–3
Law 3/2014 on Legal Practice   634
law faculties, rise of   623
lawyers as agents of the state   623–32
  court system, reorganisation   625–6
  ideology and political control   624–5
legal aid   629, 633
legal education and training   623
legal profession
  attacks on professionals   635
  contemporary Libya, lawyers in   620–3
  fragmentation   636
  lawyers as agents of the state   623–32
  nationalisation, under Gaddafi   628–30
  post-conflict pressures on practice   632–5
  post-independence period   622
  reform debates   633–4
  return of private practice   630–2
  rise of   623
  rule of law, breakdown   635
  security risks   635
  unqualified practitioners   630
Ministry of Justice   636
NGOs (non-governmental organisations)   633
oil/emergence of a plutocratic elite   621–3
People's Courts   625, 632
People's Lawyers   631–2
Petroleum Law 1955   622
Popular Committees   627
Revolutionary Command Council (RCC)   624, 625, 631
Sharia courts   622, 623, 625
suppression of professions   620–1
Supreme Court   626, 630, 634
violence   620, 624, 629, 633, 635, 636
see also Gaddafi, Muammar
licensed conveyancers   93, 121

licensing
  Brazil   394–5
  Indonesia   737–8
  Mexico   437–8
  Russia   344
  South Korea   797
  Thailand   840–1
  Vietnam   863–4
  see also unlicensed practitioners
limited liability partnerships   122, 501
Lin Ming-sheng   807–808
litigation
  Brazil   400–402, 403
  Chile   421
  India   713
  Indonesia   745
  public interest or social action litigation (PIL)   713
  'SLAPP-back'   848
  South Korea   795
  Venezuela   463–5
localisation, Taiwan   807–808
Loos, T   834, 846
López-Ayllón, S   431

MacAuslan, JPWB   495
Maduro, N   450, 454–5, 458–9, 883
magistracy, Belgium   169–70
Malaysia   832
Mamdani, M   476, 480
Mann, K   608
Marx, K   337
Master in Laws programmes
  Belgium   157, 167, 170
  Chile   416
  Germany   215–16
  Norway   188
  United States   140, 143
  Venezuela   453
Mboya, A   499, 503
Meese, Edwin (US Attorney General)   138
mega-law firms   23
Meneses, R   430
Merton, R   349
Mery, R   419–20
Mexico   429–47
  Bars and Bar associations   443, 444–5
  Constitution   431, 437
  corruption   435
  democratisation   431–2
  diversity issues in legal profession   433
  Federal Institute of the Public Defender   439
  Federal Ministry of Public Education   437
  General Law of Mexican Advocacy   444
  human rights   443

law firms 430–1
lawyers 438, 442–5
  context 442
  reforming regulation of 443–5
  regulation and disciplinary mechanisms 443
legal education and training 432–8, 887
  Bachelor of Laws Diploma 436–7
  increase in law schools and students 434–6
  law graduates 437–8
  law schools 432–6
  law students and faculty 433–4
  LLB (Bachelor of Laws) programmes 429, 434, 436–7, 440, 442
  RVOE (higher education degrees) 435, 436
Legal Practice Reform Index 442
legal profession 438–42
  female lawyers 433
  gender 433
  increase of licences to practise law 437–8
  judiciary/judges 439–40
  lawyers 438, 442–5
  notaries 438
  numbers of legal professionals 440–2
  prosecutors 439
  public administration, lawyers in 439
  public brokers 438–9
  public defenders 439
National Centre for the Evaluation of Higher Education (CENEVAL) 432
National Council of Professional Certification 444
National Survey on Employment (ENOE) 440
recent developments in the legal context 430–7
regulation of legal profession 442–5
structural reforms 431
trade liberalisation 430–1
Michelson, E 549, 702, 717
Micombero, M 484, 486
Middle Eastern countries *see* Egypt; Iran; Israel; Libya; Palestine
military rule
  Burundi 481–7
  Myanmar 779–80
  Nigeria 522–3
minority groups *see* racial/ethnic minorities
Mitterrand, French President 487
modernity, Western
  and domination relationships 2
  and professionalism 3
Moreels, R 489
Mosaddeq, M 582
Moyo, J 558
Moyo, S 557
Msipa, C 557

Mtetwa, B 559
Mubako, S 549, 550
Mubarak, H 577–8
Mudimu, V 557
multi-disciplinary partnerships (MDPs) 897
  Canada 81–2
  Germany 219
  United States 146
Mussolini, B 620
Myanmar 775–87
  advocates 776
  Bar Council 778
  Bars and Bar associations 785
  Buddhism 776–7
  Burma Laws Act 1898 777
  Burma Socialist Programme Party (BSPP) 779, 780
  commercial legislation 783
  Constituent Assembly 778
  diversity issues in legal profession 781, 891
  DULSA (Dagon University Law Association) 782
  Independent Lawyers' Association of Myanmar (ILAM) 785
  kingdoms 776
  law firms 782–5
  legal education and training 780–2, 882
    Judicial Training Institute 782
    legal career paths 782–3
    universities 781
  legal profession
    advocates 776
    career paths 782–3
    colonial state, common law profession for 777–8
    dhammathats 776
    female lawyers 781, 891
    first generation of commercial lawyers 783–5
    Higher Grade Pleader 782, 784
    new era for 780–5
    parliamentary democracy, era of 778–9
    pre-colonial 776–7
    qualifications 780
    subordinating under socialist-military rule 779–80
  Legislative Council, Rangoon 777
  NGOs (non-governmental organisations) 782, 783
  parliamentary democracy, era of 778–9
  qualified lawyers 784
  socialist-military rule 779–80
  State Law and Order Restoration Council (SLORC) 780
  Supreme Court 782

Naguib, M   575, 576
Nasser, GA   566, 567, 624, 883
Ndadaye, M   487
Nehme, N   422
neoliberalism   7, 8–9
   Australia   57
   Denmark   181
   England and Wales   90, 102
   and globalisation   45
   Netherlands   266
   Scotland   187
   United States   128, 131, 147
Netherlands   253–69
   access to justice   264–5
   Act on Advocates   263
   Bars and Bar associations   258–64
      diversity   260–1
      Dutch Bar Association   254, 259, 262
      entry to   258
      general developments within the legal profession   261
      internationalisation of law firms   260
      office size   258–9
   Committee on the Reappraisal of Compulsory Representation   262
   corruption   253
   diversity issues in legal profession   260–1, 883
   law firms
      boutique   259
      large   259
      small   258, 259, 266
   legal aid   253, 265t, 267
      Legal Aid Act 1994   264
      Legal Aid Board (LAB)   264
   legal education and training
      Bar and Bench   258
      curriculum content   257–8
      curriculum unification   256–7
      evolution   258
      law faculties, staff and student numbers   255–6
      roles   254
      student backgrounds   256
   legal profession
      attorney, role of   262–3
      court management   263–4
      female lawyers   260–1
      government sector   262–4
      liberalisation of market   262
      solo practitioners   258, 259, 261, 266
      'two hemispheres' thesis   258
   neoliberalism   266
   Supreme Court   264
new entrants, legal profession, England and Wales   95

new world order, lawyers in   5–10
   de-nationalisation   6–7
   England vs. Northern Italy   7–8
   globalisation   7, 8–9
   Lawyers in 21st-Century Societies project   12–14
   minority groups and women   9–10
   'private sector quasi states'   6
   transnational corporations (TNCs)   5–6
NewLaw, Australia   48–9
NGOs (non-governmental organisations)
   Belgium   489
   Brazil   401
   Burundi   488
   Chile   423, 424
   Egypt   571
   India   714
   Israel   602, 609–610
   Kenya   502–503
   Libya   633
   Myanmar   782, 783
   South Africa   543
   Thailand   833, 839, 845, 846
   Venezuela   464
   see also INGOs (international NGOs)
Nigeria   515–33
   Bars and Bar associations   519, 520, 521, 522
   Body of Benchers   531
   colonial period   516–19
   Committee on the Future of the Nigerian Legal Profession   519
   Council of Legal Education   519–20, 527
   developments post-independence   519–23
   diversity issues in legal profession
      age structure   528
      gender   528, 529–30t
      socio-economic backgrounds   525–6t
   geopolitical zones   522
   Lagos Law Society   520
   law firms   531
   legal aid   523
   Legal Education Act 1962   519
   legal education and training   520, 526–7
      Clinical Legal Education (CLE)   527
      National Universities Commission (NUC)   527
      Nigerian Law School   520, 524, 527
   legal profession   528, 529–30t
      age structure, changes in   528
      changes in legal practice   523–31
      female lawyers   528, 529–30t, 891
      growth in numbers   524
      socio-economic backgrounds   524, 525–6t
      solo practitioners   531

military rule   522–3
National Universities Commission (NUC)   527
Nigerian Bar Association (NBA)   519, 521, 522, 531
Nigerian Law School   520, 524, 527
Northern Nigeria   517, 518–19
One-Lawyer-One-Vote (OLOV)   531
professional associations   520–2
qualified lawyers   515, 516, 518, 523, 531, 881
Senior Advocates of Nigeria (SAN)   531
Southern Nigeria   517, 518
Supreme Court   520
Nkurunziza, P   490
non-practising lawyers   70, 71t, 146
nonprofit sector, United States   136–7
North American Free Trade Agreement (NAFTA)   430
Norway   187–8
female lawyers   891
law firms   188, 189
legal aid   188, 190
liberalism   187
notaries/notaries public
Belgium   167–8
Bosnia and Herzegovina   369
Canada   81
Czech Republic   296–7
Germany   211
Poland   314–15
Serbia   369
Nowrojee, P   512
Ntyiyankundiye, E   486–7
numerus clausus
Belgium   167, 168, 171
Czech Republic   292–3, 296, 297
Germany   209, 211

Obama, Barack   138, 144
Ojwang, JB   504
Olgiati, V   235–6, 243
Omamo, R   499
originalism (jurisprudential approach)   138
Ornstein, M   73

Pagano, V   279
Palay, T   48
Palestine
Advocates Law 1999, amended 2011   639, 642, 645, 653
Advocates Ordinances   640
Arab Lawyers Union   644, 645
Bars and Bar associations   642
Civil Bar Association Law 1966   642
division along ethno-national lines   641
Islamic Resistance Movement (Hamas)   640, 646

Israeli-Palestinian Declaration of Principles on Interim Agreement on the West Bank and Gaza Strip 1995   645
Israeli-Palestinian Declaration of Principles on Interim Self-Government Arrangement 1993   645
Law Council   640, 641
legal aid   645, 648, 655
legal education and training   648–9
apprenticeship   649–50
Bar examinations   650–1
Lawyers Apprenticeship Bye-law 2004   650–1
qualifications for law practice   648–51
legal ethics   651–4
legal profession
British era   640–1
confidentiality and privacy   652
development   639–45
Egyptian administration   641
ethics   651–4
female lawyers   650
Israeli occupation   643–5
Jordanian rule   641–3
qualifications for law practice   648–51
Minister of Justice   645
Ottoman rule   639, 640
Palestinian Authority (PA)   645
Palestinian Bar Association (PBA)   639, 645
committees   648
Council   650, 654
examinations   650–1
'federation' of two bars   647
general assembly   650–1
and legal aid   655
structure   647–8
transitional Bar Council   646
Palestinian lawyers
British era   640–1
Israeli occupation   643–5
Palestinian Legislative Council (PLC)   640
Palestinian rule, legal profession
Bar Association, structure   647–8
transitional phase   645–7
UN Partition Plan (1947)   641
West Bank lawyers   641–3
see also Egypt; Gaza; Jordan; West Bank
paralegals
Canada (changes in regulation of)   80–1
England and Wales   93–4
Scotland   118, 121
paralegals Canada (changes in regulation of)   80–1
Park Chung-hee, General/President of South Korea   789, 798
partnerships, Belgium   165–7
Peele, JJ   517

Pérez, C 452
Perez-Hurtado, L 435
Pérez-Perdomo, R 463–4
Pocar, V 235–6, 243
Poland 309–330
　advocates and attorneys 316–26
　　from 1989 to 1997 316–17
　　deregulation on basis of 2013 Act 322–3
　　efforts to open up legal profession (1997–2005) 318–21
　　evident weaknesses of statutory aims 324–6
　　expanding scope of professional rights of attorneys (1997) 317–18
　　at law 323–4
　　legal services market, situation of 323–4
　　realisation of statutory aims 324–6
　　transformation, consequences 326–8
　Association of Legal Advisers 316
　Bars and Bar associations 317, 318
　Constitutional Tribunal 319, 320, 321
　diversity issues in legal profession, gender 310–11
　judiciary/judges 312
　Law Councils 320
　Law on Higher Education 310
　Law on Notaries (1991) 314
　Law on Prosecutors (2016) 313
　Law on the System of Ordinary Courts (2001) 312
　Laws on Court Bailiffs (2018) 314
　legal education and training 310–11, 319–24, 325
　legal profession
　　advocates and attorneys 316–26
　　court bailiffs 313–14
　　earnings of lawyers 325
　　efforts to open up (1997–2005) 318–21
　　female lawyers 310–11, 891, 892
　　forms of work for lawyers 316
　　judiciary/judges 311–12
　　notaries public 314–15
　　prosecutors 312–13
　　'qualified lawyer' 309–310
　　roles 311–16
　　tax advisers 315–16
　legal services market 323–4
　Minister of Justice 312, 315, 319
　　Commission 326
　National Bailiffs Council (NBC) 313
　National Chamber of Tax Advisers 315
　National Notarial Council (NNC) 314, 315
　National School of the Judiciary and Public Prosecution, Krakow 312, 313
　Polish Workers Party 309
　Prosecutor General 312
　qualified lawyers 309–310, 311, 316, 318, 320, 323–6, 328
　self-governing councils 326
　Supreme Bar 318, 320
　Tax Advisory Services 315
　transformation, consequences 326–8
polarisation, legal profession
　France 197–8
　Switzerland 282–3
　Turkey 678–81, 682t
political liberalism 392, 406
political activism
　China 703–705
　India 721–2
　Vietnam 871–2
politics and legal profession
　Argentina 377, 382–90
　Australia 60
　England and Wales 107–108
Pridi Banomyong 835, 836
'private sector quasi states' 6
pro bono services
　Brazil 401–402
　Canada 79
　India 721–2
　South Korea 799
　Vietnam 870–3
professional associations
　England and Wales 98
　Nigeria 520–2
　Vietnam 867–9
Professional Service Firms (PSFs), England and Wales 92, 93
prosecutors
　Brazil 400
　Czech Republic 296
　Poland 312–13
　Thailand 840–1
　United States 138–9
public defenders
　Brazil 400
　United States 138–9, 144
public interest law movement/organisations
　Brazil 400–402
　Israel 607–610
　South Africa 544
　United States 136–7
public interest litigation, Brazil 400–402
public sector firms, Canada 69–70

qualified lawyers 16, 19
　Australia 56
　Brazil 394, 395
　competitors 889–90
　Denmark 185

Egypt 565
England and Wales 90, 94, 99, 101, 104
France 196
Germany 227, 888
Hong Kong 802, 810
India 891
Iran 582, 583
Israel 611
Japan 769, 772, 899
Kenya 497, 507, 510
Myanmar 784
Nigeria 515, 516, 518, 523, 531, 881
Poland 309–310, 311, 316, 318, 320, 323–6, 328
Russia 334, 337, 341, 345, 349, 889
South Korea 793
Tunisia 661, 669, 889
Turkey 680, 689
United States 138, 143
Vietnam 866
Zimbabwe 548, 550
see also unqualified practitioners

racial/ethnic minorities 9–10
Australia 57–8
Black, Asian and Minority Ethnic (BAME) law students 99, 104
Brazil 396–8, 405
Burundi
ethnic redistribution, international rules (1993–2015) 487–91
ethnic ultra-violence see Burundi
ethnicity 483, 484
geopolitics of the 'bottom-up' state 488–90
and human rights/political opposition 487–8
post-1993 crisis 488–90
India 720
Kenya 499–500
Netherlands 261
Nigeria 893
South Africa 538, 542
United States 142
Zimbabwe 551, 557
Rama V, of Siam 833
Rama VI of Siam 836
Rawal, K 498
Razaq, A 518
Reagan, Ronald 131, 138, 139
regulation of legal profession
Argentina 380
Brazil 395–7
Canada 80–1
Chile 417

Codes of Conduct
Canada 83
Chile 417
England and Wales 96
Iran 597
Italy 243, 247, 250
Scotland 122
Venezuela 456
disciplinary measures
Canada 83–4
Indonesia 747–8
Japan 768
Kenya 510–11
Mexico 442
Thailand 841
Tunisia 666
Vietnam 872
England and Wales 122–3
architecture 95–6
Codes of Conduct 96
competition, legal services market 96–8
Competition and Markets Authority (CMA) 96, 98
developments 96–8
fragmentation 96
legal education and training and academy 98–103
new entrants to the market 95
private forms 96
professional associations 98
fit and proper person requirement 49, 515, 531
Germany
authorised and unauthorised practice of law 226–7
end of self-limited self-regulation 225–6
Federal Advocates' Act 225, 226
parochialism and transregional/international lawyering 228–9
practice rules and legal ethics 225–6
Rules of Professional Conduct 225
Israel 604–605
Italy 243
Kenya 507–509
legal education 504–505
Mexico 442–5
Palestine 651–4
Russia 341
Scotland
architecture 121–2
Clementi Review (2004) 121, 123
Code of Conduct 122
competition, legal services market 122
Competition and Markets Authority (CMA) 122, 123
developments 122–3

fragmentation   122
Law Society structure   121–2
Legal Complaints Commission (SLCC)   121, 123
Legal Profession and Legal Aid (Scotland) Act 2007   121
Ombudsman, proposals for   123
reform   122–3
South Africa   541–3
United States   145–6
Vietnam   863–7
   competitive restrictions   866–7
   ethical standards   864–5
   liability and ethics   865–6
   licensing   863–4
see also competition, legal services market
Reichman, N   141
rentier class   7
Research Committee on Sociology of Law (RCSL)   vii
Rhodesia
   articled clerks   548
   historical background   547–8
   legal education and training   549
   Matabeleland Order in Council 1894   548
   Southern Rhodesian Bar   548
   see also Zimbabwe
Richter, T   300
Robinson, N   725, 786
rule of law   465–7, 635
Russia
   advocates
      contemporary, professional hallmarks   341–3
      current position   349–50
      elite   343
      exclusive jurisdiction   332
      Federal Chamber of Advocates   341
      following Perestroika   339–45
      Guild of Russian Advocates   340
      officers of the court   338
      rise of competition/failure to unify   339–41
      in Russian Empire   335–7
      in the Soviet Union   337–9
   Bars and Bar associations
      alternative Bars   344
      Federal Bar Act 2002   332, 344, 345
      qualifications   342
   Federal Chamber of Advocates   332
   forces of the legal market   343–5
   Imperial School of Jurisprudence   336
   intelligentsia   335
   Justice Ministry   335, 345, 346, 350
   legal education and training
      assistantships   342
      Bar, entry to   342

as basis of the legal profession   347–8
current position   347
entry to profession   342
internships   342
law schools   336
in the Soviet Union   345–6
theory and practice divide   348
   legal profession
      advocates   335–45
      clusters, division into   344
      earnings of lawyers   338
      fragmentation   331–2, 349
      historical background   335–9
      jurists   331
      legal education and training as the basis of   347–8
      overview   331–5
      'pocket' counsel   343
      private attorneys   337
      professionalisation from above   335–9
      public recognition problem   335–9
      rise of competition/failure to unify   339–41
      solo practitioners   342–4
      unlicensed practitioners   331–5, 340, 341, 343–5, 347, 349, 350
      unqualified practitioners   336
   Perestroika
      advocates following   339–45
      legal market   343
      regulations   340
   qualified lawyers   334, 337, 341, 345, 349, 889
   Russian Empire   335–7, 345, 349
   Soviet Union, former
      advocates   337–9, 349
      Bar associations   338, 339
      Bars and Bar associations   340
      Central Committee of the Communist Party   346
      Law on Cooperation (1988)   340
      Law on Individual Labour Activity (1986)   340
      legal education and training   345–6
      and Revolution of 1917   337
      rise of competition/failure to unify   339–41
Rwagasore, Prince   478
Rwanda   473, 479
   Congo, annexed to   480
   ethnic affiliation and violence   475, 477, 484
   genocide   474, 477, 482–3, 488–9
   see also Burundi

Sadat, MA   576–7
Salter, DR   504
Salvos Legal (Australian law firm)   48
Sánchez-Uribarri, R   458

Scandinavian countries
  Denmark *see* Denmark
  legal profession, 'two hemispheres' thesis   189
  legal professions, as 'midwives' of the state   175
  Norway   187–8
  Sweden   188–90
  see also American Bar Association (ABA)
Schuyt, CJM   253
Scotland   117–25
  Accredited Paralegal Status   121
  Act of Union 1707   117, 124
  Alternative Business Structures (ABSs)   121, 123, 124
  Bars and Bar associations   120, 123
  diversity issues in legal profession   119
  Faculty of Advocates   120
  Law Centres   117–18
  law firms   119
  Law Society of Scotland (LSS)   118
    Alternative Business Structures (ABSs)   124
    Code of Conduct   122
    Committees   121
    Council   121
    Fair Access to the Legal Profession Initiative   120
    reform   122–3
    structure   121–2
  legal academy   121
  legal aid   118
  legal education and training
    Diploma in Legal Practice   118, 119, 120
    law schools   120
    legal academy   121
    LLB (Bachelor of Laws) programmes   118
    Solicitors Qualifying Examination (SQE)   120
  legal profession   118–23
    advocates   118–19, 120
    Alternative Business Structures (ABSs)   121, 123, 124
    entry to   118
    female lawyers   119
    Legal Executives   121
    licensed conveyancers   121
    limited liability partnerships   122
    paralegals   118, 121
    regulation   121–3
    size and shape of legal services market   118–21
    solicitors   118–20
    unqualified practitioners   123
  Legal Services (Scotland) Act 2010   122
  population   117, 119
  regulation of legal profession
    architecture   121–2
    Clementi Review (2004)   121, 123
    competition, legal services market   122
    Competition and Markets Authority (CMA)   122, 123
    developments   122–3
    fragmentation   122
    Law Society structure   121–2
    Legal Profession and Legal Aid (Scotland) Act 2007   121
    Ombudsman, proposals for   123
    reform   122–3
    Scottish Legal Complaints Commission (SLCC)   121, 123
  see also England and Wales
Scott, WR   236, 248
Segatwa, F   488
Serbia   353–73
  advocates   357–9
    contemporary position   361–4
    historical background   357–9
    strikes   363
  Bars and Bar associations   363, 364, 897
  Bosnia and Herzegovina contrasted   370
  Constitution   365–6
  Constitutional Court   366, 369
  corruption   366
  diversity issues in legal profession   355
  judiciary/judges
    contemporary position   365–7
    historical background   364–5
    Judicial Academy   366
    Judicial Centre for Training and Professional Development (*later* Judicial Academy)   354–5
  law firms, large   362
  Law on Advocacy   361
  Law on Legal Representatives 1862   357
  legal academies   369
  legal aid   363
  legal education and training   354–6, 369
  legal profession
    bailiffs   369
    female lawyers   355, 364, 891
    judges   364–5
    legal academy   369
    notaries   369
    solo practitioners   370
  'Legal Professions in South Eastern Europe' project   353
  Ministry of Justice (MOJ)   357
  see also Bosnia and Herzegovina (BiH); Yugoslavia, former
Shinawatra, Thaksin   833
Siam *see* **Thailand**
Siffin, WJ   834, 836
Simbananye, A   486

Slater & Gordon   46–7
social liberalism   45, 53, 60
solicitors
   Australia   49–50
   England and Wales   90, 91–2
      Solicitors Managing Clerks Association (SMCA)   93
      Solicitors Regulation Authority (SRA)   95, 96, 97, 101, 163
   Hong Kong   819, 821, 826
   Scotland   119–20
solo practitioners   13, 27, 904, 905
   Argentina   379
   Belgium   165, 166
   Brazil   402, 403, 899
   Burundi   490
   Canada   68, 72, 74, 76, 901
   Chile   701
   Czech Republic   294, 295
   Denmark   176, 181–3, 187, 900
   England and Wales   104
   France   198–202
   Germany   211, 217, 218, 220, 223, 225
   Japan   755, 764–6
   Kenya   501
   Netherlands   258, 259, 261, 266
   Nigeria   531
   Norway   188
   Russia   342–4
   Serbia   370
   South Africa   538
   South Korea   795
   Switzerland   276, 282, 283, 901
   Tunisia   662
   Turkey   687
   United States   128, 131–3, 143, 899, 901
   see also law firms
South Africa   535–46
   access to justice   543–4
   Bars and Bar associations   535, 536, 537, 540–1
   Black Lawyers' Association   538
   Chief Litigation Office (CLO)   543
   Competition Commission   540
   competition policy   540–1
   Constitutional Court   541
   diversity issues in legal profession   883
      gender   537–8
      racial/ethnic minorities   538, 542
   General Council of the Bar (GCB)   535, 536, 537, 540–1
   Independent Association of Advocates (IAA)   540
   Law Society   539, 543
   legal aid   543–4
   Legal Aid Advice Line   543
   Legal Aid SA   543
   legal education and training
      LLB (Bachelor of Laws) programmes   538, 539
      practical legal training (PLT)   536
      School for Legal Practice   536
   Legal Practice Act   537
   Legal Practice Act 2014 (LPA)   541, 542
   Legal Practice Council   541
   legal profession
      female lawyers   537–8
      law graduates   538–40
      and political space   544
      regulatory change   541–3
      solo practitioners   538
      'two hemispheres' thesis   538
   Legal Services Charter   542
   Legal Services Ombudsman   541
   Minister of Justice   540
   National Bar Council (CNB)   542
   National Forum on the Legal Profession   543
   NGOs (non-governmental organisations)   543
   public interest law   544
   Recognition of Foreign Legal Qualifications and Legal Practice Act 1993   541
   regulatory change, legal profession   541–3
   slow pace of institutional change   540–1
   transformation in legal profession
      demographics   537–8
      educational   538–40
      regulatory   541–3
   violence   544
South Korea   789–800
   Bars and Bar associations   794, 795, 796
   Constitutional Court   798
   historical background   789–90
   human rights   798
   Judicial Research and Training Institute (JRTI)   790, 792
   Korean Bar Association   795, 796
   Korean Legal Aid Corporation   799
   Korean War (1950–53)   789
   law firms   792, 794–6, 799
   Law School Act   794
   legal aid   799
   legal education and training   791–4
      Korean Association of Law Schools   794
      Legal Education Eligibility Test (LEET)   793
      Ministry of Justice Bar examination   794
   legal profession
      earnings of lawyers   889
      new facets   795–7
      production of lawyers   792–5
      rapid growth of   790–2

social change 797–9
solo practitioners 795
licensing 797
National Human Rights Commission 798
pro bono services 799
qualified lawyers 793
Supreme Court 790, 791
Soviet Union, former
advocates 337–9
legal education and training 345–6
see also Russia
specialisation
Belgium 165–7
Germany 220–1
states
geopolitics of the 'bottom-up' state, Burundi 488–90
globalisation and legal intermediaries (Burundi) 475–6
lawyers as agents of 623–32
power of 483–5
'private sector quasi states' 6
professionalisation from above 209–210, 335–9
re-configurations and legal education and training 28–33
relations with Bar 511–12
support from, in Israel 608–609
Western formation processes and professional model 1–2
see also globalisation
Steinmetz, G 474
Sterling, JS 141
Stewart, J 551
Sun Zhigang 703
Susskind, R 48
Sweden
Bar Association 189, 190
law firms 189, 190
Switzerland 271–86
Bars and Bar associations 272, 273, 274, 282
business elites, transformation 277
diversity issues in legal profession 273–5, 283
dynamic demography 273
FATCA banking law 278, 279
Federal Law on Recovery of Illicit Assets (LRAI) 278
Federal Lawyers' Association (FSA) 273, 274
increased competition 279–83
inequality 274–5
law firms
concentration of 280–2
large 282, 283
mergers 280
polarisation 283
small 283, 284

legal education and training 277
legal profession
concentration of law firms 280–2
earnings of lawyers 271–2, 276, 889
female lawyers 273–5, 283, 892
Geneva 271, 280, 282
large firms 283
leading firms 280
polarisation 282–3
small firms 283
solo practitioners 276, 282, 283, 901
Zurich 280, 282
LLCA (federal law on free movement) 272, 273
polarisation in profession 282–3
prosperity 275–6
'real' end of bank secrecy 277–9
unified practice of law 273–4
Women's Business Society 275

Taiwan 801, 803–808
Alliance of Civilian-School Lawyers (ACL) 807–808, 815, 816
Bars and Bar associations 803–804, 805, 807, 808, 813, 814, 817
collective action in the 1990s 813–15
Democratic Progressive Party 816
diversity issues in legal profession 825–6, 827f
globalisation 801
Judicial Reform Foundation (JRF) 815, 816, 817
Judicial Yuan 816–17
KMT (Chinese Nationalists) 801–803, 805, 807, 813
Legal Aid Foundation Act (LAF) 816
legal education and training 886
legal profession
Bars, following World War II 803–804, 805f
civilian vs. military lawyer 807–808, 813
composition 803
dominance and decline of mainland lawyers 805–807
entry barriers, addressing 888
female lawyers 825–6, 827f
mainland lawyers 806
Taipei lawyers 806
lobbying in the 2000s 815–17
localisation 807–808
mainland lawyers
dominance and decline 805
migrants 803
National Judicial Reform Forum 816
separation from China 801
see also China; Hong Kong
tax advisers, Poland 315–16
Terbil, F 619

Thailand 831–53
  and Asian Financial Crisis 833, 837
  Baker McKenzie (major law firm) 841, 842
  Bangkok's largest firms 841–3
  Bars and Bar associations 833
  Constitutional Court 847, 850
  constitutionalism and new courts 847–8
  corruption 847
  diversity issues in legal profession
    class 832, 834, 835, 839, 842
    gender 839, 842–3
  elites 833
  free market capitalism 837
  global law 841–3
  Human Rights Committee 848
  independence 844–9
  KTB Law Ltd (law firm) 842
  law firms 841, 847
    small 839, 845
  Lawyers' Act 1985 840
  Lawyers Association 848
  Lawyers Council 837, 840–1, 843, 848
    Human Rights Committee 847
  legal aid 843–4
  legal education and training
    law schools 834–6
    LLB (Bachelor of Laws) programmes 837, 839
    nationwide admissions test 838–9
    nobility, training 833–6
    universities 835
  legal evolution 832
  legal profession 846–7
    class 837, 838
    female lawyers 839, 842–3, 846–7, 891
    interest in emergence of 832
    judges 840–1
    large firms 841–3
    law and development under the 'bureaucratic polity' 836–7
    lawyers for social causes 845–6
    lawyers in civic life 843–4
    legacies and prospects for change 849–50
    licensing and oversight 840–1
    politically divided legal profession 848–9
    practice as a common calling 837–9
    prosecutors 840–1
    unlicensed practitioners 840
  military coups 833
  NGOs (non-governmental organisations) 833, 839, 845, 846
  nobility, training 833–6
  October Generation 844–5, 847
  public office 843–4
  'quasi-colonial' modernisation 831–3
  Revolution of 1932 834–6
  Royal Courts of Justice 833, 834
  Siam Premier International Law Office 842
  Sor Rattanamanee Pokla 849–50
  Three Seals Law 834
  Tillike & Gibbons (law firm) 842
  violence 848
  Women Lawyers Association 846
Thaksin Shinawatra 833
Thatcher, Margaret 90
Thein Sein, President of Myanmar 784
Thomas, SJ 518
Tong, R 820
transformation, legal profession
  age structure 528
  Argentina 382–7
  balance between maintenance and change 248–9
  business elites 277
  consequences 326–8
  and continuity 549–53
  demographic 176–8, 537–8
  determining what change is possible 249–51
  educational 538–40
  external changes 180–3
  forces of change 129–31
  gender structure 528, 529–30t
  historical 392–5
  implementation of changes in Poland 321–2
  India 723–7
  instigators of change 249–51
  institutional 247–51
    slow pace of 540–1
  legal profession 46–9, 530–1
  numbers of legal professionals 524
  paralegals, regulation of 80–1
  para-professionals, legal education and training 217
  regulatory 541–3
  socio-economic backgrounds 524, 525–6t
  Tunisia 668–70
  Zimbabwe 556–7
transnational corporations (TNCs) 5–6
Trump, Donald 144
Tunisia 657–73
  Bars and Bar associations
    Bar of the State Party and commercial lawyers (RCD) 663–5, 667
    local associations 658
    Opposition Bar, under Ben Ali 667
    samsars 665–6
    see also TBA below
  corruption 663, 666
  diversity issues in legal profession 661
  High Council of the Judiciary (HCJ) 671
  Higher Bar Institute 662

independence, maintaining 670–2
judiciary/judges 670–2
knowledge economy, belief in 660
law firms 663, 664, 665
legal education and training
  entry to legal profession 661–2
  LLM (Master of Laws) Programmes 660, 661
legal profession
  CAPA (certificate of aptitude) 658, 659, 661, 662
  collective actors of the Revolution/political transition 668–70
  entry barriers, addressing 888
  entry to 661–2
  female lawyers 661
  following the rule of Ben Ali 668–70
  lawyering for defensive causes 667
  solo practitioners 662
  tutelage and emancipation, between 657–60
liberalisation 659–60
Ministry of Justice 658
political transition (2011–16) 668–70
qualified lawyers 661, 669, 889
RCD (Bar of the State Party) 663–5, 667
SMT (syndicate) 670–1
status, preserving 670–2
Supreme Court 661
TBA (Tunisian Bar Association) 658–9
  aim 672
  creation of 658–9
  judiciary before 670–2
  President 659, 668, 671
  social frustrations of 'lower echelon' 665–6
  social structure 660–3
UGTT (union) 659, 668
violence 666
see also Ben Ali, ZEA
Turkey 675–93
  AKP (Justice and Development Party) 679, 682–90
  ANAP (Motherland Party) 678
  Bars and Bar associations 676, 679, 684, 685, 691
  ÇAG (Modern Lawyers Group) 678, 679
  CHP (Republican People's Party) 675
  Civil Code 675
  Competition Council 686
  Constitutional Court 887
  corruption 683
  DSP (Democratic Left Party) 679
  early days of the Republic (1923–45) 675–6
  globalisation, liberalisation and polarisation (1980–2002) 678–81, 682t
  HDP (People's Democratic Party) 683
  Higher Education Council 887

Istanbul Bar 676, 679, 684
Izmir Bar Association 679
Kemalism 676, 677, 679, 682, 685, 690
Kurdish Human Rights Project (KHRP) 680
Kurdish nationalism 679
legal education and training 676, 681, 682t, 688–90, 887
legal profession
  female lawyers 686–7, 891
  growth 686
  practice settings 687–8
  professional developments 679–81, 685–8
  solo practitioners 687
Legal Profession Code 679
liberalism 677, 682
Ministry of Justice 679
Modern Lawyers Group (*Çağdaş Avukatlar Grubu*), ÇAG 678
modernisation 675
Muhamat Kanunu Code 676
multi-party period and military interventions (1945–80) 677–8
Öİ-ÇAG (First-Modern Lawyers Group) 679
ÖSYM (Centre for Assessment, Selection and Placement) 691
qualified lawyers 680, 689
RP (Welfare Party) 679
TBB (Union of Turkish Bar Associations) 678, 684, 685, 691
United Lawyers Group 679
violence 677, 678, 683, 684
YÖK (Higher Education Council) 688
'two hemispheres' thesis in legal profession 32
  Australia 47
  Brazil 391
  China 700, 701
  Indonesia 749
  Israel 602, 612, 613
  Netherlands 258
  Scandinavian countries 189
  South Africa 538
  United States 143, 901

U Ko Ni 783
UNCITRAL Model Law on International Commercial Arbitration 164
underrepresented racial minority (URM) 142
United Kingdom
  and Australia 47
  see also England and Wales; Scotland
United States 127–53
  Bars and Bar associations 127
    disaggregated 145–6
    entry practices 143
    private practice 129

Big Four accounting firms 134
Department of Justice (DOJ) 138, 144
diversity issues in legal profession 128, 141–6
forces of change 129–31
globalisation 127, 128, 130, 133–5, 146
inequality 141–6
   across sectors 143
   disaggregated profession 143, 145–6
   distribution of legal services 143–5
   entry to profession 141
   promotion within profession 141–3
   unequal access to lawyers 143–5
innovation 127, 128, 130–1
law firms
   boutique 133, 136
   large 133–5
   small 128, 131–3, 143
legal aid 144–5
legal education and training
   Law School Aptitude Test (LSAT) 141, 886
   law schools 137, 140, 141, 143
   legal academy 140–2
   LLM (Master of Laws) Programmes 140, 143
legal profession
   agency lawyers 139–40
   career lawyers 139–40
   differentiation and stratification patterns 127
   earnings of lawyers 132–3, 143
   entry barriers, addressing 888
   female lawyers 141
   government lawyers/sector 137–40
   immigrants 143
   inequality 128, 141–6
   internationalisation of public interest practice 130
   judiciary/judges 138
   legal process outsourcing (LPO) 130
   Legal Services Corporation (LSC) 136, 137, 144
   legal services organisations 136
   Limited License Legal Technicians 146
   nonprofit sector 136–7
   Private Attorney Involvement (PAI) 136
   private practice 131–5
   prosecutors 138–9
   public defenders 138–9, 144
   public interest law organisations 130, 133, 136–7
   scandals 135
   sectoral analysis 131–41
   size 129, 899
   solo practitioners 899, 901
   state Attorneys General (AGs) 139
   'two hemispheres' thesis 143, 901
Legal Services Corporation (LSC) 136, 137, 144
National Association for Law Placement 143
neoliberalism 128, 131, 147
Office for Access to Justice 144
private practice 131–5
   boutique firms 133
   in-house counsel 135
   large firms 133–5
qualified lawyers 138, 143
racial/ethnic minorities 142
regulation of legal profession 145–6
sectoral analysis 131–41
   government sector 137–40
   legal academy 142
   nonprofit sector 136–7
   private practice 131–5
solo practitioners 132–3
Wall Street 47
war on crime 144
unlicensed practitioners 16, 890
   Brazil 394–5, 405
   Chile 418
   Germany 227
   India 715
   Israel 603, 604, 606
   Russia 331–5, 340, 341, 343–5, 347, 349, 350
   Thailand 840
   see also licensing
unqualified practitioners 889
   Brazil 394
   England and Wales 90
   Kenya 496, 508, 509
   Libya 630
   Russia 336
   Scotland 123
Ushewokunze, H 552

Vargas, JE 419–20
Vauchez, A 197
Venezuela 449–69, 883
   Association of Administrative Law (AVEDA) 466
   Bars and Bar associations 452, 465–6
   Chavista revolution 453–6, 462, 463
   Commercial Arbitration Act (CAA) 1998 456
   Constituent Assembly 457
   Constitution 455
   COPEI (Christian-Democratic party) 451, 452
   corruption 451, 453, 457, 458
   diversity issues in legal profession 462
   Group of Public Law Professors 466
   human rights 455, 464
   Institute of Social Welfare for Lawyers 459
   judges 458
   Justice Observatory 458

law firms 452, 454, 455
legal education and training
  demography of law students/lawyers 459–63
  law schools 449–50, 455–6, 460–2
  law students and lawyers 459–63
  LLM (Master of Laws) programmes 453
legal profession
  demography 459–63
  female lawyers 462
  functional litigants 464
  instrumental litigants 464
  involuntary litigants 463–4
  professional legal careers and litigation 463–5
  and rule of law 465–7
National Assembly 457
National Council of Universities 460
NGOs (non-governmental organisations) 464
Organic Code of Criminal Procedure 1998 456
Organic Law of the Supreme Justice 457
pacted democracy, lawyers in 450–3
Planning Office of Higher Education (OPSU) 459
private law schools 461
public government-controlled law schools 461–2
rule of law 465–7
Supreme Tribunal 457
UBV (law school) 461–2
UCAB (law school) 461
UCV (law school) 460–1
Vietnam 855–78
Bars and Bar associations 857, 858, 865, 868–9
China contrasted 858
Code of Conduct and Ethics for Vietnamese Lawyers (COC) 864, 866–7
Communist Party of Vietnam (CPV) 855, 859
  Central Commission for Internal Affairs (CCIA) 868
constitutional activism 873
Criminal Procedure Code (CPC) 867
Democratic Republic of Vietnam (DRV) 856
demographics 869–70
Đổi mới (renovation) 855
  post-Đổi mới legal profession 856, 859–60
  pre-Đổi mới legal profession 856–7
Hanoi Bar Association 858, 865, 869, 873
Hanoi University of Law (HAUL) 859, 860, 862
  HAUL-UWE programme 861
historical background 856–9
Ho Chi Minh City (HCMC)
  Bar Association 858, 873
  Lawyers Association 858
  University of Law (HCMCUL) 860–3, 865, 868

Law on Lawyers (LOL) 2006 857–8
legal education and training 859–63
  curriculum 861–2
  finance and tuition fees 862–3
  LLB (Bachelor of Laws) programmes 860, 862, 863
  Master of Laws programmes 861
  revival of, post-Đổi mới era 859–60
  transformation of legal teaching and continual challenges 860–2
legal profession 859–71
  demographics 869–70
  law firms 870
  lawyering 871–3
  legal services market 871
  licensing 863–4
  post-Đổi mới legal profession 857–9
  pre-Đổi mới legal profession 856–7
  pro bono services 870–3
  professional associations 867–9
  publicly funded work 870–1
  regulation 863–7
  working practices 870
Ministry of Education and Training (MOET) 859–60
Ministry of Justice (MOJ) 855, 858, 860, 863, 865, 866, 868
Ministry of Planning and Investment (MPI) 866
qualified lawyers 866
regulation of legal profession 863–7
  competitive restrictions 866–7
  ethical standards 864–5
  liability and ethics 865–6
  licensing 863–4
Republic of Vietnam (RVN) 857, 861
socialism 855, 856, 857
Supreme People's Court (SPC) 866
Vietnam Bar Association (VBF) 867–8, 873
Vietnam Lawyers Association (VLA) 857, 867
violence
Argentina 384
Belgium 165
Burundi see Burundi
civilian 578
collective 482, 483
domestic 165, 384
Egypt 578
extreme 452, 487
gender-based 165, 384, 544
genocide 474, 477, 482–3, 488–9, 784
India 722
Libya 620, 624, 629, 633, 635, 636
machete 483
militia 620, 635
police 683, 684

political   450
South Africa   544
Thailand   848
Tunisia   666
Turkey   677, 678, 683, 684
Venezuela   450, 452

Wambua, M   499
Weber, M   103, 880, 895
West Bank
   annexation by Jordan   639
   Arab Lawyers Union   644, 645
   Bar   643
   Bar Council   647
   Civil Bar Association Law 1966   642
   civil lawyers   642
   courts   644
   Israeli occupation   640, 643
   Jordanian rule   641–3
   justice officer   643
   Union Council   644
   see also Gaza; Palestine
Western states
   formation processes and professional model   1–2
   modernity *see* modernity, Western
women lawyers   9–10
   Australia   48, 51, 58–9
   Belgium   168, 892
   Bosnia and Herzegovina (BiH)   360, 891
   Brazil   396–9, 404–405
   Canada   71, 72
   Chile   422
   China   703, 891
   Czech Republic   294, 301–302
   Denmark   184
   England and Wales   104
   France   195–6, 200
   Germany   221–4, 891, 892
   Hong Kong   825–6, 827f
   India   715–20, 719f
   Indonesia   891
   Iran   594–5
   Israel   613–14
   Japan   766, 767t, 768, 891
   Kenya   498–9
   Mexico   433
   Myanmar   781, 891
   Netherlands   260–1
   Nigeria   528, 529–30t, 891
   Norway   891
   Palestine   650
   pay differentials   223–4
   Poland   310–11, 891, 892
   Scotland   119
   Serbia   355, 364, 891

   South Africa   537–8
   South Korea   891
   Switzerland   273–5, 283, 892
   Thailand   839, 842–3, 846–7, 891
   Tunisia   661
   Turkey   686–7, 891
   United States   141
   Venezuela   462
   Zimbabwe   551, 555, 556, 891
   see also gender structure, legal profession
Working Group for the Comparative Studies of Legal Professions   vii, 880

Xi Jinping   708

Yam, Kevin   819
Youssef, SB   659
Yuen, R   820
Yugoslavia, former
   advocates   358–9
   Bars and Bar associations   358–9
   Constitution   365
   female lawyers   891
   Law on Advocacy and Legal Aid Services 1977   359
   Law on Attorney and Other Legal Aid 1971   359
   Law on Judges 1881   365
   legal academics   369
   Serbian Law on Advocacy and Other Legal Aid 1971   359
   socialism   365
   see also Bosnia and Herzegovina (BiH); Serbia

Zaghloul, S   575
Zambia   556
Zamchiya, D   552
Zheng Enchong   703
Zimbabwe
   'black letter' law   551
   broadening of civic space (1990s)   553–8
   democracy   556
   diversity issues in legal profession
      gender   555, 556, 557
      racial/ethnic minorities   551, 557
   female lawyers   891
   historical background   547–9
   human rights   553, 555, 556
   Law Faculty   553
   Law Society of Zimbabwe (LSZ)   547, 550, 552–5, 558–9
   legal education and training   882
      Council for Legal Education   550, 559
      law degree programmes   560
      University of Zimbabwe Law School   550–2

Legal Practitioners Act 1981 550, 560
legal profession
   Africanisation 550
   female lawyers 551, 555, 556
   transformation 556–7
Legal Resources Foundation 550
Movement for Democratic Change (MDC) 558
National Constitutional Assembly (NCA) 556, 558
political embeddedness 549, 550
post-2000 period 558–60
qualified lawyers 548, 550
transformation and continuity (1980s) 549–53
Zimbabwe African People's Union (PF ZAPU) 551, 555–6
Zimbabwe African People's Union (ZAPU PF) government 549, 551, 555–6, 558, 559
Zimbabwe Lawyers for Human Rights (ZLHR) 555, 559
Zimbabwe Women Lawyers Association (ZWLA) 555, 556, 557–8